Second Ed

THE Illustrated HOME

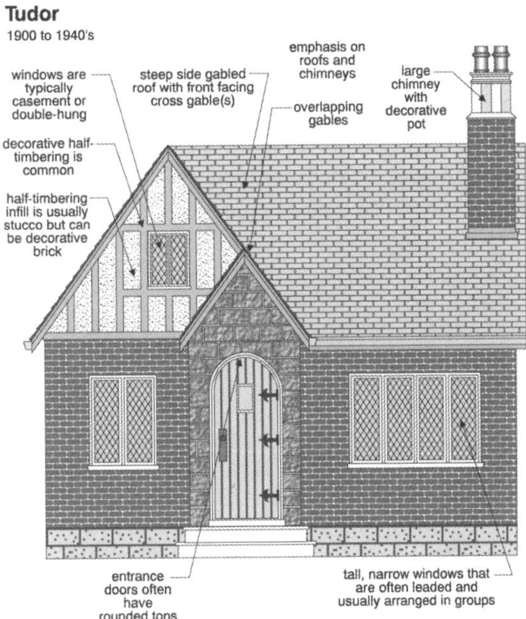

This publication is designed to provide accurate and authoritative information in regard to the subject matter covered. It is sold with the understanding that the publisher is not engaged in rendering legal, accounting, or other professional service. If legal advice or other expert assistance is required, the services of a competent professional should be sought.

President: Roy Lipner
Vice President of Product Development & Publishing: Evan Butterfield
Editorial Project Manager: Laurie McGuire
Director of Production: Daniel Frey
Senior Managing Editor, Production: Jack Kiburz
Creative Director: Lucy Jenkins
Production Artist: John Christensen

Published by Dearborn Home Inspection,
a division of Dearborn Financial Publishing, Inc.
30 South Wacker Drive, Suite 2500
Chicago, IL 60606-7481
(312) 836-4400
www.dearbornhomeinspection.com

Printed in the United States of America.

06 07 10 9 8 7 6 5 4 3 2 1

ISBN-13: 978-1-4195-8919-5

ISBN-10: 1-4195-8919-9

Table of Contents

CHAPTER ONE: ROOFING

STEEP ROOFING
9 ...... General
10 ...... Asphalt Shingles
12 ...... Wood Shingles and Shakes
13 ...... Slate
15 ...... Clay
16 ...... Concrete and Fiber Cement
17 ...... Metal
18 ...... Roll Roofing

STEEP ROOF FLASHINGS
18 ...... Valley Flashings
20 ...... Chimney Flashings
21 ...... Plumbing Stack Flashings
21 ...... Roof/Wall Flashings
22 ...... Hip and Ridge Flashings
22 ...... Skylights
23 ...... Solariums
23 ...... Drip Edge Flashings
24 ...... Dormer Flashings

FLAT ROOFING
24 ...... General
24 ...... Built-Up Roofing (Tar and Gravel)
25 ...... Modified Bitumen
26 ...... Synthetic Rubber (Elastomeric, EPDM)
26 ...... Plastic Roofing (PVC, Thermoplastic)
26 ...... Roll Roofing
26 ...... Flat Roof Flashings

CHAPTER TWO: STRUCTURE

FOOTINGS AND FOUNDATIONS
35 ...... Description
38 ...... Problems

FLOORS
47 ...... Introduction
48 ...... Sills
49 ...... Columns
50 ...... Beams
54 ...... Joists
58 ...... Subflooring
59 ...... Concrete Floor Slabs
59 ...... Steel-Framed Floors
60 ...... Old Homes
60 ...... Inspecting for Termites

WALLS
61 ...... Solid Masonry Walls
66 ...... Wood Frame Walls
70 ...... Masonry Veneer Walls
72 ...... Steel Framed Walls
72 ...... Arches and Lintels

ROOF FRAMING
74 ...... Introduction
74 ...... Rafters, Roof Joists and Ceiling Joists
78 ...... Collar Ties, Knee Walls, and Purlins
79 ...... Steel Framed Rafters, Roof Joists, and Ceiling Joists
79 ...... Trusses
80 ...... Wood "I" Joists
81 ...... Sheathing

CHAPTER THREE: ELECTRICAL

SERVICE DROP AND SERVICE ENTRANCE
85 ...... The Basics of Electricity
87 ...... Service Drop
88 ...... Service Entrance Wires
89 ...... Service Size

SERVICE BOX, GROUNDING, AND PANELS
90 ...... Service Boxes
92 ...... System Grounding
94 ...... Distribution Panels

THE DISTRIBUTION SYSTEM
99 ...... Branch Circuit Wiring (Distribution Wiring)
102..... Knob-and-Tube Wiring
103..... Aluminum Wire
103..... Lights, Outlets, Switches, and Junction Boxes

CHAPTER FOUR: HEATING

FURNACES – GAS AND OIL
115..... Introduction
117..... Heat Transfer
118..... Gas Piping and Meters
120..... Combustion Air
122..... Gas Burners
124..... Heat Exchangers
126..... Furnace Cabinets
127..... Fan/Limit Switches
127..... Thermostats
128..... Venting Gas Furnaces
130..... Distribution System
131..... Blowers
131..... Air Filters and Cleaners
132..... Humidifiers
133..... Duct Systems, Registers and Grills
134..... Mid-Efficiency Furnaces
136..... Condensing Furnaces

139..... Gravity Furnaces
139..... Combination Furnaces
140..... Oil Furnaces

HOT WATER BOILERS (HYDRONIC HEATING)
144..... Introduction
145..... Heat Exchangers
145..... Controls
149..... Distribution Systems
154..... Pulse Combustion

CHIMNEYS
155..... Introduction
156..... Masonry Chimneys
164..... Metal Chimneys or Vents

WOOD HEATING SYSTEMS
166..... Introduction
167..... Furnaces and Boilers
171..... Wood Stoves (Space Heaters)
176..... Wood Burning Fireplaces

STEAM HEATING SYSTEMS
183..... How They Work
184..... Common Steam Systems
186..... Steam Controls
187..... Steam Boiler Problems

ELECTRIC HEATING SYSTEMS
190..... Introduction
191..... Space Heaters
192..... Electric Furnaces
194..... Electric Boilers
194..... Radiant Heating

WALL AND FLOOR FURNACES, ROOM HEATERS, AND GAS FIREPLACES
194..... Wall Furnaces
196..... Floor Furnaces
196..... Room Heaters
197..... Gas Fireplaces and Gas Logs

CHAPTER FIVE: AIR CONDITIONING AND HEAT PUMPS

AIR CONDITIONING
201..... The Basics
203..... Air Conditioning Capacity
204..... Compressor
206..... Condenser Coil (Outdoor Coil)
207..... Evaporator Coil (Indoor Coil)
208..... Condensate System
210..... Refrigerant Lines
210..... Condenser Fan (Outdoor Fan)
211..... Evaporator Fan (Indoor Fan)
211..... Duct System
213..... Thermostats
213..... Life Expectancy
214..... Evaporative Coolers
214..... Whole House Fans

HEAT PUMPS
214..... Heat Pumps in Theory
216..... Heat Pumps in Practice

CHAPTER SIX: INSULATION

221..... The Basics
226..... Air/Vapor Barriers (Vapor Retarders)
228..... Venting Roofs
231..... Venting Living Spaces
234..... Attics
237..... Flat and Cathedral Roofs
238..... Walls Above Grade
239..... Basements and Crawlspaces
242..... Floors over Unheated Areas
242..... Ventilation Systems

CHAPTER SEVEN: PLUMBING

SUPPLY PLUMBING
249..... Flow and Pressure
251..... Private Water Sources
254..... Public Water Service
255..... Distribution Piping In the House

WATER HEATERS
260..... Introduction
262..... Gas Piping, Burners, and Venting
265..... Oil Tanks, Burners, and Venting
267..... Conventional Tank Type Water Heaters
269..... High Efficiency Gas Water Heaters
270..... Combination Systems
270..... Tankless Coils

DRAIN, WASTE AND VENT PLUMBING
271..... Introduction
273..... Drain Piping Materials and Problems
275..... Traps
277..... Floor Drains
277..... Venting Systems
279..... Sewage Ejector Pumps
279..... Sump Pumps
279..... Laundry Tub Pumps
279..... Septic Systems

FIXTURES AND FAUCETS
281..... Introduction
281..... Basins, Sinks and Laundry Tubs
281..... Faucets
282..... Toilets
282..... Bidets
283..... Bathtubs
283..... Tub and Shower Enclosures
284..... Shower Stalls
285..... Whirlpool Baths

CHAPTER EIGHT: EXTERIOR

ARCHITECTURAL STYLES
291..... Building Shapes and Details
294..... Windows
295..... Columns
295..... Specific House Styles

EXTERIOR CLADDING
300..... Introduction
300..... Wall Surfaces – General
302..... Masonry
305..... Stucco
309..... Wood
311..... Plywood, Hardboard and OSB
312..... Metal and Vinyl
313..... Other Sidings and Issues
315..... Soffits and Fascia
315..... Windows and Doors
316..... Trim, Flashings and Caulking

EXTERIOR STRUCTURES
317..... Introduction
317..... Porches, Decks and Balconies
322..... Garages and Carports
325..... Basement Walkouts

SURFACE WATER CONTROL AND LANDSCAPING
326..... Lot Grading
328..... Gutters and Downspouts
333..... Window Wells
334..... Walks, Driveways and Grounds
335..... Retaining Walls

CHAPTER NINE: INTERIOR

339..... Introduction
339..... Floors
341..... Walls
343..... Ceilings
344..... Trim, Counters and Cabinets
345..... Stairs
347..... Windows, Skylights and Solariums
351..... Doors
353..... Wet Basements and Crawlspaces

CHAPTER TEN: APPLIANCES

360..... Ranges
360..... Microwave Ovens
361..... Exhaust Fans
361..... Dishwashers
361..... Waste Disposals
362..... Trash Compactors
362..... Central Vacuum Systems
362..... Refrigerators
363..... Washing Machines
363..... Dryers
364..... Doorbells

INDEX

365..... Index

CHAPTER 1

STEEP ROOFING

GENERAL

9 .... 0001 Roof slopes
9 .... 0002 Steep roof types
9 .... 0003 Dormer gutters discharging onto roof
9 .... 0004 Patched roofing
9 .... 0005 Vulnerable areas
9 .... 0006 Ice dams
10 ...... 0007 Preventing ice dams with ventilation
10 ...... 0008 Eave protection against ice dams
10 ...... 0009 Avalanche guards

ASPHALT SHINGLES

10 ...... 0010 Asphalt shingle composition
10 ...... 0011 Typical asphalt shingle application – showing metal drip edge
10 ...... 0012 Self-sealing tabs
11 ...... 0013 Asphalt shingle application – showing alternate starter course arrangement
11 ...... 0014 Cutting the points
11 ...... 0015 Premature failure of fiberglass shingles
11 ...... 0016 Low slope shingle application
11 ...... 0017 Fastener problems
11 ...... 0018 Ridge shingle application

WOOD SHINGLES & SHAKES

12 ...... 0019 Shrinkage properties of wood
12 ...... 0020 Wood shingles and shakes
12 ...... 0021 Cedar shingle application
12 ...... 0022 Cedar shingles – nailing details
12 ...... 0023 Cedar shingle application – spaced-plank sheathing
12 ...... 0024 Cedar shake application
13 ...... 0025 Cedar shake – nailing details
13 ...... 0026 Cedar shake application
13 ...... 0027 Cedar shingle application
13 ...... 0028 Cedar shingle application – using synthetic ventilation layer
13 ...... 0029 Curling, cupping and splitting wood shingles

SLATE

13 ...... 0030 Slate types
14 ...... 0031 Graduated slate roof
14 ...... 0032 Slate ribbons
14 ...... 0033 Slate – nailing details
14 ...... 0034 Slate roof installation – dutch lap method
14 ...... 0035 Slate roof installation – french method
14 ...... 0036 Slate repair methods – using a slate hook
15 ...... 0037 Slate repair methods – making babies
15 ...... 0038 Slate repair methods – using a sheet metal cradle

CLAY

15 ...... 0039 Clay tile – tapered mission style
15 ...... 0040 Clay tile – barrel mission style (straight)
15 ...... 0041 Clay tile – 'S' type
15 ...... 0042 Clay tile – interlocking shingle
16 ...... 0043 How clay tiles are secured
16 ...... 0044 Eave closures for spanish or mission tiles

CONCRETE AND FIBER CEMENT

16 ...... 0045 Concrete tiles
16 ...... 0046 Cracked or broken tiles
17 ...... 0047 How concrete tiles are secured
17 ...... 0048 Fiber cement shingles

METAL

17 ...... 0049 Metal shingles
17 ...... 0050 Sheet metal roofing

ROLL ROOFING

18 ...... 0051 Roll roofing
18 ...... 0052 Roll roofing problems

CHAPTER 1

STEEP ROOF FLASHINGS

VALLEY FLASHINGS

18 ...... 0053 Roof valleys – open and closed
18 ...... 0054 Why valleys have a lower slope
18 ...... 0055 Valley flashing
18 ...... 0056 Valley flashing made of asphalt shingles
19 ...... 0057 Metal valley flashing
19 ...... 0058 Two types of metal valley flashing joints
19 ...... 0059 Metal valley secured with cleats
19 ...... 0060 Metal valley flashing – alternate application
19 ...... 0061 Metal valley flashing with upstand
19 ...... 0062 Valley flashings – cutting the poınts
20 ...... 0063 Closed cut (or half-woven) valley
20 ...... 0064 Fully woven closed valley

CHIMNEY FLASHINGS

20 ...... 0065 Chimney flashings – overview
20 ...... 0066 Chimney flashings – side flashing detail
20 ...... 0067 Chimney saddle flashings
20 ...... 0068 Chimney flashings – head flashing detail
21 ...... 0069 Chimney flashings – things to look for
21 ...... 0070 Chimney flashings – side flashing detail

PLUMBING STACK FLASHINGS

21 ...... 0071 Neoprene plumbing stack flashing
21 ...... 0072 Plumbing stack flashing – stretched or buckled

ROOF/WALL FLASHINGS

21 ...... 0073 Roof/sidewall flashings
21 ...... 0074 Roof/sidewall flashings
22 ...... 0075 Roof/sidewall flashings – clay tile
22 ...... 0076 Roof/masonry sidewall flashings
22 ...... 0077 Roof intersection with brick wall above
22 ...... 0078 Roof intersection with siding above

HIP AND RIDGE FLASHINGS

22 ...... 0079 Ridge shingle application

SKYLIGHTS

22 ...... 0080 Skylight in sloped roof – curb mount
23 ...... 0081 Skylight in sloped roof – curbless
23 ...... 0082 Skylight in sloped roof – integral curb (self-flashing skylight)
23 ...... 0083 Ice damming at skylight

SOLARIUMS

23 ...... 0084 Solariums – areas to watch for

DRIP EDGE FLASHINGS

23 ...... 0085 Typical asphalt shingle application – showing metal drip edge

DORMER FLASHINGS

23 ...... 0086 Dormer siding flashings
24 ...... 0087 Valley flashings – cutting the points

CHAPTER 1

FLAT ROOFING

GENERAL

24 ...... 0088 Flat roof drainage systems

BUILT-UP ROOFING

24 ...... 0089 Inverted roof membrane assembly
24 ...... 0090 Built-up roofing membrane – four-ply
24 ...... 0091 Damaged and patched flat roofs
24 ...... 0092 Blisters in built-up roofing membranes
25 ...... 0093 Flat roof alligatoring
25 ...... 0094 Gravel erosion (scouring) on flat roofs
25 ...... 0095 Ridging and fish mouths on flat roofs
25 ...... 0096 Ponding on flat roofs

MODIFIED BITUMEN

25 ...... 0097 Single-ply modified bitumen roof
25 ...... 0098 Two-ply modified bitumen roof
26 ...... 0099 Staggering side laps in single-ply modified bitumen roofs

SYNTHETIC RUBBER (ELASTOMERIC, EPDM)

26 ...... 0100 EPDM roof membrane

PLASTIC ROOFING (PVC, THERMOPLASTIC)

26 ...... 0101 PVC roof membrane
26 ...... 0102 PVC roof problems

ROLL ROOFING

26 ...... 0103 Wide selvage roofing

FLAT ROOF FLASHINGS

26 ...... 0104 Built-up flat roof/wall flashing
27 ...... 0105 Modified bitumen roof/wall flashing
27 ...... 0106 Two-piece counterflashings
27 ...... 0107 Built-up roofing membrane – edge details
27 ...... 0108 Built-up roof membrane – curbed edge
27 ...... 0109 Built-up flat roof/wall flashing
27 ...... 0110 Two-piece counter flashings
28 ...... 0111 Alternative attachment method for counter flashing
28 ...... 0112 Lower quality built-up flat roof/wall flashing
28 ...... 0113 EPDM (or PVC) roof/wall flashing
28 ...... 0114 Through-wall flashings
28 ...... 0115 Metal clad parapet wall
28 ...... 0116 Chimney cap details
29 ...... 0117 Skylight in flat roof
29 ...... 0118 "Stack jack" plumbing stack flashing
29 ...... 0119 Cone-style plumbing stack flashing
29 ...... 0120 Pitch pans for irregular roof penetrations
29 ...... 0121 Flat roof drainage systems
29 ...... 0122 Drain in modified bitumen roof
30 ...... 0123 Flat roof draining onto sloped roof
30 ...... 0124 Sloped roof draining onto flat roof

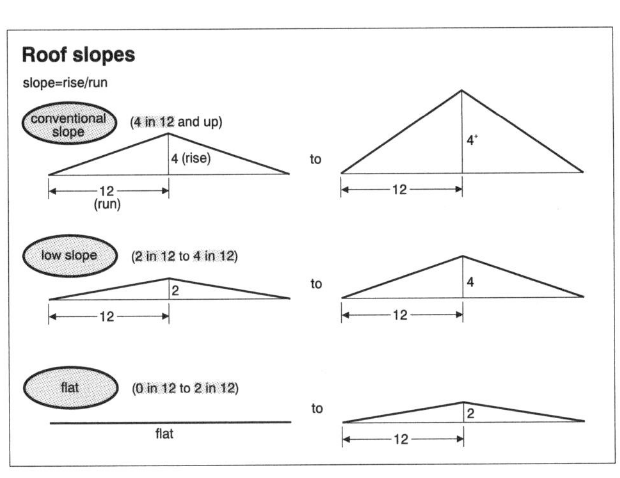

0001

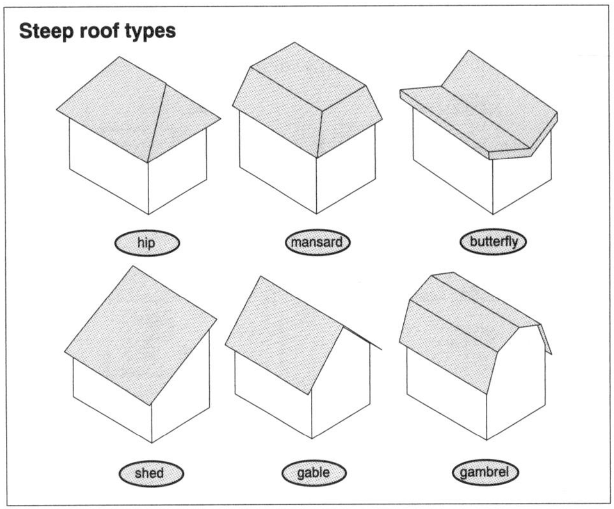

0002

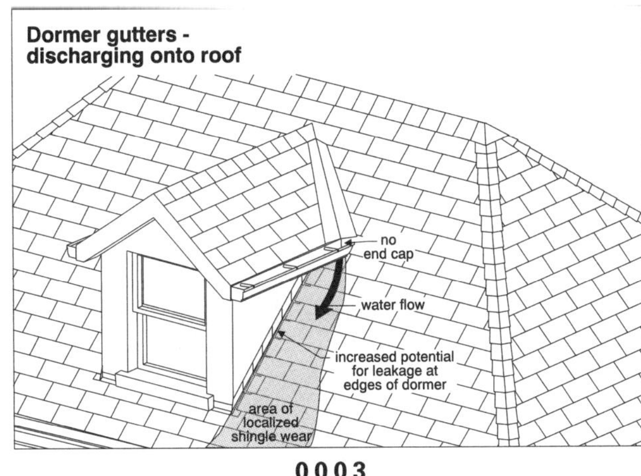

0003

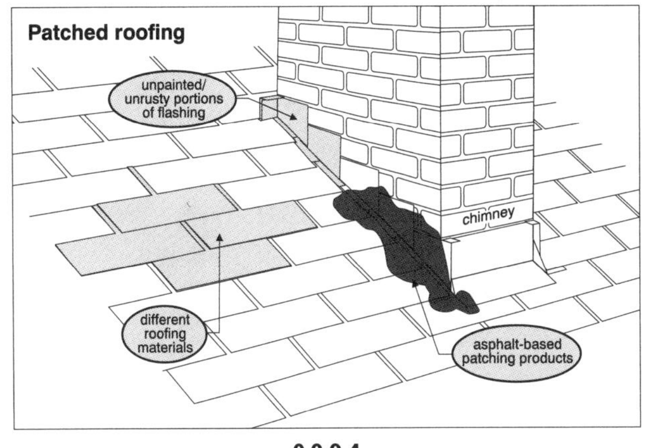

0004

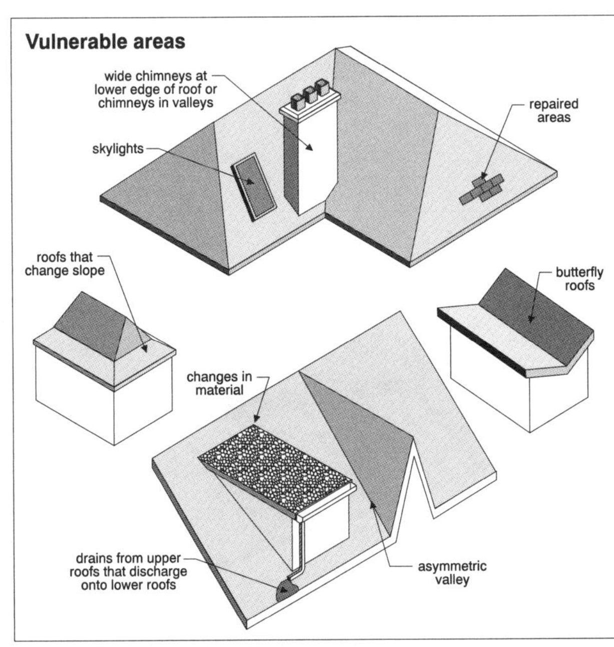

0005

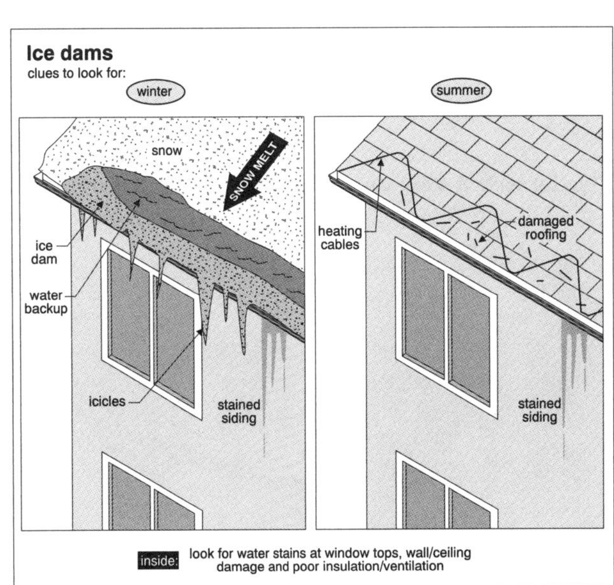

0006

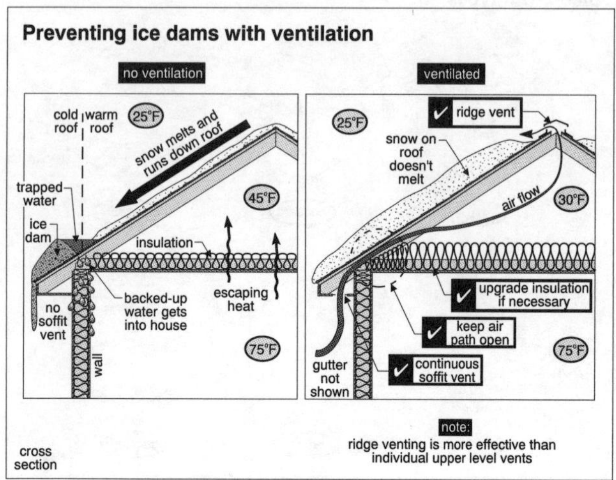

0007

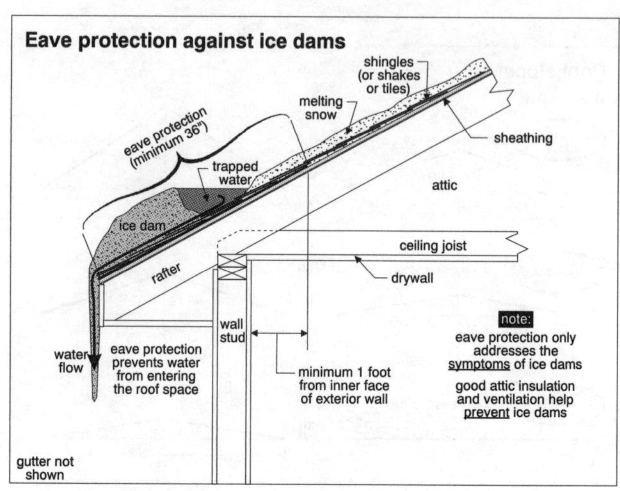

0008

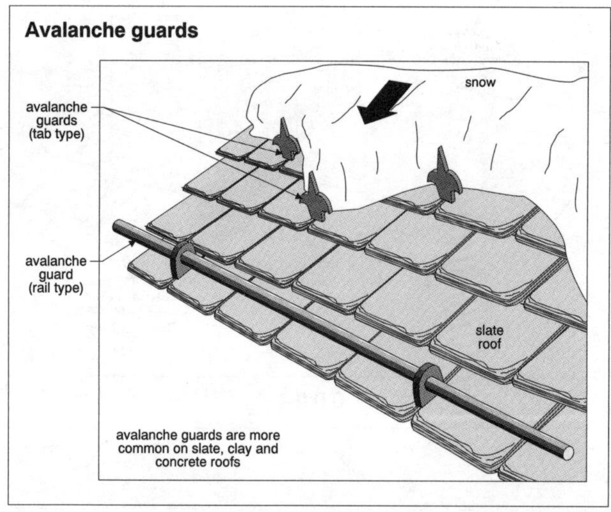

0009

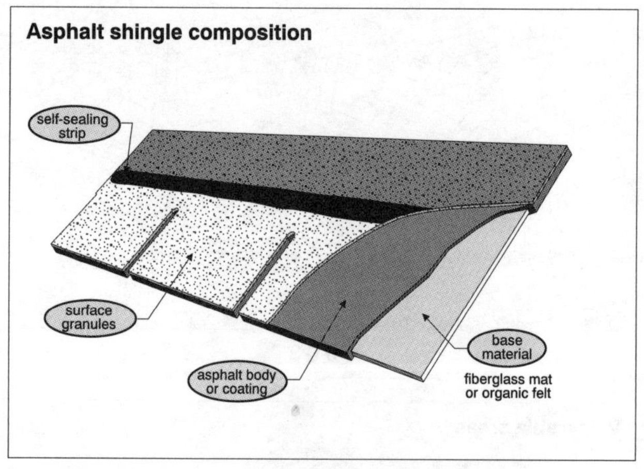

0010

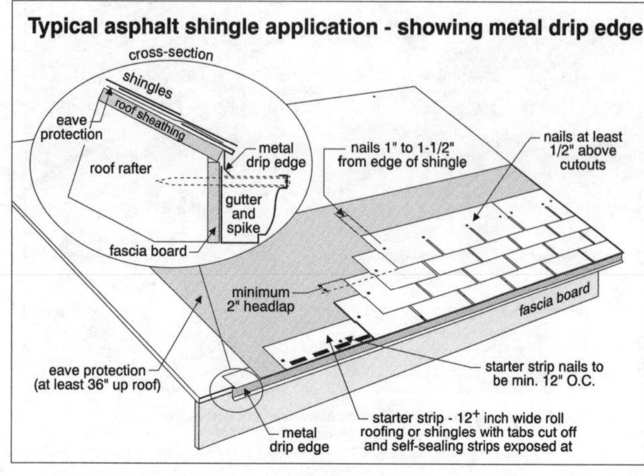

0011

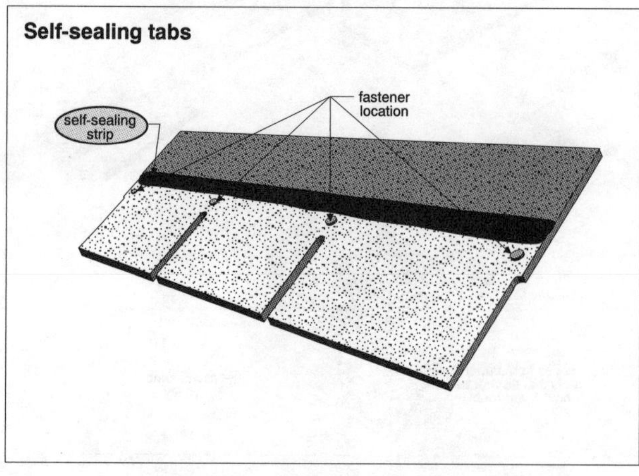

0012

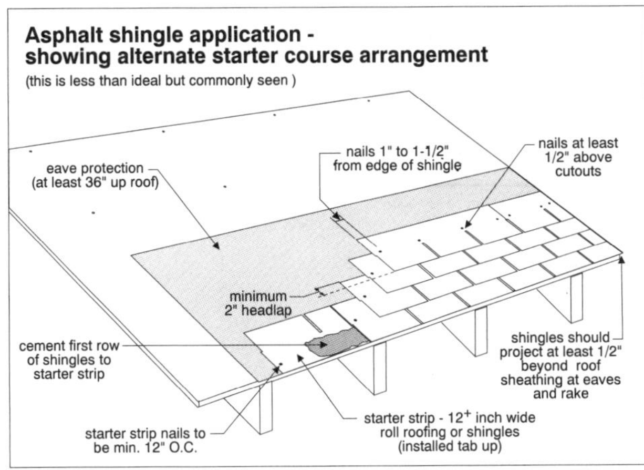

0013

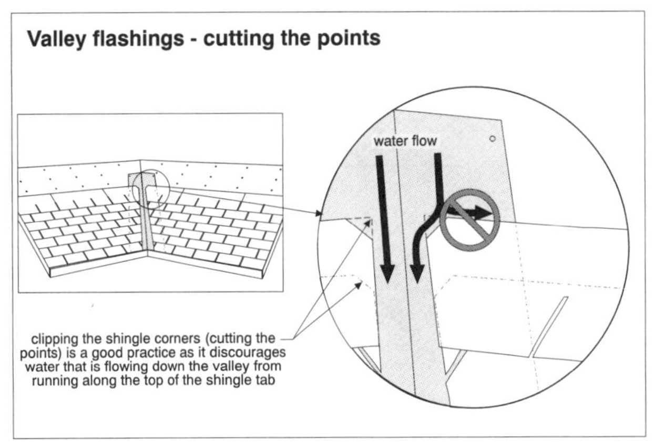

0014

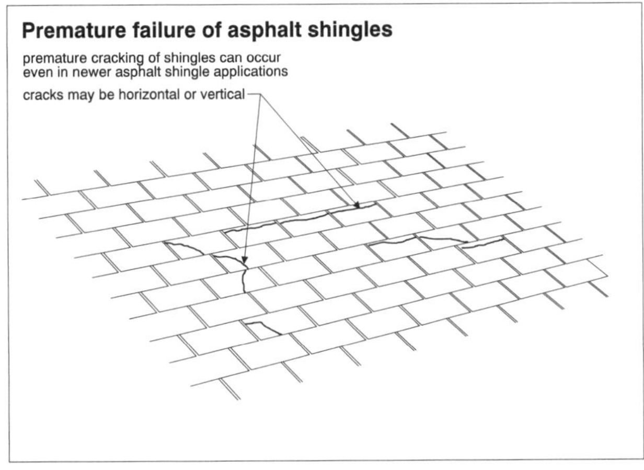

0015

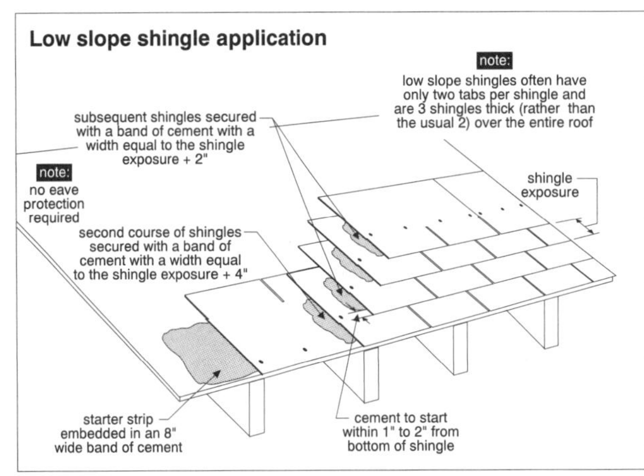

0016

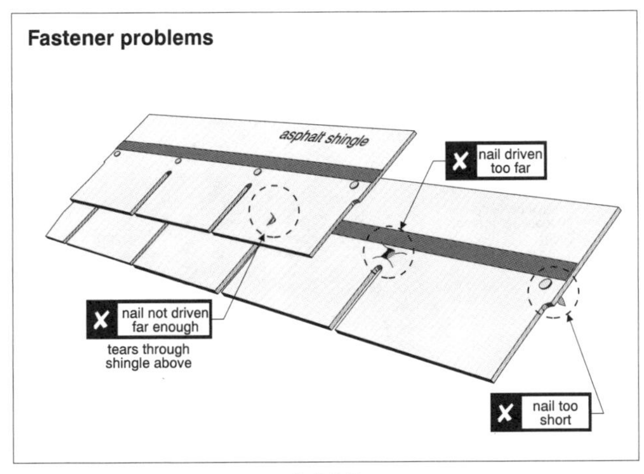

0017

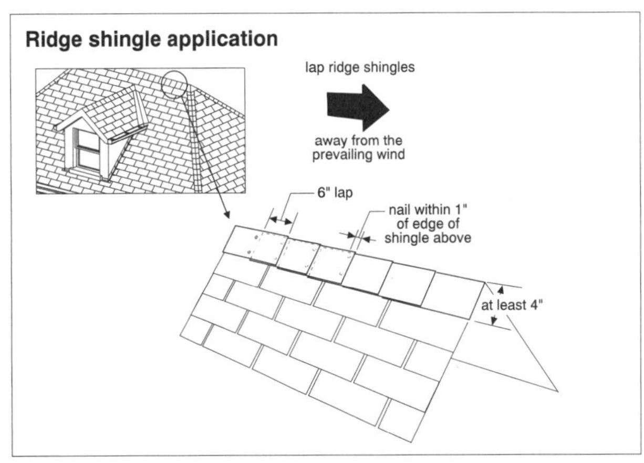

0018

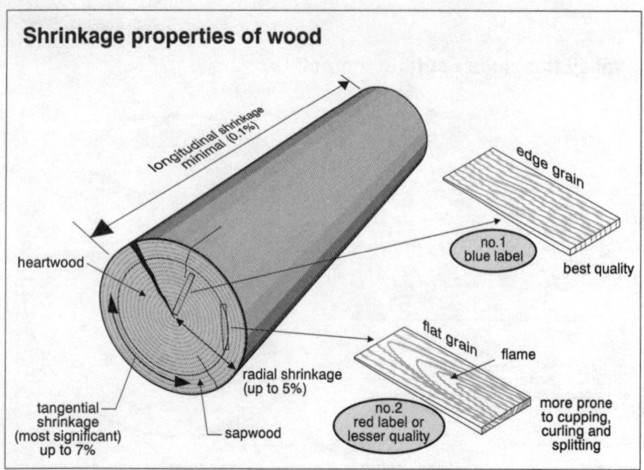

0019

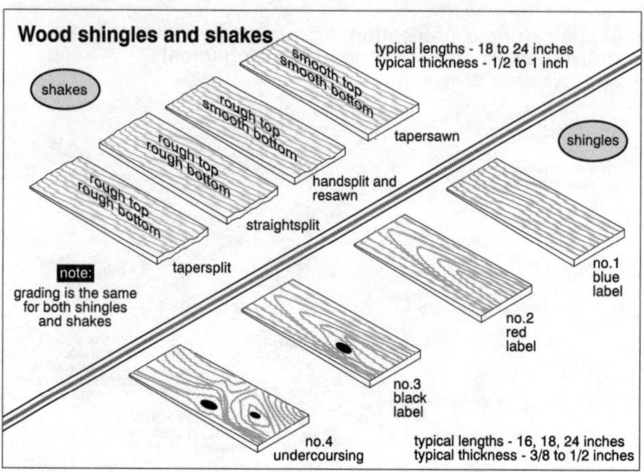

0020

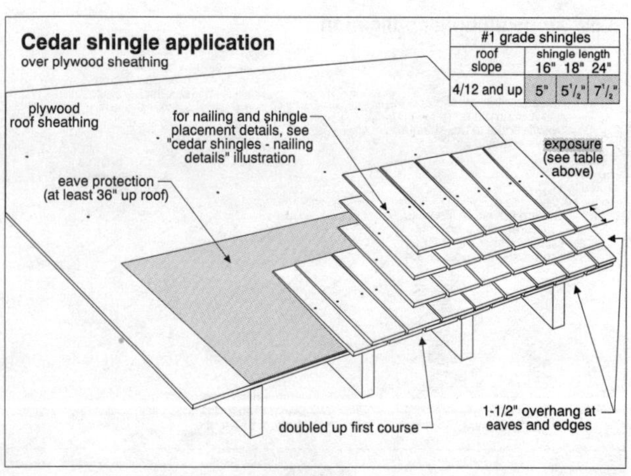

0021

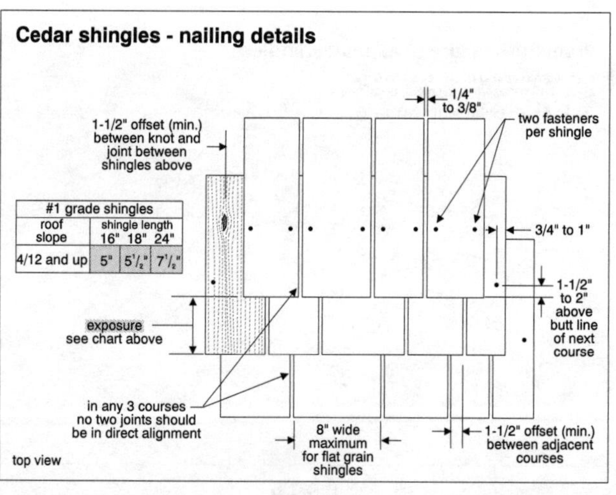

0022

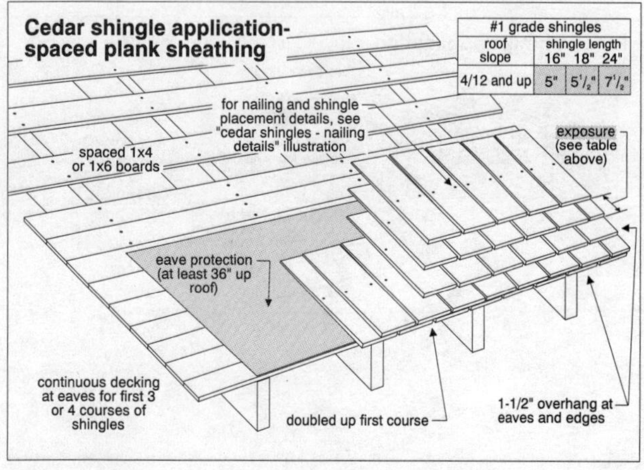

0023

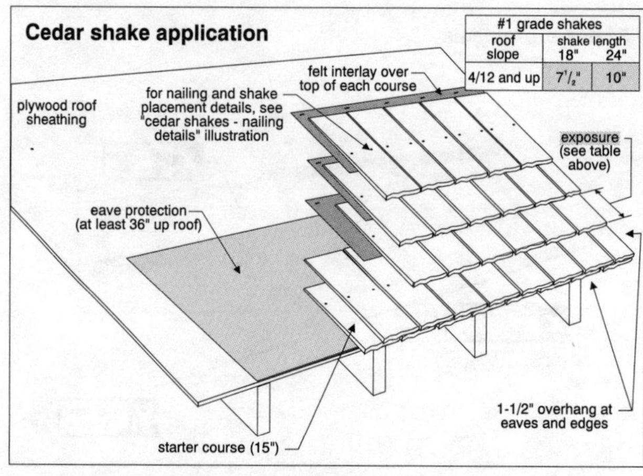

0024

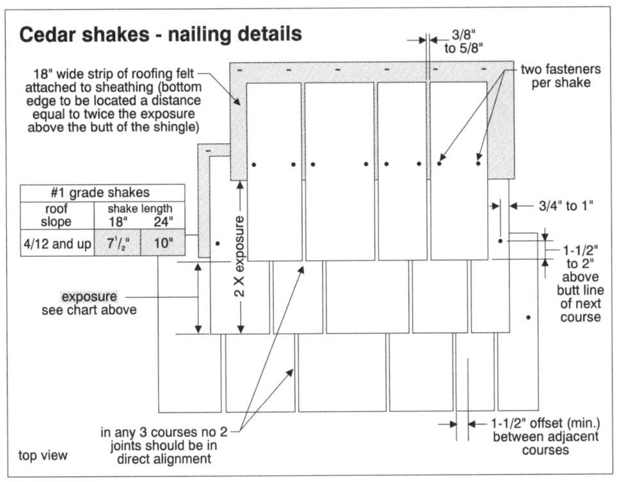

0025

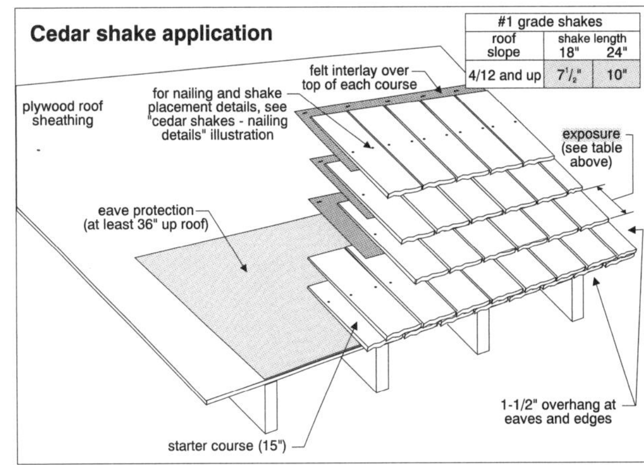

0026

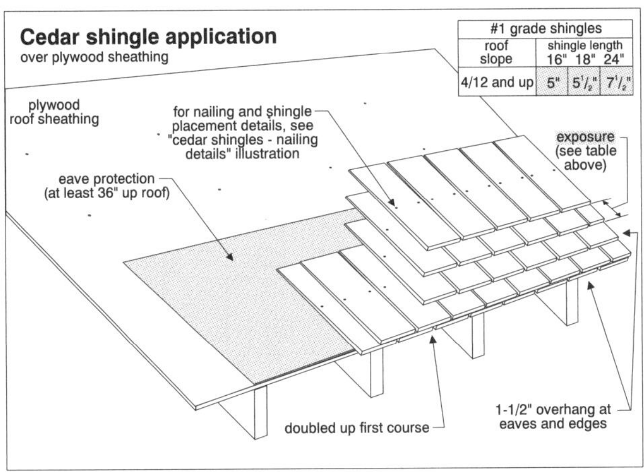

0027

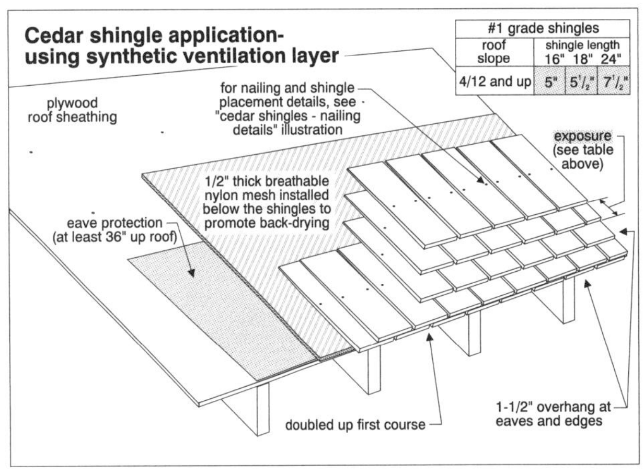

0028

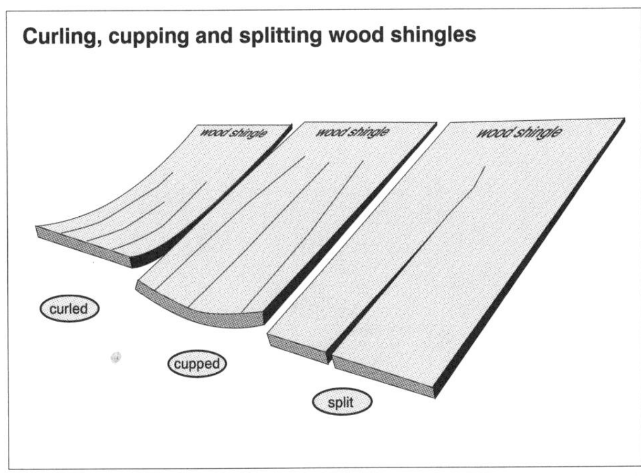

0029

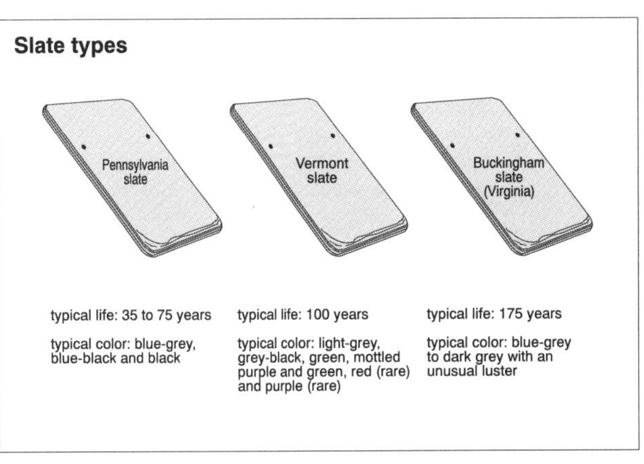

0030

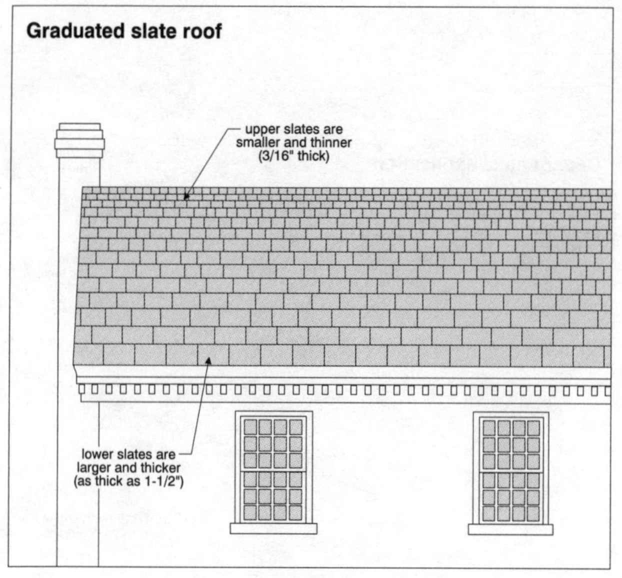

0031

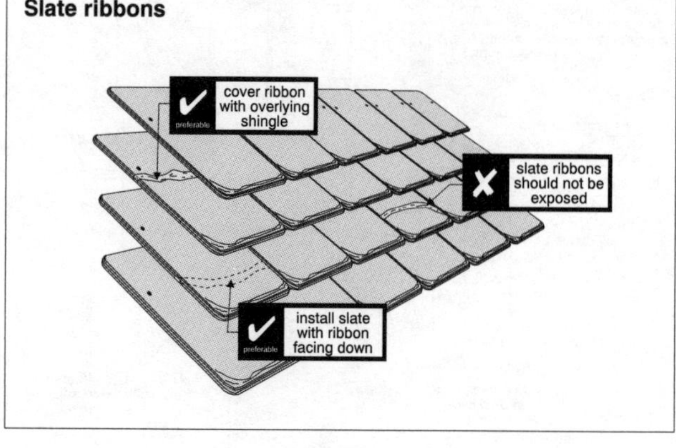

0032

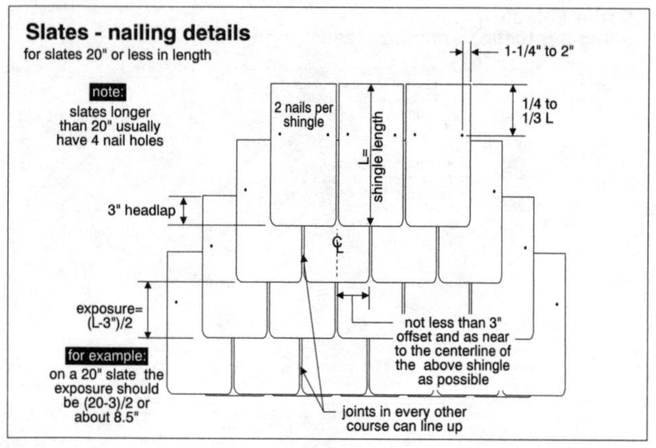

0033

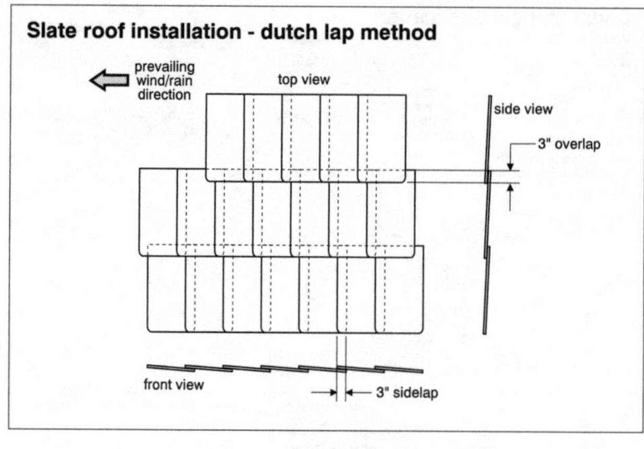

0034

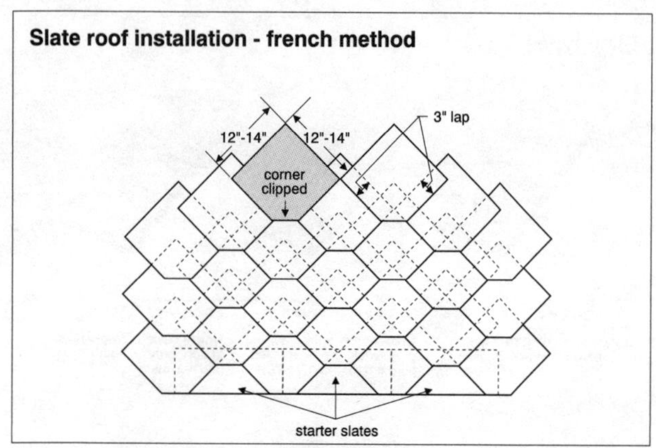

0035

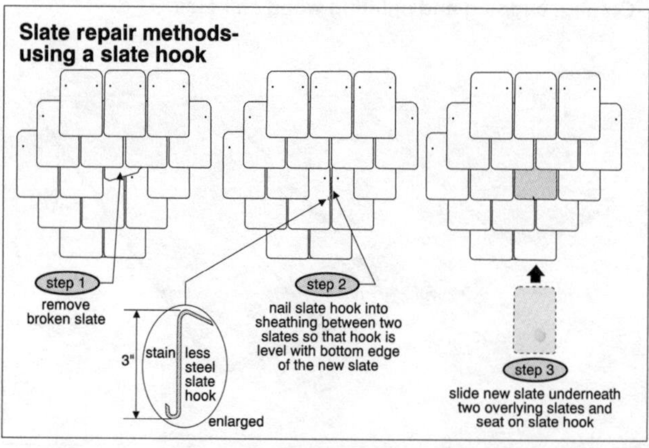

0036

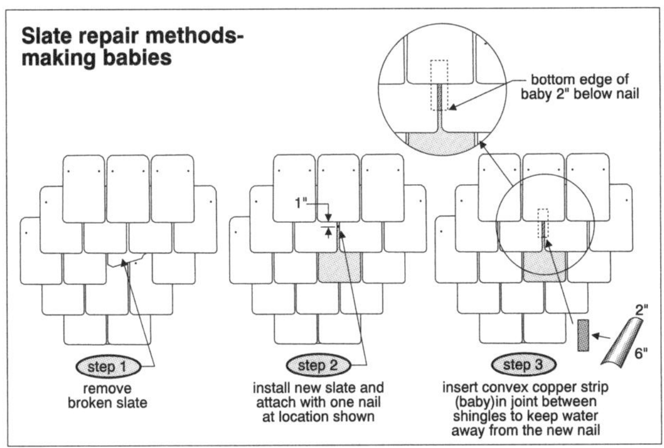

0037

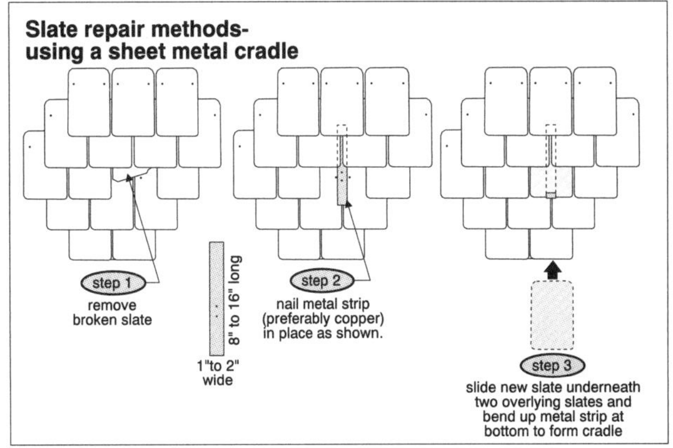

0038

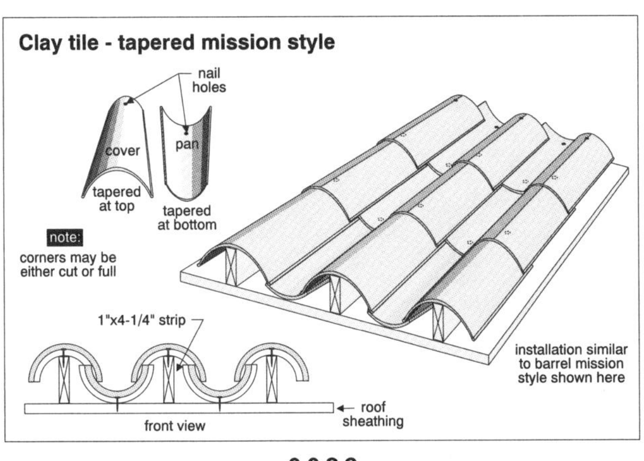

0039

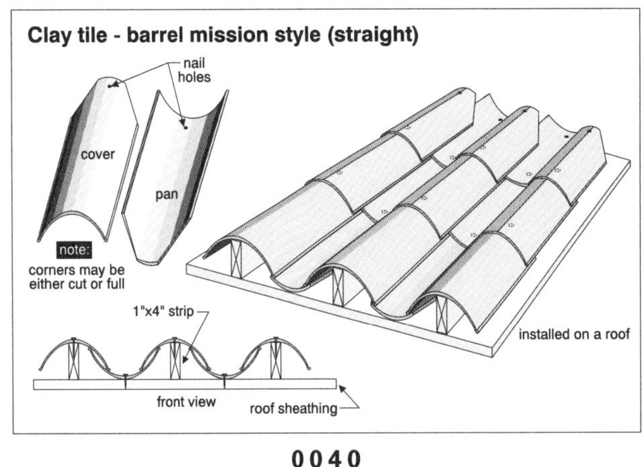

0040

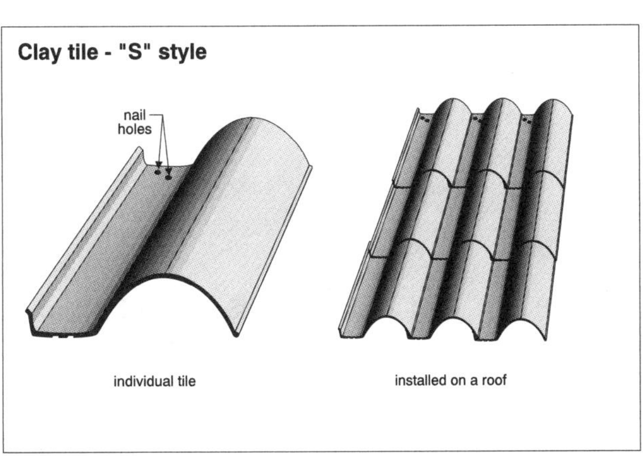

0041

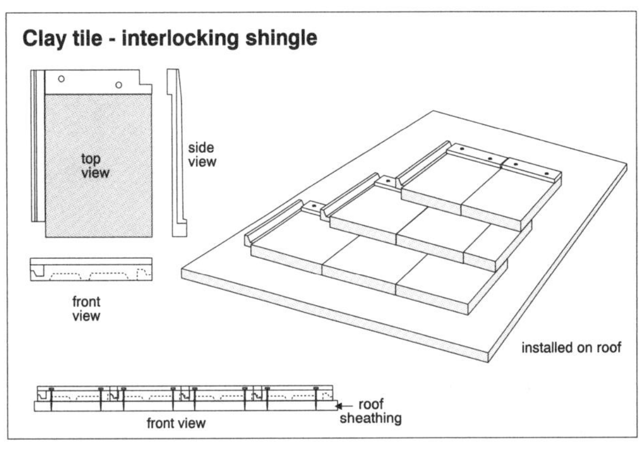

0042

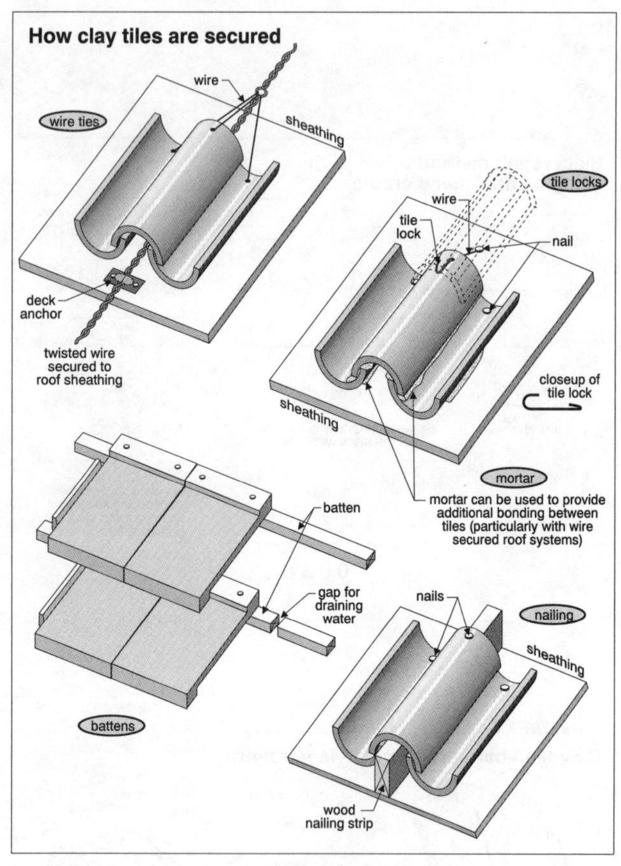

0043

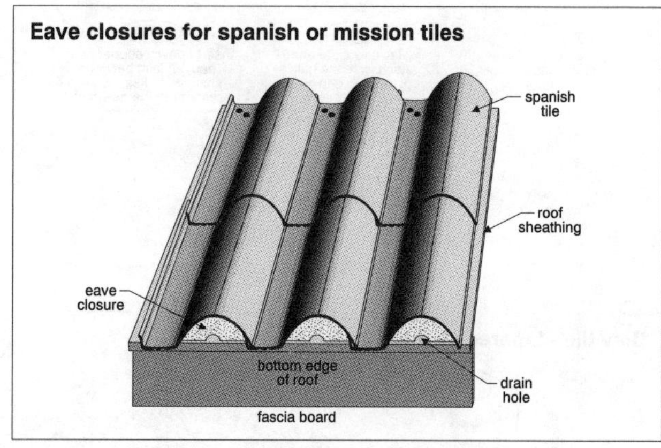

0044

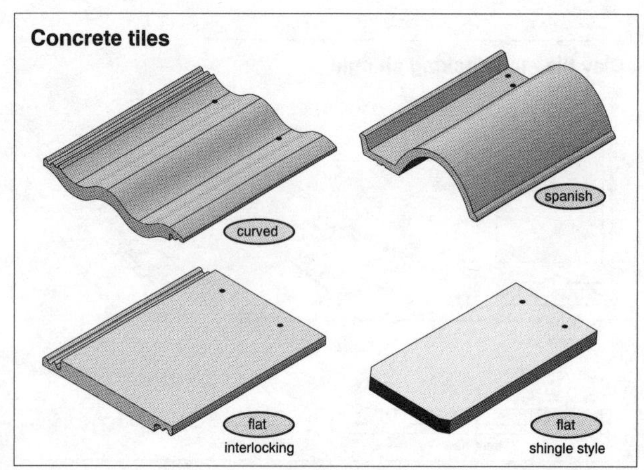

0045

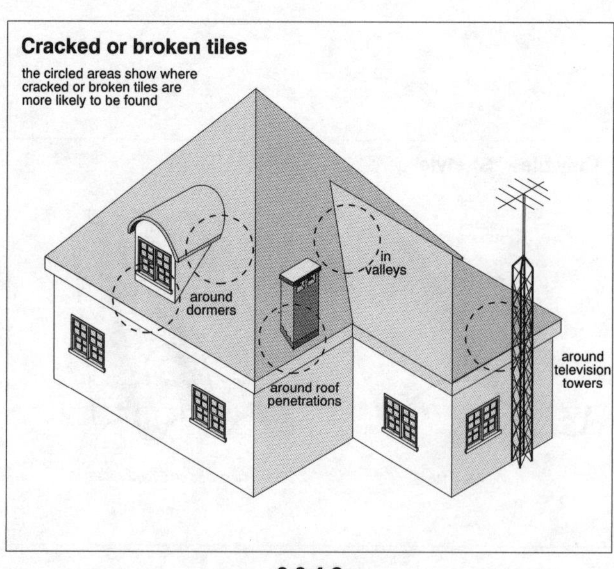

0046

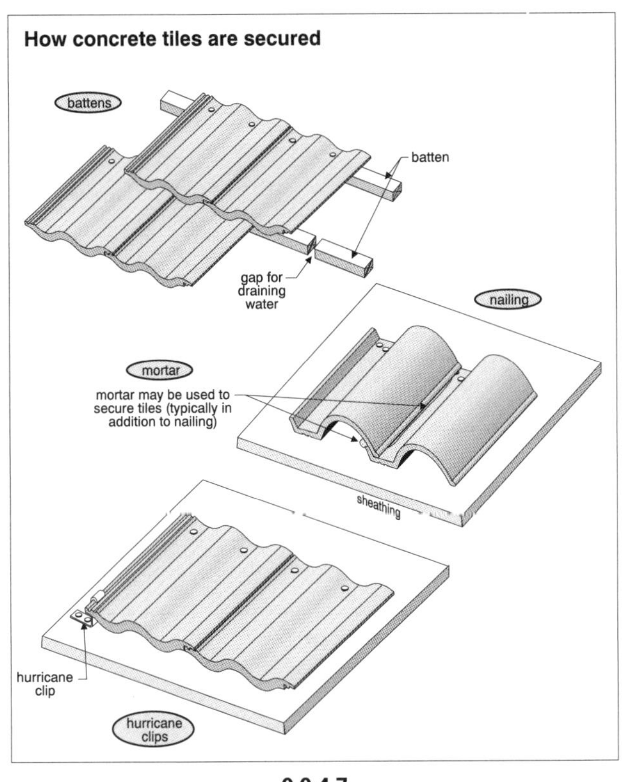

0047

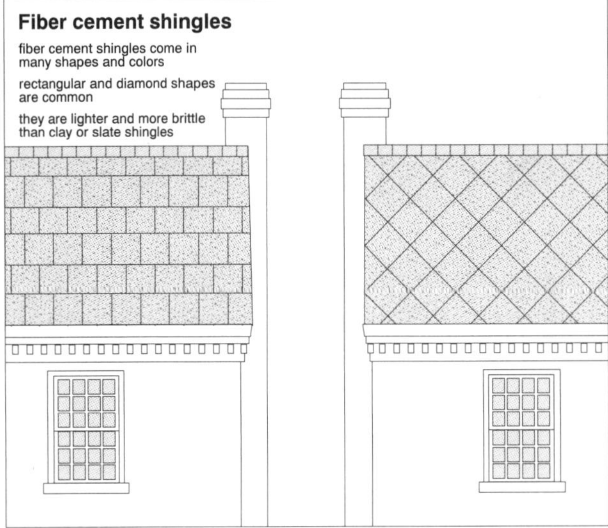

0048

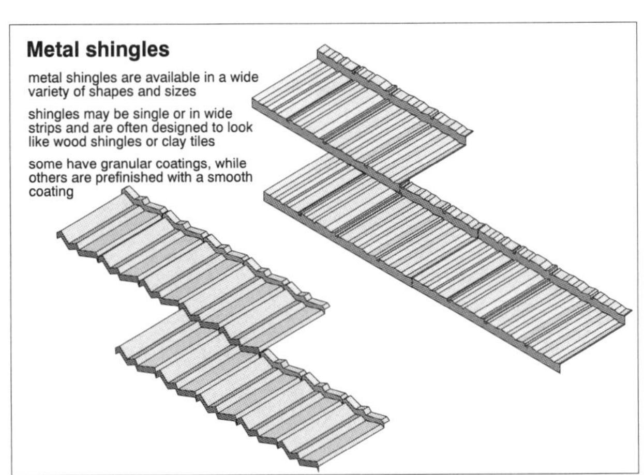

0049

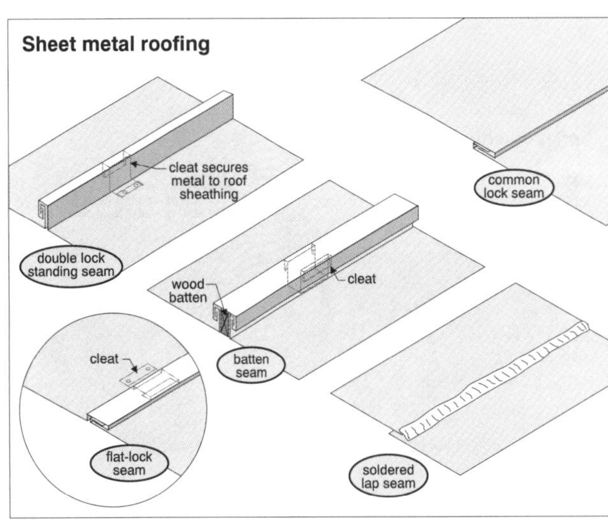

0050

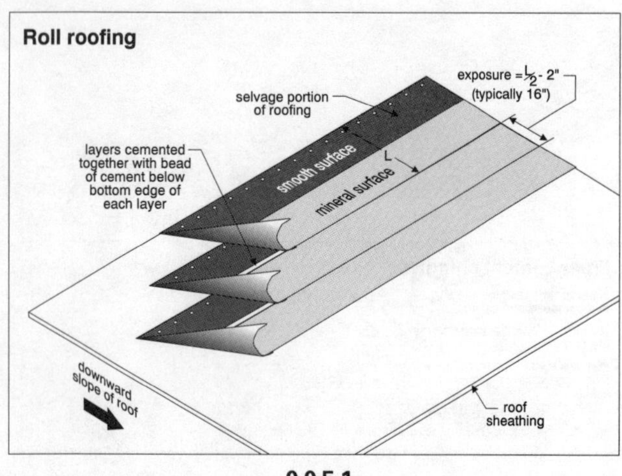

Roll roofing
exposure = L/2 - 2"
(typically 16")
selvage portion
of roofing
layers cemented
together with bead
of cement below
bottom edge of
each layer
smooth surface
mineral surface
L
downward
slope of roof
roof
sheathing

0051

Roll roofing problems
loss of
granular
material
buckling
or wrinkling
fastener
problems
blistering
open
seams

0052

Roof valleys - open and closed
open valley
with a metal
flashing
the valley should
be 4"-6" wide at
the top and
should widen out
1/8" per foot as
you move down
the valley
closed valley
still requires roll
roofing or felt
underneath
this is a closed
cut valley
see following
illustrations for
installation
details

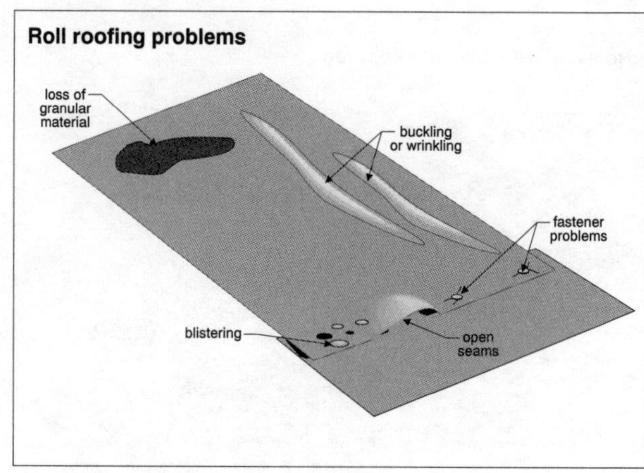

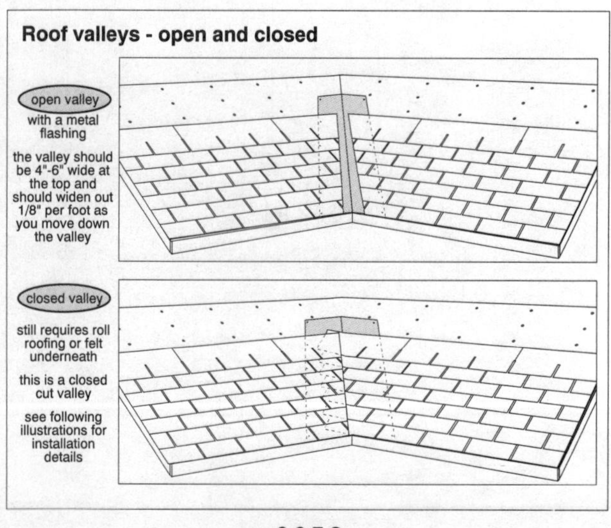

0053

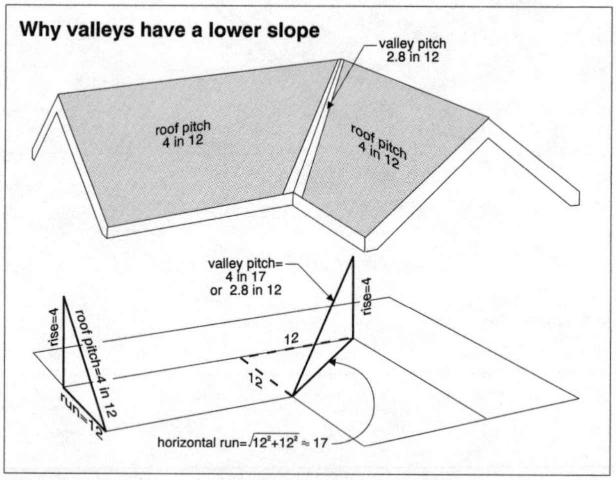

Why valleys have a lower slope
valley pitch
2.8 in 12
roof pitch
4 in 12
roof pitch
4 in 12
valley pitch=
4 in 17
or 2.8 in 12
rise=4
rise=4
roof pitch=4 in 12
run=12
12
12
horizontal run=√(12²+12²) ≈ 17

0054

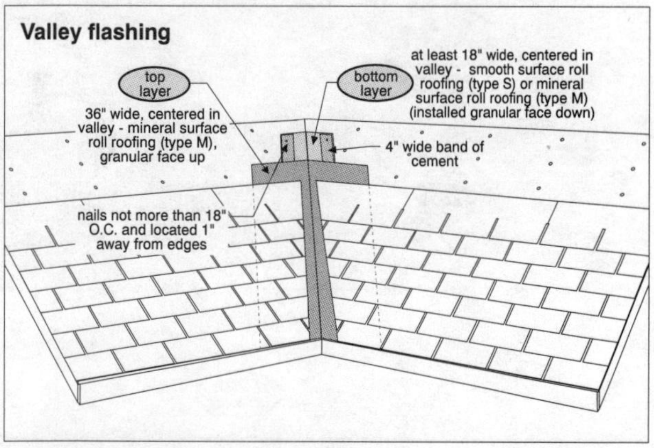

Valley flashing
top
layer
36" wide, centered in
valley - mineral surface
roll roofing (type M),
granular face up
bottom
layer
at least 18" wide, centered in
valley - smooth surface roll
roofing (type S) or mineral
surface roll roofing (type M)
(installed granular face down)
4" wide band of
cement
nails not more than 18"
O.C. and located 1"
away from edges

0055

Valley flashing made of asphalt shingles
open valleys laid with overlapped
individual shingles are likely to leak
this is poor practice

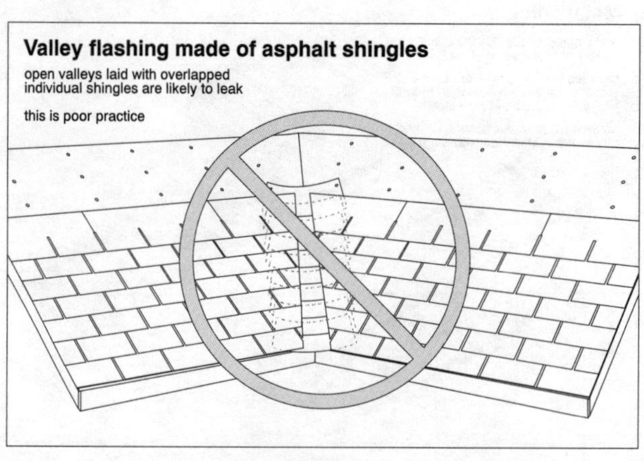

0056

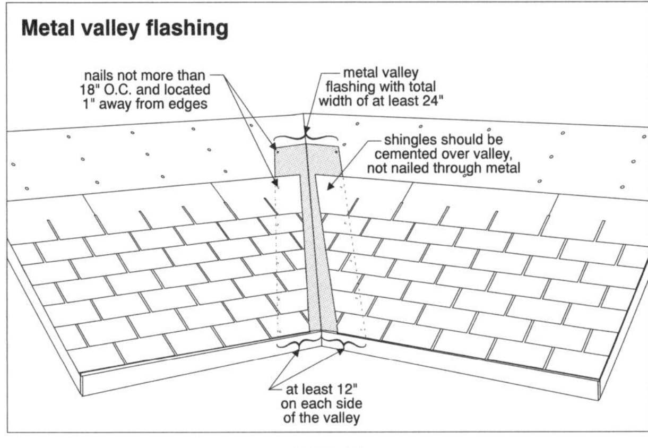

0057

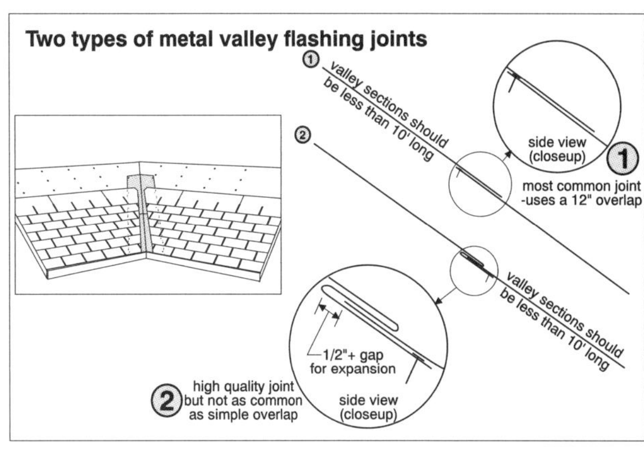

0058

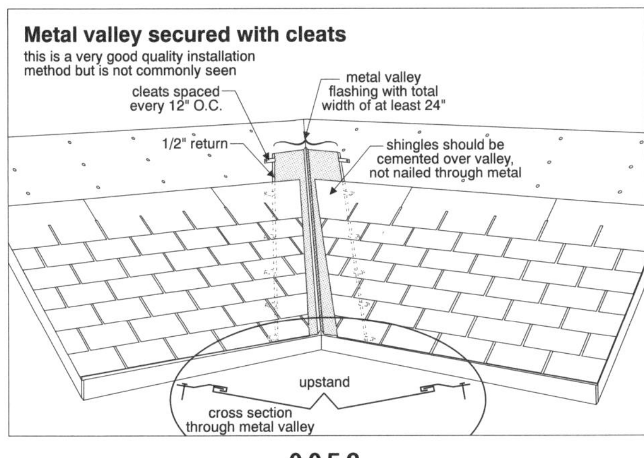

0059

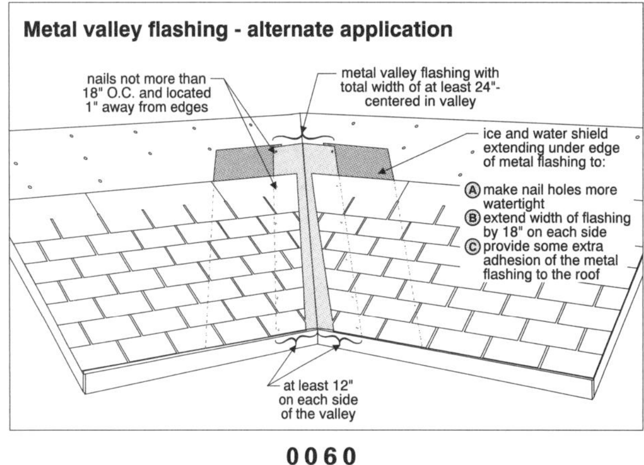

0060

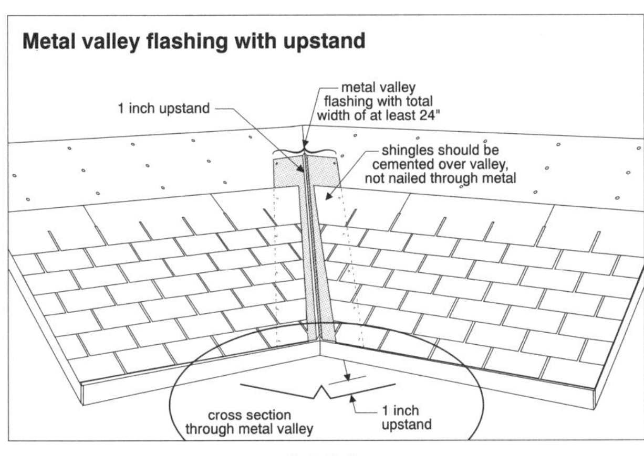

0061

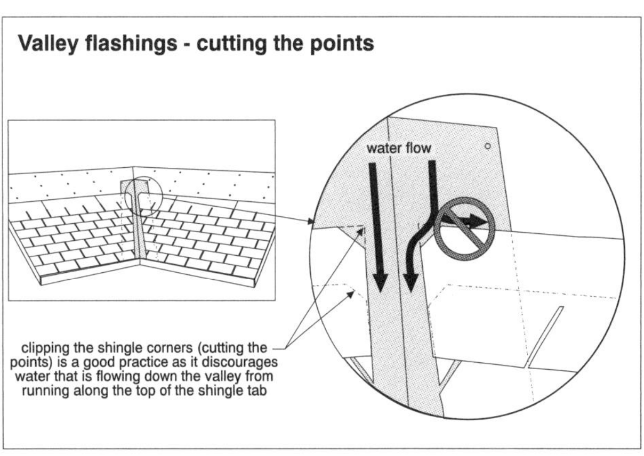

0062

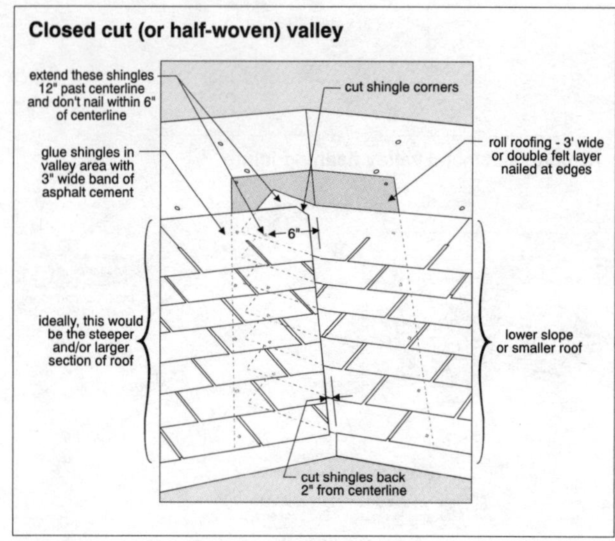

0063

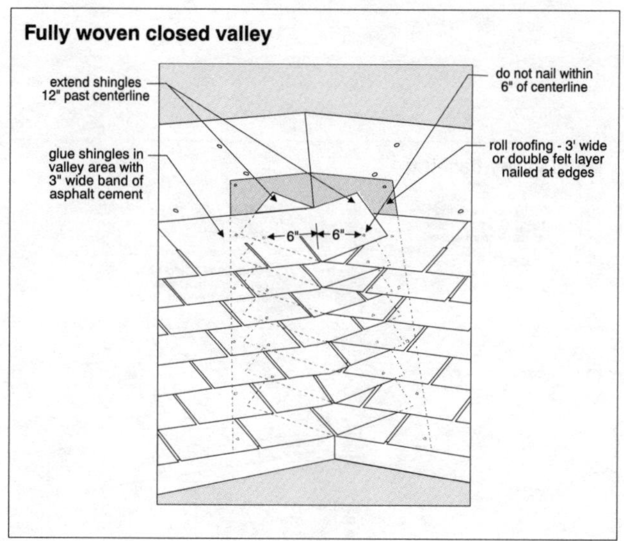

0064

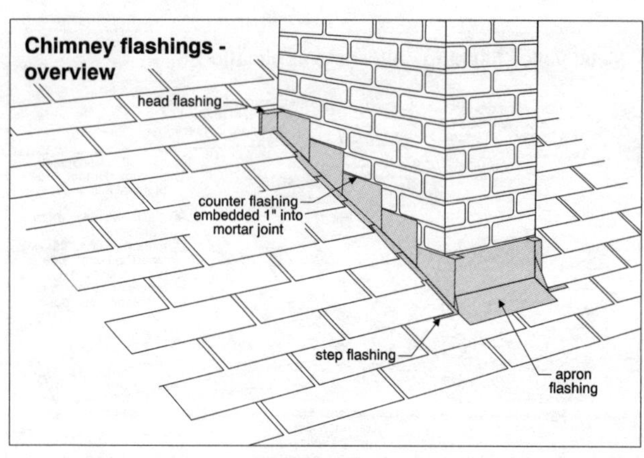

0065

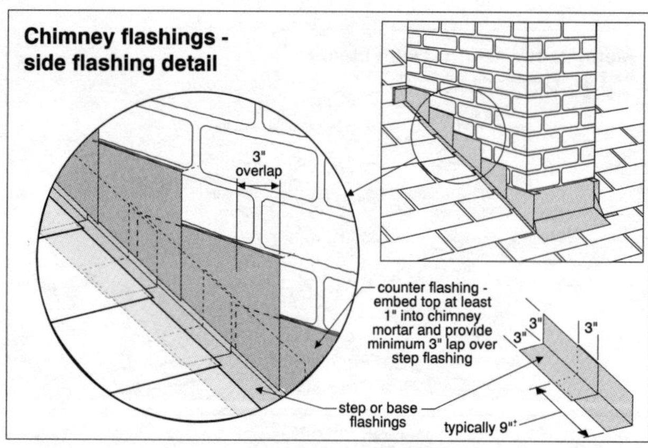

0066

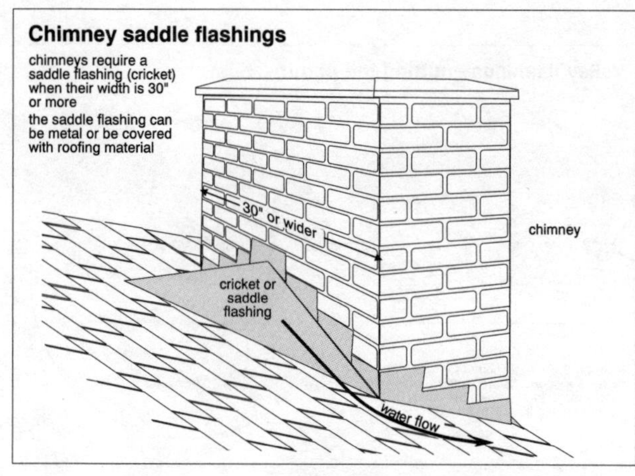

0067

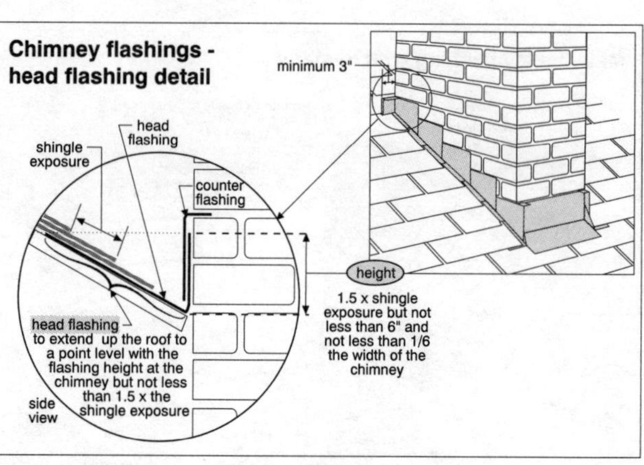

0068

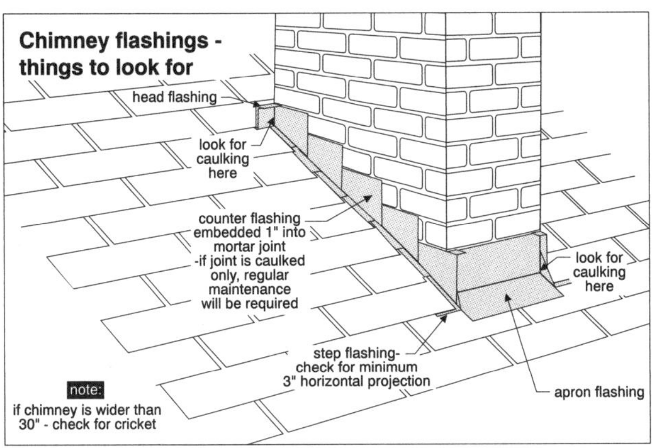

0069

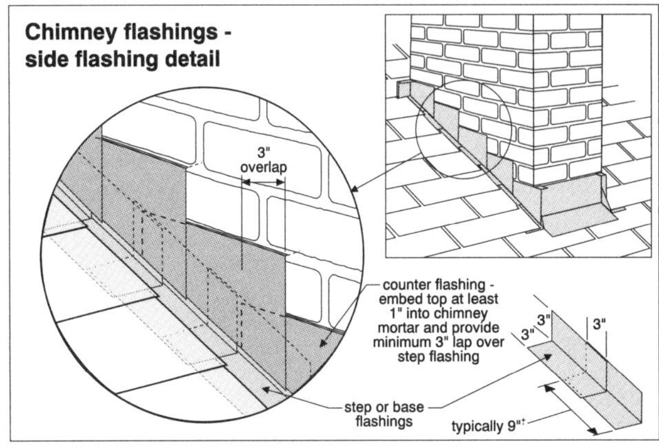

0070

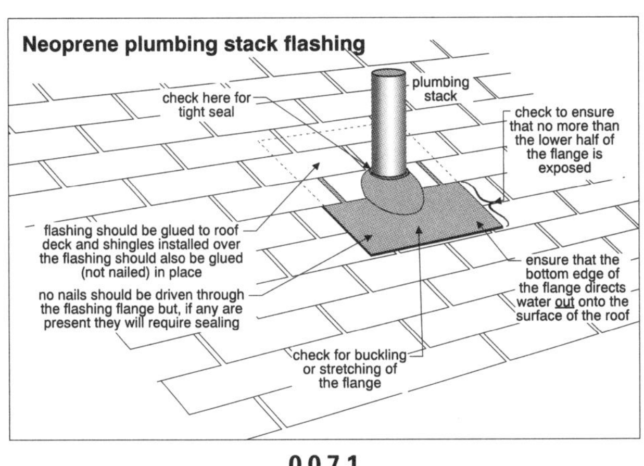

0071

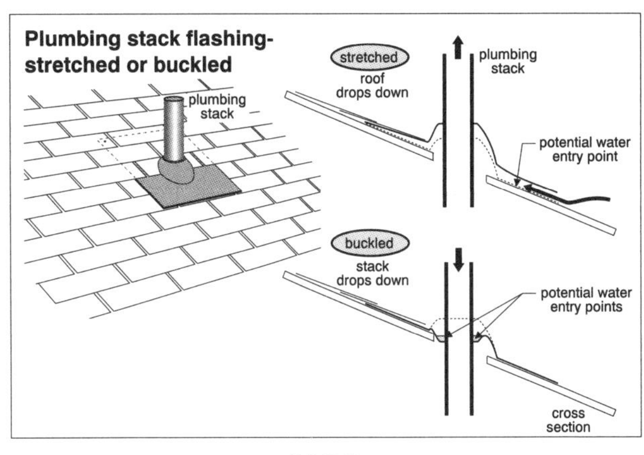

0072

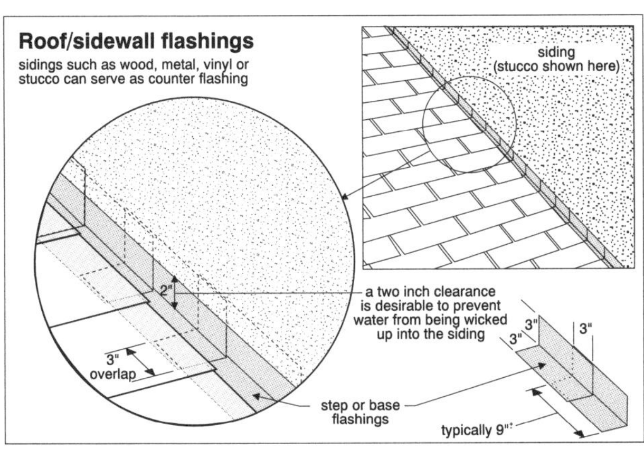

0073

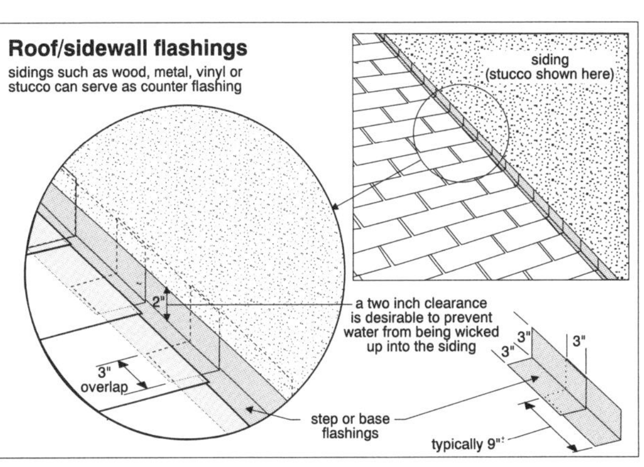

0074

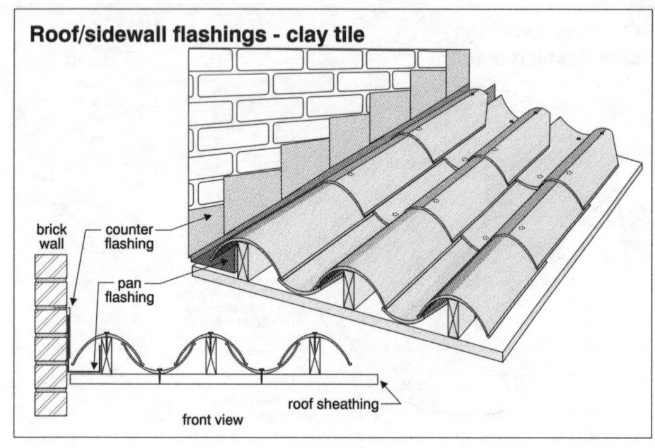

0075

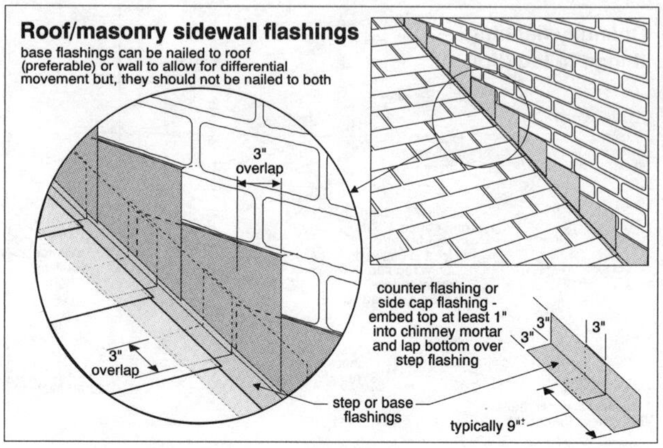

Roof/masonry sidewall flashings

base flashings can be nailed to roof (preferable) or wall to allow for differential movement but, they should not be nailed to both

3" overlap

3" overlap

counter flashing or side cap flashing - embed top at least 1" into chimney mortar and lap bottom over step flashing

3"

3"

3"

step or base flashings

typically 9"±

0076

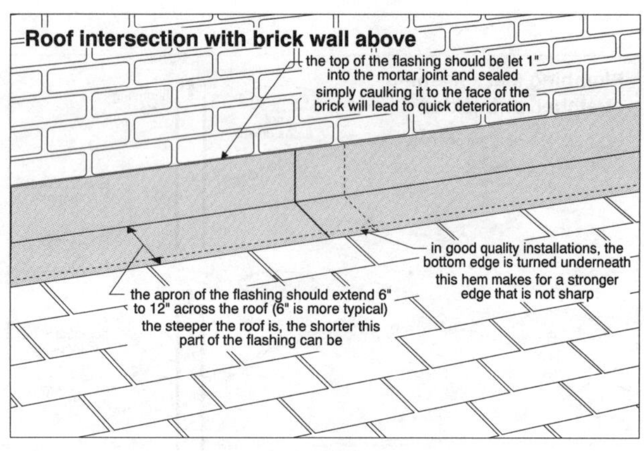

0077

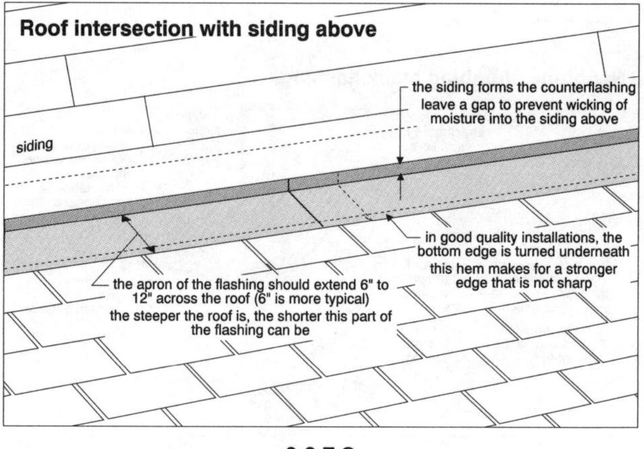

0078

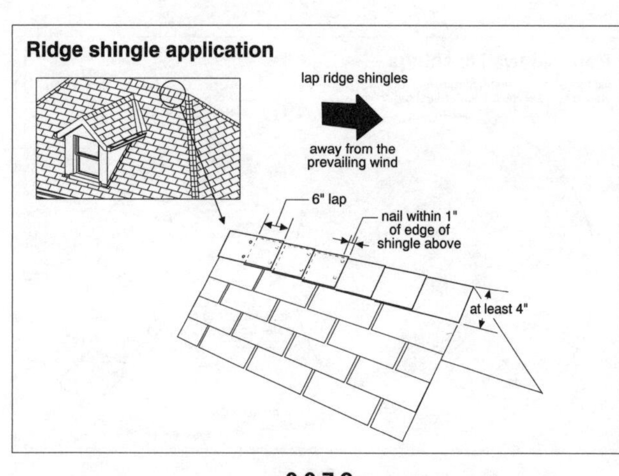

0079

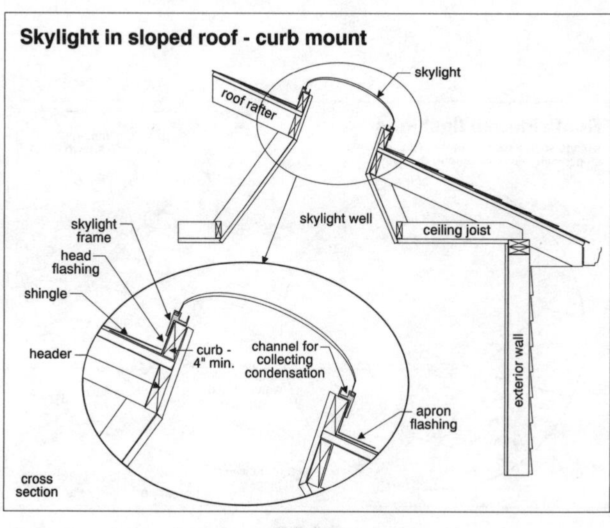

0080

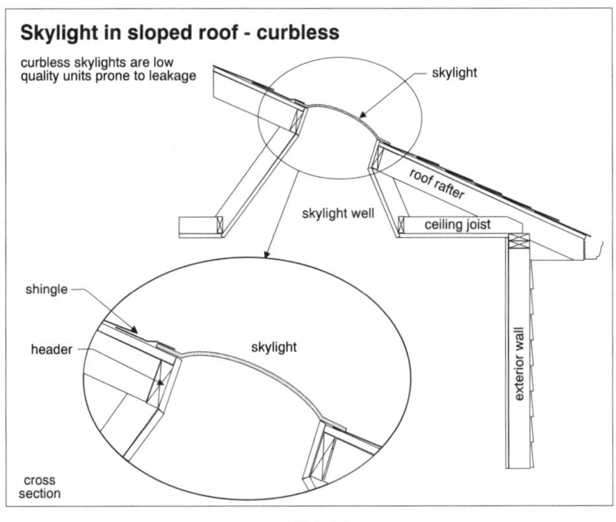

0081

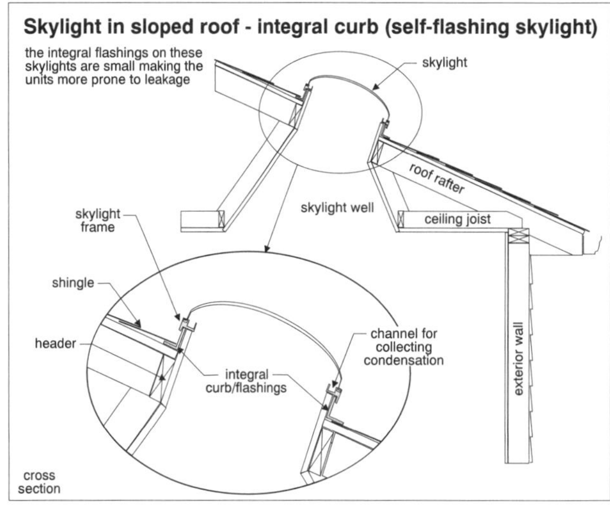

0082

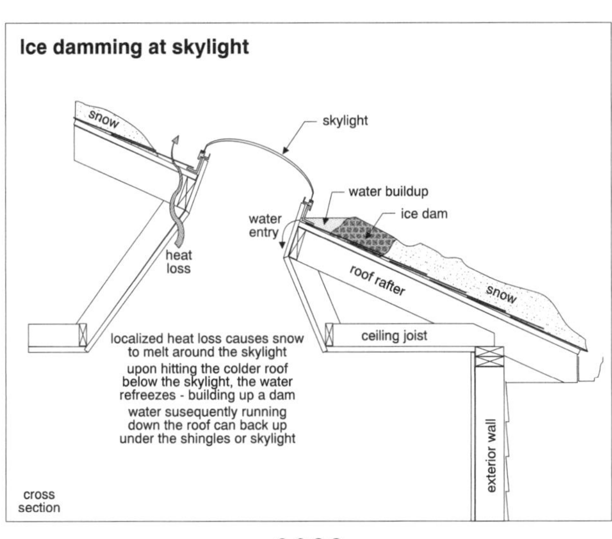

0083

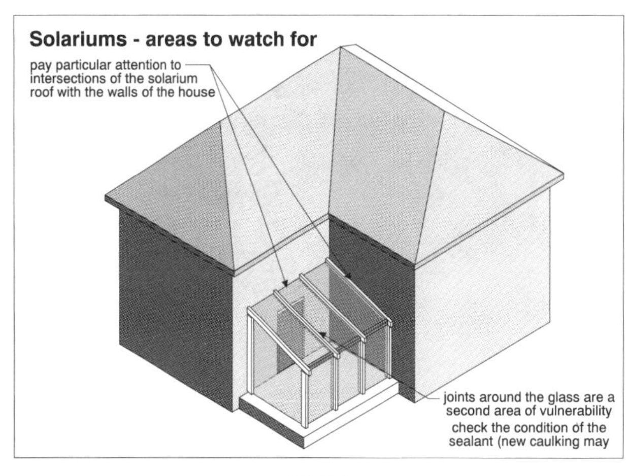

0084

Typical asphalt shingle application - showing metal drip edge

cross-section
shingles
roof sheathing
eave protection
roof rafter
metal drip edge
gutter and spike
fascia board
nails 1" to 1-1/2" from edge of shingle
nails at least 1/2" above cutouts
minimum 2" headlap
fascia board
eave protection (at least 36" up roof)
starter strip nails to be min. 12" O.C.
metal drip edge
starter strip - 12+ inch wide roll roofing or shingles with tabs cut off and self-sealing strips exposed at

0085

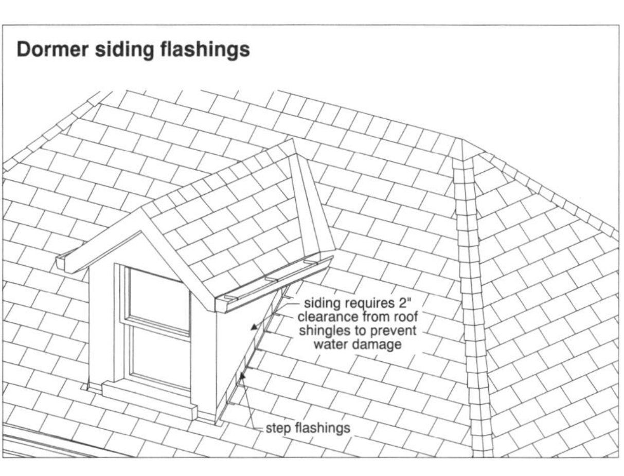

0086

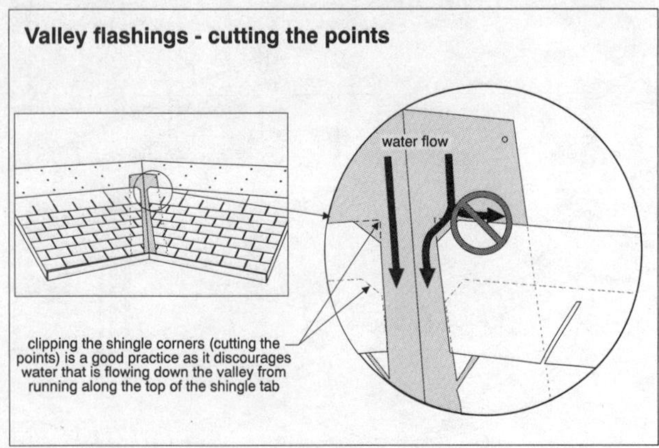

0087

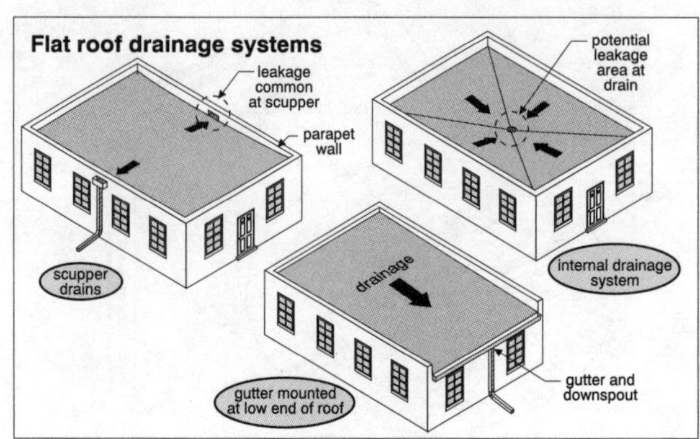

0088

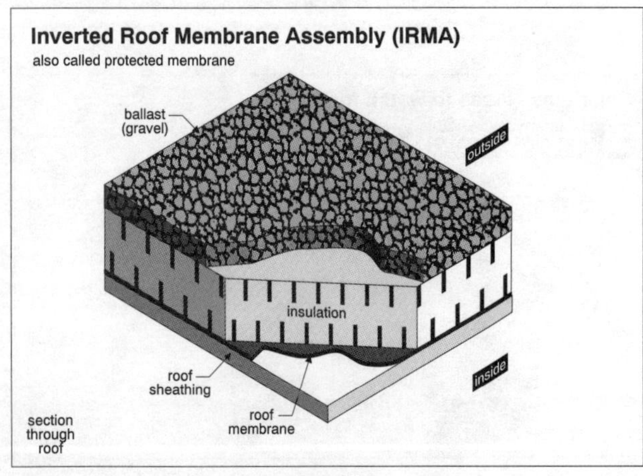

0089

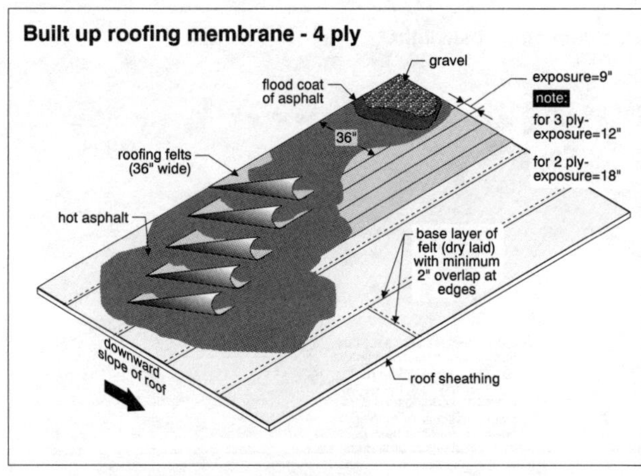

0090

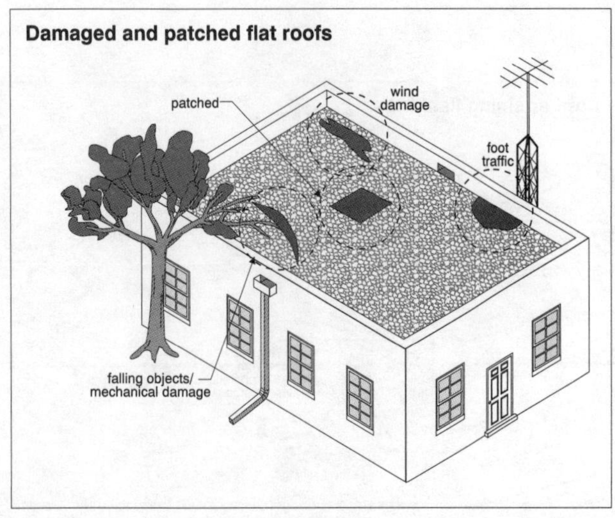

0091

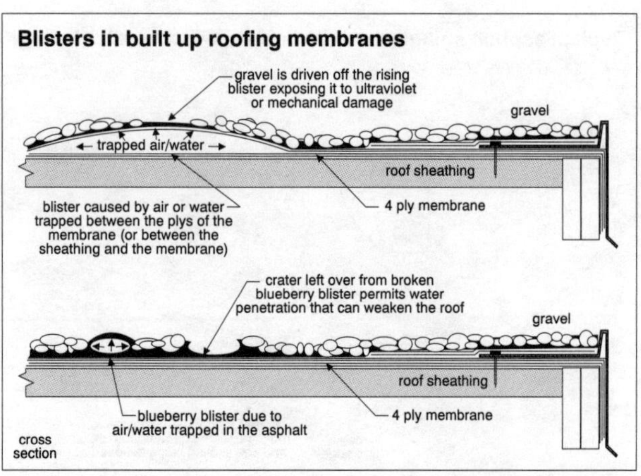

0092

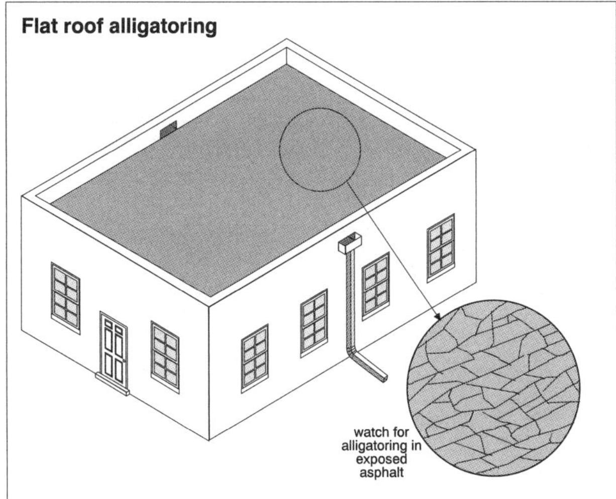

0093

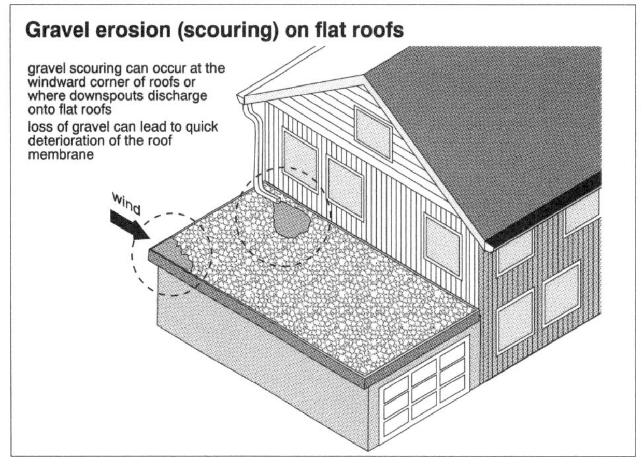

0094

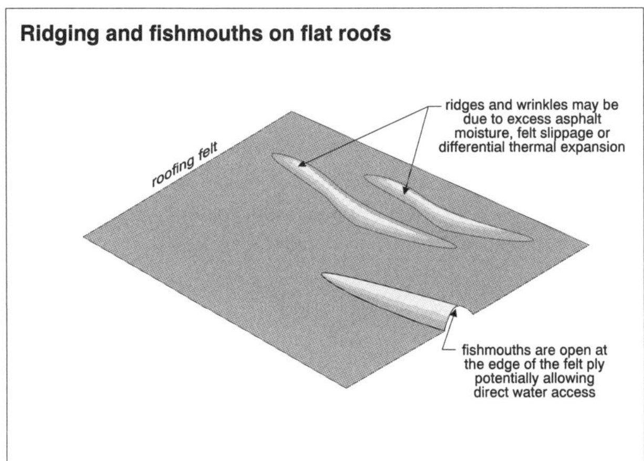

0095

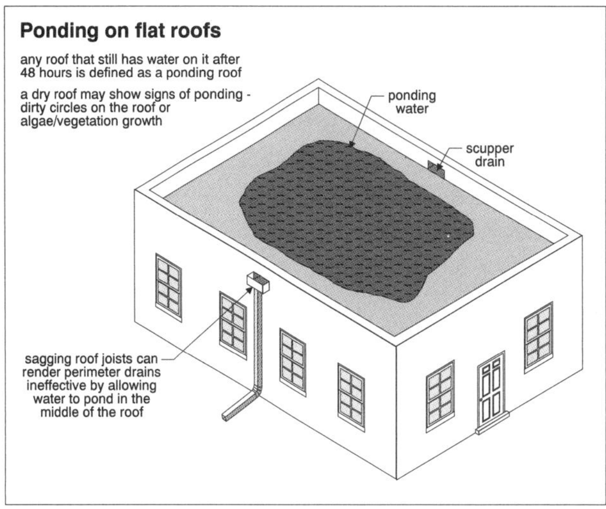

0096

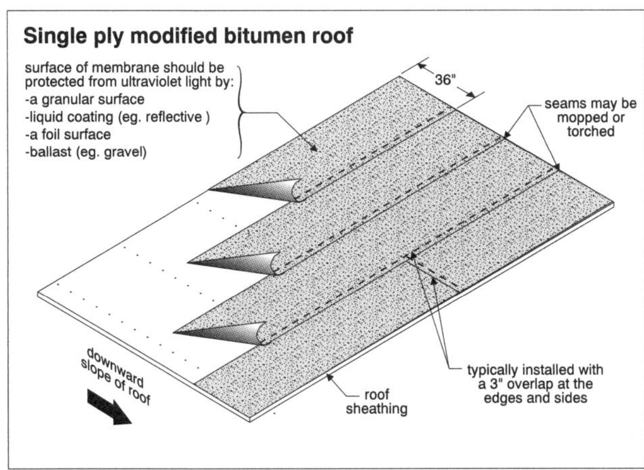

0097

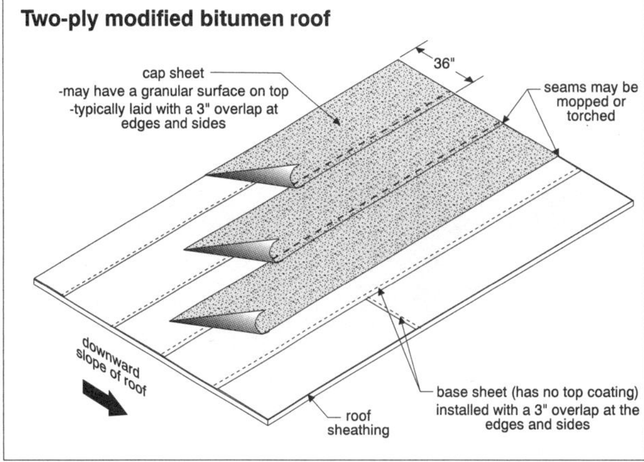

0098

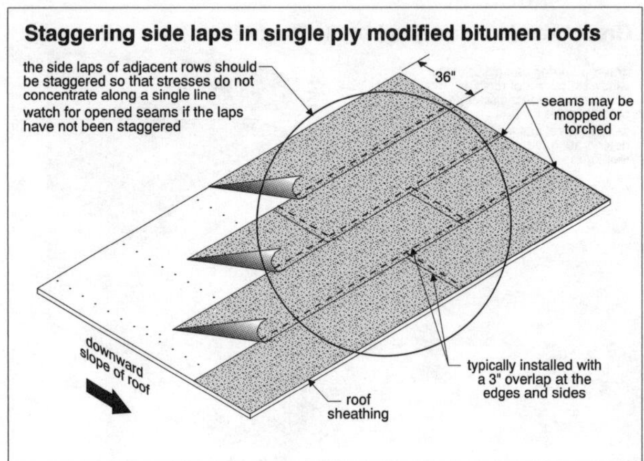

0099

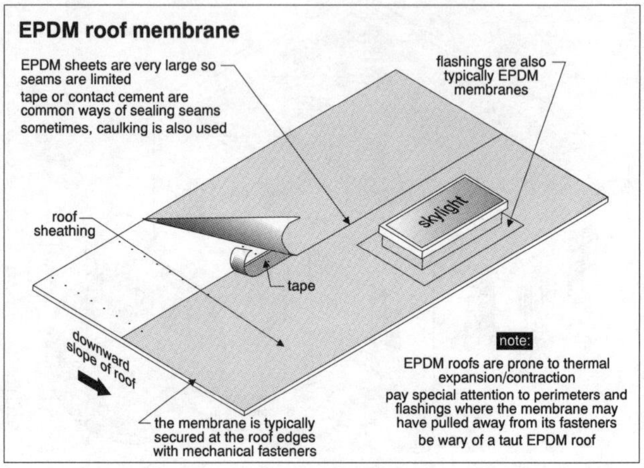

EPDM roof membrane

EPDM sheets are very large so seams are limited
tape or contact cement are common ways of sealing seams
sometimes, caulking is also used

flashings are also typically EPDM membranes

roof sheathing

skylight

tape

downward slope of roof

the membrane is typically secured at the roof edges with mechanical fasteners

note:
EPDM roofs are prone to thermal expansion/contraction
pay special attention to perimeters and flashings where the membrane may have pulled away from its fasteners
be wary of a taut EPDM roof

0100

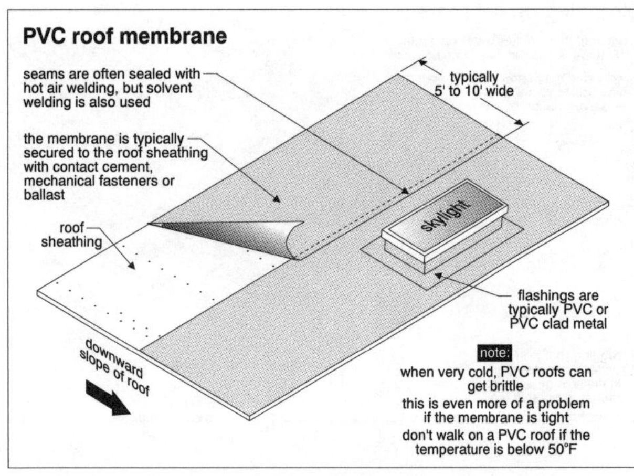

0101

PVC roof problems

shrinkage of the membrane can cause openings at flashings and perimeters as well as movement of roof projections e.g. plumbing stacks

wrinkles

skylight

fishmouth

downward slope of roof

rupture

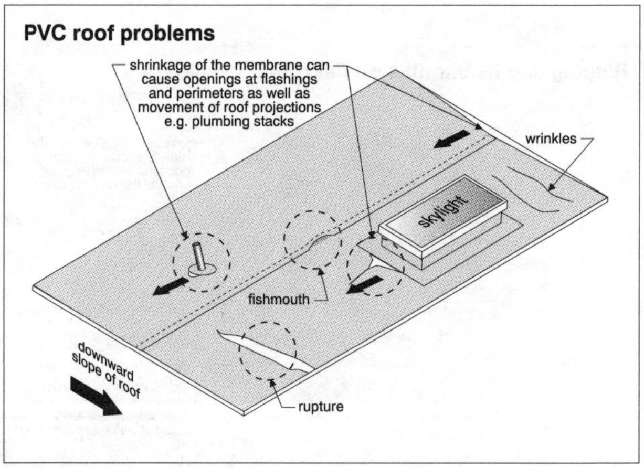

0102

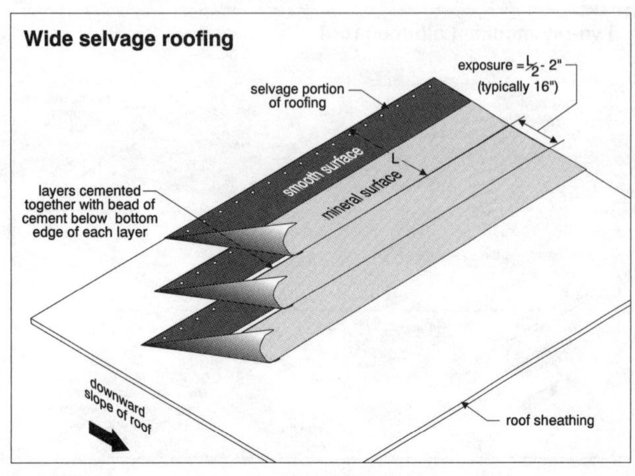

0103

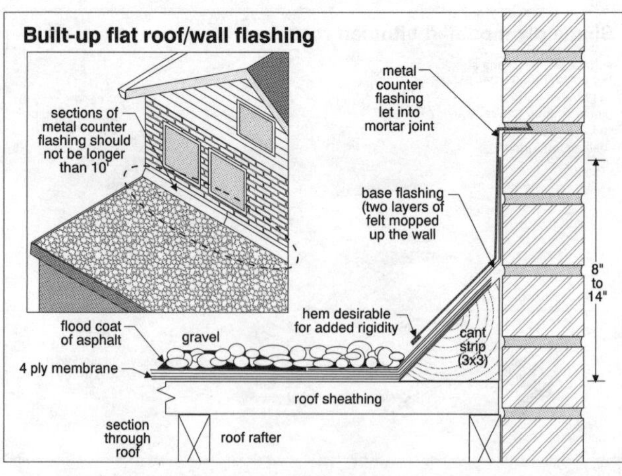

0104

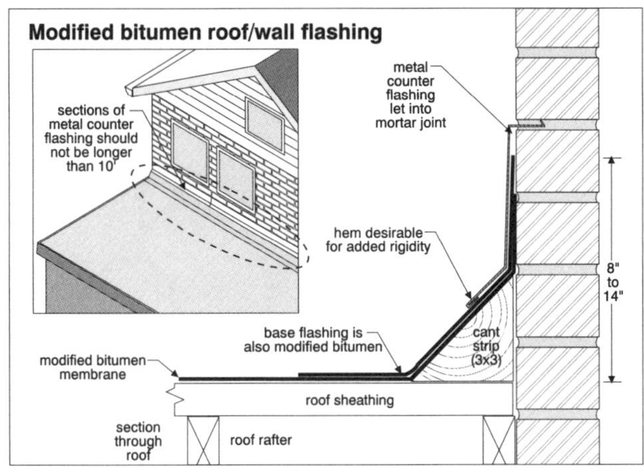

0105

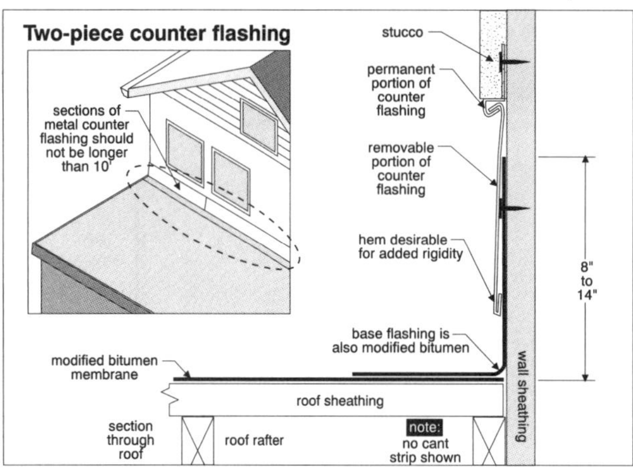

0106

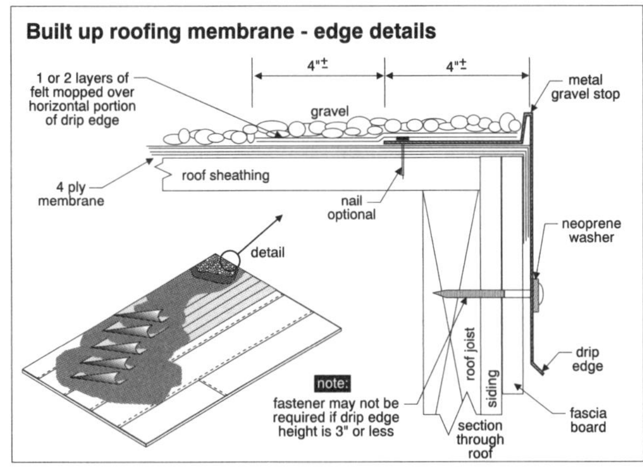

0107

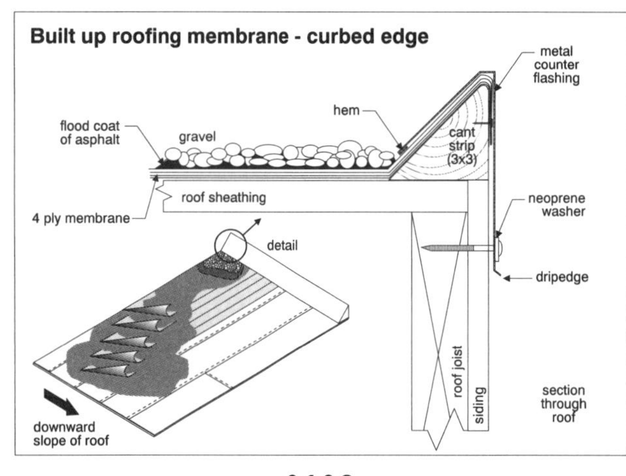

0108

Built-up flat roof/wall flashing

sections of metal counter flashing should not be longer than 10'

metal counter flashing let into mortar joint

base flashing (two layers of felt mopped up the wall

8" to 14"

hem desirable for added rigidity

flood coat of asphalt

gravel

cant strip (3x3)

4 ply membrane

roof sheathing

section through roof

roof rafter

0109

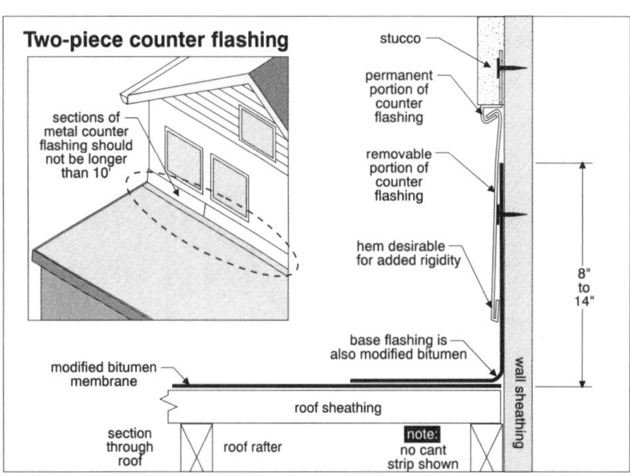

0110

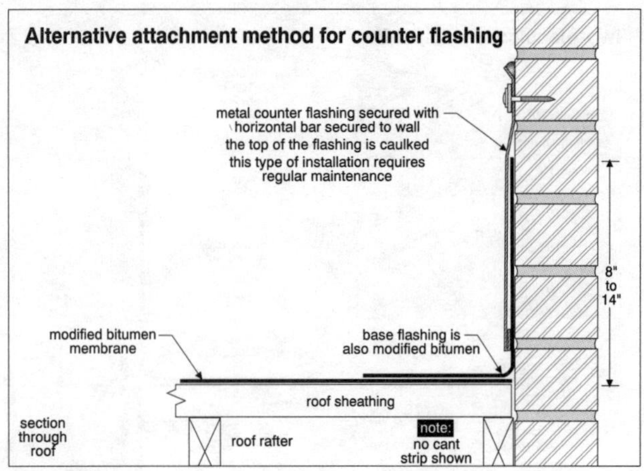

0111

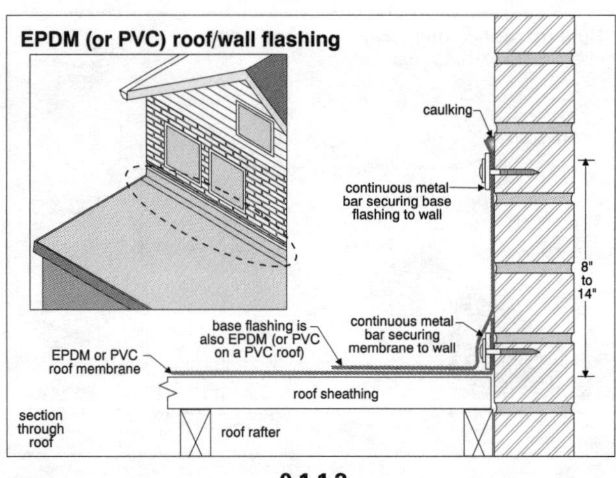

0113

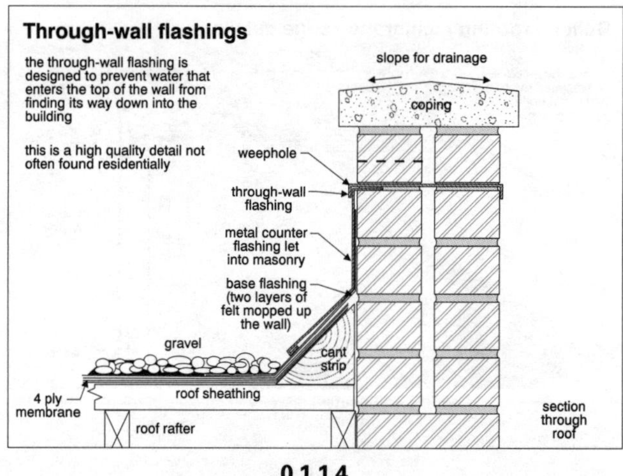

0112

0114

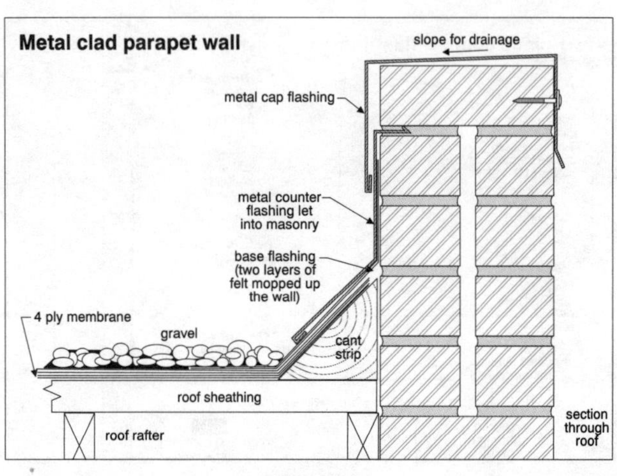

0115

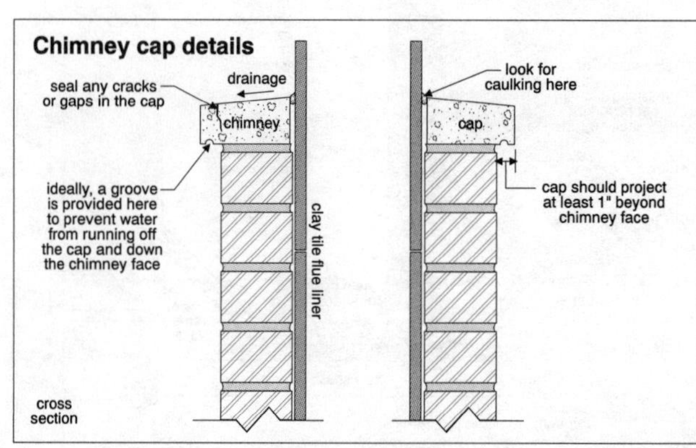

0116

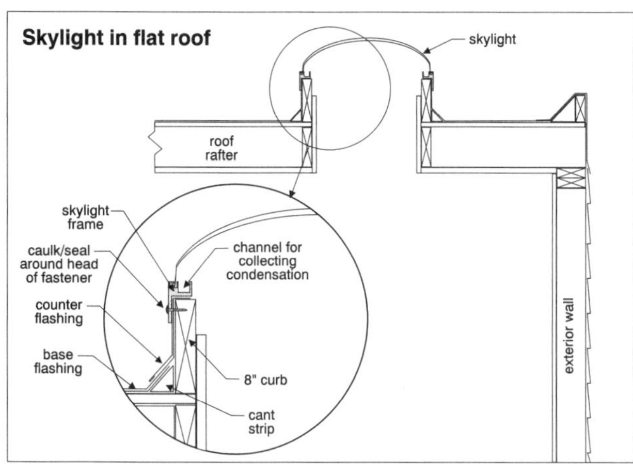

0117

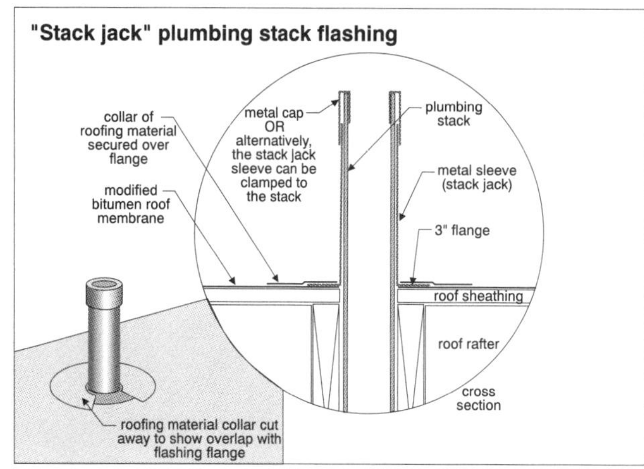

0118

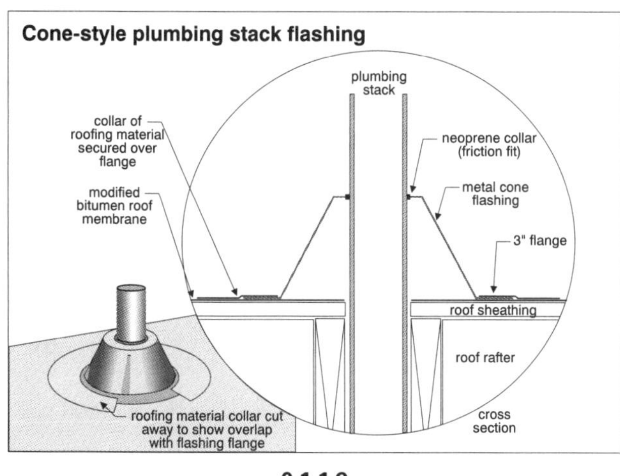

0119

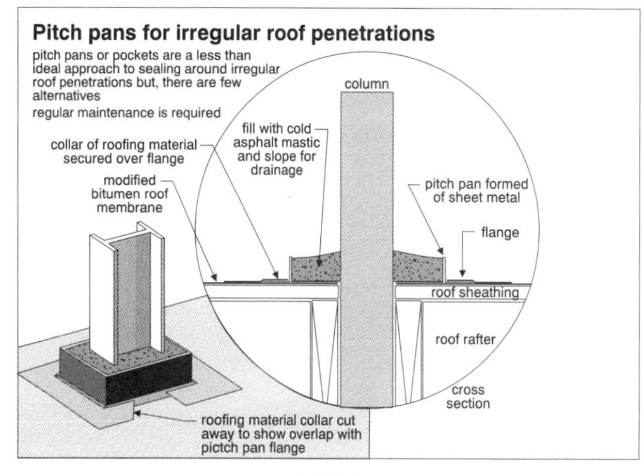

0120

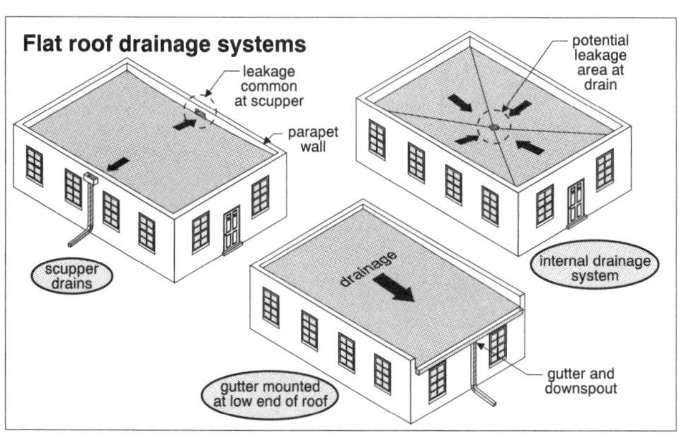

0121

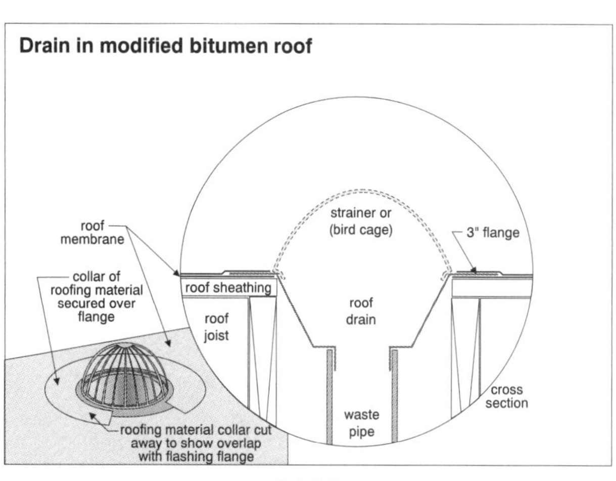

0122

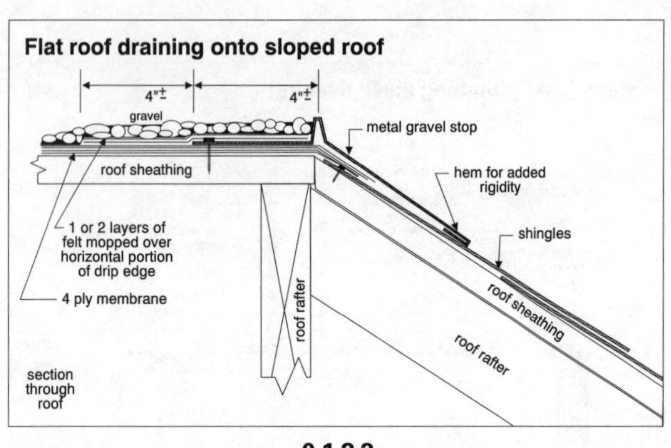
Flat roof draining onto sloped roof
4"±
4"±
gravel
metal gravel stop
roof sheathing
hem for added rigidity
1 or 2 layers of felt mopped over horizontal portion of drip edge
shingles
4 ply membrane
roof rafter
roof sheathing
roof rafter
section through roof

0123

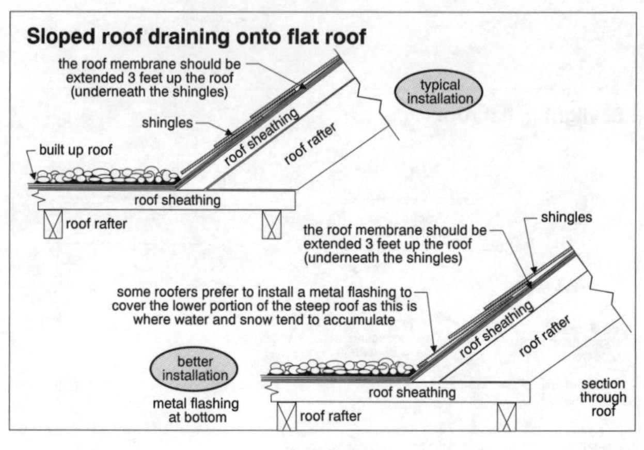
Sloped roof draining onto flat roof
the roof membrane should be extended 3 feet up the roof (underneath the shingles)
typical installation
shingles
roof sheathing
roof rafter
built up roof
roof sheathing
roof rafter
the roof membrane should be extended 3 feet up the roof (underneath the shingles)
shingles
some roofers prefer to install a metal flashing to cover the lower portion of the steep roof as this is where water and snow tend to accumulate
roof sheathing
roof rafter
better installation
roof sheathing
section through roof
metal flashing at bottom
roof rafter

0124

CHAPTER 2

FOOTINGS AND FOUNDATIONS

DESCRIPTION

35 ...... 0200 Overview of house structure
35 ...... 0201 Soil pressure on foundation walls
35 ...... 0202 Evidence of frost heaving
35 ...... 0203 Bearing strength of soils
35 ...... 0204 Two situations where frost heaving is very unlikely
35 ...... 0205 Frost heaving of unheated houses
36 ...... 0206 Slab-on-grade – floating slab
36 ...... 0207 Slab-on-grade – supported slab
36 ...... 0208 Slab-on-grade – monolithic slab
36 ...... 0209 Spread footings and pad footings
36 ...... 0210 Pile foundations
36 ...... 0211 Pier foundations
37 ...... 0212 Brick foundation with masonry exterior walls
37 ...... 0213 Stone foundation with masonry exterior walls
37 ...... 0214 Stone foundation with wood frame exterior walls
37 ...... 0215 Raft and mat foundations
37 ...... 0216 Preserved wood foundations
37 ...... 0217 Control joints in foundation walls
38 ...... 0218 Poured concrete foundation with wood frame exerior walls
38 ...... 0219 Concrete block foundation with masonry exterior walls
38 ...... 0220 Insulated concrete forms

PROBLEMS

38 ...... 0221 Types of settlement
38 ...... 0222 Differential settlement caused by variable soil types
38 ...... 0223 Ravine lots
39 .... 0224 Building settlement due to cut and fill excavation
39 ...... 0225 Analyzing crack size
39 ...... 0226 Frost heaving of footings
39 ...... 0227 Crack shapes
39 ...... 0228 Mud jacking to stabilize a settled foundation
39 ...... 0229 Using a helical anchor to stabilize a settled foundation
40 ...... 0230 Using piles to stabilize a settled foundation
40 ...... 0231 Using rods and channels to stabilize a settled house
40 ...... 0232 Step footings on sloped lots
40 ...... 0233 Lowering basement floors – bench footing
40 ...... 0234 Lowering basement floors – underpinning
40 ...... 0235 Underpinning – timing of concrete pours
41 ...... 0236 Rotational settlement cracks
41 ...... 0237 Cracking – common locations
41 ...... 0238 Frost heaving of footings
41 ...... 0239 Sources of heaving
41 ...... 0240 Evidence of frost heaving
41 ...... 0241 Exterior basement stairwell – side view
42....... 0242 Insulated exterior basement stairwell – side view
42 ...... 0243 Frost heaving of unheated houses
42 ...... 0244 Effects of adfreezing
42 ...... 0245 Adfreezing and deck piers
42 ...... 0246 Heaving of deck piers
42 ...... 0247 Foundation movement associated with horizontal cracks
43 ...... 0248 Floors provide lateral support for foundations
43 ...... 0249 Horizontal cracks and movement – 3 different possibilities
43 ...... 0250 Beam punching through foundation wall
43 ...... 0251 Excess brick overhang resulting from bowing foundation
43 ...... 0252 Lateral support for foundation walls
43 ...... 0253 Vertical foundation cracks
44 ...... 0254 Determining height of backfill
44 ...... 0255 How driveways can contribute to foundation cracking
44 ...... 0256 Foundation cracks related to tree roots
44 ...... 0257 Backfill-related foundation cracks
44 ...... 0258 Basement floors provide lateral support
44 ...... 0259 Foundation repairs – adding a buttress
45 ...... 0260 Foundation repairs – adding a pilaster
45 ...... 0261 Foundation repairs – reinforcing from inside
45 ...... 0262 Foundation repairs – using steel tie-backs
45 ...... 0263 Foundation repairs – adding an interior wall
45.......... 0264 Foundation repairs – adding a sister wall outside
45 ...... 0265 Spalling of poured concrete foundations
46 ...... 0266 The 1/3 rule for wall stability
46 ...... 0267 Piers – things to watch for
46 ...... 0268 Masonry piers – hollow channels must be vertical
46 ...... 0269 Wooden piers – things to look for
46 ...... 0270 Pilaster pulling away from wall

CHAPTER 2

46..... 0271 Cold joints in poured concrete foundations
47..... 0272 Honeycombing in poured concrete foundations
47..... 0273 Foundation wall too short (soil level too high)
47..... 0274 Lateral support for foundation walls

FLOORS

INTRODUCTION

47..... 0275 Floors provide lateral support for foundations
47..... 0276 Allowable floor deflections
47..... 0277 Distribution of floor loads
48..... 0278 Air gaps around ends of wooden beams
48..... 0279 Nails are good in shear but poor in tension

SILLS

48..... 0280 Brick veneer wall
48..... 0281 Sill anchors
48..... 0282 Sills should be above grade
48..... 0283 Mud sills
49..... 0284 Sill anchor spacing
49..... 0285 Gaps under sills
49..... 0286 Sill crushing

COLUMNS

49..... 0287 Column types
49..... 0288 Reasons for column settling
49..... 0289 Column crushing
50..... 0290 The 1/3 rule for column stability
50..... 0291 Column sizes
50..... 0292 Column buckling
50..... 0293 Column connections
50..... 0294 Rising damp in masonry columns

BEAMS

50..... 0295 Beams – shown in relation to house structure
51..... 0296 Stresses in beams
51..... 0297 Load transfer
51..... 0298 Mounting joists onto steel beams
51..... 0299 Continuous beams are stiffer than simply spanned beams
51..... 0300 Sight along beams to check for sag
51..... 0301 Support for beam ends
52..... 0302 Air gaps around ends of wooden beams
52..... 0303 Rotated or twisted beams
52..... 0304 Notches or holes not allowed in beams
52..... 0305 Nailing of built-up wooden beams
52..... 0306 Bolting of built-up wooden beams
52..... 0307 Beam bearing – simple versus continuous beams
53..... 0308 Column connections
53..... 0309 Examples of weak joist/beam connections
53..... 0310 Watch for insufficient nails in joist hangers
53..... 0311 Lateral support for steel beams
53..... 0312 Lateral support for wooden beams
53..... 0313 Concentrated loads – removing or altering walls

JOISTS

54..... 0314 Different types of floor joists
54..... 0315 Lateral support for masonry walls
54..... 0316 Bowing of masonry walls
54..... 0317 Fire cut joists
55..... 0318 Joist installation – crown up versus crown down
55..... 0319 Rim joists
55..... 0320 Two methods for improving sagging joists
55..... 0321 Strapping, bridging and blocking
55..... 0322 Hump in floor caused by excessive joist overlap
56..... 0323 Different types of joist end support
56..... 0324 Examples of weak joist/beam connections
56..... 0325 Watch for insufficient nails in joist hangers
56..... 0326 Joists attached to beams with ledger boards
56..... 0327 Mortise and tenon joints
56..... 0328 Strapping, bridging and blocking
57..... 0329 Joist notching and drilling
57..... 0330 Common causes of cracked joists
57..... 0331 Cantilevered joists
57..... 0332 Openings in floor structures
57..... 0333 Interior walls – (non-loadbearing)
57..... 0334 Wall over a trimmer
58..... 0335 Engineered wood for floors
58..... 0336 Wood "I" joist notching and drilling

SUBFLOORING

58..... 0337 Types of subflooring
58..... 0338 Plywood subflooring

CHAPTER 2

58..... 0339 Subflooring edge support
59..... 0340 Alternatives for installing ceramic tiles

CONCRETE FLOOR SLABS

59..... 0341 Pre-stressed and post-tensioned concrete floor slabs
59..... 0342 Cold joints along edge of slabs

STEEL FRAMED FLOOR

59..... 0343 Typical assembly/components for steel framed floors
60..... 0344 Typical details for steel framed floors

OLD HOMES

60..... 0345 Excessive sagging around poorly framed stair openings
60..... 0346 Hump in floor due to joists extending over solid masonry wall
60.....0347 Creep leading to sag in floor joists

INSPECTING FOR TERMITES

60..... 0348 Inspecting for subterranean termites – exterior
60..... 0349 Inspecting for subterranean termites – interior
61..... 0350 Measures to combat subterranean termites

WALL SYSTEMS

SOLID MASONRY WALLS

61..... 0351 Solid masonry walls
61..... 0352 Masonry cavity wall
61..... 0353 Brick veneer wall
61..... 0354 Brick wall terminology
61..... 0355 Masonry wall using a diagonal brick bond
62..... 0356 Lateral support for exterior masonry walls
62..... 0357 Walls that extend above ceiling joists
62..... 0358 Steel lintel in brick veneer wall
62..... 0359 Wood lintel in solid masonry wall
62..... 0360 Arch outside and wood lintel inside
62..... 0361 Crack types
63..... 0362 Cracks caused by one surface sliding against another
63..... 0363 Cracking – planes of movement
63..... 0364 Rotational settlement cracks
63..... 0365 Cracking -- common locations
63..... 0366 Roof truss uplift
63..... 0367 Garage settlement
64..... 0368 Lintel related wall cracks
64..... 0369 Bowing of masonry walls
64..... 0370 Bowed brick veneer wall – older home
64..... 0371 Walls that extend above ceiling joists
65...... 0372 Bowing of solid masonry wall due to tie failure
65..... 0373 Cracks due to clay brick expansion
65..... 0374 Using rods and channels to stabilize a settled house
65..... 0375 Corbelling
65..... 0376 Projections for veneer
65..... 0377 Blocks and bricks – hollow channels must be vertical

WOOD FRAME WALLS

66..... 0378 Platform versus balloon framing
66..... 0379 Interior walls – (non-loadbearing)
66..... 0380 Wood frame bearing wall – top plate T-connection
66..... 0381 Holes and notches in top plates of bearing walls
67..... 0382 Metal ties for connections in single top plates
67..... 0383 Load bearing wall with lintel
67..... 0384 Wall strength – stud sizes and spaces
67..... 0385 Wall plate overhangs
67..... 0386 Support for jack studs
67..... 0387 Wood frame bearing wall – in basement
68..... 0388 Wood frame wall – racking resistance
68..... 0389 Installing oriented strandboard
68..... 0390 Stud notching and drilling
68..... 0391 Identifying bearing and partition walls
68..... 0392 Common rot locations in walls
68..... 0393 Wood/soil clearances
69..... 0394 Wood frame wall – racking resistance
69..... 0395 Wood frame bearing wall – in basement
69..... 0396 Stud notching
69..... 0397 Straightening partition studs
69.......... 0398 Concentrated loads – removing or altering walls
69..... 0399 Support for jack studs on wide openings
70..... 0400 Offset bearing walls
70..... 0401 Sagging interior lintel

CHAPTER 2

MASONRY VENEER WALLS

70..... 0402 Brick veneer wall – construction detail
70..... 0403 Brick veneer wall – masonry tie detail
70..... 0404 Brick veneer wall
70..... 0405 Weep holes – vented rain screen principle
71..... 0406 Weep holes in brick veneer walls
71..... 0407 Veneer versus solid masonry
71..... 0408 Bowed brick veneer – older home
71..... 0409 Wood/soil clearances
71..... 0410 Lintel related wall cracks
71..... 0411 Steel lintel in brick veneer wall

STEEL FRAMED WALLS

72..... 0412 Typical assembly/components for light-gauge steel wall framing
72..... 0413 Lintels and bridging for light-gauge steel wall framing
72..... 0414 Bearing and bracing details for light-gauge steel walls

ARCHES AND LINTELS

72..... 0415 Lintel loads in a masonry wall
72..... 0416 Lintel loads in wood frame walls
73..... 0417 Steel lintel in brick veneer wall
73.......... 0418 Masonry arches – cracking due to lateral thrust
73..... 0419 Lintel related wall cracks
73..... 0420 End bearing for steel lintel
74..... 0421 Wood lintel bearing

ROOF FRAMING

INTRODUCTION

74..... 0422 Roof types
74..... 0423 Roof slopes
74..... 0424 Anchoring the roof to the walls
74..... 0425 Roof spreading, dishing and sagging

RAFTERS, ROOF JOISTS AND CEILING JOISTS

74..... 0426 Roof joists versus roof rafters
75..... 0427 Overlapped ceiling joist splices
75..... 0428 Plywood ceiling joist splices
75..... 0429 Rafter endbearing
75..... 0430 Hip and valley rafters
75..... 0431 Horizontal projection
76..... 0432 Ridge support
76..... 0433 Ridge boards
76..... 0434 Ridge board – not required
76..... 0435 Gable wall
76..... 0436 Gable overhang less than 16 inches
76..... 0437 Gable overhang more than 16 inches
77..... 0438 Dormer framing
77..... 0439 Soffits
77..... 0440 Roof spreading
77..... 0441 Roof spreading – remedial action
77..... 0442 Rafter endbearing
78..... 0443 Dormer framing
78..... 0444 Watch for insufficient nails in joist hangers
78..... 0445 Openings in roofs

COLLAR TIES, KNEE WALLS, AND PURLINS

78..... 0446 Methods of reducing rafter spans

STEEL FRAMED RAFTERS, ROOF JOISTS, AND CEILING JOISTS

79..... 0447 Typical assembly/components of steel framed roofs
79..... 0448 Typical details at steel framed roofs

TRUSSES

79..... 0449 Roof trusses – overview
79..... 0450 Bracing of compression webs
79..... 0451 Strapping the underside of trusses
79..... 0452 Truss types
80..... 0453 Drifting snow can cause truss sag/damage
80..... 0454 Roof truss uplift
80..... 0455 Roof truss uplift – remedial action
80..... 0456 Bracing of compression webs
80..... 0457 Roof trusses that are too long

WOOD "I" JOISTS

80..... 0458 Wood "I" joists

SHEATHING

81..... 0459 Installation of roof boards
81..... 0460 Installation of panel type roof sheathing
81..... 0461 H-clips and spacing for panel type roof sheathing

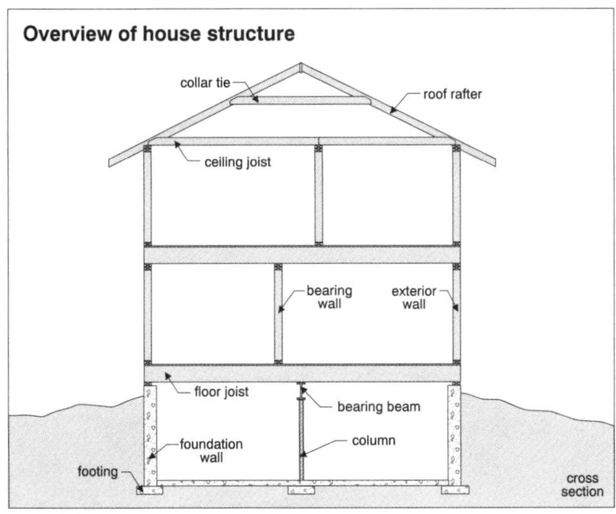

0200

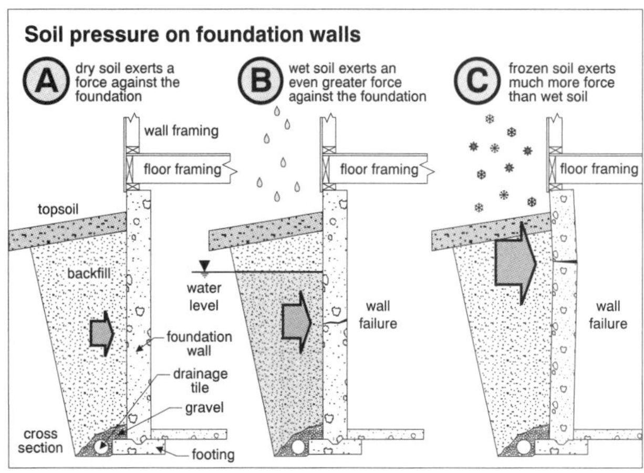

0201

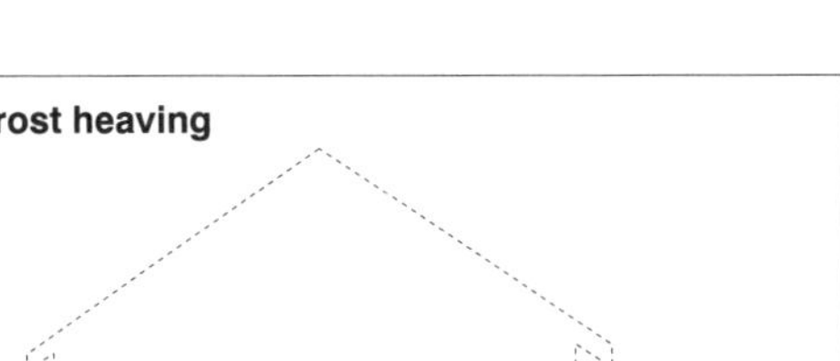

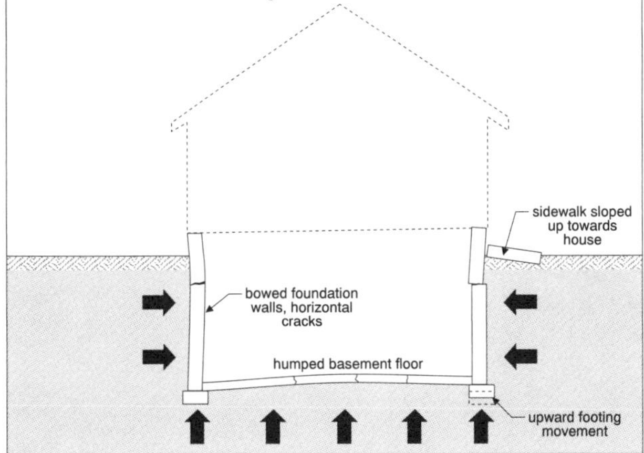

0202

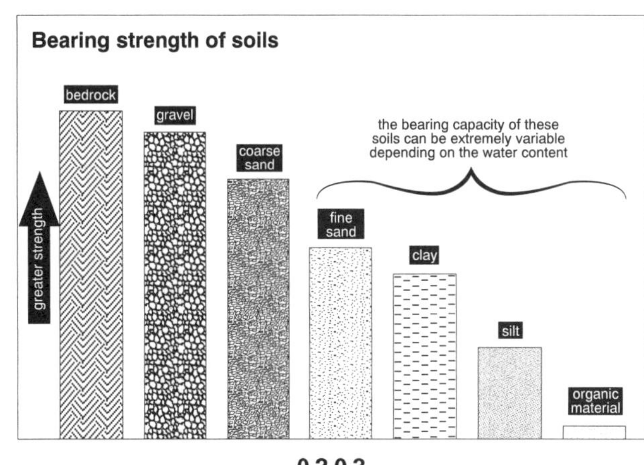

0203

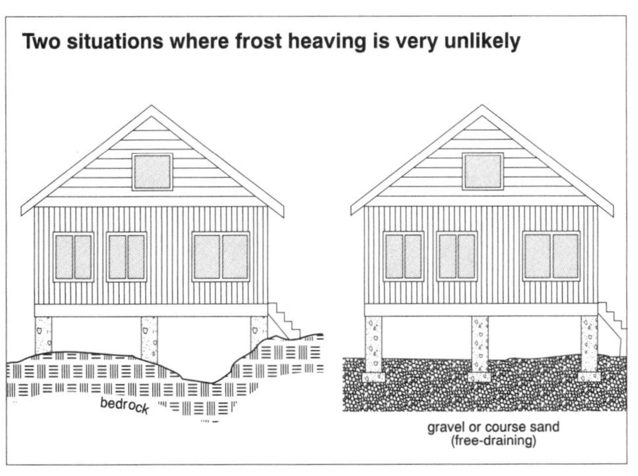

0204

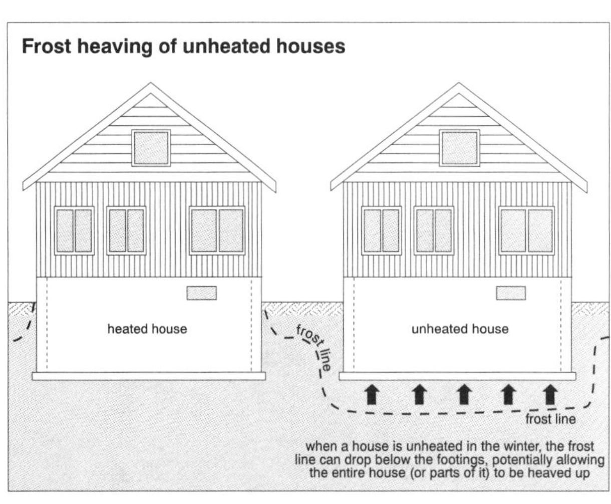

0205

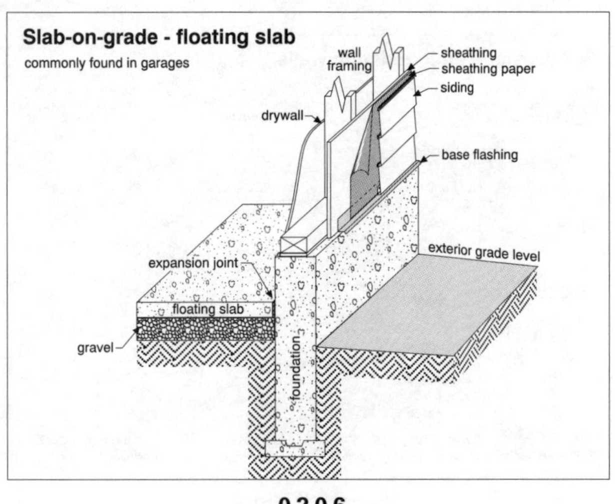

0206

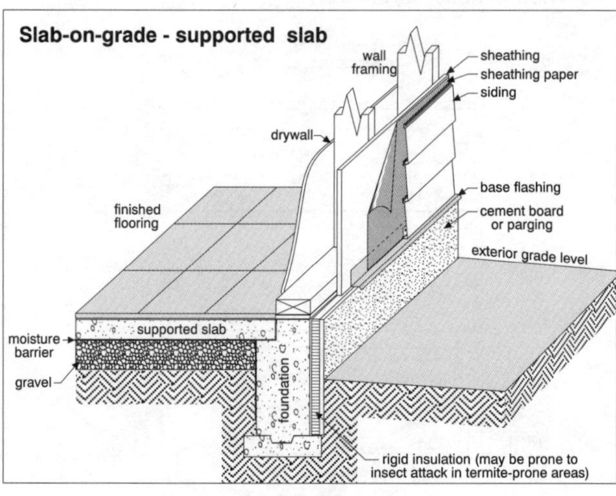

0207

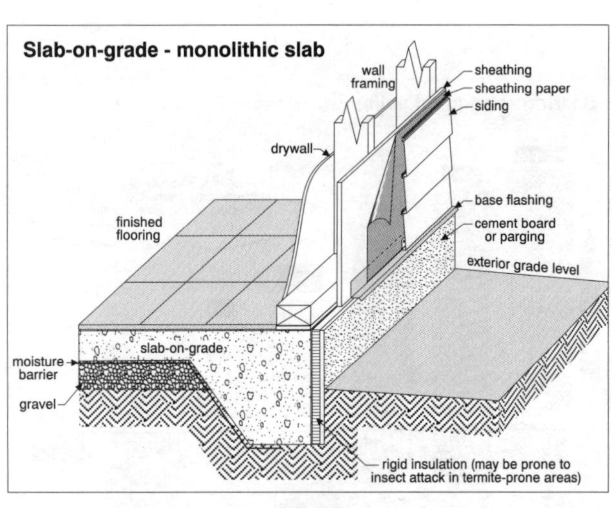

0208

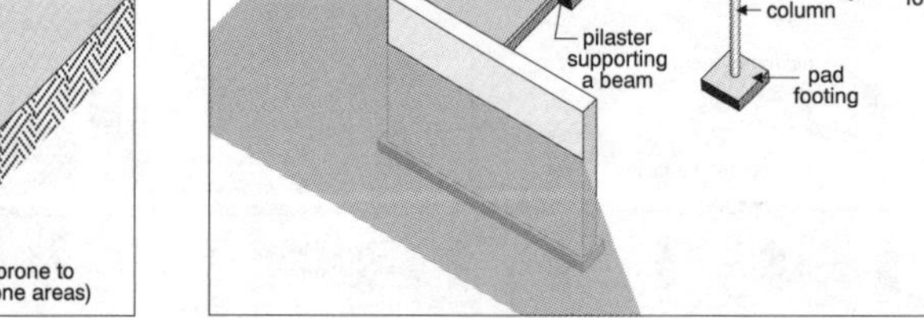

0209

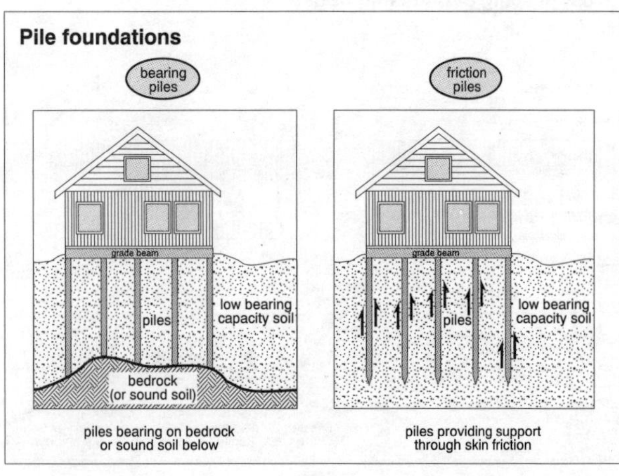

0210

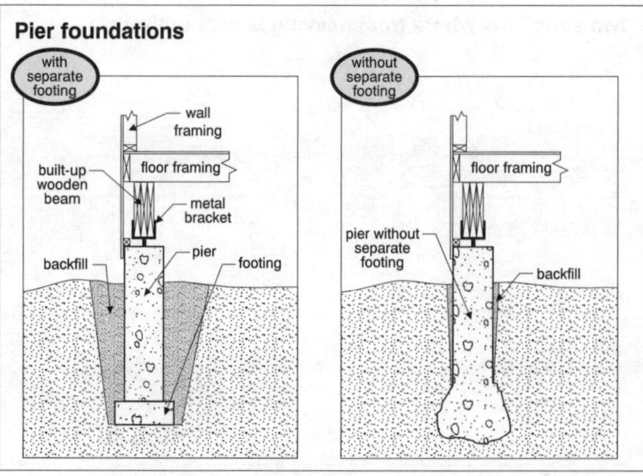

0211

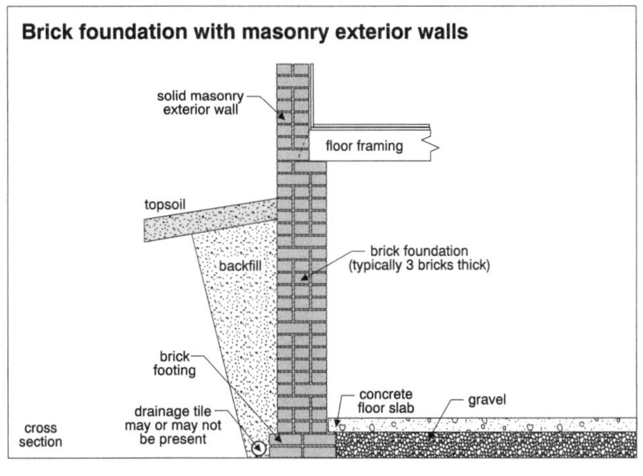

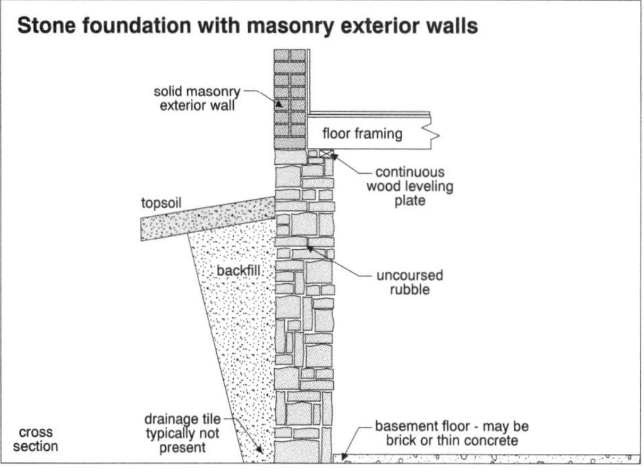

0212

0213

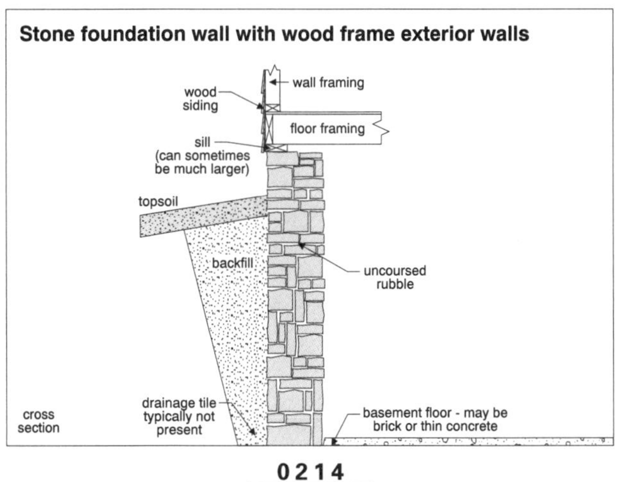

0214

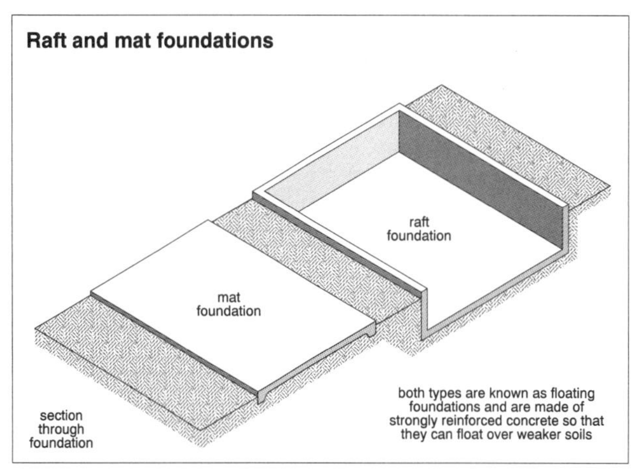

0215

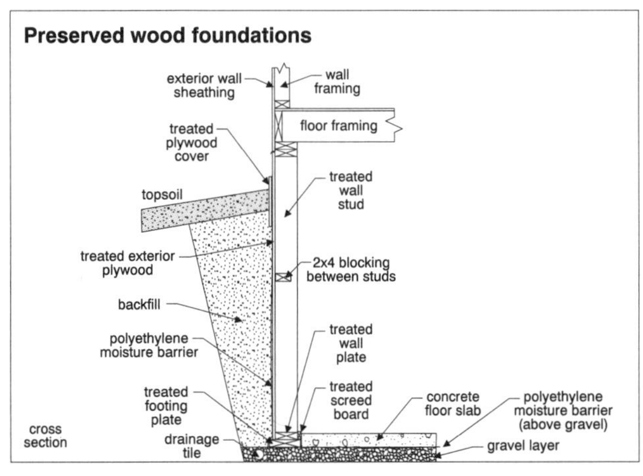

0216

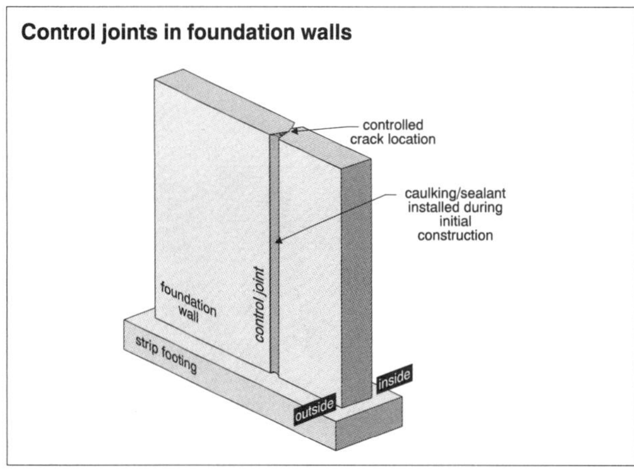

0217

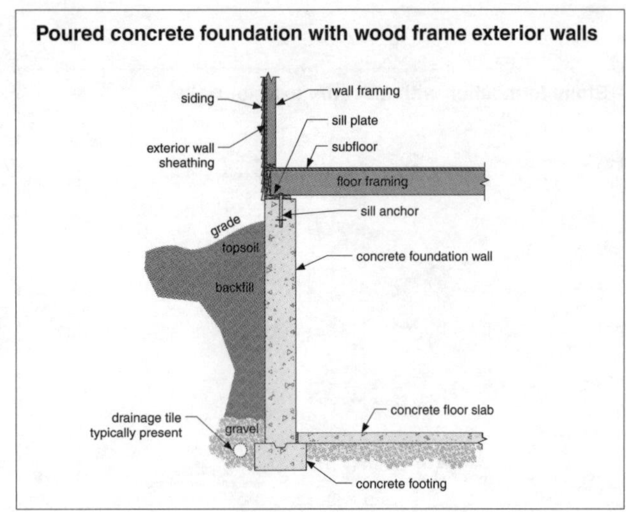

0218

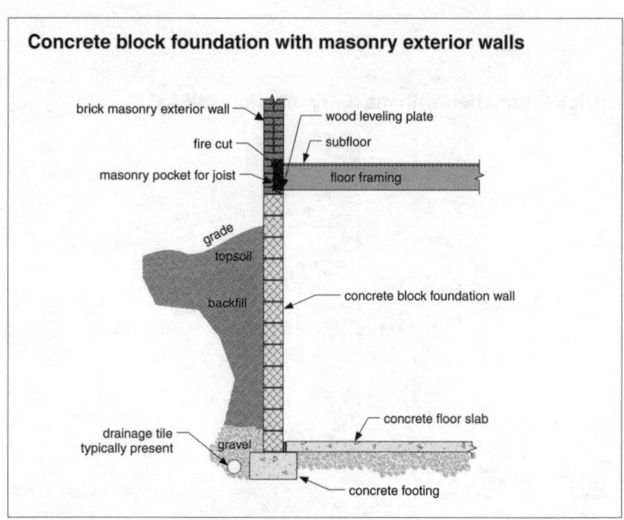

0219

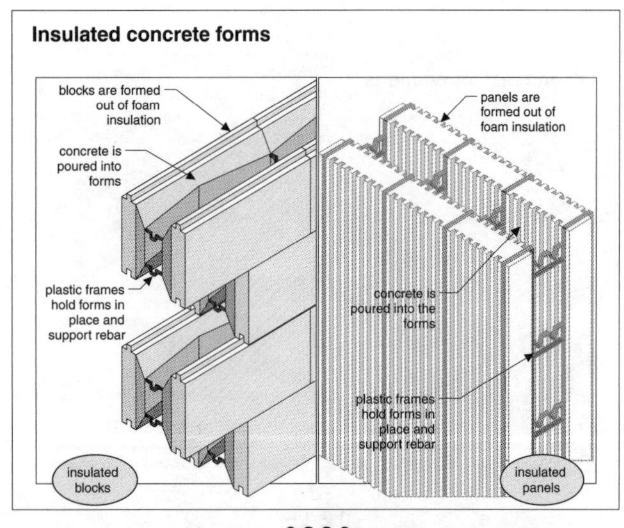

0220

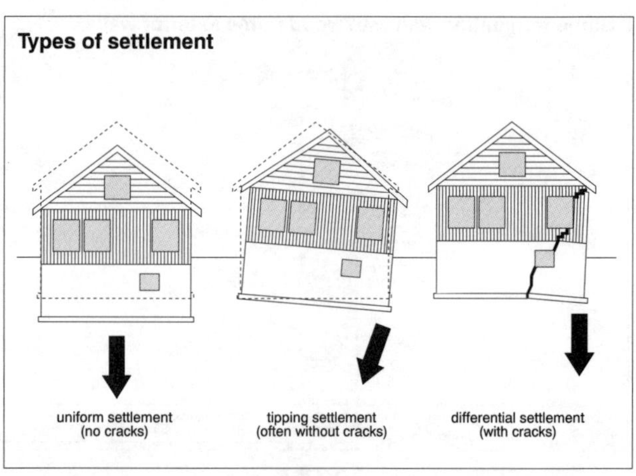

0221

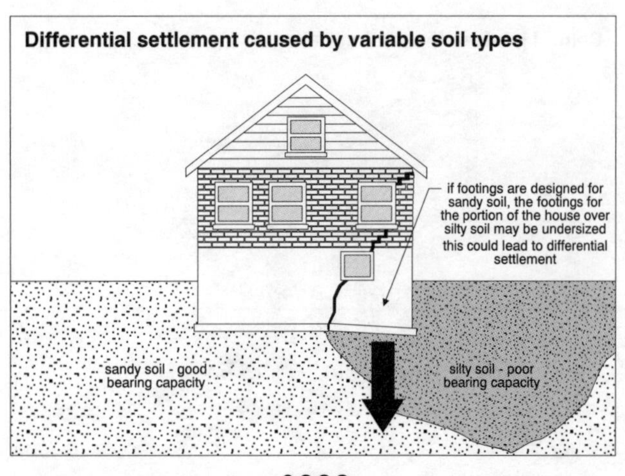

0222

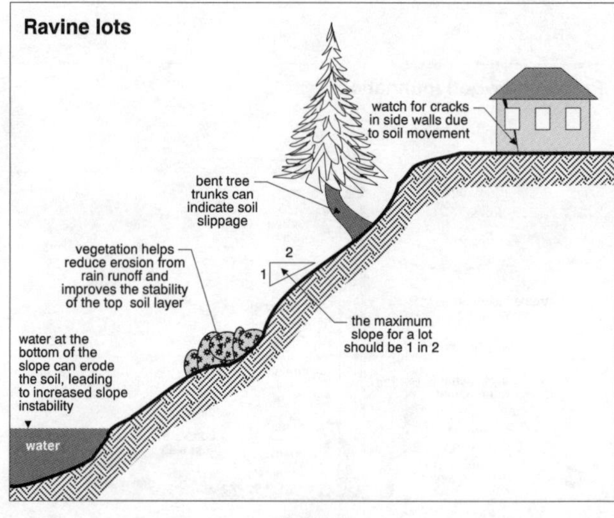

0223

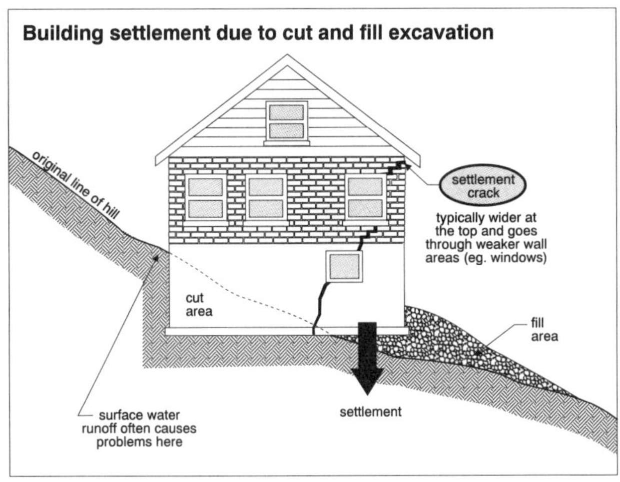

0224

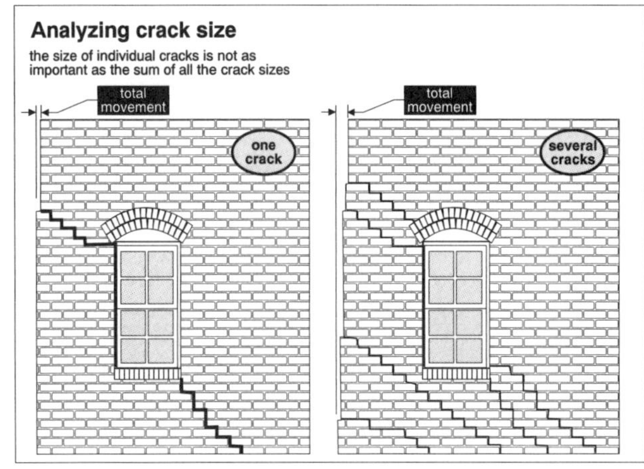

0225

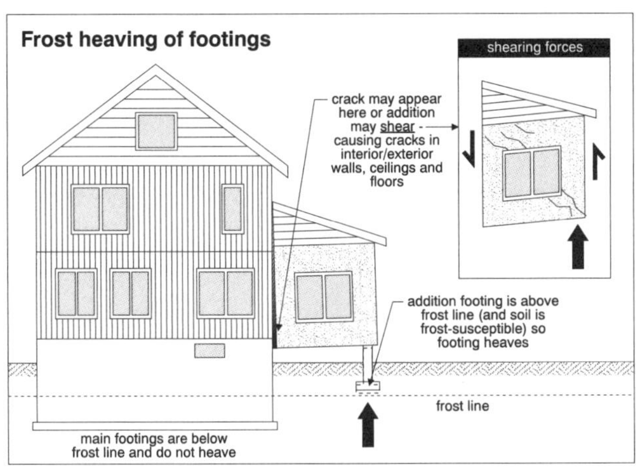

0226

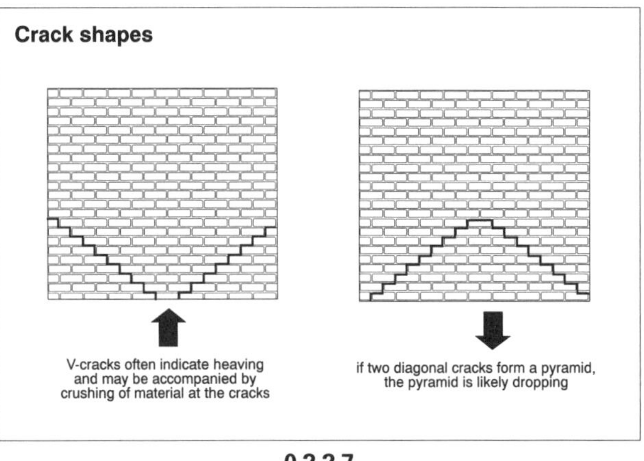

0227

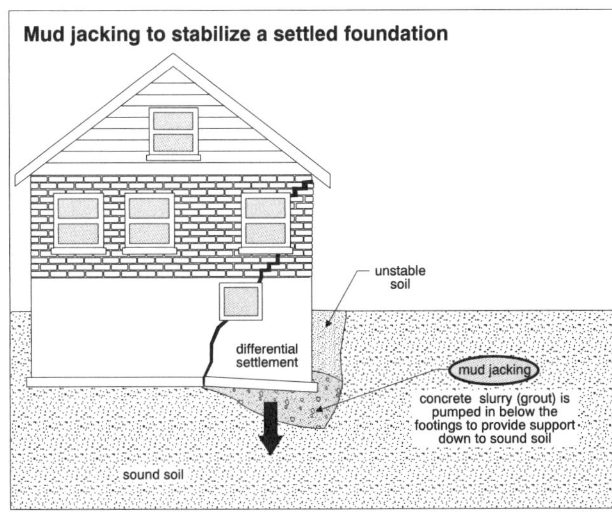

0228

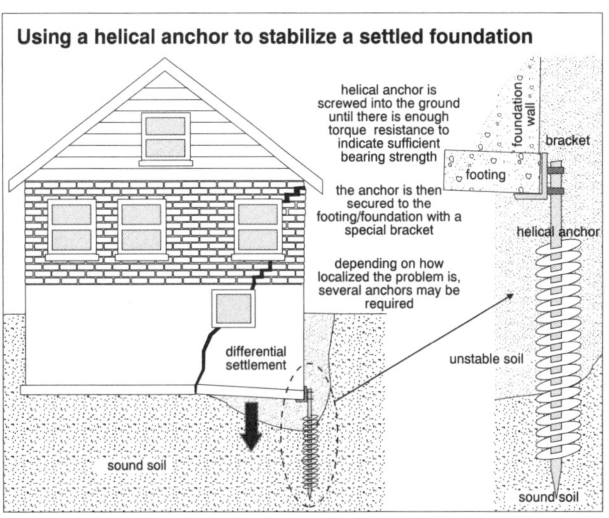

0229

Using piles to stabilize a settled foundation

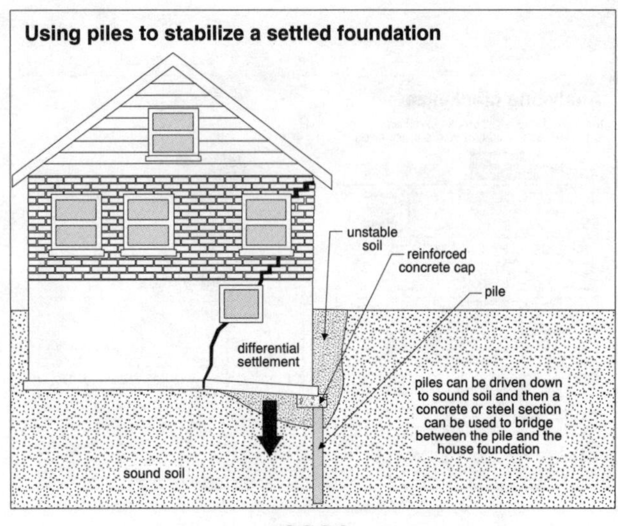

0230

Using rods and channels to stabilize a settled house

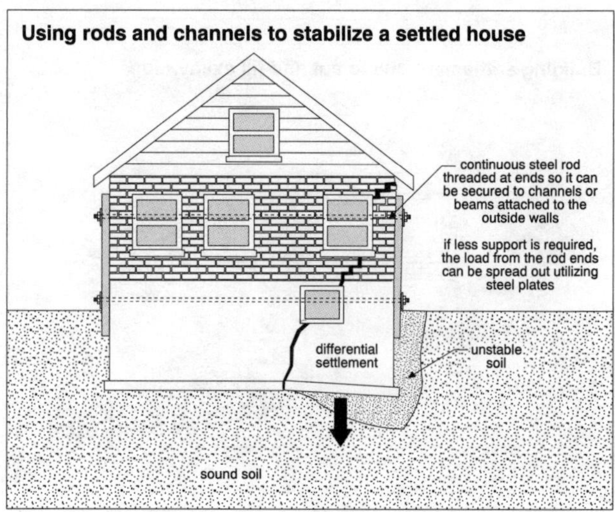

0231

Step footings on sloped lots

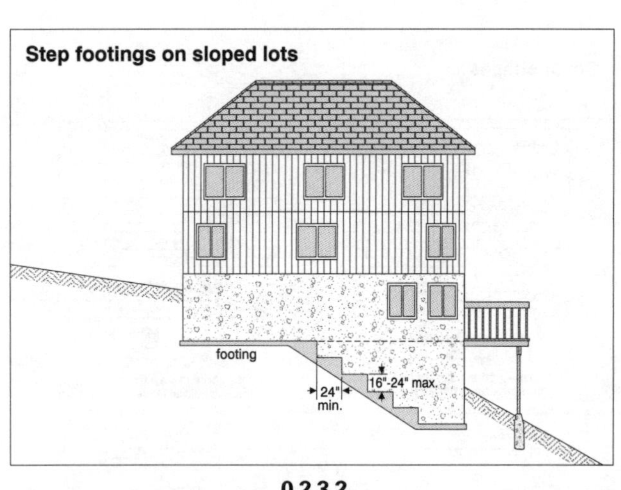

0232

Lowering basement floors - bench footing

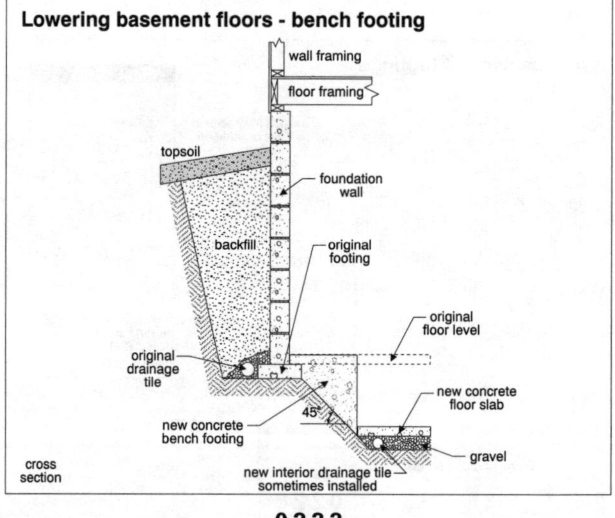

0233

Lowering basement floors - underpinning

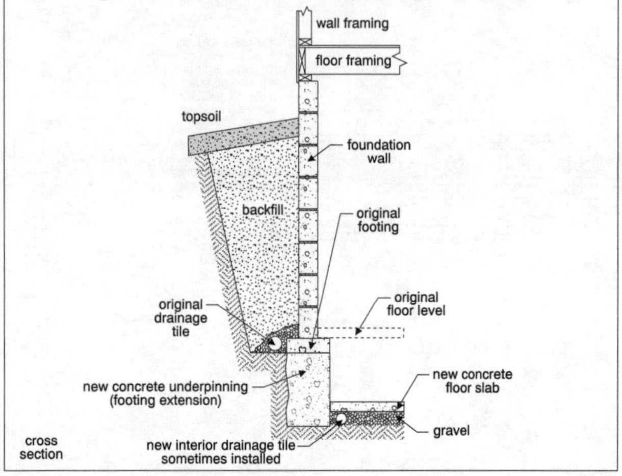

wall framing
floor framing
topsoil
foundation wall
backfill
original footing
original drainage tile
original floor level
new concrete underpinning (footing extension)
new concrete floor slab
gravel
cross section
new interior drainage tile sometimes installed

0234

Underpinning - timing of concrete pours

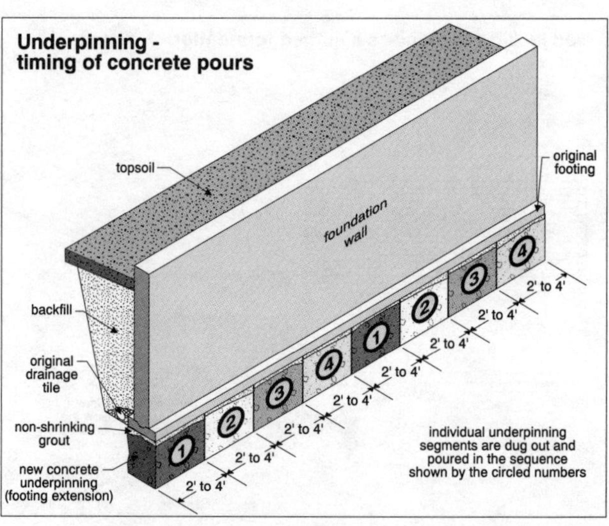

0235

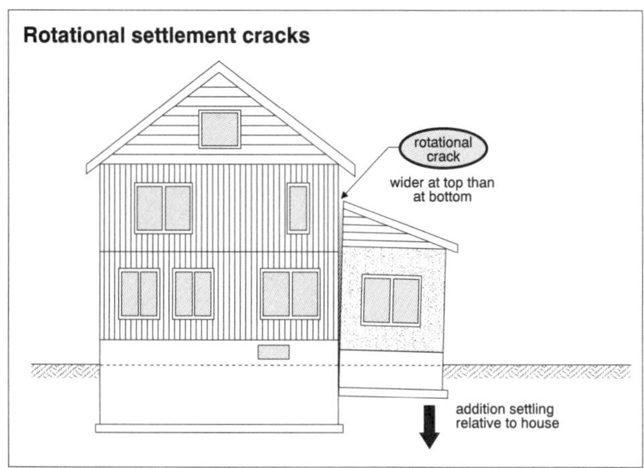

0236

Cracking - common locations

cracks often occur near high concentrated loads such as this settling column

cracks will also tend to show up at weak areas such as the line through the doors and windows

0237

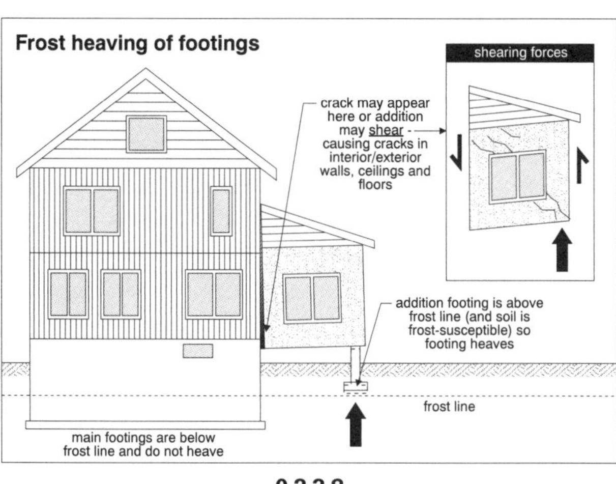

0238

Sources of heaving

frost heave

adfreezing

expansive soils

high water table

frost line

frost line

0239

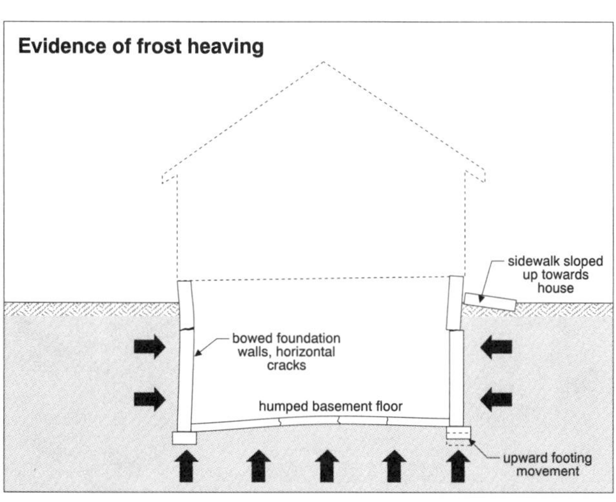

0240

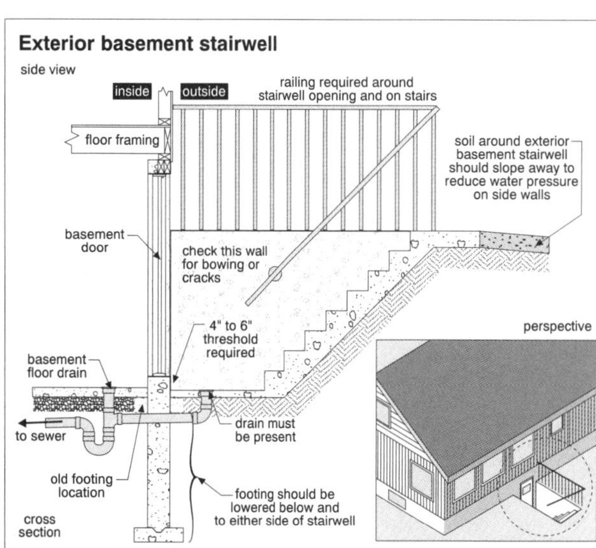

0241

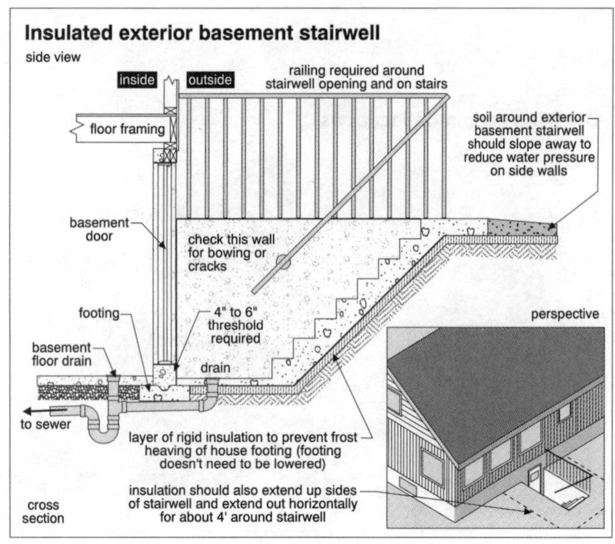

0242

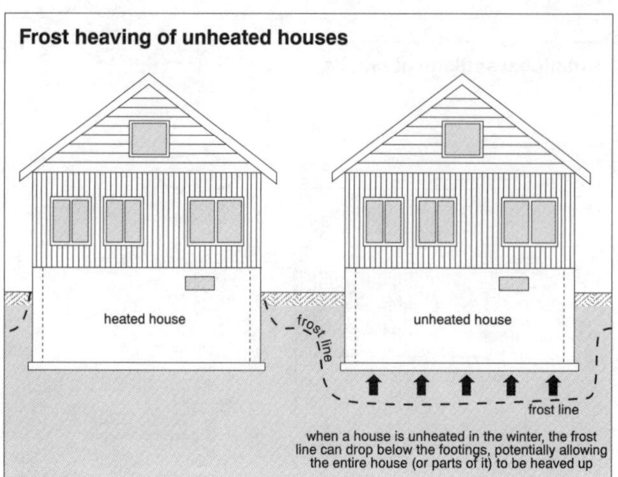

0243

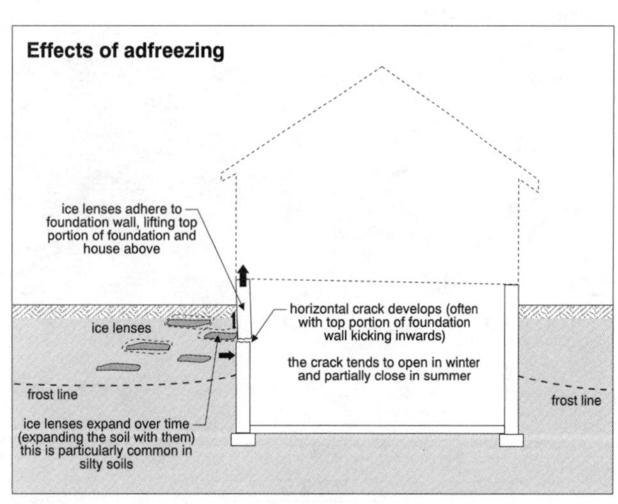

0244

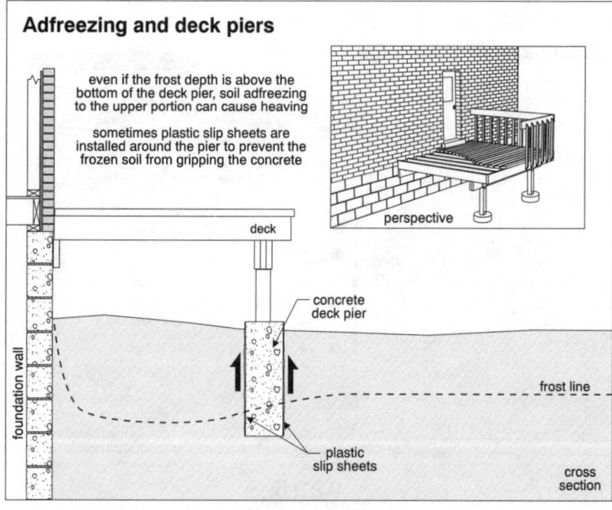

0245

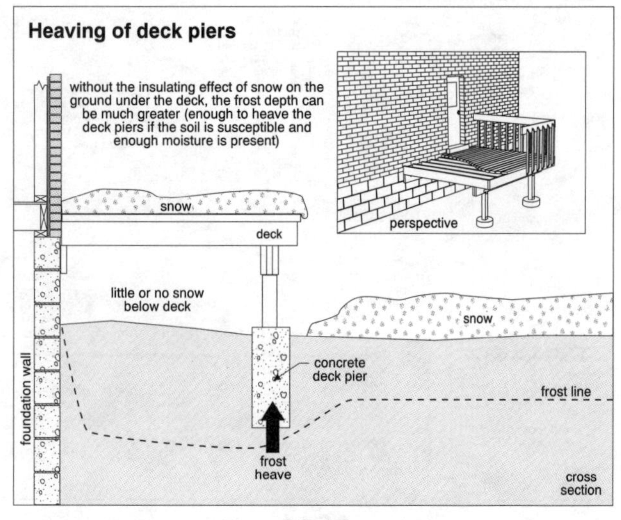

0246

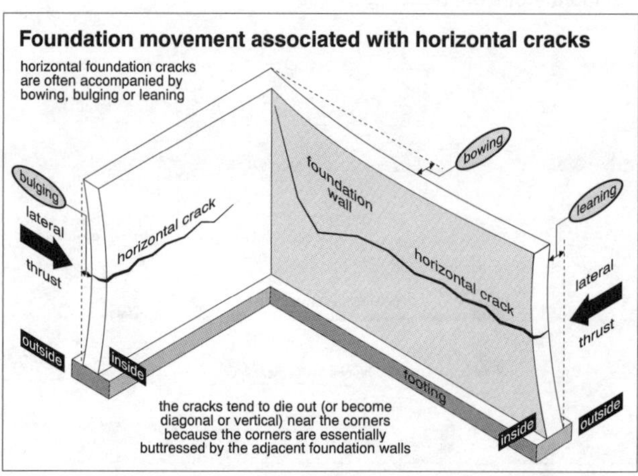

0247

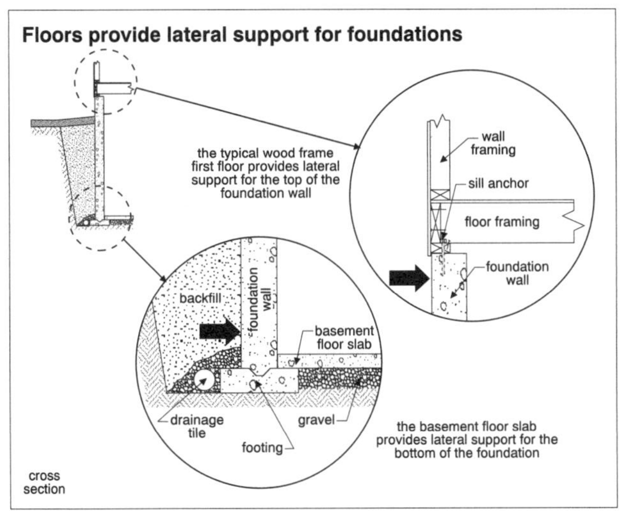

0248

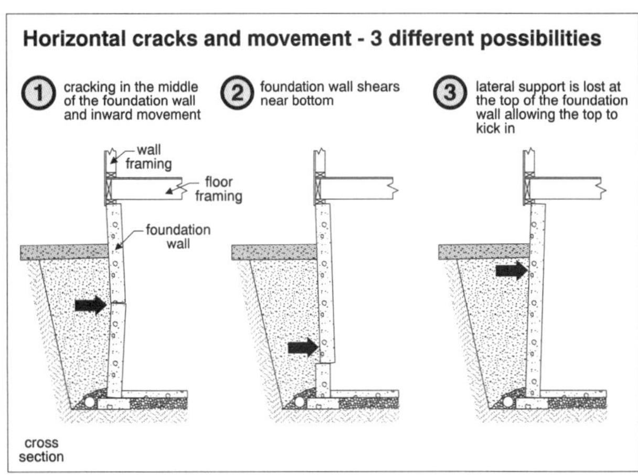

0249

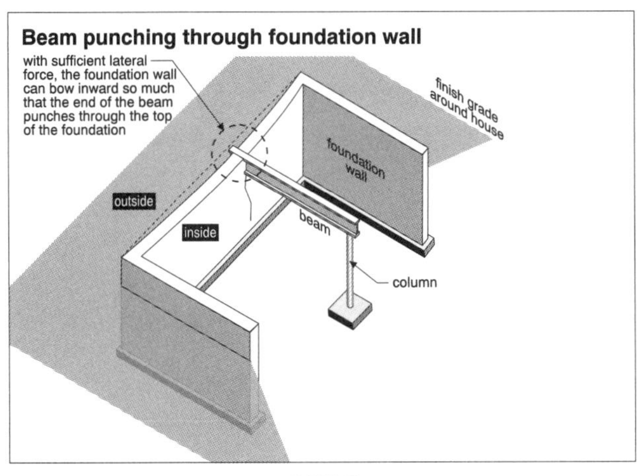

0250

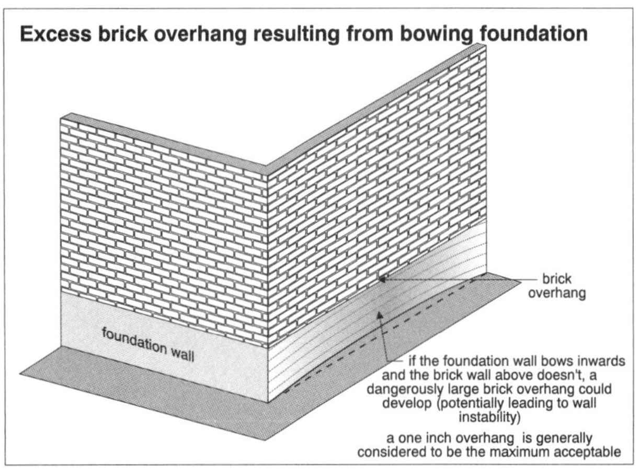

0251

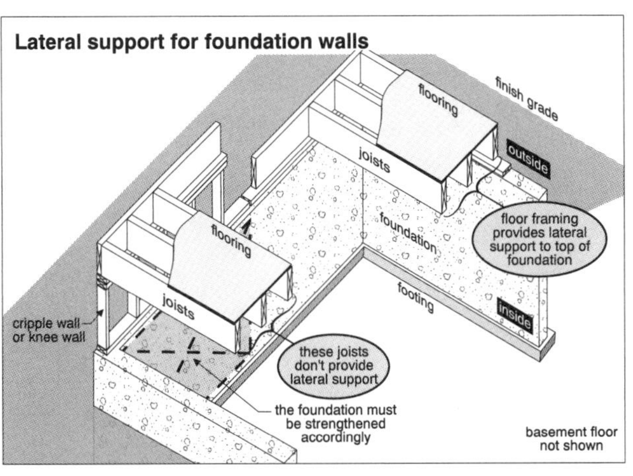

0252

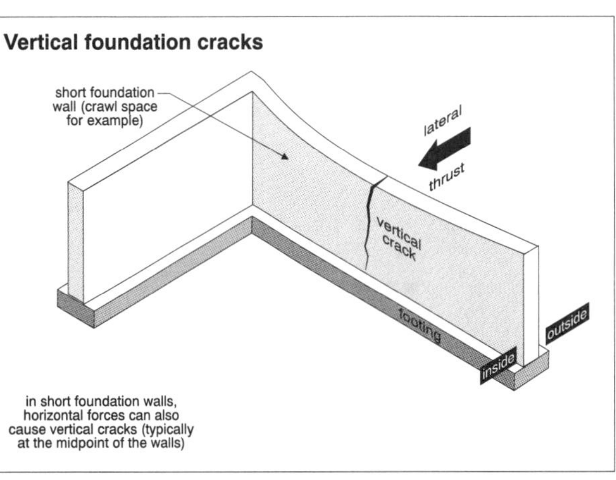

0253

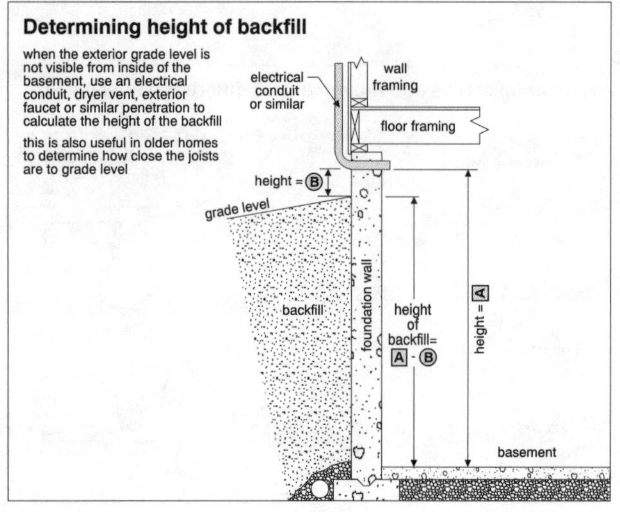

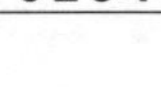

How driveways can contribute to foundation cracking

the load of heavy vehicles can be translated into horizontal forces capable of causing horizontal cracking

wall framing

floor framing

surface water flow

backfill

foundation wall

force

if the driveway slopes towards the house, large amounts of water can collect next to the foundations leading to high hydrostatic pressures and possible horizontal cracking

footing

0255

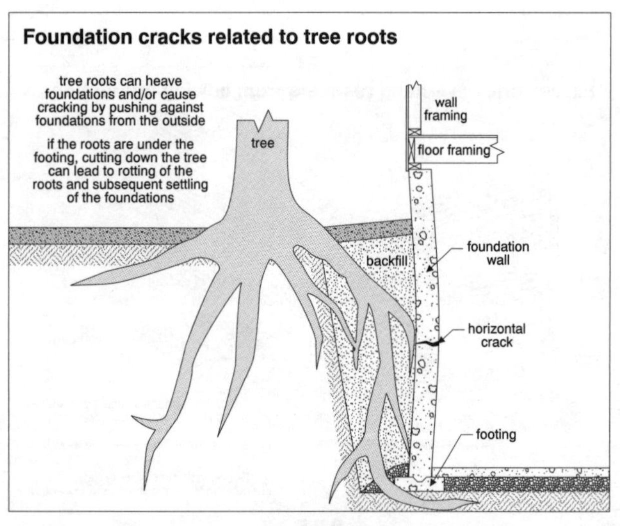

0256

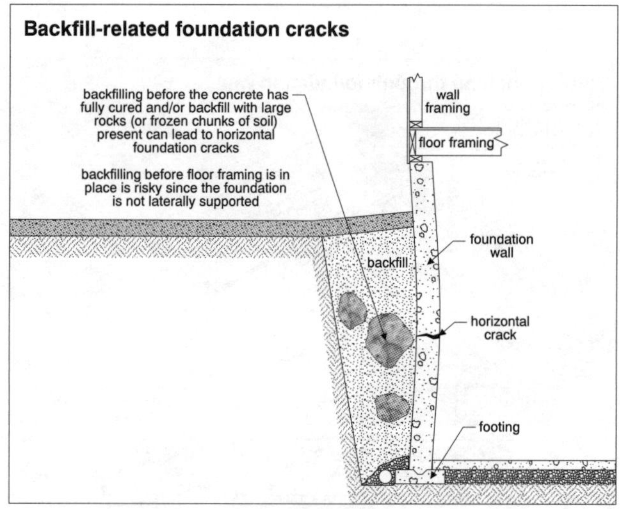

0257

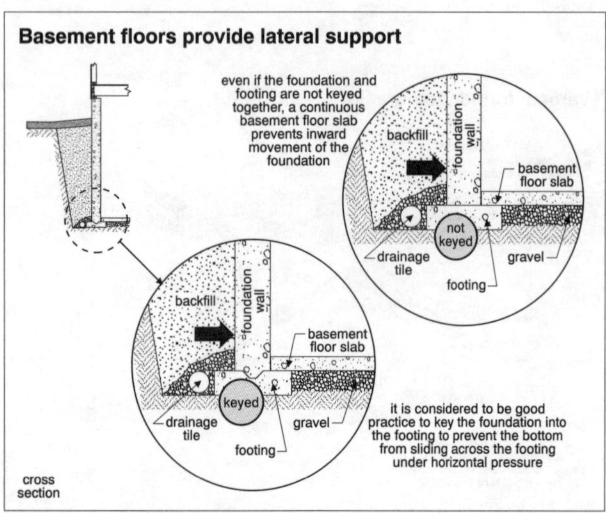

0258

Foundation repairs - adding a buttress

finish grade around house

foundation wall

outside

inside

(bsmt.)

buttress

strip footing

securing the buttress to the floor framing increases its strength

concrete floor slab

perspective

wall framing

bulging and cracked foundation wall

floor framing

topsoil

buttress

backfill

horizontal crack

additional buttress footing (if req'd)

footing

cross section

0259

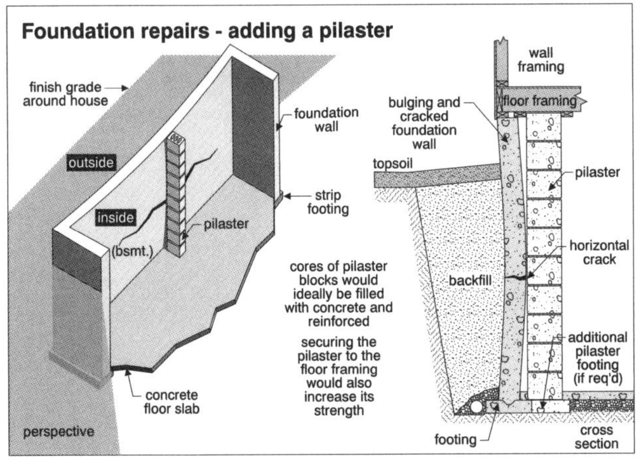

0260

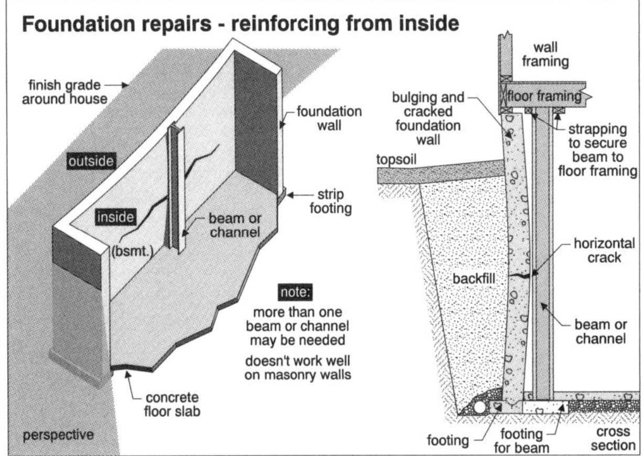

0261

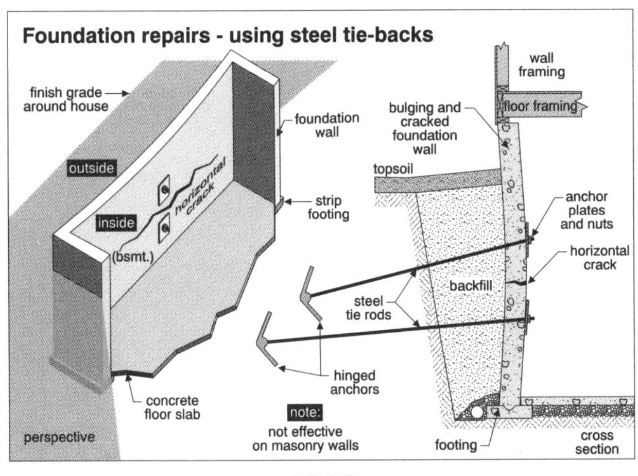

0262

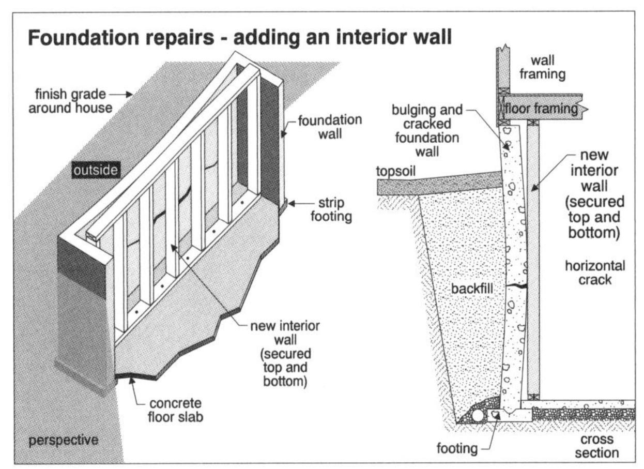

0263

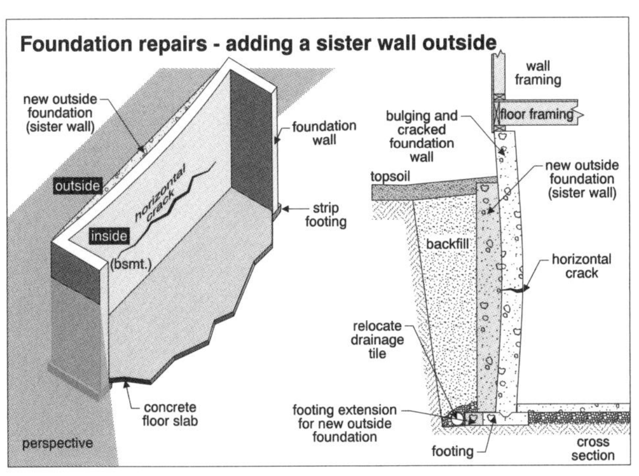

0264

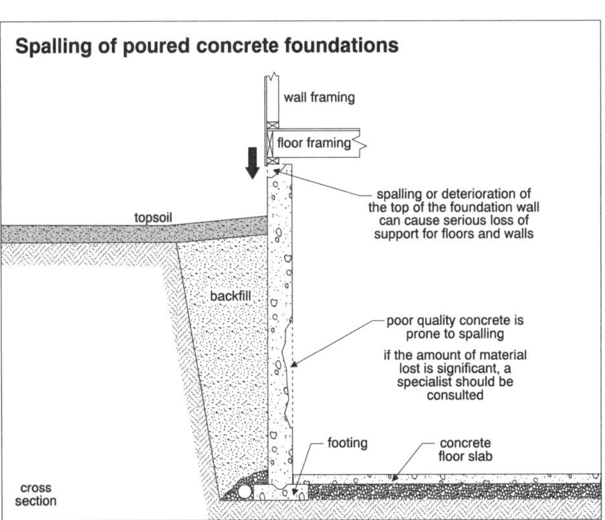

0265

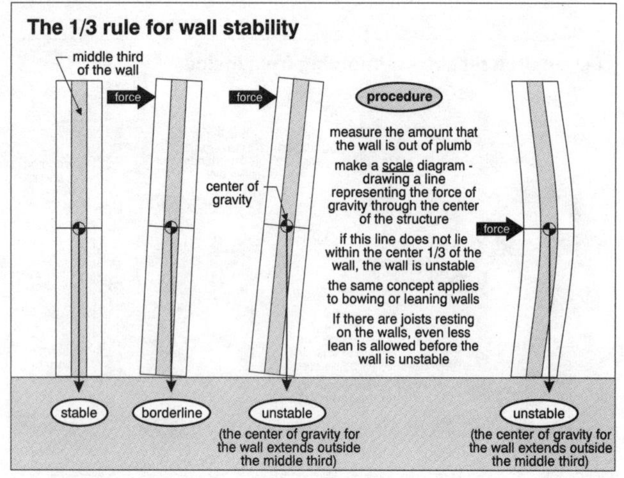

0266

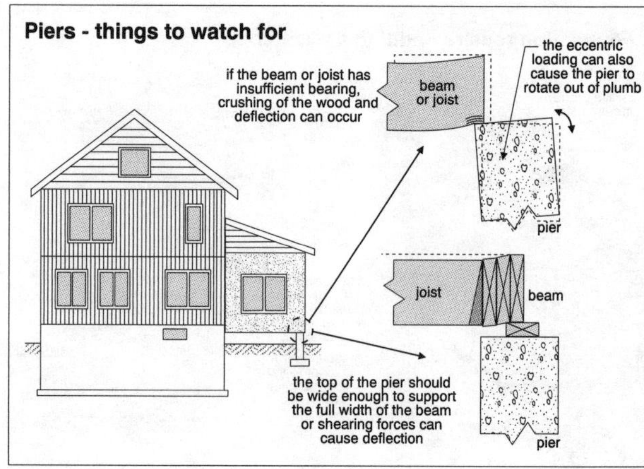

0267

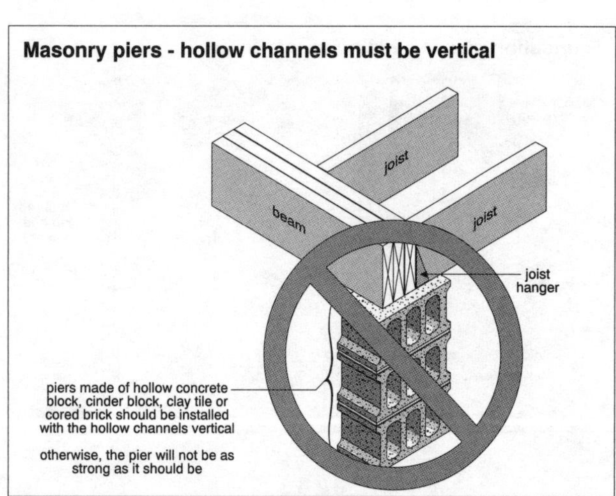

0268

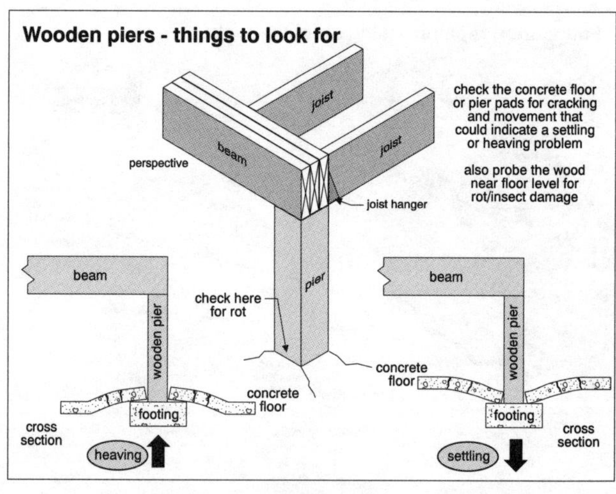

0269

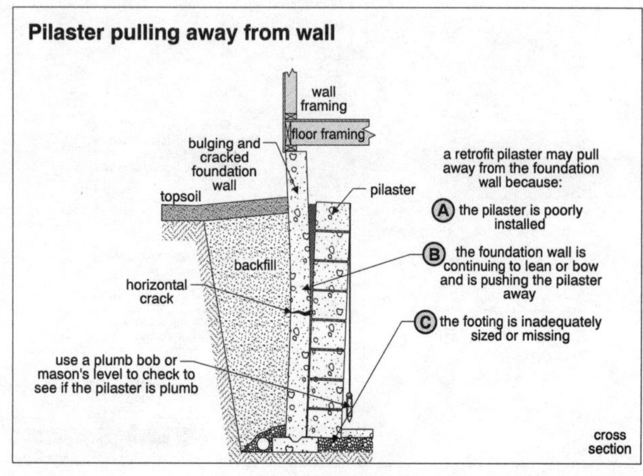

0270

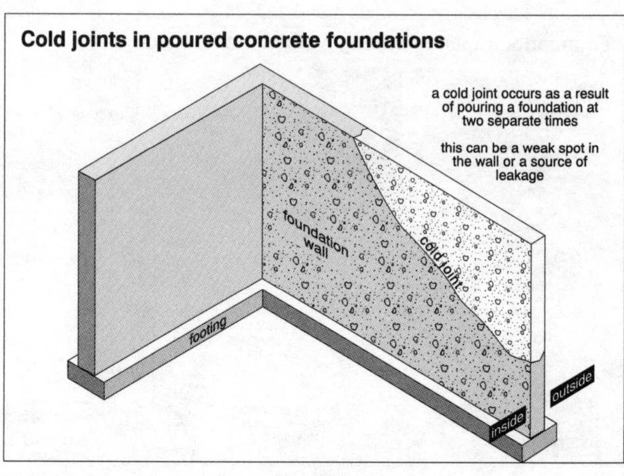

0271

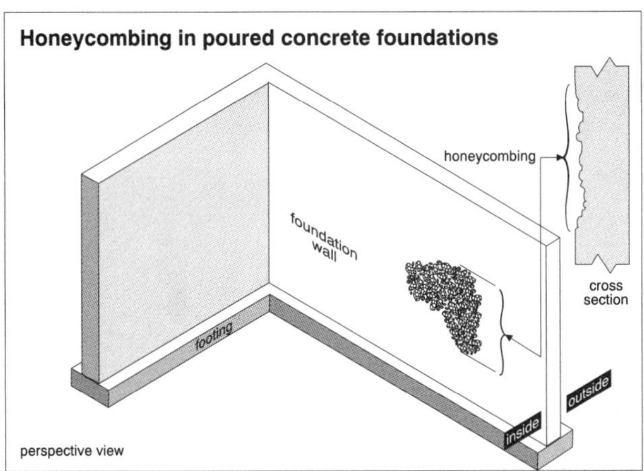

0272

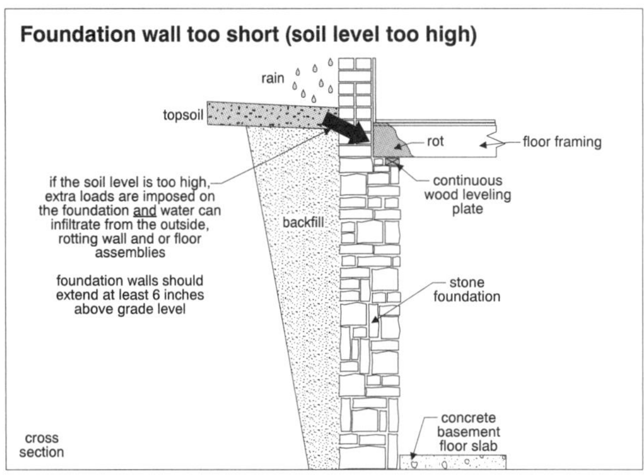

0273

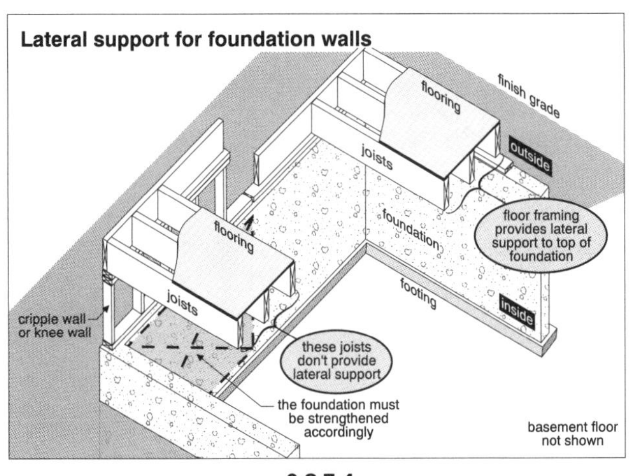

0274

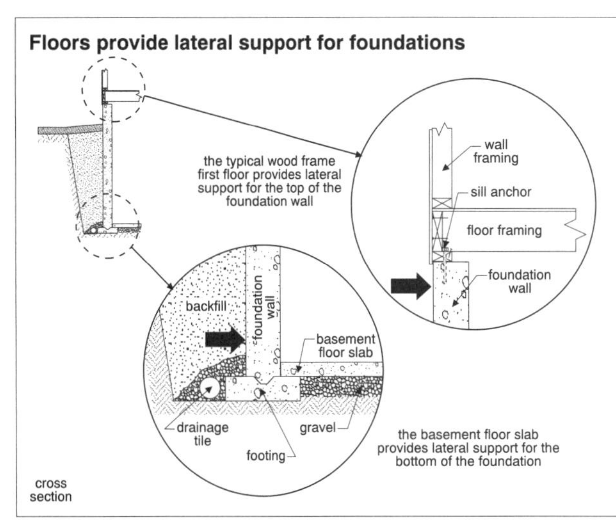

0275

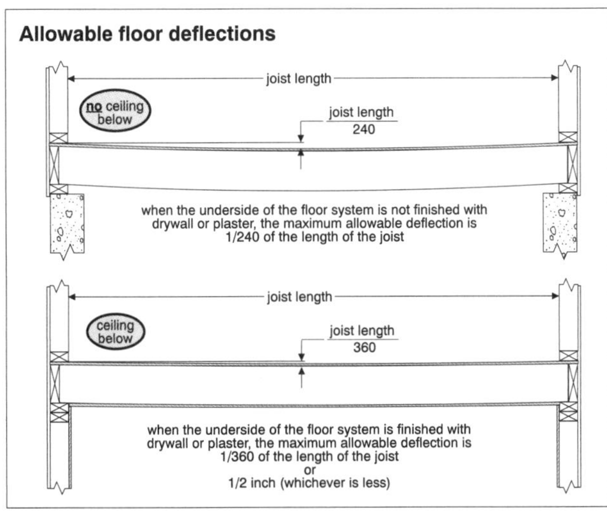

0276

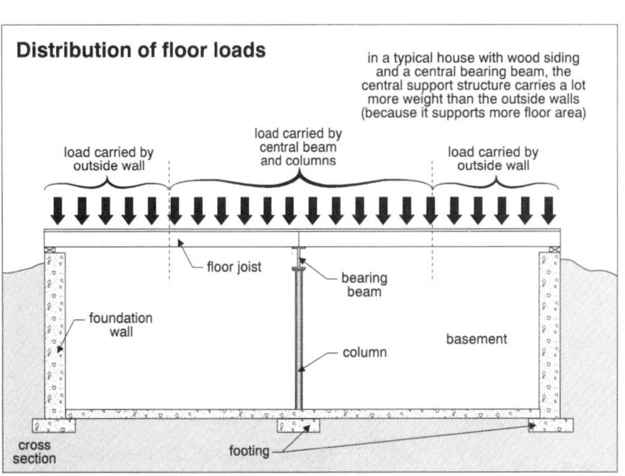

0277

Air gaps around ends of wooden beams

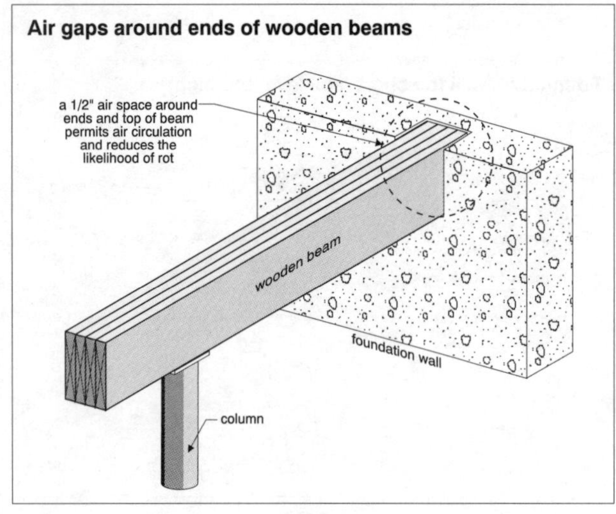

0278

Nails are good in shear but poor in tension

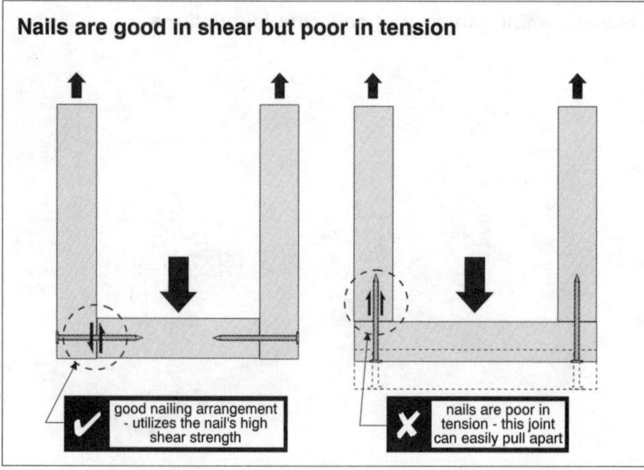

0279

Brick veneer wall

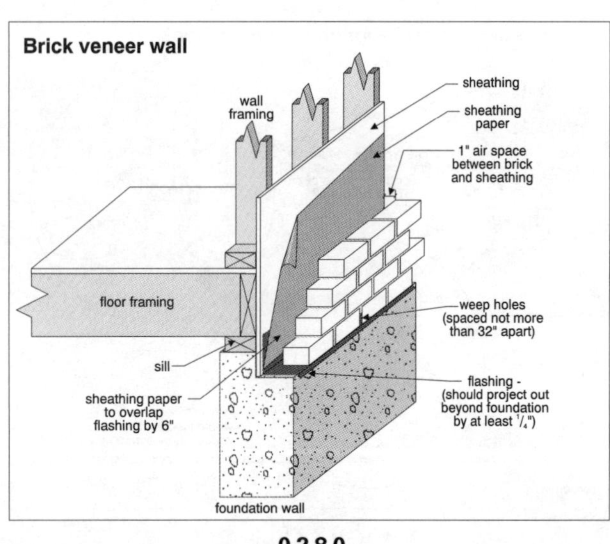

0280

Sill anchors

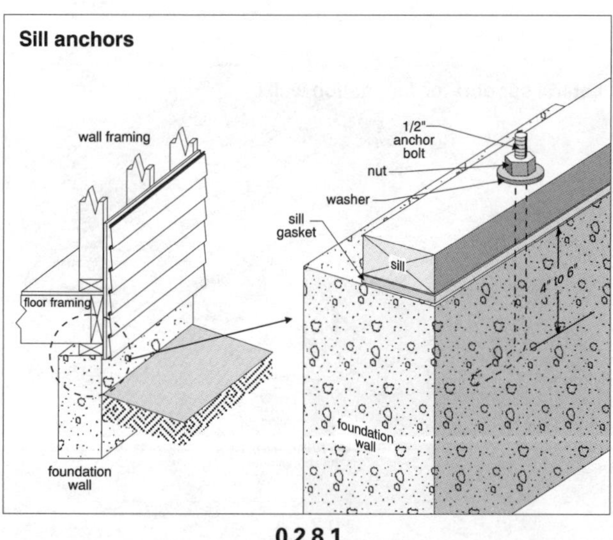

0281

Sills should be above grade

planter raises soil level next to house
rain
brick veneer
wall framing
rot
water
floor framing
water infiltration
topsoil
sill
sills should be above grade level otherwise, sills (and framing members) can rot - leading to loss of bearing and differential settlement
backfill
foundation wall
basement
drainage tile
footing
basement floor slab
gravel
cross section

0282

Mud sills

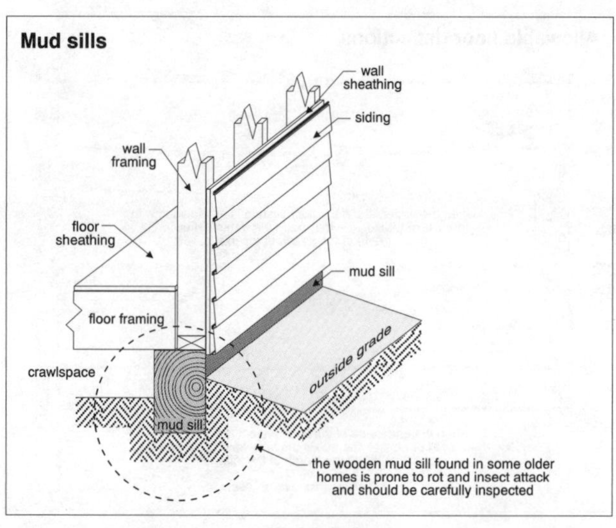

0283

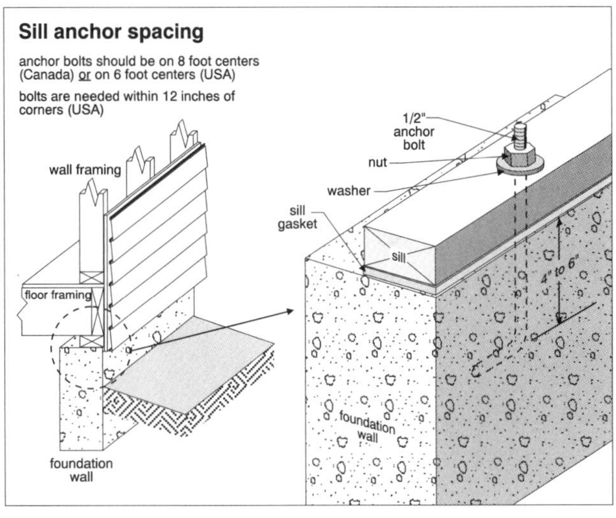

0284

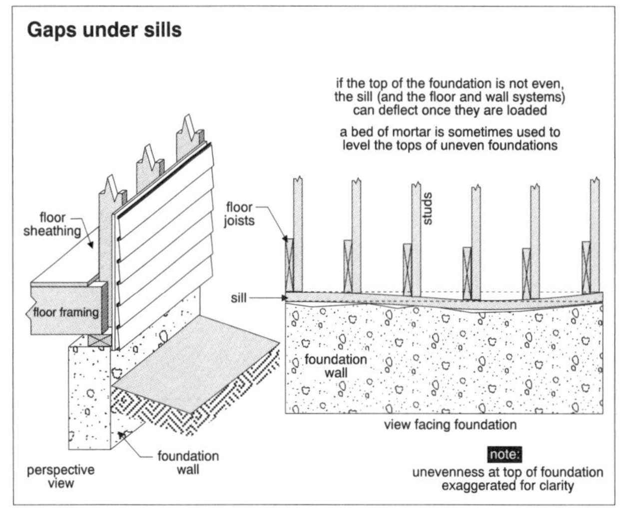

0285

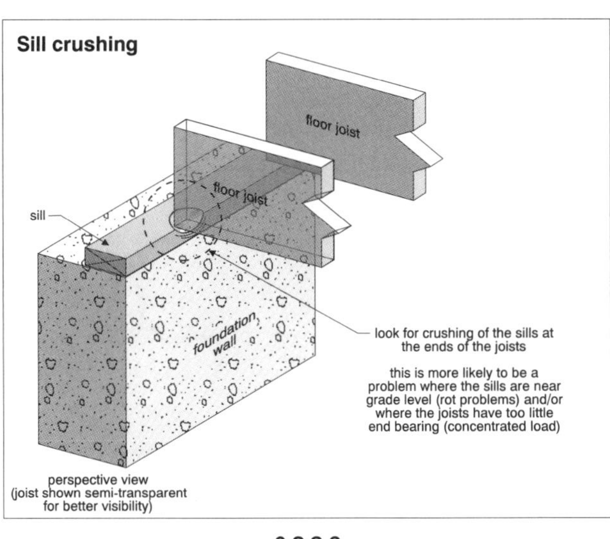

0286

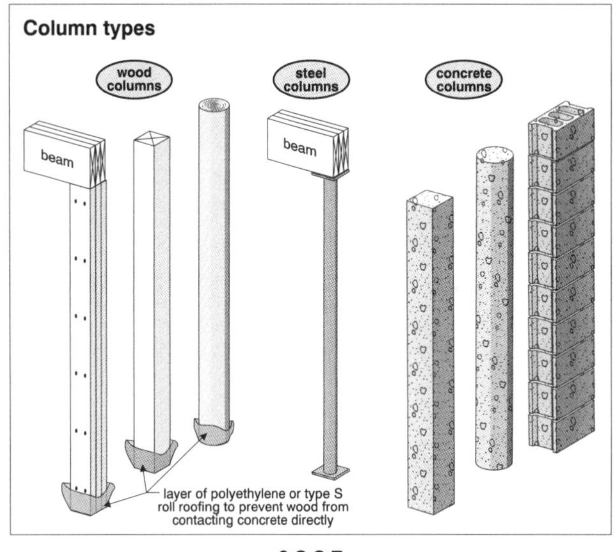

0287

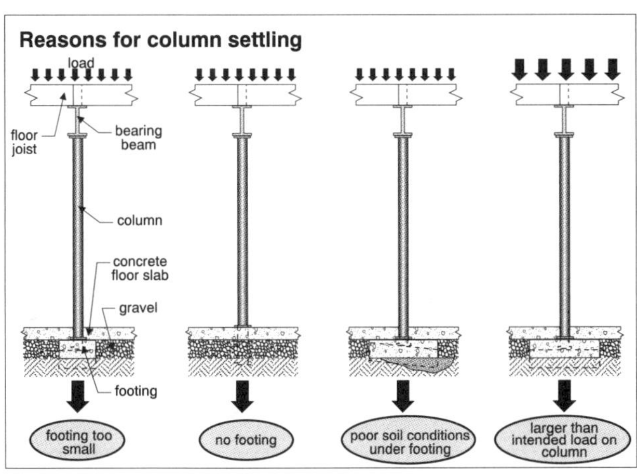

0288

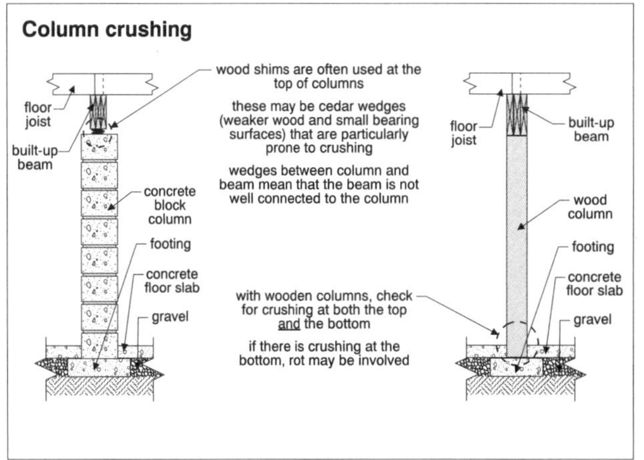

0289

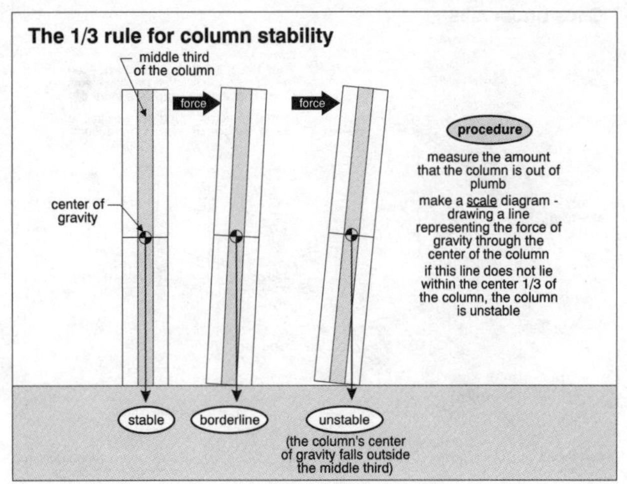

0290

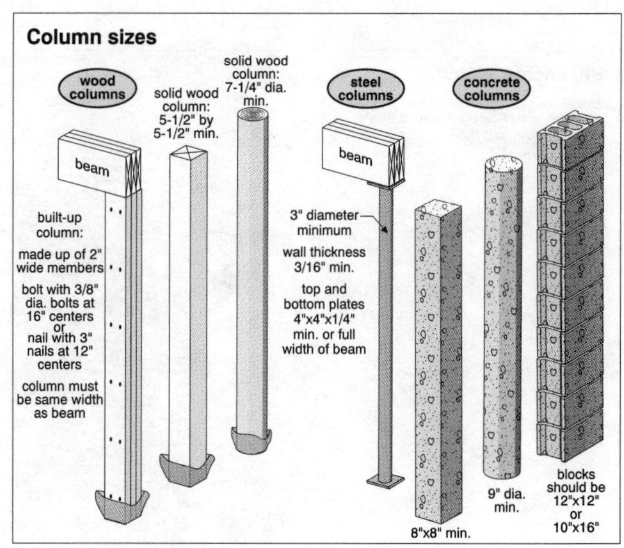

0291

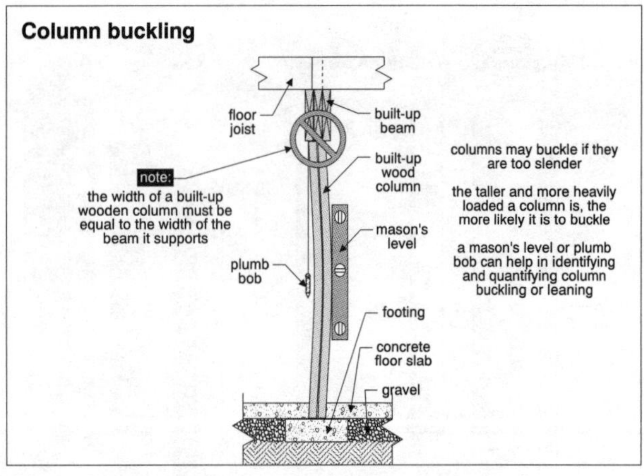

0292

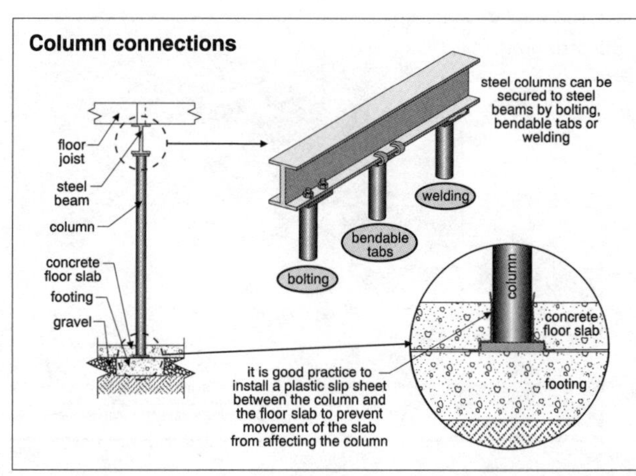

0293

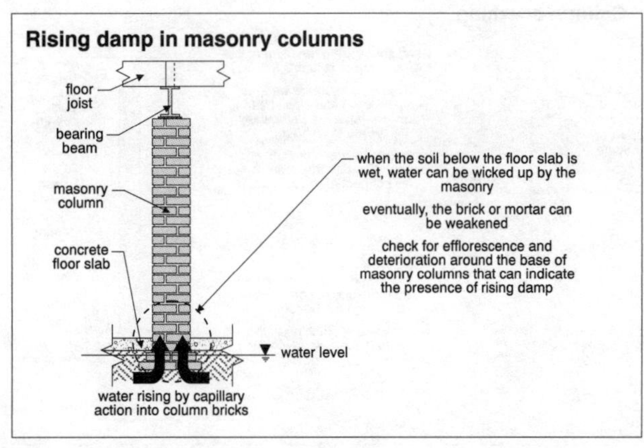

0294

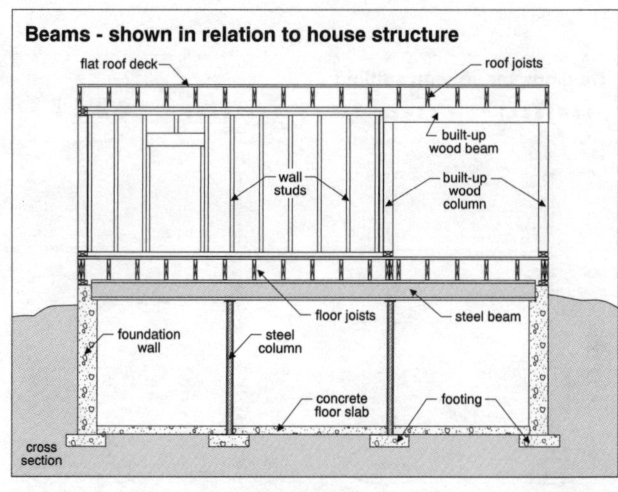

0295

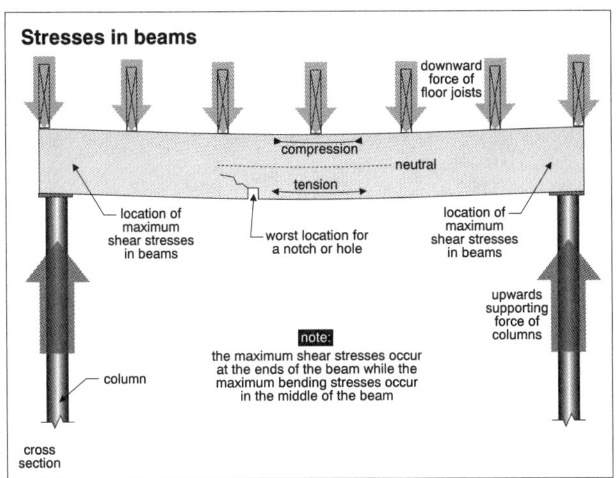

0296

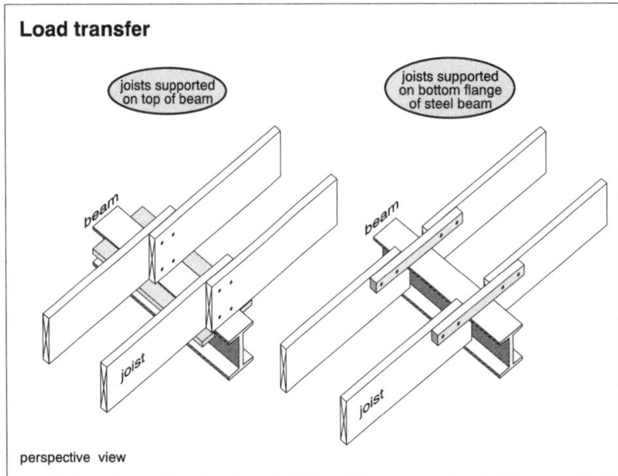

0297

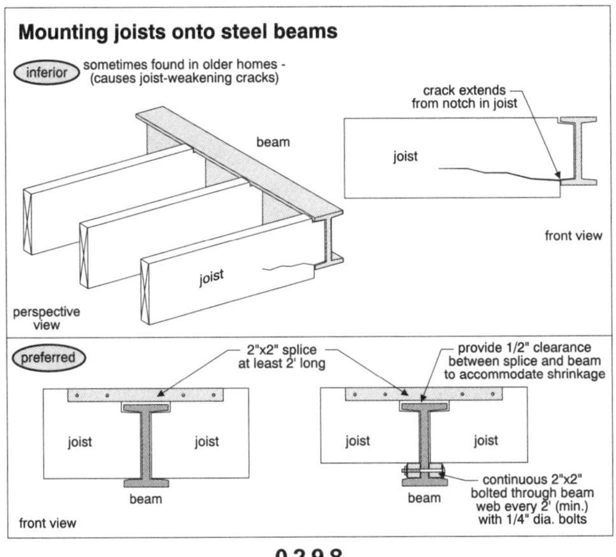

0298

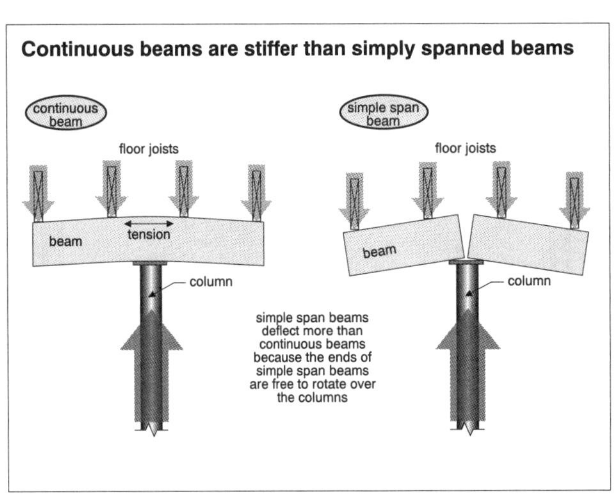

0299

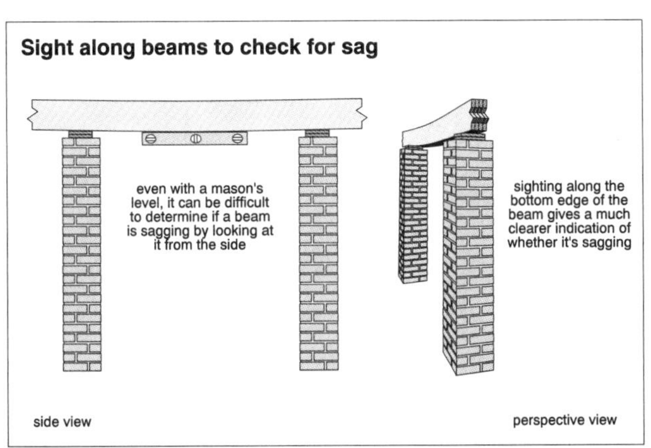

0300

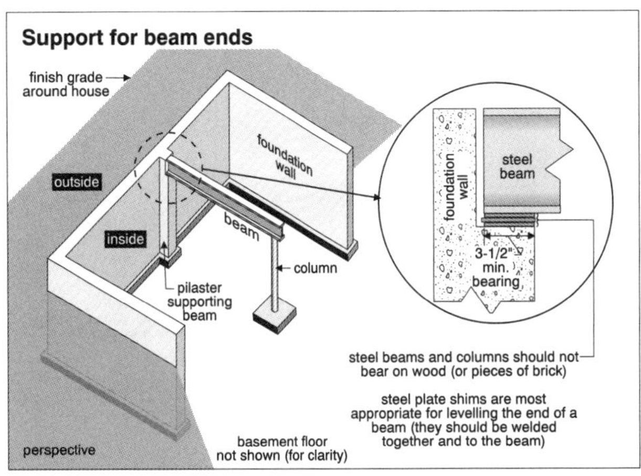

0301

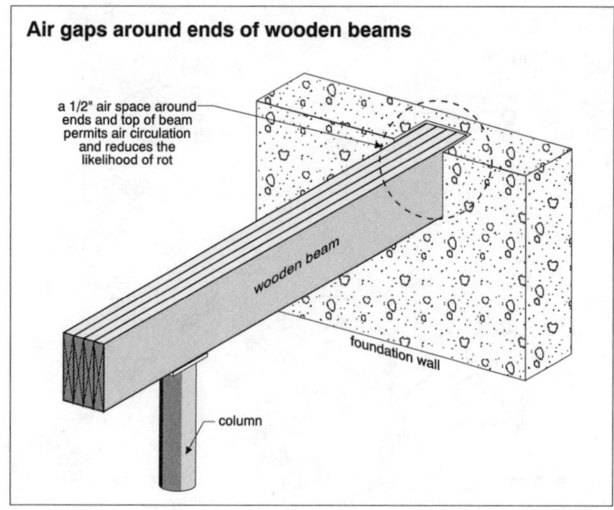

0302

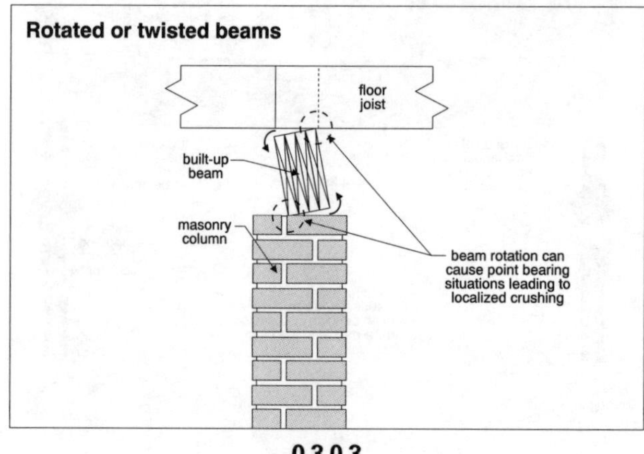

0303

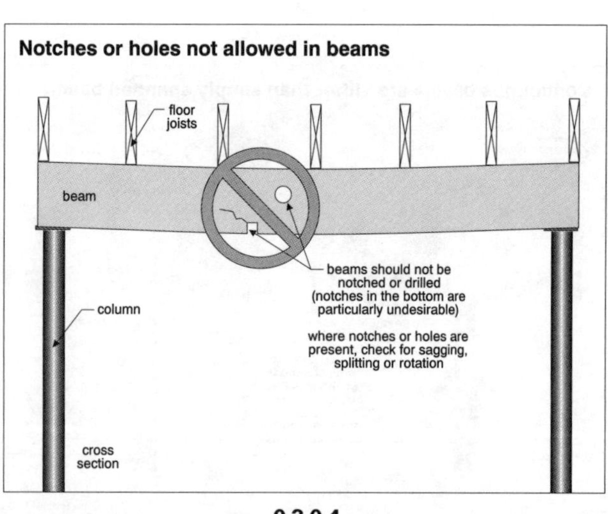

0304

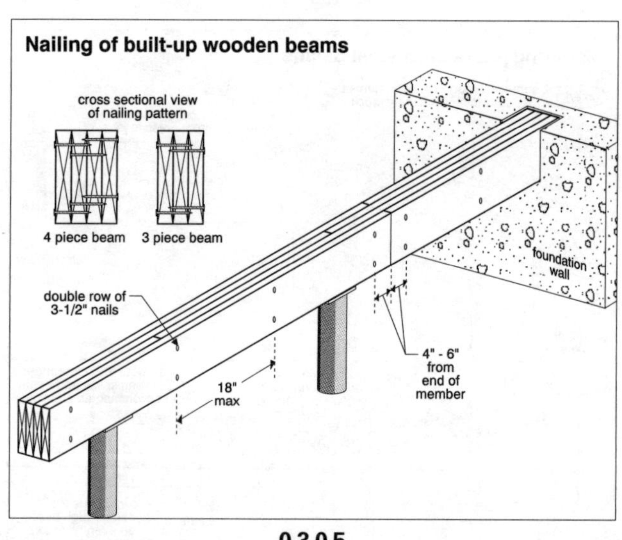

0305

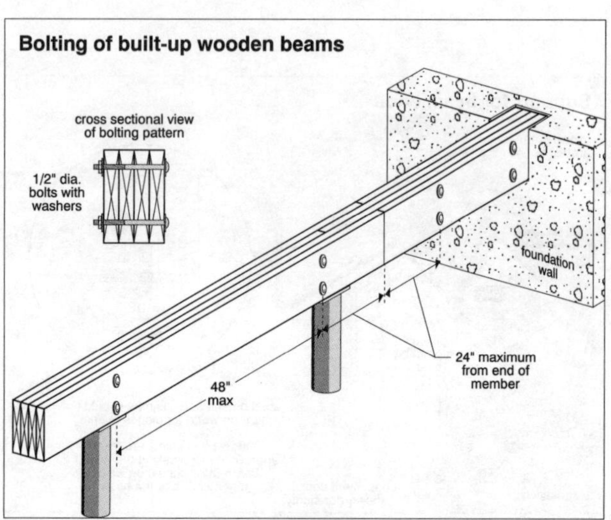

0306

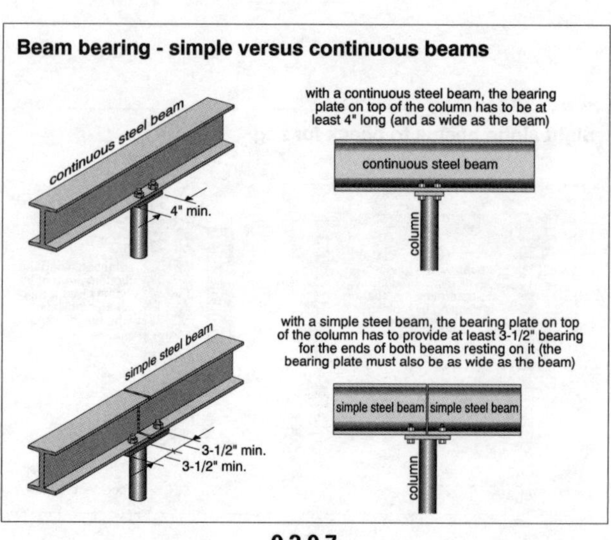

0307

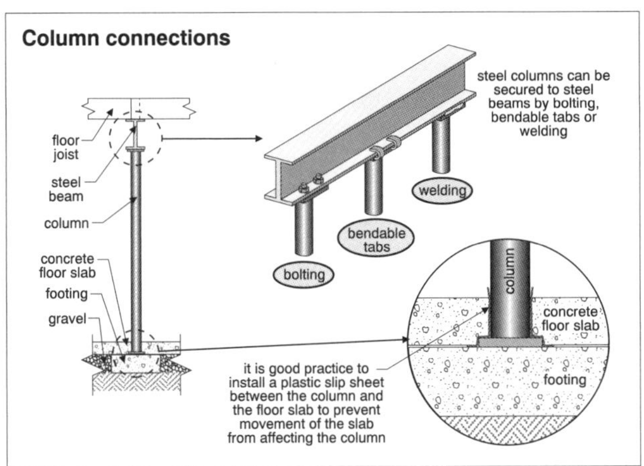

0308

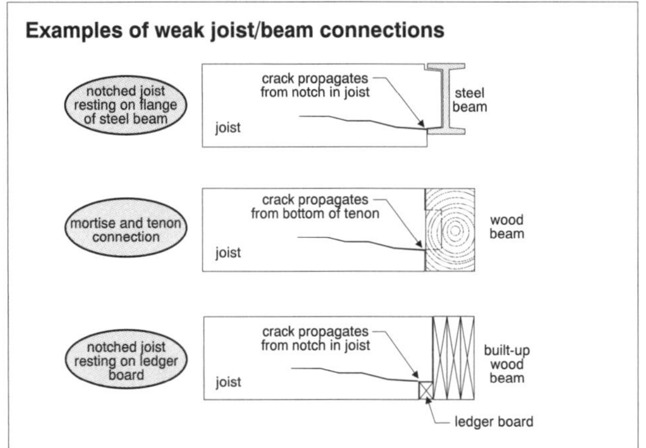

0309

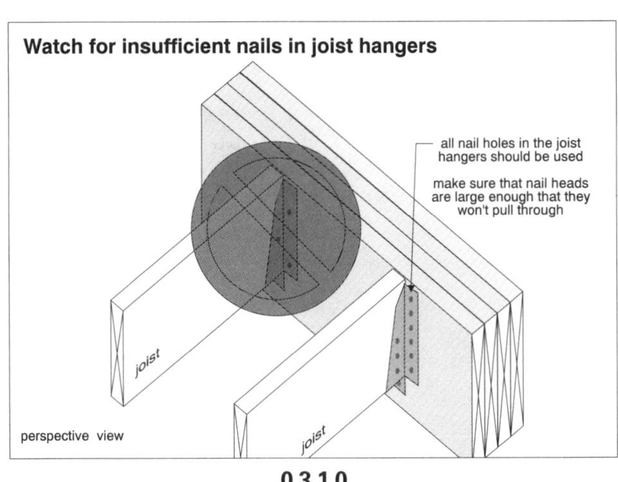

0310

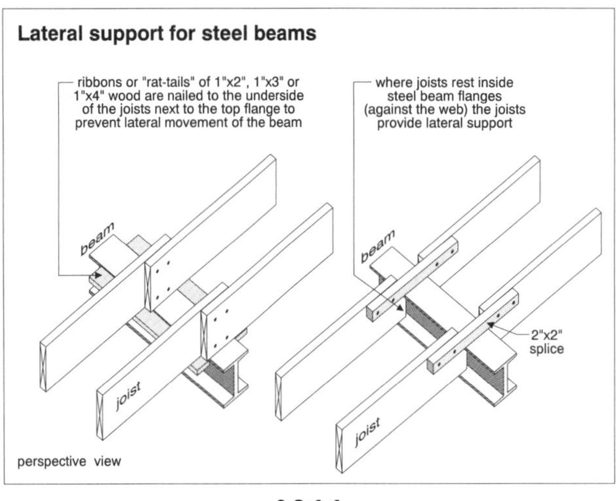

0311

Lateral support for wood beams

beam

joists nailed to beam and supported on ledger boards

joists hung off sides of beam with joist hangers

joist

beam

joist

beam

joists nailed to top of beam

joist

perspective view

0312

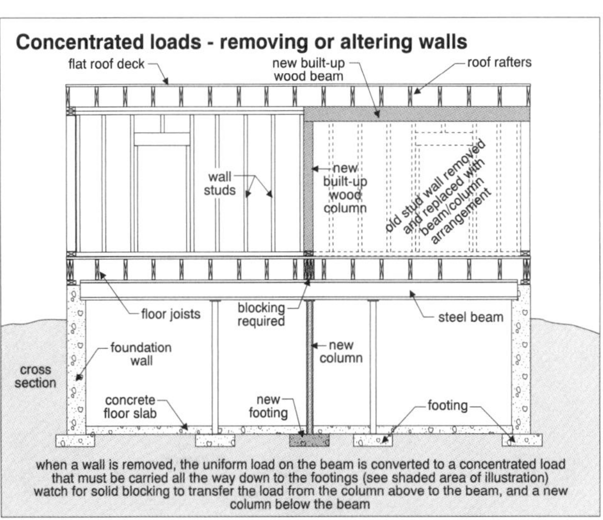

0313

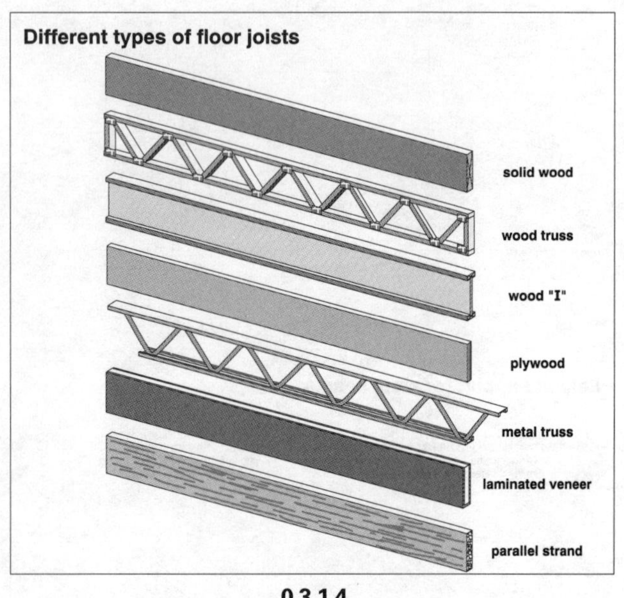

0314

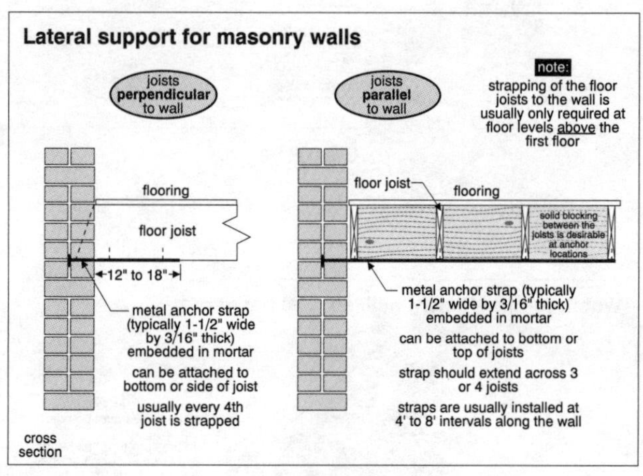

0315

Bowing of masonry walls

roof framing

masonry wall is bowing because it has not been laterally restrained at the second floor level

this is more likely to occur where the joists run parallel to the wall

second floor framing

first floor framing

foundation

cross section

0316

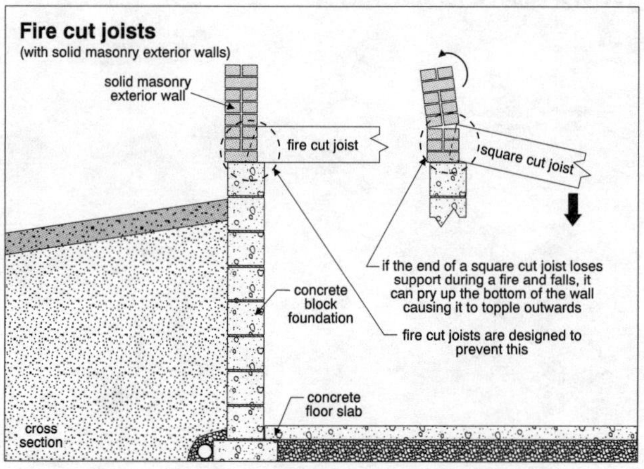

0317

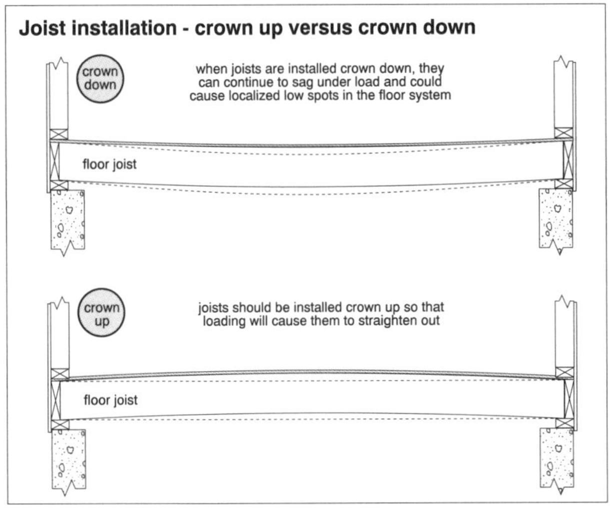

0318

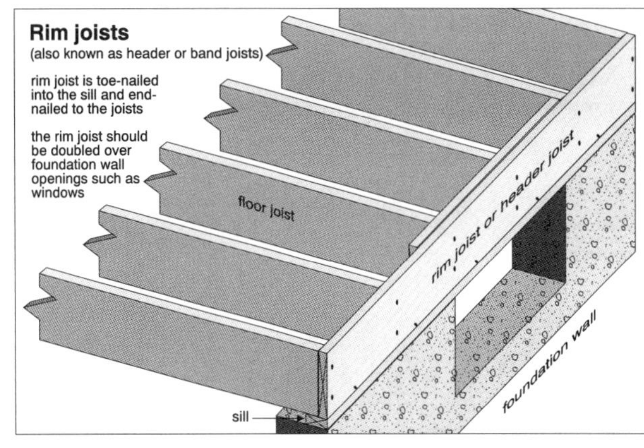

0319

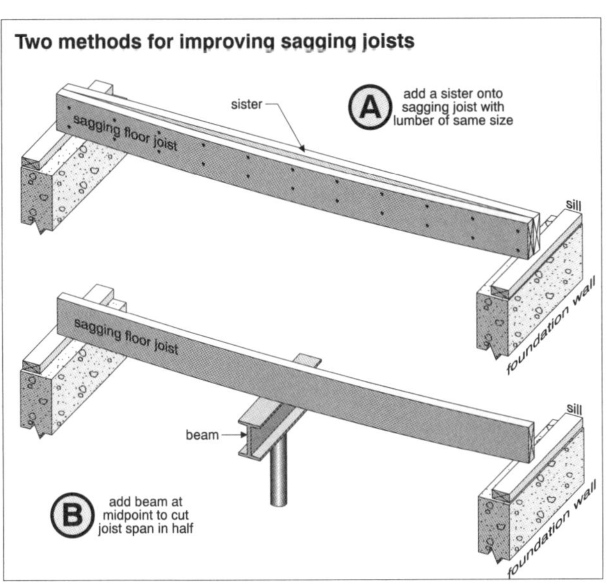

0320

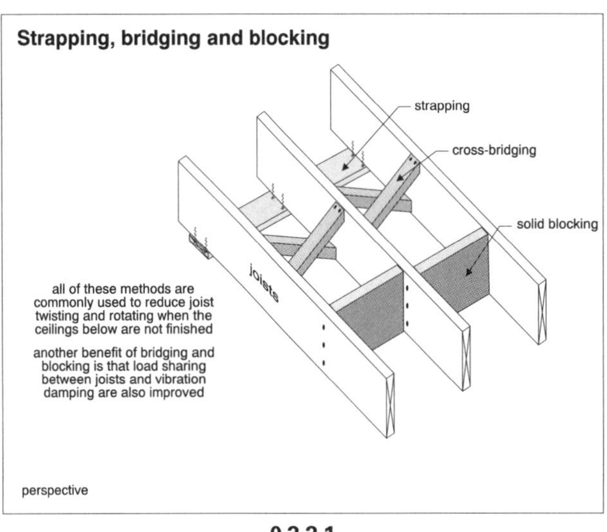

0321

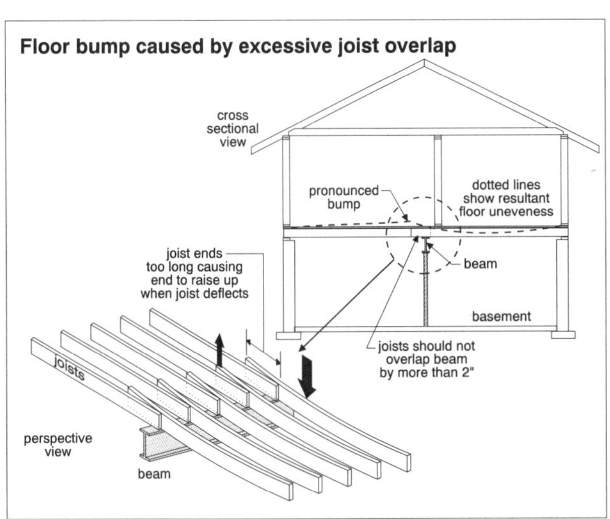

0322

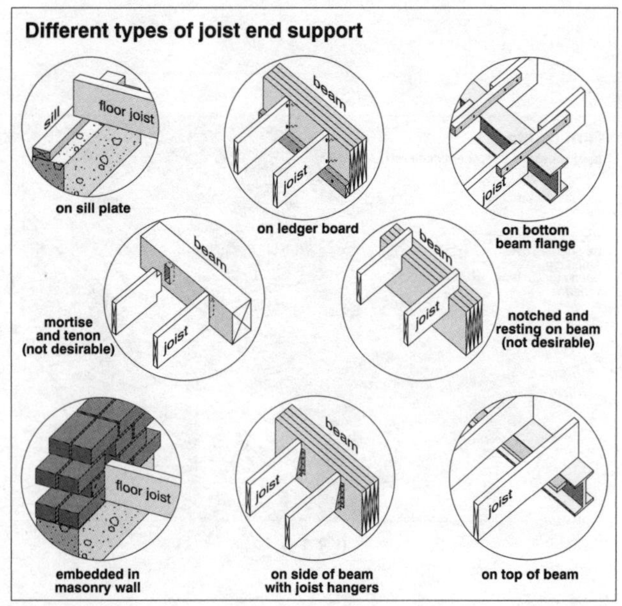

0323

Examples of weak joist/beam connections

notched joist resting on flange of steel beam
crack propagates from notch in joist
steel beam
joist

mortise and tenon connection
crack propagates from bottom of tenon
wood beam
joist

notched joist resting on ledger board
crack propagates from notch in joist
built-up wood beam
joist
ledger board

0324

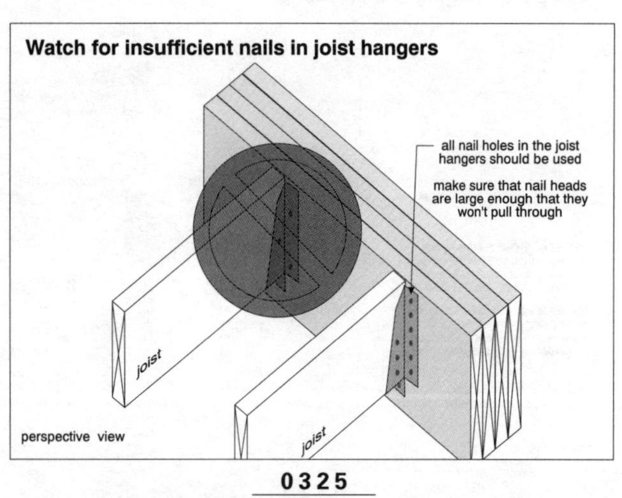

0325

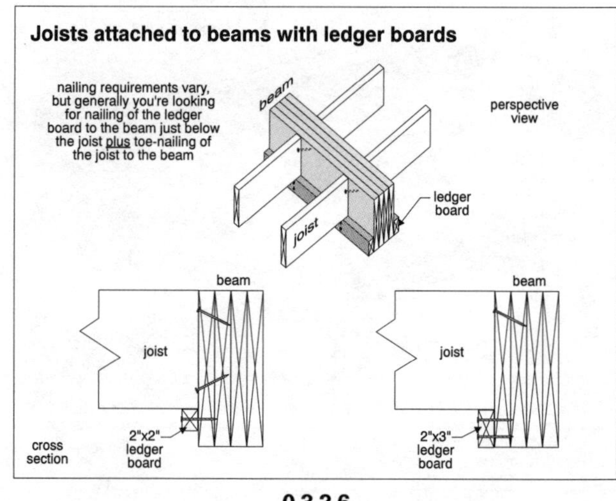

0326

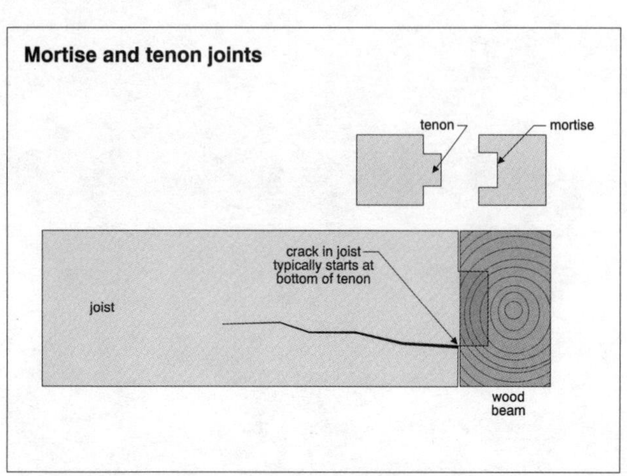

0327

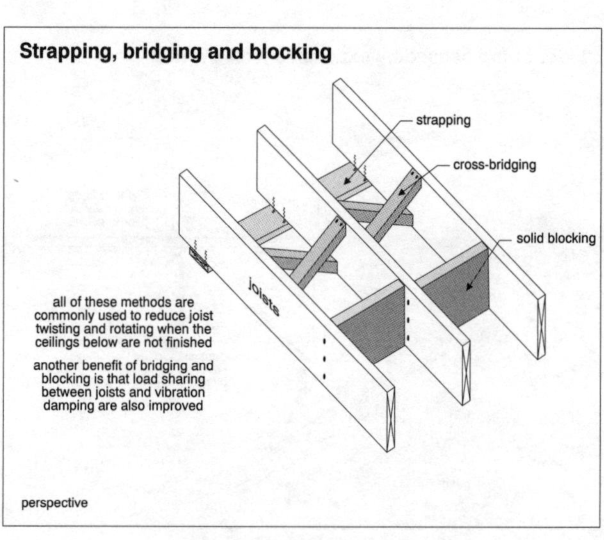

0328

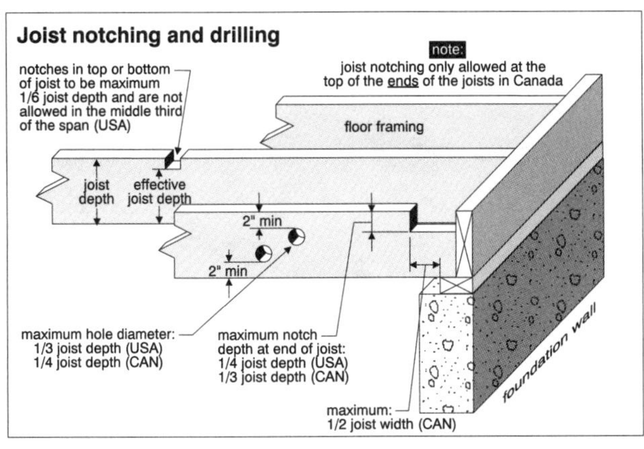

0329

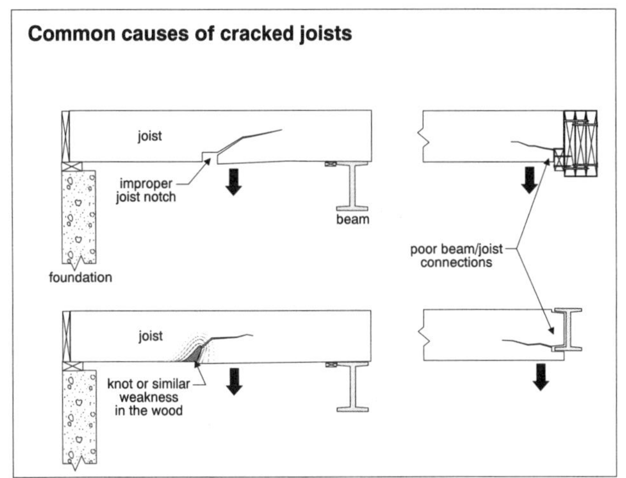

0330

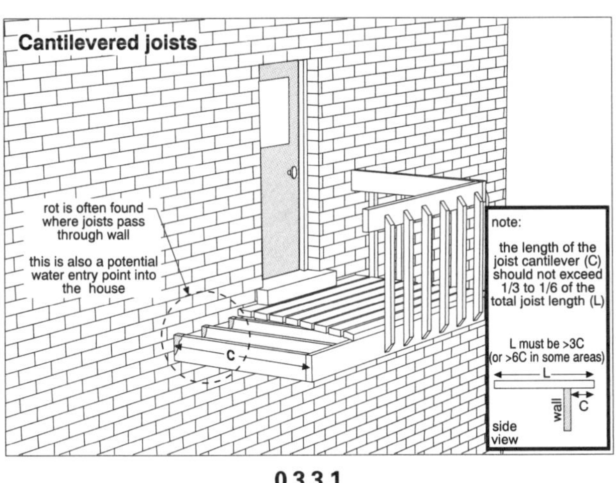

0331

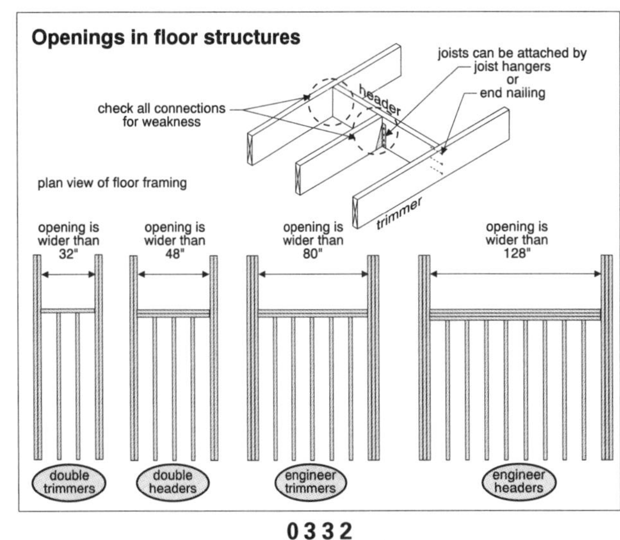

0332

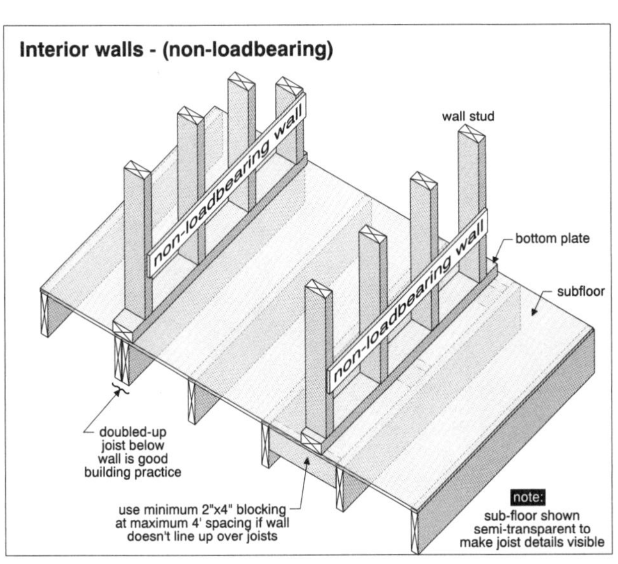

0333

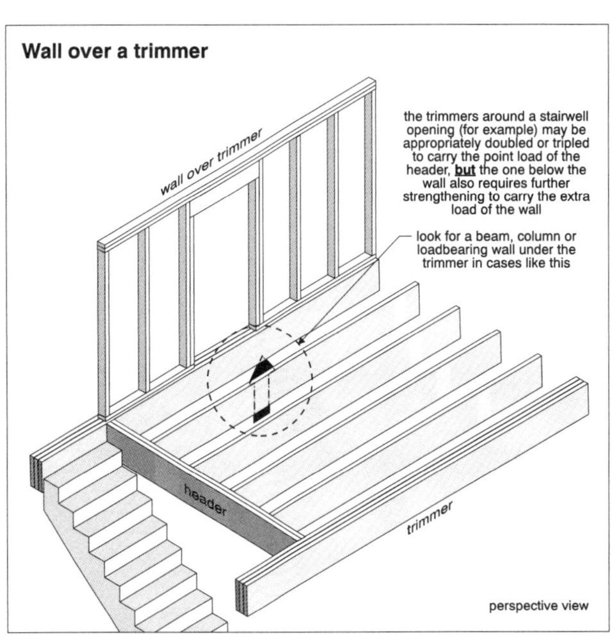

0334

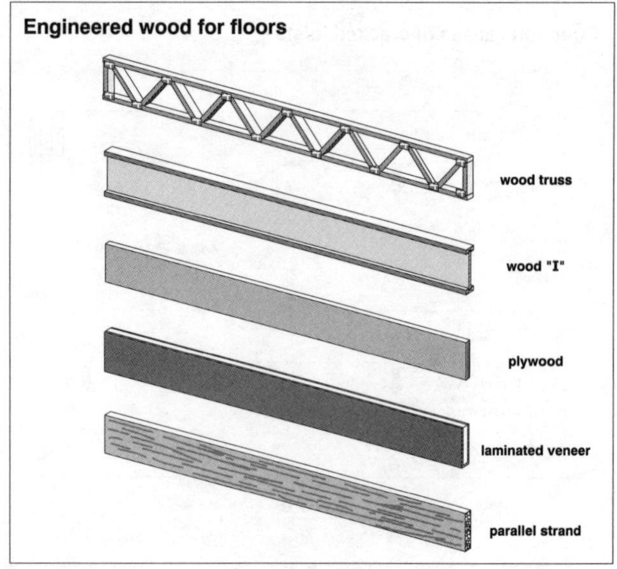

0335

Wood "I" joist notching and drilling

use prepunched knockouts, if provided

distance from support

holes should be centered

2 x D2 minimum

D1

D2

1/8" minimum

mid-span

I-joist flanges should not be notched, either fully or partially

support

reinforcement should not have holes or notches

each manufacturer has its own rules for the minimum distance between supports and holes

typically, 2 inch diameter holes may be drilled mid-height at 2 feet or more from a support

larger holes should be as close as possible to the center of the span

holes may be round or square

0336

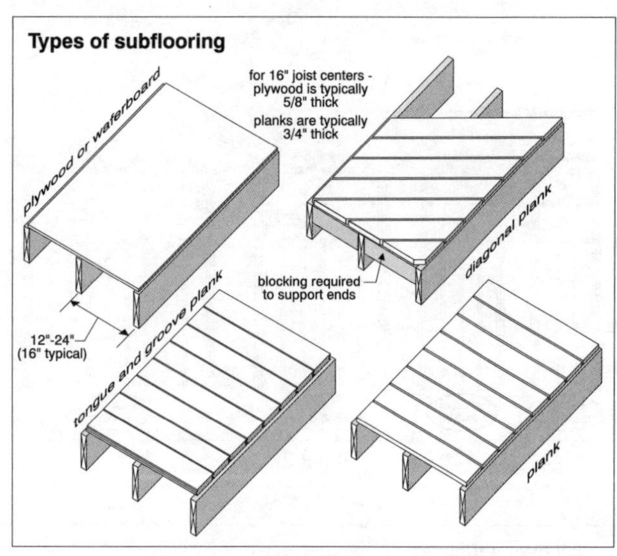

0337

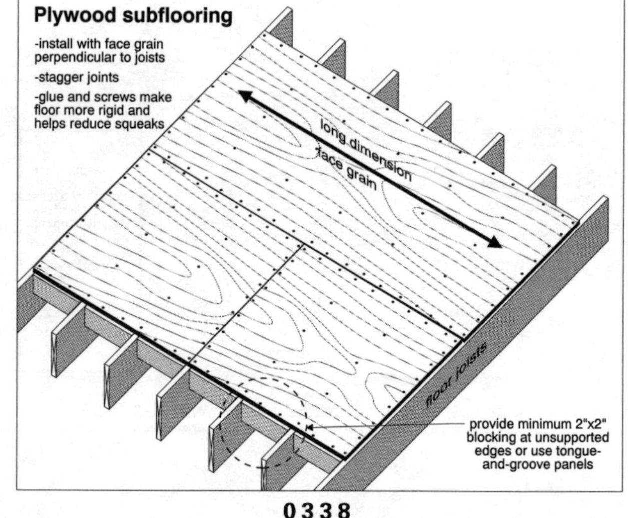

0338

Subflooring edge support

floor joists

floor joists

blocking is required below unsupported edges of plywood or waferboard (not tongue-and-groove) panel-type subflooring and diagonal plank subflooring

0339

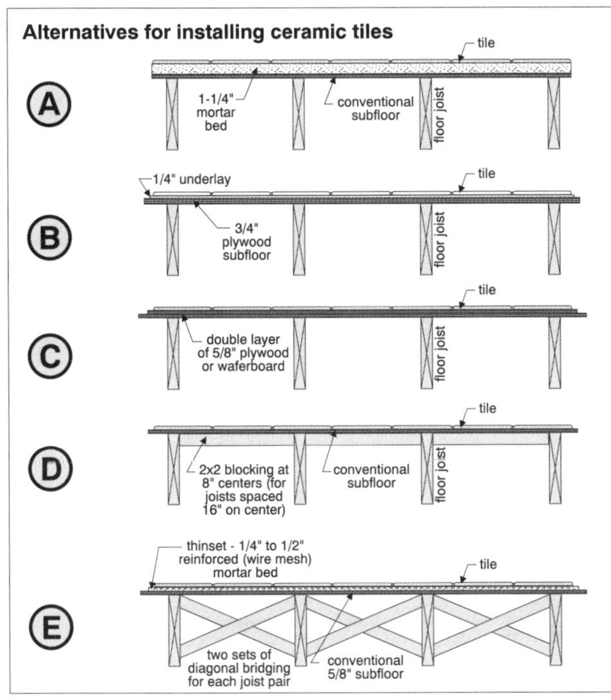

0340

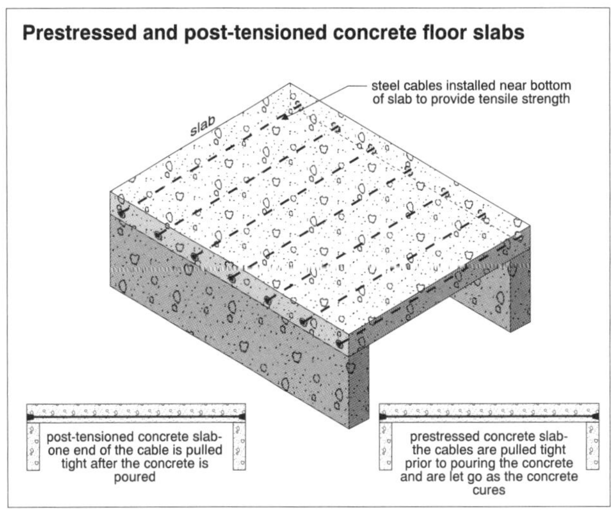

0341

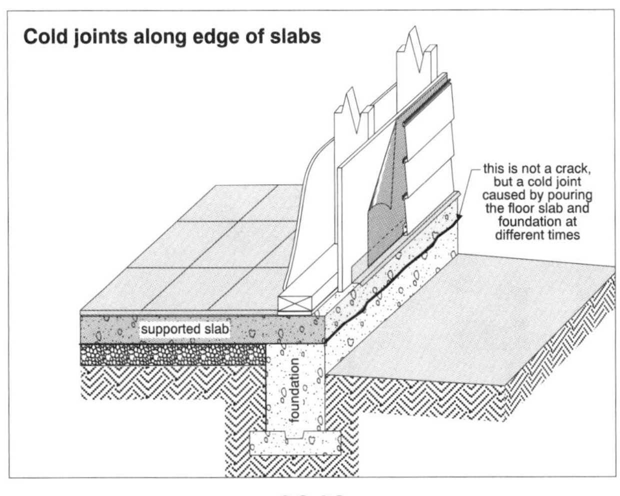

0342

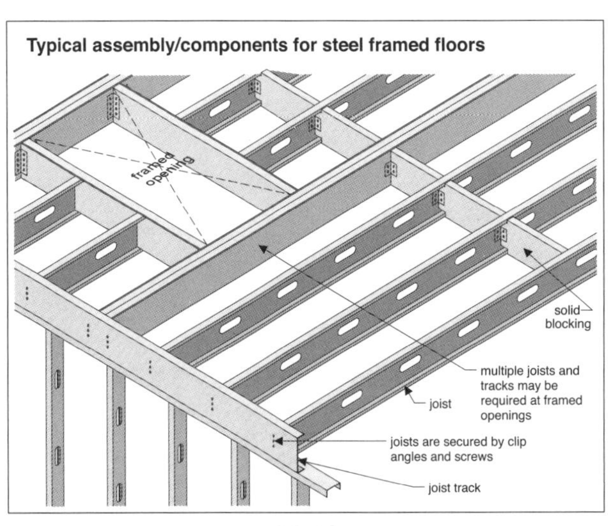

0343

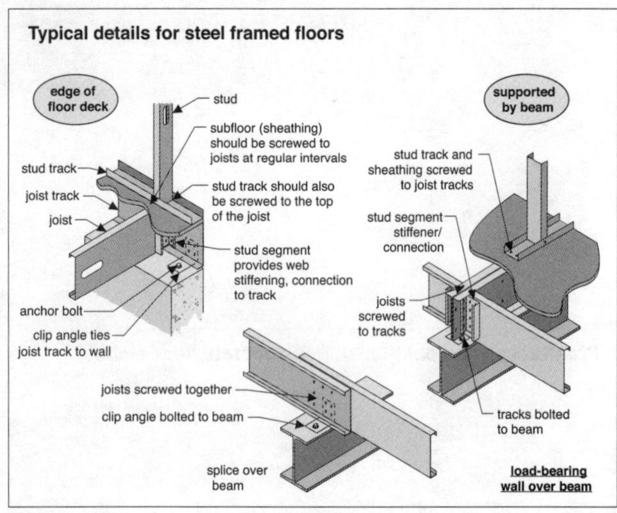

0344

Excessive sagging around poorly framed stair openings

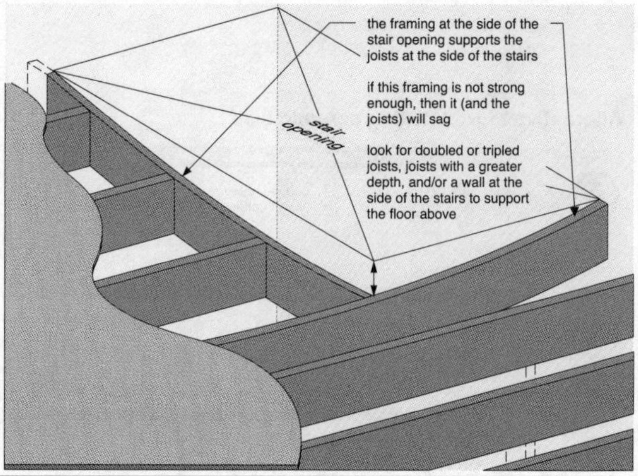

the framing at the side of the stair opening supports the joists at the side of the stairs

if this framing is not strong enough, then it (and the joists) will sag

look for doubled or tripled joists, joists with a greater depth, and/or a wall at the side of the stairs to support the floor above

stair opening

0345

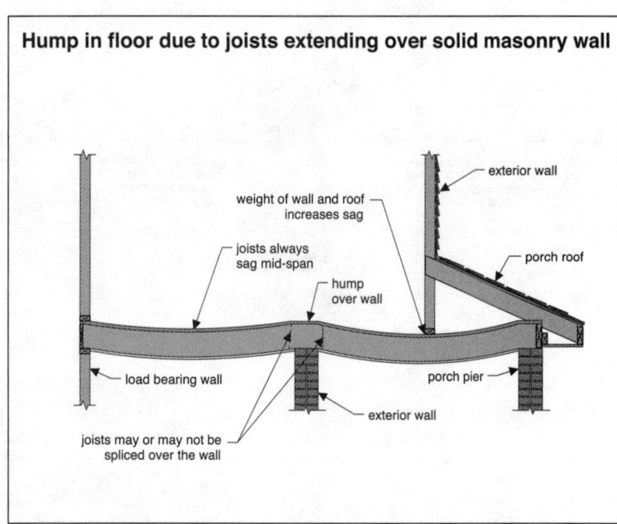

0346

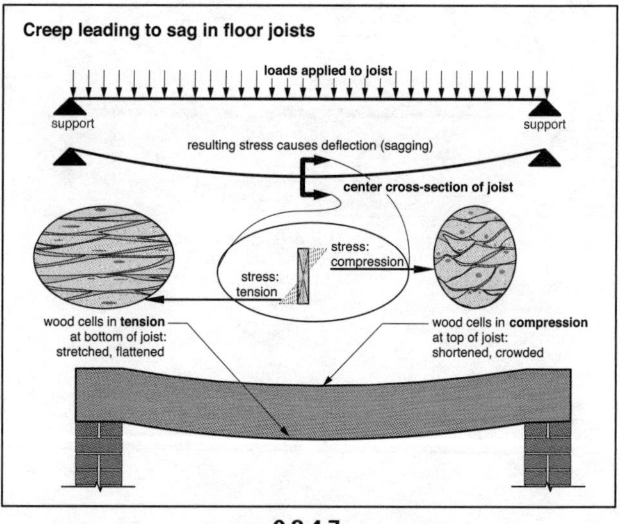

0347

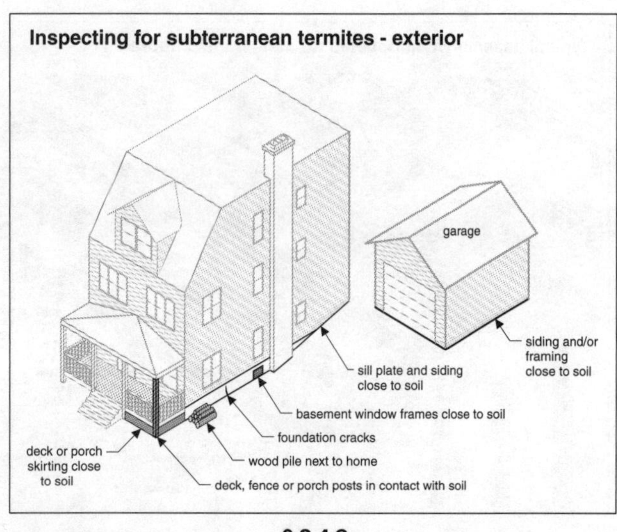

0348

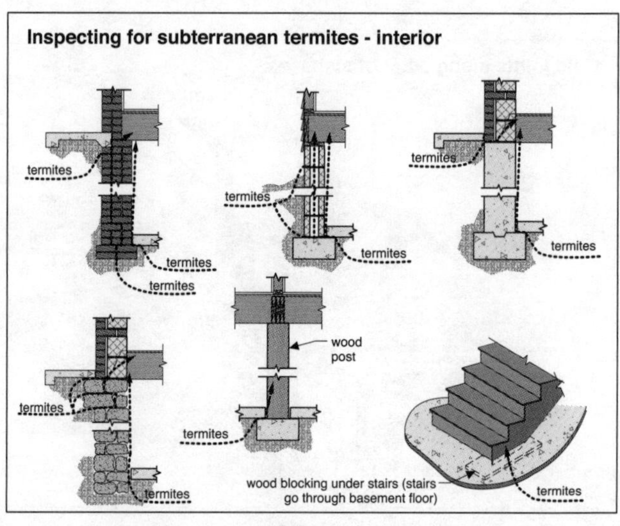

0349

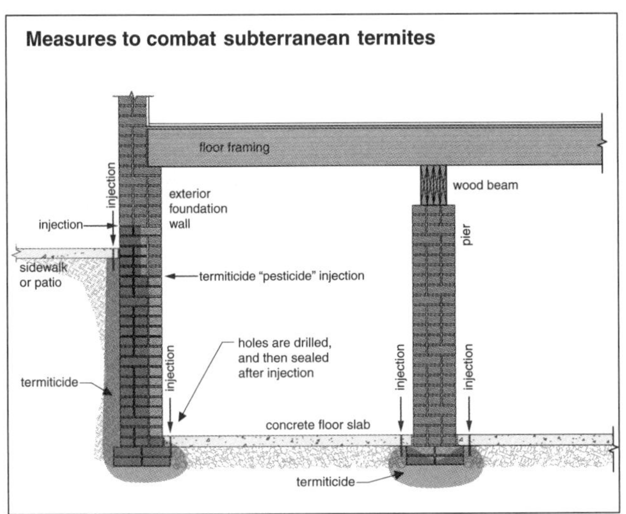

0350

Solid masonry walls

cross sectional view

metal tie

header

header

cinder block

cinder block

header

single wythe

2 wythes running bond (no headers) (uses metal ties)

2 wythes common bond (headers every 6th course)

2 wythes common bond (6th course headers) cinder block used for inside face of wall

3 wythes common bond (headers every 6th course)

0351

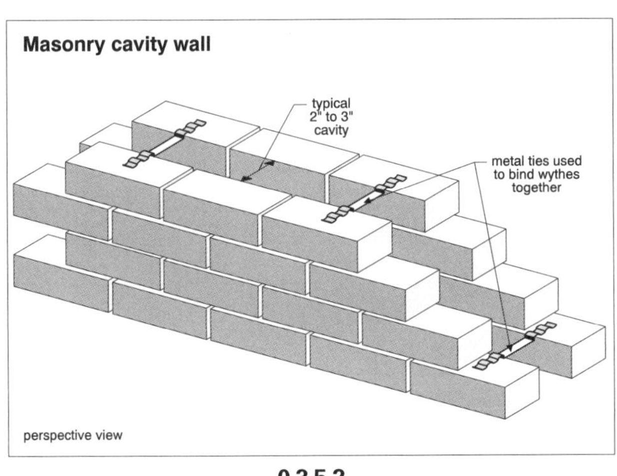

0352

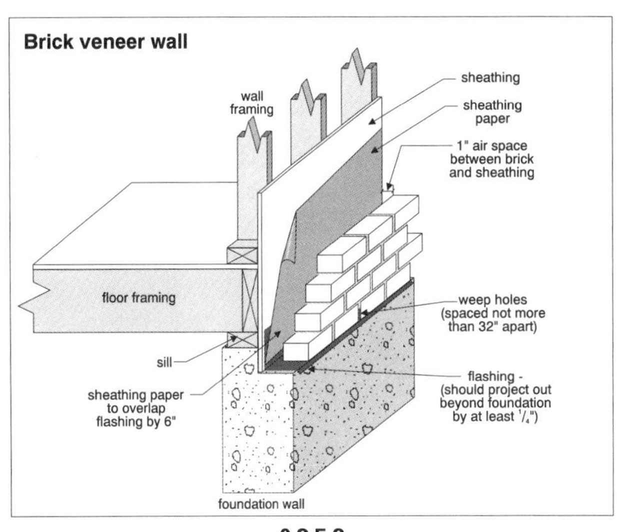

0353

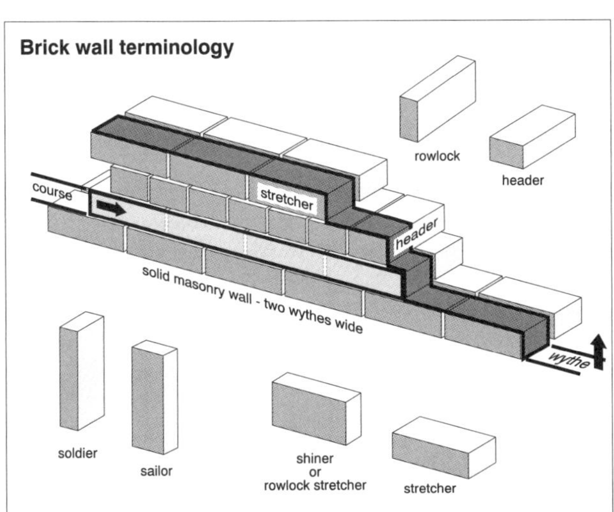

0354

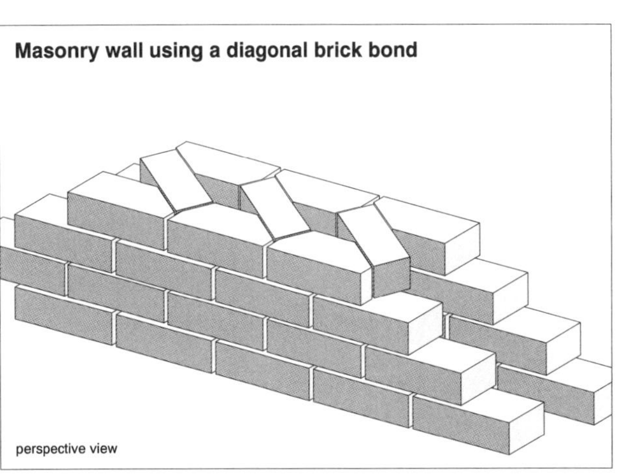

0355

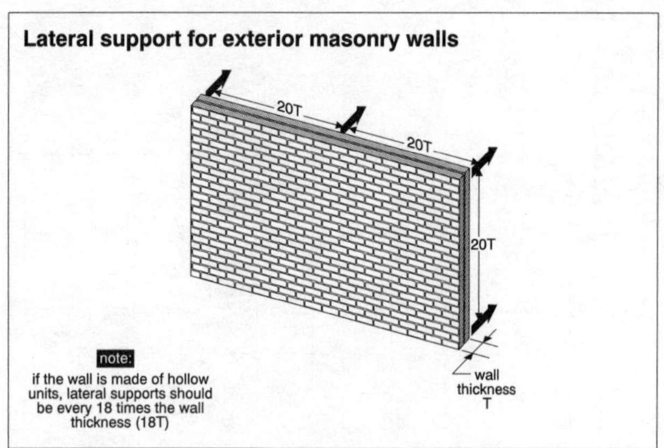

Lateral support for exterior masonry walls

0356

Walls that extend above ceiling joists

A ceiling joist and rafter bottom are same height
roof rafter
ceiling joist
when the ceiling joists are attached to the roof rafters, they help to prevent spreading

B rafter bottom above ceiling joist
roof rafter
the section of solid masonry wall above the ceiling joist can't resist the horizontal rafter force
ceiling joist

cross section

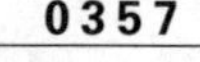

0357

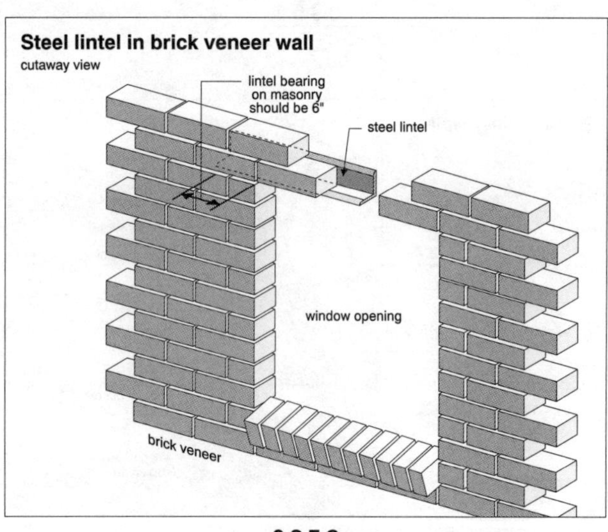

Steel lintel in brick veneer wall

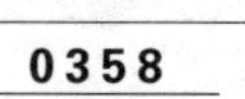

0358

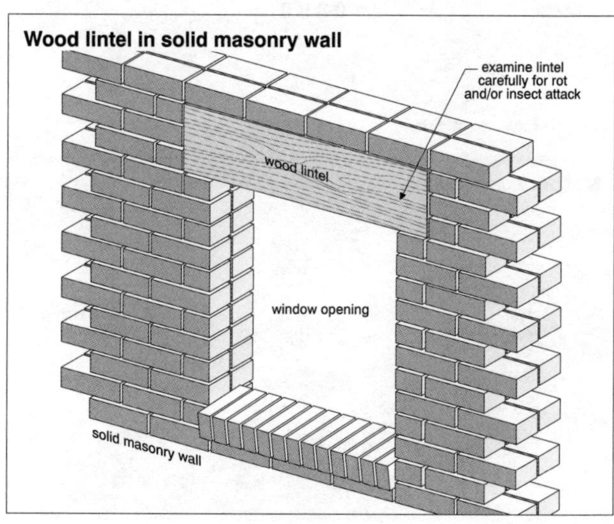

Wood lintel in solid masonry wall

0359

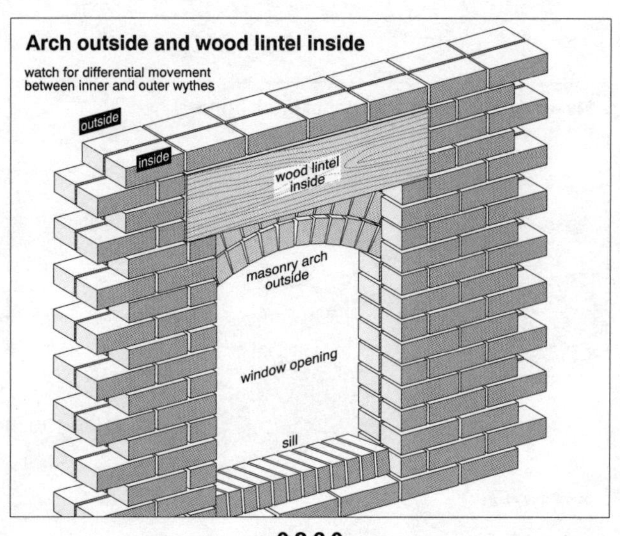

Arch outside and wood lintel inside

0360

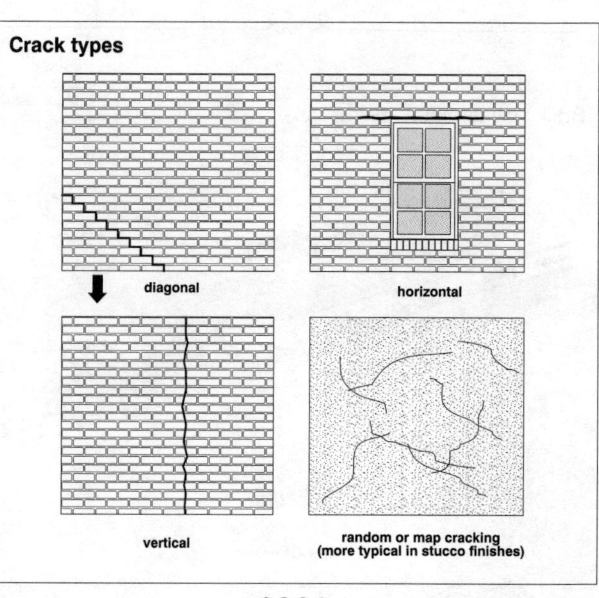

Crack types

0361

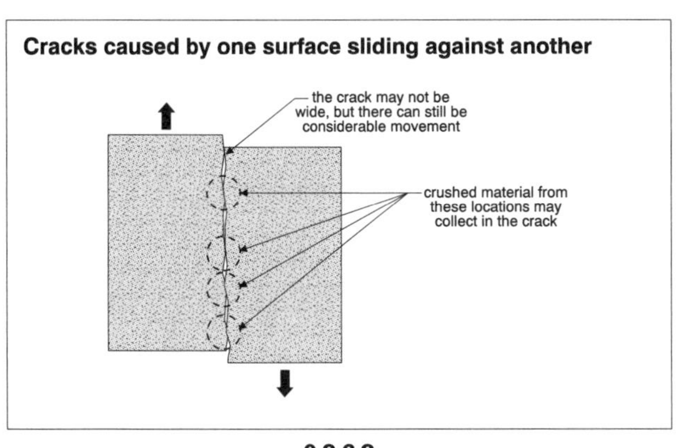

0362

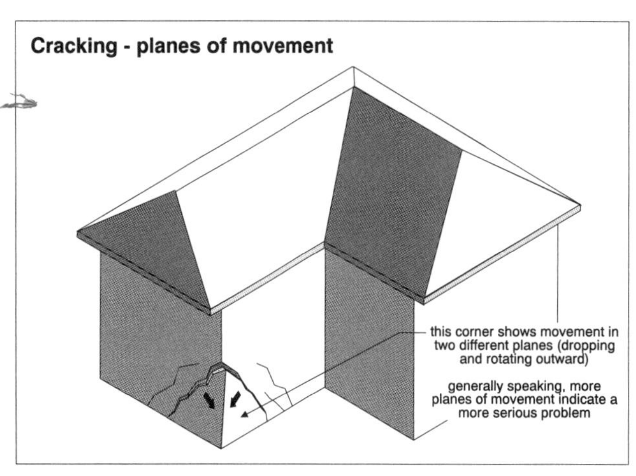

0363

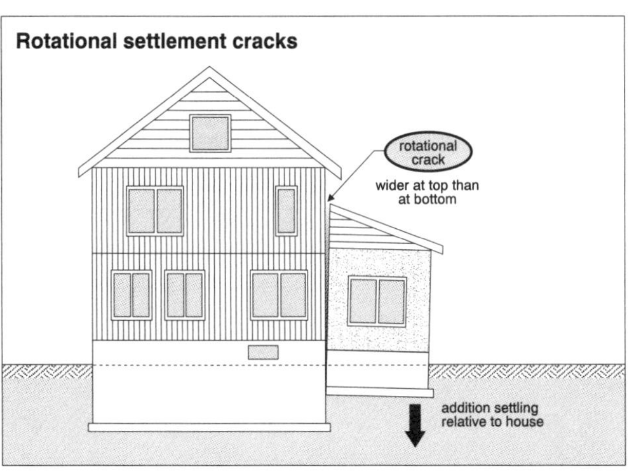

0364

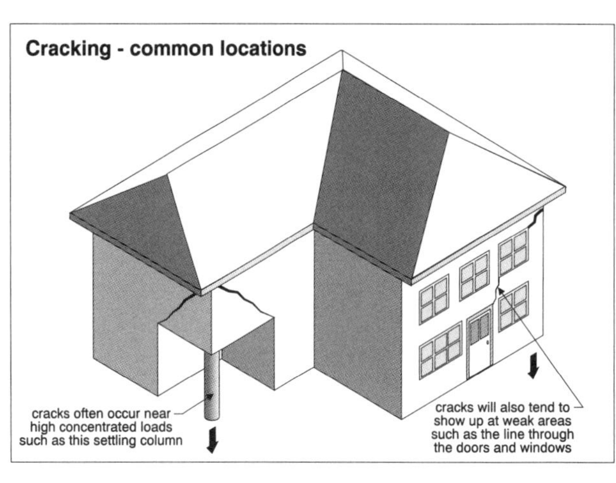

0365

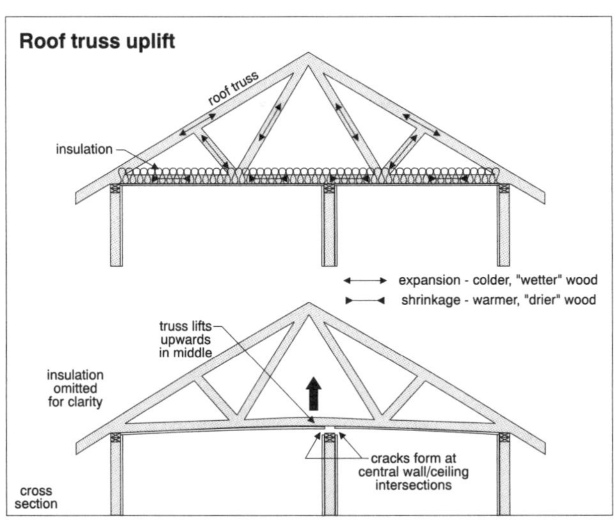

0366

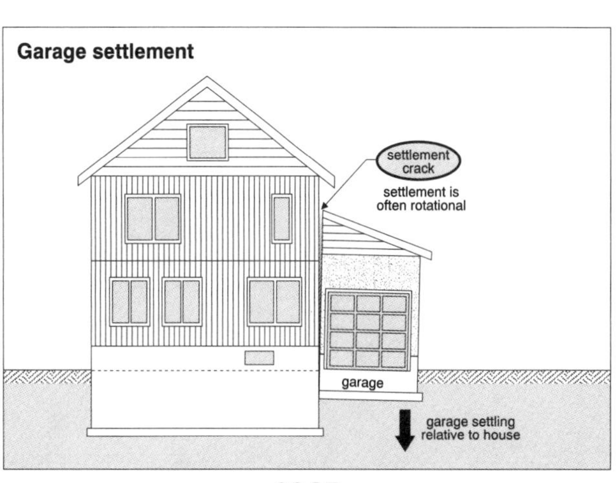

0367

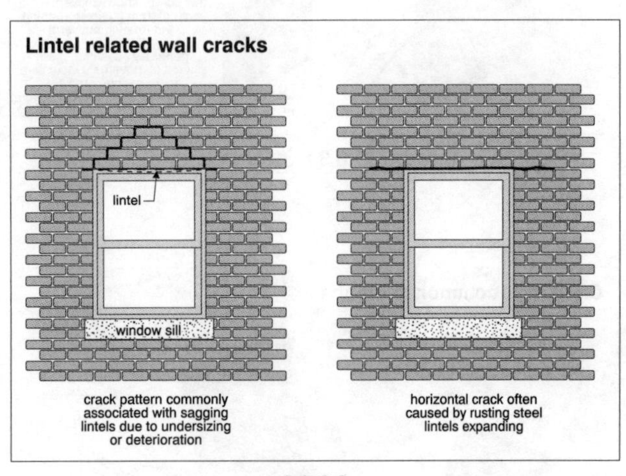

Lintel related wall cracks

0368

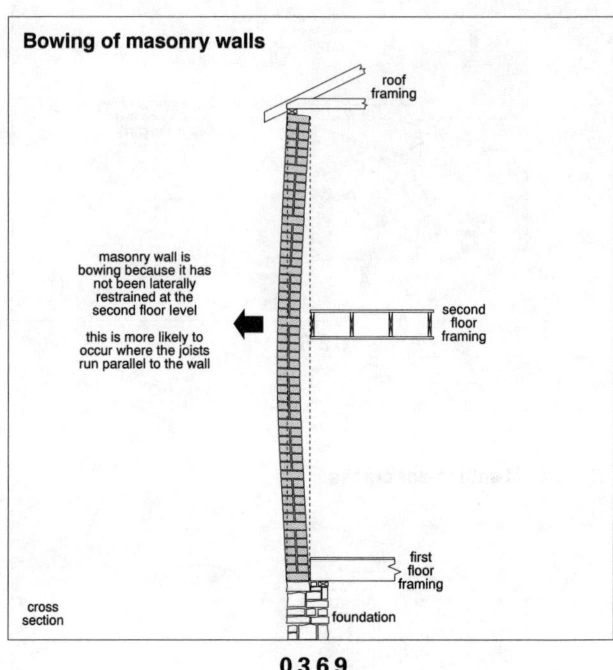

Bowing of masonry walls

0369

Bowed brick veneer wall - older home

roof framing

wall is restrained at top and bottom

wall framing

masonry ties may be rusted and/or pulled out of mortar bed

ties are often rusted below windows which are common leakage spots

second floor framing

ties on older houses (where bowing is most commonly found) are often regular framing nails

brick veneer wall

first floor framing

foundation

cross section

0370

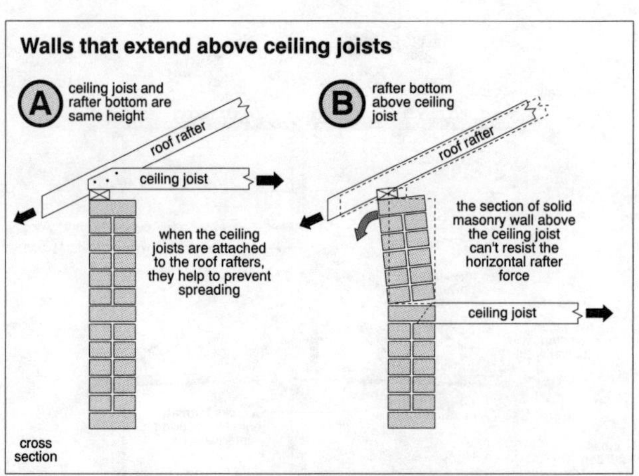

Walls that extend above ceiling joists

0371

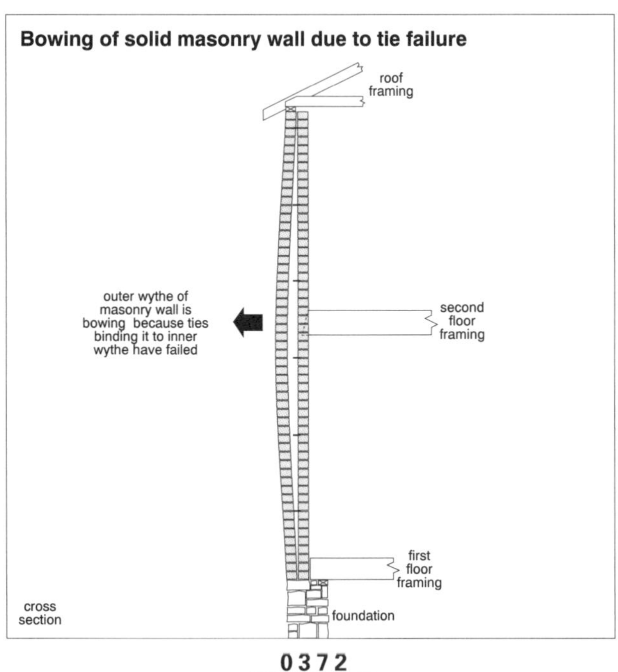

0372

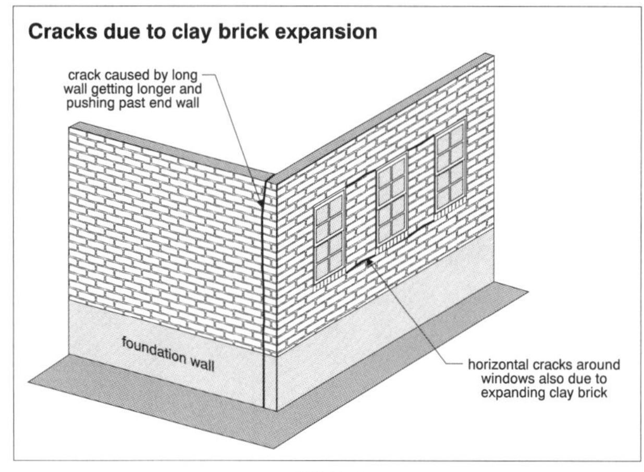

0373

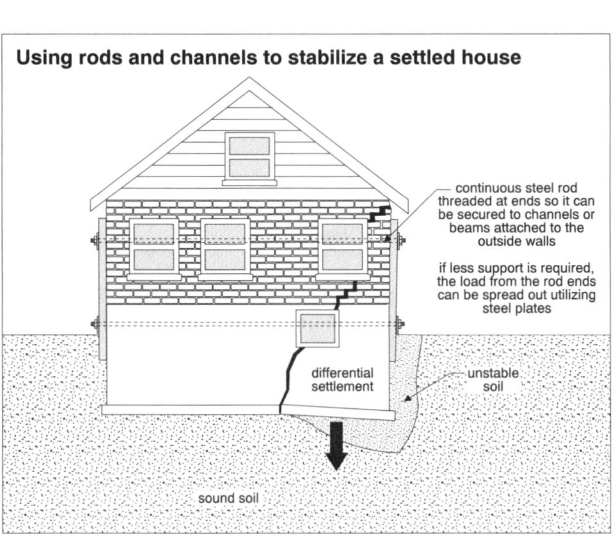

0374

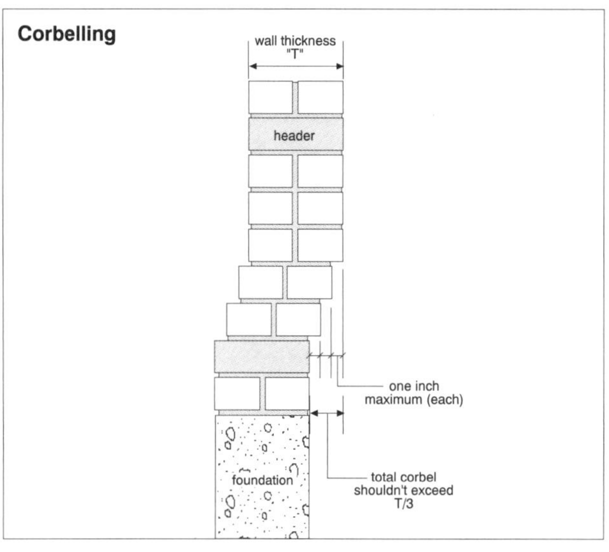

0375

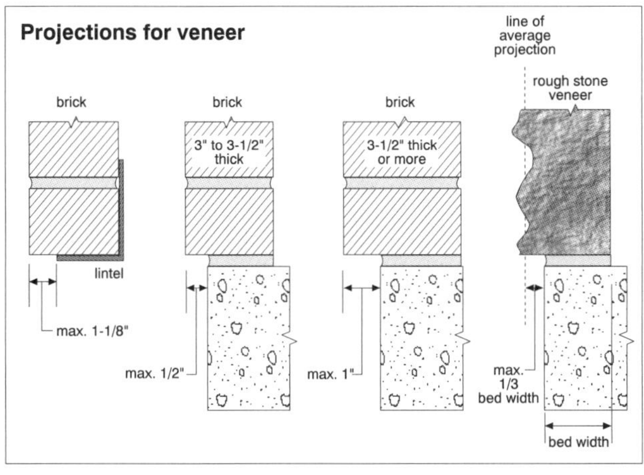

0376

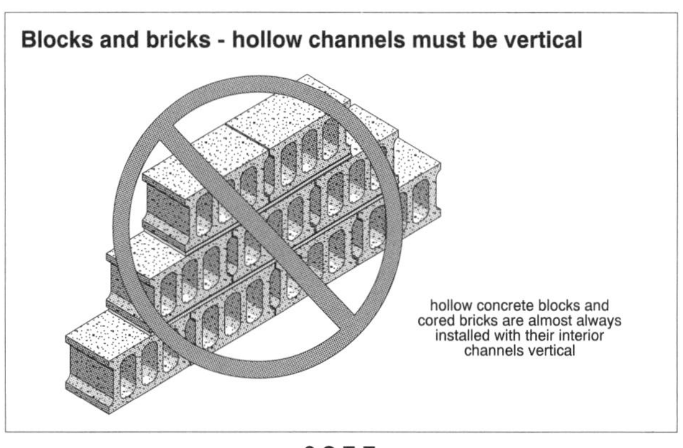

0377

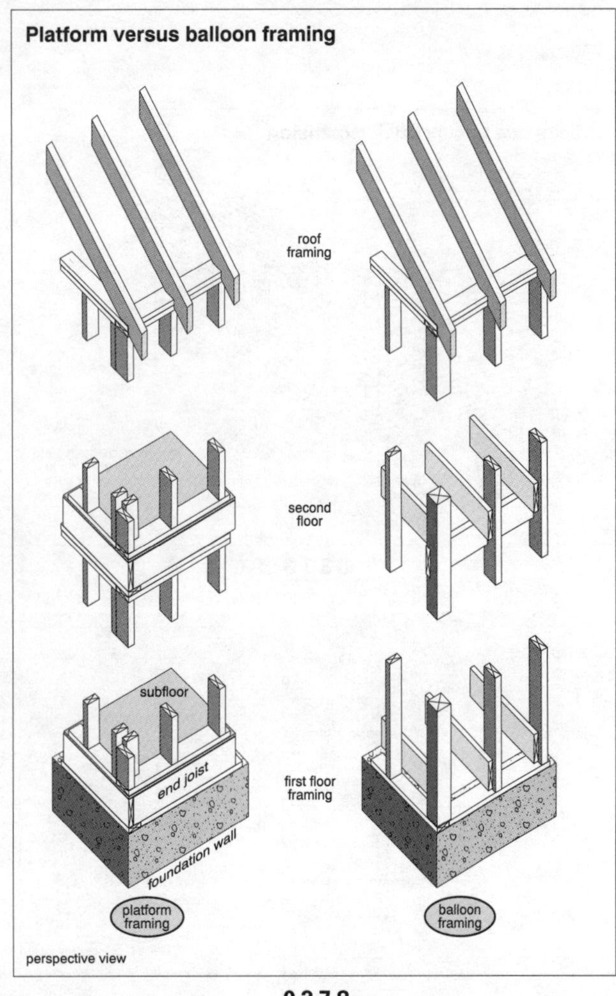

0378

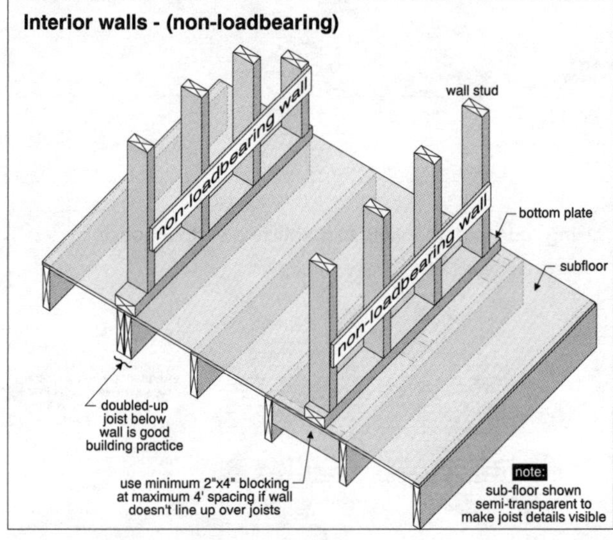

0379

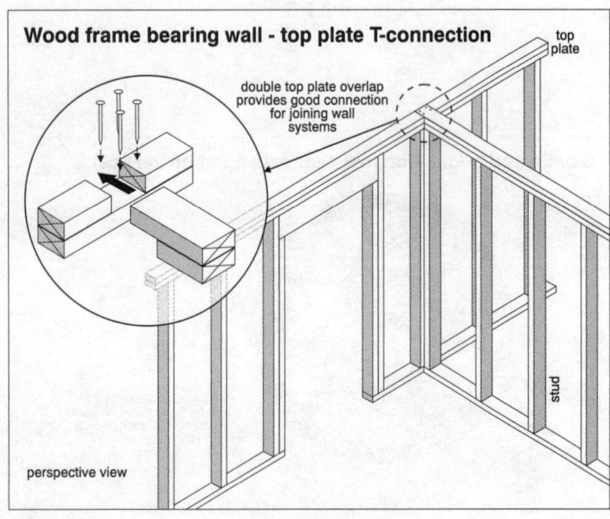

0380

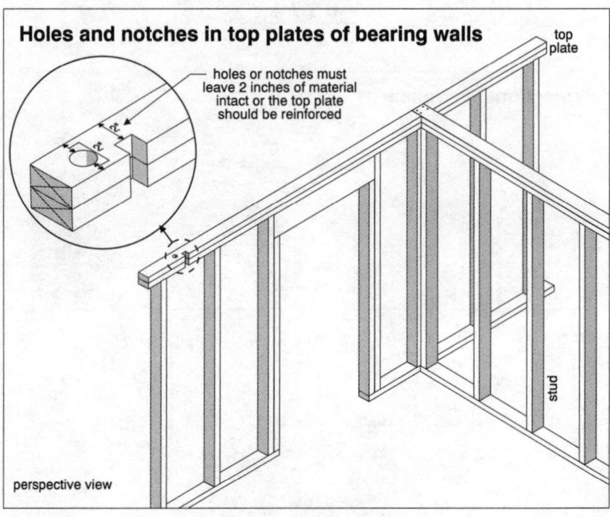

0381

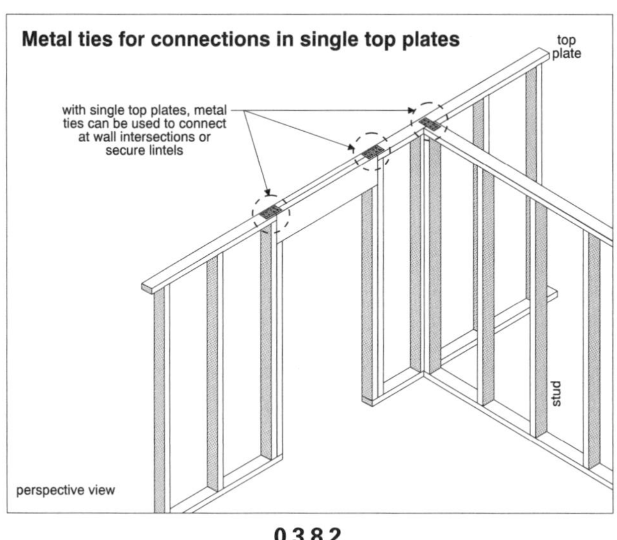

0382

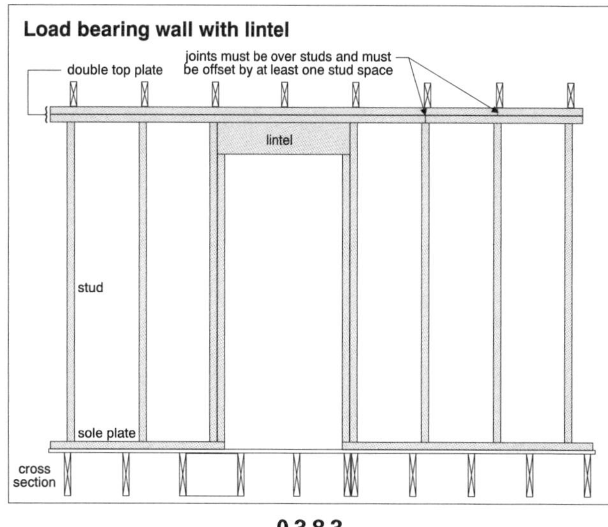

0383

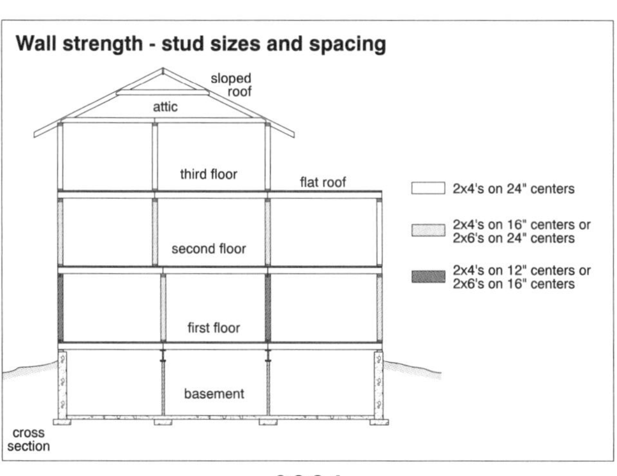

0384

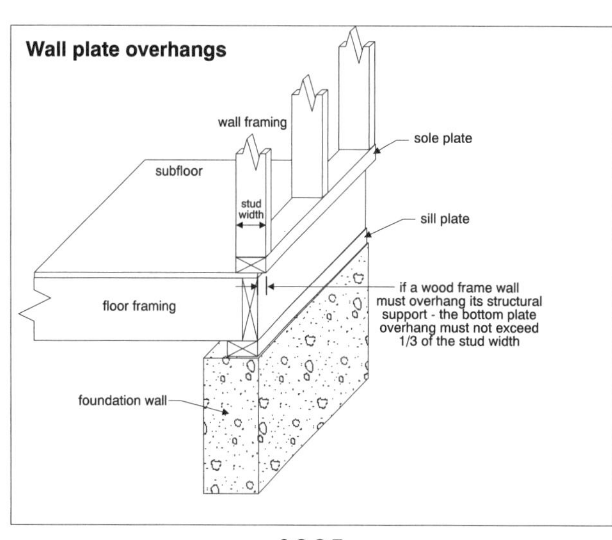

0385

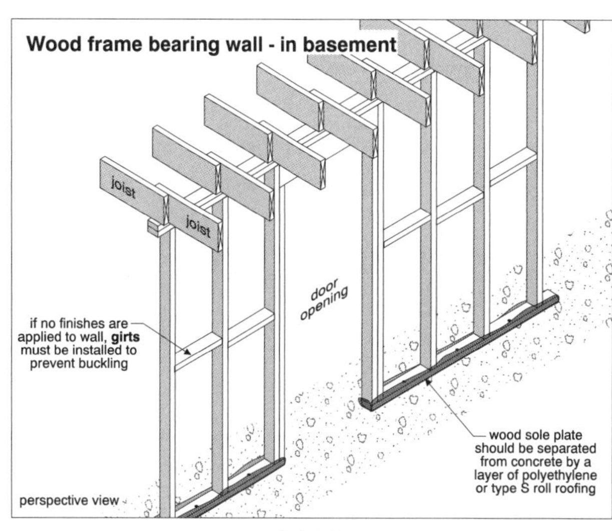

0386

0387

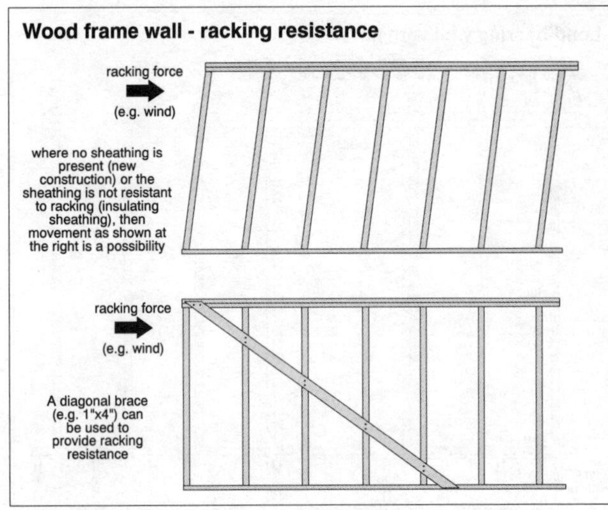

0388

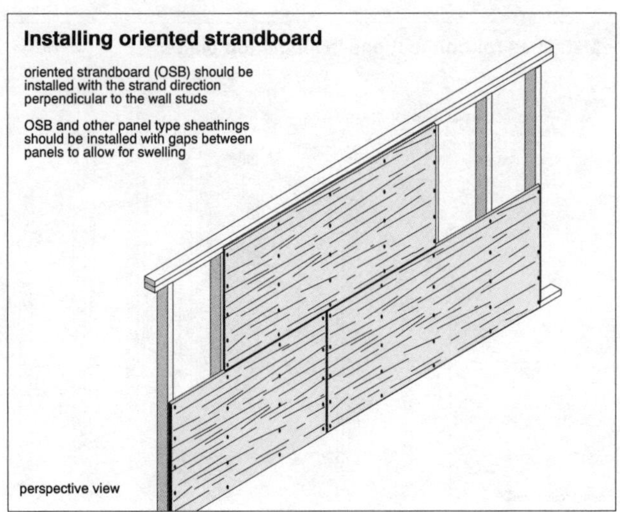

0389

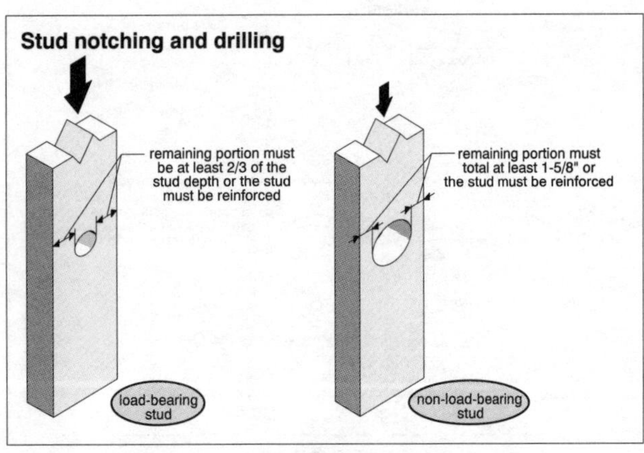

0390

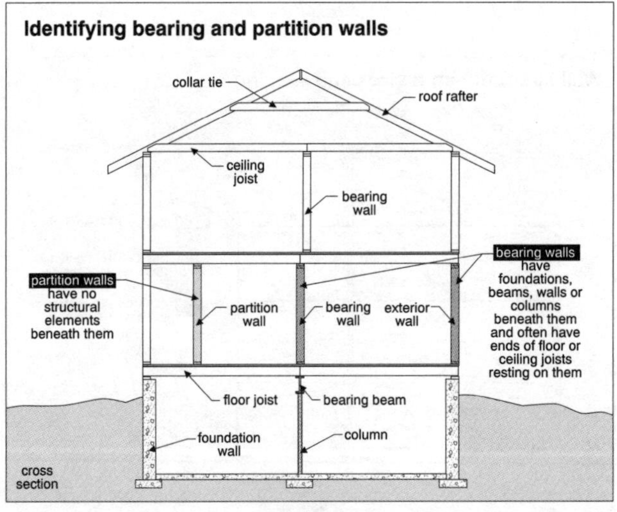

0391

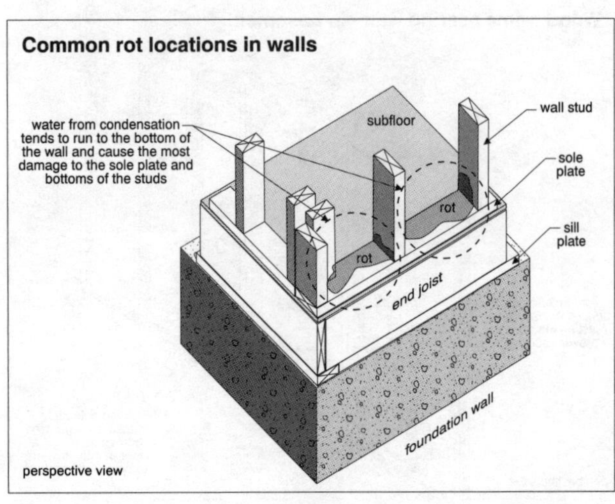

0392

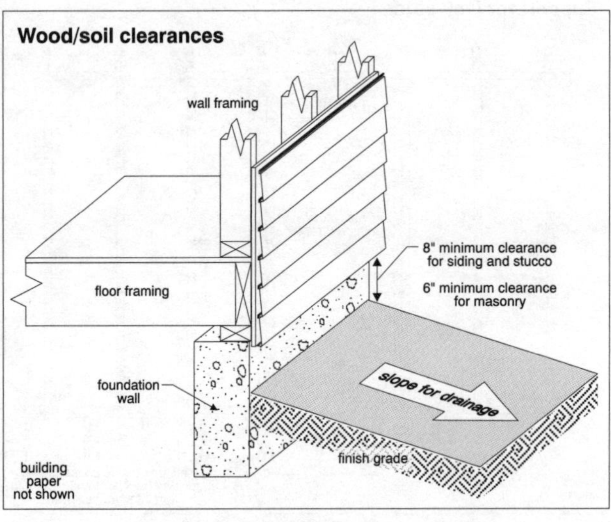

0393

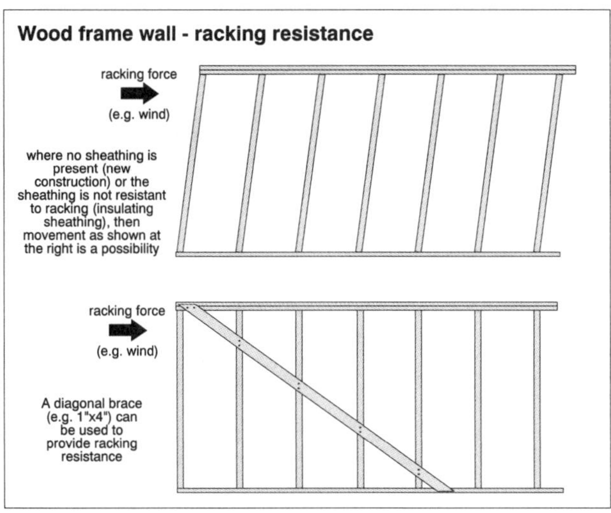

0394

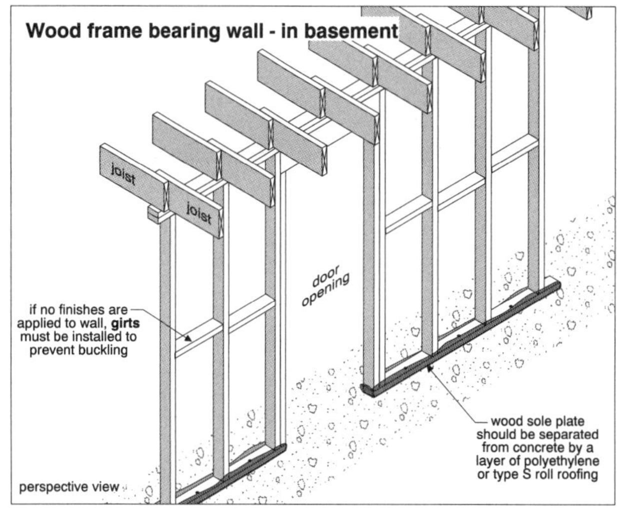

0395

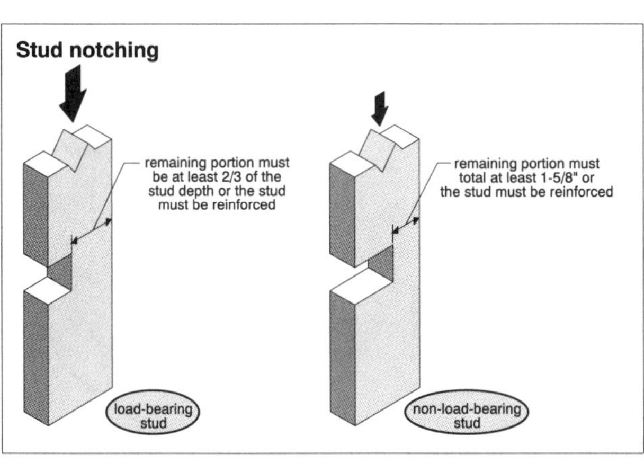

0396

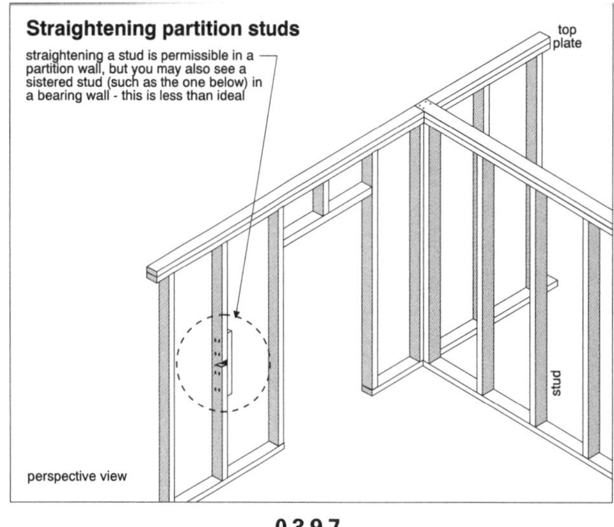

0397

Concentrated loads - removing or altering walls

flat roof deck
new built-up wood beam
roof rafters
wall studs
new built-up wood column
old stud wall removed and replaced with beam/column arrangement
floor joists
blocking required
steel beam
foundation wall
new column
cross section
concrete floor slab
new footing
footing

when a wall is removed, the uniform load on the beam is converted to a concentrated load that must be carried all the way down to the footings (see shaded area of illustration) watch for solid blocking to transfer the load from the column above to the beam, and a new column below the beam

0398

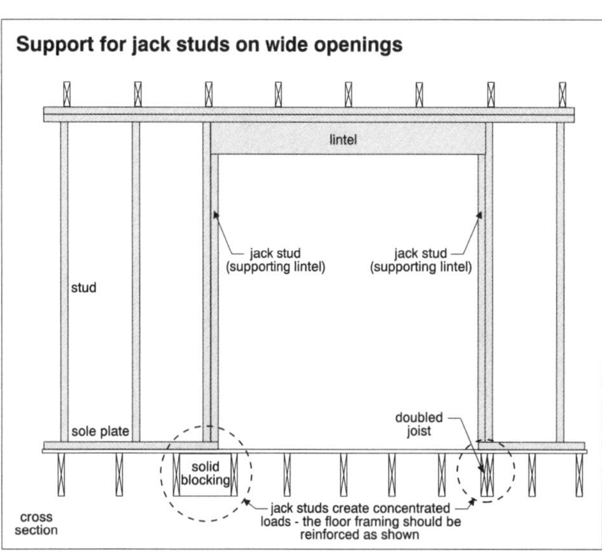

0399

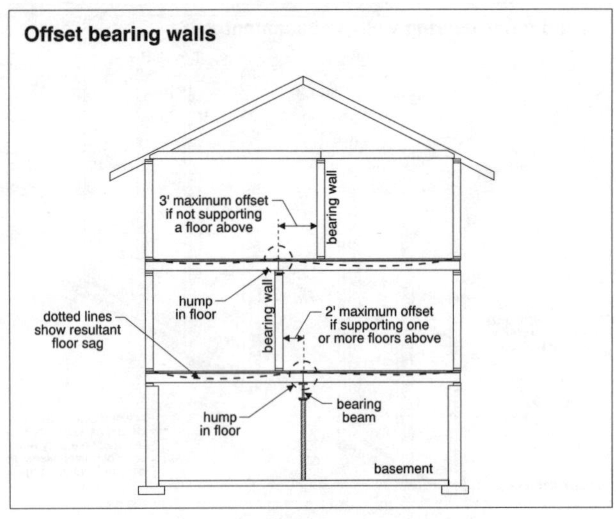

0400

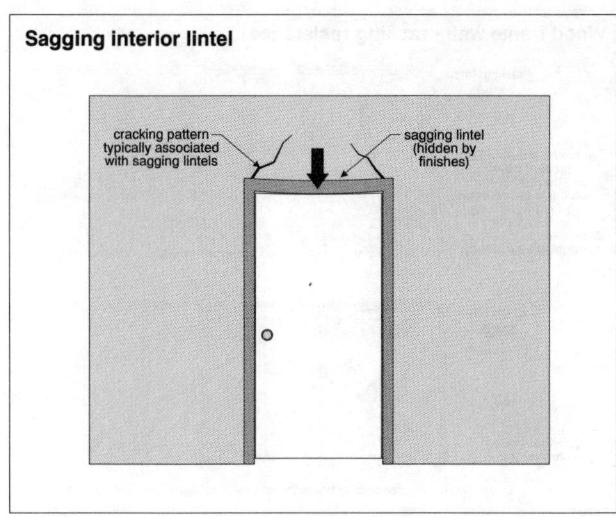

0401

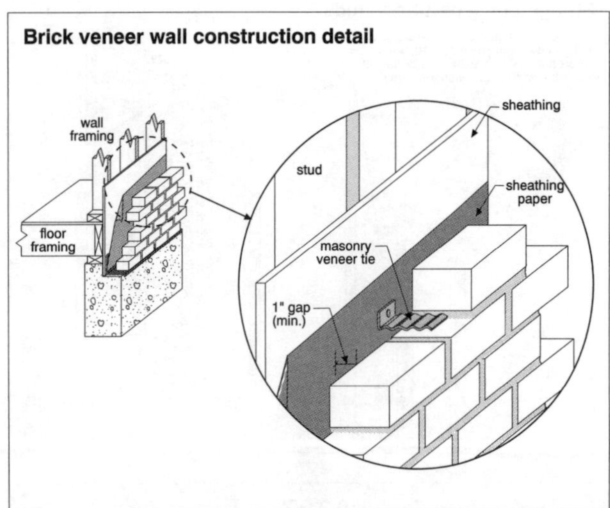

0402

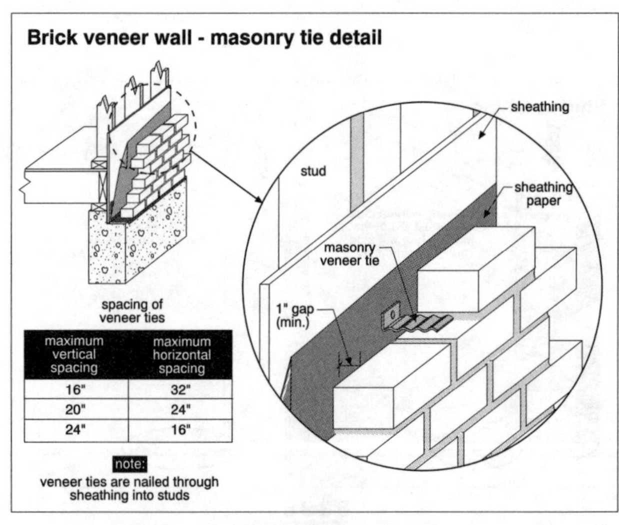

maximum vertical spacing	maximum horizontal spacing
16"	32"
20"	24"
24"	16"

0403

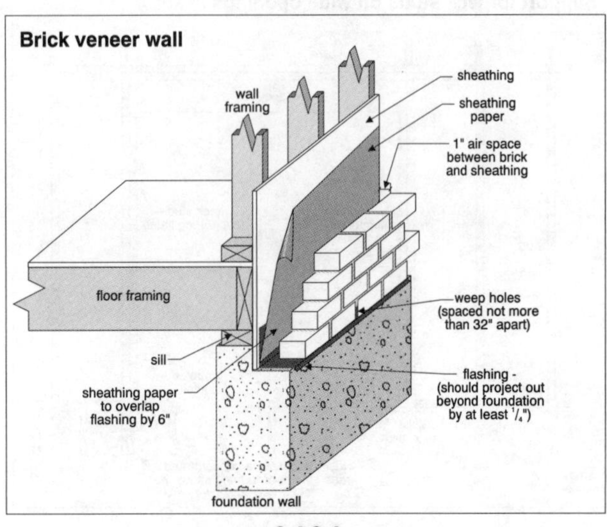

0404

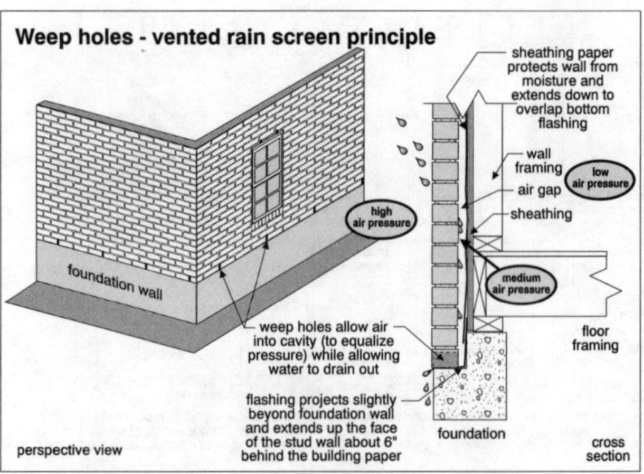

0405

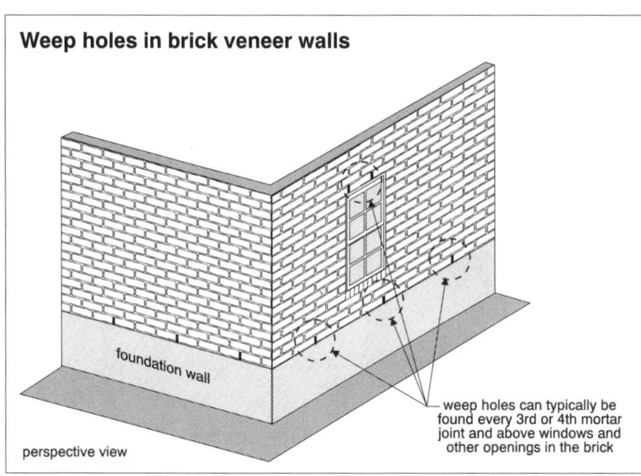

0406

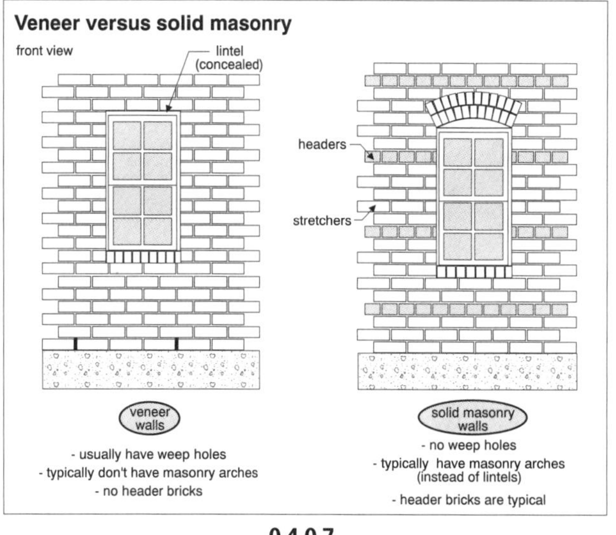

0407

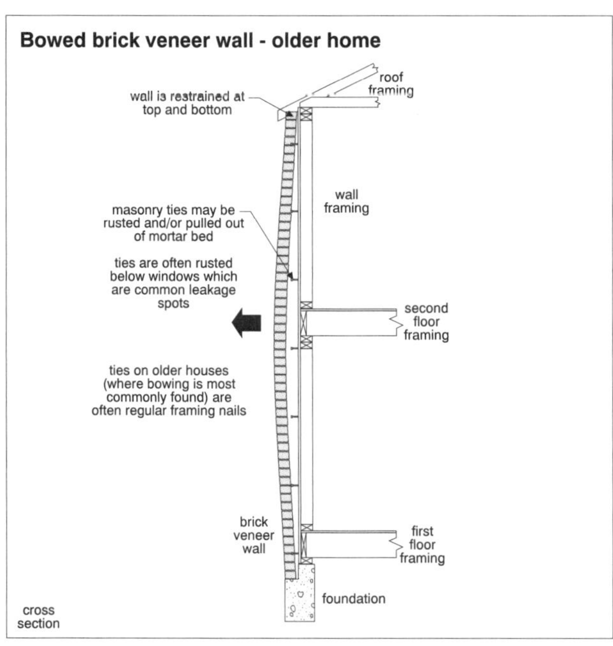

0408

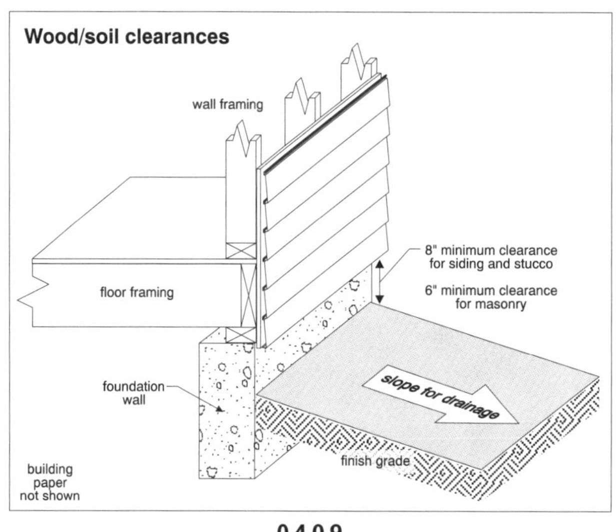

0409

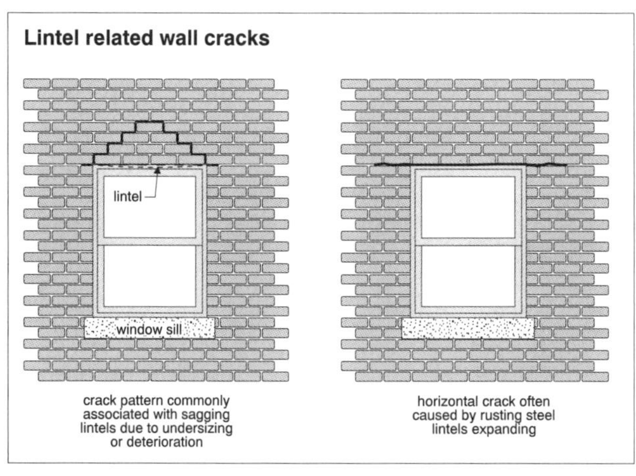

0410

Steel lintel in brick veneer wall

cutaway view

lintel bearing on masonry should be 6"

steel lintel

window opening

brick veneer

0411

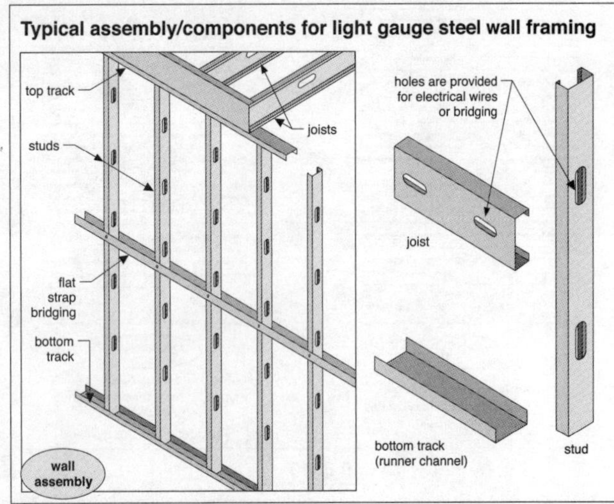

0412

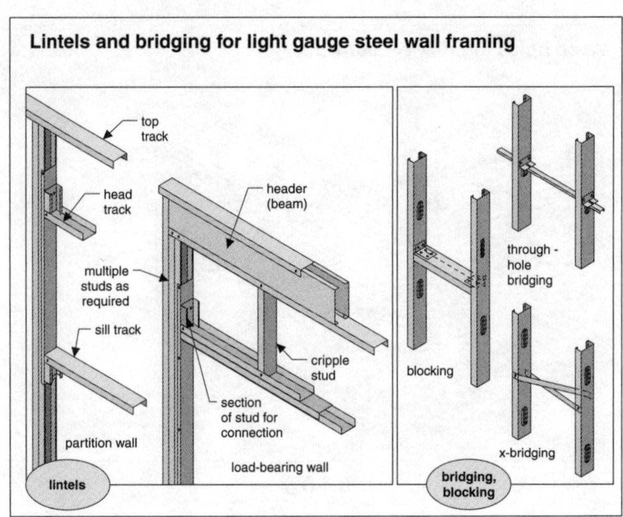

0413

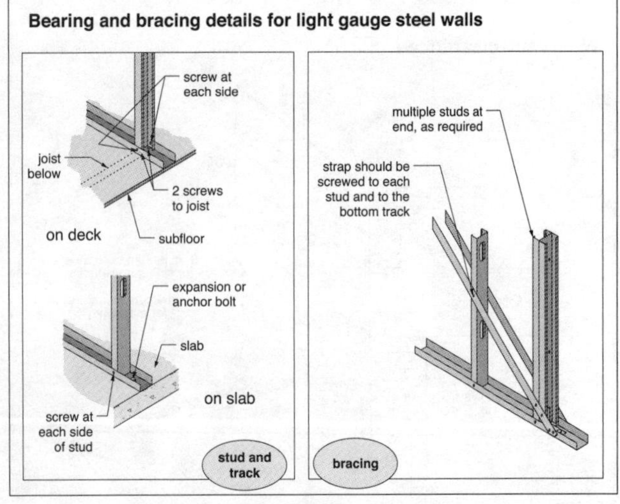

0414

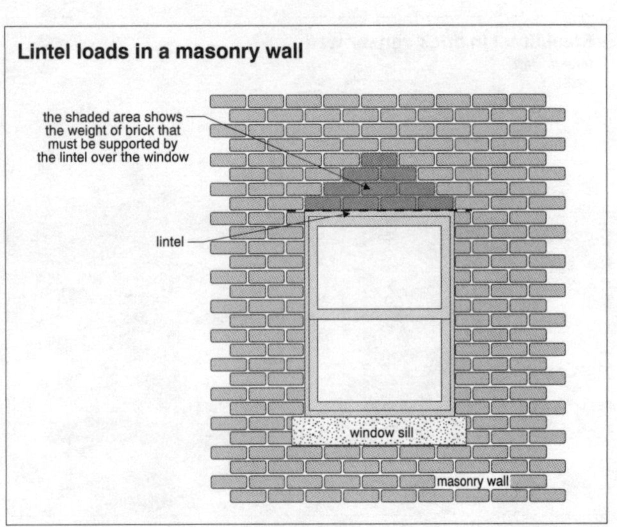

0415

Lintel loads in wood frame walls

lintel

lintels in masonry walls support only the weight of the pyramid of bricks above the lintel

lintels in wood frame walls may carry loads from many floors above and need to be strengthened accordingly

stud

sole plate

cross section

0416

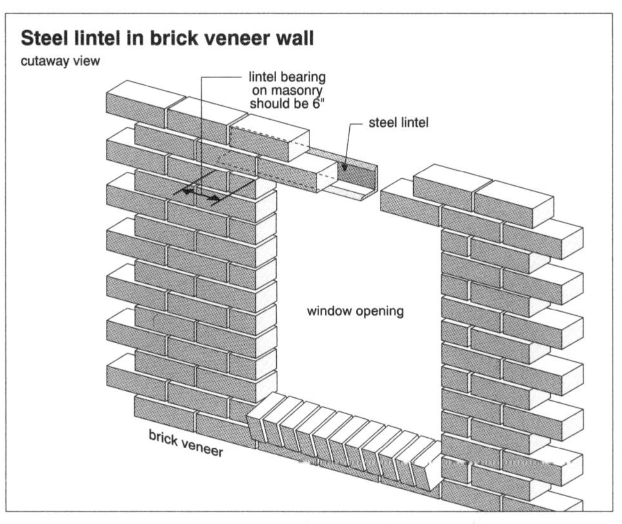

0417

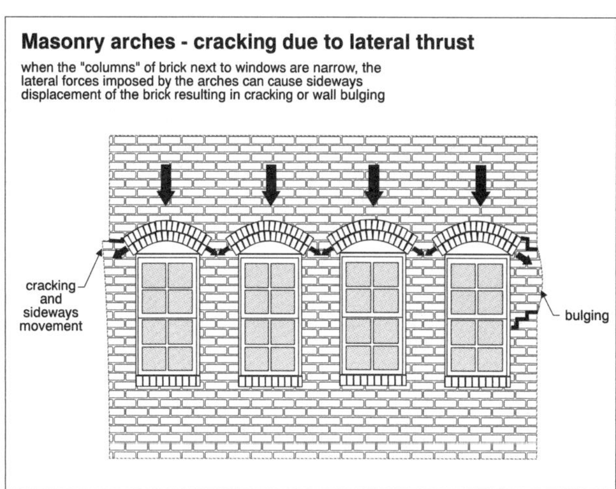

0418

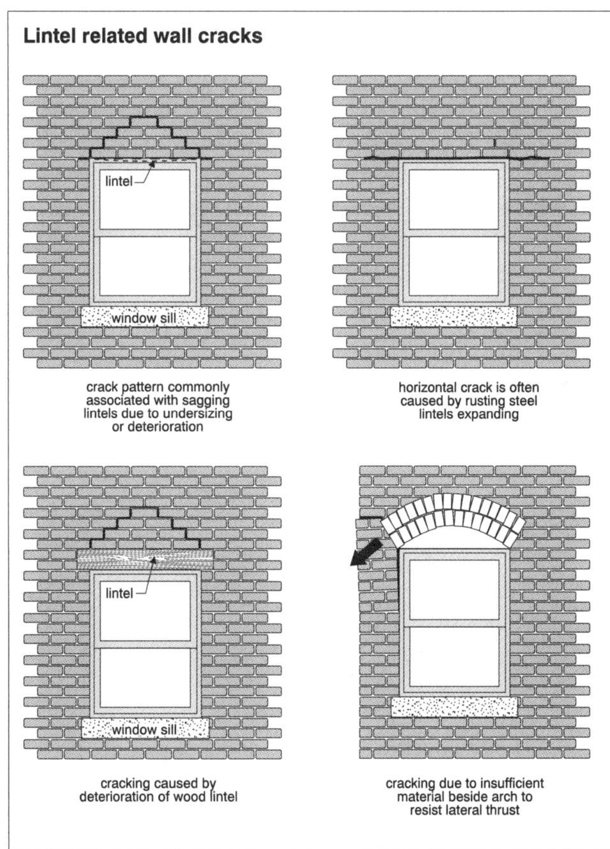

0419

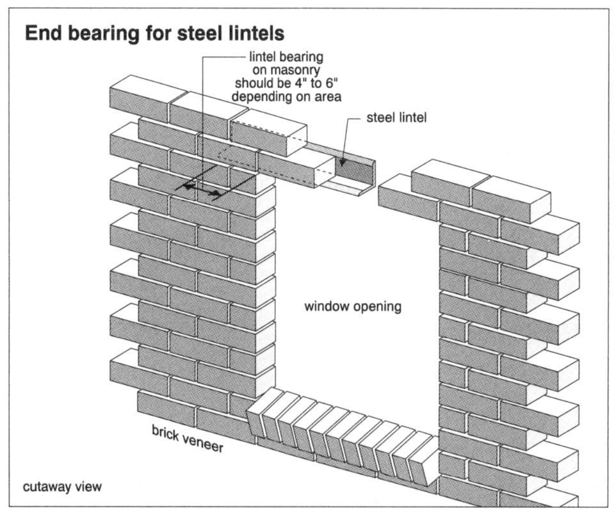

0420

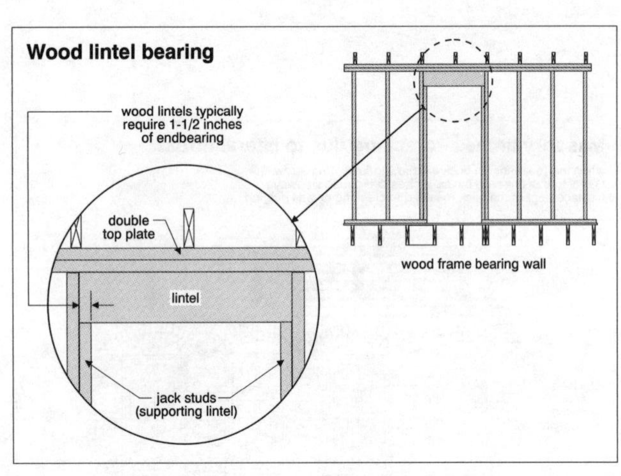

0421

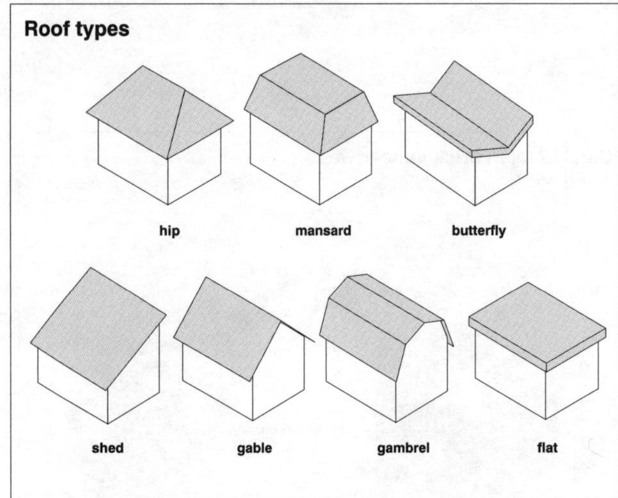

0422

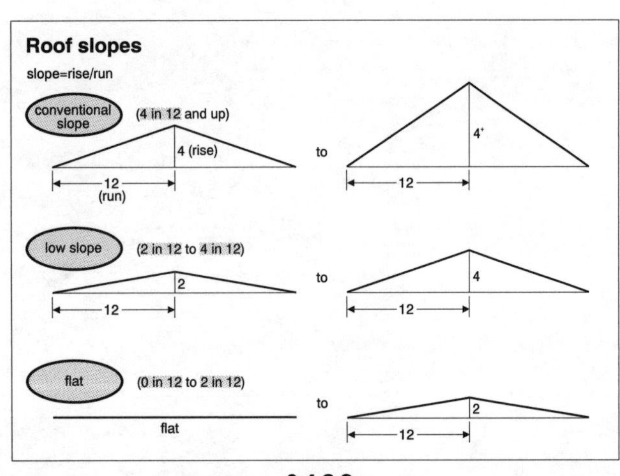

0423

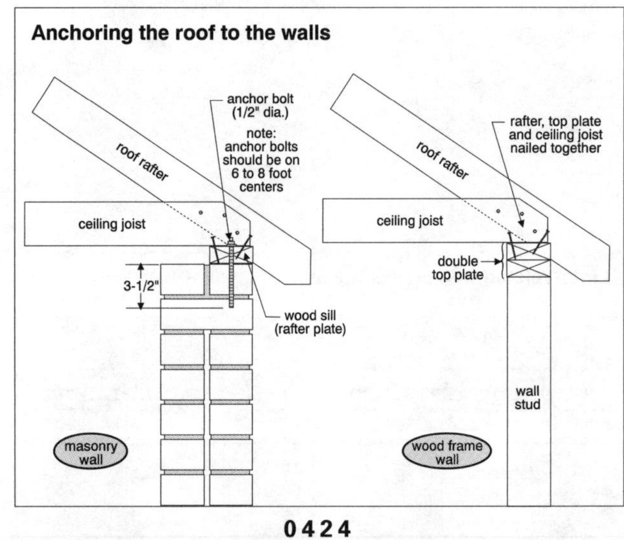

0424

Roof spreading, dishing and sagging

roof spreading

dishing in the field of the roof

sagging of the rafter or ridge system

perspective view

0425

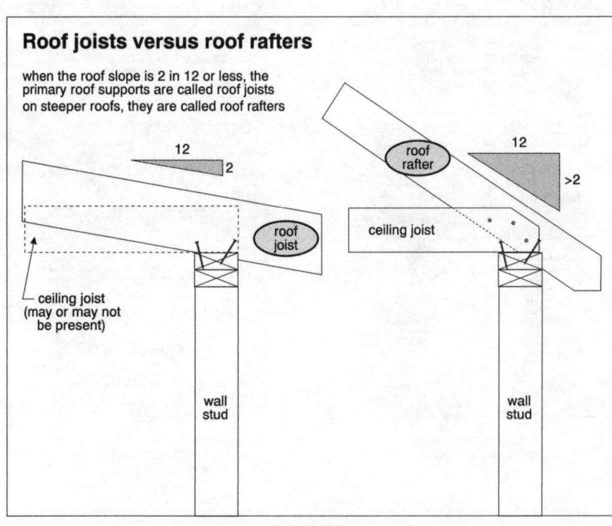

0426

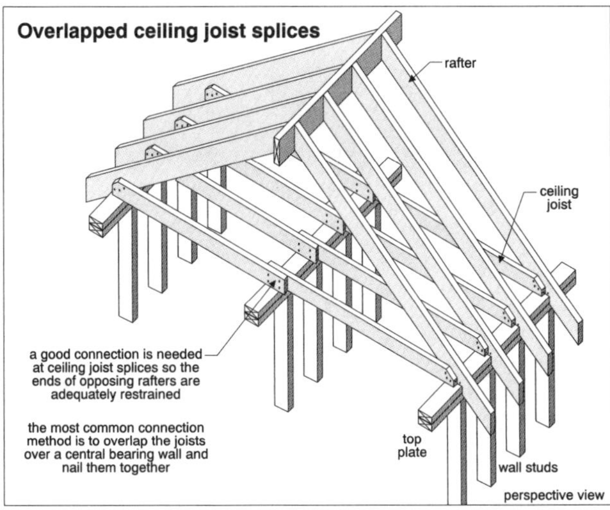

0427

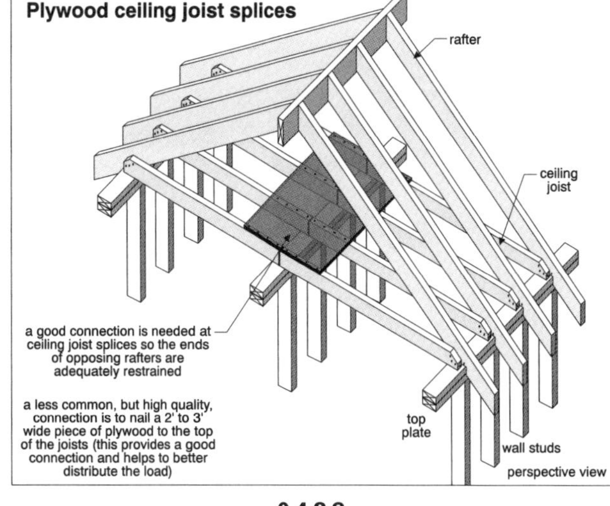

0428

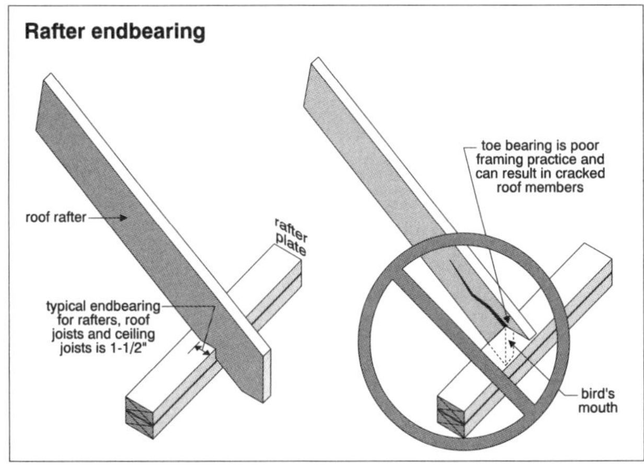

0429

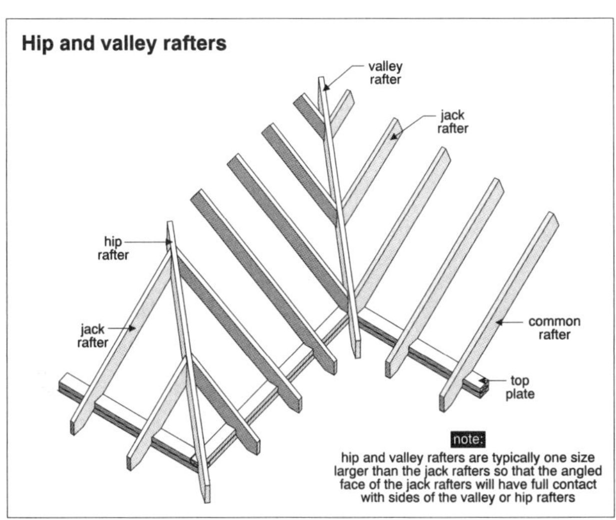

0430

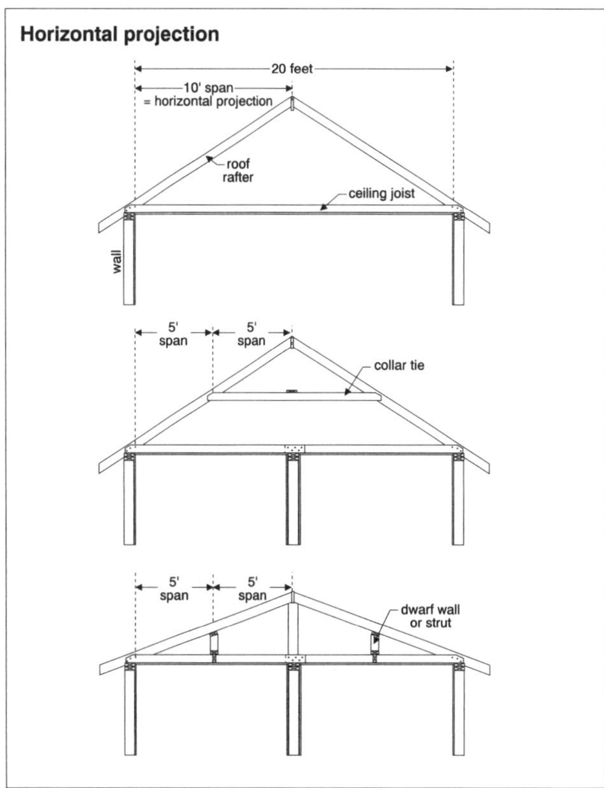

0431

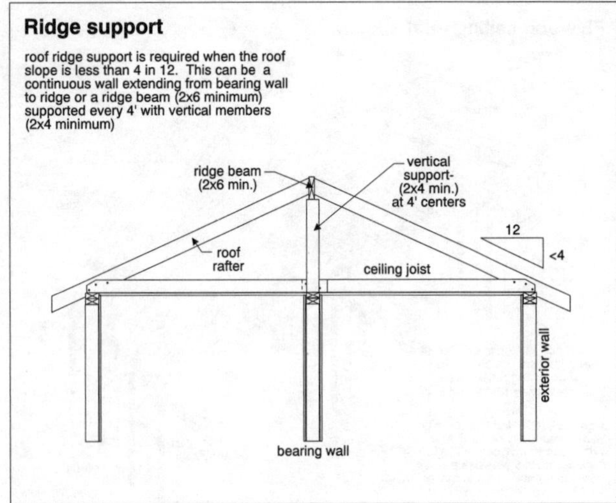

0432

Ridge boards

rafter

ceiling joist

ridge boards are used on roofs with a slope of 4 in 12 or more

typically they are nominal 1" boards one size larger than the roof rafters

top plate

wall studs

perspective view

0433

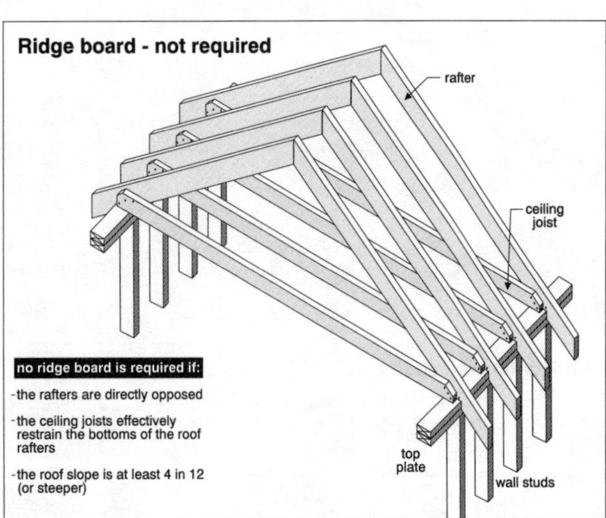

0434

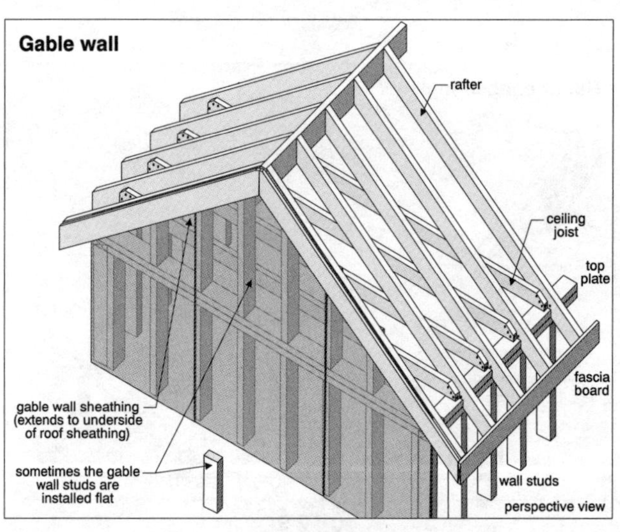

0435

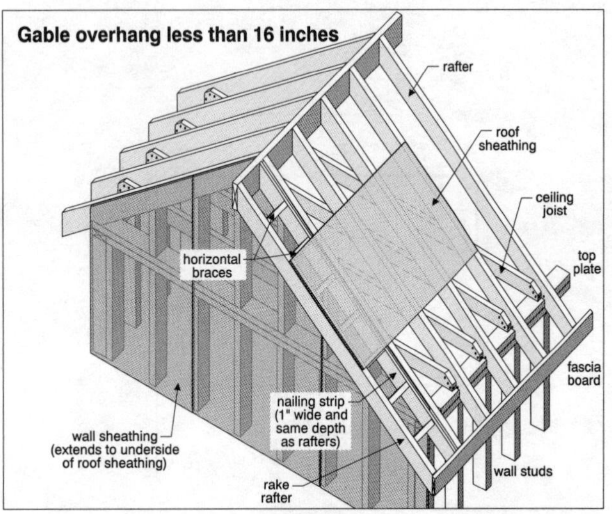

0436

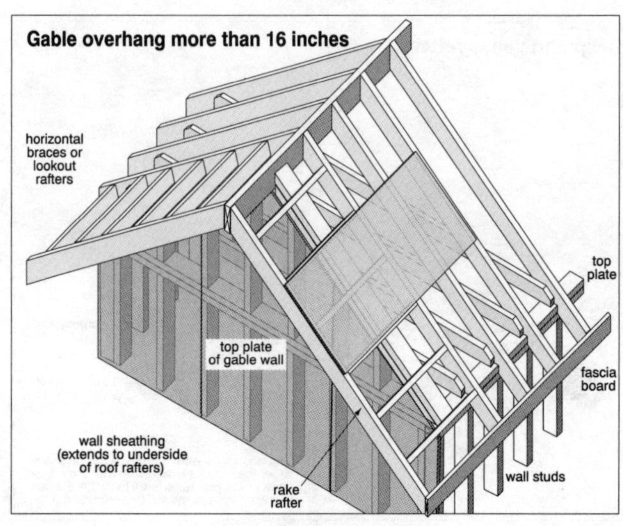

0437

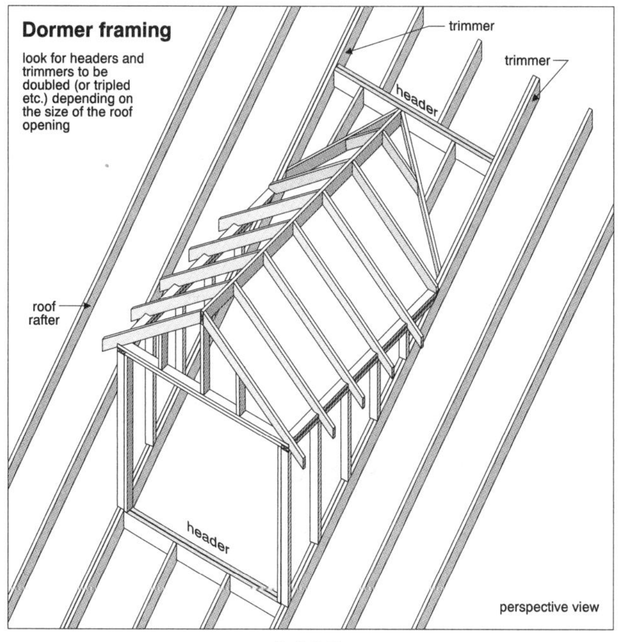

0438

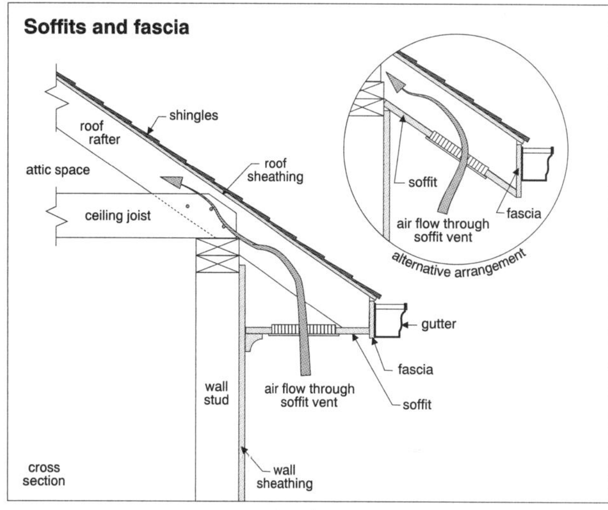

0439

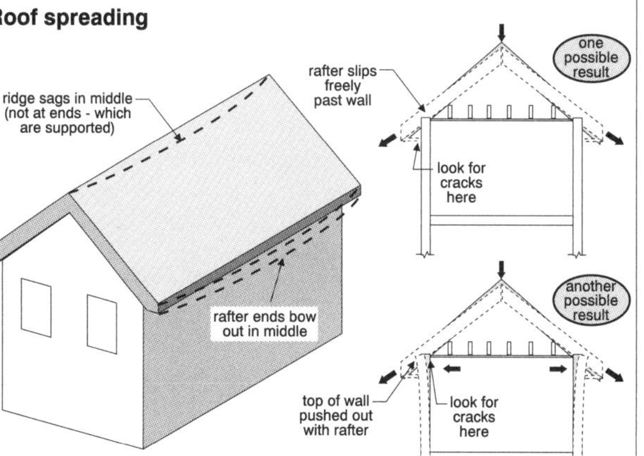

0440

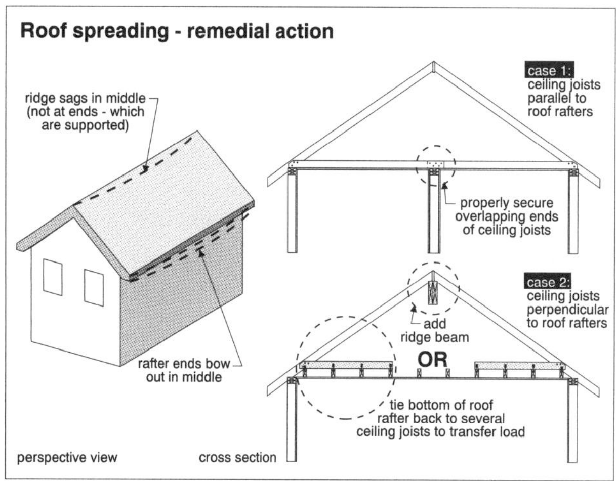

0441

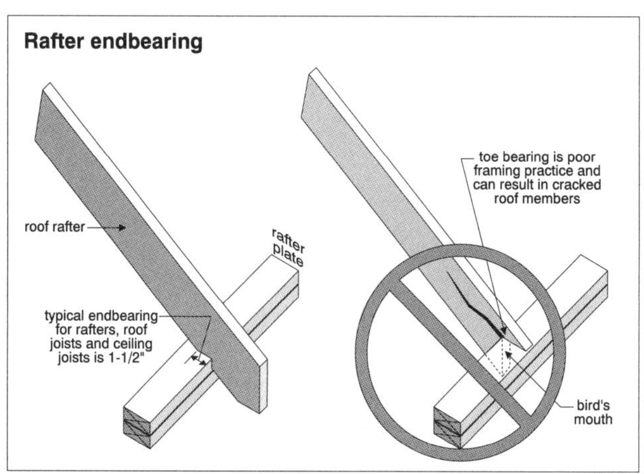

0442

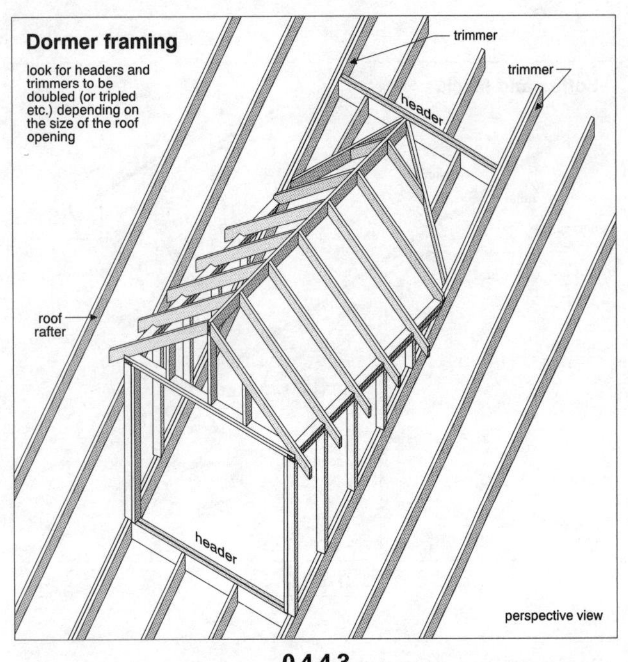

0443

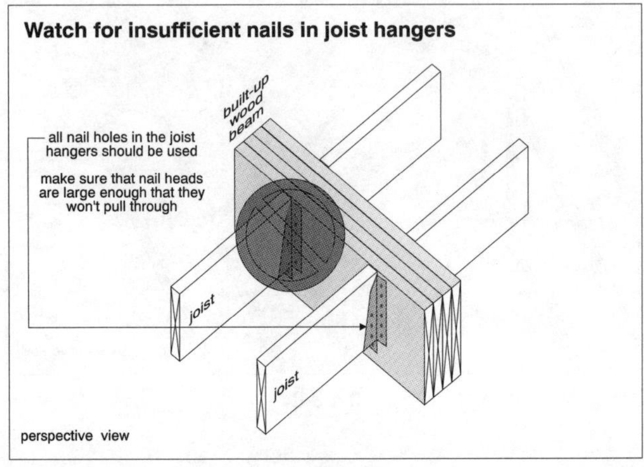

0444

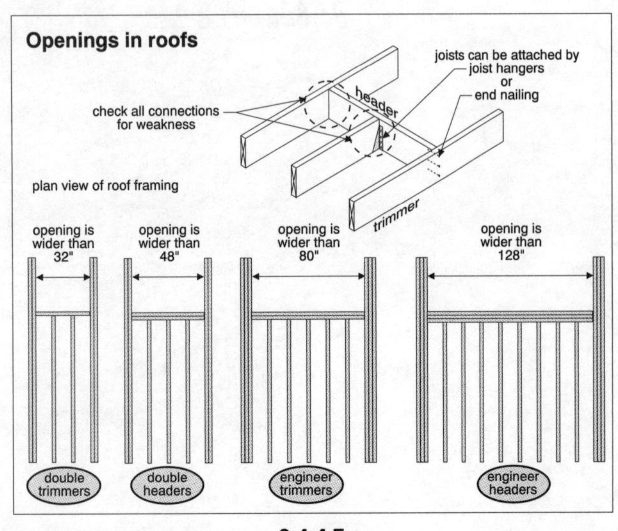

0445

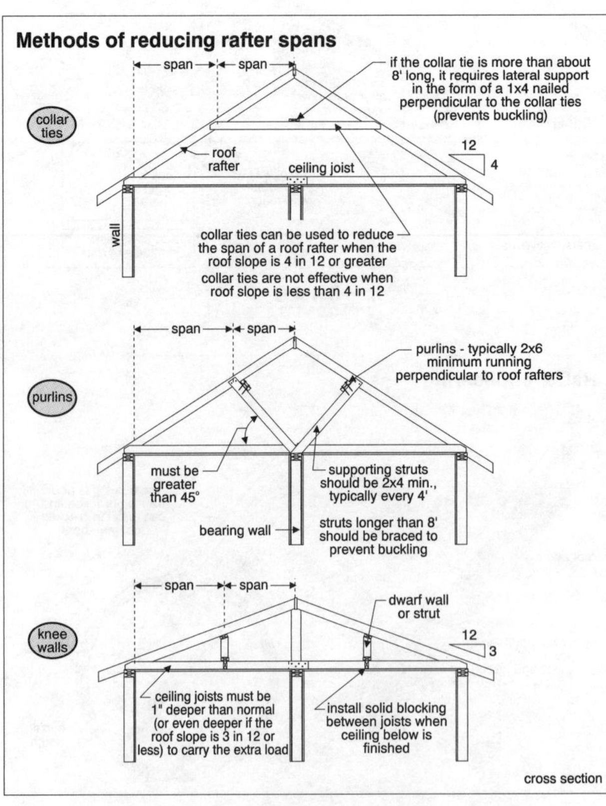

0446

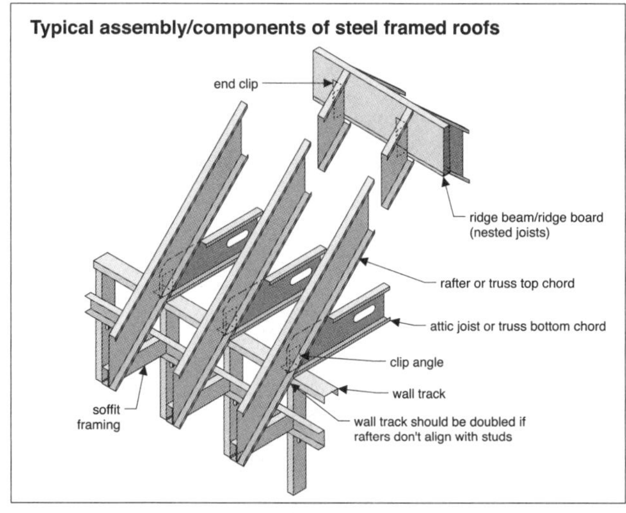

0447

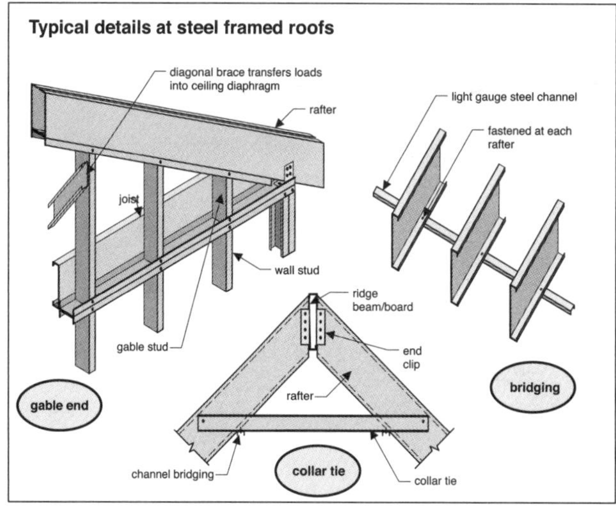

0448

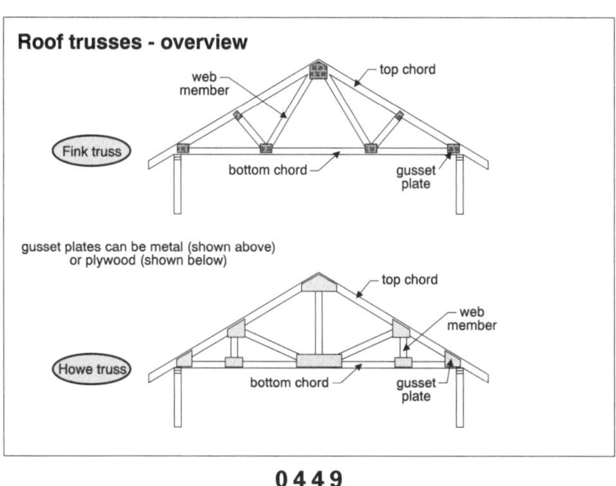

0449

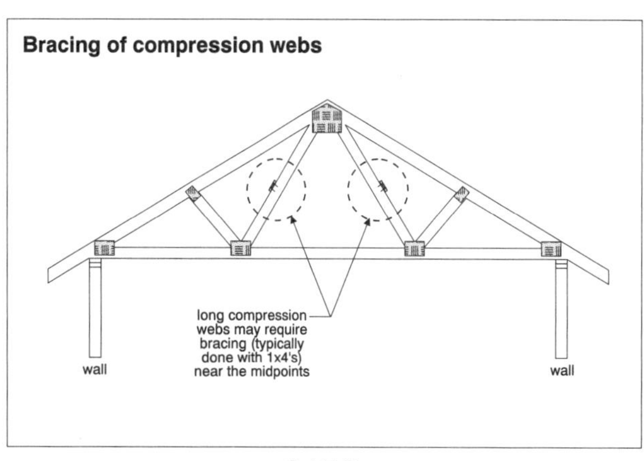

0450

Strapping the underside of trusses

trusses

sagging drywall

A common practice - drywall attached directly to trusses on 24" centers can cause drywall sagging

trusses

drywall applied to strapping

B better practice - install strapping (e.g. 1x3's or 2x2's) perpendicular to trusses every 16" before installing drywall

note:
some builders use 5/8" drywall instead of strapping to help reduce sagging while others use both methods

front view | side view

0451

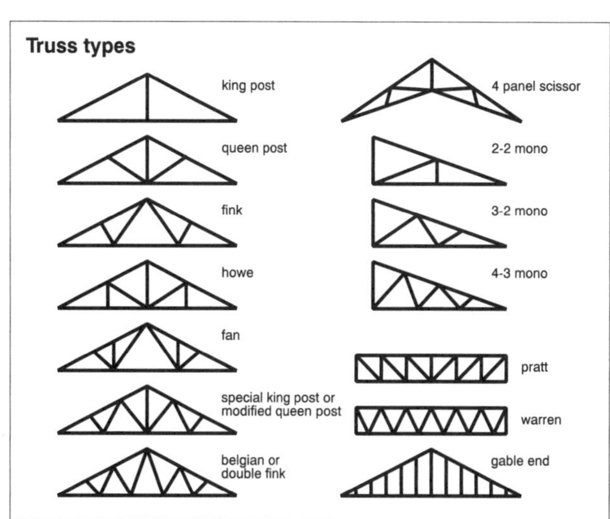

0452

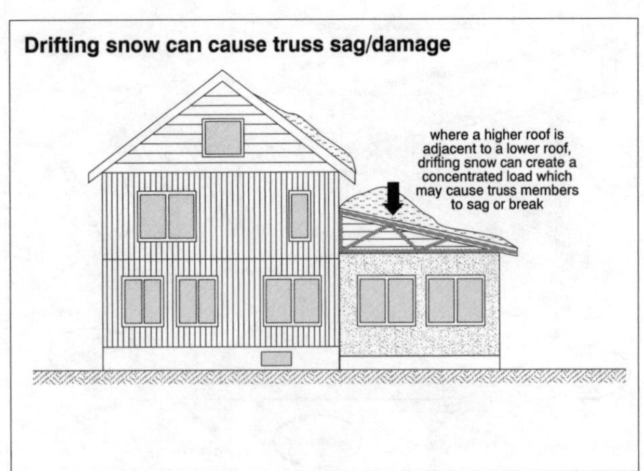

0453

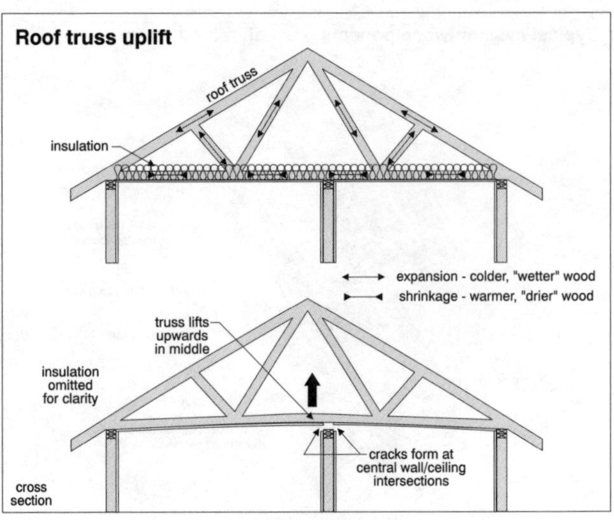

0454

Roof truss uplift - remedial action

1x6 installed between trusses to anchor edge of drywall (clips are also available for the same purpose)

A OR B

bottom chord of truss

drywall

install first ceiling fastener about 18" away from wall to allow the drywall to flex

bottom chord of truss

drywall

top plate

molding secured to ceiling (not wall) can float up and down with truss movement

wall stud typ. 2x4

0455

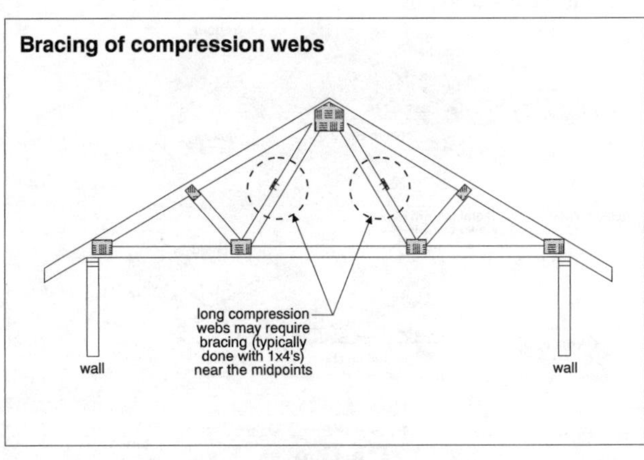

0456

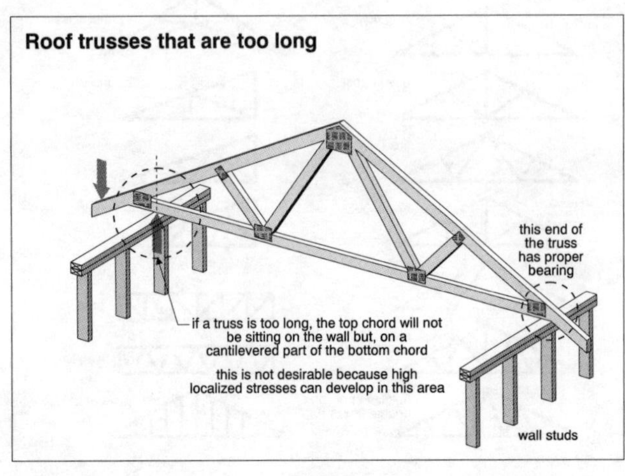

0457

Wood "I" joists

DO's
- use joist hangers to connect wood "I" joists to ridge beam
- provide 1-3/4" end bearing

DON'Ts
- don't notch bottom plate (e.g. for birds' mouth)
- don't butt top of wood "I" against opposing joist at peak
- don't bear wood "I" on its toe

ridge beam

wood "I" joist

0458

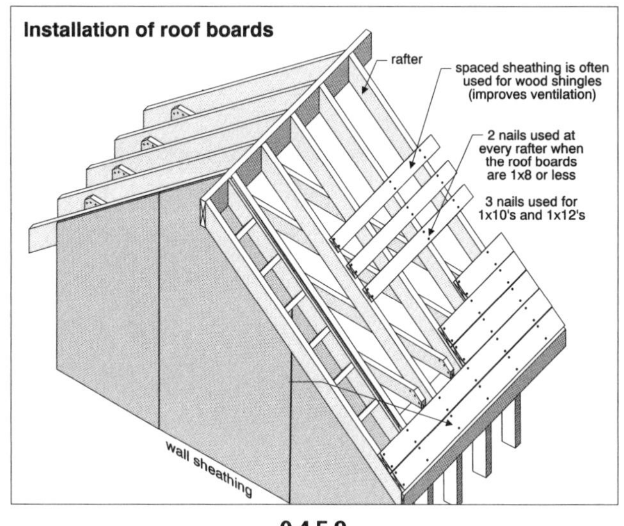

0459

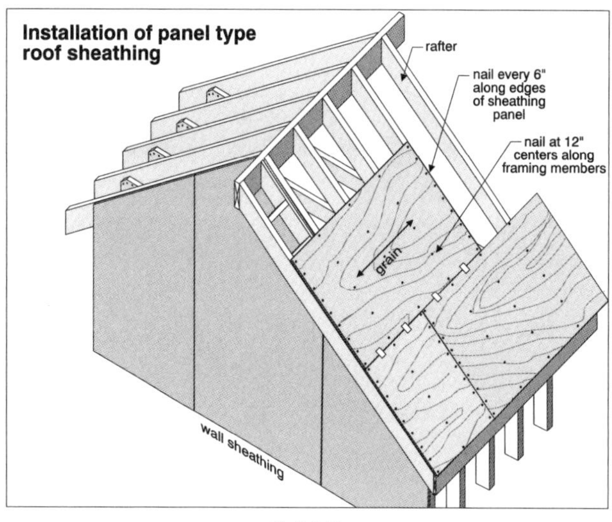

0460

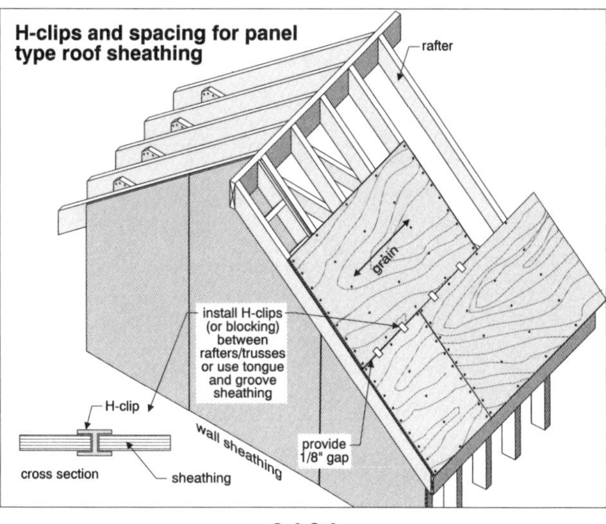

0461

CHAPTER 3

SERVICE DROP & SERVICE ENTRANCE

THE BASICS OF ELECTRICITY

85 ...... 0500 Where does the electrical inspection start?
85 ...... 0501 Electricity – basic concepts
85 ...... 0502 Electrical potential
85 ...... 0503 Electrical resistance
85 ...... 0504 Current flow equals amperage
85 ...... 0505 120/240 volts
86 ...... 0506 Color-coding for typical 120-volt circuit
86 ...... 0507 A simple electrical circuit
86 ...... 0508 Short circuit
86 ...... 0509 Fuses and breakers
86 ...... 0510 Fuses provide protection against
86 ...... 0511 Household wiring is done in parallel
87 ...... 0512 Damaged wire

SERVICE DROP

87 ...... 0513 Service drop
87 ...... 0514 Underground electrical service
87 ...... 0515 Service drop clearances (United States)
87 ...... 0516 Service drop clearances (Canada)
87 ...... 0517 Wire clearances around windows
88 ...... 0518 Wires not well secured to the house
88 ...... 0519 Inadequate wire clearance over roofs

SERVICE ENTRANCE WIRES

88 ...... 0520 Drip loop
88 ...... 0521 Service entrance wires
88 ...... 0522 Drip loop
88 ...... 0523 Using service entrance cable
89 ...... 0524 Bent service masts
89 ...... 0525 Support requirements for service entrances
89 ...... 0526 Service entrance – areas of potential water entry
89 ...... 0527 Poor seal at house/wall penetration
89 ...... 0528 Service entrance cable should not be covered by siding

SERVICE SIZE

89 ...... 0529 Common wire sizes
90 ...... 0530 Determining service size by the service entrance wires
90 ...... 0531 Determining service size by the main disconnect

SERVICE BOX, GROUNDING & PANELS

SERVICE BOXES

90 ...... 0532 Service equipment (service box, main panel or service panel)
90 ...... 0533 Grounding equipment
90 ...... 0534 Panels
90 ...... 0535 Branch circuit overcurrent devices
91 ...... 0536 Breaker and fuse type service boxes
91 ...... 0537 Meter location
91 ...... 0538 Panel clearances
91 ...... 0539 Securing the panel
91 ...... 0540 Panel openings
91 ...... 0541 Panel mounting
92 ...... 0542 Main fuses must be properly sized
92 ...... 0543 Illegal taps
92 ...... 0544 Neutral wires shouldn't by-pass the service box
92 ...... 0545 The main fuses must be downstream of the disconnect switch

SYSTEM GROUNDING

92 ...... 0546 Ground wires let fuses blow
92 ...... 0547 Electrical path for ground and neutral wires
93 ...... 0548 Grounding the gas piping
93 ...... 0549 Arcing and sparks
93 ...... 0550 Electrical path for ground and neutral wires
93 ...... 0551 Where do ground wires go?
94 ...... 0552 Jumper wires
94 ...... 0553 Jumper wires needed
94 ...... 0554 Don't bond neutral and ground wires downstream of service box
94 ...... 0555 Bond service box to ground
94 ...... 0556 Need ground in subpanel feeder wires

DISTRIBUTION PANELS

94 ...... 0557 Typical arrangement of panel wires
95 ...... 0558 120/240 volts
95 ...... 0559 Pull-out fuse blocks for 240-volt circuits
95 ...... 0560 Special circuit breakers for 240 volts
95 ...... 0561 Common household wire and fuses sizes
95 ...... 0562 Inspecting the service box and panels
95 ...... 0563 Panel clearances

CHAPTER 3

96..... 0564 Fuse types
96..... 0565 Inspecting the service box and panels
96..... 0566 Fused neutrals and old wiring systems
96..... 0567 Securing the panel
96..... 0568 Panel mounting
96..... 0569 Panel openings
97..... 0570 Panel clearances
97..... 0571 Subpanel wiring – no separate disconnect switch
97..... 0572 Subpanel wiring – disconnect by subpanel
97..... 0573 Subpanel wiring – disconnect by main panel
97..... 0574 Don't bond neutral and ground wires downstream of service box
97..... 0575 Need ground in subpanel feeder wires
98..... 0576 Double tapping (double lugging)
98..... 0577 Pig-tailing to avoid double taps
98..... 0578 Overcurrent protection for multi-wire branch circuits
98..... 0579 Staggered bus bars on circuit breaker panels
98..... 0580 Bus bars in fuse panels
98..... 0581 Pull-out fuse blocks for multi-wire branch circuits and 240-volt circuits
99..... 0582 Special circuit breakers for 240 volts
99..... 0583 Excess sheathing on panel wires
99..... 0584 Securing wires
99..... 0585 Wires shouldn't cross bus bars
99..... 0586 Arc fault circuit interrupter

THE DISTRIBUTION SYSTEM

BRANCH CIRCUIT WIRING (DISTRIBUTION WIRING)

99..... 0587 Common household wire and fuse sizes
100..... 0588 Stranded wire for overhead runs
100..... 0589 Number of conductors
100..... 0590 Common household wire and fuse sizes
100..... 0591 Types of connections
100..... 0592 Securing wires
100..... 0593 Cable support
101..... 0594 Wire installations below floors
101..... 0595 Wire support with steel studs
101..... 0596 Wire clearances from hot ducts and pipes
101..... 0597 Edge clearance for wires in studs and joists
101..... 0598 Wire support with steel studs
101..... 0599 Exposed wiring
102..... 0600 Exposed wiring in attics
102..... 0601 Stranded wire for overhead runs

KNOB-AND-TUBE WIRING

102..... 0602 Knob-and-tube
102..... 0603 Knob-and-tube connections
102..... 0604 Knob-and-tube wiring – connecting a new branch circuit
102..... 0605 Fused neutrals in old wiring systems

ALUMINUM WIRE

103..... 0606 CUAL designation

LIGHTS, OUTLETS, SWITCHES AND JUNCTION BOXES

103..... 0607 Stairway lighting
103..... 0608 How 3-way switches work
103..... 0609 Potlights in insulated ceilings
103..... 0610 Use proper bulbs for potlights
103..... 0611 Poor heat lamp locations
104..... 0612 Isolating links needed on pull chains
104..... 0613 Reversed polarity
104..... 0614 Importance of correct polarity with light fixtures
104..... 0615 Wrong-type receptacle
104..... 0616 Ground-fault interrupter
104..... 0617 GFI's can protect ordinary outlets downstream
105..... 0618 Wiring for multi-wire branch circuits
105..... 0619 Load miser
105..... 0620 Bathroom outlets and switches
105..... 0621 Outlets near basins
105..... 0622 Outlets should not be above electric baseboard heaters
105..... 0623 Outlets in floors or countertops
106..... 0624 Garage outlets should be at least 18 inches off the floor
106..... 0625 Old push-button switches are obsolete
106..... 0626 Furnace switches
106..... 0627 How 3-way switches work
106..... 0628 Garbage disposal switches
106..... 0629 Garbage disposal wiring

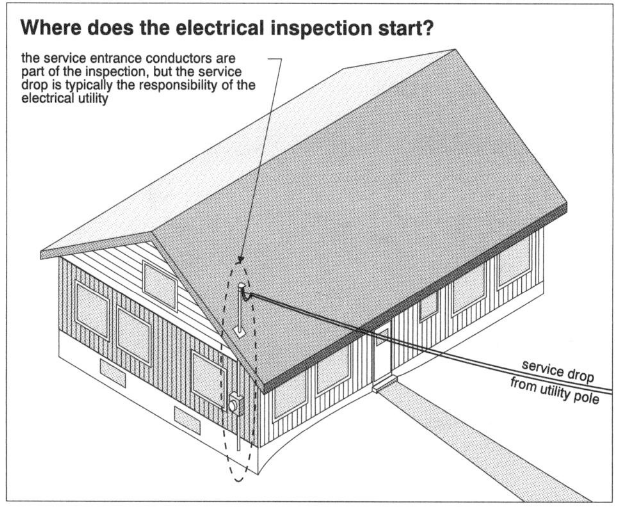

0500

Electricity - basic concepts

electrons (electricity) travelling along a wire

electricity flow can be compared to water flow - if pressure is applied at one end of a pipe (or wire) then, water (or electricity) will flow out the other end

water flowing through a pipe

0501

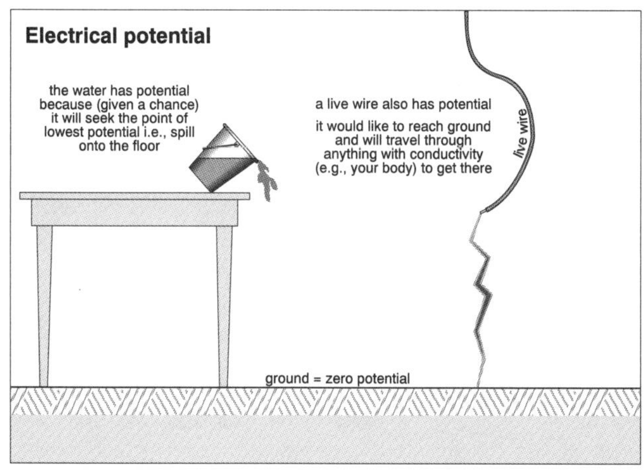

0502

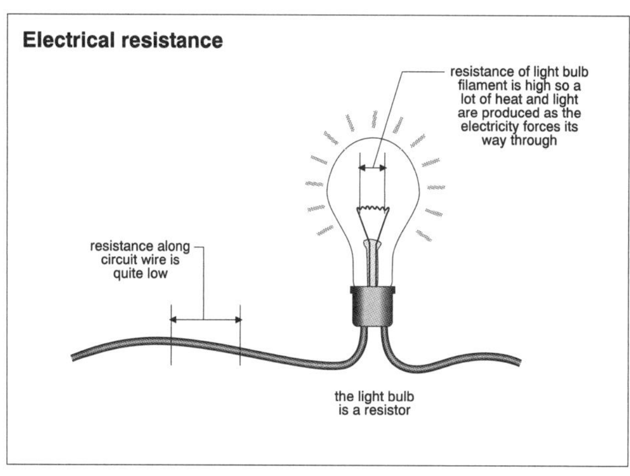

0503

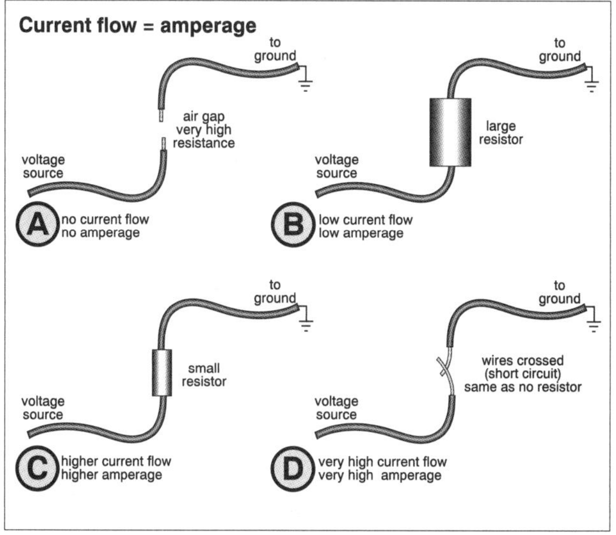

0504

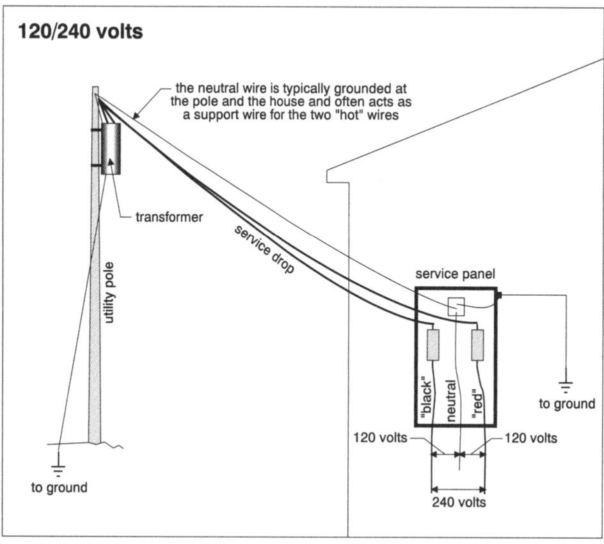

0505

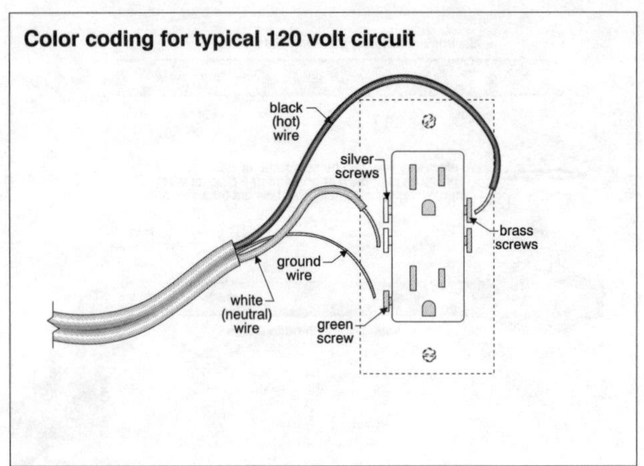

0506

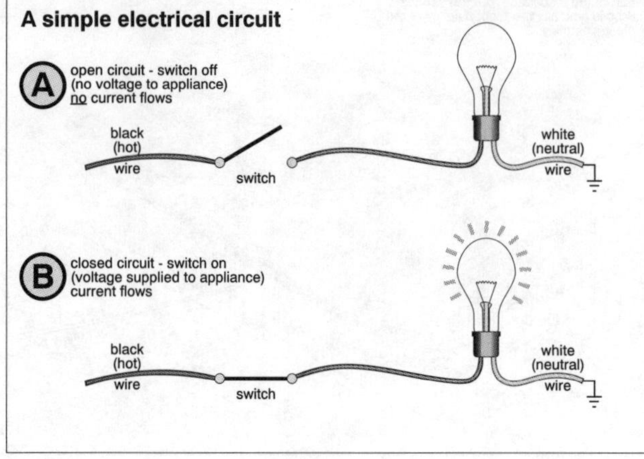

0507

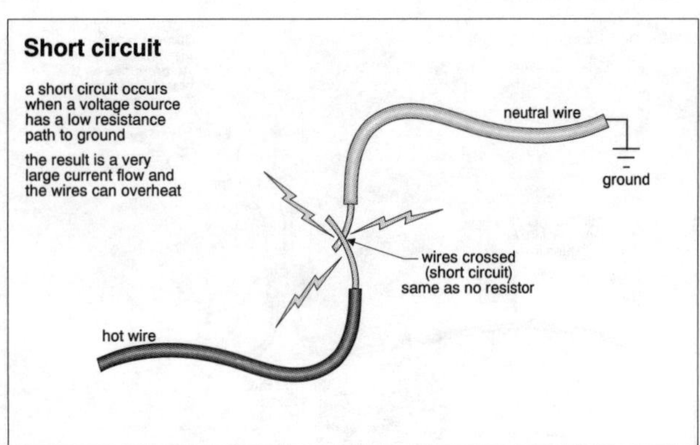

0508

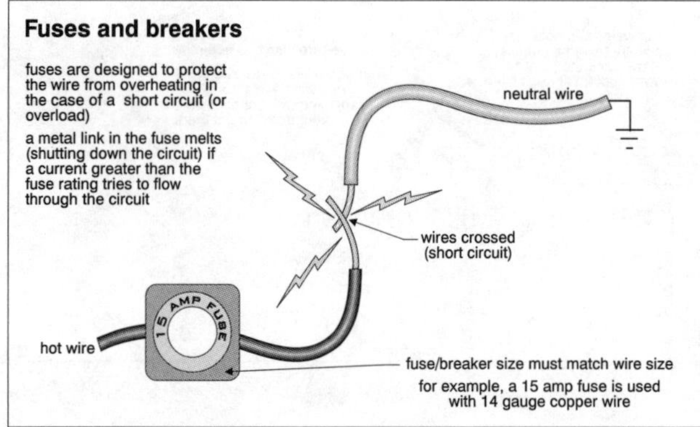

0509

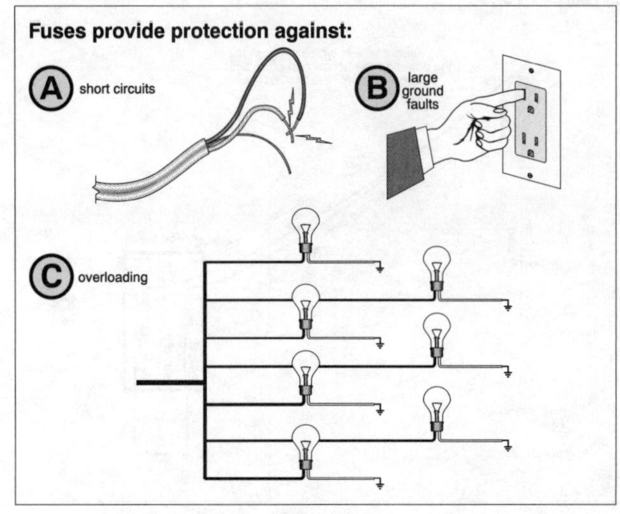

0510

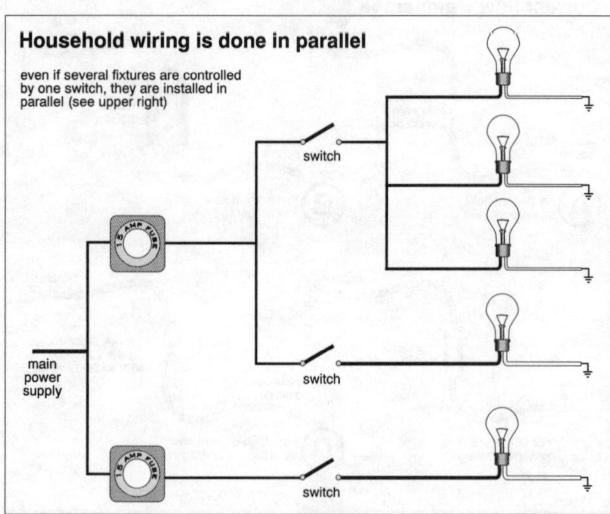

0511

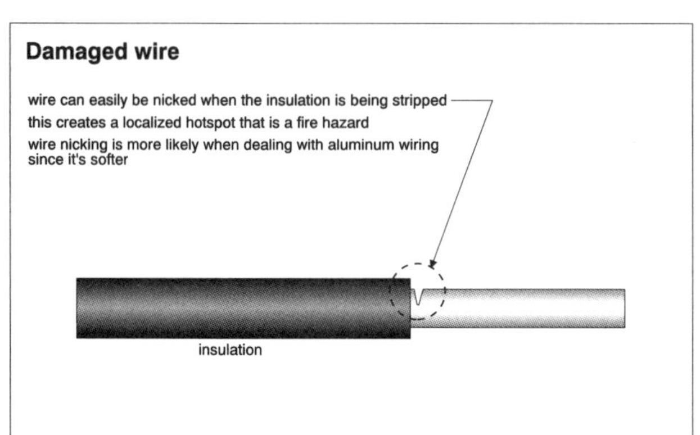

0512

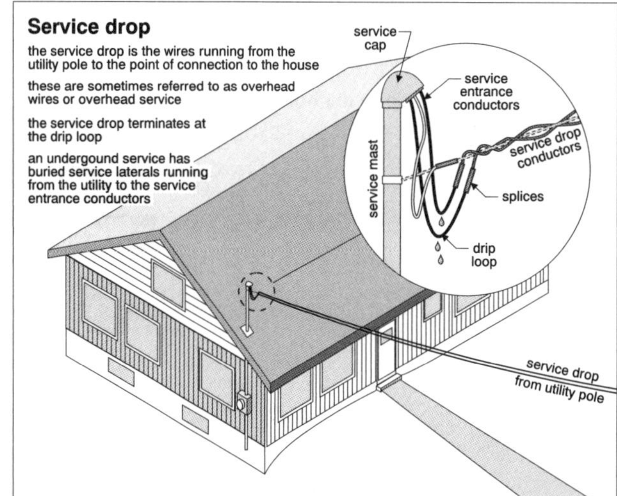

0513

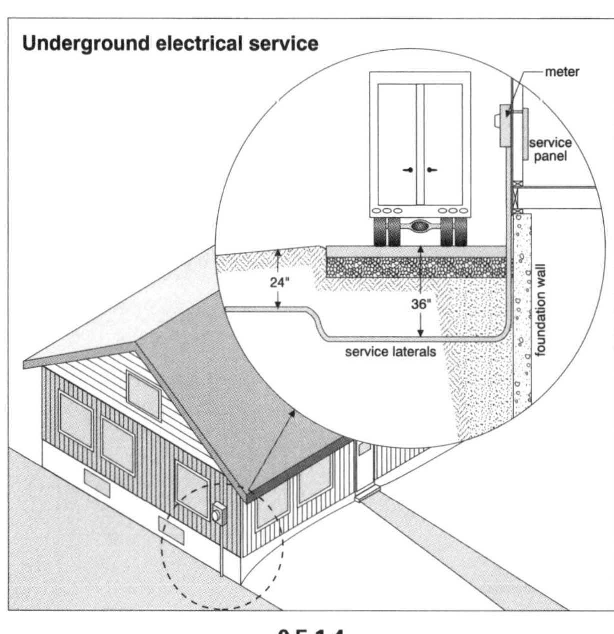

0514

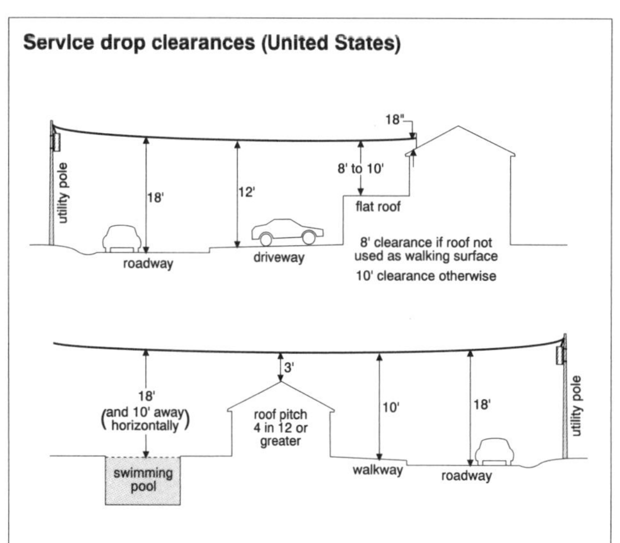

0515

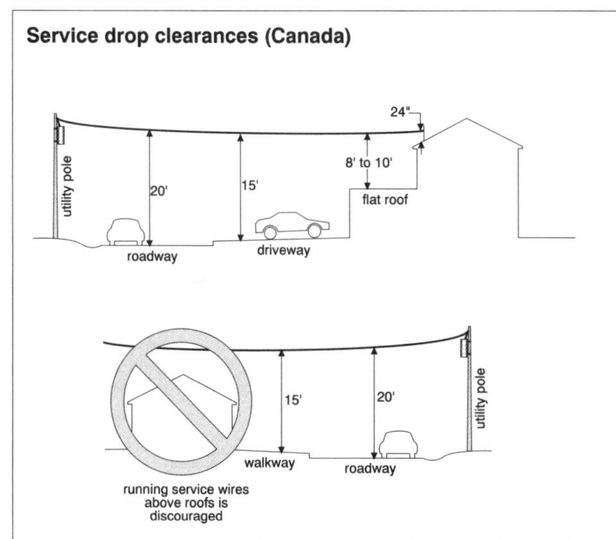

0516

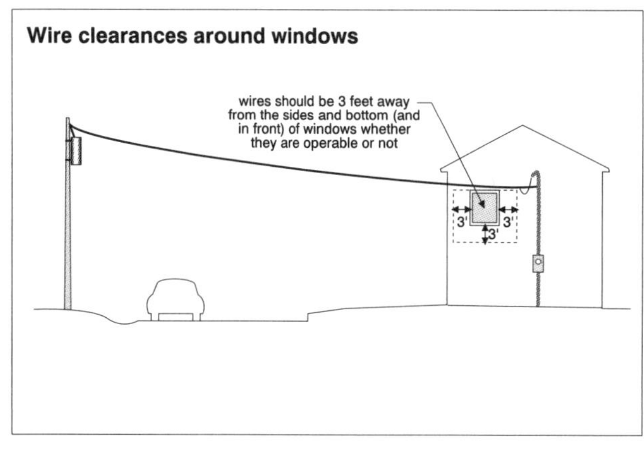

0517

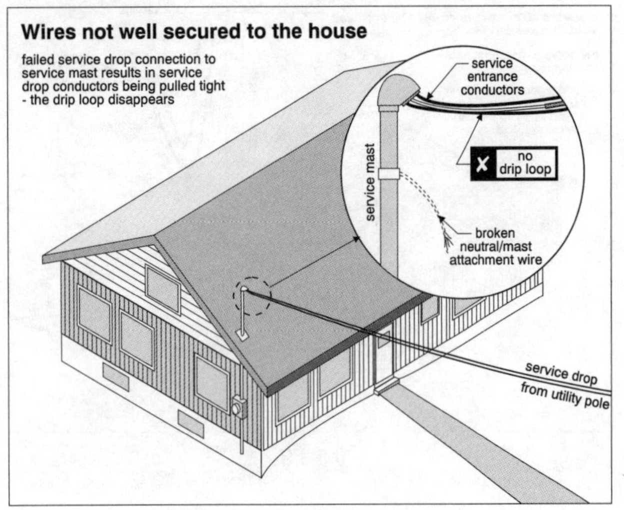

0518

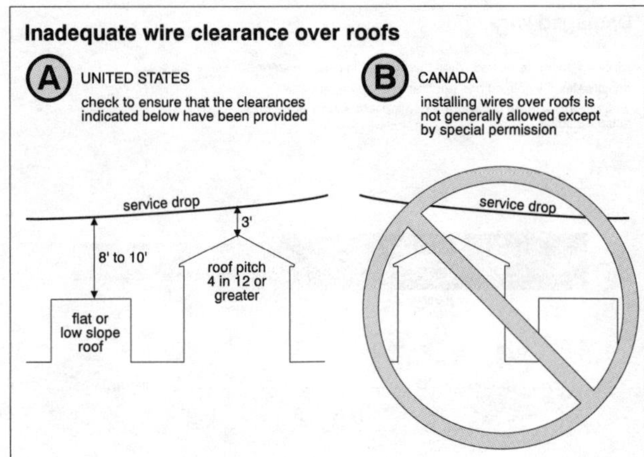

0519

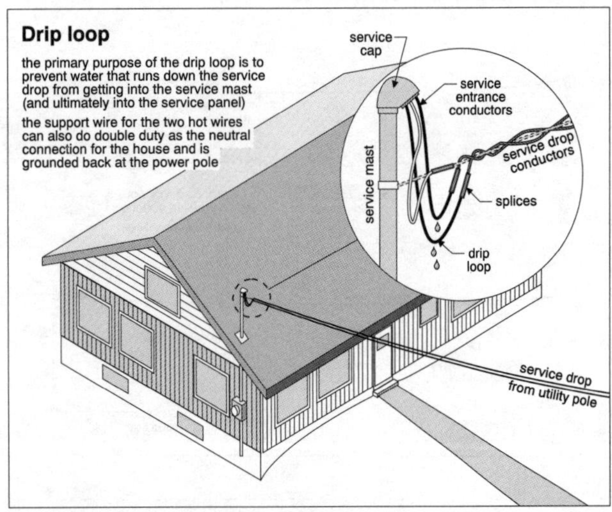

0520

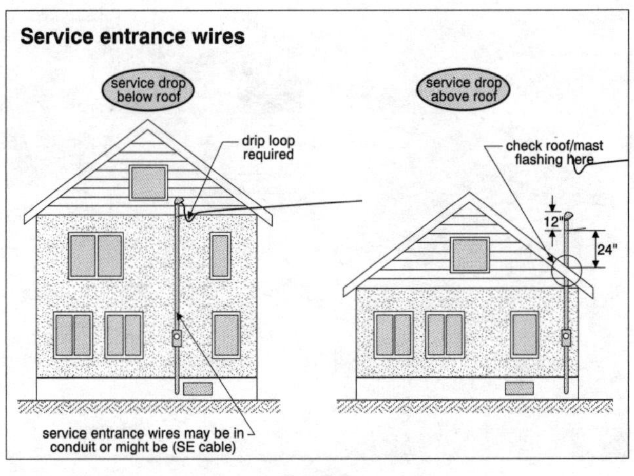

0521

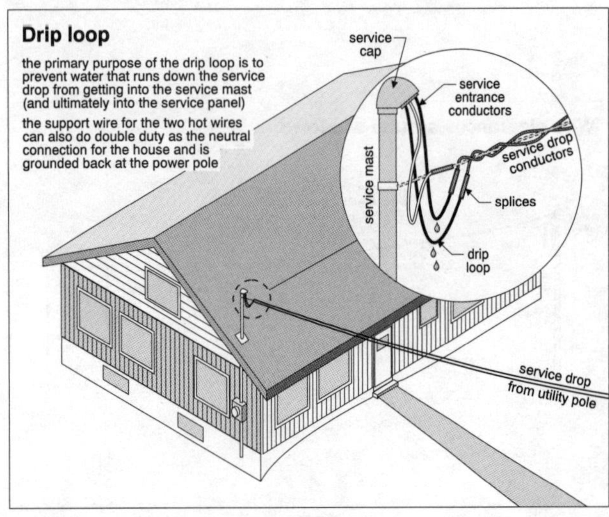

0522

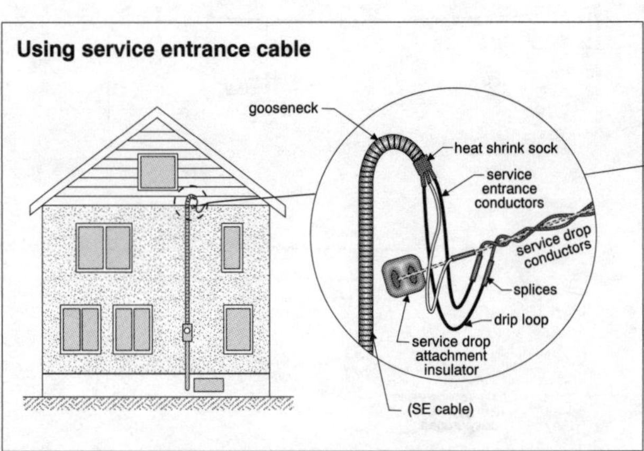

0523

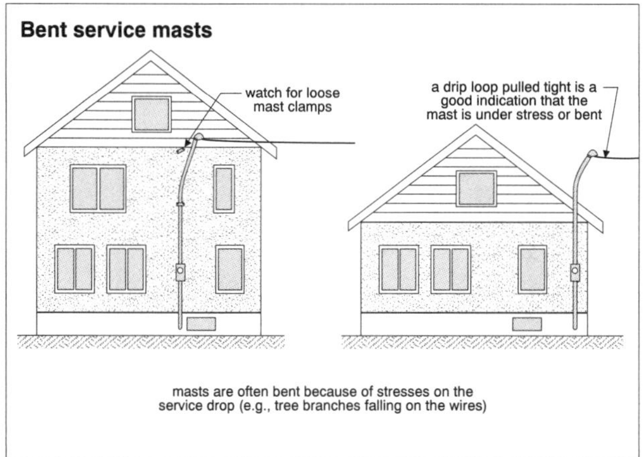

0524

Support requirements for service entrances

cables should be secured every 30" to 5'

conduit should be secured every 5' to 6'

masts over 5' tall should have guy wires for extra support

0525

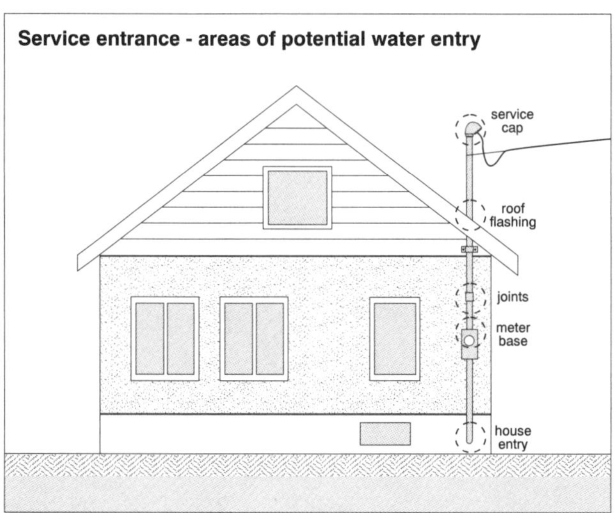

0526

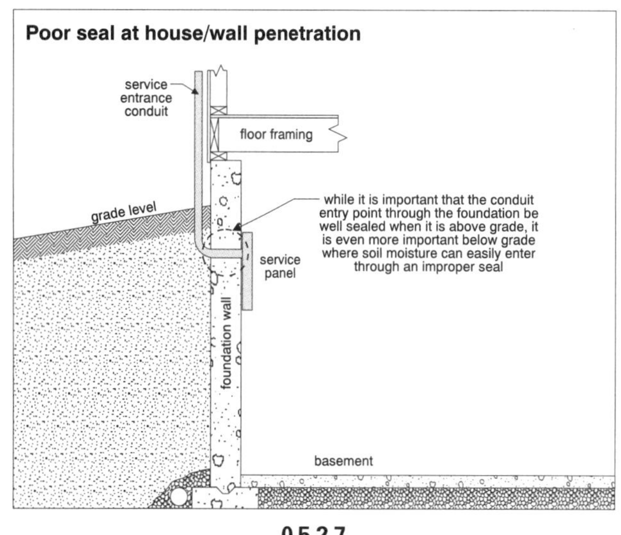

0527

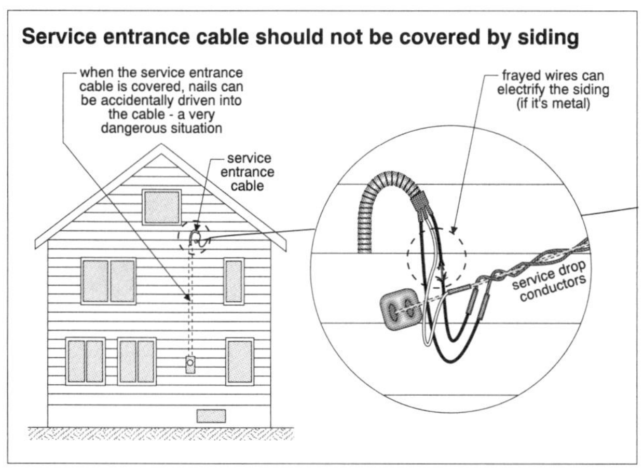

0528

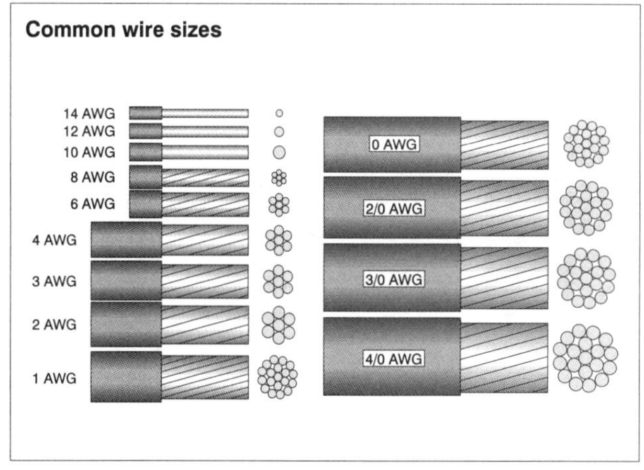

0529

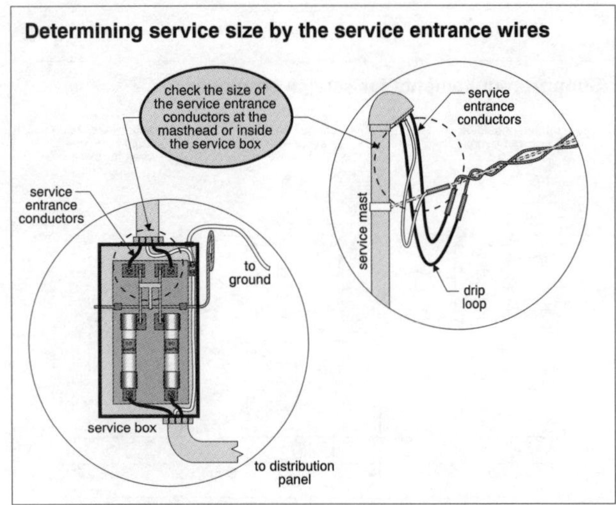

0530

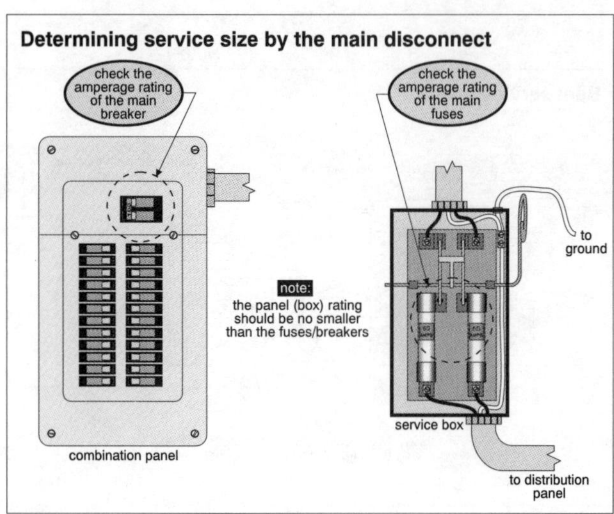

0531

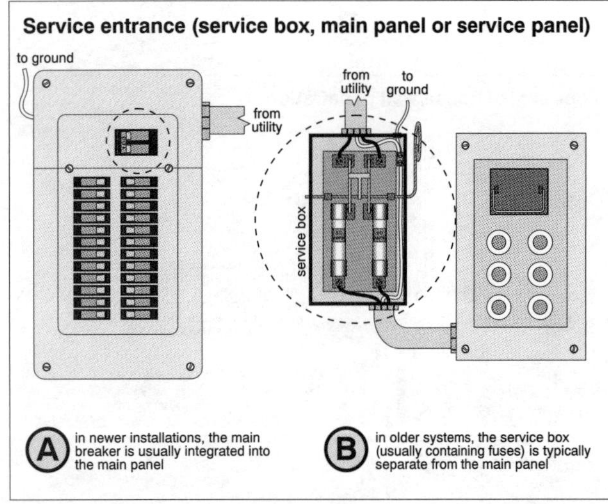

0532

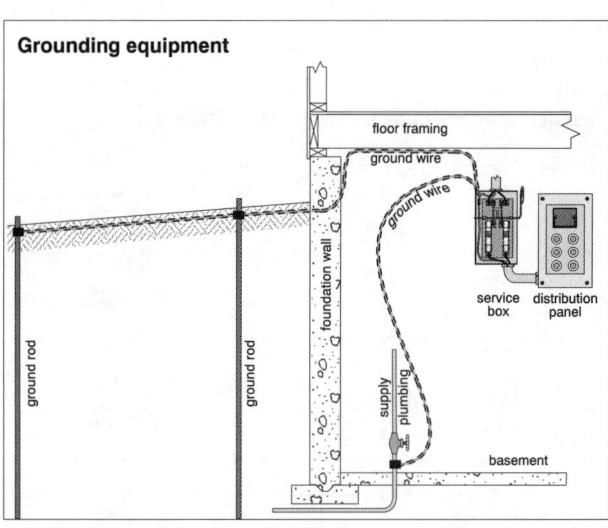

0533

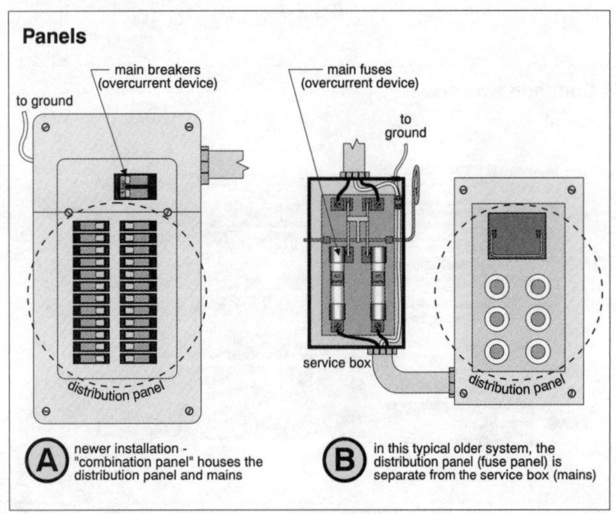

0534

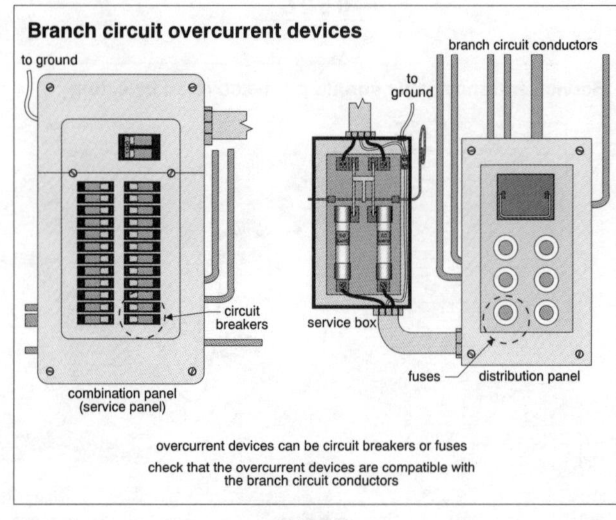

0535

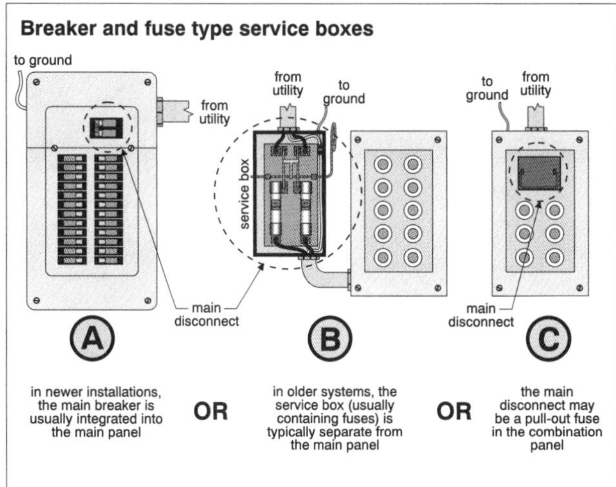

0536

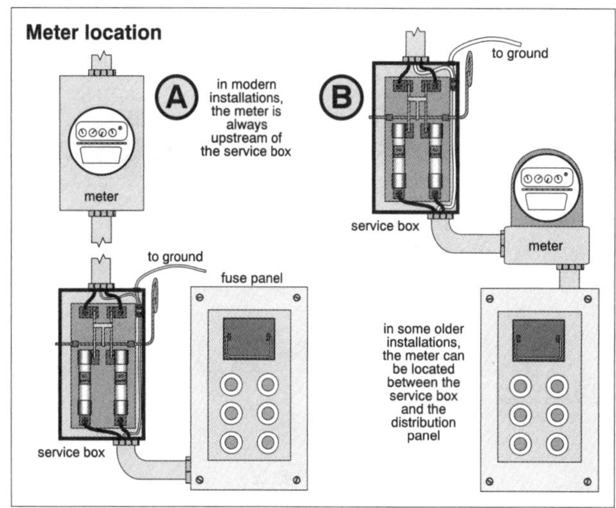

0537

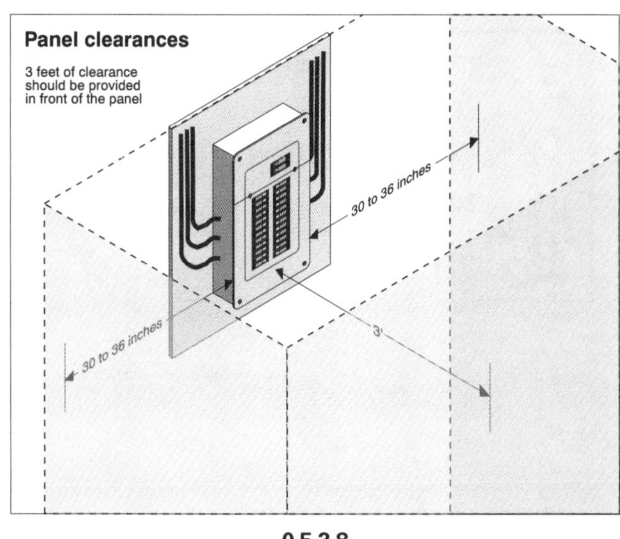

0538

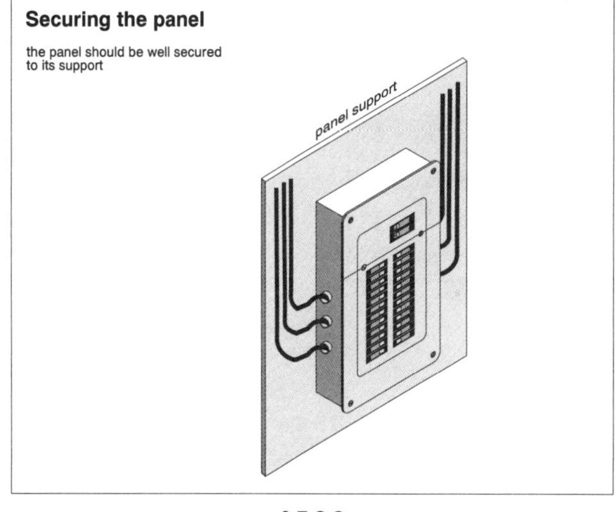

0539

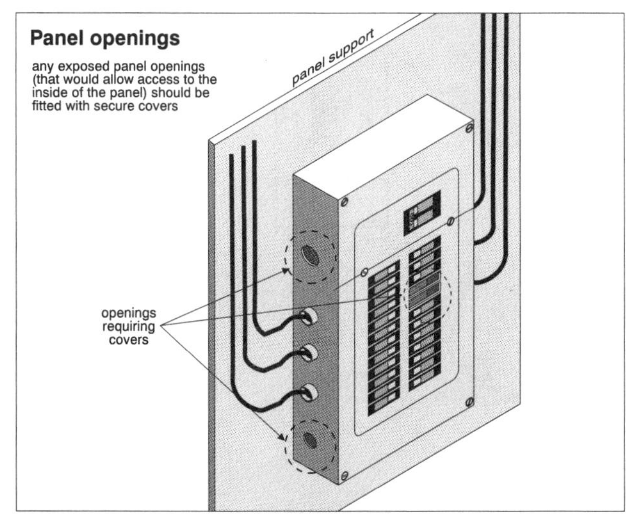

0540

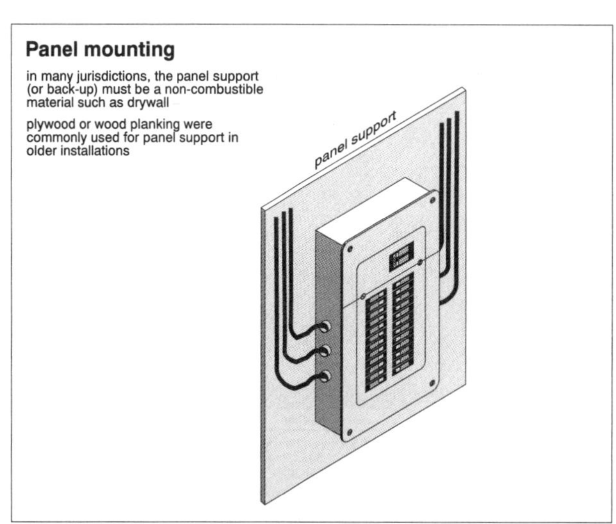

0541

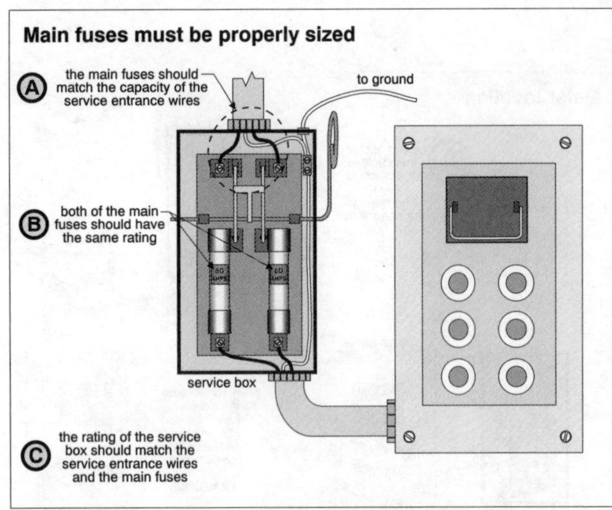

0542

Illegal taps

to ground

illegal tap

service box

meter

watch for illegal taps where household circuits are tapped off the service box directly (upstream of the meter)

distribution panel

0543

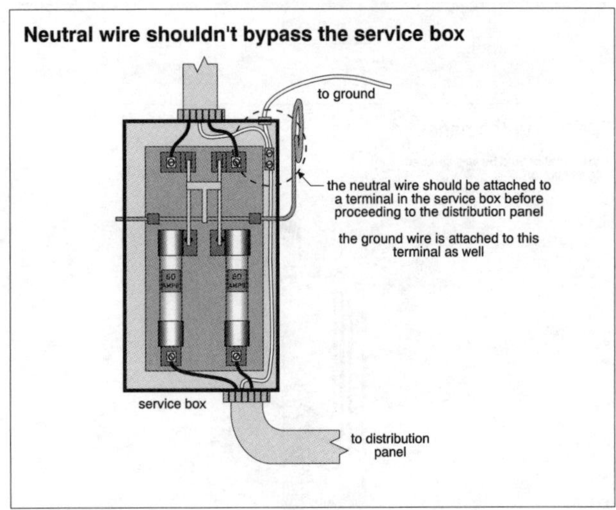

0544

The main fuses must be downstream of the disconnect switch

to ground

to ground

60 AMPS

service box

to distribution panel

even if the main switch is off, the fuses are still energized - a dangerous situation when changing fuses

0545

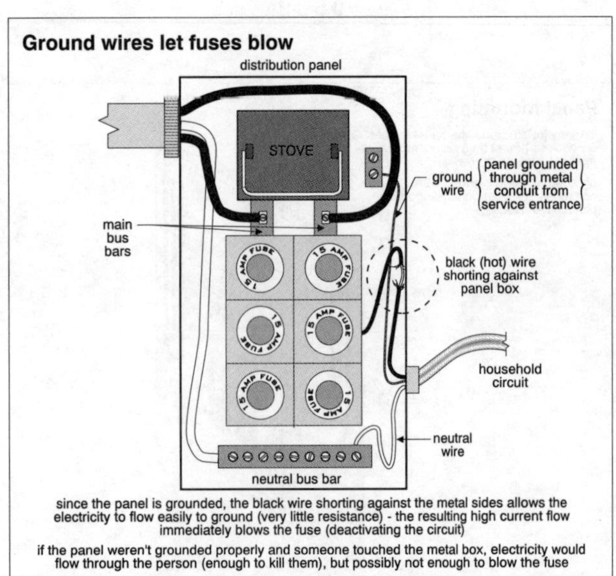

0546

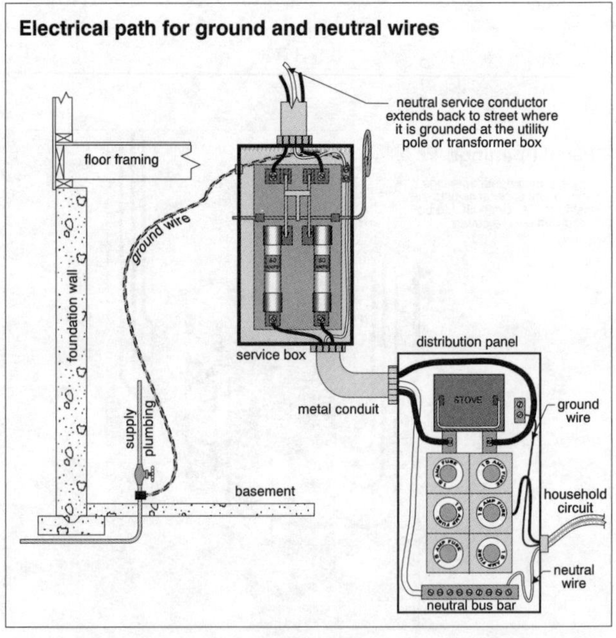

0547

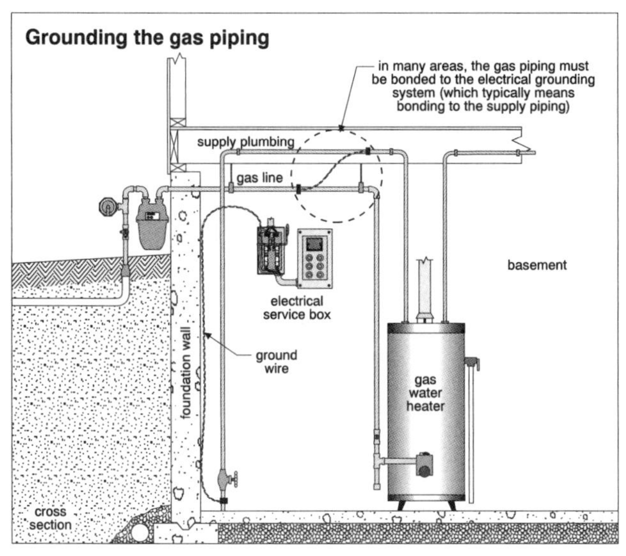

0548

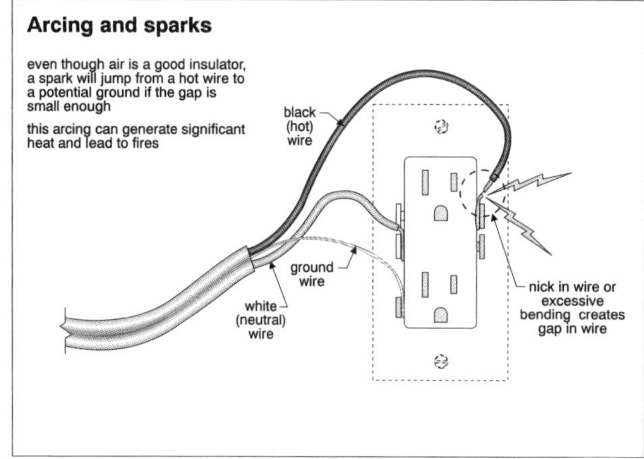

0549

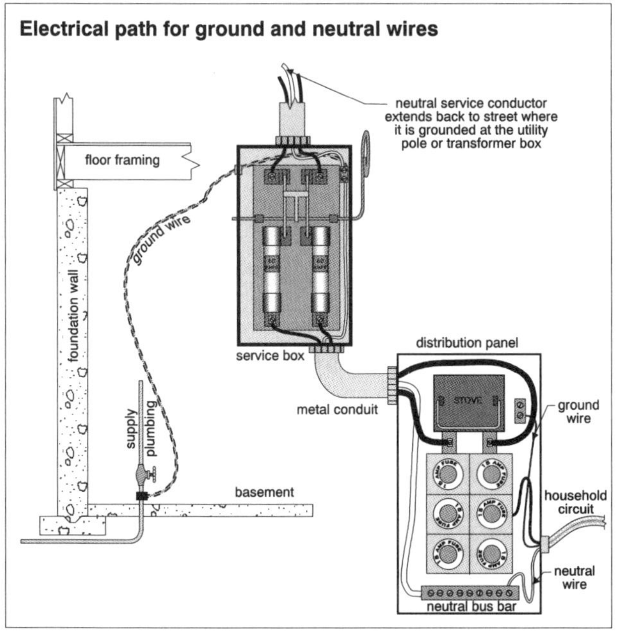

0550

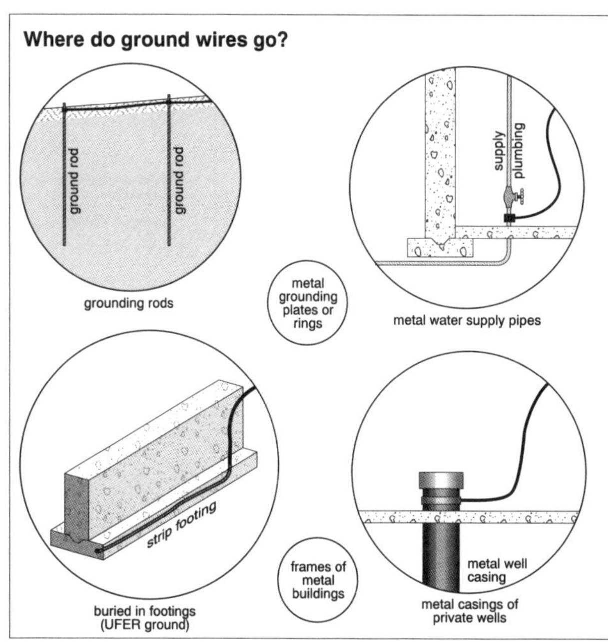

0551

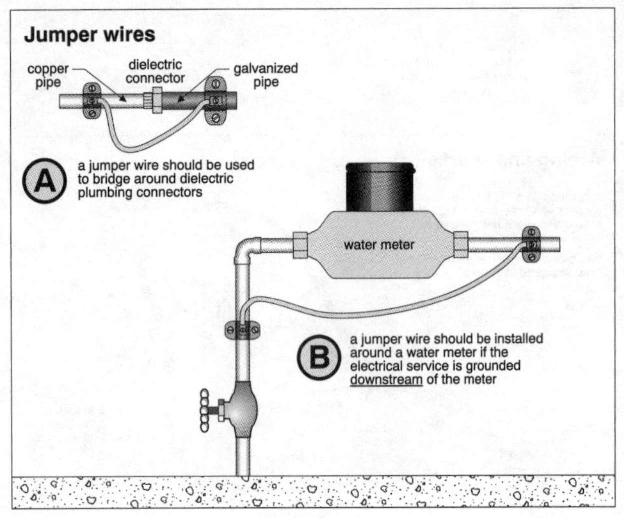

0552

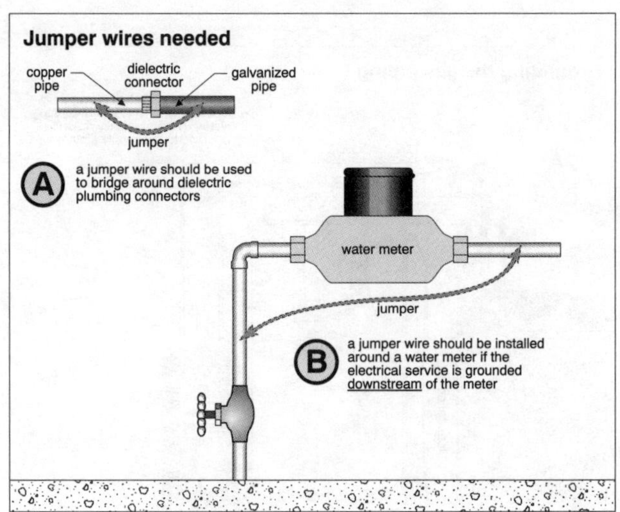

0553

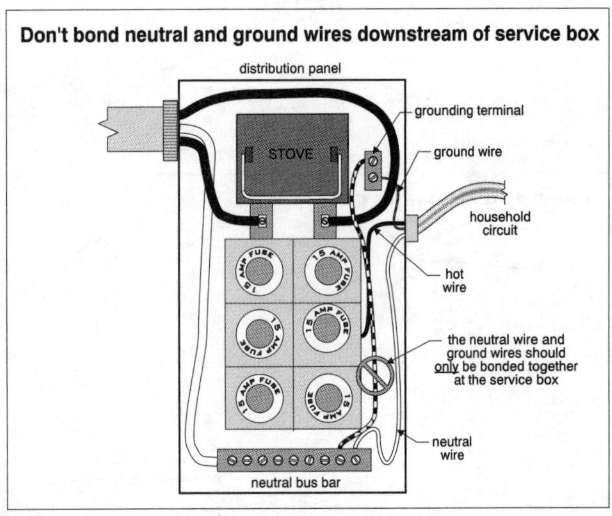

0554

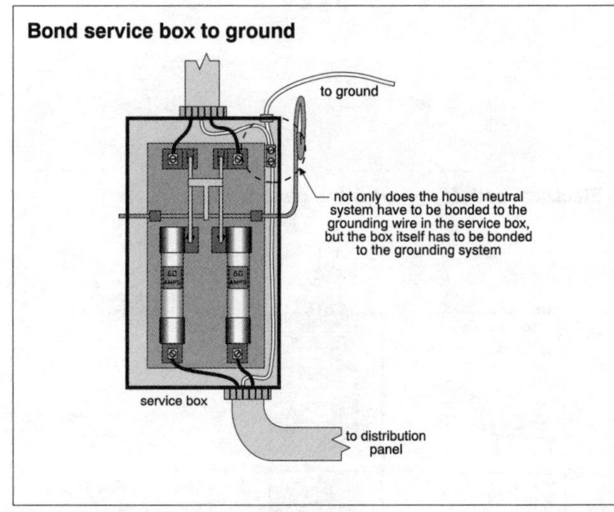

0555

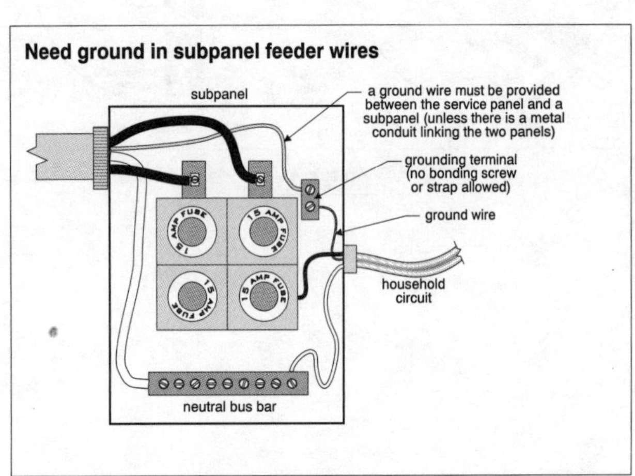

0556

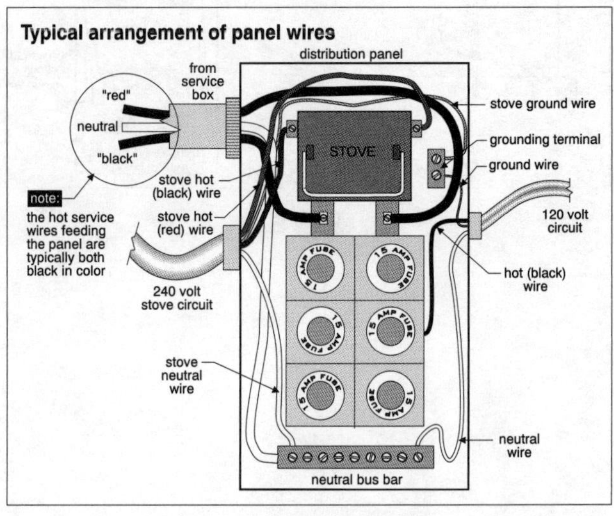

0557

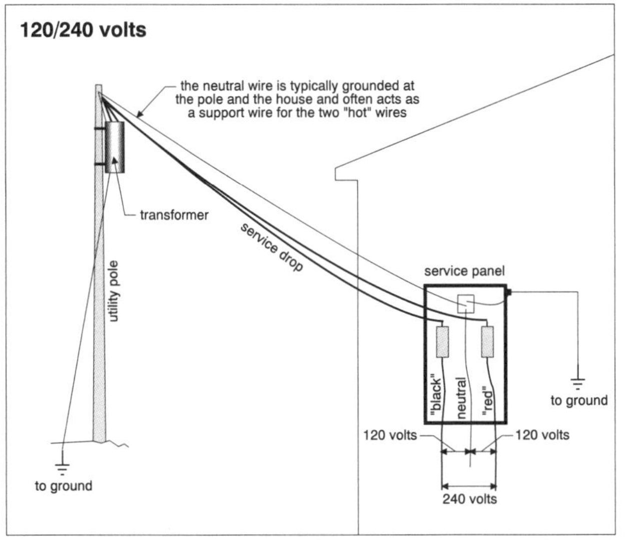

0558

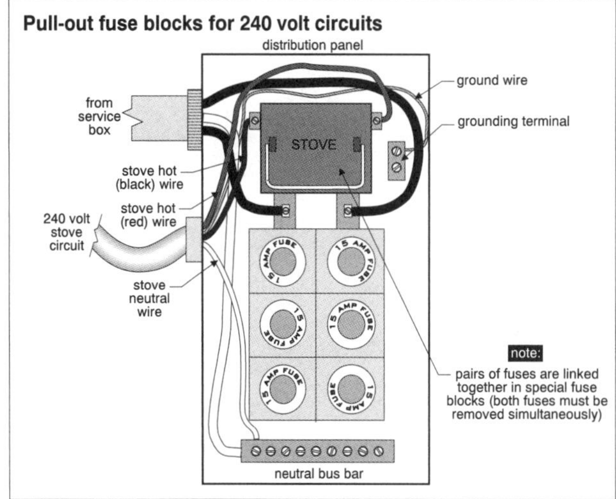

0559

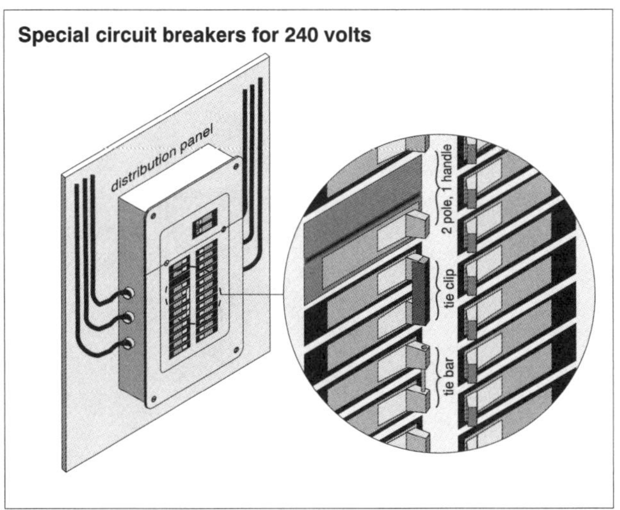

0560

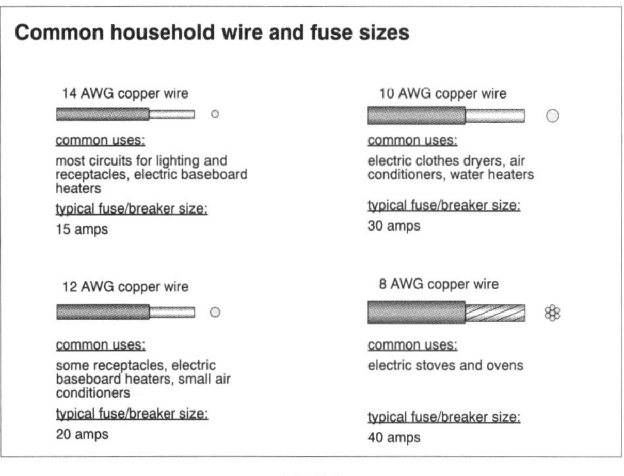

0561

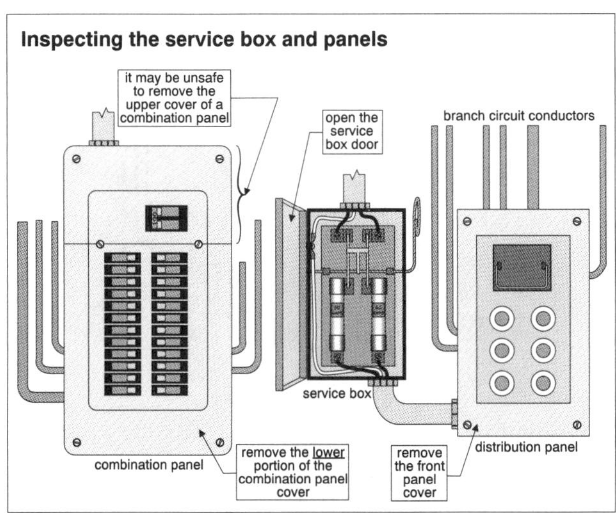

0562

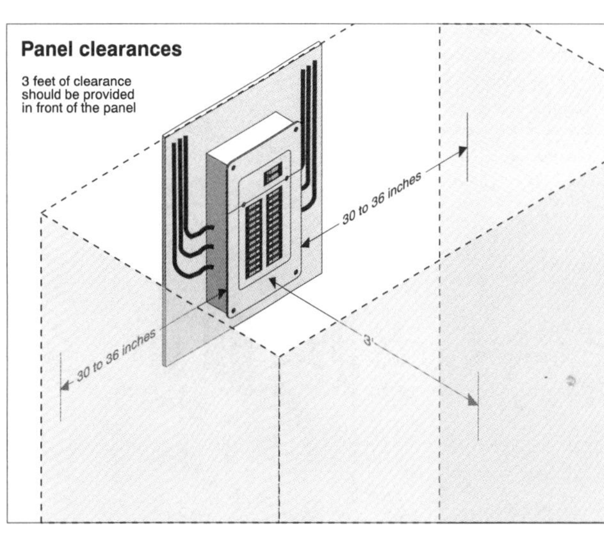

0563

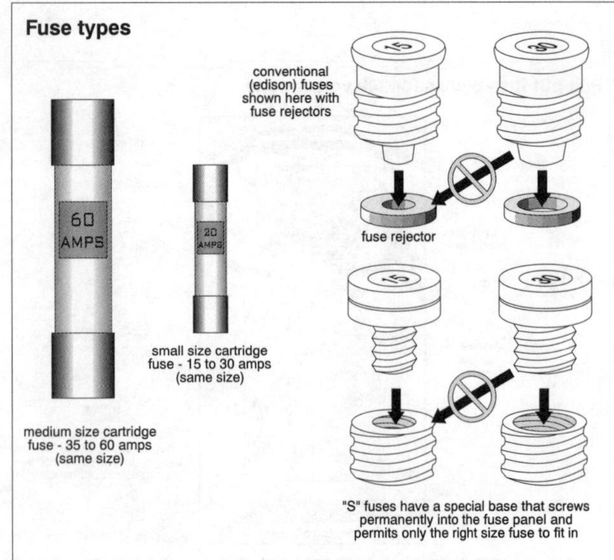

0564

0565

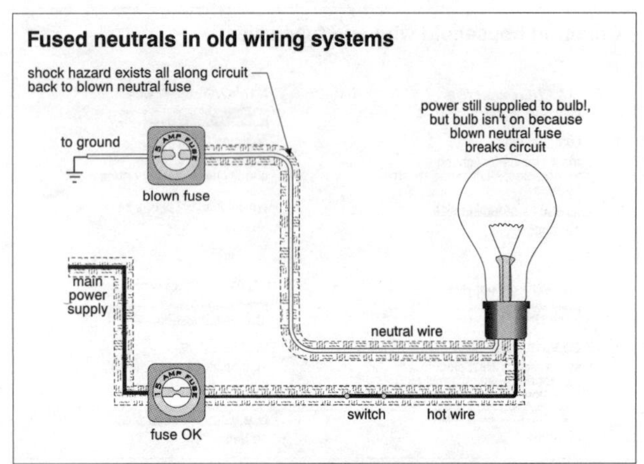

0566

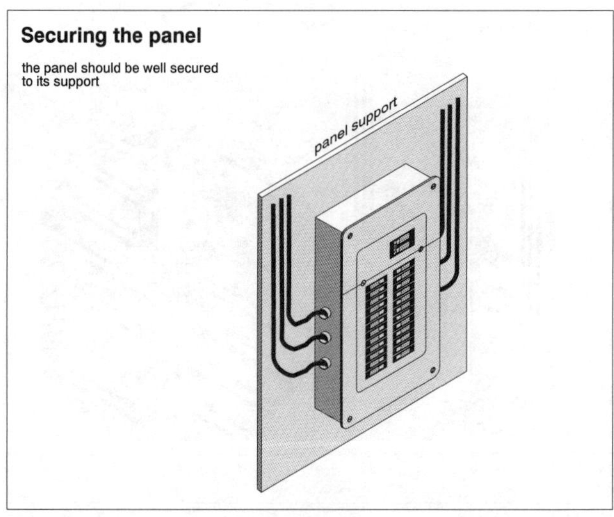

0567

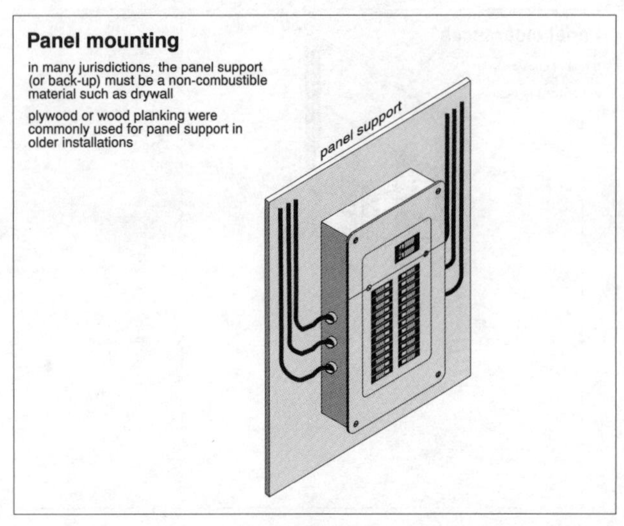

0568

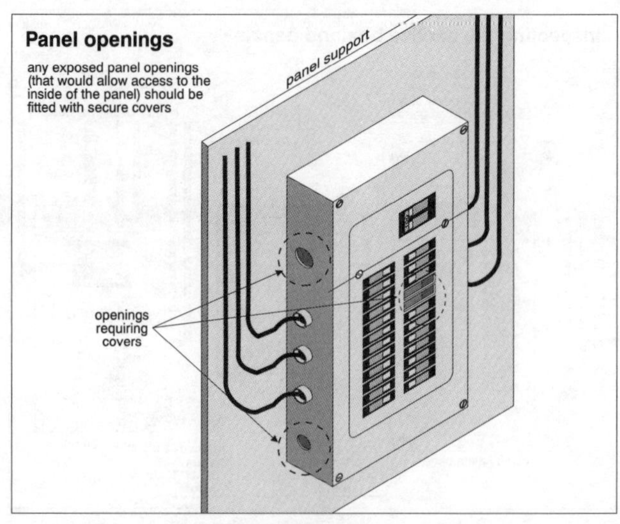

0569

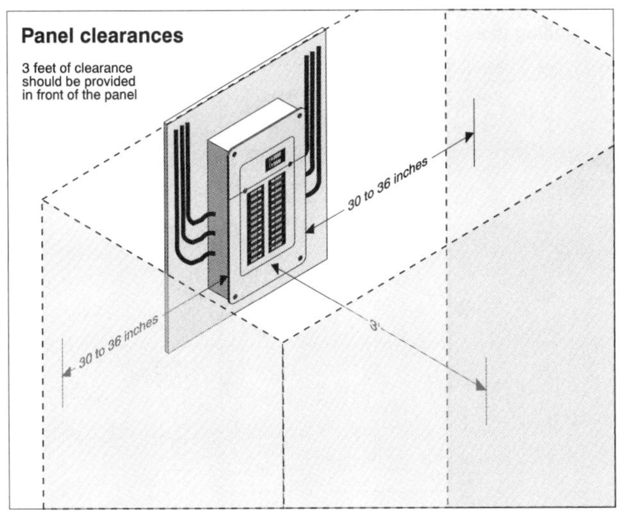

0570

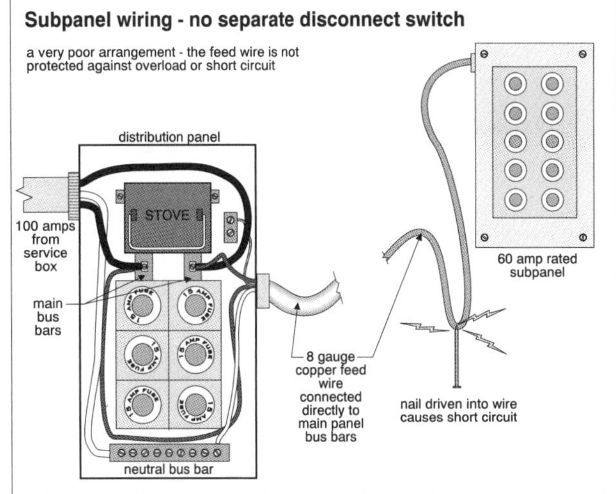

0571

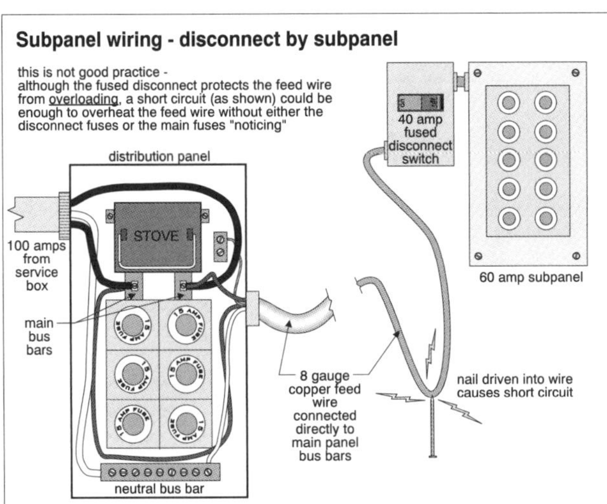

0572

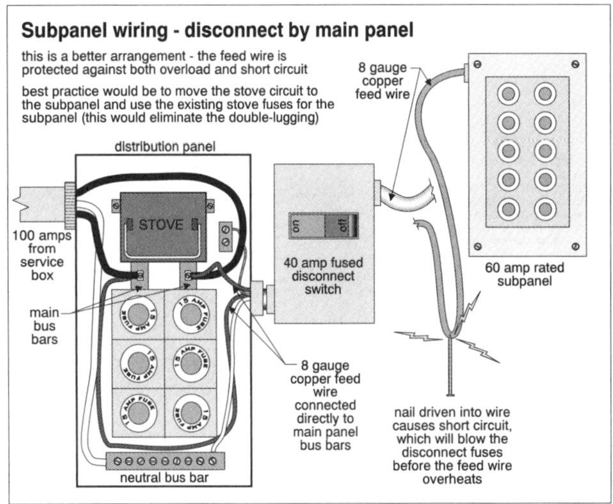

0573

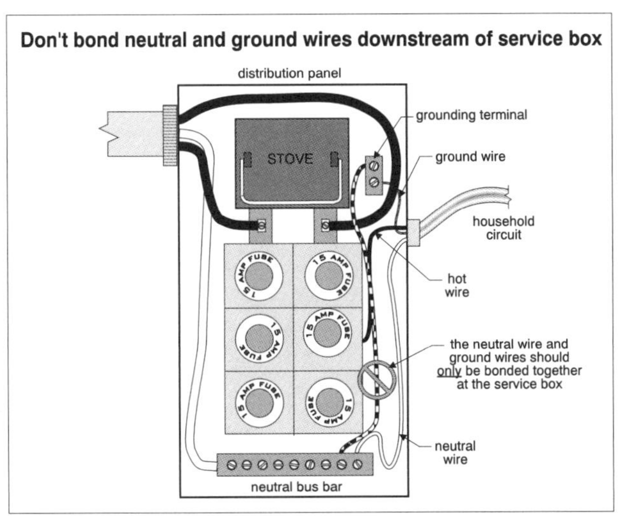

0574

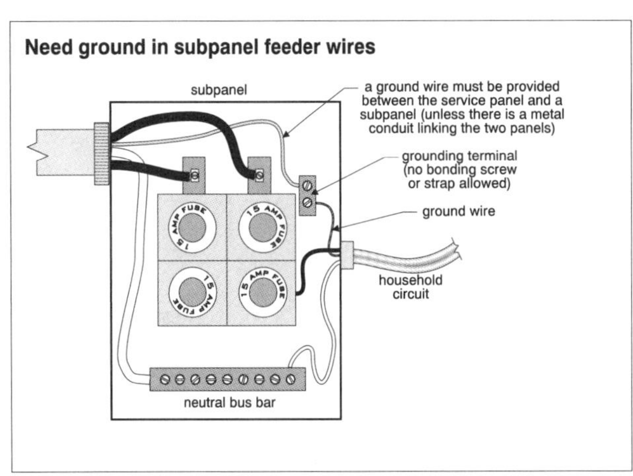

0575

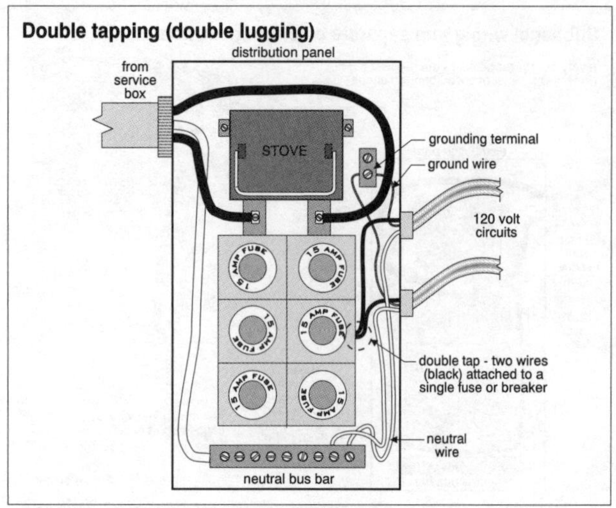

Double tapping (double lugging)

distribution panel
from service box
STOVE
grounding terminal
ground wire
120 volt circuits
double tap - two wires (black) attached to a single fuse or breaker
neutral wire
neutral bus bar

0576

Pigtailing to avoid double taps

distribution panel
from service box
STOVE
grounding terminal
ground wire
120 volt circuits
pigtail connection
neutral wire
neutral bus bar

0577

Overcurrent protection for multi-wire branch circuits

distribution panel
from service box
note:
pairs of fuses are linked together in special fuse blocks intended for split receptacles and other multi-wire branch circuits (both fuses must be removed simultaneously)
in some areas, not all multi-wire branch circuits require special fuse blocks
red and black wires are fed from different bus bars
red and black wires are fed from same bus bar
STOVE
red wire
grounding terminal
ground wire
to split receptacle (properly wired)
to split receptacle (improperly wired)
black wire
red wire
neutral wire
neutral bus bar

0578

Staggered bus bars on circuit breaker panels

to ground
main breaker
service conductors
red wire
black wire
240 volt circuit
neutral wire
ground wire
neutral bus bar
bus bars
grounding terminal
bus bars on circuit breaker panels are typically (but not always) staggered so that adjacent breakers are on different poles
this makes it easier to tie together breakers for 240 volt circuits and split receptacles

0579

Bus bars in fuse panels

distribution panel
from service box
grounding terminal
ground wire
240 volt circuit
red wire
black wire
neutral wire
bus bar
empty fuse sockets
bus bars in fuse panels are typically not staggered
in order to wire a 240 volt circuit, special fuse blocks are used to tie together opposite (rather than adjacent) fuses
neutral bus bar

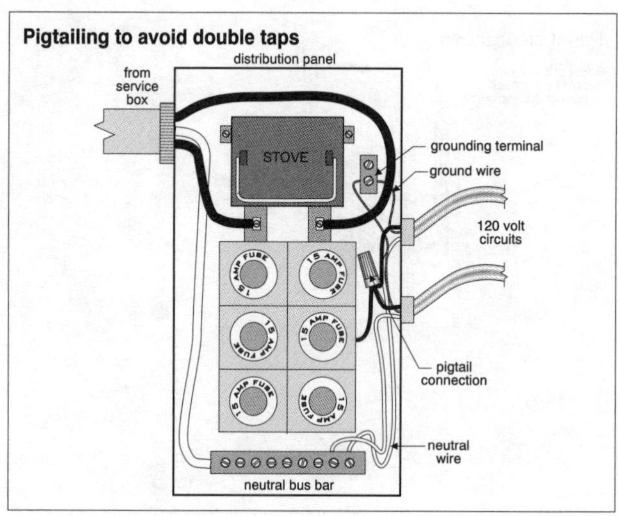

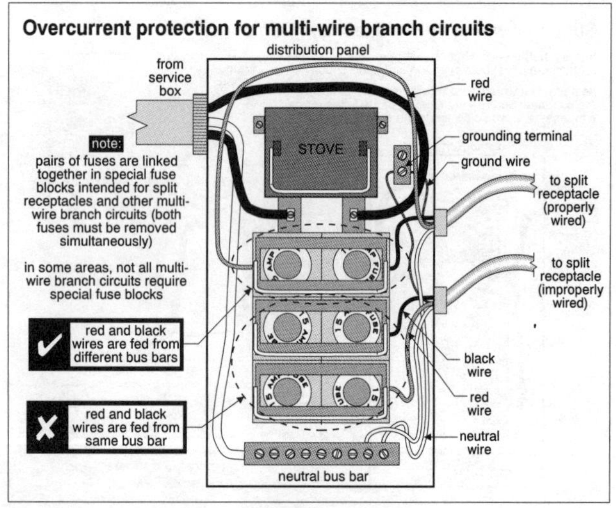

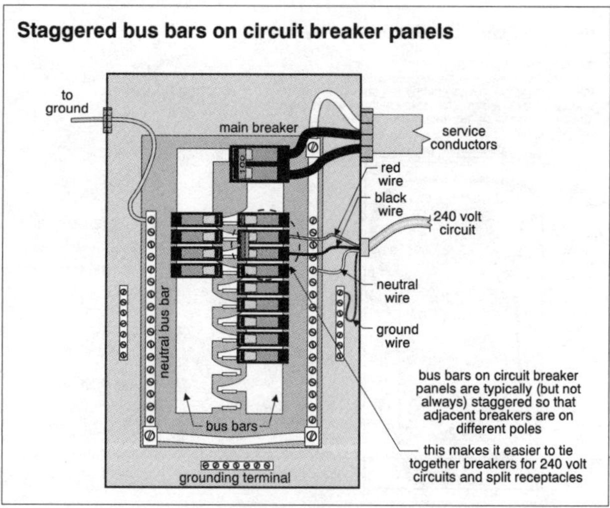

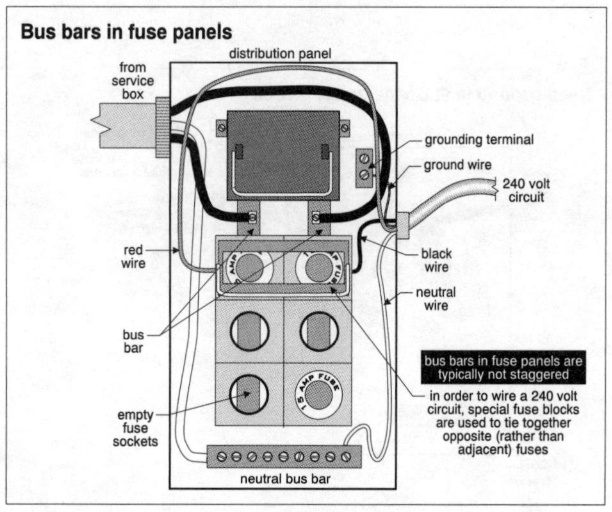

0580

Pull-out fuse blocks for multi-wire branch circuits and 240 volt circuits

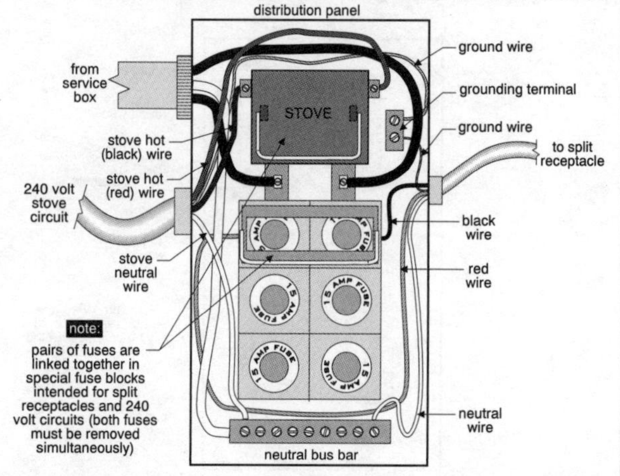

distribution panel
from service box
STOVE
ground wire
grounding terminal
ground wire
to split receptacle
stove hot (black) wire
stove hot (red) wire
240 volt stove circuit
stove neutral wire
black wire
red wire
note:
pairs of fuses are linked together in special fuse blocks intended for split receptacles and 240 volt circuits (both fuses must be removed simultaneously)
neutral wire
neutral bus bar

0581

Special circuit breakers for 240 volts

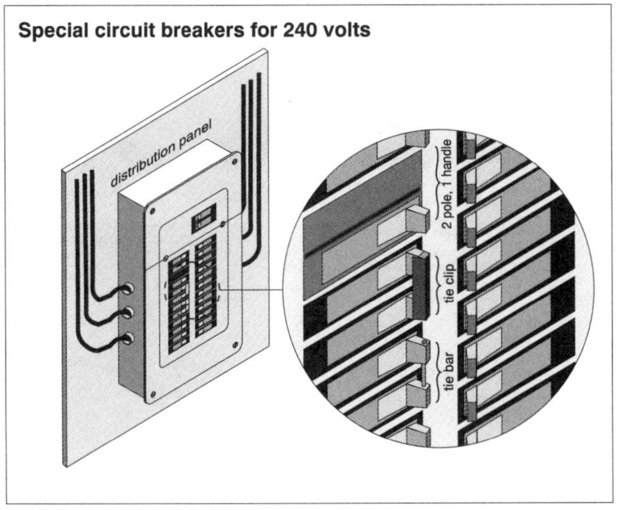

0582

Excess sheathing on panel wires

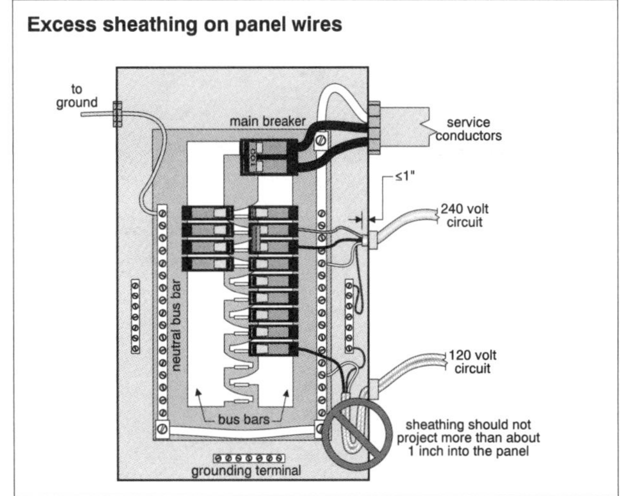

0583

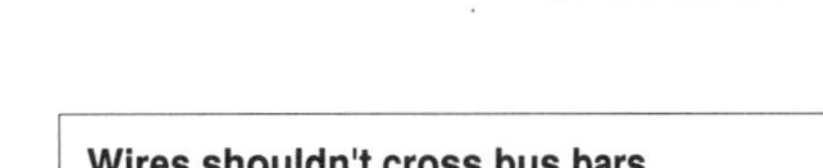

Securing wires

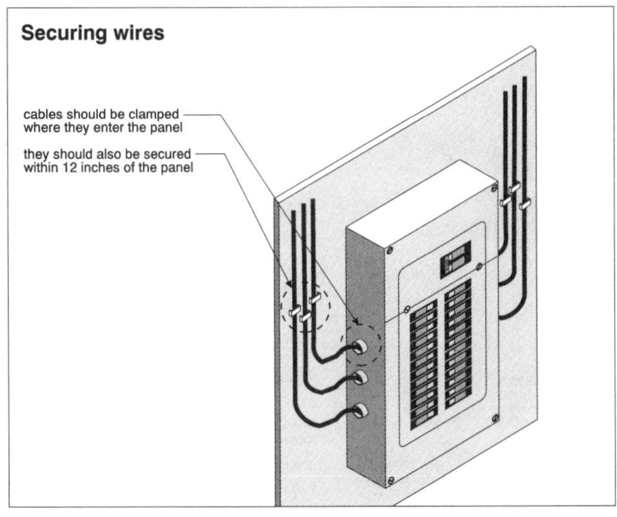

0584

Wires shouldn't cross bus bars

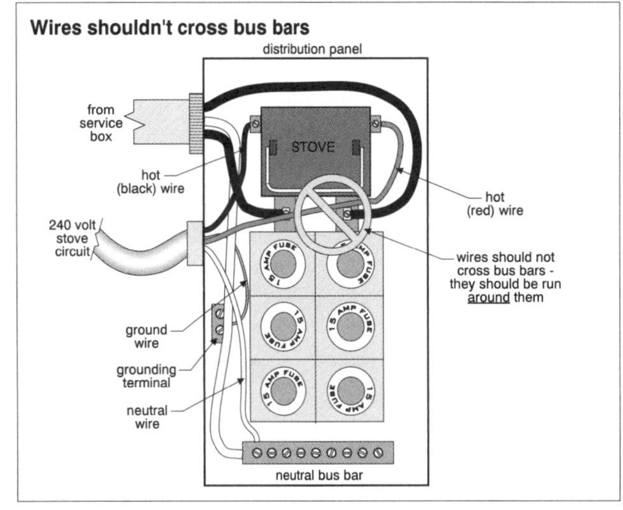

0585

Arc fault circuit interrupter

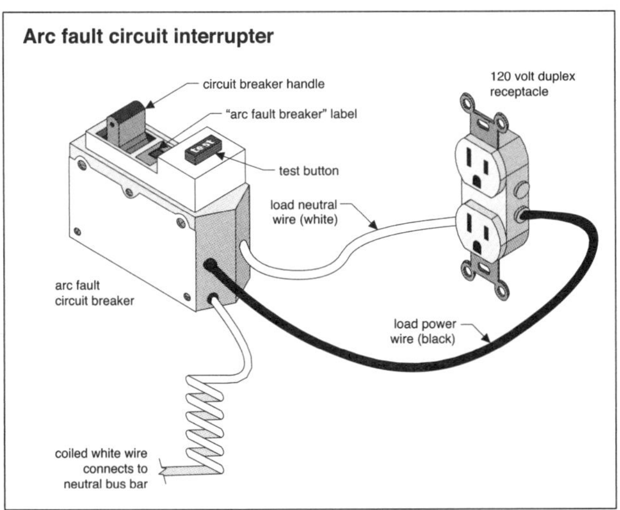

0586

Common household wire and fuse sizes

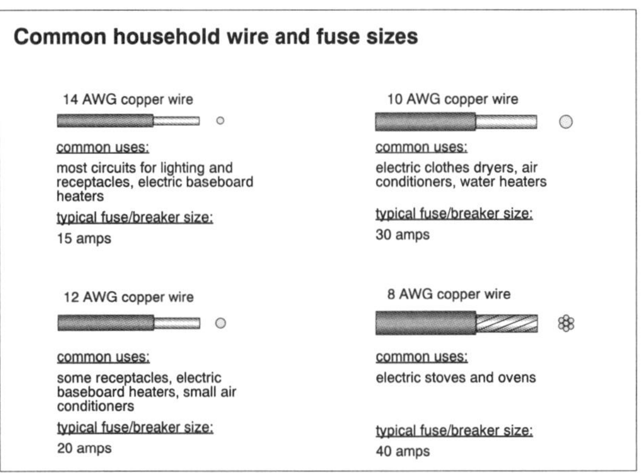

14 AWG copper wire

common uses:
most circuits for lighting and receptacles, electric baseboard heaters

typical fuse/breaker size:
15 amps

10 AWG copper wire

common uses:
electric clothes dryers, air conditioners, water heaters

typical fuse/breaker size:
30 amps

12 AWG copper wire

common uses:
some receptacles, electric baseboard heaters, small air conditioners

typical fuse/breaker size:
20 amps

8 AWG copper wire

common uses:
electric stoves and ovens

typical fuse/breaker size:
40 amps

0587

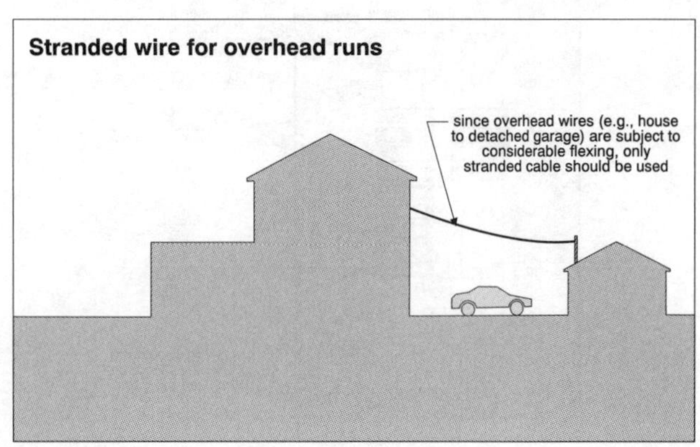

0588

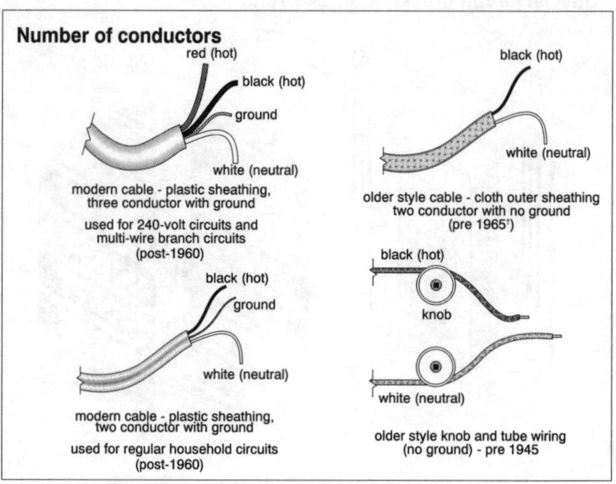

0589

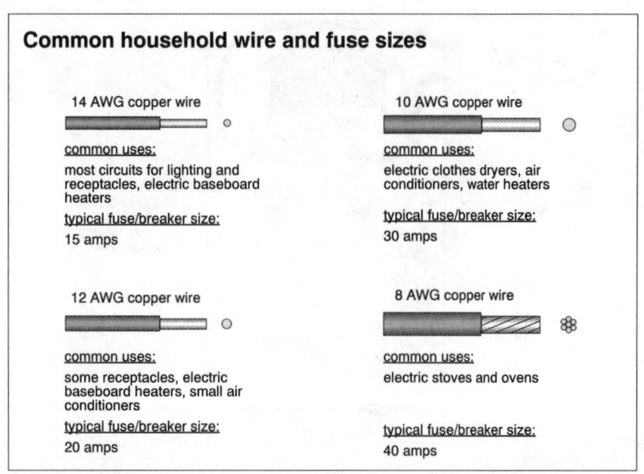

0590

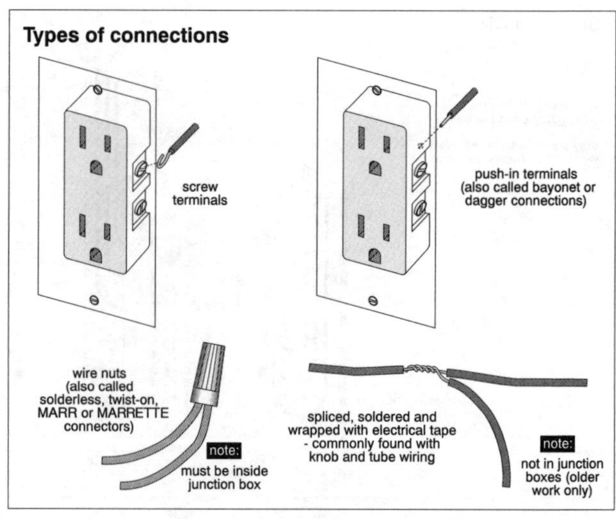

0591

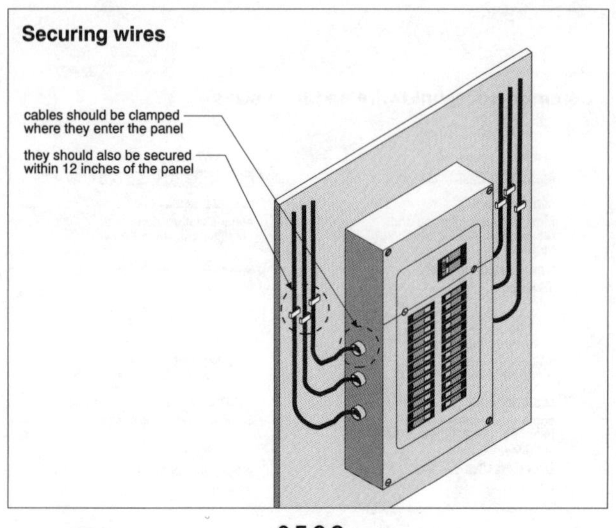

0592

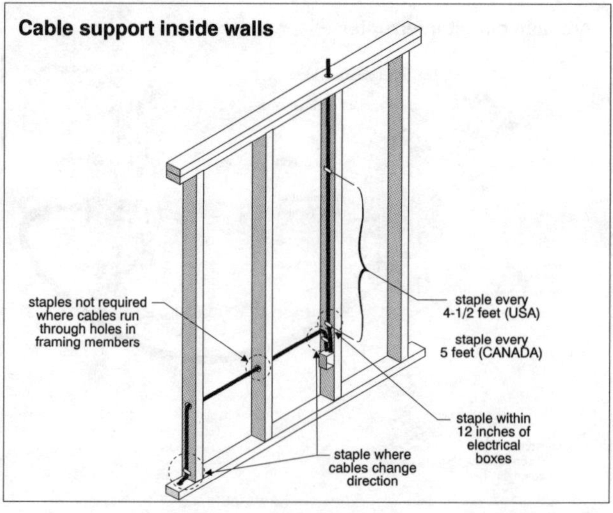

0593

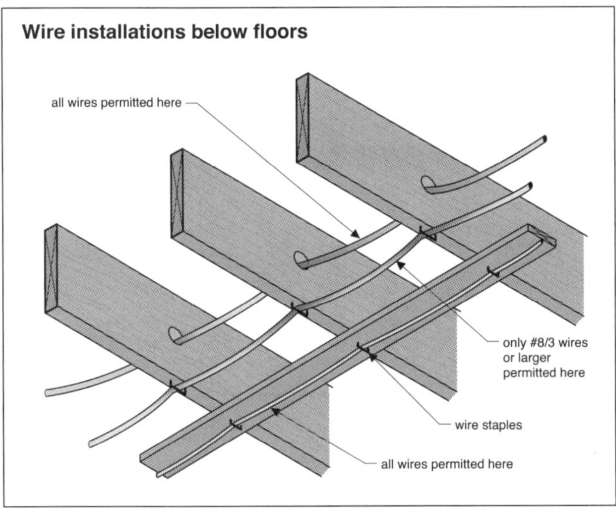

0594

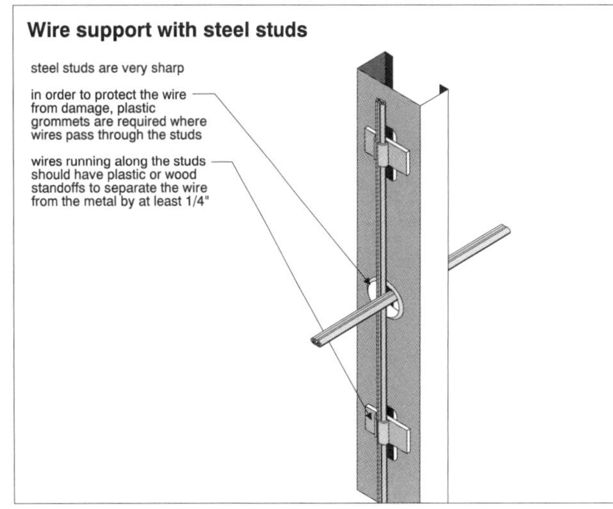

0595

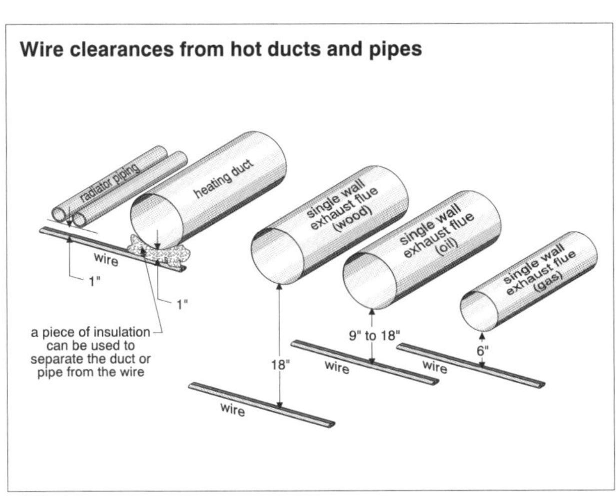

0596

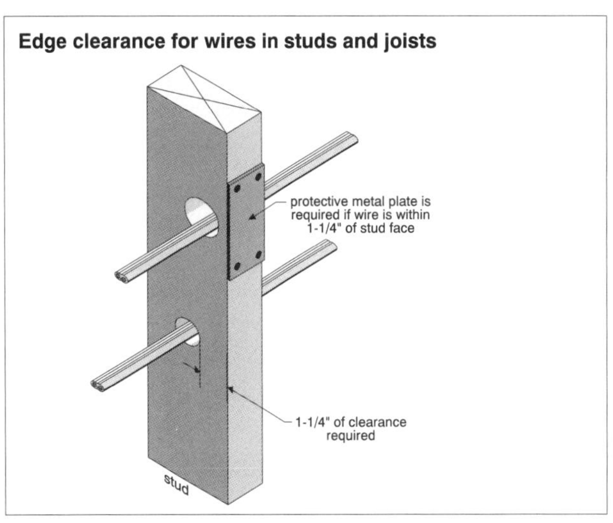

0597

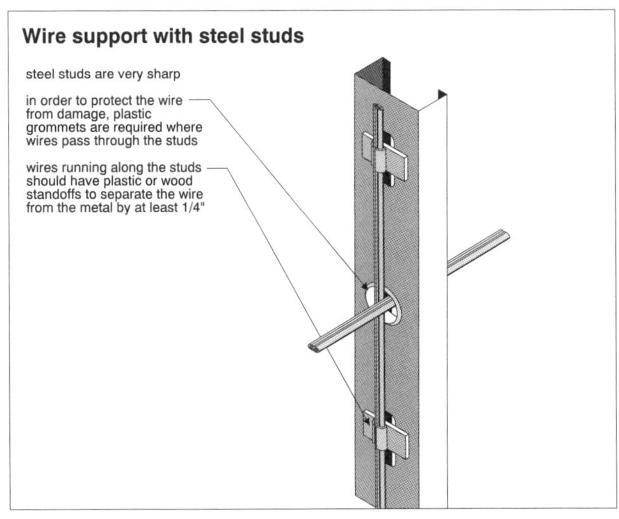

0598

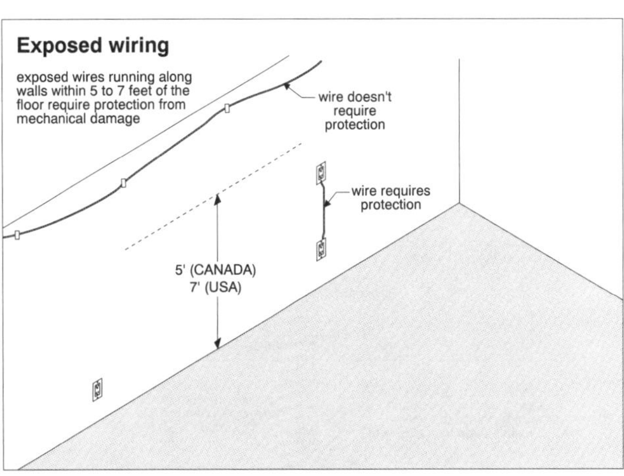

0599

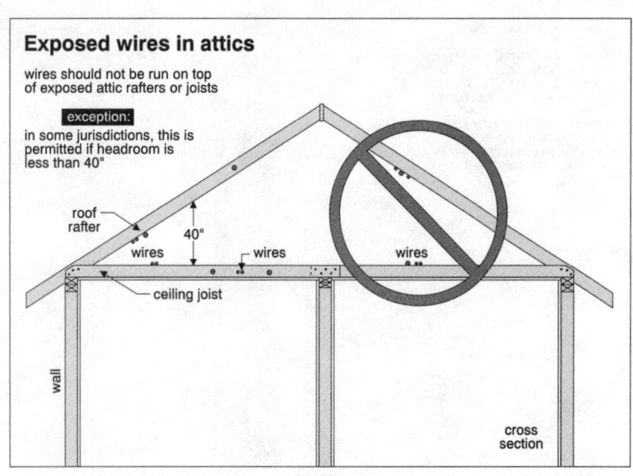

0600

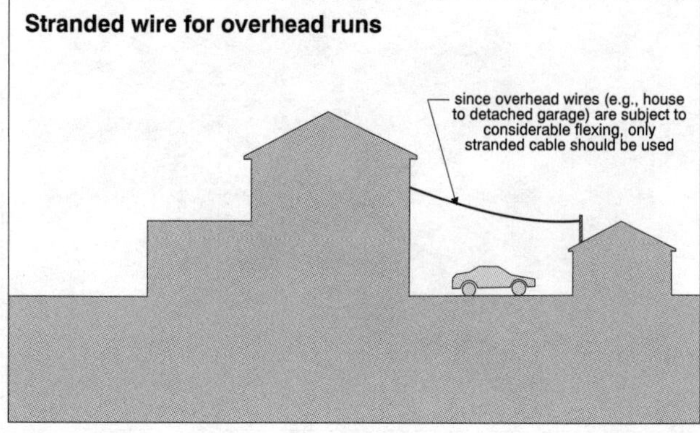

0601

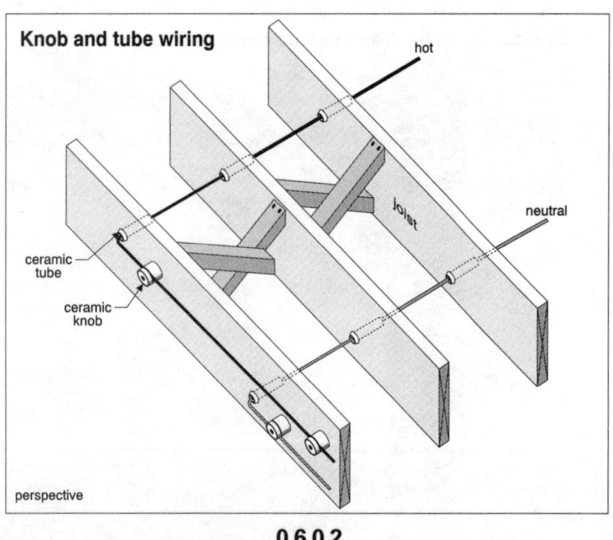

0602

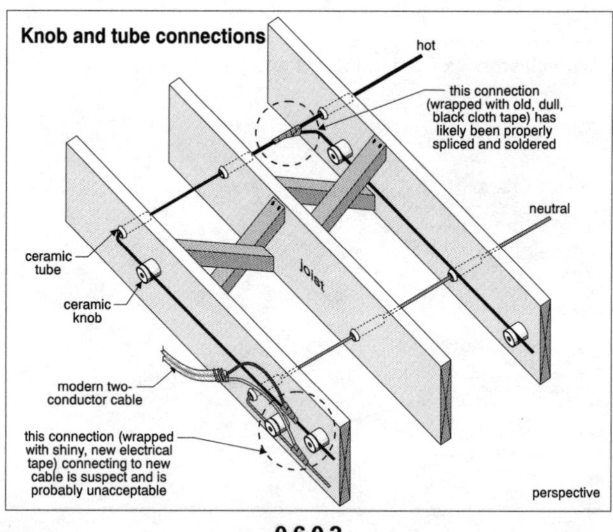

0603

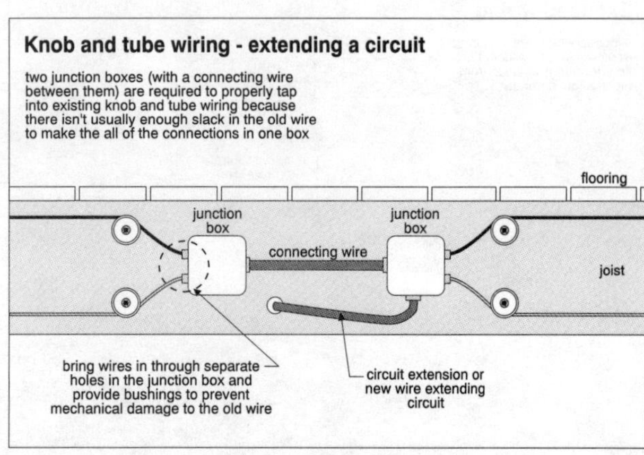

0604

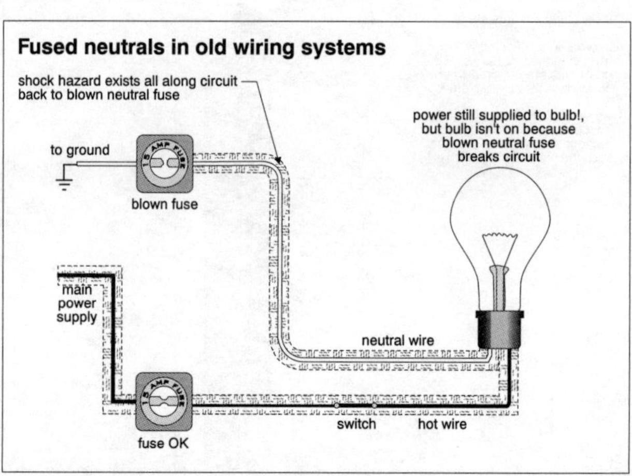

0605

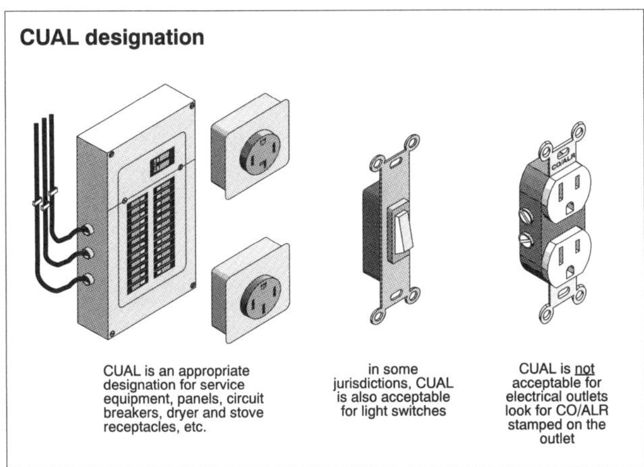

0606

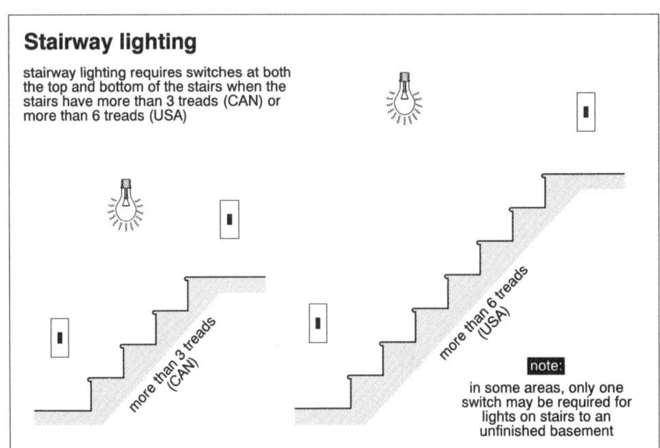

0607

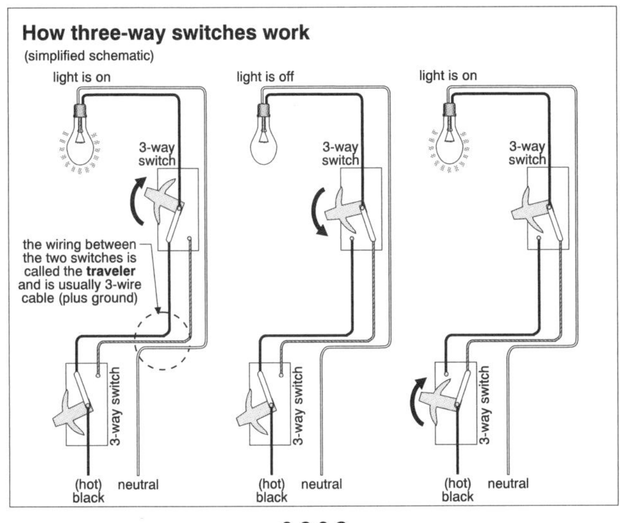

0608

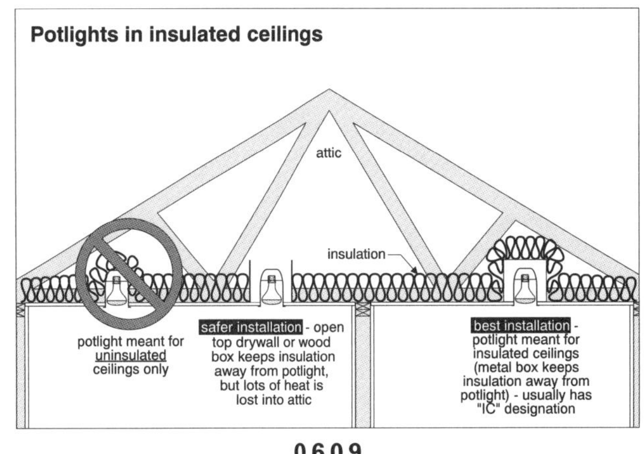

0609

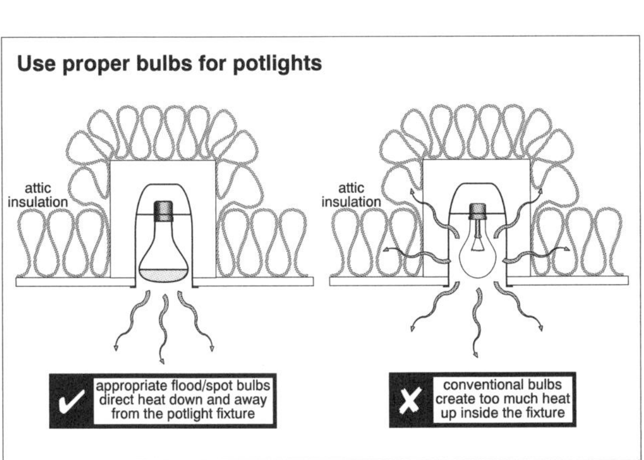

0610

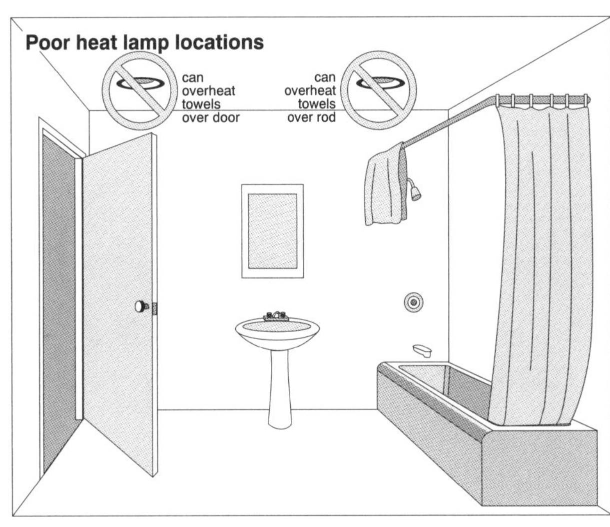

0611

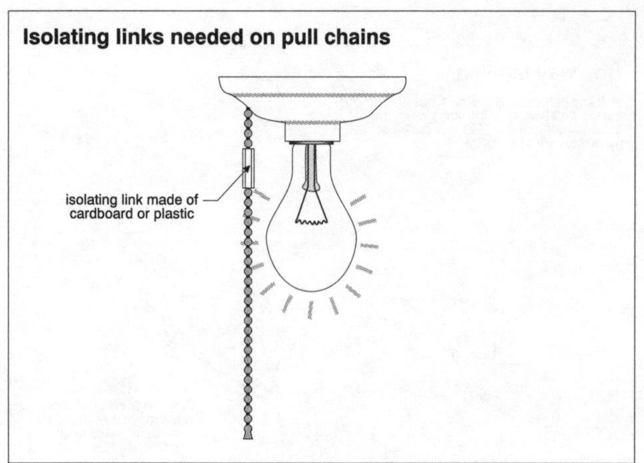

0612

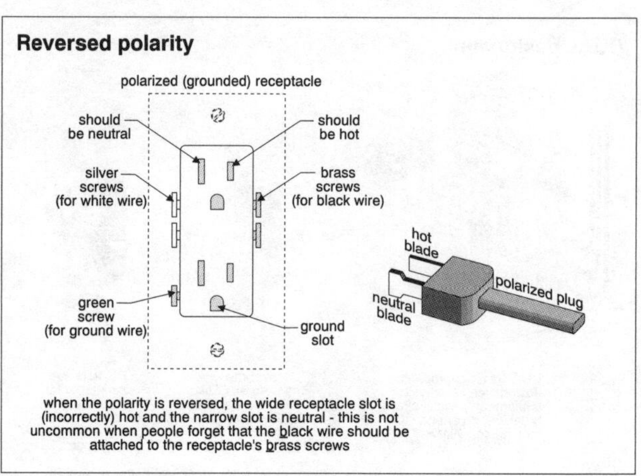

0613

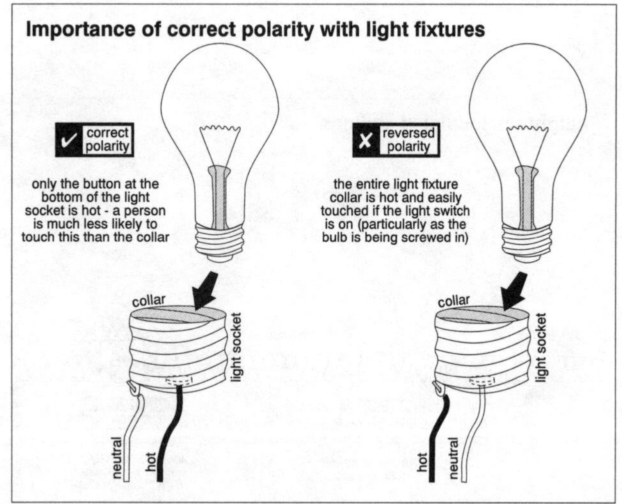

0614

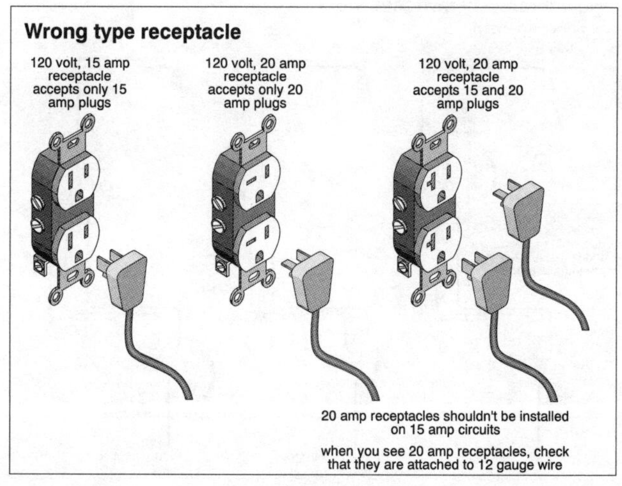

0615

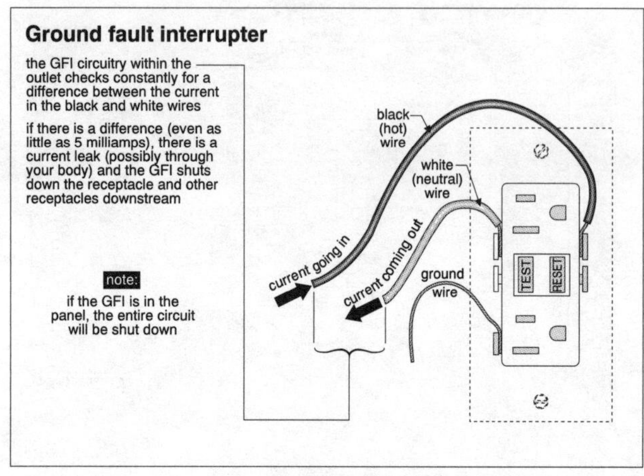

0616

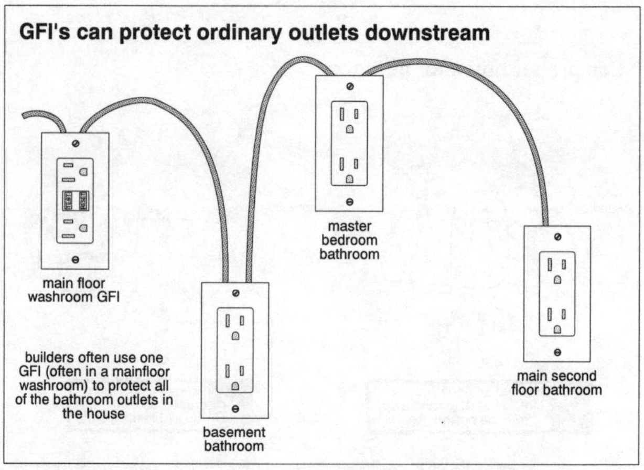

GFI's can protect ordinary outlets downstream

main floor washroom GFI

master bedroom bathroom

basement bathroom

main second floor bathroom

builders often use one GFI (often in a mainfloor washroom) to protect all of the bathroom outlets in the house

0617

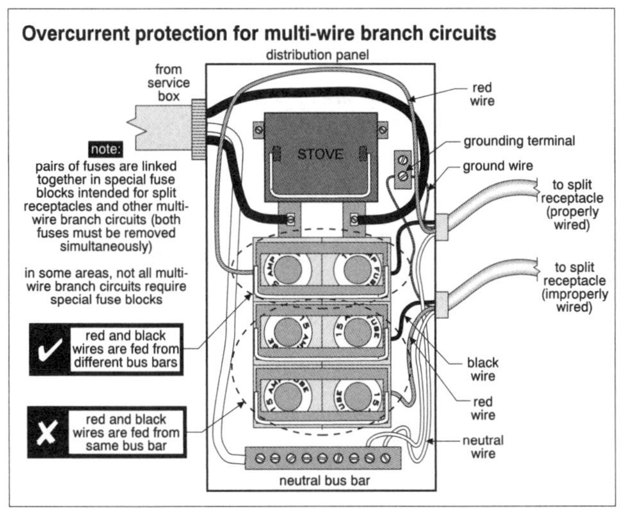

0618

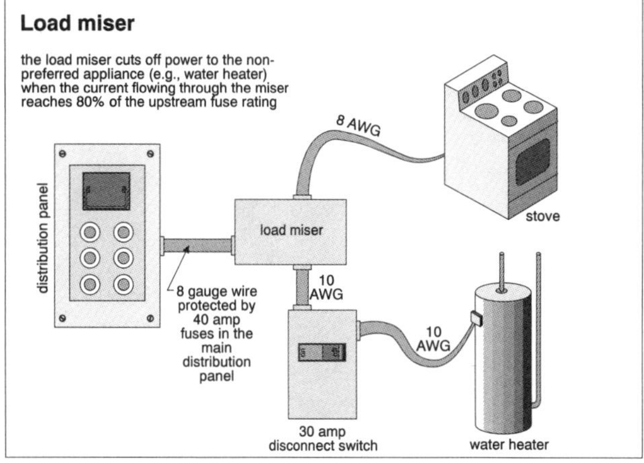

0619

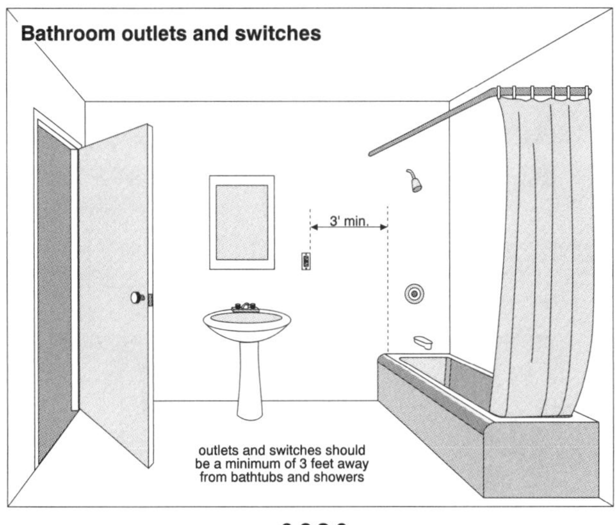

0620

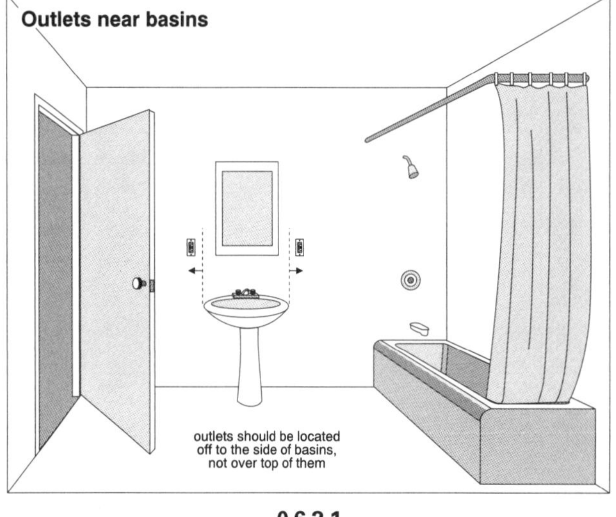

0621

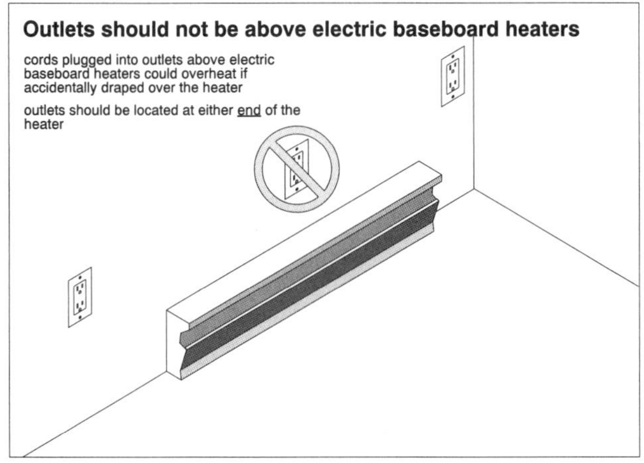

0622

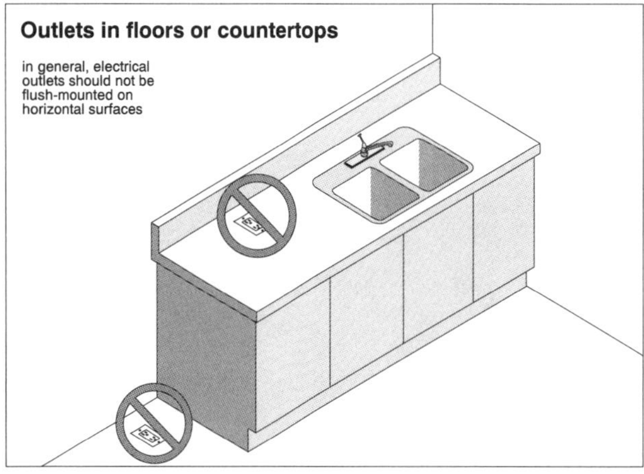

0623

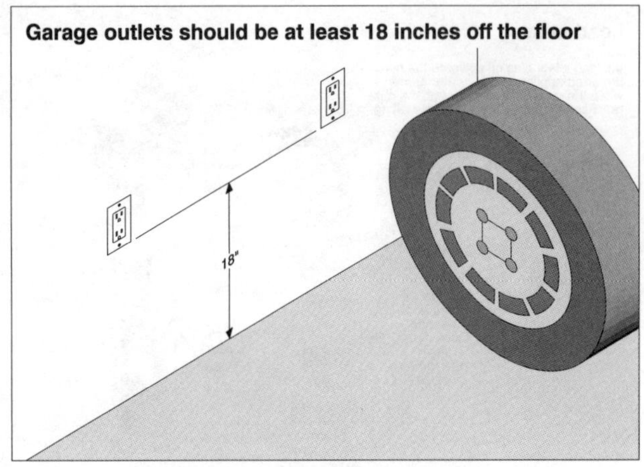

0624

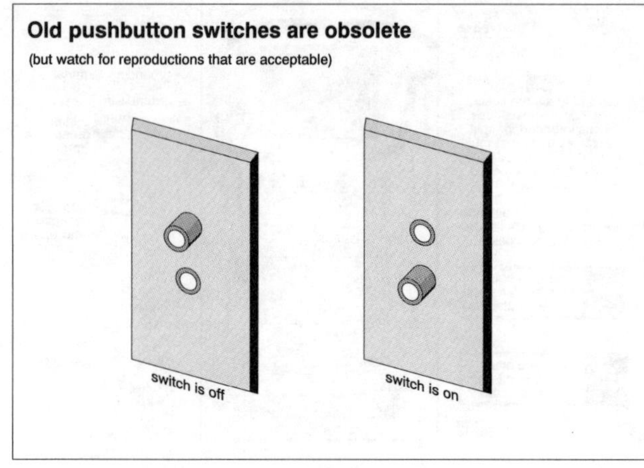

0625

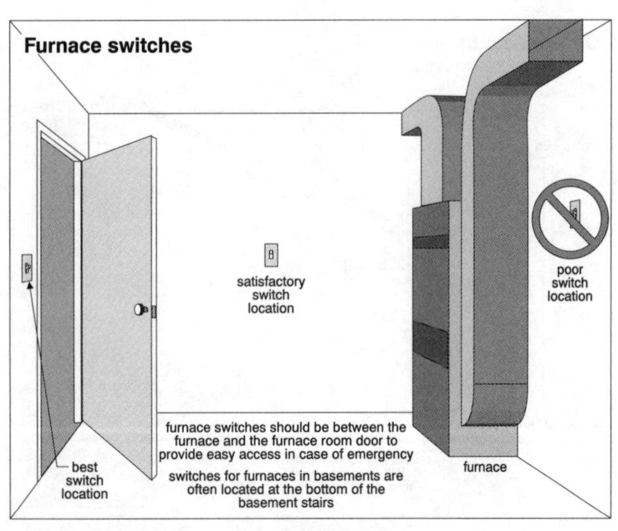

0626

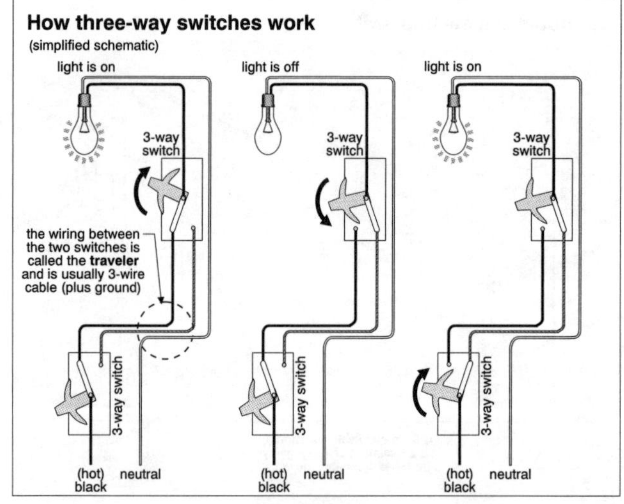

0627

Garbage disposal switches

the garbage disposal switch is best mounted above the counter or in the cupboard below the sink rather than on the front face of the base cabinets where it is prone to damage

best location

garbage disposal

better location

0628

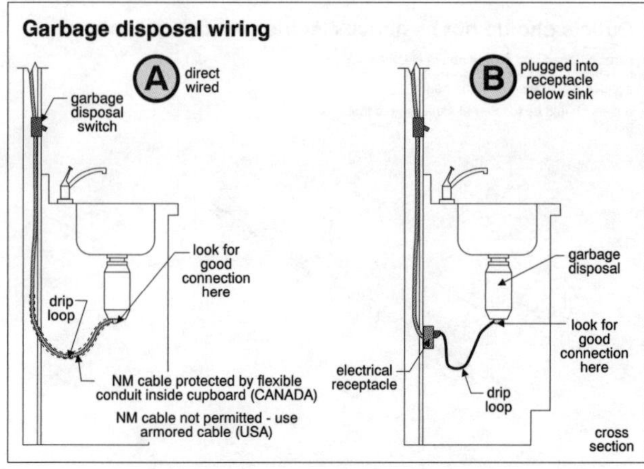

0629

CHAPTER 4

FURNACES – GAS & OIL

INTRODUCTION

115 ... 0700 How heat is generated
115 ... 0701 British Thermal Unit (BTU's)
115 ... 0702 Cool spots
115 ... 0703 Cold floors
115 ... 0704 The outdoor fire
115 ... 0705 Fire comes inside
116 ... 0706 The hole in the roof
116 ... 0707 Homes built with holes
116 ... 0708 Fire gets contained
116 ... 0709 Building a chimney
116 ... 0710 Gravity furnace
116 ... 0711 House air flow
117 ... 0712 The fire triangle

HEAT TRANSFER

117 ... 0713 Methods of heat transfer
117 ... 0714 Electric radiant heat
117 ... 0715 Insulation behind radiators
117 ... 0716 Radiator covers
117 ... 0717 Conventional gas furnace
118 ... 0718 Mid-efficiency gas furnace
118 ... 0719 High efficiency gas furnace

GAS PIPING AND METERS

118 ... 0720 Gas service line and outdoor meter
118 ... 0721 Ice on regulator
118 ... 0722 Poor meter locations
118 ... 0723 Gas piping terminology
119 ... 0724 Flexible gas appliance connectors
119 ... 0725 Teflon tape at connections
119 ... 0726 Flexible copper tubing for gas piping
119 ... 0727 Gas shut off valves
119 ... 0728 Grounding the gas piping
120 ... 0729 Gas piping support
120 ... 0730 Drip leg
120 ... 0731 Gas service line and outdoor meter

COMBUSTION AIR

120 ... 0732 Combustion air
121 ... 0733 Three kinds of draft
121 ... 0734 Natural draft burners
121 ... 0735 Draft hoods
121 ... 0736 Backdrafting
122 ... 0737 Furnace room air openings
122 ... 0738 Outside air supply
122 ... 0739 Backdrafting
122 ... 0740 Gas burners

GAS BURNERS

122 ... 0741 Monoport burners
122 ... 0742 Gas supply to burners
123 ... 0743 Crossover igniters
123 ... 0744 Refractory/fire pot
123 ... 0745 Gas supply to burners
123 ... 0746 Thermostat – bi-metallic (mercury bulb)
123 ... 0747 Continuous pilot light
124 ... 0748 Pilot light – relighting
124 ... 0749 Scorching
124 ... 0750 Heat shield or flame rollout shield

HEAT EXCHANGERS

124 ... 0751 Heat exchanger heat flow
125 ... 0752 Draft hoods
125 ... 0753 House air flow
125 ... 0754 Exhaust breech through cold air return
125 ... 0755 Heat pump coil upstream of heat exchanger
125 ... 0756 Downflow and upflow furnaces
125 ... 0757 Horizontal gas-fired furnace

FURNACE CABINETS

126 ... 0758 Fan cover missing
126 ... 0759 Furnace covers
126 ... 0760 Draft hoods
126 ... 0761 Furnace clearances

FAN/LIMIT SWITCHES

127 ... 0762 Fan switch
127 ... 0763 Fan/limit switch
127 ... 0764 Fan/limit switch set wrong or defective

CHAPTER 4

THERMOSTATS

127 ... 0765 Thermostat – bi-metallic (mercury bulb)
127 ... 0766 Themostat – bi-metallic (snap-action)
127 ... 0767 Variable thermostat anticipator
128 ... 0768 Thermostat must be level

VENTING GAS FURNACES

128 ... 0769 Draft hoods
128 ... 0770 Vent connector slope
128 ... 0771 Vent connector length
128 ... 0772 Vent connector support
128 ... 0773 Combustible clearances for vent connectors and B-vents
129 ... 0774 Size of vent connector
129 ... 0775 Chimney/vent connections
129 ... 0776 Vent connector extends too far into chimney
129 ... 0777 Backdrafting

DISTRIBUTION SYSTEM

130 ... 0778 House air flow
130 ... 0779 Typical supply and return register locations
130 ... 0780 Distribution components for forced air heating
130 ... 0781 Factors affecting air supply

BLOWERS

131 ... 0782 Blowers – belt drive and direct drive
131 ... 0783 Fan belts on furnace blowers

AIR FILTERS AND CLEANERS

131 ... 0784 Air filter orientation
131 ... 0785 Electronic air cleaner
132 ... 0786 Electronic air cleaner problems
132 ... 0787 Electronic air cleaner – installed backwards/parts missing

HUMIDIFIERS

132 ... 0788 Drum-type humidifier
132 ... 0789 Trickle humidifier
133 ... 0790 Air flow through humidifier
133 ... 0791 Humdifier above heat exchanger

DUCT SYSTEMS, REGISTERS AND GRILLS

133 ... 0792 Return ducts in floor joists
133 ... 0793 Supply air registers, diffusers and grills
133 ... 0794 Renovations remove ducts
133 ... 0795 High and low returns
134 ... 0796 Ducts in concrete floor slabs
134 ... 0797 Supply and return registers poorly located
134 ... 0798 Basement heat registers
134 ... 0799 Return grill in furnace room
134 ... 0800 Air return outside room

MID-EFFICIENCY FURNACES

134 ... 0801 Intermittent pilot light
135 ... 0802 Hot surface ignition
135 ... 0803 Three kinds of draft
135 ... 0804 Blockage switches
135 ... 0805 Improper side wall venting of gas appliances

CONDENSING FURNACES

136 ... 0806 High efficiency furnaces have long heat exchangers
136 ... 0807 Condensation in high efficiency furnaces
136 ... 0808 Maximizing temperature differences
136 ... 0809 Venting for high efficiency furnaces
137 ... 0810 Improper side wall vent locations
137 ... 0811 Safety devices for high efficiency furnaces
137 ... 0812 Pulse furnace – how it works
137 ... 0813 Pulse furnace heat exchanger components
138 ... 0814 High efficiency furnaces and duct sizes
138 ... 0815 Automatic vent dampers
138 ... 0816 Inspecting high efficiency furnaces
138 ... 0817 Inspecting high efficiency furnaces
138 ... 0818 Improper side wall vent locations
139 ... 0819 Venting for high efficiency furnaces

CHAPTER 4

HOT WATER BOILERS

GRAVITY FURNACES

139 ... 0820 Gravity furnaces

COMBINATION FURNACES

139 ... 0821 Combination furnace/water heater system
139 ... 0822 Tempering valve – combination system

OIL FURNACES

140 ... 0823 Buried oil storage tank
140 ... 0824 Exterior above ground oil storage tank
140 ... 0825 Oil storage tanks – clearance from oil burner
140 ... 0826 Oil storage tank leaks
140 ... 0827 Underground oil storage tank
140 ... 0828 Fill and vent piping
141 ... 0829 Caps for fill and vent pipes on oil storage tanks
141 ... 0830 Undersized fill lines
141 ... 0831 Oil furnace emergency shutoffs
141 ... 0832 Atomizing oil burner
141 ... 0833 Oil burner with flame retention head
141 ... 0834 Primary control
142 ... 0835 Inspecting an oil burner
142 ... 0836 Refractory/fire pot
142 ... 0837 Primary control
142 ... 0838 Flame sensor
142 ... 0839 Barometric damper
142 ... 0840 Barometric damper (draft regulator) problems
143 ... 0841 Spillage from barometric damper
143 ... 0842 Exhaust flue slope
143 ... 0843 Exhaust flue support
143 ... 0844 Exhaust flue length
143 ... 0845 Exhaust flue clearances –
143 ... 0846 Obstruction in exhaust flue
144 ... 0847 Mid-efficiency oil furnace (sidewall vented)
144 ... 0848 Improper side wall vent locations for oil furnaces

INTRODUCTION

144 ... 0849 How boilers work
144 ... 0850 How radiators heat the air through convection
144 ... 0851 Radiator covers
144 ... 0852 Superheated water
145 ... 0853 Conventional gas boiler
145 ... 0854 High efficiency gas boiler

HEAT EXCHANGERS

145 ... 0855 Heat exchangers
145 ... 0856 Copper tube heat exchangers

CONTROLS

145 ... 0857 Pressure relief valve
145 ... 0858 Pressure relief valve location
146 ... 0859 Inspecting pressure relief valves
146 ... 0860 High temperature limit switch
146 ... 0861 Low water cut out
146 ... 0862 Backflow preventer
146 ... 0863 Pressure reducing valve location
146 ... 0864 Backflow preventer installed backwards
147 ... 0865 Temperature and pressure gauge
147 ... 0866 Pressure reducing valve
147 ... 0867 Combined pressure reducing valve and pressure relief valve
147 ... 0868 Pressure set too low
147 ... 0869 Don't operate air bleed valves
147 ... 0870 Pressure reducing/relief valve installed backwards
148 ... 0871 Air separators
148 ... 0872 Aquastat – primary control
148 ... 0873 Inoperative aquastat
148 ... 0874 Pump control (combined with high limit)
148 ... 0875 Zone control with pumps
148 ... 0876 Zone control with valves
149 ... 0877 Outdoor air temperature sensor
149 ... 0878 Flow control valves

CHAPTER 4

DISTRIBUTION SYSTEMS

149 ... 0879 Open hydronic system
149 ... 0880 Closed hydronic system
149 ... 0881 Series loop
149 ... 0882 One-pipe system
150 ... 0883 Two-pipe system (direct return)
150 ... 0884 Two-pipe system (reverse return)
150 ... 0885 Balancing methods
150 ... 0886 Expansion tank water levels
150 ... 0887 Overflow pipe
150 ... 0888 Conventional expansion tank
151 ... 0889 Diaphragm tank
151 ... 0890 Circulating pump
151 ... 0891 Zone control with pumps
151 ... 0892 Flow control valves
151 ... 0893 Pipe corrosion
151 ... 0894 Extending hot water systems
152 ... 0895 Covering radiators reduces efficiency
152 ... 0896 Convector
152 ... 0897 Finned tube baseboard
152 ... 0898 Cast iron baseboard
152 ... 0899 Mixing systems
152 ... 0900 Radiators on ceilings or high on walls
153 ... 0901 Radiator valve leaks
153 ... 0902 Don't operate air bleed valves
153 ... 0903 Hot water radiant heat
153 ... 0904 Controls and mixing valve layout for radiant floor heat
153 ... 0905 Water blender on radiant system
153 ... 0906 Tankless coil
154 ... 0907 Side arm heater
154 ... 0908 Spillage switch
154 ... 0909 Bypass loop

PULSE COMBUSTION

154 ... 0910 Pulse combustion – how it works

CHIMNEYS

INTRODUCTION

155 ... 0950 Not required to inspect fireplace insert flue connections
155 ... 0951 Chimneys
155 ... 0952 Vents
155 ... 0953 Chimneys are not supporting structures
155 ... 0954 Warm chimneys are best
155 ... 0955 Three kinds of draft
156 ... 0956 Chimney extender
156 ... 0957 Masonry chimneys

MASONRY CHIMNEYS

156 ... 0958 Basic masonry chimney components
156 ... 0959 Basic masonry chimney and fireplace components
157 ... 0960 Chimney walls
157 ... 0961 Lateral support for masonry chimneys
157 ... 0962 Clay tile flue liners
157 ... 0963 Chimney offsets
157 ... 0964 Miter the flue liners
157 ... 0965 Chimney clearances
158 ... 0966 Chimneys supporting framing members
158 ... 0967 What makes a good chimney cap?
158 ... 0968 Chimney deterioration
158 ... 0969 Removing abandoned chimneys
158 ... 0970 Causes of chimney settling or leaning
158 ... 0971 Tall masonry chimneys
159 ... 0972 3-sided chimneys
159 ... 0973 Bracket chimneys
159 ... 0974 Flue divider missing
159 ... 0975 Chimney leaning above roof line
160 ... 0976 Chimney offsets
160 ... 0977 Proper chimney height
160 ... 0978 Chimney height above appliance
160 ... 0979 Fireplace cleanout - door too close to combustibles
161 ... 0980 Incomplete liner
161 ... 0981 Fire stopping
161 ... 0982 What makes a good chimney cap?
161 ... 0983 Rain caps and spark arresters
161 ... 0984 Improper slope on cap
161 ... 0985 Drip edge on cap

CHAPTER 4

162 ... 0986 Creosote deposits
162 ... 0987 Vent connector extends too far into chimney
162 ... 0988 Vent connector loose at chimney
162 ... 0989 Flue or vent connector obstructed
163 ... 0990 Abandoned flue openings
163 ... 0991 Chimney extender
163 ... 0992 Two fireplaces on one flue
163 ... 0993 Two gas appliances on one flue
163 ... 0994 Wood below oil on same floor level
163 ... 0995 Deteriorated clay chimney liner

METAL CHIMNEYS OR VENTS

164 ... 0996 Type "B" vent
164 ... 0997 Type "L" vent
164 ... 0998 Class "A" chimney
164 ... 0999 Triple-wall metal chimney
164 ... 1000 650°C chimneys
164 ... 1001 Connections of metal vent pieces
165 ... 1002 Metal chimney bracing
165 ... 1003 Metal chimney combustible clearances
165 ... 1004 Fire stopping
165 ... 1005 Missing chimney cap
165 ... 1006 Rusting and/or pitting metal chimneys
165 ... 1007 Chimney height
166 ... 1008 Excessive offset from vertical
166 ... 1009 Metal chimney not continuous through roof
166 ... 1010 Adjacent chimneys of different heights

WOOD HEATING SYSTEMS

INTRODUCTION

166 ... 1011 Not required to inspect fireplace insert flue connections
166 ... 1012 Wood burning furnaces, boilers, fireplaces and stoves
166 ... 1013 Heat content of various fuels

FURNACES AND BOILERS

167 ... 1014 Components of wood furnaces
167 ... 1015 Ventilation/cooling air for wood furnaces
167 ... 1016 Combustion air damper arrangement
167 ... 1017 How a combustion air damper works
167 ... 1018 Forced draft combustion for wood furnace
167 ... 1019 Combustion chamber (firebox)
168 ... 1020 Two combustion chambers
168 ... 1021 Heat exchangers shouldn't have nooks and crannys
168 ... 1022 Checking the barometric damper
168 ... 1023 Vent connector combustible clearances
168 ... 1024 Joining vent connector sections
168 ... 1025 Vent connector support and slope
169 ... 1026 Thermostat conditions to watch for
169 ... 1027 Fan/limit switch
169 ... 1028 Duct clearances - typical
169 ... 1029 Combustible return ducts
170 ... 1030 Add-on wood furnace (downstream series)
170 ... 1031 Add-on wood furnace (divider plate method)
170 ... 1032 Wood furnace not downstream
170 ... 1033 Duct arrangement allows reverse flow
171 ... 1034 Dual fuel furnace (wood/oil)

CHAPTER 4

WOOD STOVES (SPACE HEATERS)

171 ... 1035 Wood stove components
171 ... 1036 Wood below oil on same floor level
171 ... 1037 Don't confine wood
171 ... 1038 Chimney liners often required for fireplace inserts
171 ... 1039 Convective wood stoves
172 ... 1040 Advanced combustion wood stoves
172 ... 1041 Catalytic combustors
172 ... 1042 Bypass damper on catalytic wood stove
172 ... 1043 Pellet stoves
172 ... 1044 Wood stove floor protection – masonry (legs less than 3″ tall)
172 ... 1045 Wood stove floor protection – masonry (legs 3″ to 7″ tall)
173 ... 1046 Wood stove floor protection – steel (legs 3″ to 7″ tall)
173 ... 1047 Wood stove floor protection – masonry (legs more than 7″ tall)
173 ... 1048 Wood stove floor protection – steel (legs more than 7″ tall)
173 ... 1049 Clearances for unlisted wood stoves
174 ... 1050 Vent connector clearances
174 ... 1051 Wall shields – metal
174 ... 1052 Wall shields
174 ... 1053 Firewood is combustible
175 ... 1054 Clearance from oil tanks
175 ... 1055 Wood stove vent connector slope
175 ... 1056 Wood stove vent connections
175 ... 1057 Draw bands or adjustible connectors
175 ... 1058 Poor vent connection at chimney
175 ... 1059 Wood below oil on same floor level
176 ... 1060 Testing dampers

WOOD BURNING FIREPLACES

176 ... 1061 Three kinds of fireplaces
176 ... 1062 Masonry fireplace components
176 ... 1063 Combustible clearance requirements
177 ... 1064 Basement fireplaces
177 ... 1065 Problematic fireplace designs
177 ... 1066 Fireplace footings
177 ... 1067 Causes of chimney settling
178 ... 1068 Hearth materials
178 ... 1069 Metal spark strip
178 ... 1070 Hearth extension dimensions
178 ... 1071 Raised hearths
178 ... 1072 Hearth extensions for factory built fireplaces
178 ... 1073 Remove hearth extension forming boards
179 ... 1074 Firebrick on walls
179 ... 1075 Metal firebox clearance
179 ... 1076 Flue liner shouldn't rest on metal firebox
179 ... 1077 Coal burning fireplaces
179 ... 1078 Lintel rusting, sagging or loose
179 ... 1079 Firebox damper
180 ... 1080 Damper at top of chimney
180 ... 1081 Missing damper
180 ... 1082 Low damper
180 ... 1083 Throat, smokeshelf and smoke chamber
180 ... 1084 Smoke chamber – wall slope
180 ... 1085 Smoke chamber forms must be removed
181 ... 1086 Fireplace breast
181 ... 1087 Settled (gap at wall)
181 ... 1088 Clearance from fireplace opening
181 ... 1089 Ashpit
182 ... 1090 Outdoor combustion air
182 ... 1091 Insulating combustion air ducts
182 ... 1092 Outdoor intake screening
182 ... 1093 Combustion air duct clearances
182 ... 1094 Glass doors
182 ... 1095 Heat circulators
183 ... 1096 Gas igniters

STEAM HEATING SYSTEMS

HOW THEY WORK

183 ... 1097 How steam systems work
183 ... 1098 Steam system operation: at rest
183 ... 1099 Steam system operation: call for heat
183 ... 1100 Air vents
183 ... 1101 Dimension "A"
184 ... 1102 Equalizer pipe
184 ... 1103 Steam system operation: thermostat is satisfied
184 ... 1104 Hartford loop

CHAPTER 4

COMMON STEAM SYSTEMS

184 ... 1105 One pipe counterflow system
184 ... 1106 One pipe parallel flow system
184 ... 1107 Two pipe system
185 ... 1108 Thermostatic trap
185 ... 1109 F & T trap (float and thermostat trap)
185 ... 1110 Location of condensate pump
185 ... 1111 Condensate pump
186 ... 1112 Location of boiler feed pump
186 ... 1113 Boiler feed pump

STEAM CONTROLS: KEEPING IT SAFE

186 ... 1114 Location of low water cut-out
186 ... 1115 Pressure relief valve
187 ... 1116 Location of pressuretrol
187 ... 1117 Hartford Loop and equalizer

STEAM BOILER PROBLEMS

187 ... 1118 Water hammer
187 ... 1119 Low water cut-out for steam boiler
188 ... 1120 Water level gauge
188 ... 1121 Pressuretrol
188 ... 1122 Hartford Loop and equalizer – details
188 ... 1123 Hartford Loop – close nipple missing
188 ... 1124 Air vents
188 ... 1125 Main air vent
189 ... 1126 F & T trap (float and thermostat trap)
189 ... 1127 Condensate pump
189 ... 1128 Boiler feed pump
189 ... 1129 One pipe parallel flow system
190 ... 1130 Two pipe system
190 ... 1131 Low water cut-out for steam boiler

ELECTRIC HEATING SYSTEMS

INTRODUCTION

190 ... 1132 Current flow = amperage
190 ... 1133 BTU's per hour compared to Kilowatts
191 ... 1134 Equivalent furnaces
191 ... 1135 5 to 8 watts per square foot
191 ... 1136 Wire, fuse and heater sizing

SPACE HEATERS

191 ... 1137 Floor mounted electric heaters
191 ... 1138 Toekick electric heaters
191 ... 1139 Electric wall heater – fan operated
192 ... 1140 Best location for electric heaters
192 ... 1141 Wiring for electric space heaters
192 ... 1142 Determining baseboard heater wattage – rule of thumb
192 ... 1143 Electric baseboard heaters – clearances to draperies
192 ... 1144 Outlets should not be above electric baseboard heaters

ELECTRIC FURNACES

192 ... 1145 Sequencers
193 ... 1146 Fan limit switch
193 ... 1147 Plenum heater
193 ... 1148 Ampmeter testing of electric furnace
193 ... 1149 Excess temperature rise

ELECTRIC BOILERS

194 ... 1150 Electric boiler

RADIANT HEATING

194 ... 1151 Electric radiant heat – ceilings
194 ... 1152 Electric radiant heat – floors

CHAPTER 4

WALL & FLOOR FURNACES, ROOM HEATERS & GAS FIREPLACES

WALL FURNACES

194 ... 1153 Wall furnace
195 ... 1154 Minimum wall furnace clearances
195 ... 1155 Wall furnace venting
195 ... 1156 Firestop spacers
195 ... 1157 Minimum vent height
196 ... 1158 Wall furnace – direct vent

FLOOR FURNACES

196 ... 1159 Unvented wall furnace
196 ... 1160 Minimum floor furnace clearances
196 ... 1161 Inspection cap missing or damaged

ROOM HEATERS

196 ... 1162 Room heaters – combustible clearances
196 ... 1163 Wall furnace – direct vent
197 ... 1164 Unvented space heater
197 ... 1165 Fireplace damper not fixed open

GAS FIREPLACES AND GAS LOGS

197 ... 1166 Gas fireplace location restrictions
197 ... 1167 Gas fireplace – direct vent
197 ... 1168 Gas fireplace – combustible clearances

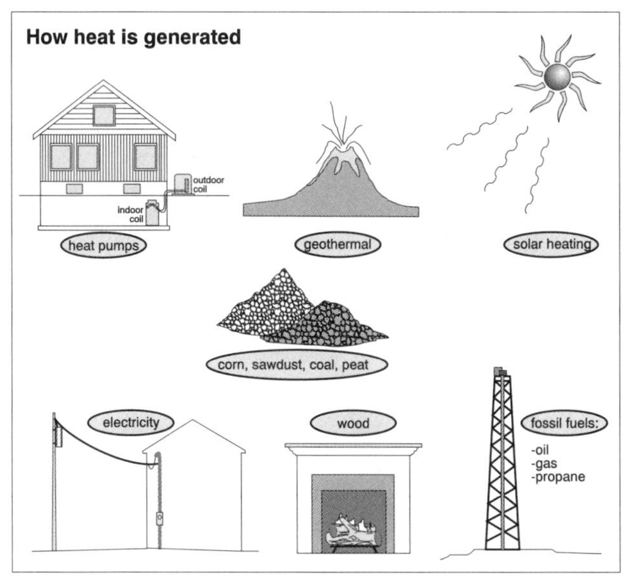

0700

British Thermal Unit (BTU's)

1° Fahrenheit

1 pound of water

one BTU is the amount of heat required to raise the temperature of 1 pound of water by 1° Fahrenheit

0701

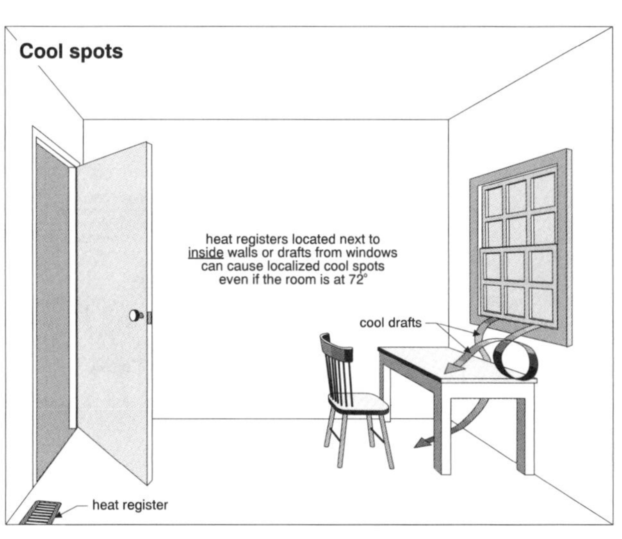

0702

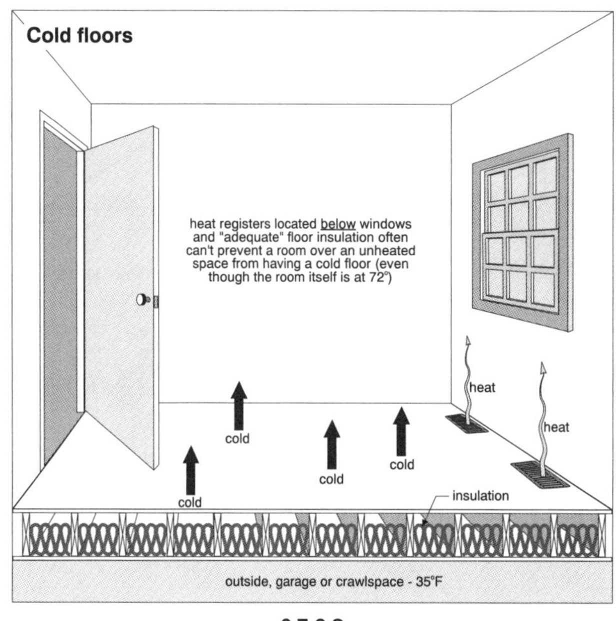

0703

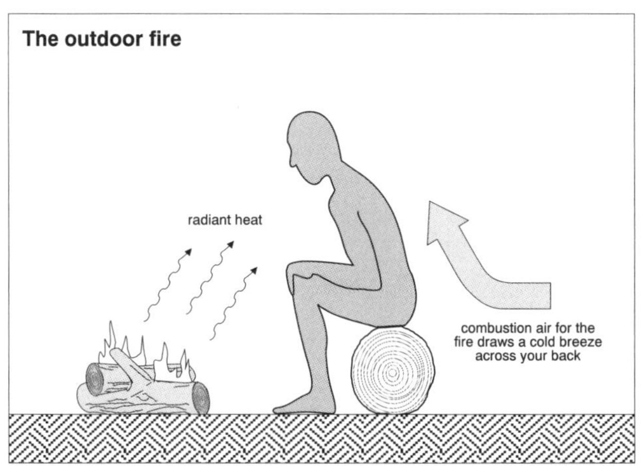

0704

Fire comes inside

radiant heat

radiant heat

radiant heat bounces back off the cave walls - keeping your back warmer

unfortunately smoke is a problem

0705

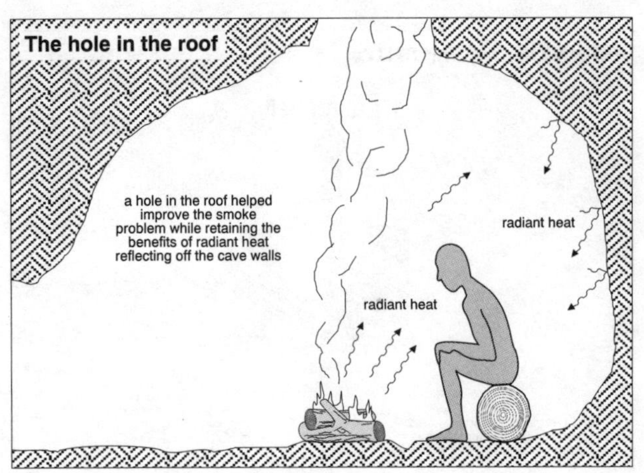

0706

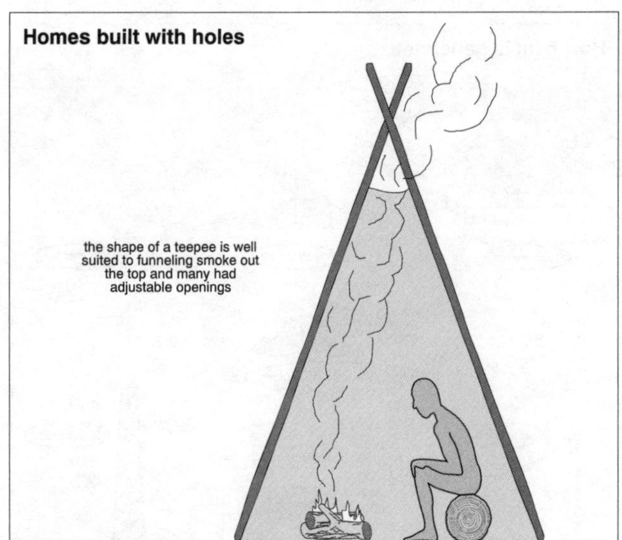

0707

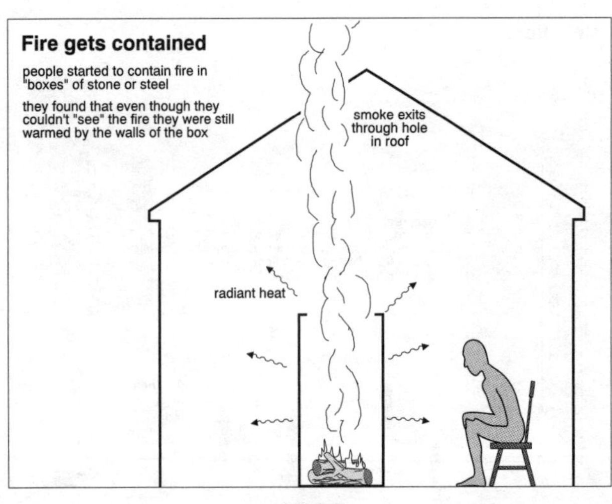

0708

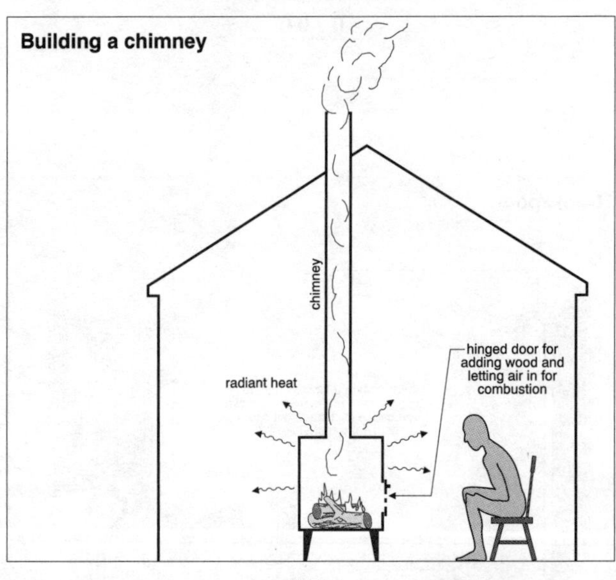

0709

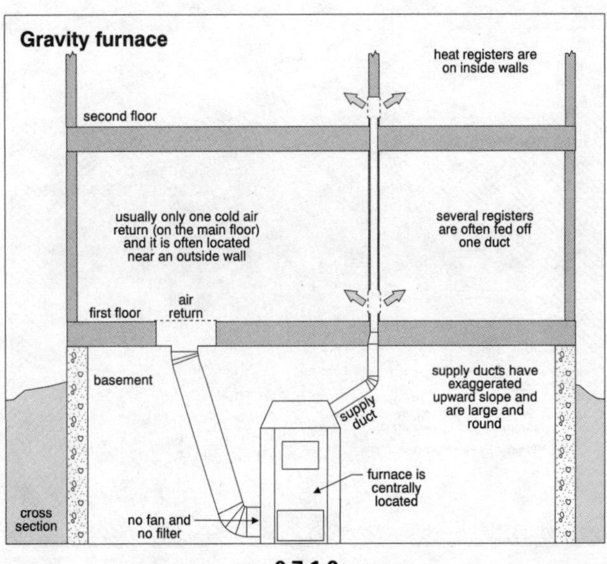

0710

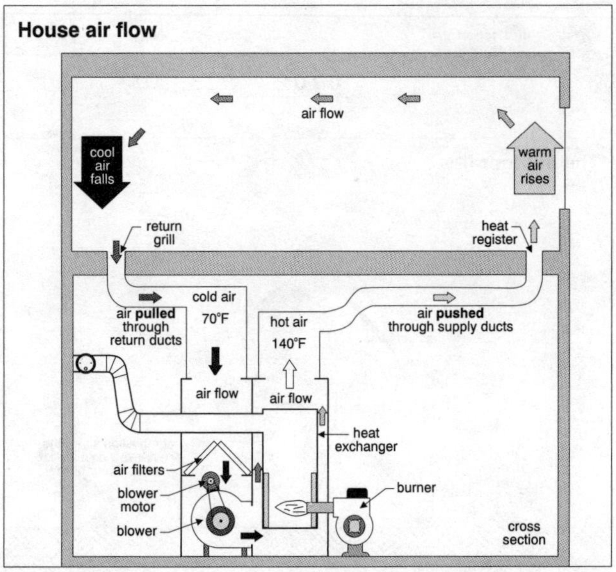

0711

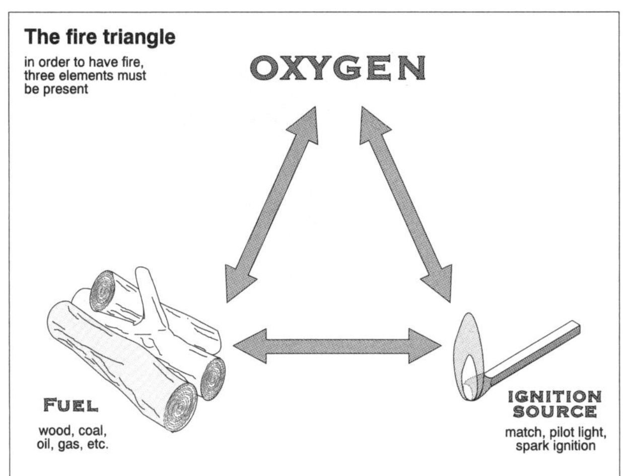

0712

Methods of heat transfer

air above the pot warms up (becomes less dense) and rises - drawing more cool air in from the sides to be heated up

outside (cold)

inside (warm)

heat

radiation

heat transferred through electromagnetic waves e.g. thermal infrared energy (sunlight)

convection

heat transfer within a gas or liquid

conduction

heat transfer through a solid material

0713

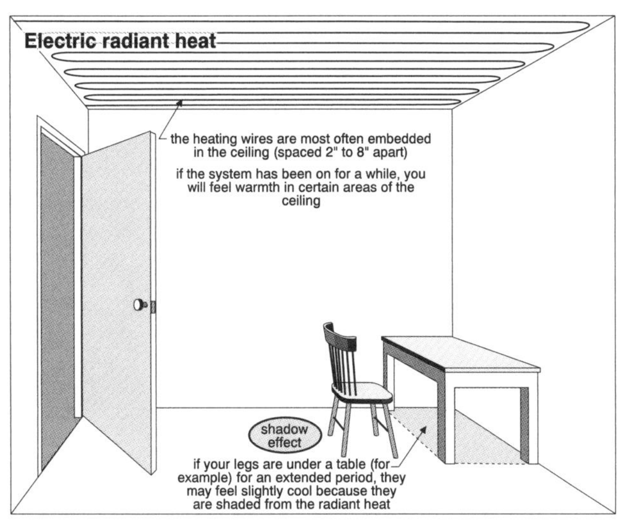

0714

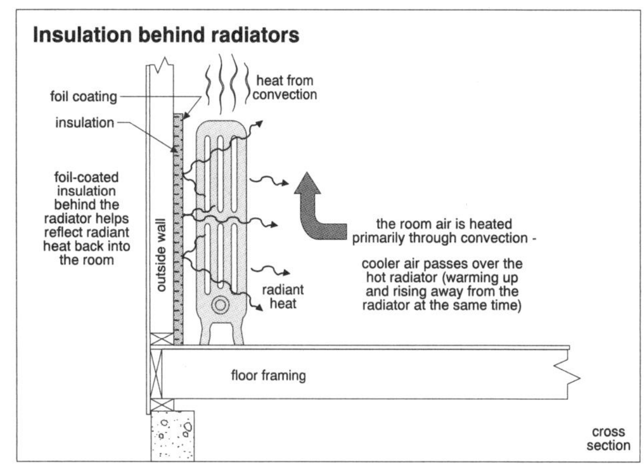

0715

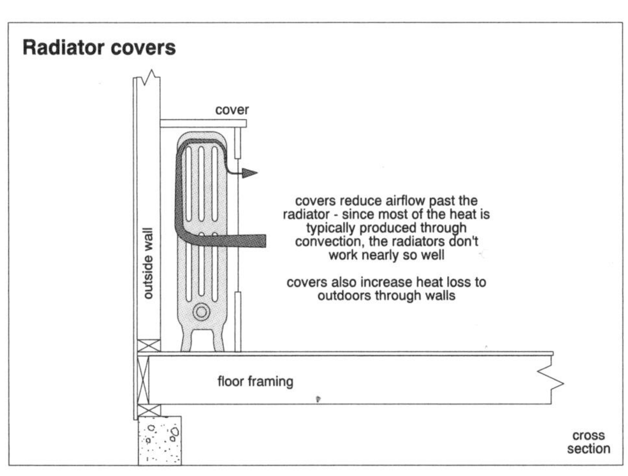

0716

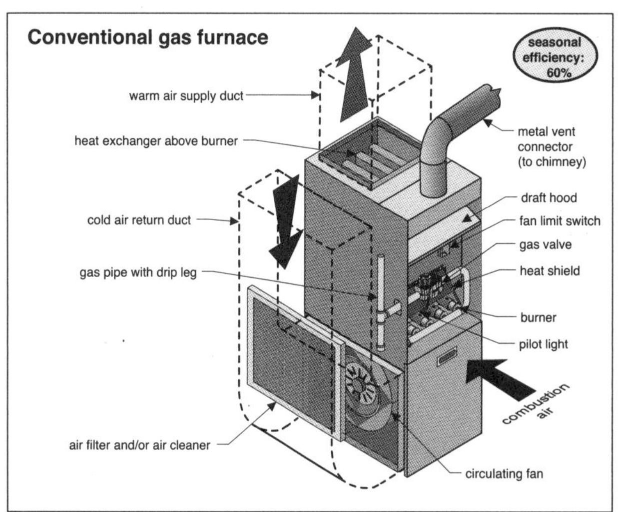

0717

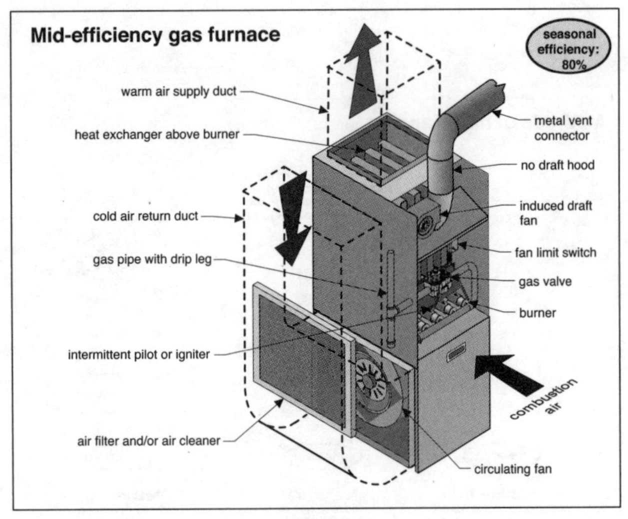

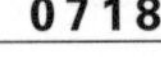

0718

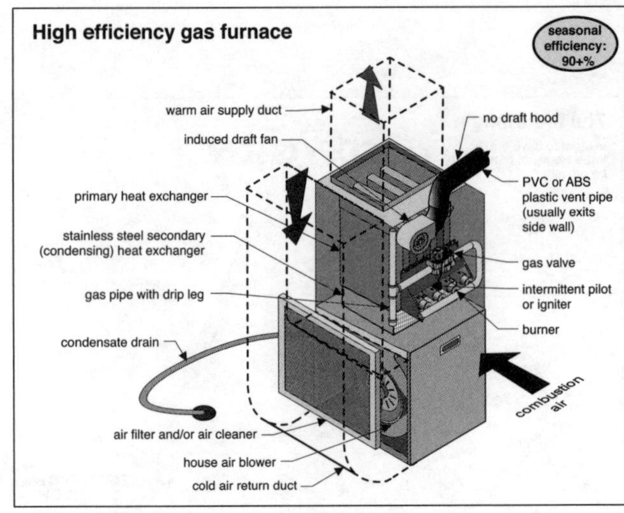

0719

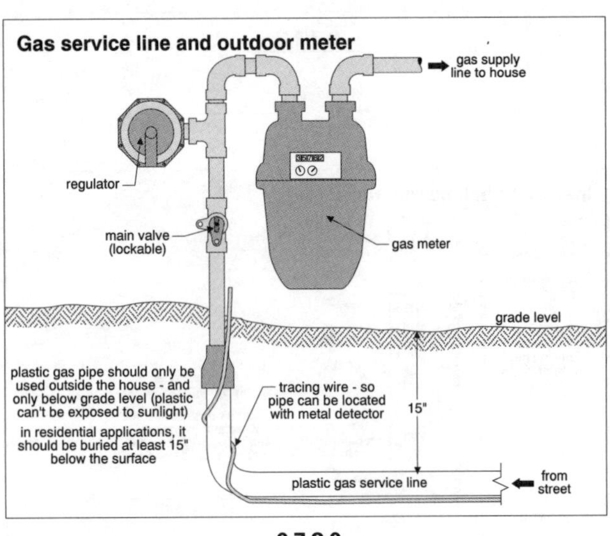

0720

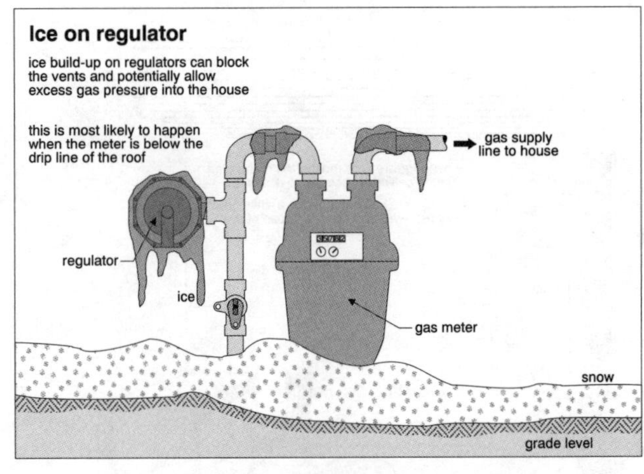

0721

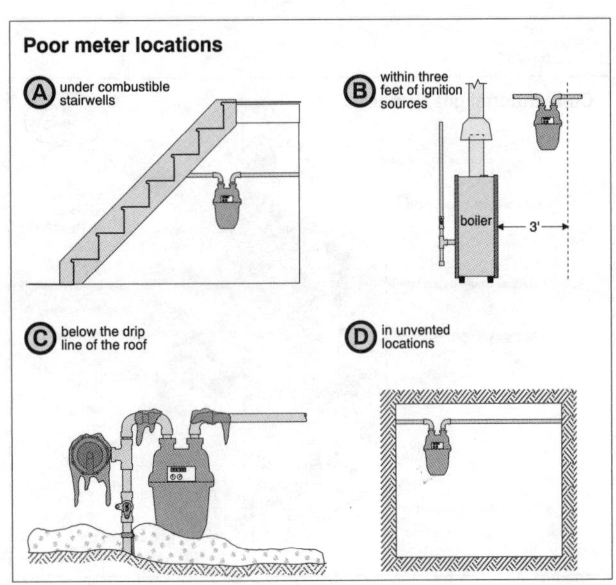

0722

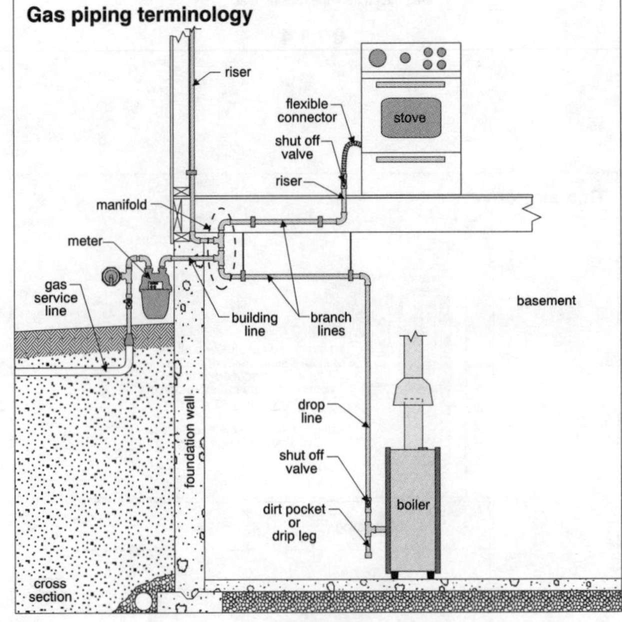

0723

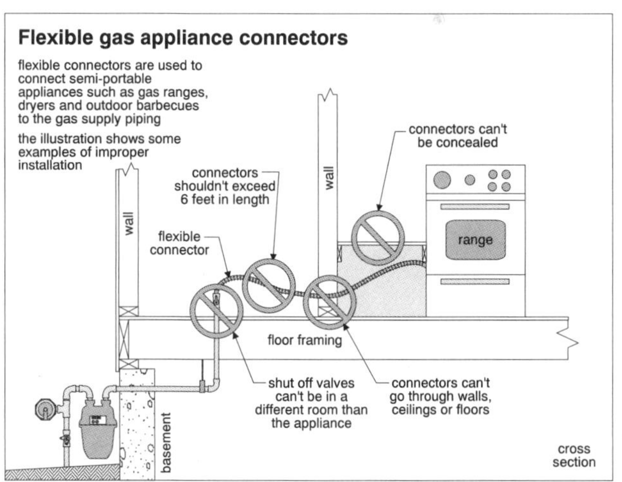

0724

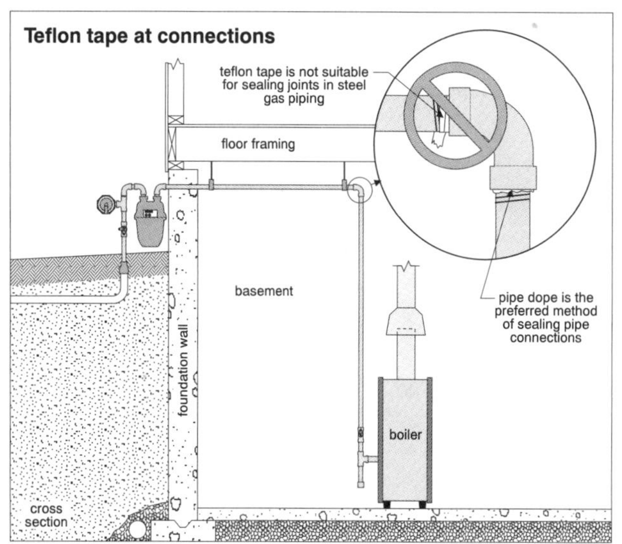

0725

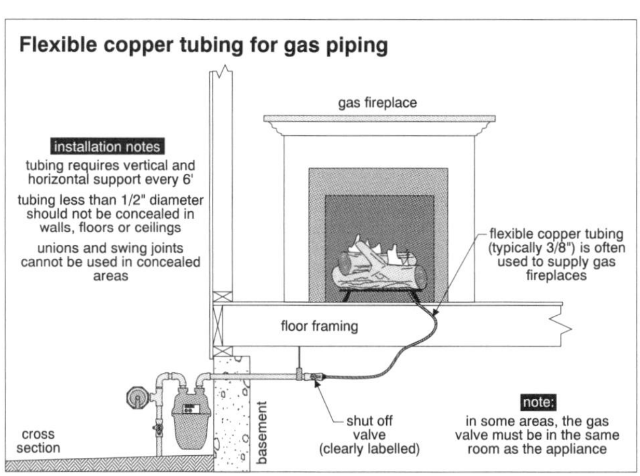

0726

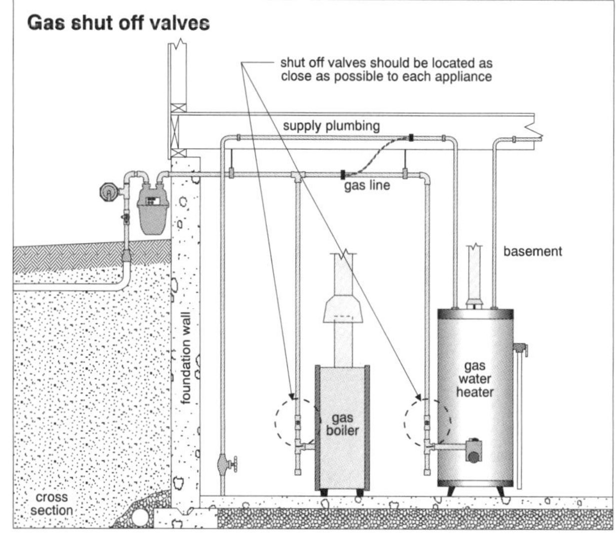

0727

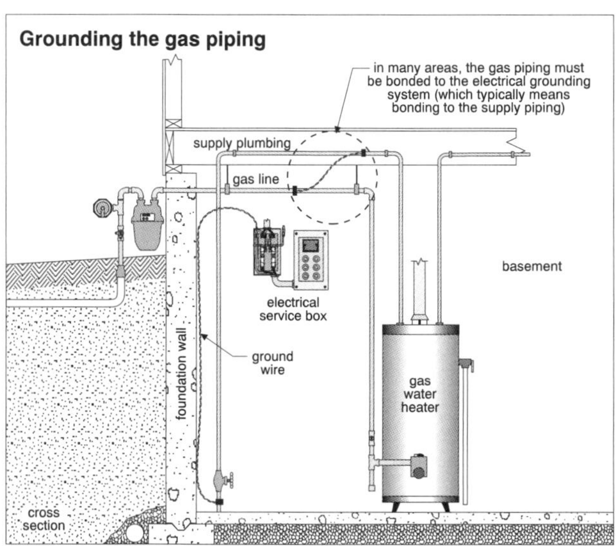

0728

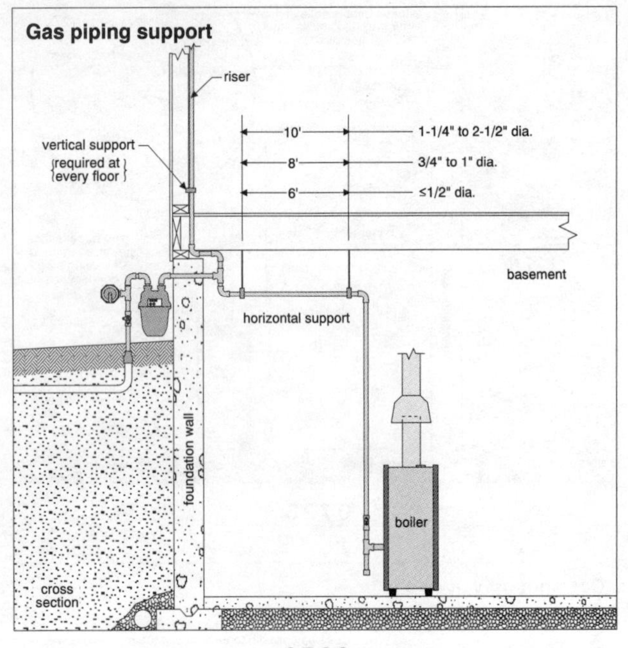

0729

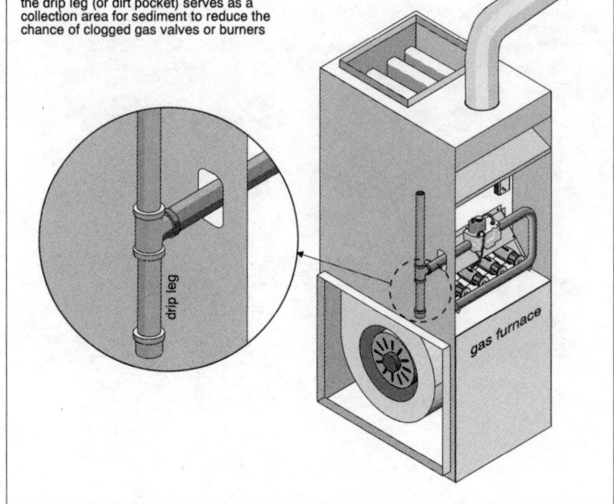

0730

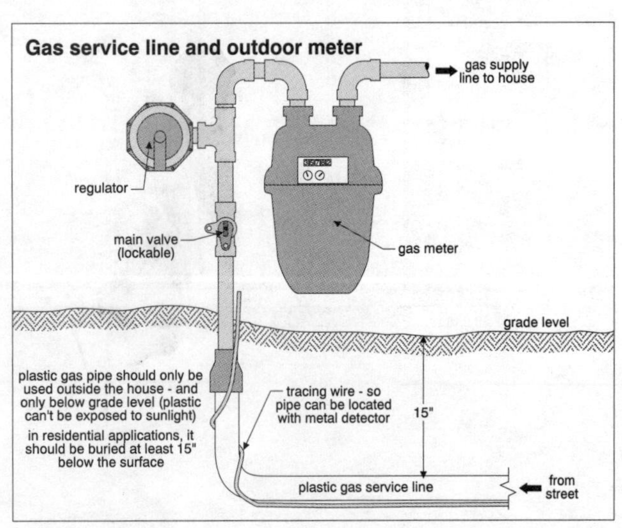

0731

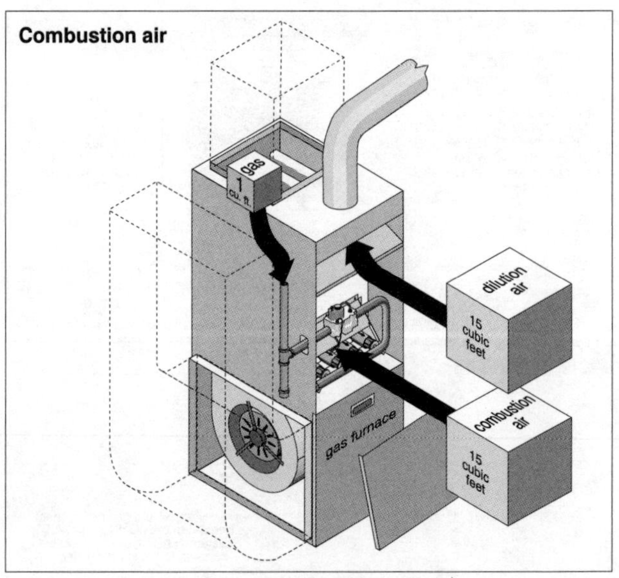

0732

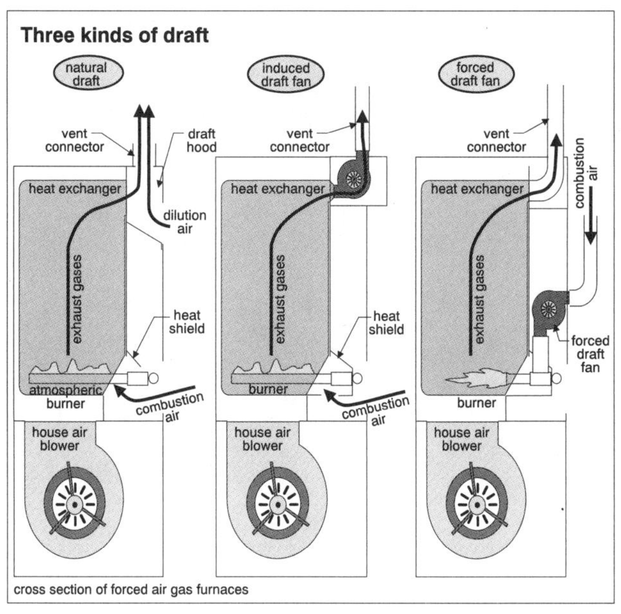

0733

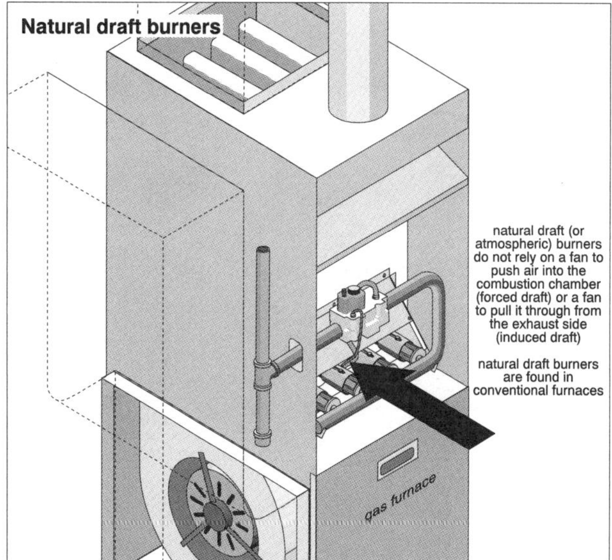

0734

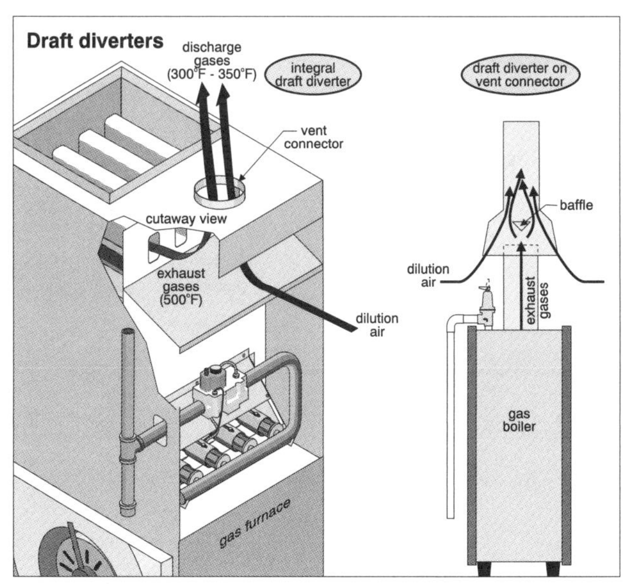

0735

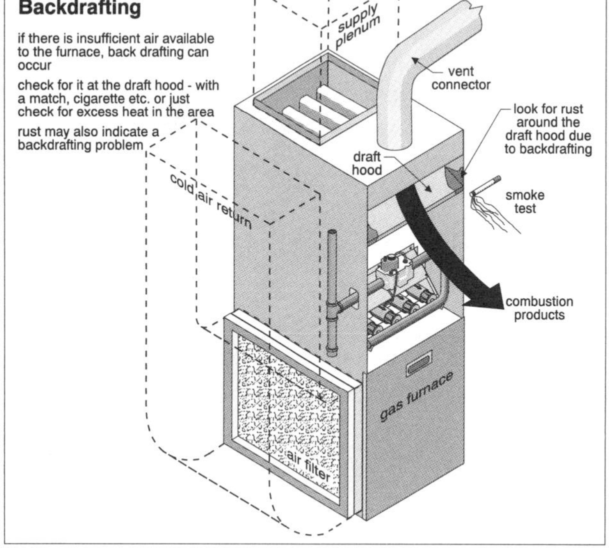

0736

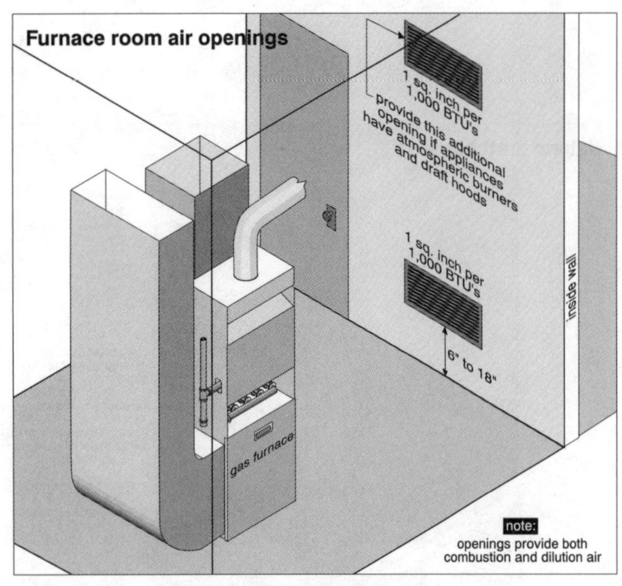

0737

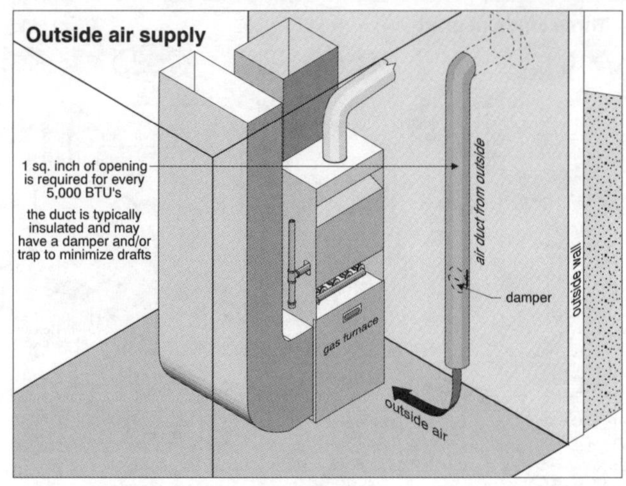

0738

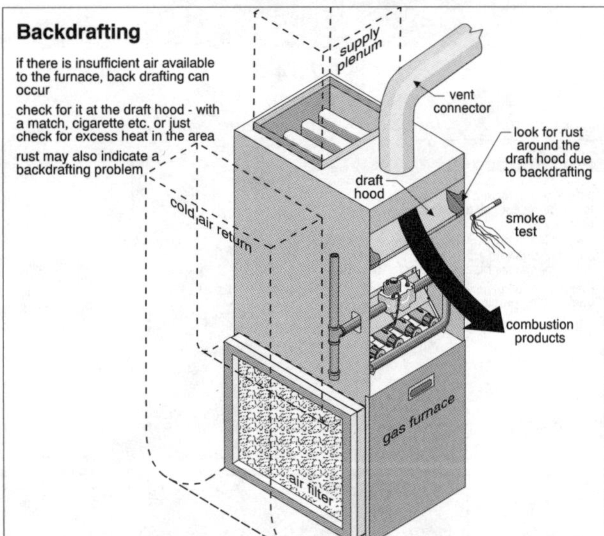

0739

Gas burners

gas

pilot

ribbon burners

mixing tube

manifold

the shutter on the mixing tube can be adjusted to provide the best air/gas ratio for a good flame at the burner

air

shutter

manifold

gas flow

gas

burner

cross section

note: crossover igniters omitted for clarity

gas orifice

0740

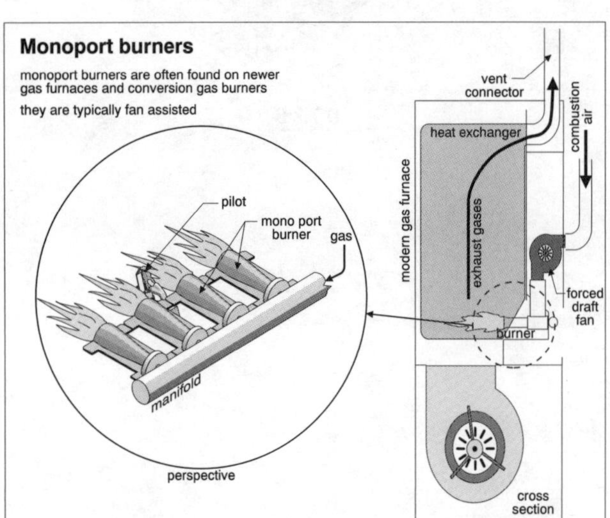

0741

Gas supply to burners

gas pipe

gas supply to pilot

pilot

gas valve

ribbon burners

to thermocouple

drip leg (collects water/debris)

manifold

note: crossover igniters omitted for clarity

0742

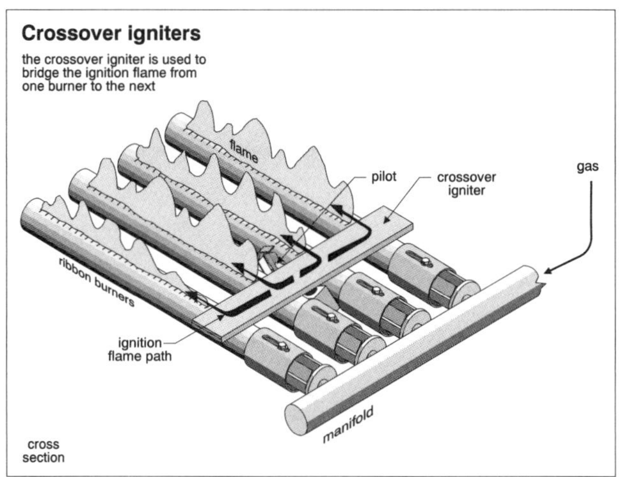

0743

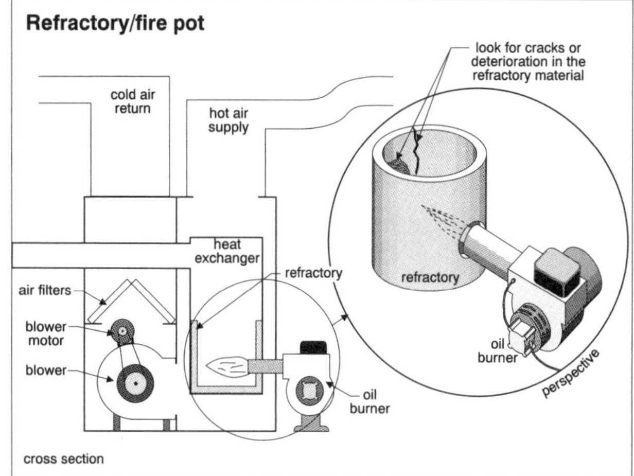

0744

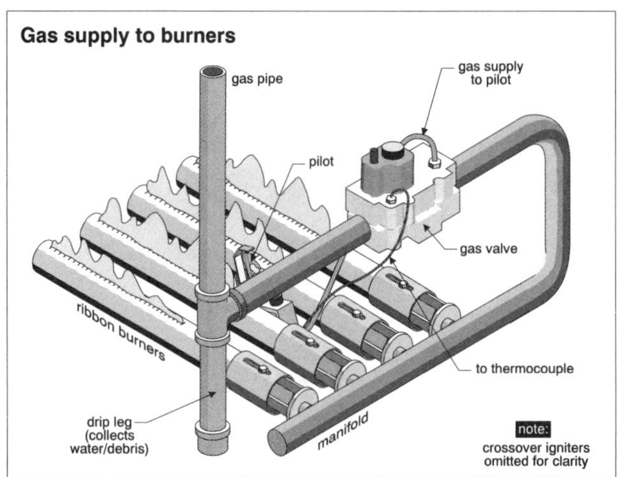

0745

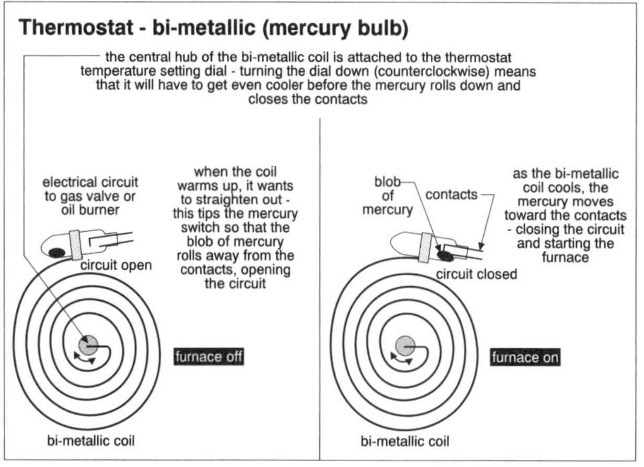

0746

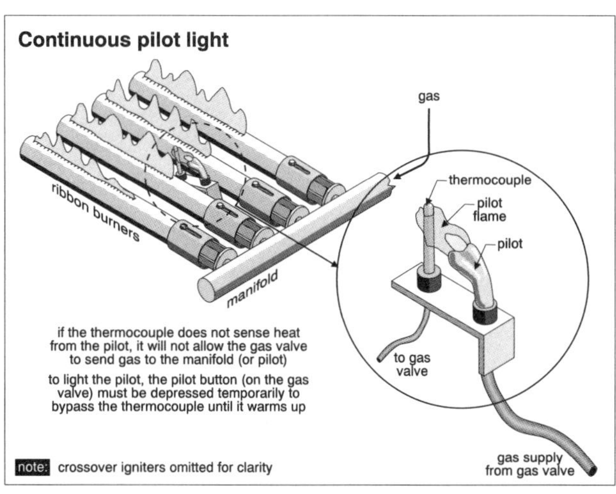

0747

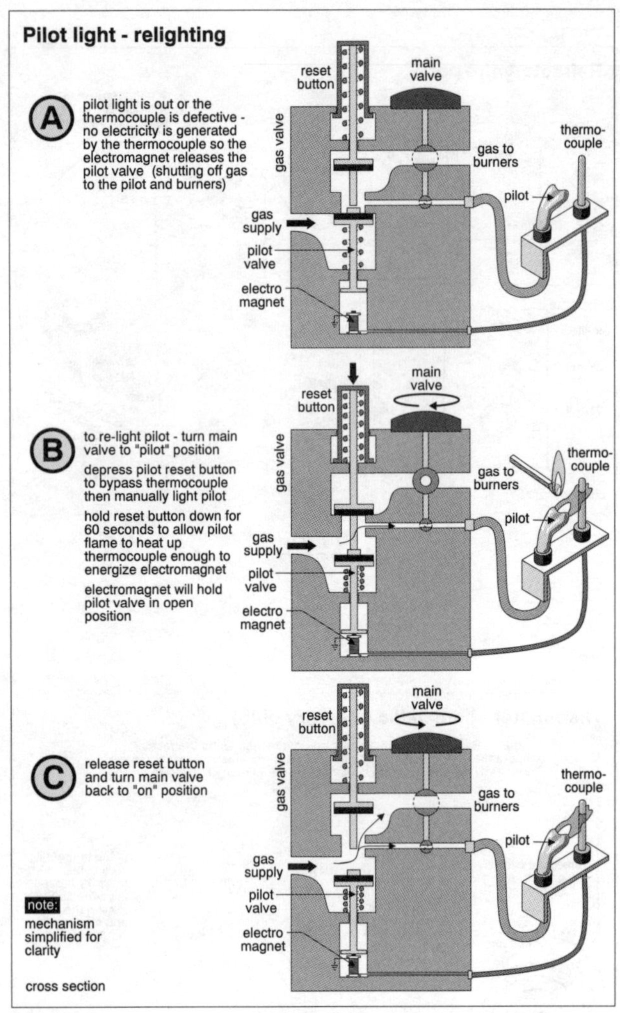

0748

Scorching

locations to look for evidence of scorching:

- wiring
- heat exchanger face plate
- gas valve
- heat shield (flame rollout shield)
- cabinetry or cover

gas furnace

0749

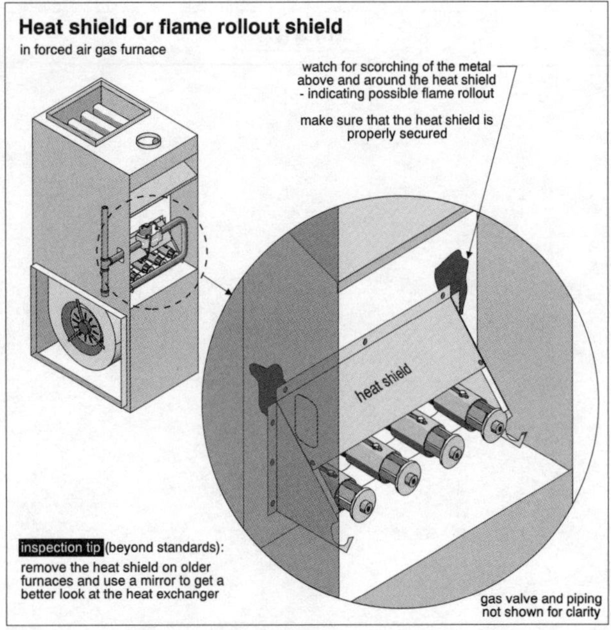

0750

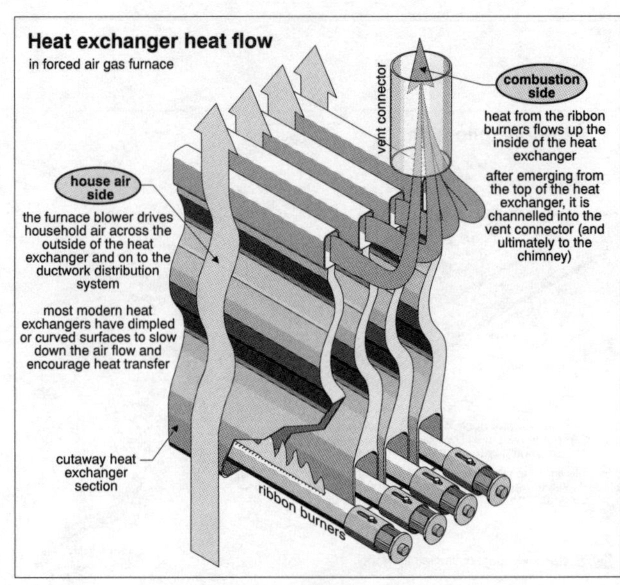

0751

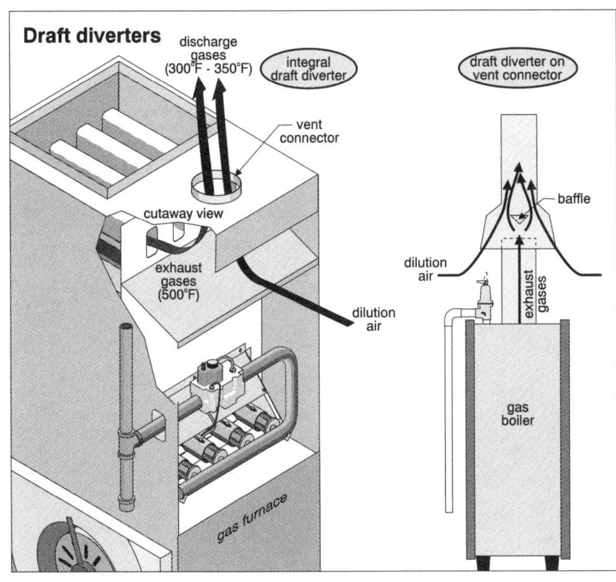

0752

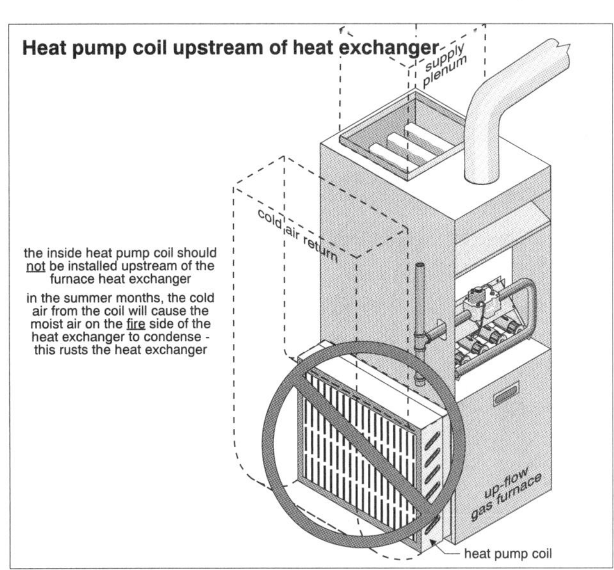

0753

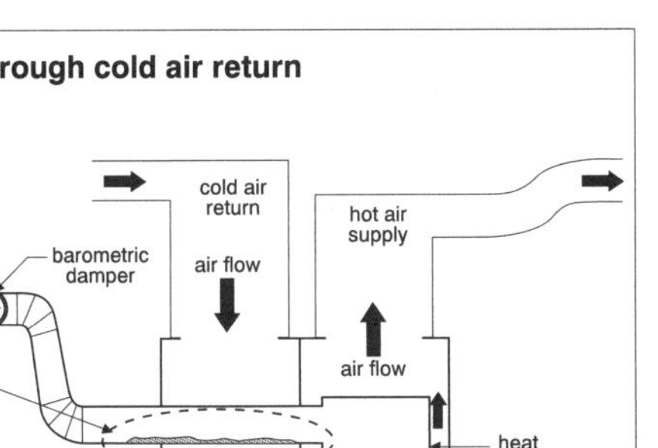

0754

0755

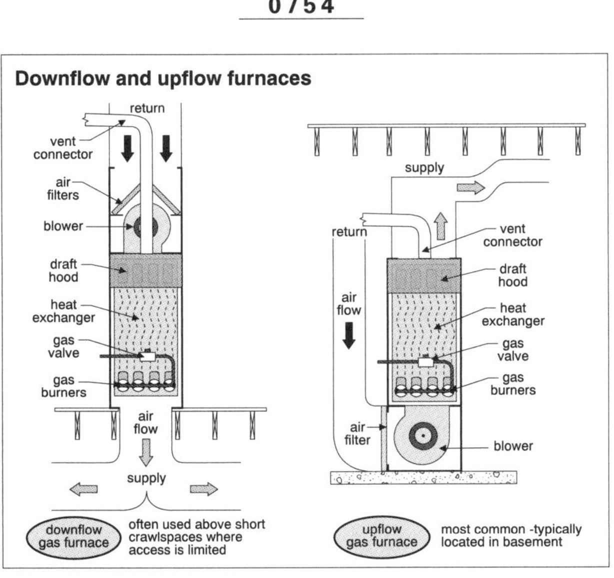

0756

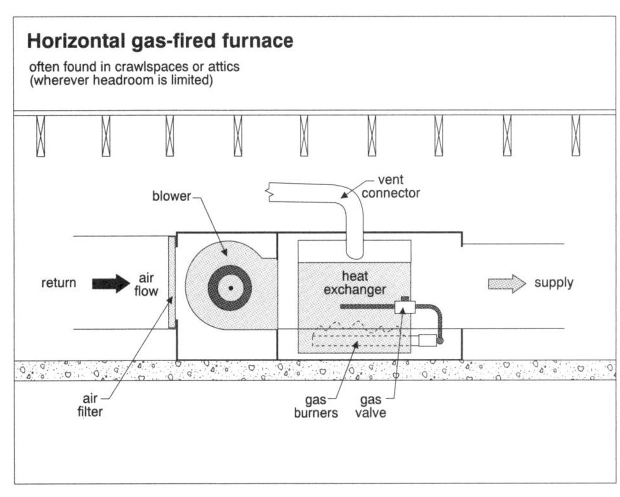

0757

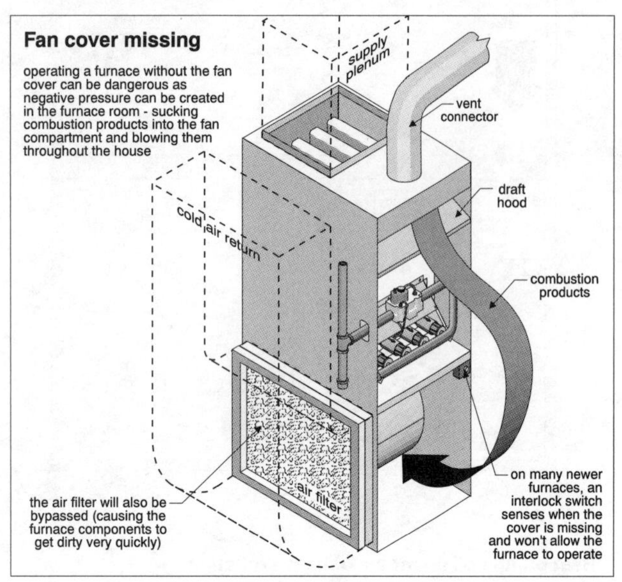

0758

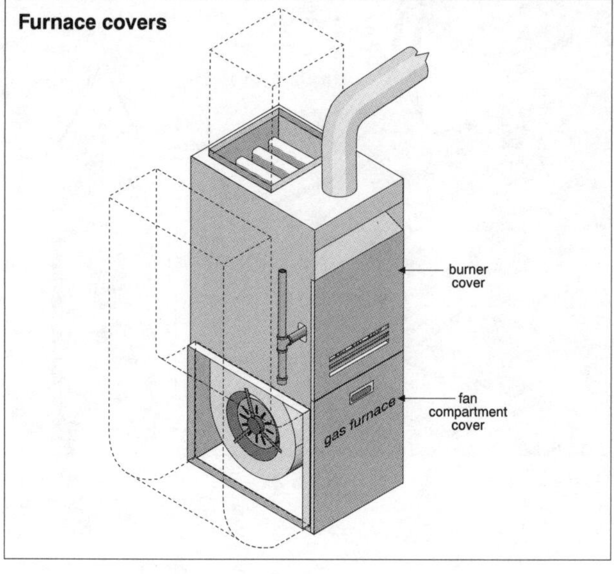

0759

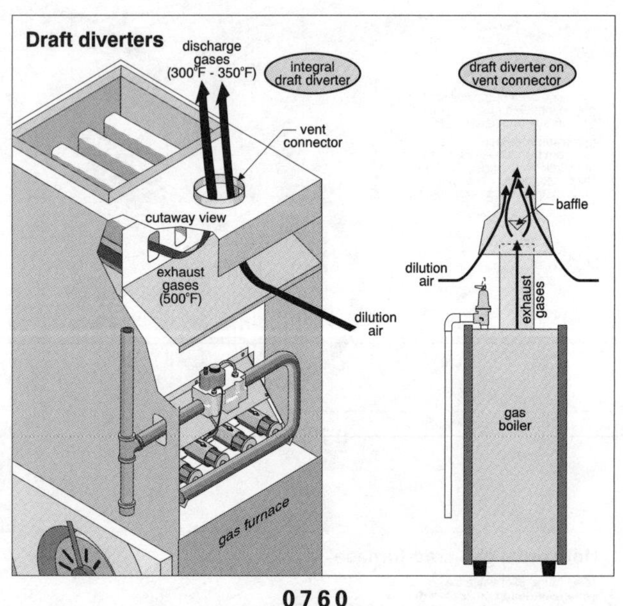

0760

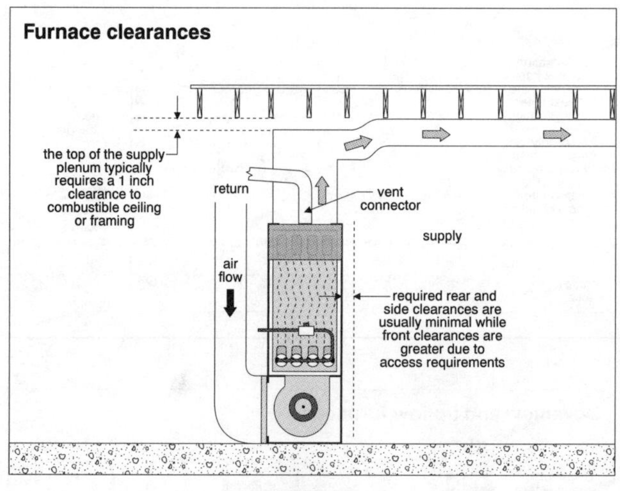

0761

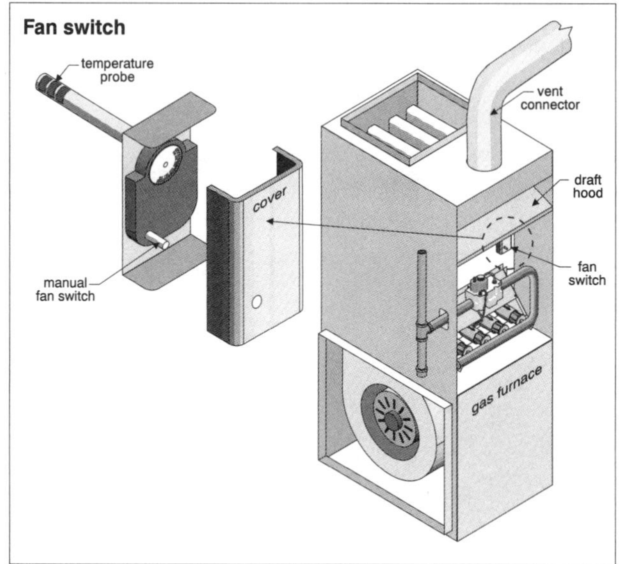

0762

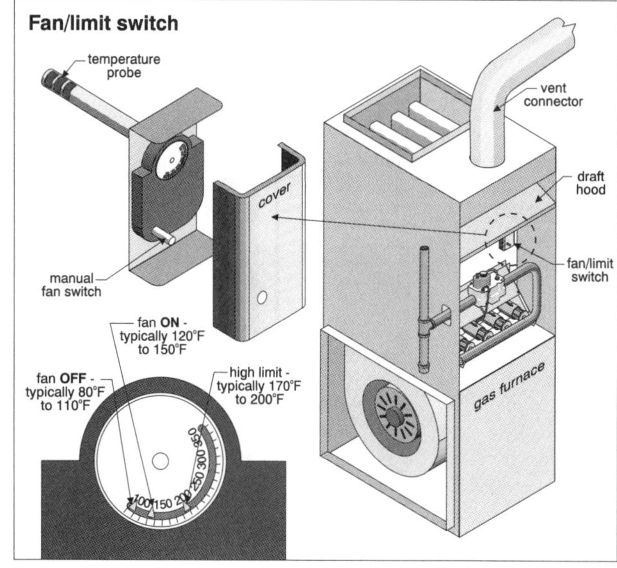

0763

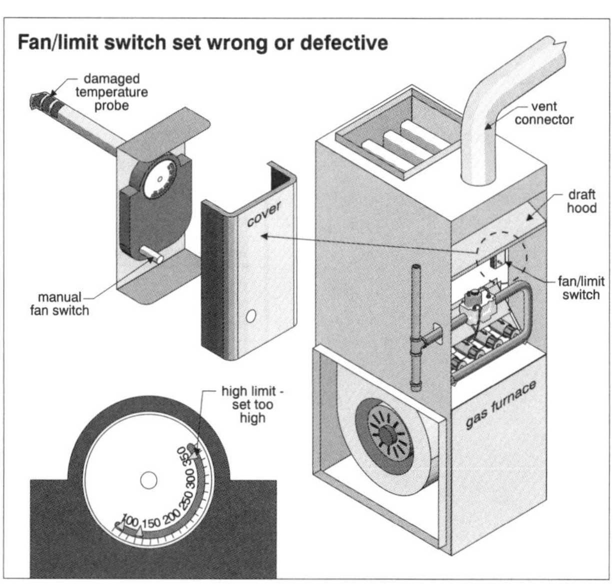

0764

Thermostat - bi-metallic (mercury bulb)

the central hub of the bi-metallic coil is attached to the thermostat temperature setting dial - turning the dial down (counterclockwise) means that it will have to get even cooler before the mercury rolls down and closes the contacts

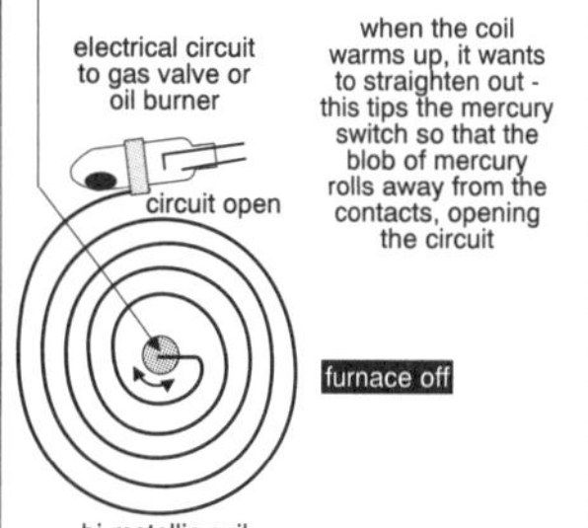

0765

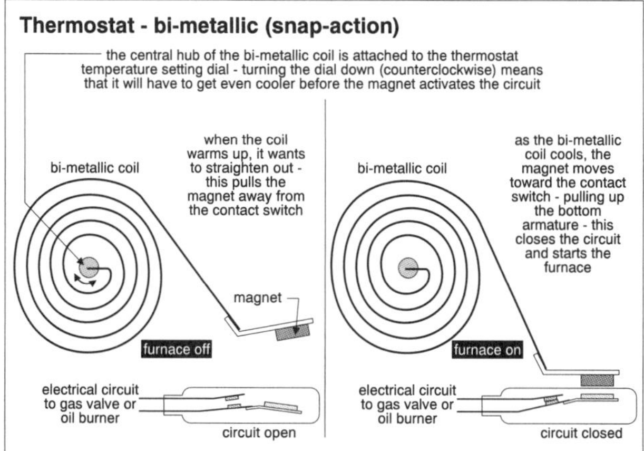

0766

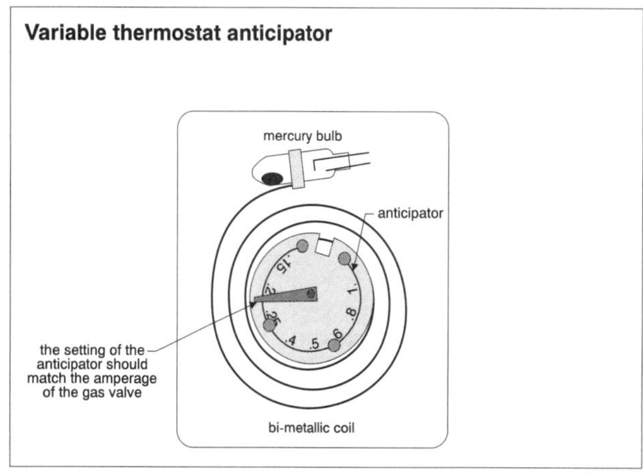

0767

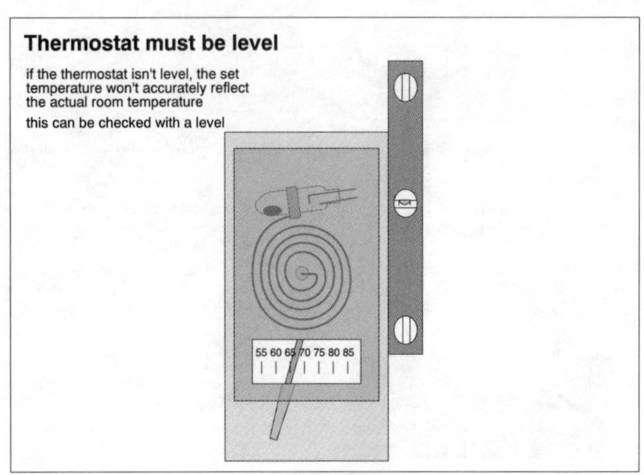

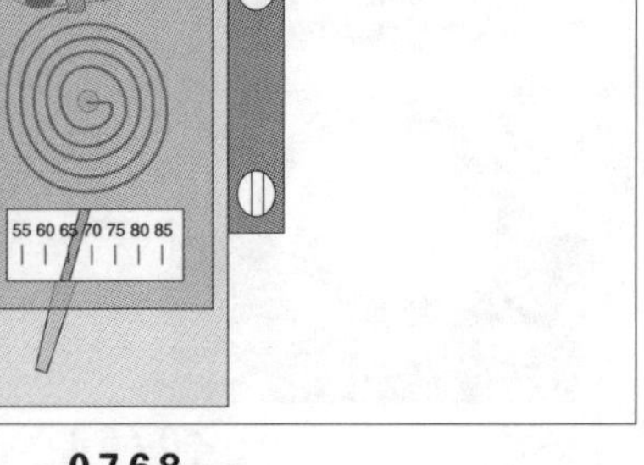

0768

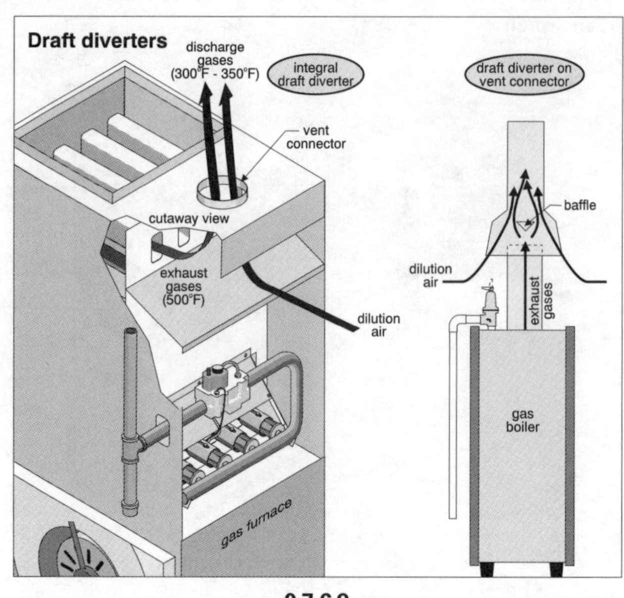

0769

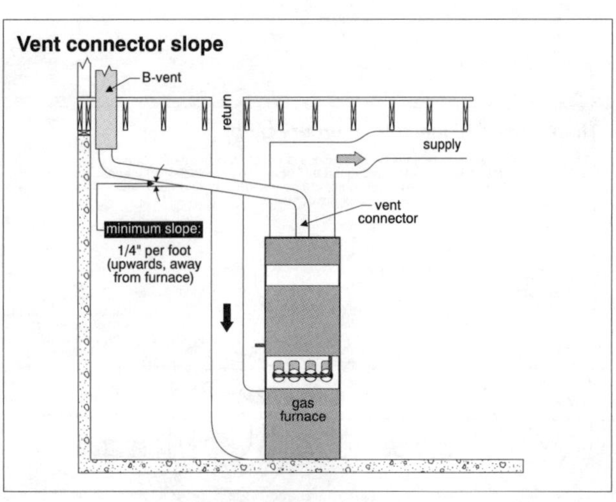

0770

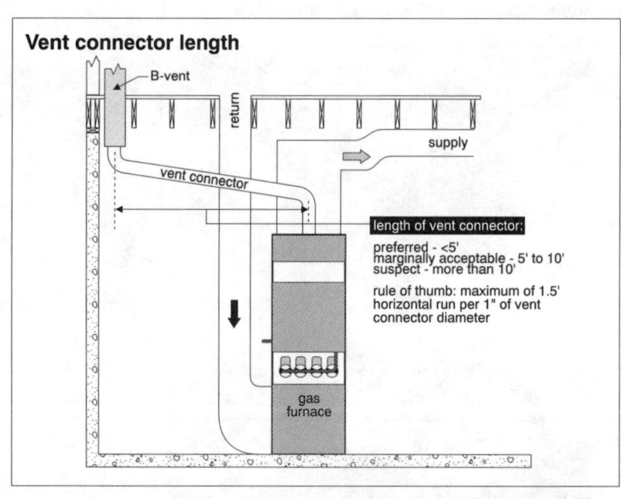

0771

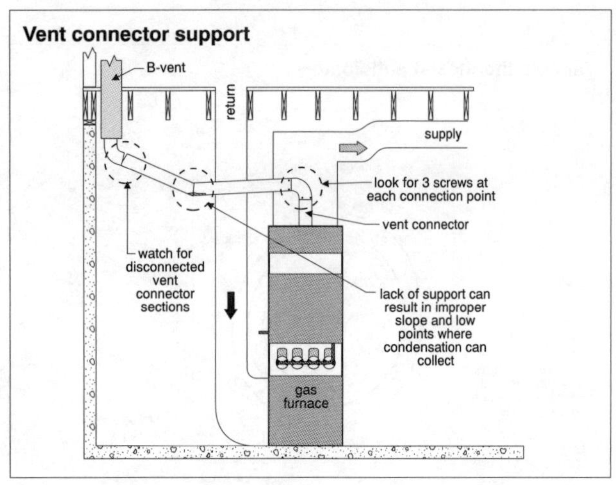

0772

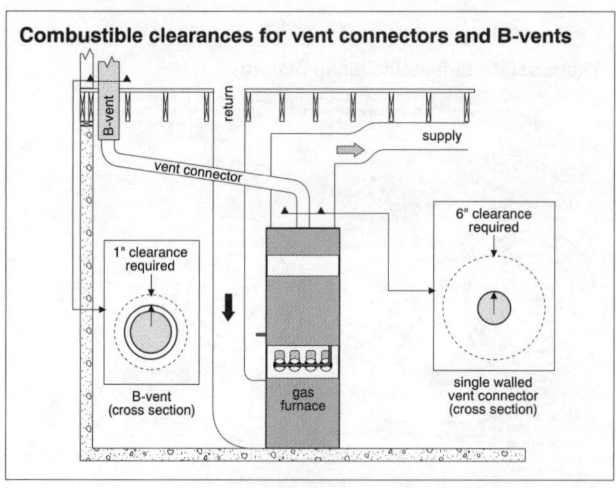

0773

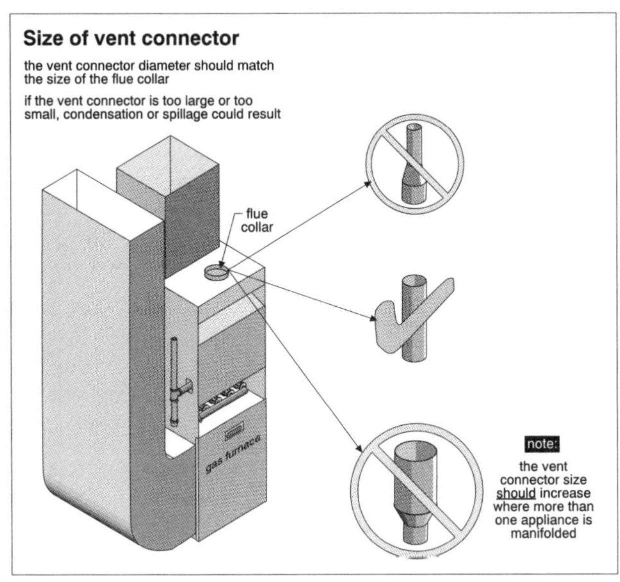

0774

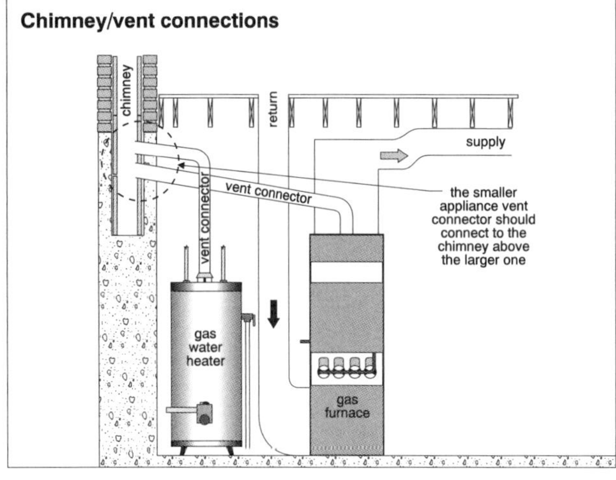

0775

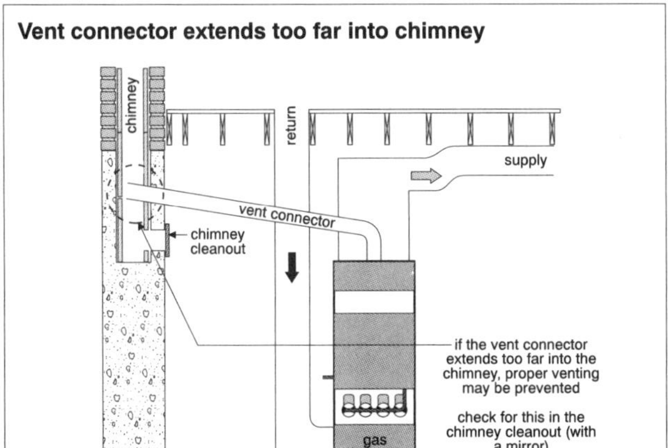

0776

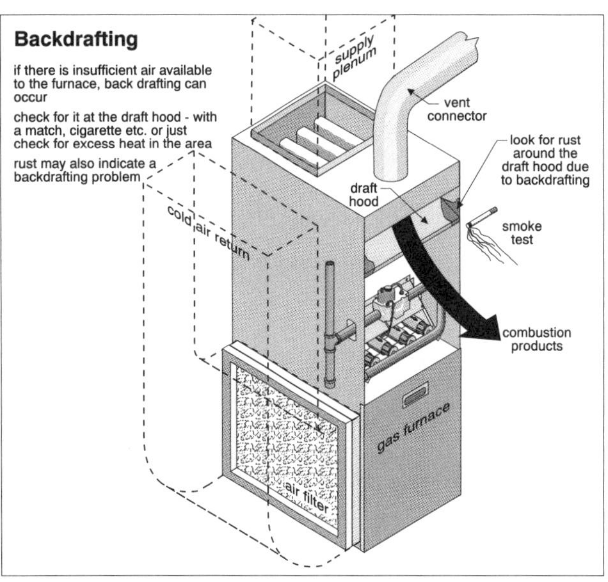

0777

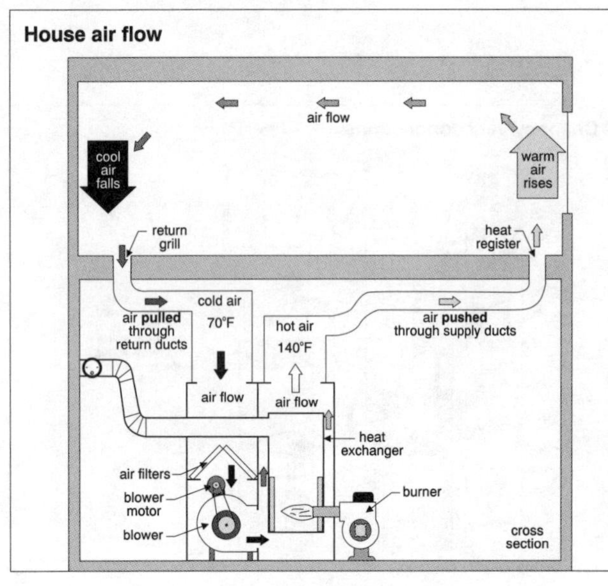

0778

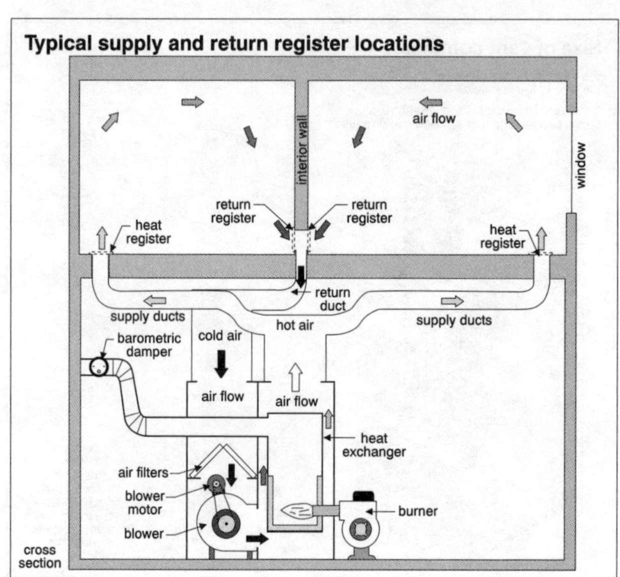

0779

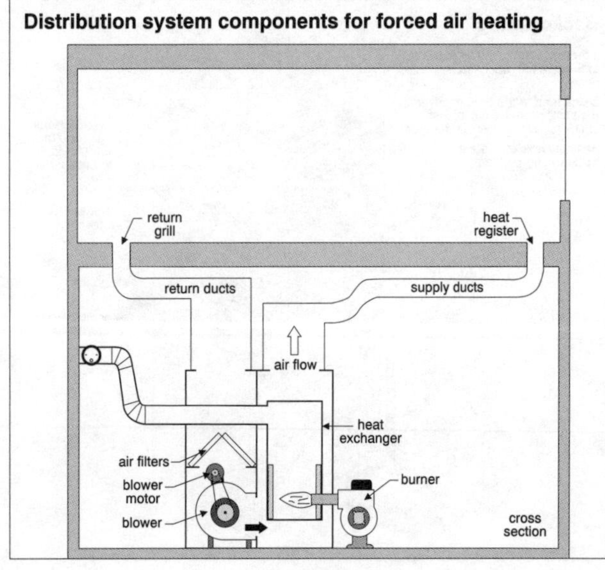

0780

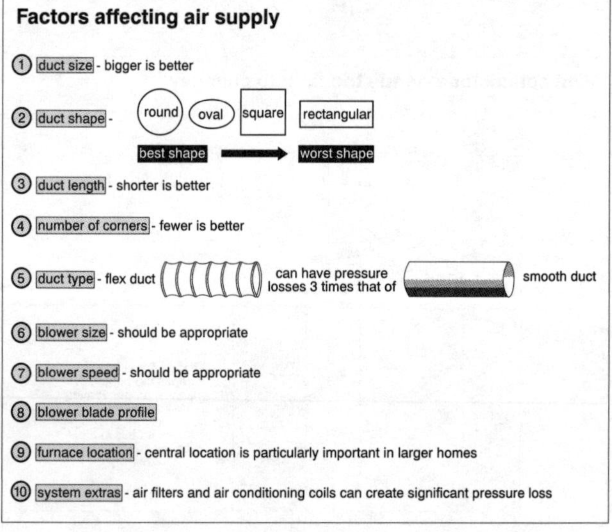

0781

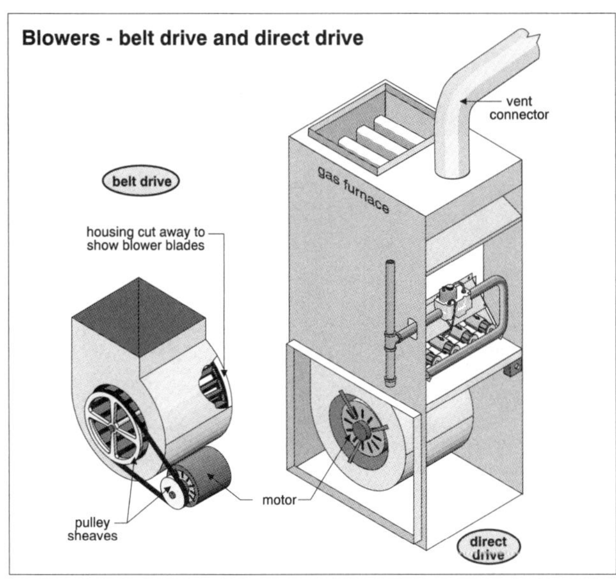

0782

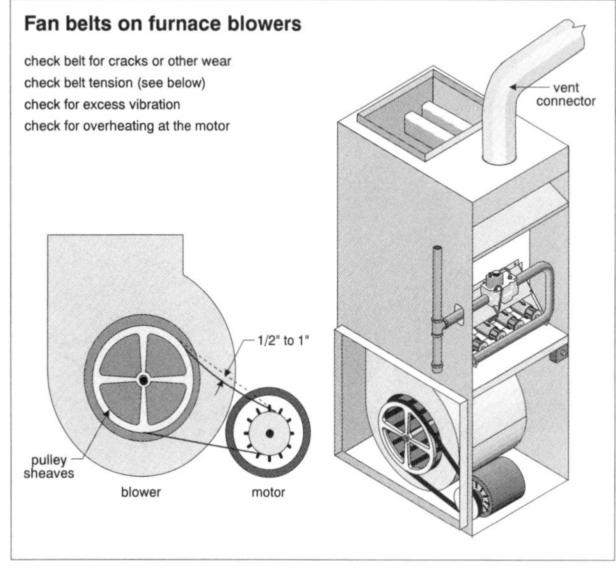

0783

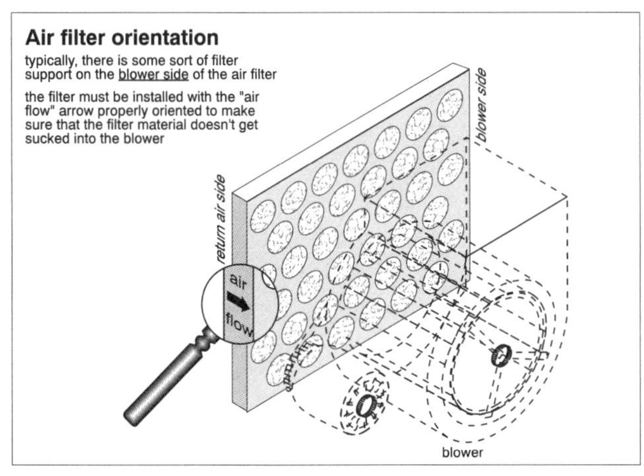

0784

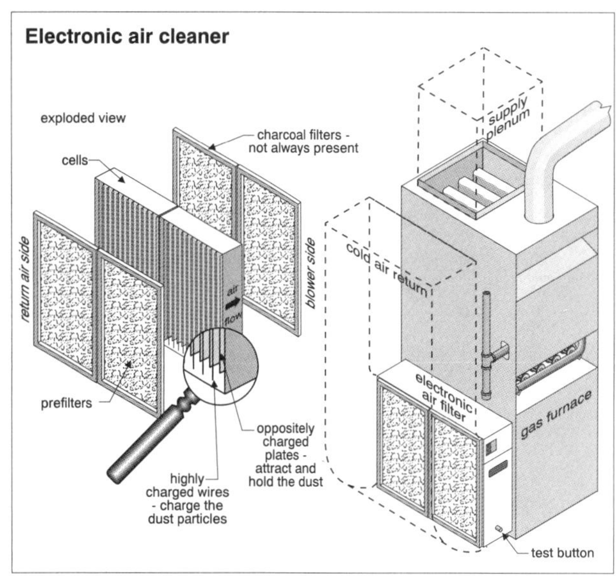

0785

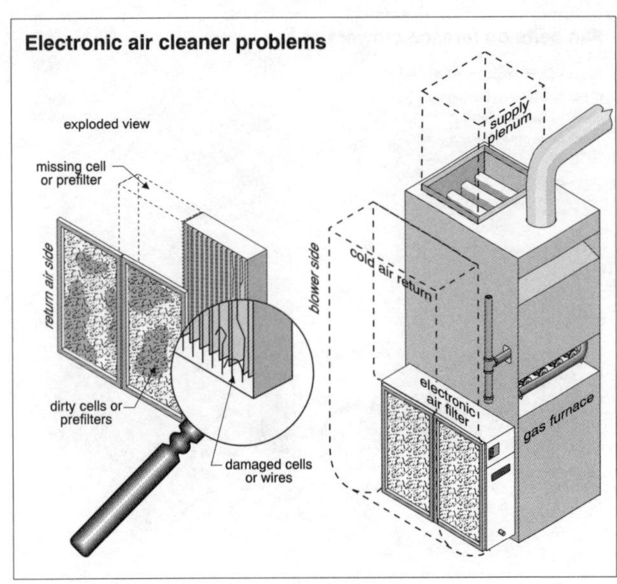

0786

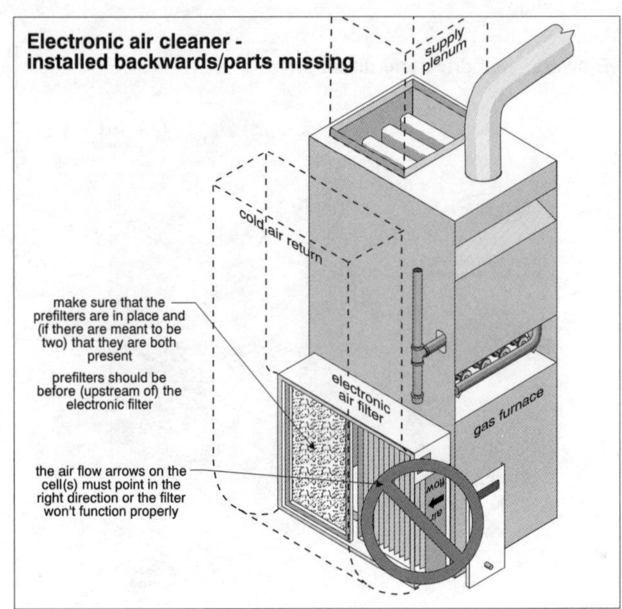

0787

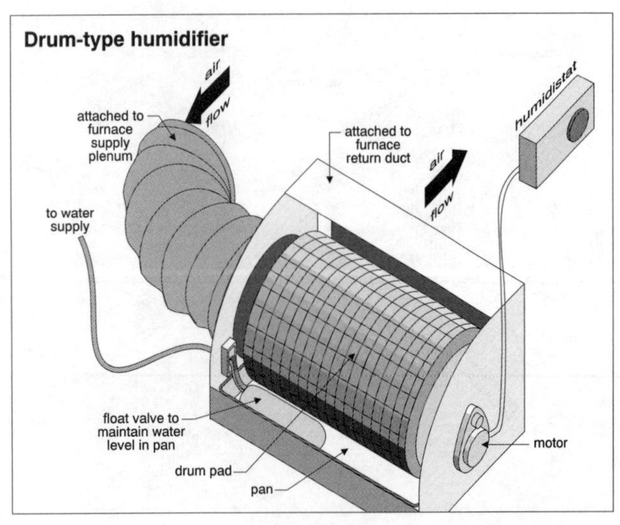

0788

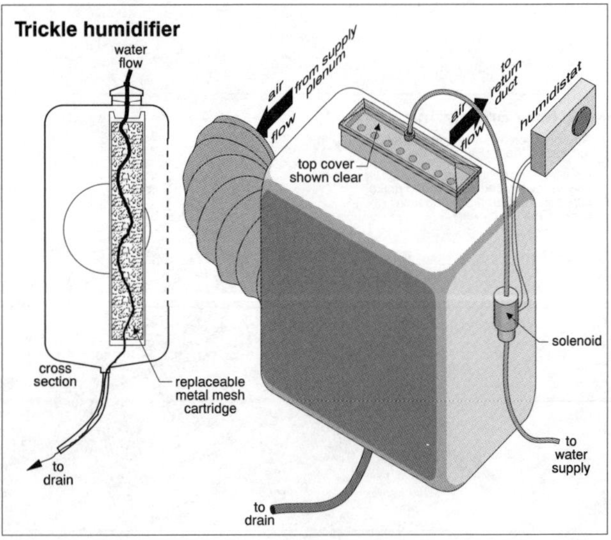

0789

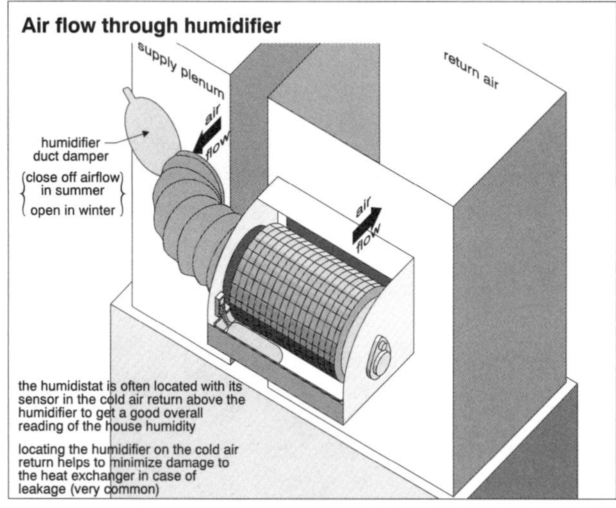

0790

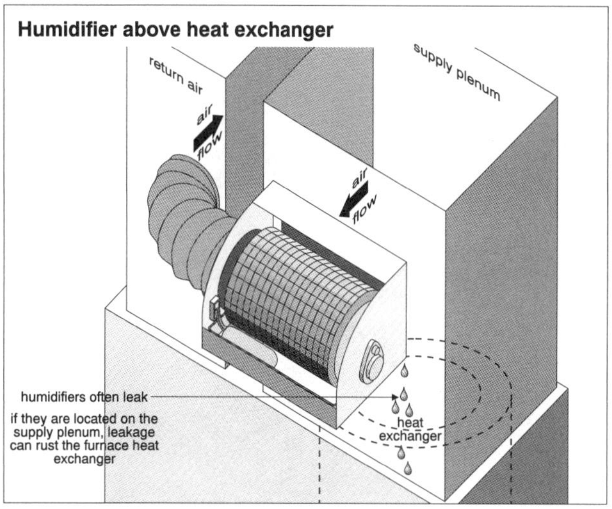

Humidifier above heat exchanger
supply plenum
return air
air flow
air flow
humidifiers often leak
if they are located on the supply plenum, leakage can rust the furnace heat exchanger
heat exchanger

0791

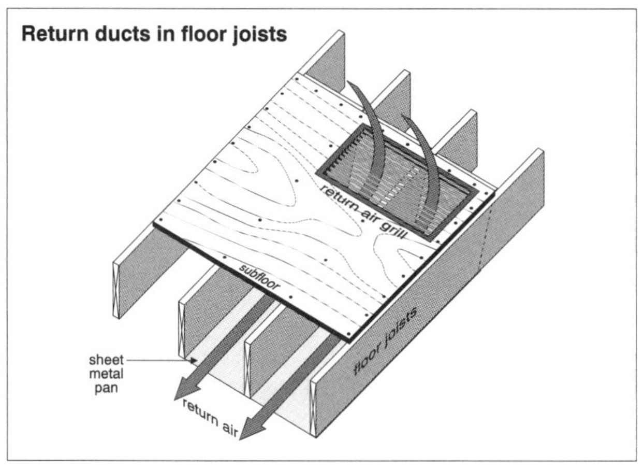

0792

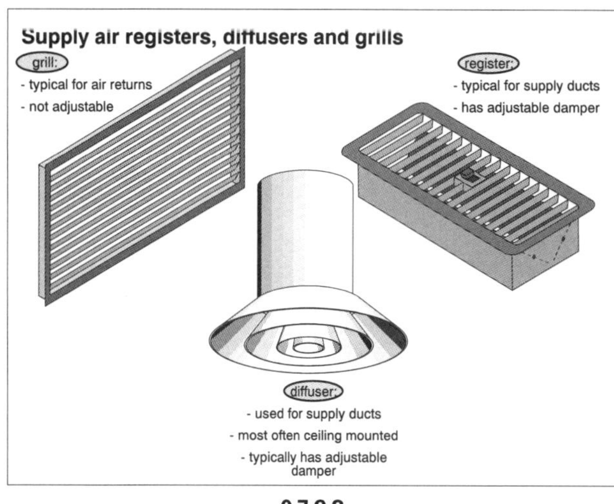

0793

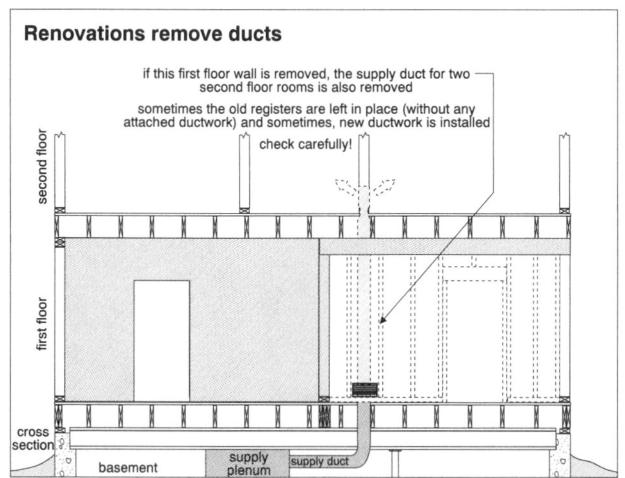

0794

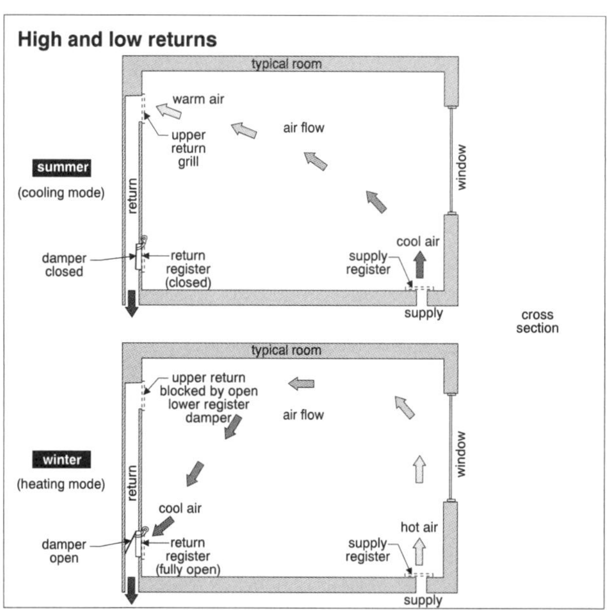

0795

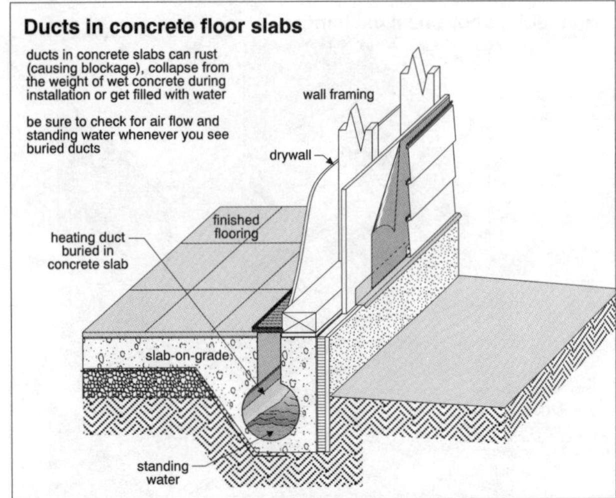

0796

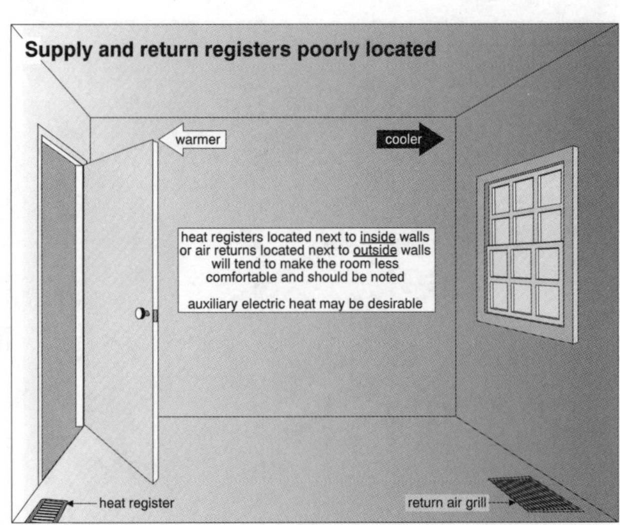

0797

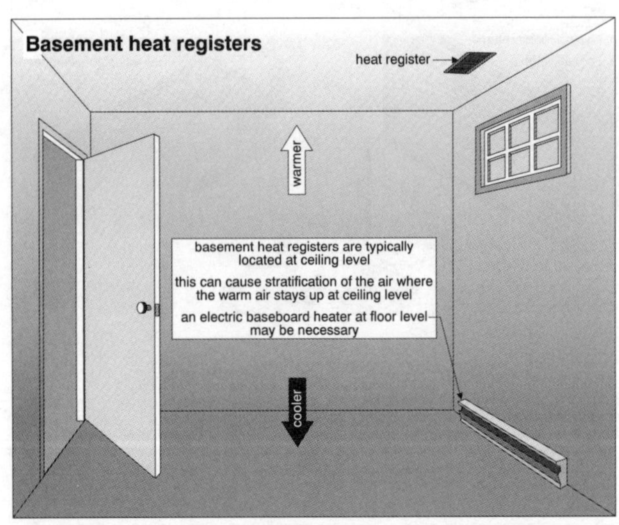

0798

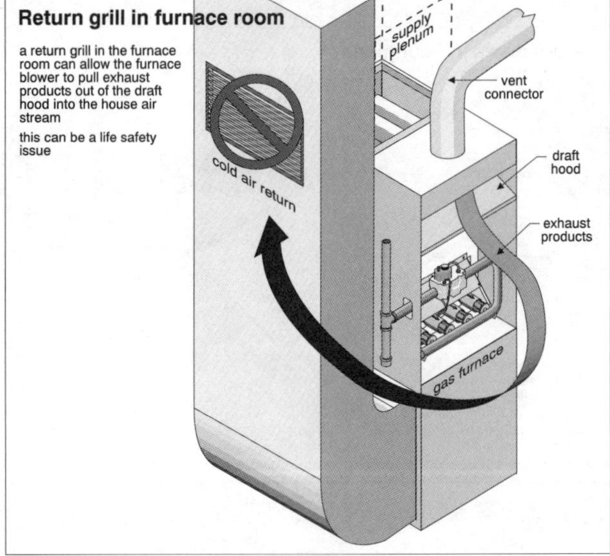

0799

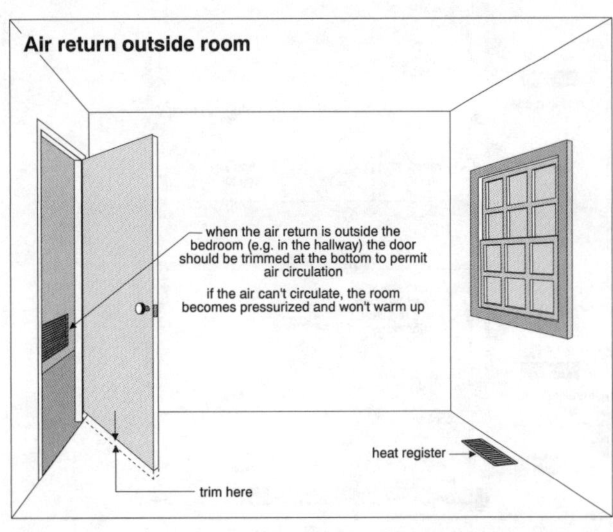

0800

Intermittent pilot light

the igniter is very much like a spark plug - the spark jumping across the air gap lights the pilot flame

gas

ribbon burners

manifold

igniter

pilot

the flame sensor in an intermittent pilot system may be located near the pilot light or may be near one of the ribbon burners

to ignite power supply

gas supply from gas valve

note: crossover igniters omitted for clarity

0801

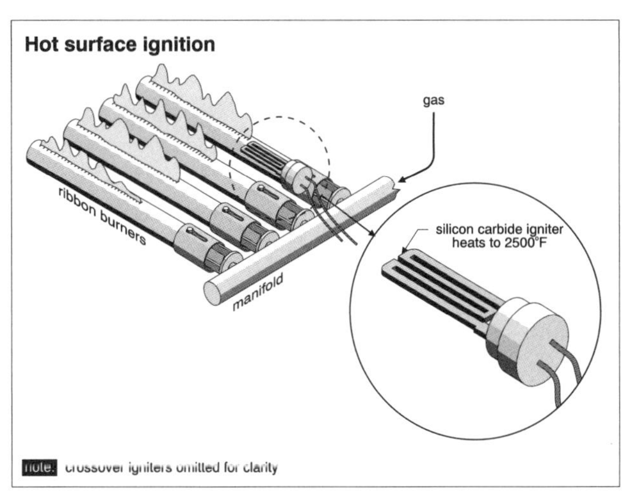

0802

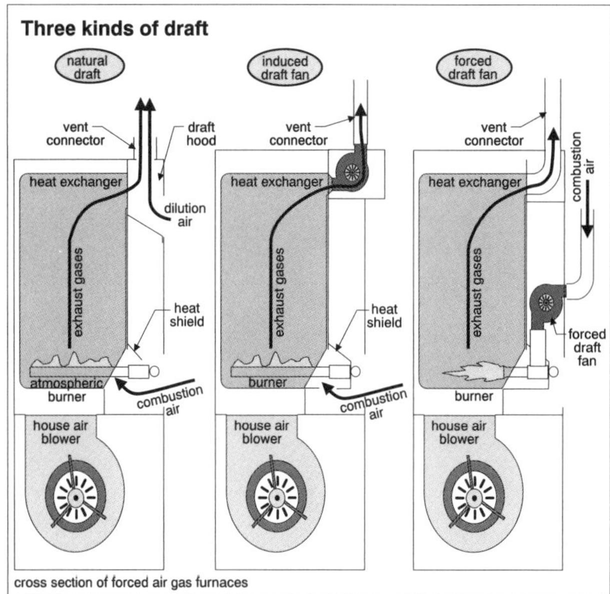

0803

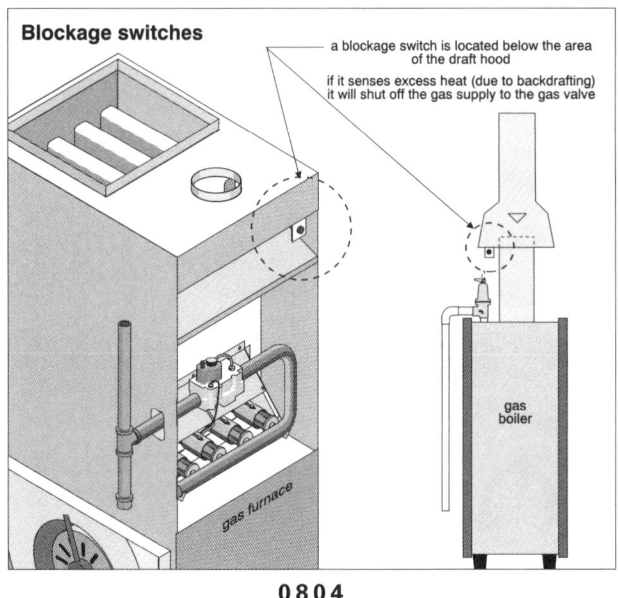

0804

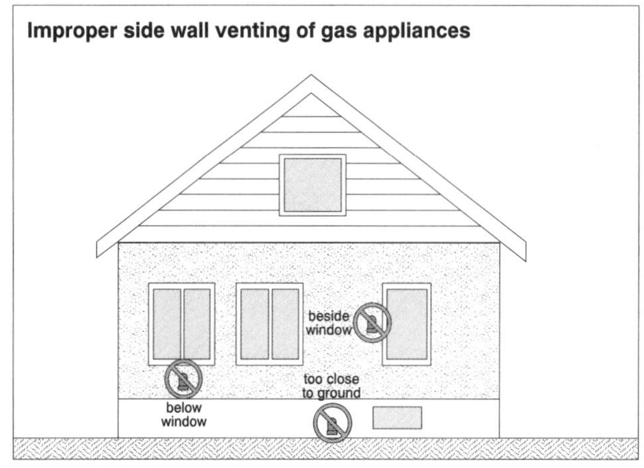

0805

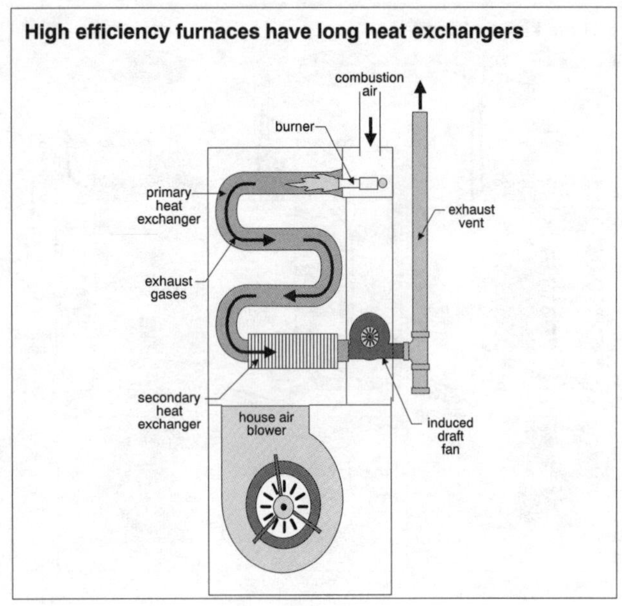

0806

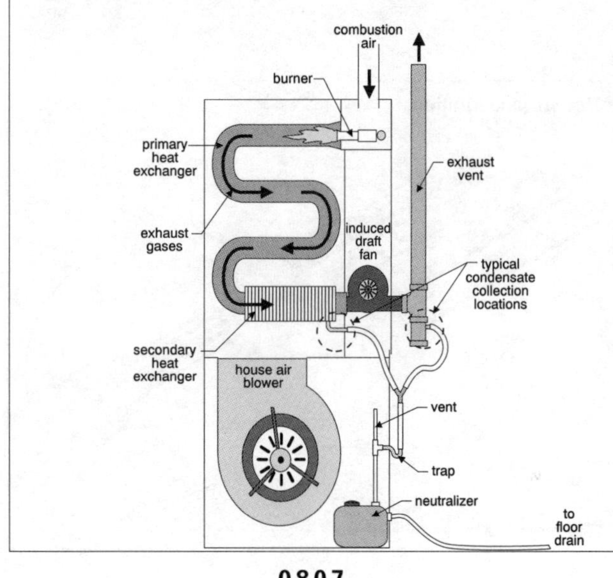

0807

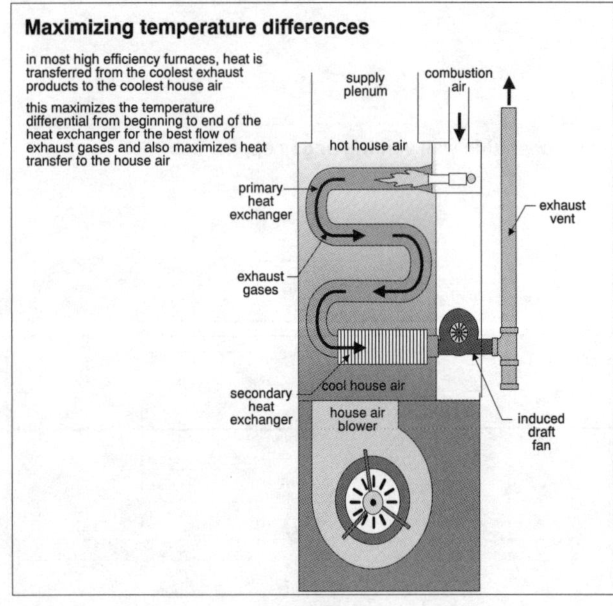

0808

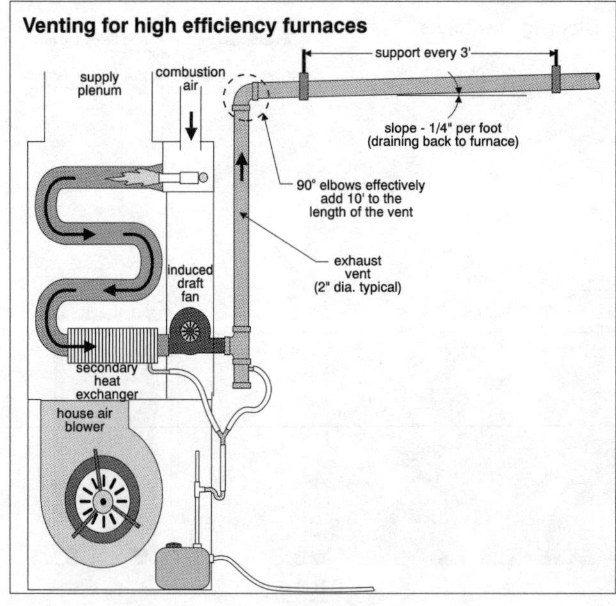

0809

Improper sidewall vent locations - high efficiency furnaces

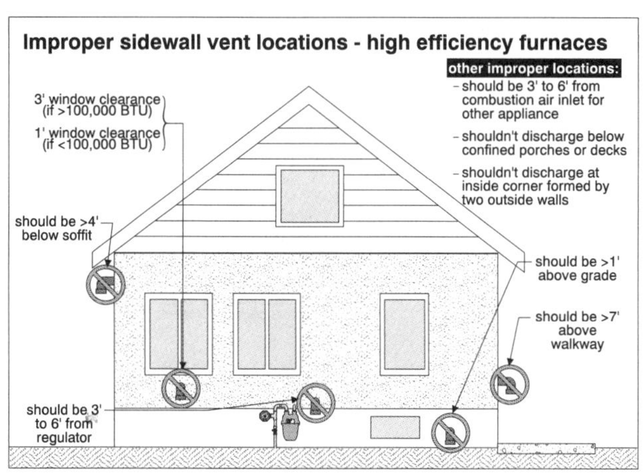

0810

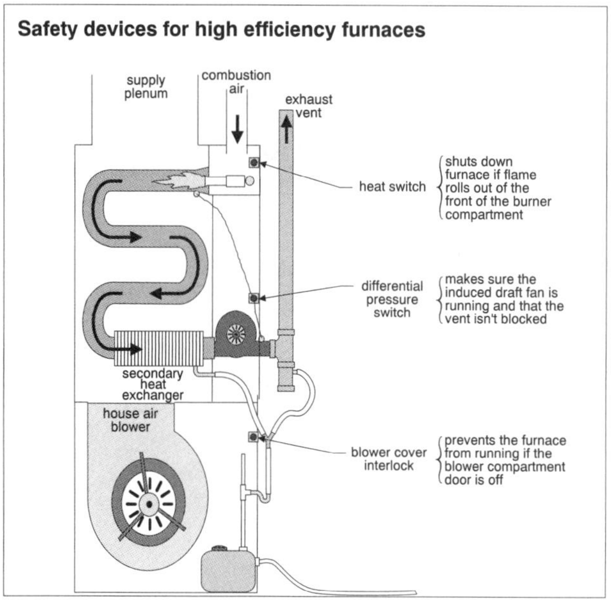

Safety devices for high efficiency furnaces

supply plenum
combustion air
exhaust vent
heat switch
shuts down furnace if flame rolls out of the front of the burner compartment
differential pressure switch
makes sure the induced draft fan is running and that the vent isn't blocked
secondary heat exchanger
house air blower
blower cover interlock
prevents the furnace from running if the blower compartment door is off

0811

Pulse furnace - how it works

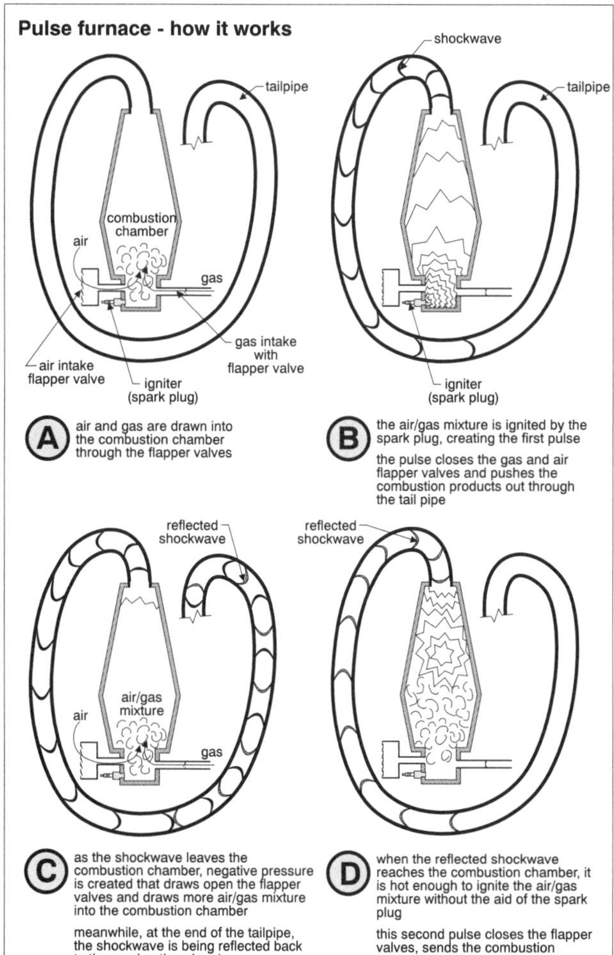

0812

Pulse furnace heat exchanger components

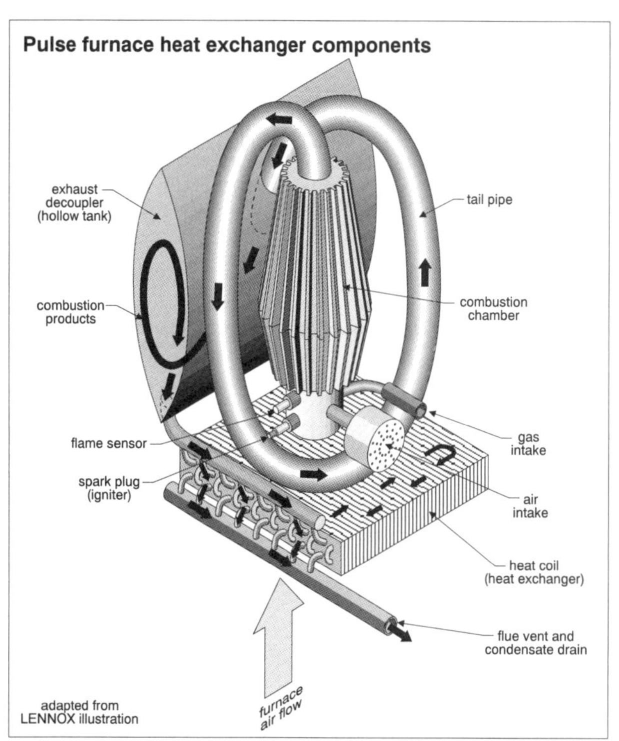

0813

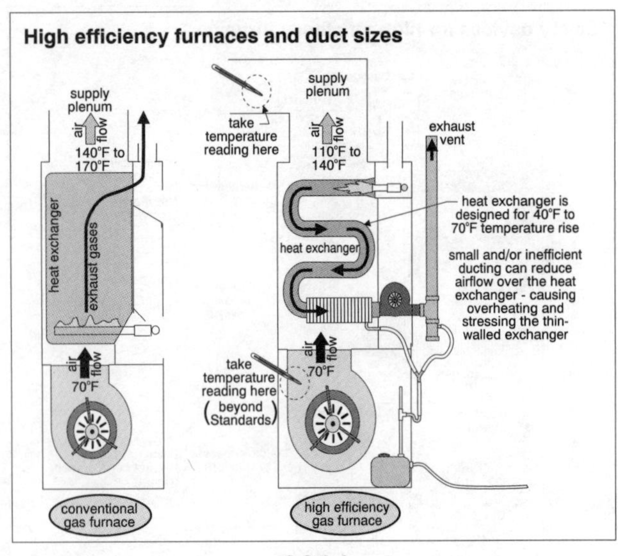

0814

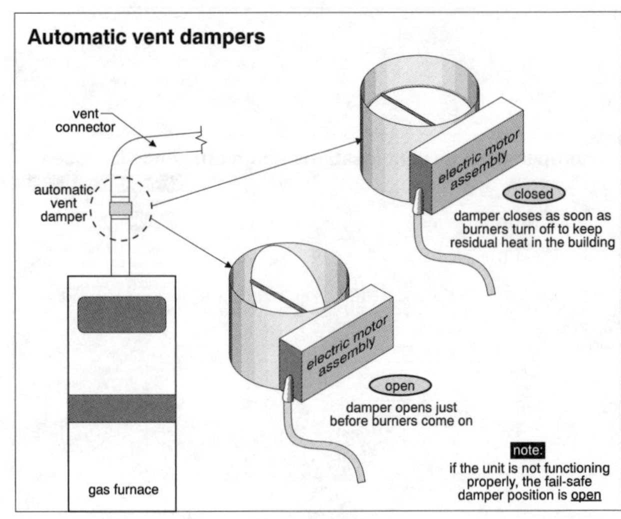

0815

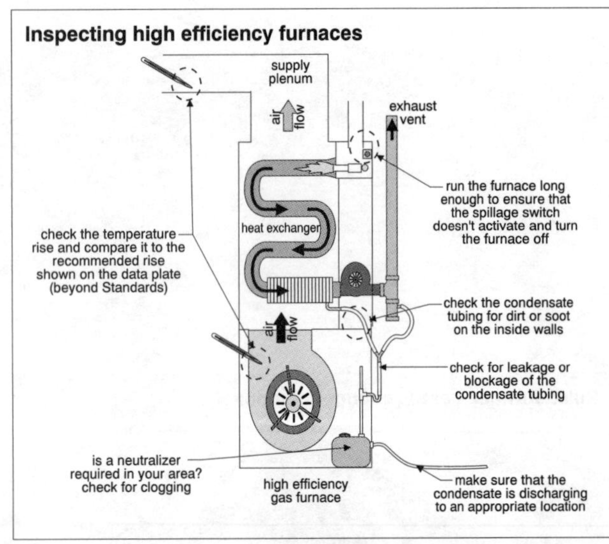

0816

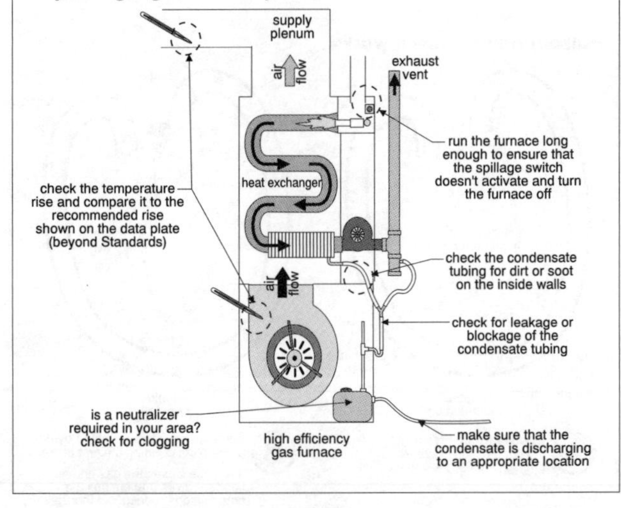

0817

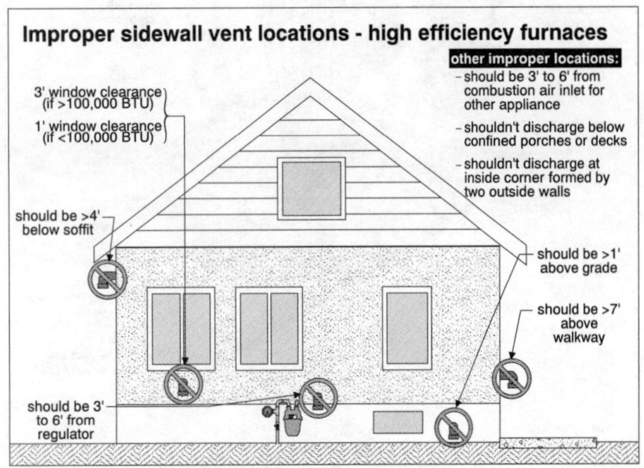

0818

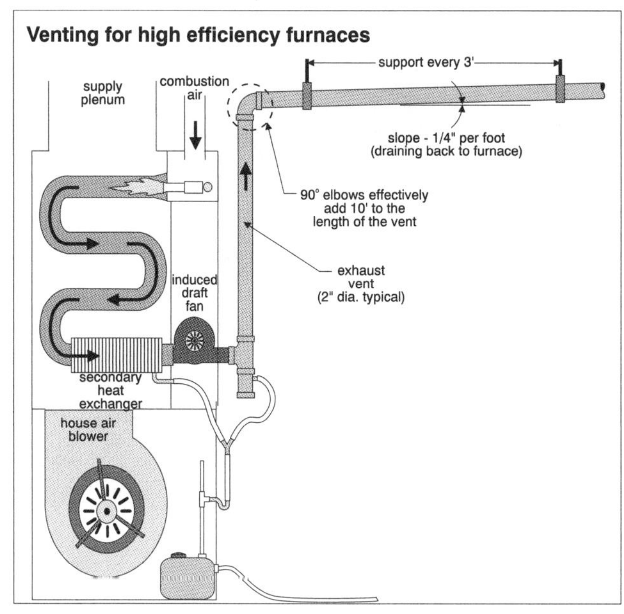

0819

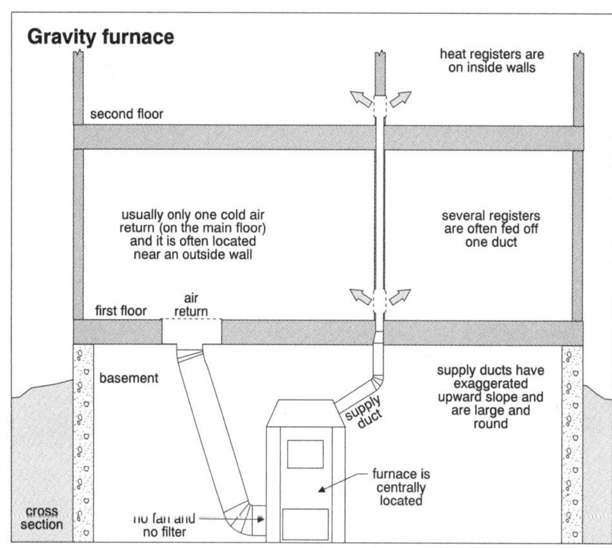

0820

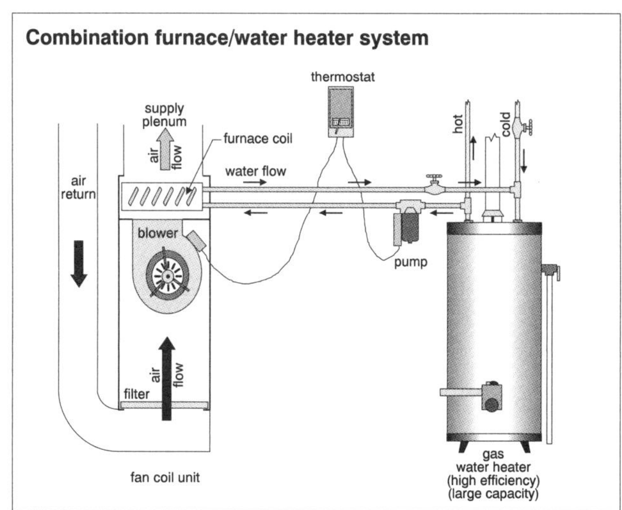

0821

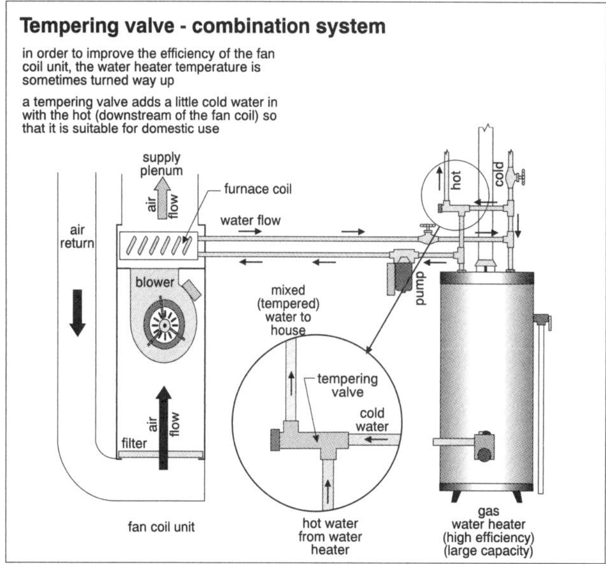

0822

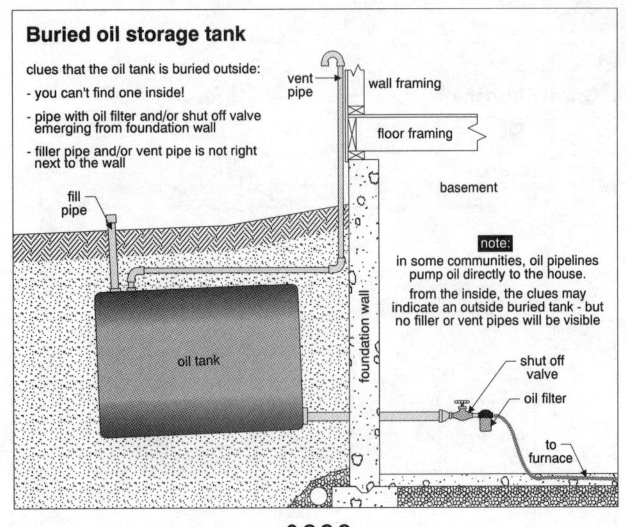

0823

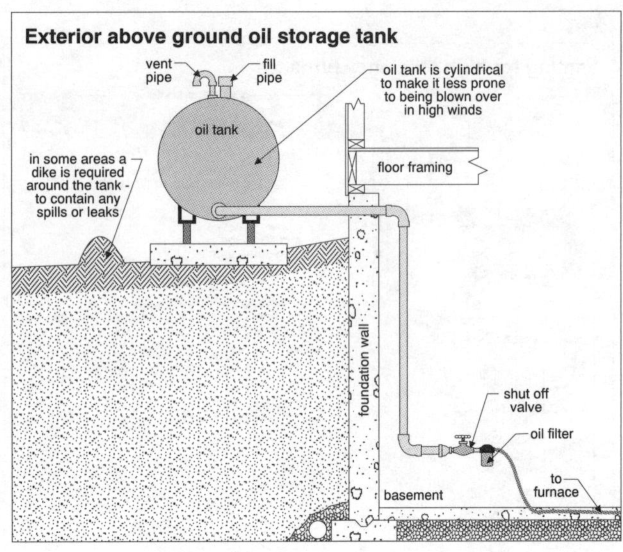

0824

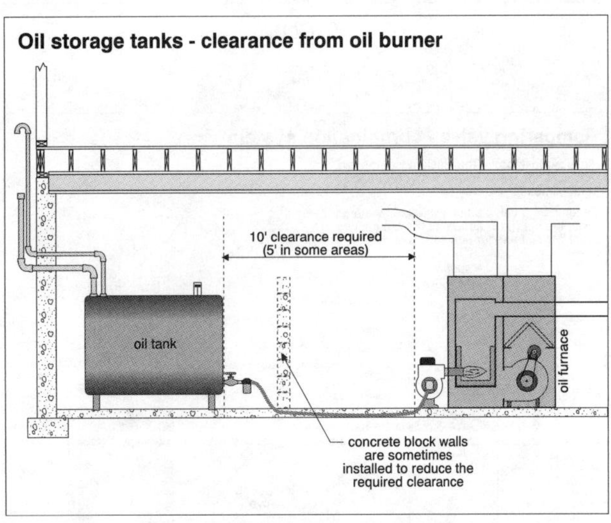

0825

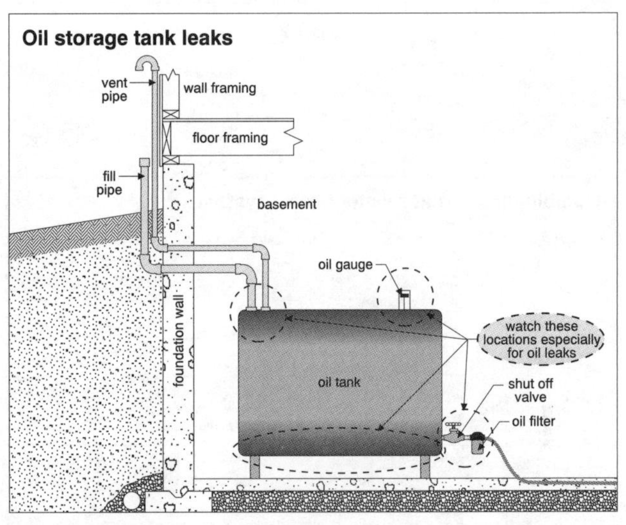

0826

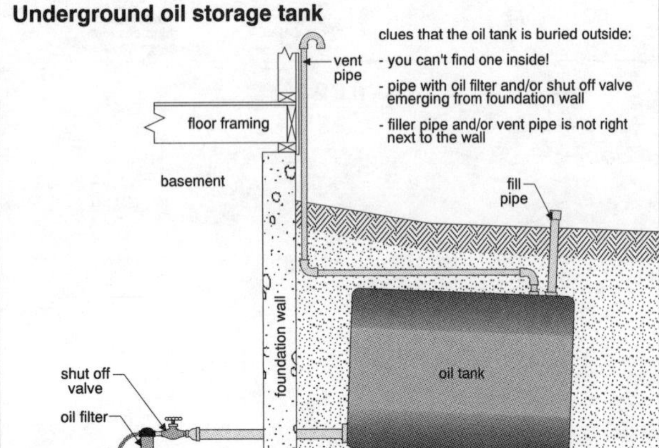

0827

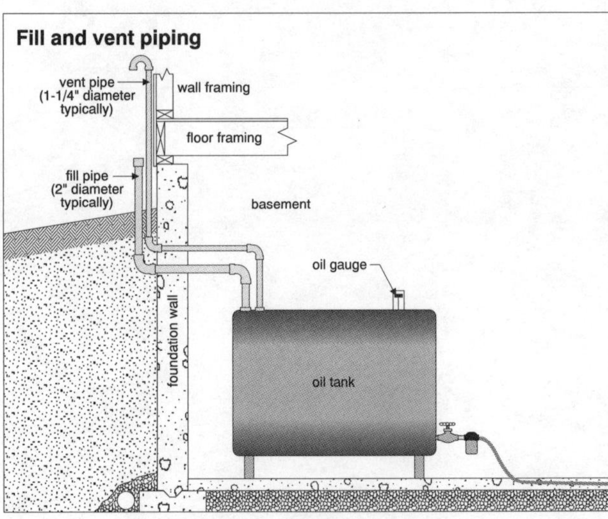

0828

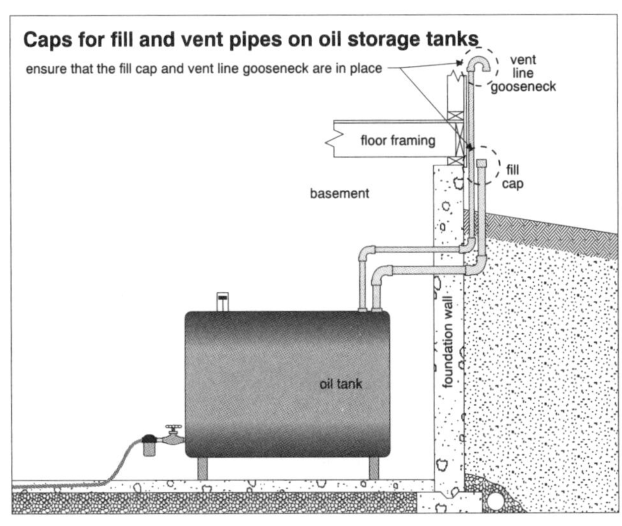

0829

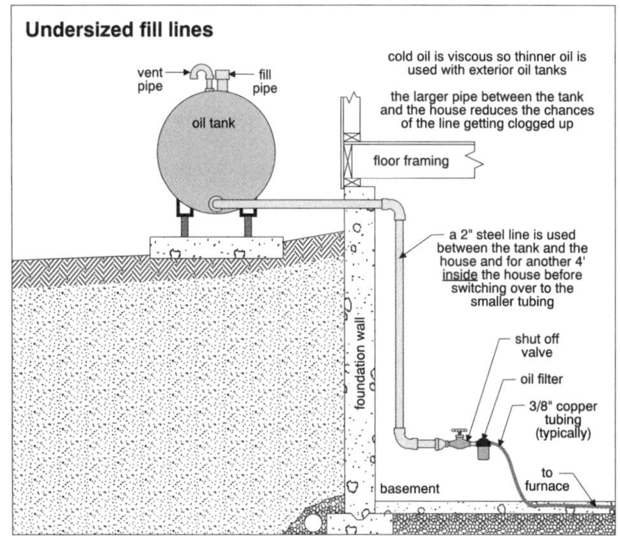

0830

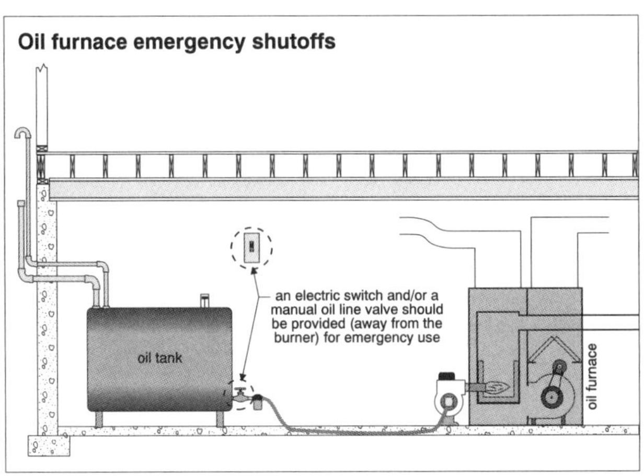

0831

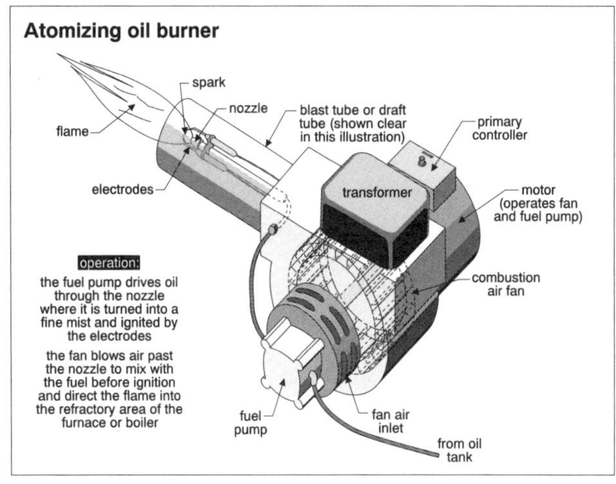

0832

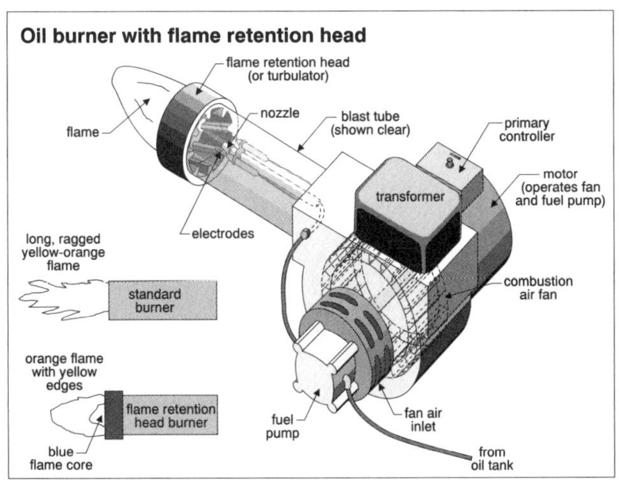

0833

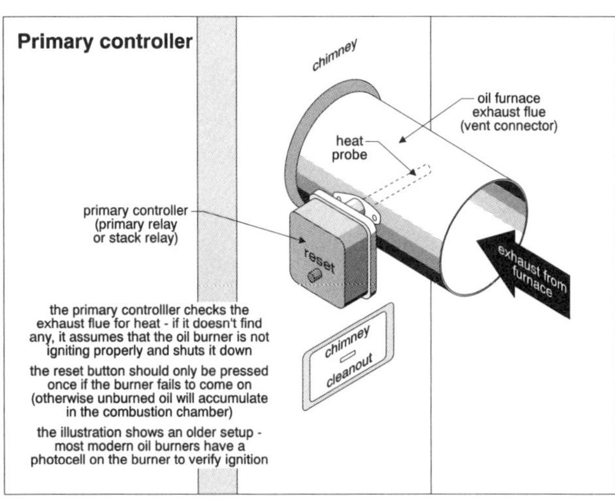

0834

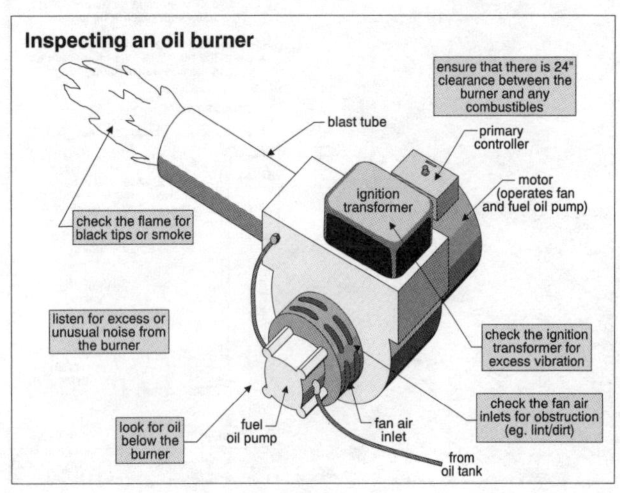

0835

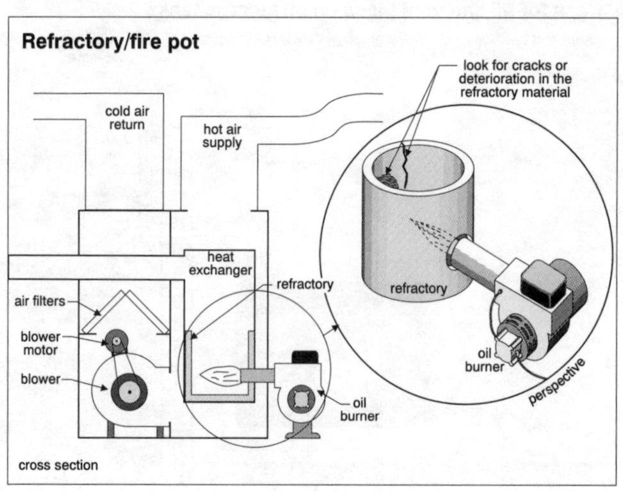

0836

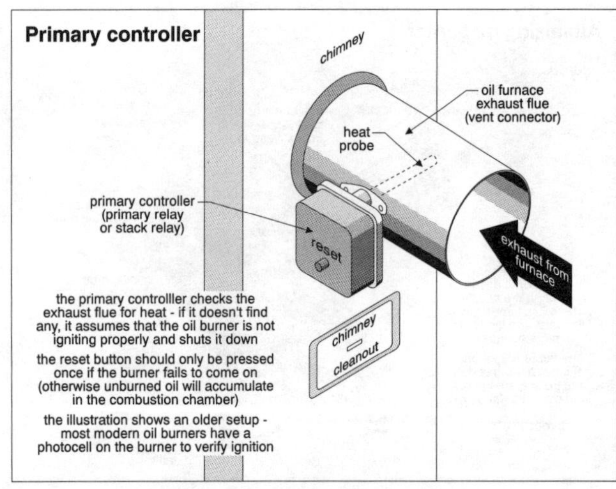

0837

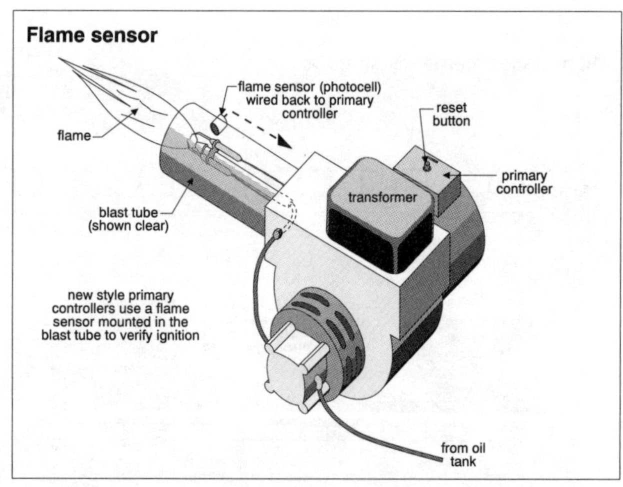

0838

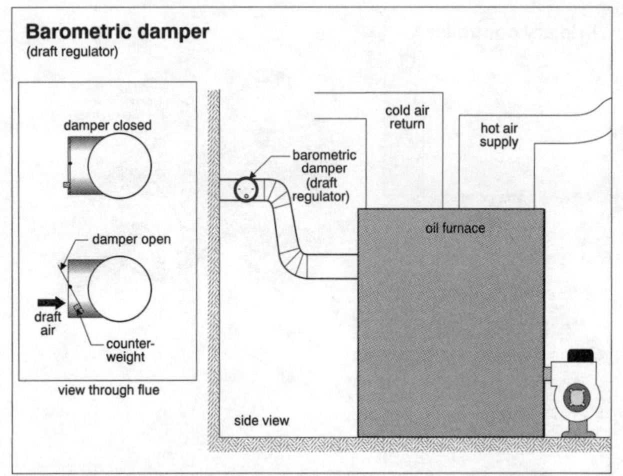

0839

Barometric damper (draft regulator) problems

furnace off
damper closed
furnace running
damper open
draft air
view through flue
cold air return
hot air supply
barometric damper (draft regulator)
oil furnace
check operation with screwdriver (damper should move freely)
side view

0840

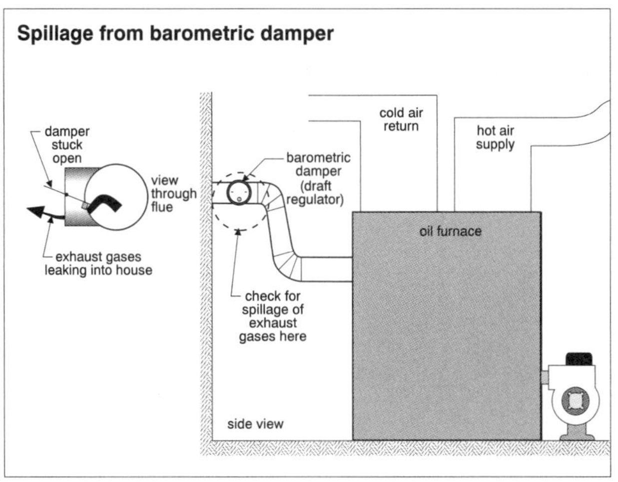

0841

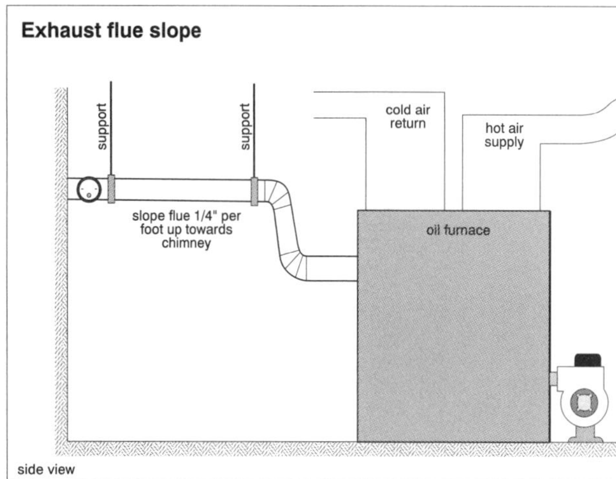

0842

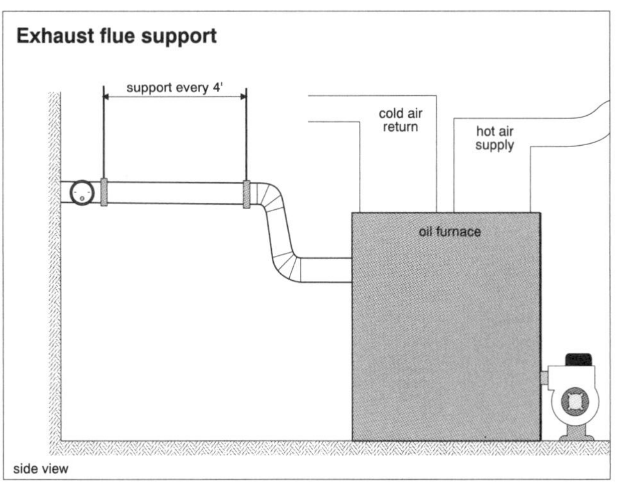

0843

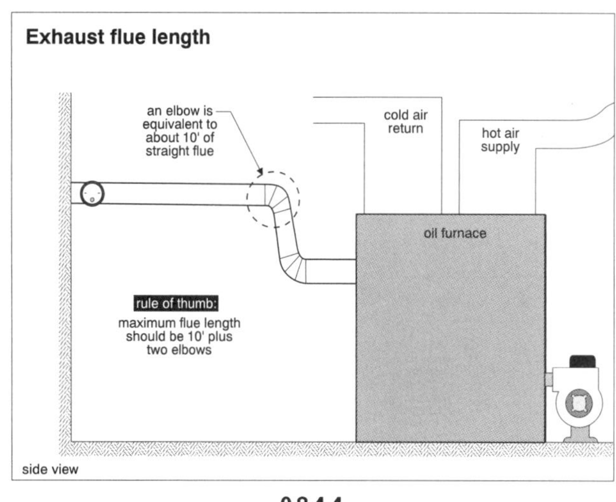

0844

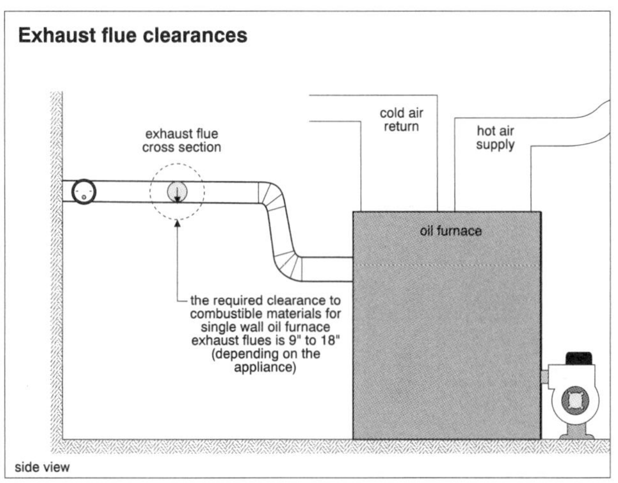

0845

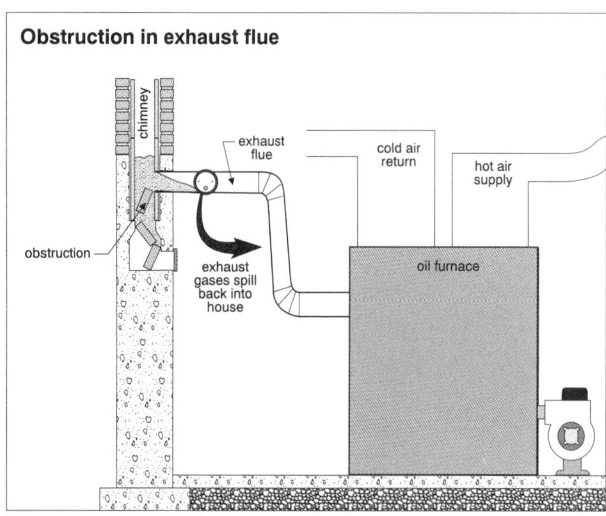

0846

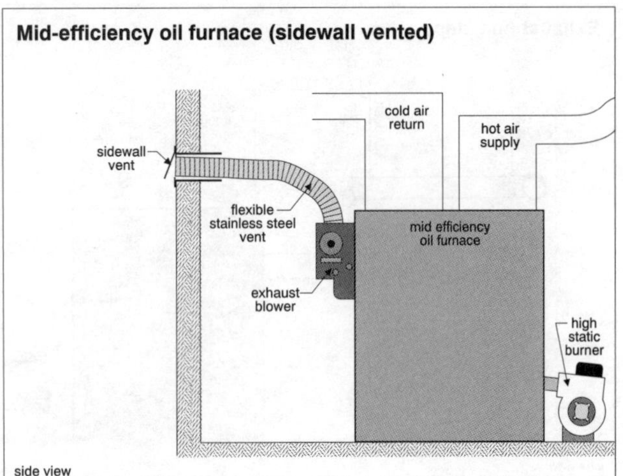

0847

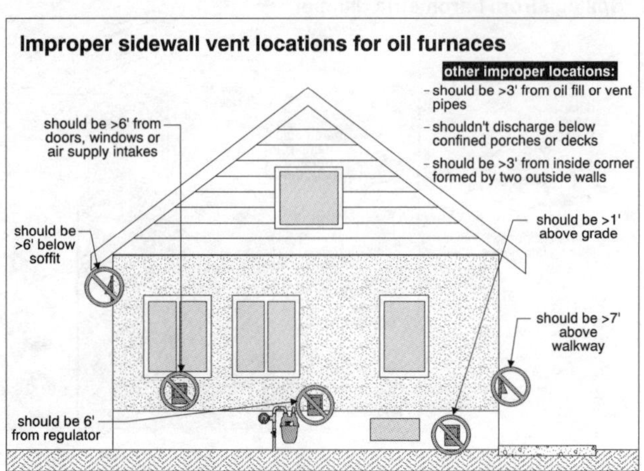

0848

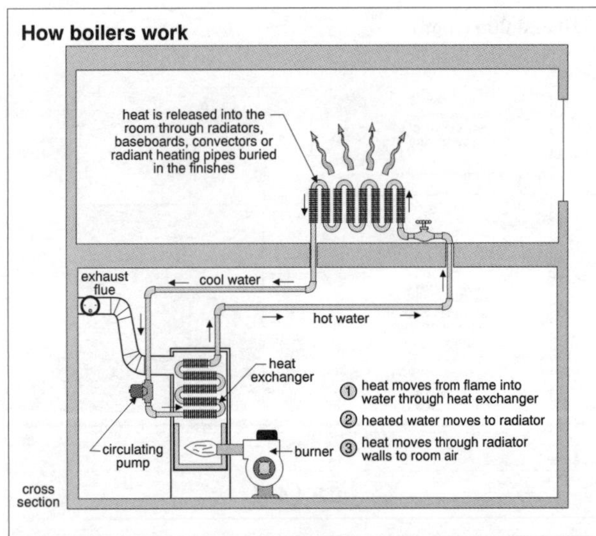

0849

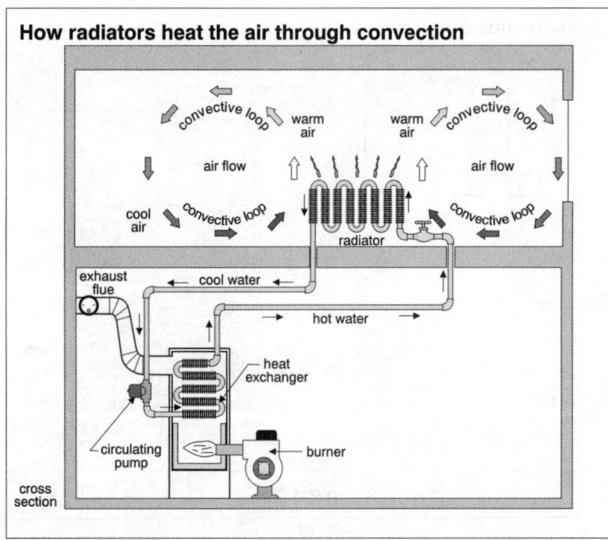

0850

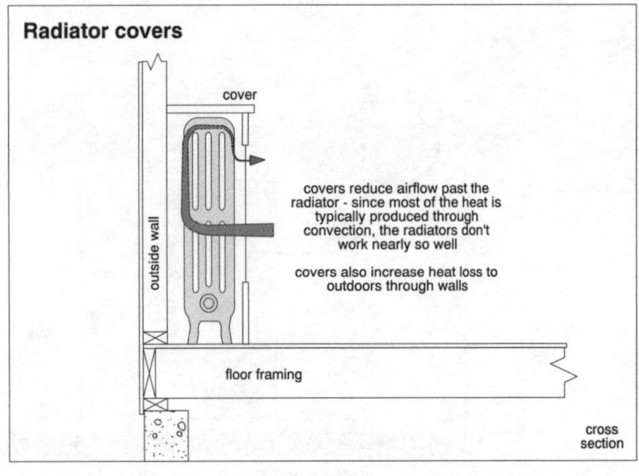

0851

Superheated water

hot water - 300°F or more under high pressure

if this vessel is ruptured, the resultant drop in pressure will cause the superheated water to turn instantaneously into steam with explosive outwards force

0852

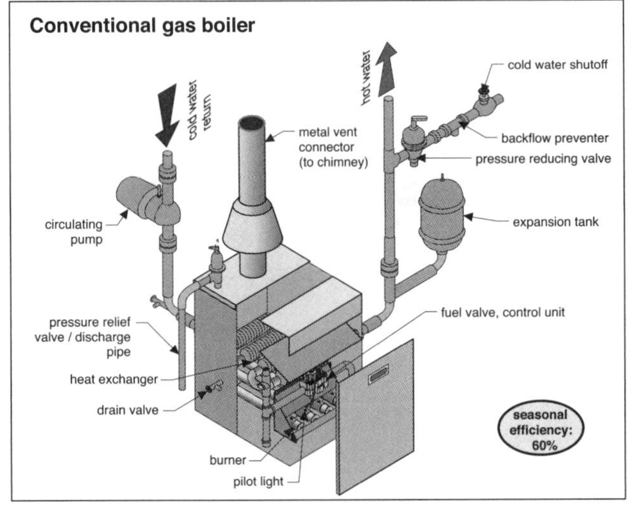

0853

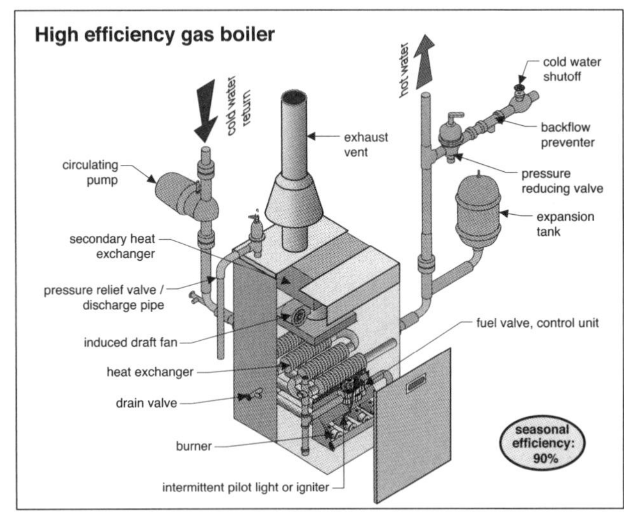

0854

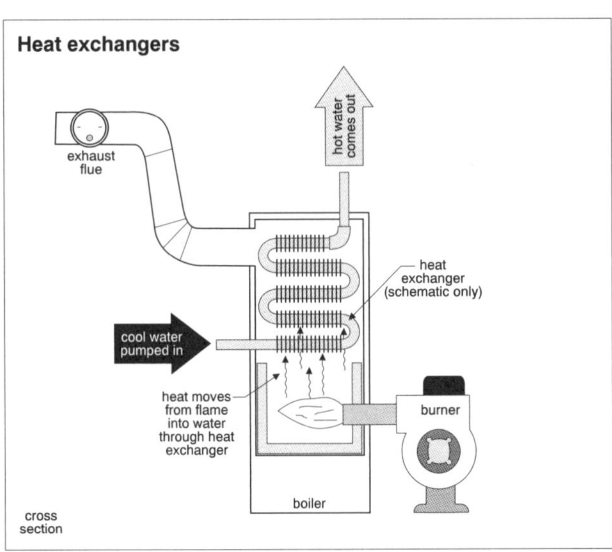

0855

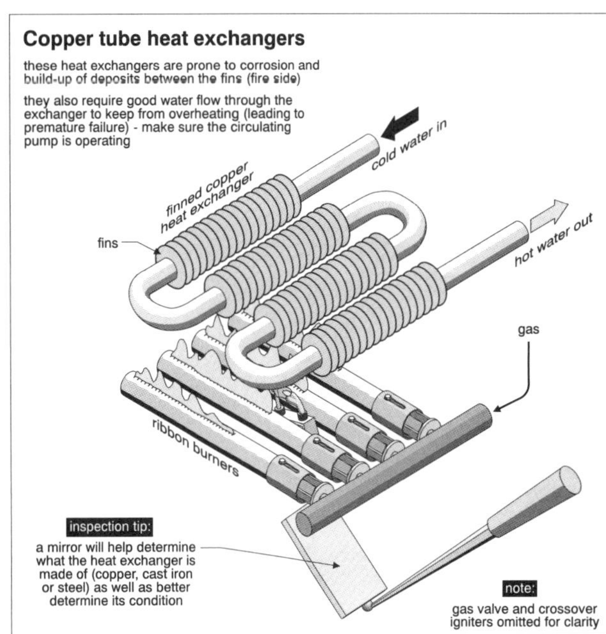

0856

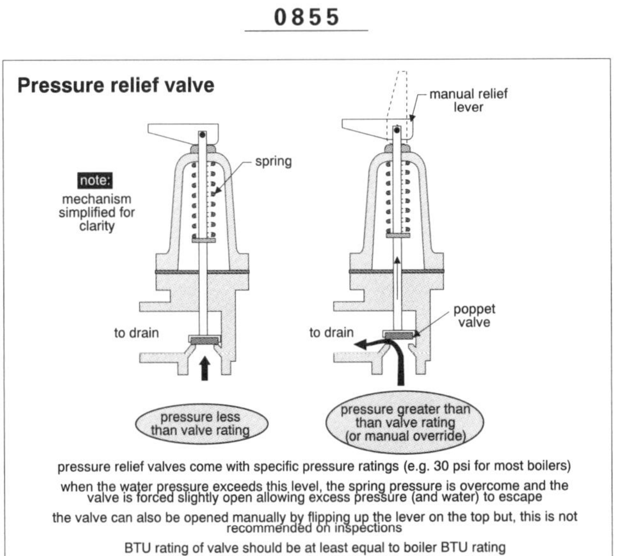

0857

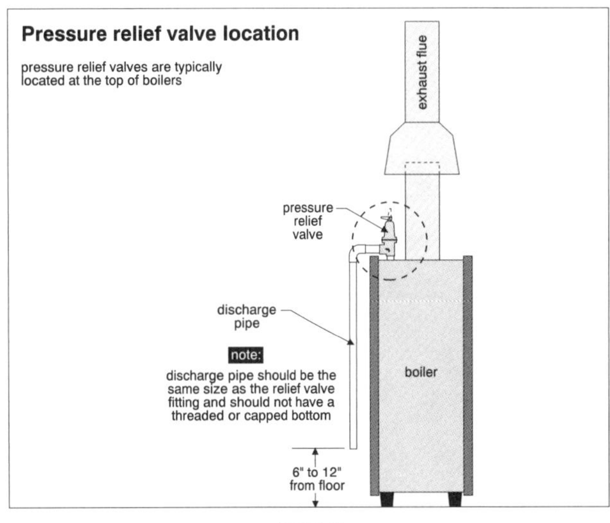

0858

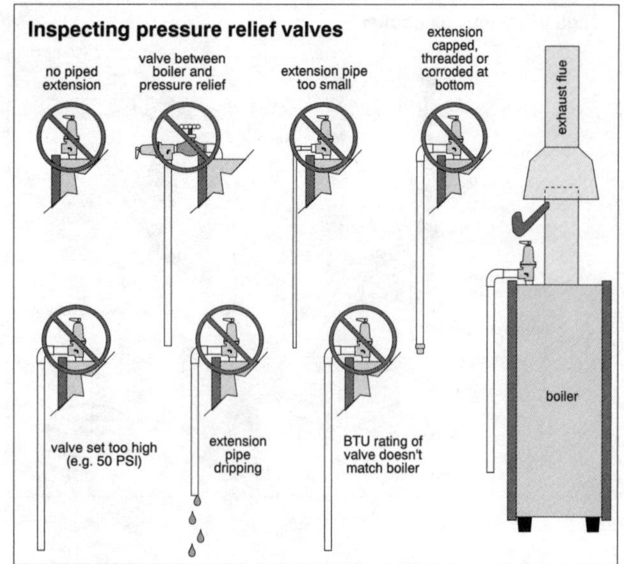

0859

High temperature limit switch

0860

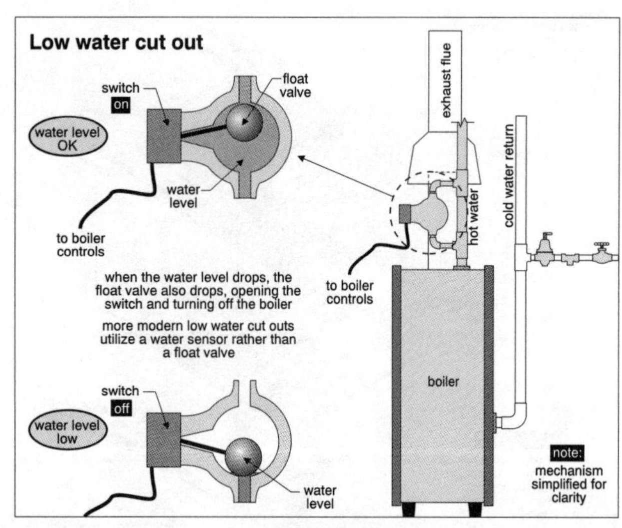

0861

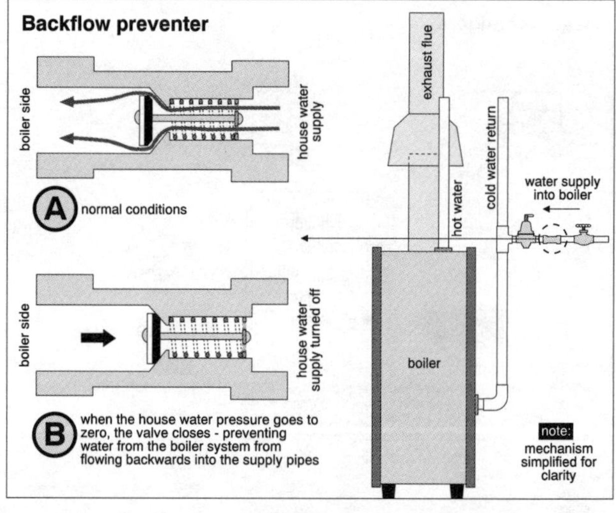

0862

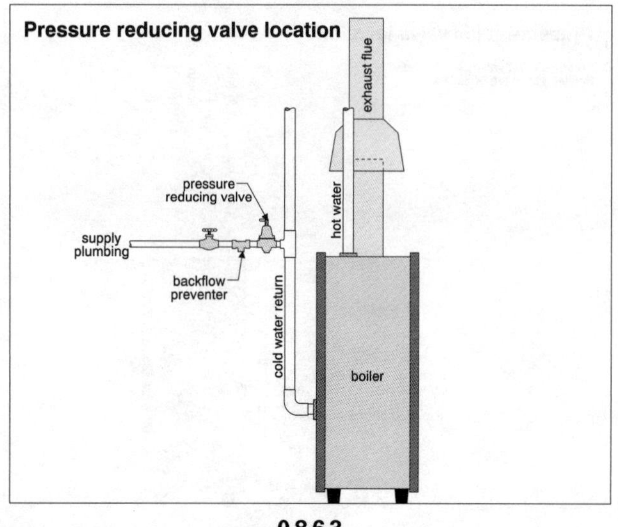

0863

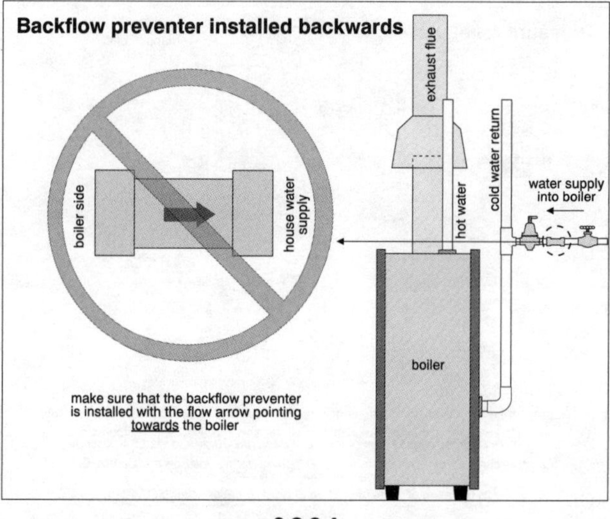

0864

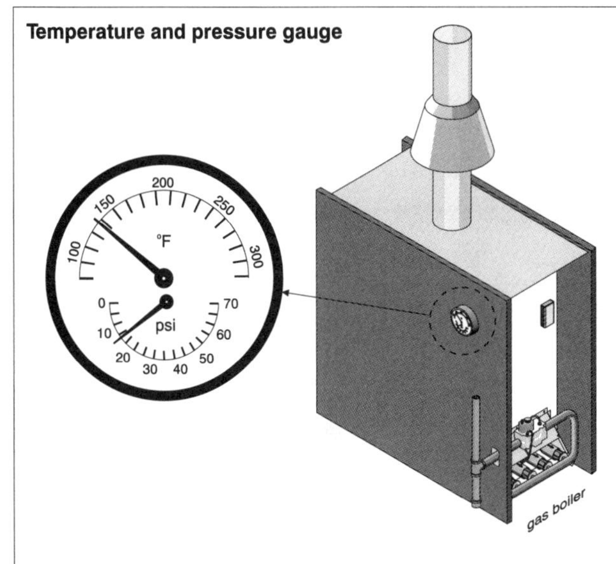

0865

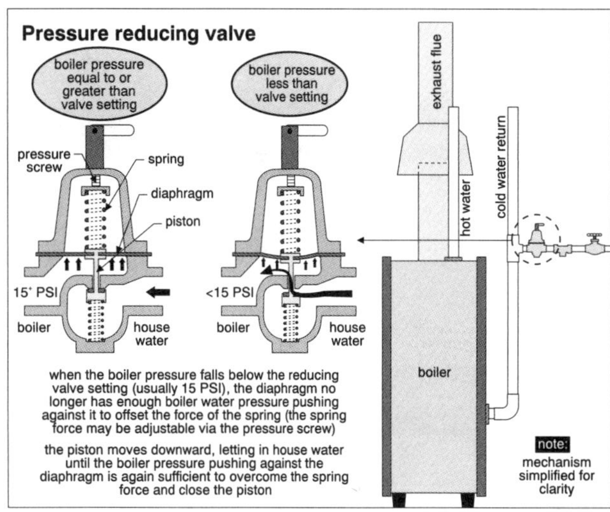

0866

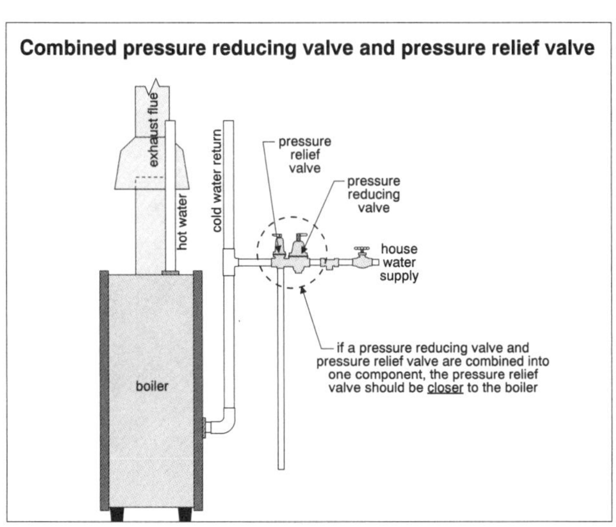

0867

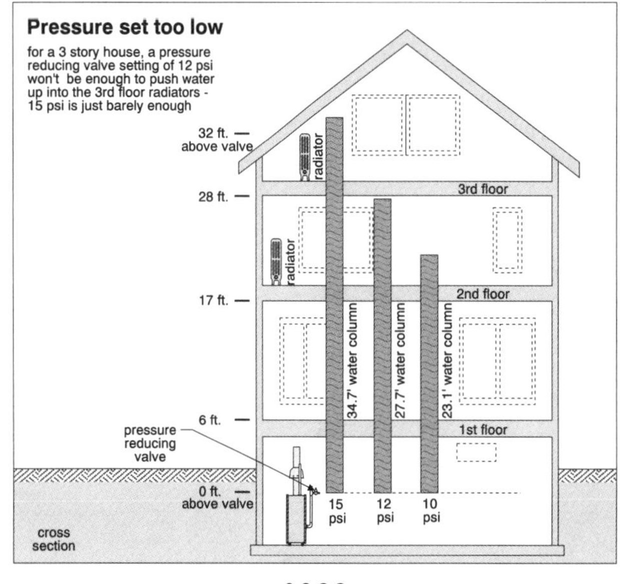

0868

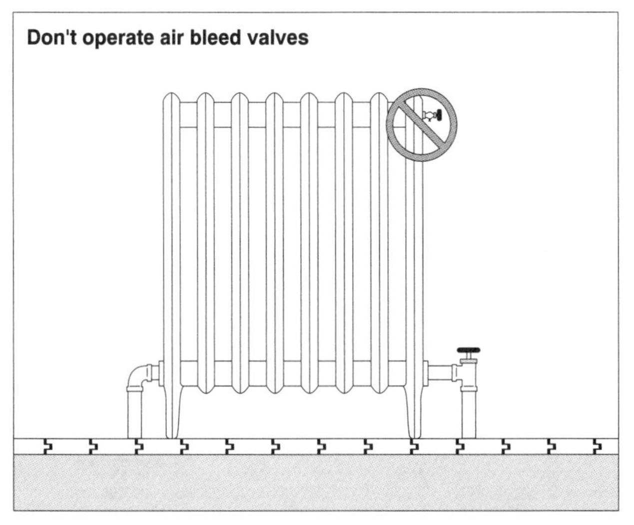

0869

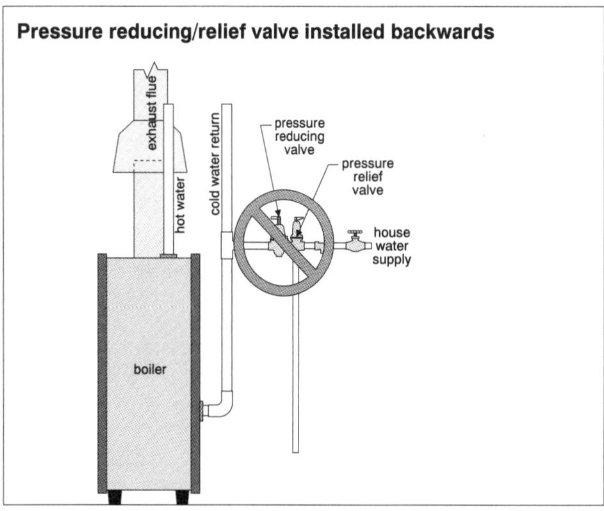

0870

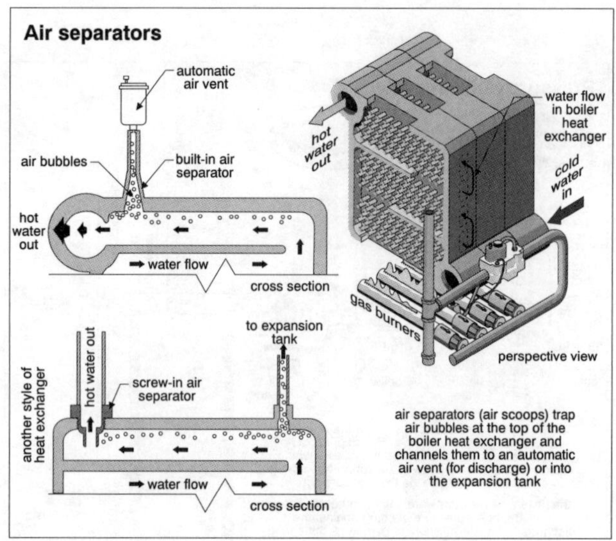

0871

Aquastat - primary control

an aquastat is a primary control that is typically strapped to the hot water piping above the boiler

it must be tightly secured to the pipe to function properly

cool water

exhaust flue

hot water

securing strap

aquastat

boiler

circulating pump

burner

0872

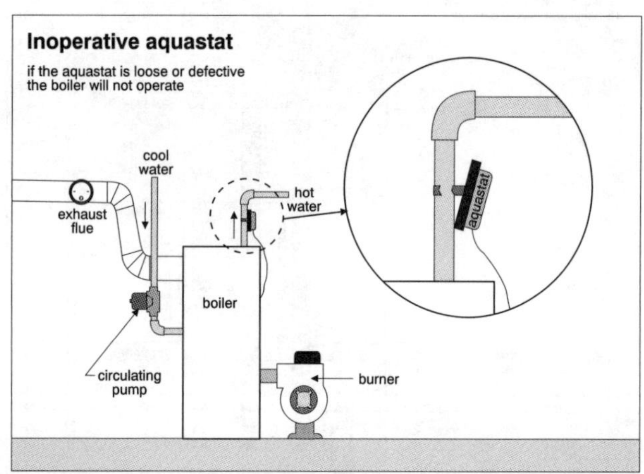

0873

Pump control

temperature probe

LO

cover

high limit/ pump control

LO

220 200 180 160 140 120

pump control - "ON" temperature for circulating pump - typically 110°F to 130°F

note:

pump control can be combined with high limit switch

an alternate location for the pump control is on the hot water piping near the boiler

gas boiler

0874

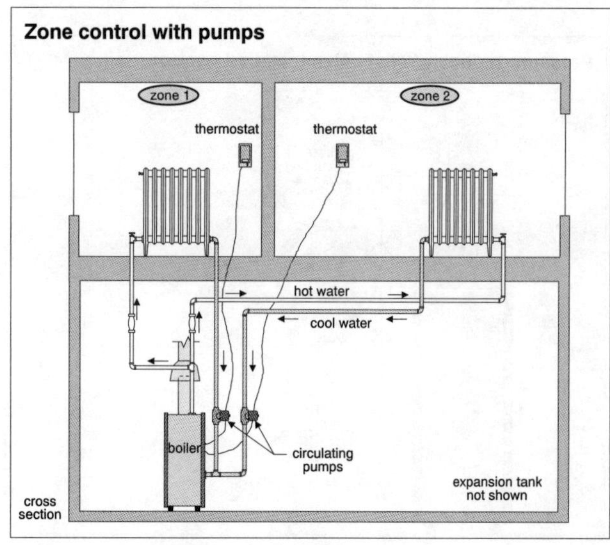

0875

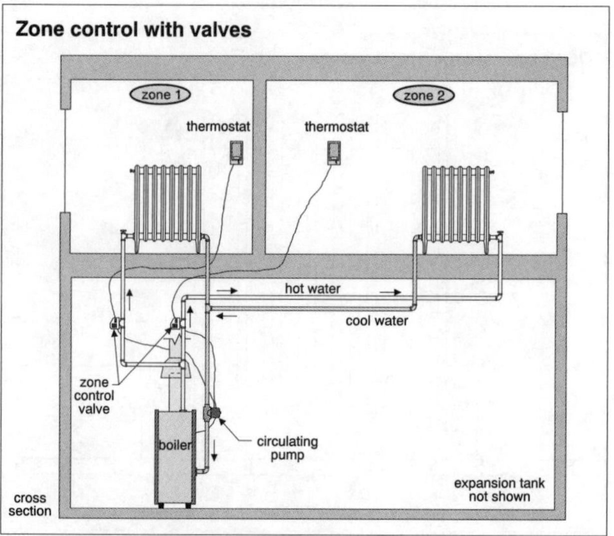

0876

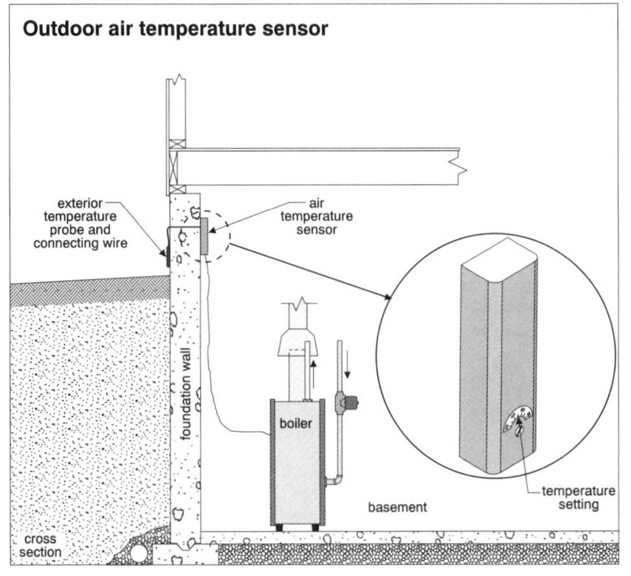

0877

Flow control valves

zone 1
zone 2
thermostat
thermostat
hot water
cool water
flow control valves prevent the circulation of hot water by convection when the circulating pump(s) are not running
these valves are typically found on multi-zone (pump control) systems and systems where hot standby temperatures are maintained
boiler
circulating pumps
cross section

0878

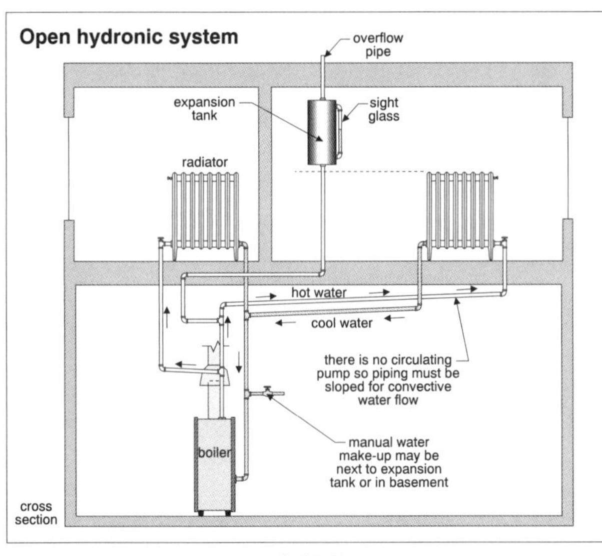

0879

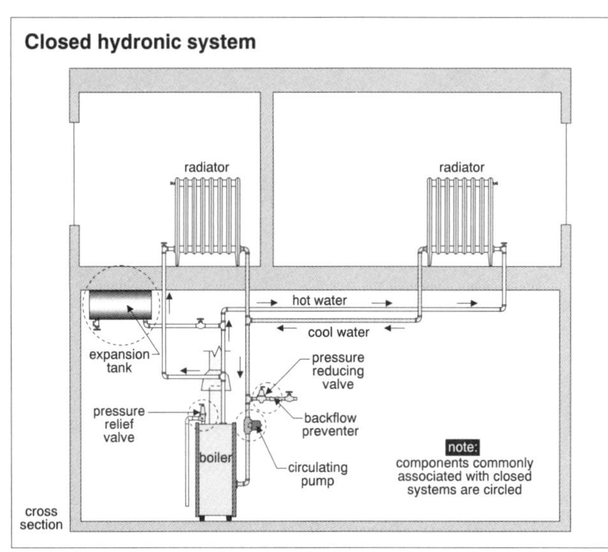

0880

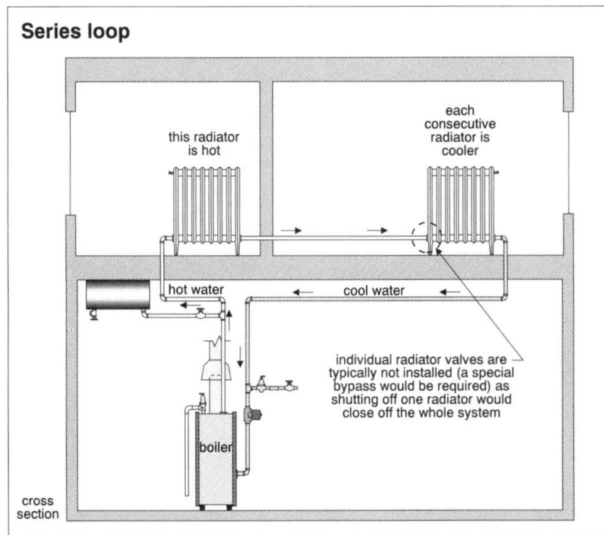

0881

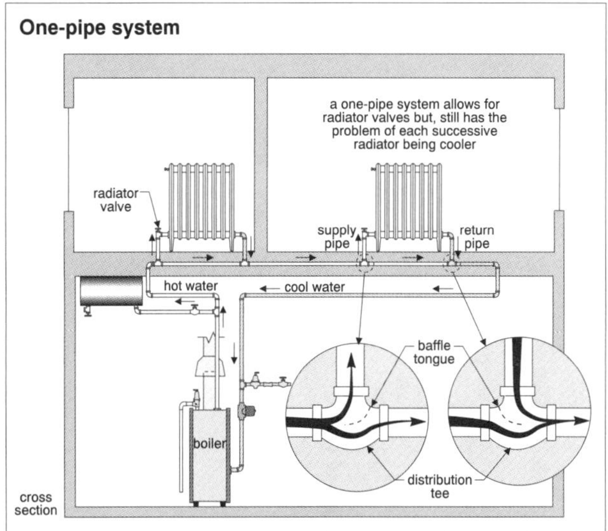

0882

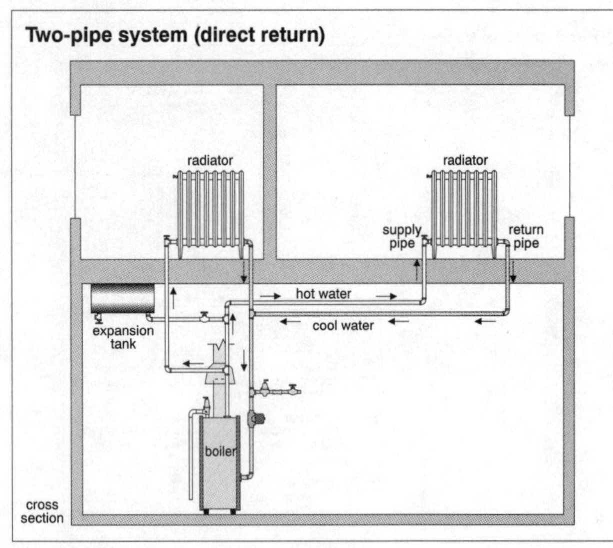

0883

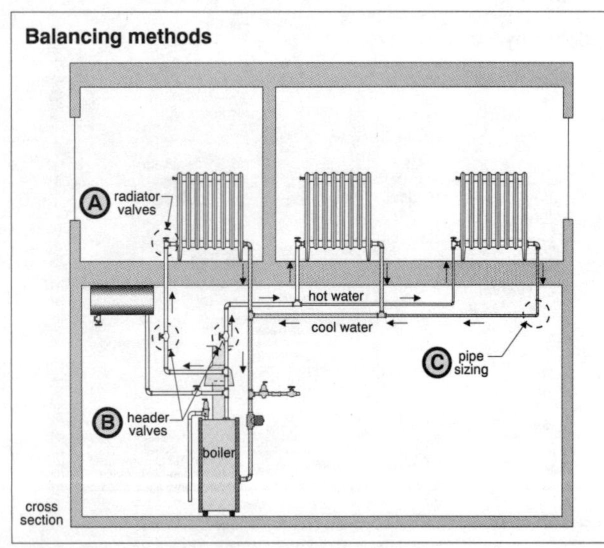

0885

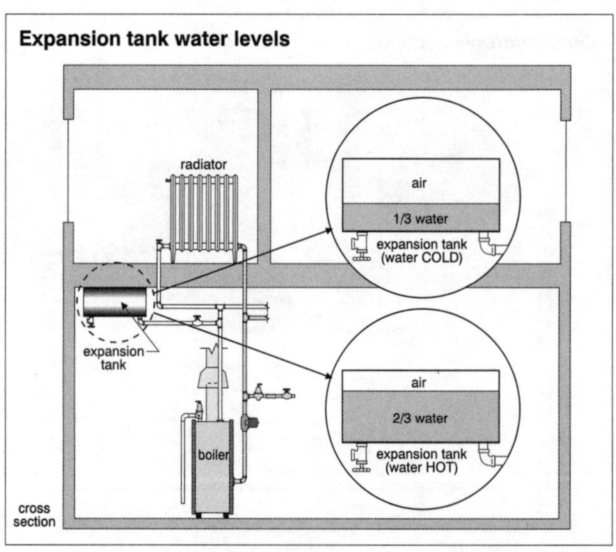

0886

Two-pipe system (reverse return)

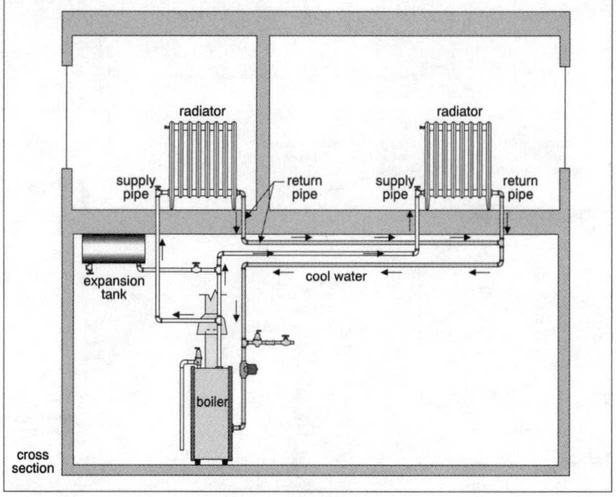

radiator · radiator · supply pipe · return pipe · supply pipe · return pipe · cool water · expansion tank · boiler · cross section

0884

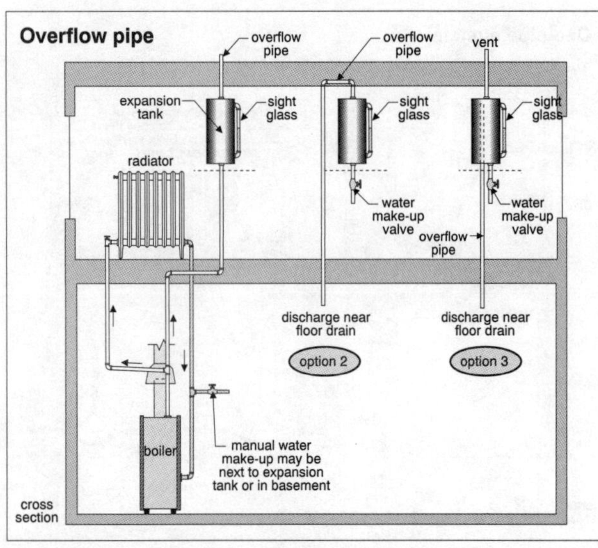

0887

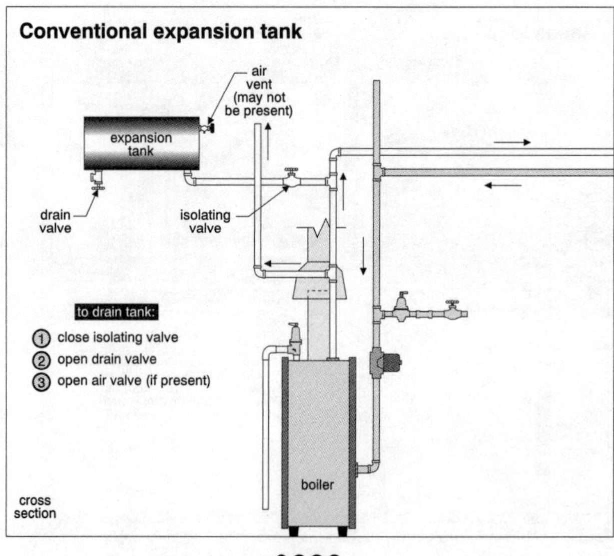

0888

Diaphragm tank

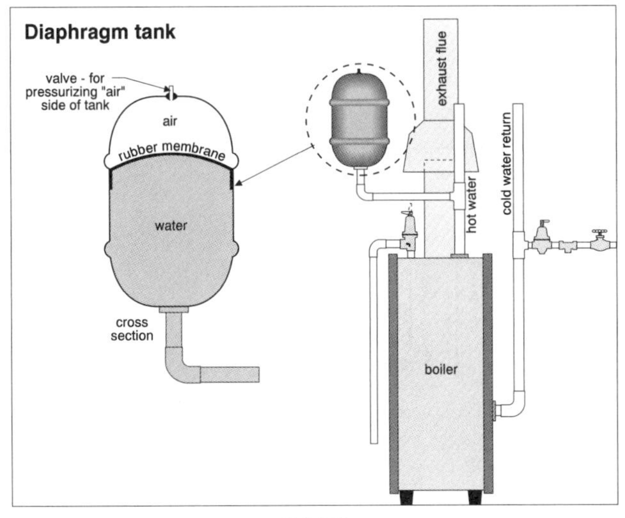

0889

Circulating pump

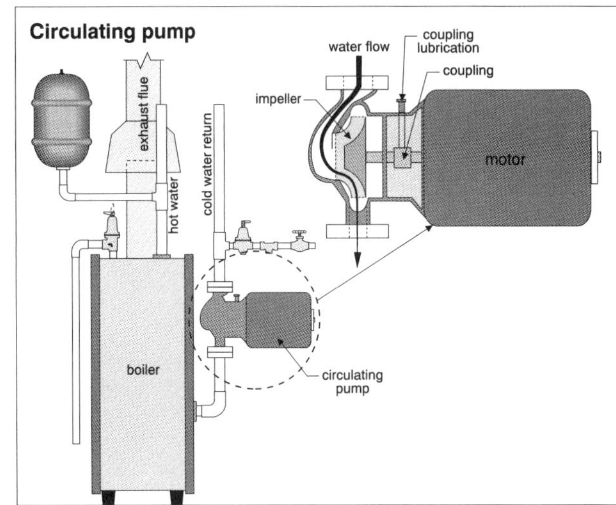

0890

Zone control with pumps

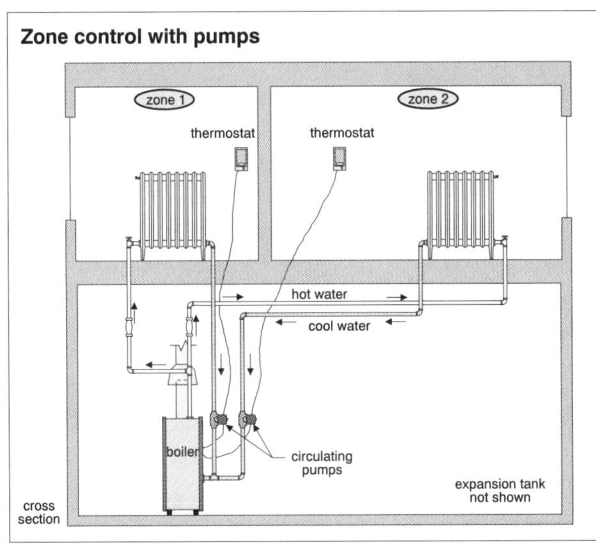

0891

Flow control valves

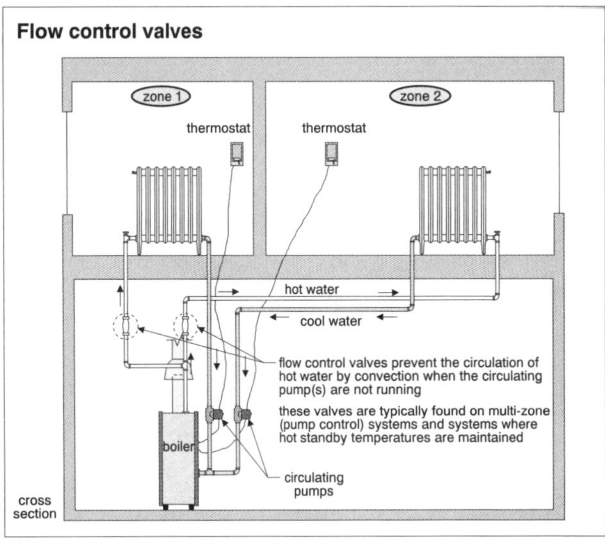

0892

Pipe corrosion

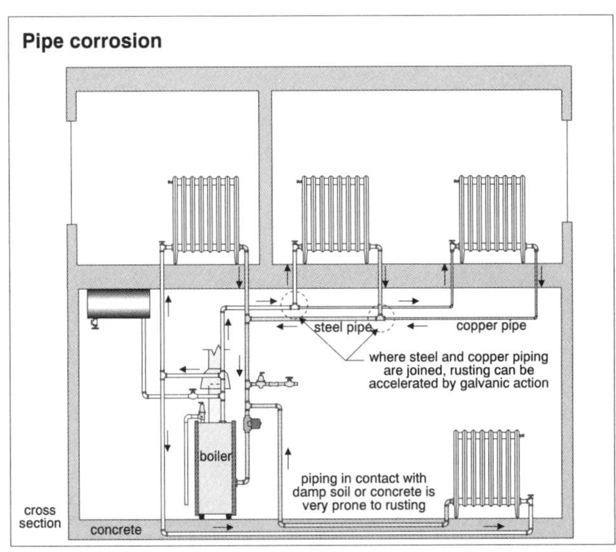

0893

Extending hot water systems

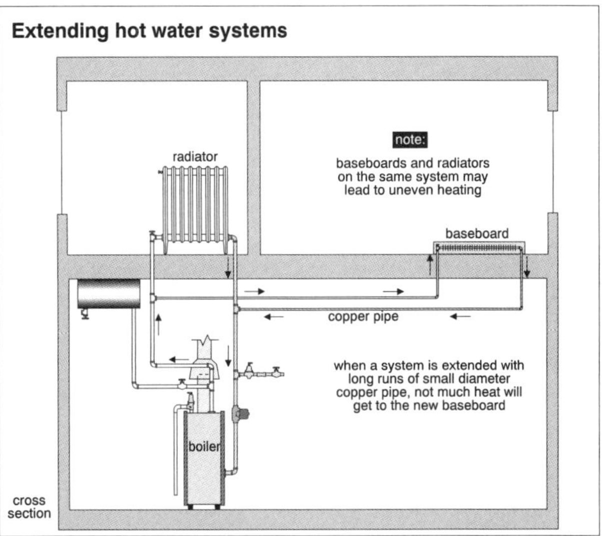

0894

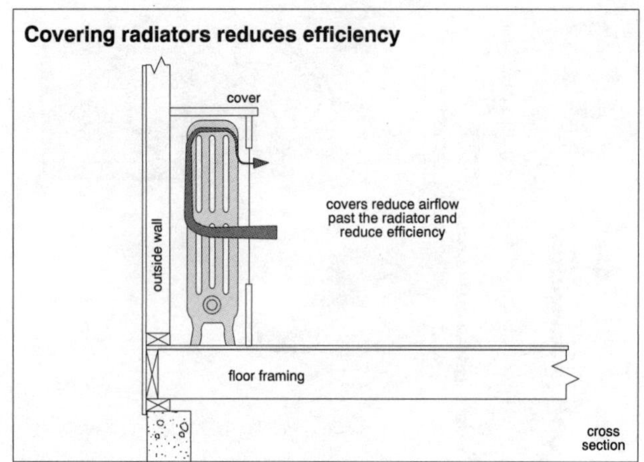

0895

Convector

sheet metal cover

warm air out

cast iron convector (finned tube convectors are also used)

air is heated as it passes by convector

outside wall

cool air in

floor framing

cross-section

0896

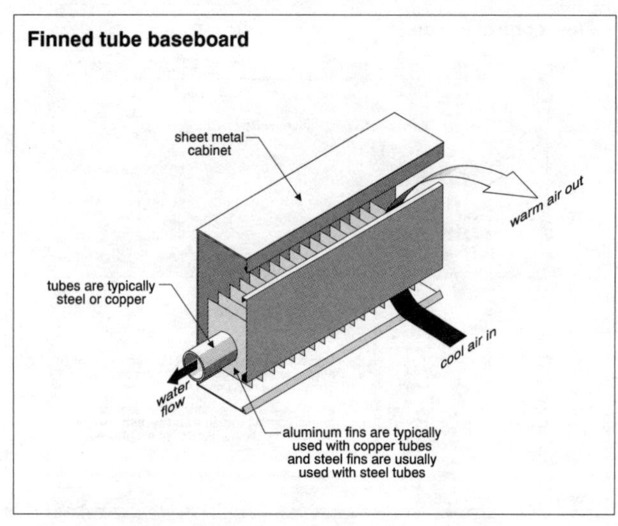

0897

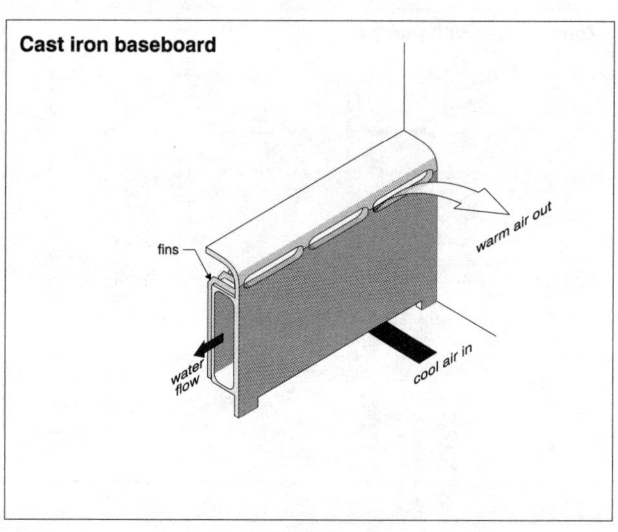

0898

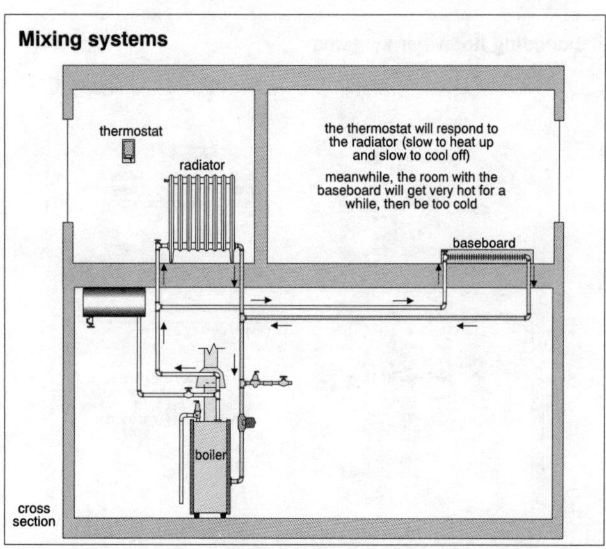

0899

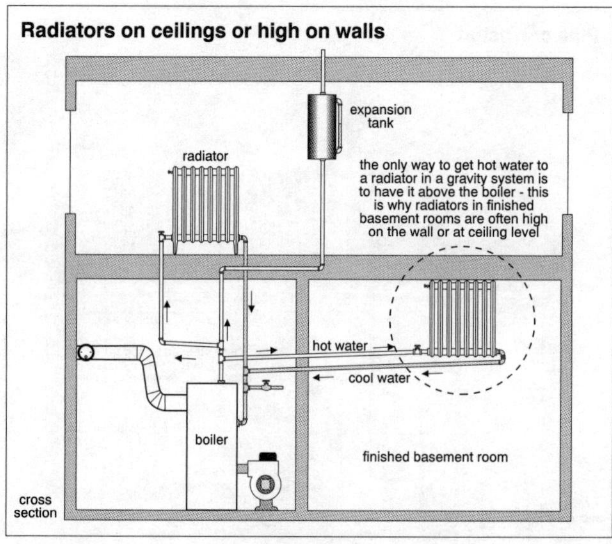

0900

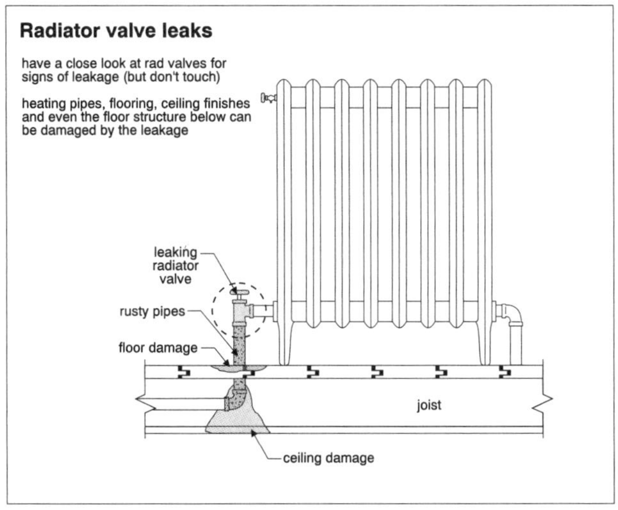

0901

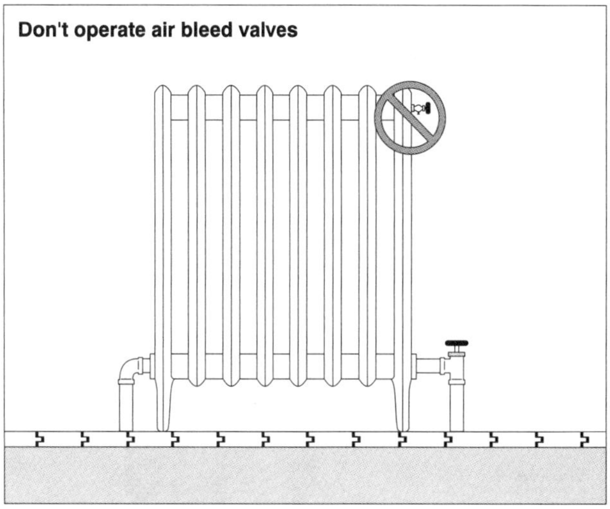

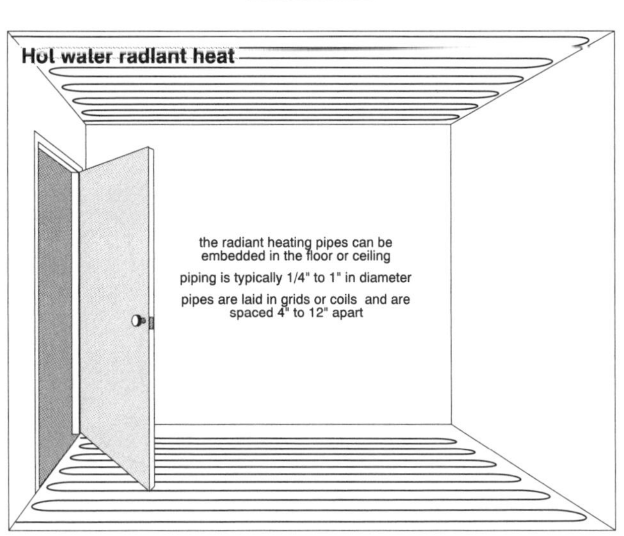

0903

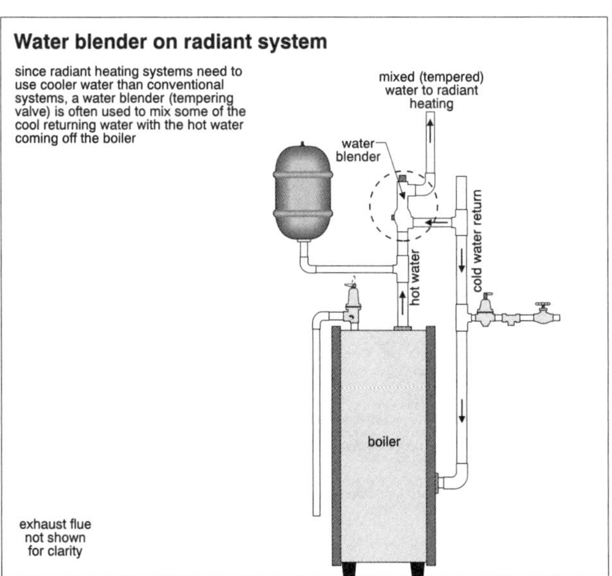

0905

Don't operate air bleed valves

0902

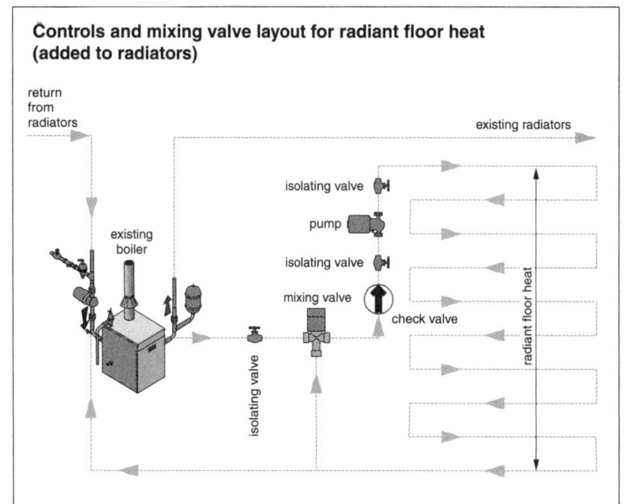

0904

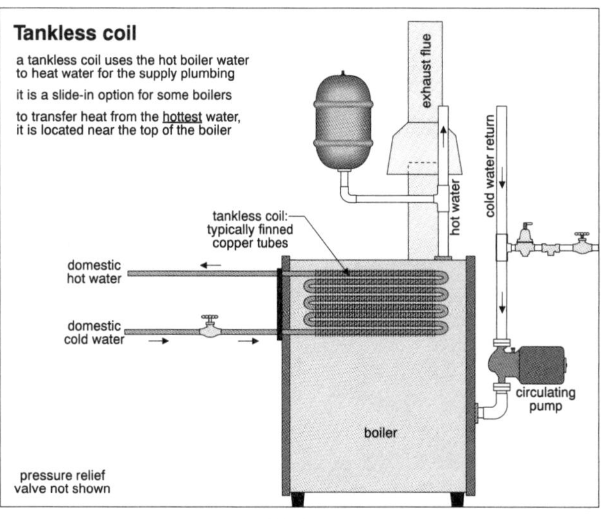

0906

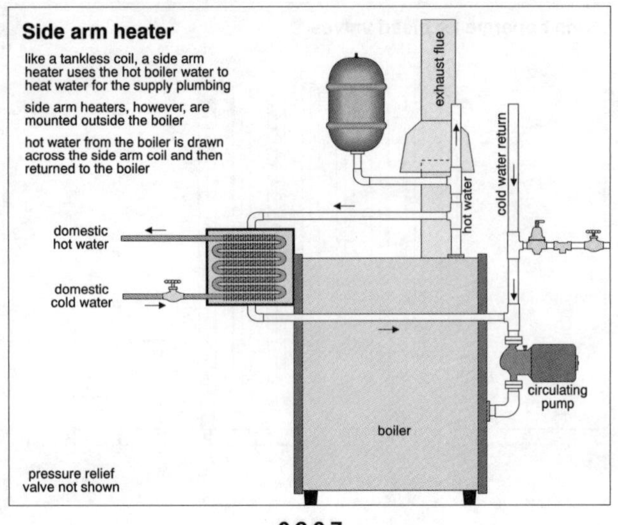

0907

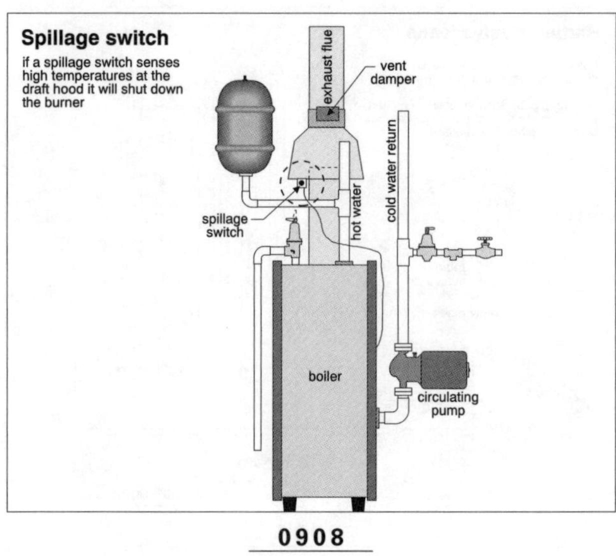

0908

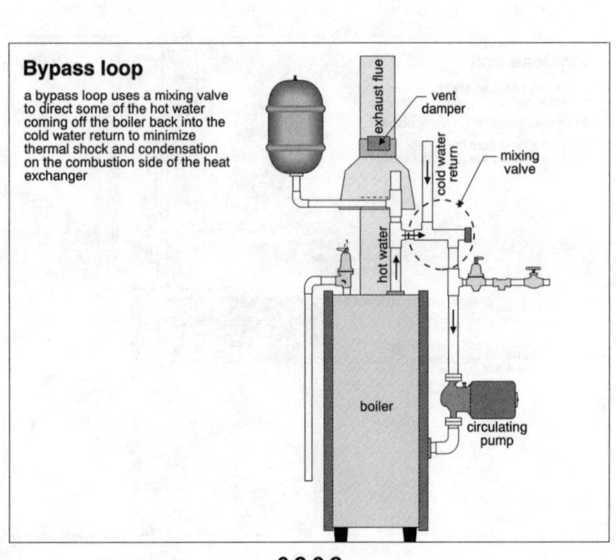

0909

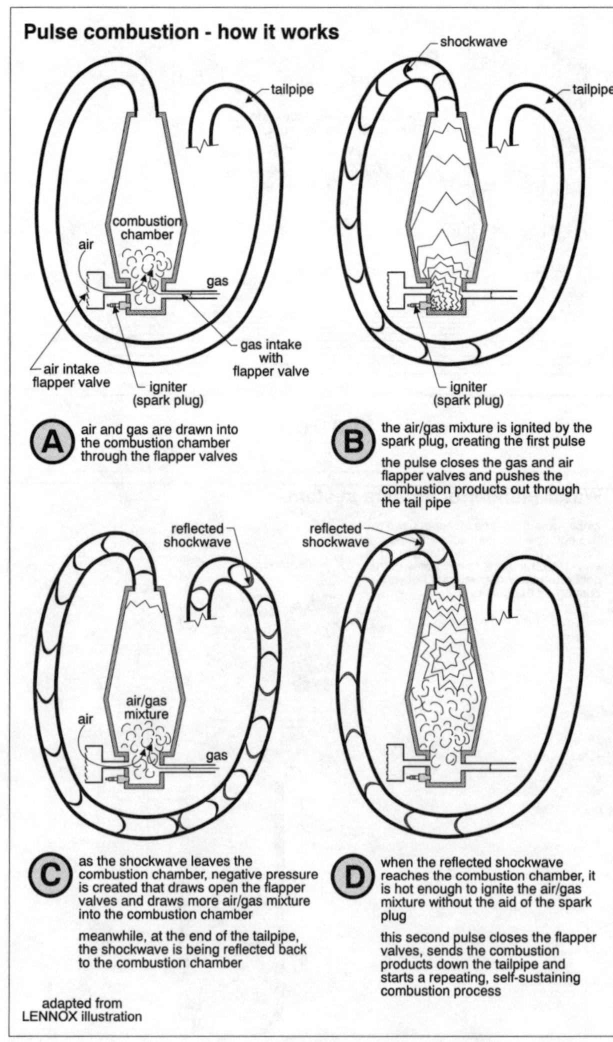

0910

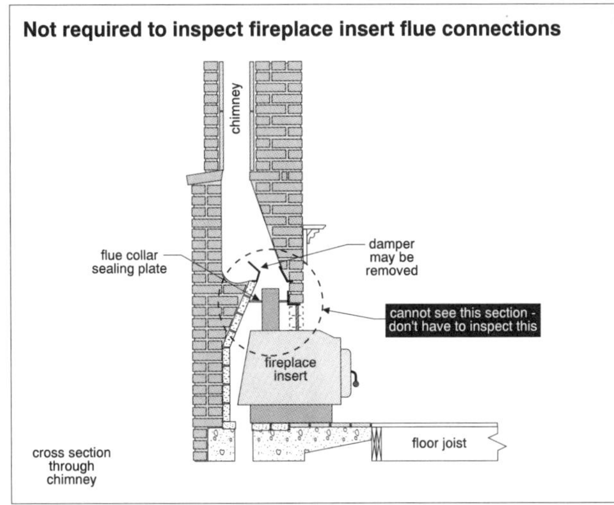

0950

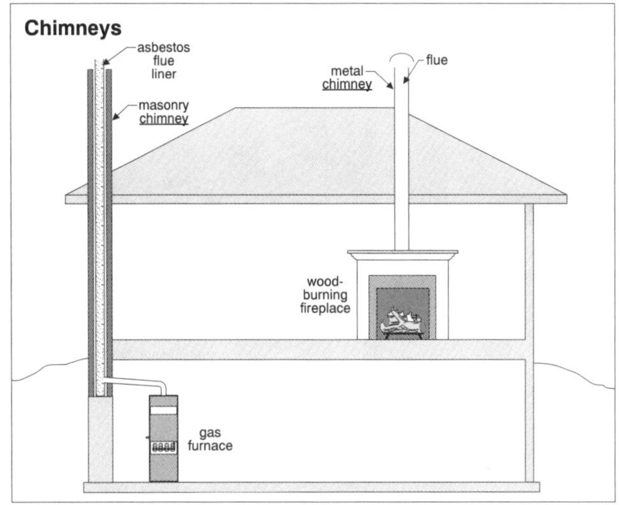

0951

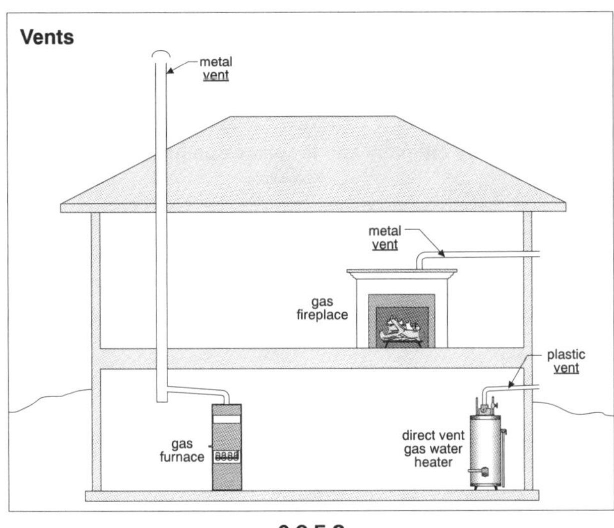

0952

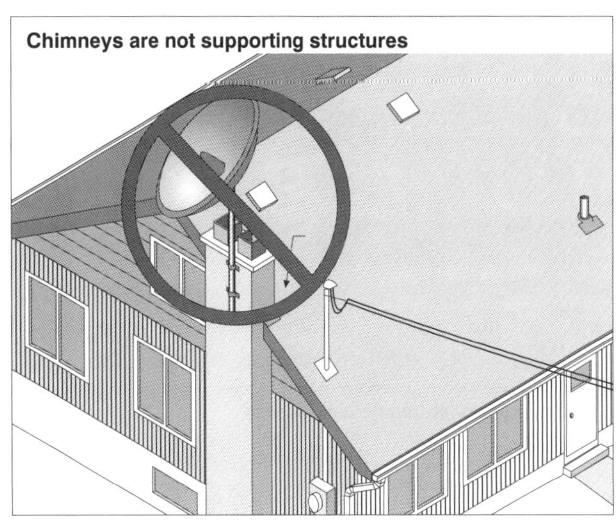

0953

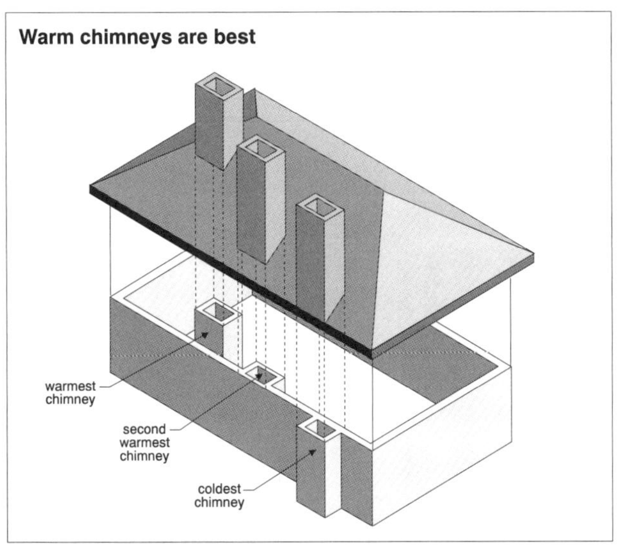

0954

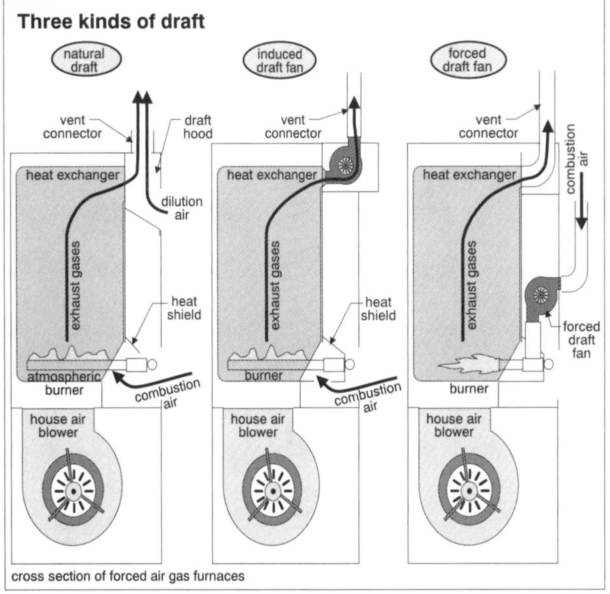

0955

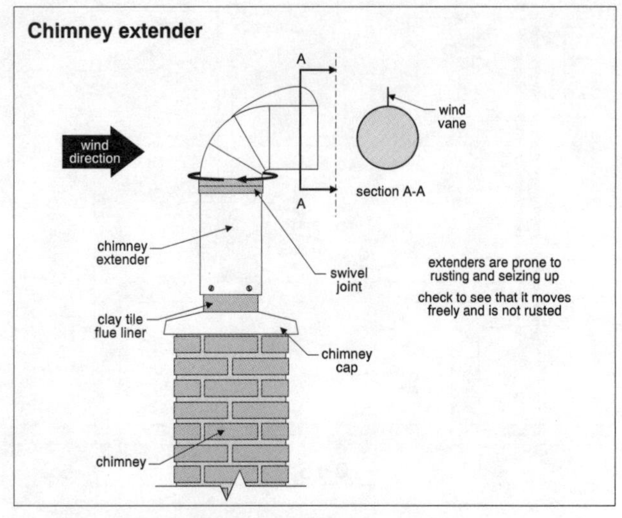

0956

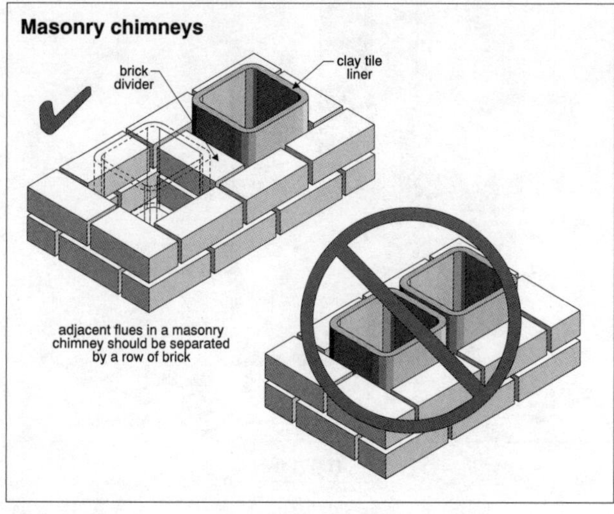

0957

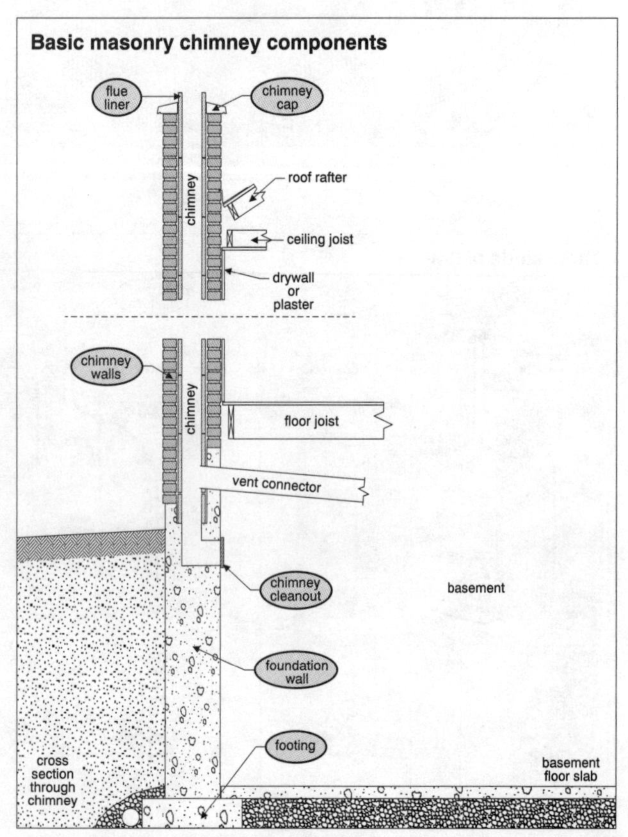

0958

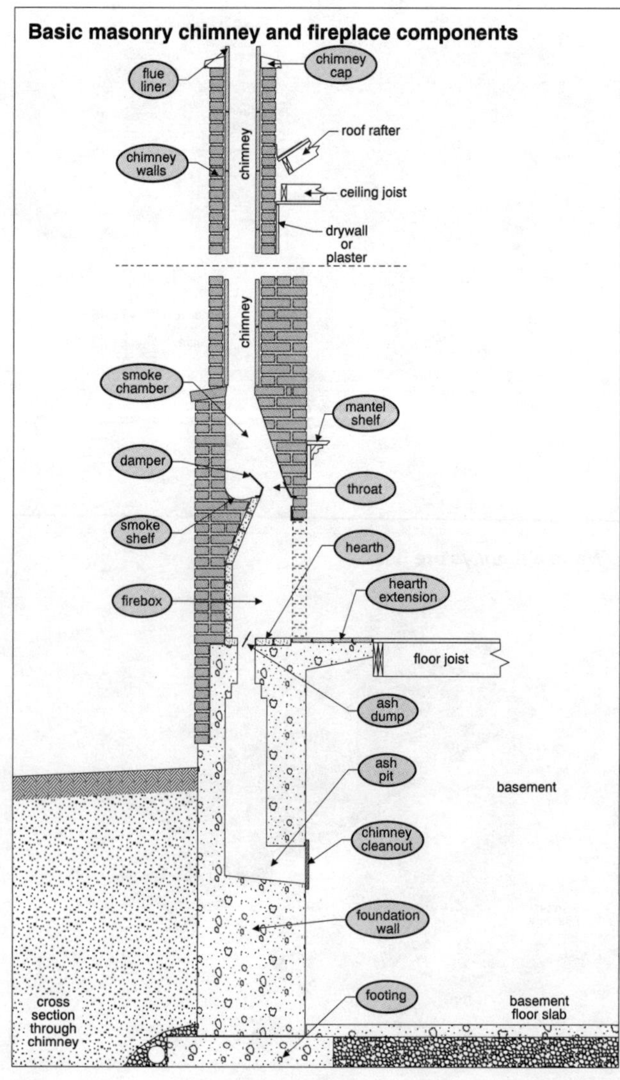

0959

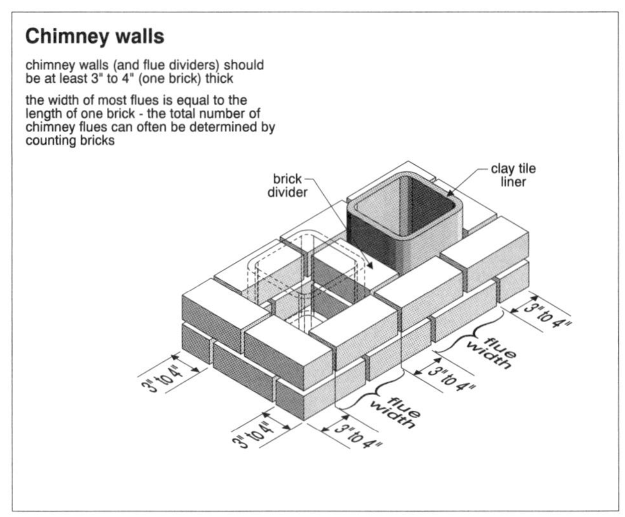

0960

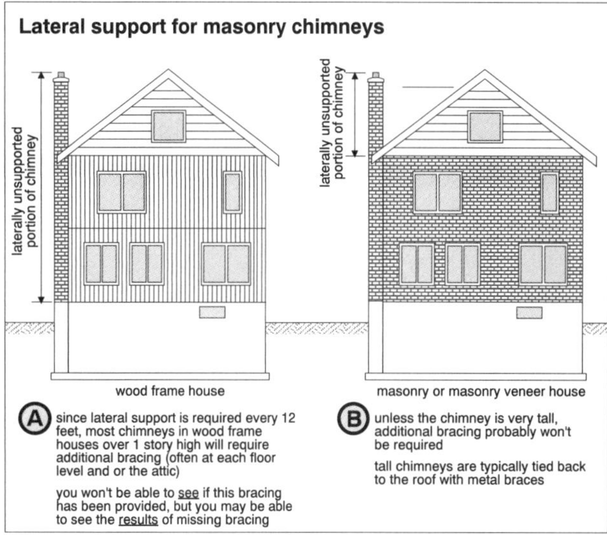

0961

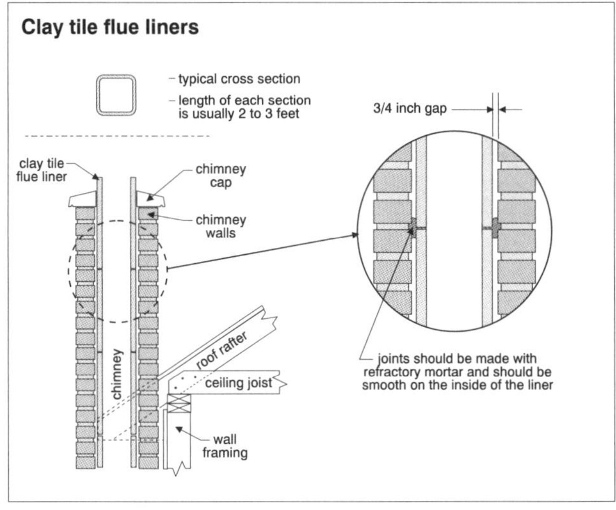

0962

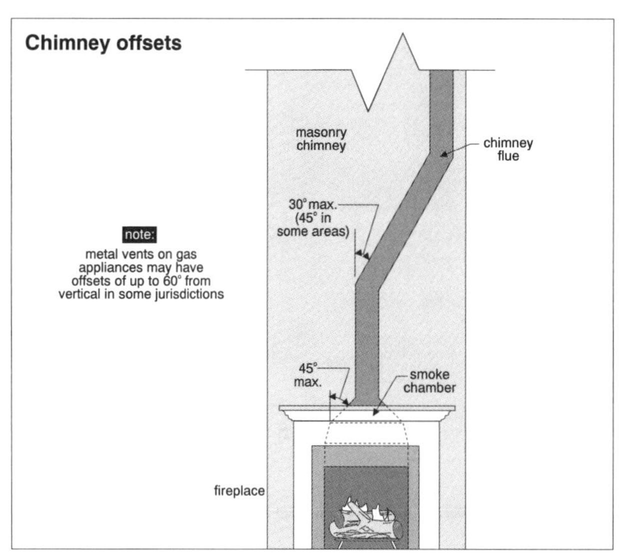

0963

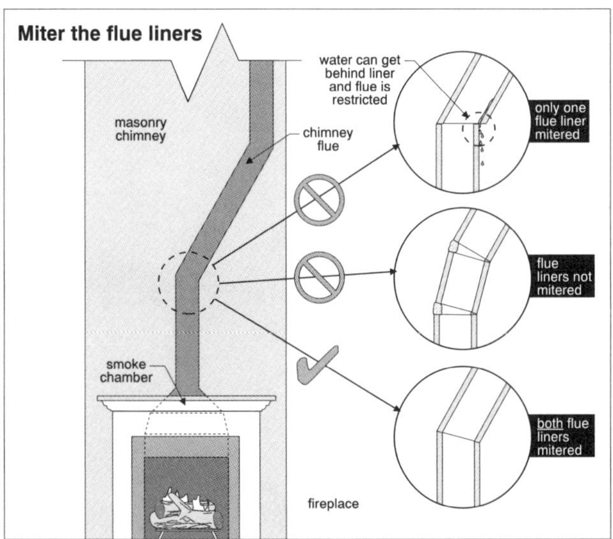

0964

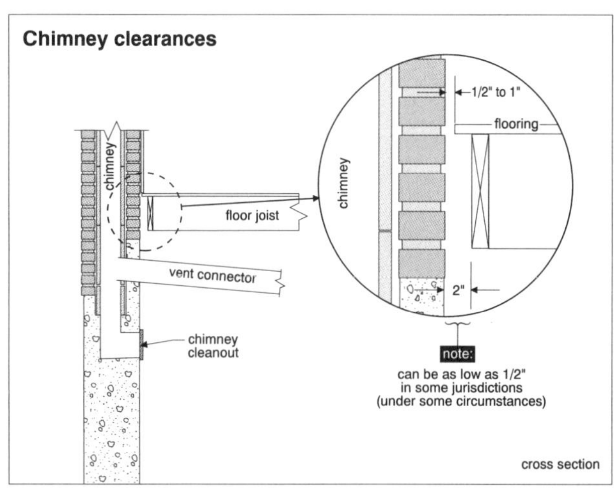

0965

Chimneys supporting framing members

floor joist
12" of solid masonry
chimney
floor joist
chimney
smoke chamber
firebox
fireplace
framing members should not rest in or on chimneys unless there is at least 12 inches of solid masonry between the wood framing member and the flue
floor joist
cross section through chimney

0966

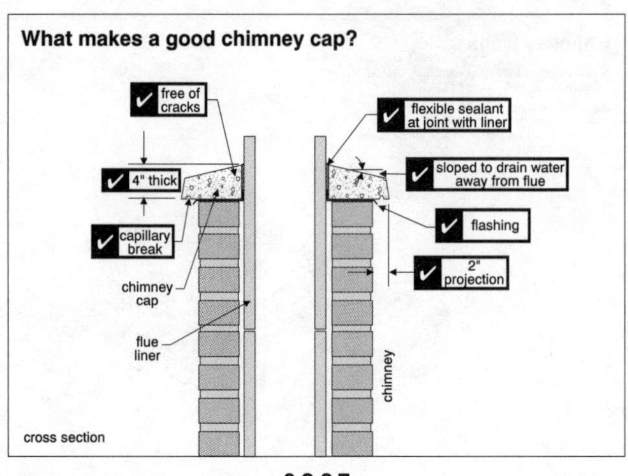

0967

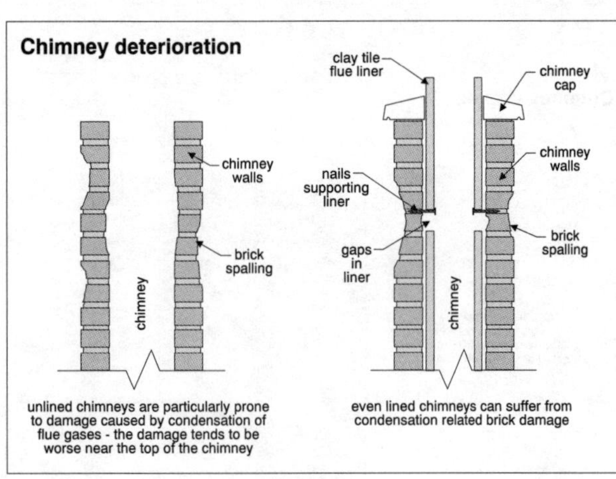

0968

Removing abandoned chimneys

new shingles
roof rafter
fill in roof supports and add new sheathing
attic
ceiling joist
attic
wall
wall
cross section

0969

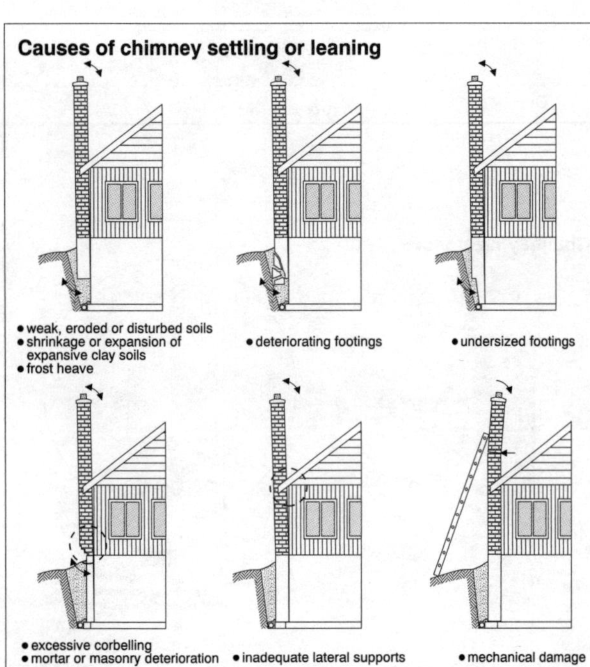

0970

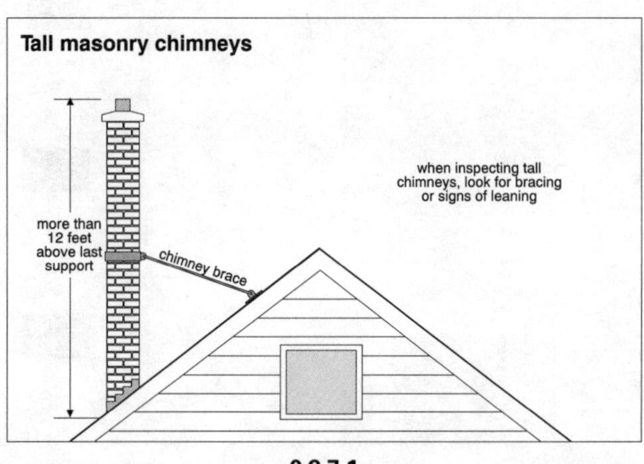

0971

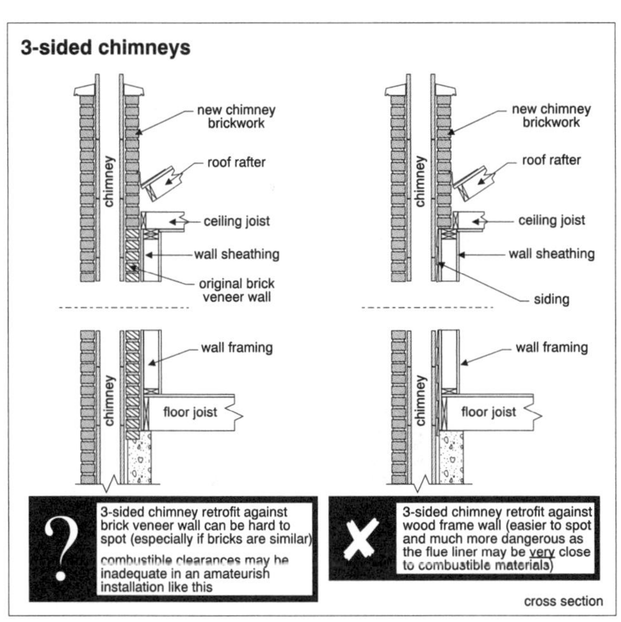

0972

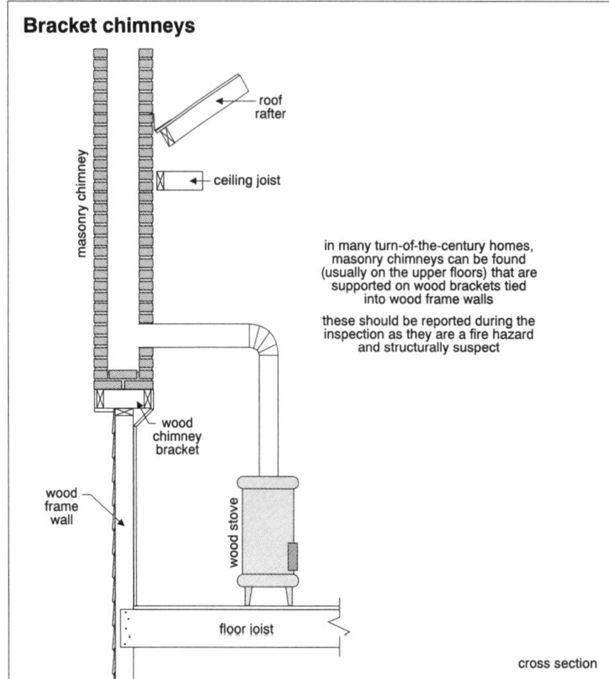

0973

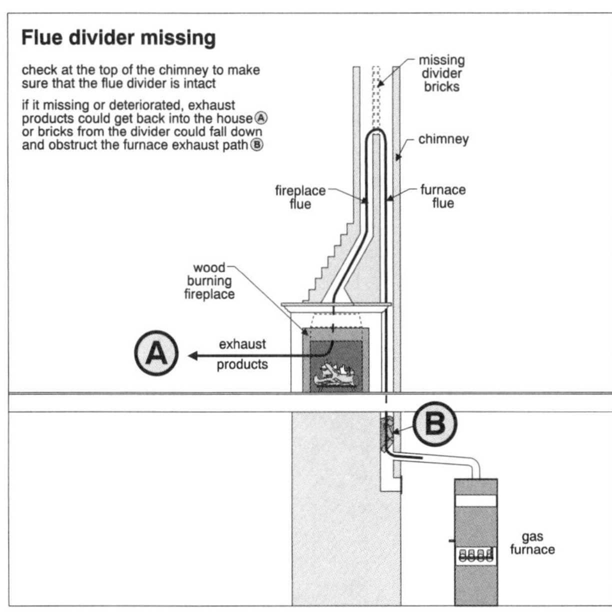

0974

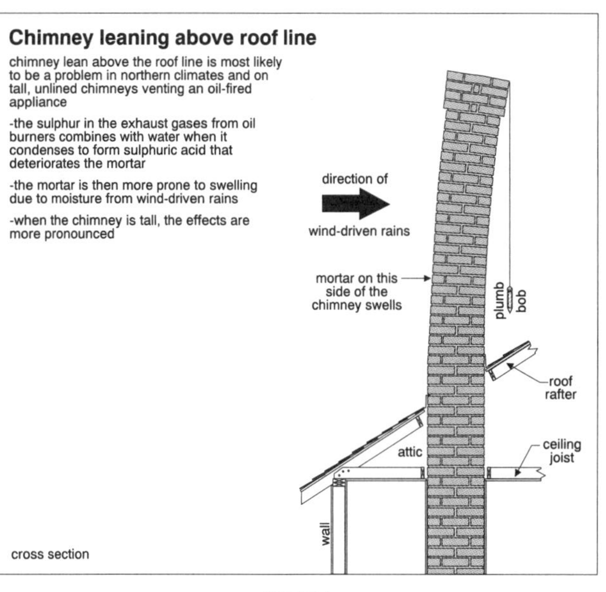

0975

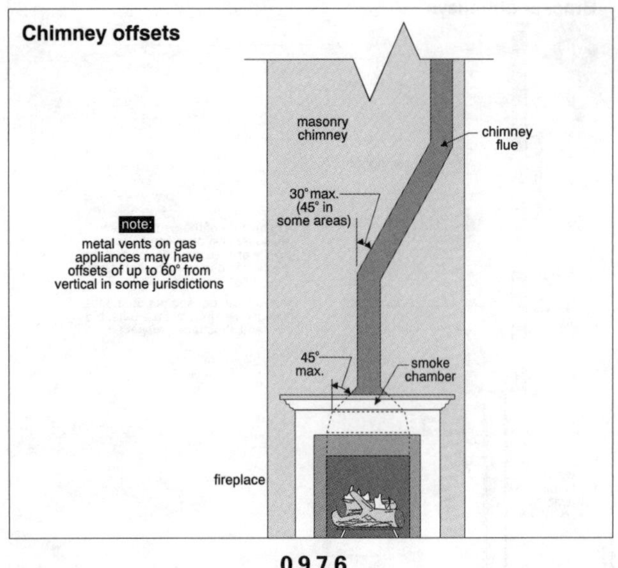

0976

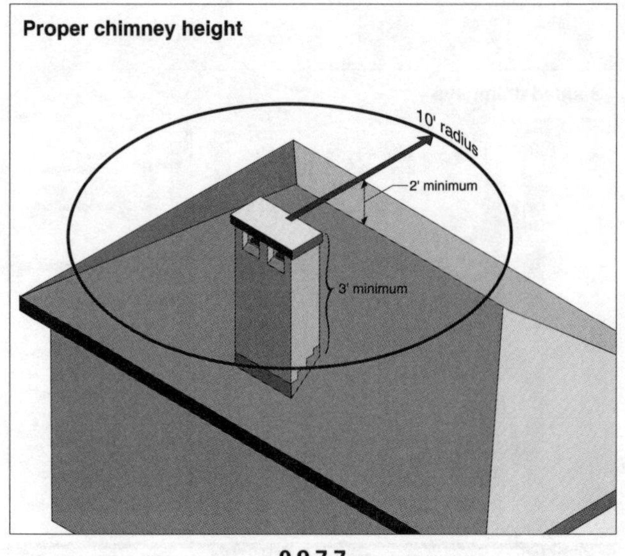

0977

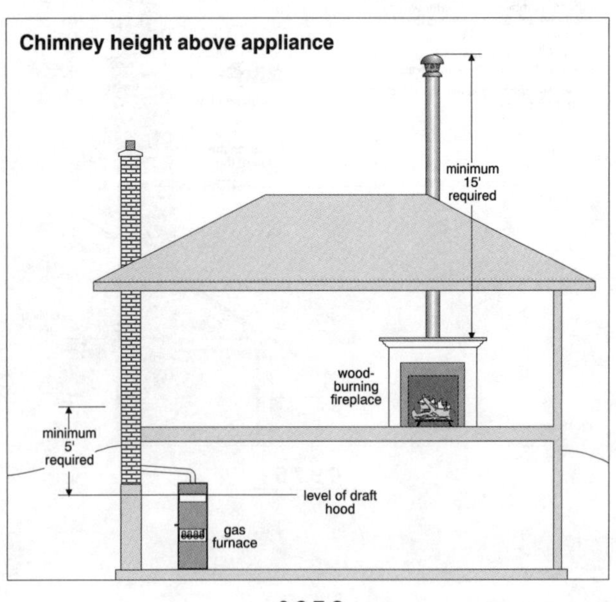

0978

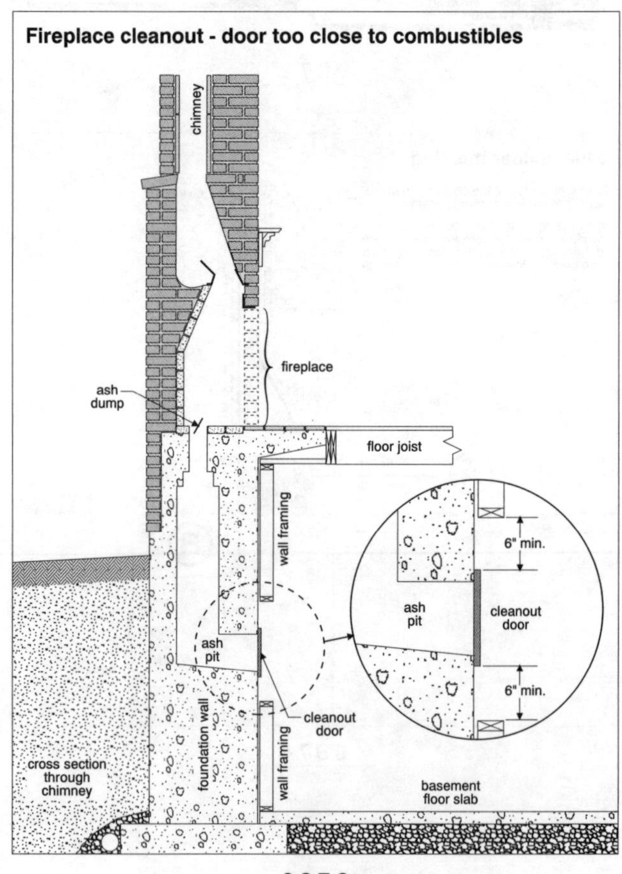

0979

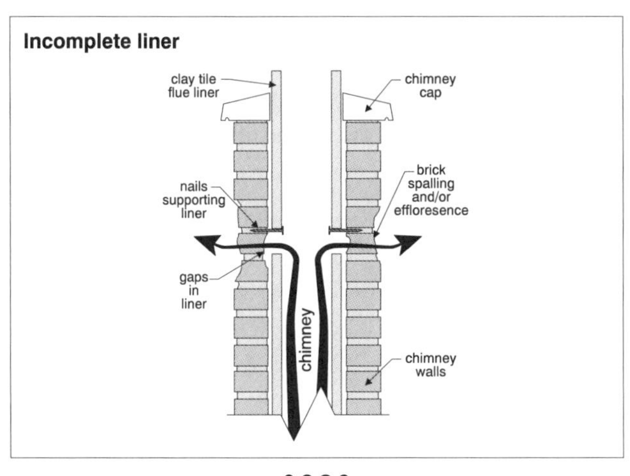

0980

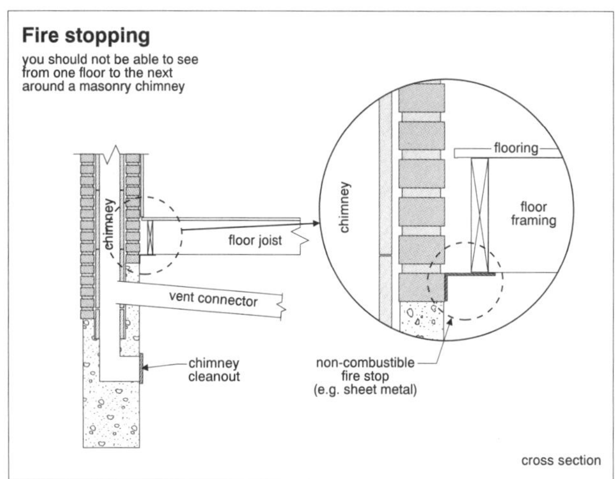

0981

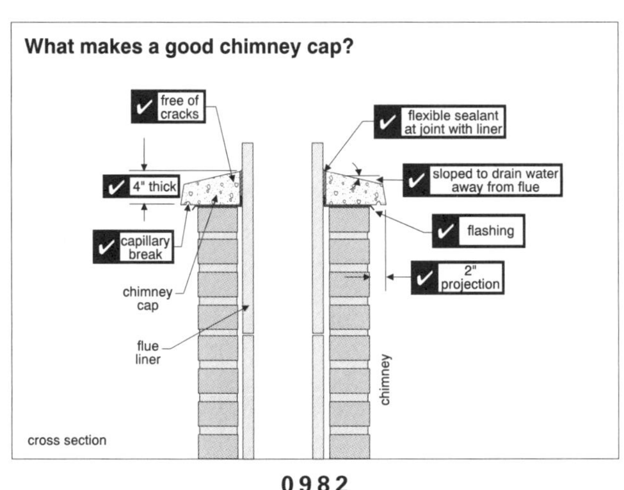

0982

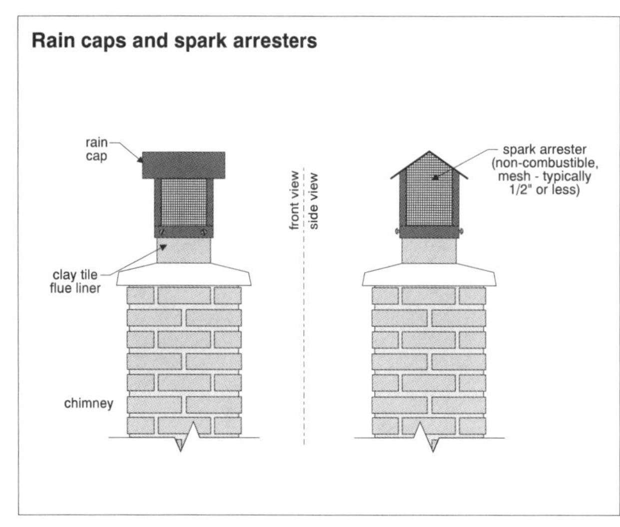

0983

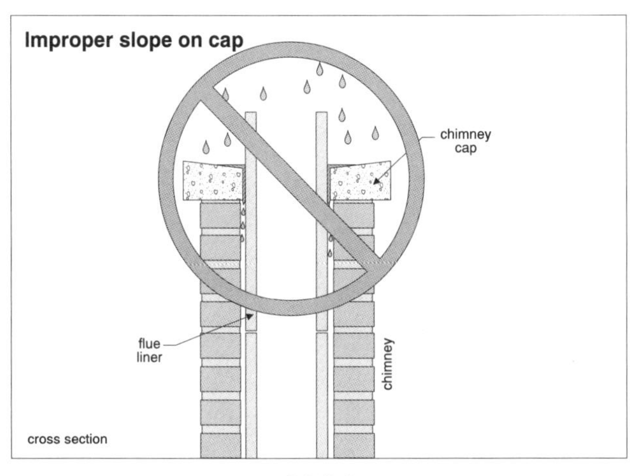

0984

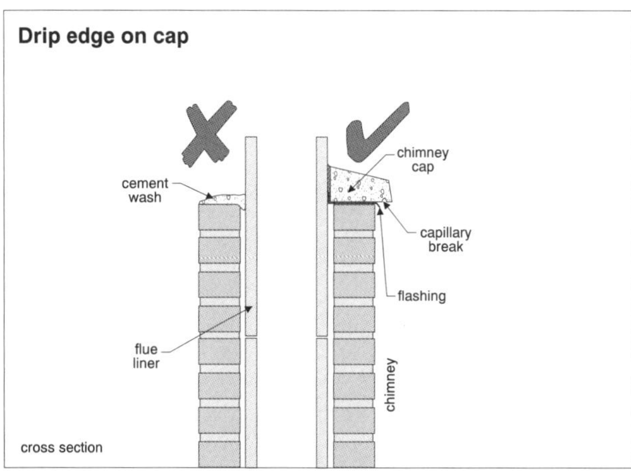

0985

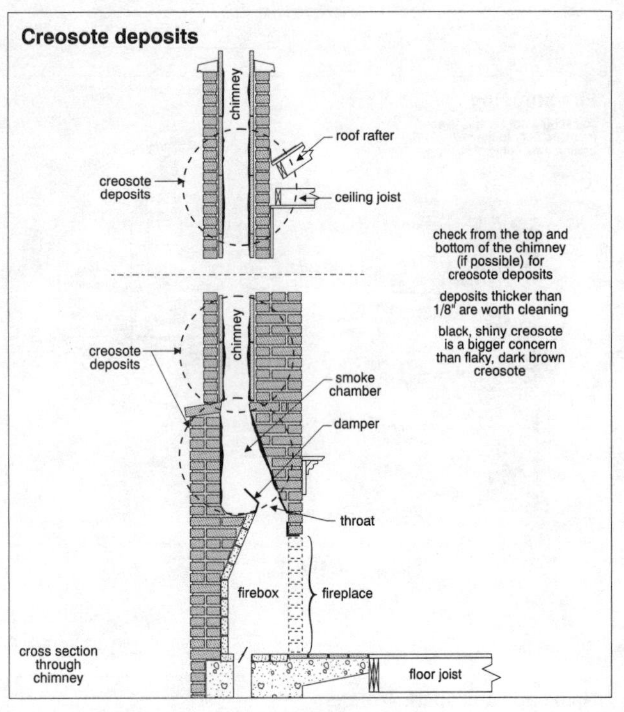

0986

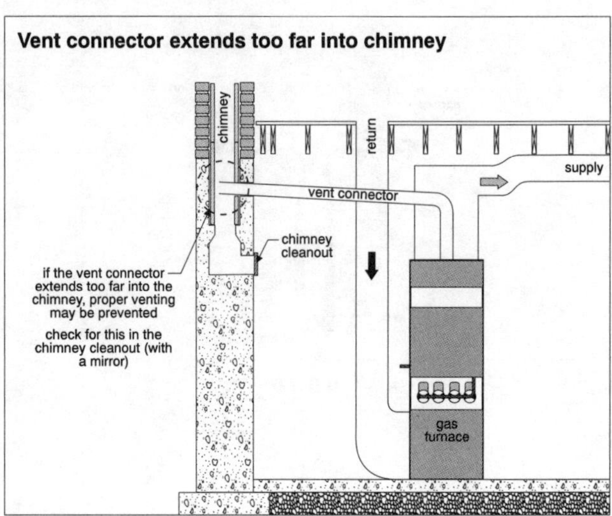

0987

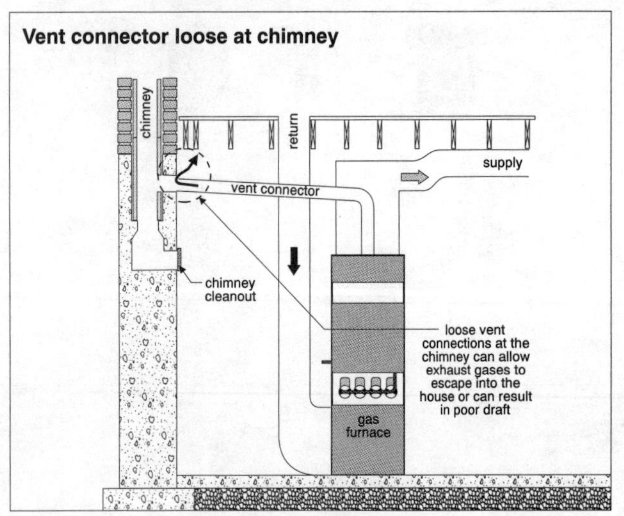

0988

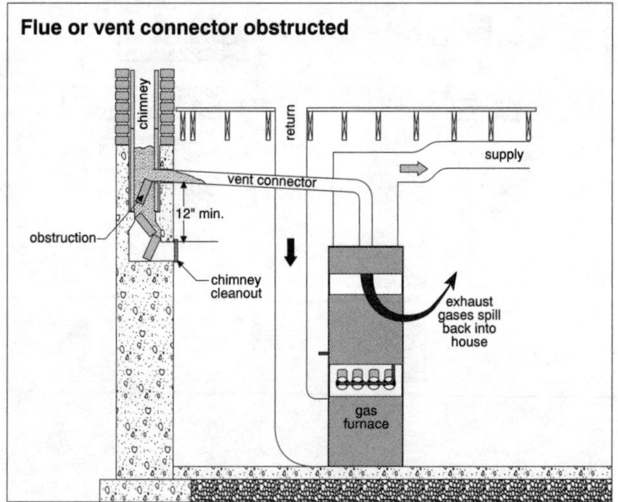

0989

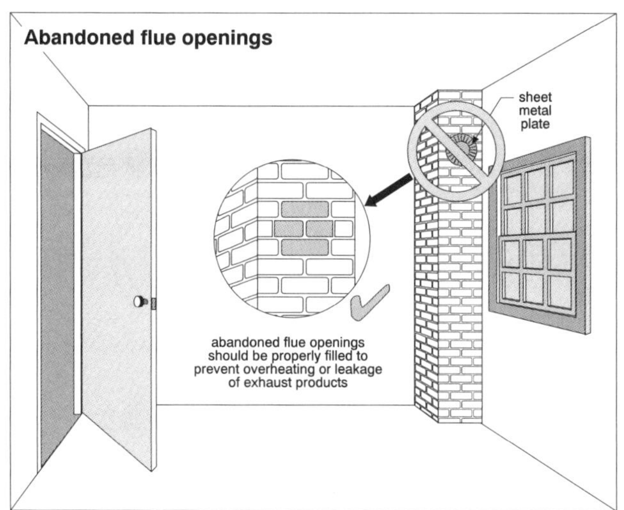

0990

Chimney extender

wind direction
A
A
wind vane
section A-A
chimney extender
swivel joint
clay tile flue liner
chimney cap
chimney
extenders are prone to rusting and seizing up
check to see that it moves freely and is not rusted

0991

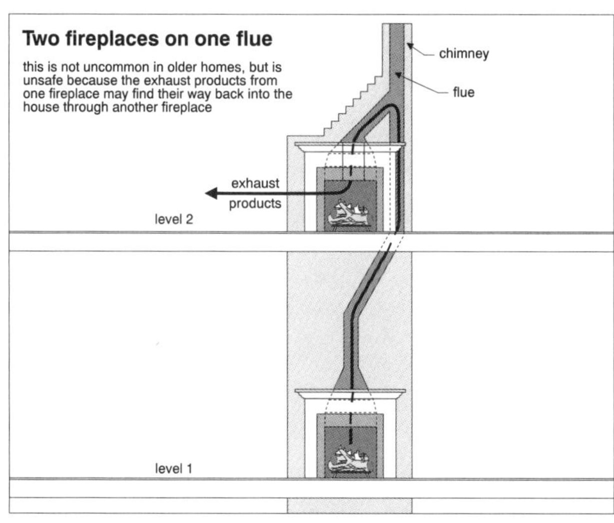

0992

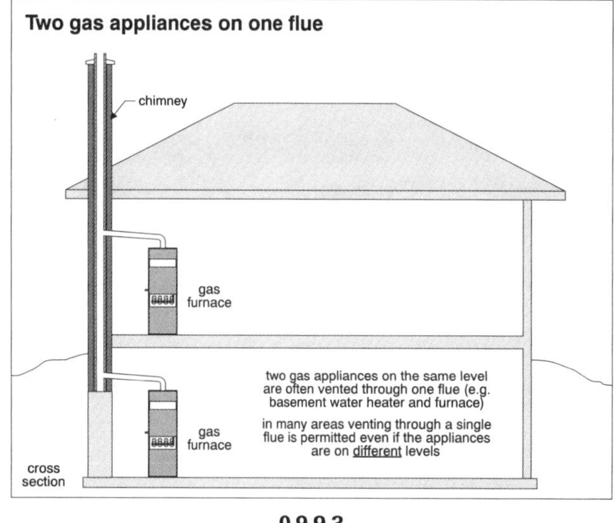

0993

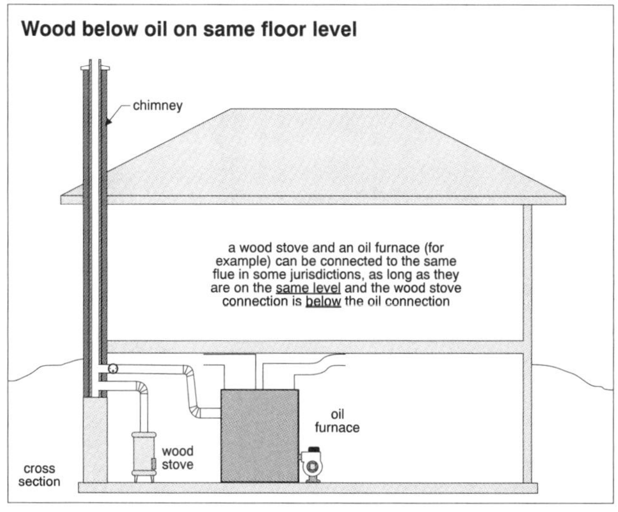

0994

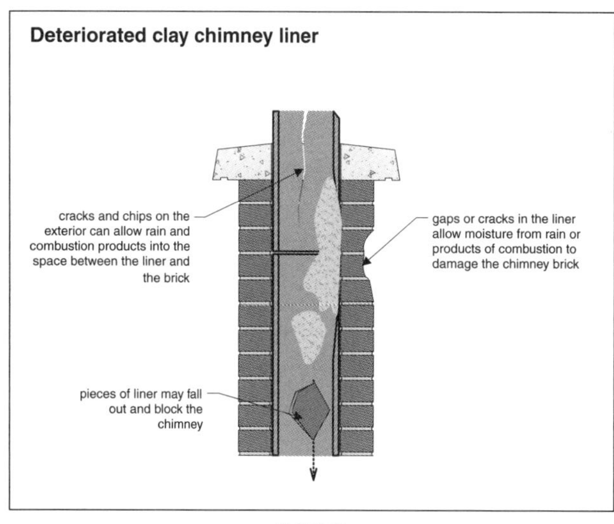

0995

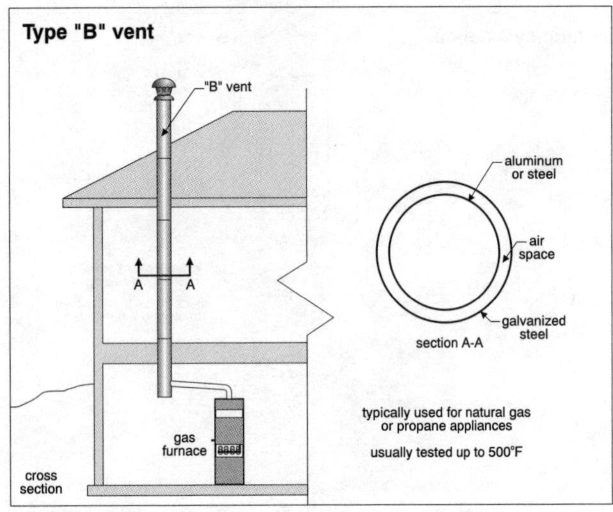

0996

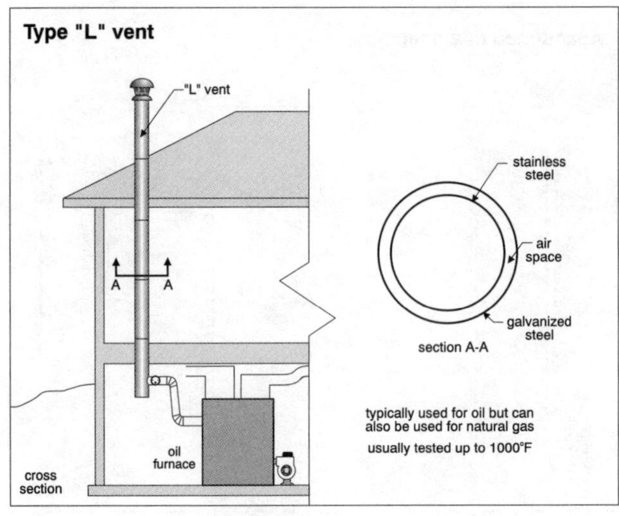

0997

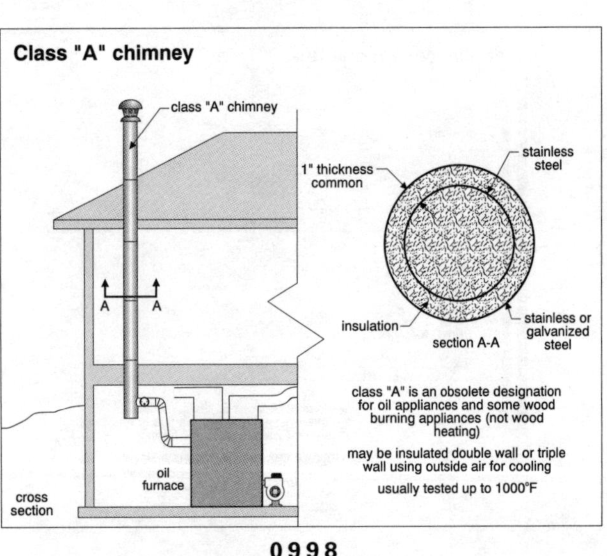

0998

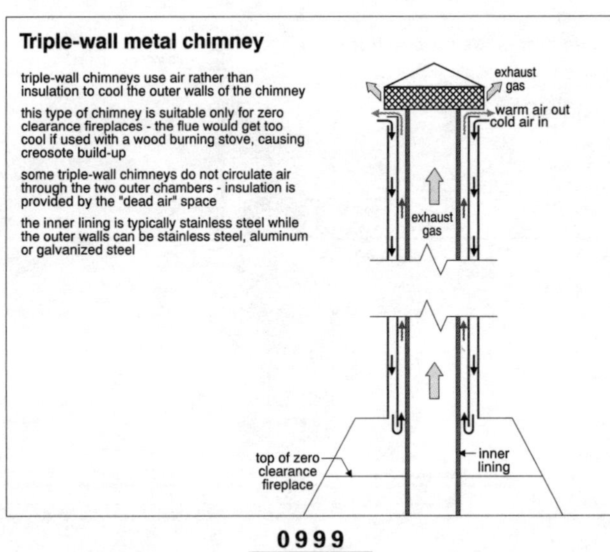

0999

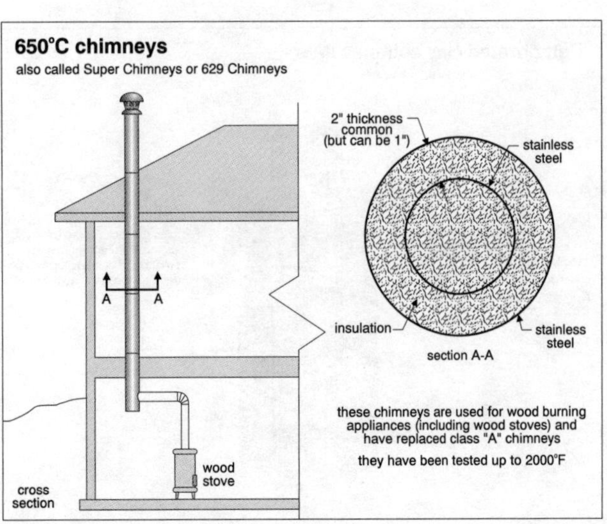

1000

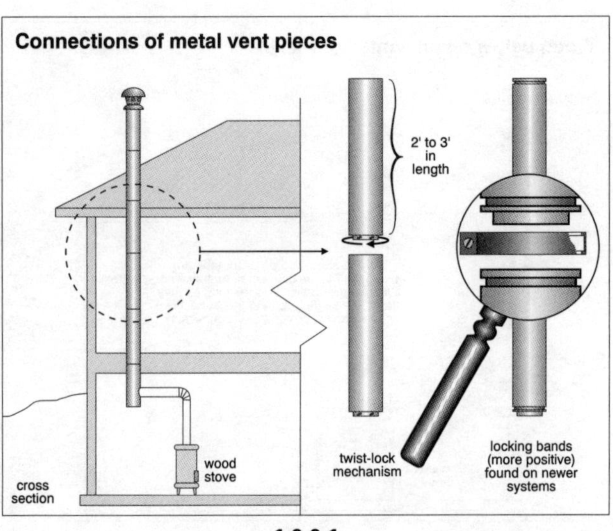

1001

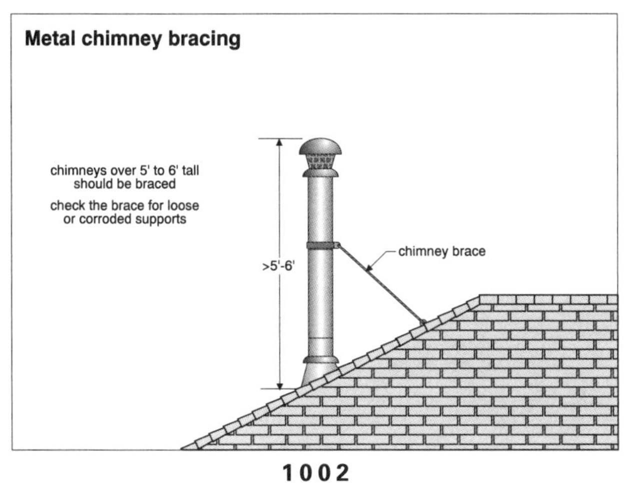

1002

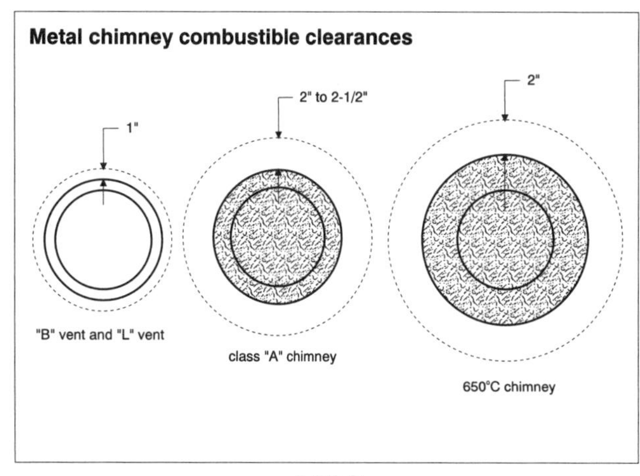

1003

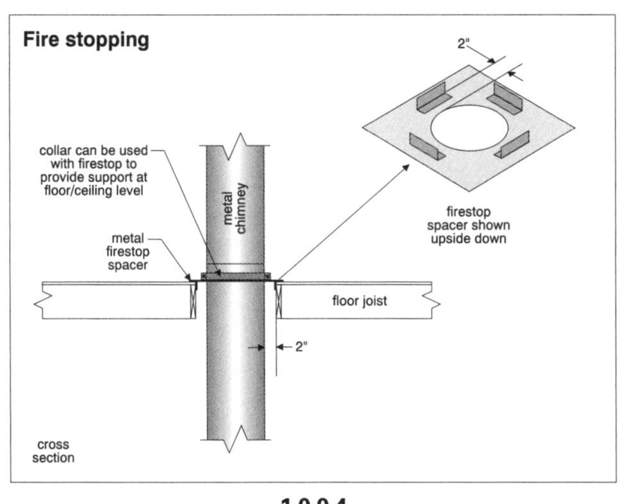

1004

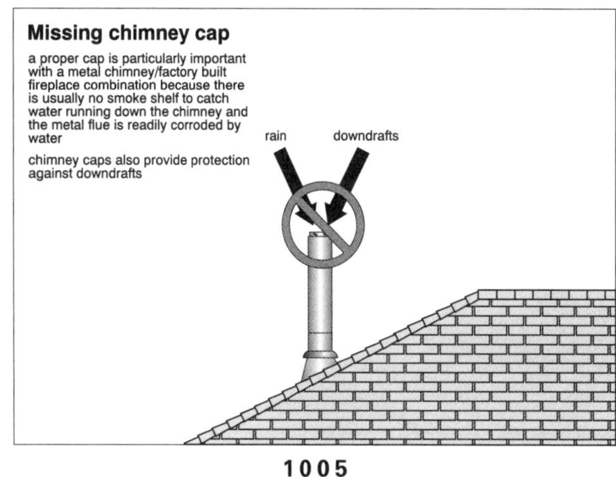

1005

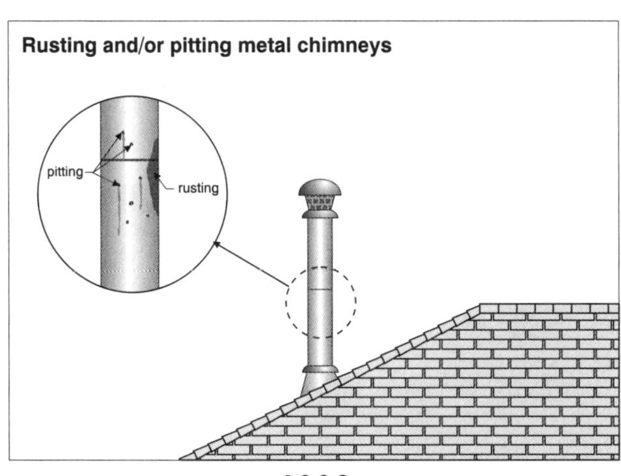

1006

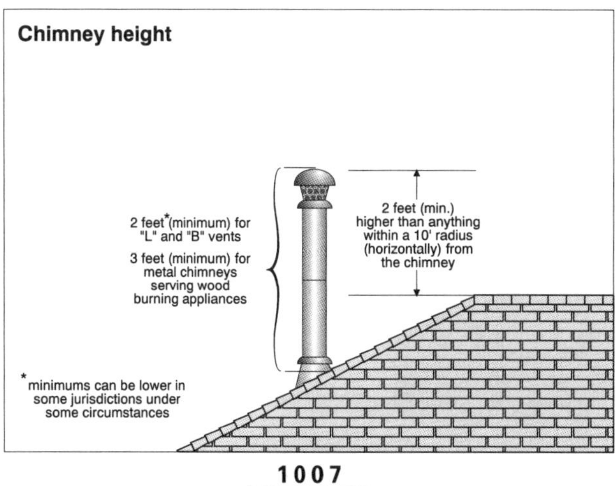

1007

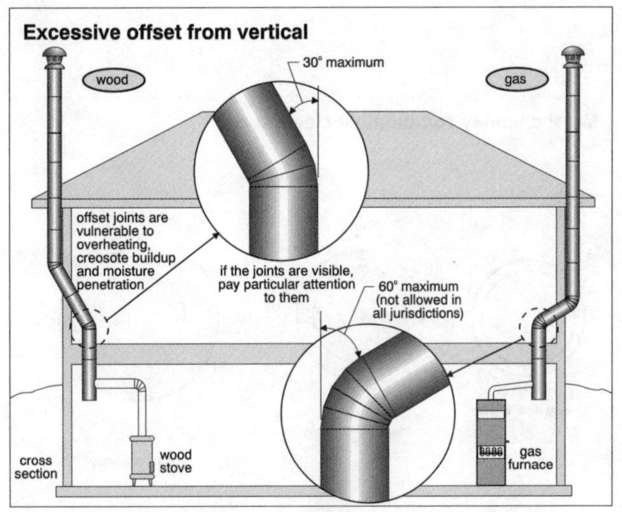

1008

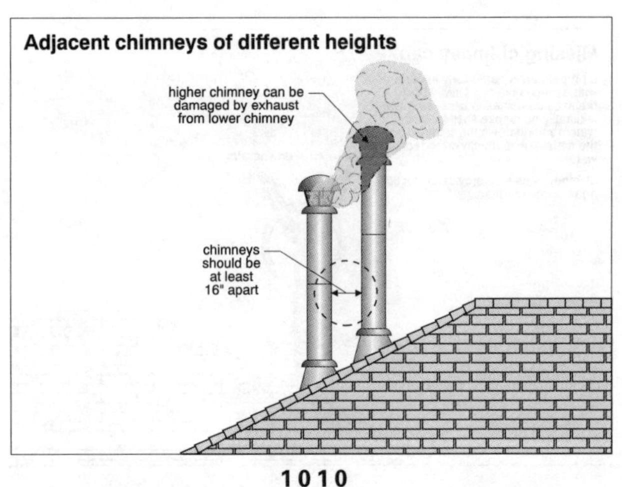

1009

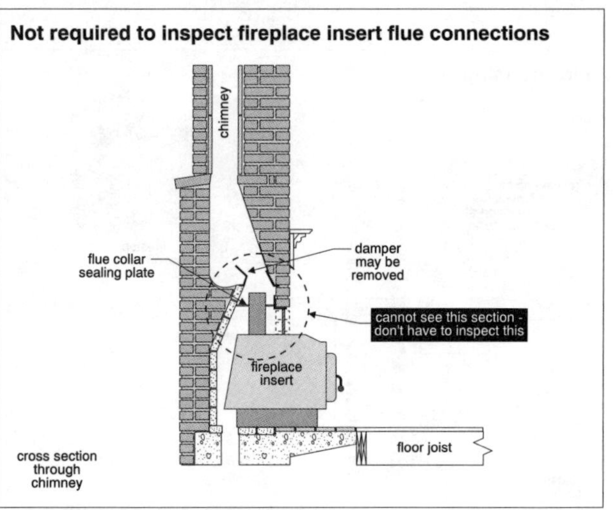

1010

1011

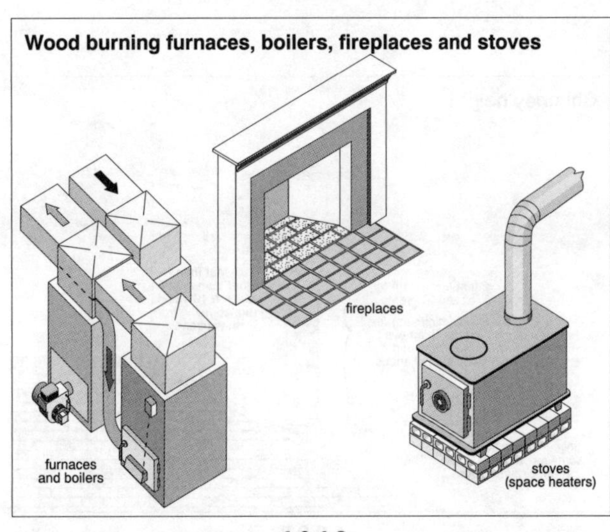

1012

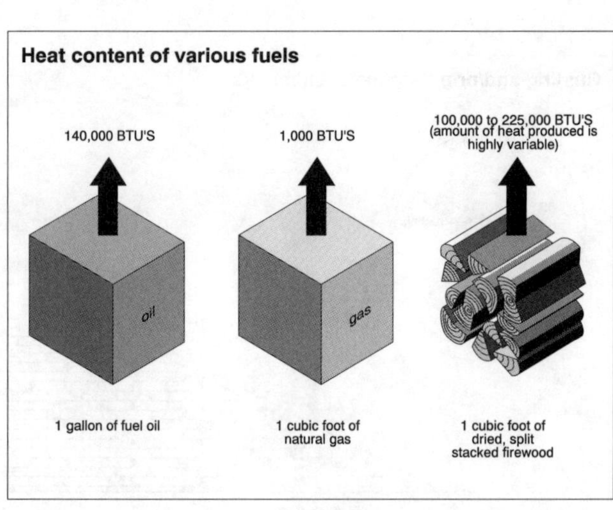

1013

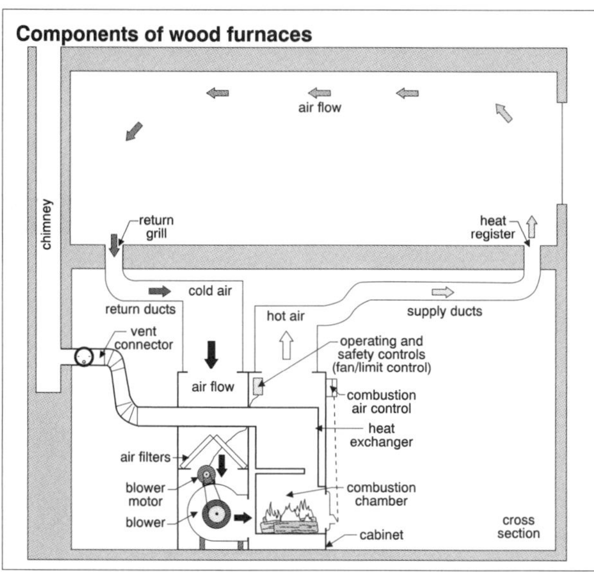

1014

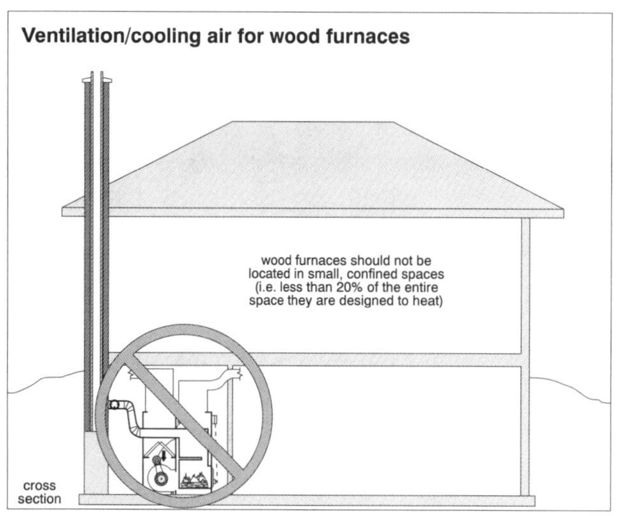

1015

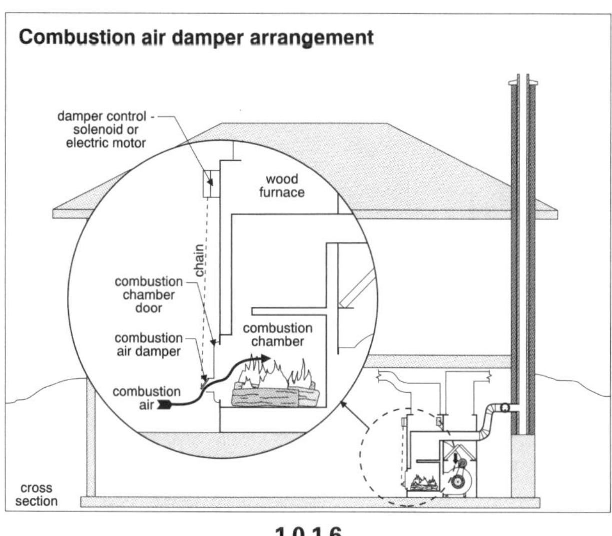

1016

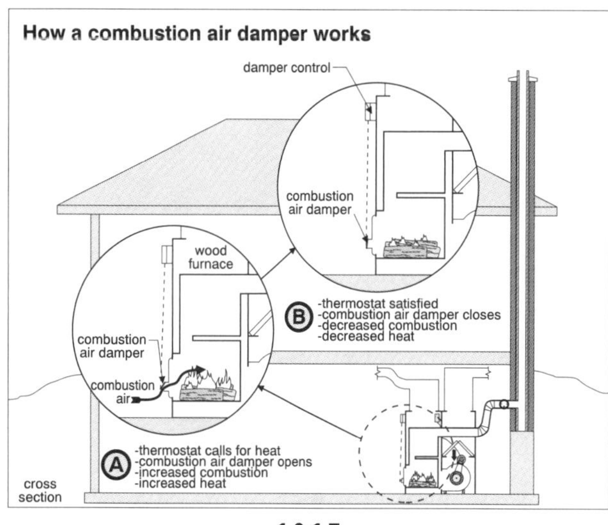

1017

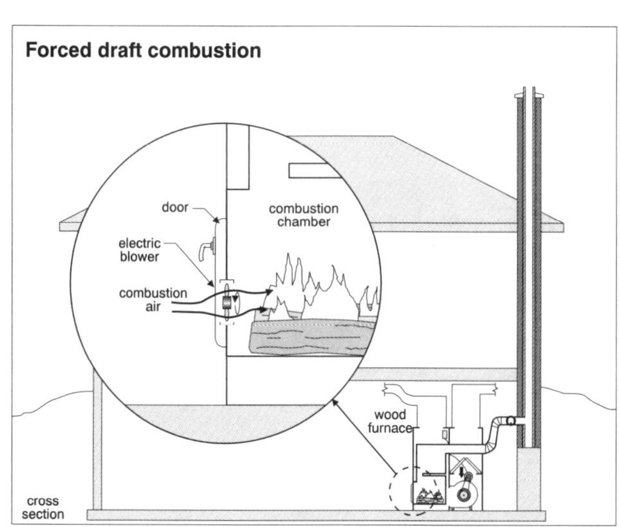

1018

Combustion chamber (firebox)

cold air

hot air

air flow

operating and safety controls

wood furnace

air filters

combustion chamber

walls of combustion chamber are typically heavy steel plate (1/4" thick)

on older units, the firebox may be lined with brick

blower motor

blower

can be designed to accommodate 16", 24" or 48" pieces of wood

cross section

1019

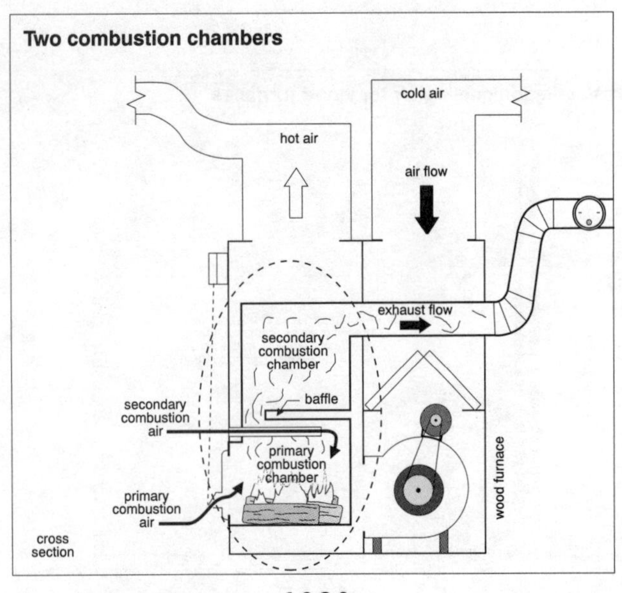

1020

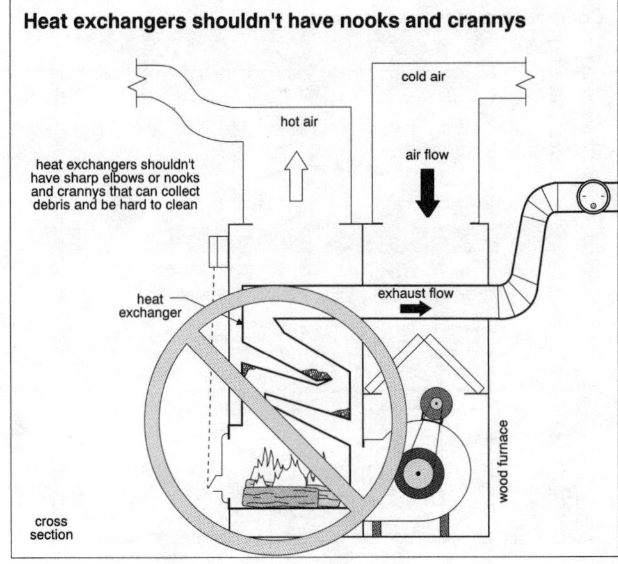

1021

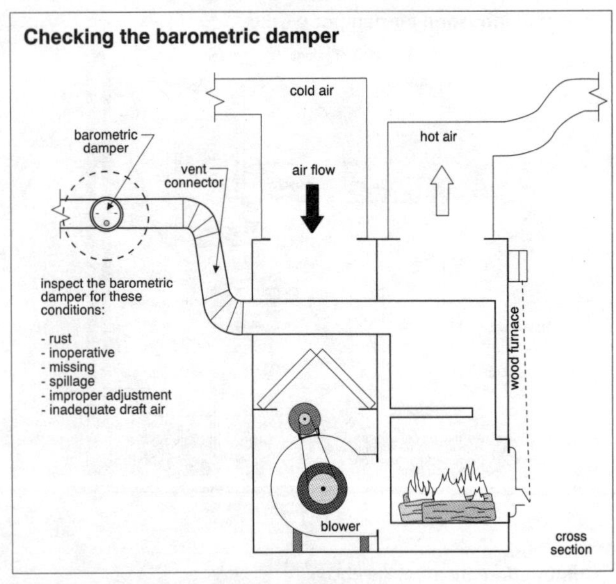

1022

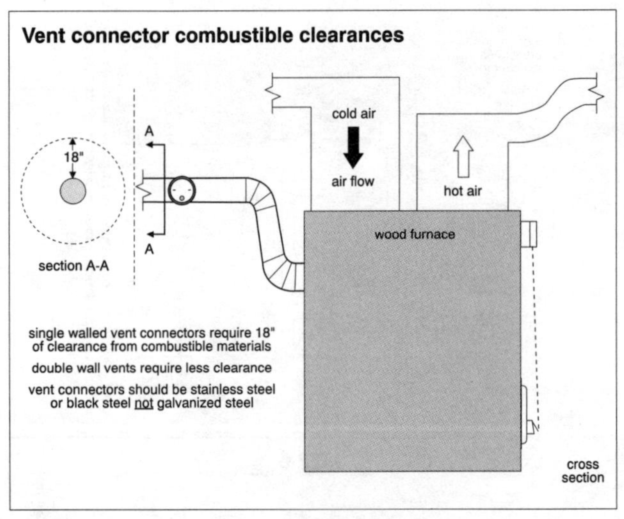

1023

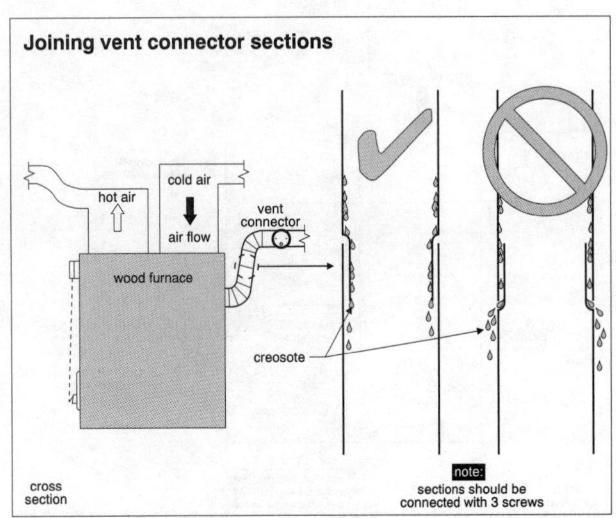

1024

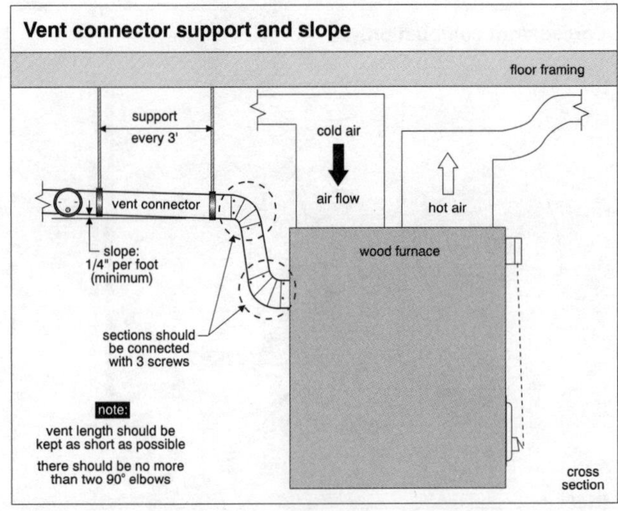

1025

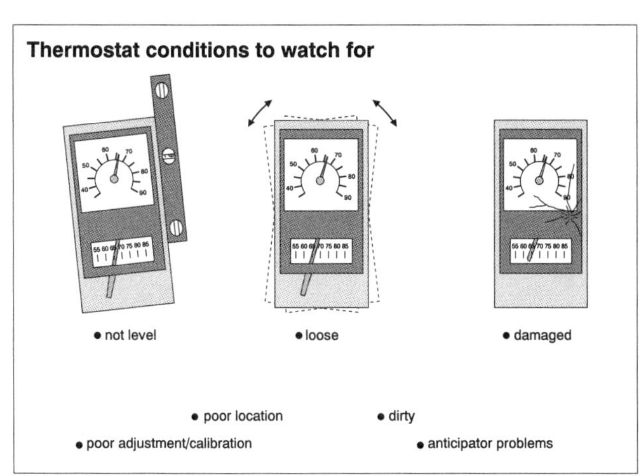

1026

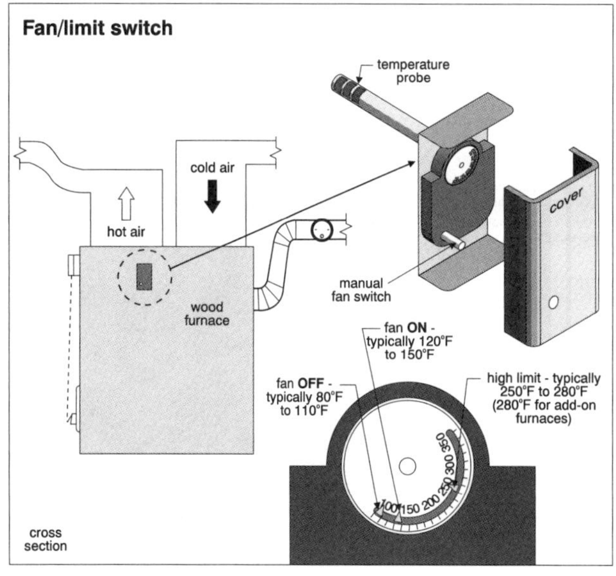

1027

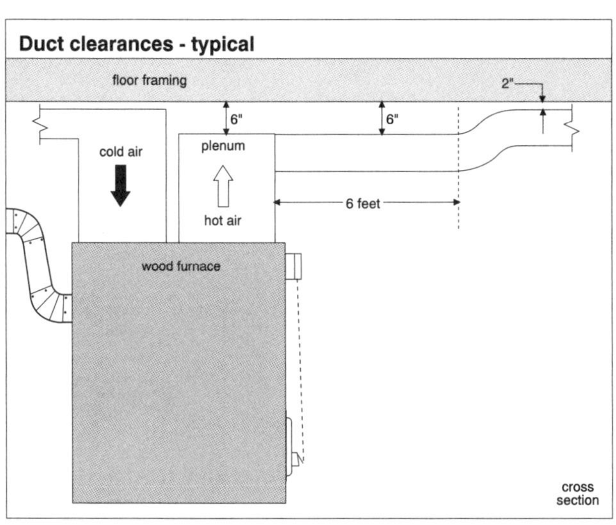

1028

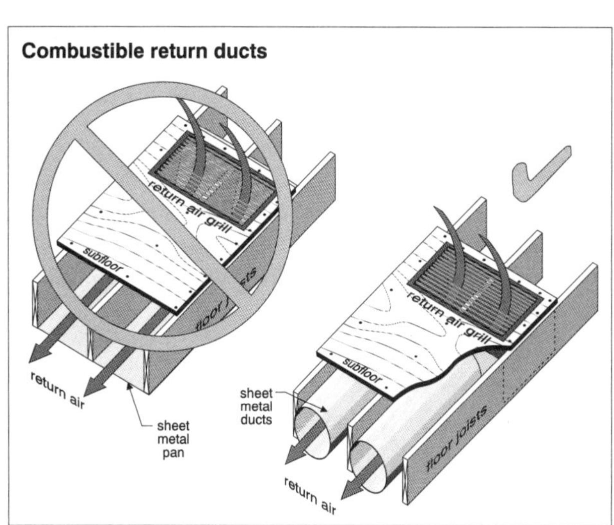

1029

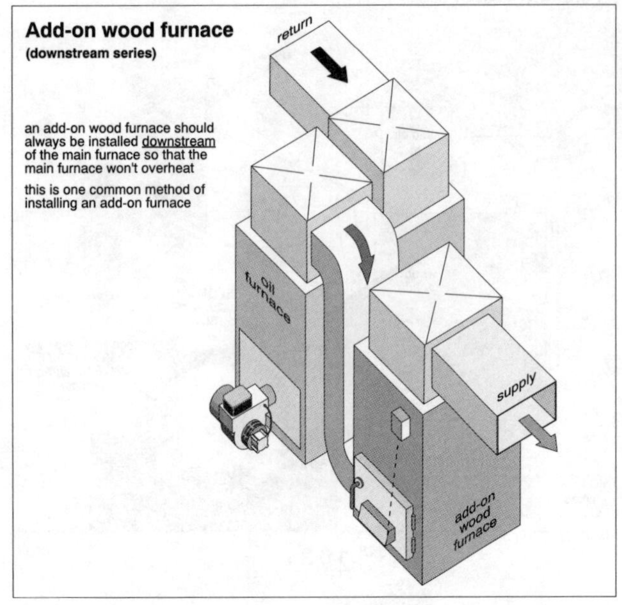

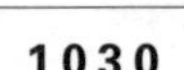
1030

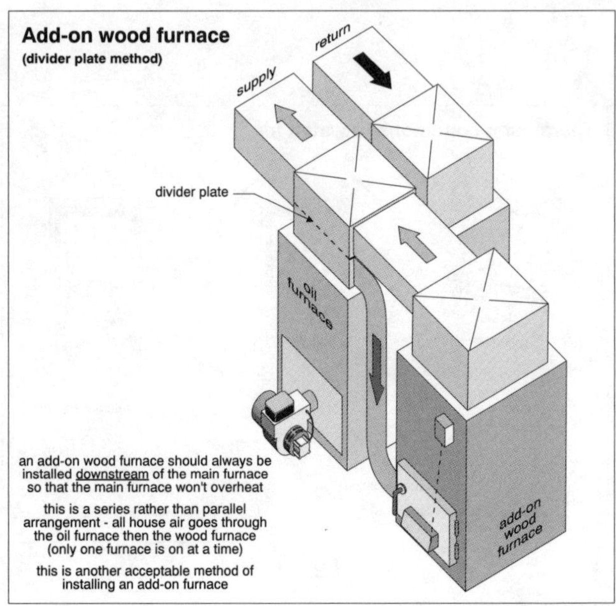

1031

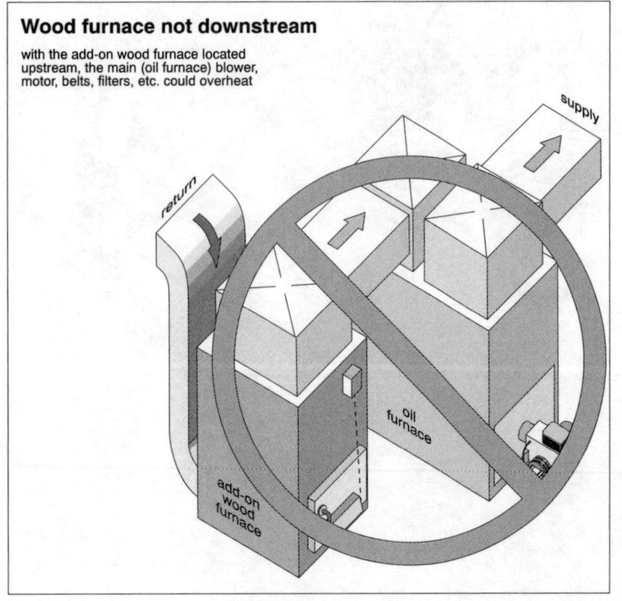

1032

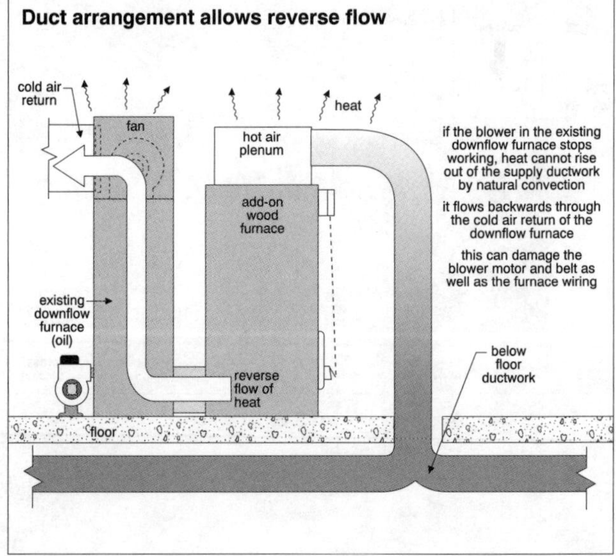

1033

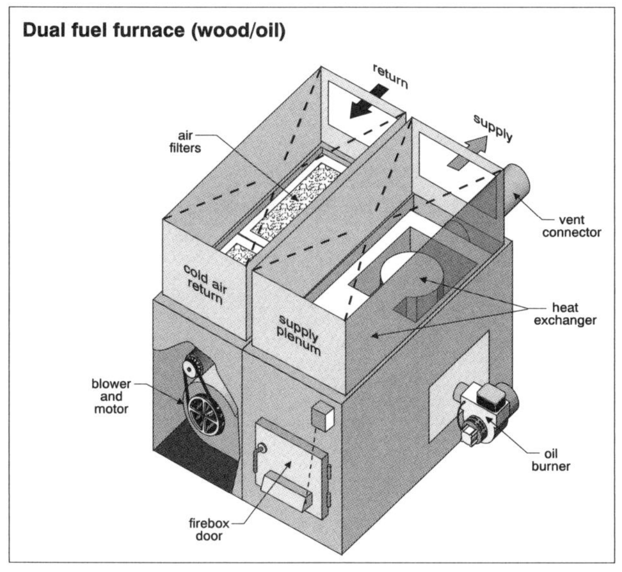

1034

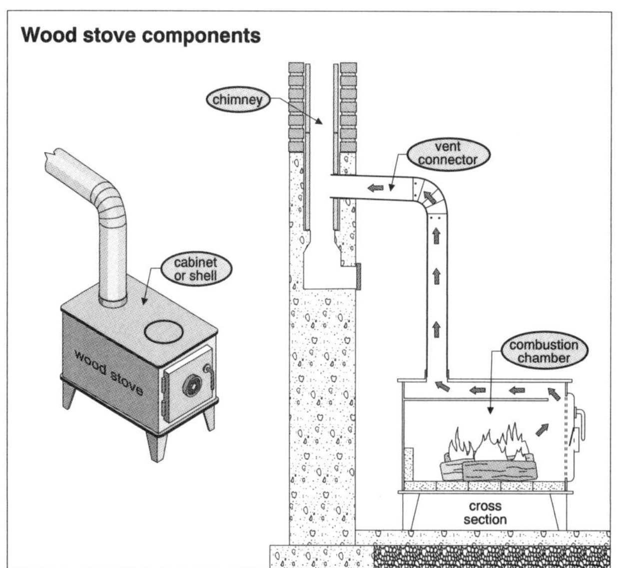

1035

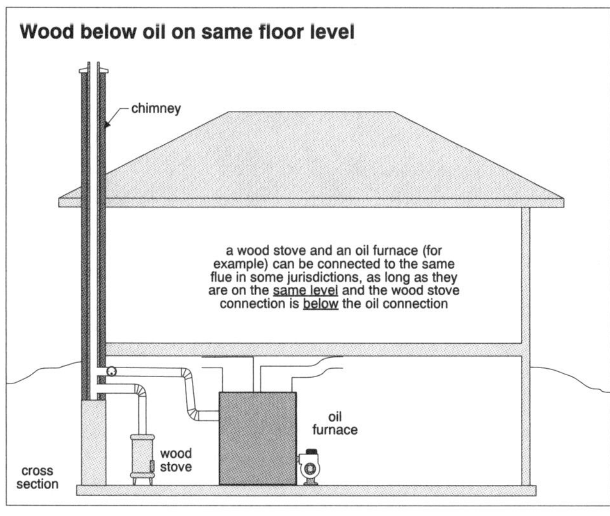

1036

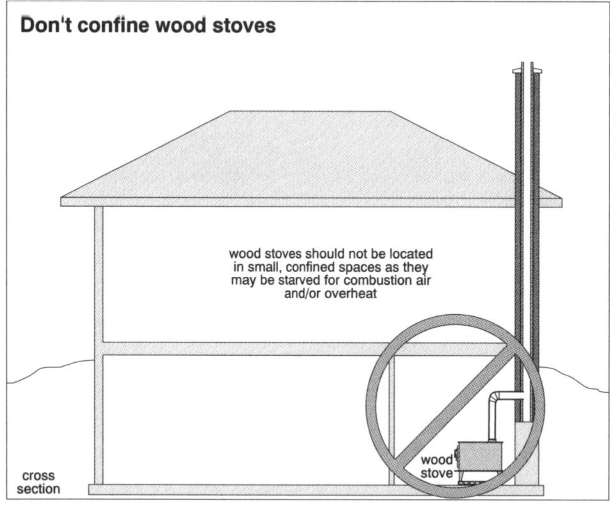

1037

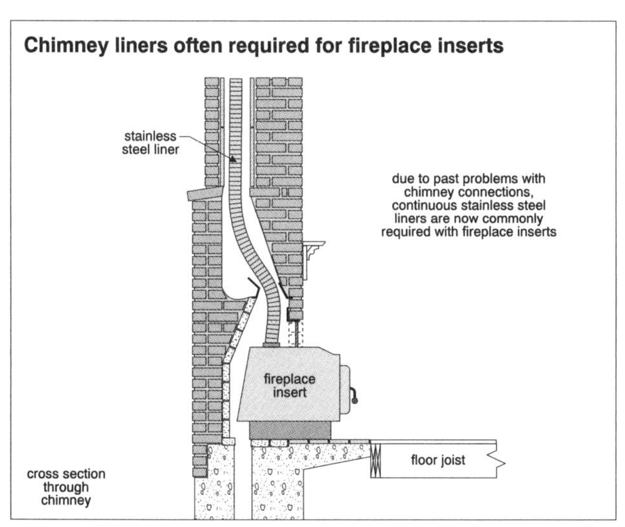

1038

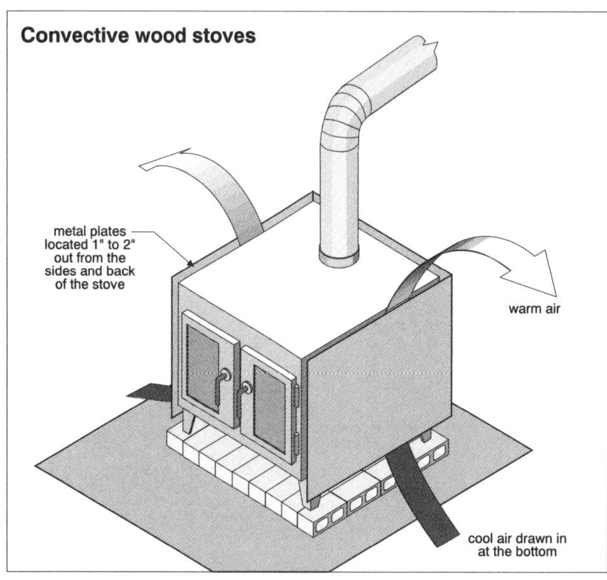

1039

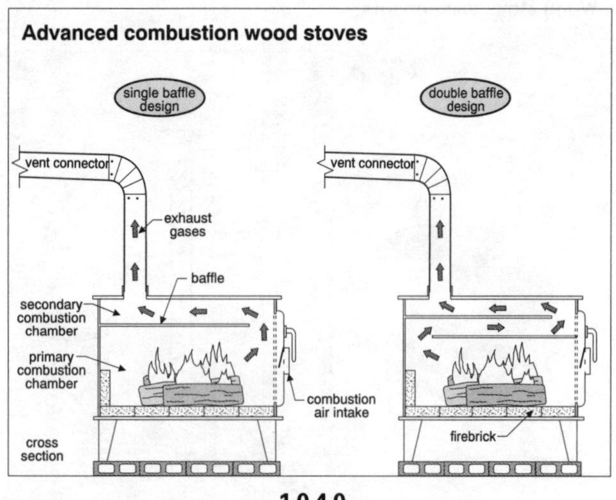

1040

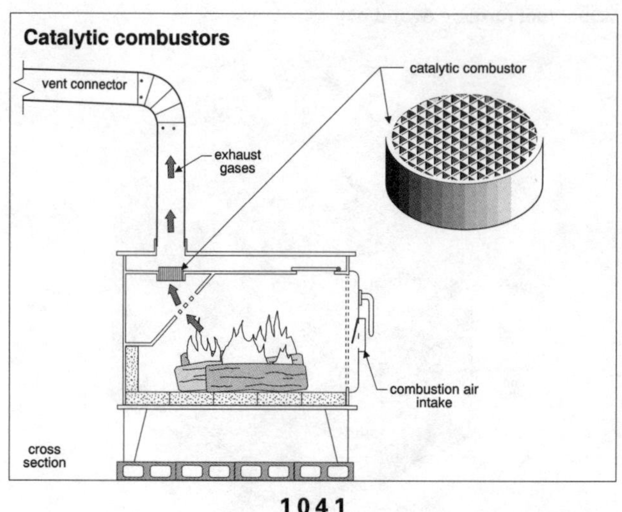

1041

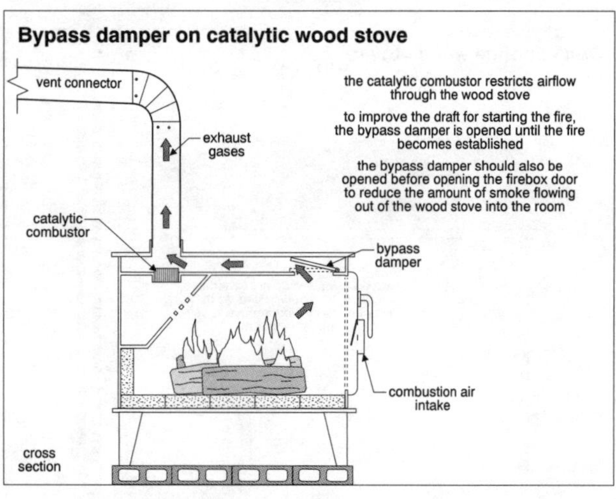

1042

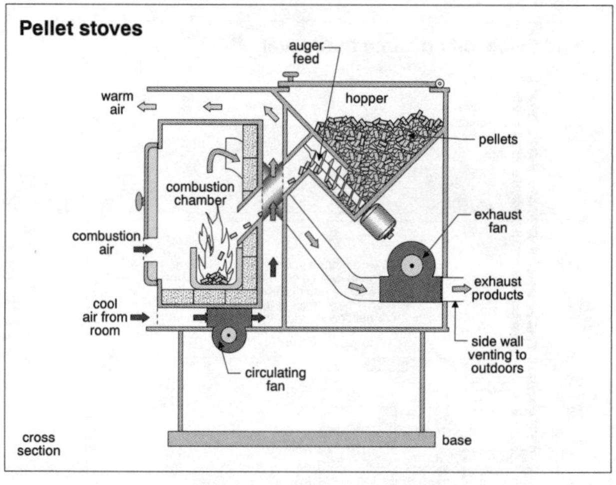

1043

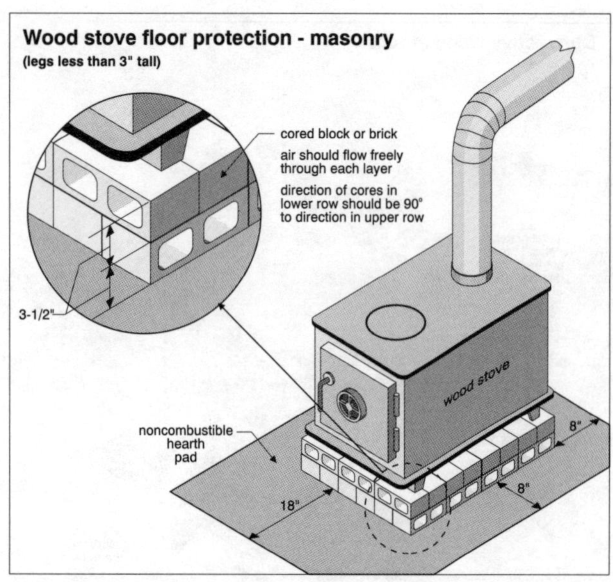

1044

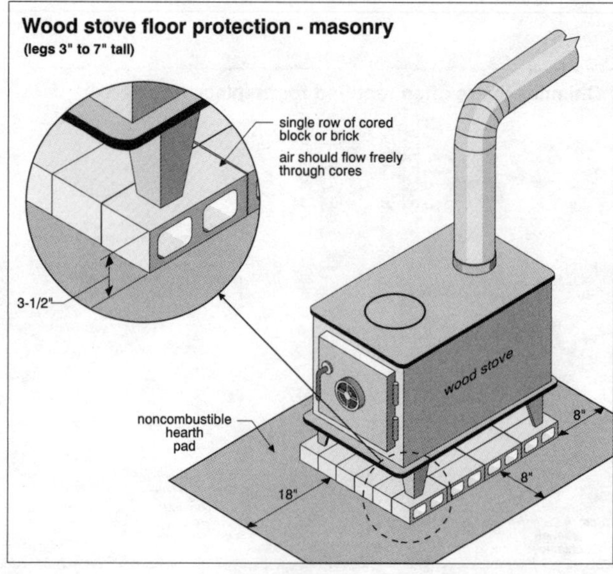

1045

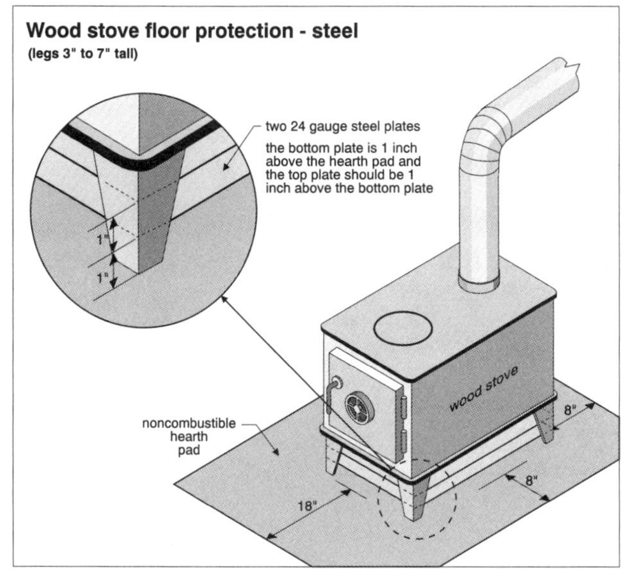

1046

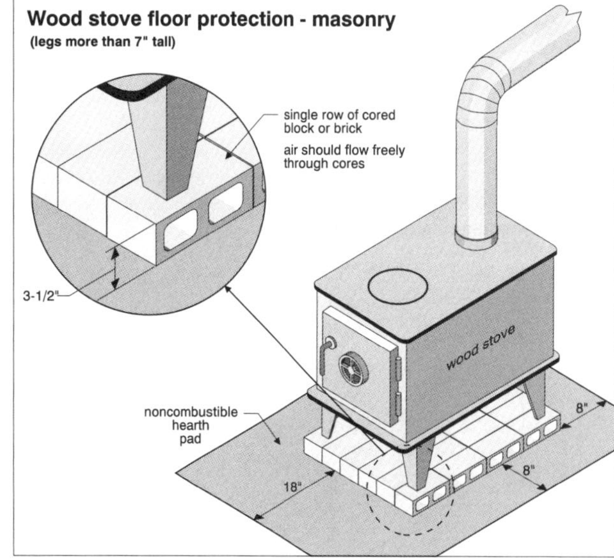

1047

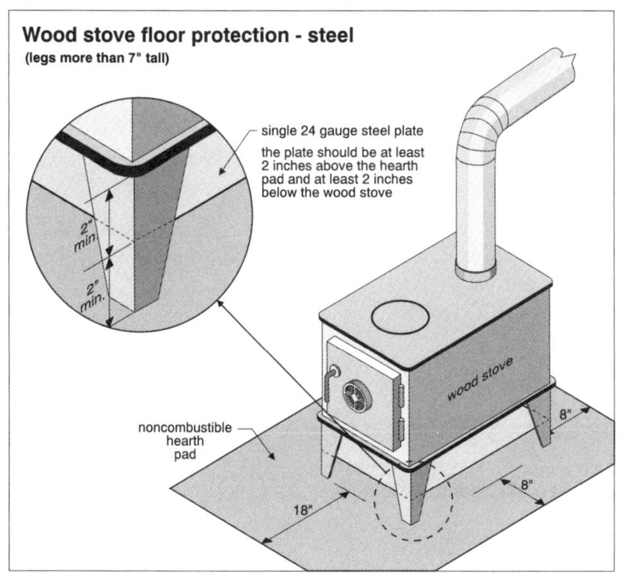

1048

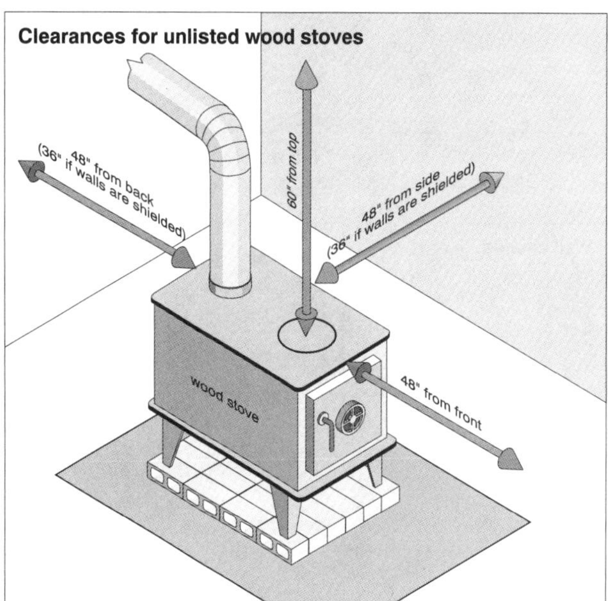

1049

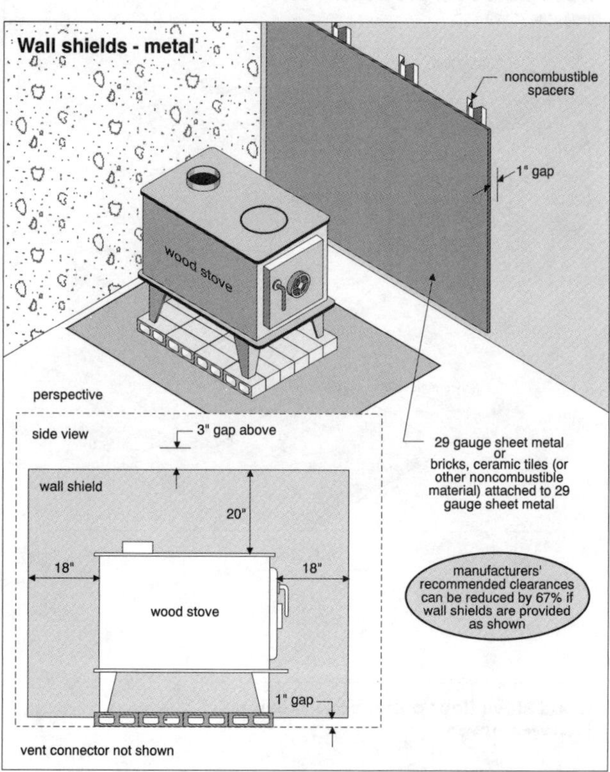

1051

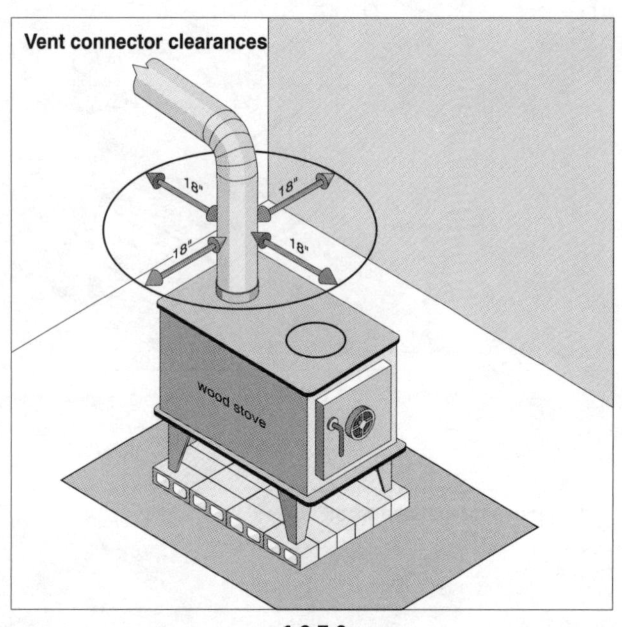

1050

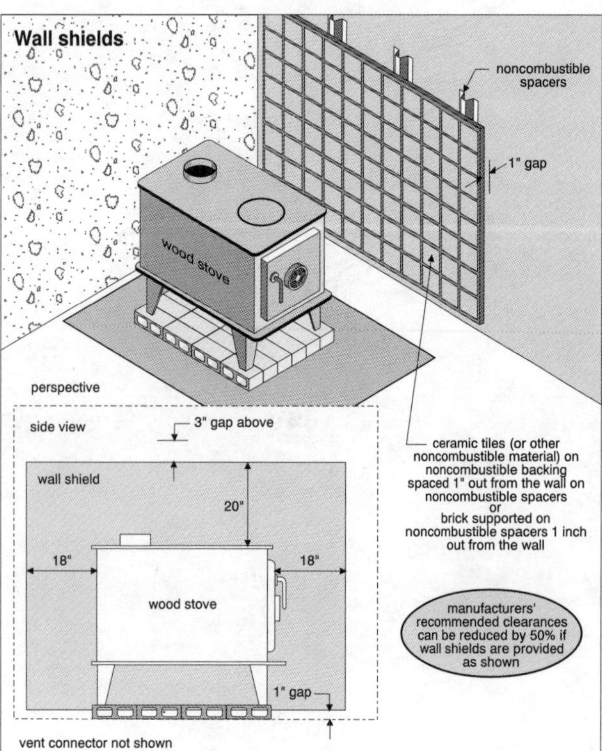

1052

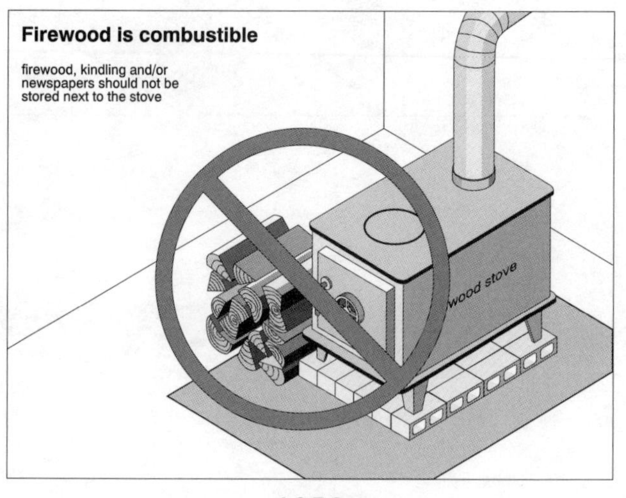

1053

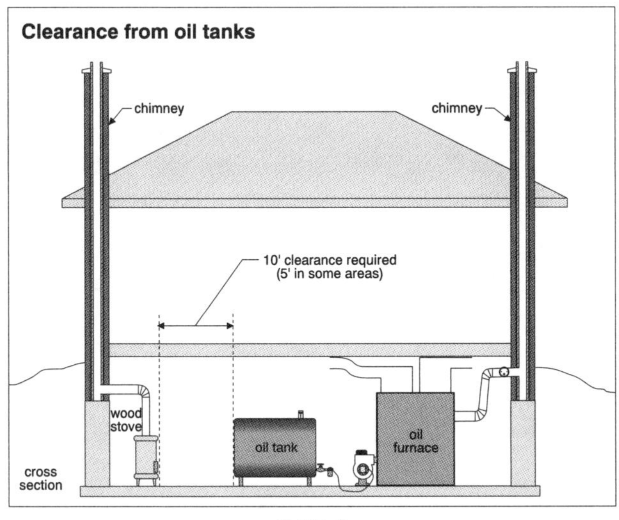

Clearance from oil tanks

1054

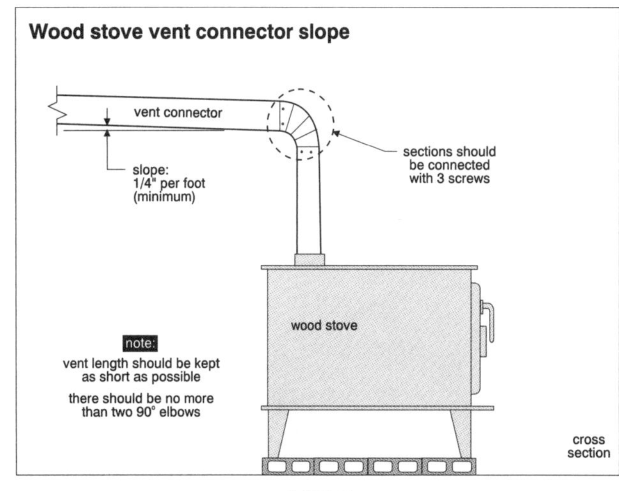

Wood stove vent connector slope

1055

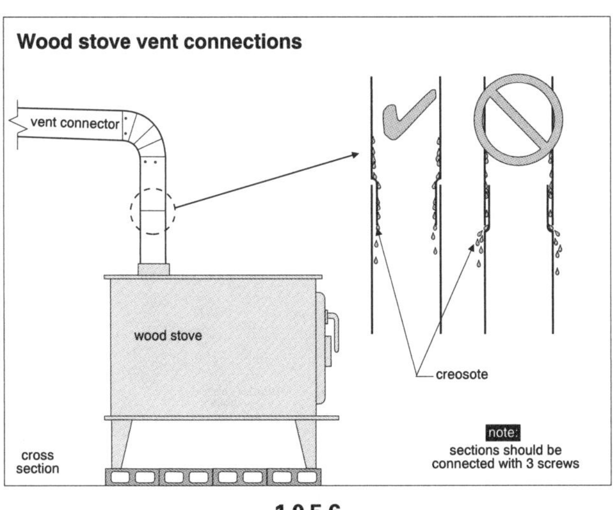

Wood stove vent connections

1056

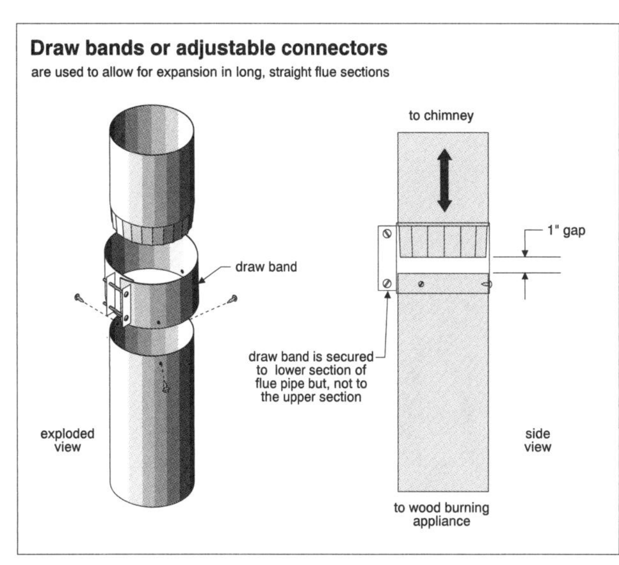

Draw bands or adjustable connectors
are used to allow for expansion in long, straight flue sections

1057

Poor vent connection at chimney

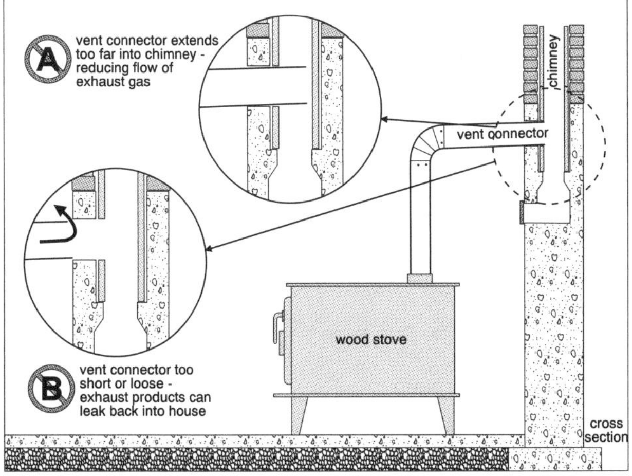

A vent connector extends too far into chimney - reducing flow of exhaust gas

chimney

vent connector

wood stove

B vent connector too short or loose - exhaust products can leak back into house

cross section

1058

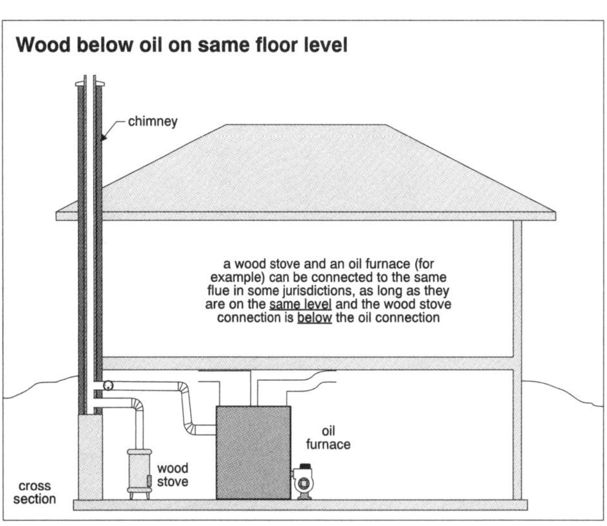

Wood below oil on same floor level

1059

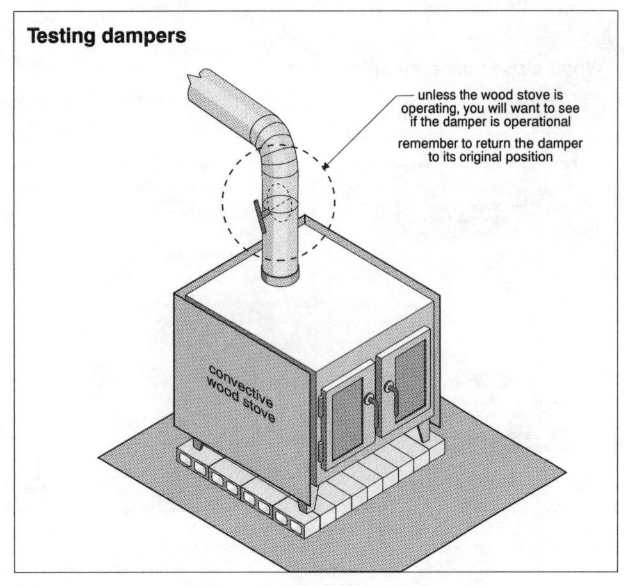

1060

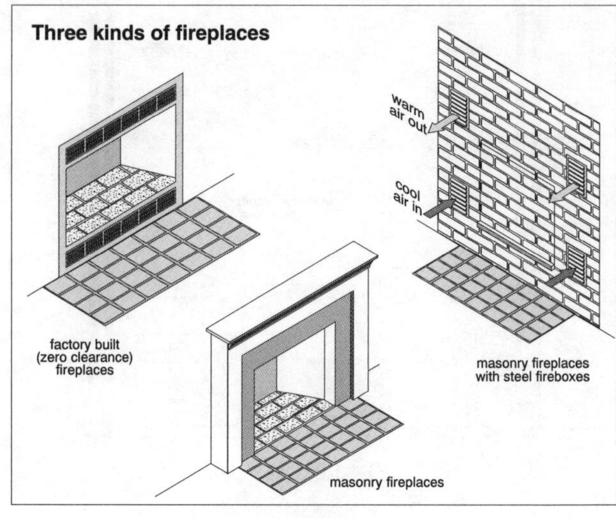

1061

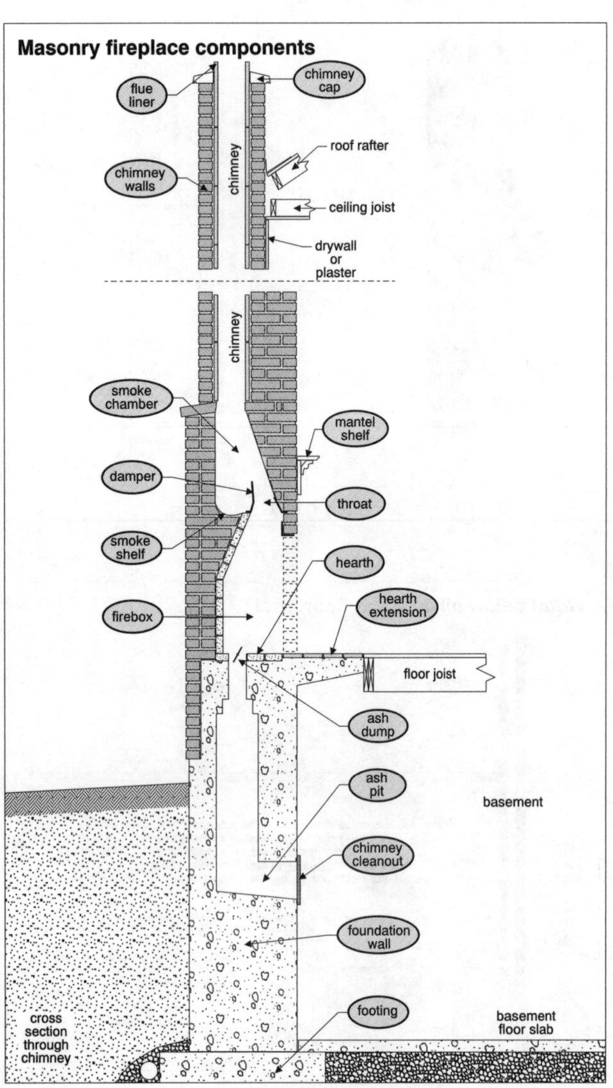

1062

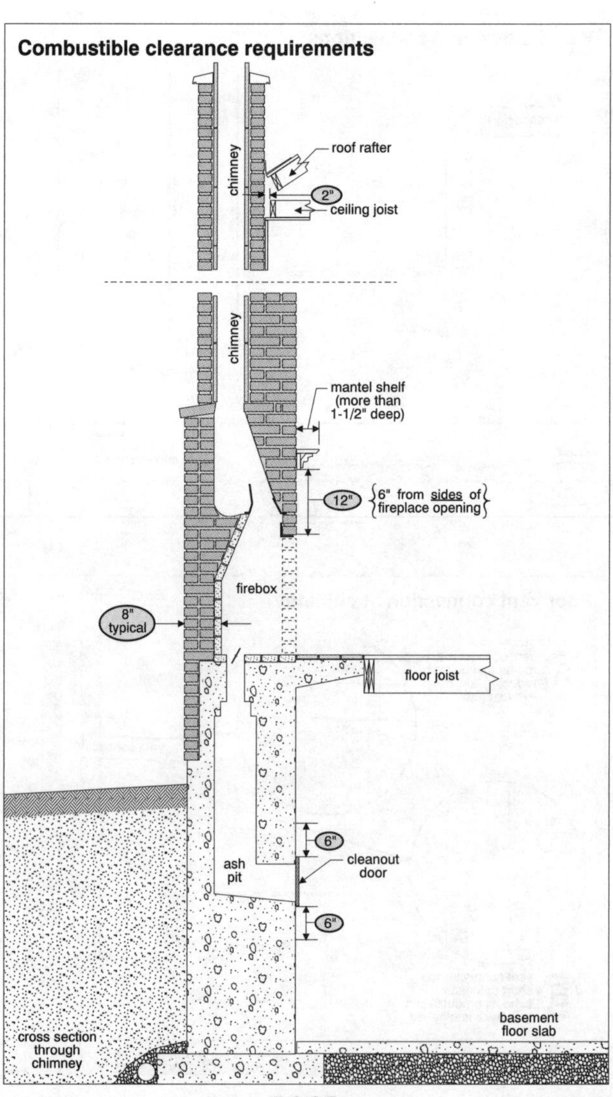

1063

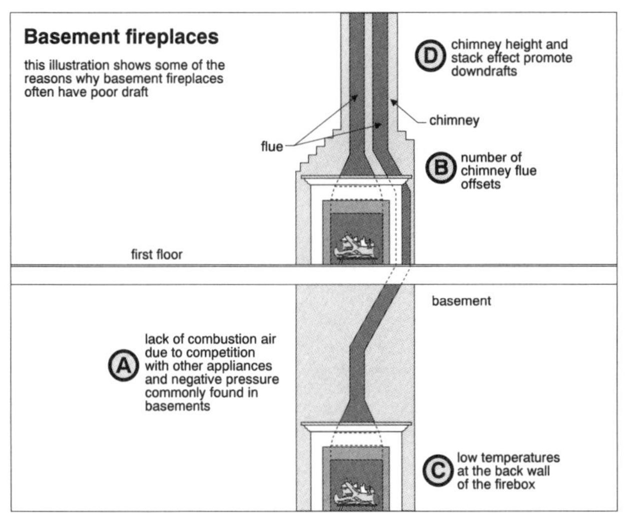

1064

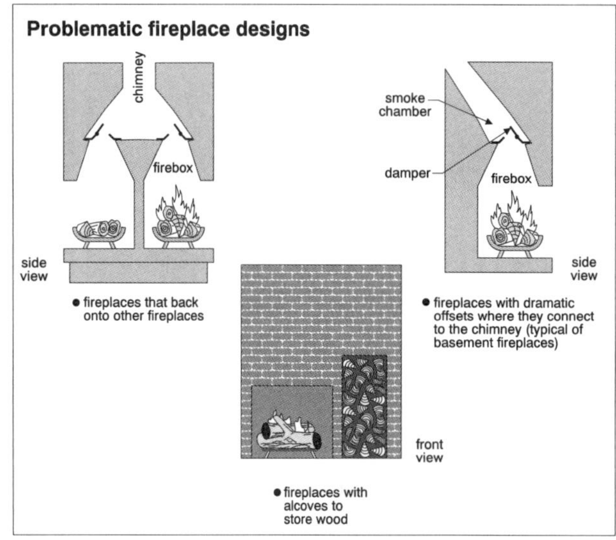

1065

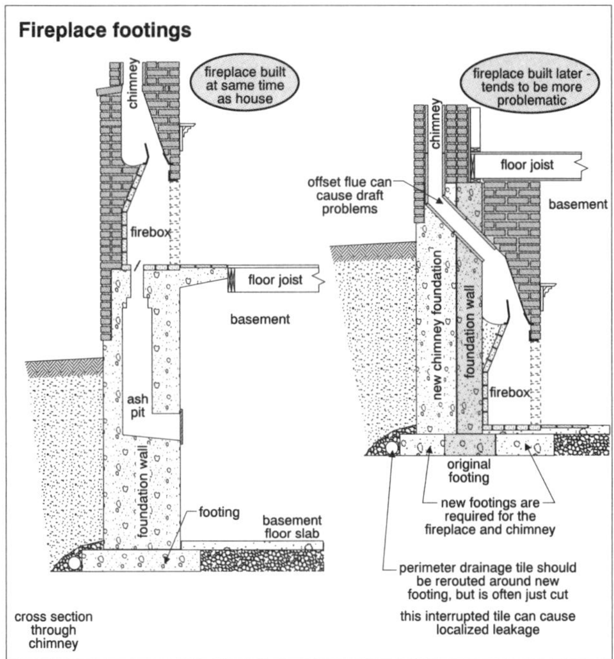

1066

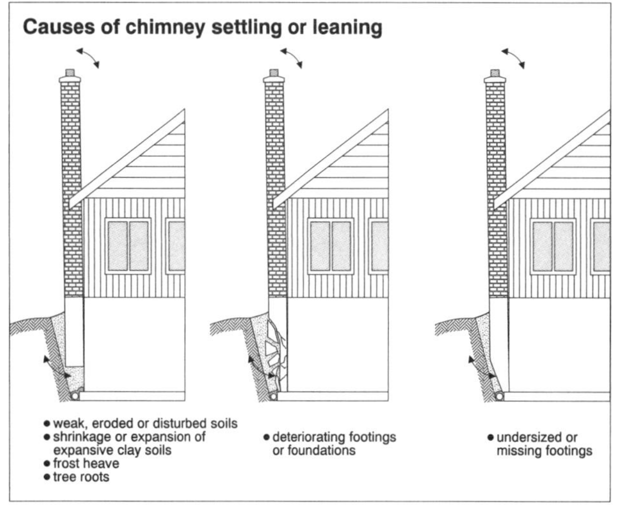

1067

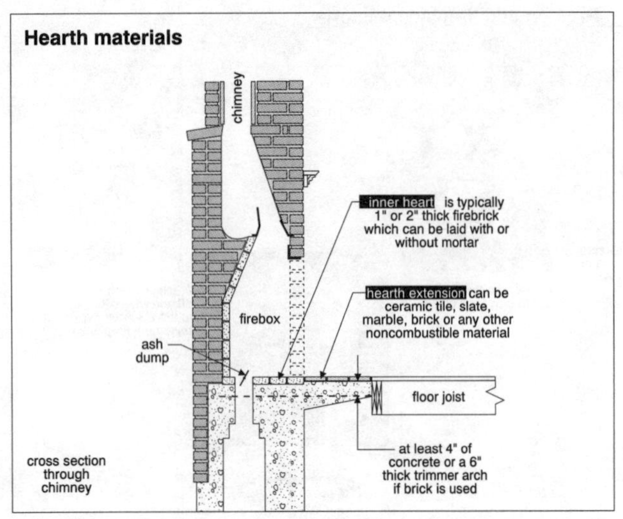

1068

1069

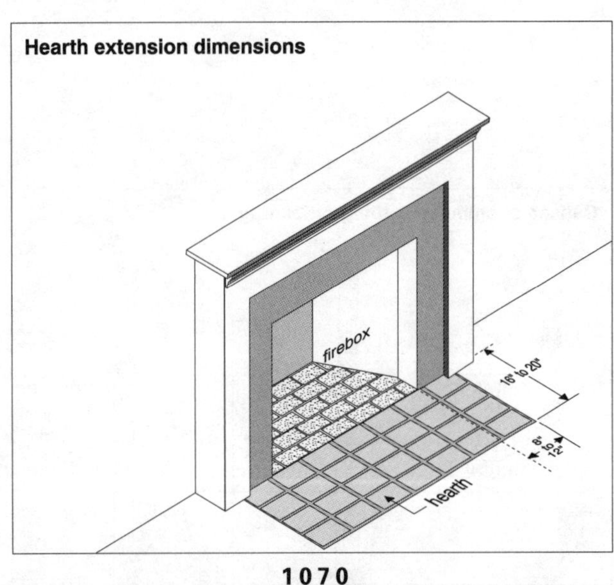

1070

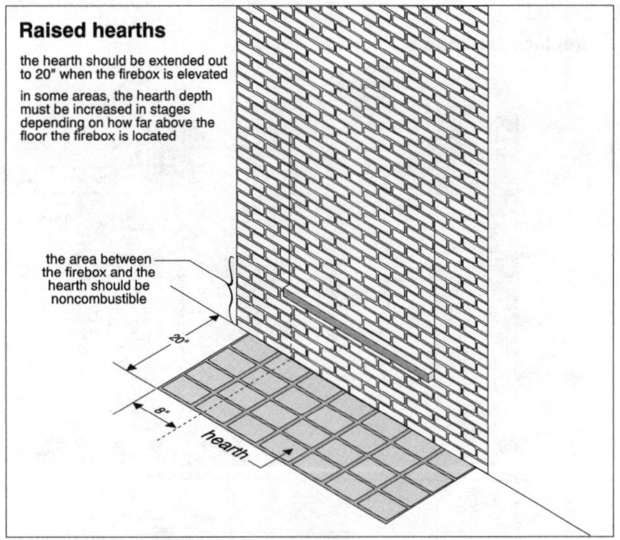

1071

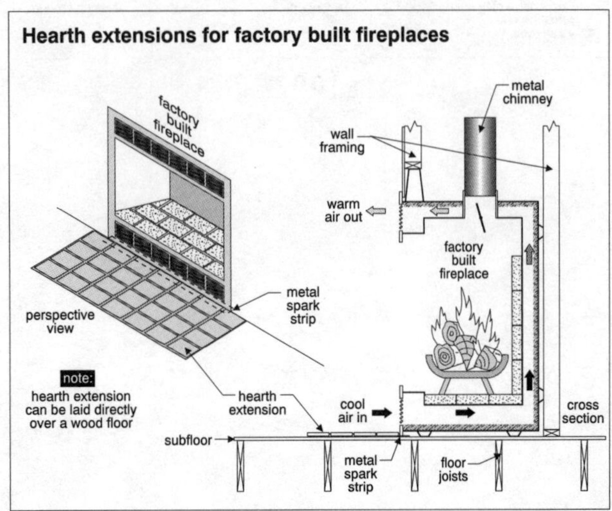

1072

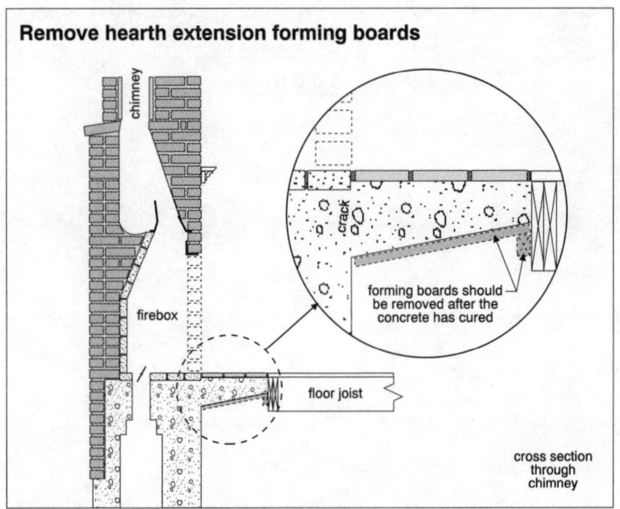

1073

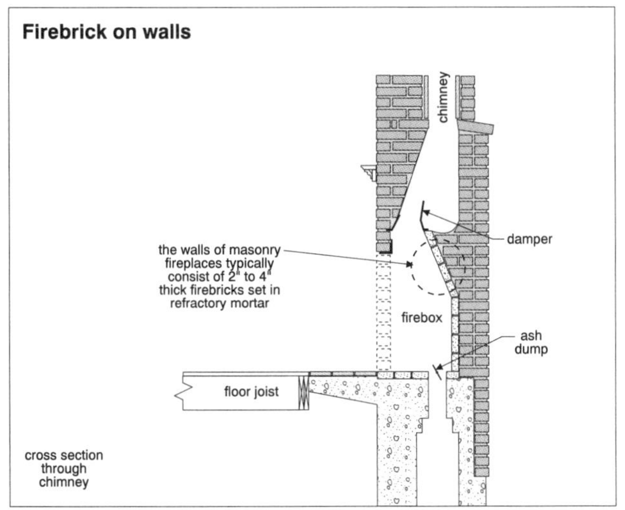

1074

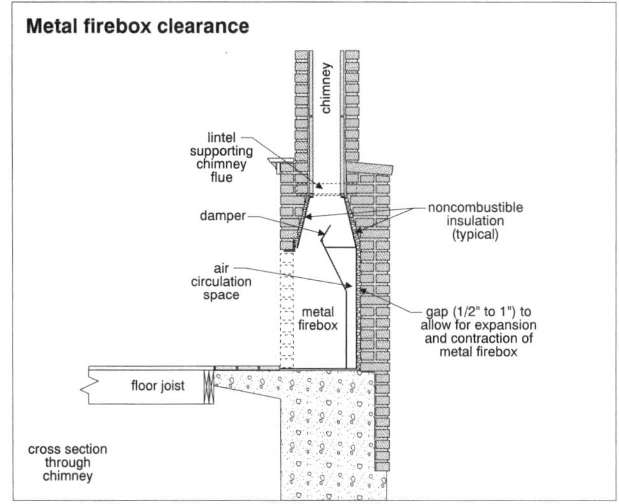

1075

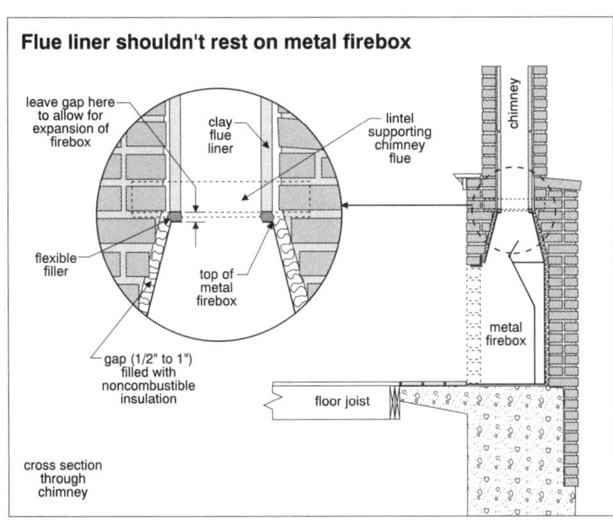

1076

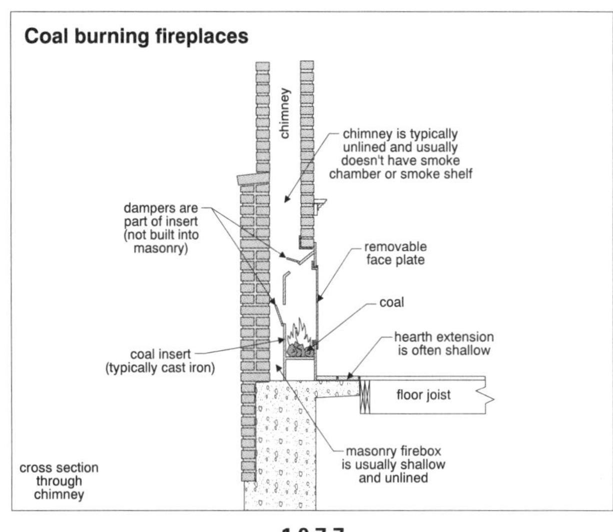

1077

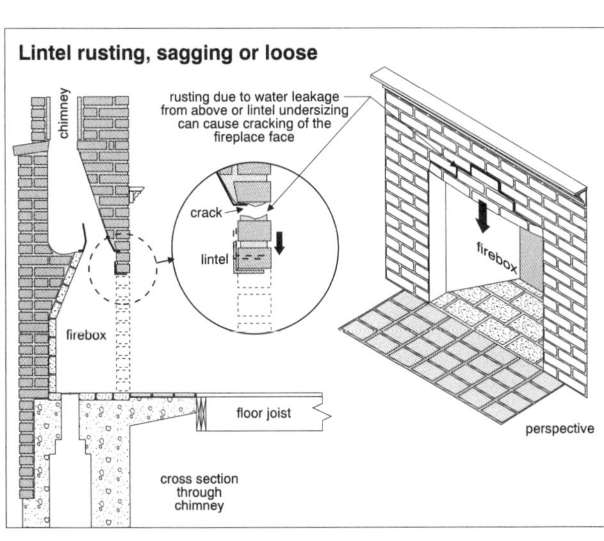

1078

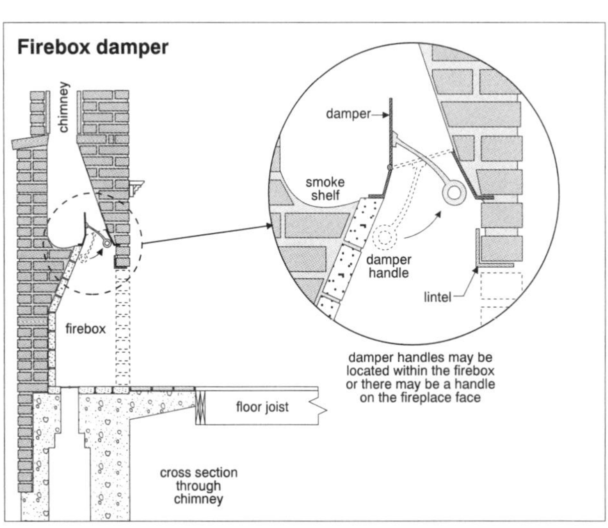

1079

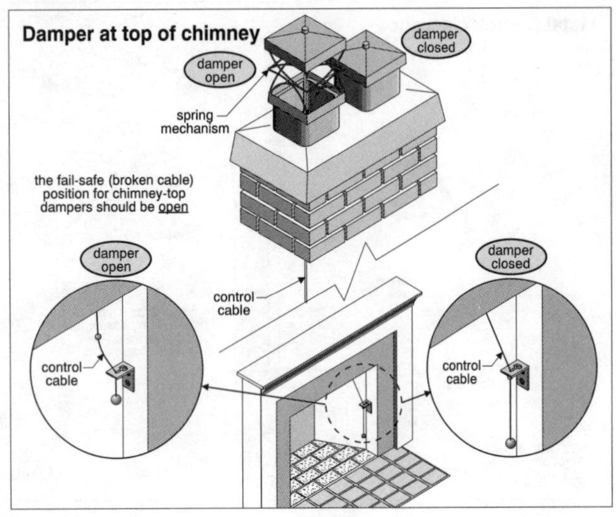

1080

Missing damper

chimney

dampers must sometimes be removed to install fireplace inserts

if the insert is removed later, the fireplace will be without a damper - resulting in heat loss and possible downdraft problems

damper may have been removed

fireplace insert

floor joist

cross section through chimney

1081

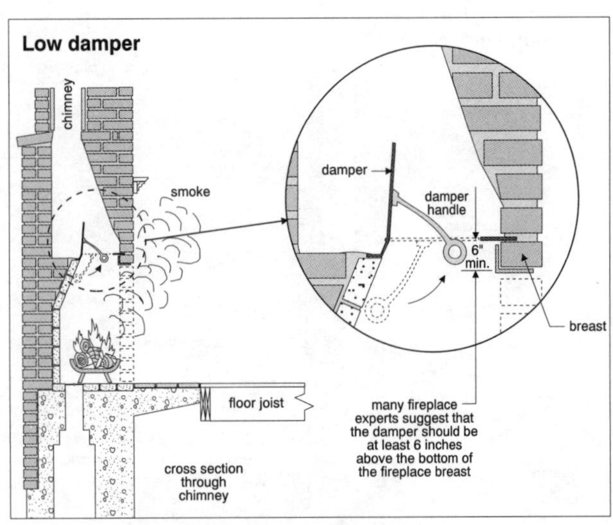

1082

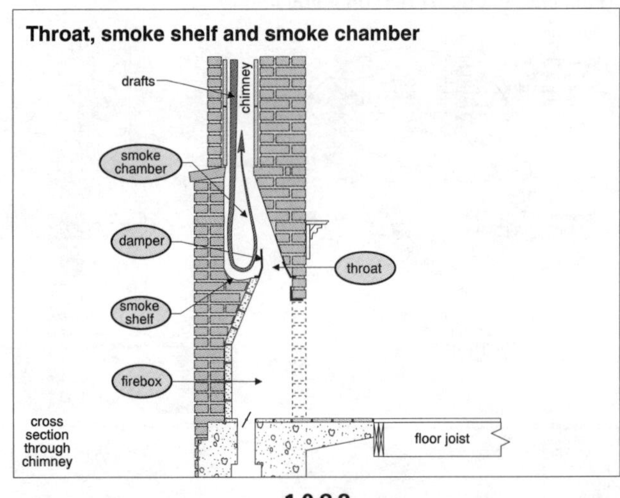

1083

Smoke chamber - wall slope

masonry chimney

chimney flue

45° max.- 30° is preferable

smoke chamber

damper

fireplace

a symmetrical smoke chamber with side and front slopes not exceeding 45° off vertical (30° is better) is the best design

masonry chimney

chimney flue

45° max.- 30° is preferable

smoke chamber

damper

fireplace

an asymmetrical smoke chamber (especially with one side vertical and the other steeply angled off vertical) can lead to draft problems

1084

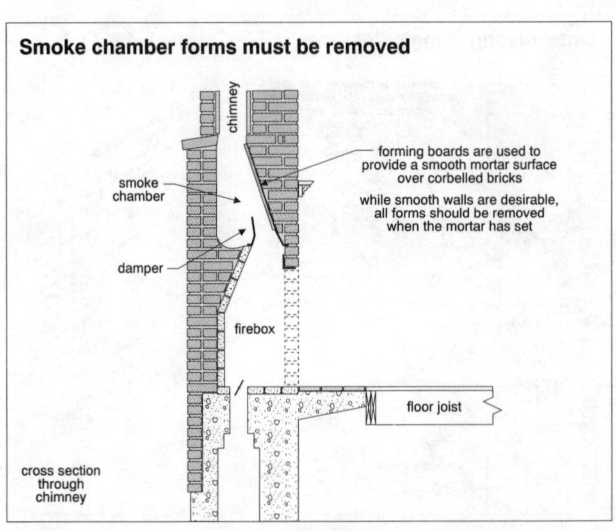

1085

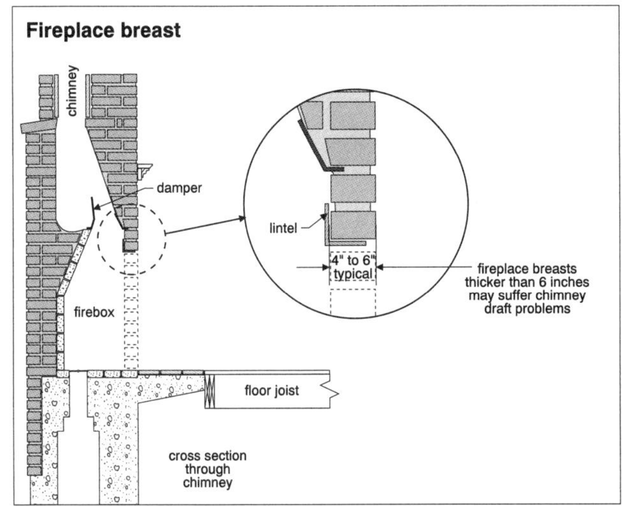

1086

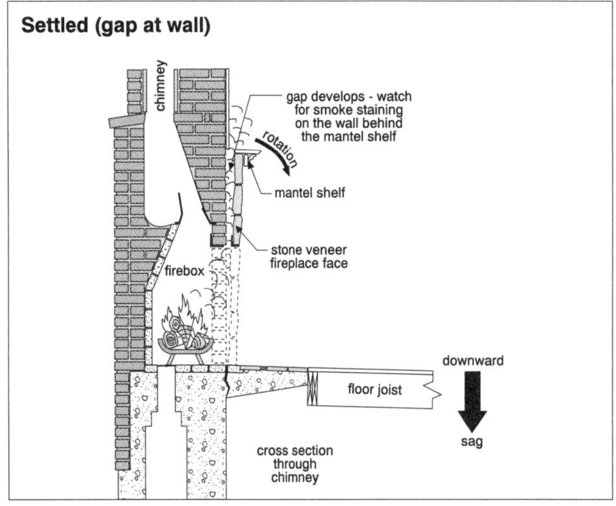

1087

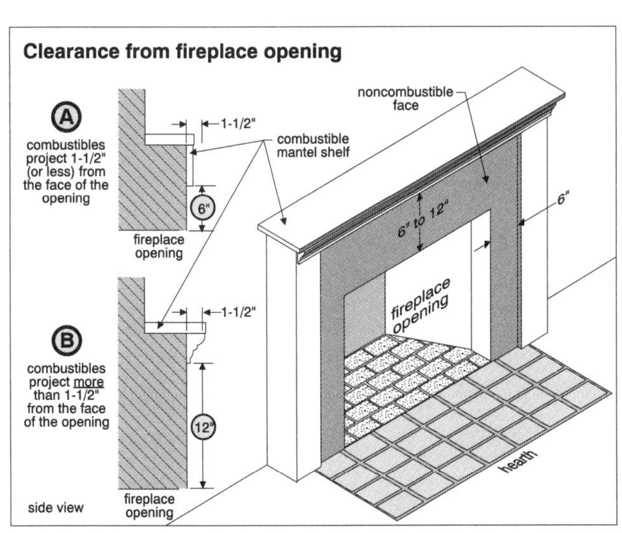

1088

Ashpit
chimney
ashpit walls should be at least 4" thick
any wood forms should be removed
ideally, the ashpit doesn't extend below the level of the cleanout door (to make cleaning easier)
fireplace
ash dump
floor joist
wall framing
6" min. (clearance to combustibles)
ash pit
cleanout door
6" min.
ash pit
cleanout door
foundation wall
wall framing
cross section through chimney
basement floor slab

1089

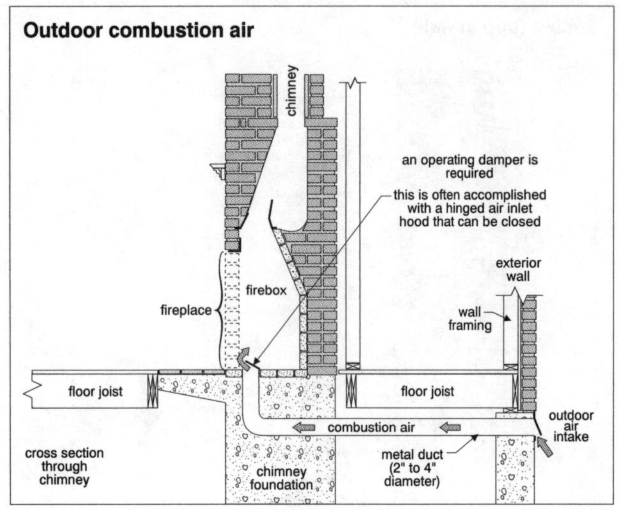

1090

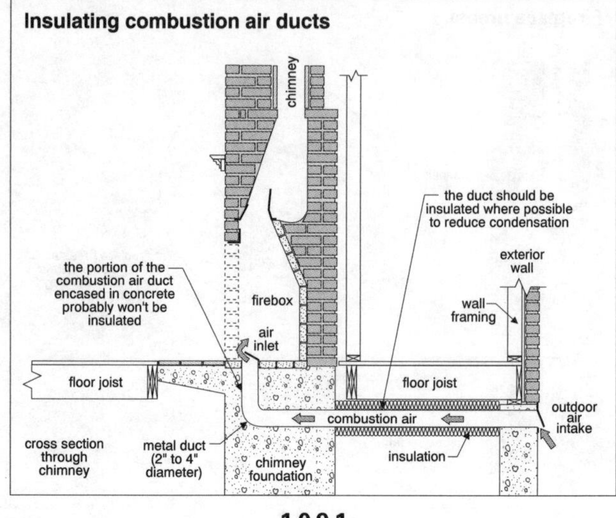

1091

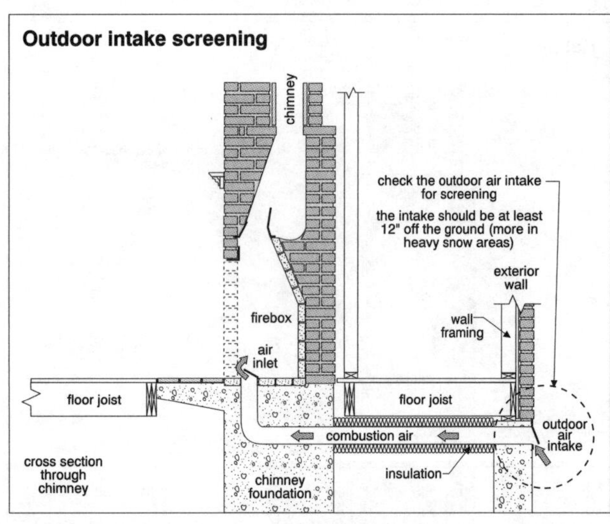

1092

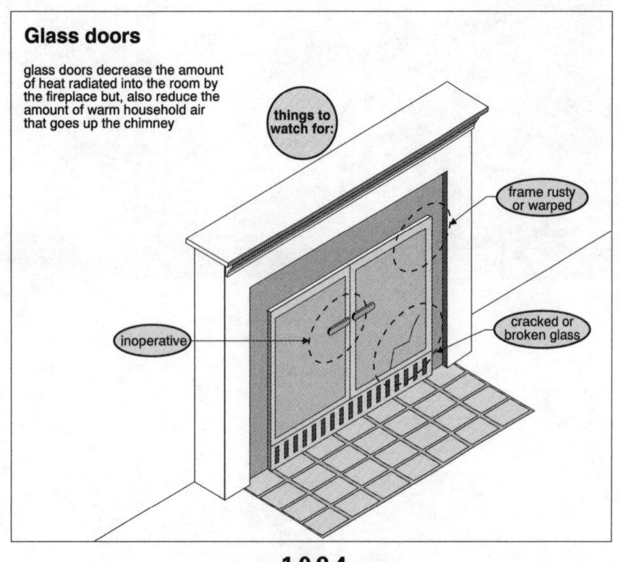

1093

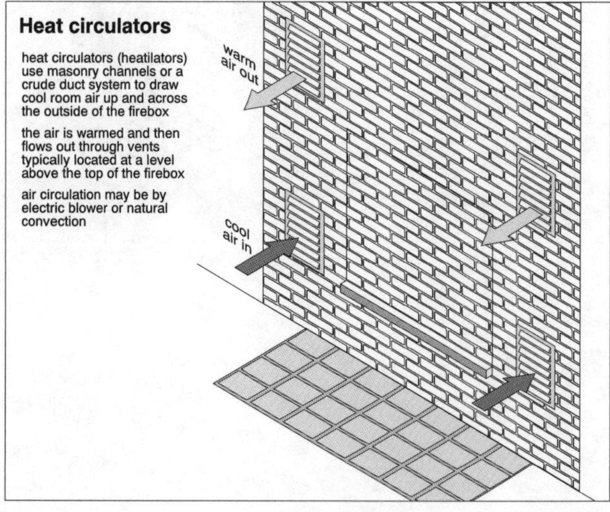

1094

1095

Gas igniters

most gas igniters have few safety features and may not be permitted in some areas - find out if they are allowed in *your* area

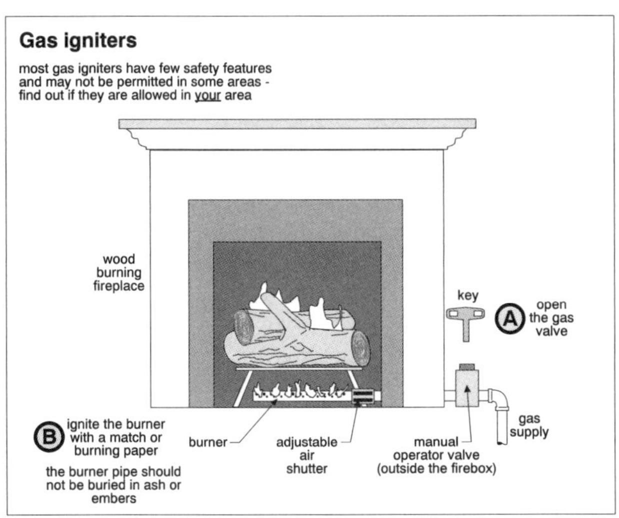

1096

How steam systems work

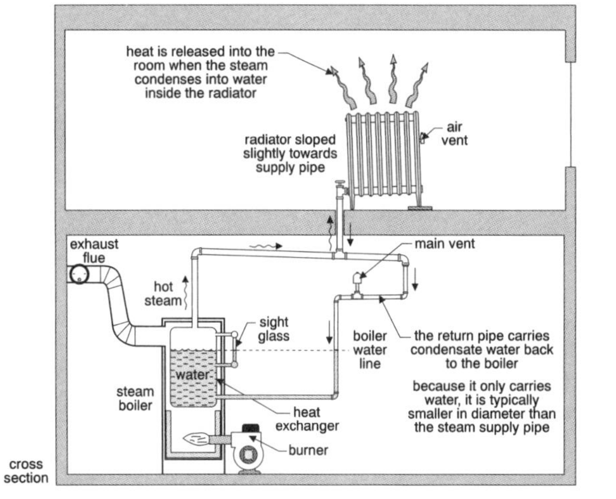

1097

Steam system operation: at rest

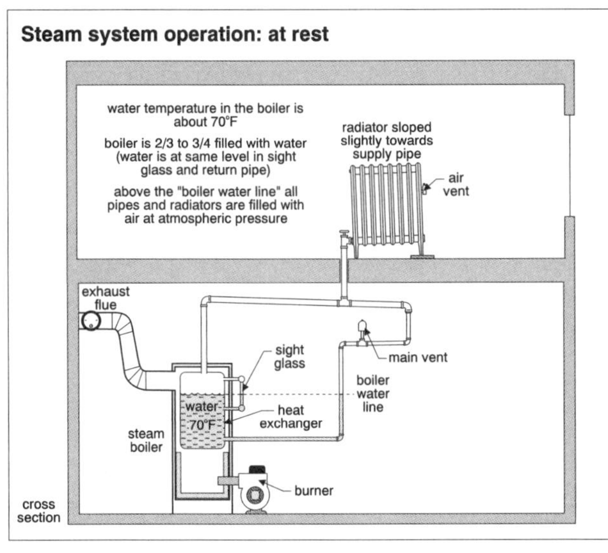

1098

Steam system operation: call for heat

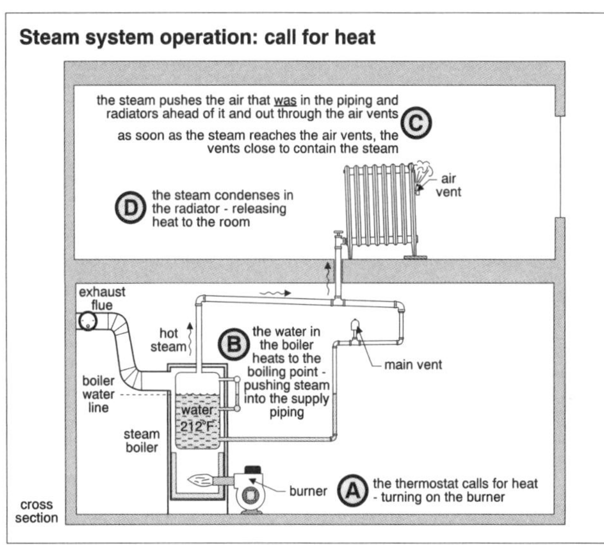

1099

Air vents

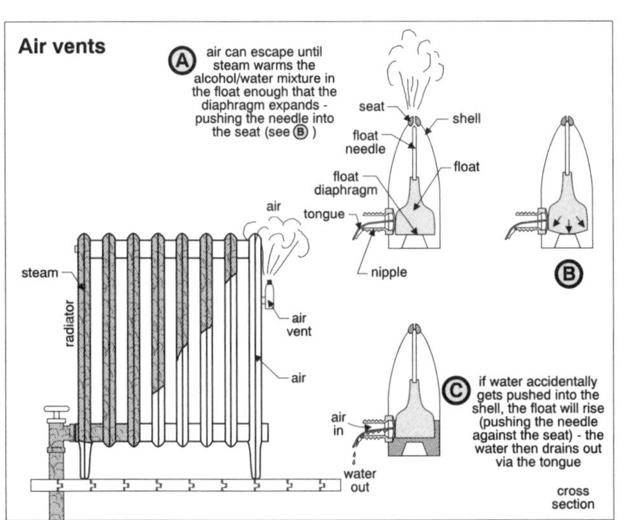

1100

Dimension "A"

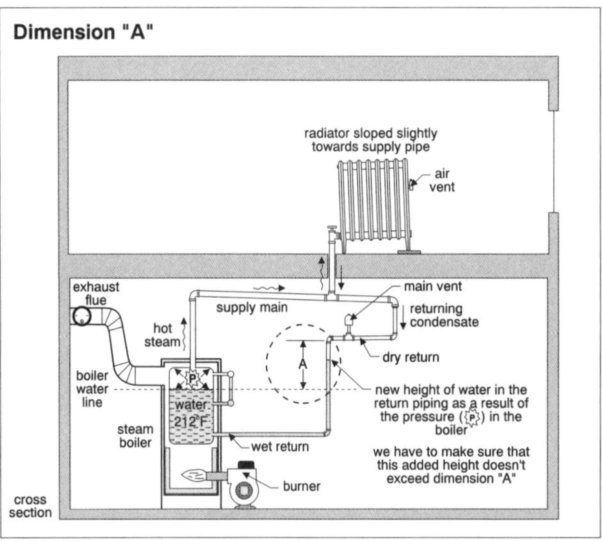

1101

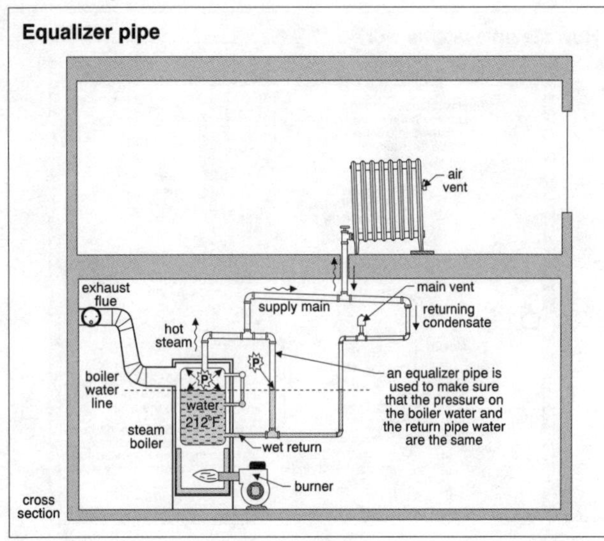

1102

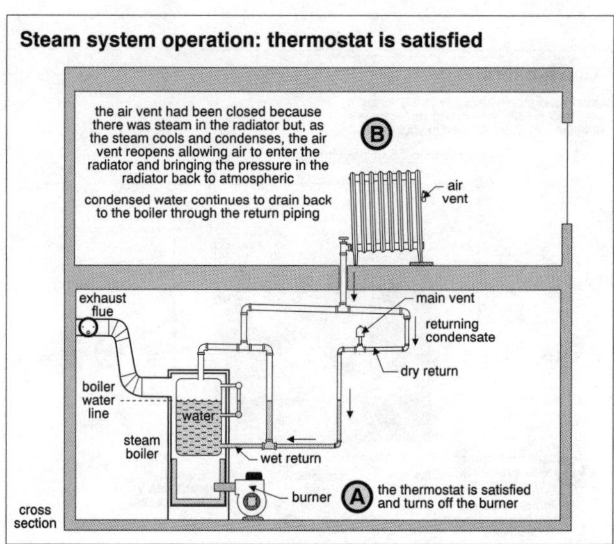

1103

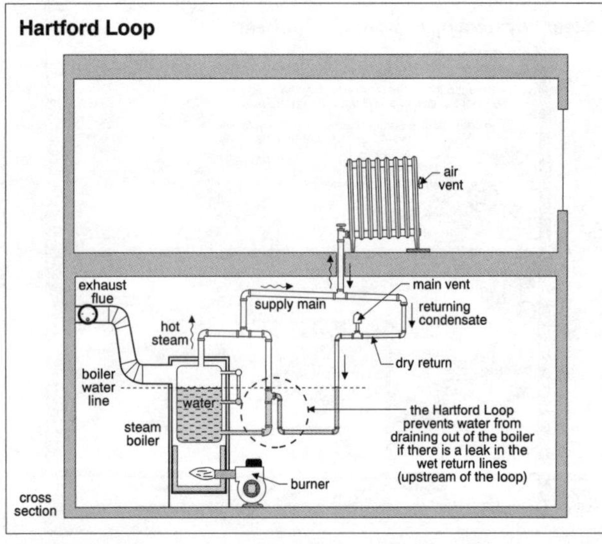

1104

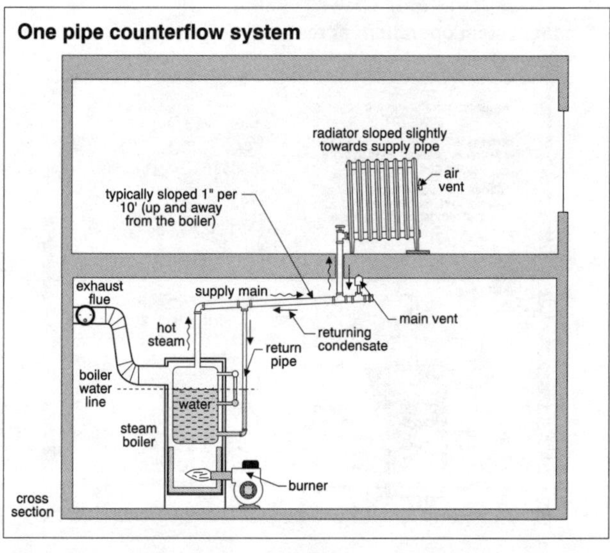

1105

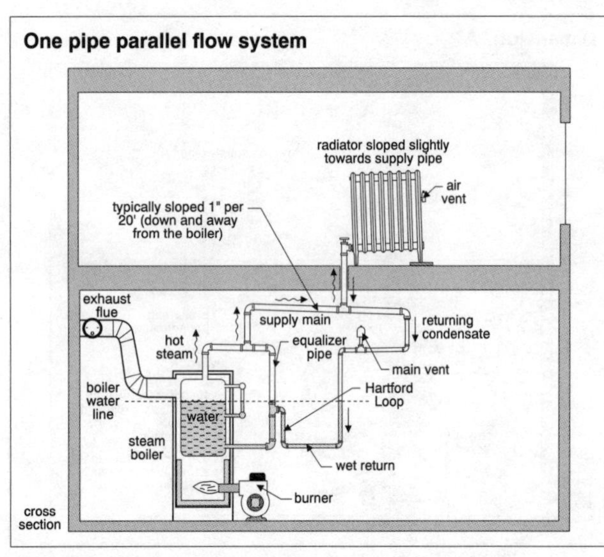

1106

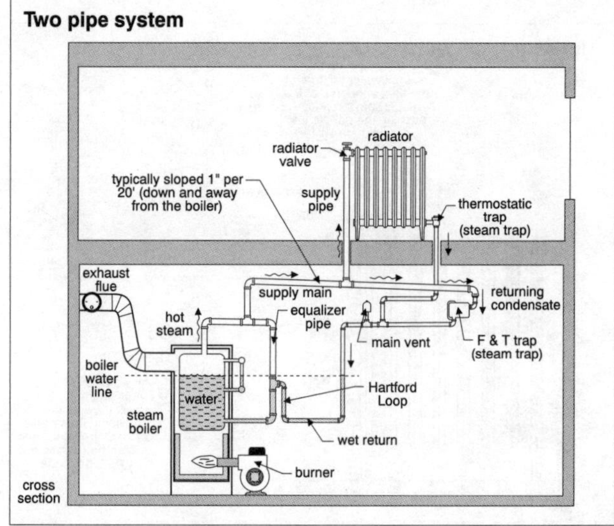

1107

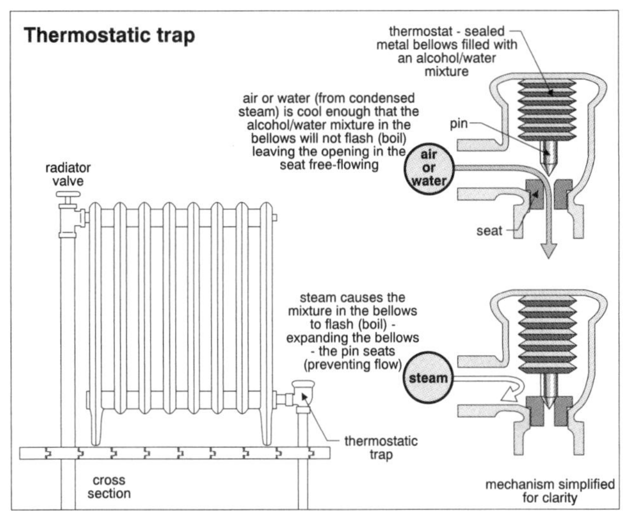

1108

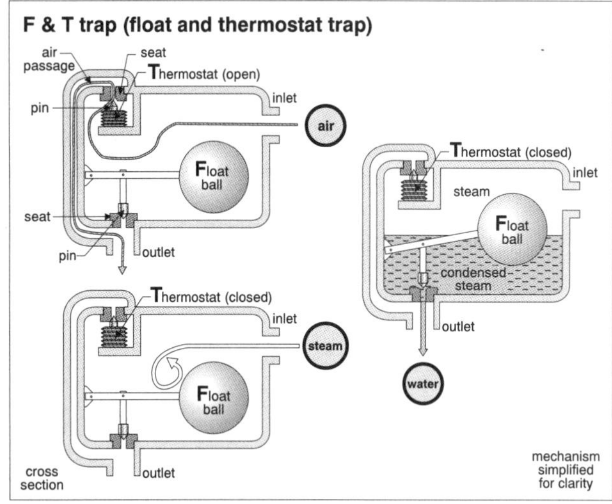

1109

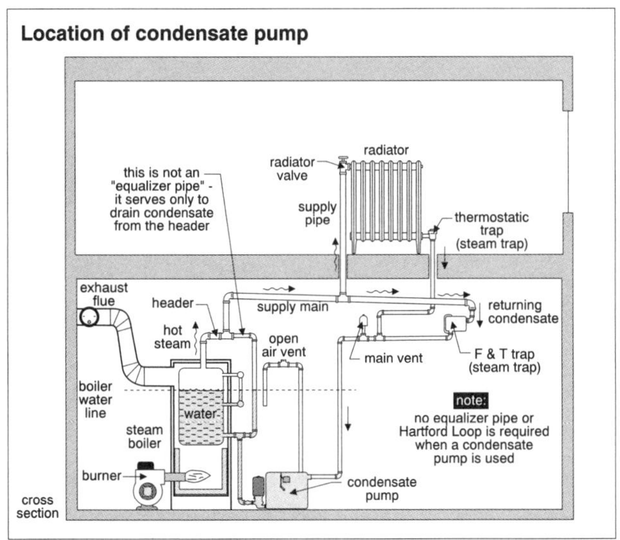

1110

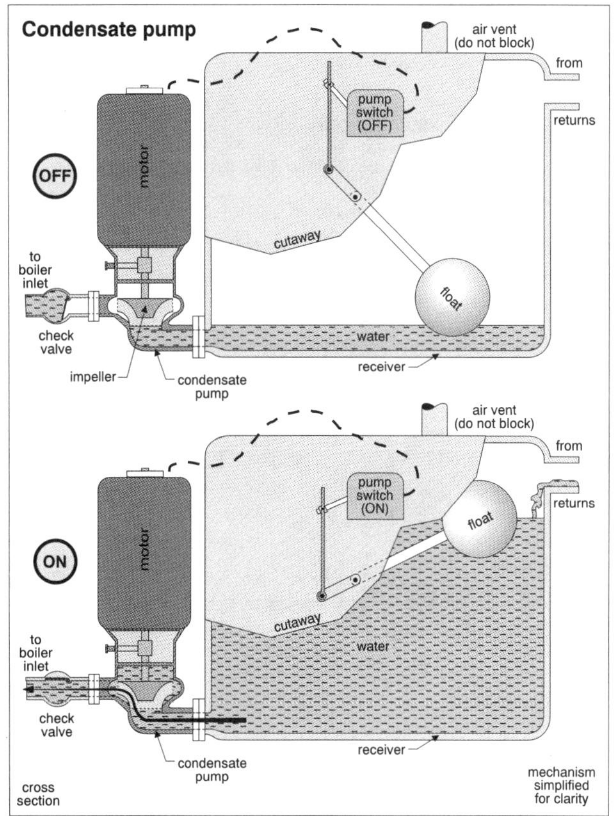

1111

Location of boiler feed pump
radiator
radiator valve
this is not an "equalizer pipe" - it serves only to drain condensate from the header
supply pipe
thermostatic trap (steam trap)
exhaust flue
header
supply main
returning condensate
hot steam
open air vent
main vent
F & T trap (steam trap)
boiler water line
water
note:
no equalizer pipe or Hartford Loop is required when a boiler feed pump is used
steam boiler
burner
to supply plumbing system
boiler feed pump
cross section

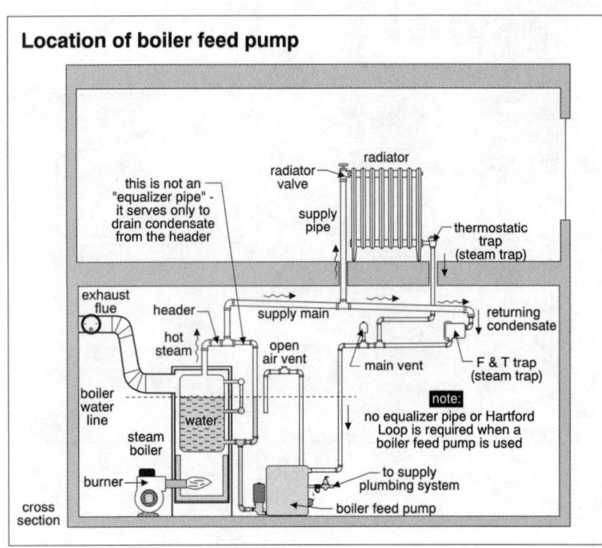

1112

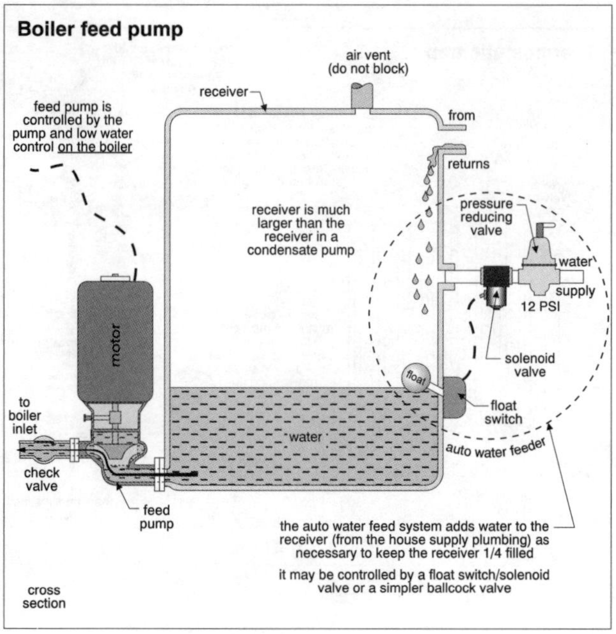

Boiler feed pump
air vent (do not block)
receiver
from
returns
feed pump is controlled by the pump and low water control on the boiler
receiver is much larger than the receiver in a condensate pump
pressure reducing valve
water supply
12 PSI
solenoid valve
motor
float
float switch
to boiler inlet
water
auto water feeder
check valve
feed pump
the auto water feed system adds water to the receiver (from the house supply plumbing) as necessary to keep the receiver 1/4 filled
it may be controlled by a float switch/solenoid valve or a simpler ballcock valve
cross section

1113

Location of low water cut-out
water level gauge
low water cut-out
switch (to boiler)
radiator
house supply plumbing
automatic water feeder
blowdown valve
supply main
returning condensate
equalizer pipe
main vent
F & T trap (steam trap)
boiler water line
Hartford Loop
water
steam boiler
wet return
burner
cross section

1114

Pressure relief valve
radiator
the pressure relief valve is typically set to discharge steam pressure in excess of 15 PSI
supply main
returning condensate
equalizer pipe
main vent
F & T trap (steam trap)
boiler water line
Hartford Loop
water
steam boiler
wet return
burner
cross section

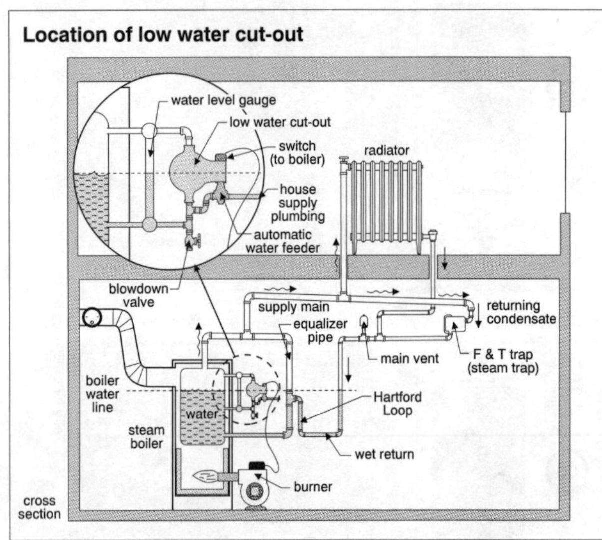

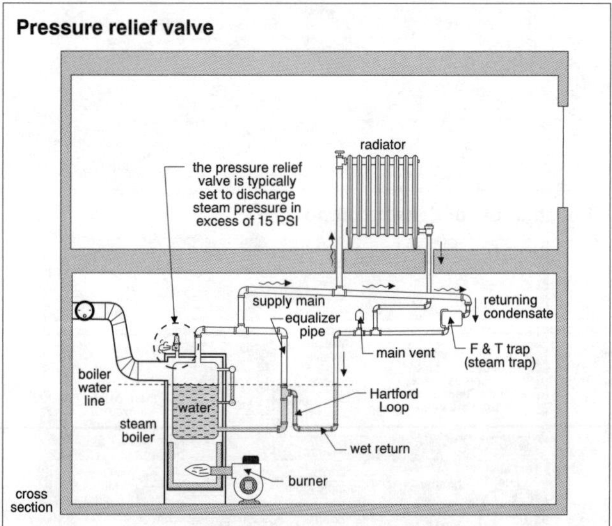

1115

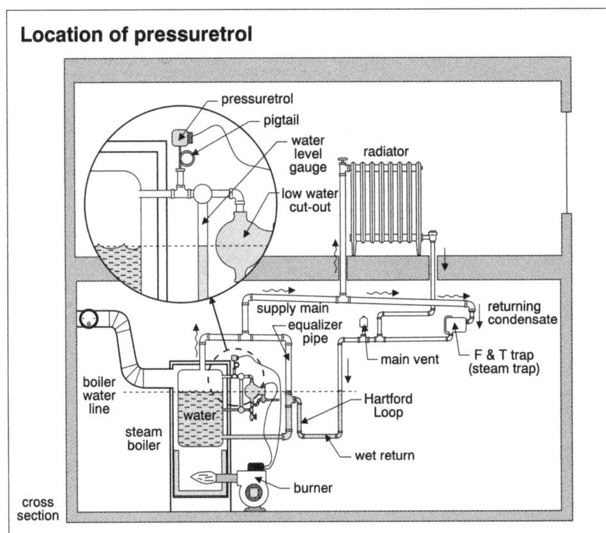

1116

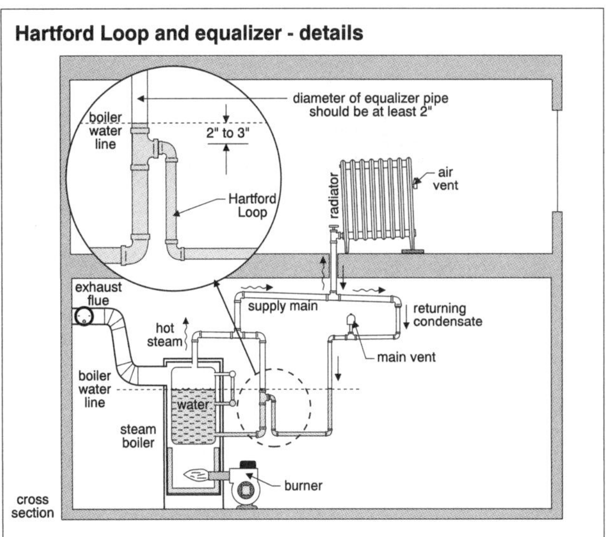

1117

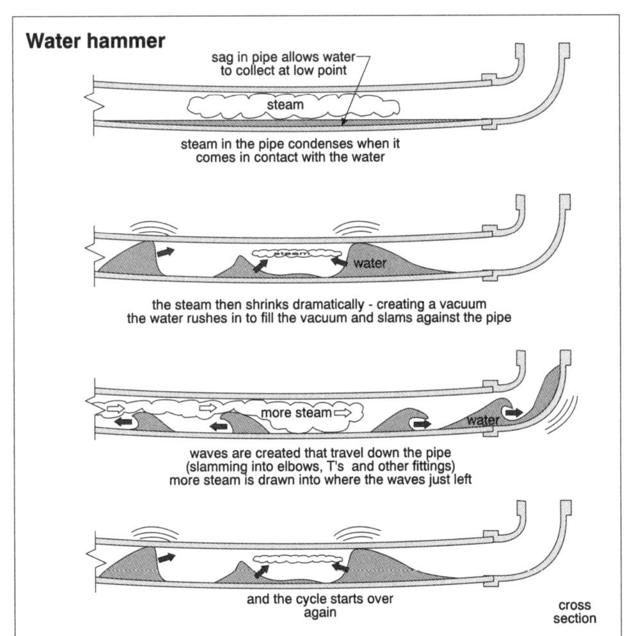

1118

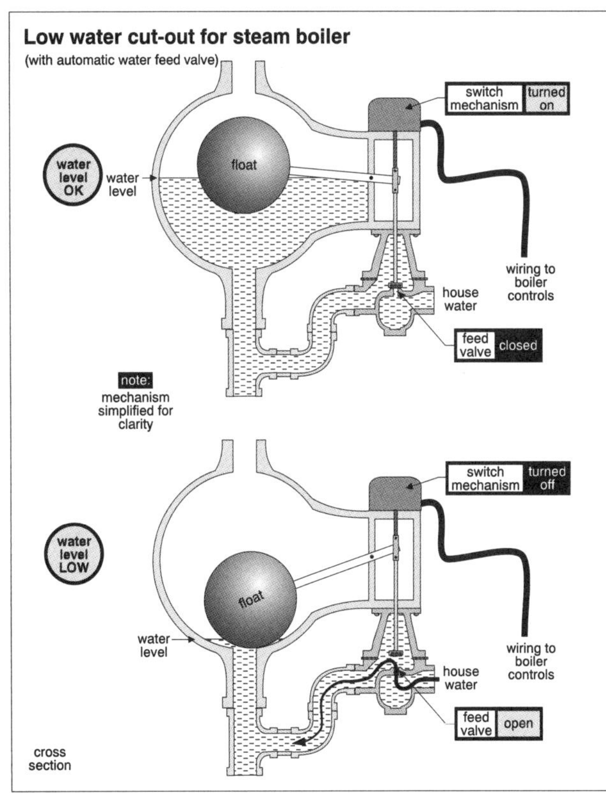

1119

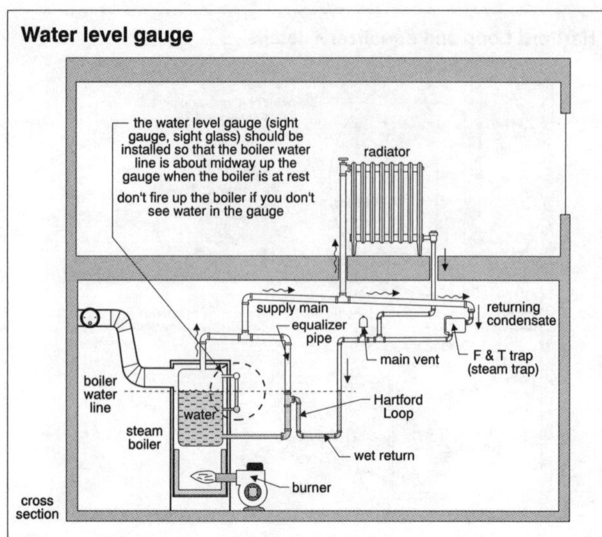

1120

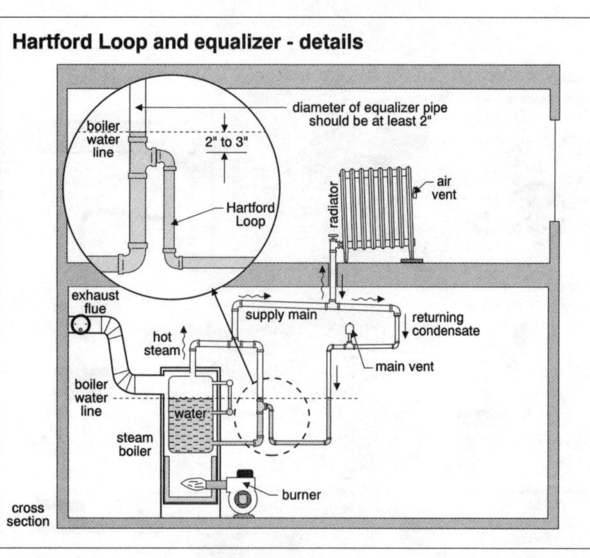

1122

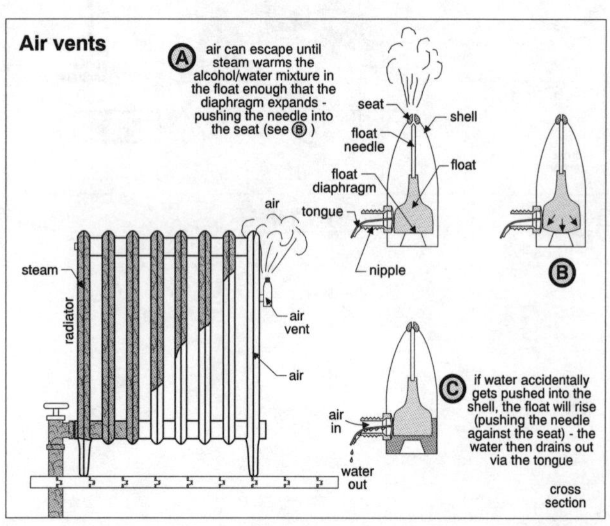

1124

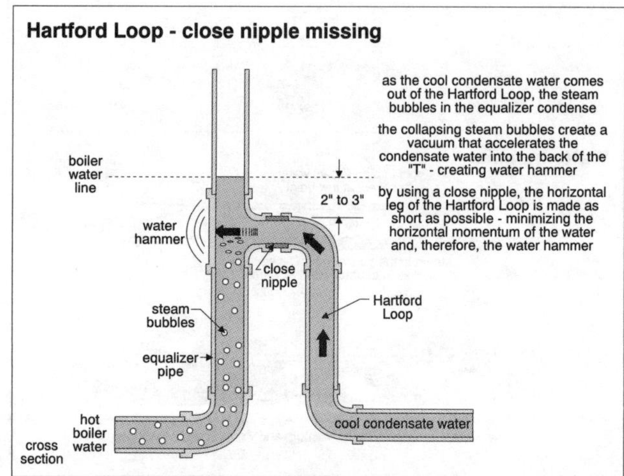

1121

1123

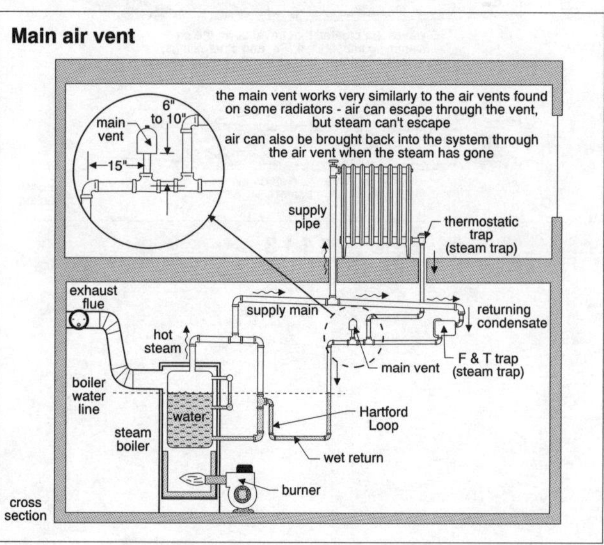

1125

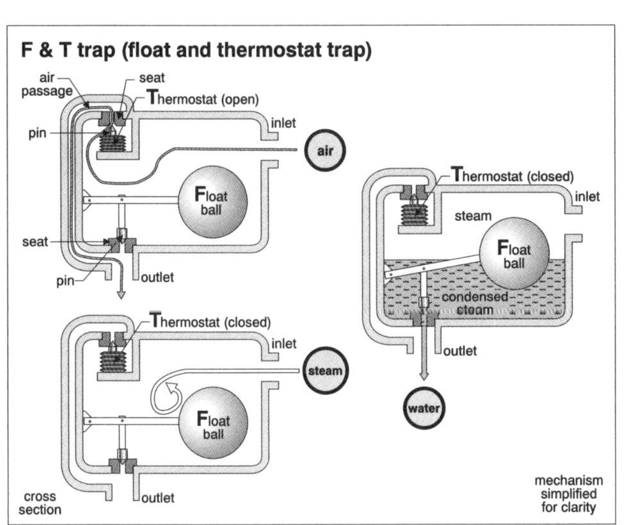

1126

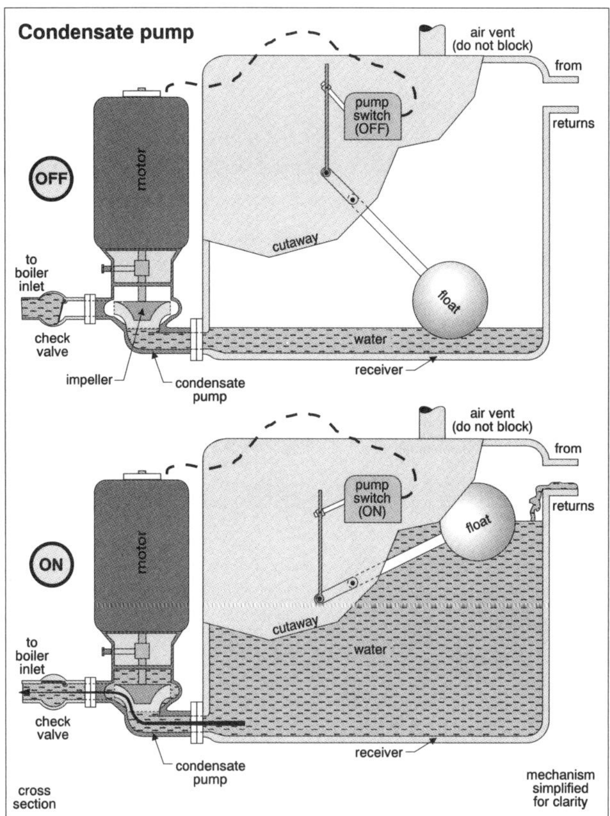

1127

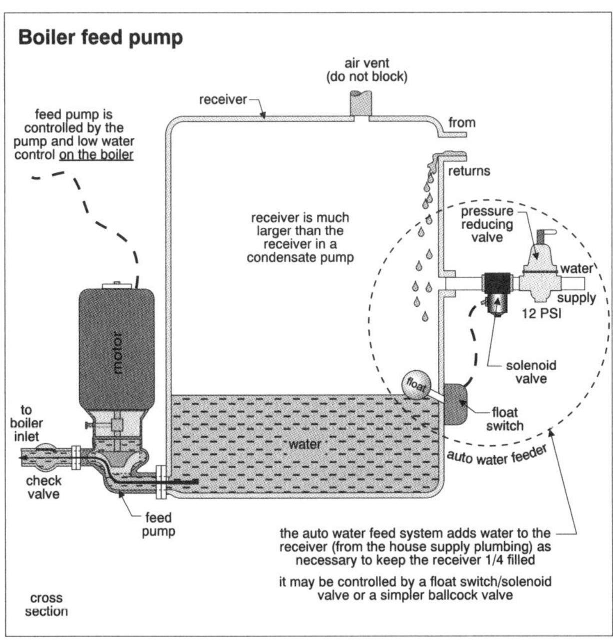

1128

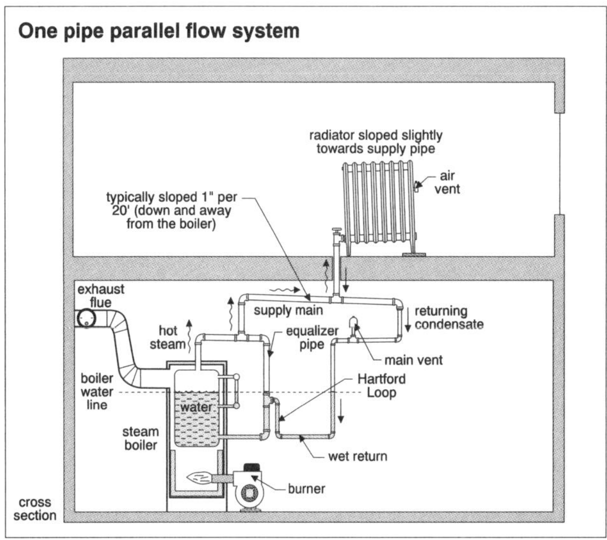

1129

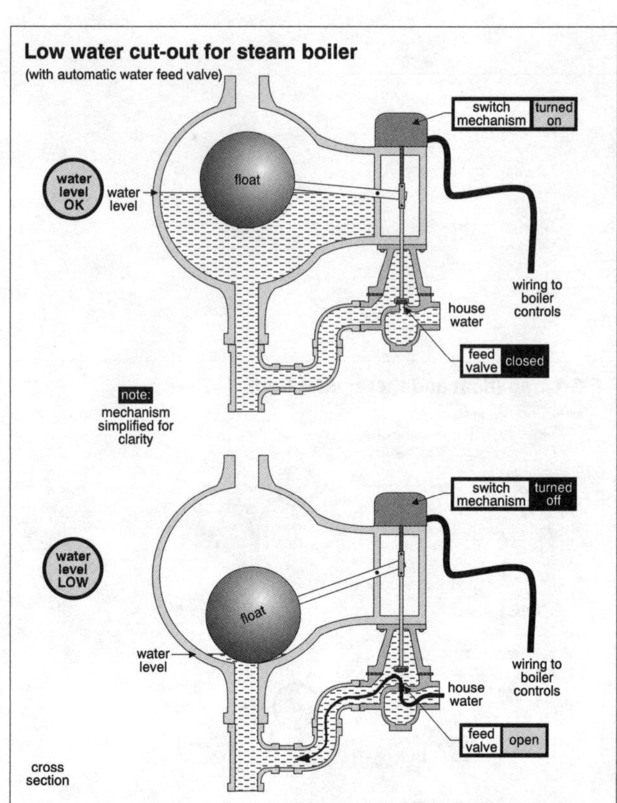

1131

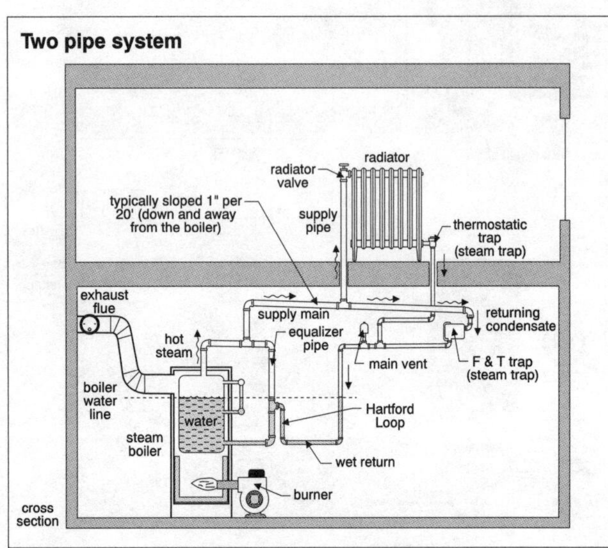

1130

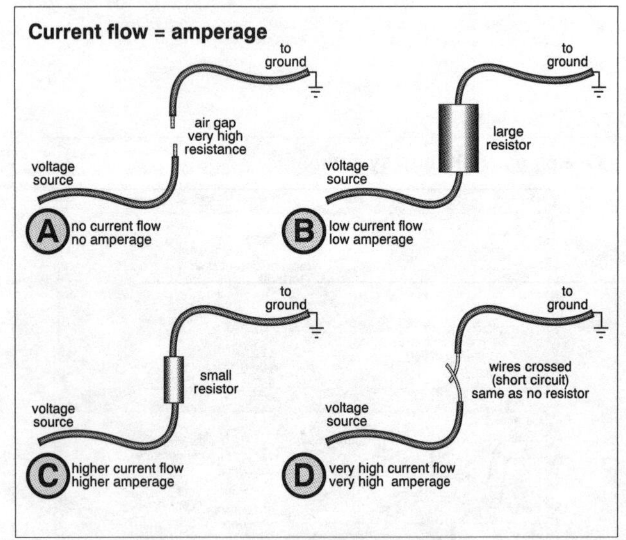

1132

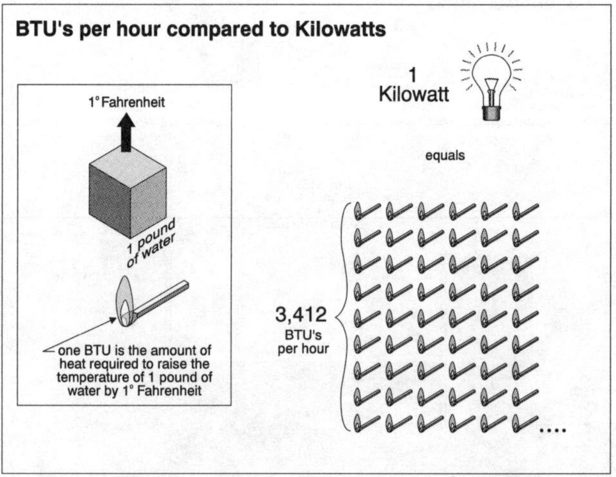

1133

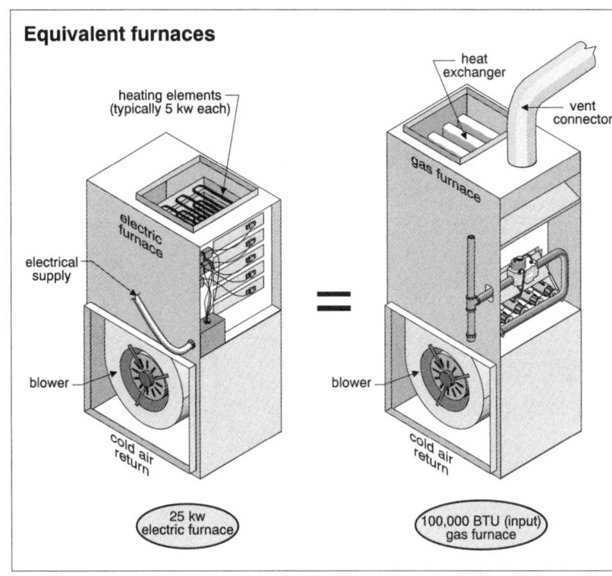

1134

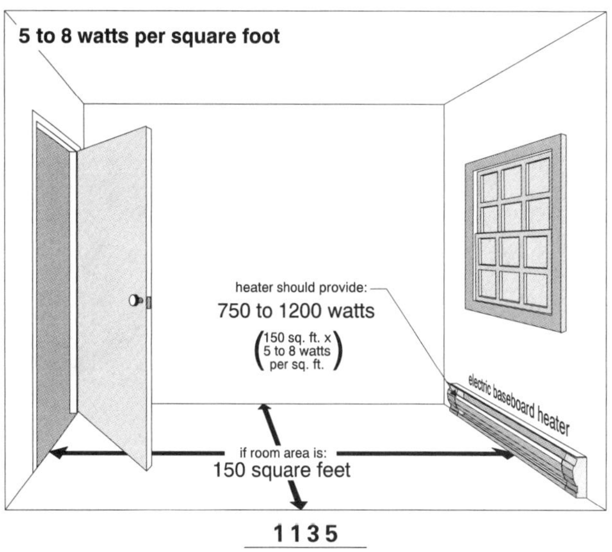

1135

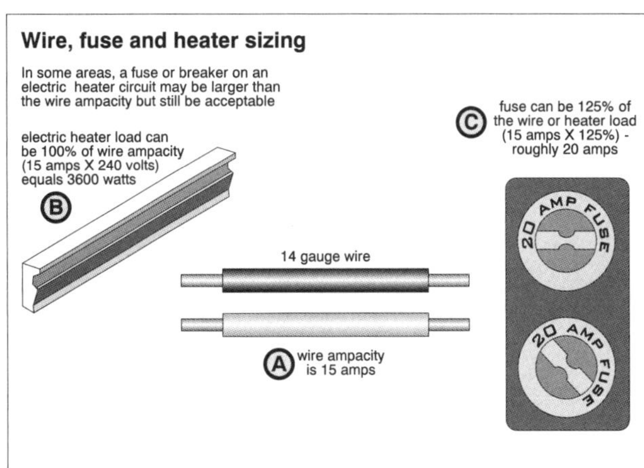

1136

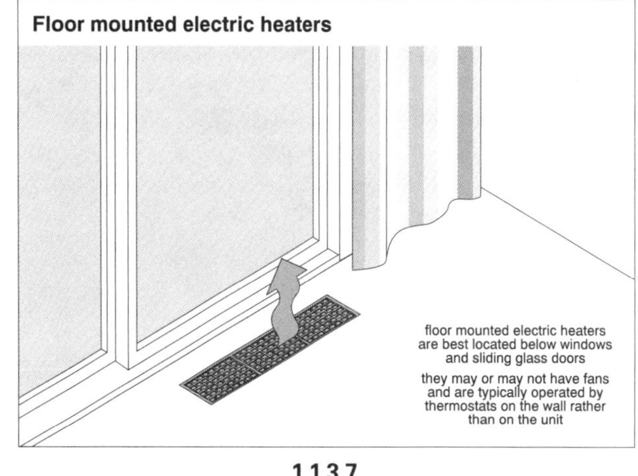

1137

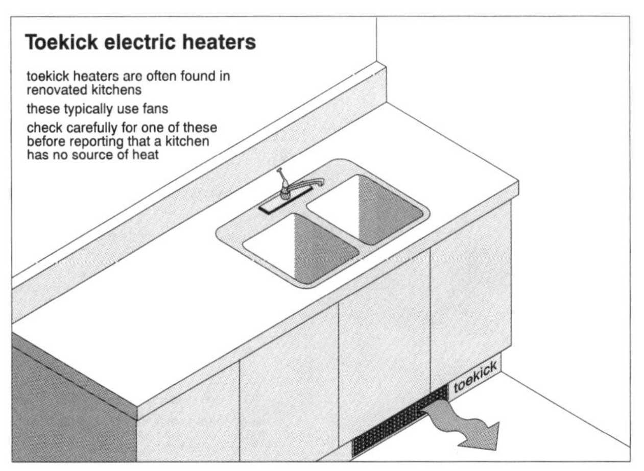

1138

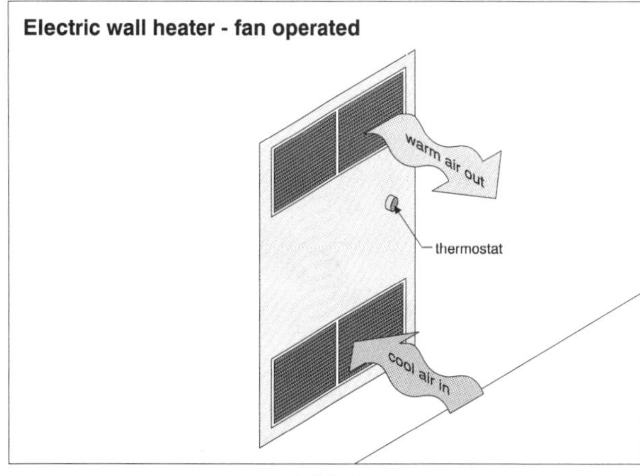

1139

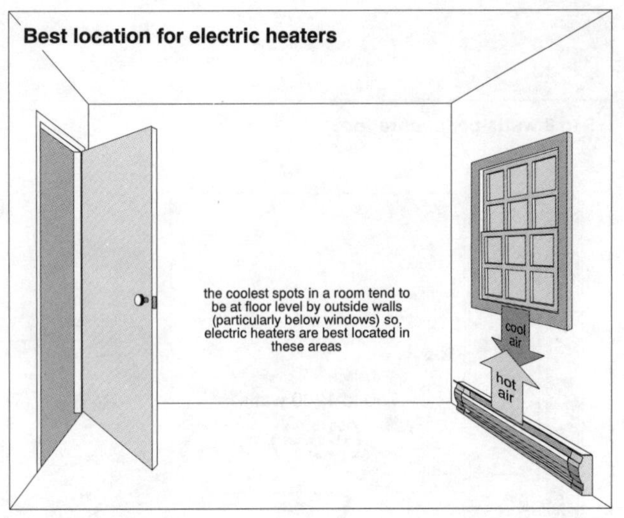

1140

Wiring for electric space heaters

distribution panel
from service box
STOVE
grounding terminal
ground wire
to electric heater
to electric heater
if conventional wiring is used for electric heater circuits, the white wire should be wrapped with black electrical tape to show that it is a hot wire
wiring intended specifically for electric heater circuits typically has red or orange sheathing and contains one black and one red wire
black wire
red wire
the fuses/breakers for 240 volt electric heaters must be linked together
wrap white wire with black tape
neutral bus bar

1141

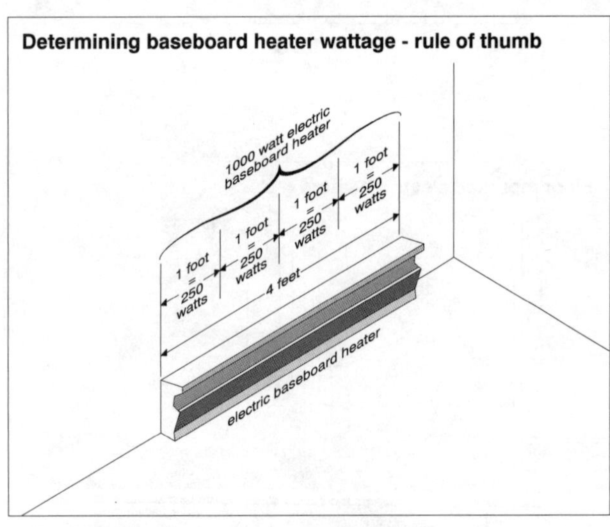

1142

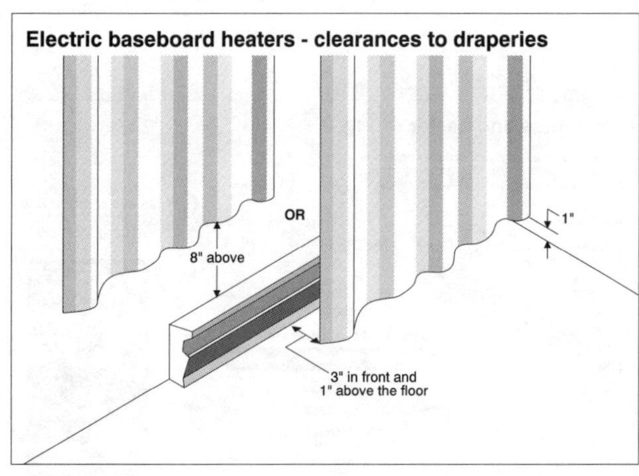

1143

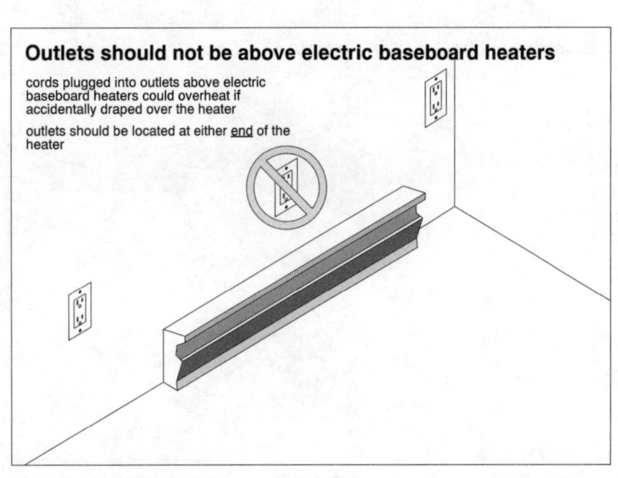

1144

Sequencers

hot air plenum
heating elements (typically 5 kw each)
elements turned on
25 kw electric furnace
5 120 to 360 seconds later
4 90 to 270 seconds later
3 60 to 180 seconds later
2 30 to 90 seconds later
1 thermostat calls for heat
electrical supply
blower
cold air return

the sequencers control when the heating elements come on

the elements are activated at 30 - 90 second intervals to avoid demand surges on the electrical system

in a **staged furnace**, the heating elements come on in sequence as long as the temperature at the thermostat continues to drop

once the temperature starts to rise, no more elements are turned on

when there is minimal demand for heat, the furnace may be utilizing only one or two heating elements

1145

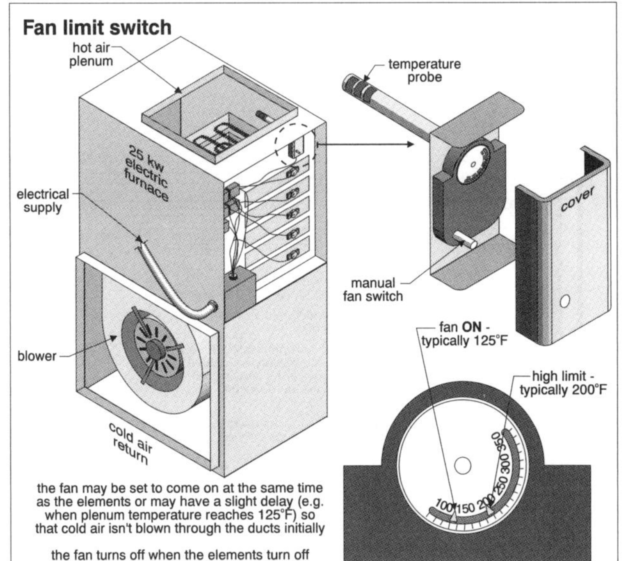

1146

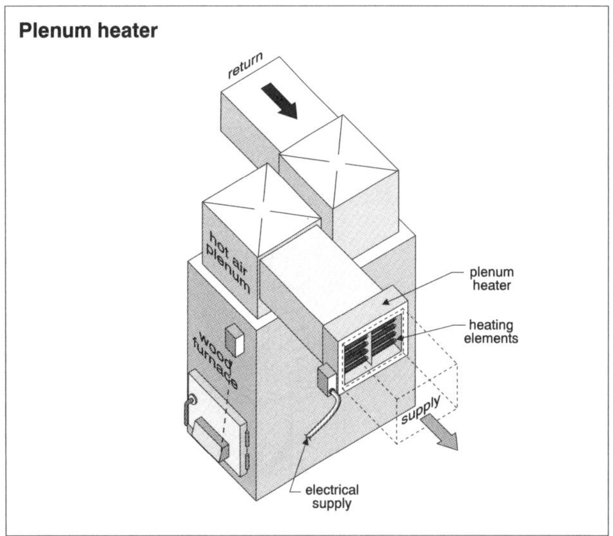

1147

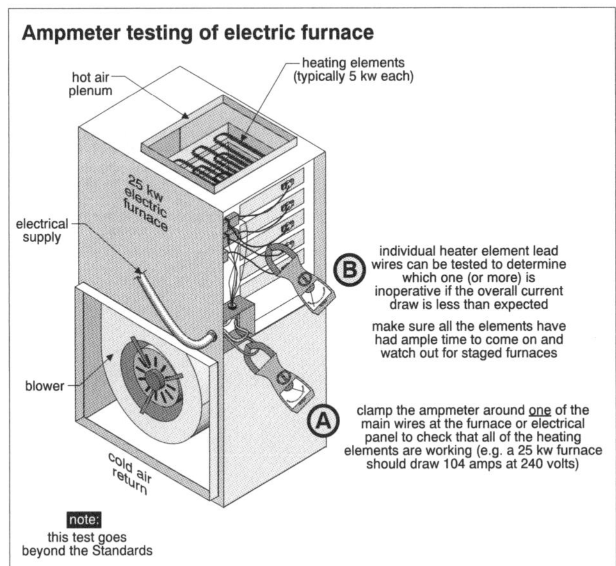

1148

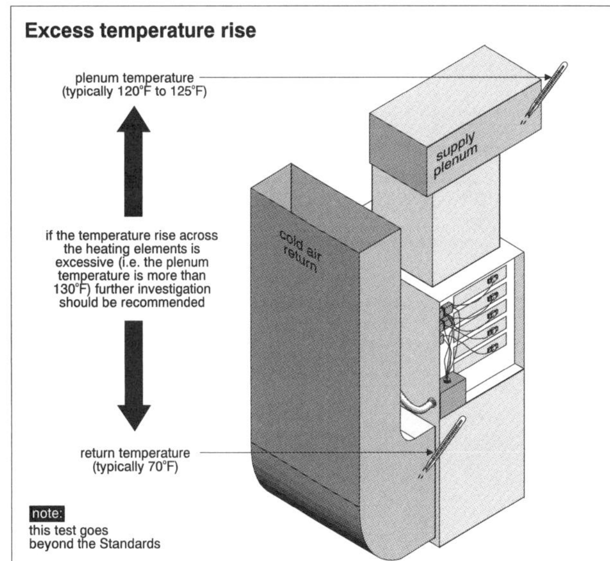

1149

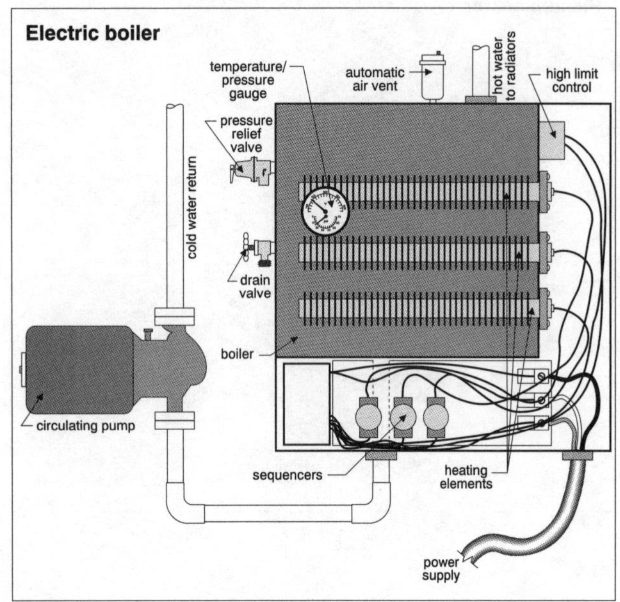

1150

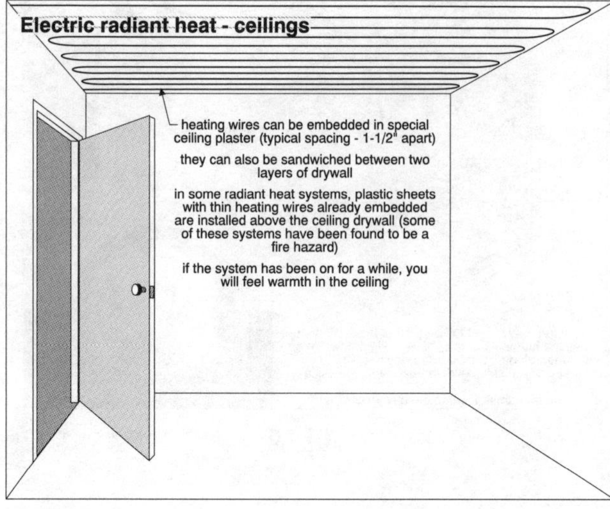

1151

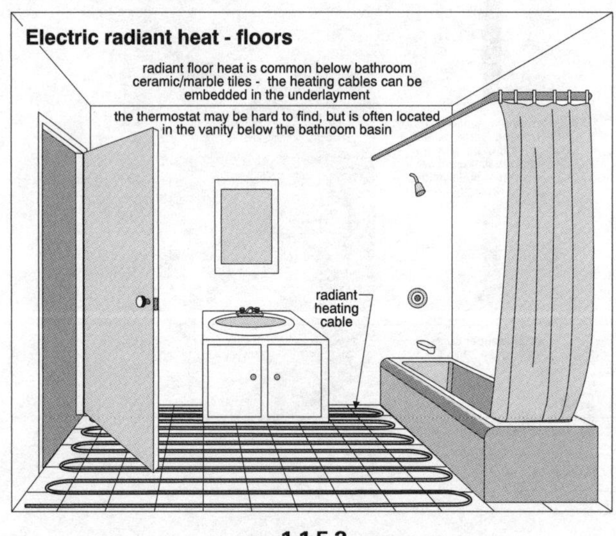

1152

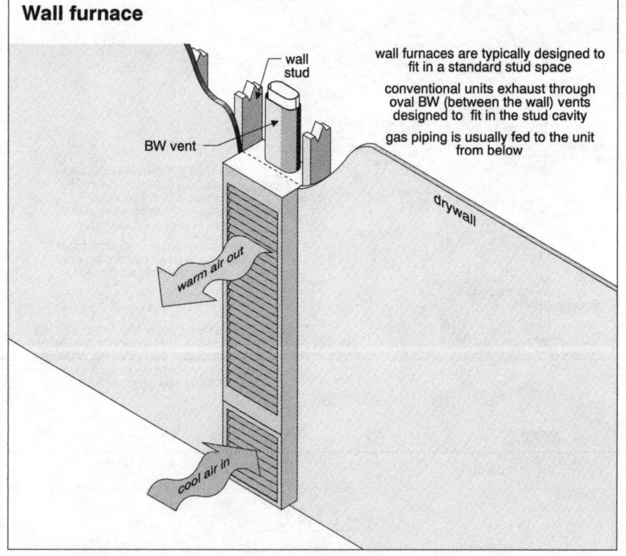

1153

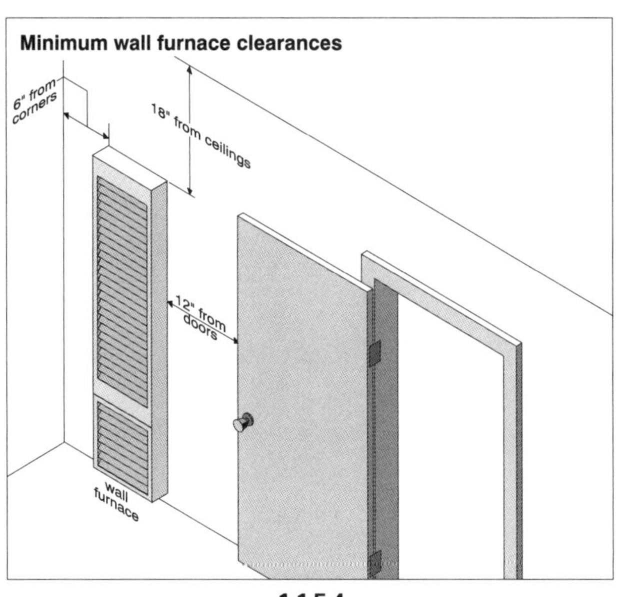

1154

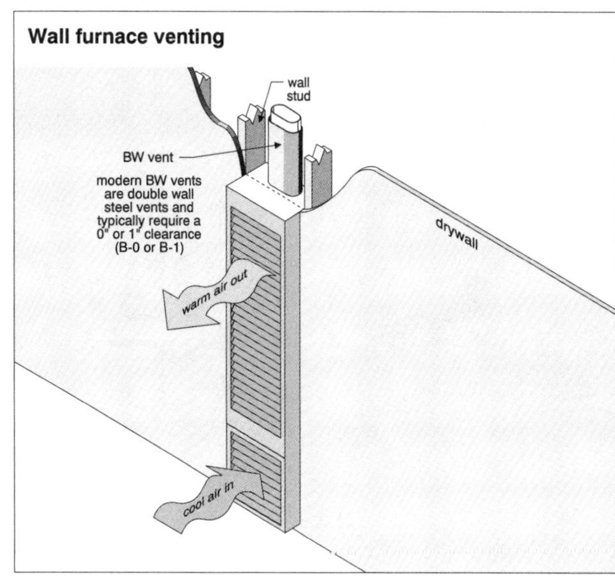

1155

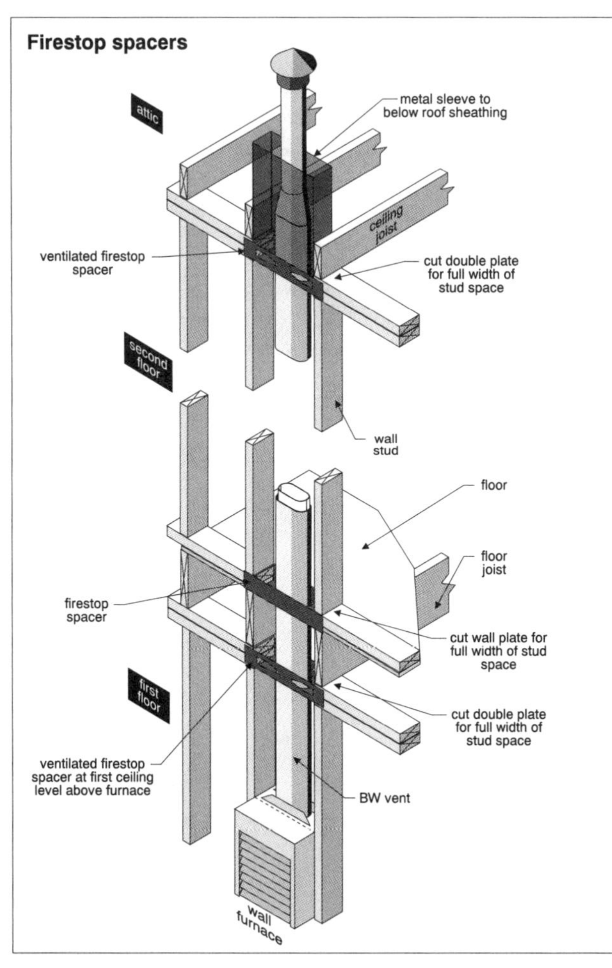

1156

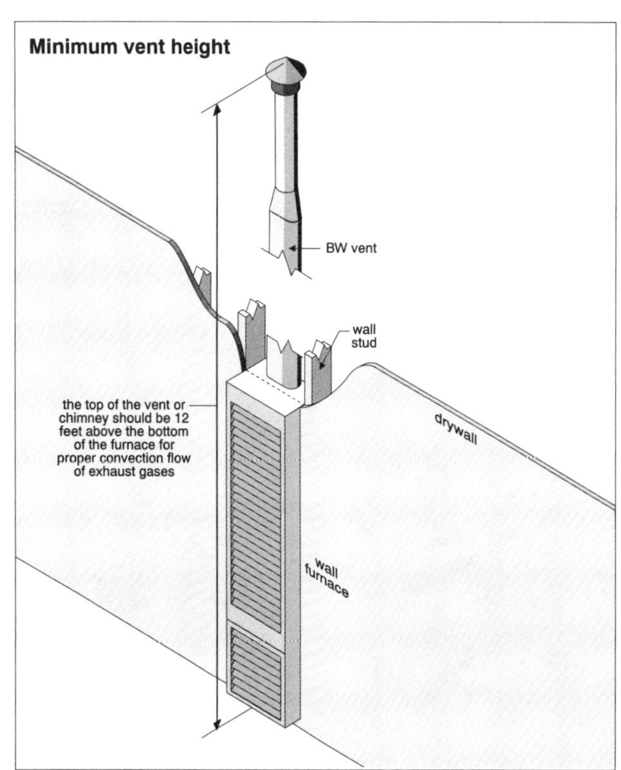

1157

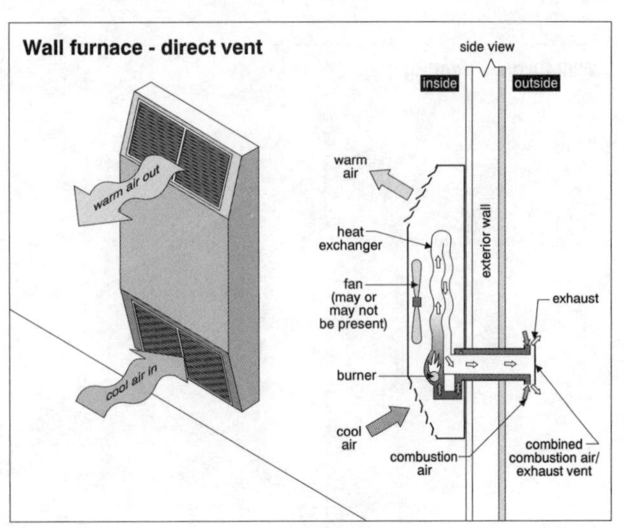

1158

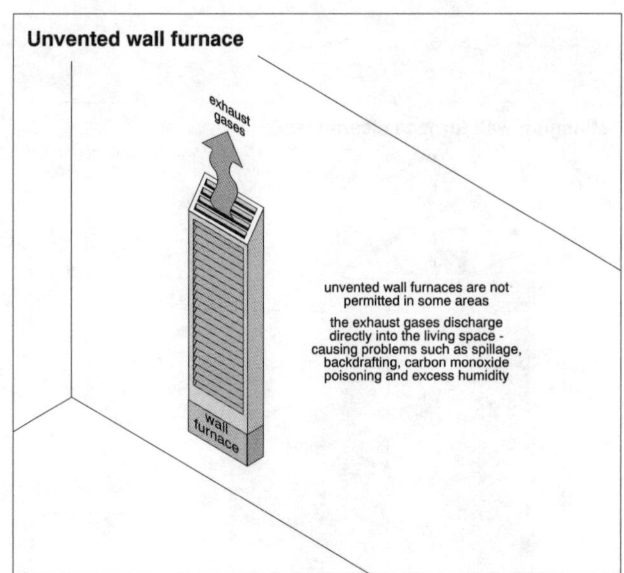

1159

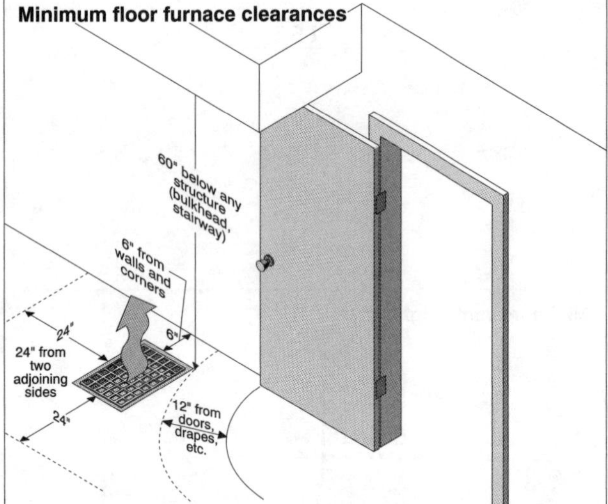

1160

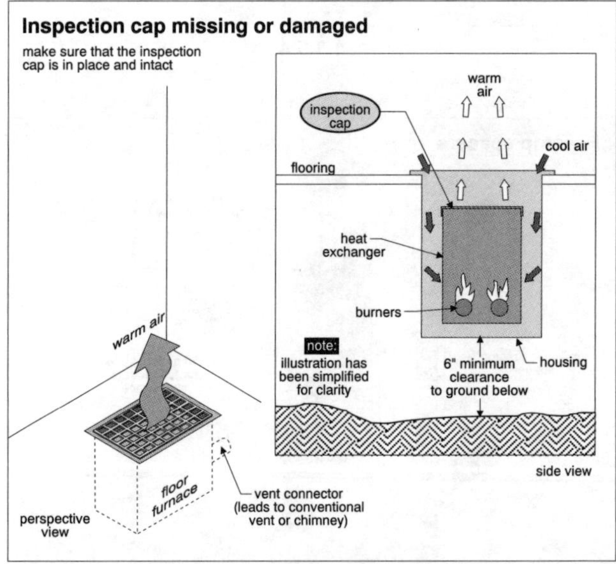

1161

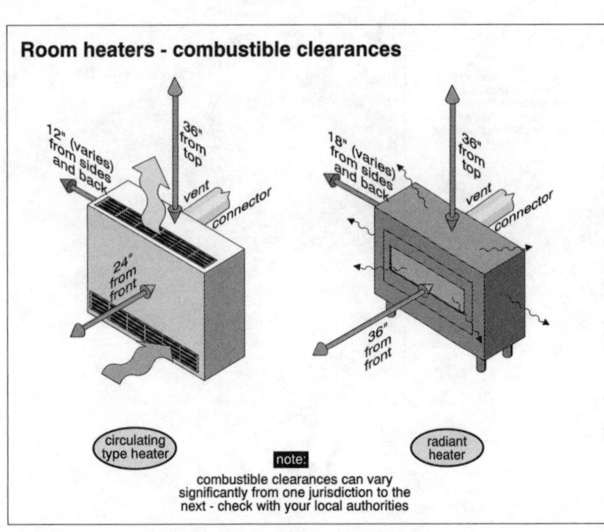

1162

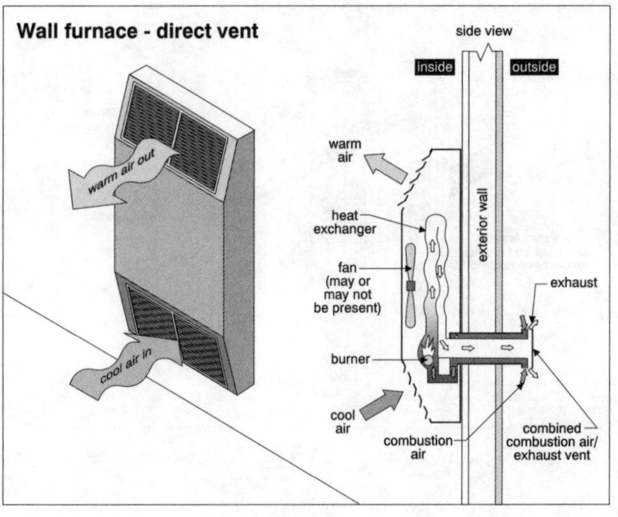

1163

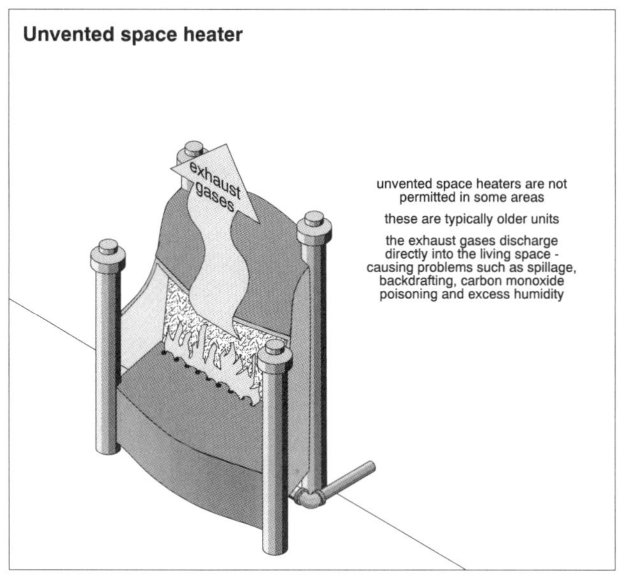

1164

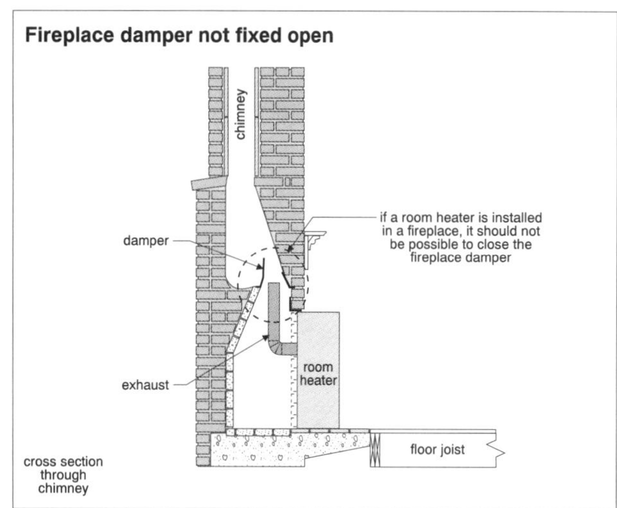

1165

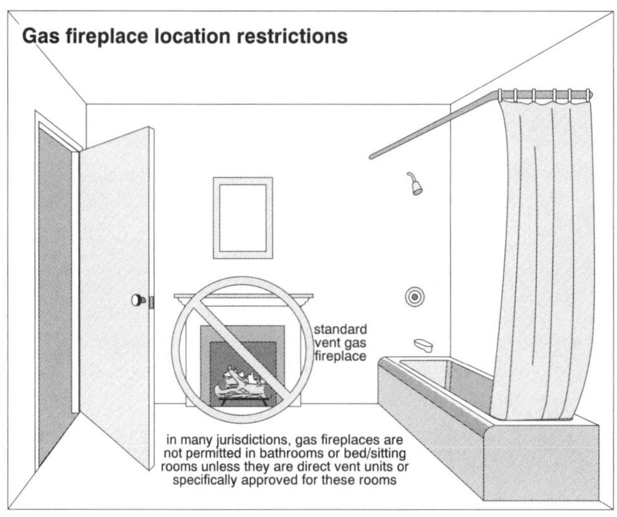

1166

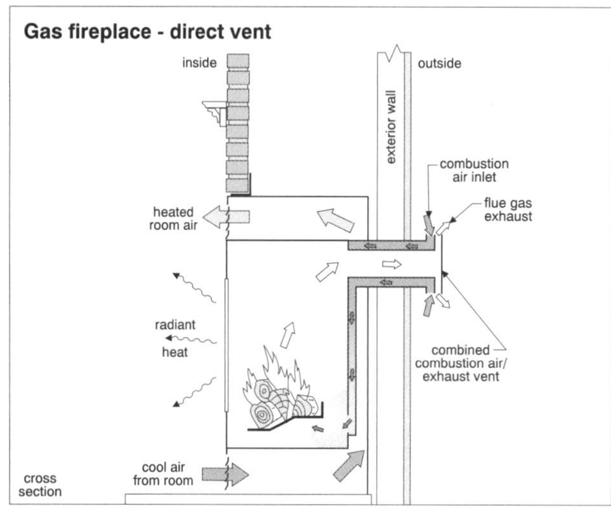

1167

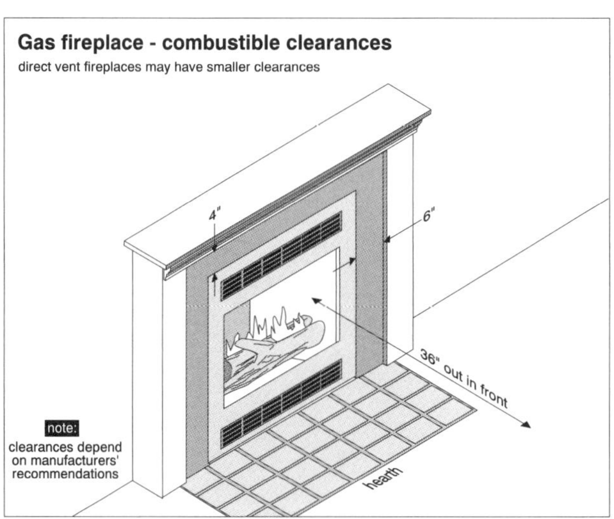

1168

CHAPTER 5

AIR CONDITIONING

THE BASICS

201..... 1200 Moving heat from the inside to the outside
201..... 1201 Heat transfer at the inside coil
201..... 1202 Evaporator coil – collecting hot air inside the house
201..... 1203 The Freon gas goes outside
201..... 1204 Compressors – heating up Freon gas
201..... 1205 Condenser coil – exhausting hot air to the outside
202..... 1206 Hot liquid back to the house
202..... 1207 Expansion devices – cooling hot liquid Freon
202..... 1208 Air conditioning – schematic of system
202..... 1209 Latent heat of vaporization
202..... 1210 Discharging condensate
202..... 1211 High pressure and low pressure sides
203..... 1212 Inspecting the condenser unit
203..... 1213 Air conditioning – schematic of system
203..... 1214 Water-cooled air conditioning – schematic of system
203..... 1215 Central air conditioning vs. ductless air conditioning
203..... 1216 Ductless air conditioning system

AIR CONDITIONING CAPACITY

203..... 1217 One ton of cooling
204..... 1218 How much area can one ton cool?
204..... 1219 Larger ducts are required for air conditioning
204..... 1220 Bigger is not better
204..... 1221 Guessing the size
204..... 1222 Measure temperature drop across inside coil

COMPRESSOR

204..... 1223 Don't test when it's cold
205..... 1224 Wait before restarting a compressor
205..... 1225 Slugging
205..... 1226 Condensing unit out of level
205..... 1227 Excess electric current draw (beyond the Standards)
205..... 1228 Missing electrical shut-off
205..... 1229 Scroll compressor
206..... 1230 Scroll vs. standard compressor

CONDENSER COIL (OUTDOOR COIL)

206..... 1231 Water heater exhaust vent too close to condenser
206..... 1232 Dryer vent too close to condenser
206..... 1233 Water-cooled air conditioning – schematic of system
207..... 1234 Testing water-cooled air conditioners
207..... 1235 Missing backflow preventer

EVAPORATOR COIL (INDOOR COIL)

207..... 1236 A-coil
207..... 1237 Slab coil
208..... 1238 Attic evaporator coil
208..... 1239 Coil upstream of heat exchanger
208..... 1240 Evaporator coil – inspection procedures
208..... 1241 Thermostatic expansion valve
208..... 1242 Capillary tube defects

CONDENSATE SYSTEM

208..... 1243 Leaking condensate tray
209..... 1244 Auxiliary condensate line from attic evaporator coil
209..... 1245 Trap required in condensate line
209..... 1246 Condensate discharge locations
209..... 1247 Condensate pump

REFRIGERANT LINES

210..... 1248 Refrigerant lines
210..... 1249 Filter/dryer
210..... 1250 Sight glass
210..... 1251 Leaking refrigerant lines – vulnerable areas

CONDENSER FAN (OUTDOOR FAN)

210..... 1252 Condenser fan
210..... 1253 Condenser coil location requirements

CHAPTER 5

EVAPORATOR FAN (INDOOR FAN)

211..... 1254 Evaporator fan
211..... 1255 Belt or pulley adjustment

DUCT SYSTEM

211..... 1256 General rule for duct work adequacy
211..... 1257 Flow of cooled air – older-style ductwork
212..... 1258 Flow of cooled air – modern ductwork
212..... 1259 High and low returns
212..... 1260 Testing cold air returns
212..... 1261 Ducts in concrete floor slabs
212..... 1262 Air return outside room
212..... 1263 Close humidifier damper in summer
213..... 1264 Vapor barriers and air conditioning ductwork
213..... 1265 Flexible ductwork

THERMOSTATS

213..... 1266 Thermostat – bi-metallic (mercury bulb)
213..... 1267 Thermostat – bi-metallic (snap action)
213..... 1268 Poor location for thermostat

LIFE EXPECTANCY

213..... 1269 Typical compressor life

EVAPORATIVE COOLERS

214..... 1270 Three types of evaporative coolers
214..... 1271 Single stage evaporative cooler (swamp cooler)
214..... 1272 Two stage evaporative cooler (swamp cooler)

WHOLE HOUSE FANS

214..... 1273 Whole house fan
214..... 1274 Whole house fan – inadequate attic venting

HEAT PUMPS

HEAT PUMPS IN THEORY

214..... 1275 Heat pump principles
215..... 1276 Heat pump evaporator coil – grabbing heat from the outside air
215..... 1277 Heat pump condenser coil – giving off warm air to the inside
215..... 1278 Heat pump schematic – summer mode
215..... 1279 Co-efficient of performance (COP & balance point)
215..... 1280 Balance point
215..... 1281 All-electric heat pump system
216..... 1282 Water source heat pump – open loop system (well-based)
216..... 1283 Ground source heat pump – horizontal closed loop

HEAT PUMPS IN PRACTICE

216..... 1284 How much area can one ton cool?
216..... 1285 Triple split system heat pump (old systems)
216..... 1286 Two expansion devices
216..... 1287 Defrost cycle
217..... 1288 Poor outdoor coil location
217..... 1289 Flow of cooled air – modern ductwork
217..... 1290 Testing back-up heat
217..... 1291 Water source heat pump – open loop system (well-based)
218..... 1292 Ground source heat pump – horizontal closed loop
218..... 1293 Ground source heat pump – vertical closed loop
218..... 1294 Bivalent schematic

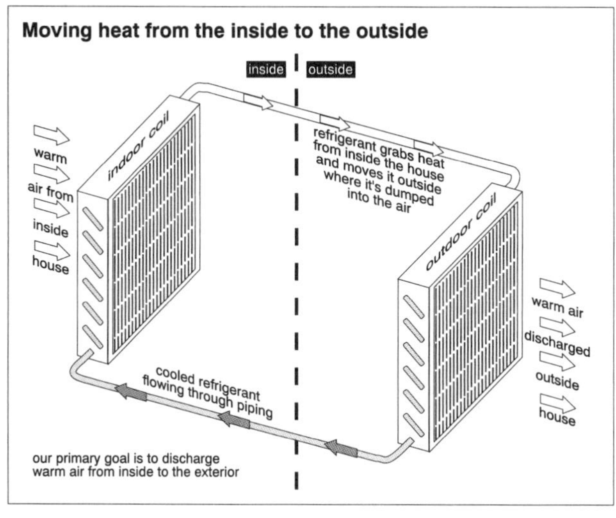

1200

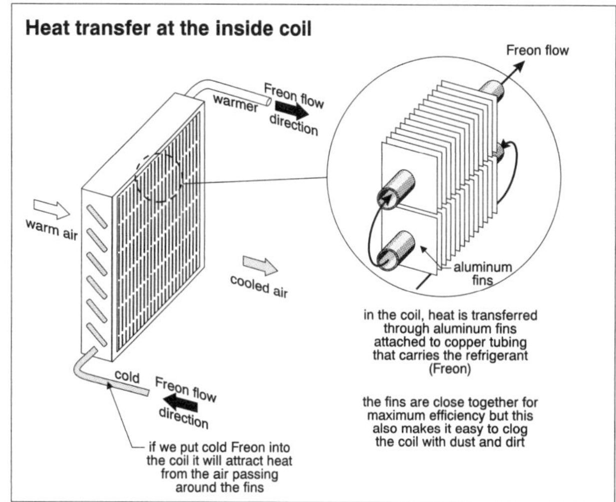

1201

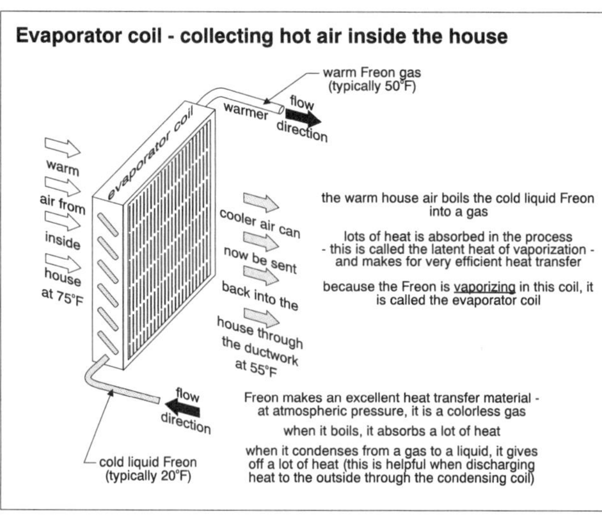

1202

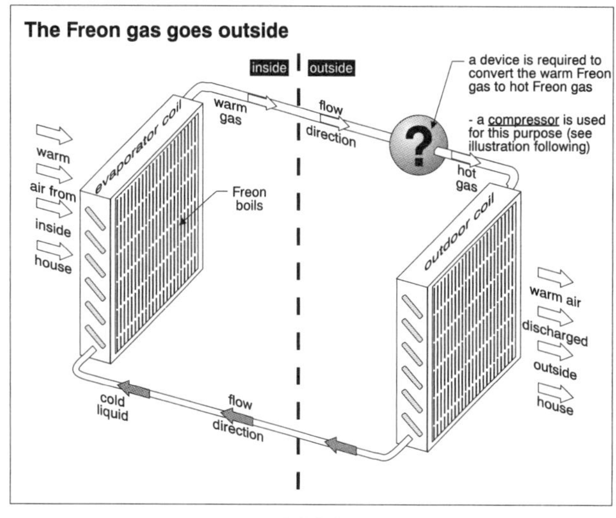

1203

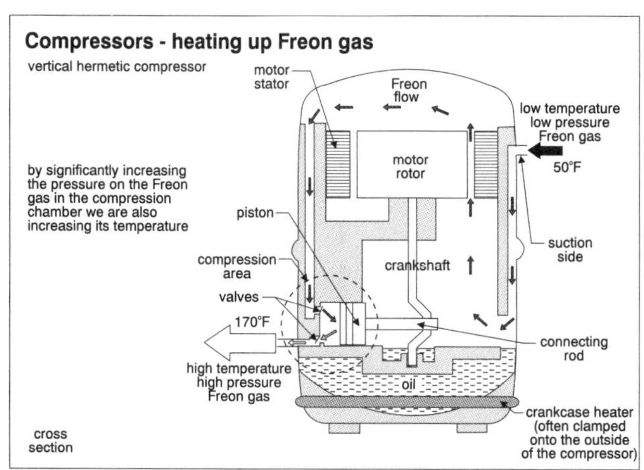

1204

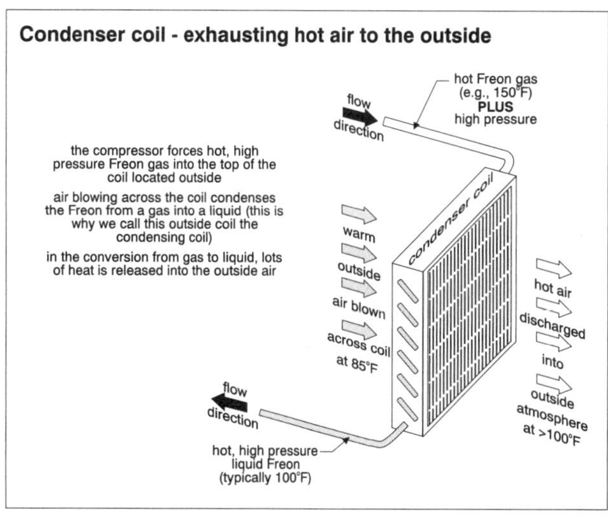

1205

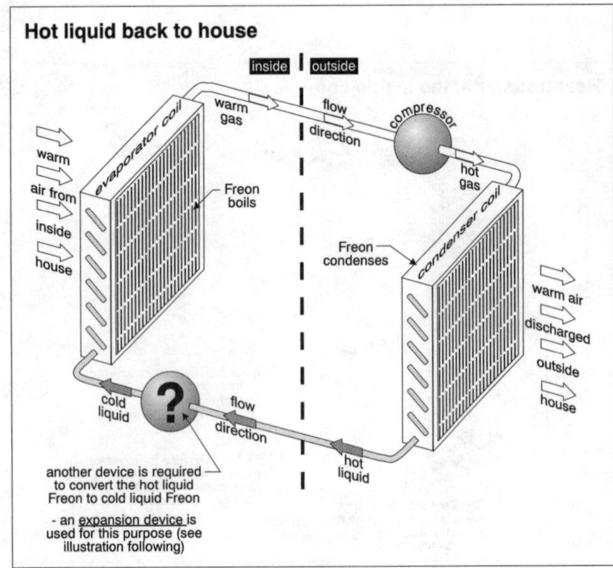

1206

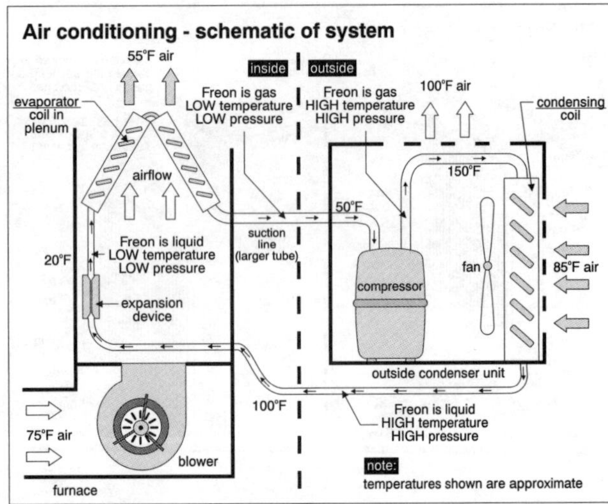

1208

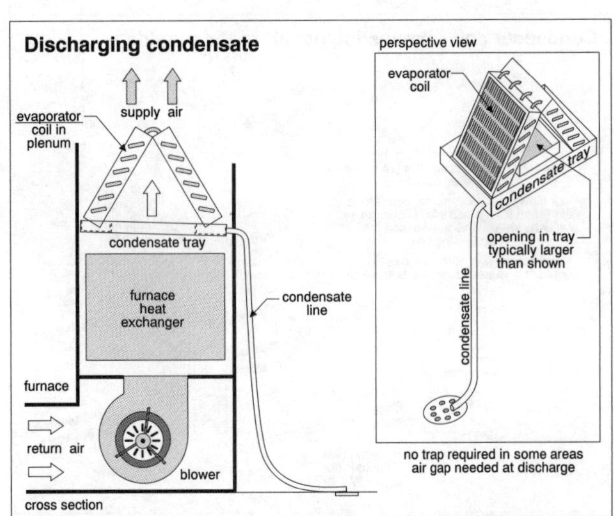

1210

Expansion devices - cooling hot liquid Freon

the capillary tube is a bottleneck designed to restrict the flow of liquid Freon

at the discharge point of the bottleneck, the Freon is at a much lower pressure

when the pressure is reduced the temperature also goes down

the Freon coming out of the tube may be about 20°F and is ready to go into the evaporator coil to collect more heat

the expansion device is typically just upstream of the evaporator coil

low temperature
low pressure Freon liquid

high temperature
high pressure Freon liquid

restriction

Freon

flow

20°F

Freon

flow

100°F

metering (or expansion) device

1207

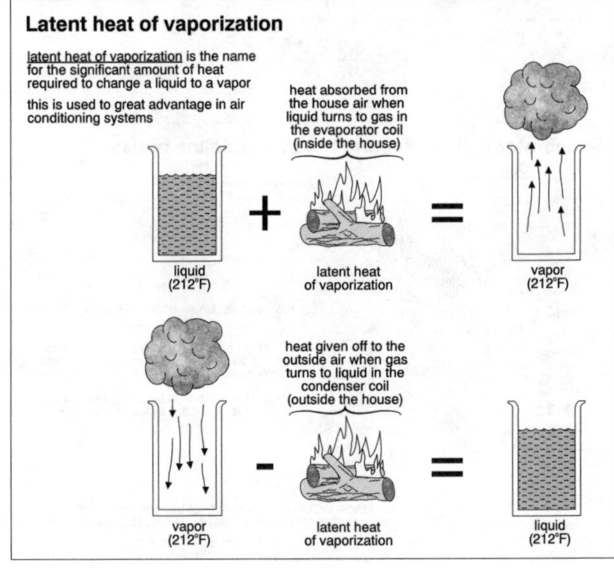

1209

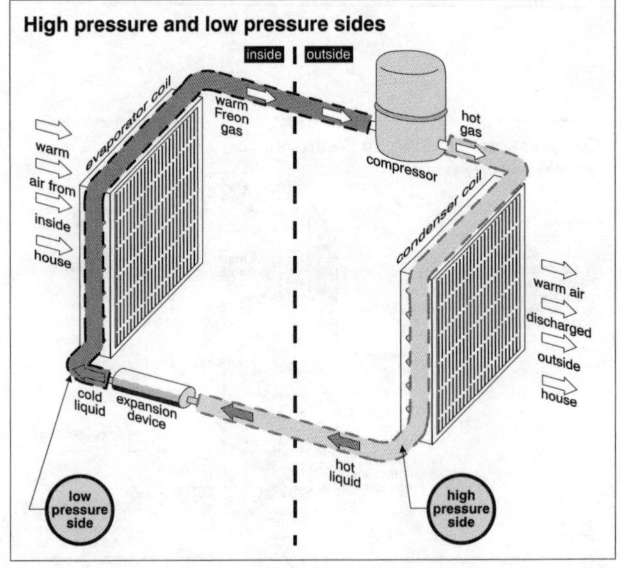

1211

Inspecting the condenser unit

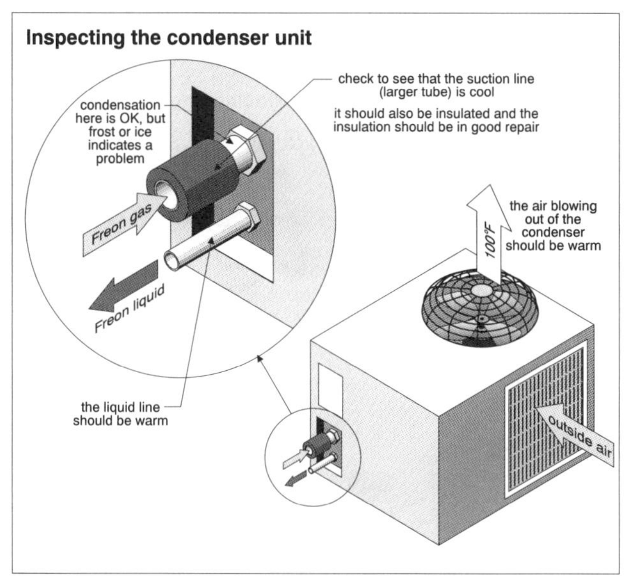

1212

Air conditioning - schematic of system

55°F air
inside
outside
evaporator coil in plenum
Freon is gas LOW temperature LOW pressure
Freon is gas HIGH temperature HIGH pressure
100°F air
condensing coil
airflow
150°F
50°F
suction line (larger tube)
Freon is liquid LOW temperature LOW pressure
20°F
compressor
fan
85°F air
expansion device
outside condenser unit
100°F
Freon is liquid HIGH temperature HIGH pressure
75°F air
blower
furnace
note:
temperatures shown are approximate

1213

Water-cooled air conditioning - schematic of system

55°F air
inside
outside
evaporator coil in plenum
Freon is gas LOW temperature LOW pressure
Freon is gas HIGH temperature HIGH pressure
warm water out (to drain)
airflow
150°F
50°F
suction line (larger tube)
70°F
Freon is liquid LOW temperature LOW pressure
20°F
compressor
cold water in
expansion device
50°F
inside condenser unit
100°F
Freon is liquid HIGH temperature HIGH pressure
condensing coil
75°F air
blower
furnace
note:
-temperatures shown are approximate
-mechanics simplified for clarity

1214

Central air conditioning vs. ductless air conditioning

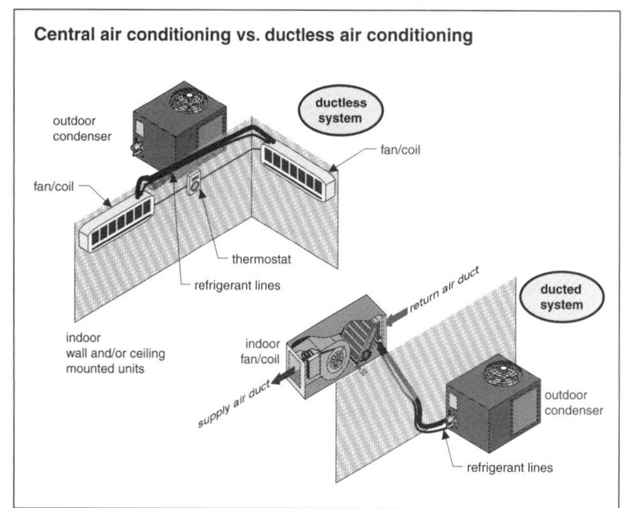

1215

Ductless (mini split) air conditioning system

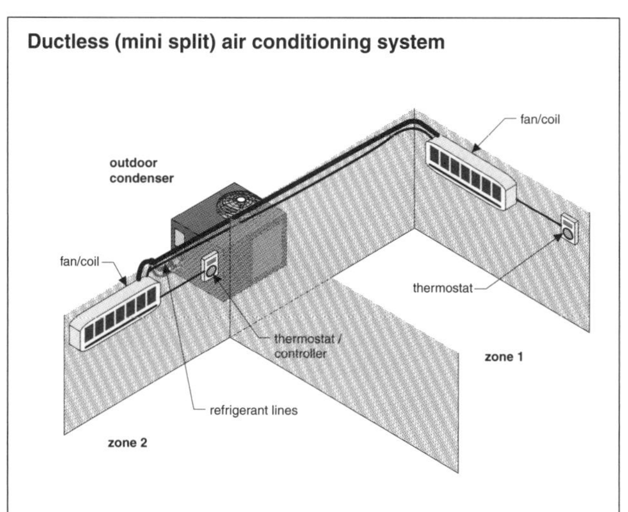

1216

One ton of cooling

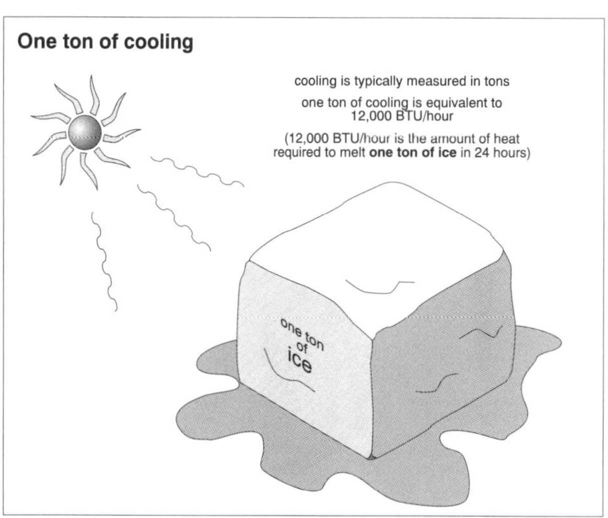

1217

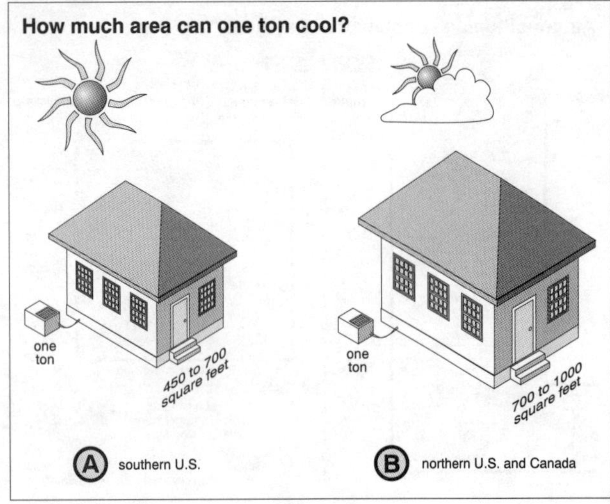

1218

Larger ducts are required for air conditioning

cold air is denser and harder to push through ductwork

larger ducts are required for air conditioned houses

look for updated ductwork where air conditioning has been retrofit in an older house (if it hasn't been updated the performance of the system may be poor)

cold air

50°F

airflow

ductwork

140°F

hot air

airflow

ductwork

1219

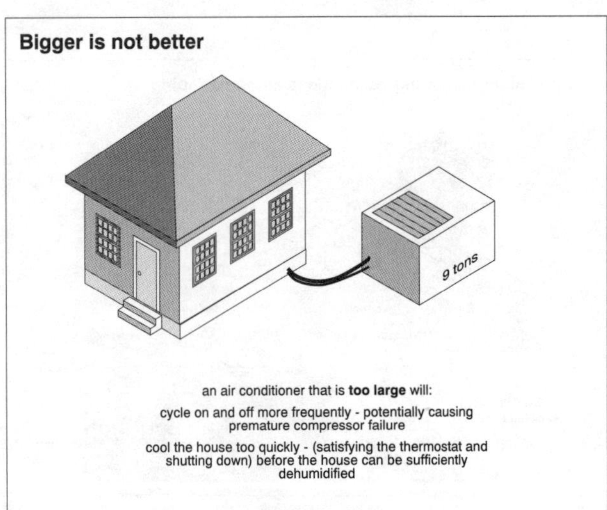

1220

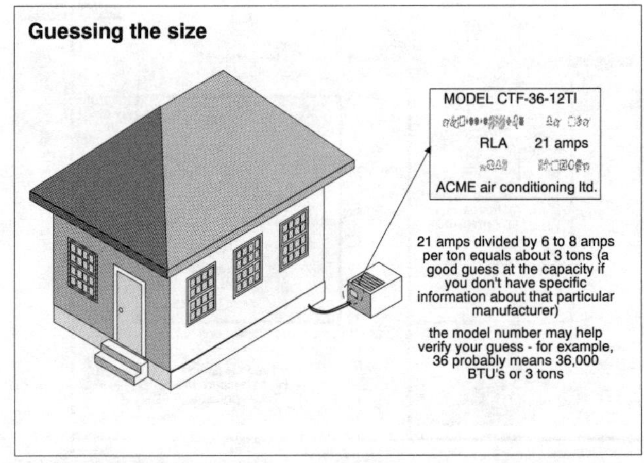

1221

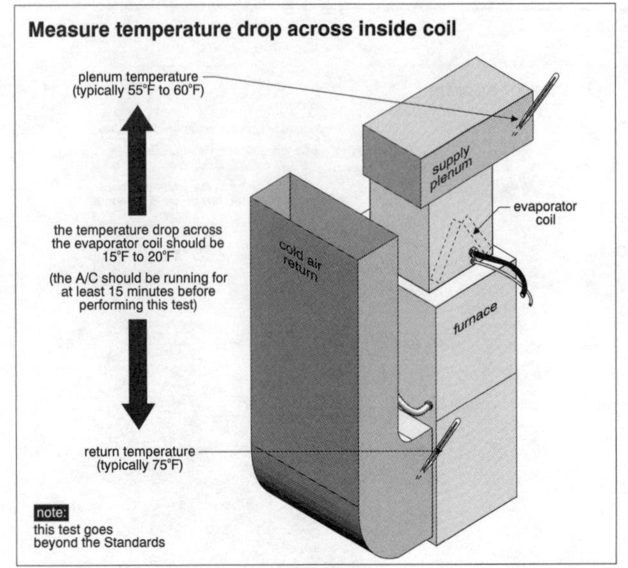

1222

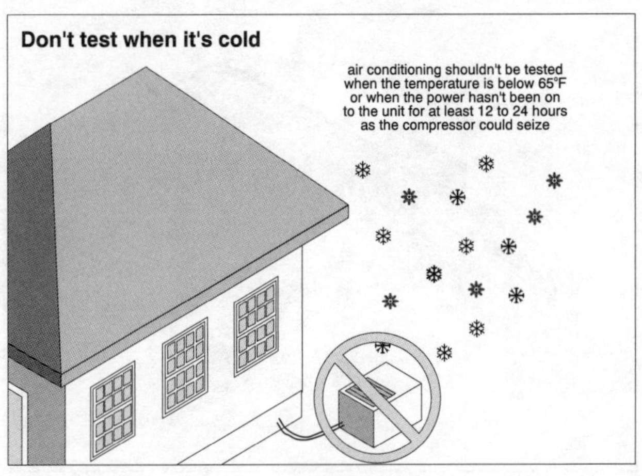

1223

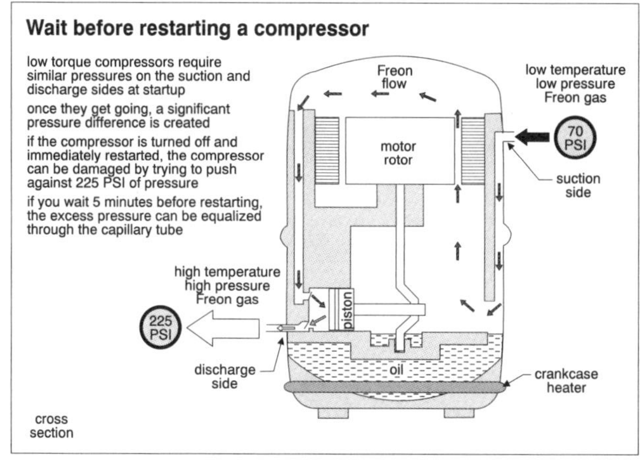

1224

Slugging

slugging is the term for the problem that occurs when Freon liquid instead of gas enters the compressor

this is very hard on the valves and is most often caused by the Freon not getting heated up enough at the evaporator (perhaps due to low airflow, dirty coil, furnace fan problems etc.)

Freon flow

motor rotor

suction side

valves

discharge side

oil

cross section

1225

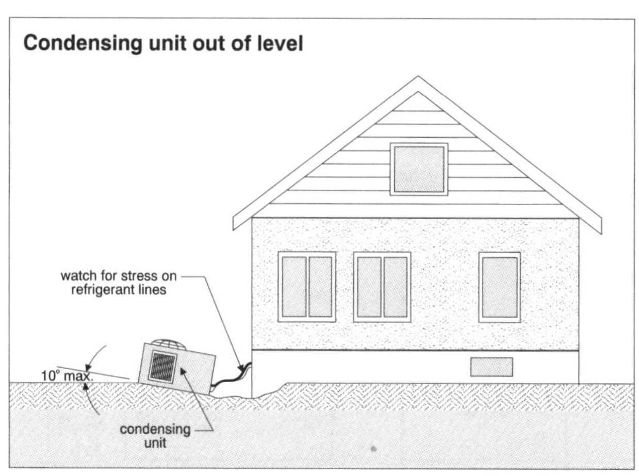

1226

Excess electric current draw (beyond the Standards)

using an amp-meter, measure the draw of the air conditioner at the electrical panel (be sure to subtract the amperage related to the condenser fan)

the measured amperage should be 60% to 90% of the **rated load amperage** (RLA) indicated on the data plate

if the current draw is at or above the RLA, the compressor may be near the end of its life

STOVE

distribution panel

to A/C

black wire

red wire

the current can be measured at either the red or black wire

neutral bus bar

neutral wire

amp meter

1227

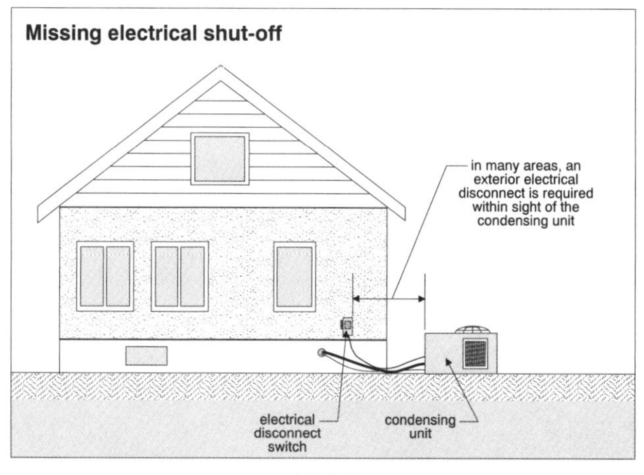

1228

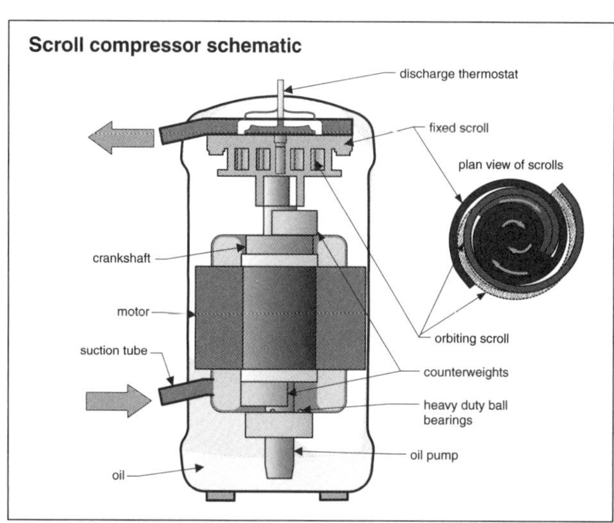

1229

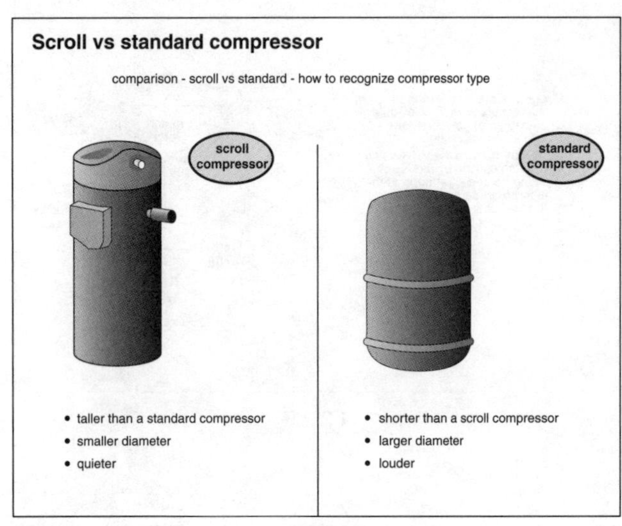

1230

Water heater exhaust vent too close to condenser

side wall vented water heaters discharging warm air near the condenser can reduce the capacity and efficiency of the air conditioning system

warm air

heat

1231

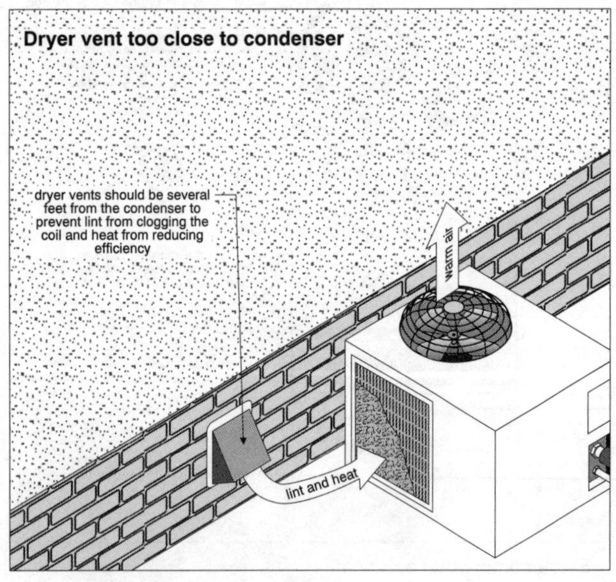

1232

Water-cooled air conditioning - schematic of system

inside | outside

55°F air

evaporator coil in plenum

airflow

Freon is gas LOW temperature LOW pressure

Freon is gas HIGH temperature HIGH pressure

150°F

warm water out (to drain)

70°F

50°F

suction line (larger tube)

20°F

Freon is liquid LOW temperature LOW pressure

expansion device

compressor

cold water in

50°F

inside condenser unit

100°F

Freon is liquid HIGH temperature HIGH pressure

condensing coil

75°F air

blower

furnace

note:
-temperatures shown are approximate
-mechanics simplified for clarity

1233

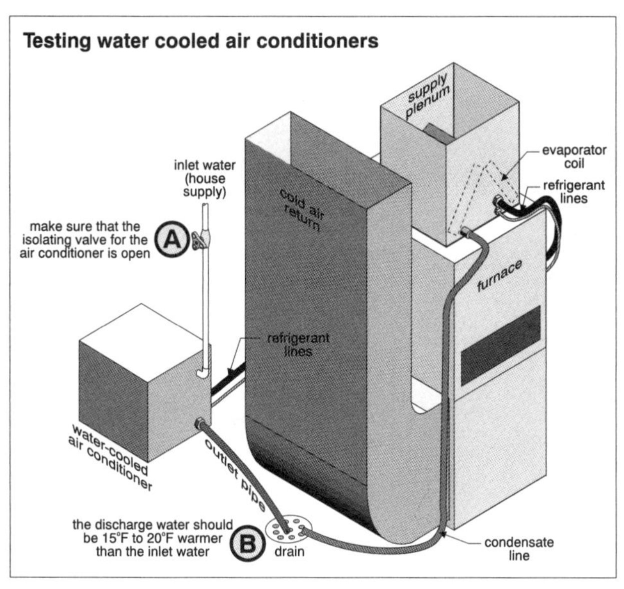

1234

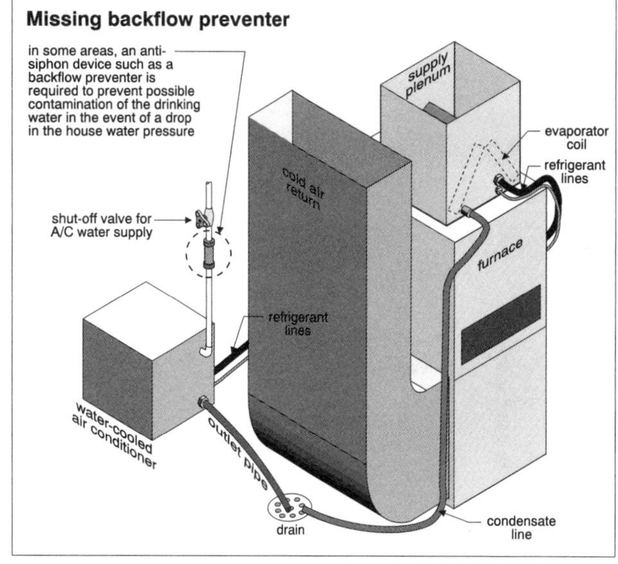

1235

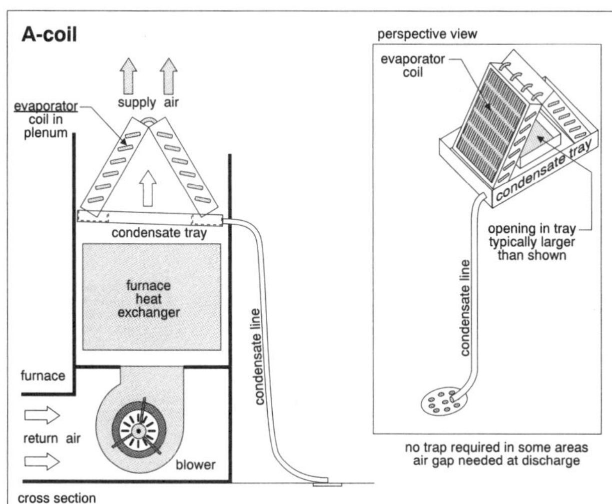

1236

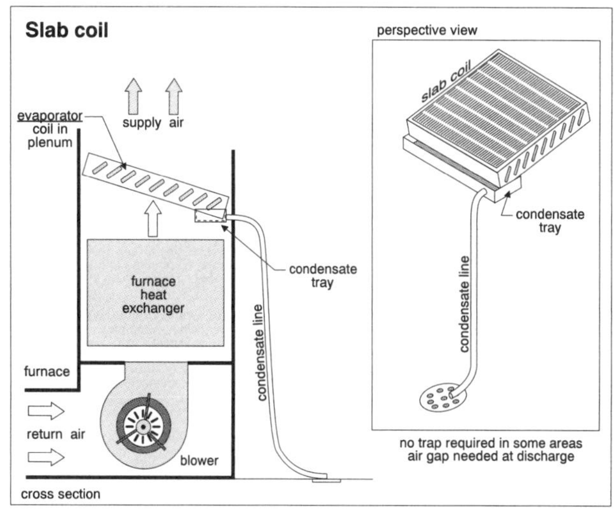

1237

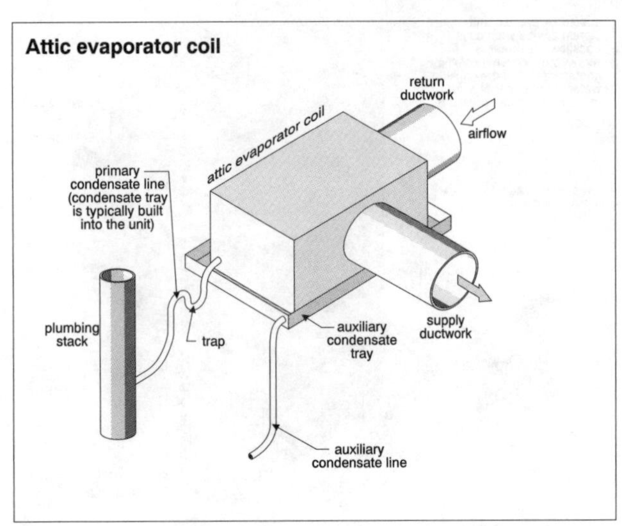

1238

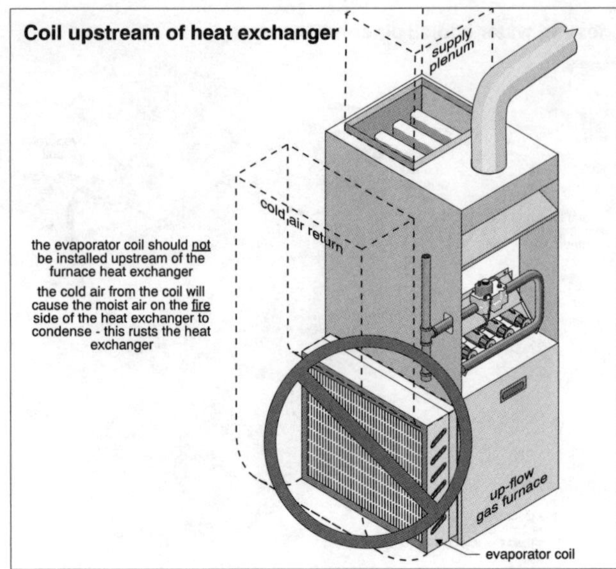

1239

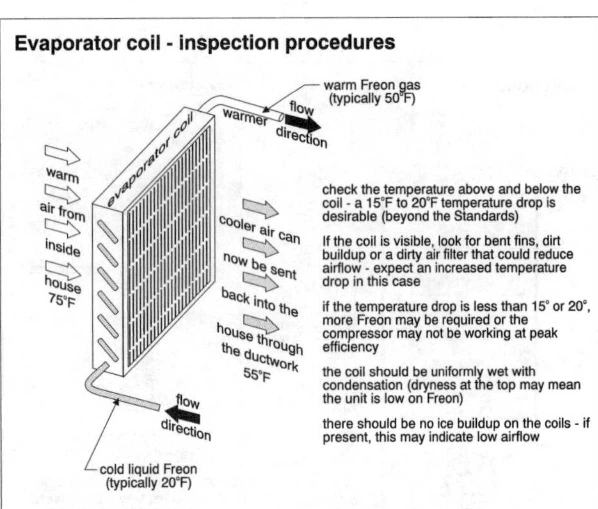

1240

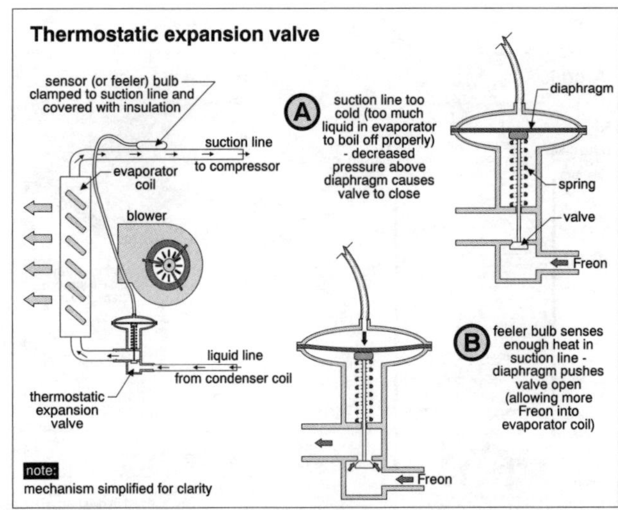

1241

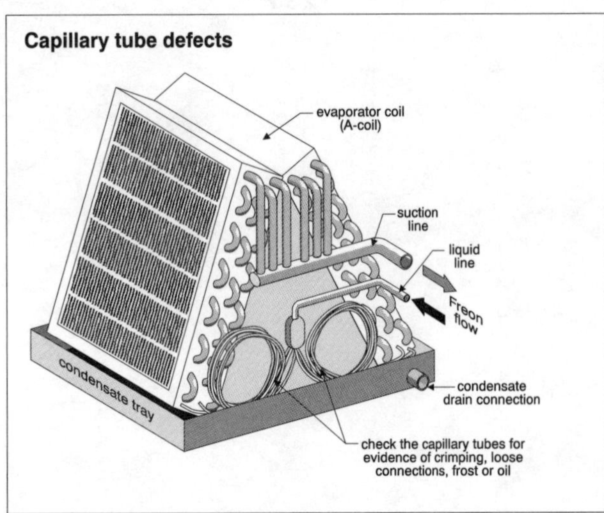

1242

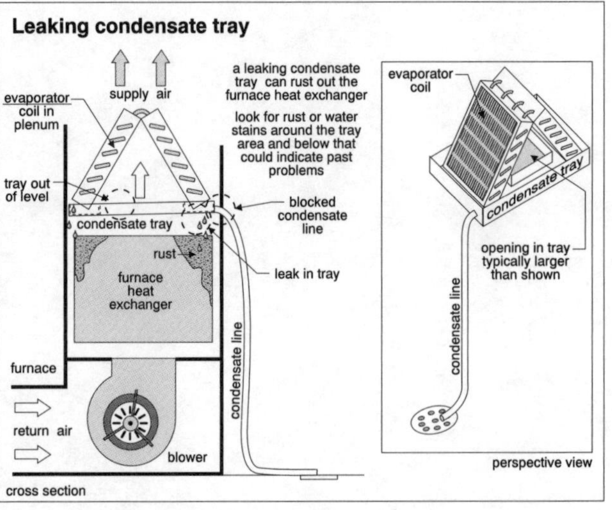

1243

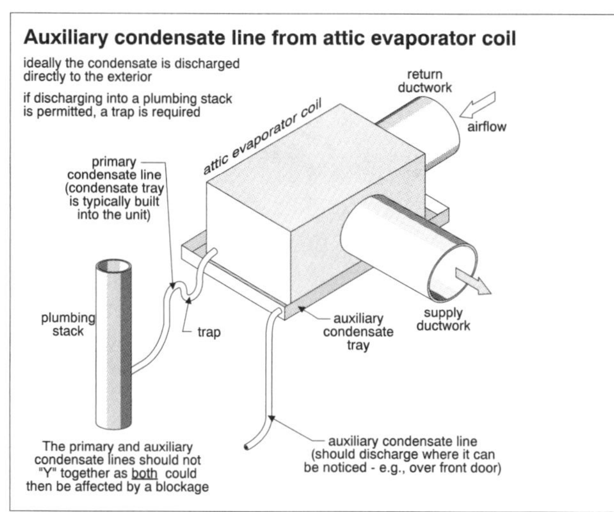

1244

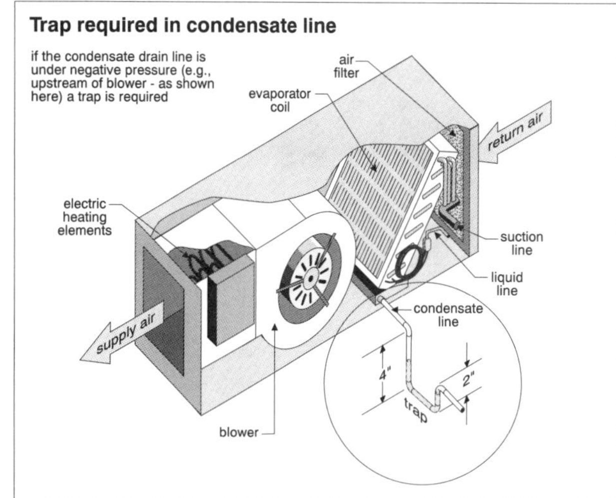

1245

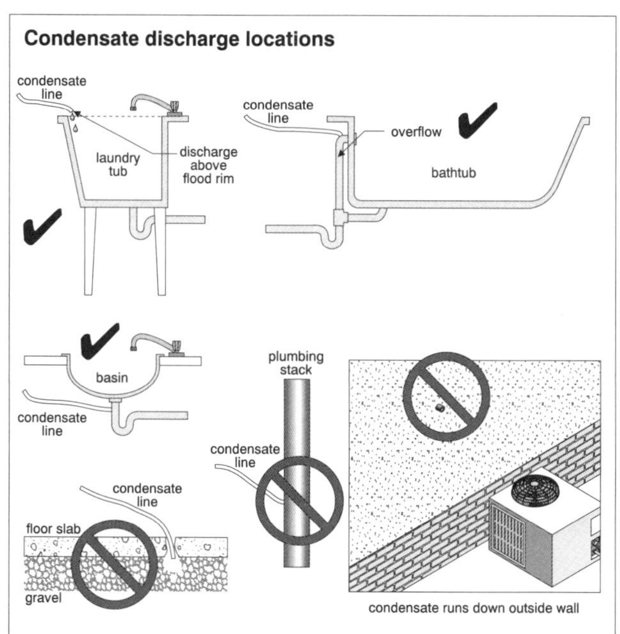

1246

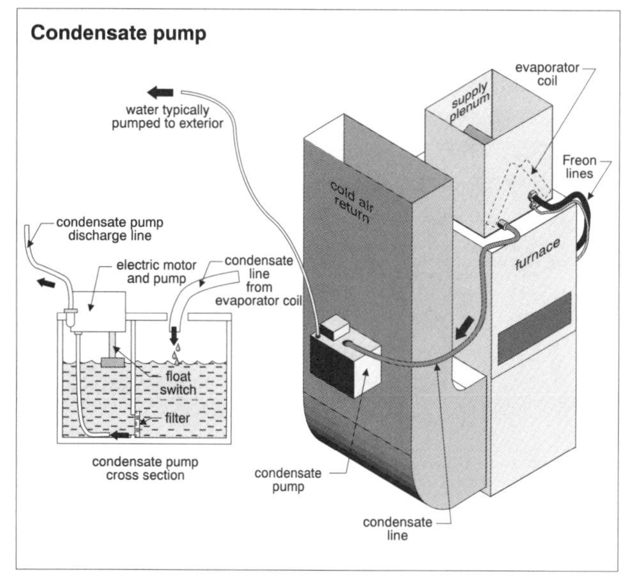

1247

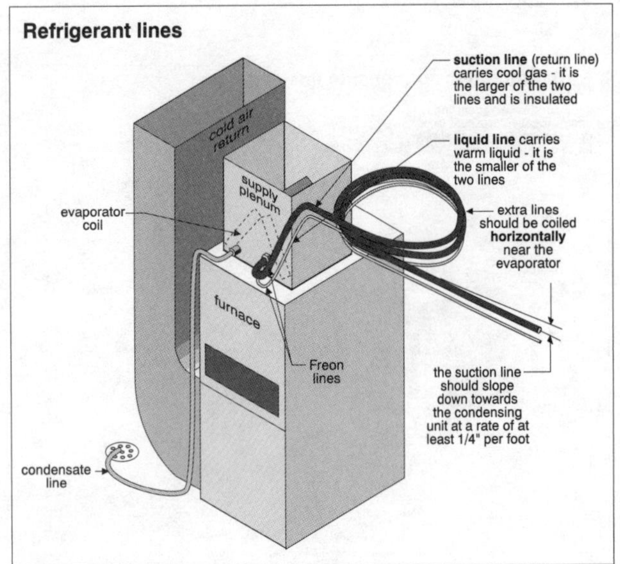

1248

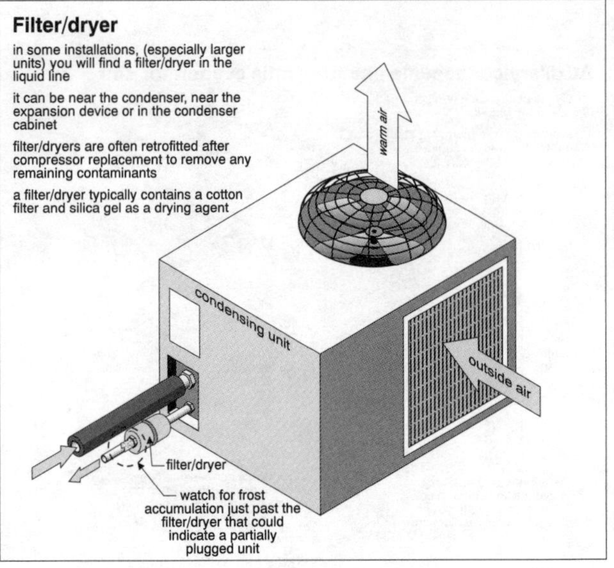

1249

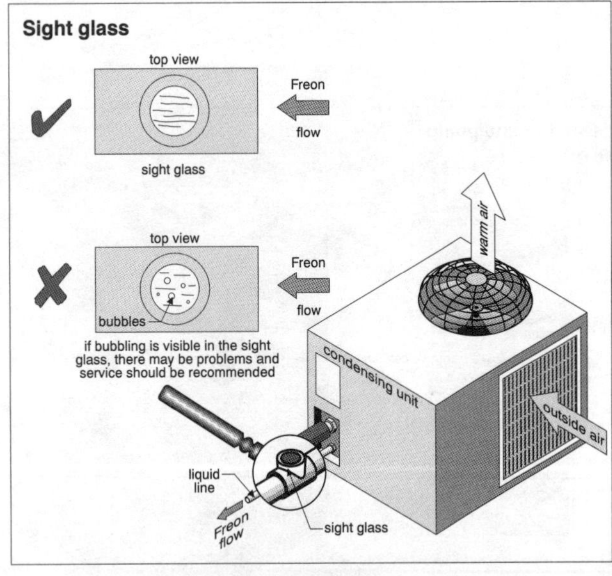

1250

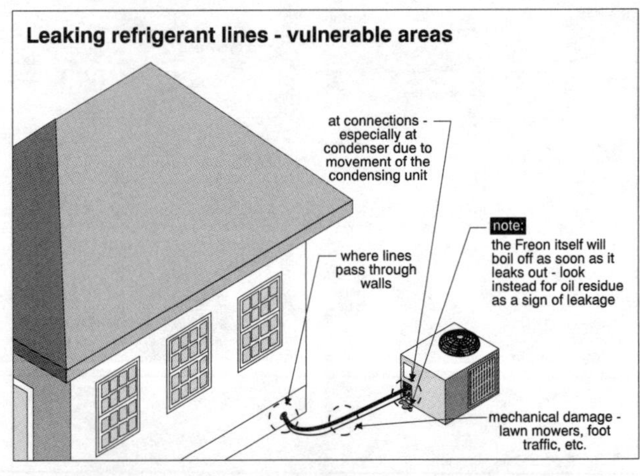

1251

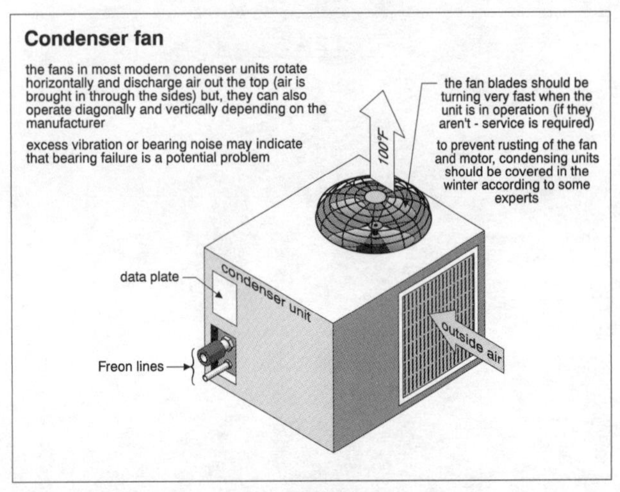

1252

Condenser coil location requirements

A/C

below deck installation may result in excessive heat build-up and restricted air flow

deck and tree are obstructing airflow

4' to 6' vertical clearance recommended

house wall

deck

airflow

condenser coil

tree

side view

1' to 3' horizontal clearance recommended

1253

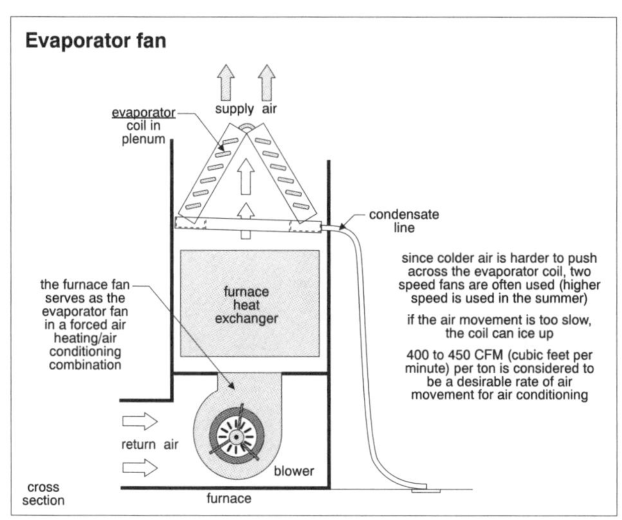

1254

Belt or pulley adjustment

a loose or misaligned fan belt can reduce the amount of air flowing past the evaporator coil and degrade system performance

- check belt for cracks or other wear
- check belt tension (see below)
- check for excess vibration
- check for overheating at the motor

1/2" to 1"

pulley sheaves

blower

motor

1255

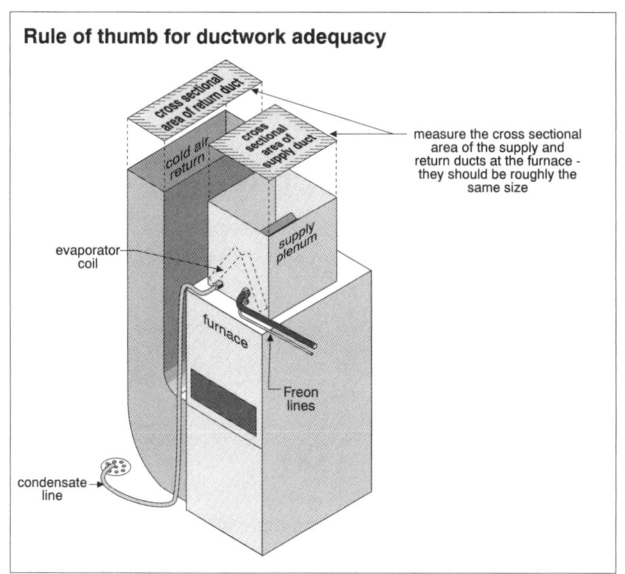

1256

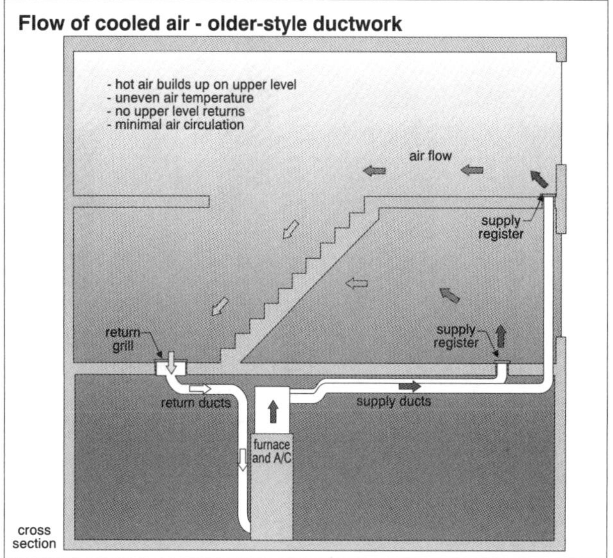

1257

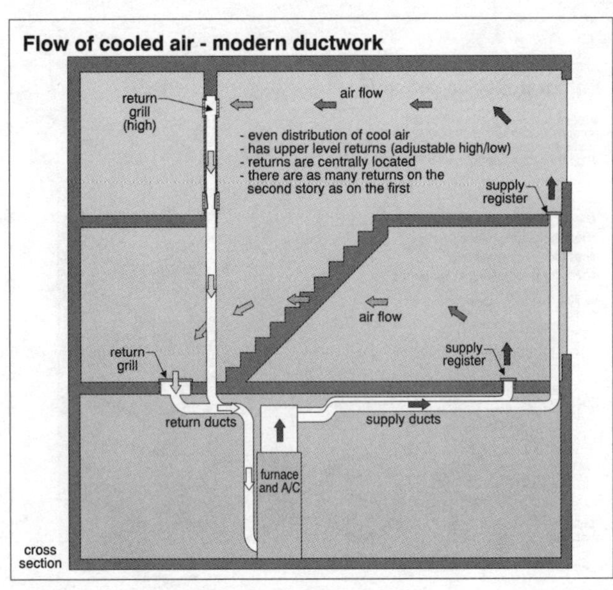

1258

High and low returns

typical room
warm air
upper return grill
air flow
summer
(cooling mode)
return
window
return register (closed)
cool air
supply register
supply

typical room
upper return grill blocked by open lower register
air flow
winter
(heating mode)
return
window
cool air
return register (fully open)
hot air
supply register
supply
cross section

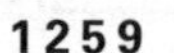

1259

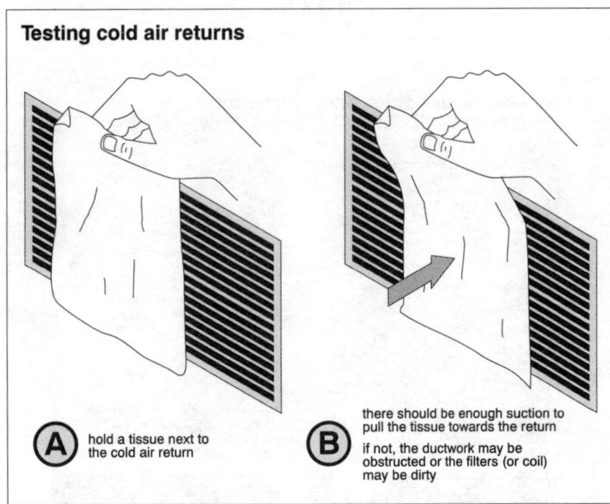

1260

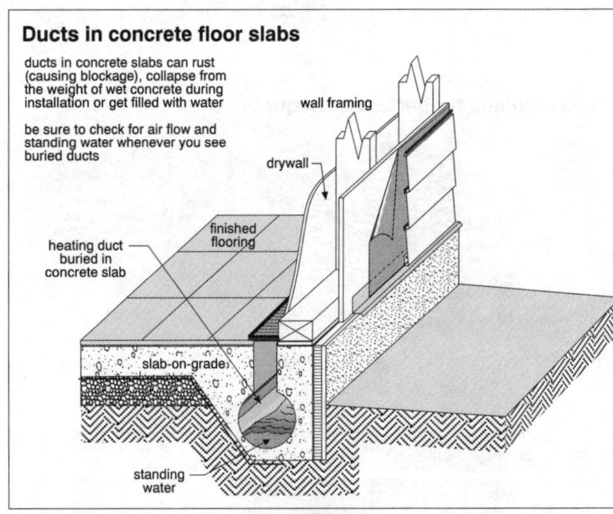

1261

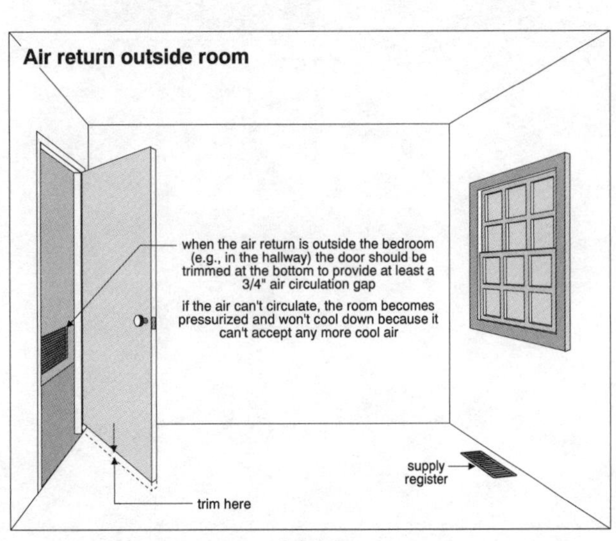

1262

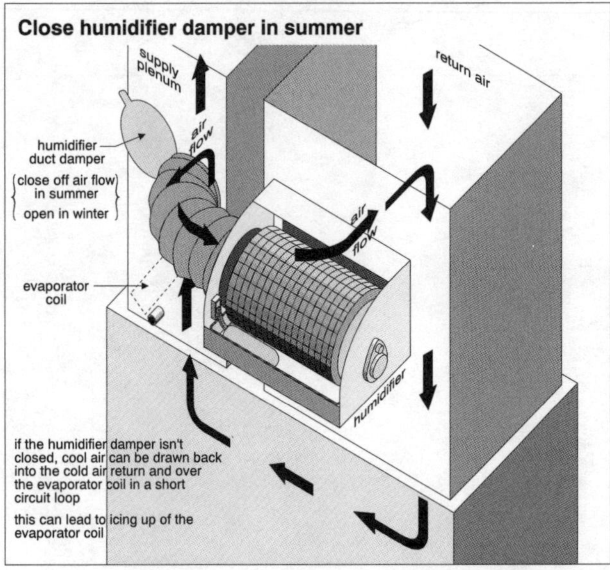

1263

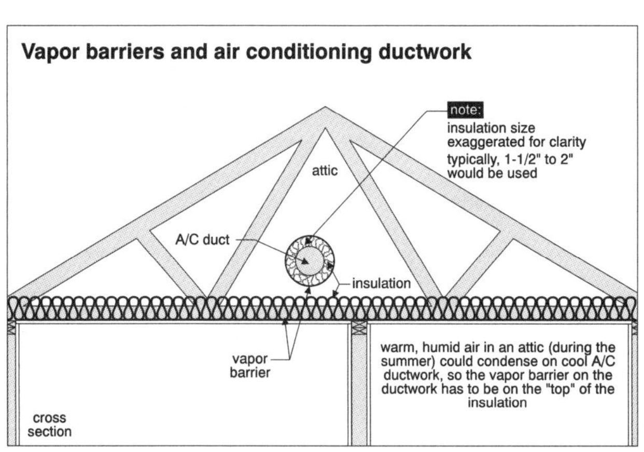

1264

Flexible ductwork

rigid ducts are best for vertical runs; a "tree and branch" structure with rigid ducts as the main runs is best

horizontals should be supported every 5' and at connections

25' maximum length

tight corners and contact with metal objects should be avoided

radius should be more than one duct diameter

termination devices should be independently supported

verticals should be supported every 6"

flexible ducts should be at least 4" from hot equipment

should not be installed:

on the exterior | in contact with soil | in direct sunlight | in concrete

1265

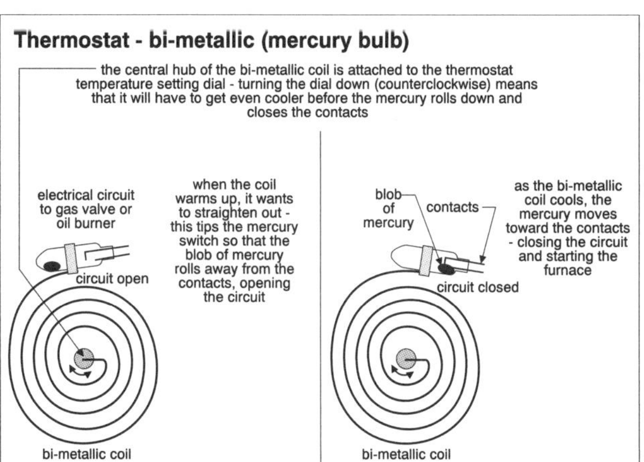

1266

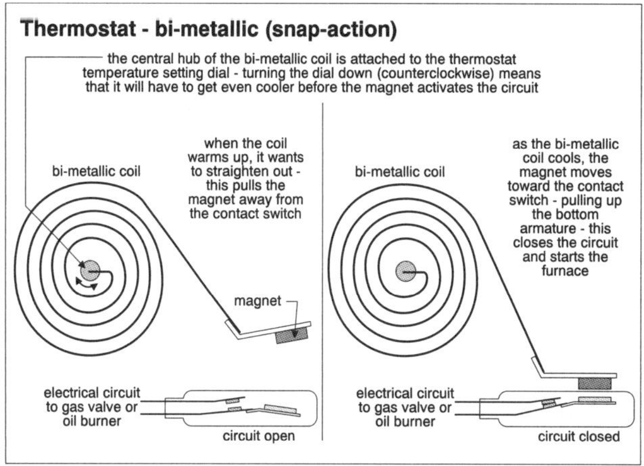

1267

Poor location for thermostat

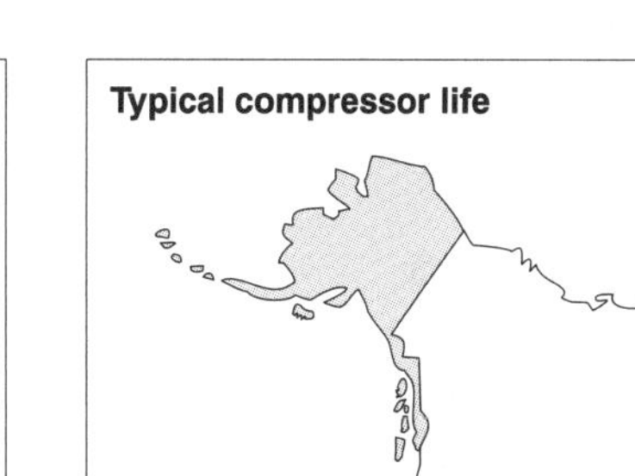

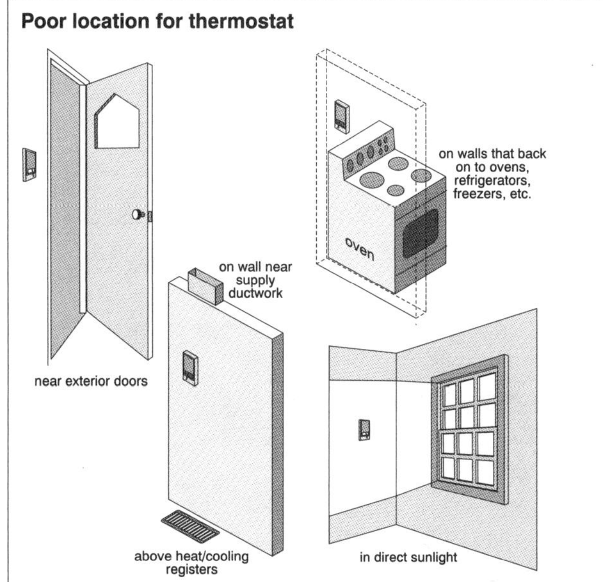

1268

Typical compressor life

Canada

United States

15 to 20 years

10 to 15 years

8 to 10 years

note:
illustration is intended to show general trends only and is not to be taken literally

1269

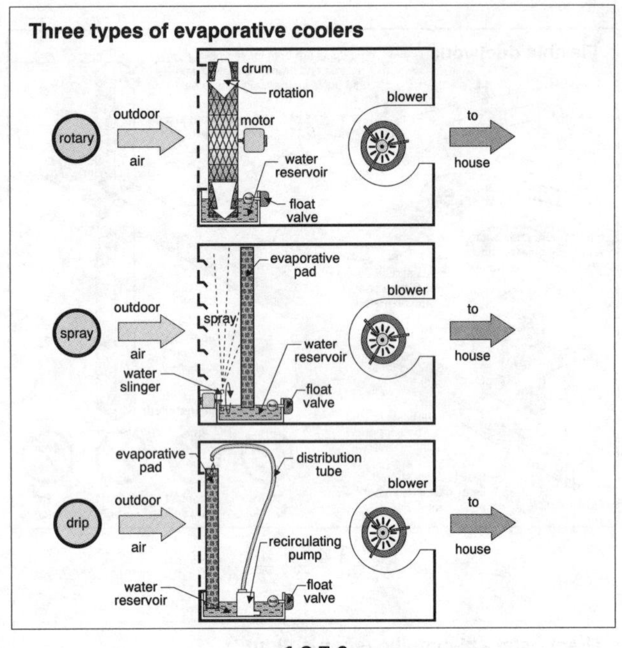

1270

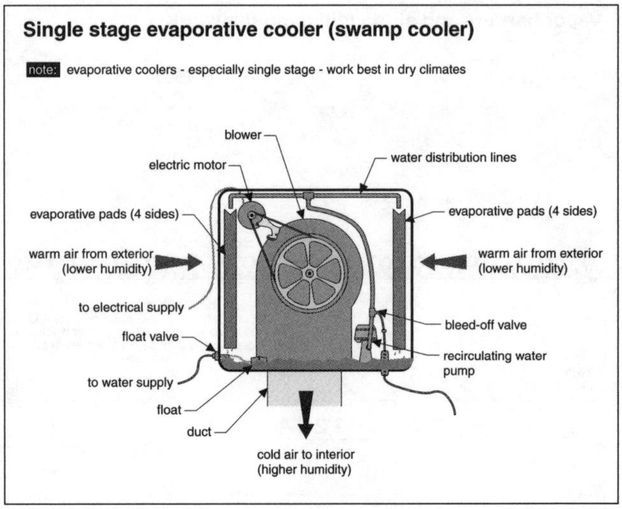

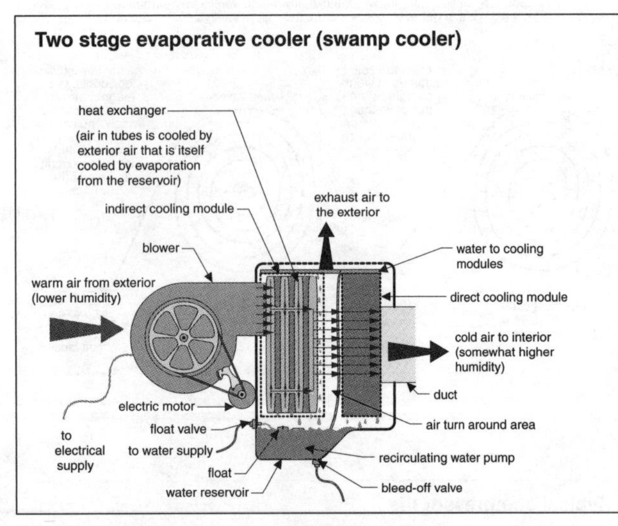

1272

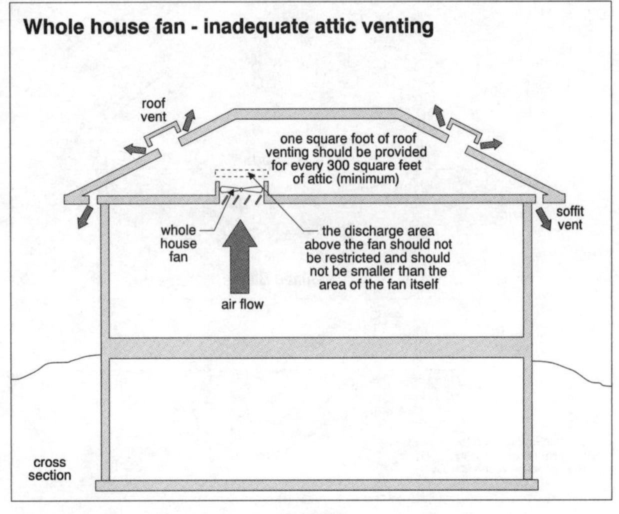

1274

Single stage evaporative cooler (swamp cooler)

note: evaporative coolers - especially single stage - work best in dry climates

1271

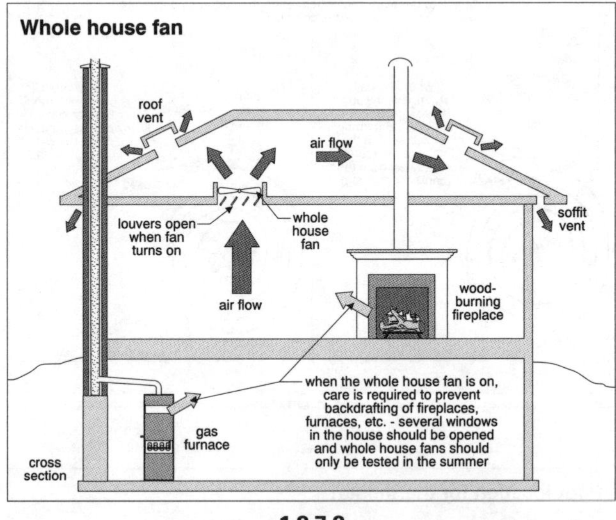

1273

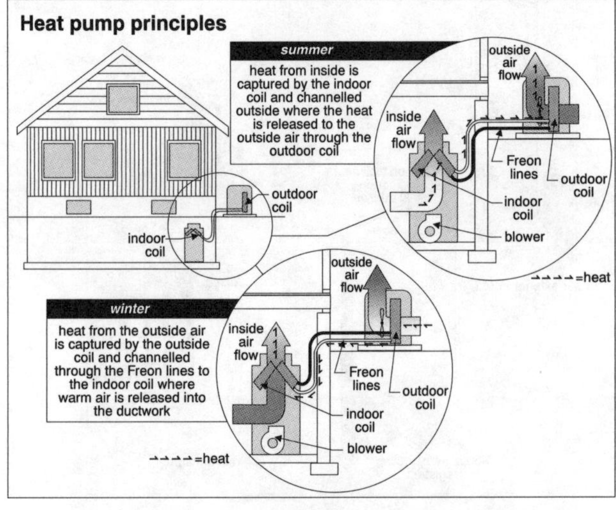

1275

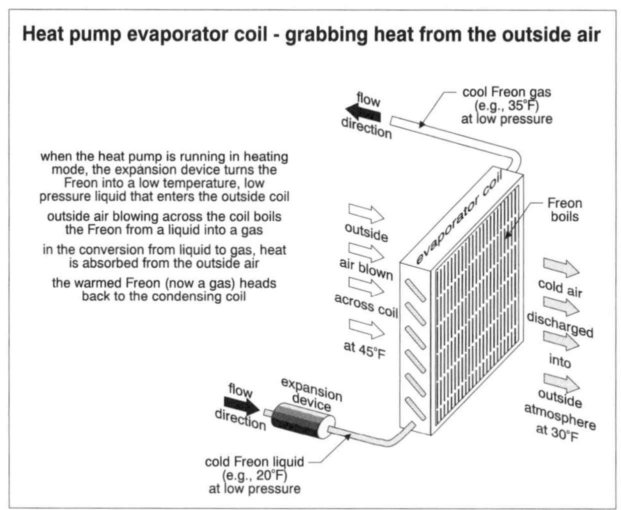

1276

Heat pump condenser coil - giving off warm air to the inside

compressor

hot Freon gas (e.g., 160°F) at high pressure

flow direction

cool air from inside house at 70°F

condenser coil

Freon condenses

warm air can now be sent back into the house through the ductwork at 90°F

the compressor converts cool Freon gas to hot Freon gas which is forced into the indoor coil

air blowing across the coil condenses the Freon from a gas into a liquid (this is why we call the heat pump's inside coil the condensing coil)

in the conversion from gas to liquid, heat is released into the supply air

warm liquid Freon (e.g., 110°F) at high pressure

flow direction

1277

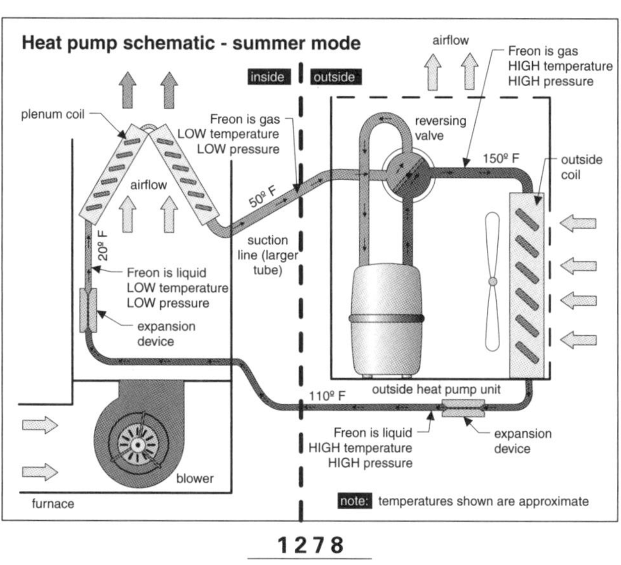

1278

Co-efficient of performance (COP) and balance point

energy (kw)

20, 15, 10, 5, 0

-20°F, -5°F, 15°F, 32°F, 50°F, 70°F

outdoor temperature (°F)

3.0, 2.0, 1.0, 0

CO-EFFICIENT OF PERFORMANCE

co-efficient of performance

heat pump output

below balance point, heat pump can't keep up

balance point

house heat loss

modern heat pumps have COP's greater than 1.0 down to -25°F

1279

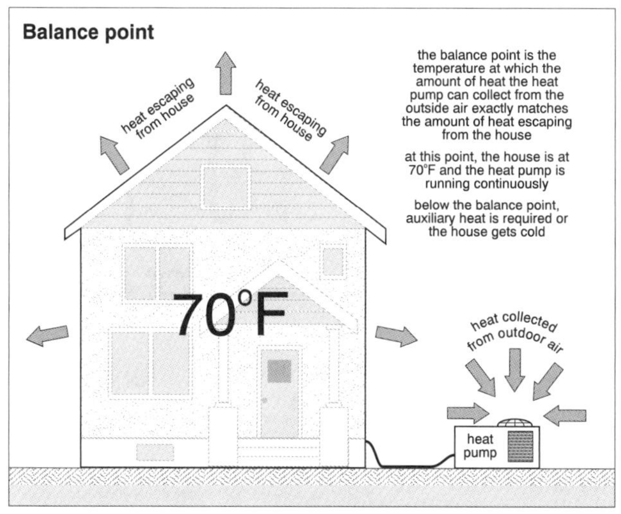

1280

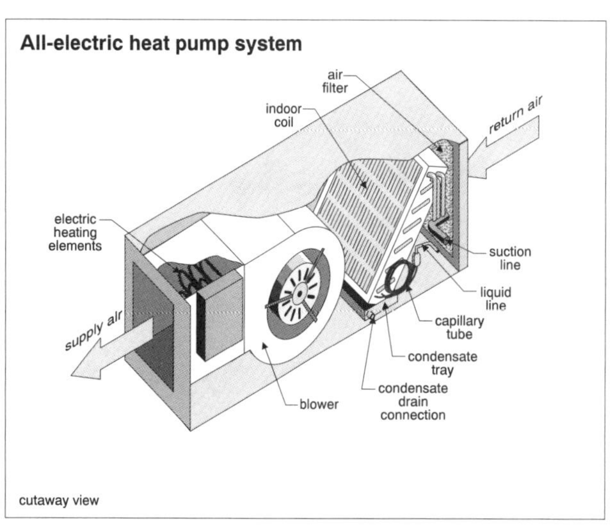

1281

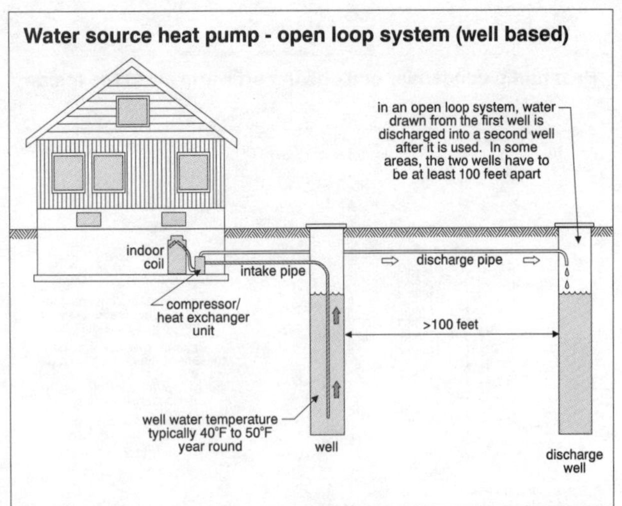

1282

1283

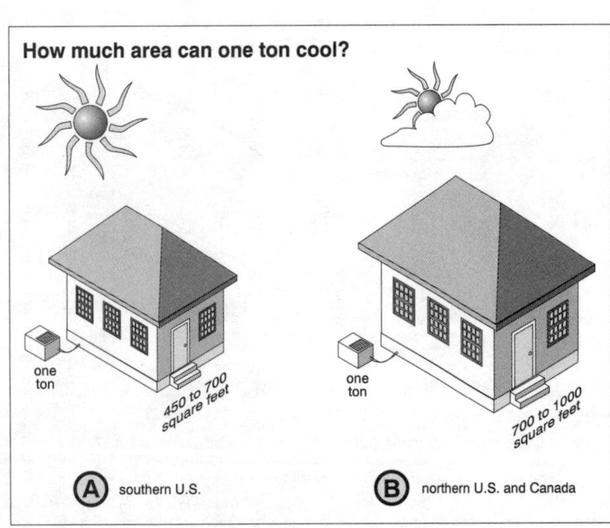

1284

1285

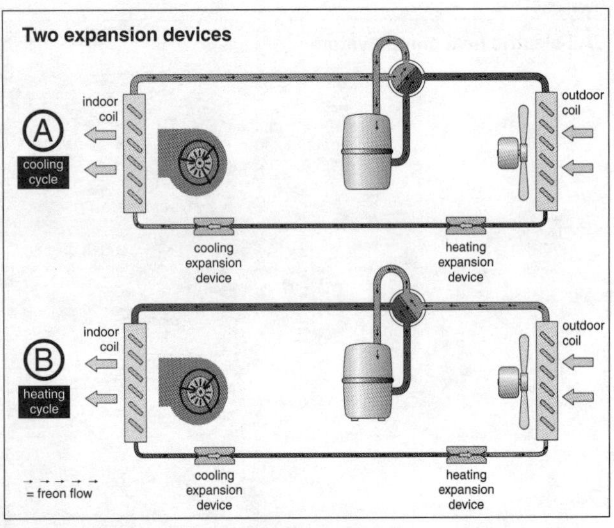

1286

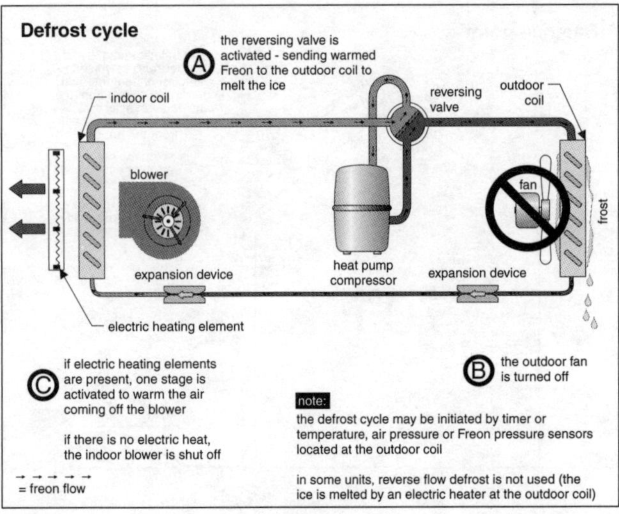

1287

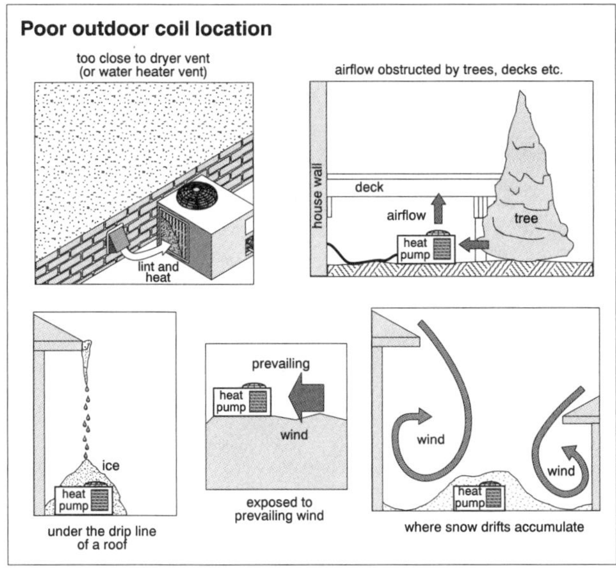

1288

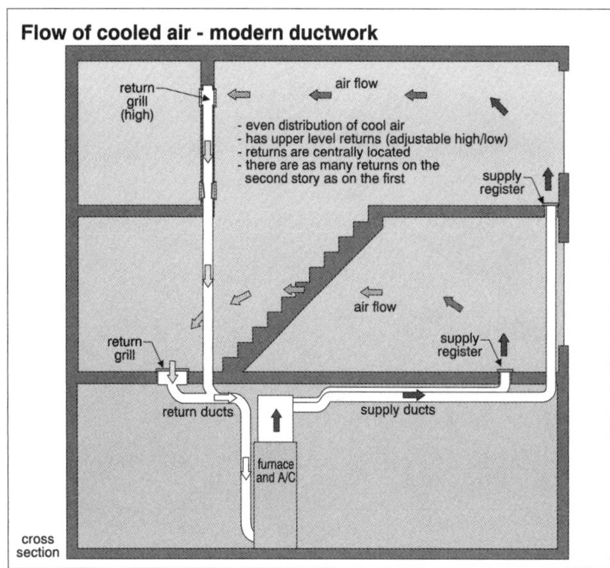

1289

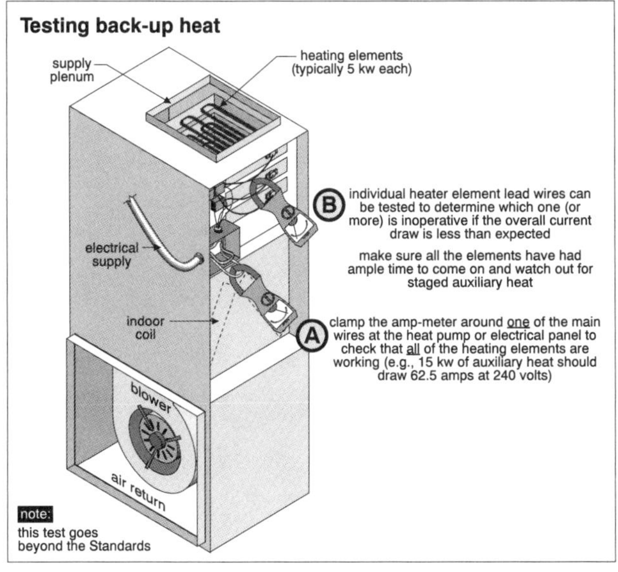

1290

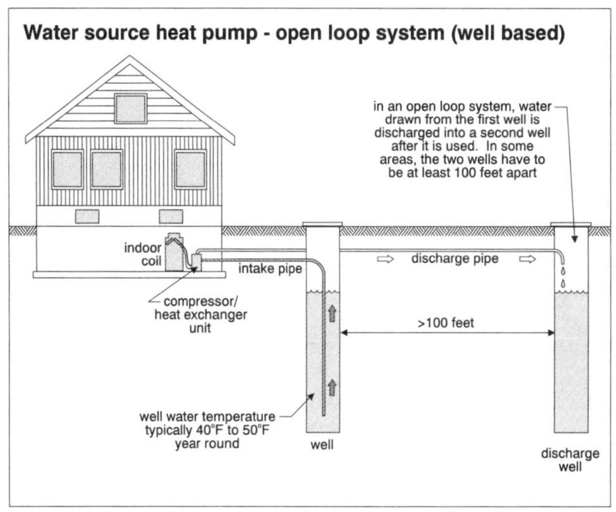

1291

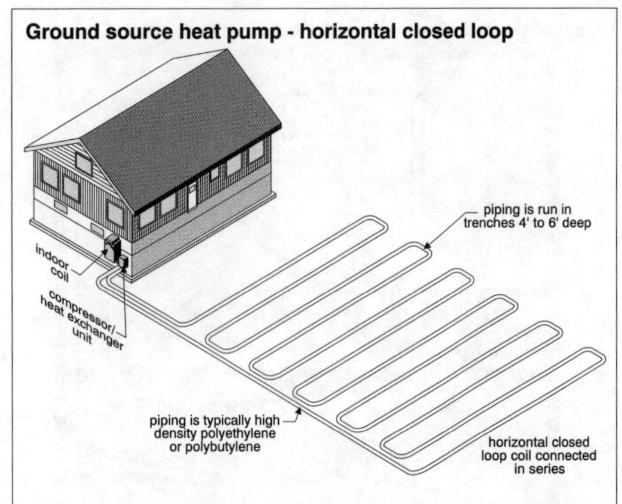

1292

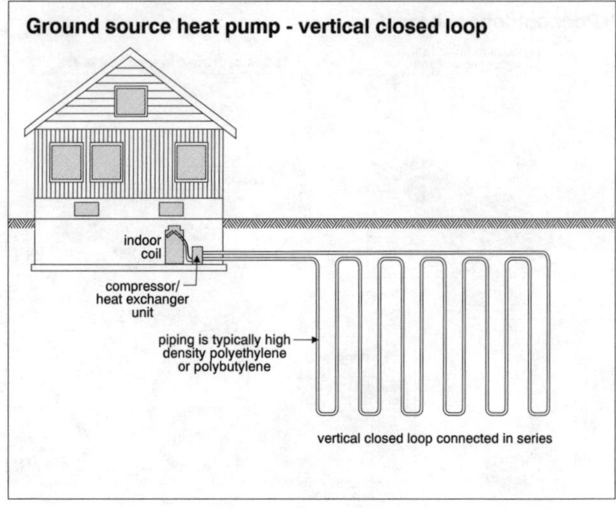

1293

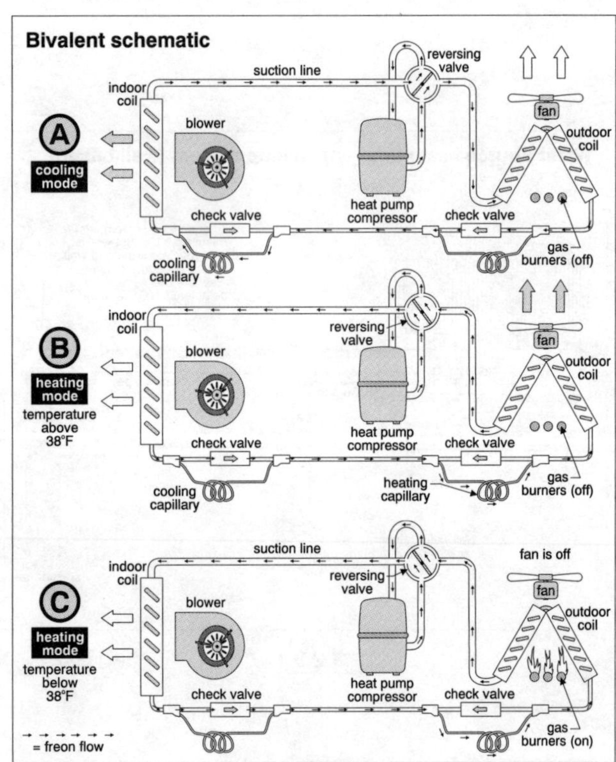

1294

CHAPTER 6

THE BASICS

221 ... 1300 British Thermal Unit (BTU's)
221 ... 1301 Latent heat of vaporization
221 ... 1302 Mechanisms of heat transfer
221 ... 1303 People releasing heat
221 ... 1304 Thermal conductivity
221 ... 1305 Conductance
222 ... 1306 Two comfort strategies
222 ... 1307 Convective loop
222 ... 1308 R-value per inch
222 ... 1309 Recommended insulation levels
222 ... 1310 Balanced air changes
222 ... 1311 Absolute and relative humidity
223 ... 1312 How moisture moves
223 ... 1313 Stack effect
223 ... 1314 Neutral pressure plane
223 ... 1315 Dew point
223 ... 1316 Vapor diffusion
223 ... 1317 Drafty is good (for houses)
224 ... 1318 Adding new siding can trap moisture
224 ... 1319 Moisture control in hot climates
224 ... 1320 Differences between old and new construction
224 ... 1321 Exhaust fans
224 ... 1322 Direct vent appliances
224 ... 1323 Heat recovery ventilator
225 ... 1324 How depressurization can occur in houses
225 ... 1325 Controlling moisture in hot climates

225 ... 1326 Wall marks due to thermal bridging
225 ... 1327 Insulation voids and convective loops
225 ... 1328 Wind washing
226 ... 1329 Forms of insulation
226 ... 1330 Other types of polystyrene insulation
226 ... 1331 Radiant barriers

AIR/VAPOR BARRIER (VAPOR RETARDERS)

226 ... 1332 Air barrier versus vapor barrier
227 ... 1333 Housewrap versus building paper
227 ... 1334 Sill gaskets and electrical box enclosures
227 ... 1335 Gaskets for electrical boxes
227 ... 1336 Backer rods
227 ... 1337 Caulking – indoors or out?
227 ... 1338 Pot lights
228 ... 1339 Vapor barrier location
228 ... 1340 Cover crawlspace floor

VENTING ROOFS

228 ... 1341 Reducing attic heat with ventilation
228 ... 1342 Preventing ice dams with ventilation
229 ... 1343 Types and locations of vents
229 ... 1344 Turbine vents
229 ... 1345 Baffles for soffit vents
229 ... 1346 Recommended amount of attic ventilation
230 ... 1347 Venting cathedral roofs
230 ... 1348 Venting mansard and gambrel roofs

VENTING LIVING SPACES

231 ... 1349 Three approaches to ventilation
231 ... 1350 Exhaust system components
231 ... 1351 Supply systems
231 ... 1352 Heat recovery ventilators (basic components)
232 ... 1353 HRV and ERV heat exchangers
232 ... 1354 HRV (heat recovery ventilator) components
232 ... 1355 HRV intake and exhaust locations
232 ... 1356 Filters and condensate drains
233 ... 1357 Defrost control
233 ... 1358 HRV – integrated intake and exhaust
233 ... 1359 HRV connections to furnace ductwork
233 ... 1360 HRV attic installation

CHAPTER 6

ATTICS

234 ... 1361 Attic access hatch
234 ... 1362 Stairwells to attic
234 ... 1363 Pull-down stairs
234 ... 1364 Secondary attics
234 ... 1365 Risks of adding more insulation
234 ... 1366 Wet insulation below vents
235 ... 1367 Missing insulation at dropped ceiling
235 ... 1368 Insulating knee walls
235 ... 1369 Insulating skylight wells
235 ... 1370 Ducts in attics
235 ... 1371 Insulation too close to chimneys
235 ... 1372 Air/vapor barrier incomplete or wrong location
236 ... 1373 Potential air leakage locations
236 ... 1374 Recommended amount of attic ventilation
236 ... 1375 Wet insulation below vents
236 ... 1376 Turbine vents
237 ... 1377 Attic power vents
237 ... 1378 Delaminating sheathing -
237 ... 1379 Whole house fan with no insulating cover

FLAT AND CATHEDRAL ROOFS

237 ... 1380 Insulating flat (and cathedral) roofs
238 ... 1381 Evidence of insulation added
238 ... 1382 Two different strategies for insulating cathedral/flat roofs
238 ... 1383 Channeled vents versus cross ventilation

WALLS ABOVE GRADE

238 ... 1384 Insulation short circuit
239 ... 1385 Adding insulation to solid masonry walls
239 ... 1386 Cold wall effect
239 ... 1387 Drying potential of walls

BASEMENTS AND CRAWLSPACES

239 ... 1388 Adding exterior basement insulation
240 ... 1389 Adding interior basement insulation
240 ... 1390 Basement moisture control
240 ... 1391 Insulating crawlspaces
240 ... 1392 Clues – has insulation been added?
241 ... 1393 Rim joist insulation
241 ... 1394 Don't insulate embedded joists
241 ... 1395 Exposed combustible insulation
241 ... 1396 Cover crawlspace floor

FLOORS OVER UNHEATED AREAS

242 ... 1397 Insulation in floors over unheated areas

VENTILATION SYSTEMS

242 ... 1398 Reducing moisture
242 ... 1399 Exhaust fan conditions
242 ... 1400 Cold-side ducts not insulated
243 ... 1401 HRV intake and exhaust locations
243 ... 1402 Furnace duct/HRV connection
243 ... 1403 HRV exhaust grille locations
243 ... 1404 Flow collars and balancing dampers
243 ... 1405 HRV not interlocked with furnace fan
243 ... 1406 Filters dirty or missing
244 ... 1407 HRV core missing or dirty
244 ... 1408 Trap in condensate drain

British Thermal Unit (BTU's)

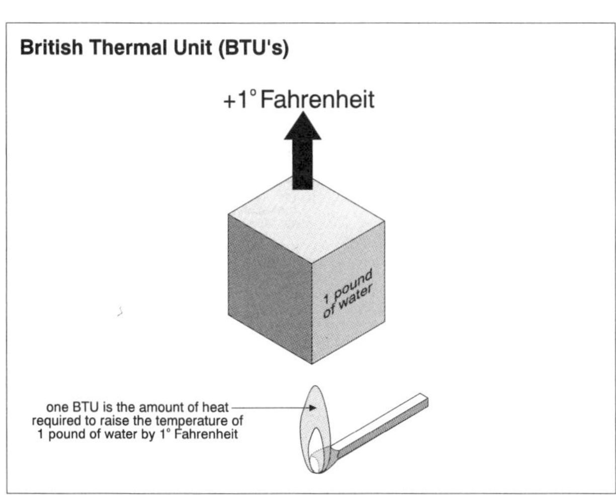

1300

Latent heat of vaporization

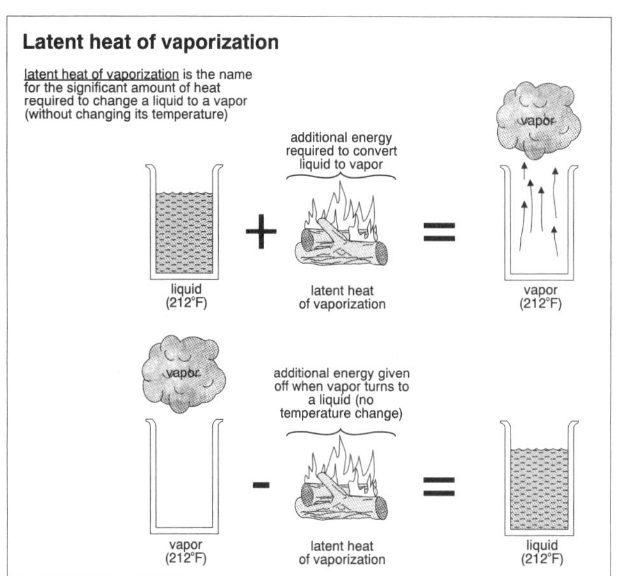

1301

Mechanisms of heat transfer

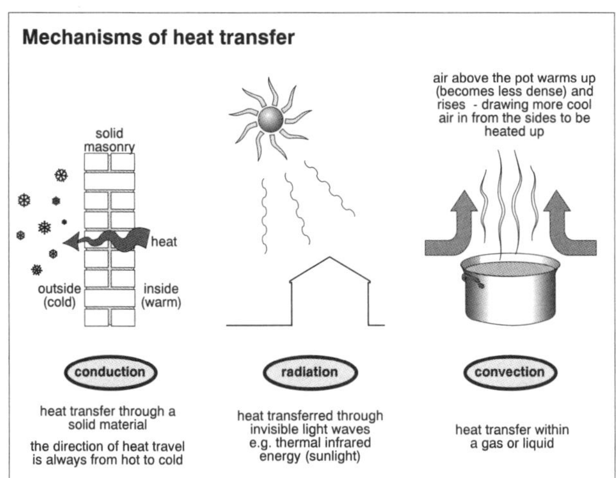

1302

People and homes release heat

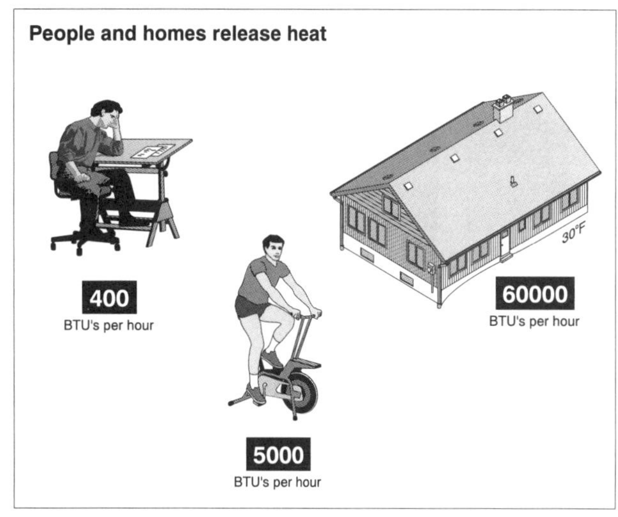

1303

Thermal conductivity

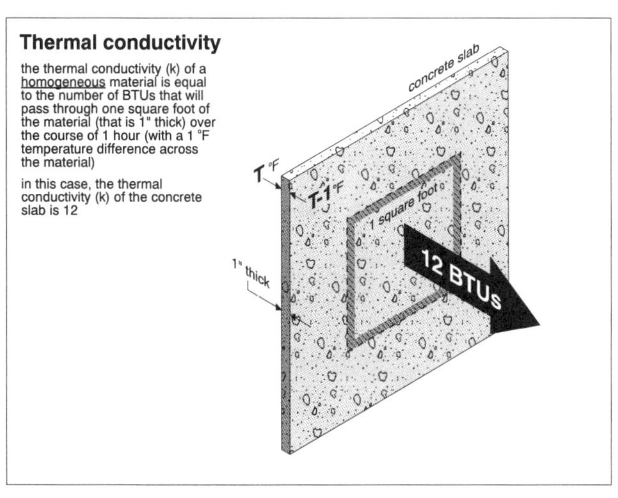

1304

Conductance

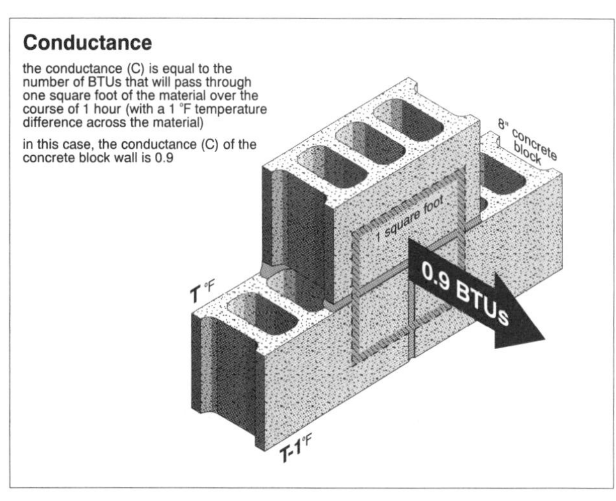

1305

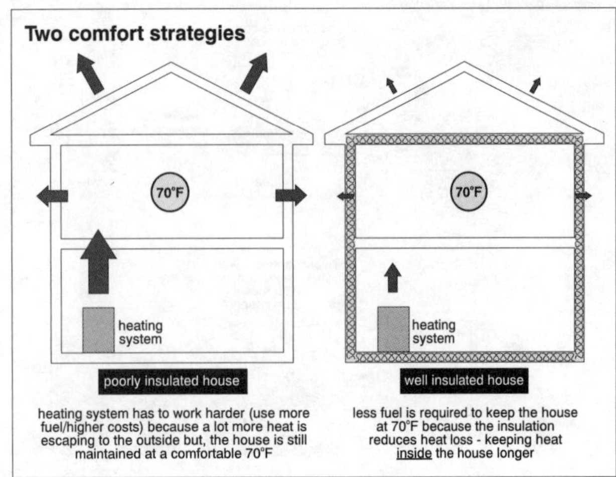

1306

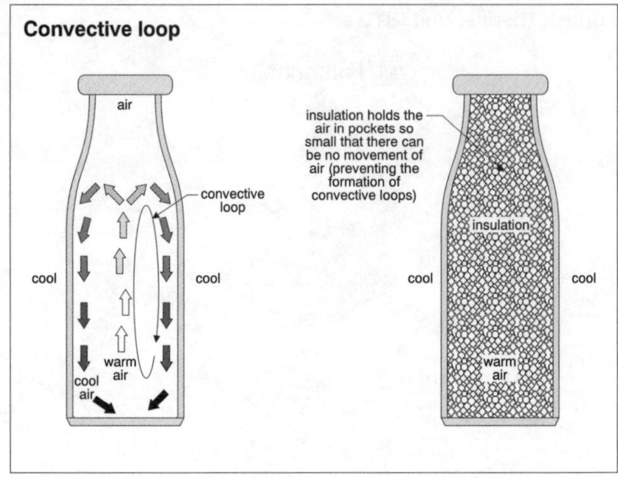

1307

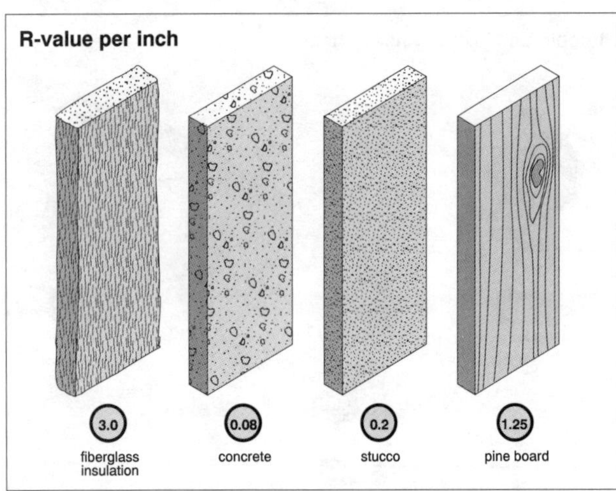

1308

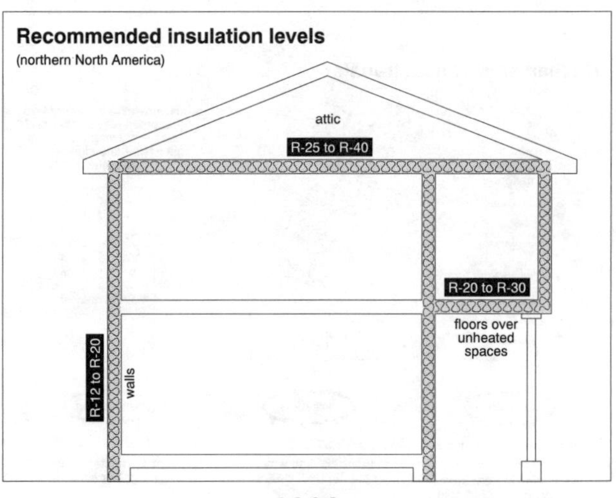

1309

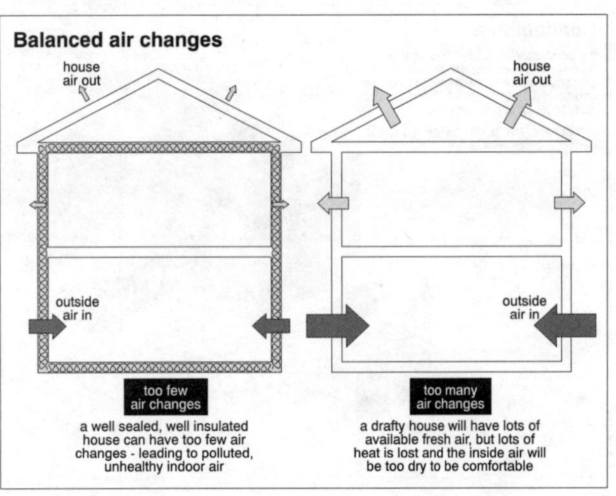

1310

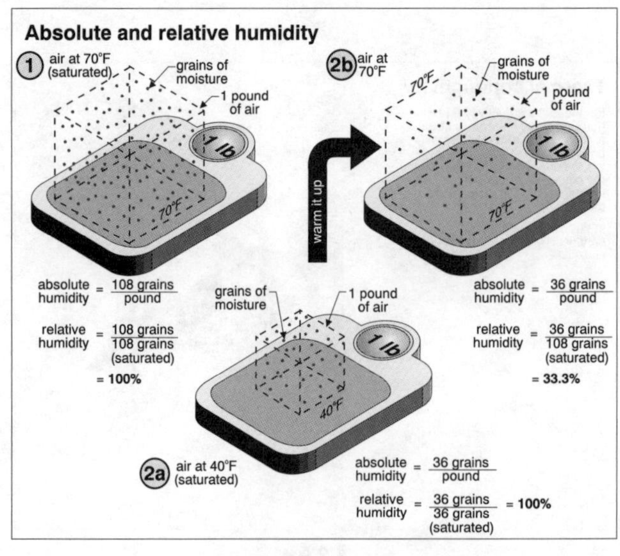

1311

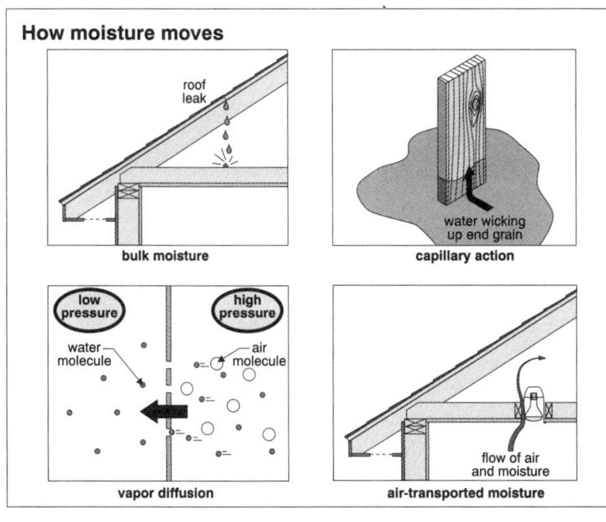

1312

Stack effect

B additional warm air expands, increasing pressure and pushing household air out through cracks/gaps

A warm (less dense) air rises

C air leaving the house creates negative pressure in the cooler, lower levels - outdoor air is drawn in through any cracks or gaps

note: assumes calm conditions (no wind)

1313

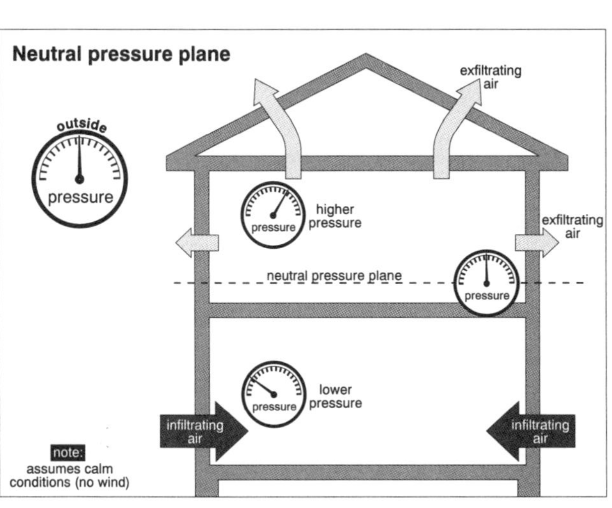

1314

Dew point

example 1

50% relative humidity

vapor

80°F

cool 20°F

100% relative humidity

dew point temperature is 60°F

example 2

90% relative humidity

vapor

80°F

cool 2°F

100% relative humidity

dew point temperature is 78°F

1315

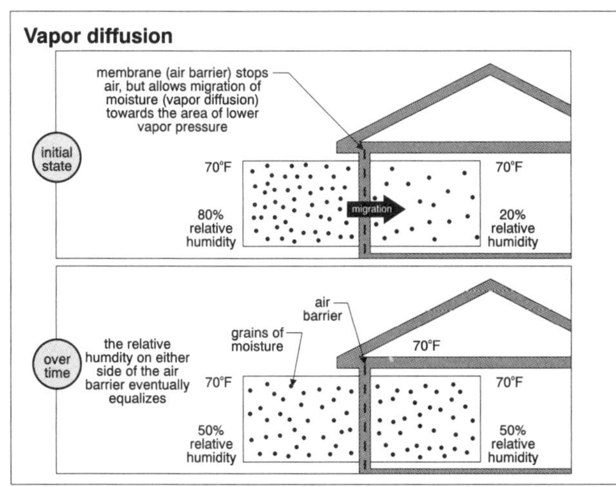

1316

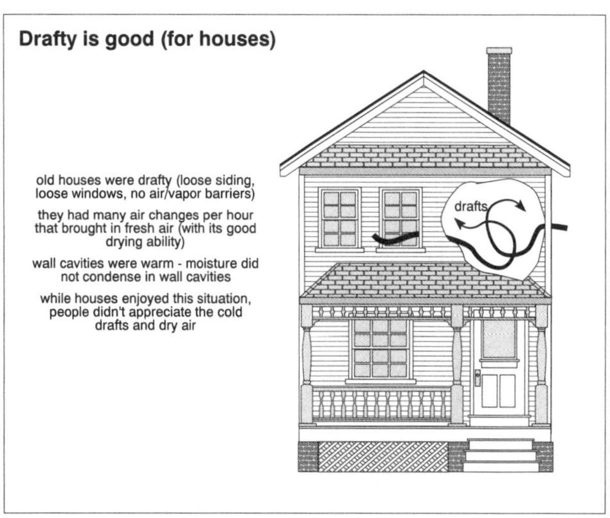

1317

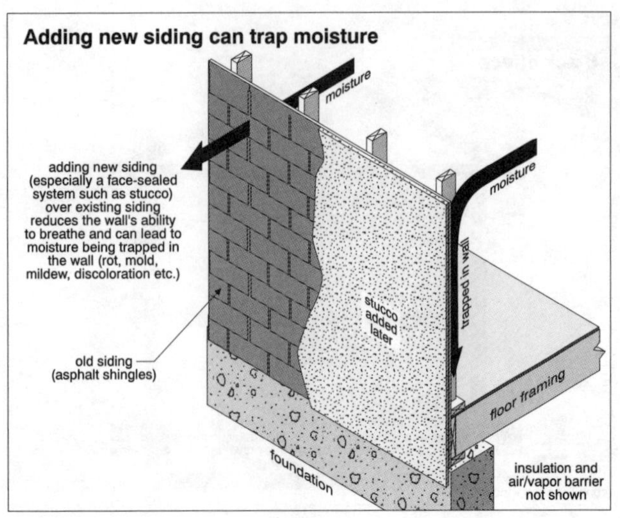

1318

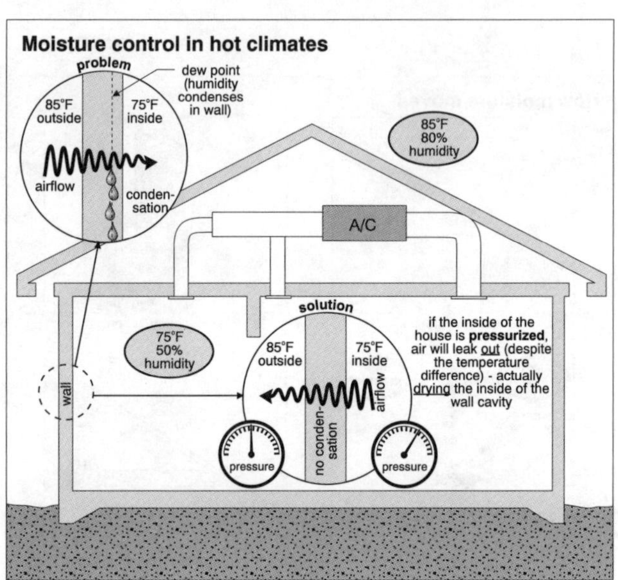

1319

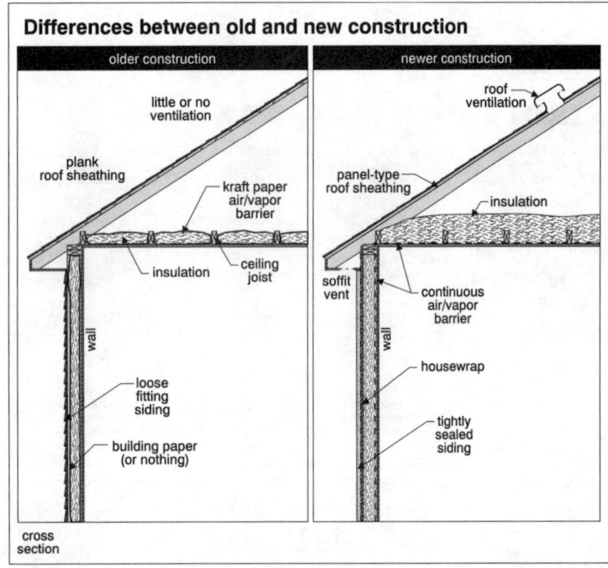

1320

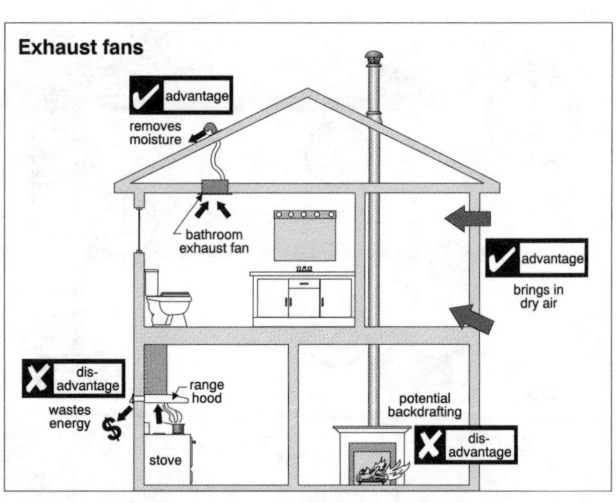

1321

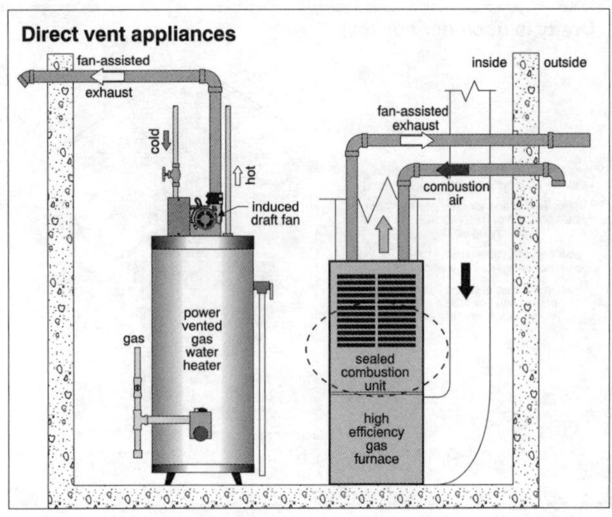

1322

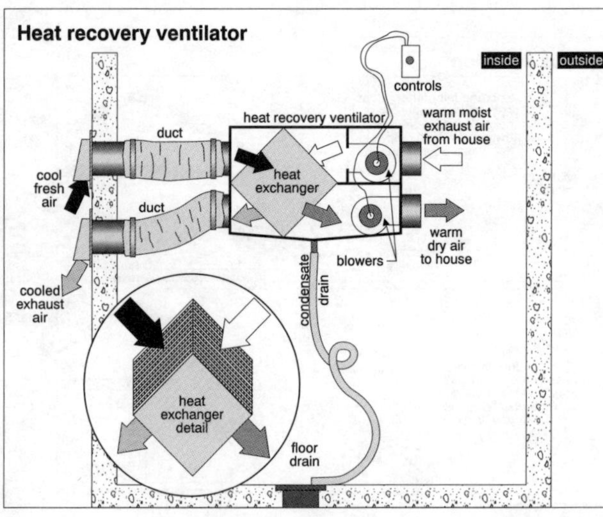

1323

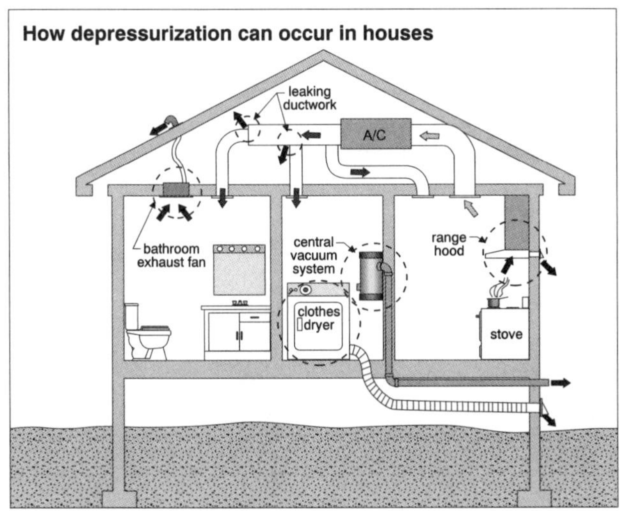

1324

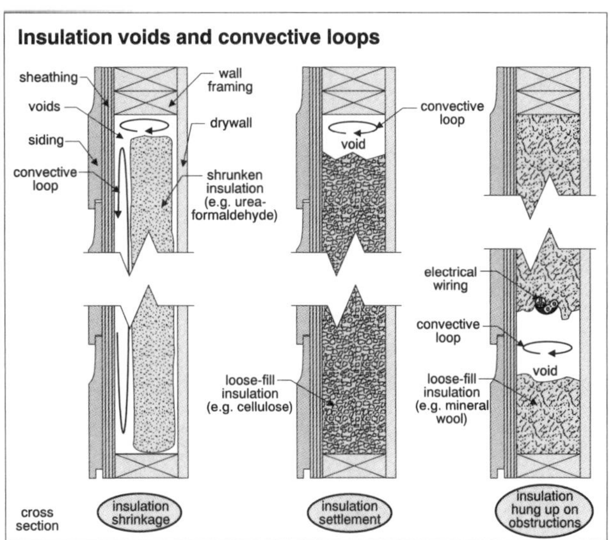

1325

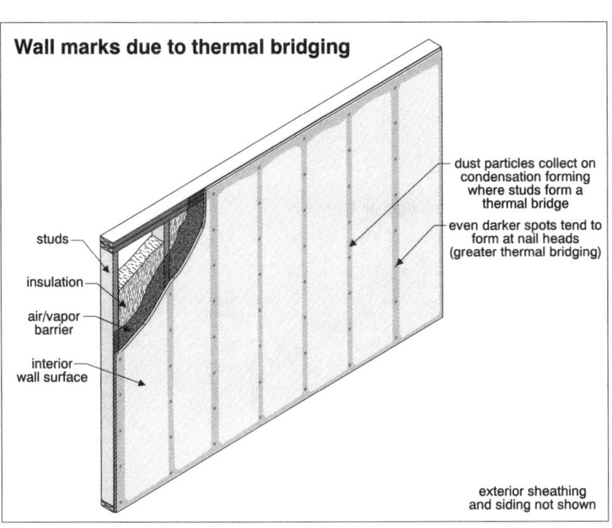

1326

1327

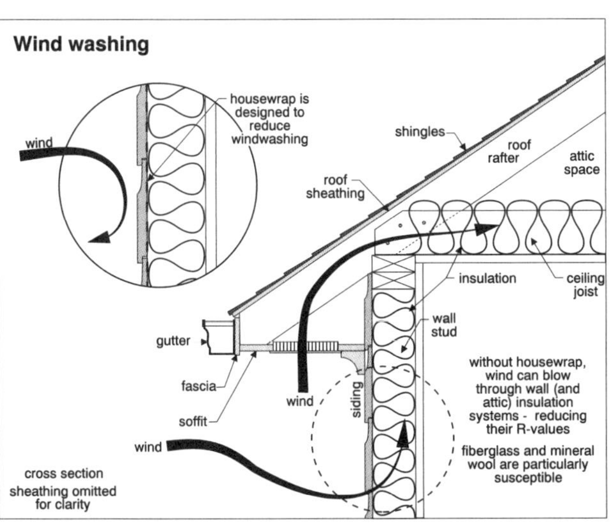

1328

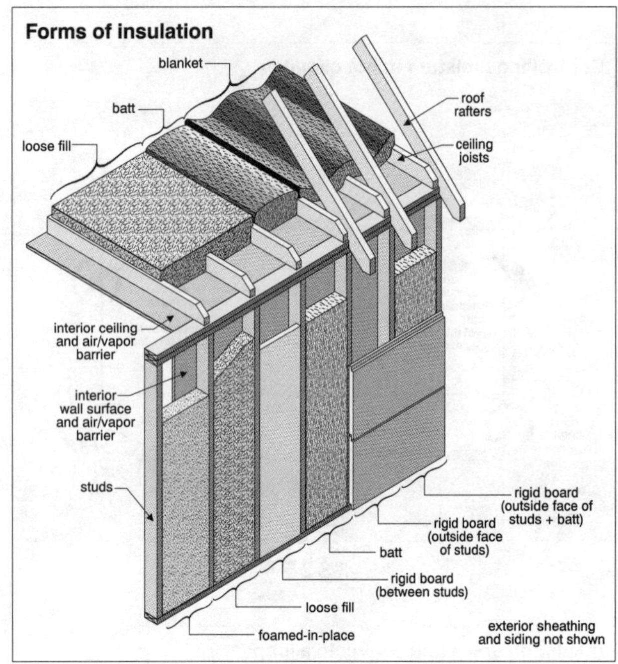

1329

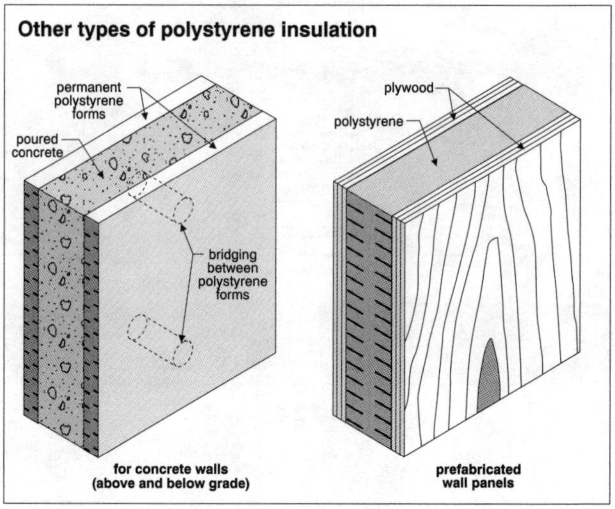

Other types of polystyrene insulation

permanent polystyrene forms
poured concrete
bridging between polystyrene forms
plywood
polystyrene

for concrete walls (above and below grade)

prefabricated wall panels

1330

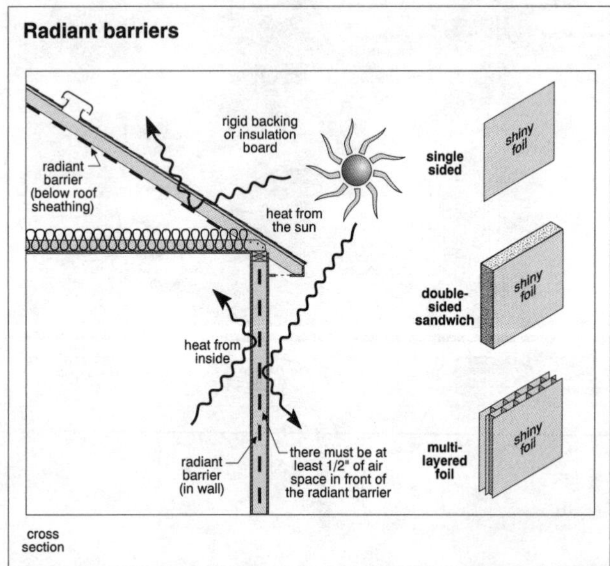

1331

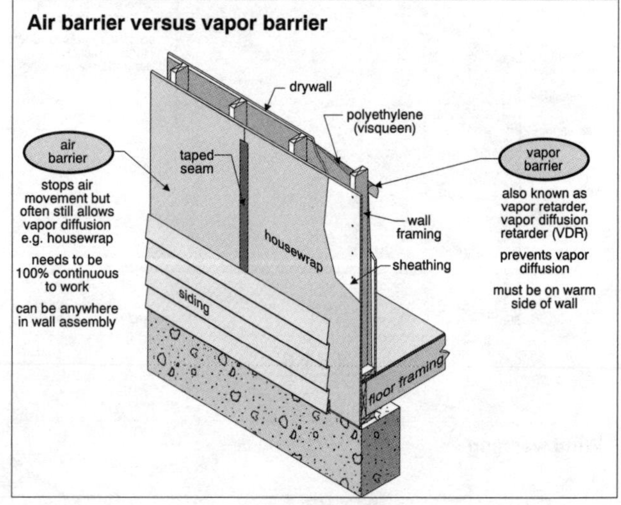

1332

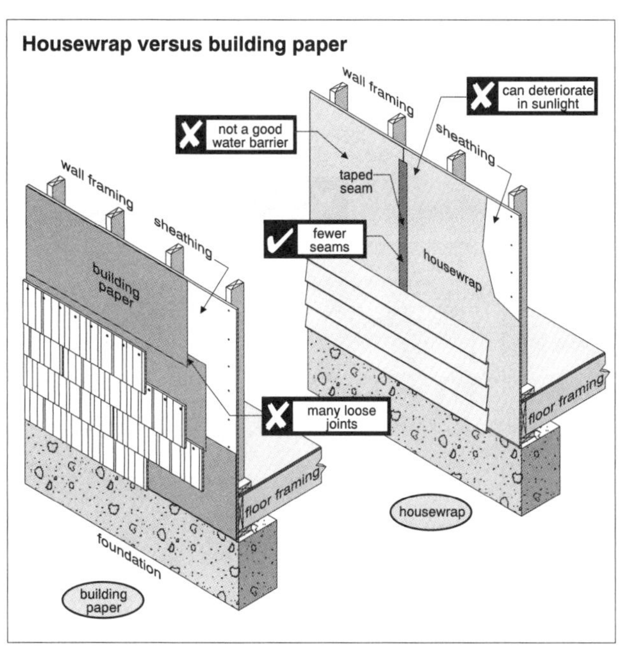

1333

Sill gaskets and electrical box enclosures

manufactured enclosure sealed to air barrier

sill gasket

sealant

wall framing

air barrier

sheathing

floor framing

foundation

electrical box enclosure made on site (of polyethylene) and sealed to air barrier

insulation, drywall not shown

1334

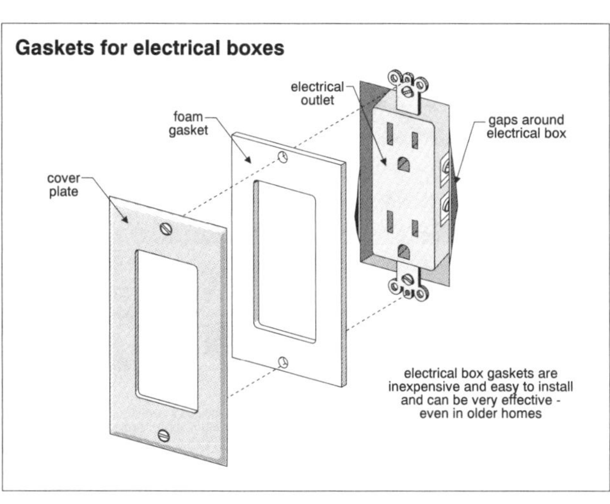

1335

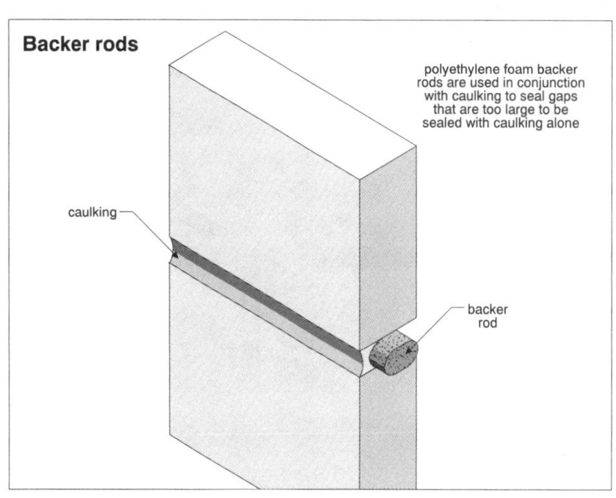

1336

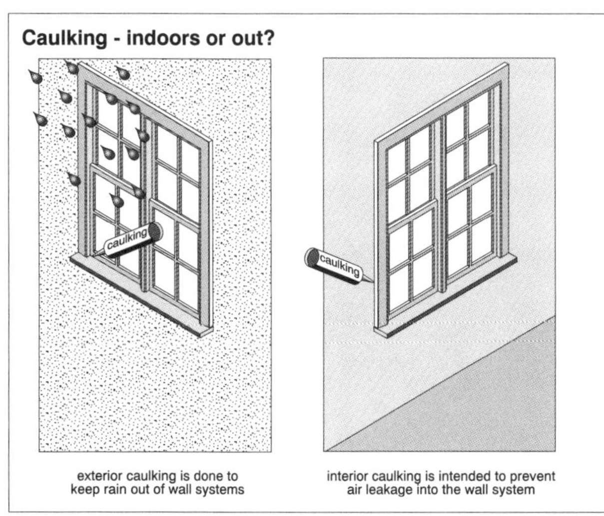

1337

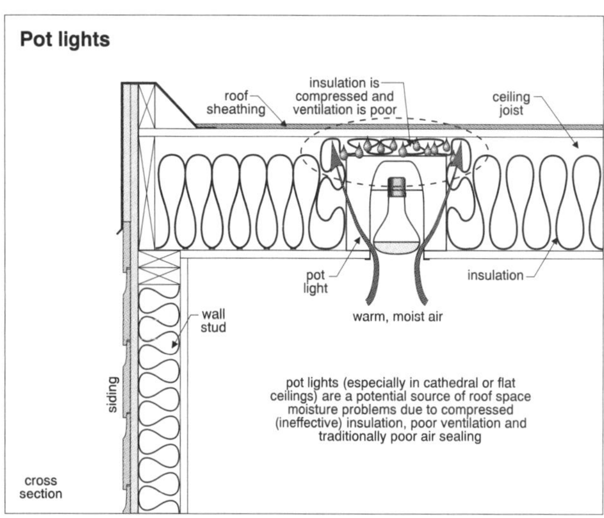

1338

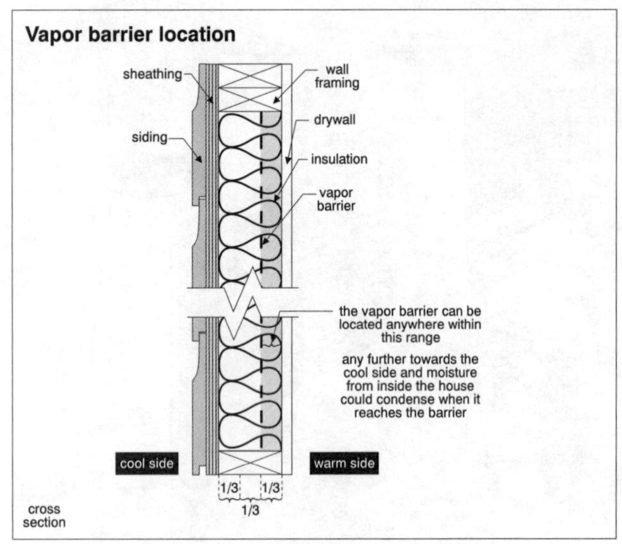

1339

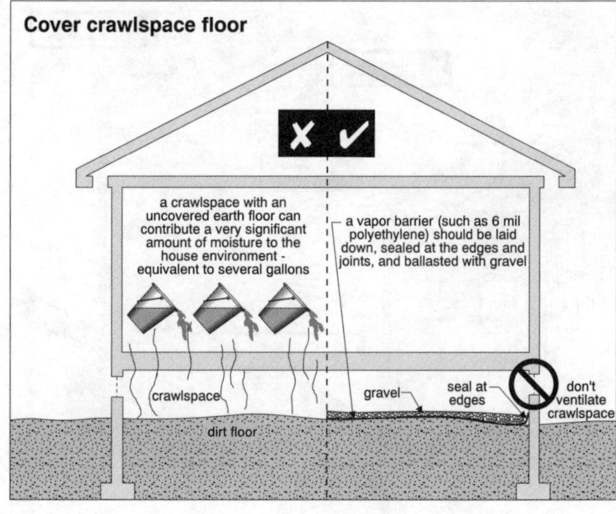

1340

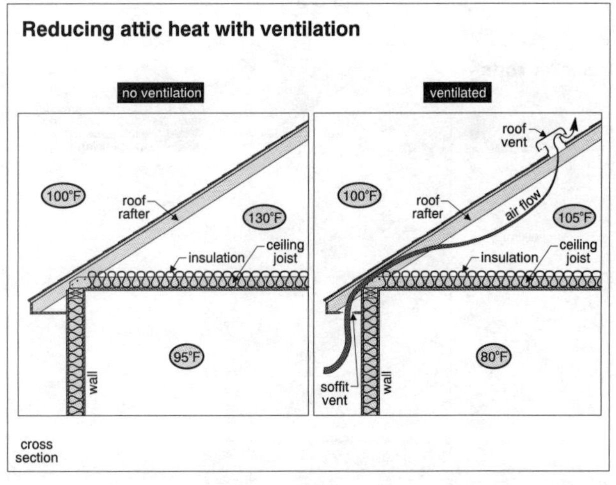

1341

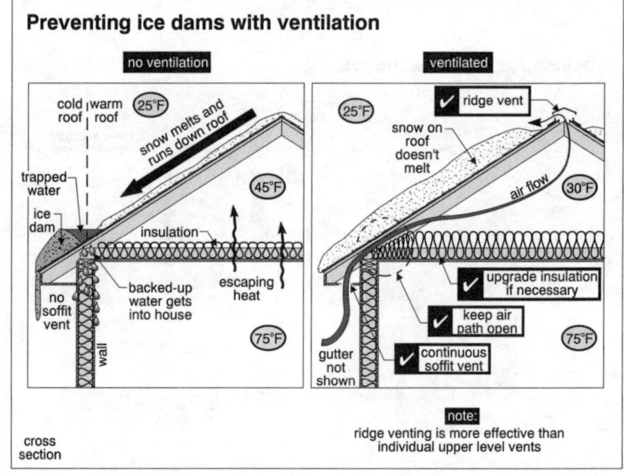

1342

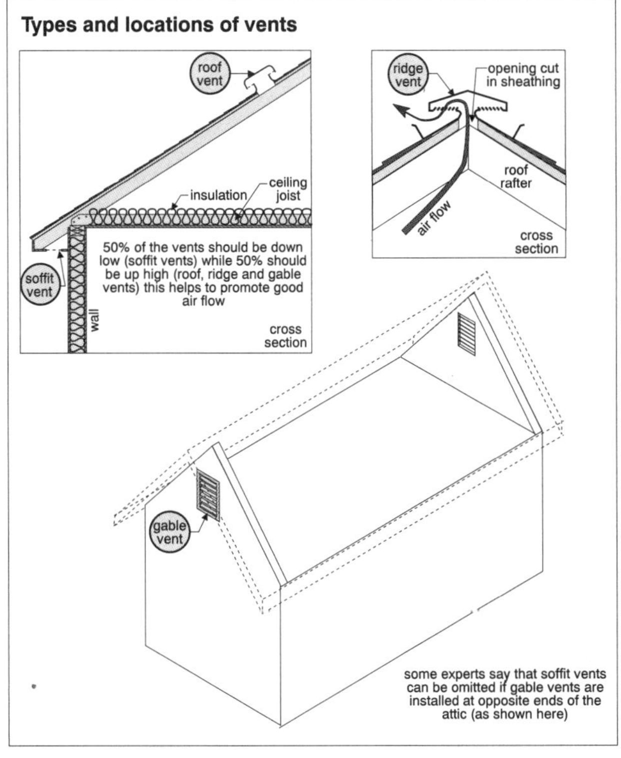

1343

Turbine vents

turbine vent

roof rafter

air flow

insulation

ceiling joist

soffit vent

cross section

turbine vents:

- don't work without wind
- can depressurize the attic on windy days
- can be noisy
- often seize
- often leak

1344

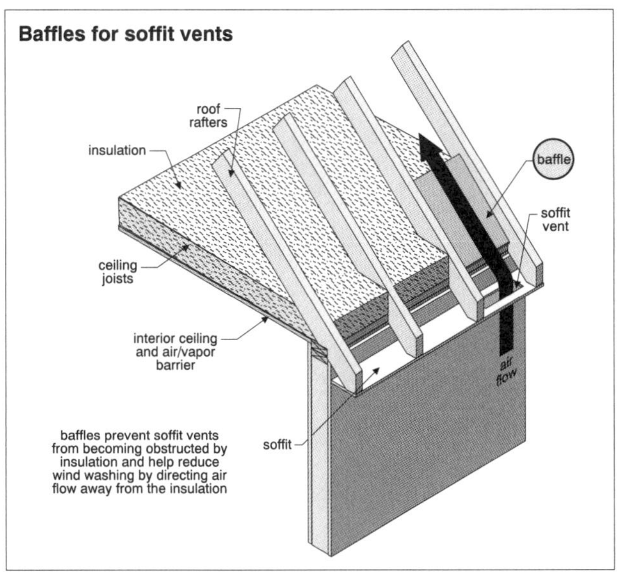

1345

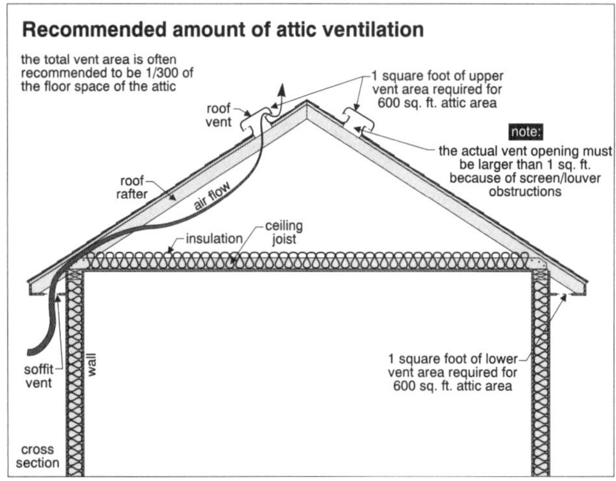

1346

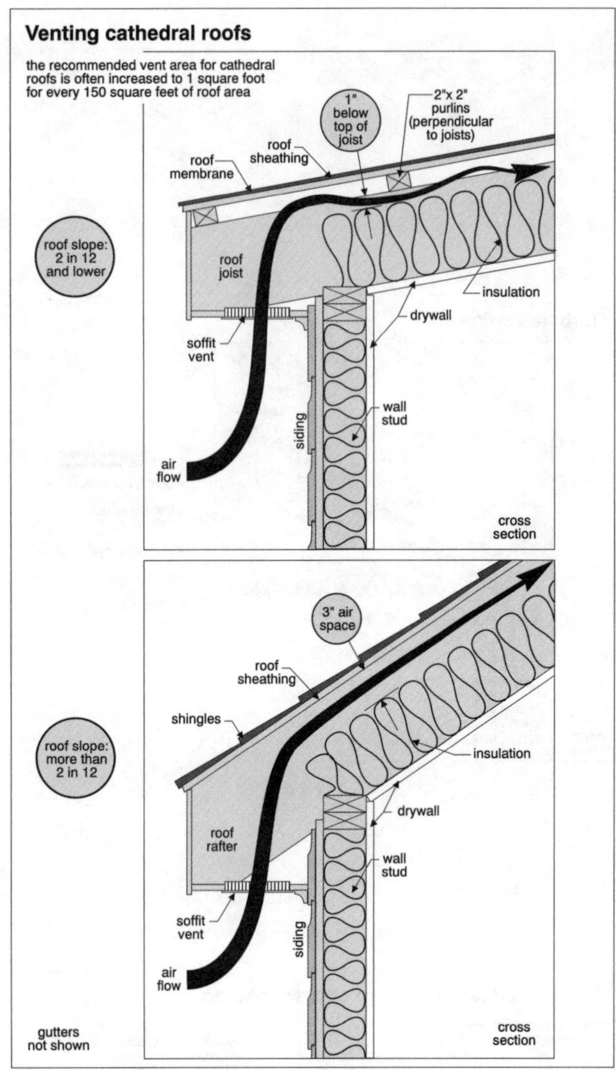
Venting cathedral roofs
the recommended vent area for cathedral roofs is often increased to 1 square foot for every 150 square feet of roof area
1" below top of joist
2"x 2" purlins (perpendicular to joists)
roof sheathing
roof membrane
roof slope: 2 in 12 and lower
roof joist
insulation
drywall
soffit vent
wall stud
siding
air flow
cross section
3" air space
roof sheathing
shingles
roof slope: more than 2 in 12
insulation
drywall
roof rafter
wall stud
soffit vent
siding
air flow
gutters not shown
cross section

1347

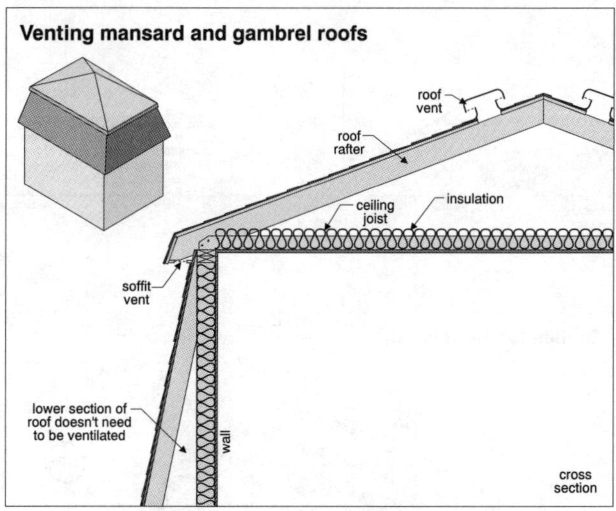
Venting mansard and gambrel roofs
roof vent
roof rafter
ceiling joist
insulation
soffit vent
lower section of roof doesn't need to be ventilated
wall
cross section

1348

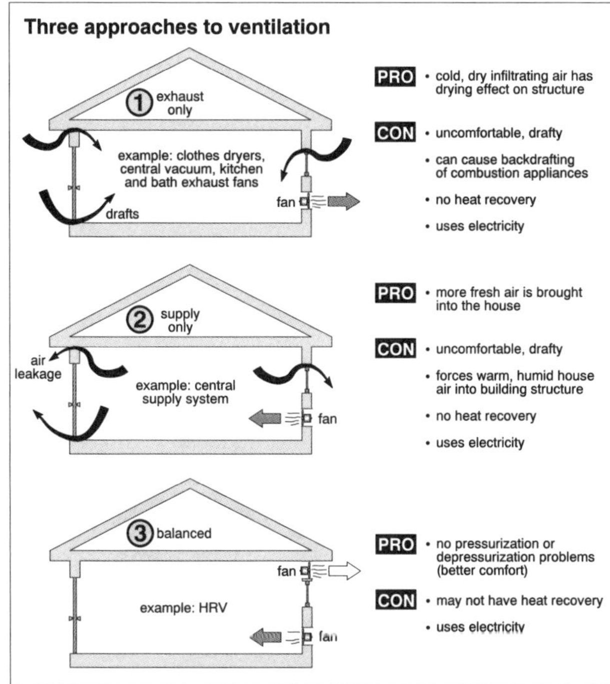

1349

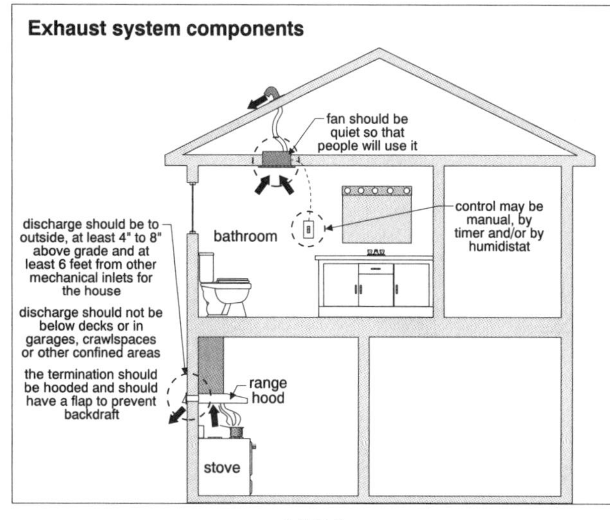

1350

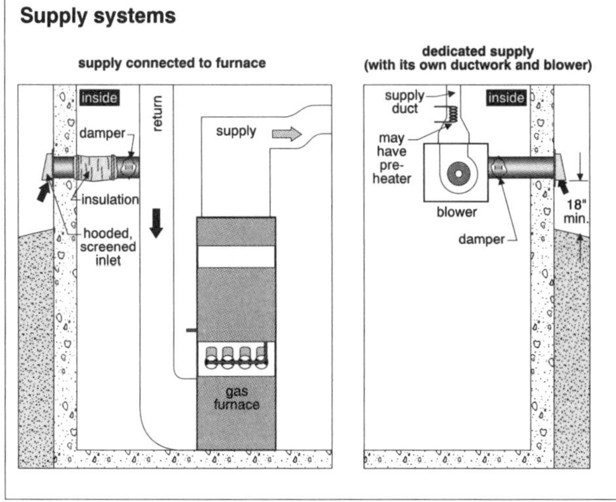

1351

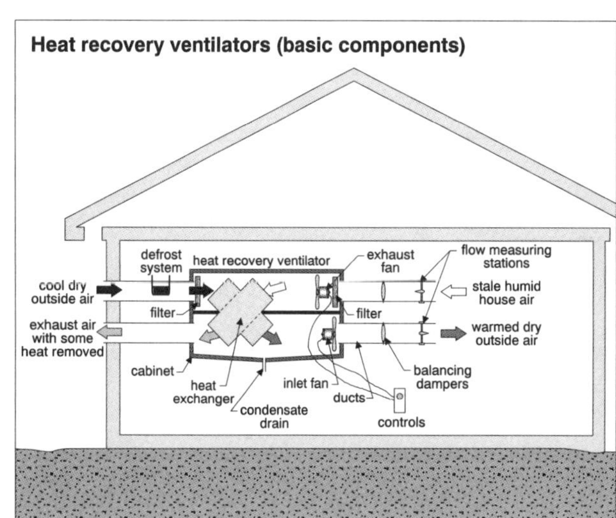

1352

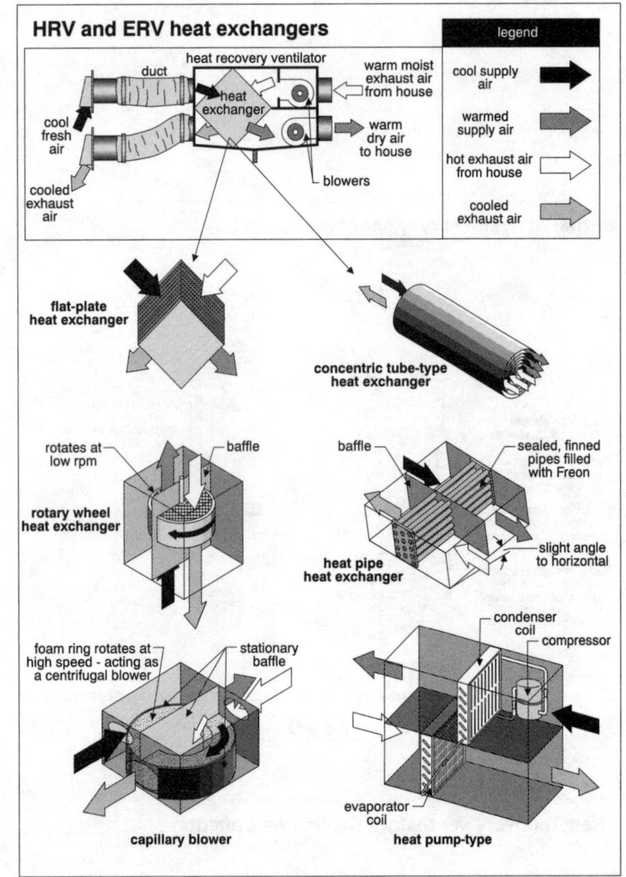

1353

HRV (heat recovery ventilator) components

outside
inside
controls
heat recovery ventilator
12" min.
warm moist exhaust air from house
cool fresh air
supply
heat exchanger
exhaust
warm dry air to house
blowers
cutaway showing balancing damper
flow collar
cooled exhaust air
condensate drain
cold-side ducts should be:
- short
- straight (supported every 3 feet)
- insulated
- sloped down to drain condensation (exhaust duct only)

floor drain

1354

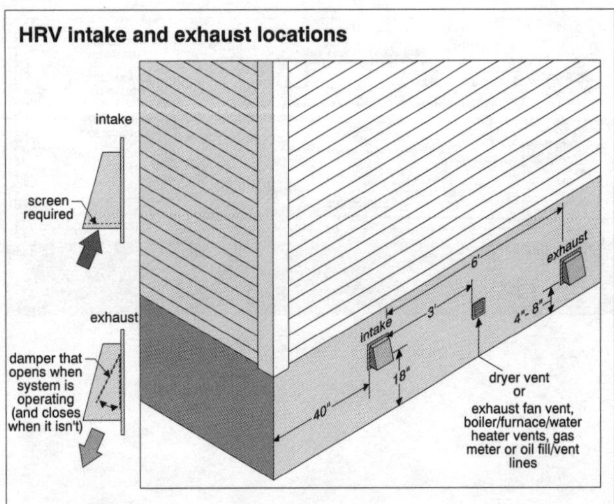

1355

Filters and condensate drains

outside
inside
intake filter
filters are similar to furnace filters (but smaller)
exhaust filter
heat recovery ventilator
cool fresh air
supply
heat exchanger
warm moist exhaust air from house
warm dry air to house
exhaust
cooled exhaust air
condensate pan
plumbing stack
condensate line
condensate drain (1/2" typ.)
trap
condensate line
air gap
laundry tub
floor drain

1356

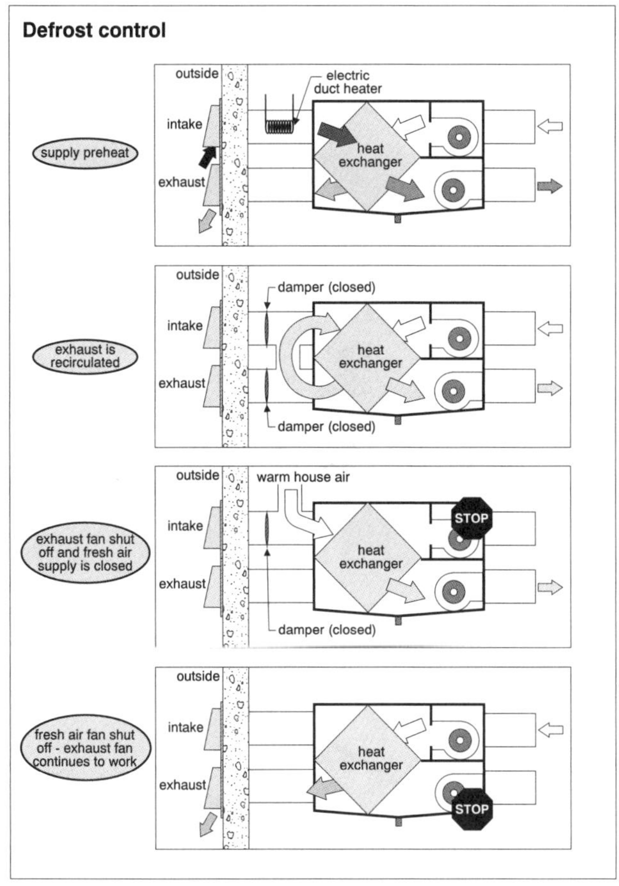

1357

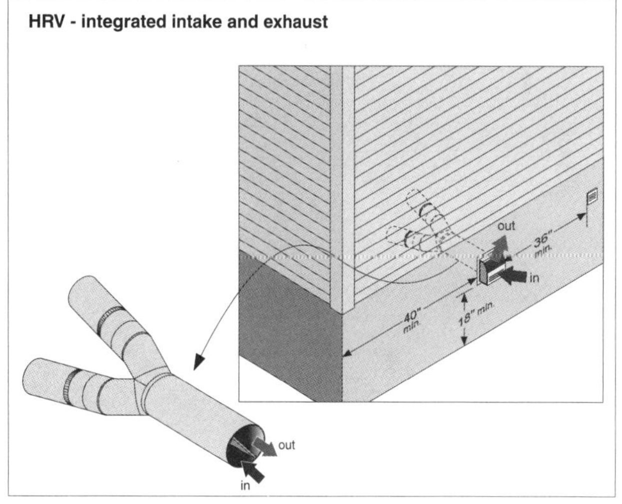

1358

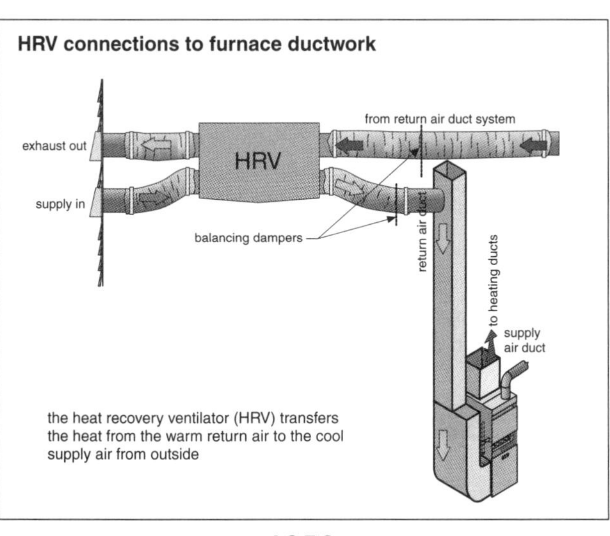

1359

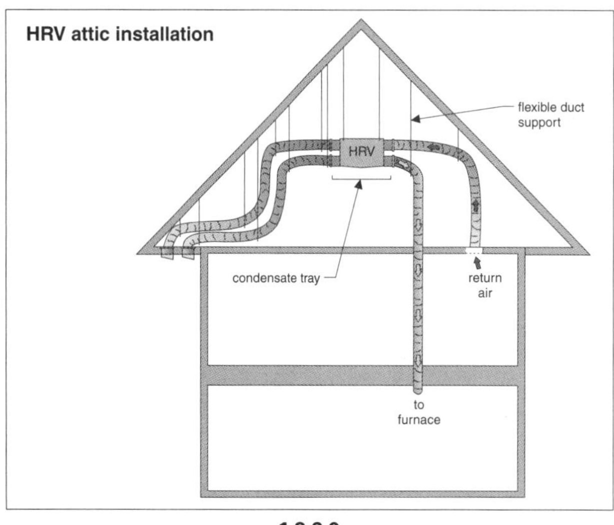

1360

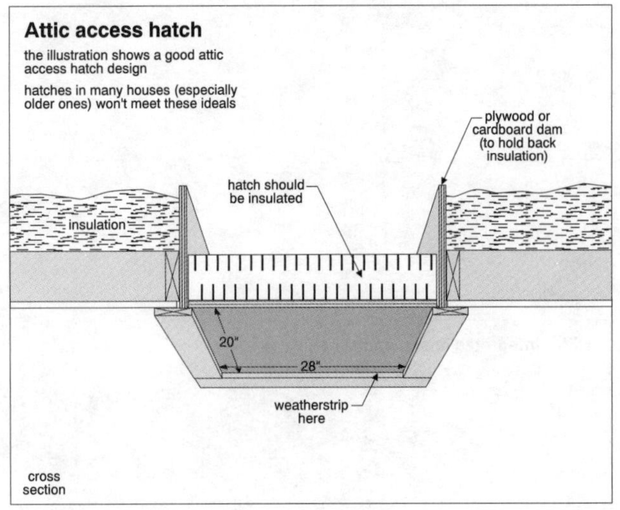

1361

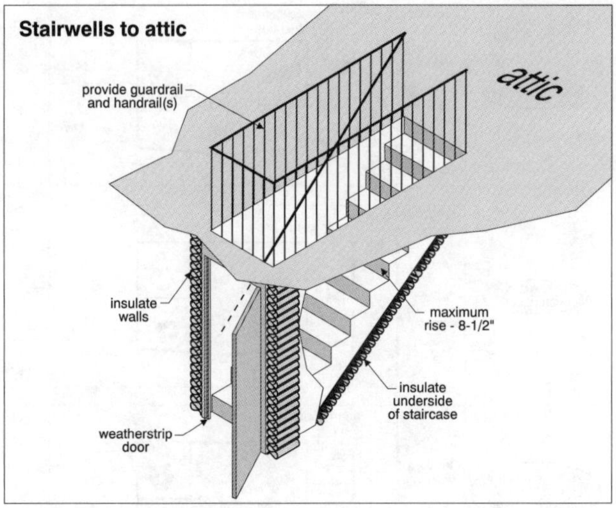

Stairwells to attic

attic

provide guardrail and handrail(s)

insulate walls

maximum rise - 8-1/2"

insulate underside of staircase

weatherstrip door

1362

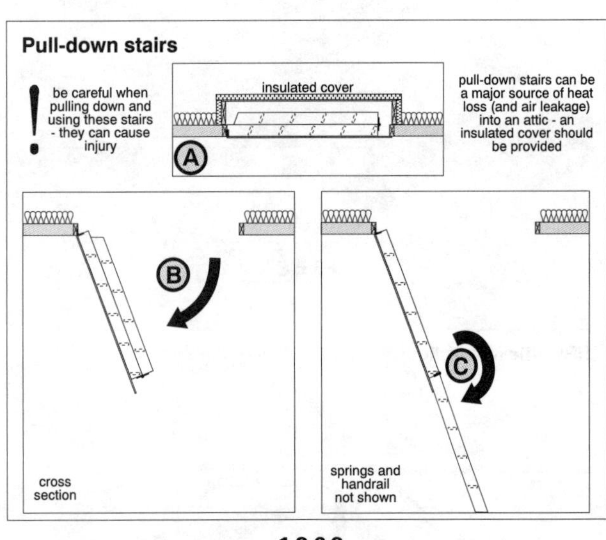

1363

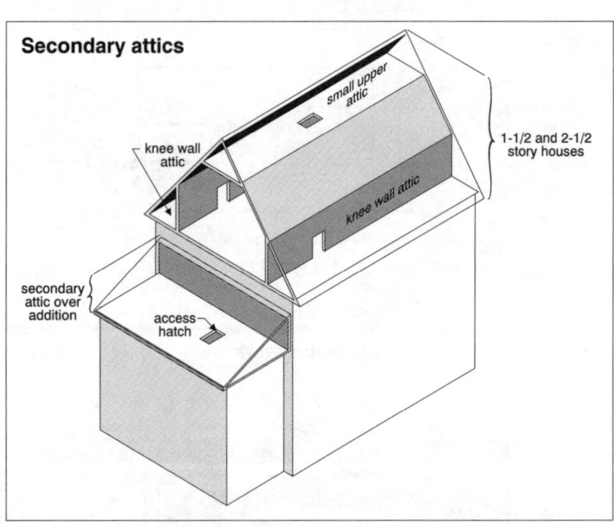

1364

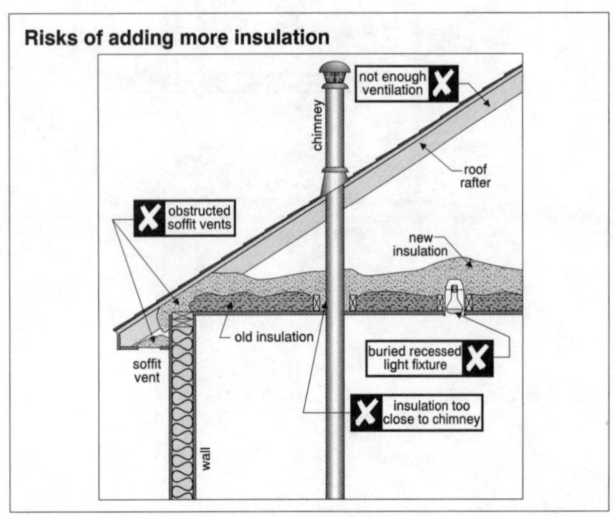

1365

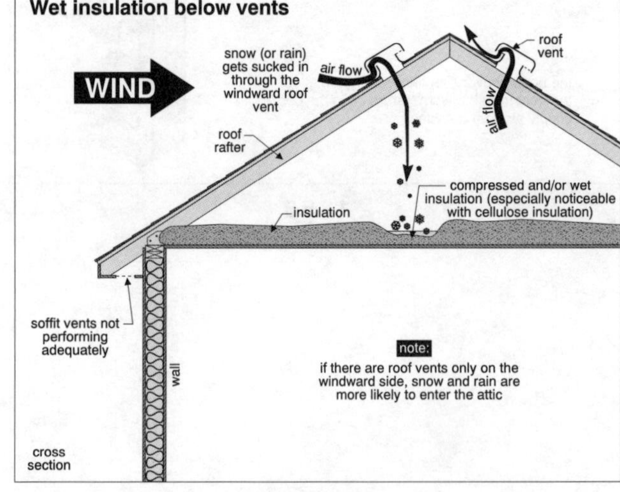

1366

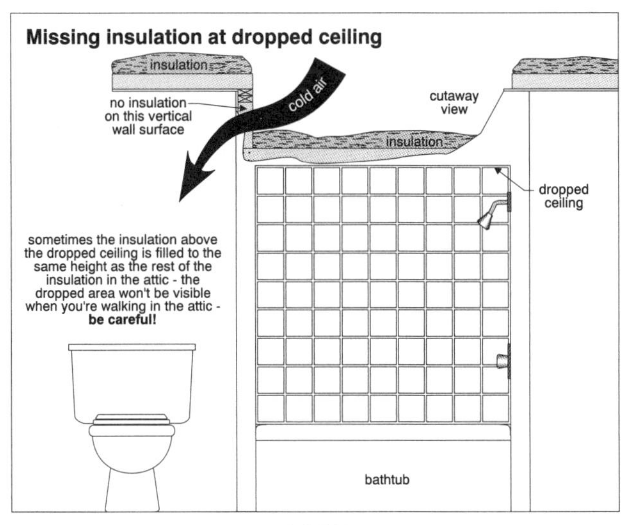

1367

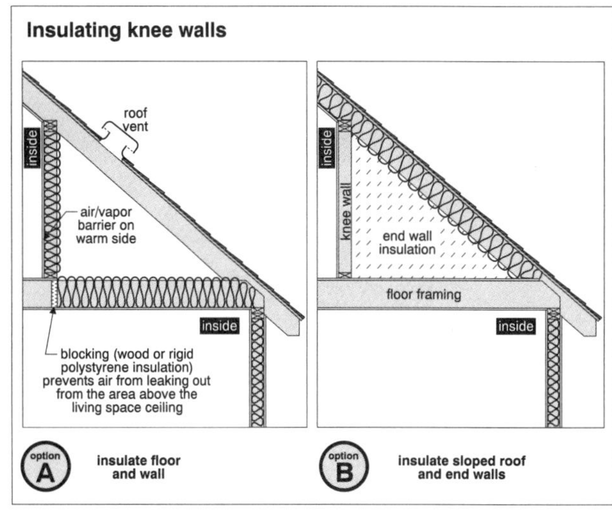

1368

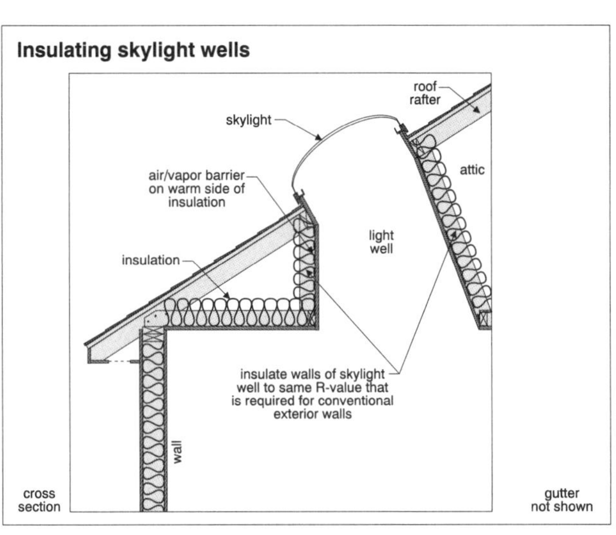

1369

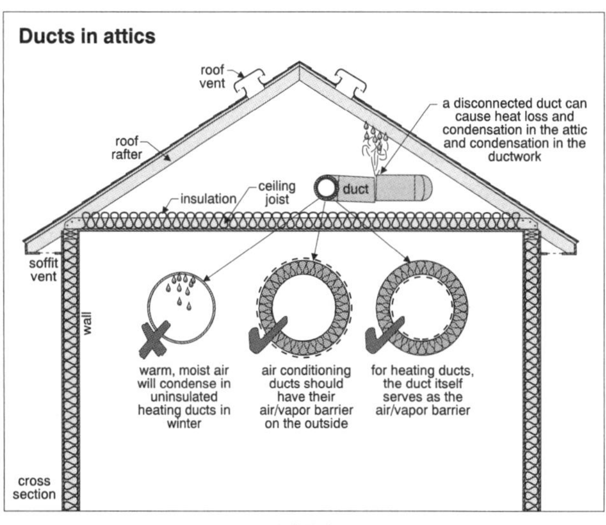

1370

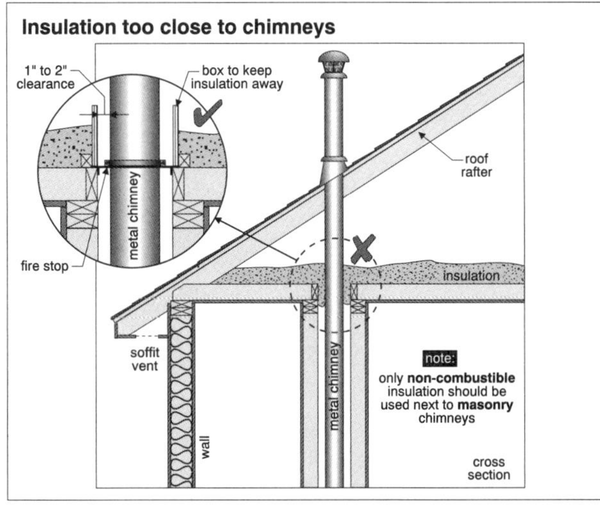

1371

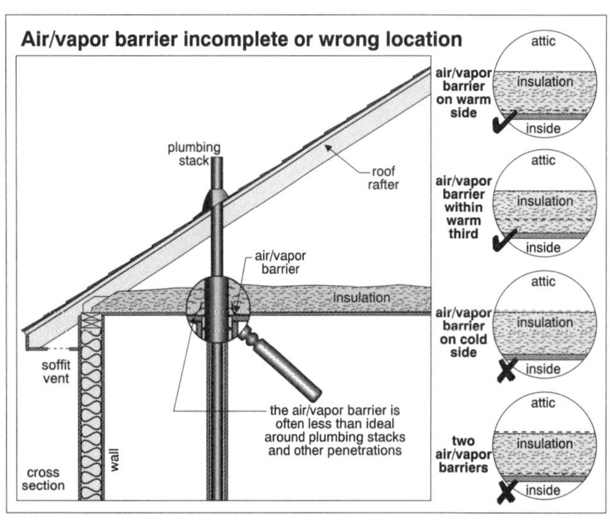

1372

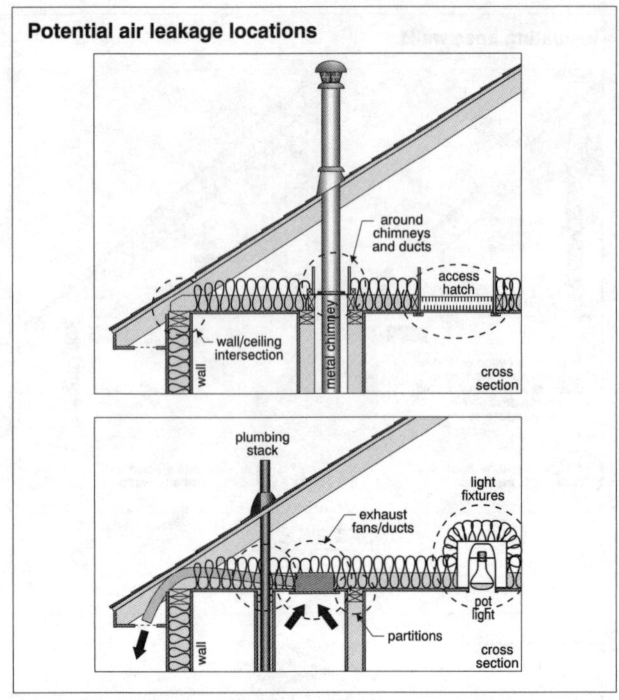

1373

Recommended amount of attic ventilation

the total vent area is often recommended to be 1/300 of the floor space of the attic

1 square foot of upper vent area required for 600 sq. ft. attic area

roof vent

note: the actual vent opening must be larger than 1 sq. ft. because of screen/louver obstructions

roof rafter

air flow

ceiling joist

insulation

soffit vent

wall

1 square foot of lower vent area required for 600 sq. ft. attic area

cross section

1374

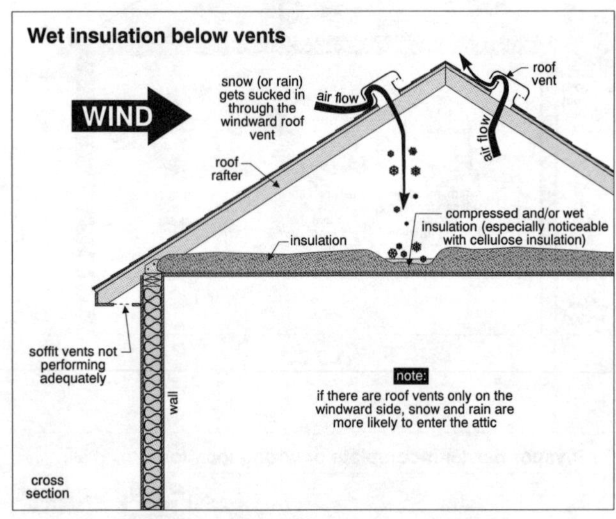

1375

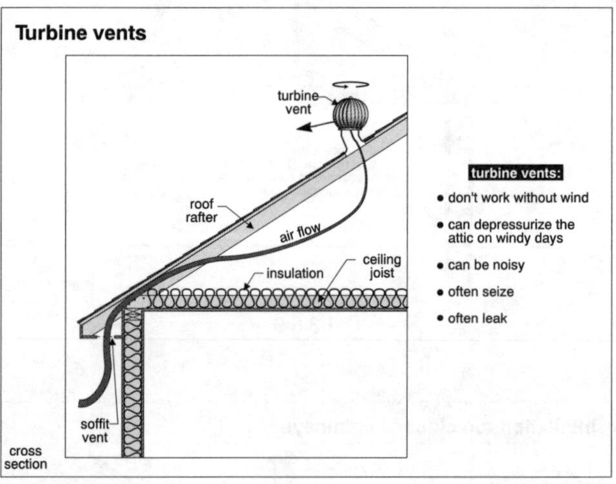

1376

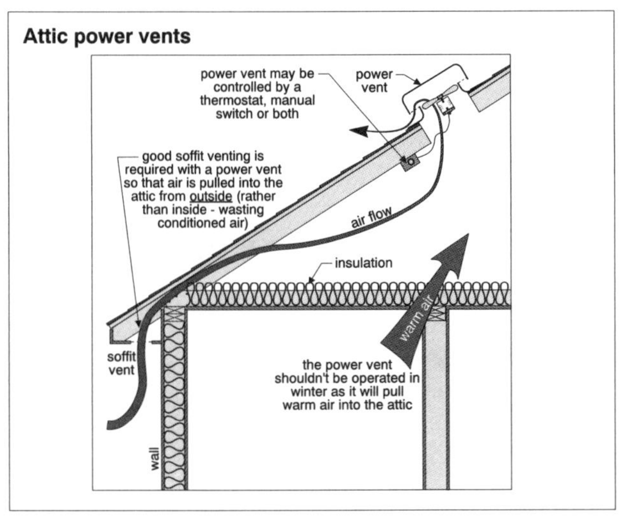

1377

Delaminating sheathing

H-clip
sheathing
rafter
cross section
rafter
sheathing
provide 1/8" gap
fasteners can pull through the delaminated sheathing
an H-clip here (or blocking, etc.) helps to prevent panel buckling
sheathing
cross section
install H-clips (or blocking) between rafters/trusses or use tongue and groove sheathing

1378

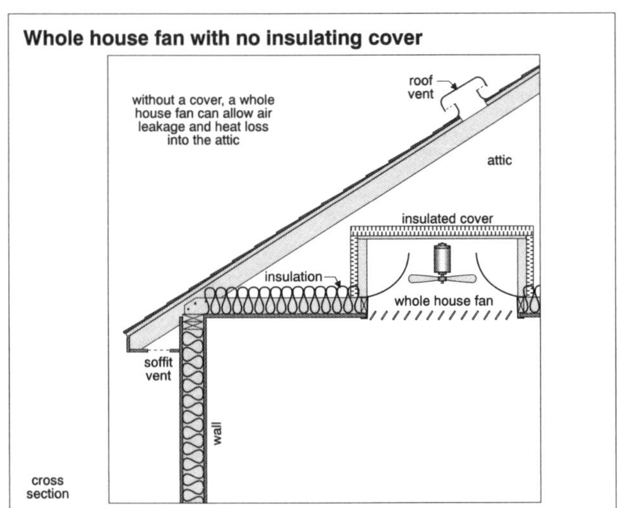

1379

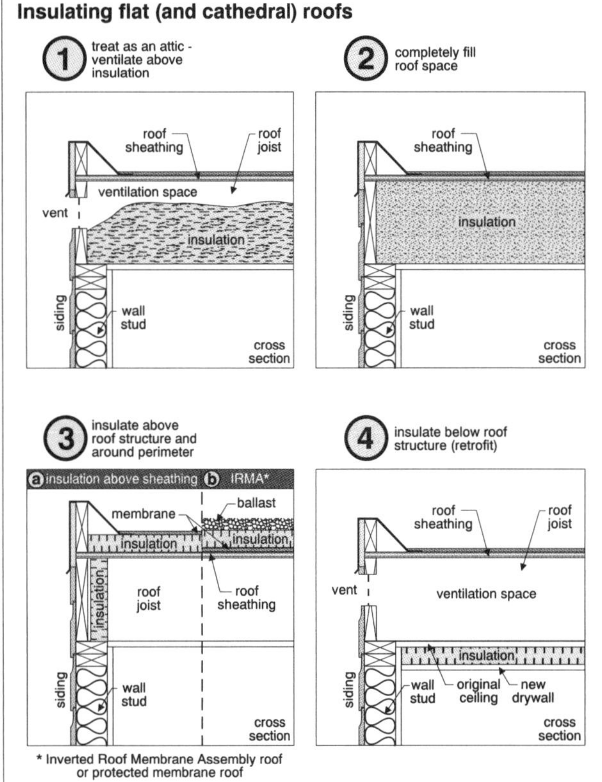

1380

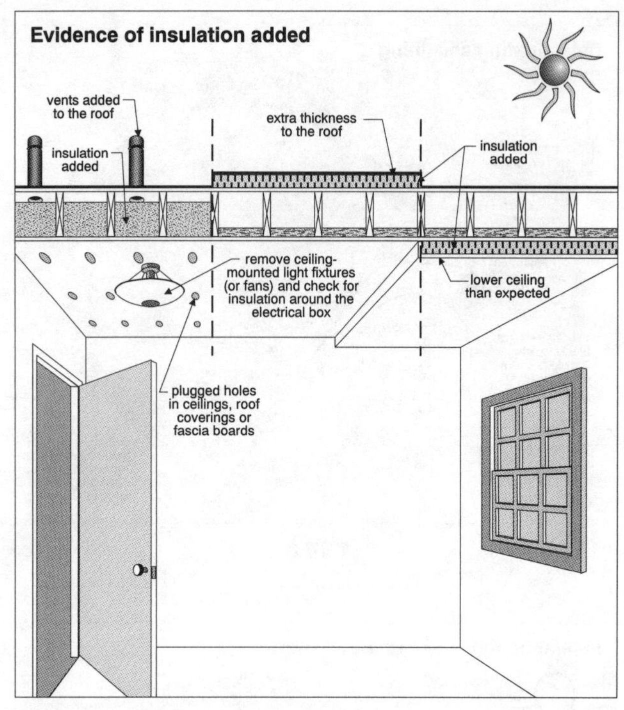

Evidence of insulation added
vents added to the roof
insulation added
extra thickness to the roof
insulation added
remove ceiling-mounted light fixtures (or fans) and check for insulation around the electrical box
lower ceiling than expected
plugged holes in ceilings, roof coverings or fascia boards

1381

Two different strategies for insulating cathedral/flat roofs
any warm, moist air that gets into the roof space is carried away by the ventilation
roof vent
roof rafter
insulation
cathedral ceiling
soffit vent
air flow
wall
insulation
cross section
vented roof space
since no air can escape the roof space, moist humid air from inside the house can't be drawn into the roof space
insulation
cathedral ceiling
wall
insulation
cross section
sealed roof space

1382

Channeled vents versus cross ventilation
for cathedral ceilings and flat roofs the recommended vent area is 1 square foot for every 150 square feet of roof area
3" air space
roof sheathing
shingles
insulation
roof rafter
drywall
soffit vent
wall stud
air flow
siding
insulation
cross section
channeled vents
1" below top of joist
2"x 2" purlins (perpendicular to joists)
roof sheathing
roof membrane
roof joist
insulation
drywall
soffit vent
wall stud
air flow
siding
cross section
cross ventilation
open web trusses also permit cross ventilation

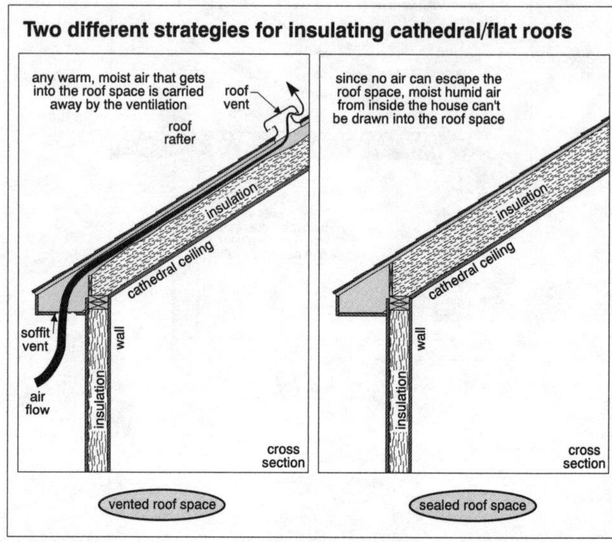

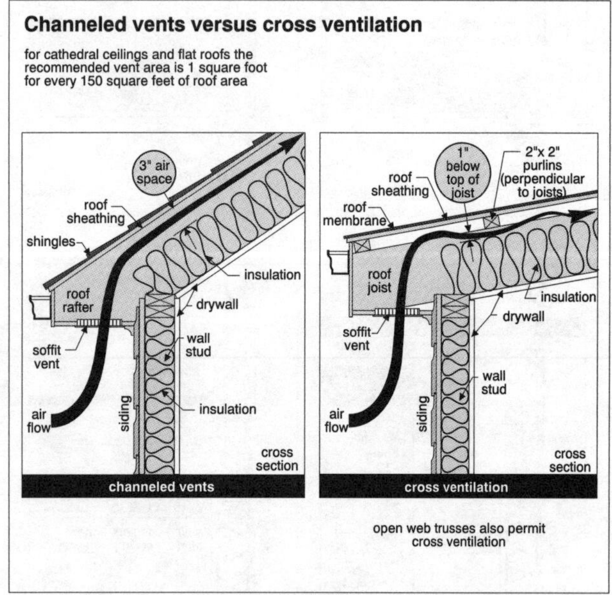

1383

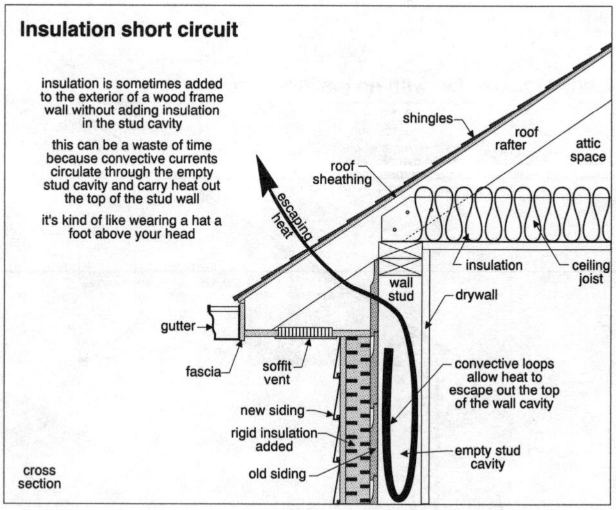

Insulation short circuit
insulation is sometimes added to the exterior of a wood frame wall without adding insulation in the stud cavity
this can be a waste of time because convective currents circulate through the empty stud cavity and carry heat out the top of the stud wall
it's kind of like wearing a hat a foot above your head
shingles
roof rafter
attic space
roof sheathing
escaping heat
insulation
ceiling joist
wall stud
drywall
gutter
fascia
soffit vent
convective loops allow heat to escape out the top of the wall cavity
new siding
rigid insulation added
old siding
empty stud cavity
cross section

1384

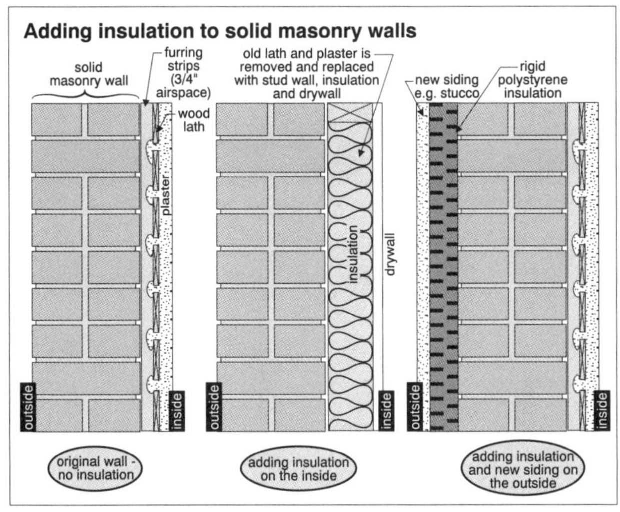

1385

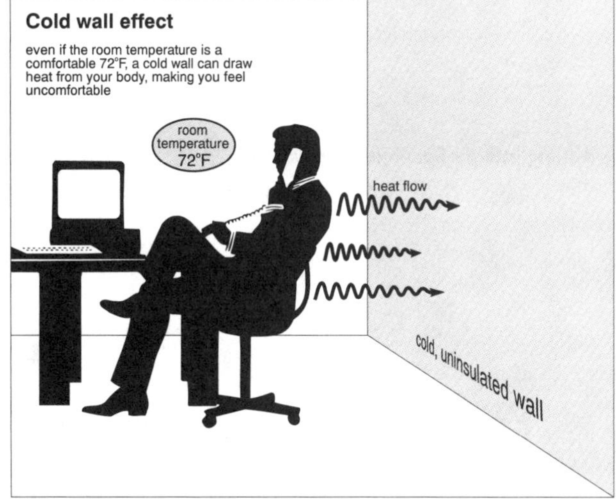

1386

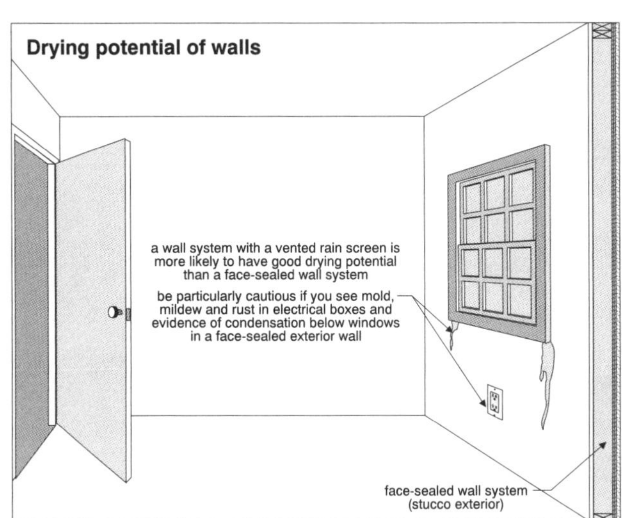

1387

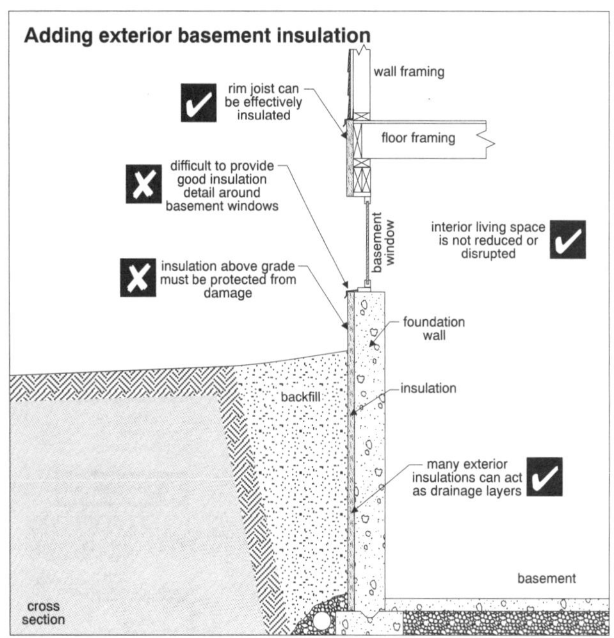

1388

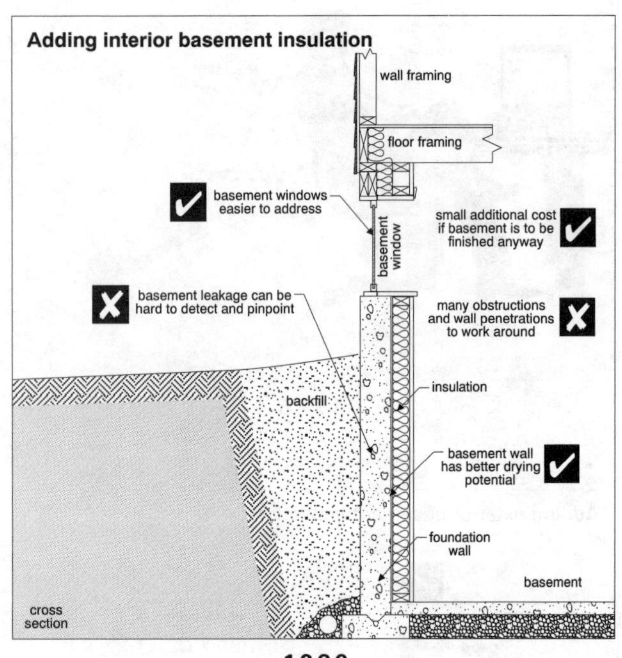

1389

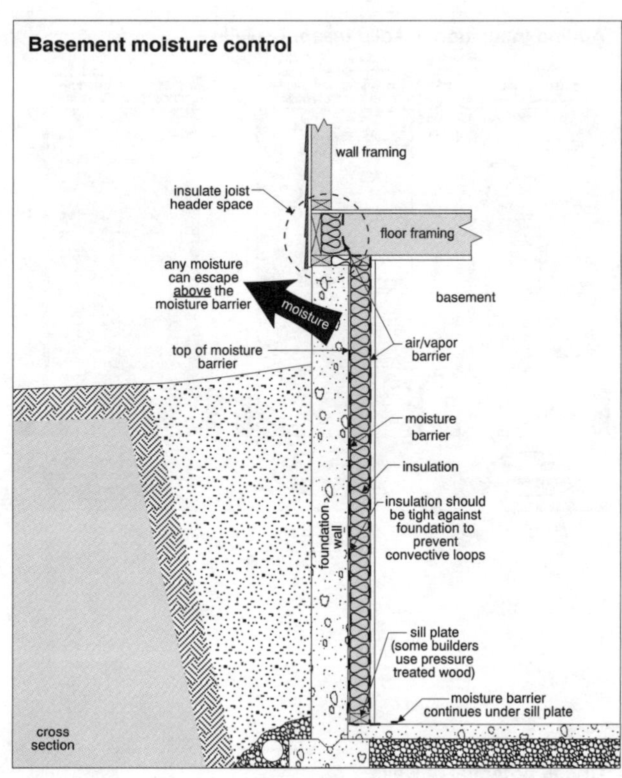

1390

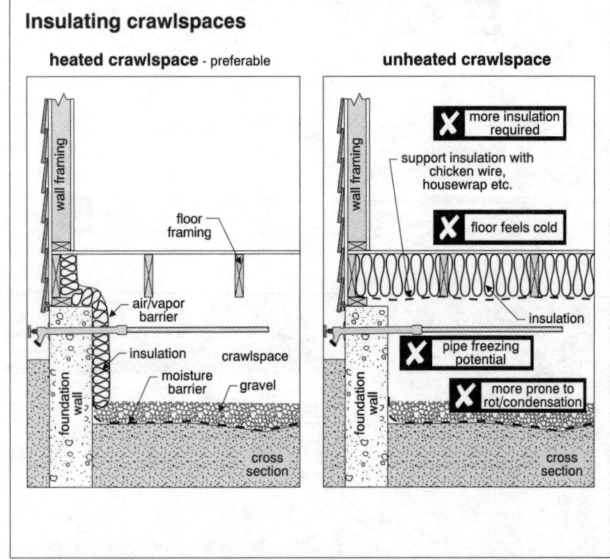

1391

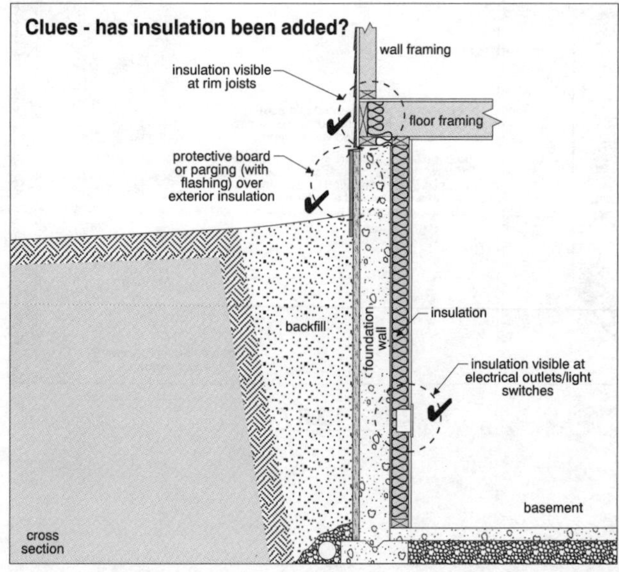

1392

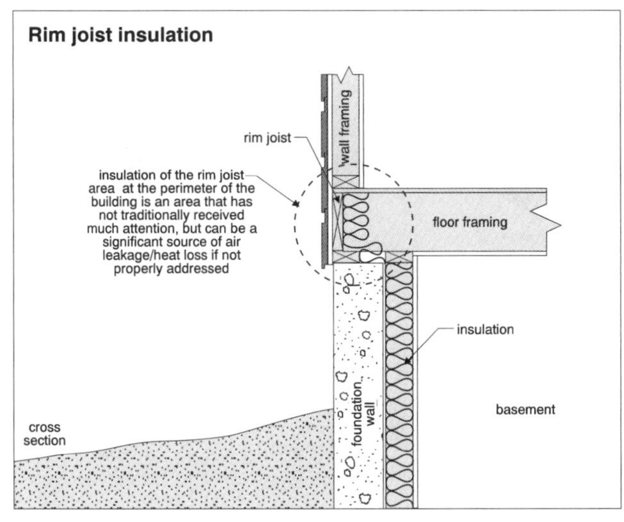

1393

Don't insulate embedded joists

insulating around embedded joists can lead to rotting

good air sealing with caulking is a better alternative

insulation

caulking

foundation

floor joist

1394

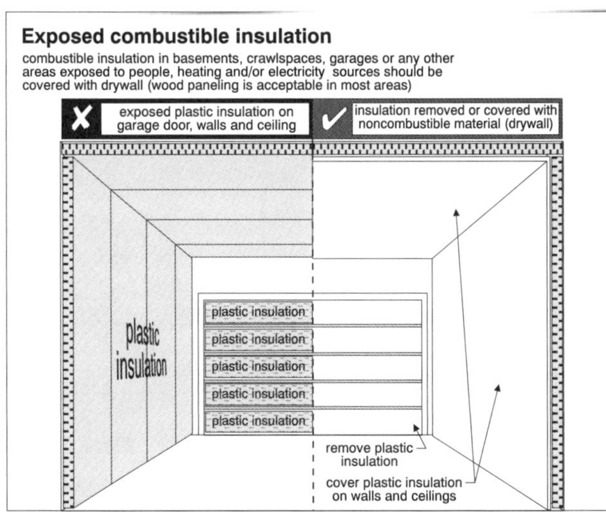

1395

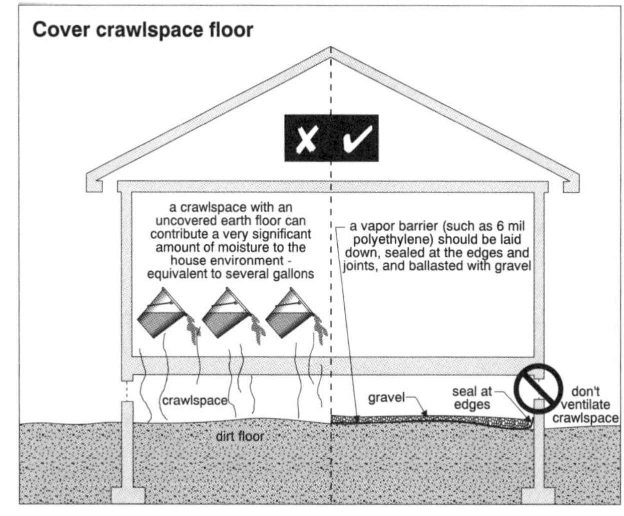

1396

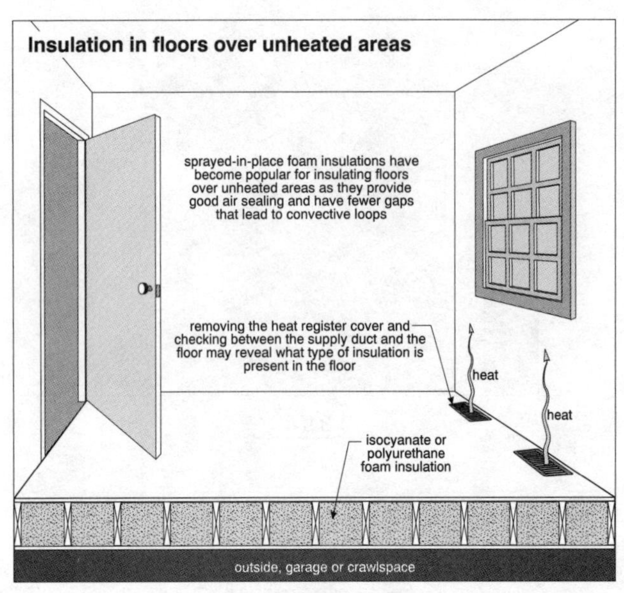

1397

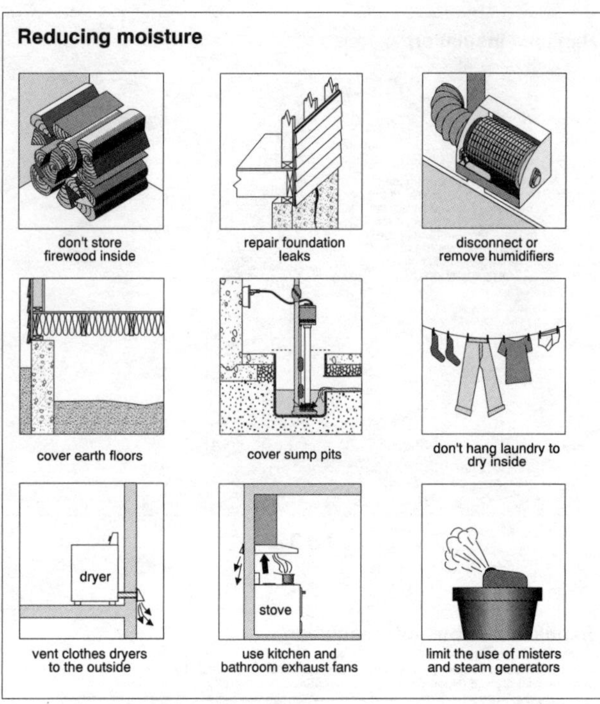

1398

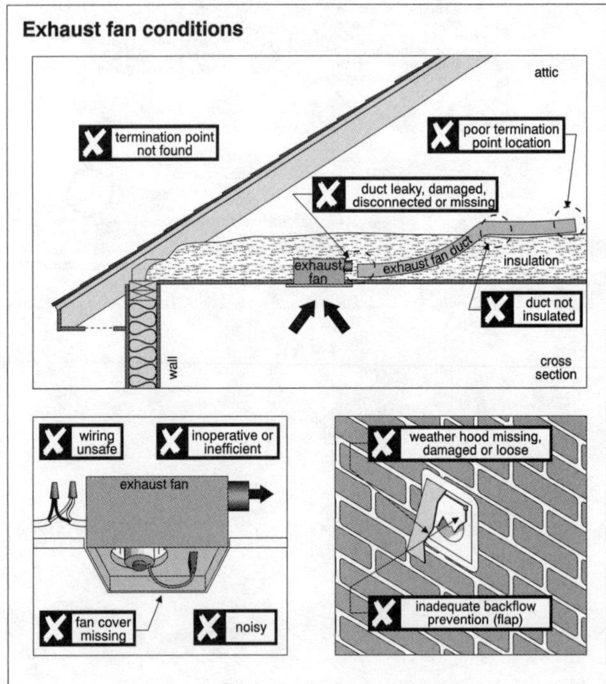

1399

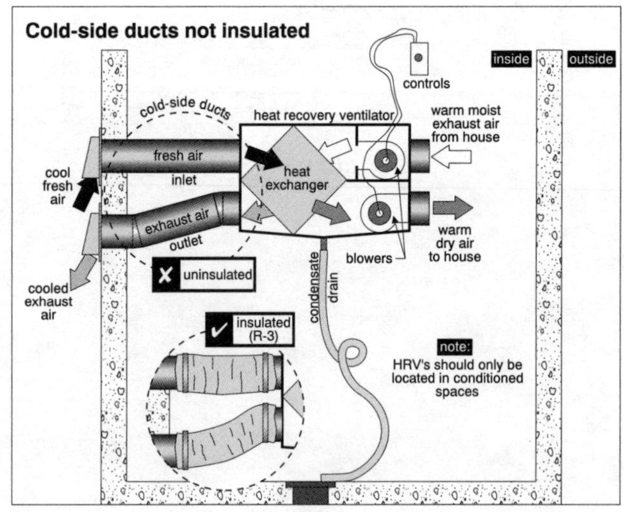

1400

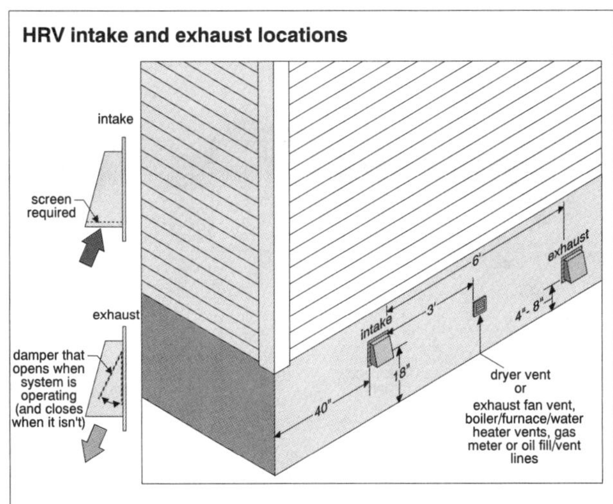

1401

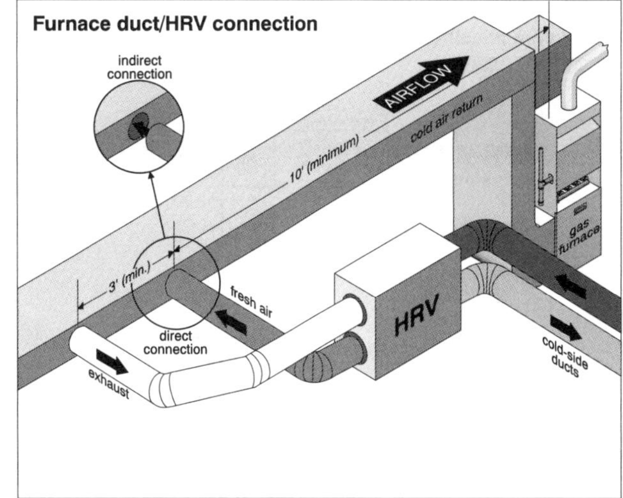

1402

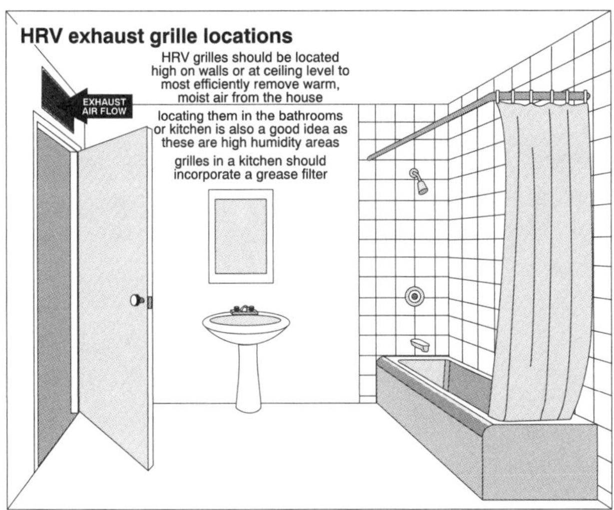

1403

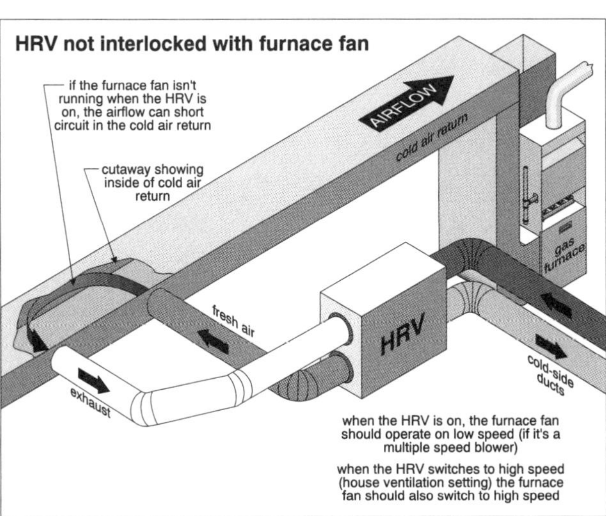

1404

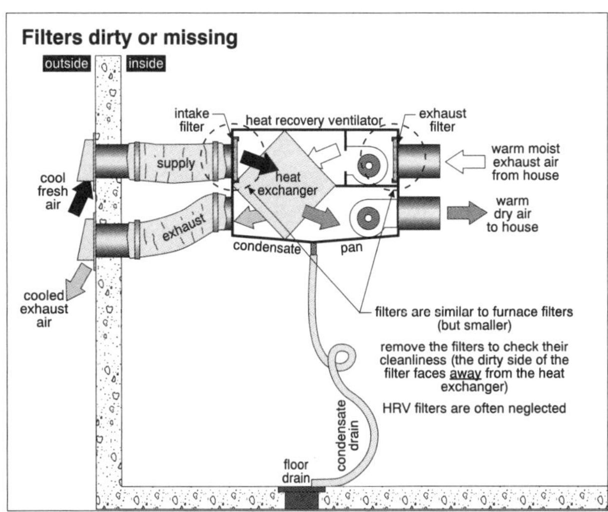

1405

1406

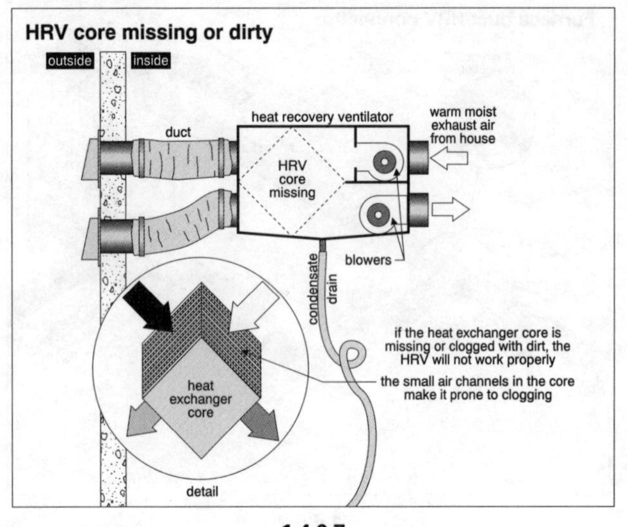
HRV core missing or dirty
outside
inside
duct
heat recovery ventilator
warm moist exhaust air from house
HRV core missing
blowers
condensate drain
if the heat exchanger core is missing or clogged with dirt, the HRV will not work properly
heat exchanger core
the small air channels in the core make it prone to clogging
detail

1407

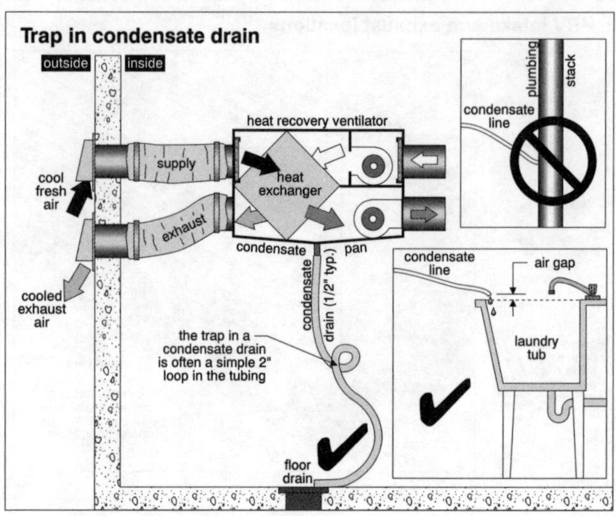
Trap in condensate drain
outside
inside
heat recovery ventilator
supply
heat exchanger
exhaust
cool fresh air
cooled exhaust air
condensate
pan
condensate drain (1/2" typ.)
the trap in a condensate drain is often a simple 2" loop in the tubing
floor drain
plumbing stack
condensate line
air gap
laundry tub

1408

CHAPTER 7

SUPPLY PLUMBING

FLOW AND PRESSURE

249..... 1500 Factors affecting supply of water
249..... 1501 Pressure drop as flow rate increases
249..... 1502 Static water pressure
249..... 1503 3/4″ pipe is more than twice as big as 1/2″ pipe!
249..... 1504 Galvanized steel pipe
249..... 1505 Downstream versus upstream pipe replacement
250..... 1506 Elbows and tees reduce pressure
250..... 1507 Pressure regulator required
250..... 1508 Constant water flow (velocity) can wear out pipes
250..... 1509 Pressure decreases with height
250..... 1510 Larger diameter pipe to water heater
250..... 1511 Pressure decreases with height

PRIVATE WATER SOURCES

251..... 1512 Draw down test
251..... 1513 Dug wells
251..... 1514 Bored wells
251..... 1515 Drilled wells
251..... 1516 Casings for drilled wells
251..... 1517 Well pits
252..... 1518 Static head
252..... 1519 Well location
252..... 1520 Deep wells and shallow wells
252..... 1521 Foot valve
252..... 1522 Types of pumps
252..... 1523 Centrifugal pump
253..... 1524 Shallow well with single line jet pump
253..... 1525 Two line jet pump
253..... 1526 Piston pump
253..... 1527 Drilled well with submersible pump
253..... 1528 Pressure tank components and pump controls
254..... 1529 Bladder-type pressure tank
254..... 1530 Waterlogged pressure tank – short-cycling

PUBLIC WATER SERVICE

254..... 1531 Service piping – when different types were used
254..... 1532 Separate water service from sewer pipe
255..... 1533 Main shut off valve – stop and waste
255..... 1534 Globe valve
255..... 1535 Gate valve
255..... 1536 Ball valve
255..... 1537 Pressure regulator required

DISTRIBUTION PIPING IN THE HOUSE

255..... 1538 Types of copper supply pipe
256..... 1539 Soldered pipe connection
256..... 1540 Flare fitting
256..... 1541 Compression fitting
256..... 1542 Galvanized steel pipe
256..... 1543 Dielectric union
256..... 1544 Hangers for copper pipe
257..... 1545 Cross connections
257..... 1546 Air gap
257..... 1547 Atmospheric vacuum breaker
257..... 1548 Pressure type vacuum breaker
257..... 1549 Double check valve assembly
257..... 1550 Reduce pressure principle device
258..... 1551 Dishwasher air gap
258..... 1552 Atmospheric vacuum breaker
258..... 1553 Correcting water hammer
258..... 1554 Vent connectors and clearances to plastic supply pipe
259..... 1555 Polybutylene pipe should be at least 18″ from water heaters
259..... 1556 Polybutylene pipe – crimp fitting
259..... 1557 Polybutylene pipe – compression (grip) fitting
259..... 1558 Bend radius for polybutylene pipe

CHAPTER 7

WATER HEATERS

INTRODUCTION

260..... 1559 Sacrificial anode
260..... 1560 Vacuum relief valve
260..... 1561 Oil-fired water heater
260..... 1562 Gas water heater
261........ 1563 External (floating) tank water heater (oil-fired)
261..... 1564 Dip tube
261..... 1565 Sacrificial anode
261..... 1566 Recovery rate
262..... 1567 Electric water heater
262..... 1568 Electric water heater – element sequencing

GAS PIPING, BURNERS, AND VENTING

262..... 1569 Ice on regulator
262..... 1570 Poor meter locations
263..... 1571 Gas piping support
263..... 1572 Drip leg
263..... 1573 Gas shut off valves
263..... 1574 Teflon tape at connections
264..... 1575 Scorching
264..... 1576 Vent connector length
264..... 1577 Poor connections
264..... 1578 Vent clearances
264..... 1579 Size of vent connector
264..... 1580 Chimney/vent connections
265........ 1581 Vent connector extends too far into chimney
265..... 1582 Poor location of pressure relief valve

OIL TANKS, BURNERS, AND VENTING

265..... 1583 Oil storage tanks – clearance from oil burner
265..... 1584 Oil storage tanks (leaks)
265..... 1585 Buried oil storage tank
265..... 1586 Undersized fill lines
266..... 1587 Primary control
266..... 1588 Refractory/fire pot
266..... 1589 Primary control
266..... 1590 Barometric damper
266..... 1591 Exhaust flue support
266..... 1592 Exhaust flue length
267..... 1593 Exhaust flue clearances

CONVENTIONAL TANK TYPE WATER HEATERS

267..... 1594 Relative recovery rates
267..... 1595 BTU's per hour compared to Kilowatts
267..... 1596 Gas burner cover and roll out shield
267..... 1597 Working space around water heaters
267..... 1598 Water heaters in garages
268..... 1599 Superheated water
268..... 1600 Temperature/pressure relief valve
268..... 1601 Gas shut off on high temperature
268..... 1602 Baffle collapsed or missing
269..... 1603 Isolating and drain valves
269..... 1604 Multiple water heaters are installed in parallel
269..... 1605 Circulating hot water system
269..... 1606 Power vented water heater
269..... 1607 Improper side wall vent locations

HIGH EFFICIENCY GAS WATER HEATERS

269..... 1608 High-efficiency gas water heaters

COMBINATION SYSTEMS

270..... 1609 Combination systems
270..... 1610 Tempering valve required
270..... 1611 Boilers heat domestic water

TANKLESS COILS

270..... 1612 Tankless coil
270..... 1613 Side arm heater
270..... 1614 Tempering valve with tankless coil
271..... 1615 Instantaneous water heater

CHAPTER 7

DRAIN, WASTE AND VENT PLUMBING

INTRODUCTION

271..... 1616 Too little or too much slope isn't good
271..... 1617 Trap terminology
271..... 1618 Trap cleanout required
272..... 1619 No traps for toilets
272..... 1620 Trap Primer
272..... 1621 Vent terminology
272..... 1622 Soil stack versus waste stack
272..... 1623 Stack vent
272..... 1624 Proper vent location relative to trap
273..... 1625 Direct venting
273..... 1626 Wet venting

DRAIN PIPING MATERIALS AND PROBLEMS

273..... 1627 Connecting cast iron waste pipe – hubless
273..... 1628 Cast iron waste pipe – bell and spigot
273..... 1629 Hangers for copper pipe
273..... 1630 Cross connections
274..... 1631 Dishwasher air gap
274..... 1632 Standpipe
274..... 1633 Condensate discharge locations
274..... 1634 Connecting vertical drain pipes to horizontal drain pipes
274..... 1635 Pinholing and cracks in cast iron stacks
274..... 1636 Issues with old clay pipe sewer

TRAPS

275..... 1637 Trap cleanout required
275..... 1638 Building trap – older installation
275..... 1639 Building trap – new installation
275..... 1640 Illegal traps
275..... 1641 Double trapping doesn't work
276..... 1642 Tail piece too long
276..... 1643 Venting an island sink (below-floor trap permitted)
276..... 1644 Loop vent or circuit vent for an island sink
276..... 1645 Proper vent location relative to trap
277..... 1646 Trap terminology
277..... 1647 Trap Primer
277..... 1648 S-traps can lead to siphoning

FLOOR DRAINS

277..... 1649 Backwater valve
277..... 1650 Downspout connection upstream of trap

VENTING SYSTEMS

277..... 1651 Flashing problems
278..... 1652 Horizontal vent offset
278..... 1653 Vent on the wrong side of the trap
278..... 1654 Wet venting
278..... 1655 Venting an island sink (if below-floor trap not permitted)
278..... 1656 Another alternate island venting arrangement
278..... 1657 Vent too tall
279..... 1658 Plumbing vent clearances
279..... 1659 Automatic air vent

SEWAGE EJECTOR PUMPS

279..... 1660 Sewage ejector pump

SUMP PUMPS

279..... 1661 Sump pump

LAUNDRY TUB PUMPS

279..... 1662 Laundry tub pump

SEPTIC SYSTEMS

279..... 1663 Septic tank (two compartment)
280..... 1664 Tile beds
280..... 1665 Tile bed location
280..... 1666 Dosing chamber
280..... 1667 Seepage pit
280..... 1668 Septic tank pump-out
280..... 1669 Warning signs for tile beds

CHAPTER 7

FIXTURES AND FAUCETS

INTRODUCTION

281..... 1670 Hot/cold conventions

BASINS, SINKS AND LAUNDRY TUBS

281..... 1671 Rusting overflow

FAUCETS

281..... 1672 Compression faucet
281..... 1673 Correcting water hammer
281..... 1674 Hot/cold conventions
281..... 1675 Shut off valves for outside faucets
282..... 1676 Atmospheric vacuum breaker

TOILETS

282..... 1677 Toilet flushing actions
282..... 1678 Supply tubes
282..... 1679 Loose toilet
282..... 1680 Toilet flush mechanism

BIDETS

282..... 1681 Bidets

BATHTUBS

283..... 1682 Tubs without tile lips more prone to leakage
283..... 1683 Don't test overflows
283..... 1684 Inspecting a bathtub

TUB AND SHOWER STALL ENCLOSURES

283..... 1685 Bathtubs on exterior walls
283..... 1686 Windows over bathtubs aren't a good idea
283..... 1687 Bathroom outlets and switches

SHOWER STALLS

284..... 1688 One-piece shower stalls
284..... 1689 Acrylic base
284..... 1690 Metal showers are bad
284..... 1691 Tiled mortar base
284..... 1692 Cement board installation
284..... 1693 Expansion and debonding of tile due to moisture

WHIRLPOOL BATHS

285..... 1694 Whirlpool bath
285..... 1695 Make sure the jets are submerged before testing
285..... 1696 Bathroom outlets and switches

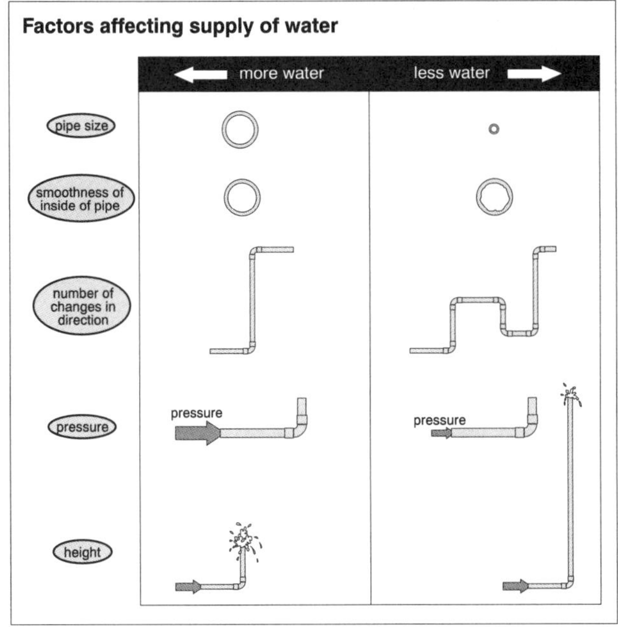

1500

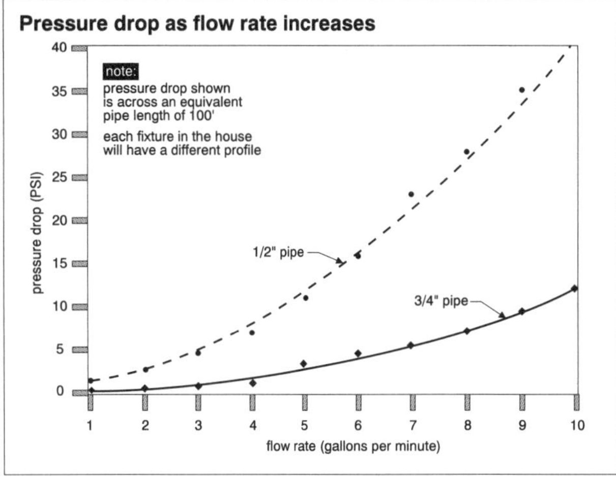

1501

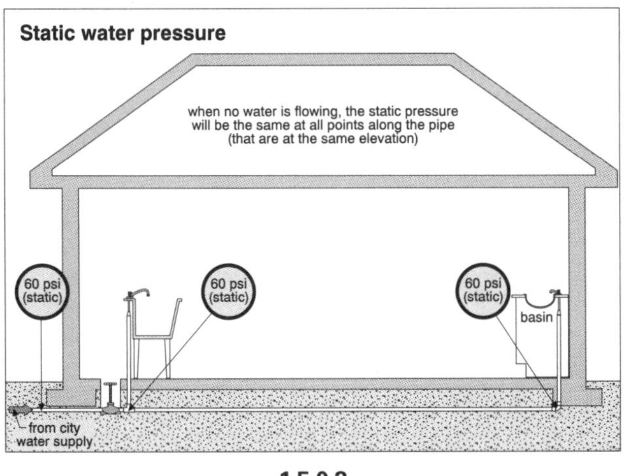

1502

3/4" pipe is more than twice as big as 1/2" pipe!

r=radius=0.25"

1/2"

diameter

1/2" pipe

cross sectional area
= pi x r^2
= 3.14x$(0.25)^2$
= 0.2 square inches

r=radius=0.375"

3/4"

diameter

3/4" pipe

cross sectional area
= pi x r^2
= 3.14x$(0.375)^2$
= 0.44 square inches

1503

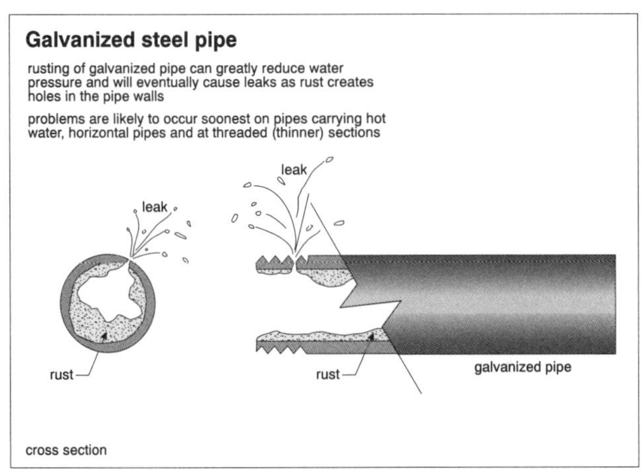

1504

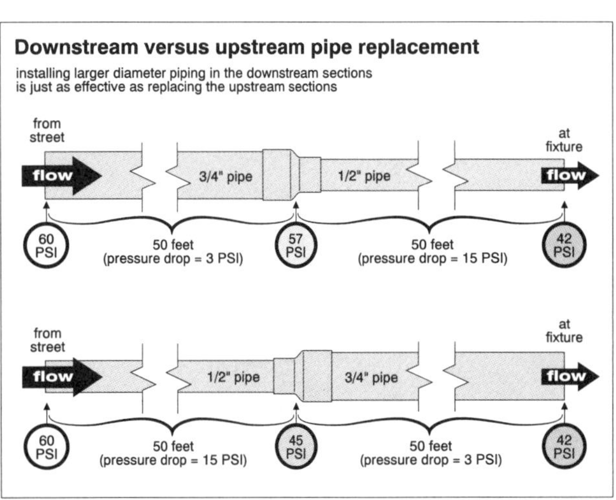

1505

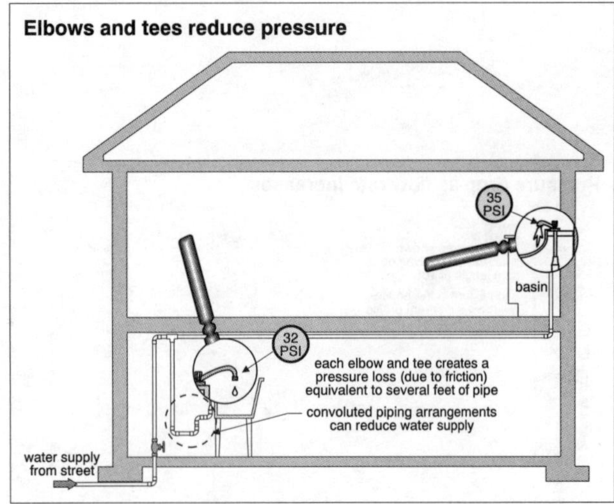

1506

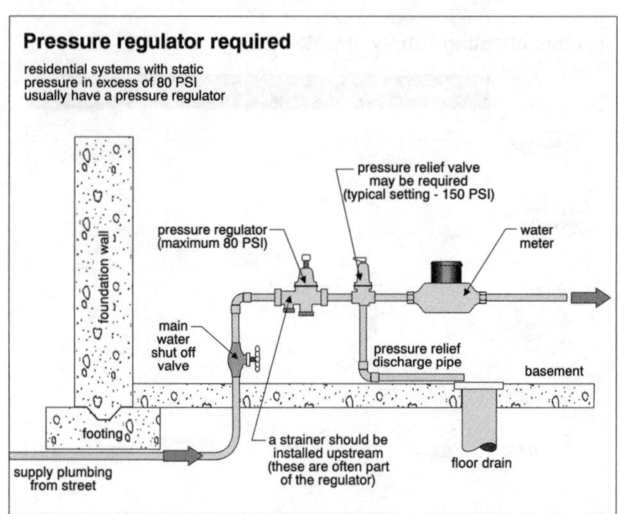

1507

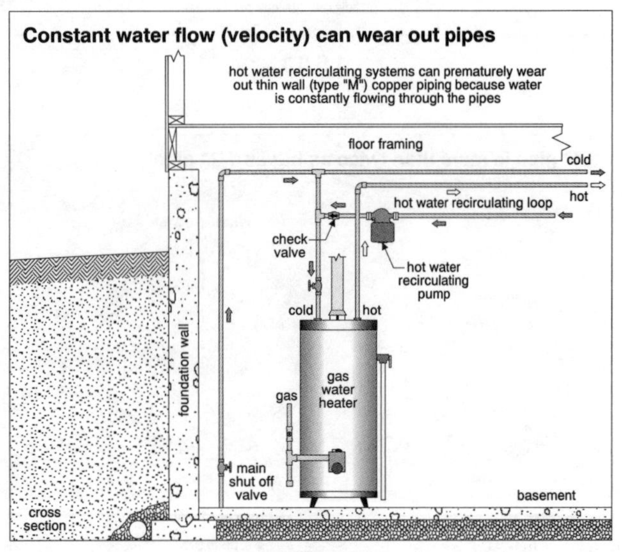

1508

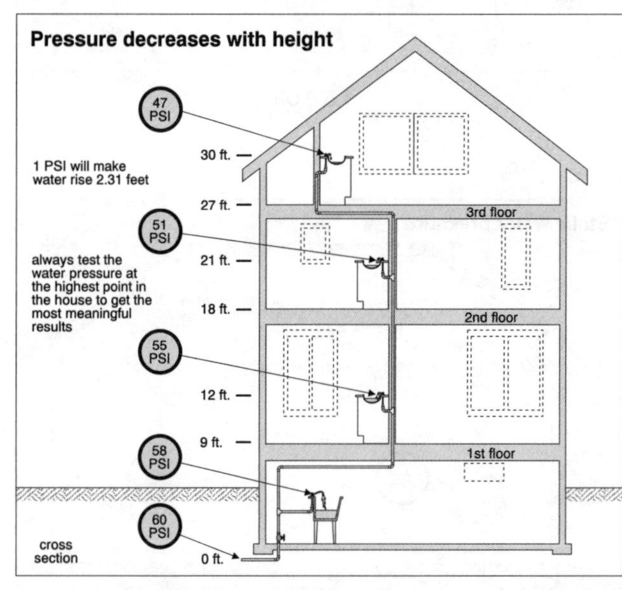

1509

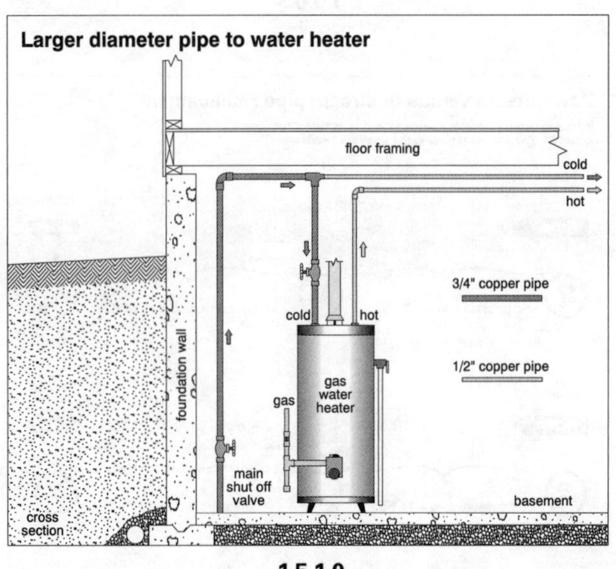

1510

Pressure decreases with height

47 PSI
30 ft.
1 PSI will make water rise 2.31 feet
27 ft.
3rd floor
51 PSI
always test the water pressure at the highest point in the house to get the most meaningful results
21 ft.
18 ft.
2nd floor
55 PSI
12 ft.
9 ft.
1st floor
58 PSI
60 PSI
cross section
0 ft.

1511

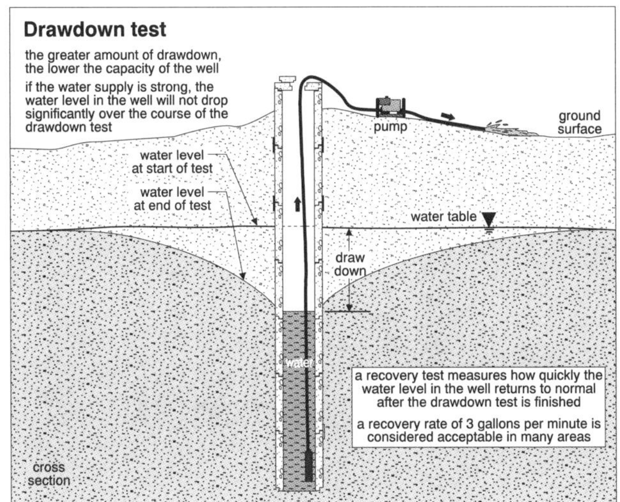

1512

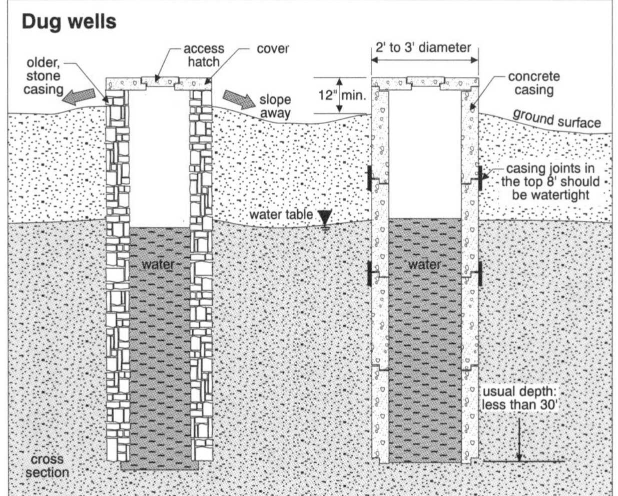

1513

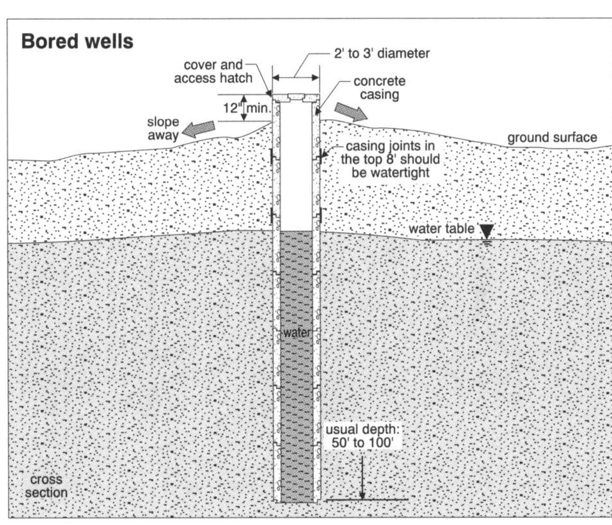

1514

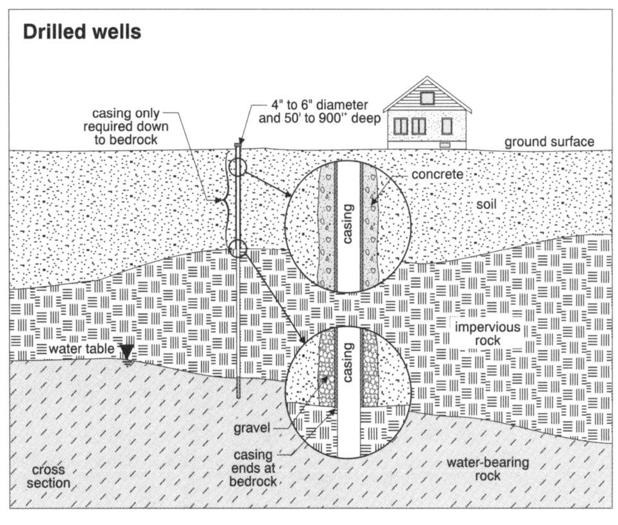

1515

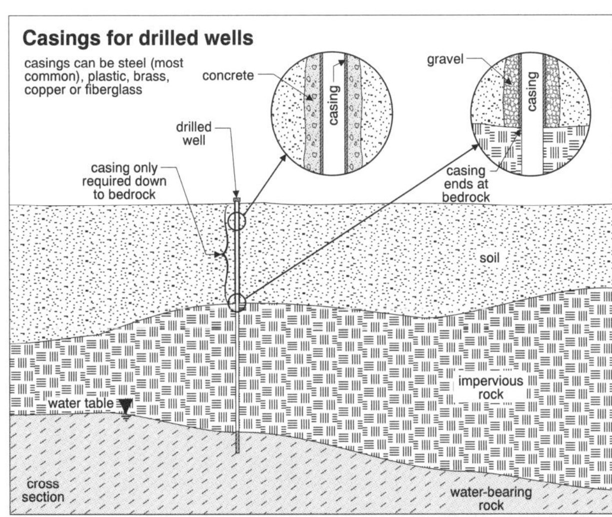

1516

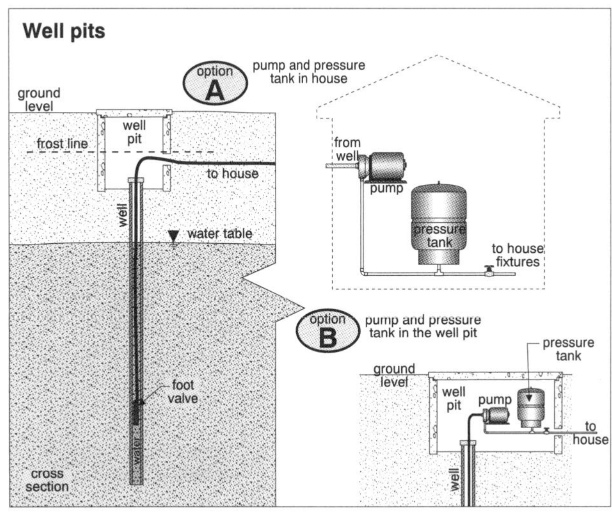

1517

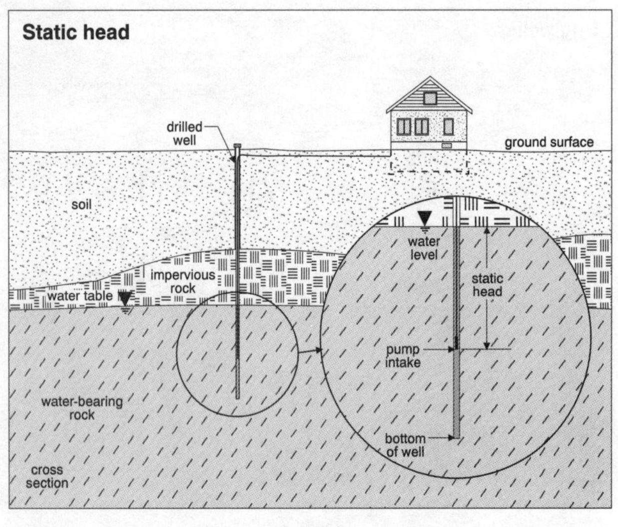

1518

Well location

1519

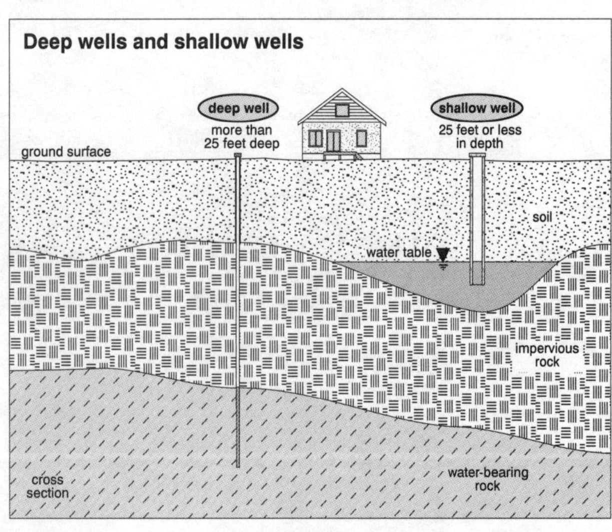

1520

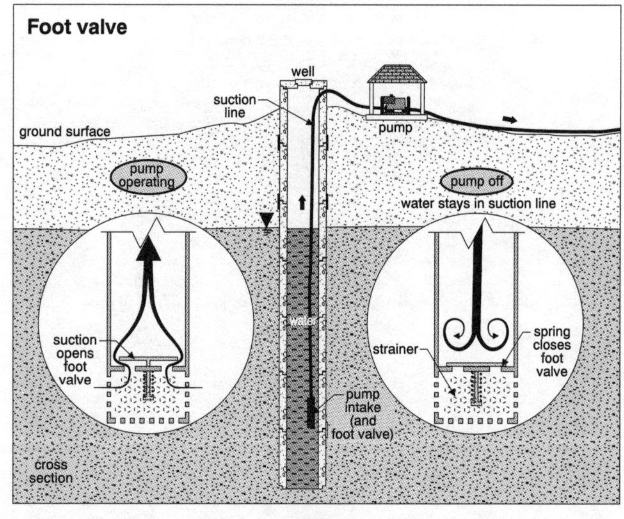

1521

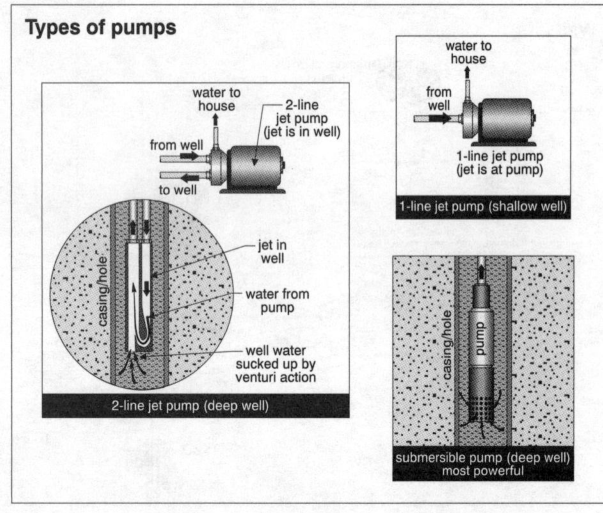

1522

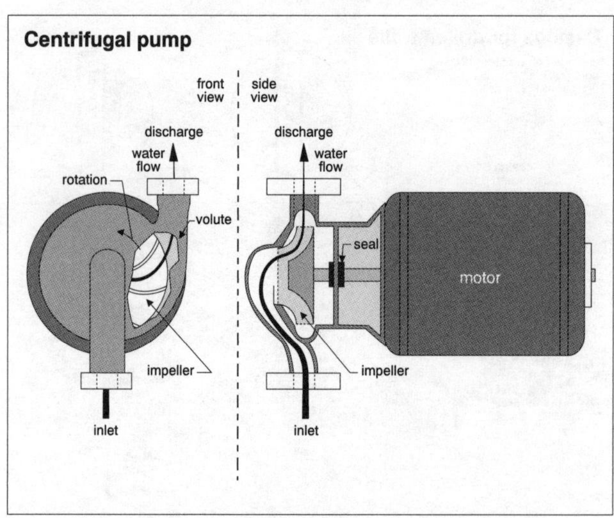

1523

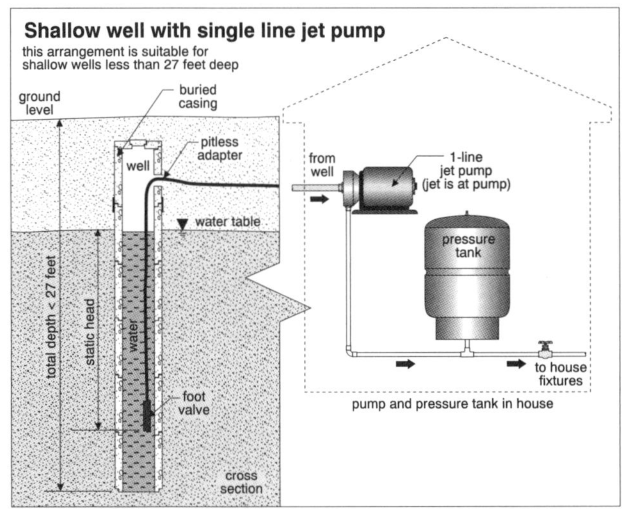

1524

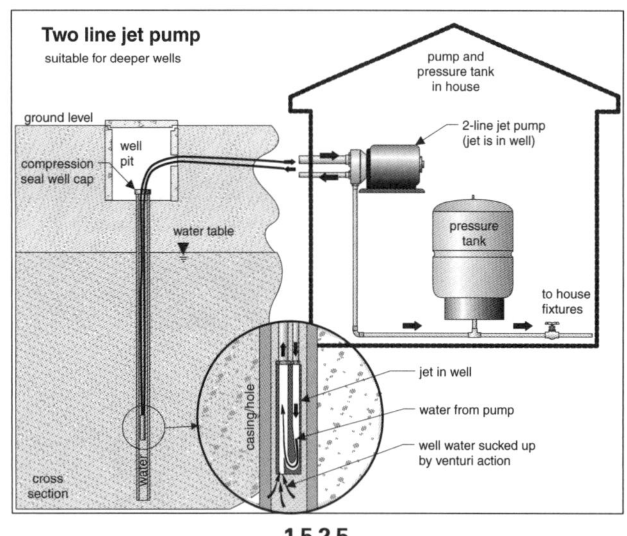

1525

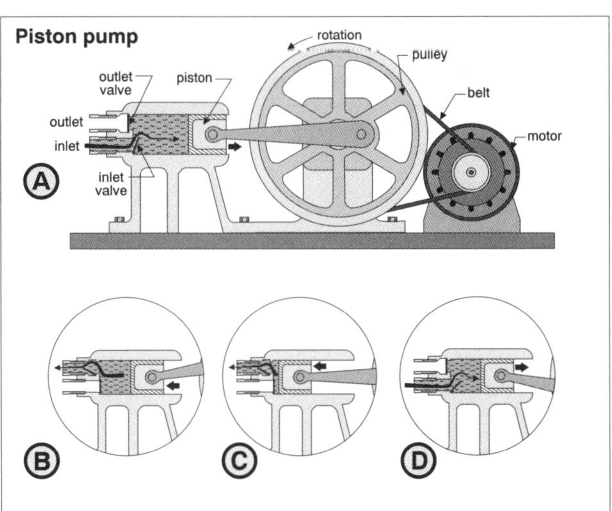

1526

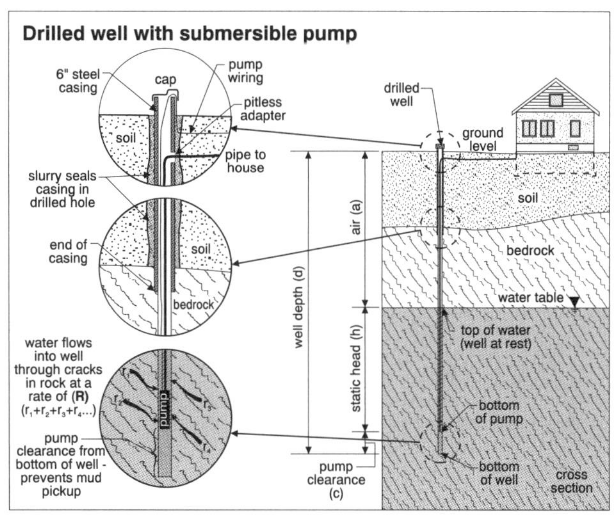

1527

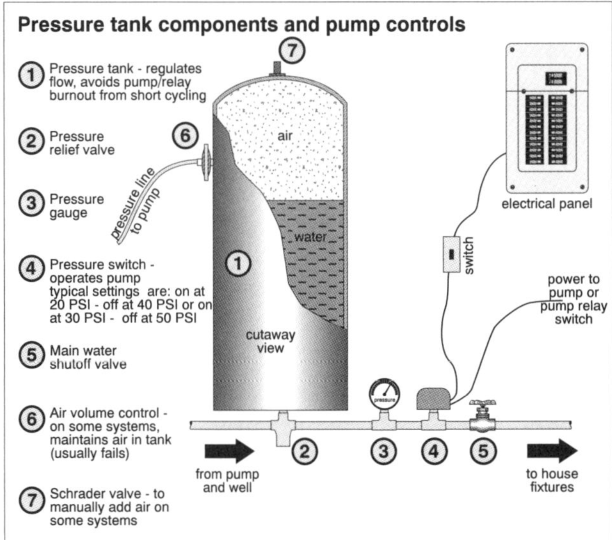

1528

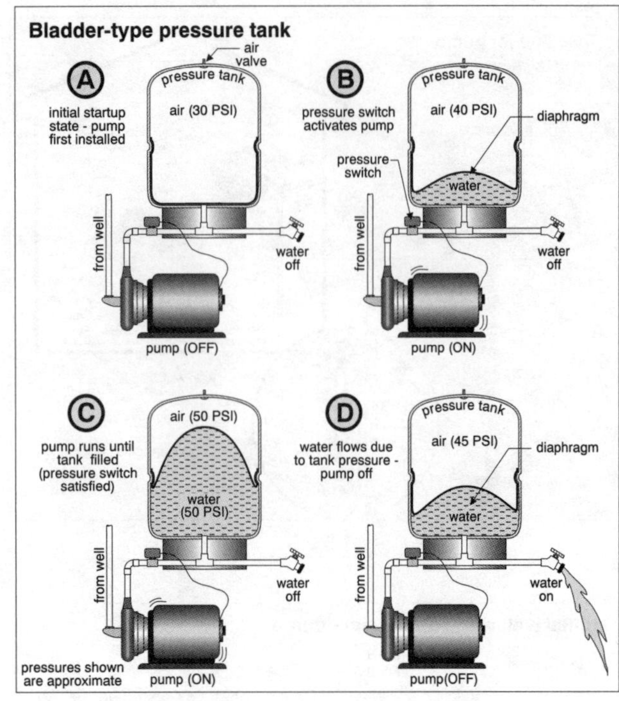

1529

Waterlogged pressure tank - short-cycling

start of run-down PUMP IS OFF

end of run-down PUMP TURNS ON

Schrader valve

air @ 40 PSI

condensation or stains show normal water level

water

air @ 30 PSI

water level

pressure tank

air @ 20 PSI

water level

water

pressure tank

this is the rest position with the tank charged

the pump has just shut off

as water is drawn off, the air expands slowly, maintaininga relatively constant pressure in the piping

when the pressure drops to 20 psi, the pump kicks in

water level

waterlogged tank - insufficient air will cause short pump cycle - air may have leaked out or have been absorbed by the water

for a typical 20 to 40 gallon tank and one fixture running, it takes 1/2 to 2 minutes to draw down the water enough for the pump to cut in

if the pump cuts in after only 5 to 10 seconds and keeps cycling at that rate, more air is needed in the tank or another problem exists and must be repaired promptly

from pump and well

to house fixtures

cutaway view

1530

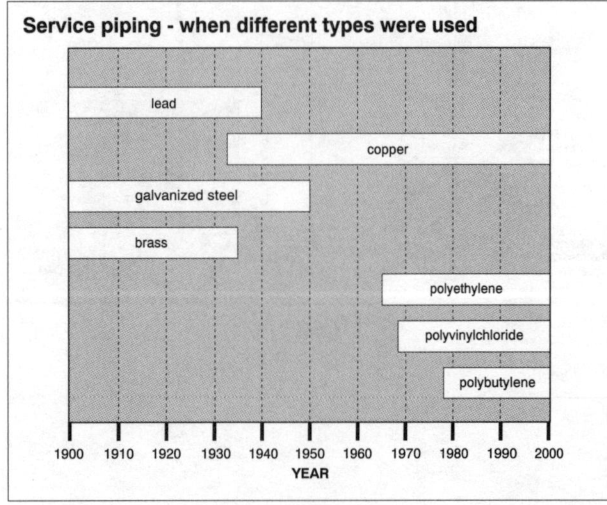

1531

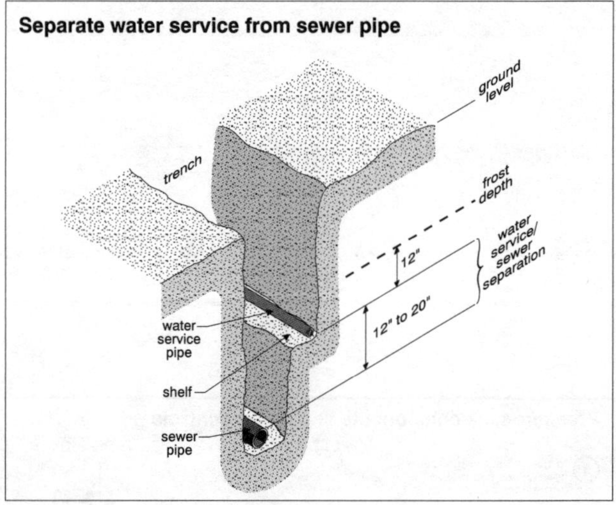

1532

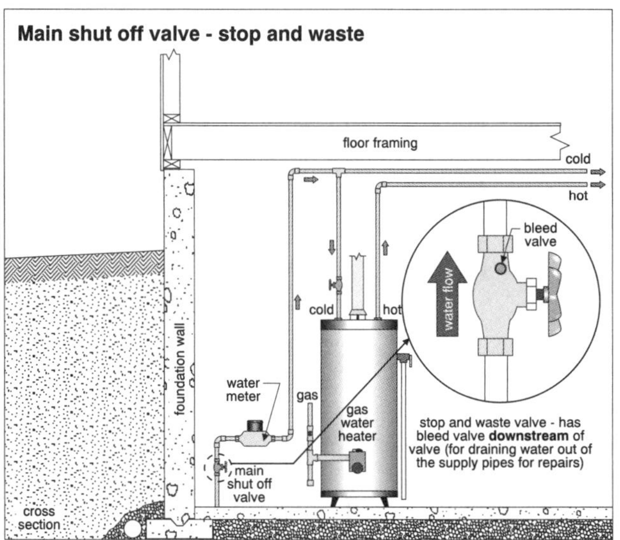

1533

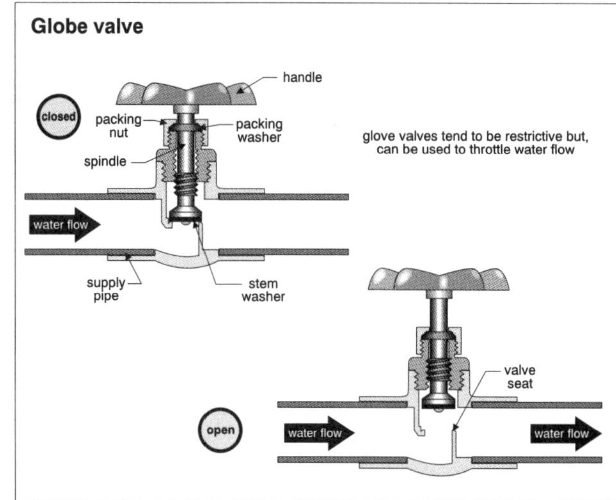

1534

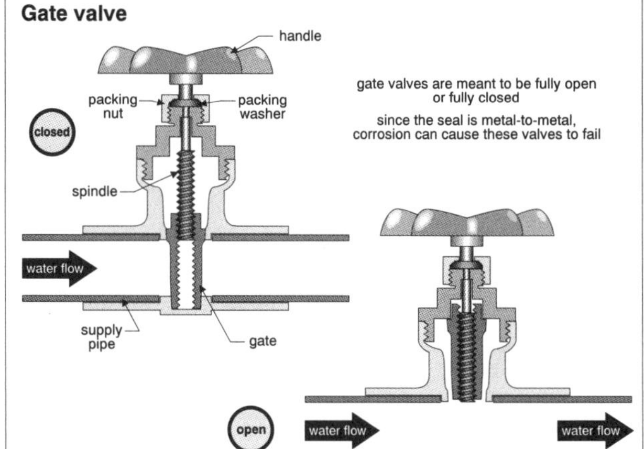

1535

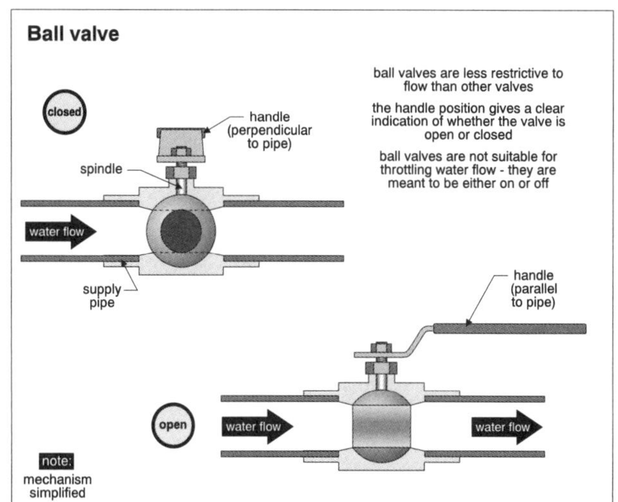

1536

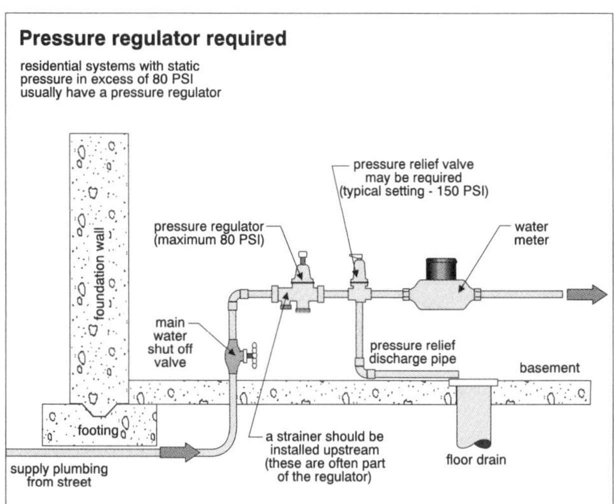

1537

Types of copper supply pipe

for general plumbing (not for underground) - available in hard temper only

outside diameter - .625"

TYPE M (printed in red)

wall thickness .028"

for general plumbing and heating - available in soft or hard temper

outside diameter - .625"

TYPE L (printed in blue)

wall thickness .040"

outside diameter - .625"

TYPE K (printed in green)

wall thickness .049"

for underground service (as well as plumbing, heating and gas lines) - available in soft or hard temper

1/2" copper pipe shown for comparison purposes

1538

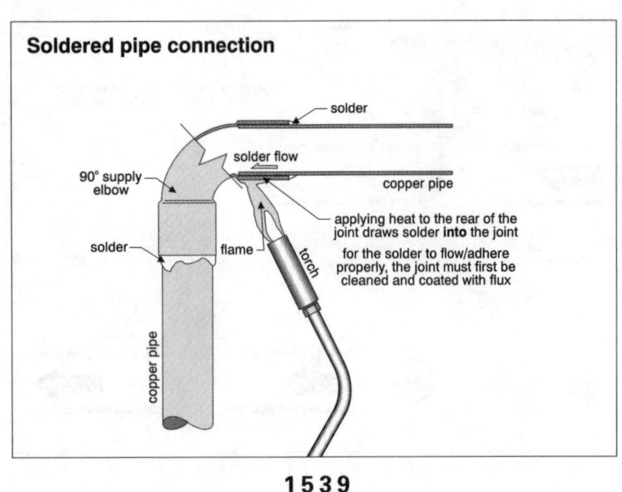

1539

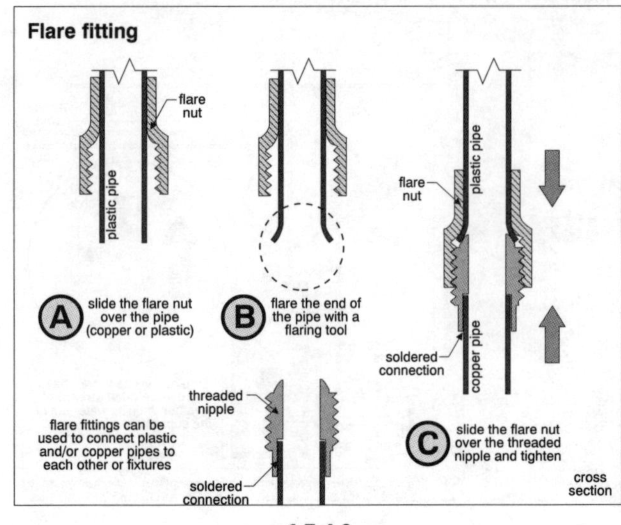

1540

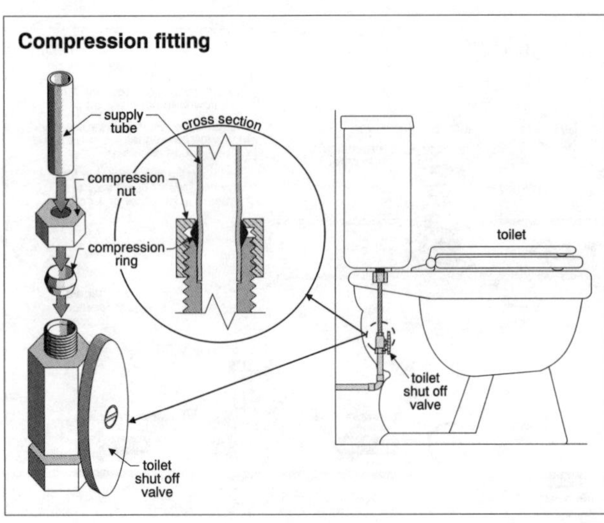

1541

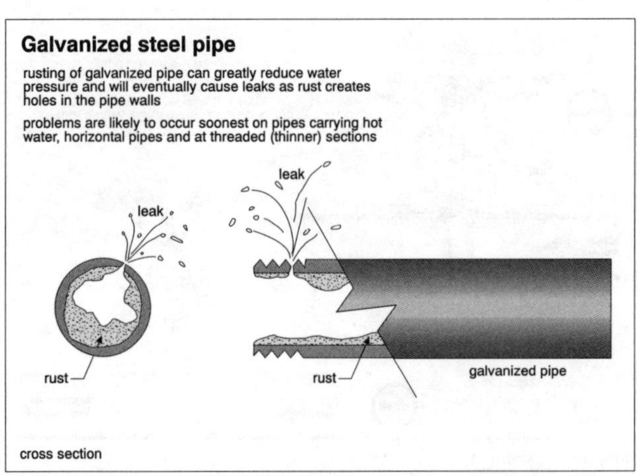

1542

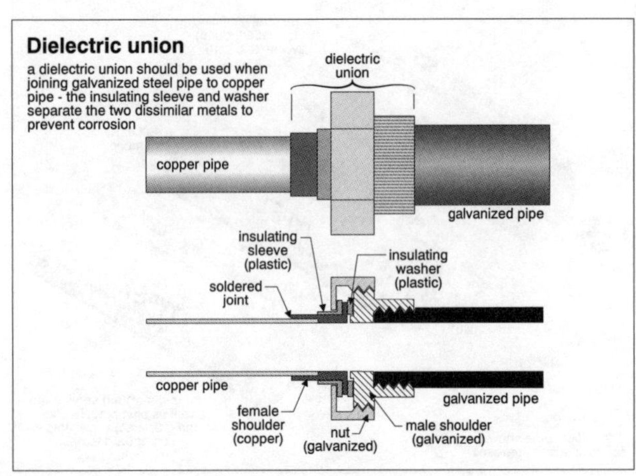

1543

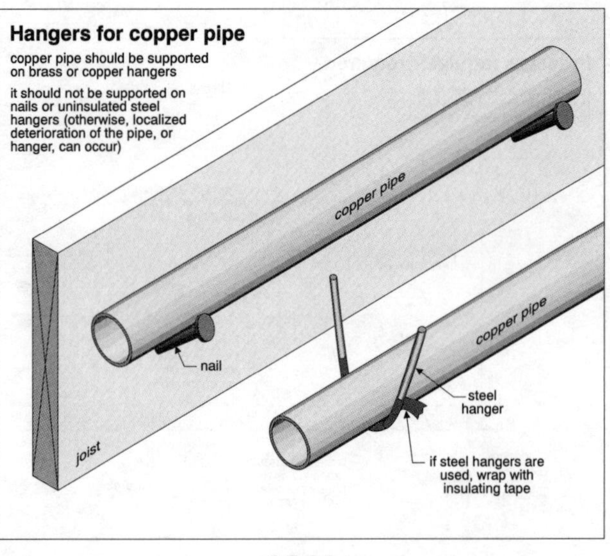

1544

Cross connections

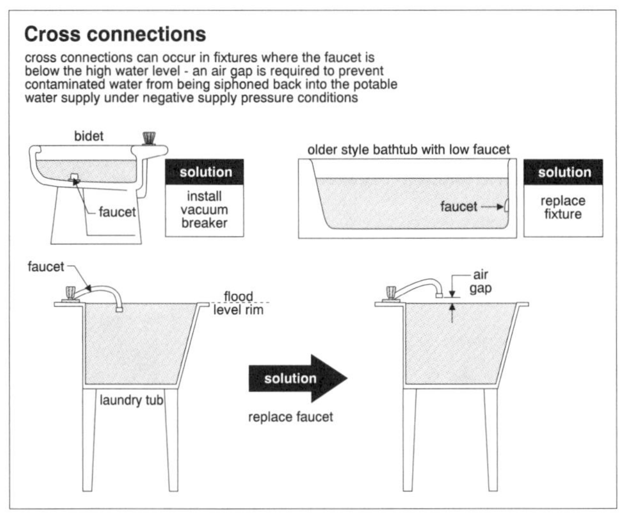

1545

Air gap

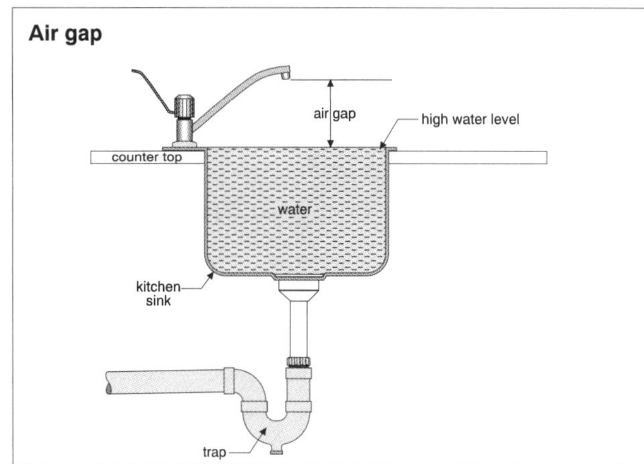

1546

Atmospheric vacuum breaker

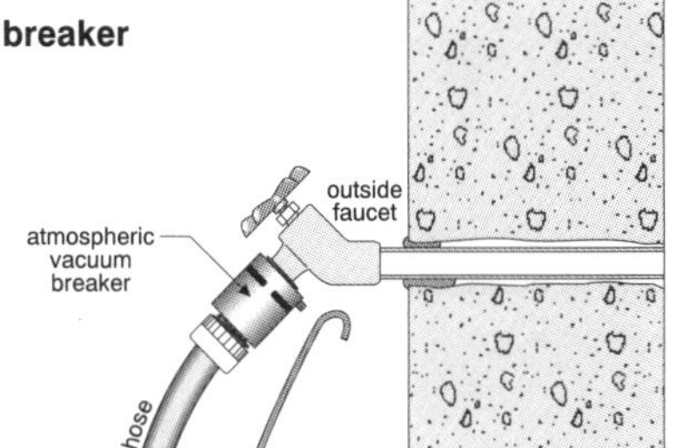

1547

Pressure type vacuum breaker

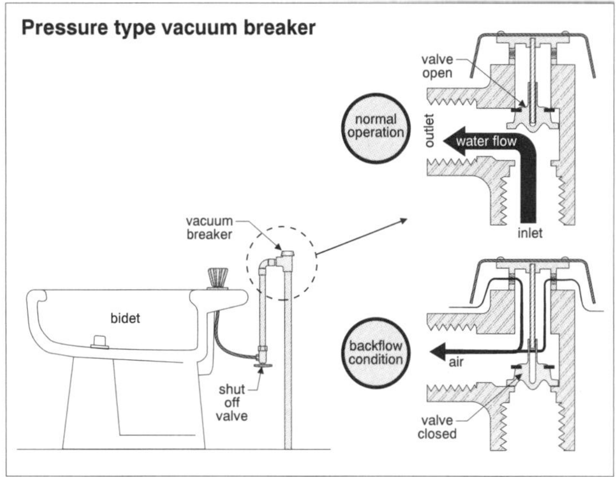

1548

Double check valve assembly

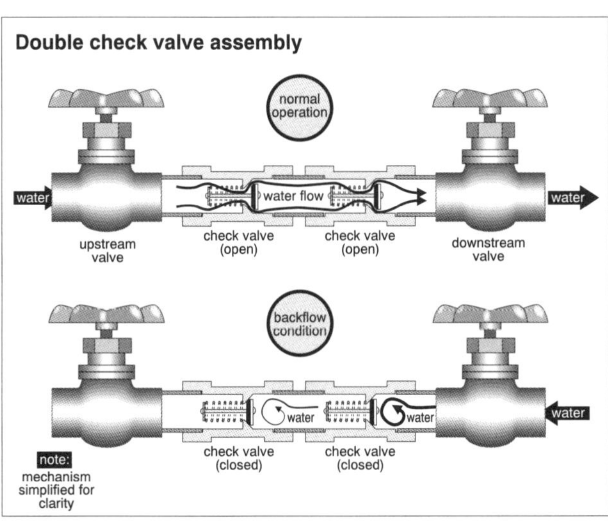

1549

Reduce pressure principle device

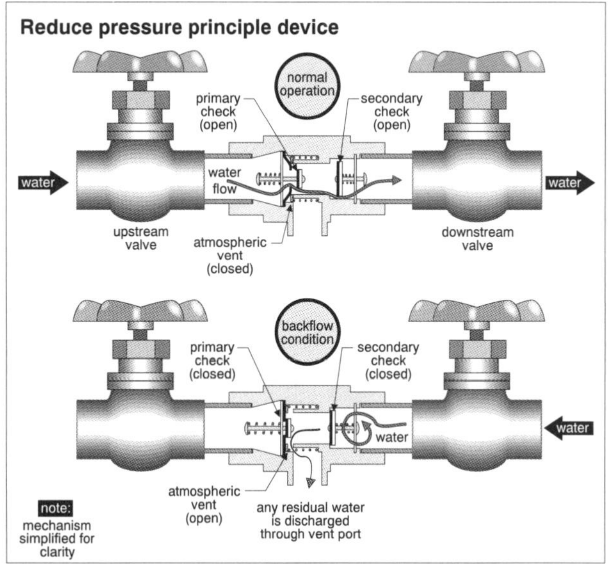

1550

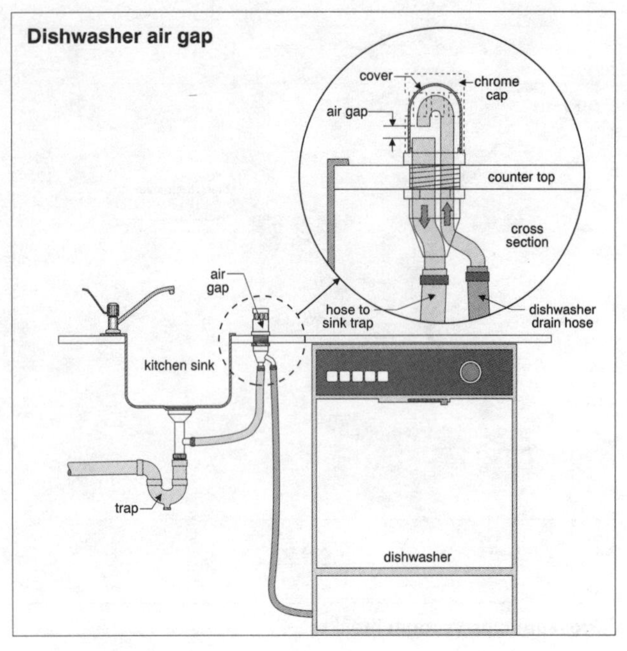

1551

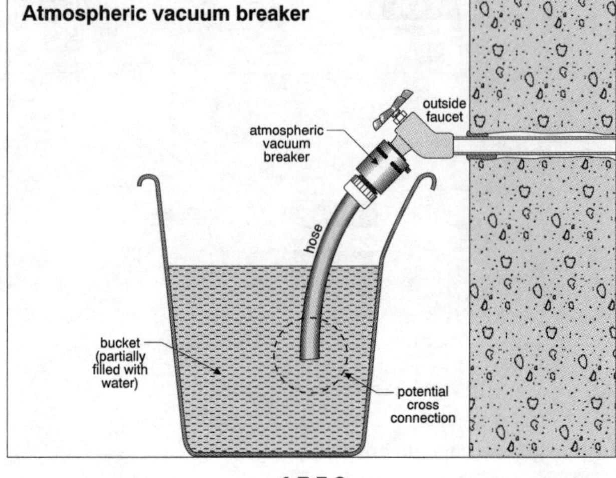

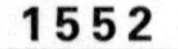

1552

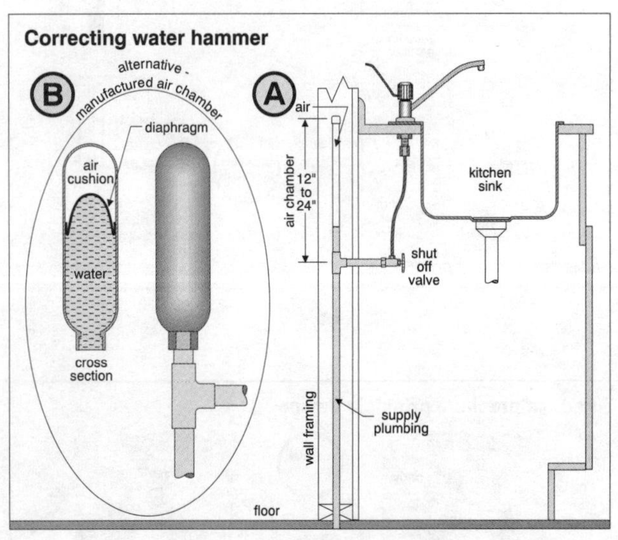

1553

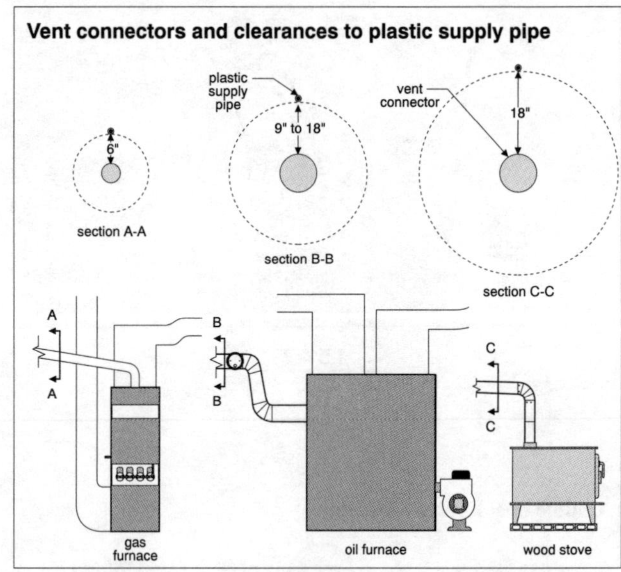

1554

Polybutylene pipe should be at least 18" from water heaters
floor framing
cold
hot
6" min. from vent connector
polybutylene pipe
18" min. from water heater
cold
hot
copper pipe
foundation wall
water meter
gas
gas water heater
main shut off valve
cross section

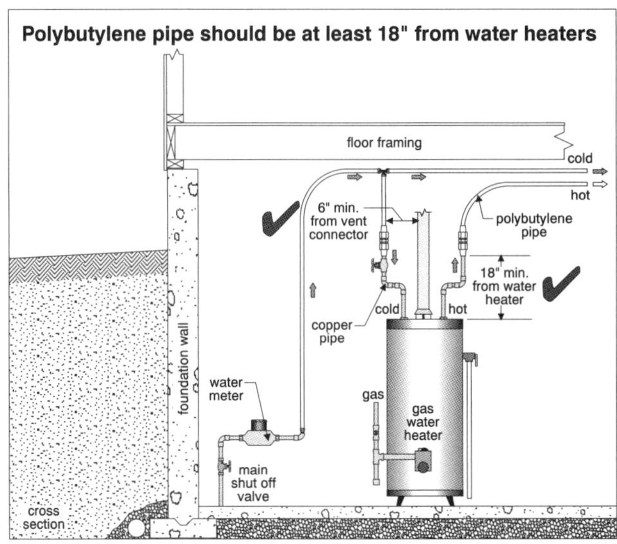

1555

Polybutylene pipe - crimp fitting
the crimp ring should be copper - older aluminum crimp rings have been problematic
coupling
1/8" to 1/4" from end
polybutylene pipe
crimp ring
polybutylene pipe
barbed insert fittings should be copper or brass - older polyacetyl (plastic) fittings were more likely to cause leaks at connections
after the crimp ring is installed, its diameter is checked with a special gauge to ensure that it hasn't been overtightened or undertightened

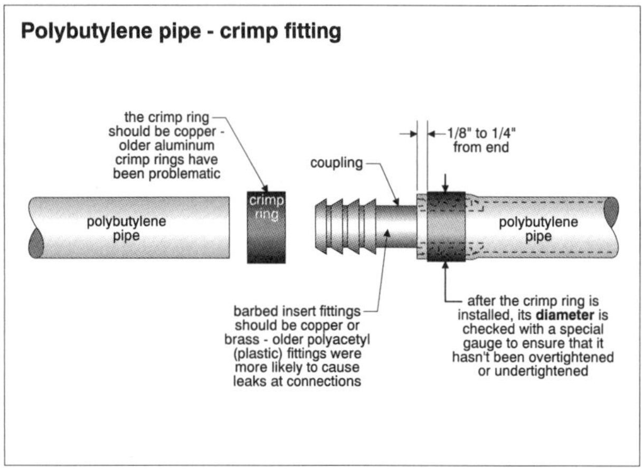

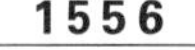

1556

Polybutylene pipe - compression (grip) fitting
same arrangement on this side
compression ring
grip ring
coupling nut
polybutylene pipe
cross section
compression ring
grip ring
polybutylene pipe
coupling nut
note:
grip fittings work well with both polybutylene and copper pipe

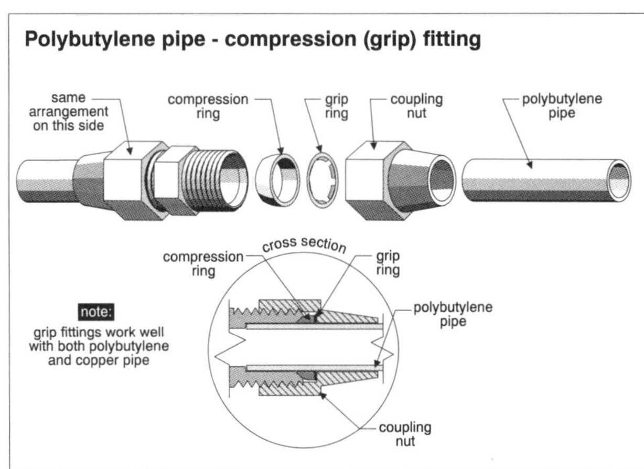

1557

Bend radius for polybutylene pipe
supports for horizontal piping should be every 32 inches according to some
floor framing
polybutylene pipe
D (pipe diameter)
bend radius 12 x D
a bend radius of at least 12 times the diameter of the pipe will help prevent the pipe (especially the hot water piping) from collapsing at the middle of the bend
foundation wall
water meter
main shut off valve
cross section

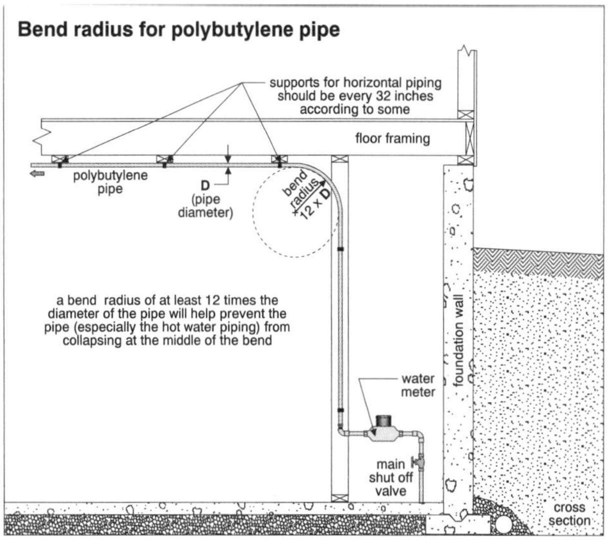

1558

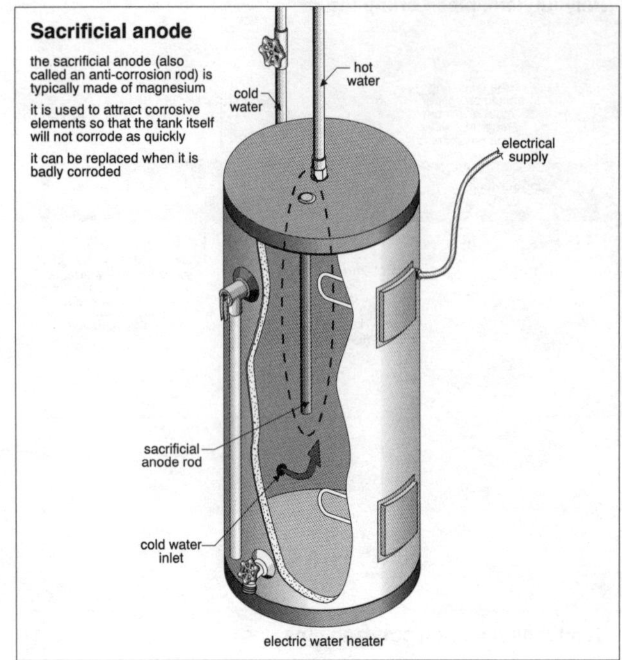

1559

Vacuum relief valve

vacuum relief valves are installed in some jurisdictions to prevent hot water from backing into the cold water lines in the event of a cold water pressure drop

they also protect against possible collapse of the storage tank by preventing a vacuum from forming inside

floor framing
cold
hot
cold
hot
foundation wall
water meter
gas
gas water heater
cold water supply valve
vacuum relief valve
cross section

1560

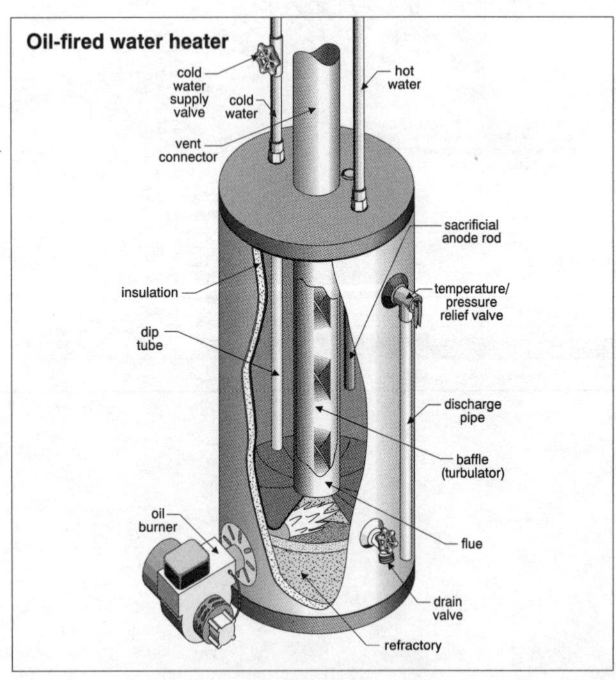

1561

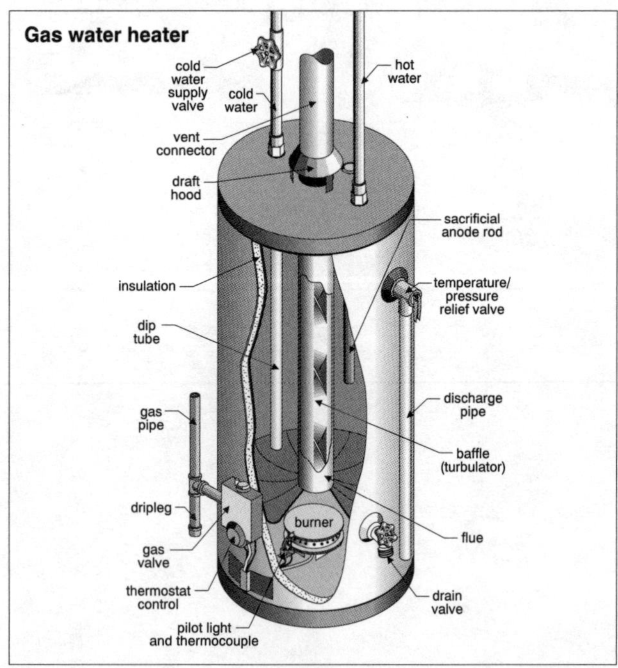

1562

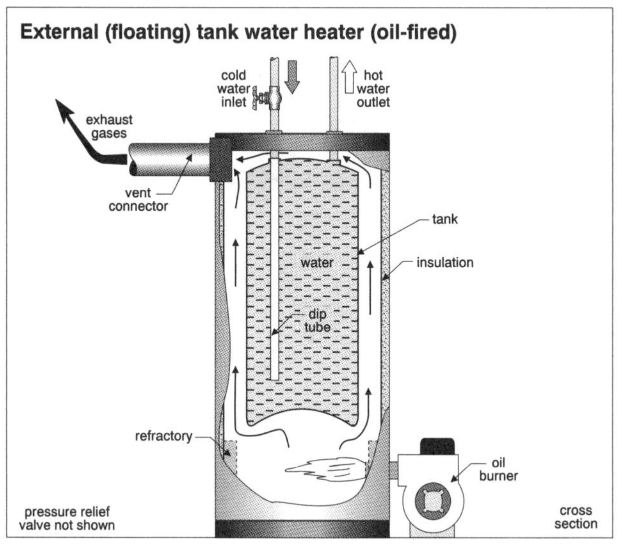

1563

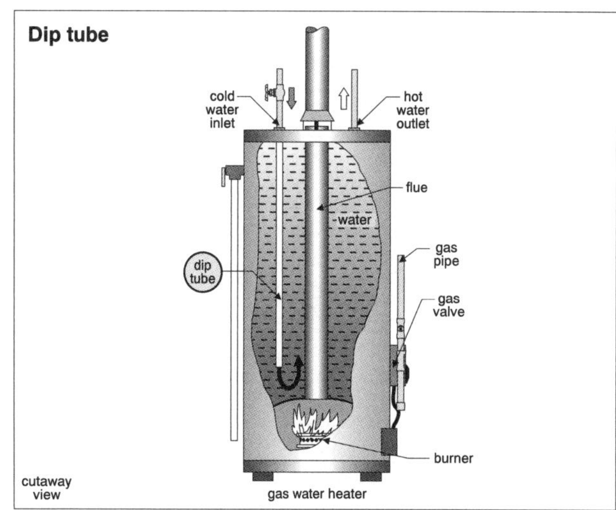

1564

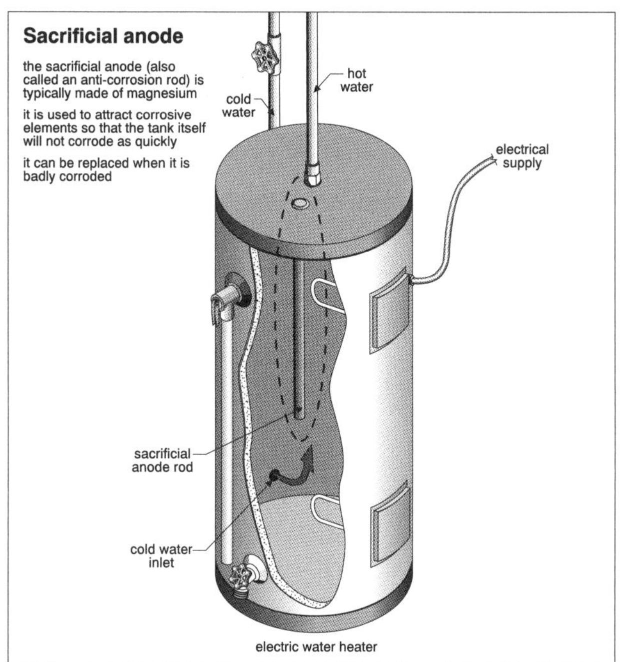

1565

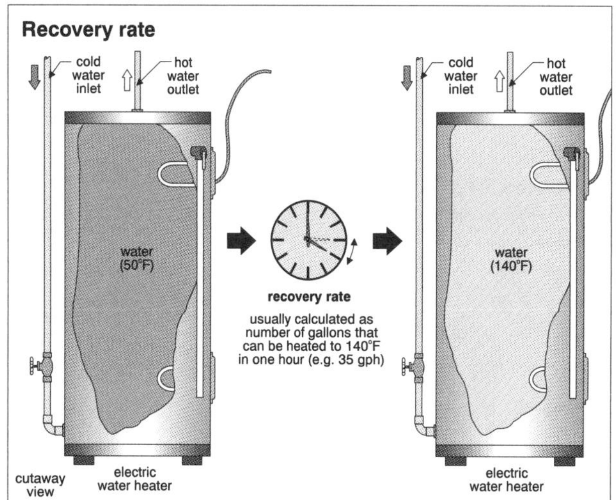

1566

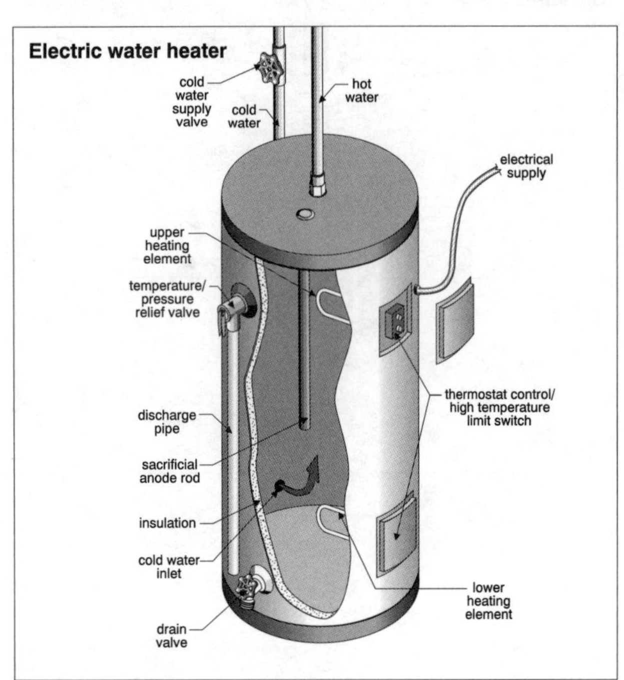

1567

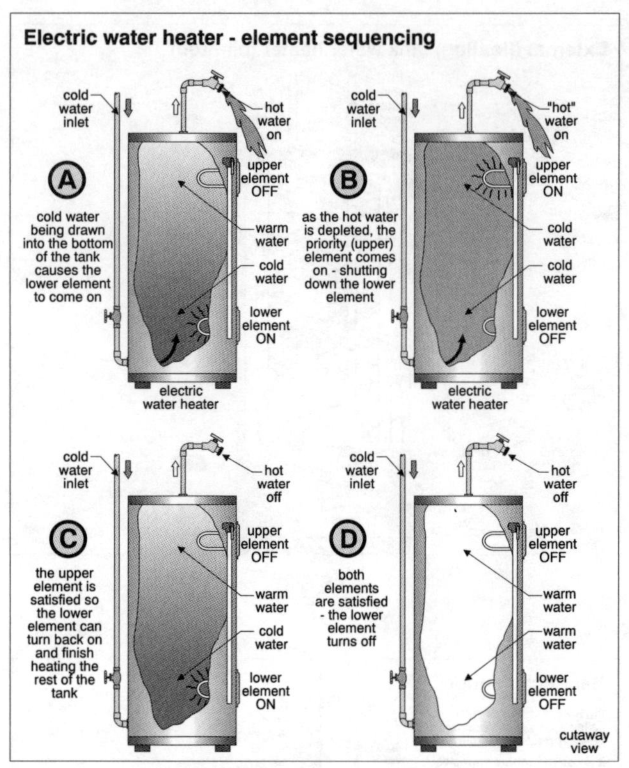

1568

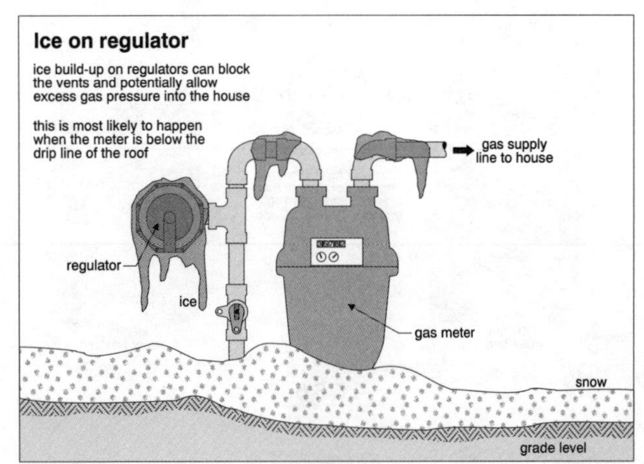

1569

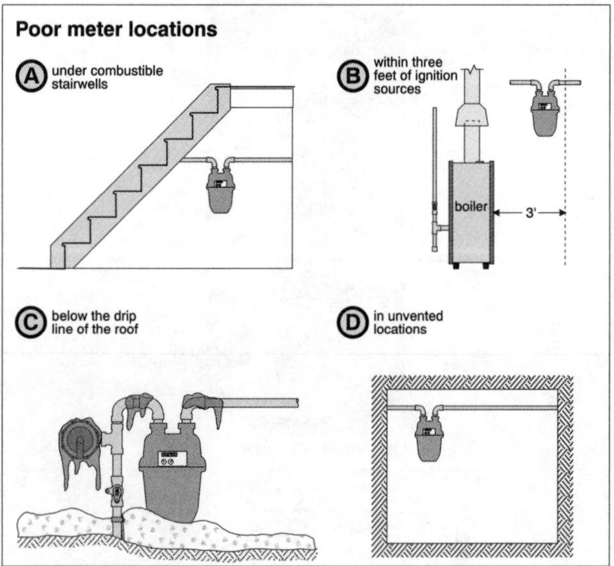

1570

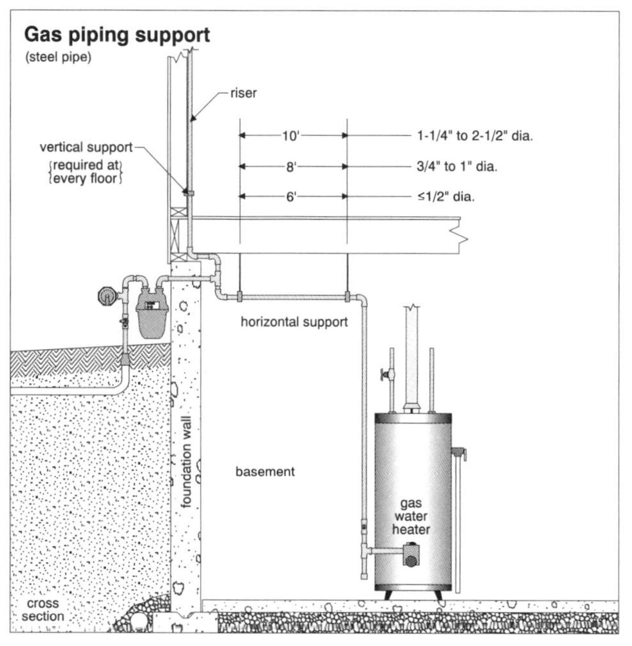

1571

Drip leg

the drip leg (or dirt pocket) serves as a collection area for sediment to reduce the chance of clogged gas valves or burners

cold water supply valve
cold water
hot water
vent connector
draft hood
drip leg
gas pipe
gas water heater
gas valve
thermostat control

1572

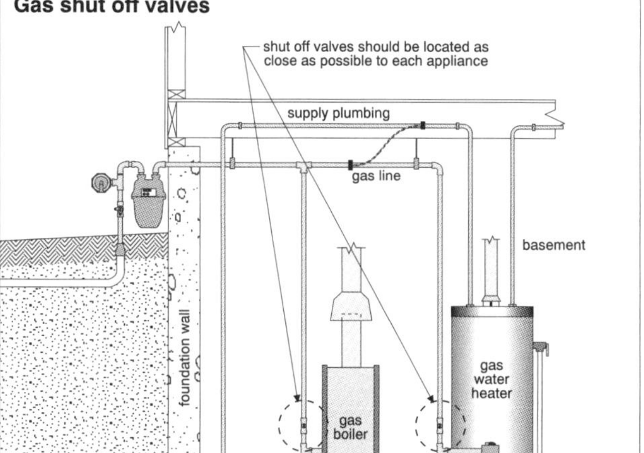

1573

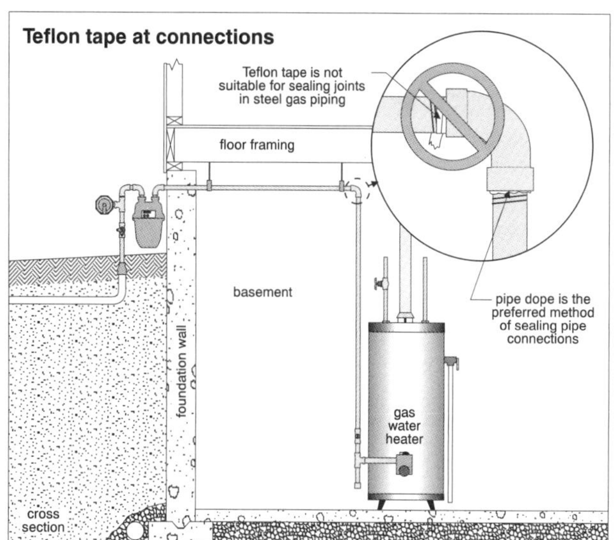

1574

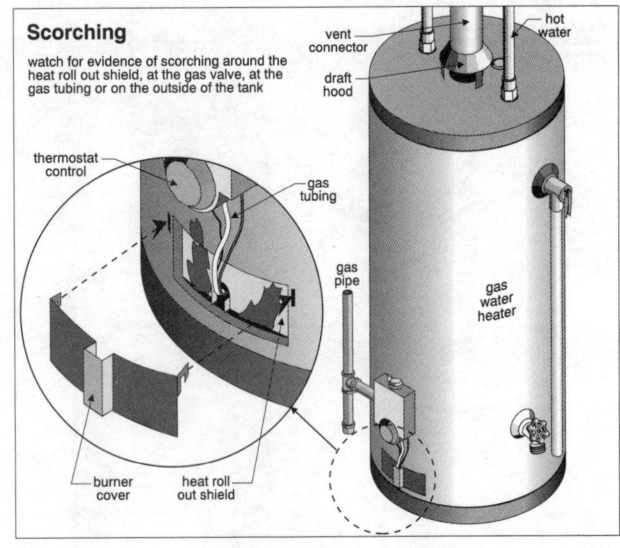

1575

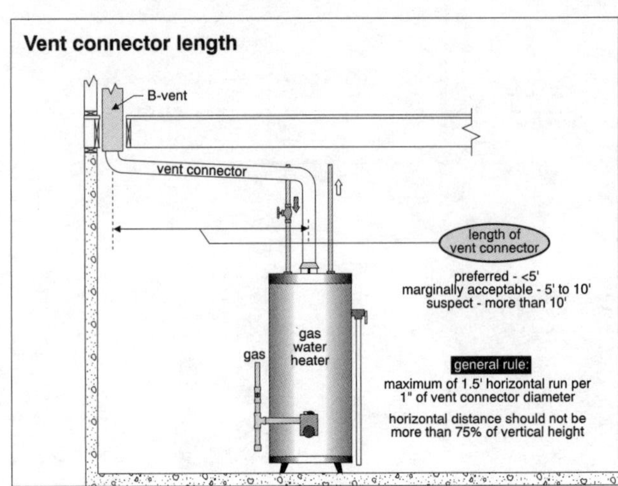

1576

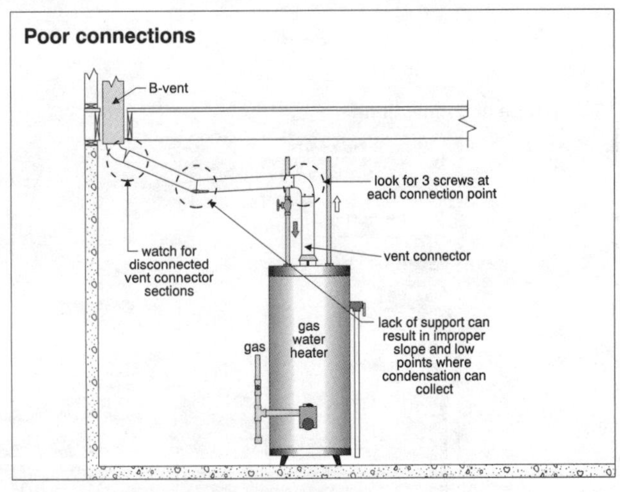

1577

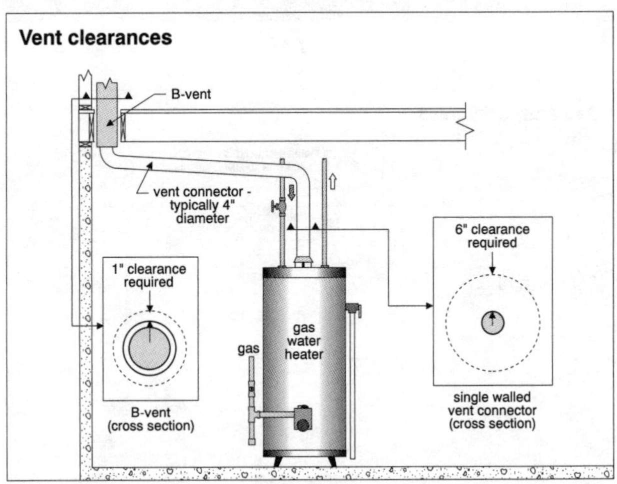

1578

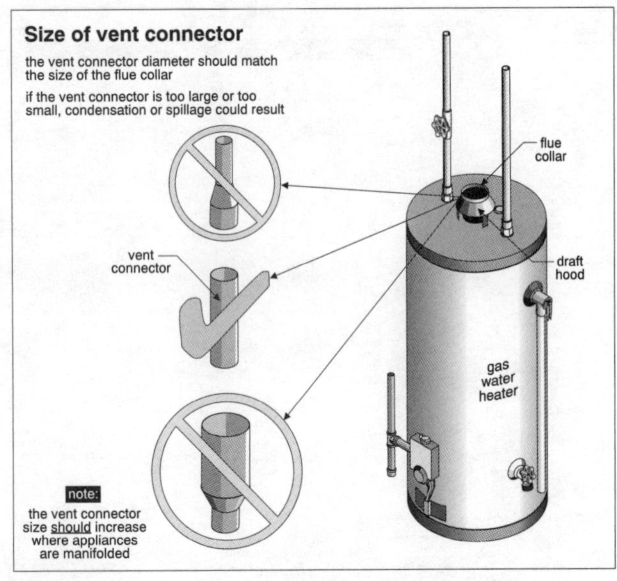

1579

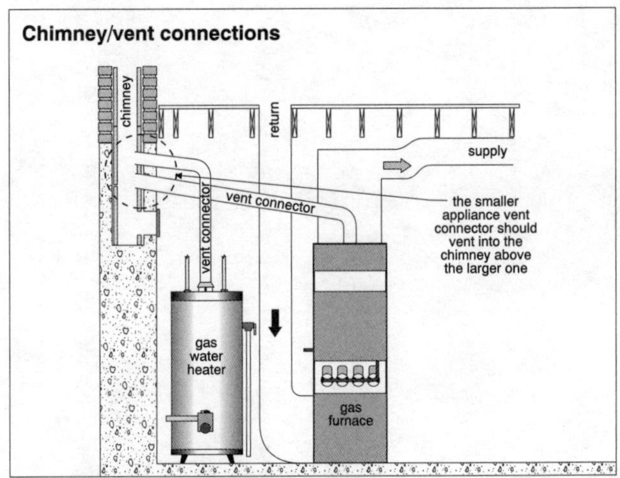

1580

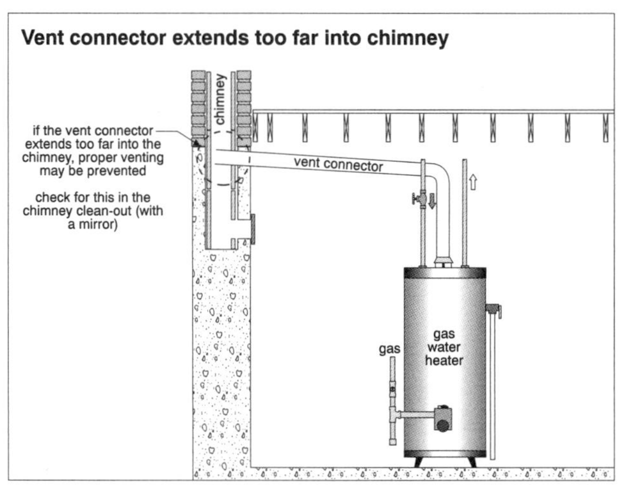

1581

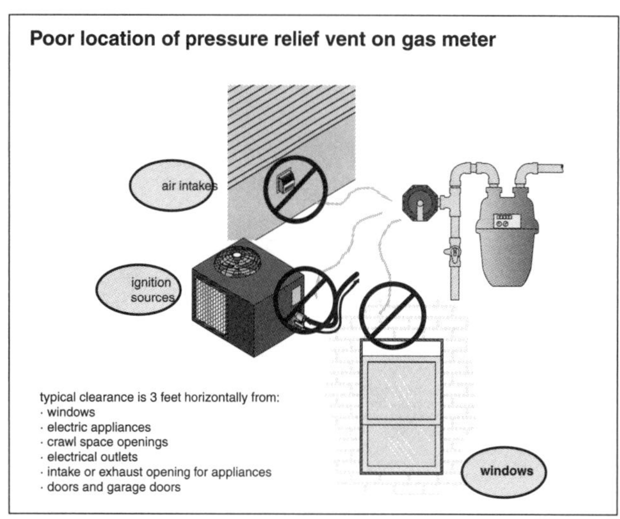

1582

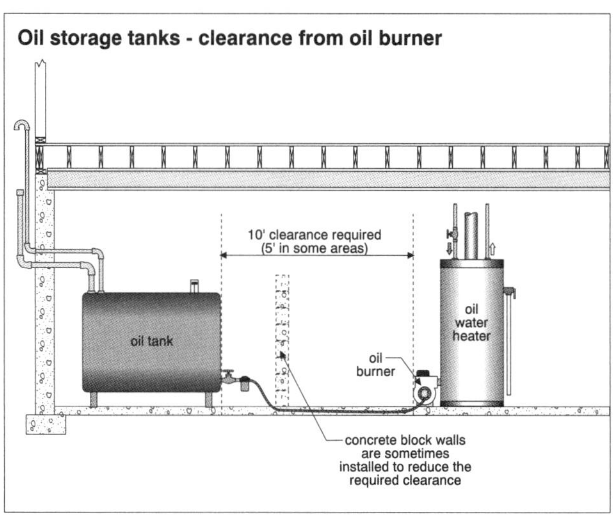

1583

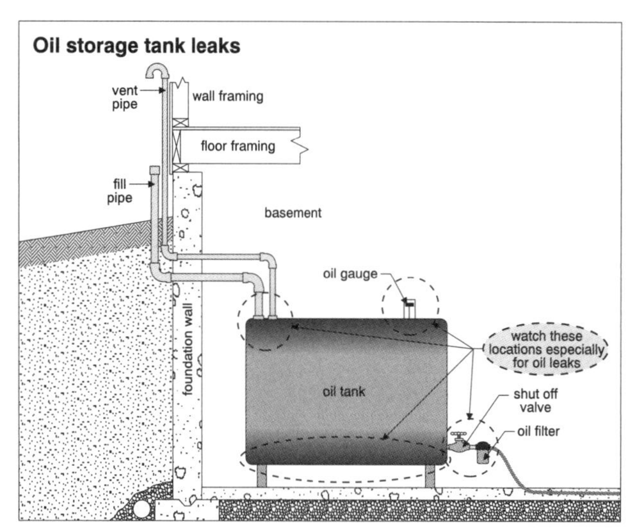

1584

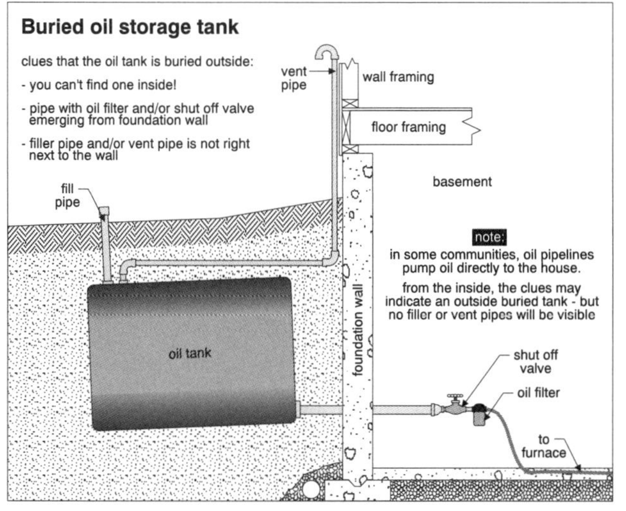

1585

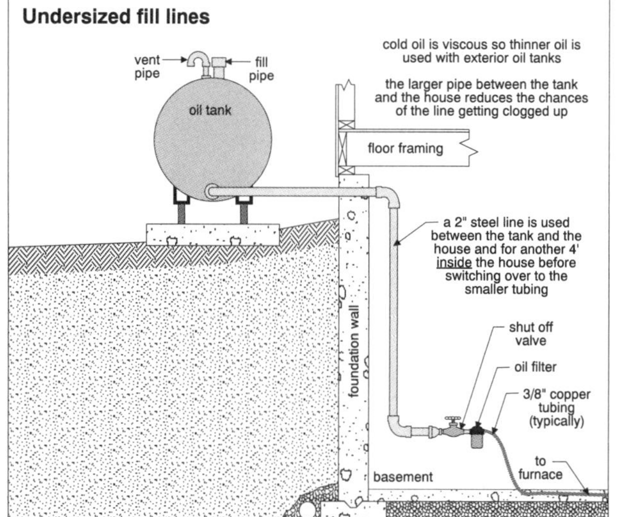

1586

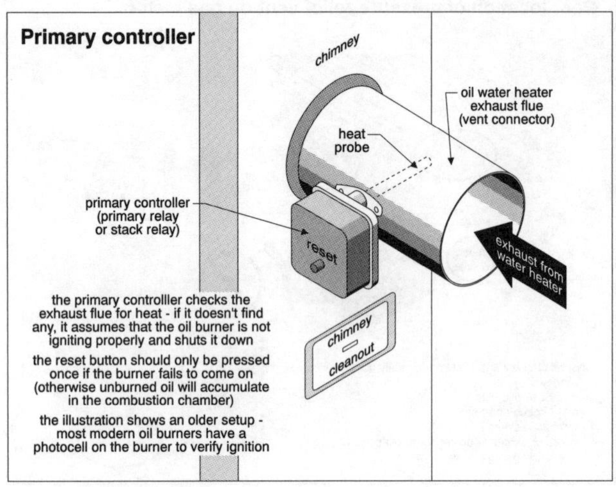

1587

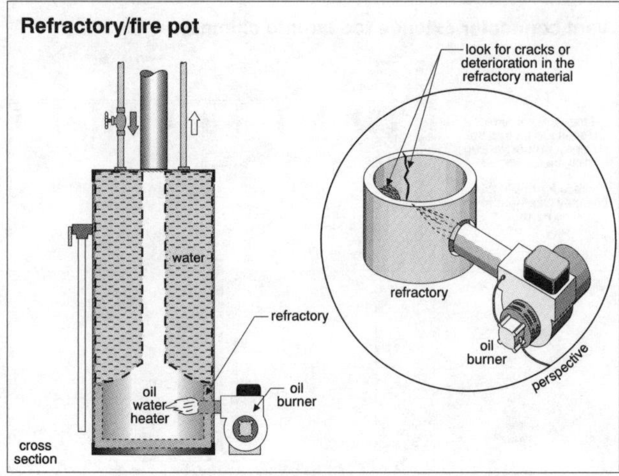

1588

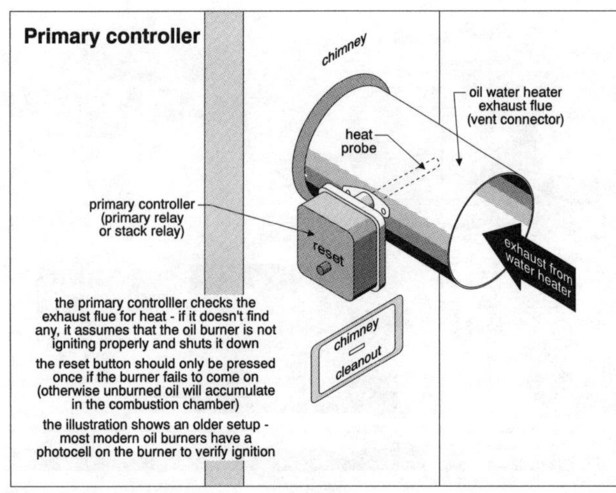

1589

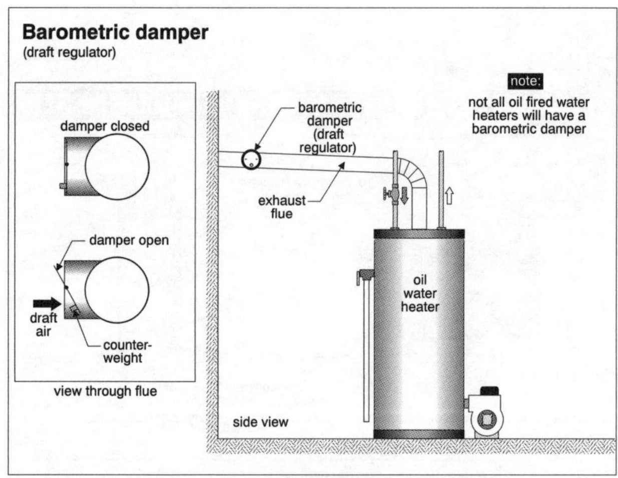

1590

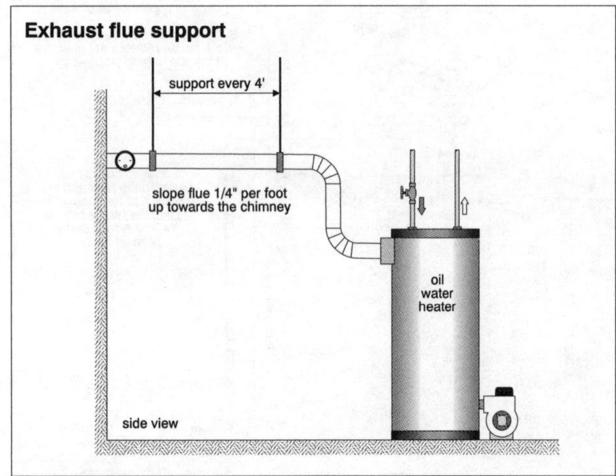

1591

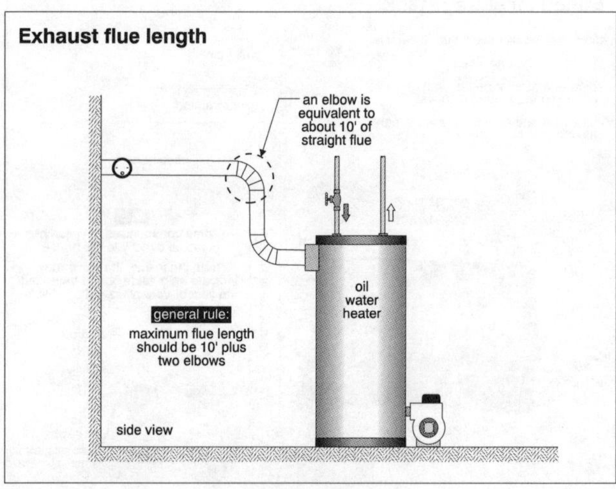

1592

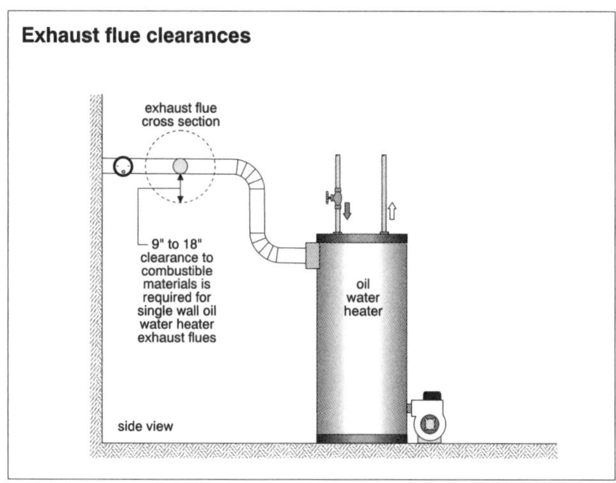

1593

Relative recovery rates

higher

lower

ELECTRIC

GAS

OIL

1594

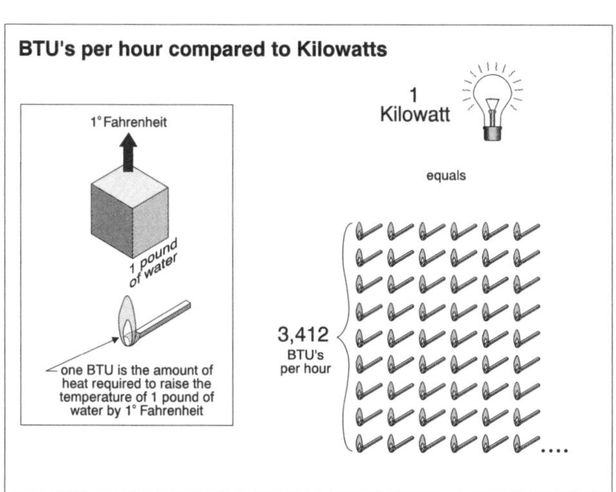

1595

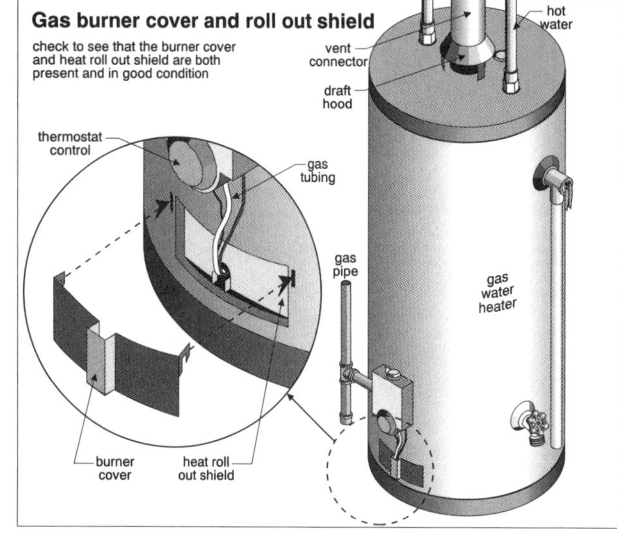

1596

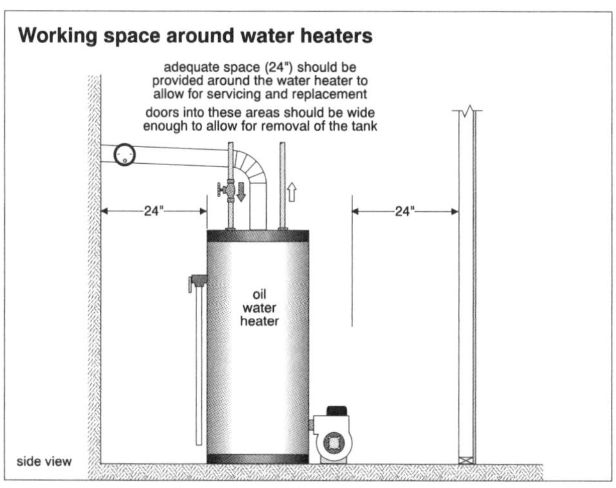

1597

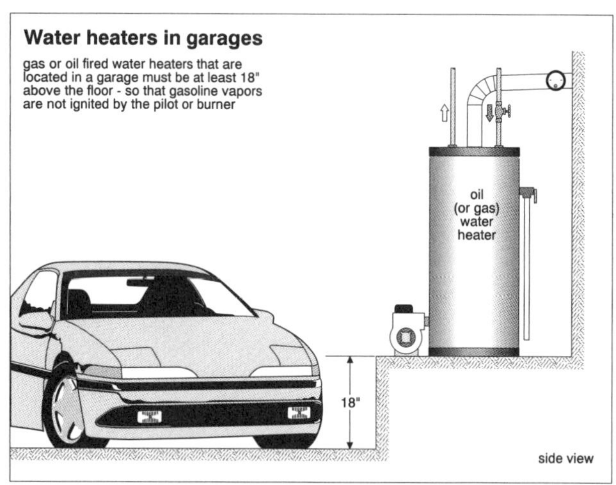

1598

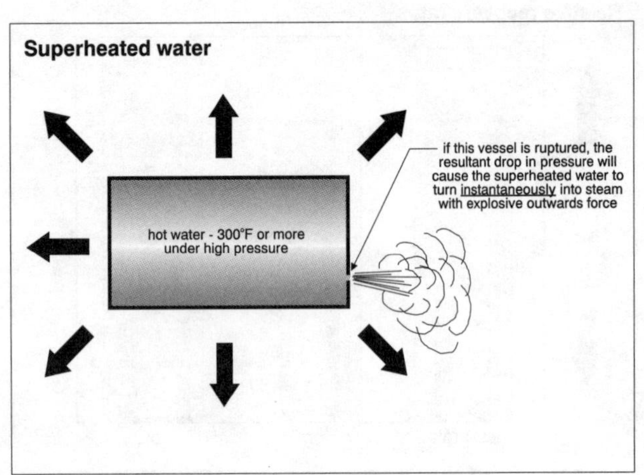

1599

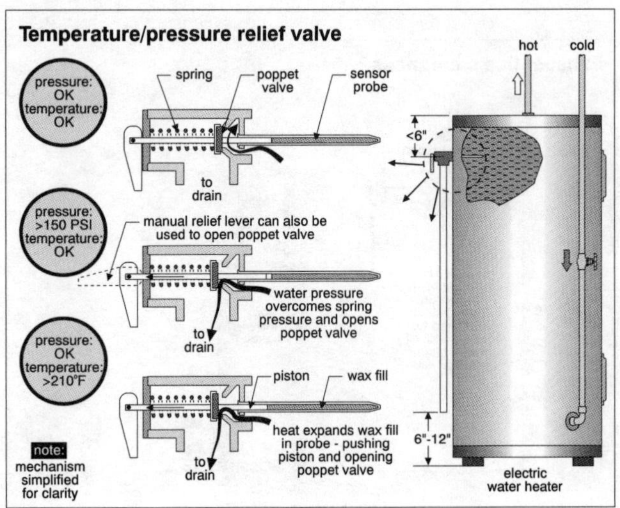

1600

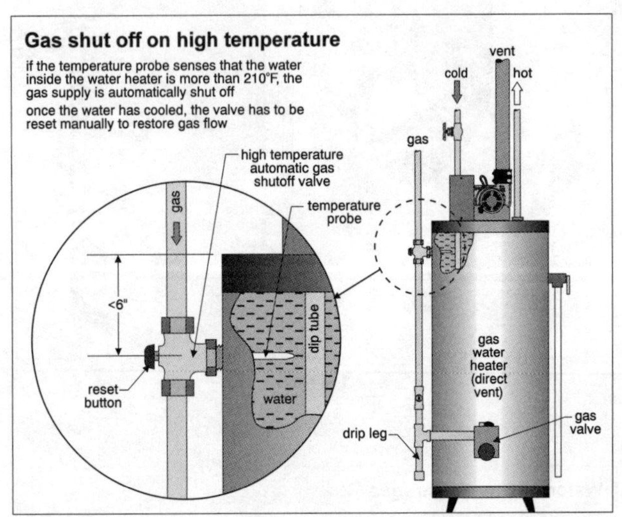

1601

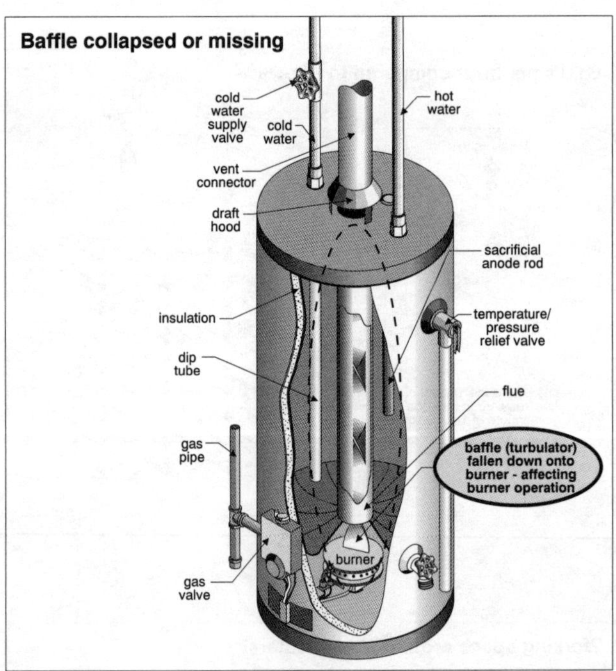

1602

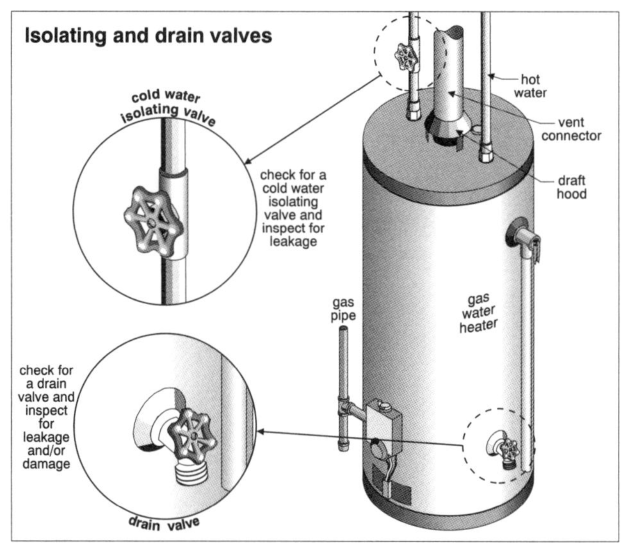

1603

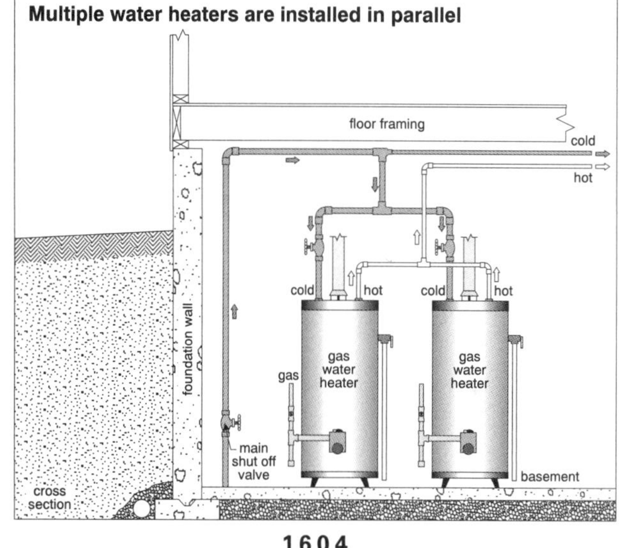

1604

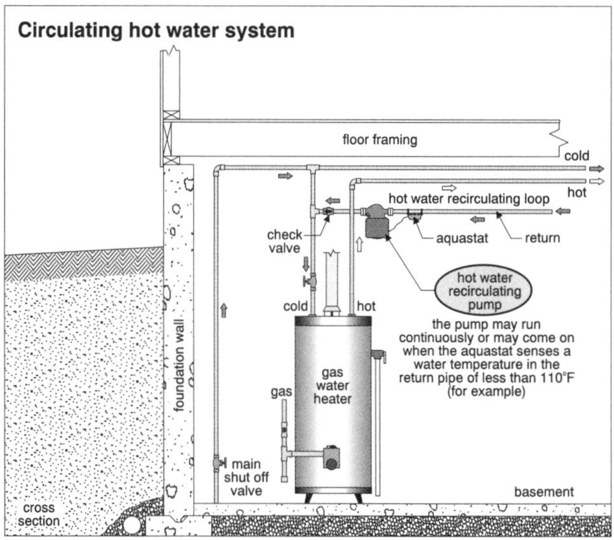

1605

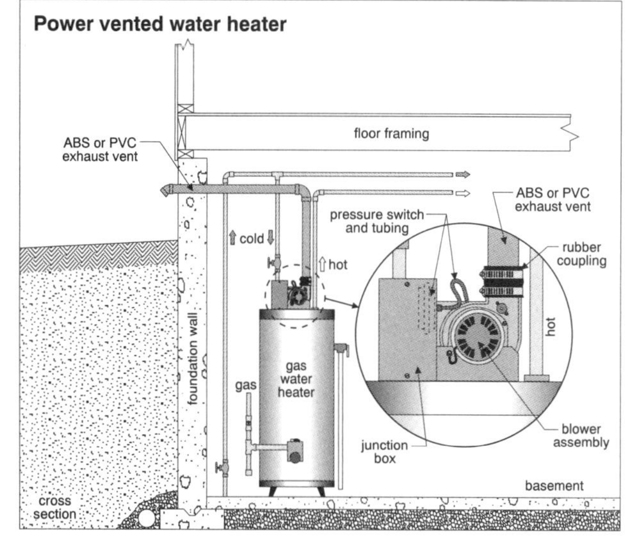

1606

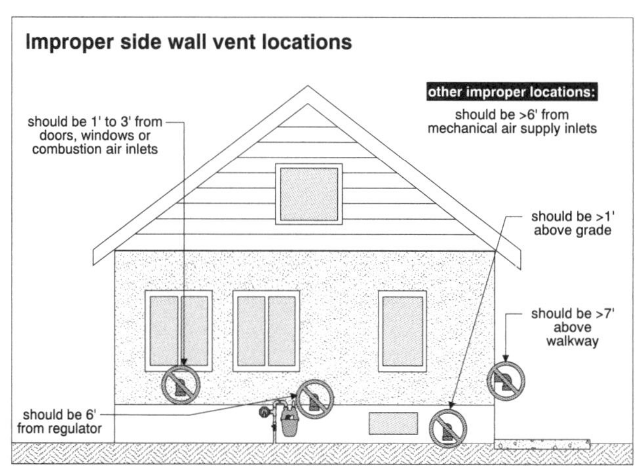

1607

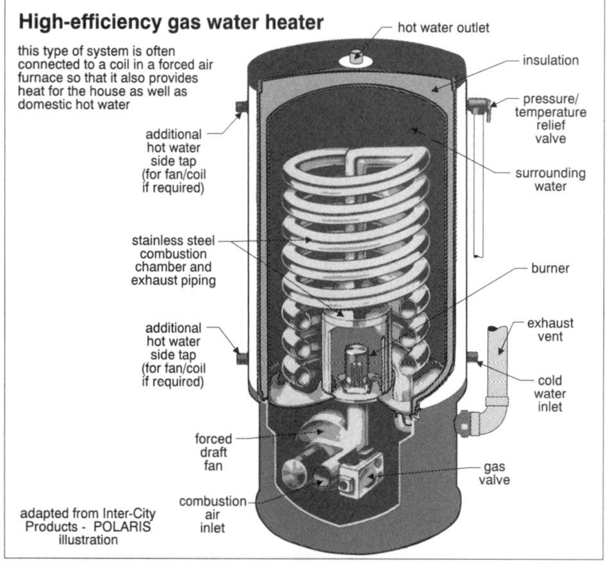

1608

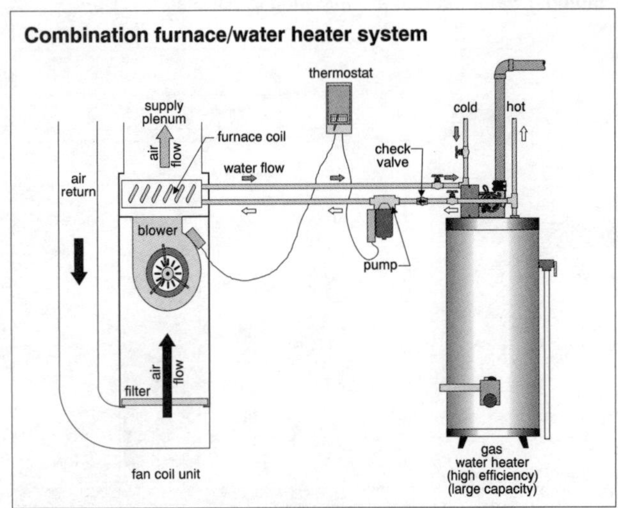

1609

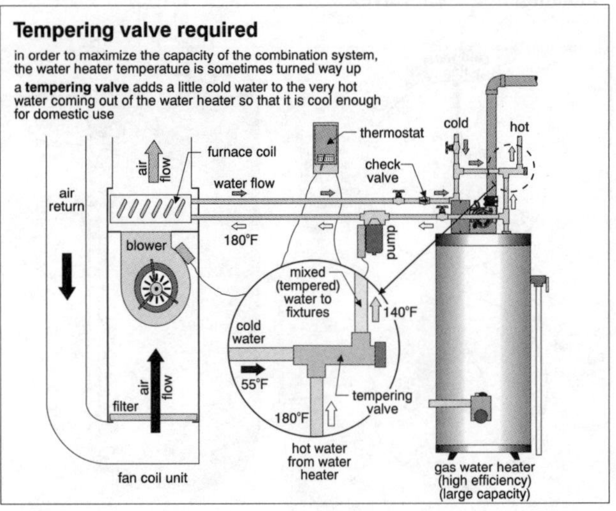

1610

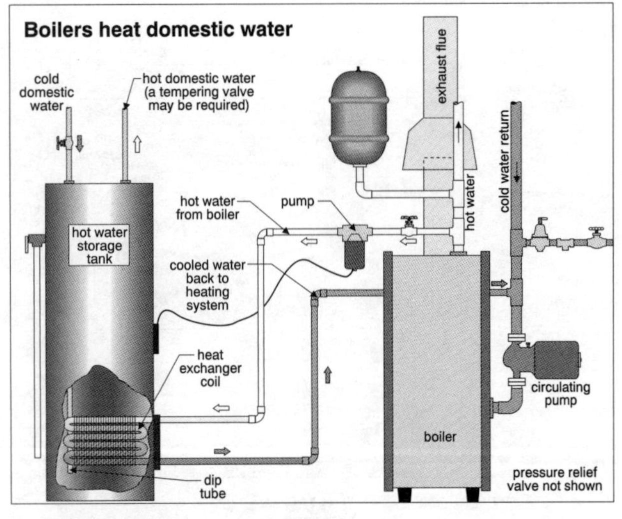

1611

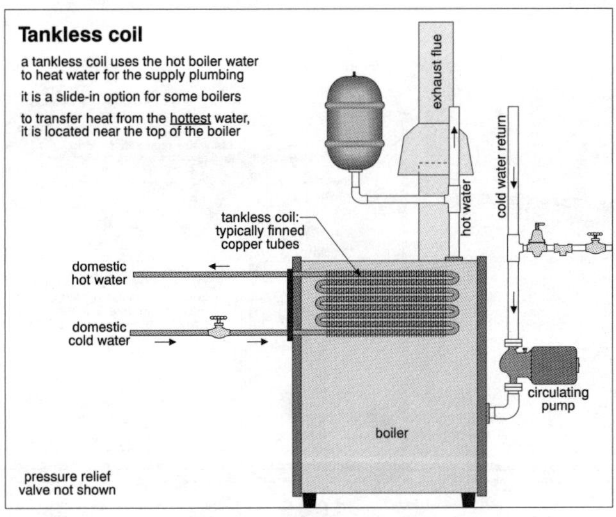

1612

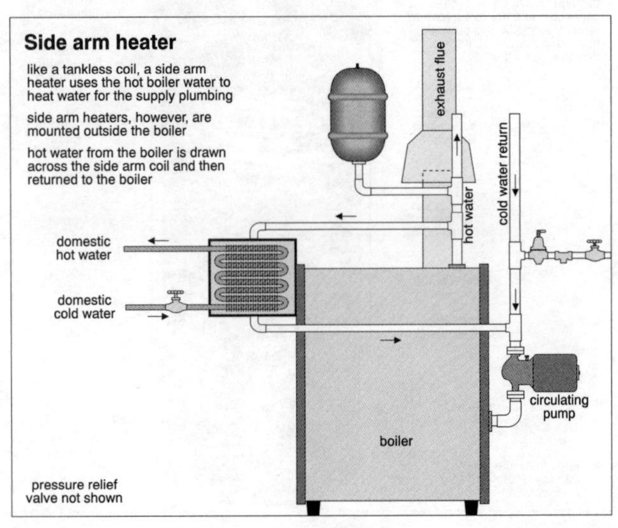

1613

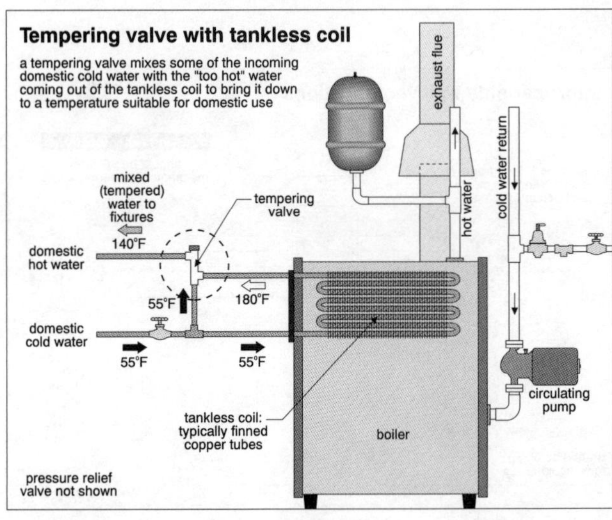

1614

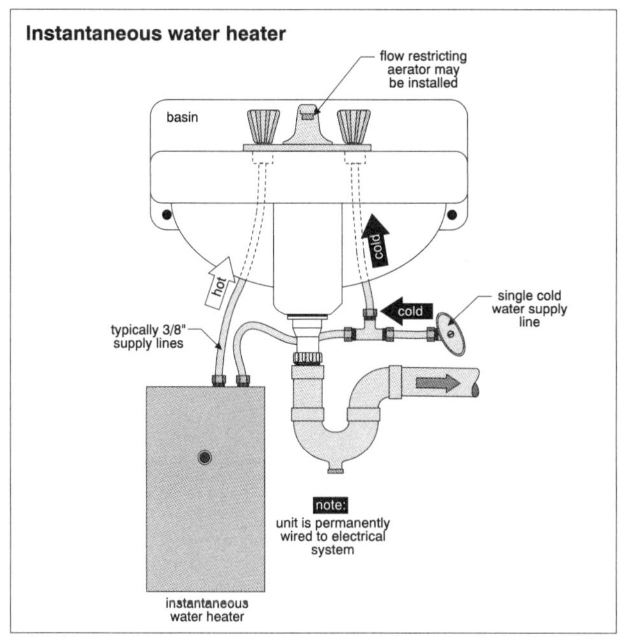

1615

Too little or too much slope isn't good

no drainage
no slope
1/4" to 1/2"
1 foot
both liquids and solids drain out
liquid drains too quickly (solids left behind)
more than 1/2"
1 foot

1616

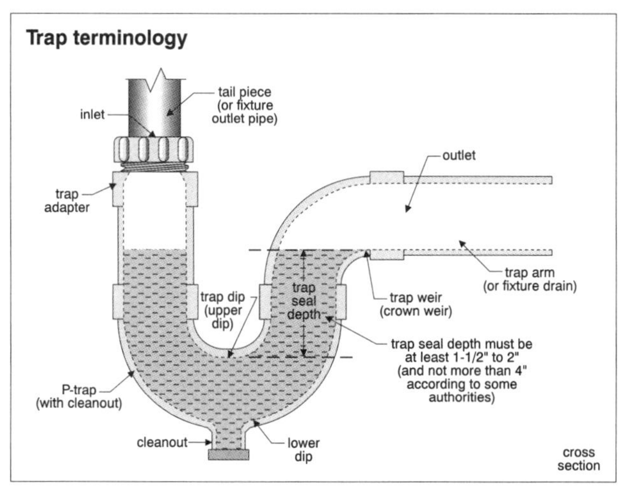

1617

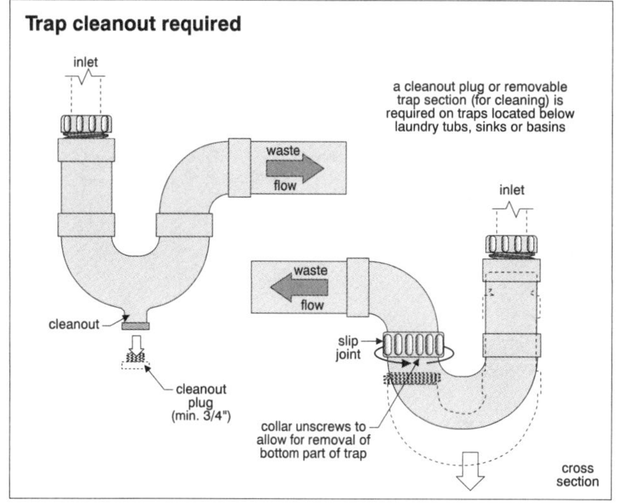

1618

No traps for toilets

in cross section, the similarities between a P-trap and the "built-in" trap of a toilet bowl are visible

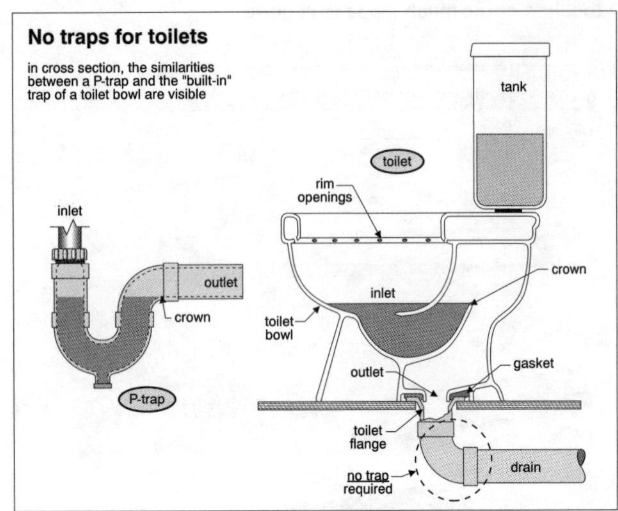

1619

Trap primer

the trap primer is typically a 3/8" diameter plastic tube attached to a fixture (e.g. laundry tub)

whenever the fixture is used, some water is sent to the floor drain trap to keep it filled

the trap primer is often fed into a piece of polyethylene pipe when it must pass through a concrete floor

trap primer
cross section
floor drain
trap seal
waste stack
faucet
foundation wall
loose fit
air gap
trap primer
laundry tub
polyethylene pipe (extension of trap primer)

1620

Vent terminology

branch vent
slope
basin
vent stack
stack vent
toilet
wet vent
slope 1/4" per ft.
soil stack

1621

Soil stack versus waste stack

toilet
basin
soil stack
vertical drain pipe that carries soil waste from sanitary units (i.e. toilets)
often also referred to as the main stack in houses with only one soil stack
soil stack
waste stack
waste stack
any other vertical drain pipe (that doesn't carry soil from a sanitary fixture)

1622

Stack vent

the stack vent is an extension of the waste stack that runs up through the roof to the exterior - for venting of exhaust gases and to maintain atmospheric pressure in the waste system

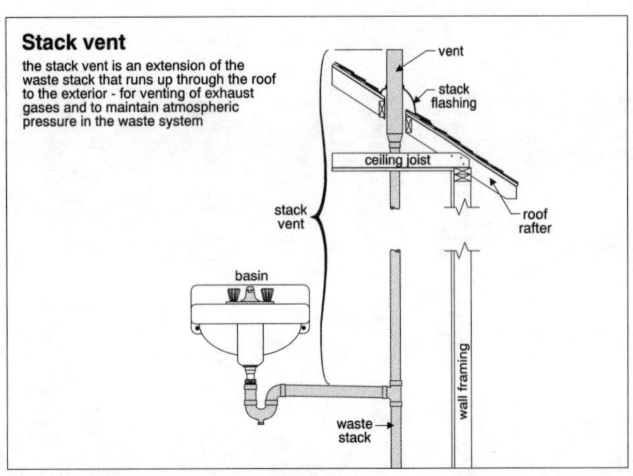

1623

Proper vent location relative to trap

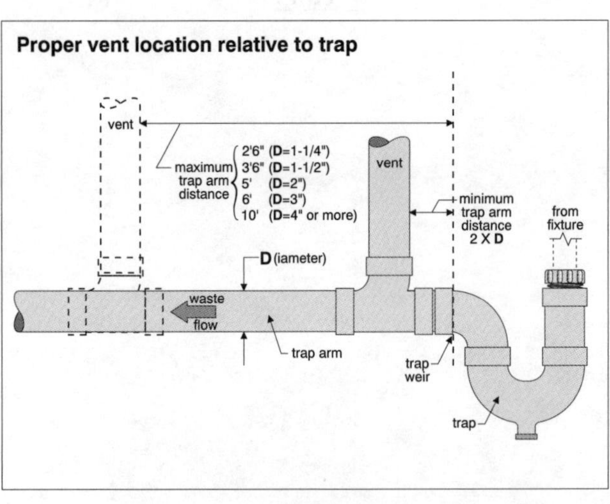

1624

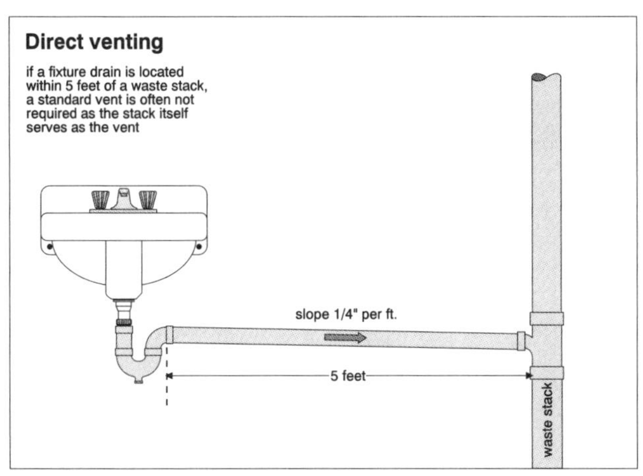

1625

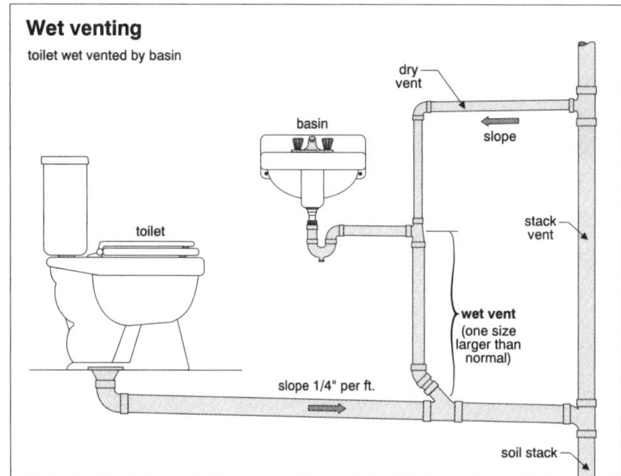

1626

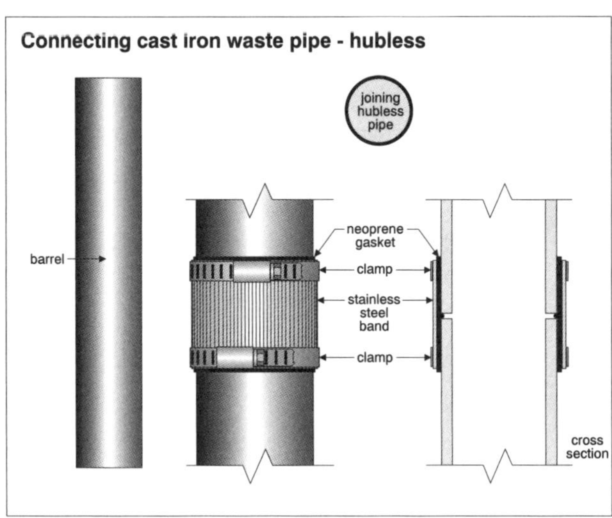

1627

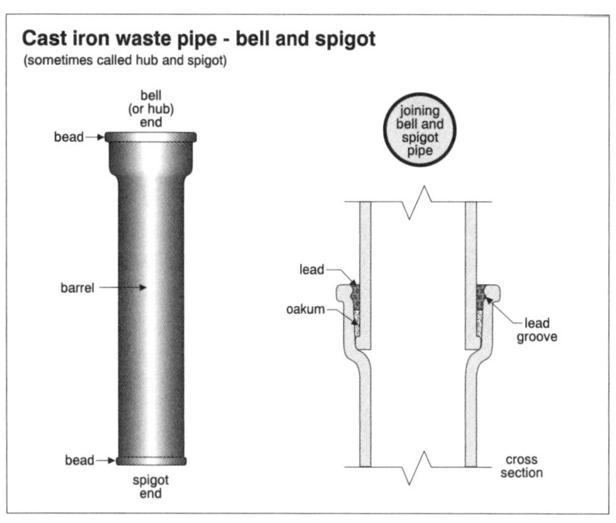

1628

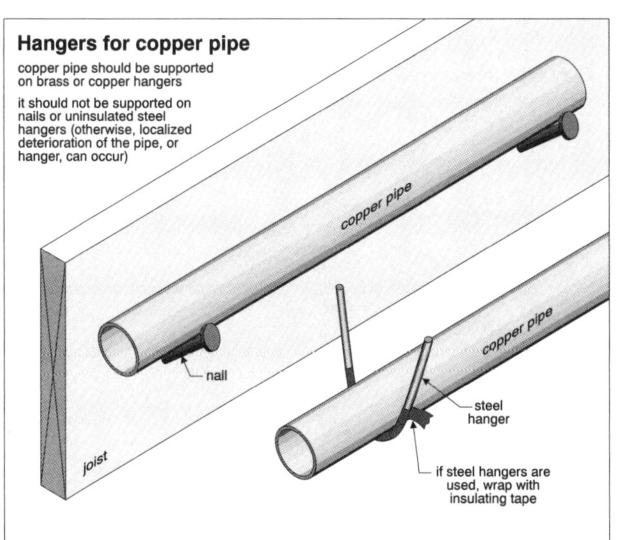

1629

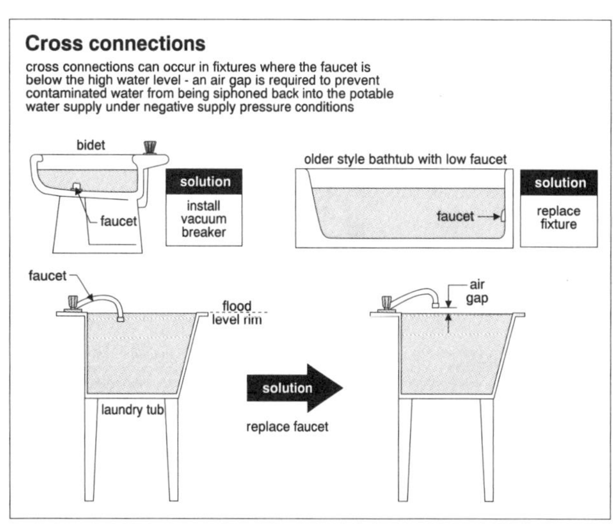

1630

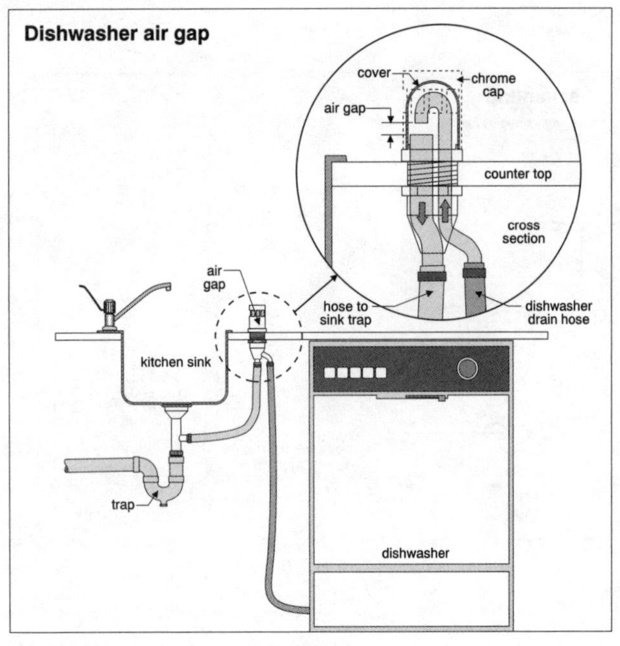

1631

Standpipe

indirect connection
clothes washer
clothes washer drain hose
18" min. to 30" max. (some areas)
standpipe
trap (may not be permitted below floor)
6" min. to 18" max.
waste stack

1632

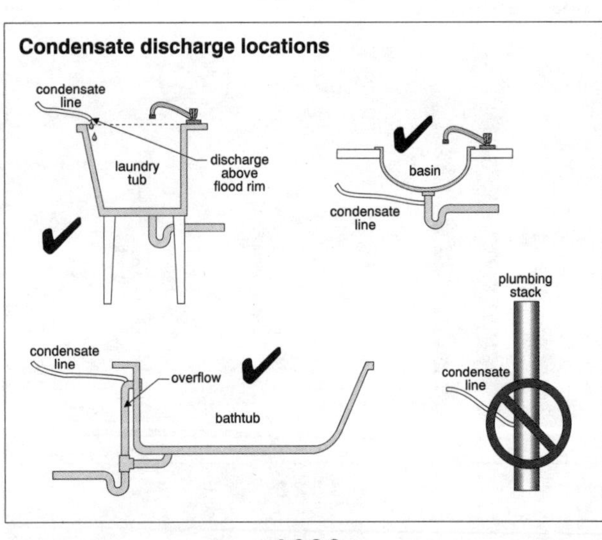

1633

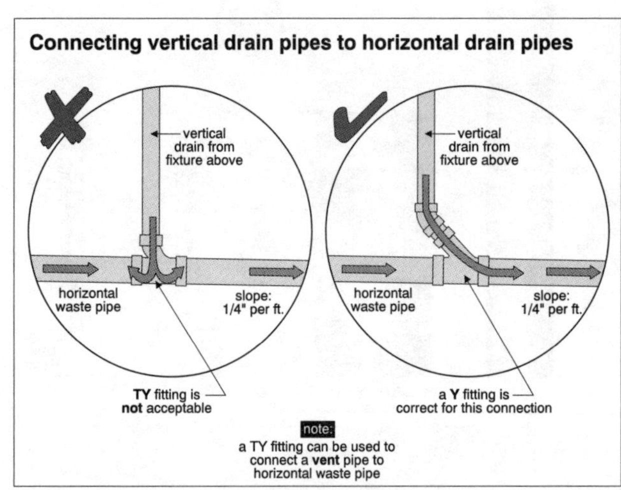

1634

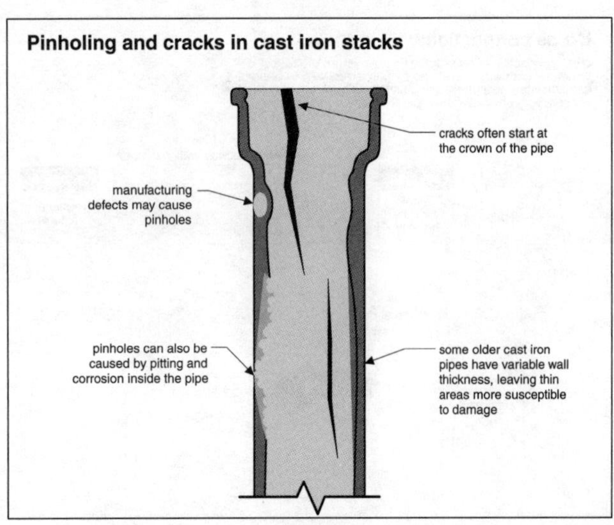

1635

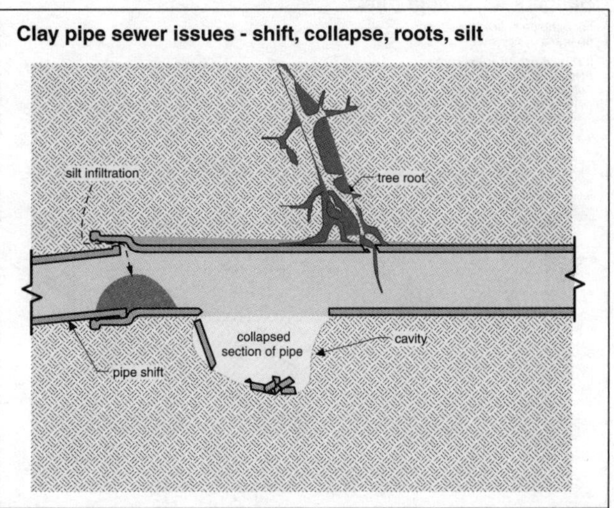

1636

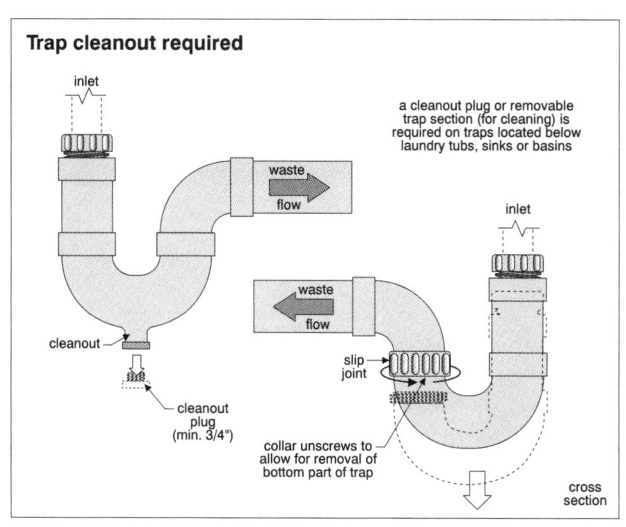

1637

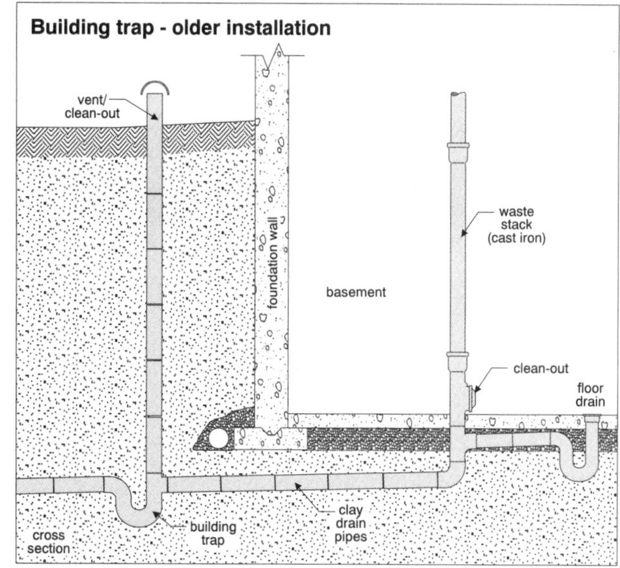

1638

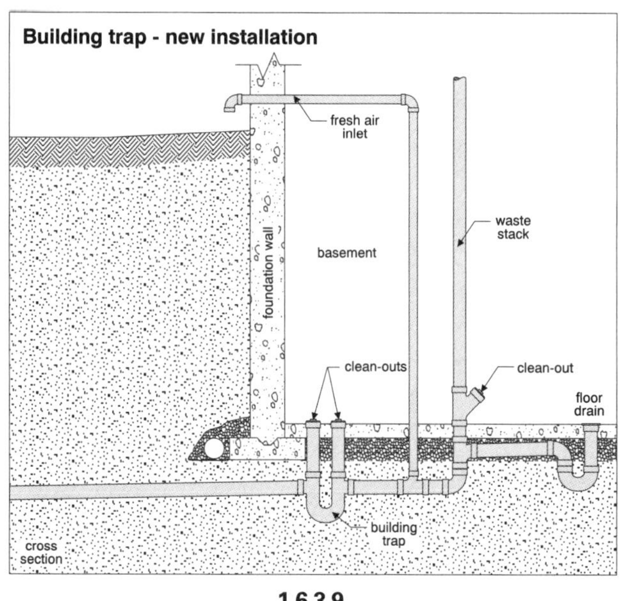

1639

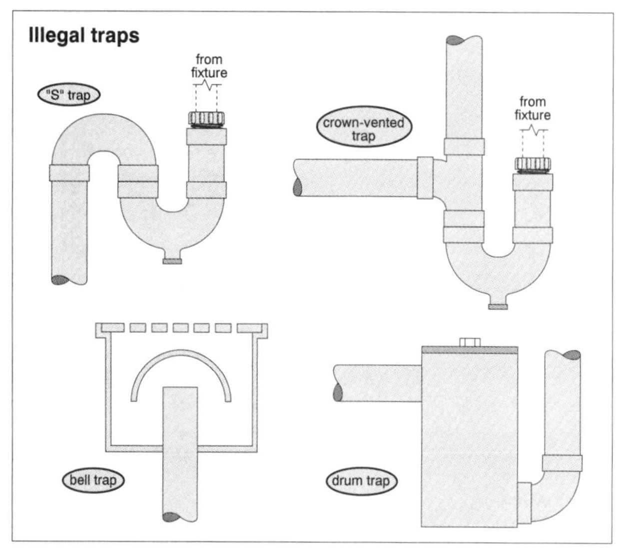

1640

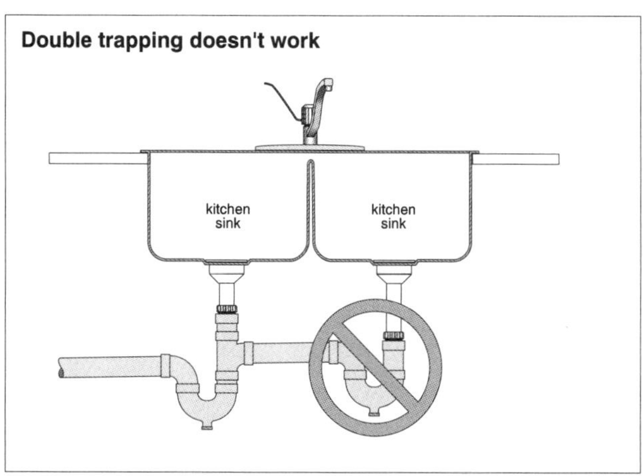

1641

Tail piece too long

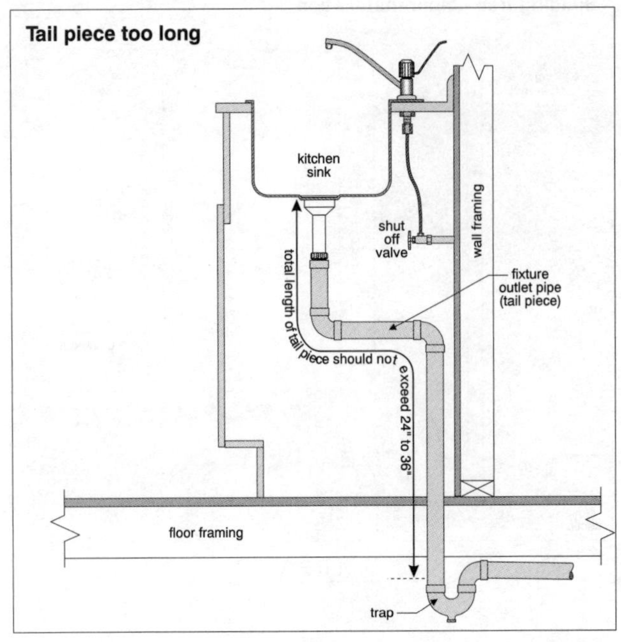

1642

Venting an island sink (below-floor trap permitted)

wall
vent
island sink
if local codes permit long (i.e. 36") tail pieces, an island sink can be vented relatively easily by installing the trap below floor level
floor framing
trap accessible from below
drain

1643

Loop vent or circuit vent for an island sink

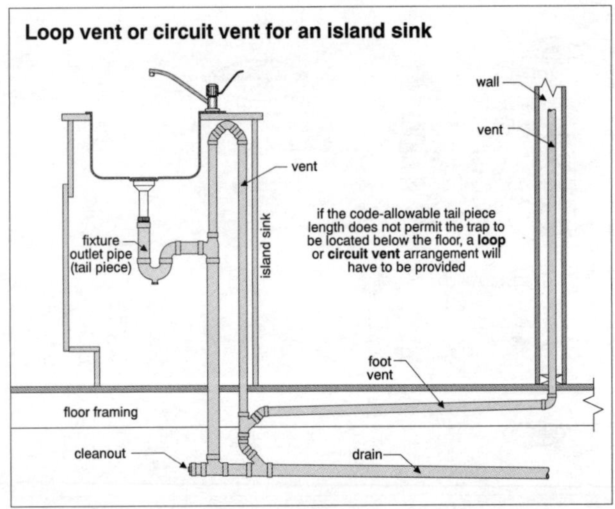

1644

Proper vent location relative to trap

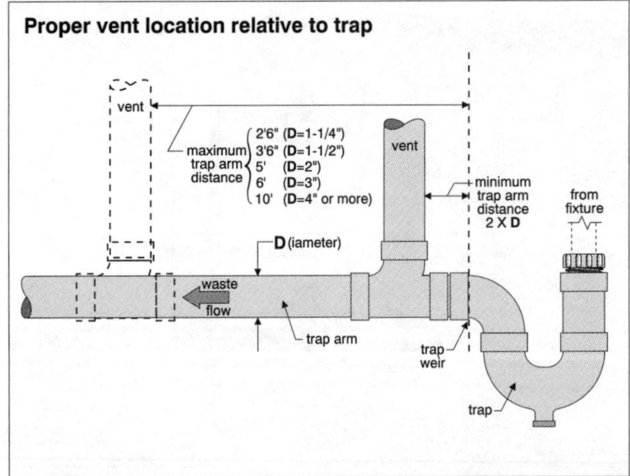

1645

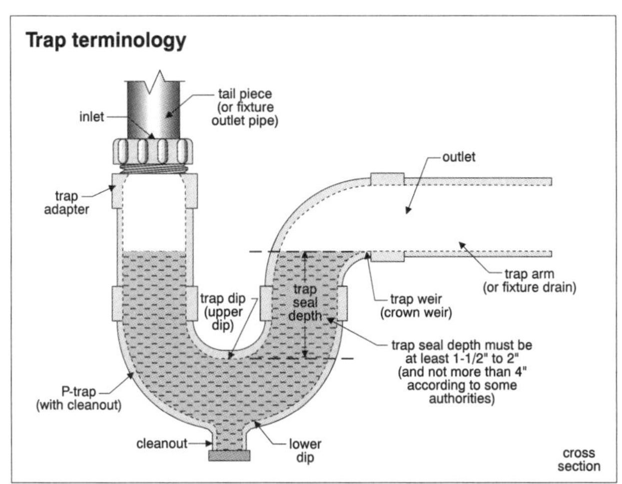

1646

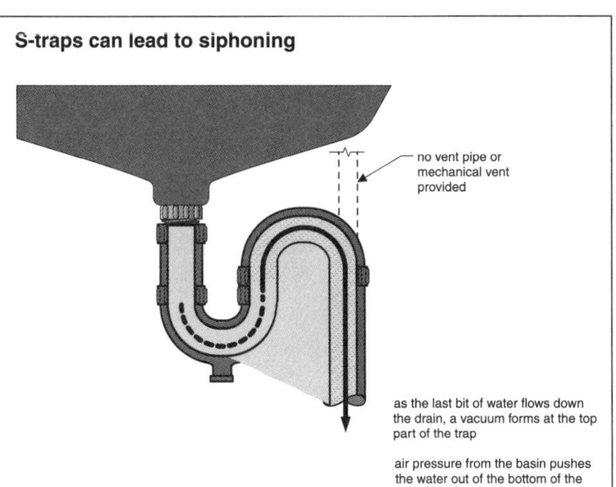

1648

Trap primer

the trap primer is typically a 3/8" diameter plastic tube attached to a fixture (e.g. laundry tub)

whenever the fixture is used, some water is sent to the floor drain trap to keep it filled

the trap primer is often fed into a piece of polyethylene pipe when it must pass through a concrete floor

1647

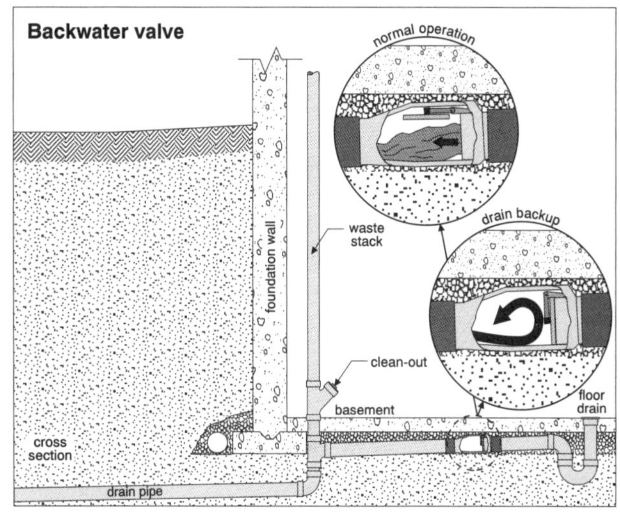

1649

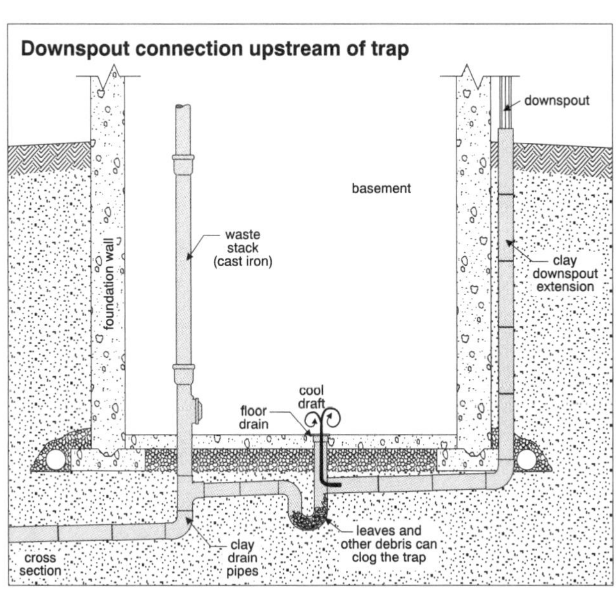

1650

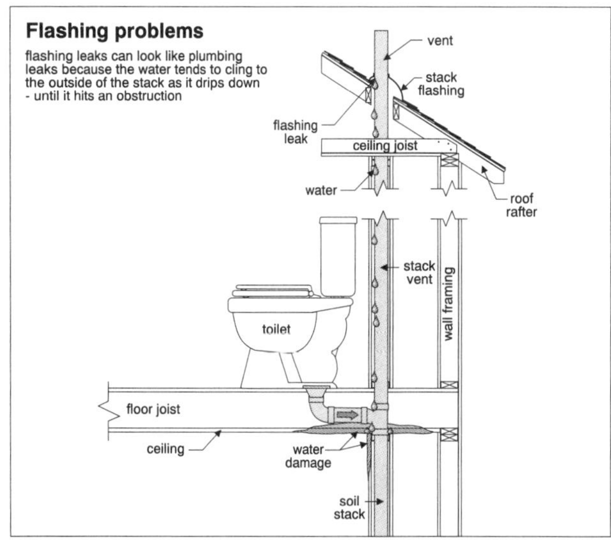

1651

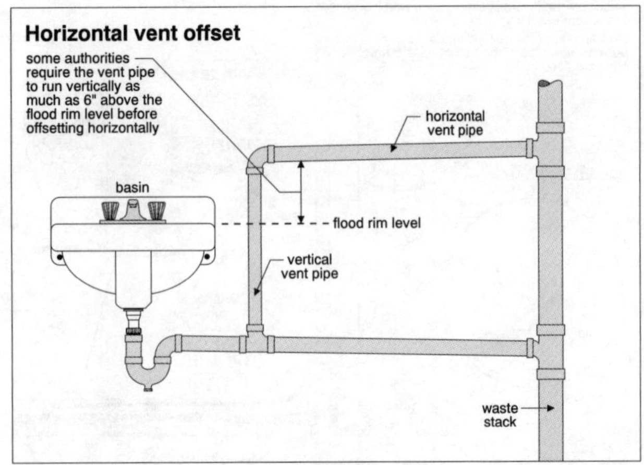

1652

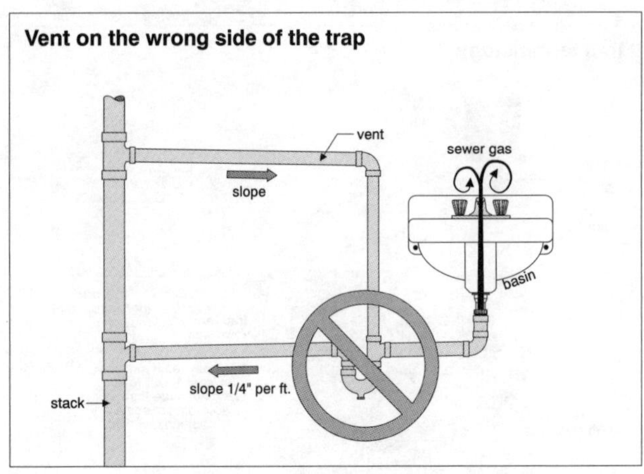

1653

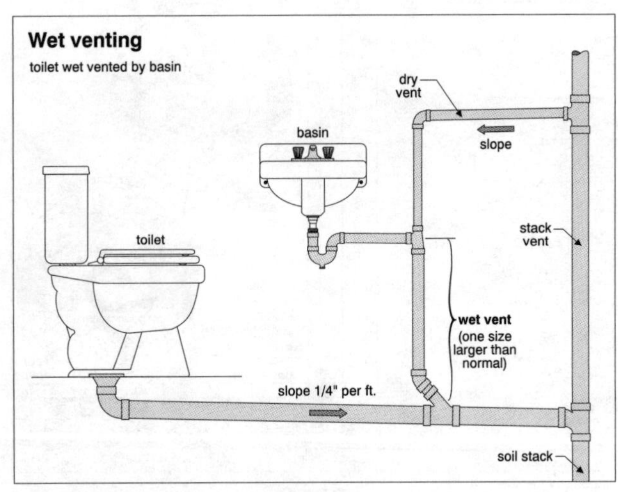

1654

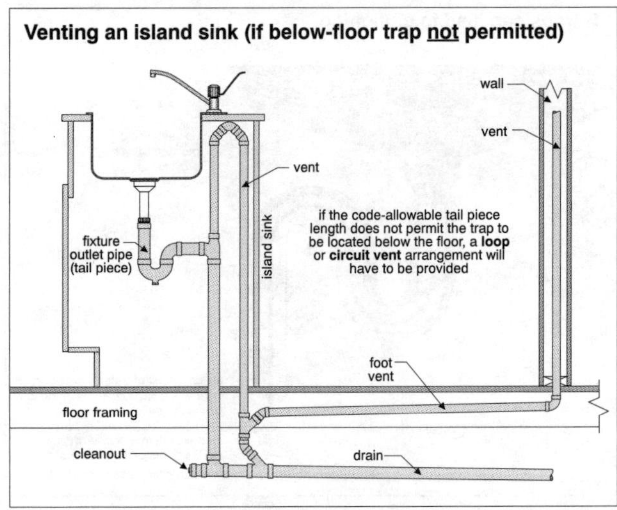

1655

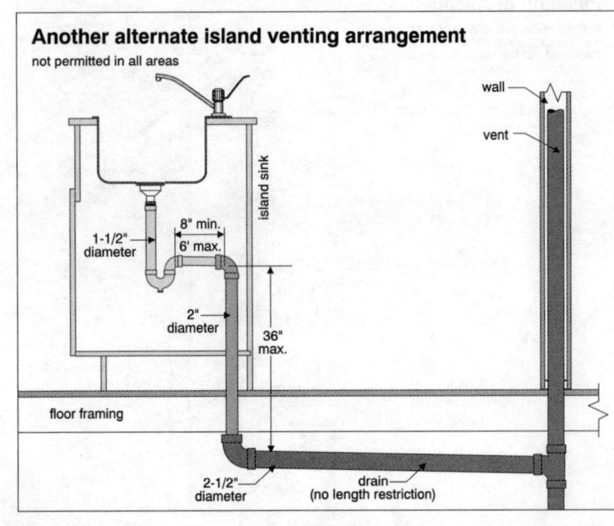

1656

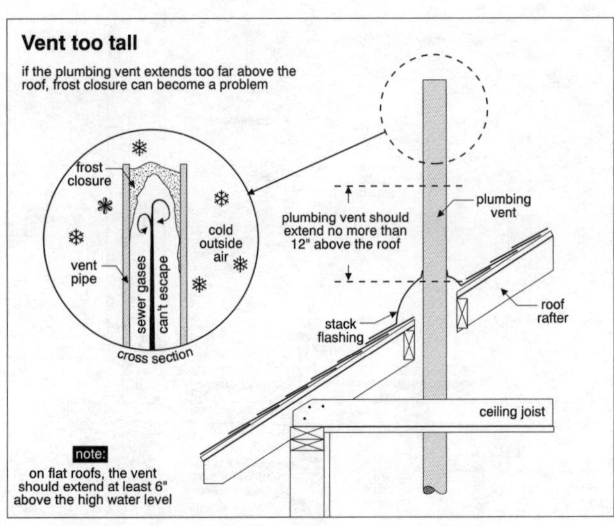

1657

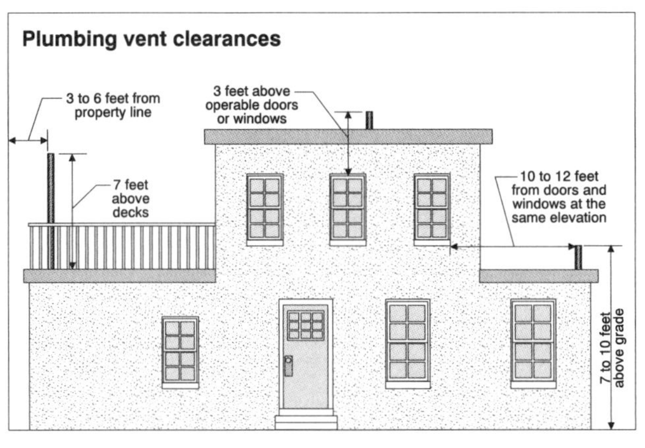

1658

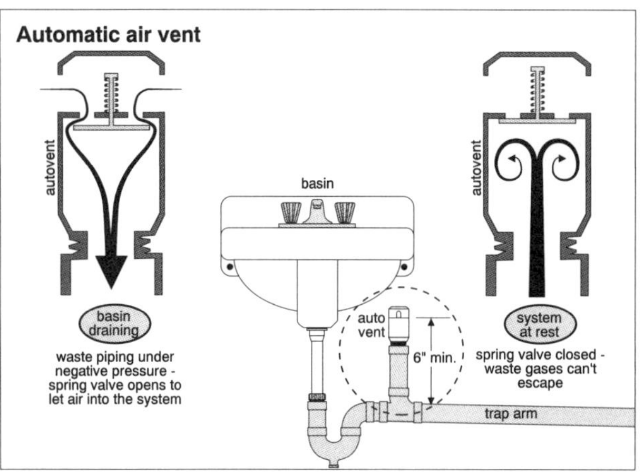

1659

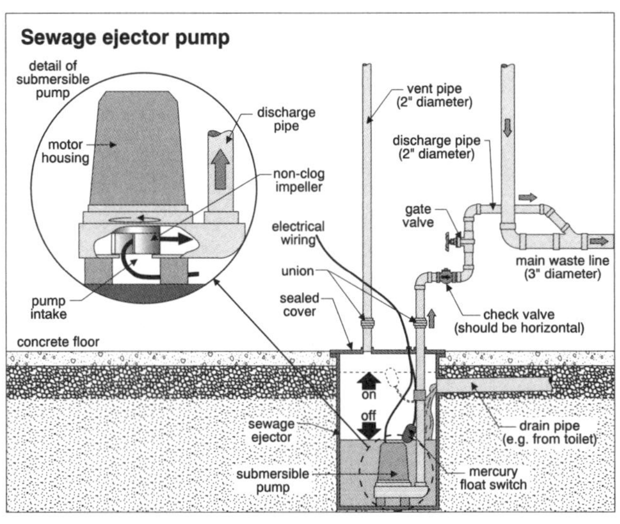

1660

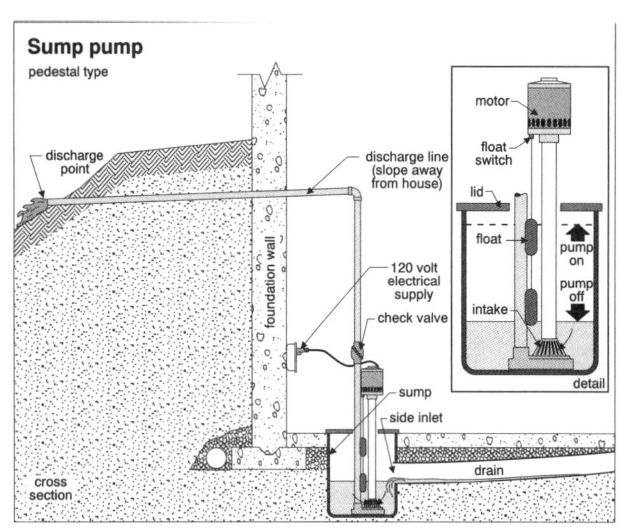

1661

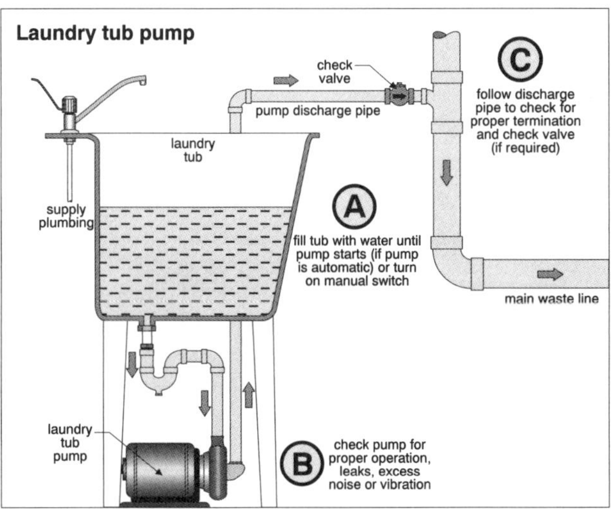

1662

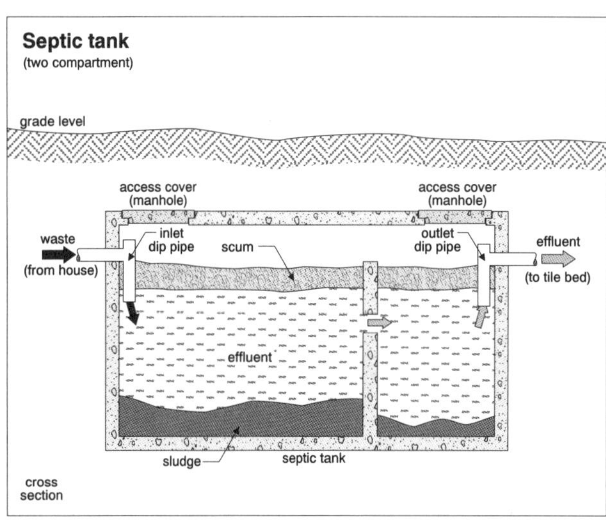

1663

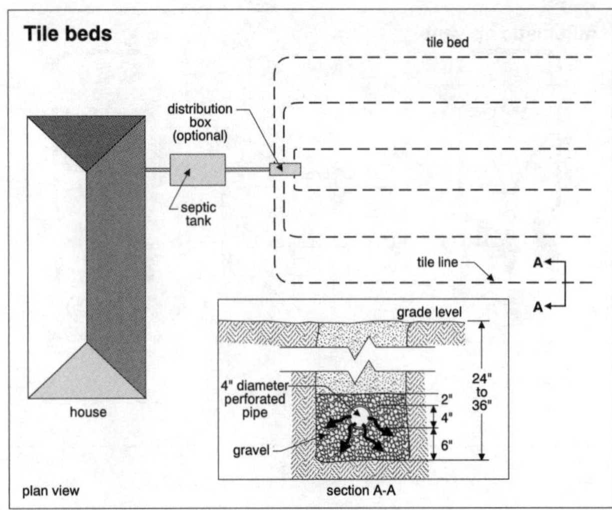

1664

Tile bed location

property line
10' min.
5' min.
10' min.
tile bed
50' min.
6' to 10'
septic tank
tile line - 100' max.
lake
15' min.
house
50' minimum if well has a casing
100' minimum if well has no casing
well
plan view

1665

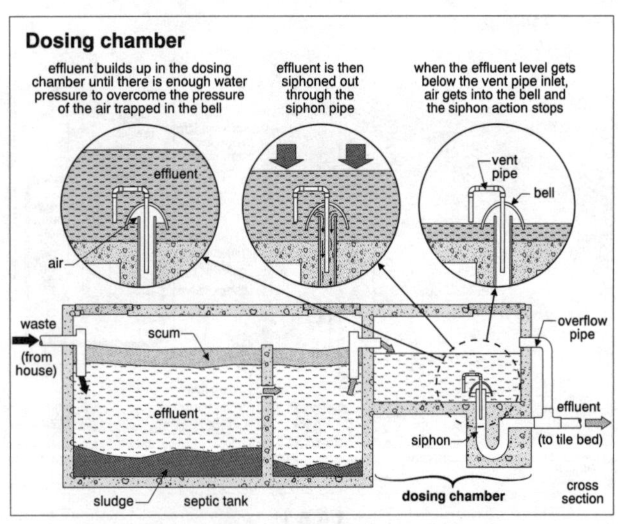

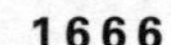
1666

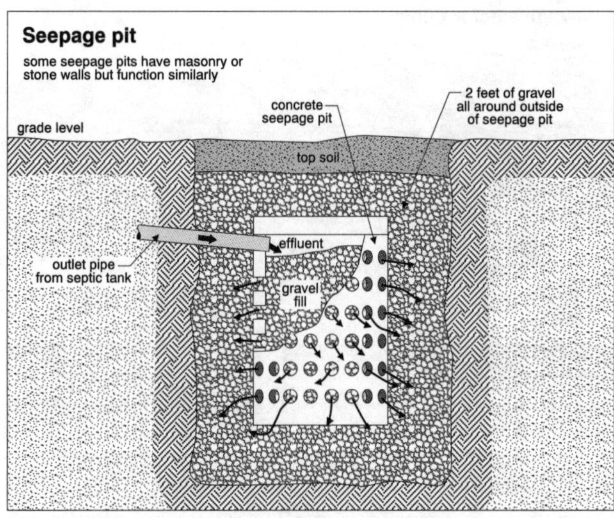

1667

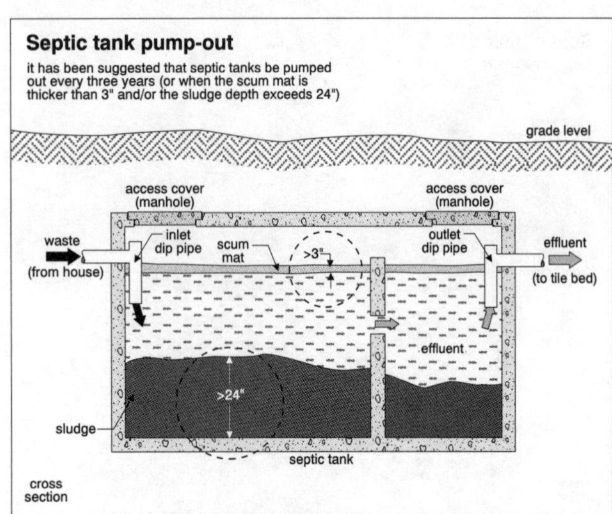

1668

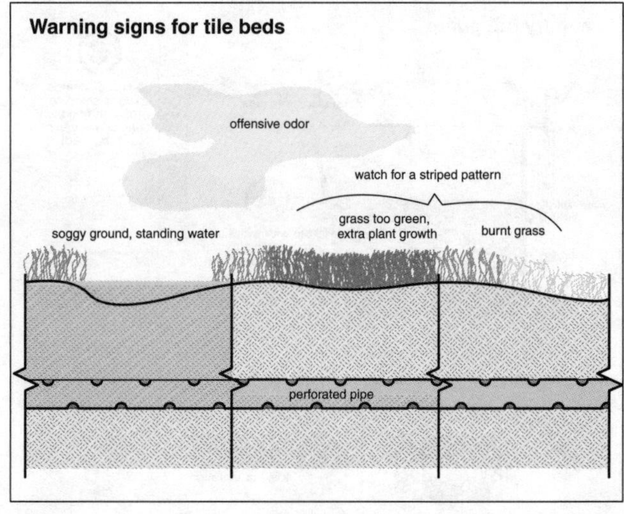

1669

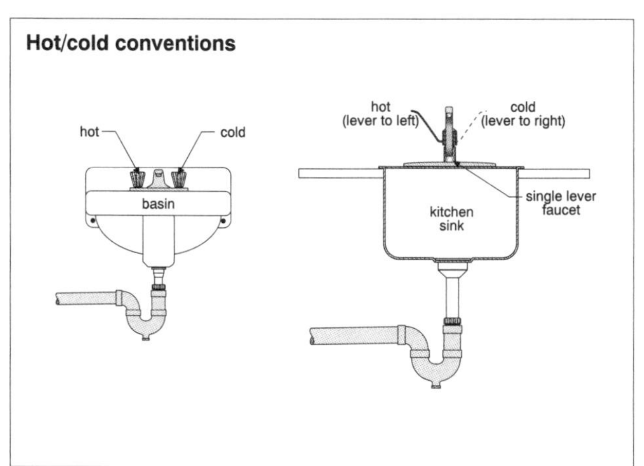

1670

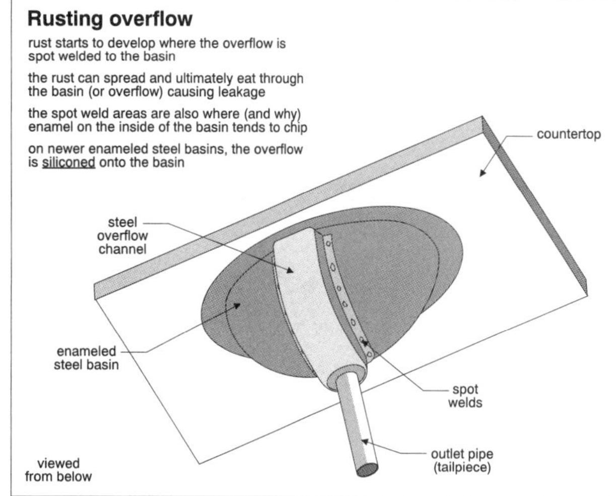

1671

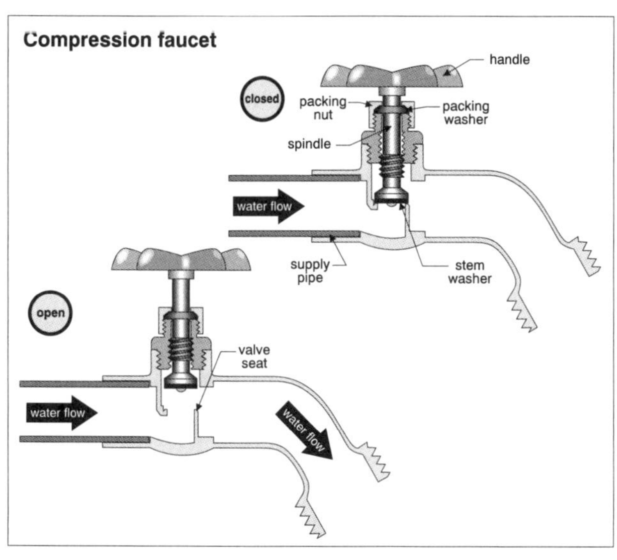

1672

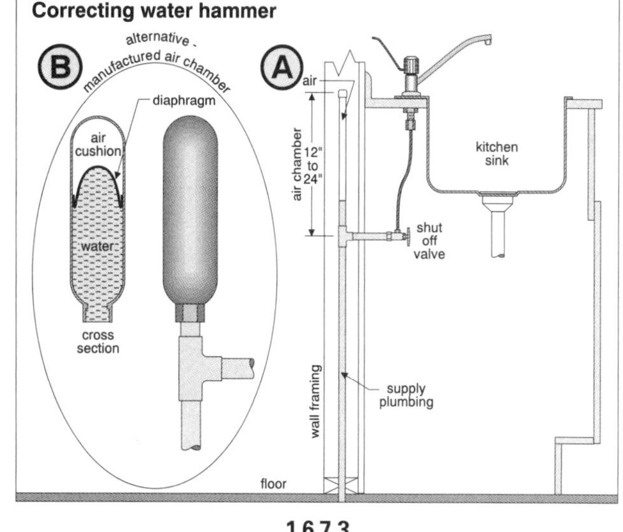

1673

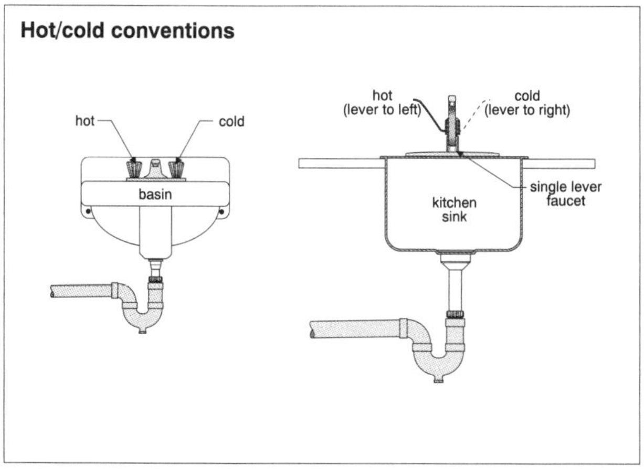

Hot/cold conventions
hot
cold
basin
hot (lever to left)
cold (lever to right)
kitchen sink
single lever faucet

1674

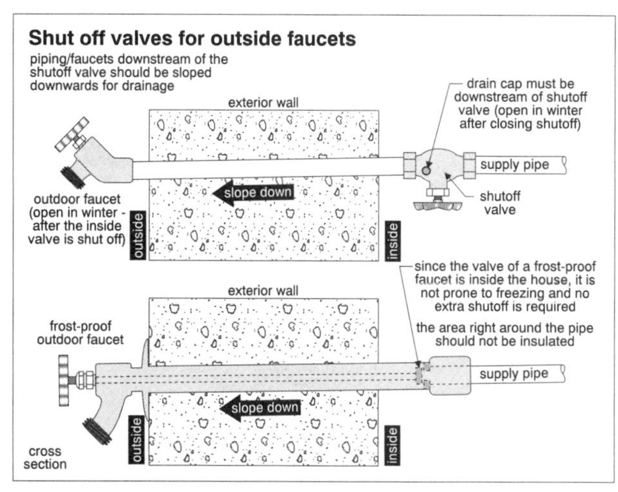

1675

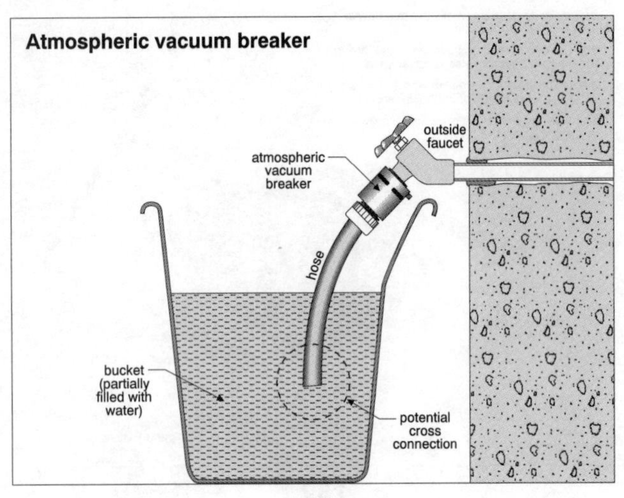

1676

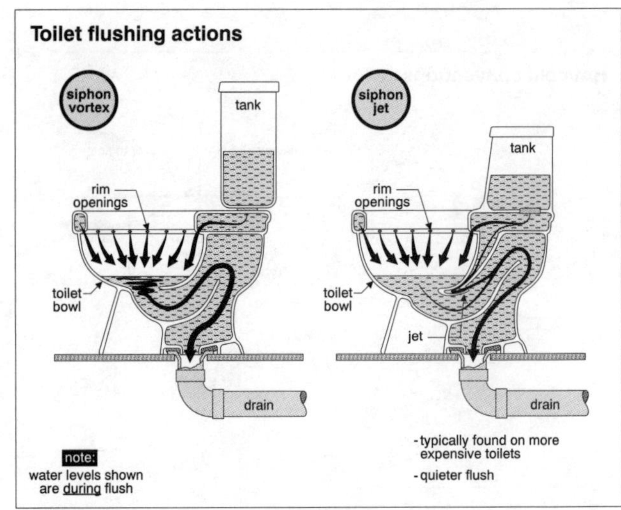

1677

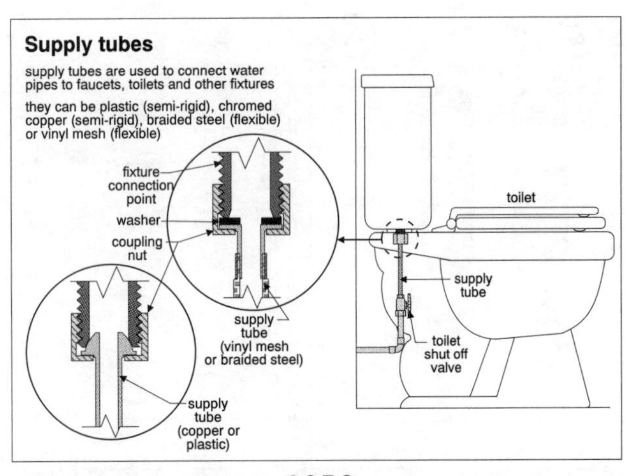

1678

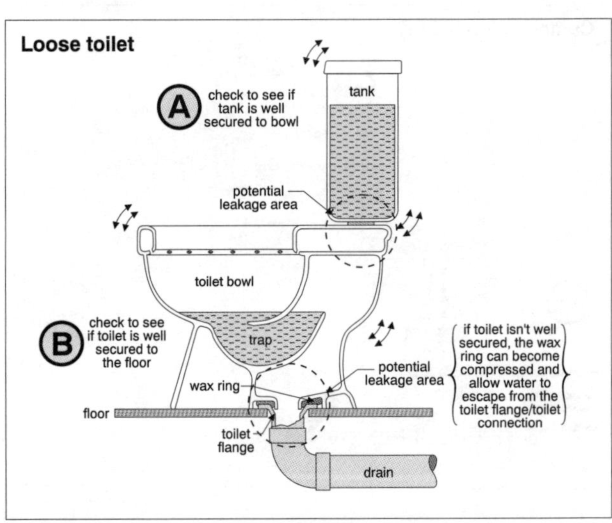

1679

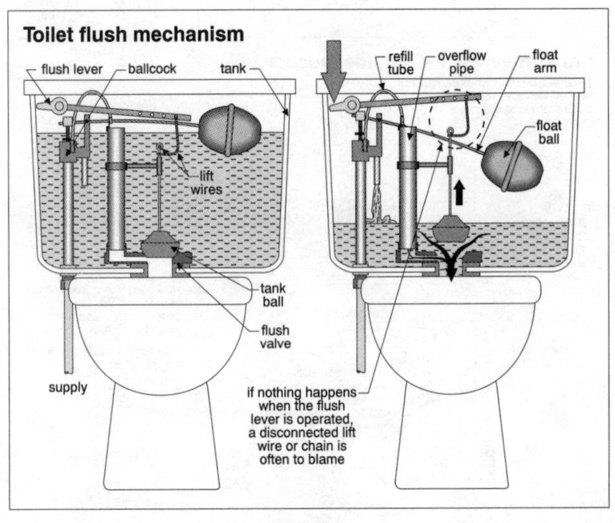

1680

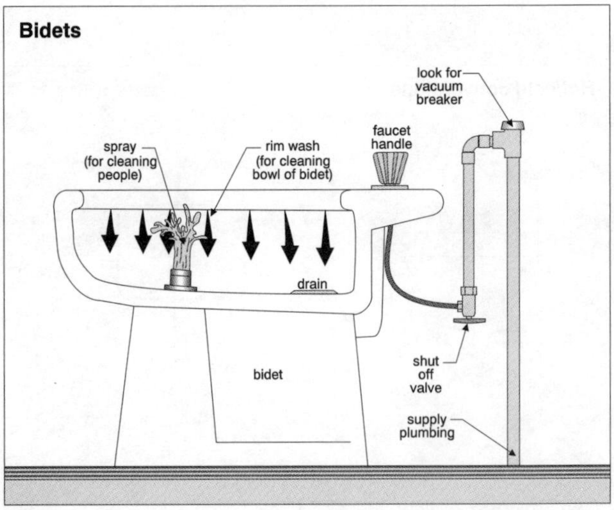

Bidets

look for vacuum breaker

faucet handle

spray (for cleaning people)

rim wash (for cleaning bowl of bidet)

drain

bidet

shut off valve

supply plumbing

1681

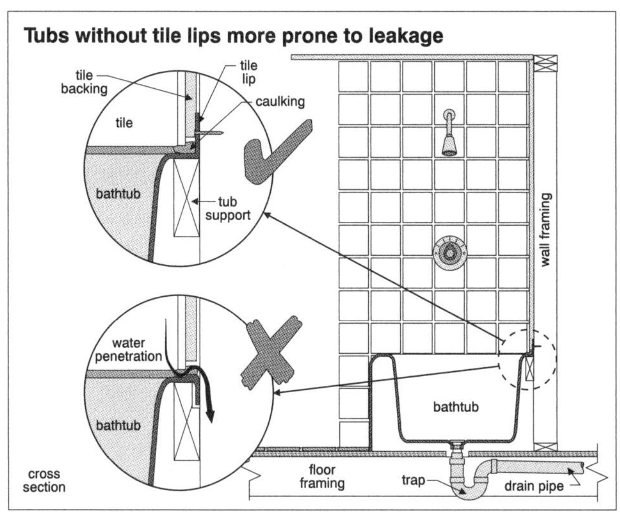

1682

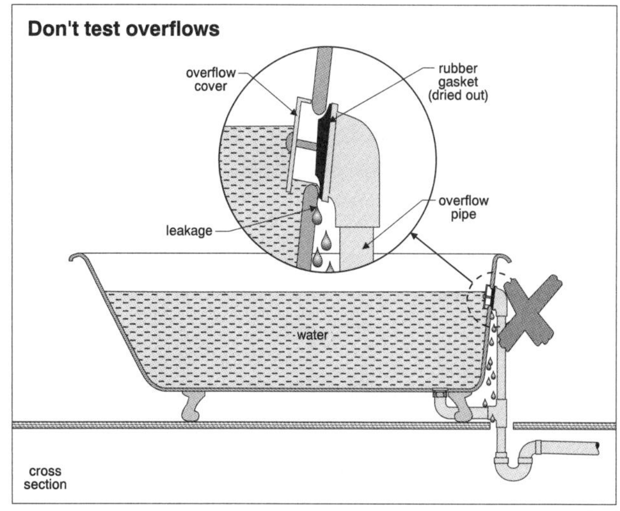

1683

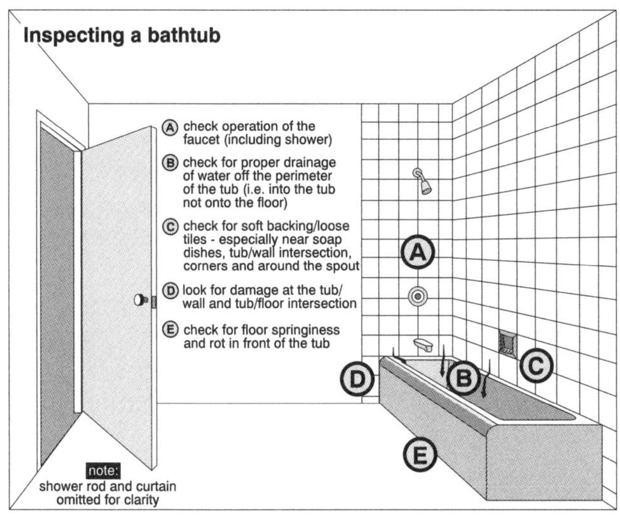

1684

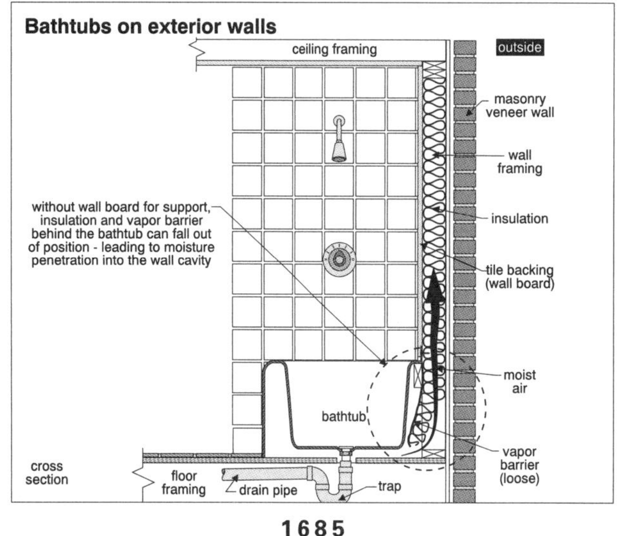

1685

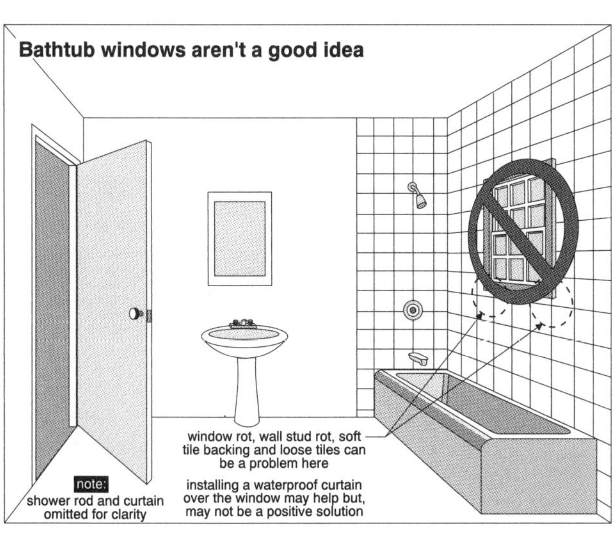

1686

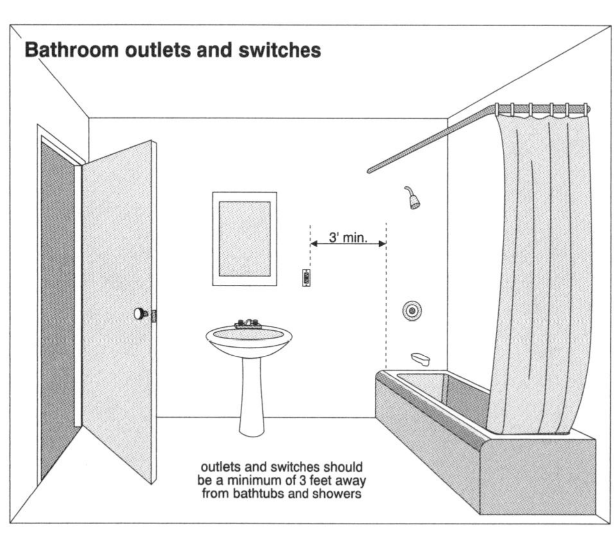

1687

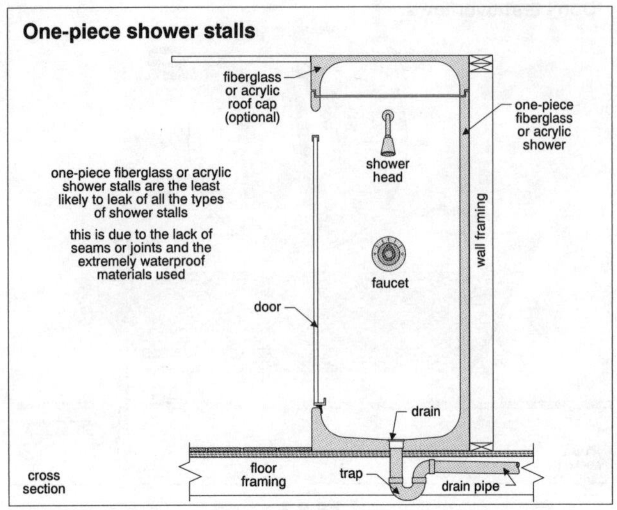

1688

1689

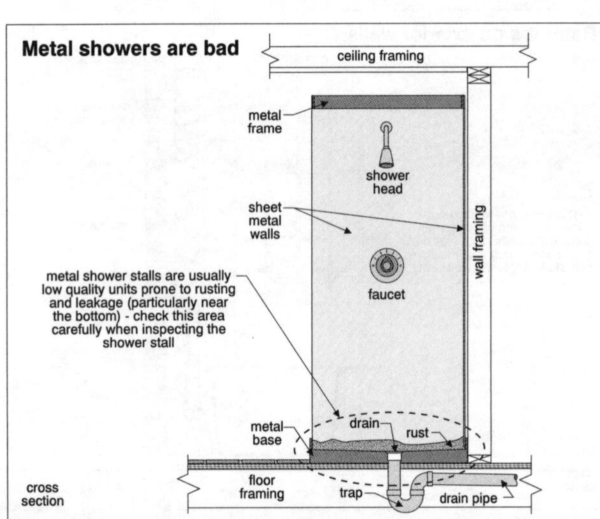

1690

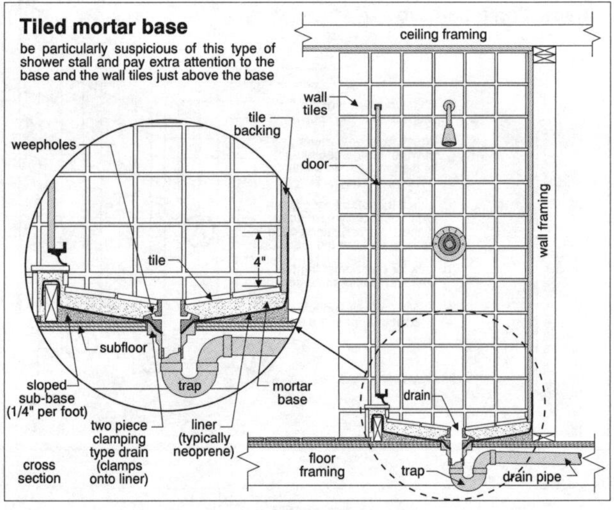

1691

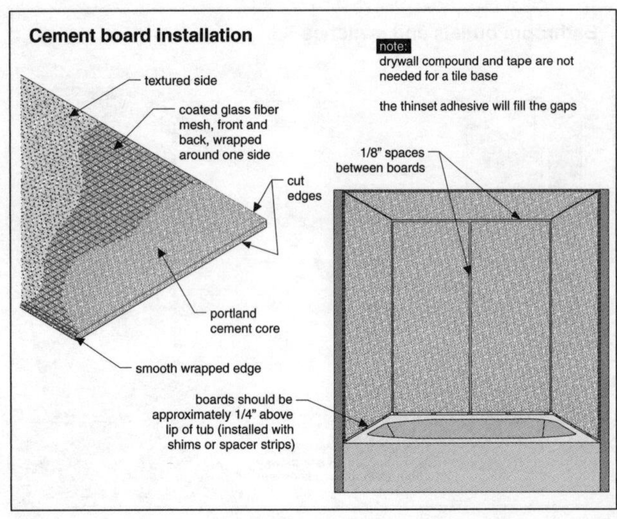

1692

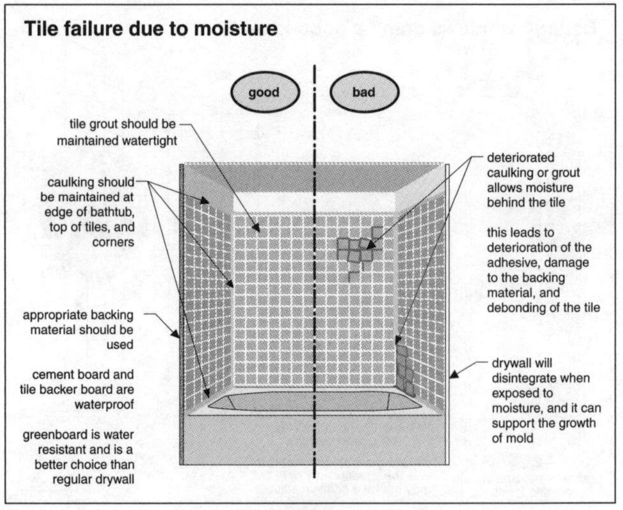

1693

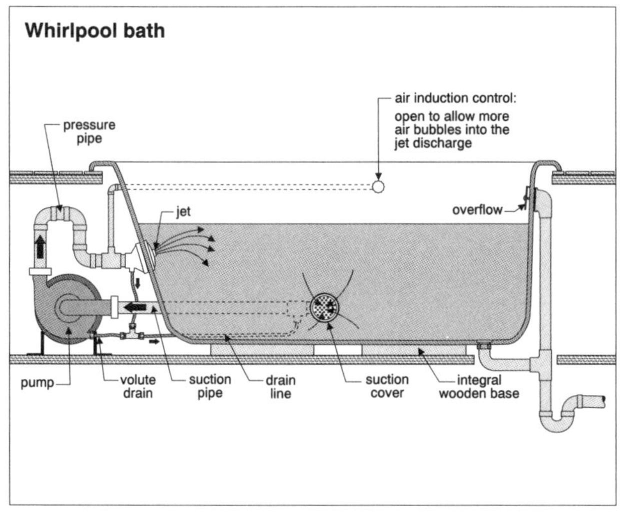

1694

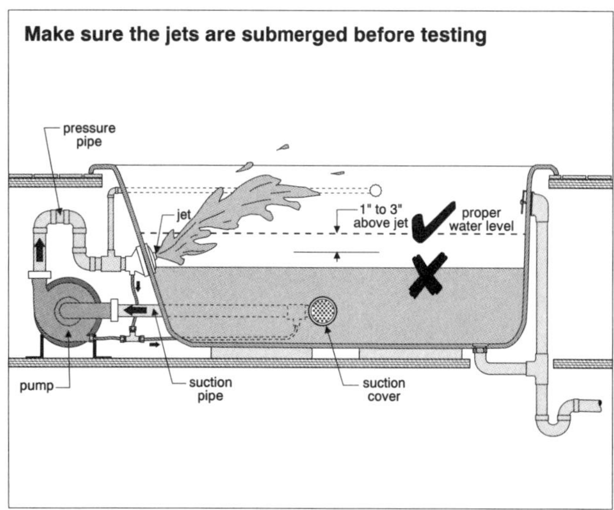

1695

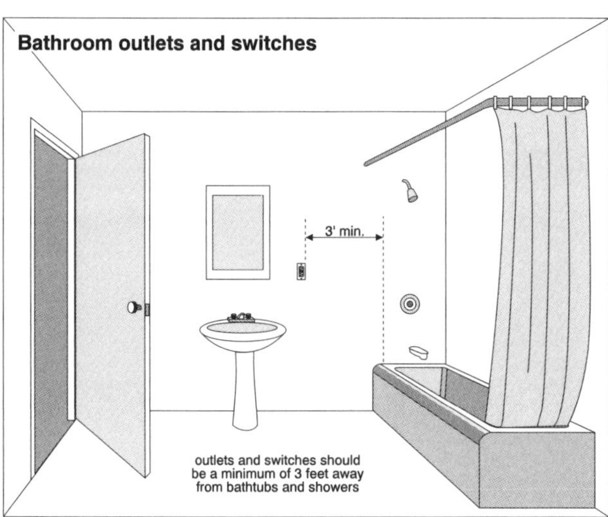

1696

CHAPTER 8

ARCHITECTURAL STYLES

BUILDING SHAPES AND DETAILS

291 ... 1700 Linear plan vs. massed plan
291 ... 1701 Saltbox, four-square and compound plans
291 ... 1702 Flat roofs
291 ... 1703 Sloped roof shapes
291 ... 1704 Bell-cast eave
291 ... 1705 Roof details
292 ... 1706 Gable details
292 ... 1707 Decorative chimneys
293 ... 1708 Dormer types
293 ... 1709 Cornice terms
293 ... 1710 Brackets versus dentils
293 ... 1711 Half-timbering

WINDOWS

294 ... 1712 Quoining
294 ... 1713 Double and single-hung windows
294 ... 1714 Casement windows
294 ... 1715 Sliders
294 ... 1716 Awning and hopper windows
294 ... 1717 Jalousie (or louver) windows
295 ... 1718 Window terms
295 ... 1719 Window shapes
295 ... 1720 Bow, bay and oriel windows
295 ... 1721 Door lights

COLUMNS

295 ... 1722 Columns

SPECIFIC HOUSE STYLES

295 ... 1723 Early Classical Revival
296 ... 1724 Greek Revival
296 ... 1725 Georgian
296 ... 1726 Adam
296 ... 1727 Colonial Revival
297 ... 1728 Italian Renaissance
297 ... 1729 Italianate
297 ... 1730 Gothic Revival
297 ... 1731 Stick
298 ... 1732 Queen Anne
298 ... 1733 Additional Queen Anne details
298 ... 1734 Shingle
298 ... 1735 Tudor
299 ... 1736 Prairie
299 ... 1737 Craftsman
299 ... 1738 Modernistic
299 ... 1739 International
300 ... 1740 Spanish Colonial
300 ... 1741 Mission
300 ... 1742 Cape Cod
300 ... 1743 Saltbox

EXTERIOR CLADDING

INTRODUCTION

300 ... 1744 Exterior inspection includes other systems

WALL SURFACES – GENERAL

300 ... 1745 Wall assemblies
301 ... 1746 Support for siding
301 ... 1747 Condensation in walls
301 ... 1748 Too close to grade
301 ... 1749 Weep holes below grade
301 ... 1750 Siding too close to roof
301 ... 1751 Watch for planters or gardens against walls
302 ... 1752 Insulation holes

MASONRY

302 ... 1753 Veneer versus solid masonry
302 ... 1754 Parapet walls prone to damage
302 ... 1755 Chimney deterioration due to condensation
302 ... 1756 Rising damp
302 ... 1757 Freezing water spalls bricks
303 ... 1758 Repointing
303 ... 1759 Rusting lintels
303 ... 1760 Toothed in masonry on additions
303 ... 1761 Common mortar joints
303 ... 1762 Mortar joints in brick walls
303 ... 1763 Weep holes – vented rain screen principle
304 ... 1764 Bowed brick veneer wall – older home
304 ... 1765 Brick veneer wall – masonry tie detail
304 ... 1766 Lateral support for masonry walls
304 ... 1767 Bowing of masonry walls

CHAPTER 8

STUCCO

305 ... 1768 Stucco – three coat process
305 ... 1769 Stucco – two coat process
305 ... 1770 Drip screed
305 ... 1771 Stucco cracking
305 ... 1772 Tudor style stucco problems
305 ... 1773 Nail popping
306 ... 1774 Synthetic stucco (EIFS)
306 ... 1775 EIFS installation details
306 ... 1776 Kickout prevents stucco damage
306 ... 1777 EIFS – reinforcing mesh layout around window openings
306 ... 1778 EIFS – common problems at decks
306 ... 1779 EIFS – window flashing detail (fully flashed)
307 ... 1780 EIFS – window flashing detail (simple)
307 ... 1781 EIFS – wire penetration
307 ... 1782 EIFS – above grade termination
307 ... 1783 EIFS – flashings around decks
307 ... 1784 EIFS – light fixture detailing
307 ... 1785 EIFS – hosebib or railing attachment detail
308 ... 1786 EIFS – drainage layer
308 ... 1787 EIFS – ideal caulking configurations
308 ... 1788 Exterior inspection strategy for EIFS
308 ... 1789 Interior inspection strategy for EIFS

WOOD

309 ... 1790 Horizontal wood siding
309 ... 1791 Board-and-batten siding
309 ... 1792 Nailing controversy
309 ... 1793 Concealed nails
310 ... 1794 Inside and outside corners
310 ... 1795 Wood shingles and shakes
310 ... 1796 Cedar shingles – nailing details
310 ... 1797 Wood shingle siding
310 ... 1798 Cut back bottom of siding
310 ... 1799 Mitered corners
311 ... 1800 Vertical siding – butt joint detail
311 ... 1801 Joints in siding boards
311 ... 1802 Concealed nails
311 ... 1803 Strapping for vertical siding

PLYWOOD, HARDBOARD, AND OSB

311 ... 1804 Plywood and composite siding
311 ... 1805 Hardboard siding
312 ... 1806 Oriented strandboard (OSB) siding
312 ... 1807 Vertical joints in panel siding
312 ... 1808 Siding too close to roof
312 ... 1809 Z flashings
312 ... 1810 Identifying Inner-Seal® siding

METAL AND VINYL

312 ... 1811 Metal and vinyl
313 ... 1812 Nailing too tightly
313 ... 1813 Mounting blocks
313 ... 1814 Flashings below windows
313 ... 1815 J moldings around windows

OTHER SIDINGS AND ISSUES

313 ... 1816 Asbestos cement siding
313 ... 1817 Clay and slate shingles
314 ... 1818 Six nails per shingle
314 ... 1819 Insulbrick
314 ... 1820 Foundation height
314 ... 1821 Areas to check for wood/soil contact include:
314 ... 1822 Preserved wood foundations
314 ... 1823 Parging

SOFFITS AND FASCIA

315 ... 1824 Soffits and fascia
315 ... 1825 Rotting soffit and fascia

WINDOWS AND DOORS

315 ... 1826 Putty (glazing compound)
315 ... 1827 Capillary break
315 ... 1828 Windows move
315 ... 1829 Frame deformation

TRIM, FLASHINGS, AND CAULKING

316 ... 1830 Flashings over windows
316 ... 1831 Kickout flashing
316 ... 1832 Kickout prevents siding/wall damage
316 ... 1833 Dormer flashing
316 ... 1834 Missing kickout flashing
316 ... 1835 Macro approach

CHAPTER 8

EXTERIOR STRUCTURES

INTRODUCTION

317 ... 1836 Porches
317 ... 1837 Decks
317 ... 1838 Balconies
317 ... 1839 Garages versus carports
317 ... 1840 Basement walkout

PORCHES, DECKS, AND BALCONIES

317 ... 1841 Support for concrete steps
318 ... 1842 Rise, run and tread width
318 ... 1843 Landings
318 ... 1844 Settled or heaved steps
318 ... 1845 Rot in wood stairs
318 ... 1846 Designing steps that aren't springy
318 ... 1847 Handrails and guards
319 ... 1848 Handrail design
319 ... 1849 Spindle spacing
319 ... 1850 Handrails or guards too low
319 ... 1851 Common column materials
319 ... 1852 Column hinge point
319 ... 1853 Beams
320 ... 1854 Inspecting for beam sag
320 ... 1855 Poor end support
320 ... 1856 Beam rotation (twisting)
320 ... 1857 Joist support
320 ... 1858 Porch floor sag
320 ... 1859 Securing ledgerboards
321 ... 1860 Ledgerboard flashing
321 ... 1861 Cantilevered decks
321 ... 1862 Canvas duck
321 ... 1863 Deck board installation details
321 ... 1864 Sagging deck or porch boards
321 ... 1865 Threshold
322 ... 1866 Hinged pillars affect roof structure
322 ... 1867 Skirting

GARAGES AND CARPORTS

322 ... 1868 Garages versus carports
322 ... 1869 Fire and gas proofing in attached garages
322 ... 1870 Heating ductwork in garages
322 ... 1871 Man door (attached garage)
323 ... 1872 Combustible insulation in garages
323 ... 1873 Structural garage floor
323 ... 1874 Poor garage floor drainage
323 ... 1875 Slab is partly on disturbed soil
323 ... 1876 Mud jacking (pressure grouting)
323 ... 1877 Drains for below-grade garages
324 ... 1878 Drain pipe should face down
324 ... 1879 Garage door types
324 ... 1880 Garage door conditions
324 ... 1881 Automatic garage door openers
324 ... 1882 Manual operation of automatic garage door openers
324 ... 1883 Check electrical connection
325 ... 1884 Testing automatic reverse
325 ... 1885 Check photo-eye
325 ... 1886 Water heaters in garages

BASEMENT WALKOUTS

325 ... 1887 Basement walkouts
325 ... 1888 Lowered footings around basement walkouts
325 ... 1889 Insulated exterior basement stairwell
326 ... 1890 Perimeter drainage tile
326 ... 1891 No outside traps
326 ... 1892 Door threshold
326 ... 1893 Walkout cover or roof

SURFACE WATER CONTROL AND LANDSCAPING

LOT GRADING

326 ... 1894 Recommended grading slopes
326 ... 1895 Water penetration due to subgrade soil conditions
327 ... 1896 Swales
327 ... 1897 Maximum slopes
327 ... 1898 Evidence of exterior insulation installation
327 ... 1899 Drainage layer
327 ... 1900 Foundation cracks – repair methods
327 ... 1901 Settled backfill
328 ... 1902 Swales
328 ... 1903 French
328 ... 1904 Excavation, dampproofing and drainage tile
328 ... 1905 Catch basins – drain pipe should face down
328 ... 1906 Water penetration due to subgrade soil conditions

CHAPTER 8

GUTTERS AND DOWNSPOUTS

328 ... 1907 Interior flat roof drains
329 ... 1908 Integral gutter
329 ... 1909 Yankee gutter
329 ... 1910 Identifying aluminum and galvanized steel gutters
329 ... 1911 Excess shingle overhang
329 ... 1912 Gutters – common reasons for leakage
329 ... 1913 Repairing an integral gutter
330 ... 1914 Gutter attachment methods
330 ... 1915 Screens on gutters
330 ... 1916 Gutter and downspout installation
330 ... 1917 No downspout on secondary roof
330 ... 1918 Downspout running across roof
330 ... 1919 No downspouts on small roofs
331 ... 1920 Downspouts – common leakage areas
332 ... 1921 Downspouts – proper connection of sections
331 ... 1922 35 feet per downspout
331 ... 1923 Baskets/strainers at the top of downspouts
331 ... 1924 Downspout extension too short
331 ... 1925 Downspouts discharge into floor drain
332 ... 1926 Does the downspout drain into the floor drain trap?
332 ... 1927 French drain
332 ... 1928 Abandon below grade downspouts
332 ... 1929 Flat roof drainage systems
332 ... 1930 Scupper drains
332 ... 1931 Weight of water
333 ... 1932 Clogged interior flat roof drain
333 ... 1933 Drains in columns and walls
333 ... 1934 Adding a roof drain

WINDOW WELLS

333 ... 1935 Window well
333 ... 1936 Add or extend wells when re-grading
333 ... 1937 Damaged window wells
334 ... 1938 Wood soil contact
334 ... 1939 Drain problems

WALKS, DRIVEWAYS, AND GROUNDS

334 ... 1940 Concrete and asphalt driveways
334 ... 1941 Walkway steps
334 ... 1942 Trees and shrubs too close to house
334 ... 1943 Raised patios
335 ... 1944 Walk/patio sloping toward house

RETAINING WALLS

335 ... 1945 Gabion retaining wall
335 ... 1946 Precast concrete retaining wall systems
335 ... 1947 Cantilevered concrete retaining wall
335 ... 1948 Pile retaining walls (shoring)
335 ... 1949 Wood retaining wall
336 ... 1950 Drainage is important
336 ... 1951 Movement or cracking
336 ... 1952 Block walls need rebar and cap
336 ... 1953 Inspecting retaining walls – things to watch for
336 ... 1954 Weep holes

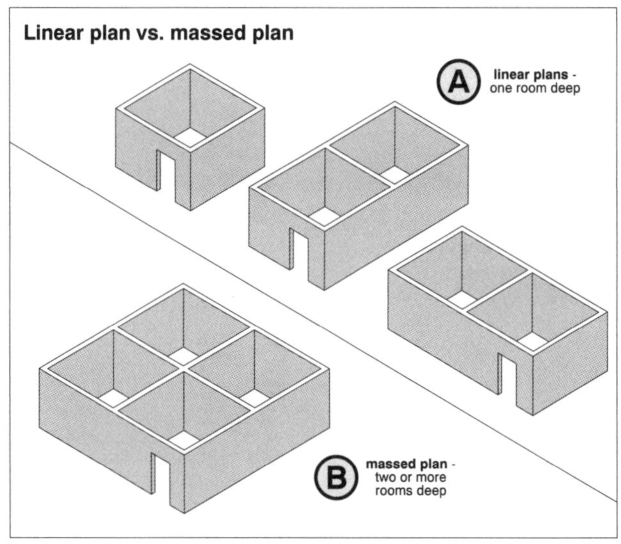

1700

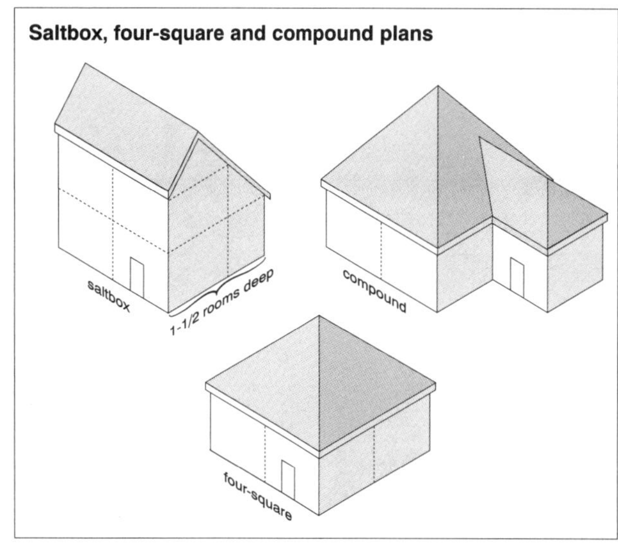

1701

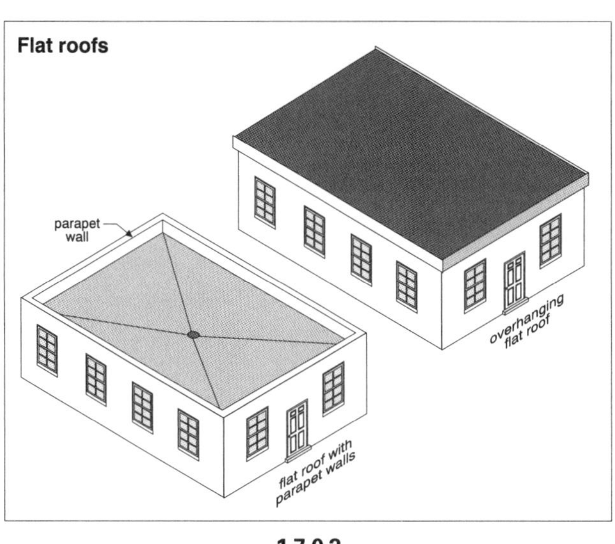

1702

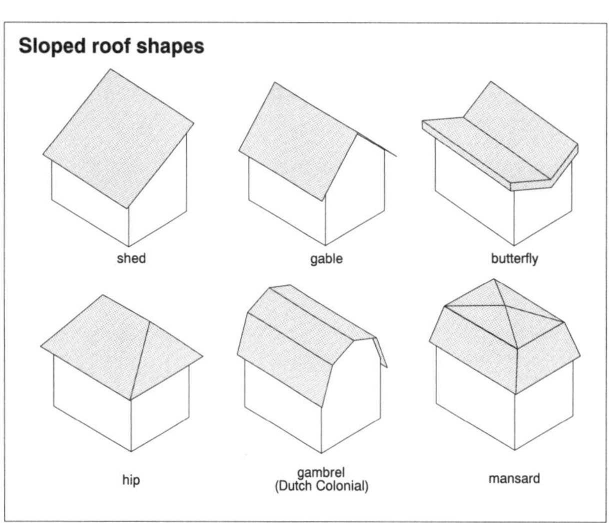

1703

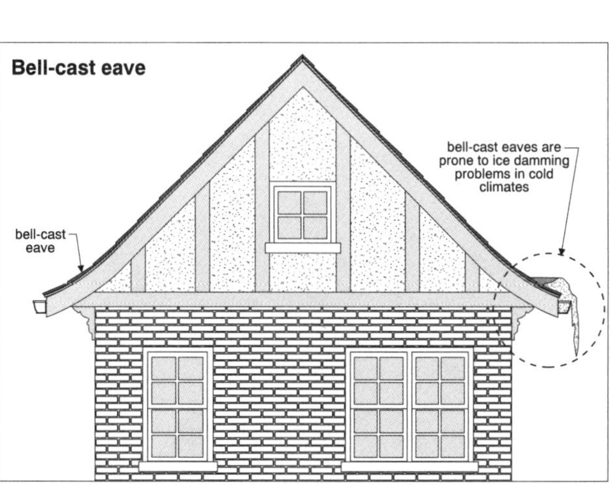

1704

Roof details

widow's walk

turret

pinnacle

cupola

cresting

1705

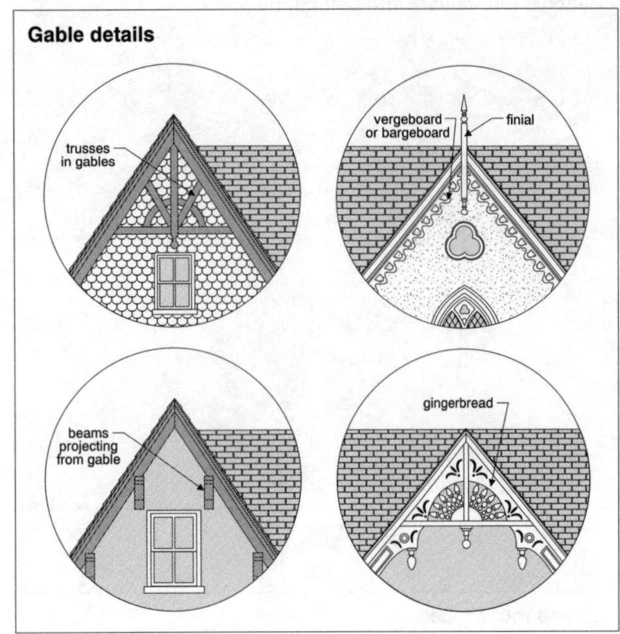
Gable details
trusses in gables
vergeboard or bargeboard
finial
beams projecting from gable
gingerbread

1706

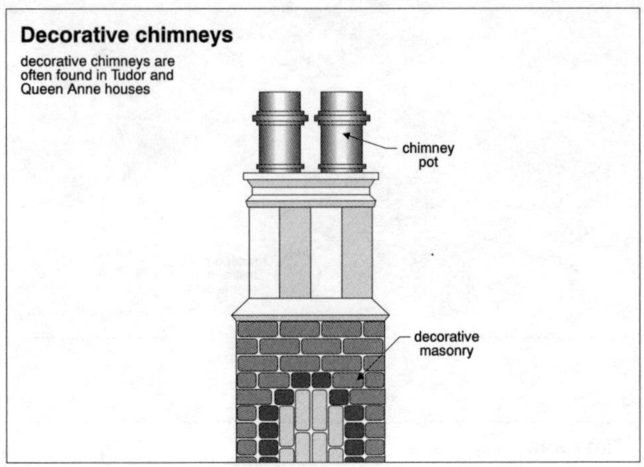
Decorative chimneys
decorative chimneys are often found in Tudor and Queen Anne houses
chimney pot
decorative masonry

1707

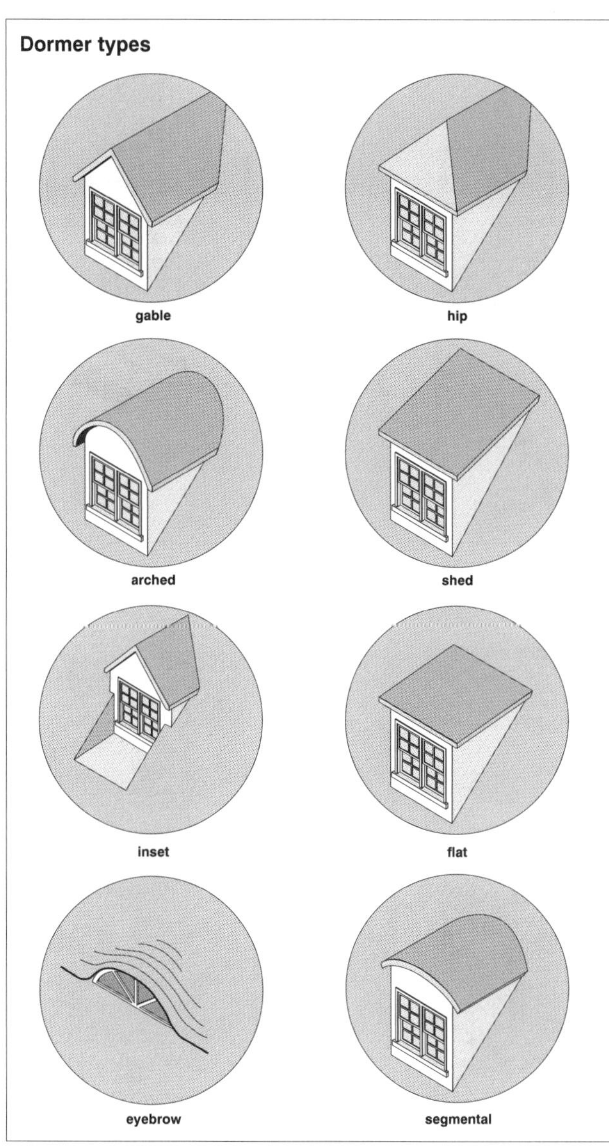

1708

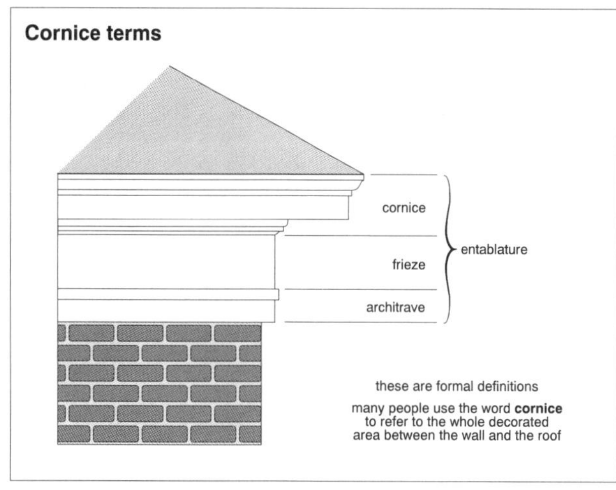

1709

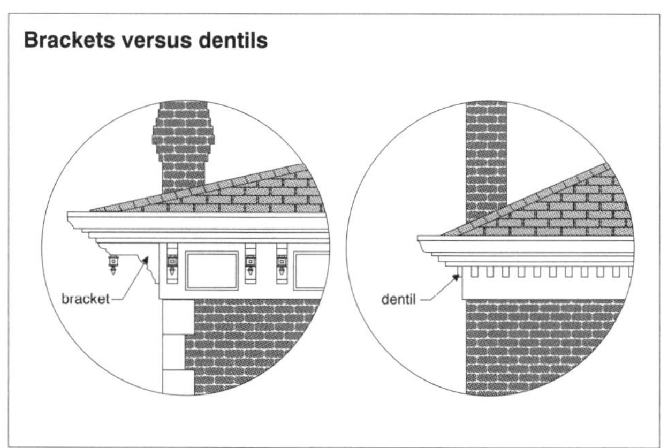

1710

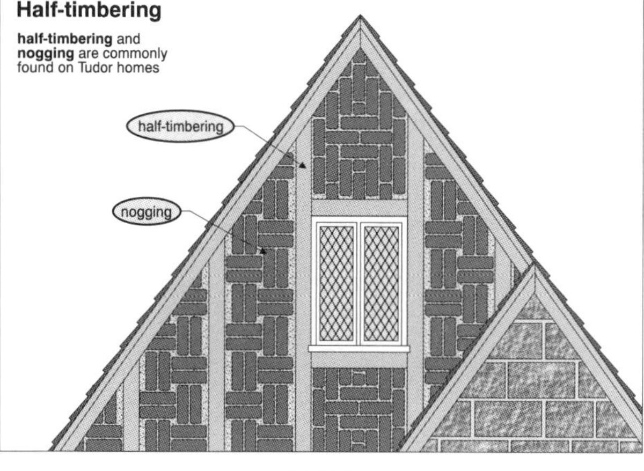

1711

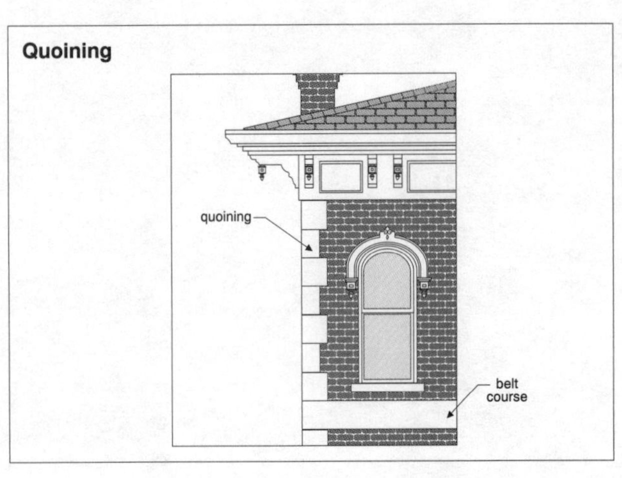

1712

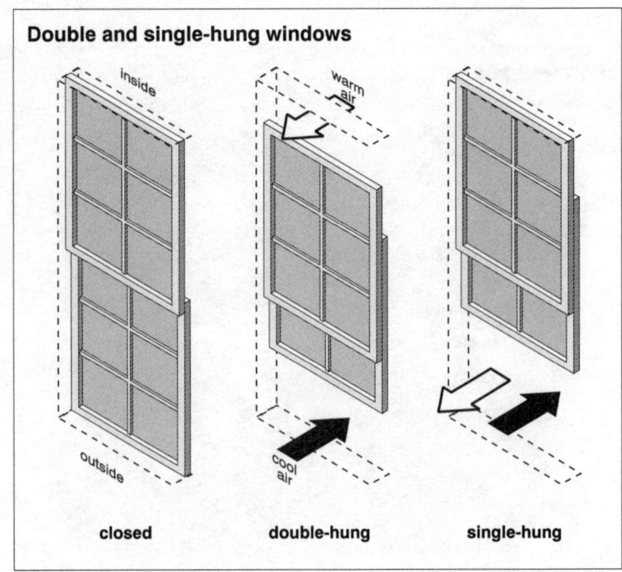

1713

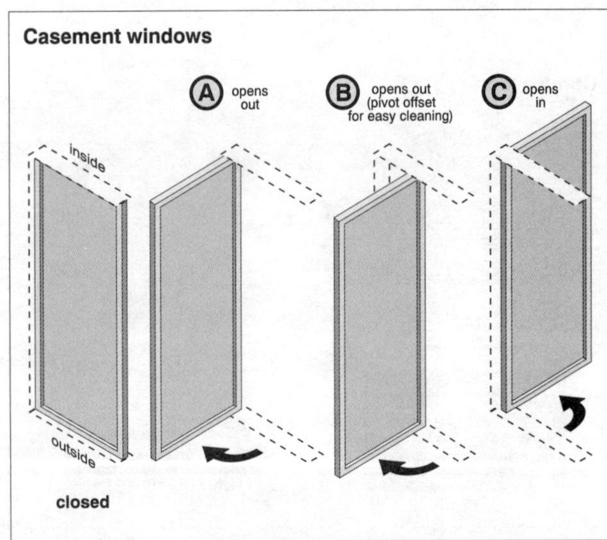

1714

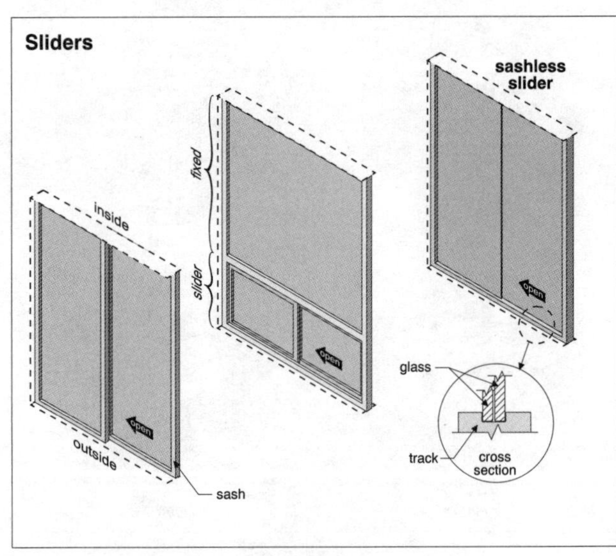

1715

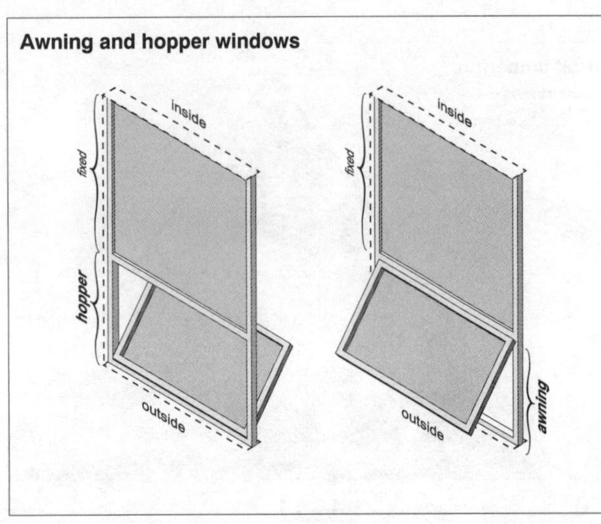

1716

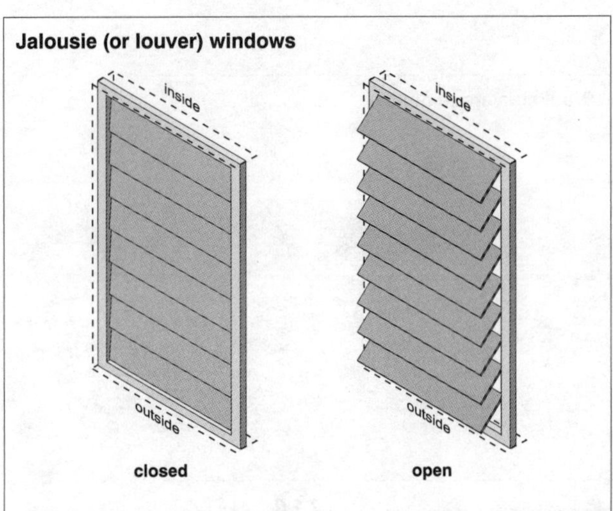

1717

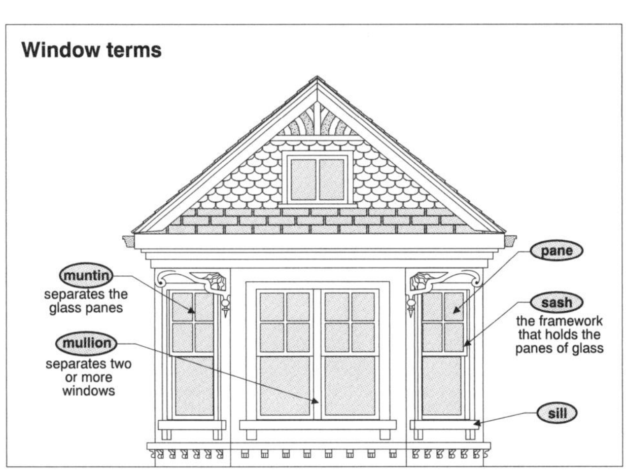

1718

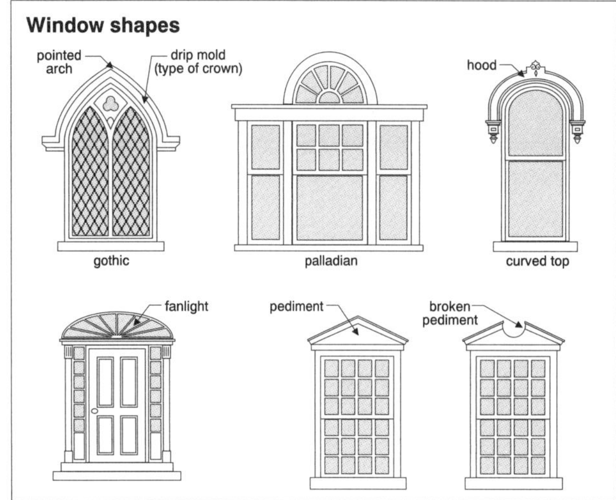

1719

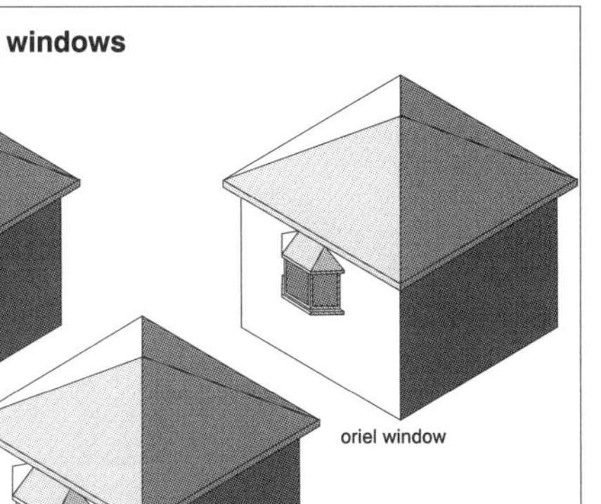
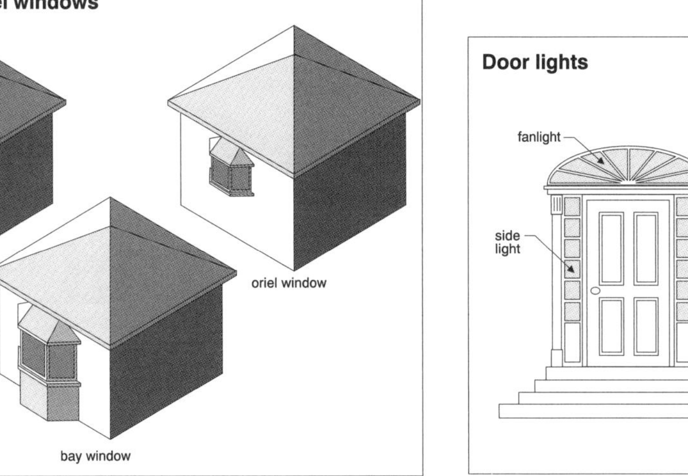

1720

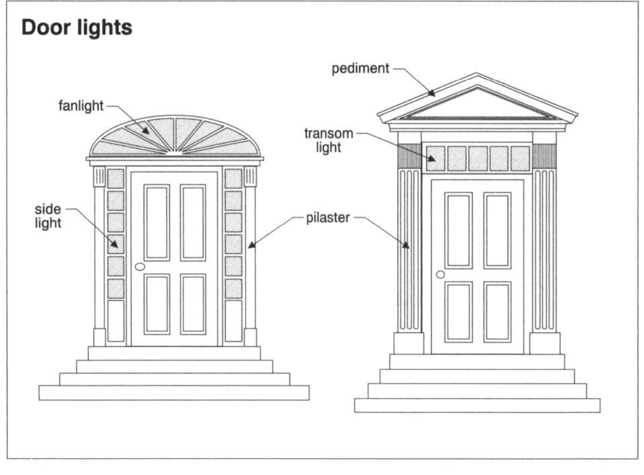

1721

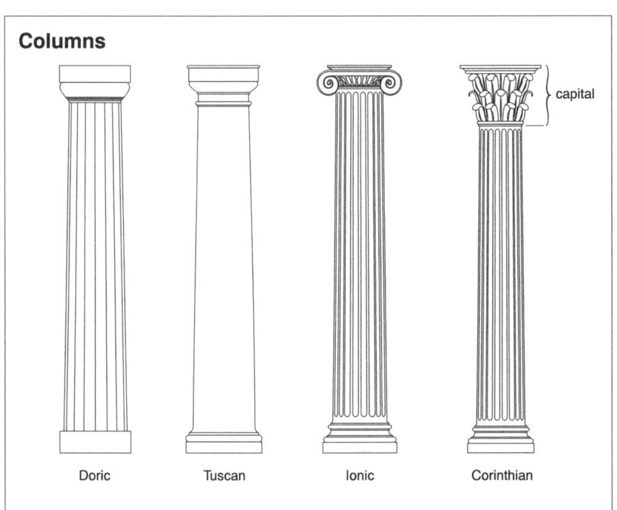

1722

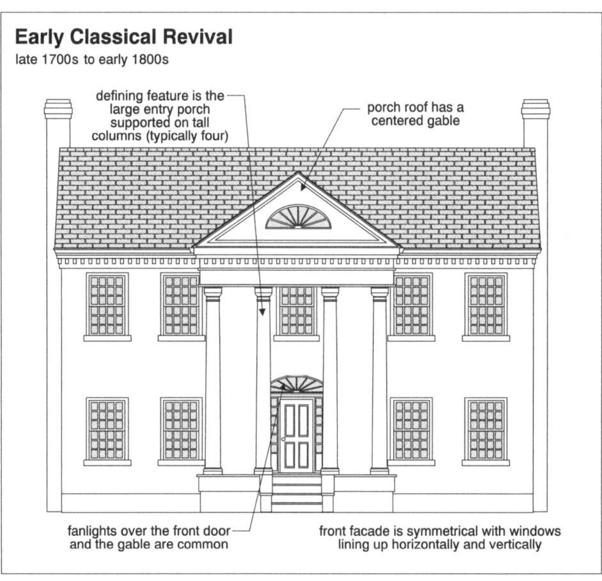

1723

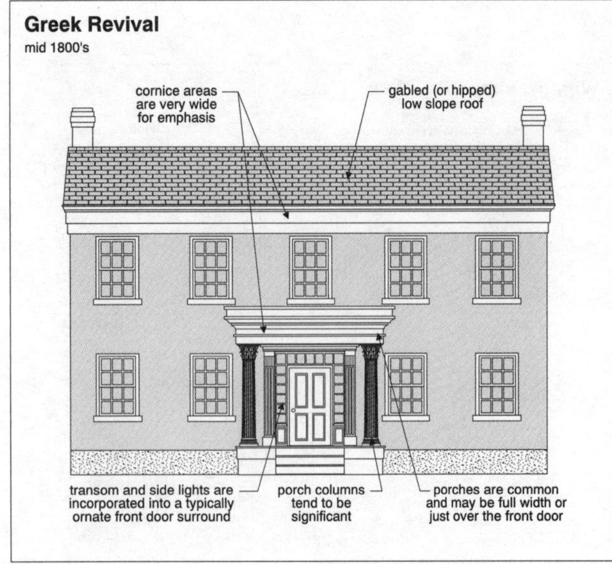

1724

Georgian

throughout the 1700's

windows are not grouped in pairs and are symmetrically placed about center door

cornice often decorated with dentils

pedimented window

paneled door typically capped with crown (entablature) and small horizontally placed panes of glass

double-hung windows (typically 9 to 12 panes per sash)

muntins are wide

1725

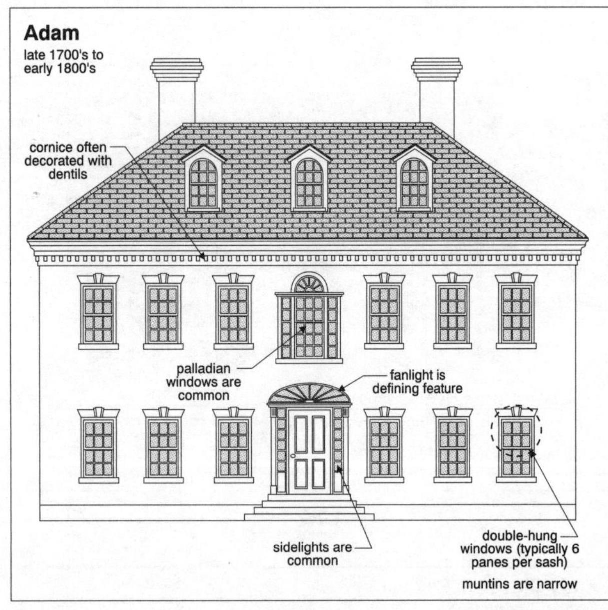

1726

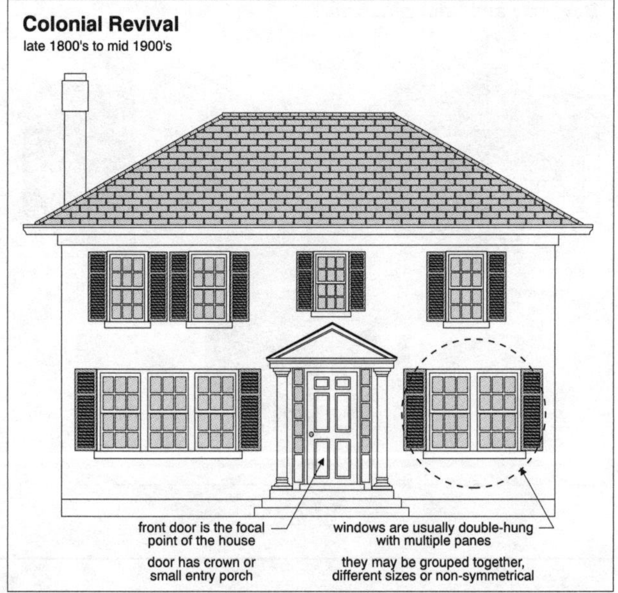

1727

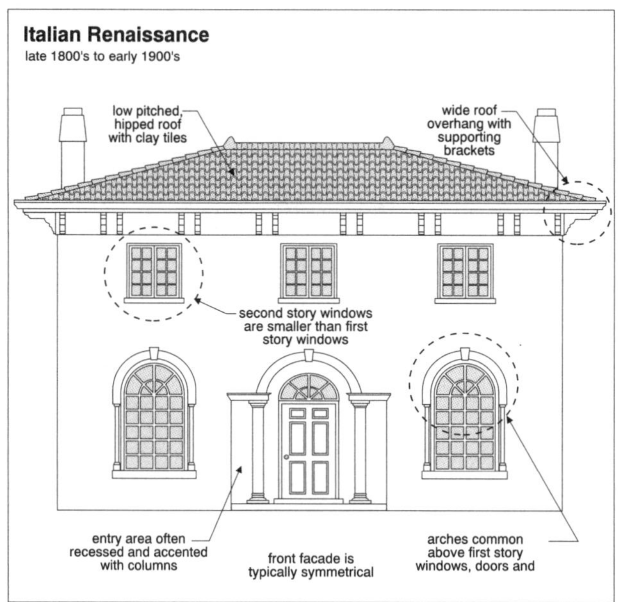

1728

Italianate

mid 1800's

typically low sloped, hipped roof

cupola or tower often present

wide overhang with decorative brackets

tall, narrow windows often have curved or rounded tops

belt course

window pairing is common

quoining

porch columns are slender and often used in groups of two or three

1729

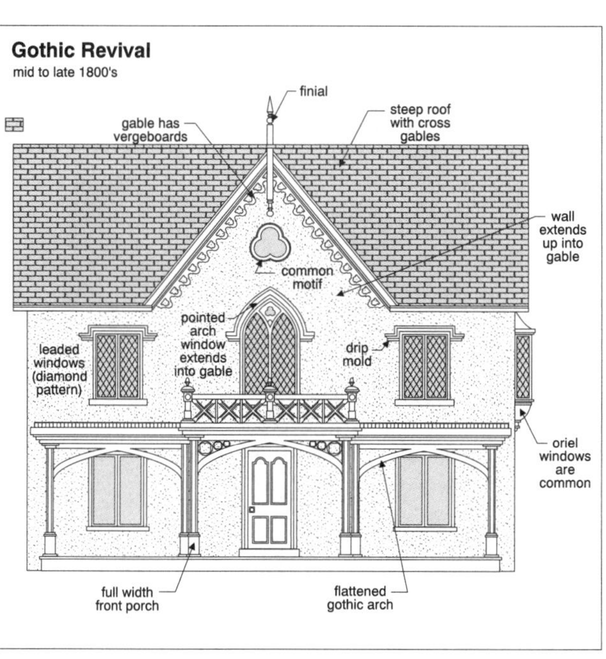

1730

Stick

latter half of the 1800's

decorative gable truss

steep gable roof (usually with cross gables)

multi-textured wall surfaces

raised horizontal and vertical boards

wooden siding

siding and trim in contrasting colors

diagonal porch-support braces

overhanging eaves with exposed rafter ends and braces

1731

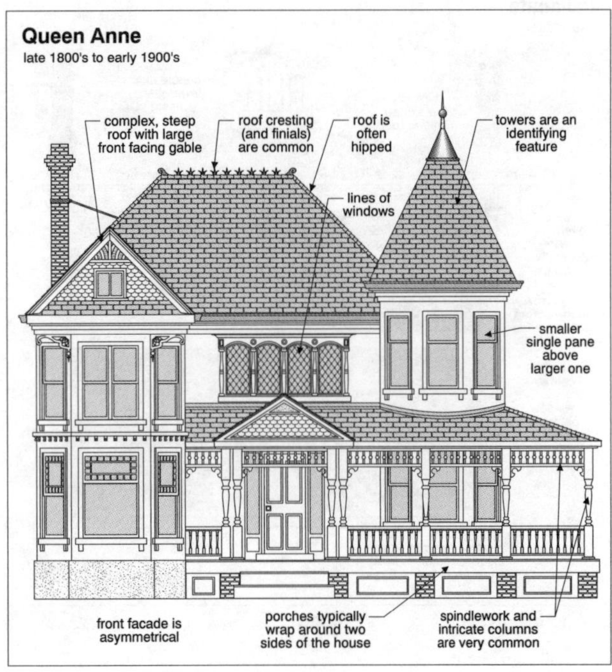

1732

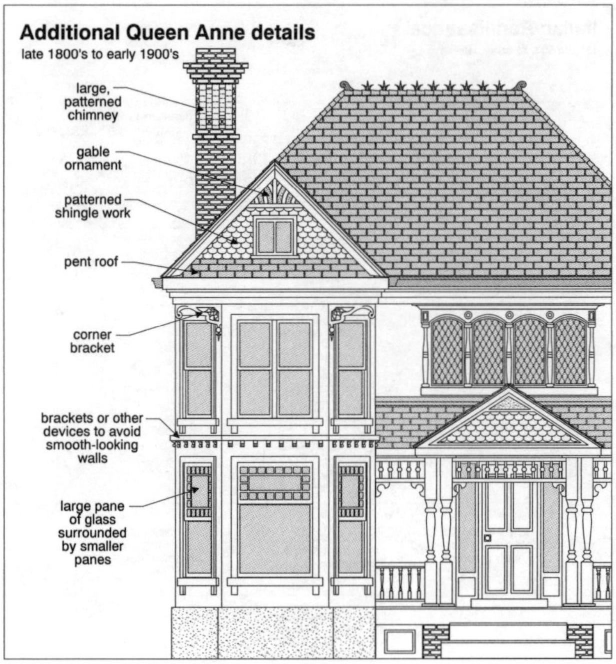

Additional Queen Anne details

late 1800's to early 1900's

large, patterned chimney

gable ornament

patterned shingle work

pent roof

corner bracket

brackets or other devices to avoid smooth-looking walls

large pane of glass surrounded by smaller panes

1733

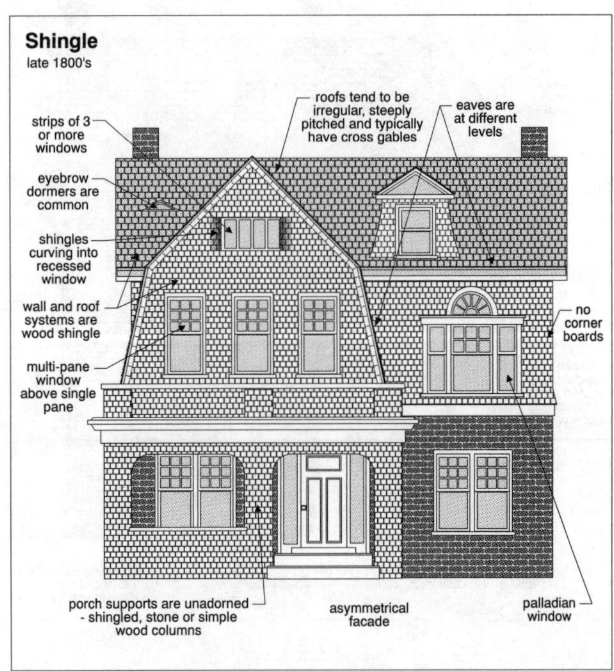

1734

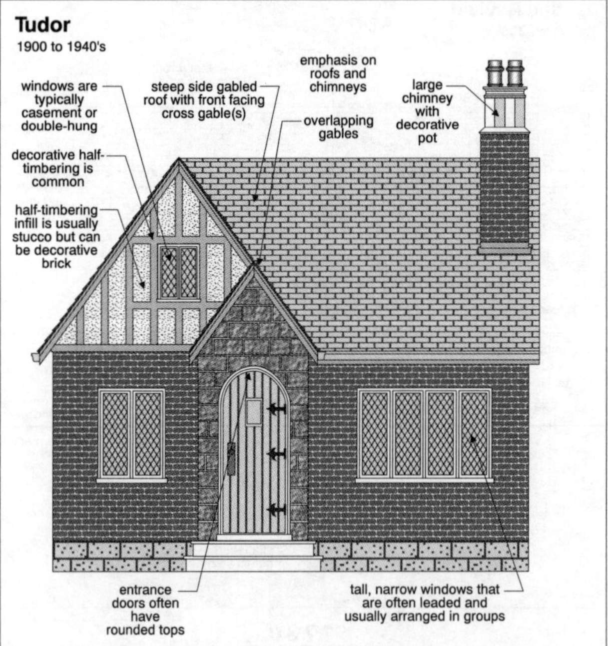

1735

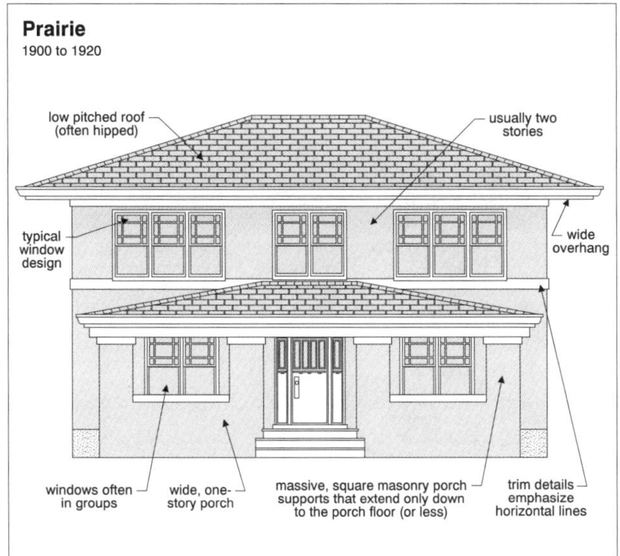

1736

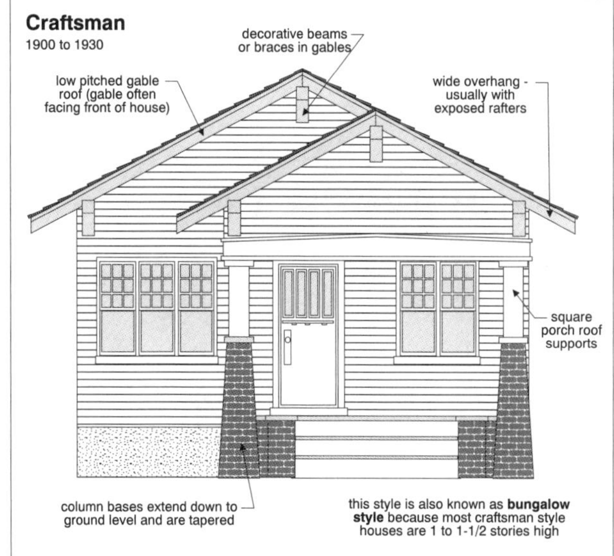

1737

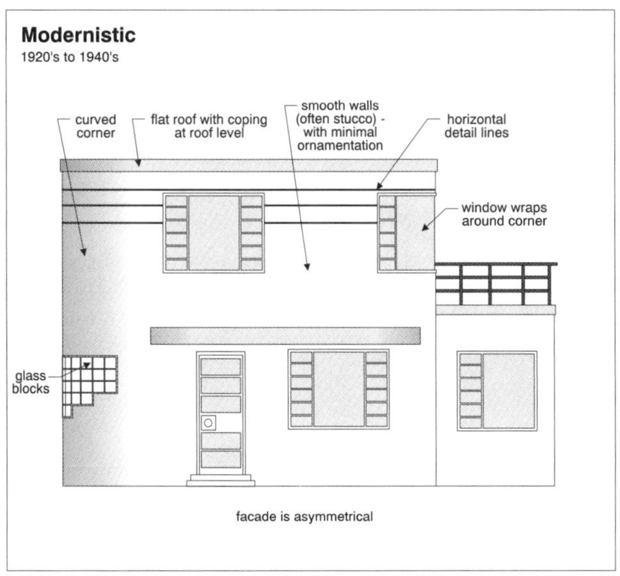

1738

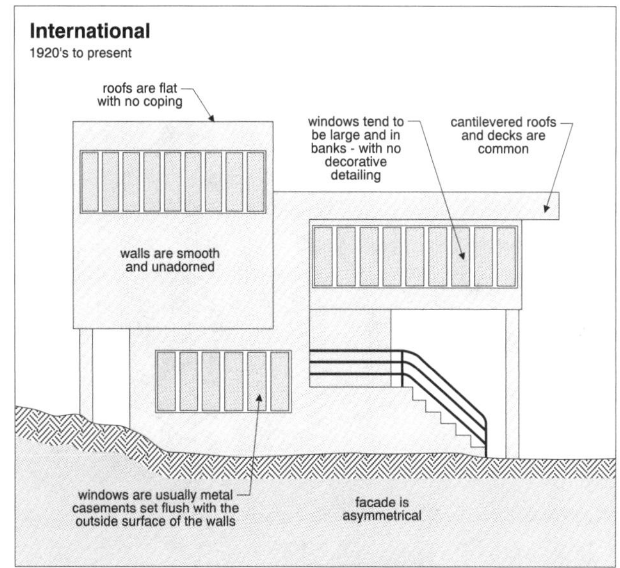

1739

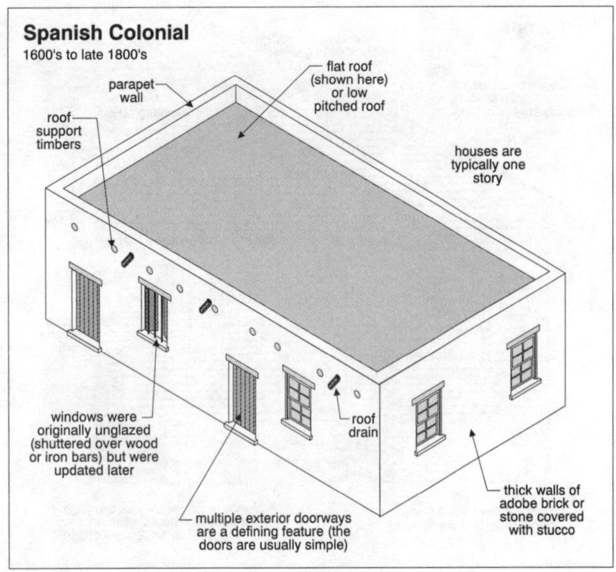

1740

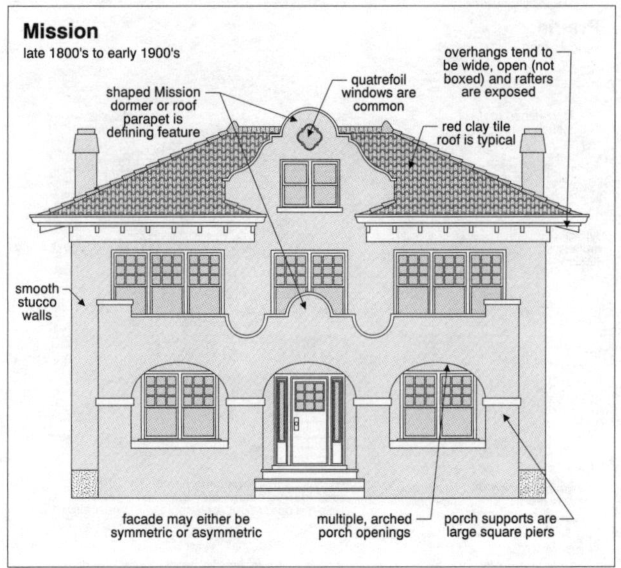

1741

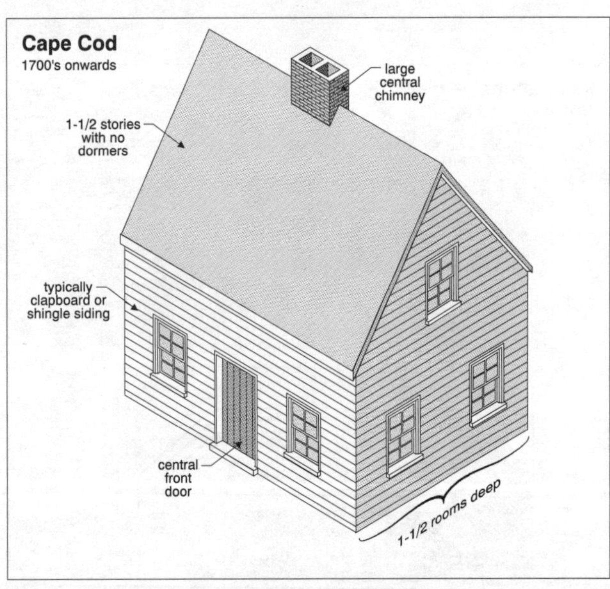

1742

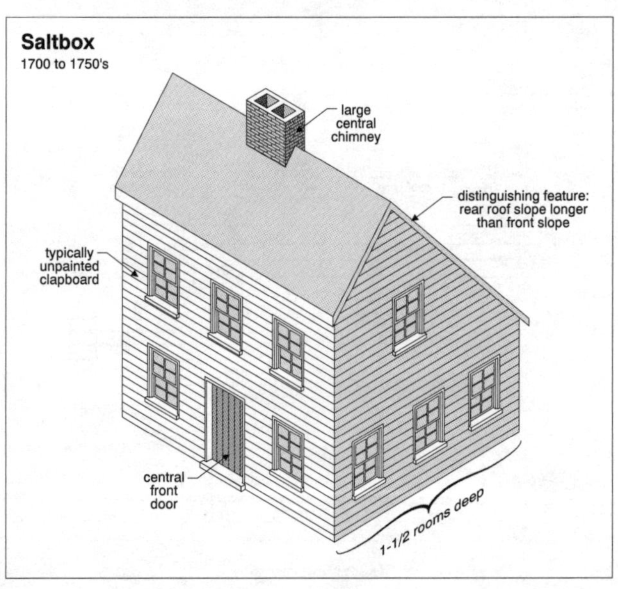

1743

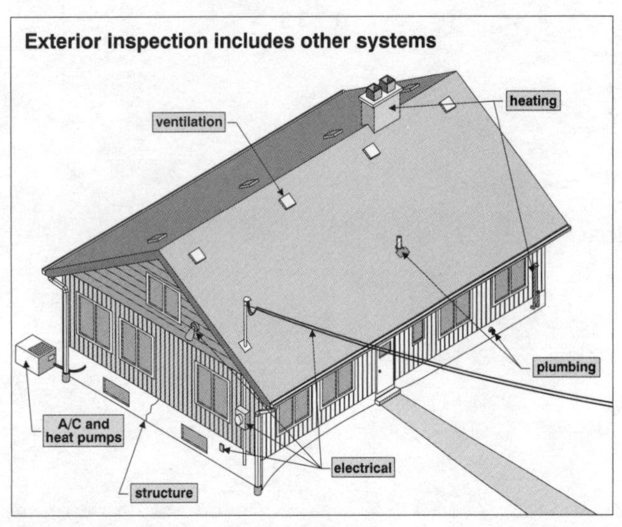

1744

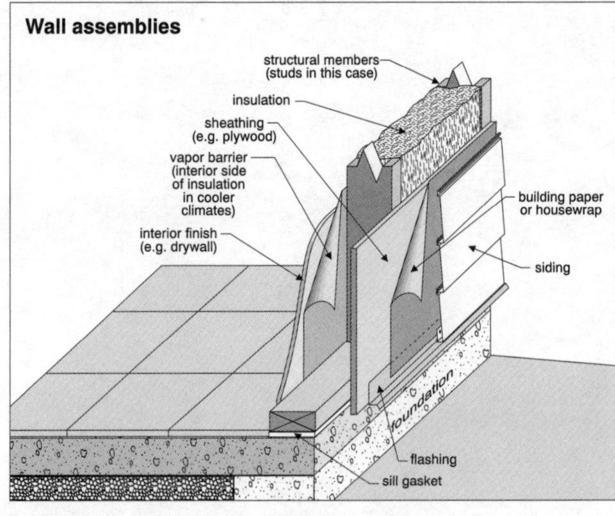

1745

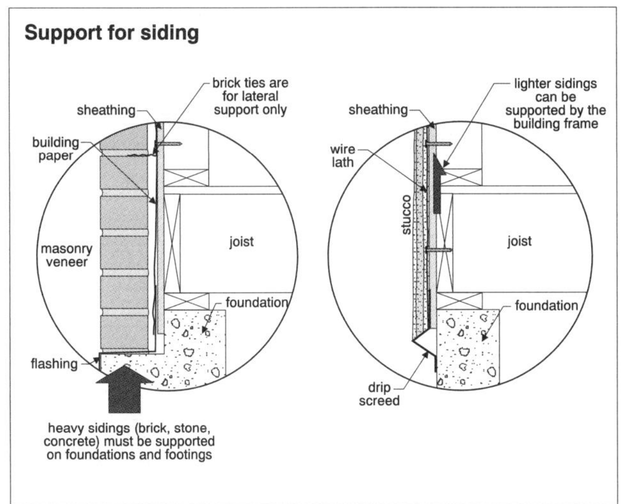

1746

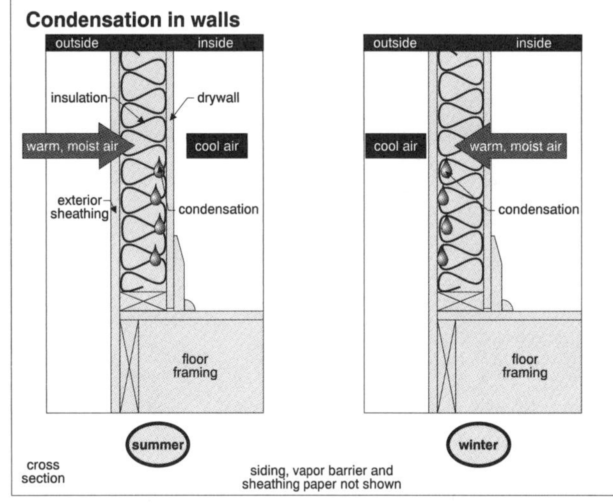

1747

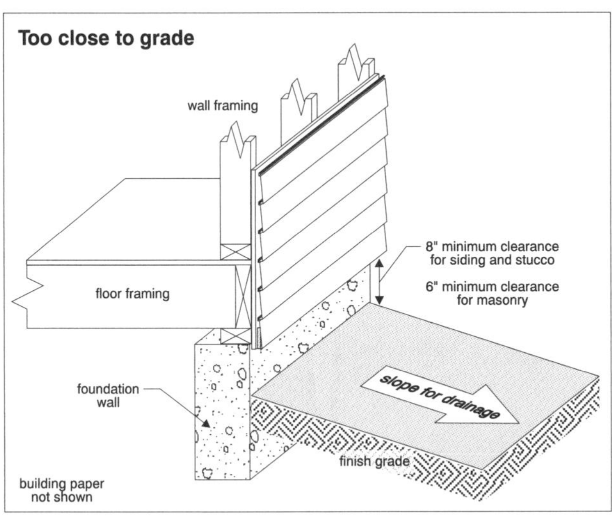

1748

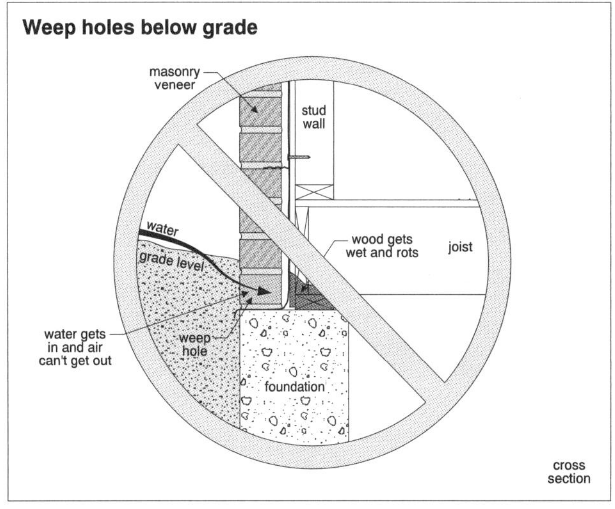

1749

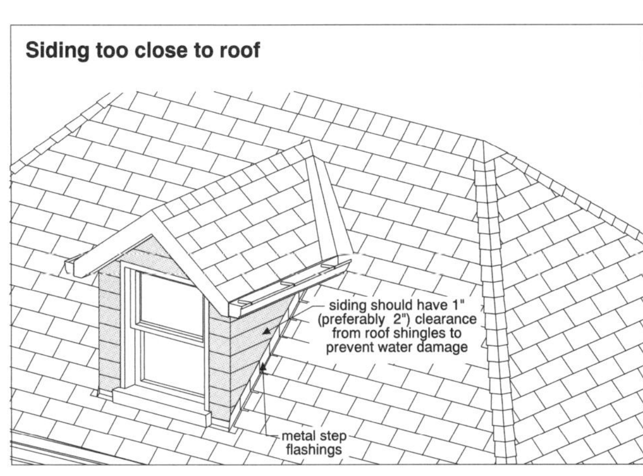

1750

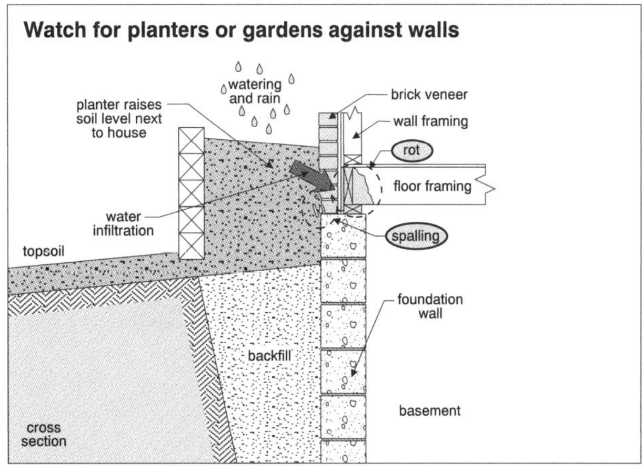

1751

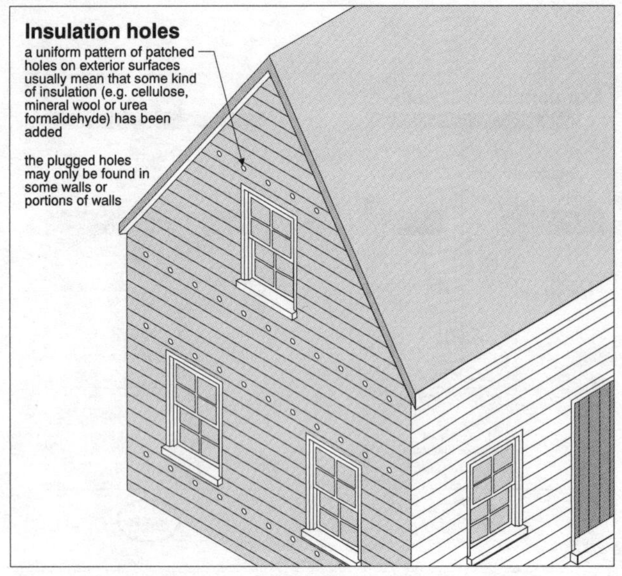

1752

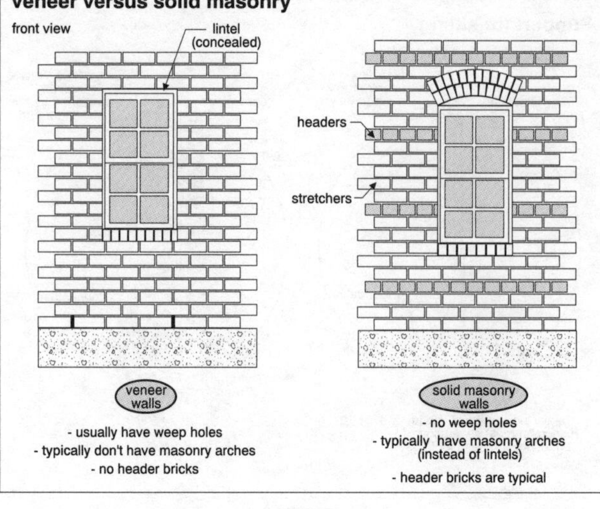

1753

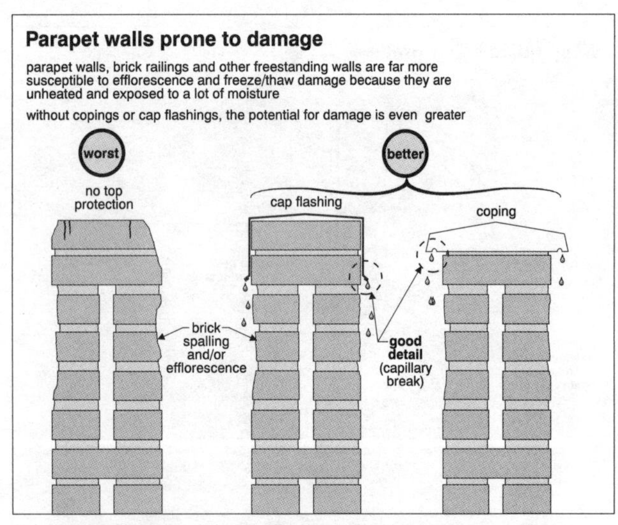

1754

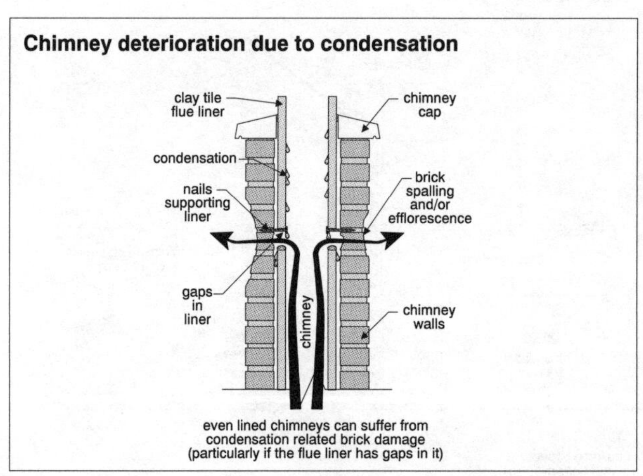

1755

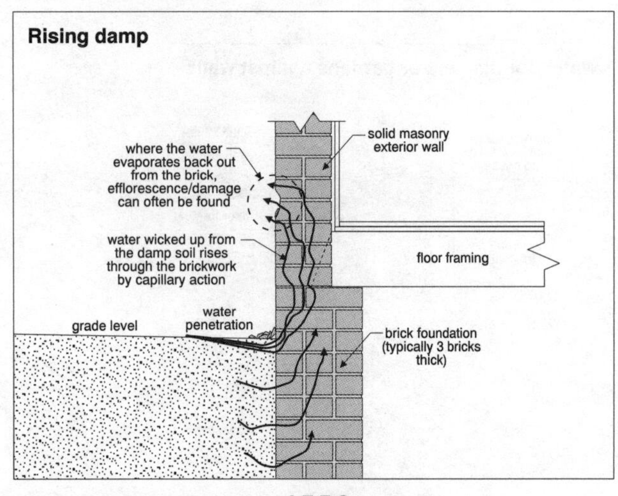

1756

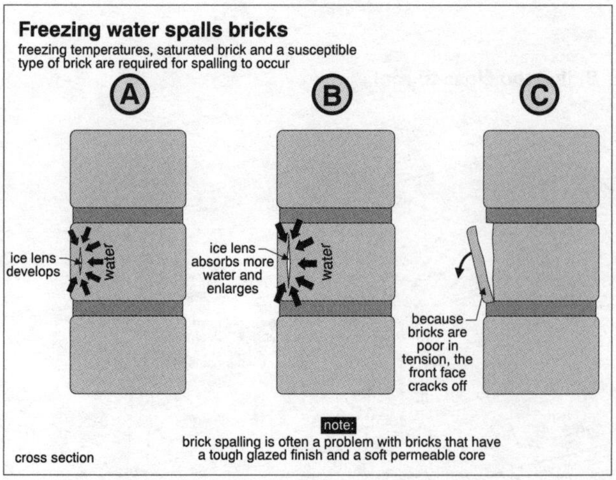

Freezing water spalls bricks

freezing temperatures, saturated brick and a susceptible type of brick are required for spalling to occur

A

ice lens develops

water

B

ice lens absorbs more water and enlarges

water

C

because bricks are poor in tension, the front face cracks off

note:

brick spalling is often a problem with bricks that have a tough glazed finish and a soft permeable core

cross section

1757

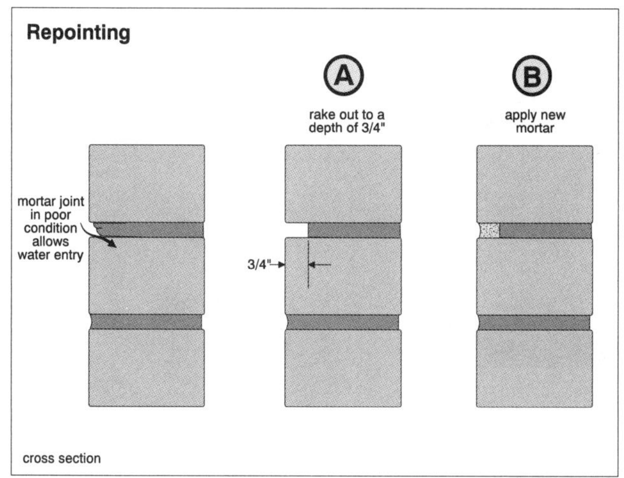

1758

Rusting lintels

the expansion of rusting steel lintels can cause horizontal cracks above windows

1759

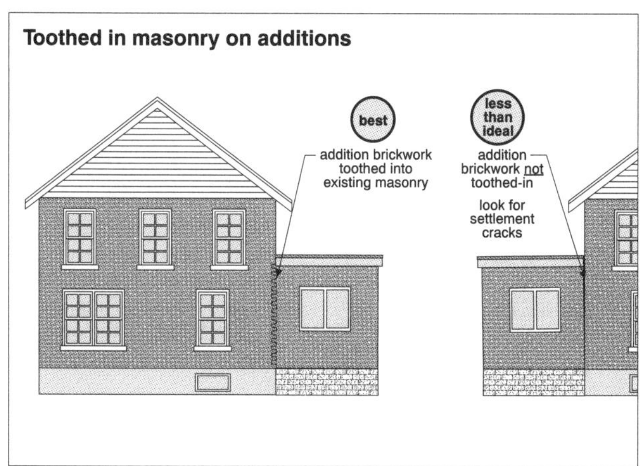

1760

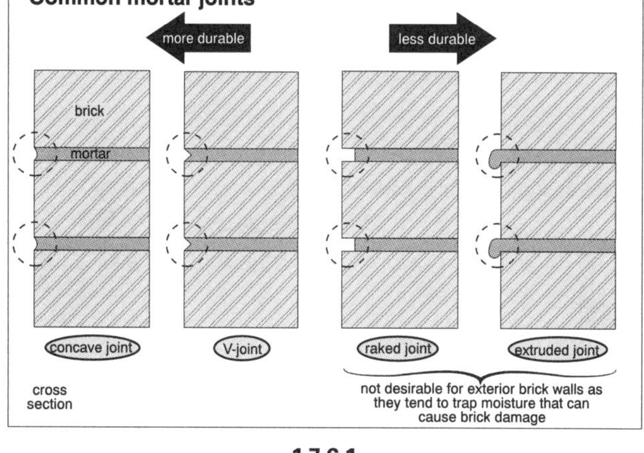

1761

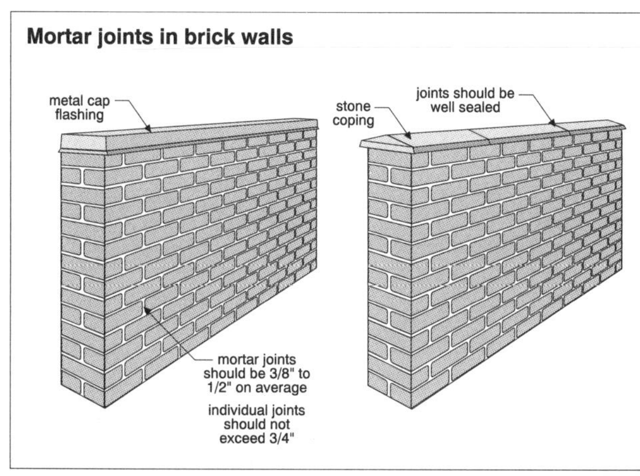

1762

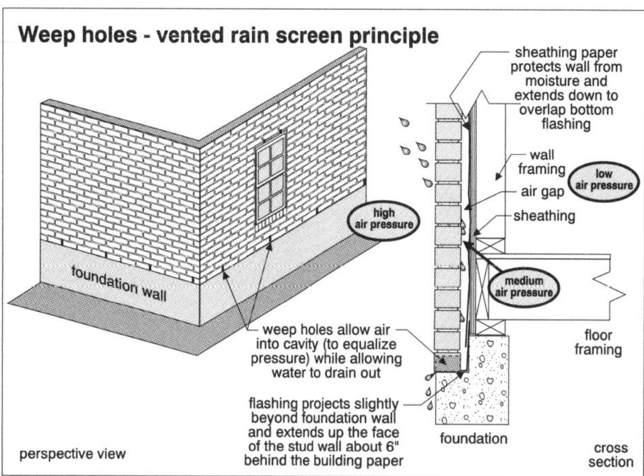

1763

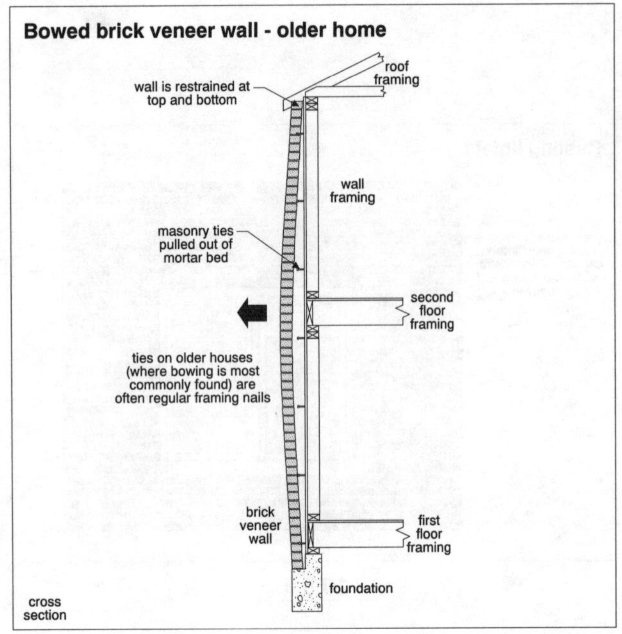

Bowed brick veneer wall - older home
roof framing
wall is restrained at top and bottom
wall framing
masonry ties pulled out of mortar bed
second floor framing
ties on older houses (where bowing is most commonly found) are often regular framing nails
brick veneer wall
first floor framing
foundation
cross section

1764

Brick veneer wall - masonry tie detail
wall framing
floor framing
sheathing
stud
sheathing paper
masonry veneer tie
1" gap (min.)
spacing of veneer ties
note:
veneer ties are nailed into studs

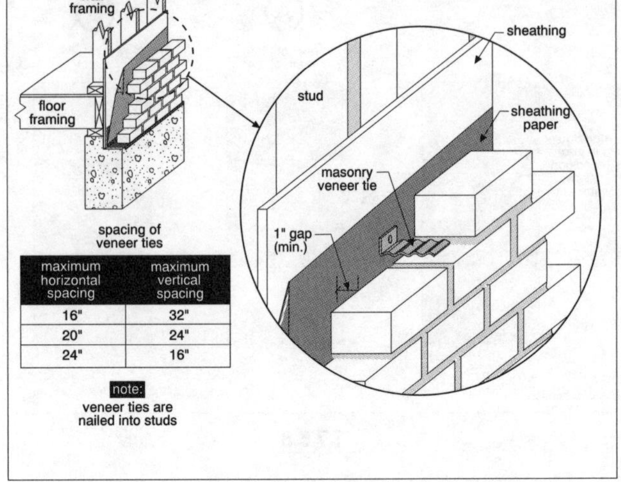

maximum horizontal spacing	maximum vertical spacing
16"	32"
20"	24"
24"	16"

1765

Lateral support for masonry walls
joists perpendicular to wall
joists parallel to wall
note:
strapping of the floor joists to the wall is usually only required at floor levels above the first floor
flooring
floor joist
12" to 18"
metal anchor strap (typically 1-1/2" wide by 3/16" thick) embedded in mortar
can be attached to bottom or side of joist
usually every 4th joist is strapped
floor joist
flooring
solid blocking between the joists is desirable at anchor locations
metal anchor strap (typically 1-1/2" wide by 3/16" thick) embedded in mortar
can be attached to bottom or top of joists
strap should extend across 3 or 4 joists
straps are usually installed at 4' to 8' intervals along the wall
cross-section

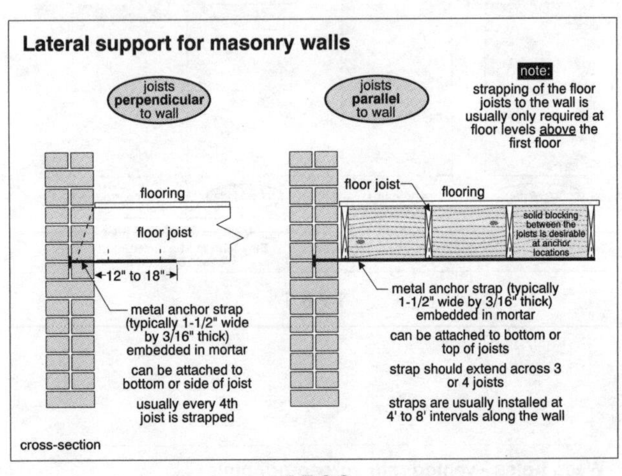

1766

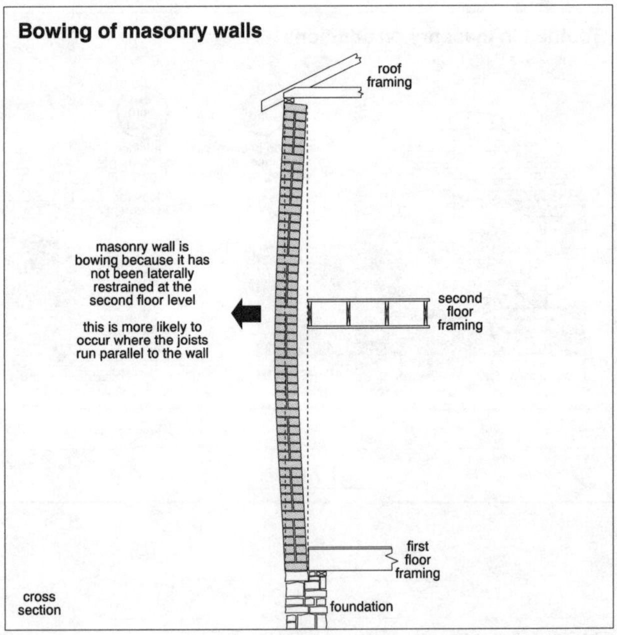

Bowing of masonry walls
roof framing
masonry wall is bowing because it has not been laterally restrained at the second floor level
this is more likely to occur where the joists run parallel to the wall
second floor framing
first floor framing
foundation
cross section

1767

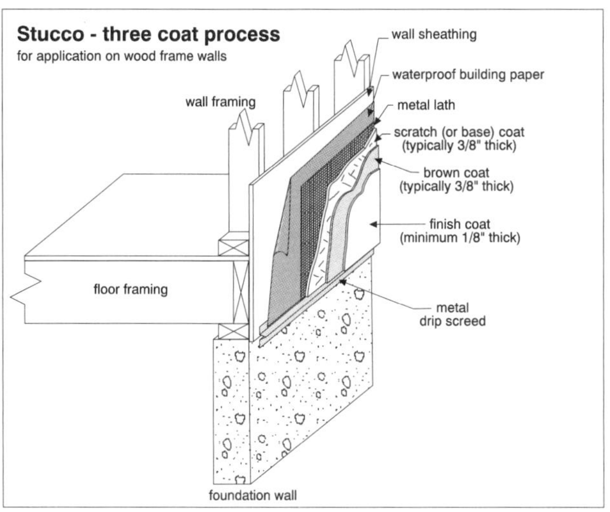

1768

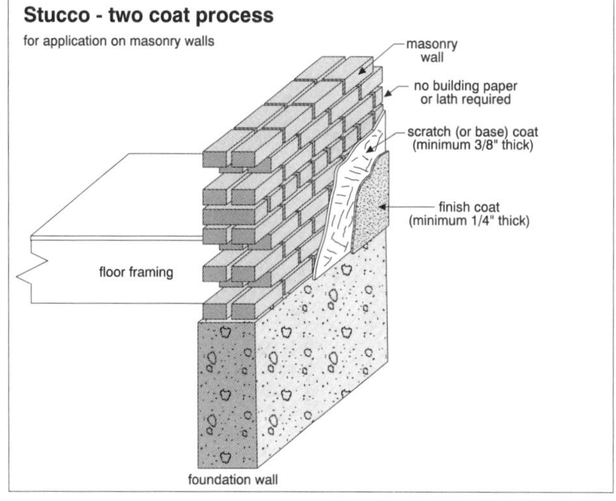

1769

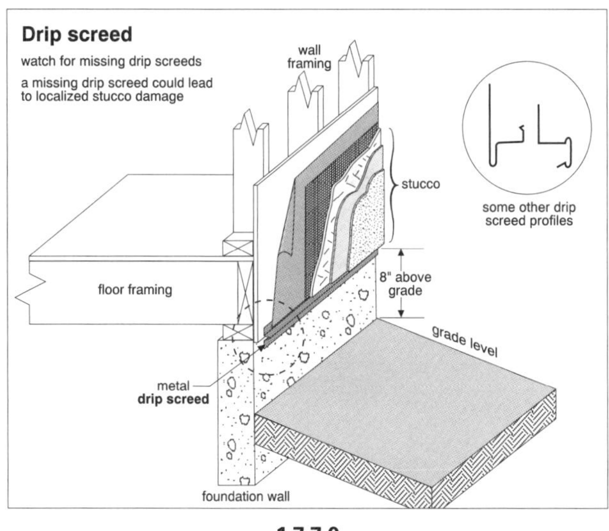

1770

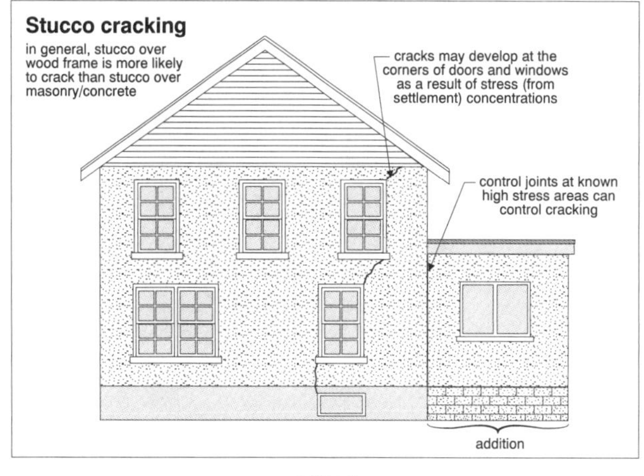

1771

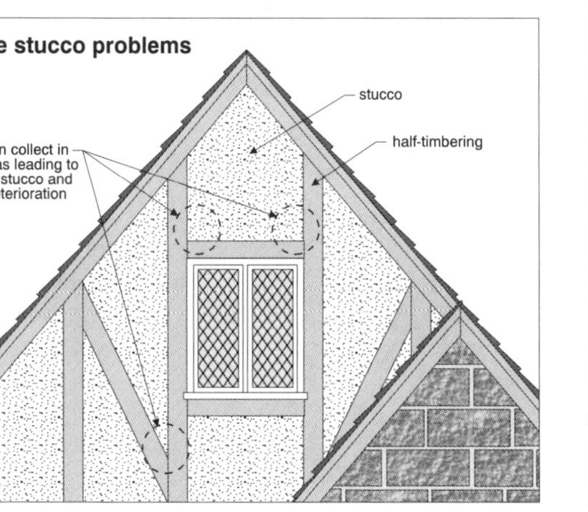

1772

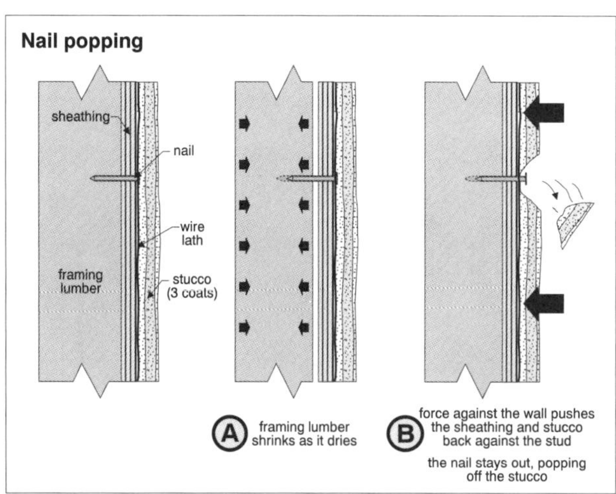

1773

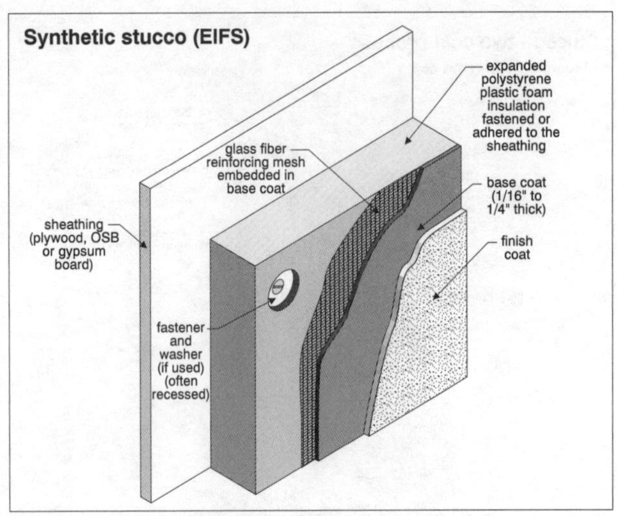

1774

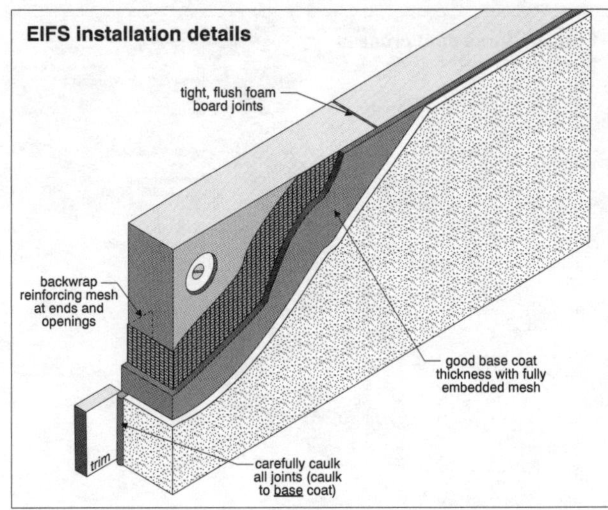

1775

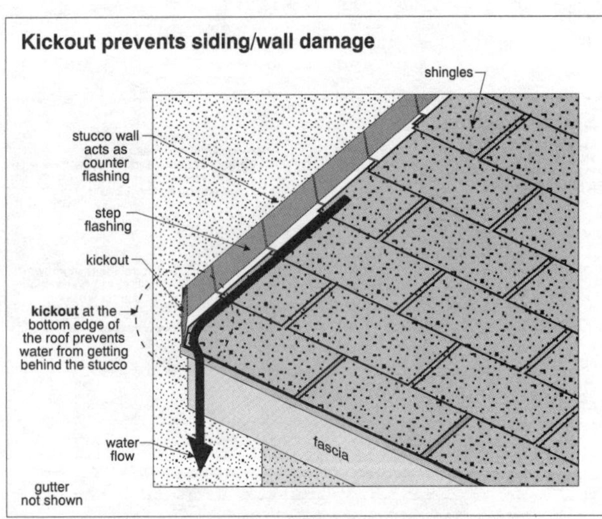

1776

EIFS - reinforcing mesh layout around window openings

cracking may occur if the mesh is not reinforced at the corners of openings

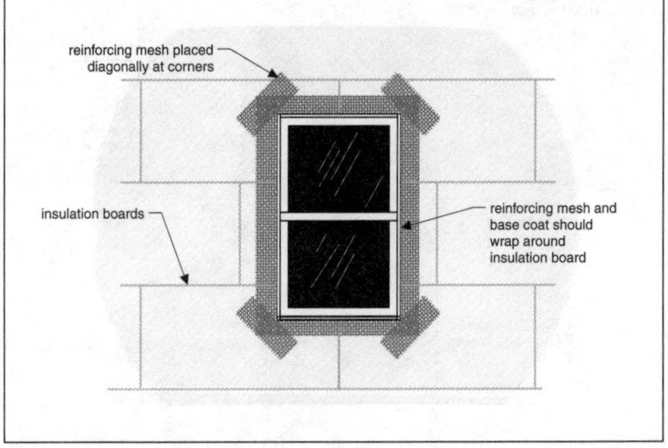

reinforcing mesh placed diagonally at corners

insulation boards

reinforcing mesh and base coat should wrap around insulation board

1777

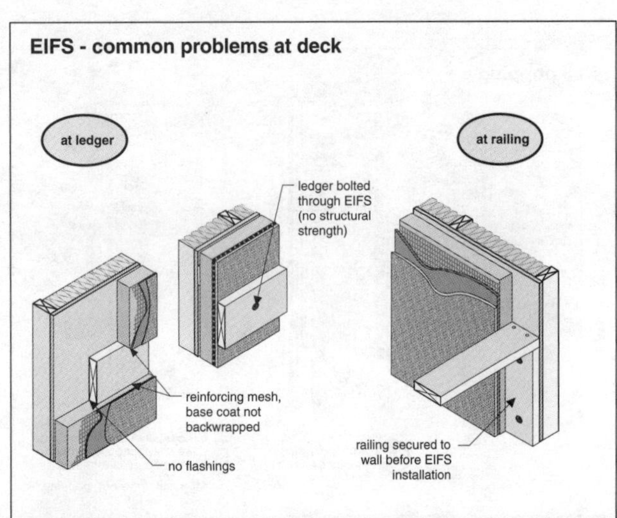

1778

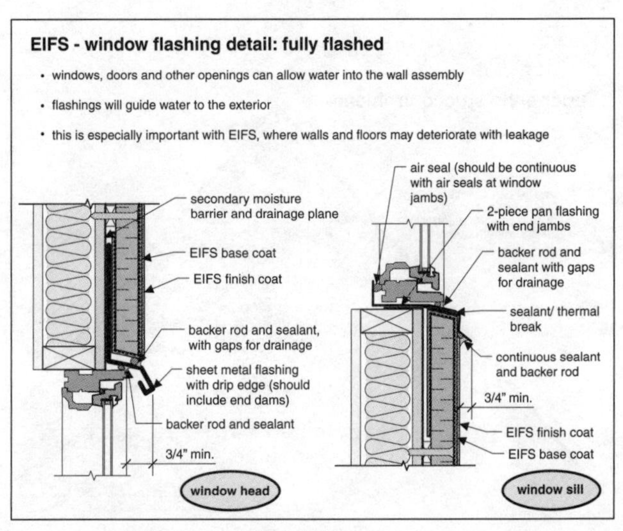

1779

EIFS - window flashing detail: simple

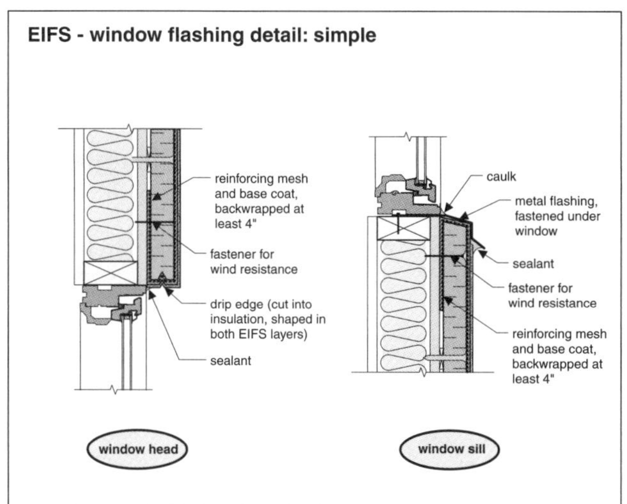

1780

EIFS - wire penetration

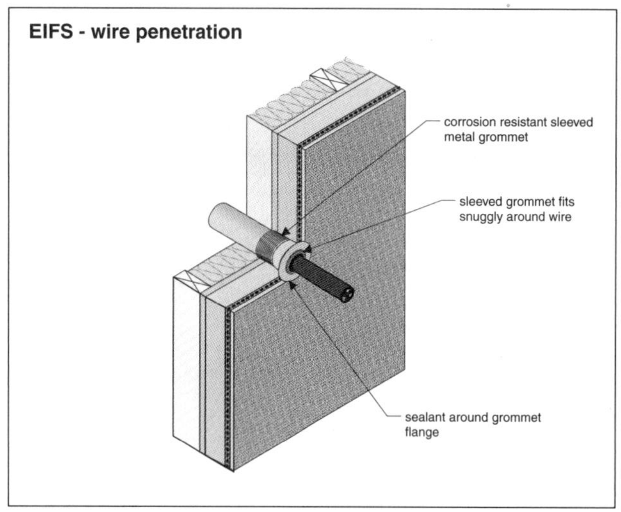

1781

EIFS - above grade termination

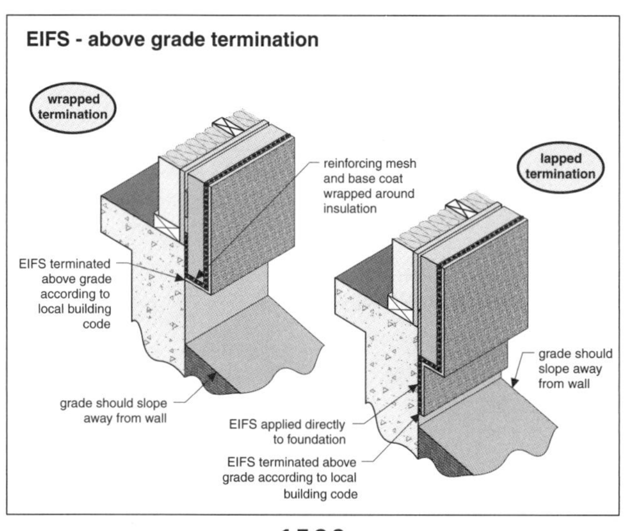

1782

EIFS - flashings around decks

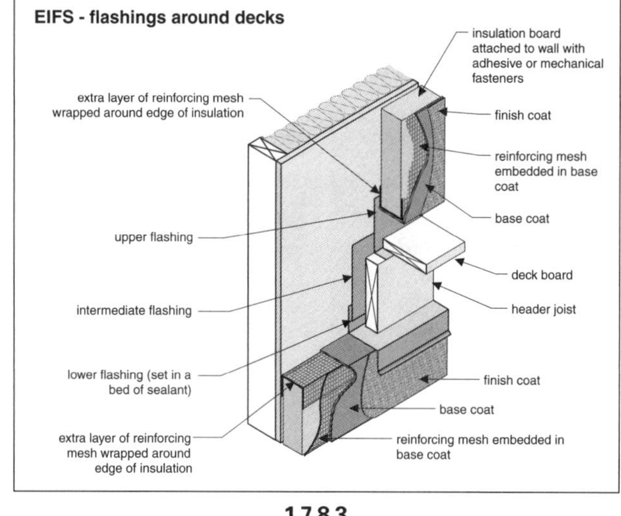

1783

EIFS - light fixture detailing

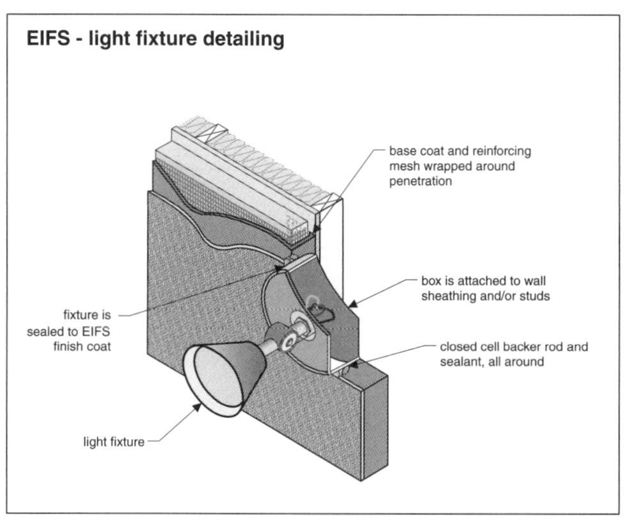

1784

EIFS - railing detail

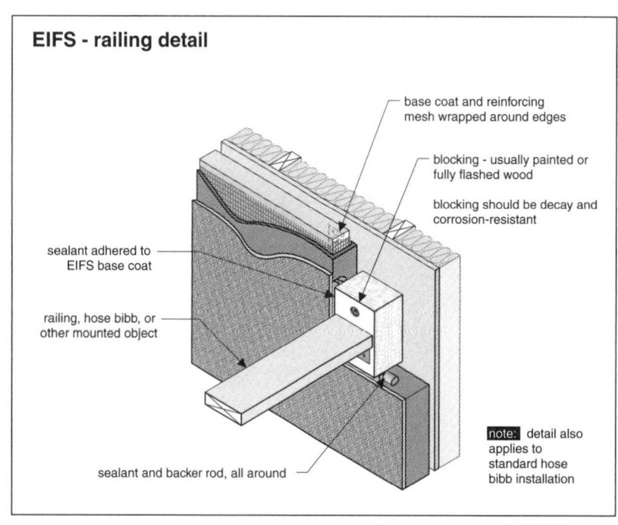

1785

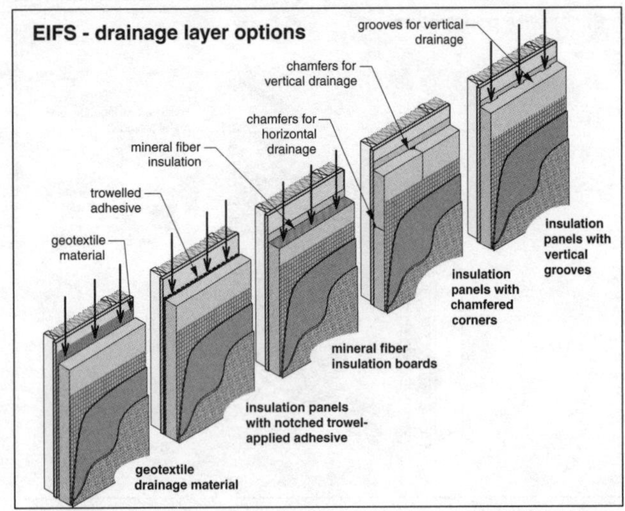

1786

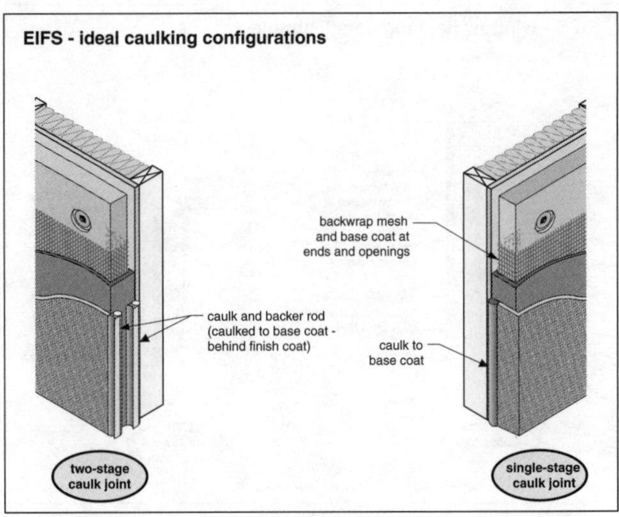

1787

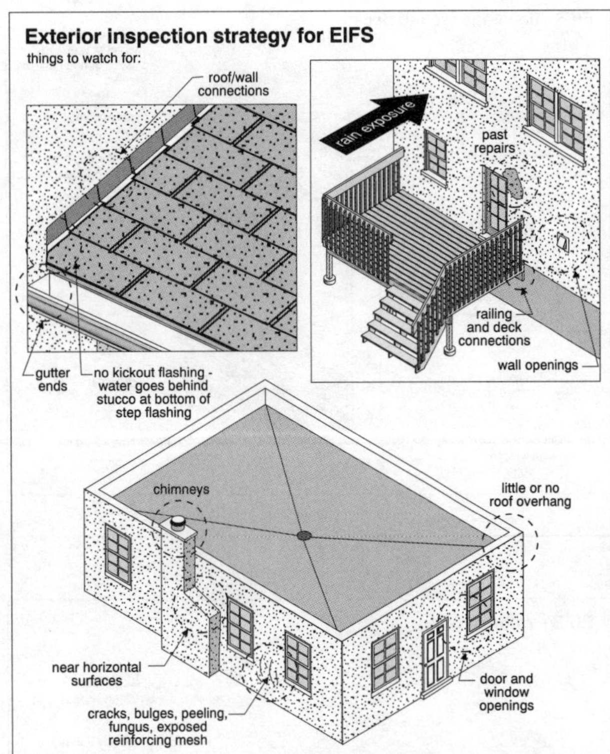

1788

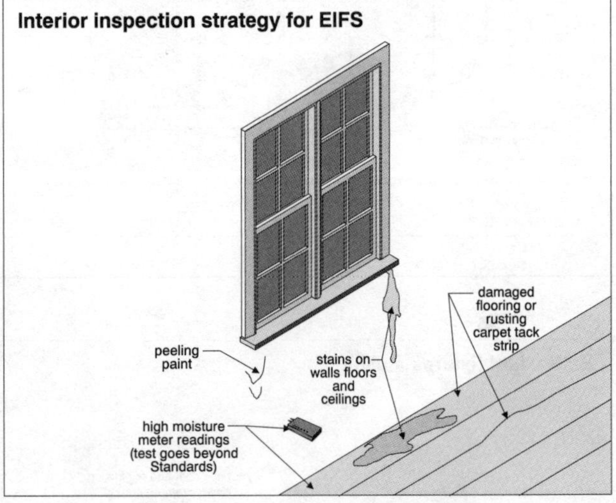

1789

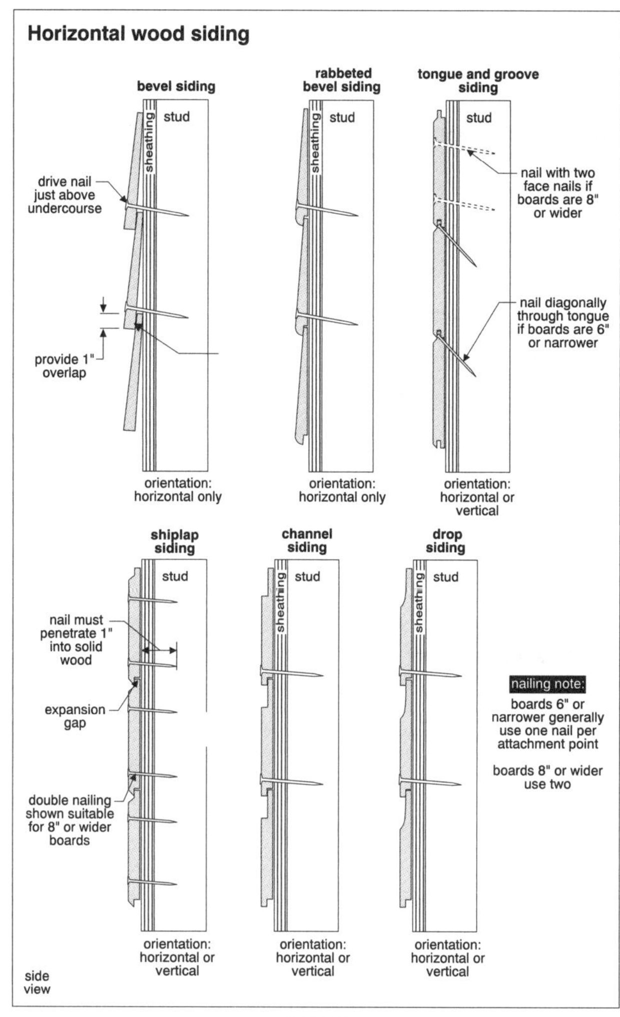

1790

Board-and-batten siding

board-and-batten siding is always installed vertically

as with horizontal siding, one nail is used per nailing point with boards 6" or narrower while 2 nails are used with boards 8" and wider

stud
1/2"
1-1/2"
1"
sheathing
batten
board
horizontal blocking
batten-on-board
board-on-board
board-on-batten
top view

1791

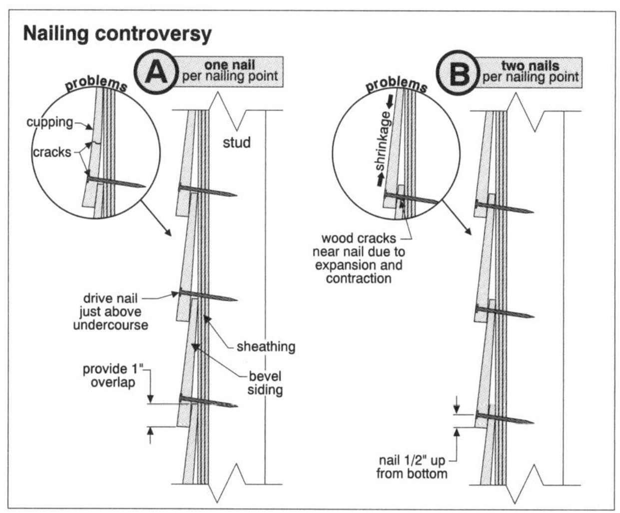

1792

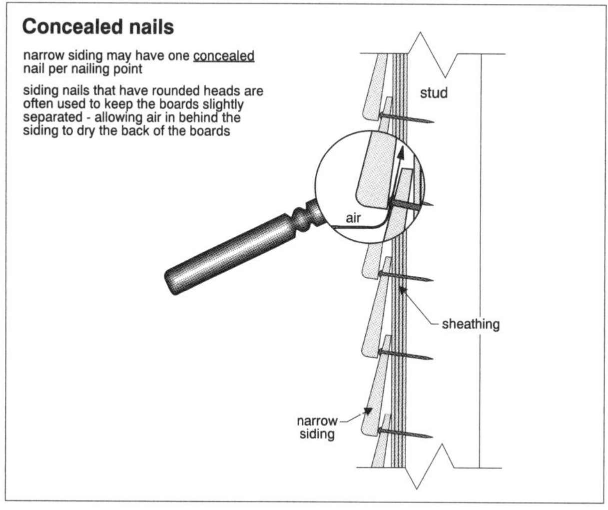

1793

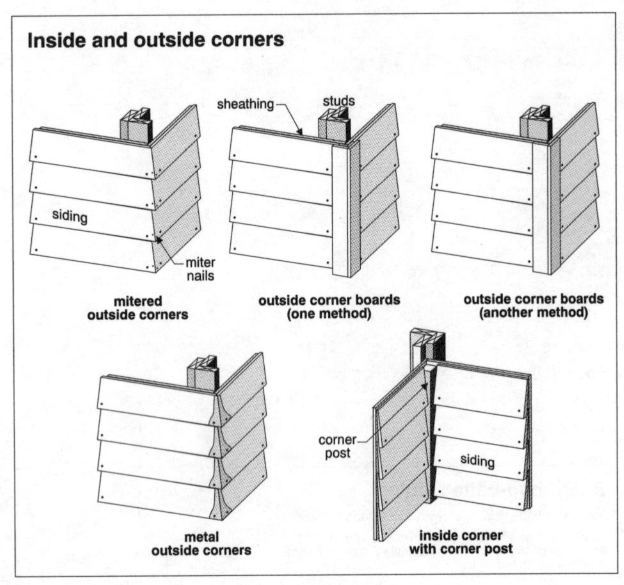

1794

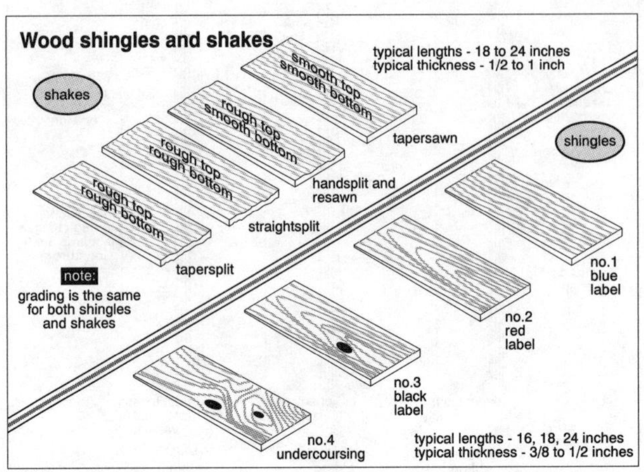

1795

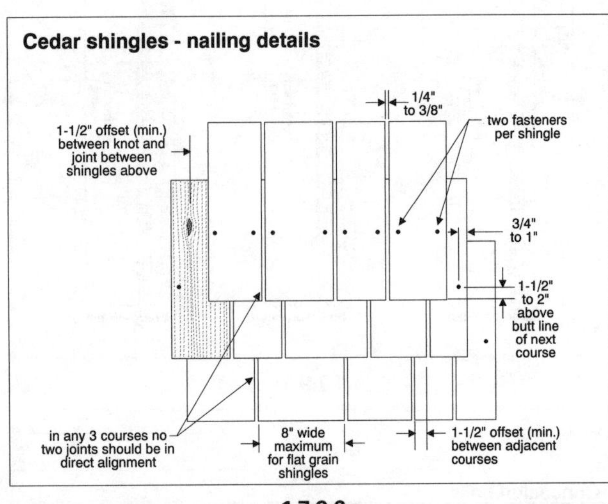

1796

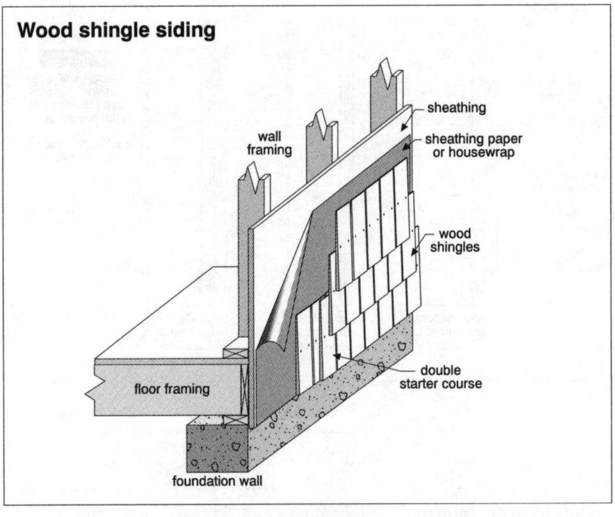

1797

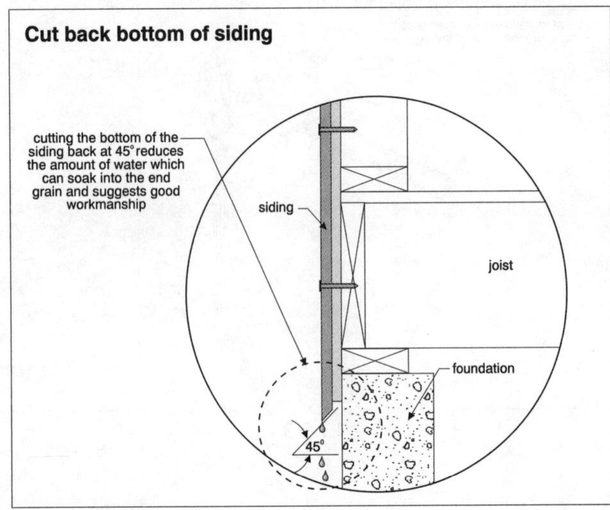

1798

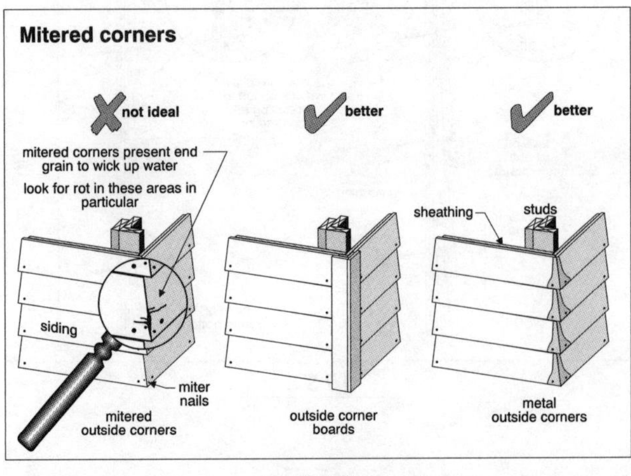

1799

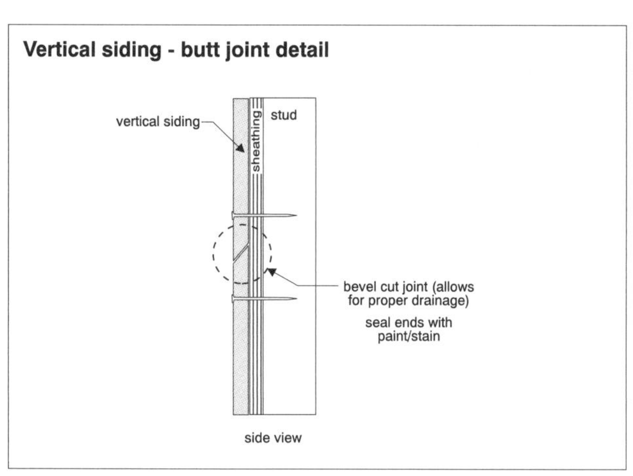

1800

Joints in siding boards

1801

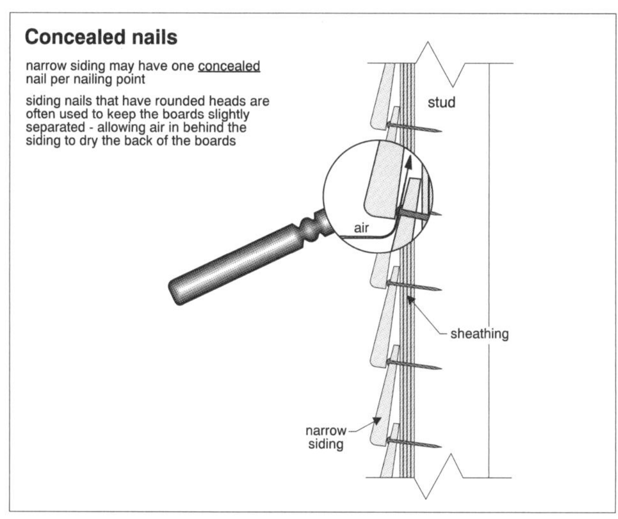

1802

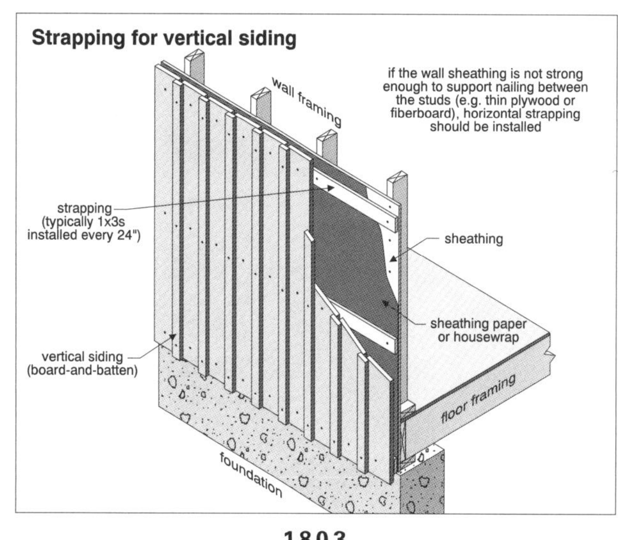

1803

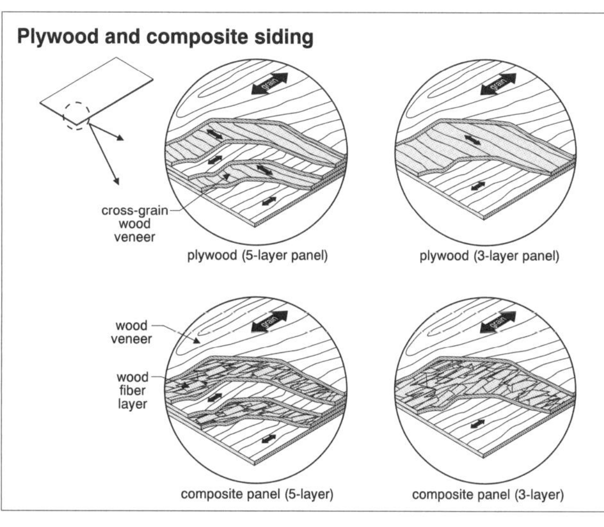

1804

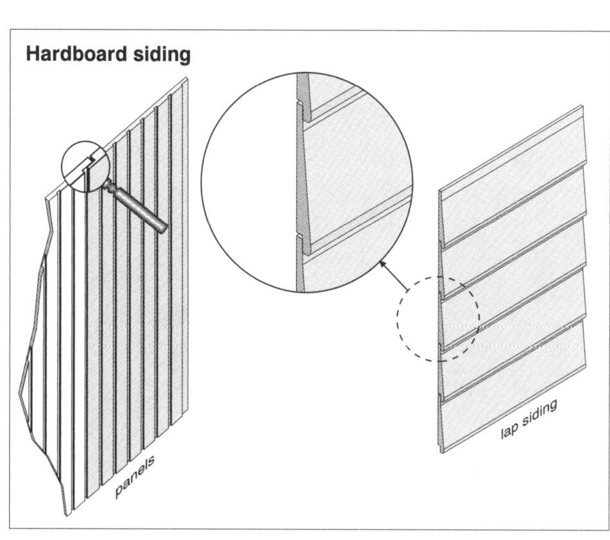

1805

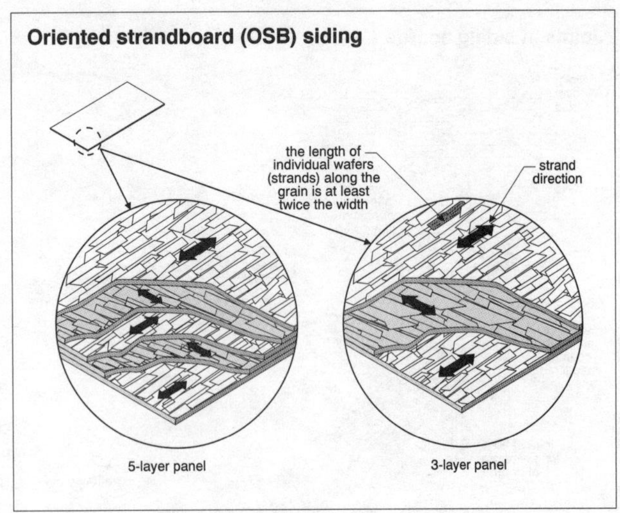

Oriented strandboard (OSB) siding
the length of individual wafers (strands) along the grain is at least twice the width
strand direction
5-layer panel
3-layer panel

1806

Vertical joints in panel siding
cover with batten
tongue-and-groove
caulking
OR
OR
sheathing
corner post
panel siding
outside corner molding
inside corner
outside corner

1807

Siding too close to roof
siding should have 1" (preferably 2") clearance from roof shingles to prevent water damage
metal step flashings

1808

Z flashings
panel siding
sheathing
horizontal joint
Z flashing
panel siding
sheathing paper or housewrap omitted for clarity

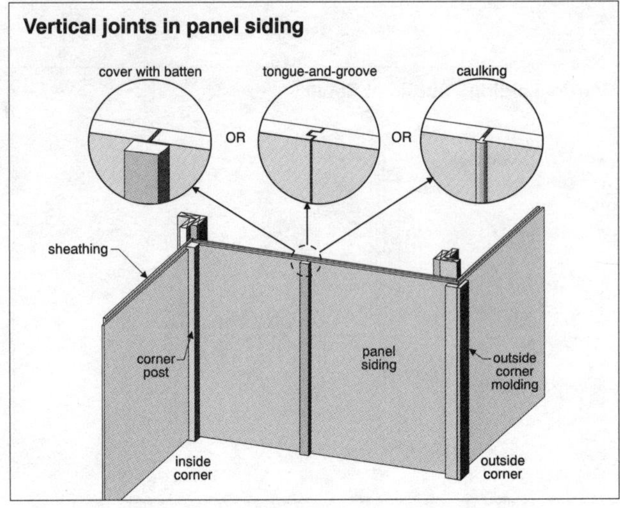

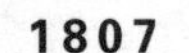

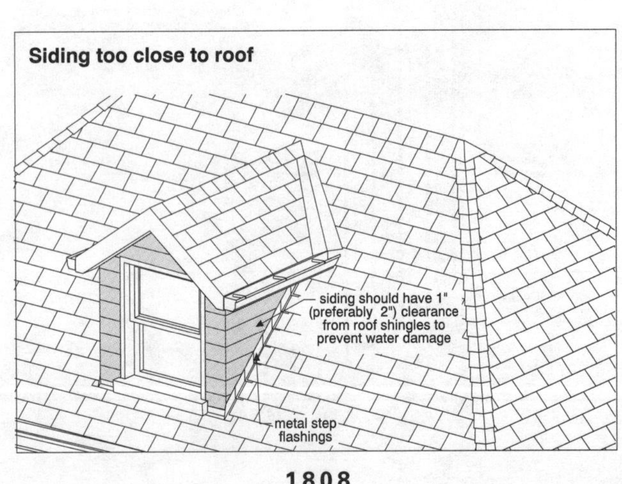

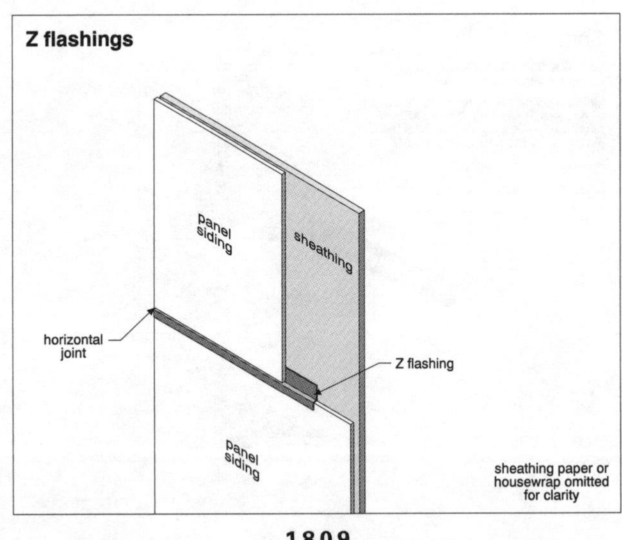

1809

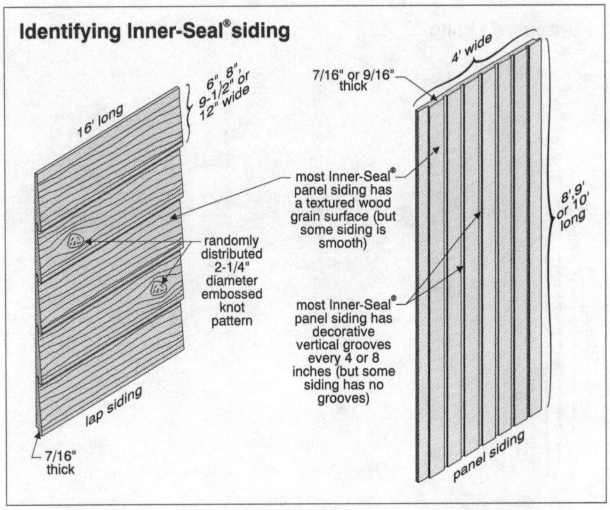

Identifying Inner-Seal® siding
6", 8", 9-1/2" or 12" wide
16' long
7/16" or 9/16" thick
4' wide
most Inner-Seal® panel siding has a textured wood grain surface (but some siding is smooth)
8', 9' or 10' long
randomly distributed 2-1/4" diameter embossed knot pattern
most Inner-Seal® panel siding has decorative vertical grooves every 4 or 8 inches (but some siding has no grooves)
lap siding
7/16" thick
panel siding

1810

Metal and vinyl siding
steel siding can look like aluminum siding and have a prepainted finish
it may even have a vinyl coating
older steel siding often had patterns such as brick or stone pressed into it
steel siding
aluminum siding can come in the form of boards, sheets, panels or shingles
the prepainted finish can be scratched to reveal the relatively soft aluminum underneath
the color in vinyl siding goes right through the material so scratching it won't reveal a different color beneath
aluminum siding
vinyl siding

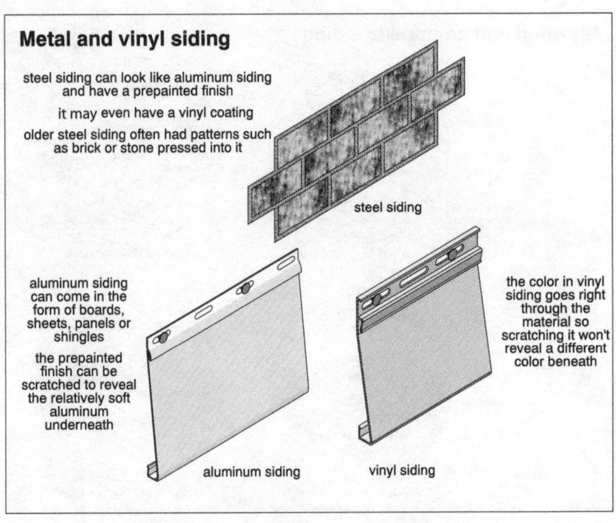

1811

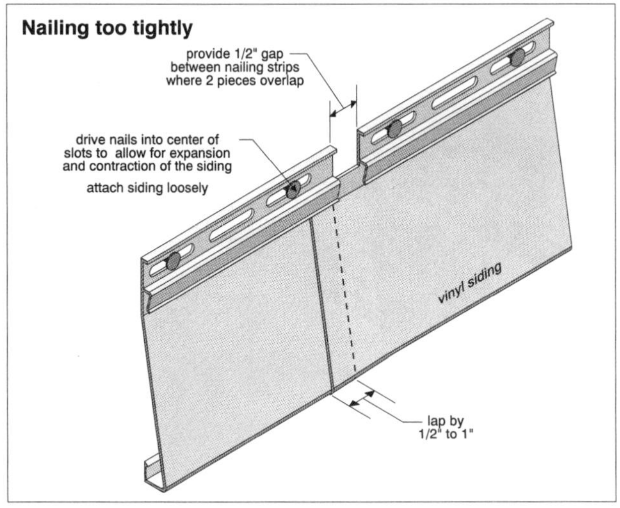

1812

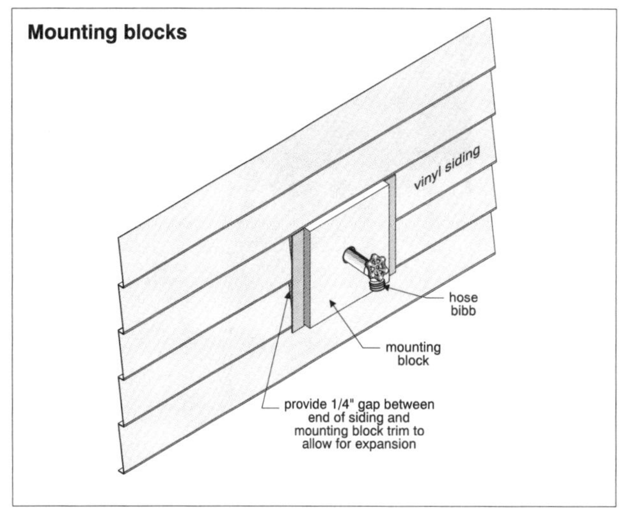

1813

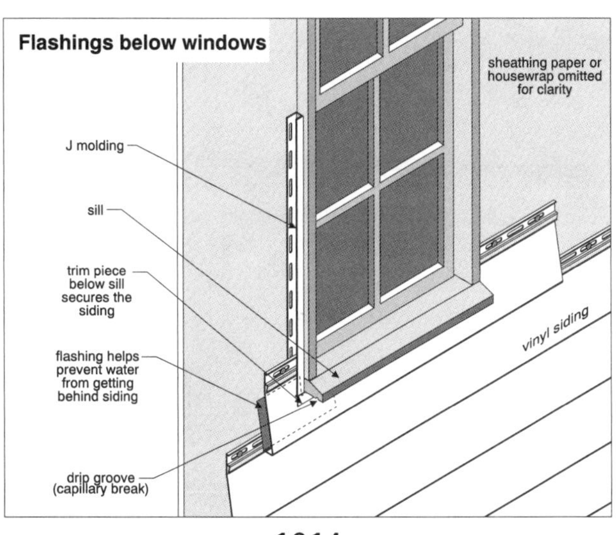

1814

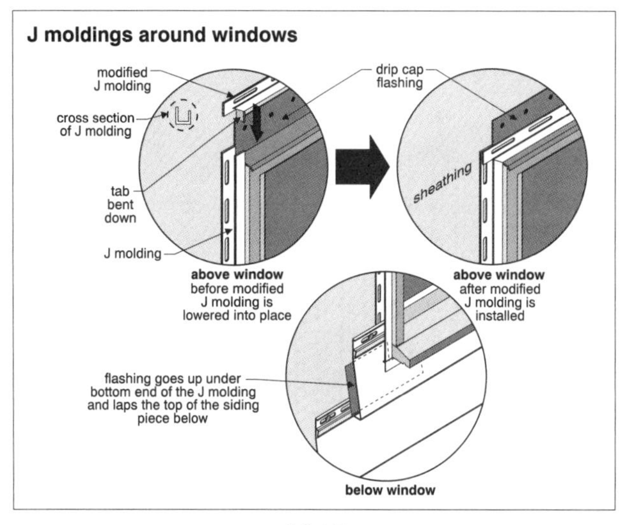

1815

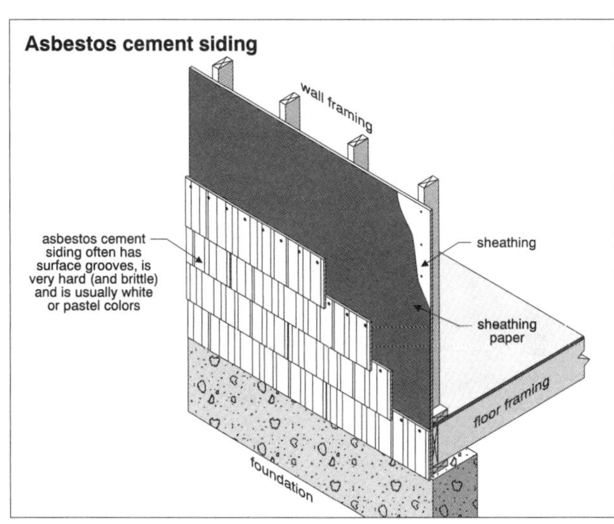

1816

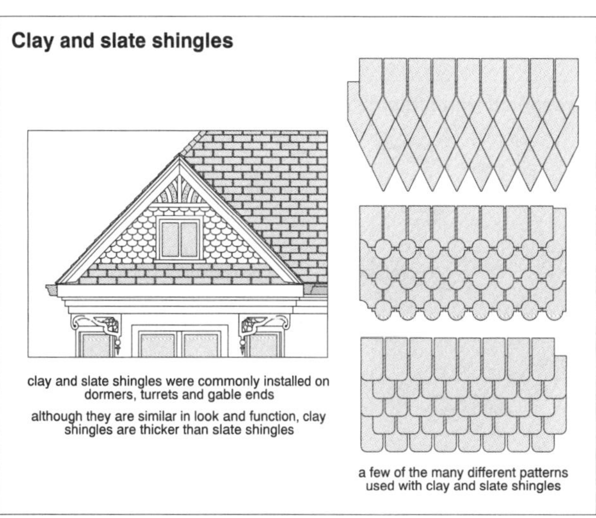

1817

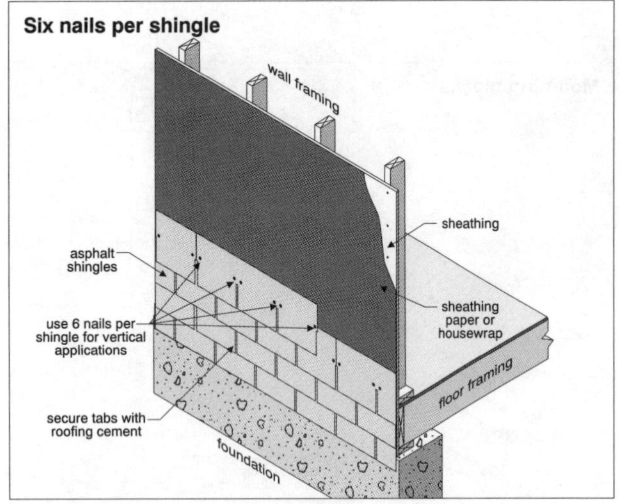

1818

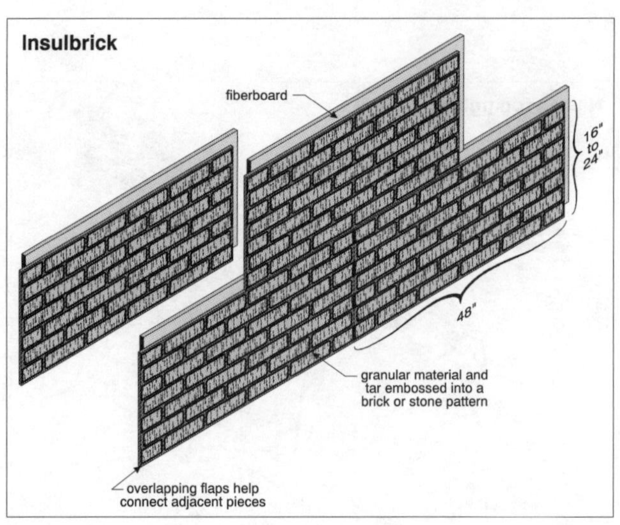

1819

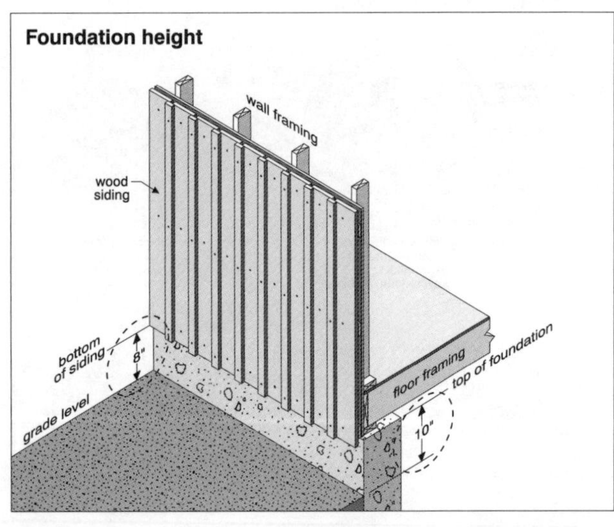

1820

1821

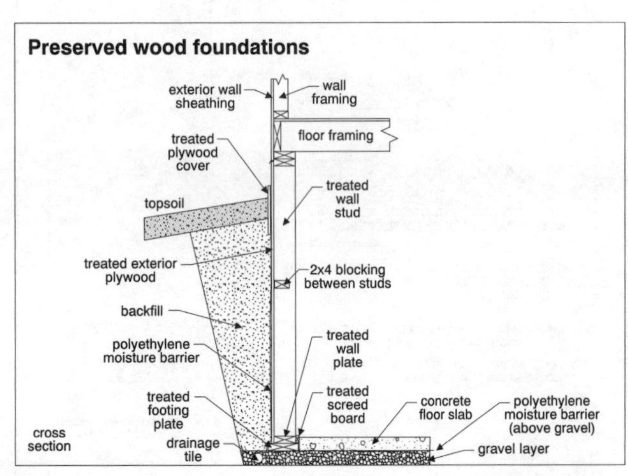

1822

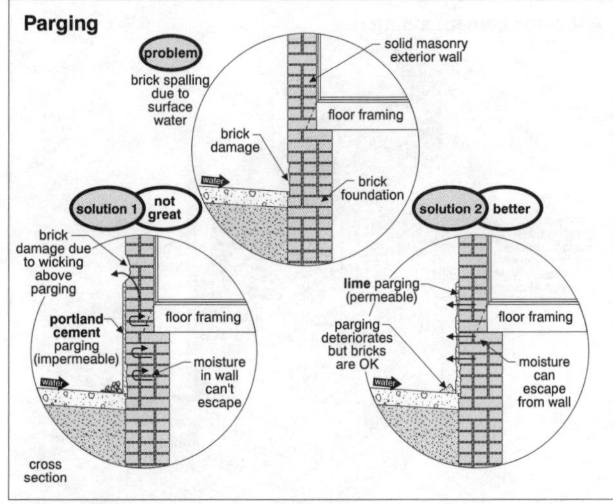

1823

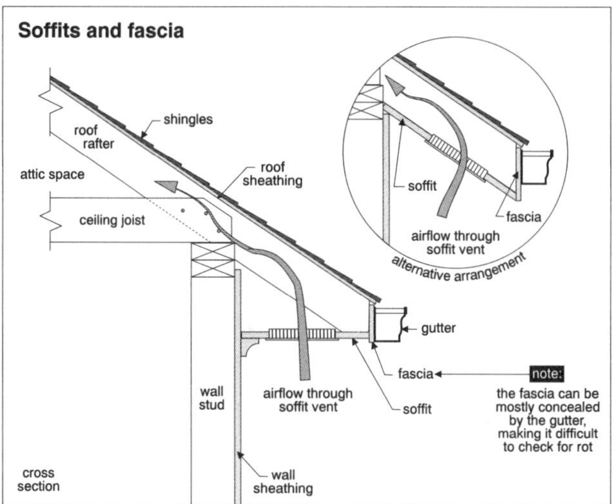

1824

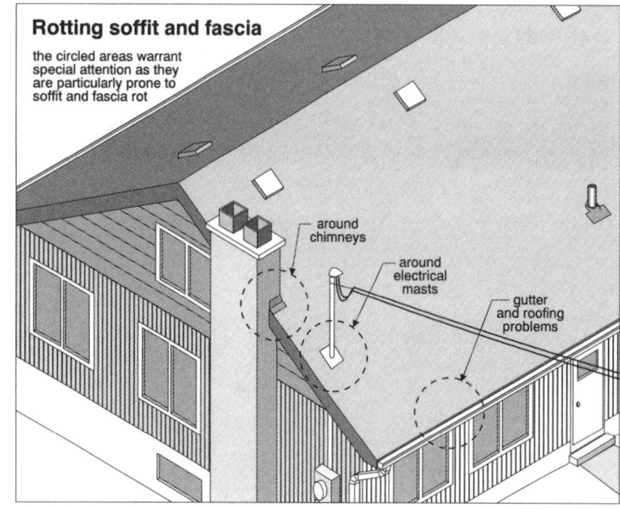

1825

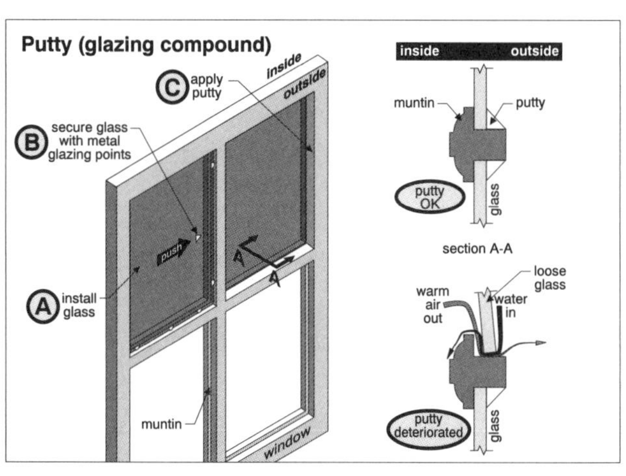

1826

Capillary break

water flow
sill
no groove in sill underside allows water penetration and brick damage below window sill
window
poor
water flow
properly grooved sill
sill
capillary break
water flow
sill
best
wall framing
brick veneer
sheathing paper
sheathing
caulking added at underside of sill to break surface tension and redirect water flow
better

1827

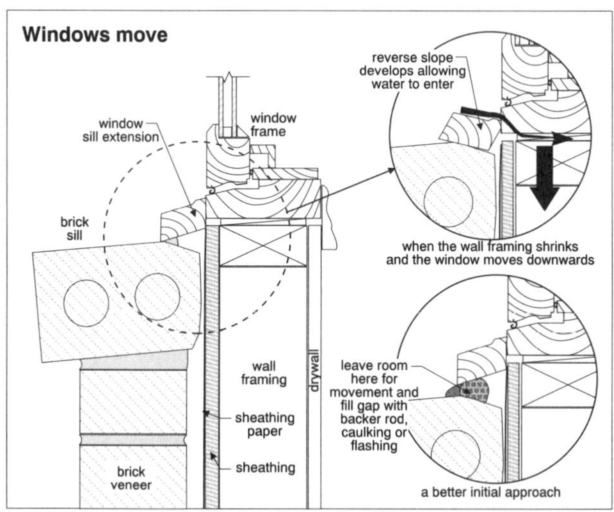

1828

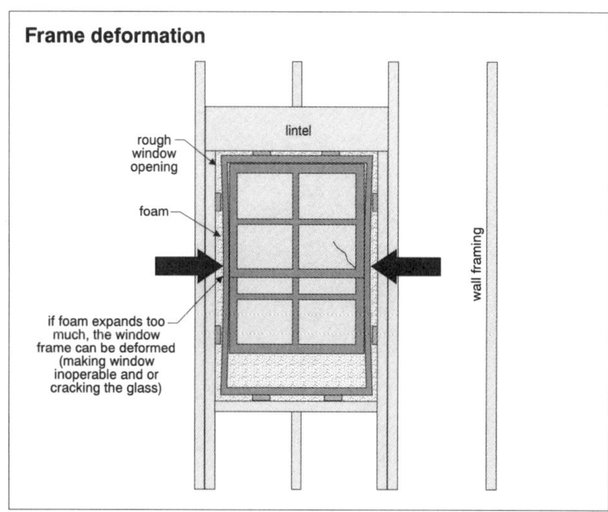

1829

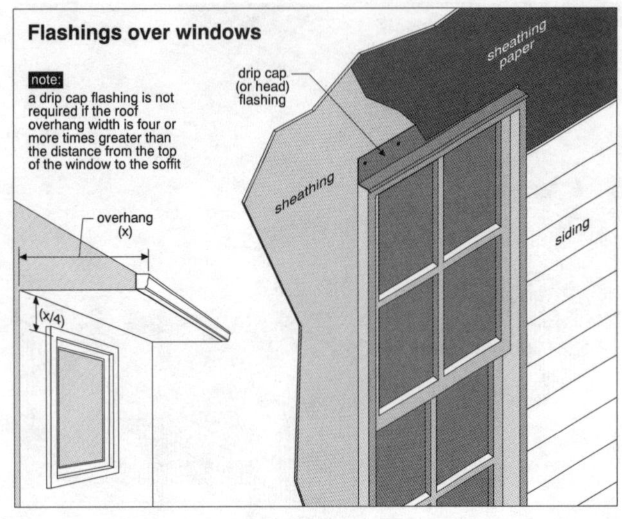

1830

Kickout flashing
siding
step flashings
shingles
sheathing paper/house wrap
kickout flashing
cladding
wall continues past edge of roof
gutter
eave protection
drip edge
note: lower shingles and siding not shown for clarity

1831

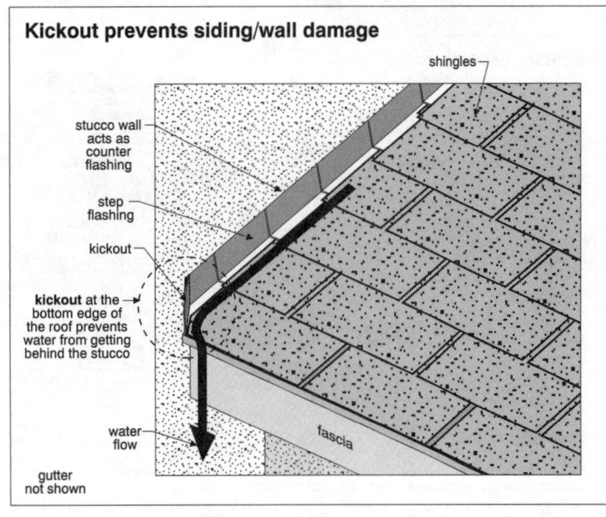

1832

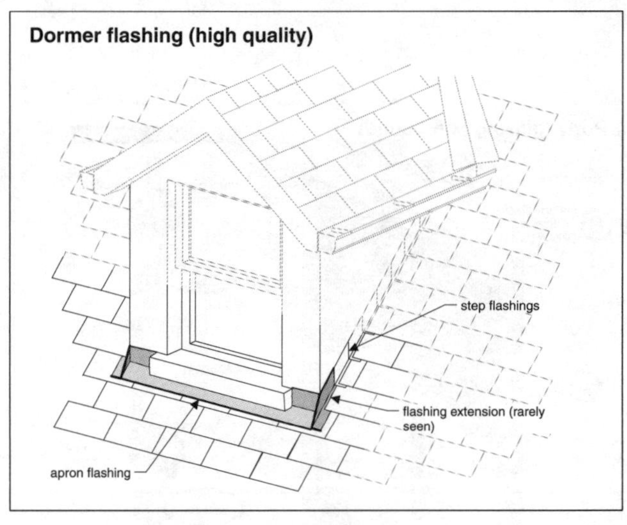

1833

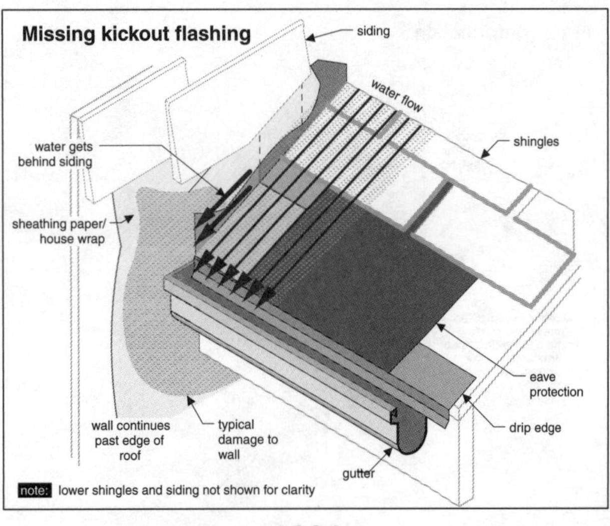

1834

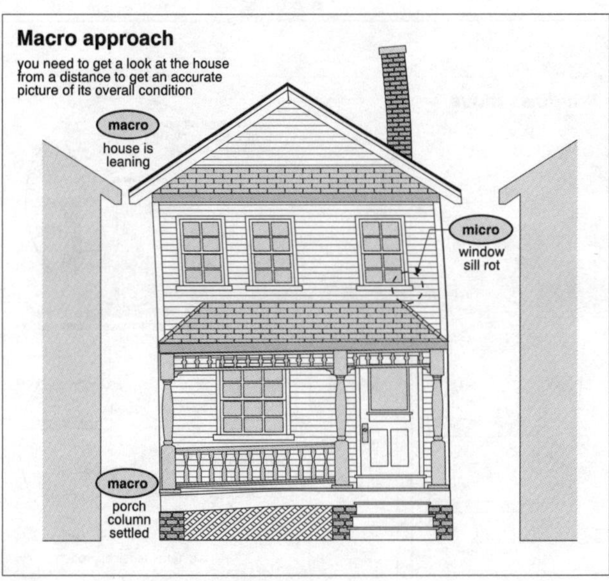

1835

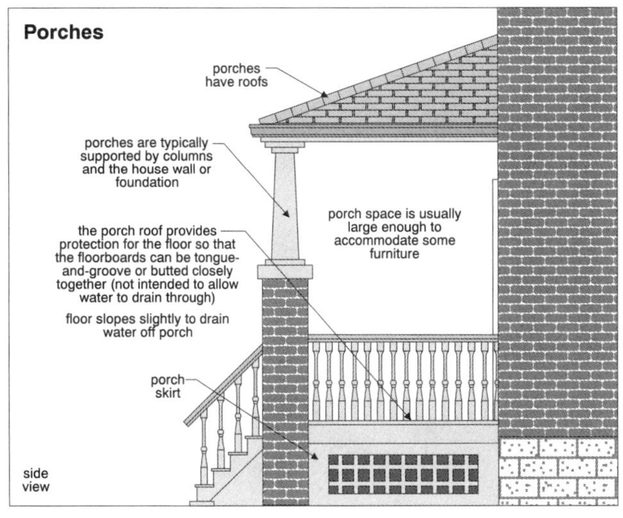

1836

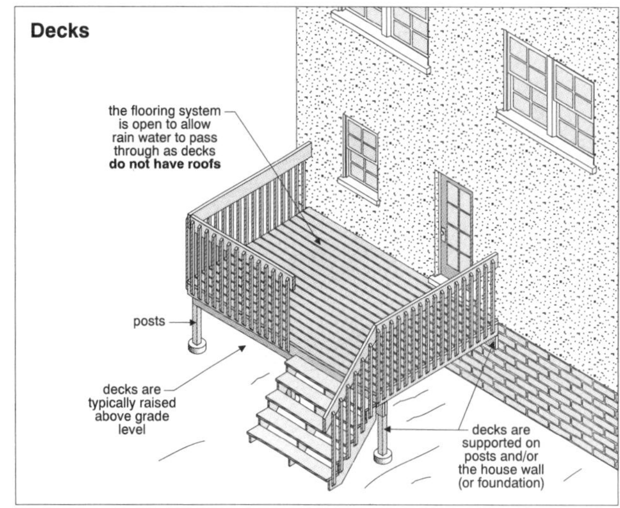

1837

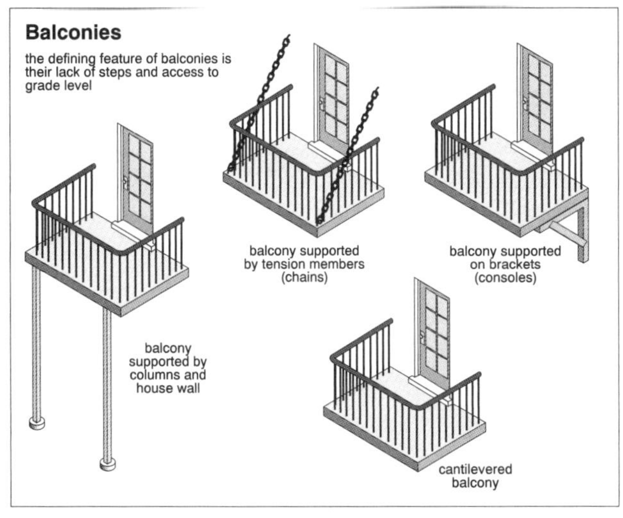

1838

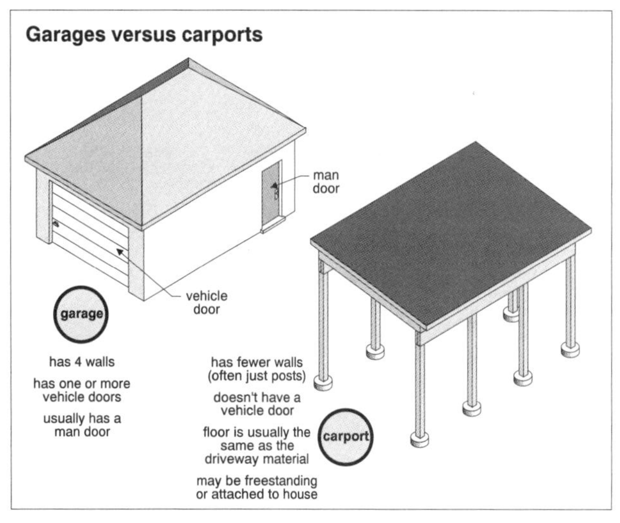

1839

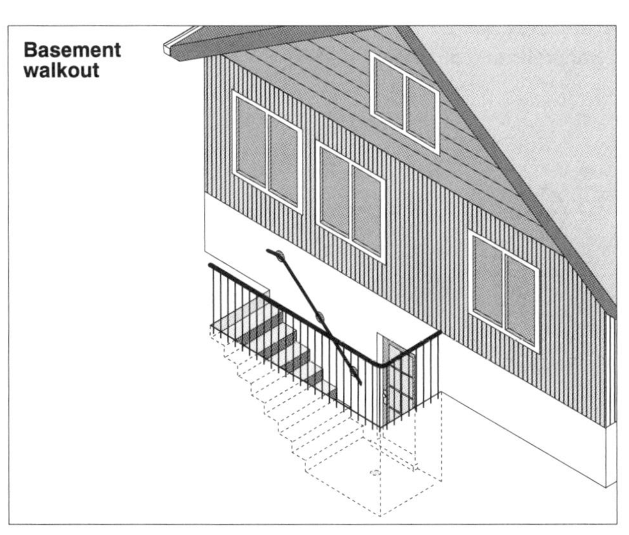

1840

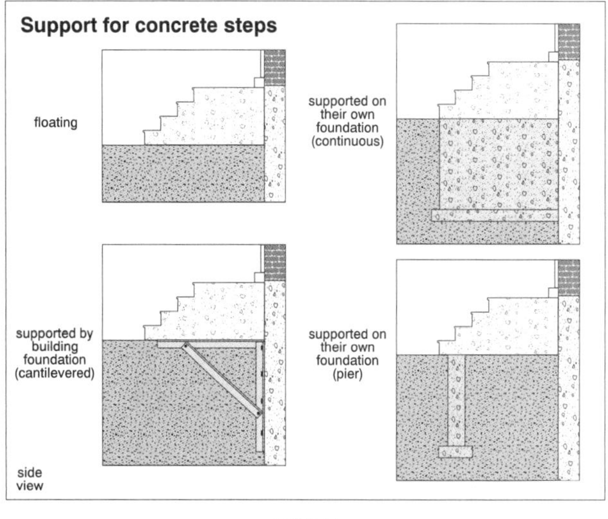

1841

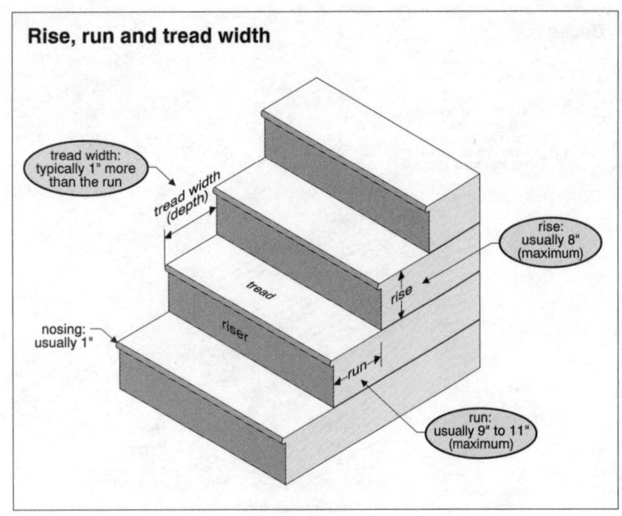

1842

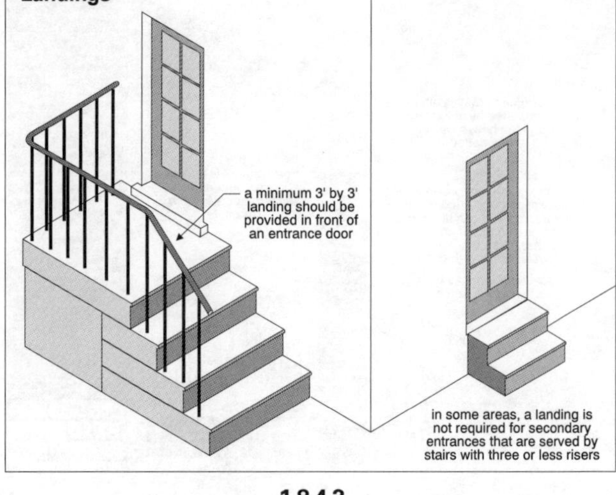

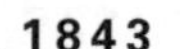
1843

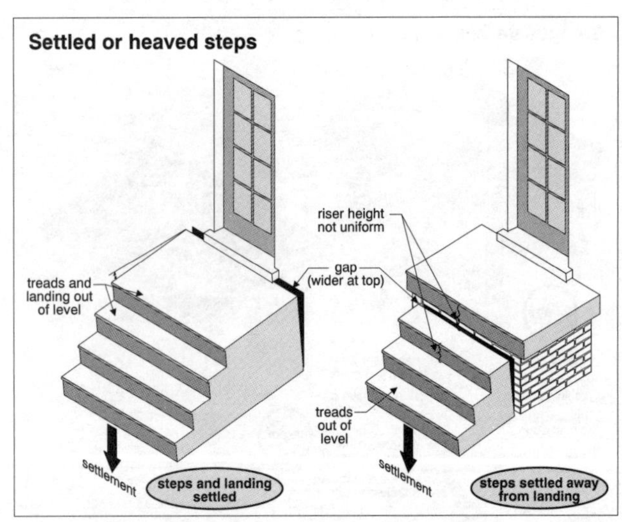

1844

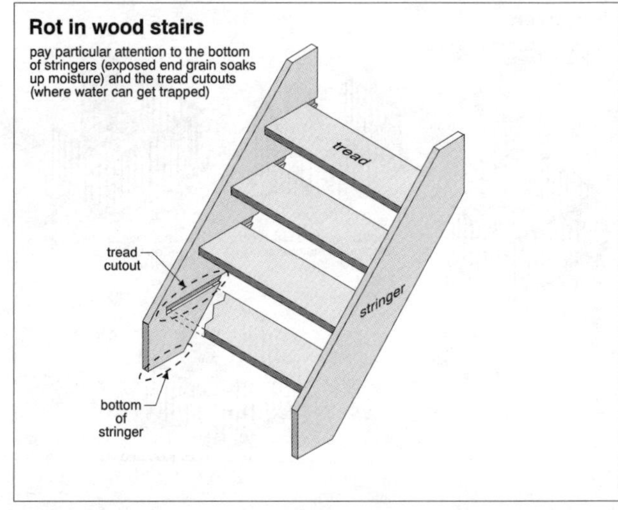

1845

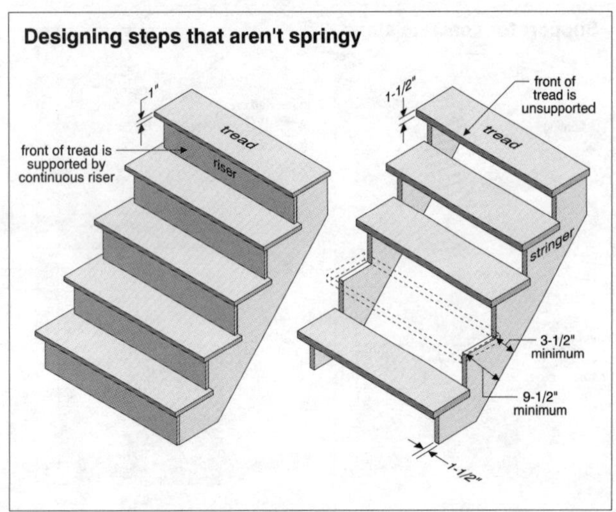

1846

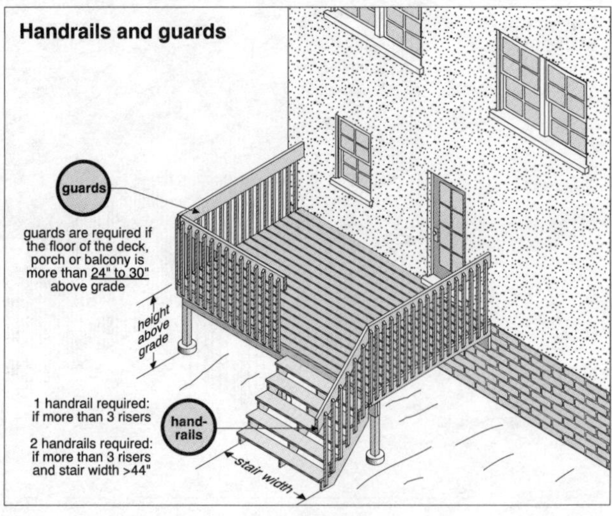

1847

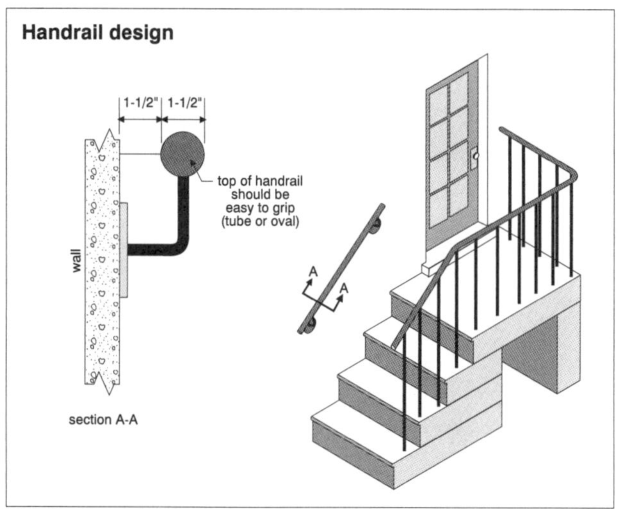

1848

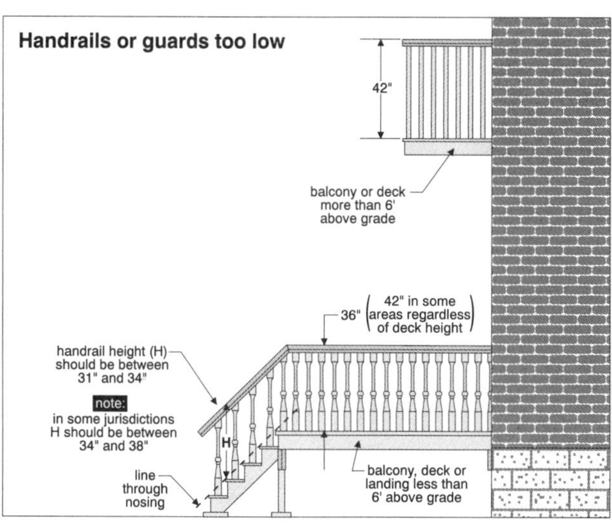

1849

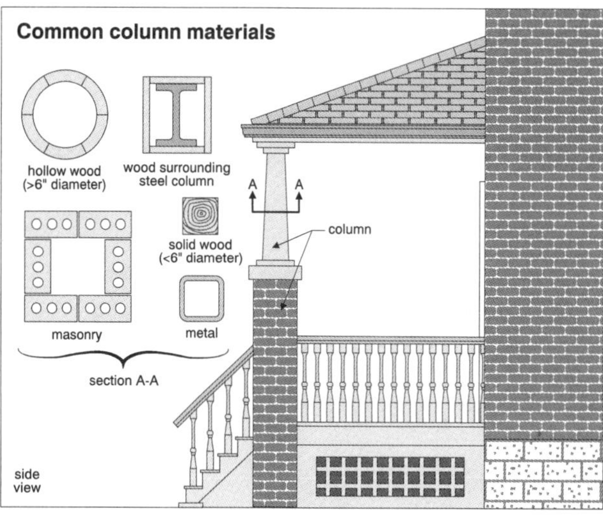

1850

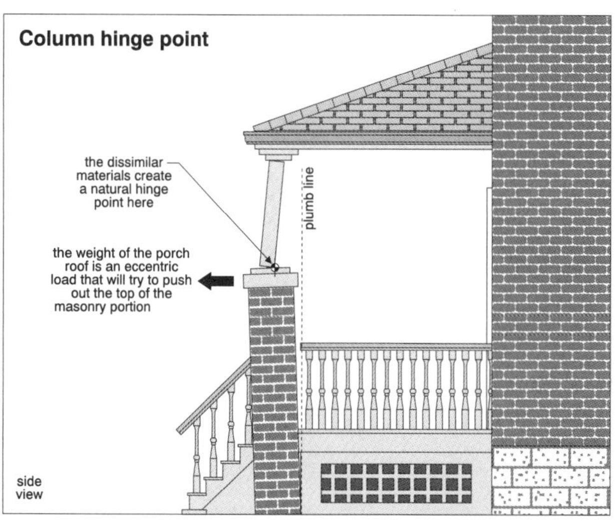

1851

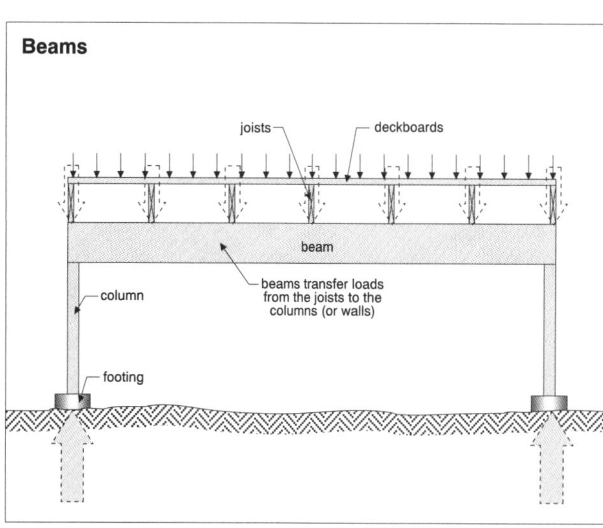

1852

1853

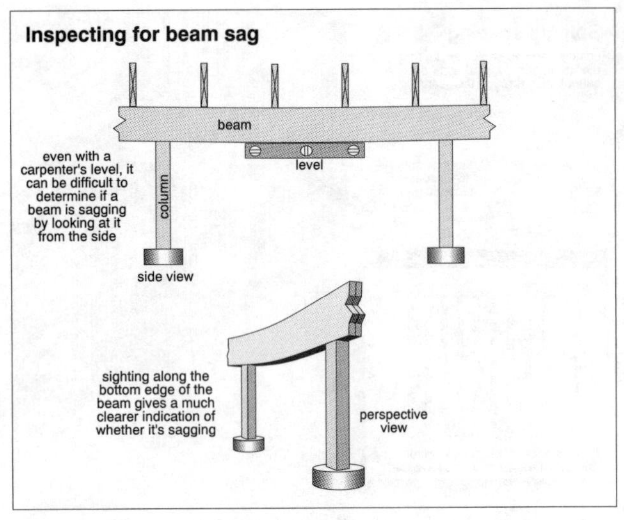

1854

1855

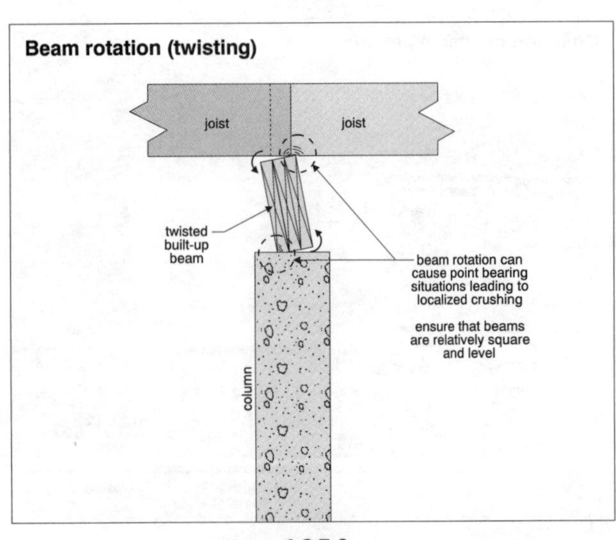

1856

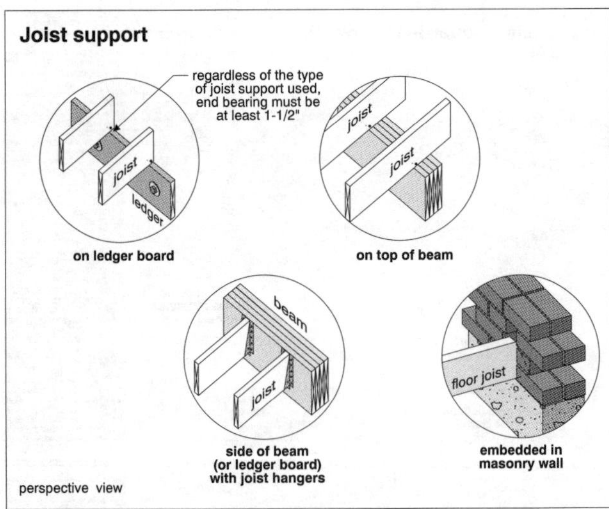

1857

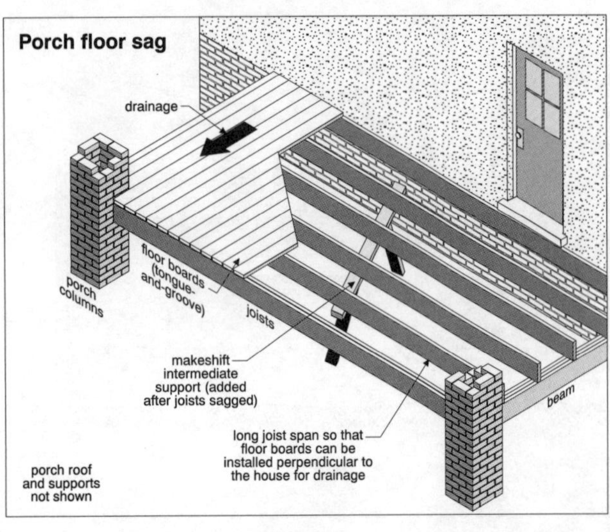

1858

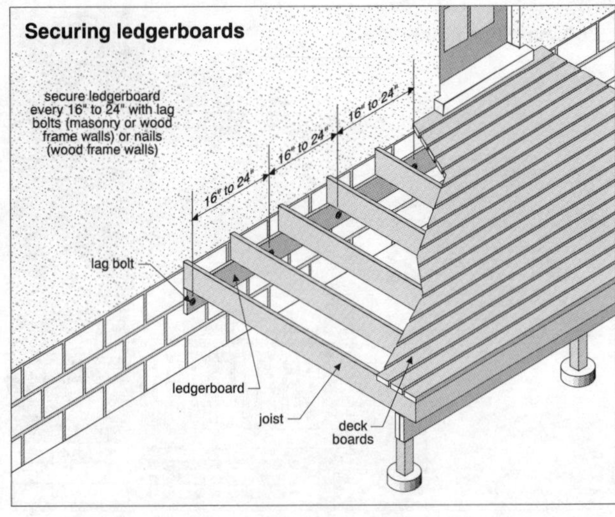

1859

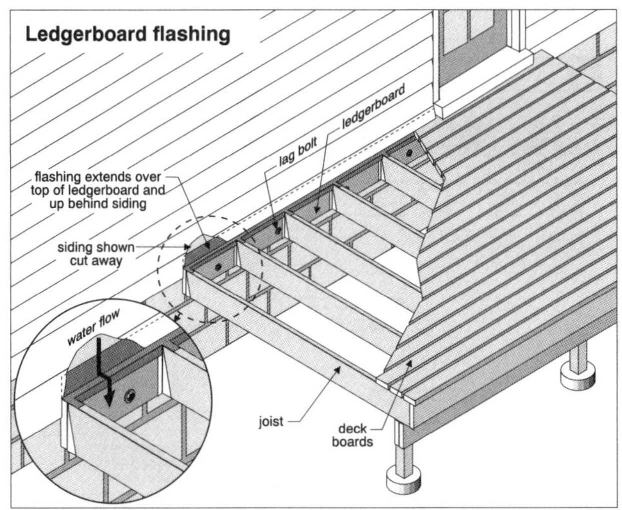

1860

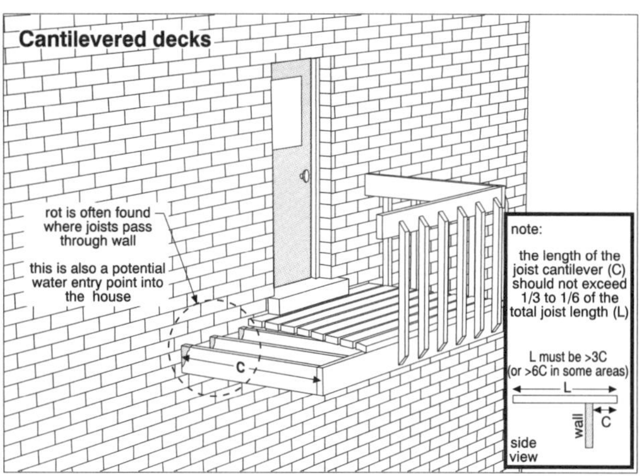

1861

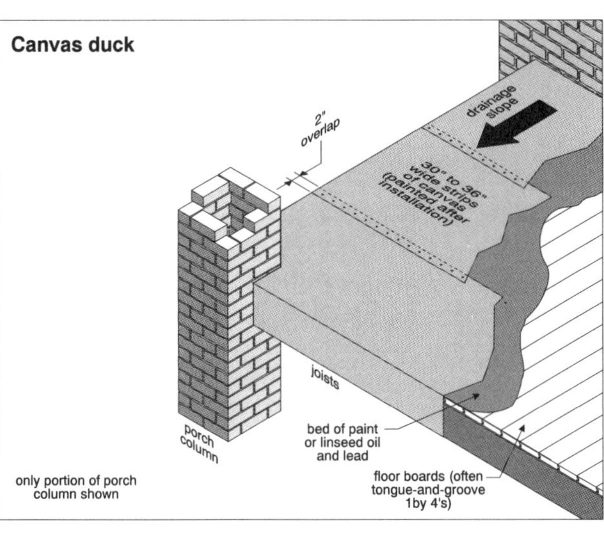

1862

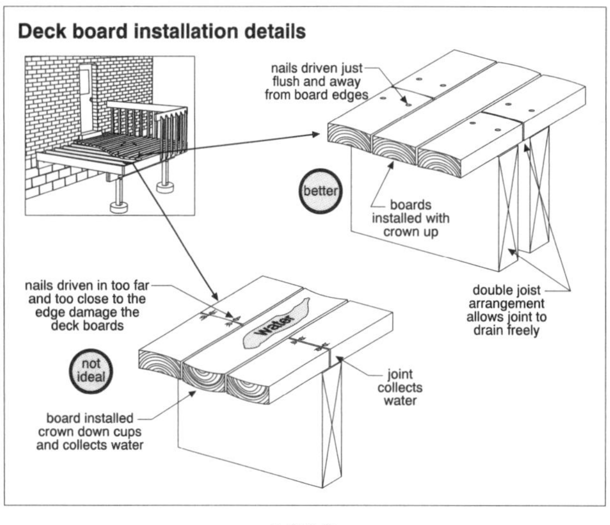

1863

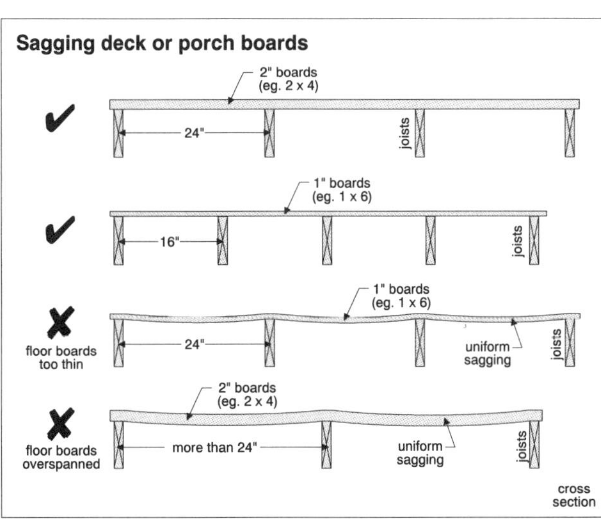

1864

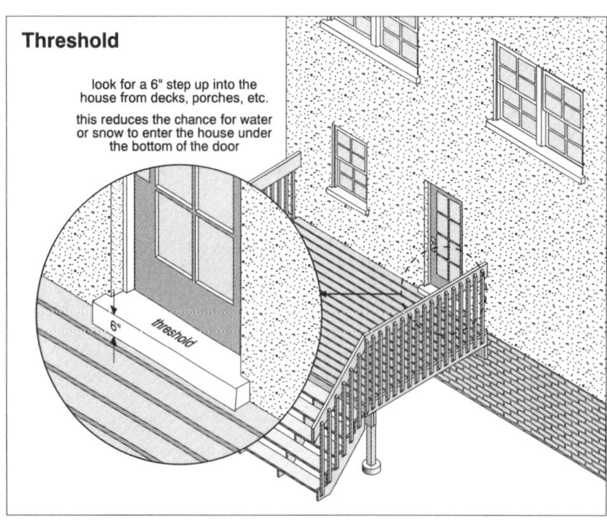

1865

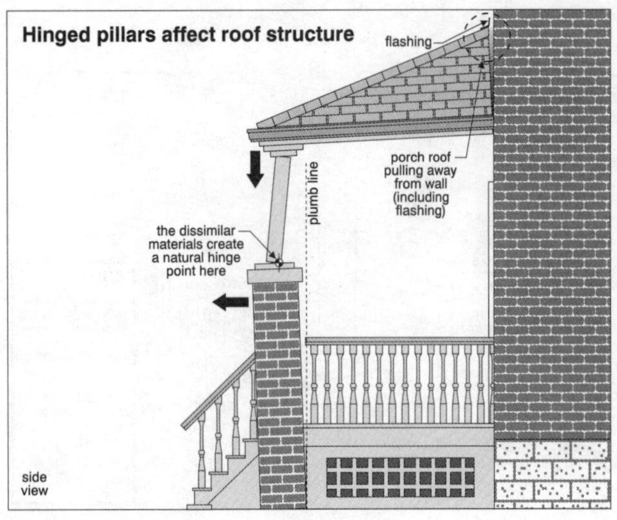

1866

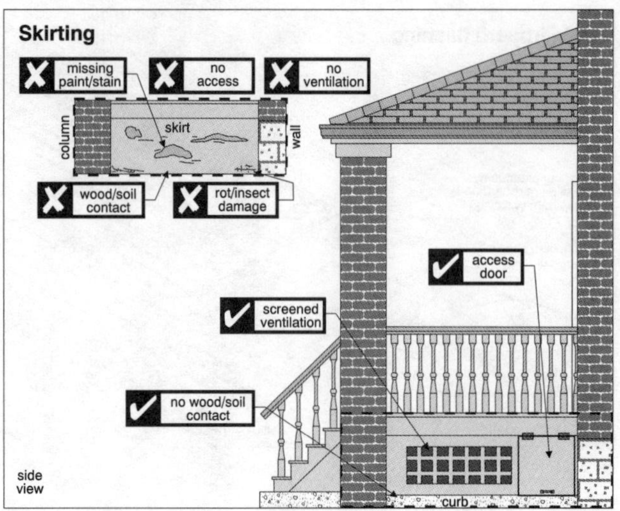

1867

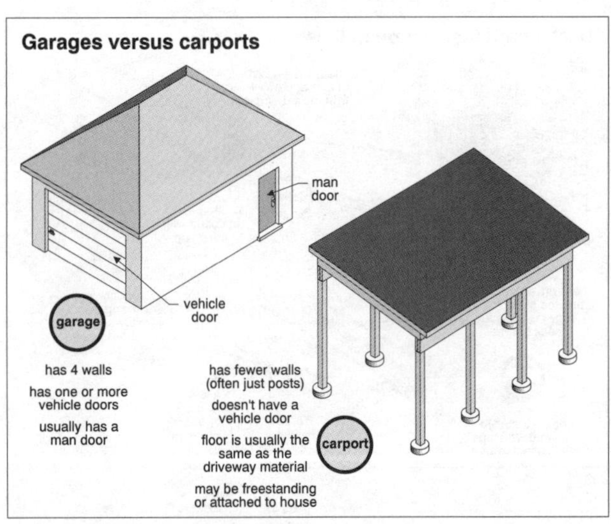

1868

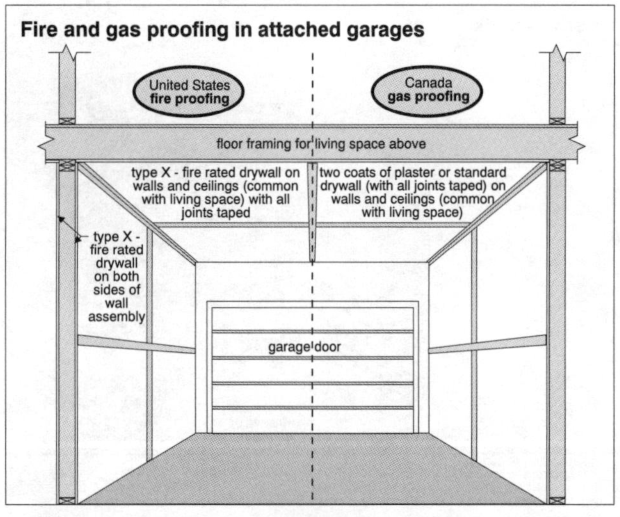

1869

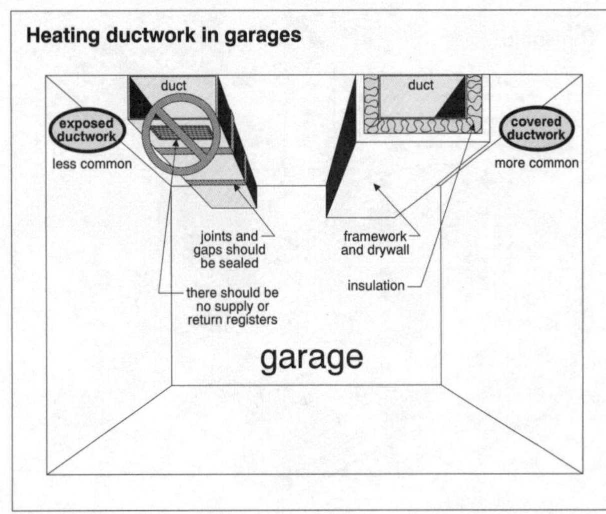

1870

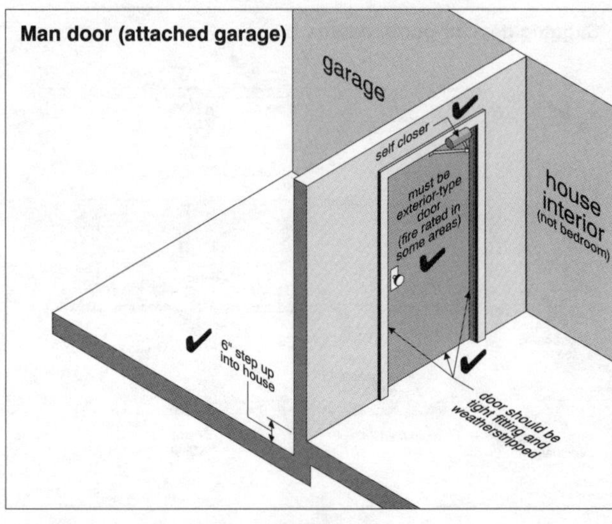

1871

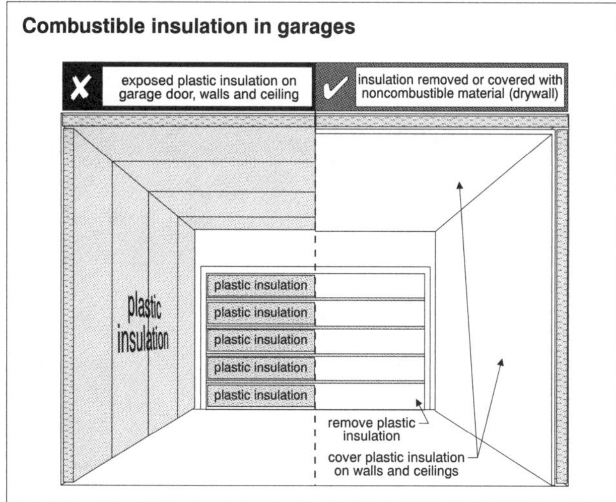

1872

Structural garage floor

1873

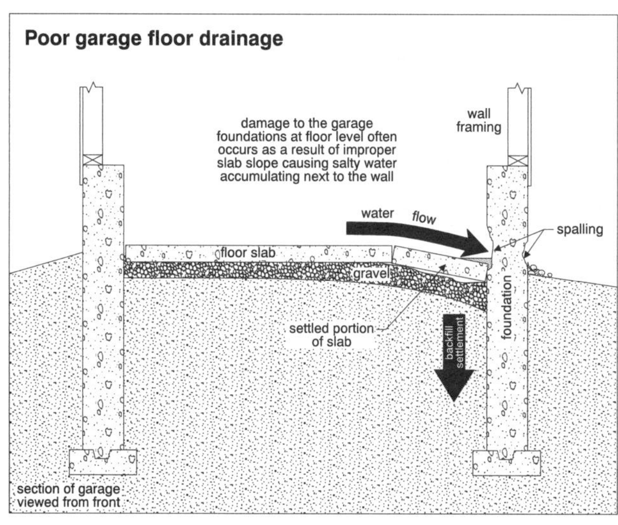

1874

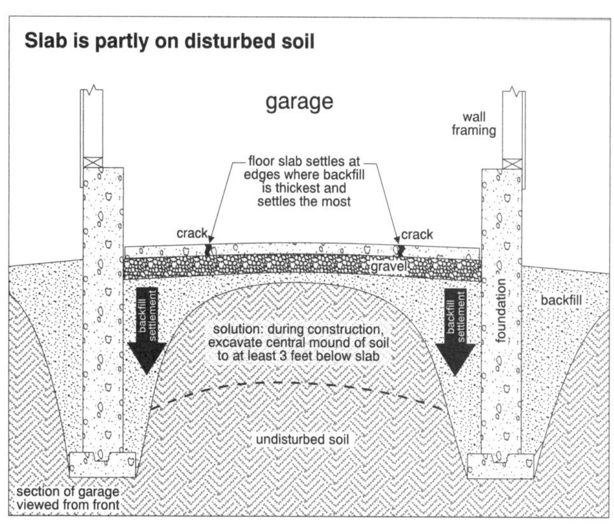

1875

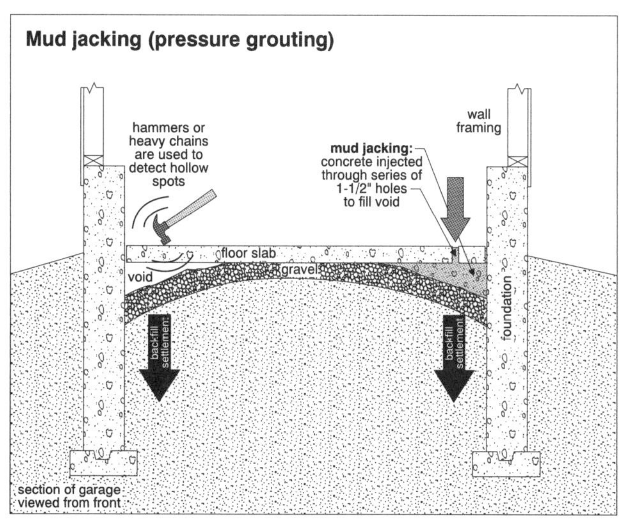

1876

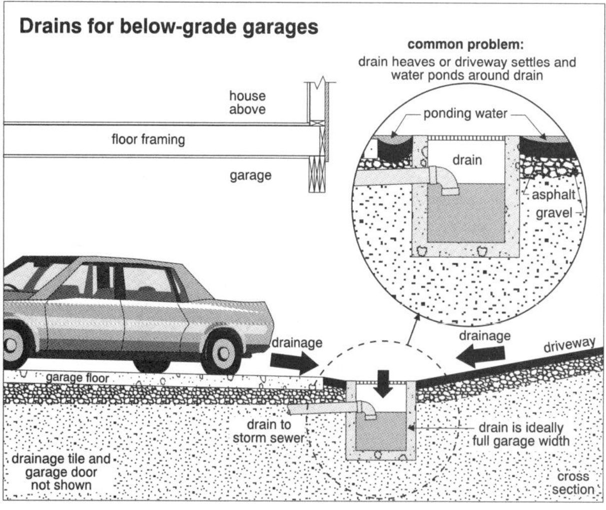

1877

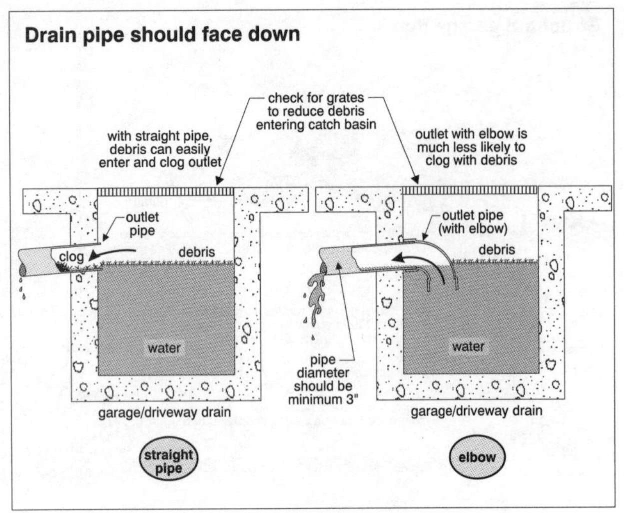

1878

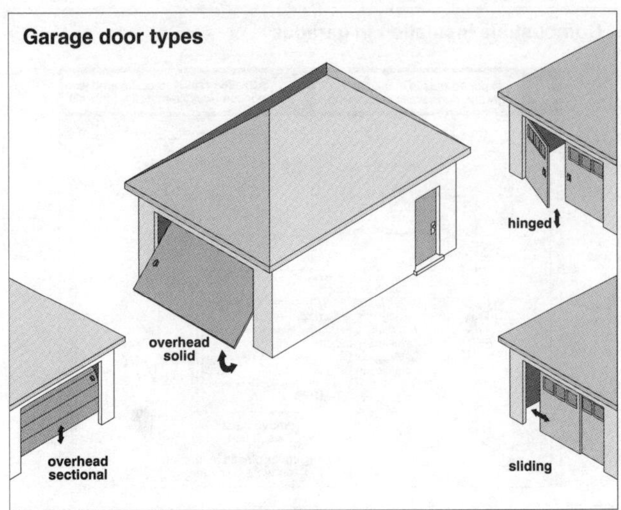

1879

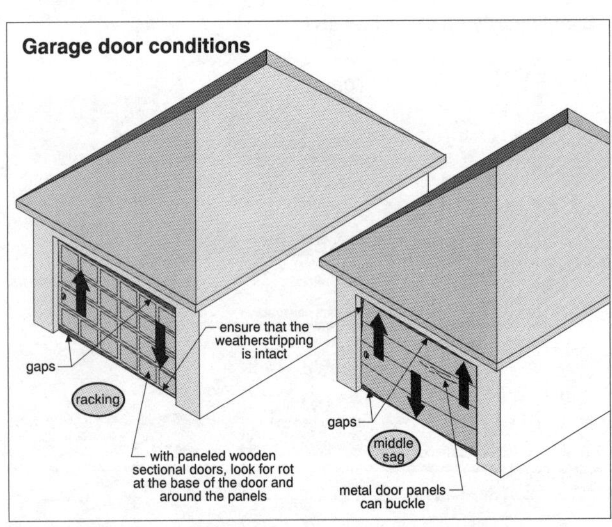

1880

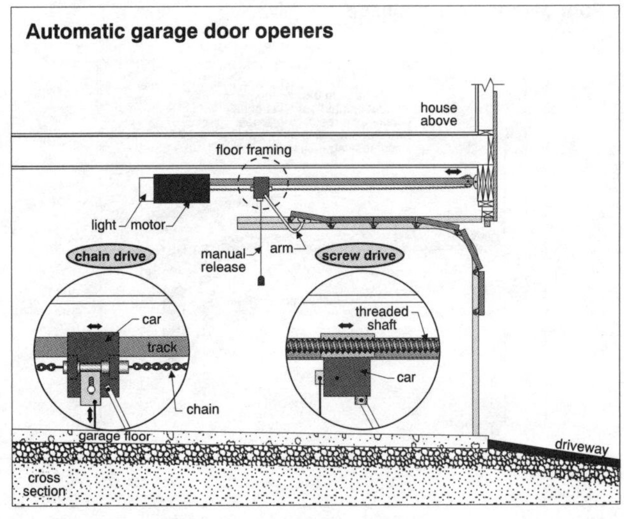

1881

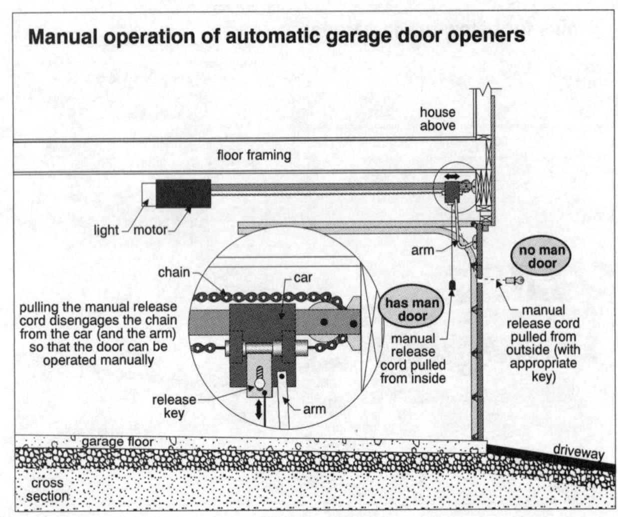

1882

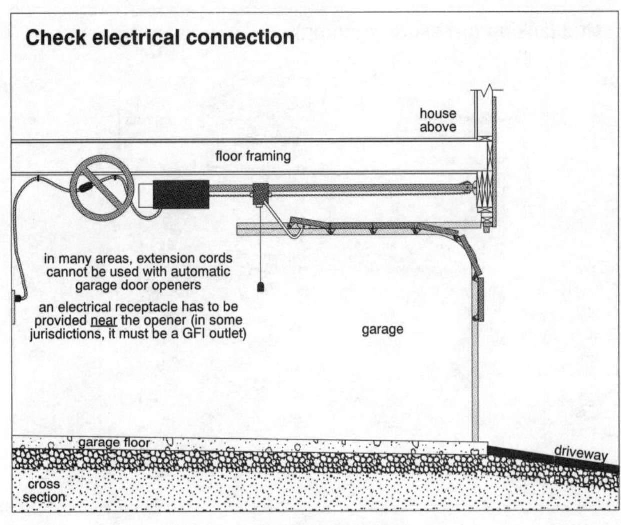

1883

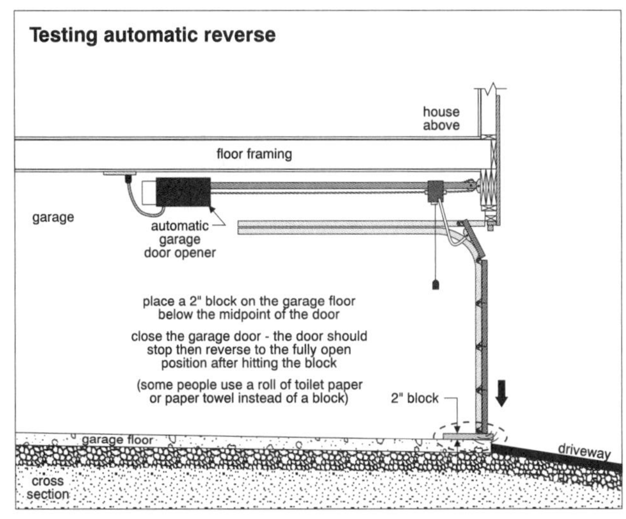

1884

1885

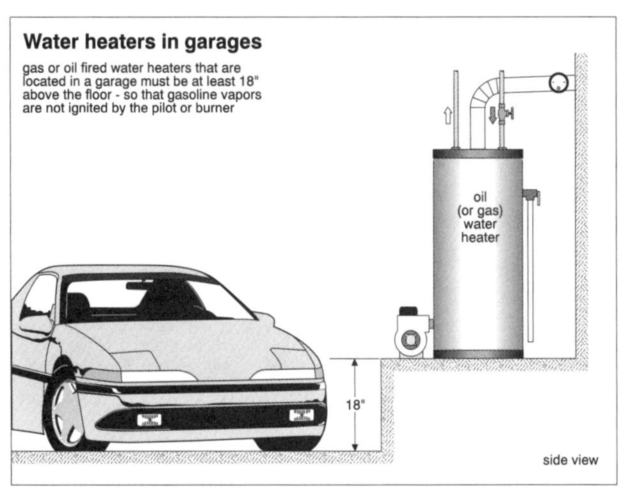

1886

Basement walkouts

common problem areas

covers/ roofs

steps and railings

door thresholds

drains

frost

walls cracking, leaning, bowing or spalling

1887

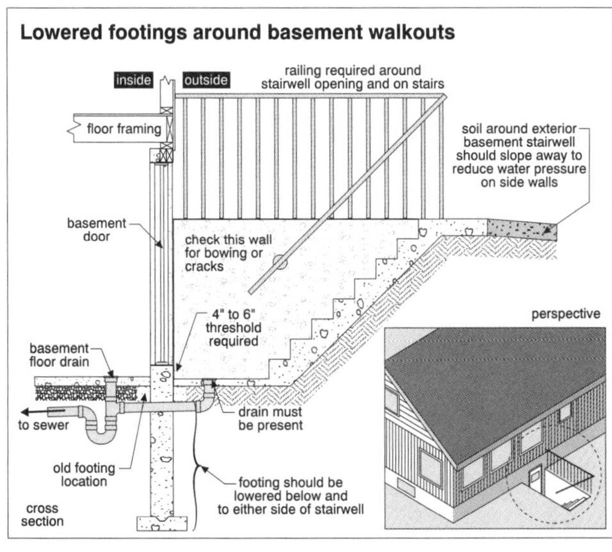

1888

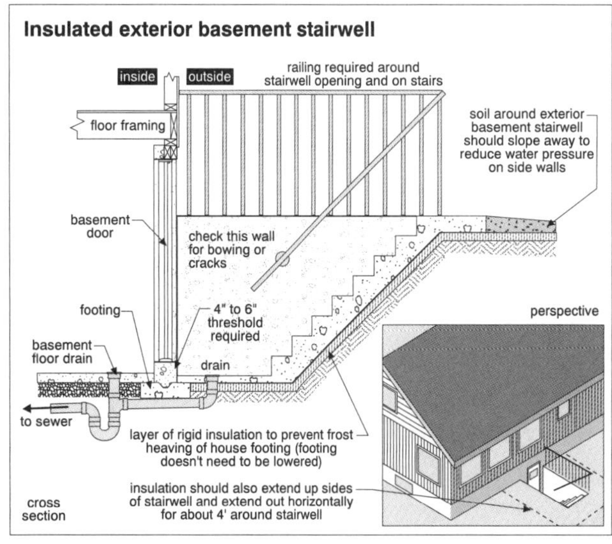

1889

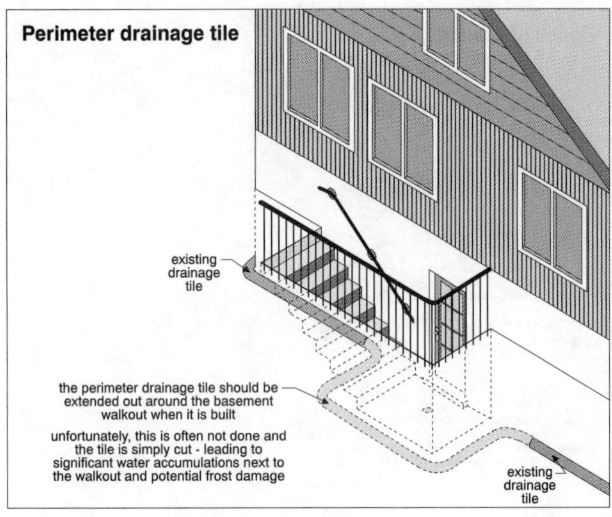

1890

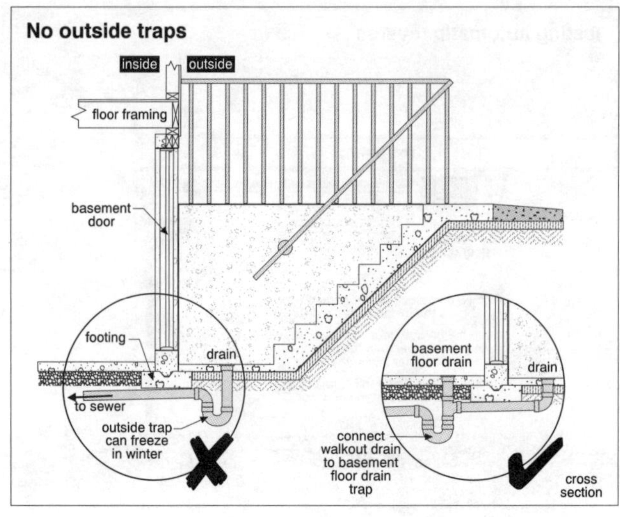

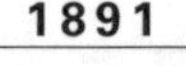

1891

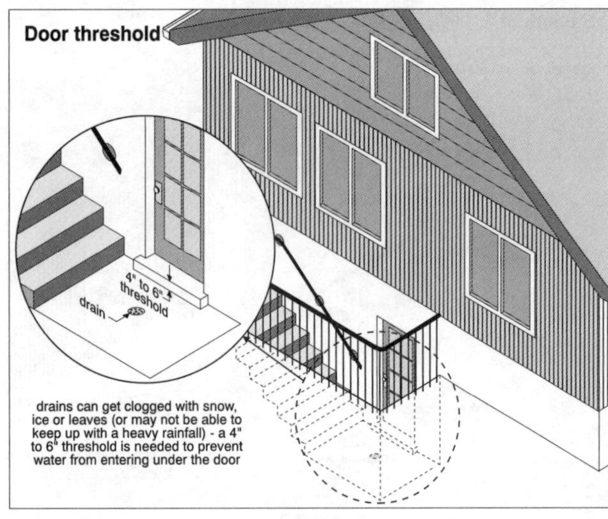

1892

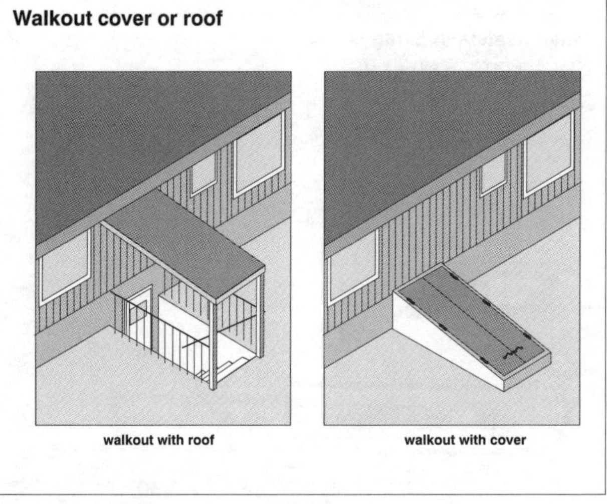

1893

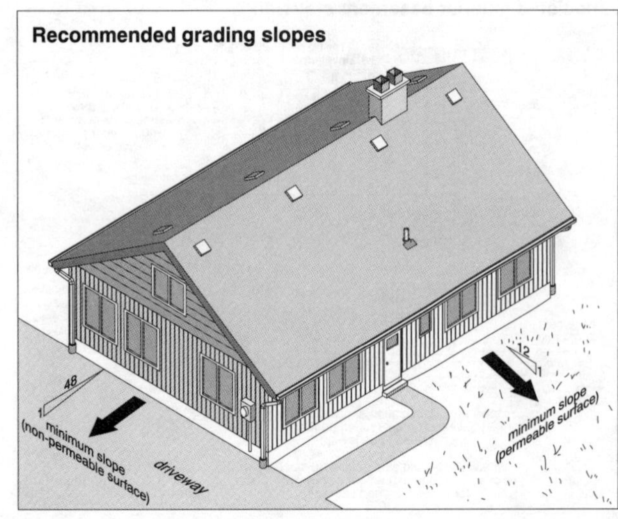

1894

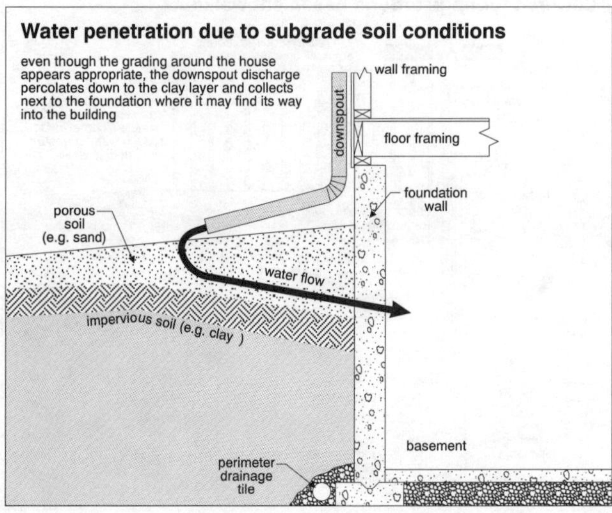

1895

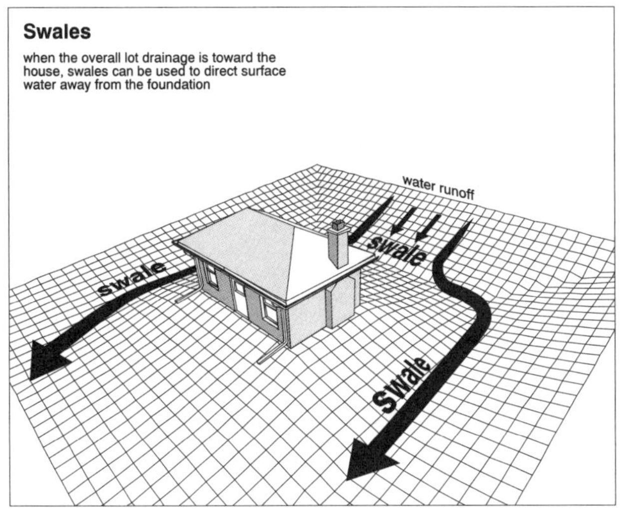

1896

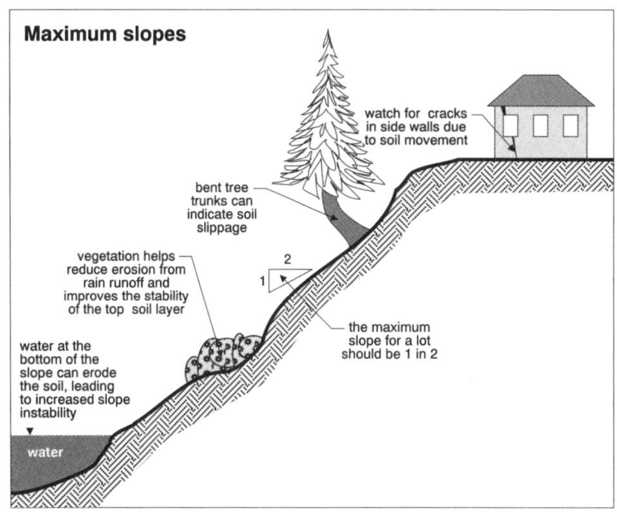

1897

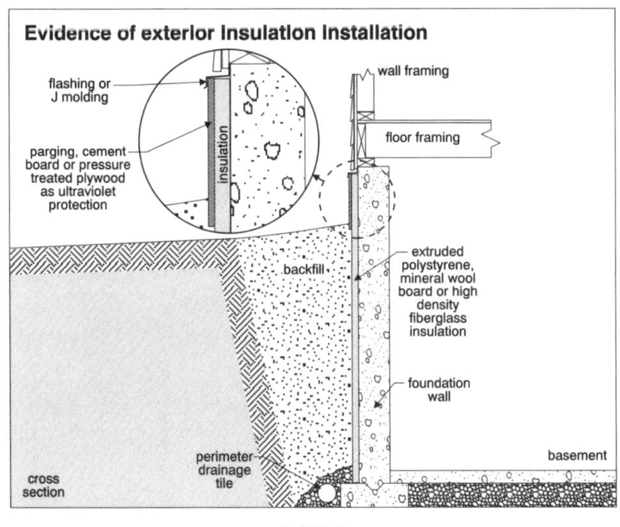

1898

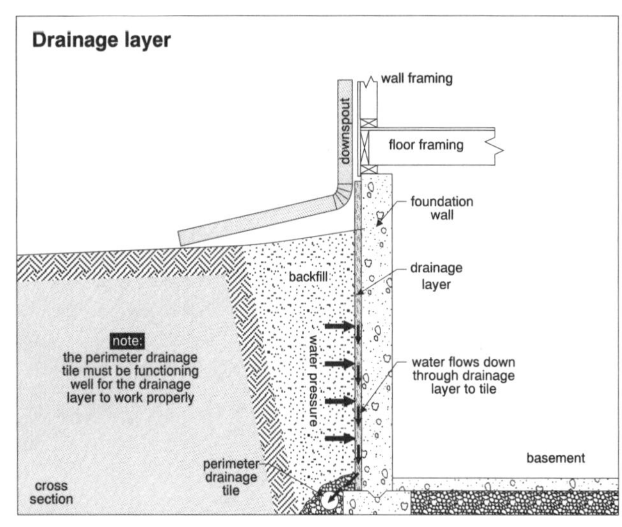

1899

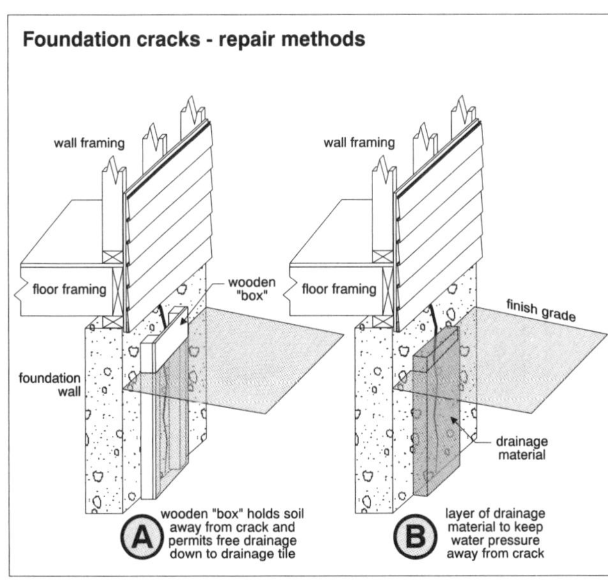

1900

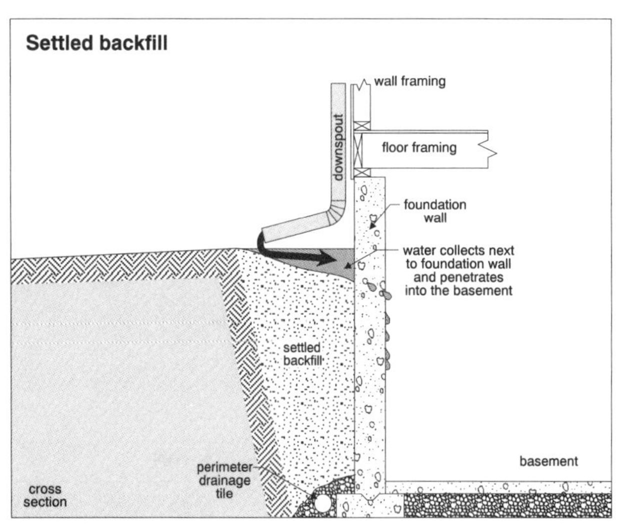

1901

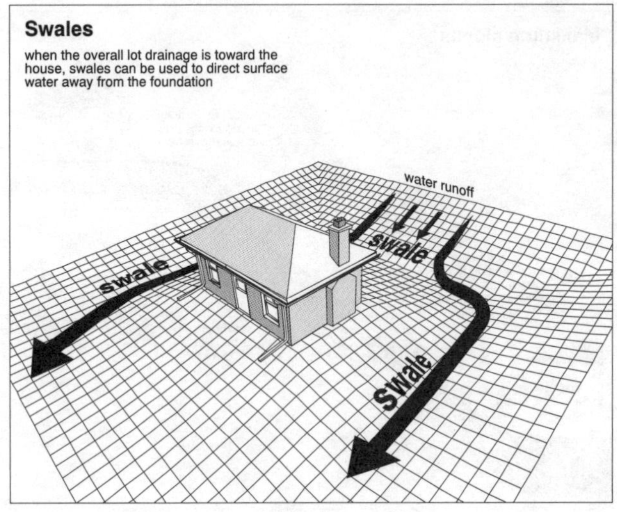

1902

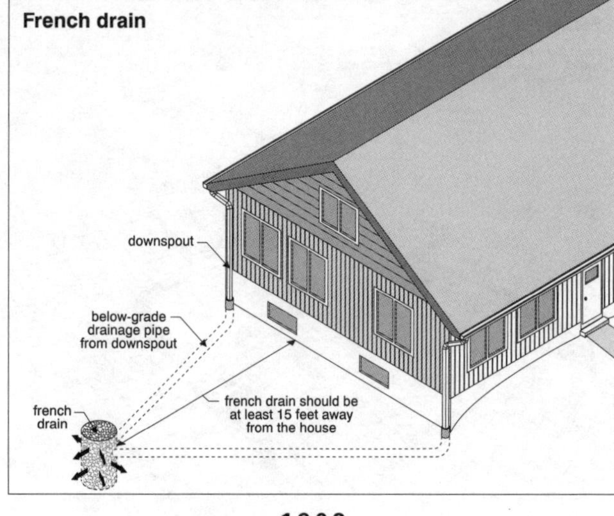

1903

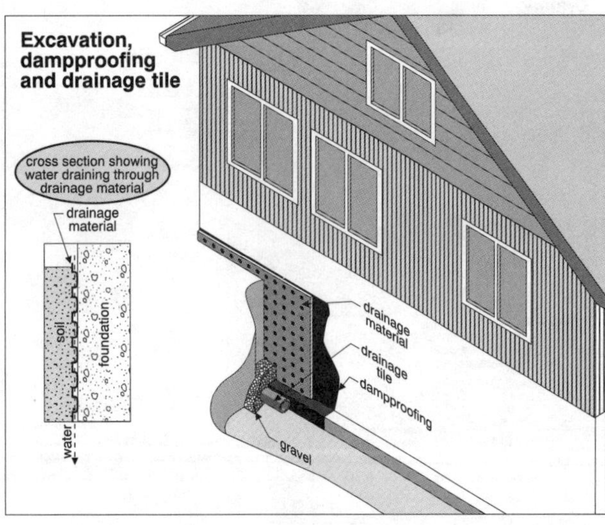

1904

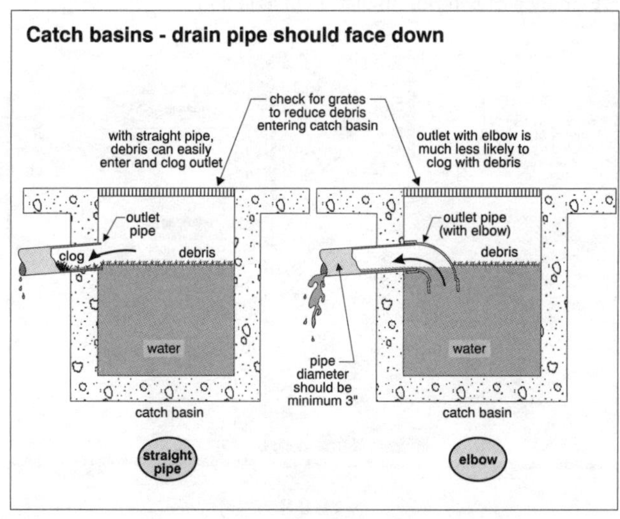

1905

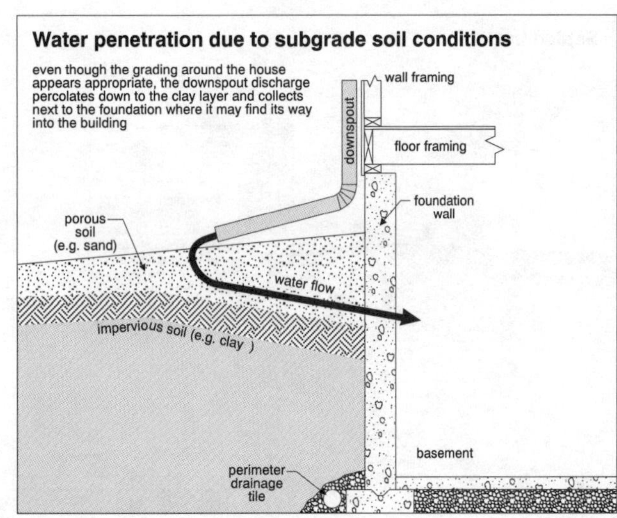

1906

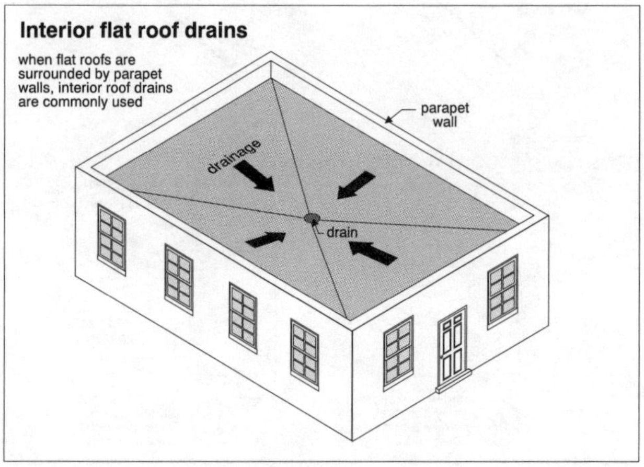

Interior flat roof drains

when flat roofs are surrounded by parapet walls, interior roof drains are commonly used

parapet wall

drainage

drain

1907

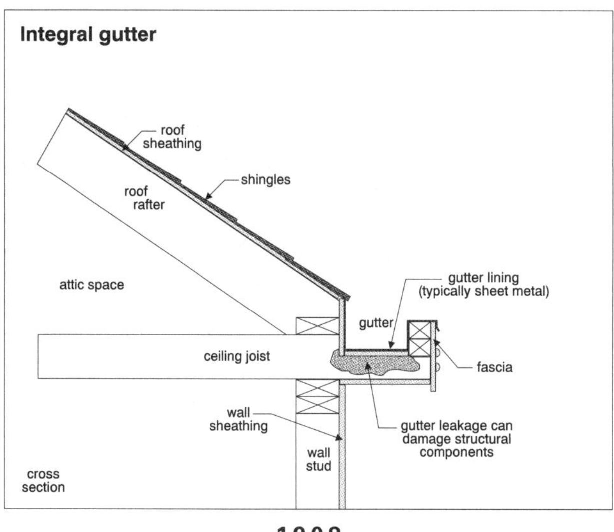

1908

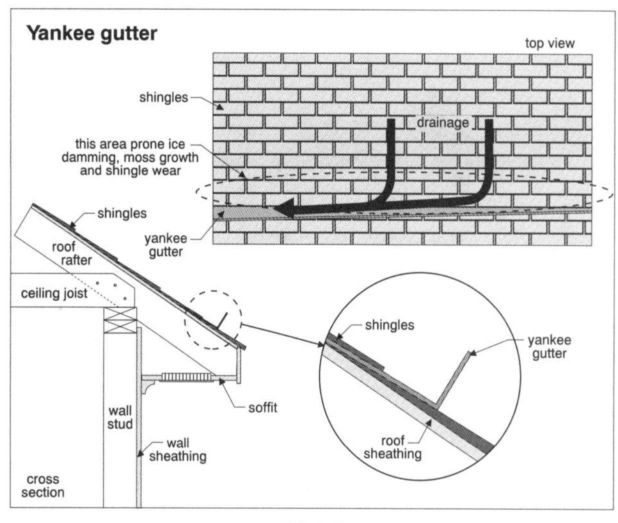

1909

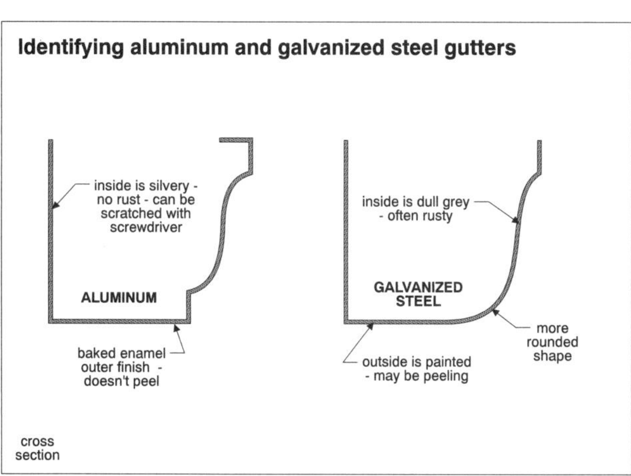

1910

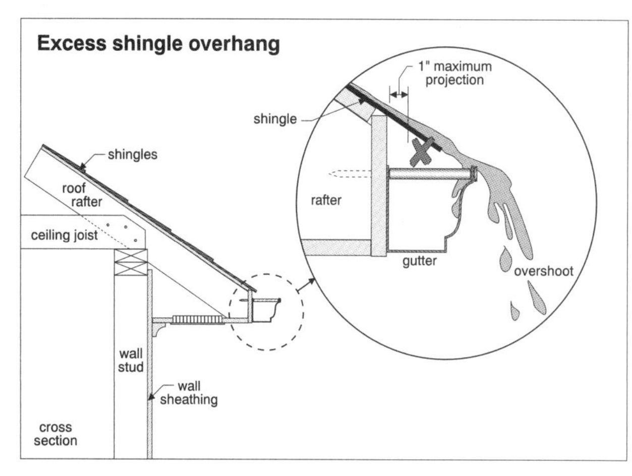

1911

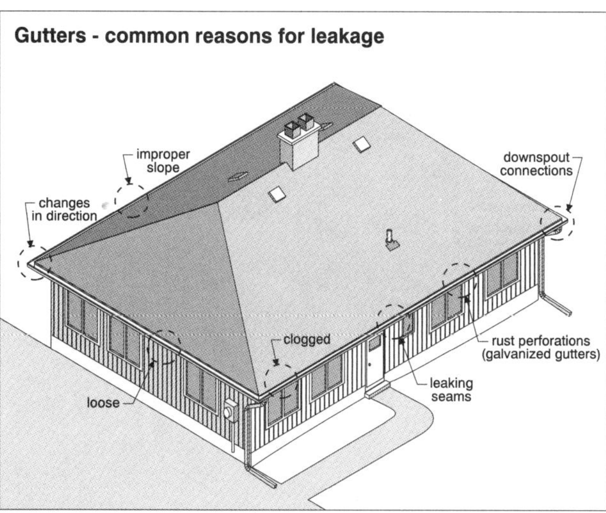

1912

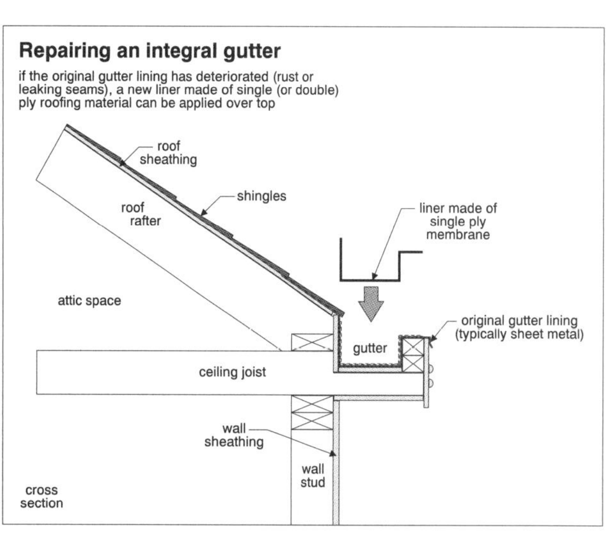

1913

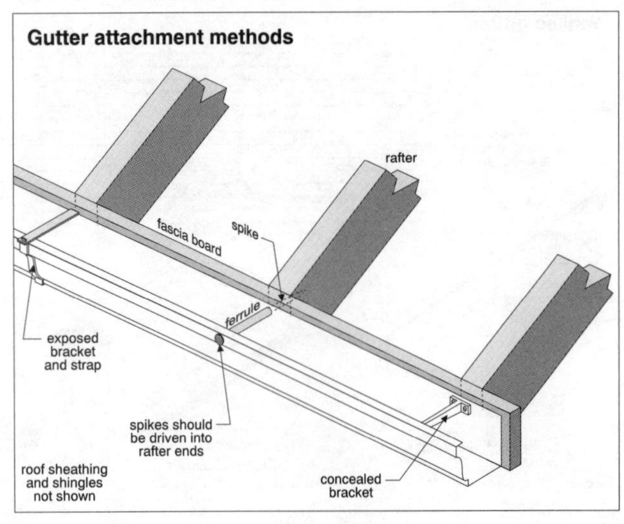

1914

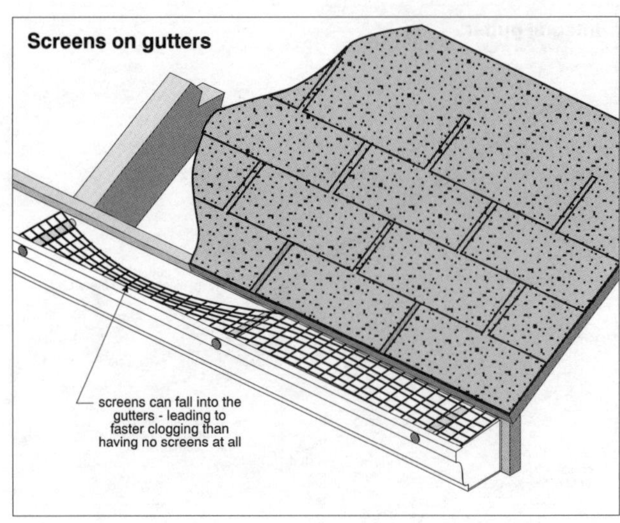

1915

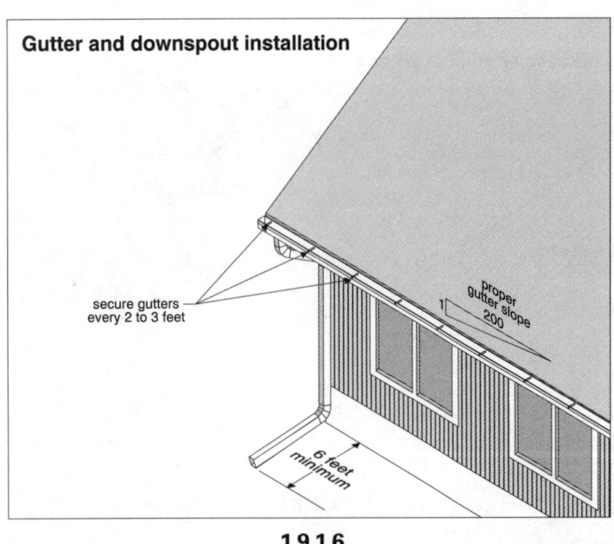

1916

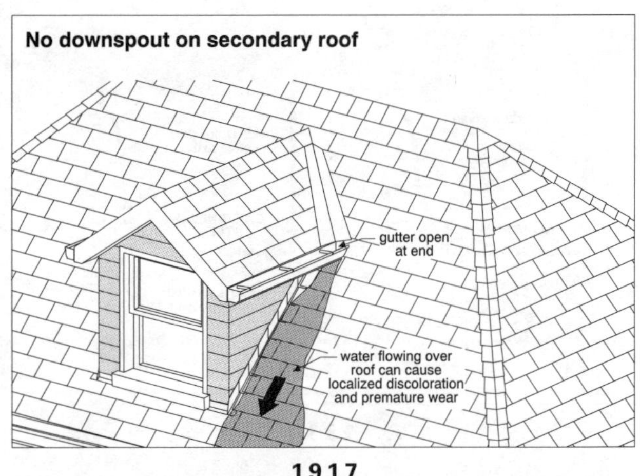

1917

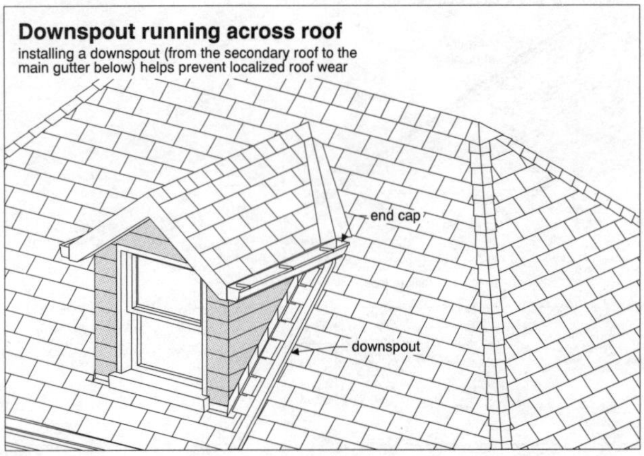

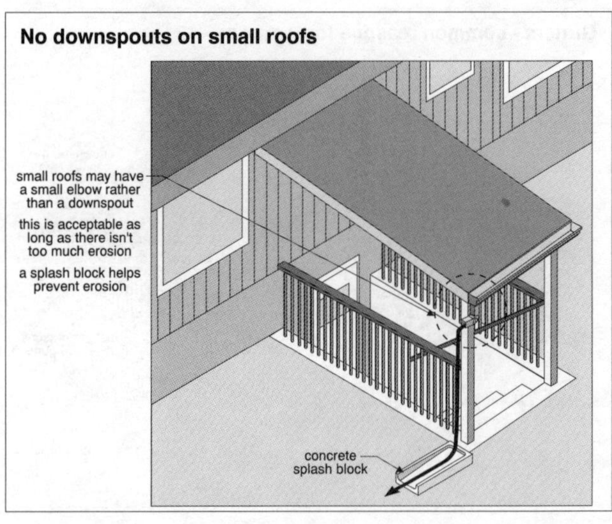

1919

1918

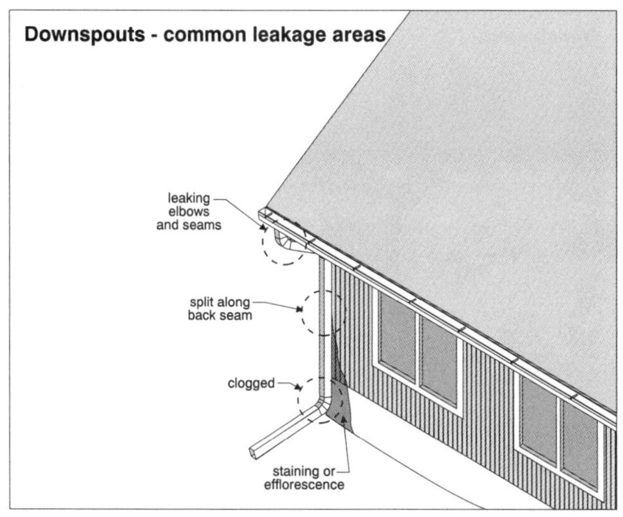

1920

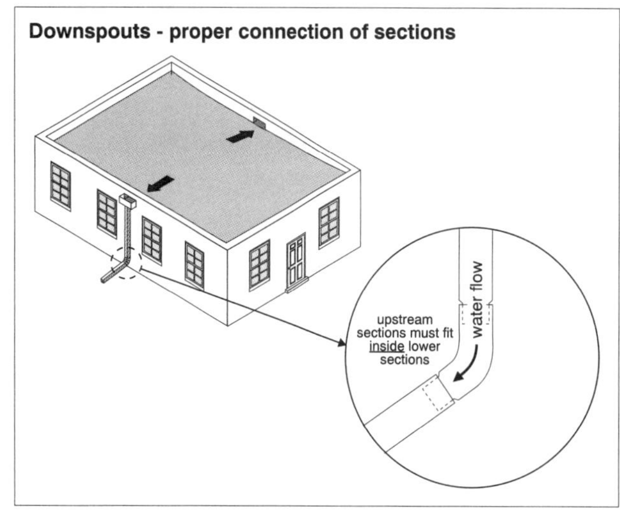

1921

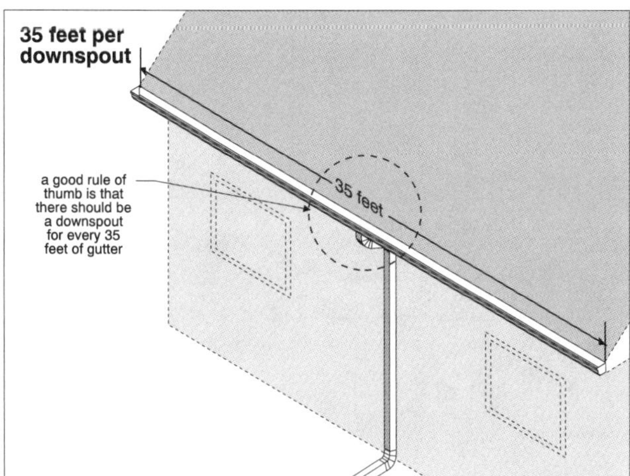

1922

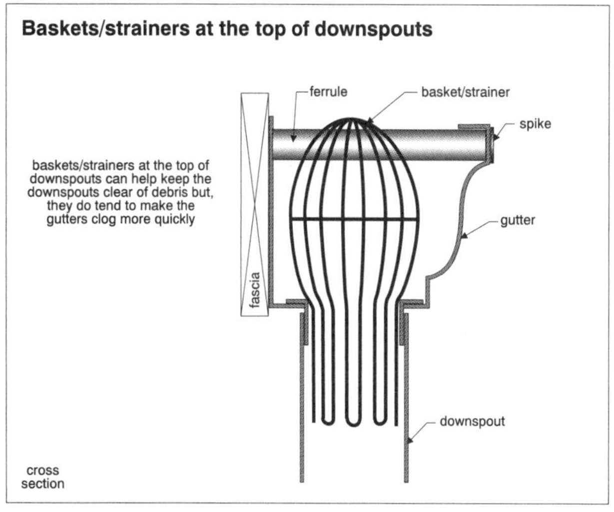

1923

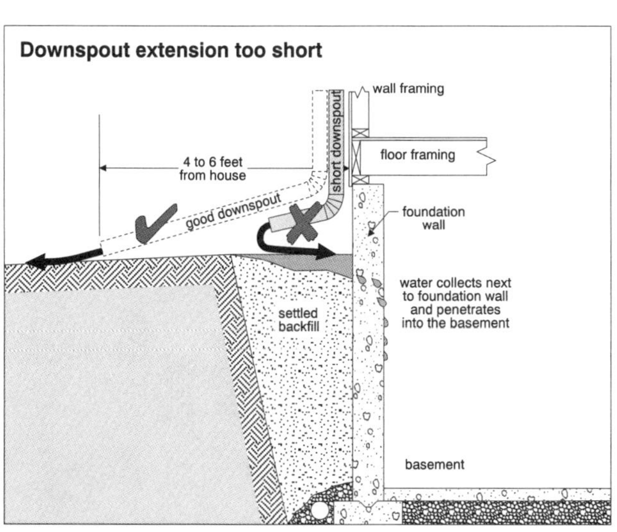

1924

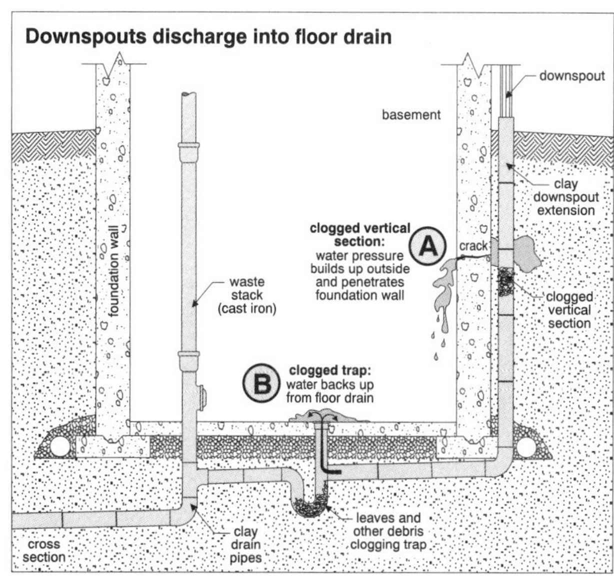

1925

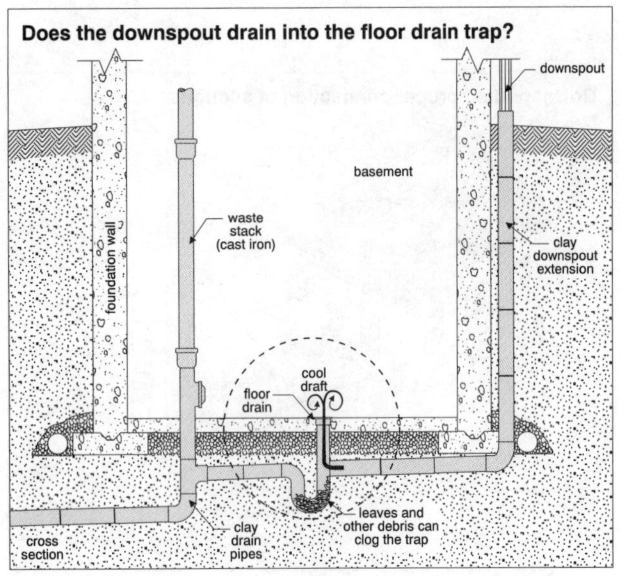

1926

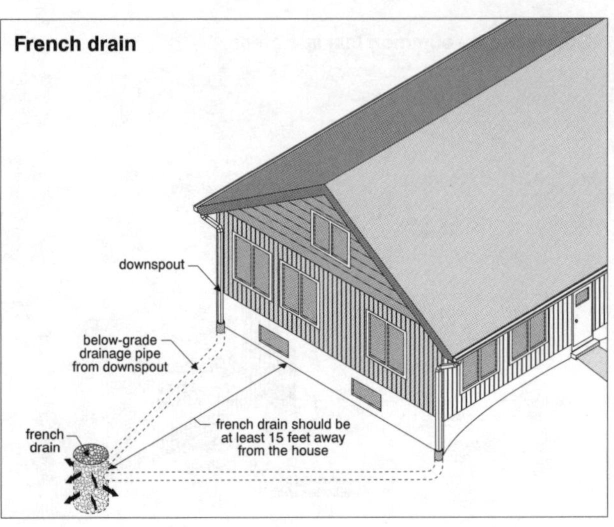

1927

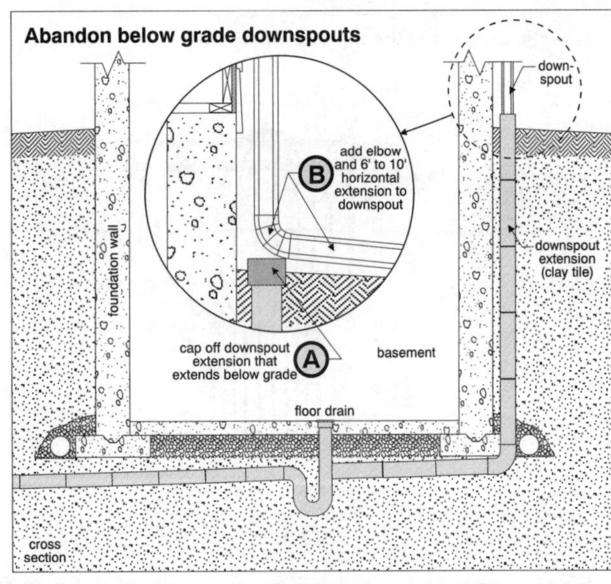

1928

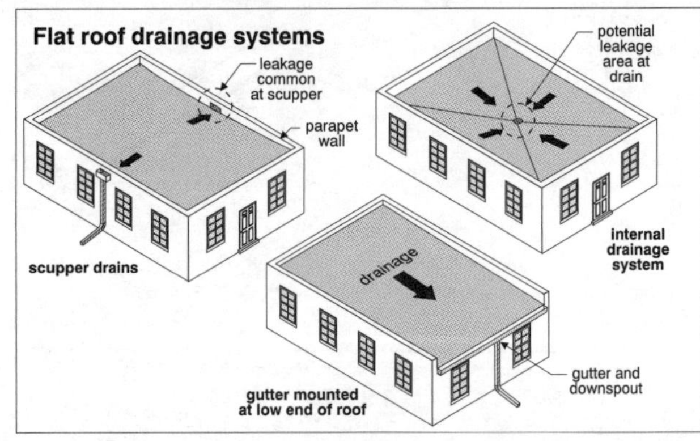

1929

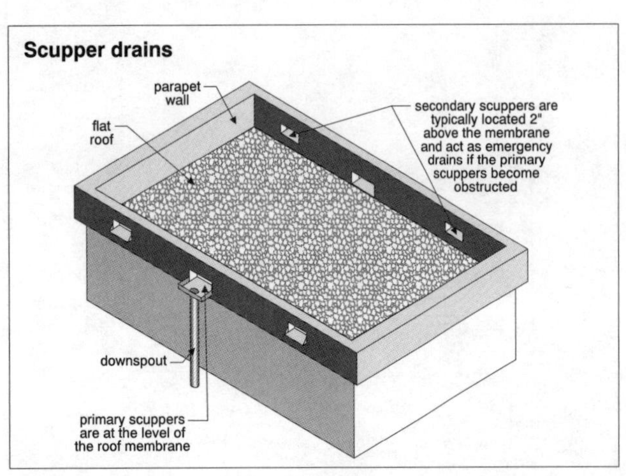

1930

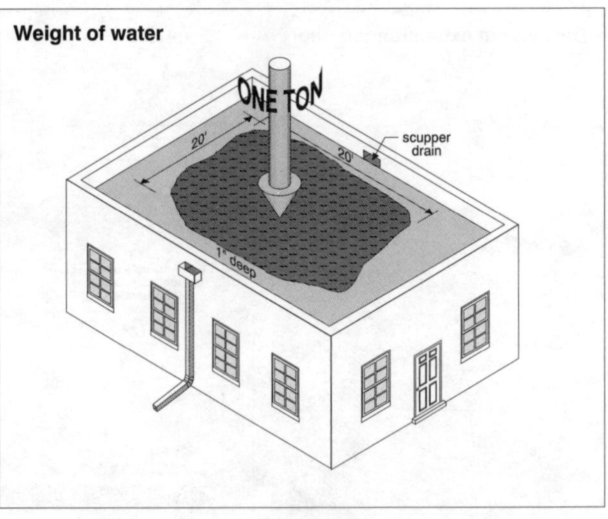

1931

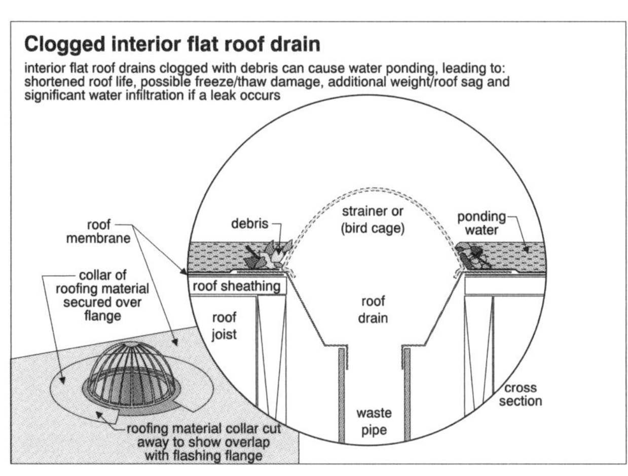

1932

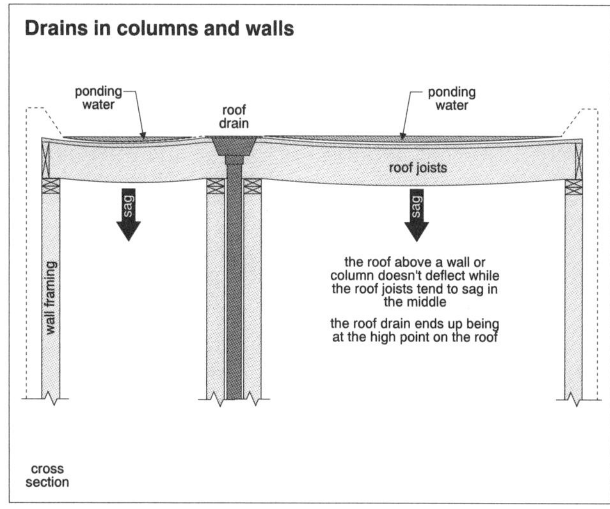

1933

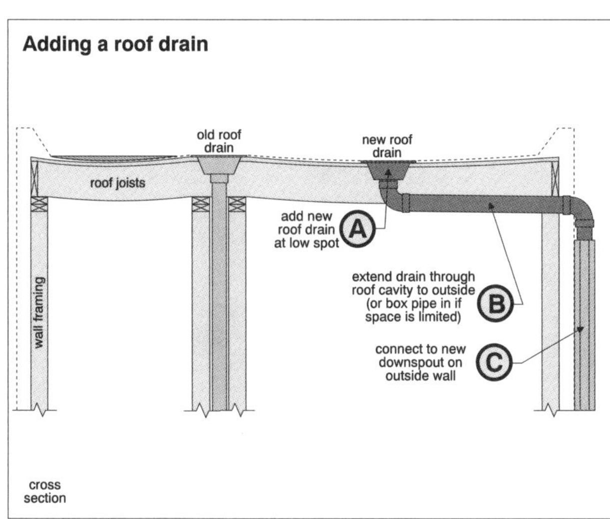

1934

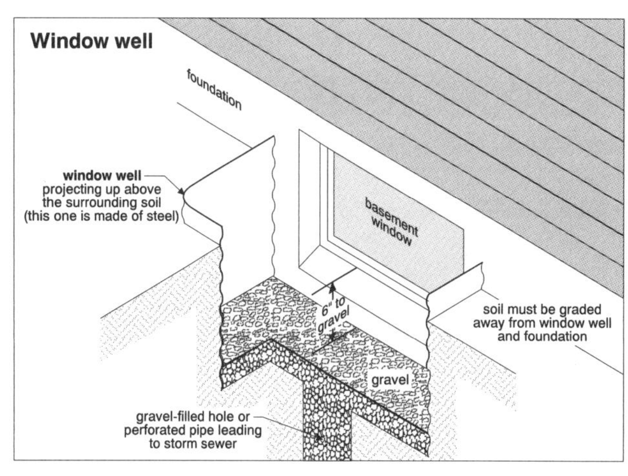

1935

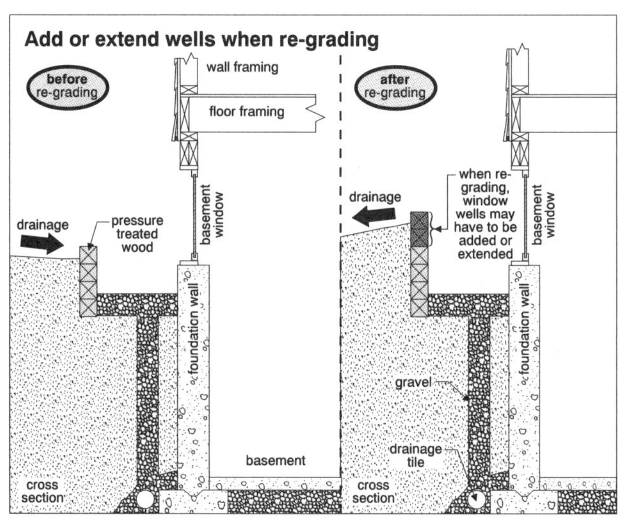

1936

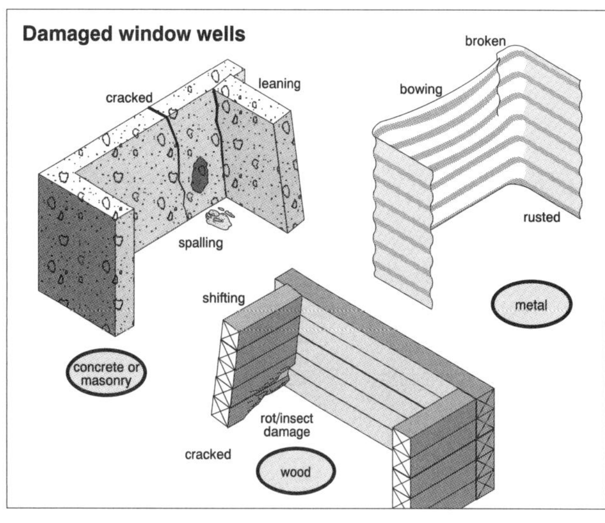

1937

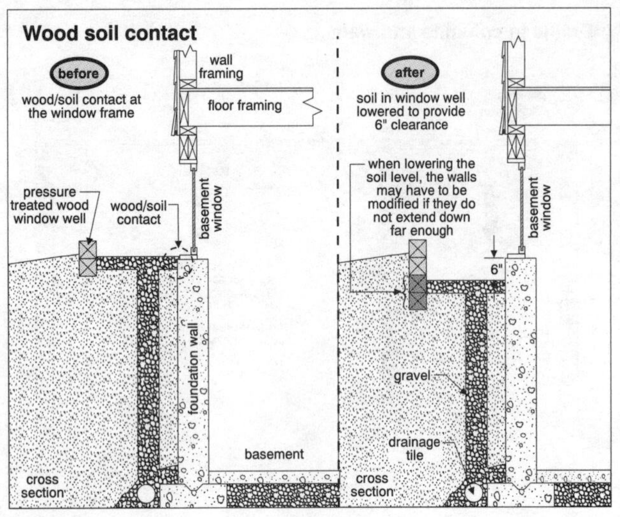

1938

Drain problems

wall framing

floor framing

basement window

pressure treated wood window well

water level if drain isn't working

check for water stains/damage here

water

the drain pipe may be visible above the gravel or there may not be a pipe at all

cutaway

drain pipe filled with gravel

foundation wall

basement

cross section

window well cover

a clear cover can be a cost-effective answer to many window well drain problems

1939

Concrete and asphalt driveways

concrete driveways should have expansion and/or control joints so that cracking occurs in predetermined locations

sealant

5" bed of gravel for both concrete and asphalt driveways

1940

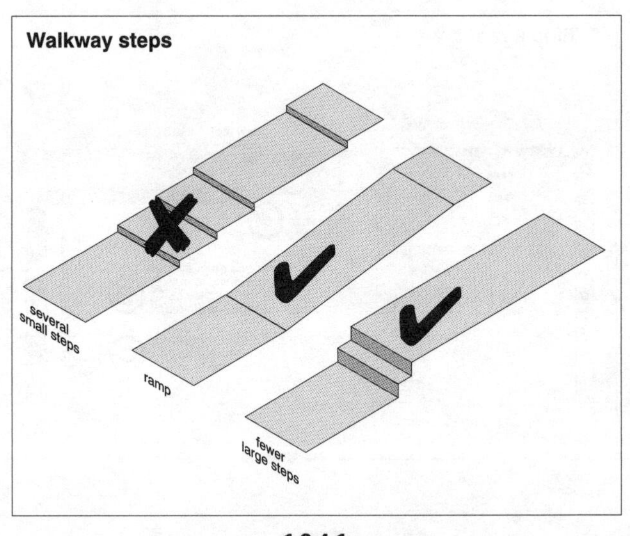

1941

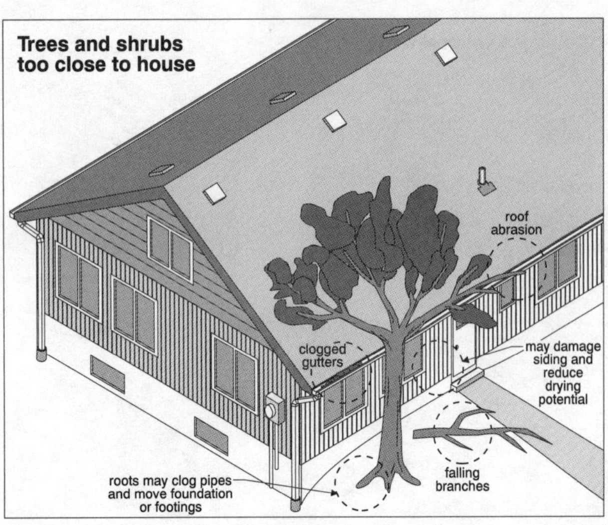

1942

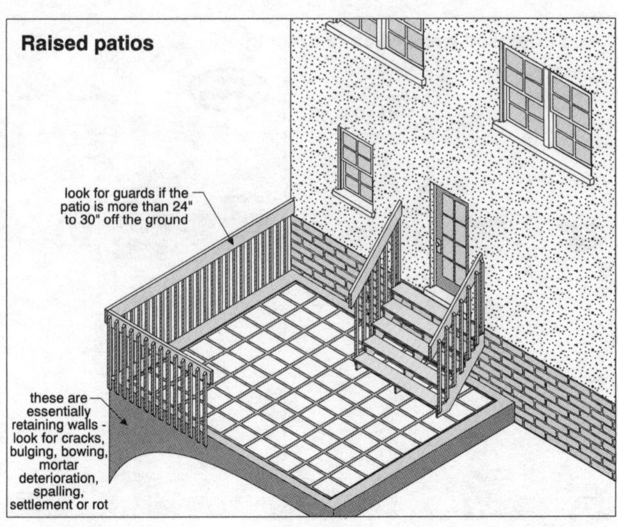

1943

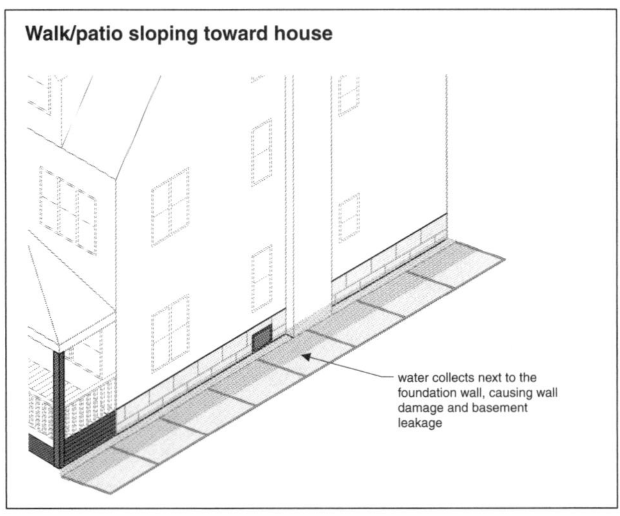

1944

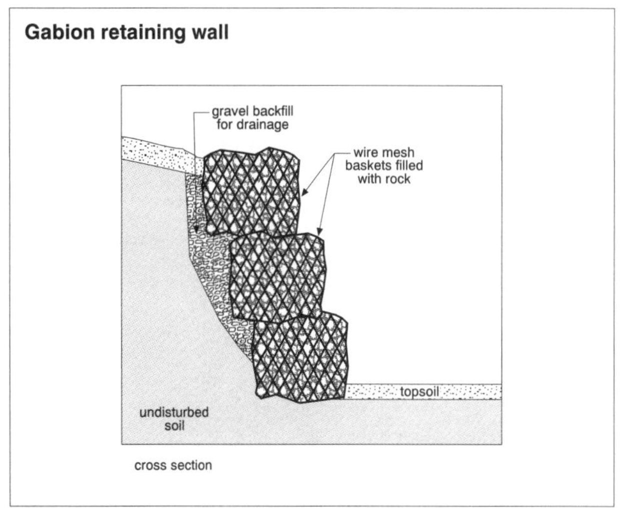

1945

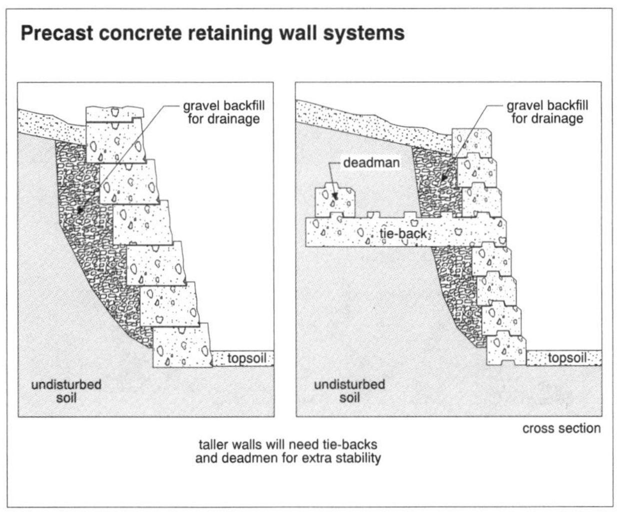

1946

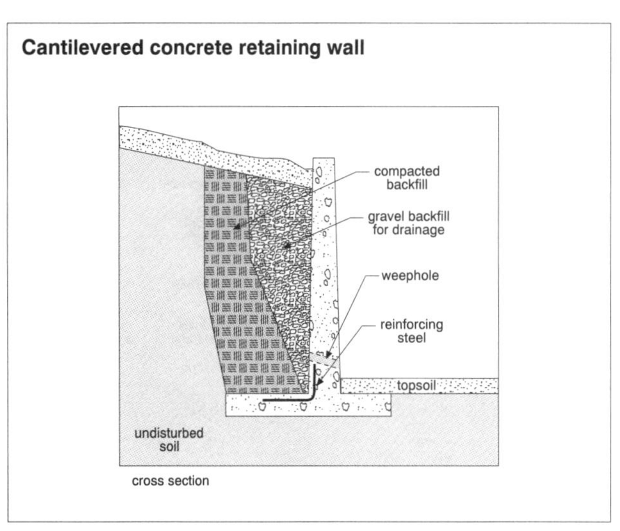

1947

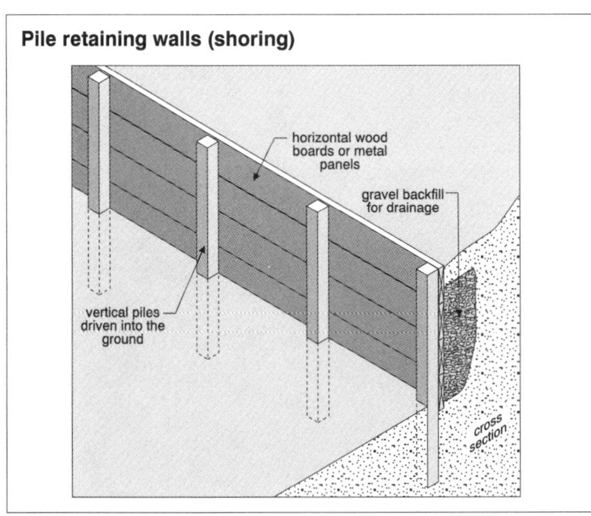

1948

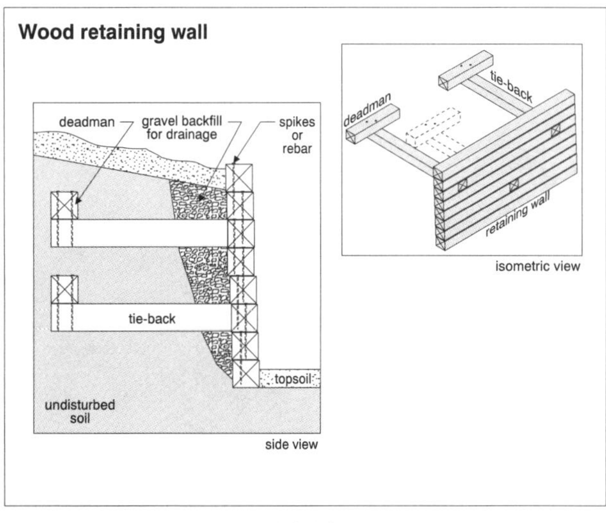

1949

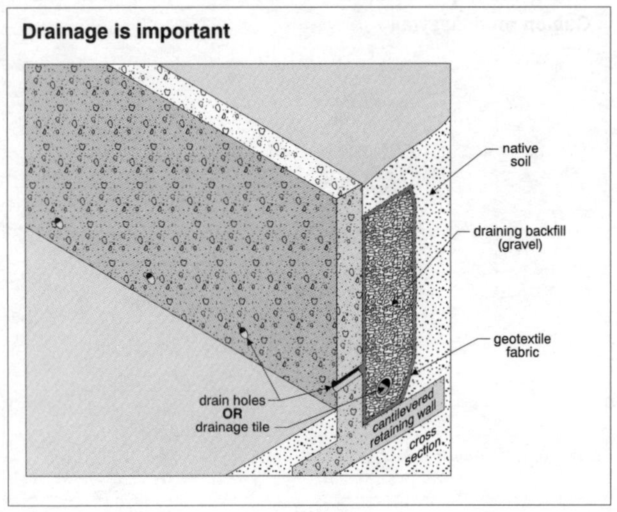

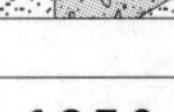

1950

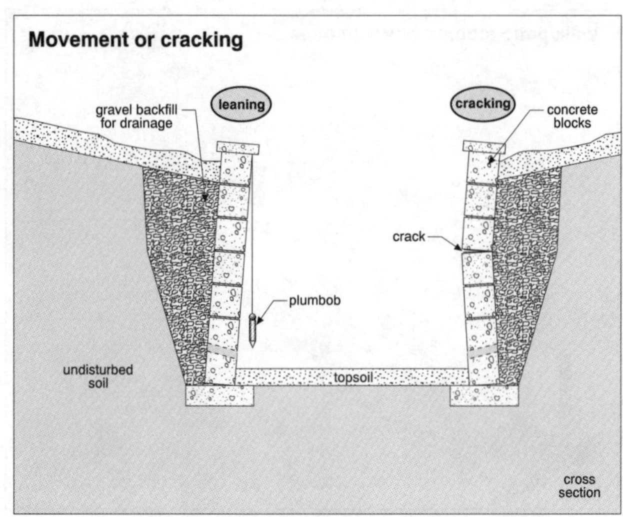

1951

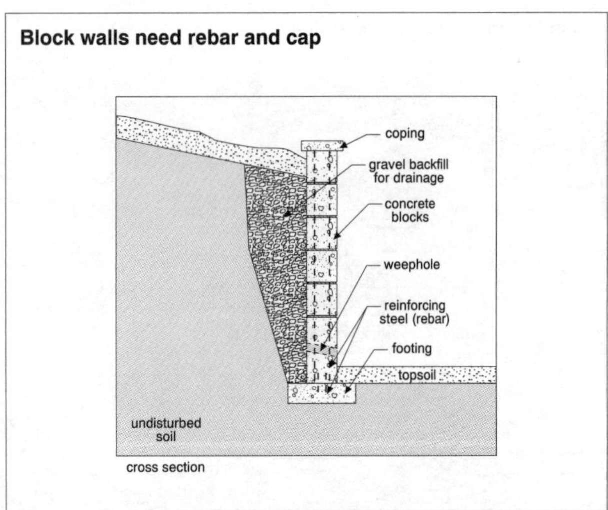

1952

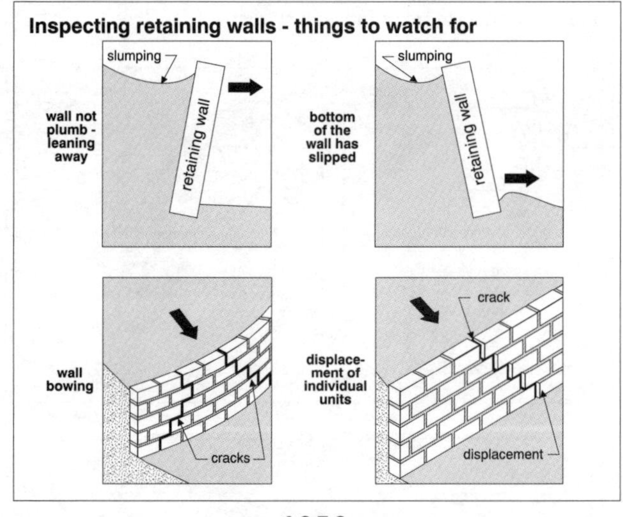

1953

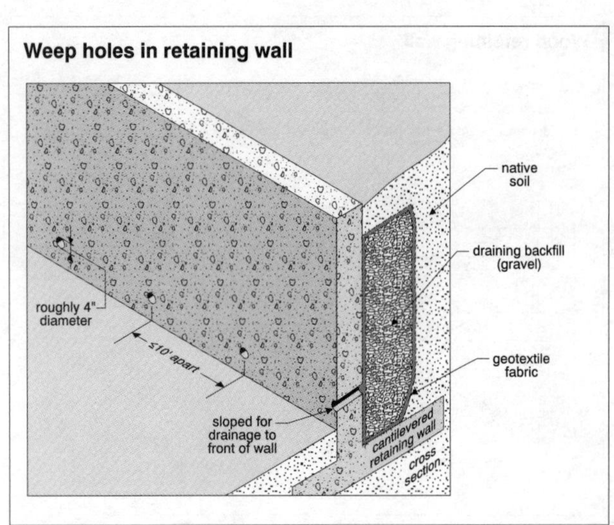

1954

CHAPTER 9

INTERIOR

INTRODUCTION

339 ... 2000 Fire and gas proofing in attached garages
339 ... 2001 Look behind window treatments

FLOORS

339 ... 2002 Control joints in concrete floors
339 ... 2003 Rot around plumbing fixtures
340 ... 2004 Sources of interior water damage
340 ... 2005 Concrete floor problems
340 ... 2006 Hollows
340 ... 2007 Causes of rot
341 ... 2008 Alternatives for installing ceramic tiles

WALLS

341 ... 2009 Gypsum lath versus drywall
341 ... 2010 Inspecting walls
341 ... 2011 Common locations for water damage
342 ... 2012 Structural clues
342 ... 2013 Shadow effect
342 ... 2014 Nail pop mechanism
342 ... 2015 Wood frame party wall
343 ... 2016 Ice dams
343 ... 2017 Plaster with wood lathe
343 ... 2018 Bulging of plaster due to creep in wood-frame walls

CEILINGS

343 ... 2019 Roof truss uplift
343 ... 2020 Roof truss uplift – remedial action
343 ... 2021 Strapping the underside of trusses
344 ... 2022 Stairway lighting
344 ... 2023 Sagging ceilings – broken keys

TRIM, COUNTERS, AND CABINETS

344 ... 2024 Kinds of trim
344 ... 2025 Counter problems
344 ... 2026 Loose cabinets can seriously injure people
344 ... 2027 Cabinet defects

STAIRS

345 ... 2028 Stair dimensions (straight stairs)
345 ... 2029 Curved treads
345 ... 2030 Winders
345 ... 2031 Stringers
345 ... 2032 Stairwell width
346 ... 2033 Handrails and guards
346 ... 2034 Rot in wood stairs
346 ... 2035 Tread/stringer connections
346 ... 2036 Stringer movement
347 ... 2037 Handrail support
347 ... 2038 Fire stopping for stairs
347 ... 2039 Stairway lighting

WINDOWS, SKYLIGHTS, AND SOLARIUMS

347 ... 2040 Glazing types
347 ... 2041 Window types
348 ... 2042 Window components
348 ... 2043 Fall protection
348 ... 2044 Drain holes
348 ... 2045 Flashing pan
348 ... 2046 Energy efficiency
348 ... 2047 Low-E glass
349 ... 2048 Move glass inboard
349 ... 2049 Spacing between layers of glass
349 ... 2050 Thermal breaks in frames
349 ... 2051 Look behind window treatments
349 ... 2052 Sloped glazing
349 ... 2053 Skylight and solarium leaks
350 ... 2054 Lintels sagging or missing
350 ... 2055 Window frame deformation
350 ... 2056 Window installed backwards
350 ... 2057 Flashings over windows
350 ... 2058 Watch for faulty windows
350 ... 2059 Don't push on upper sash
351 ... 2060 Fall protection
351 ... 2061 Exit window sizes
351 ... 2062 Ice damming below skylight
351 ... 2063 Leaking corner of vinyl or aluminum window frame
351 ... 2064 Blinds and shutters can contribute to window condensation

CHAPTER 9

DOORS

351 ... 2065 Door cores
352 ... 2066 Door operation
352 ... 2067 French doors
352 ... 2068 Lintels sagging or missing
352 ... 2069 Insulated metal doors shouldn't have a storm door
352 ... 2070 Doorsill support
352 ... 2071 Staining below exterior doors
353 ... 2072 Man door (attached garage)
353 ... 2073 Racking door openings due to sloping floors

WET BASEMENTS AND CRAWLSPACES

353 ... 2074 Causes of wet basement problems
353 ... 2075 Roof and surface water control
353 ... 2076 Basement windows and stairs
353 ... 2077 Swales
354 ... 2078 Concrete flaws
354 ... 2079 Where cracks appear
354 ... 2080 Concrete block walls
354 ... 2081 High water table
355 ... 2082 Depth of foundation
355 ... 2083 Wet basement clues – part 1
355 ... 2084 Wet basement clues – part 2
355 ... 2085 Why is there a sump pump in the basement?
355 ... 2086 Control surface water
355 ... 2087 Patching cracks
356 ... 2088 Interior drainage system
356 ... 2089 Excavation, dampproofing and drainage tile
356 ... 2090 Crack repair – epoxy and polyurethane injection
356 ... 2091 Crack repair – drainage layer
356 ... 2092 Crack repair – exterior patching
356 ... 2093 Interior drainage system – different approaches
357 ... 2094 Basement leakage clues – efflorescence
357 ... 2095 Basement leakage clues – rot, stains and water marks
357 ... 2096 Basement leakage clues – rust
357 ... 2097 Basement leakage clues – crumbling plaster, drywall or masonry

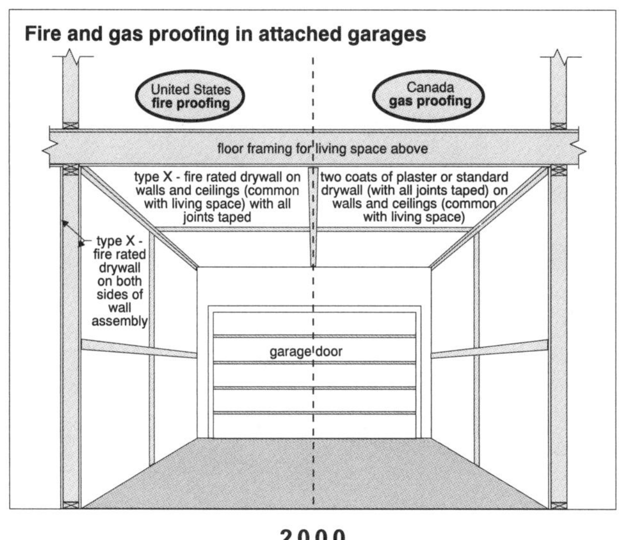

2000

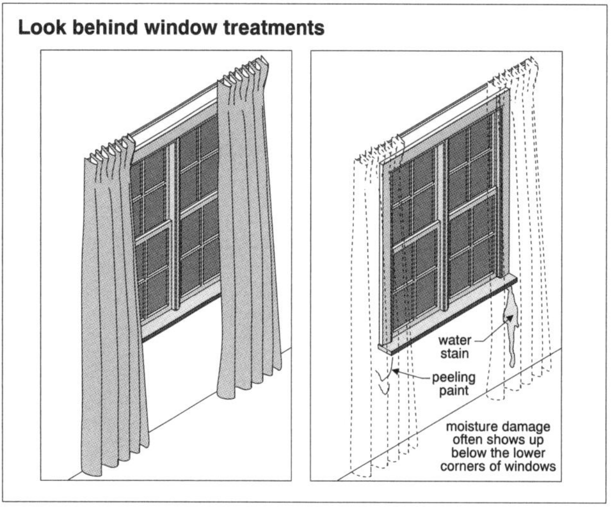

2001

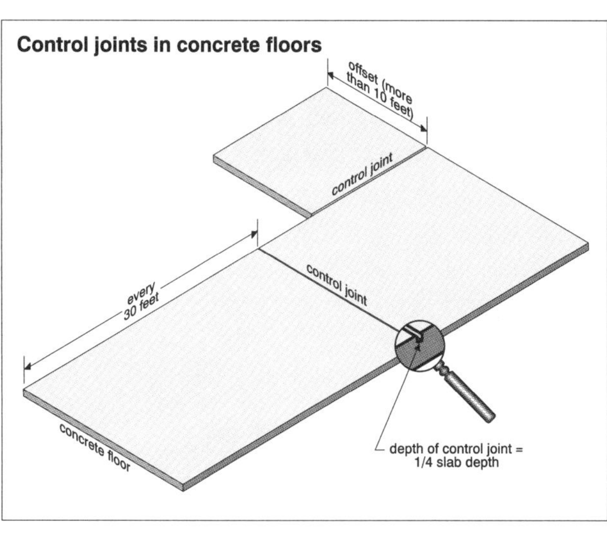

2002

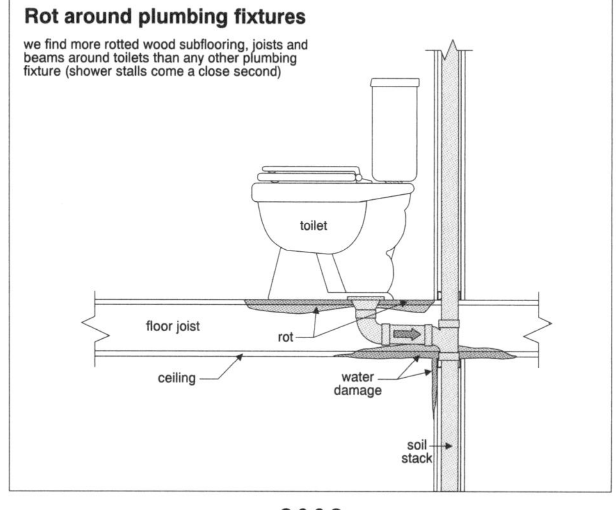

2003

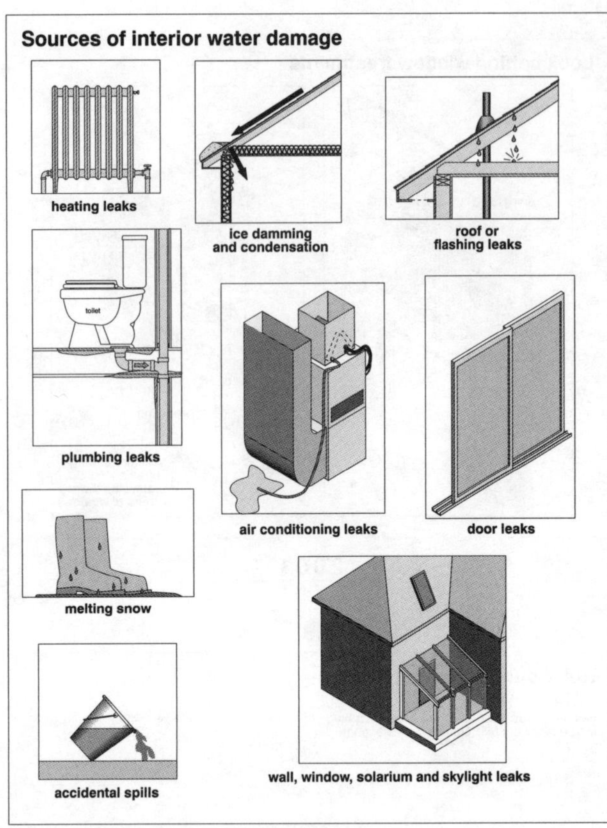

2004

Concrete floor problems

hollow below
heaved
water penetration
cracked
gravel
cross section
settled
sloped away from drain
efflorescence
gravel
cross section

2005

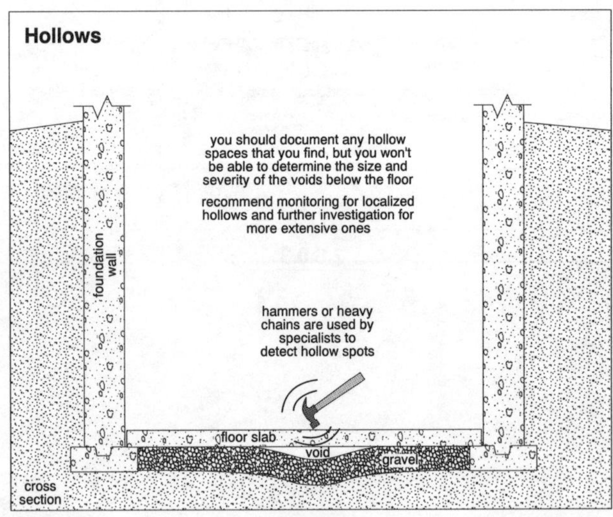

2006

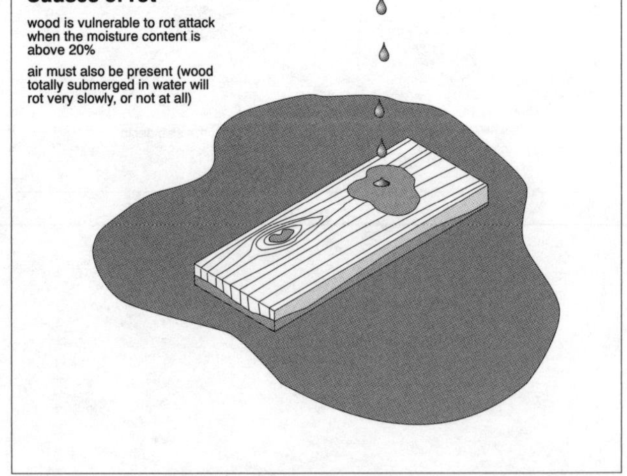

2007

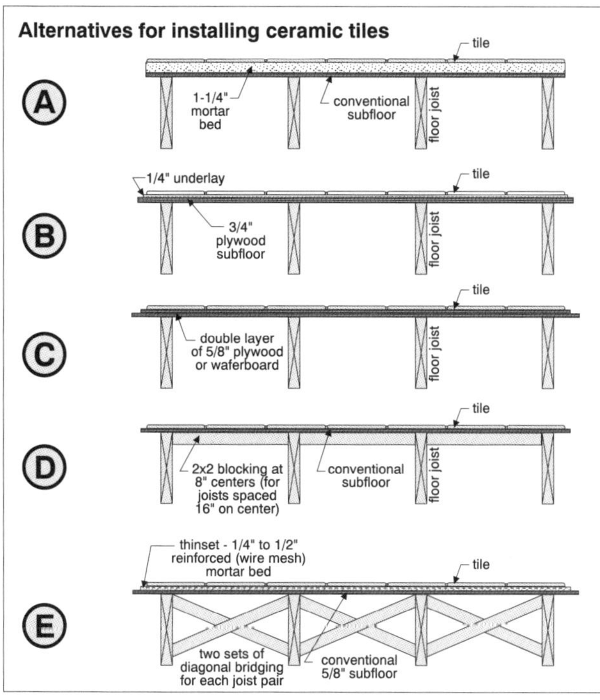

2008

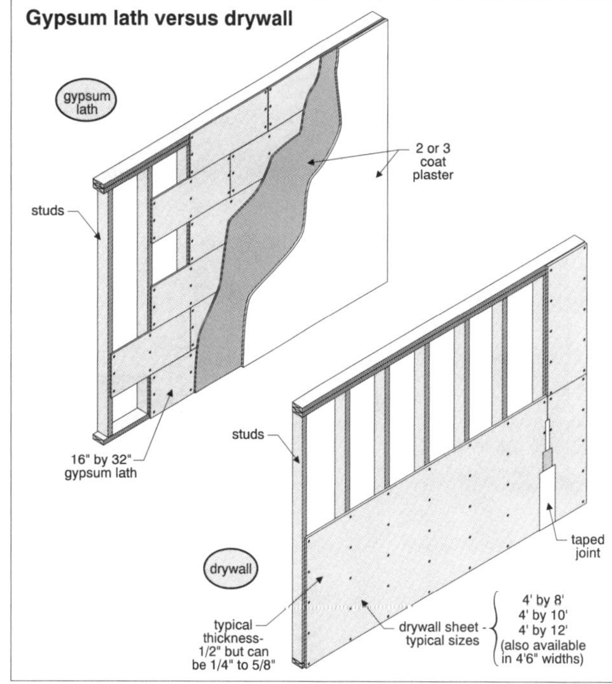

2009

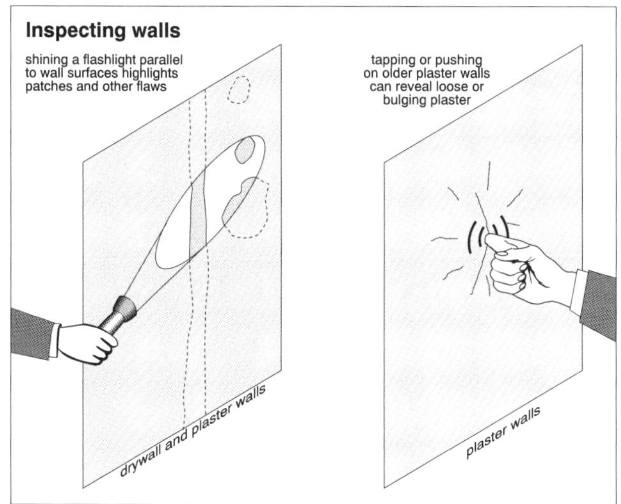

2010

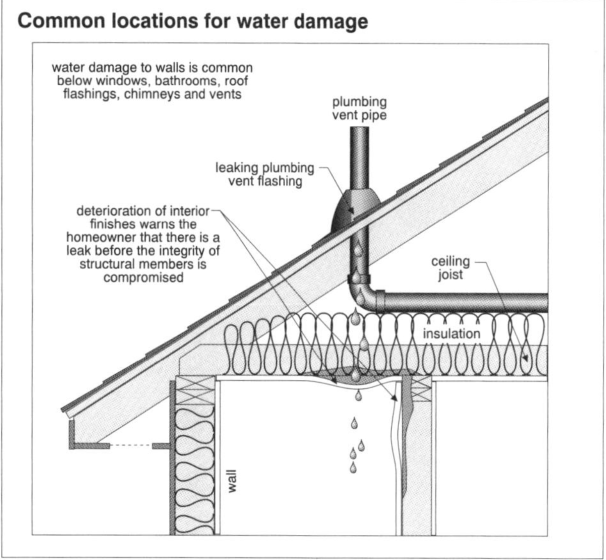

2011

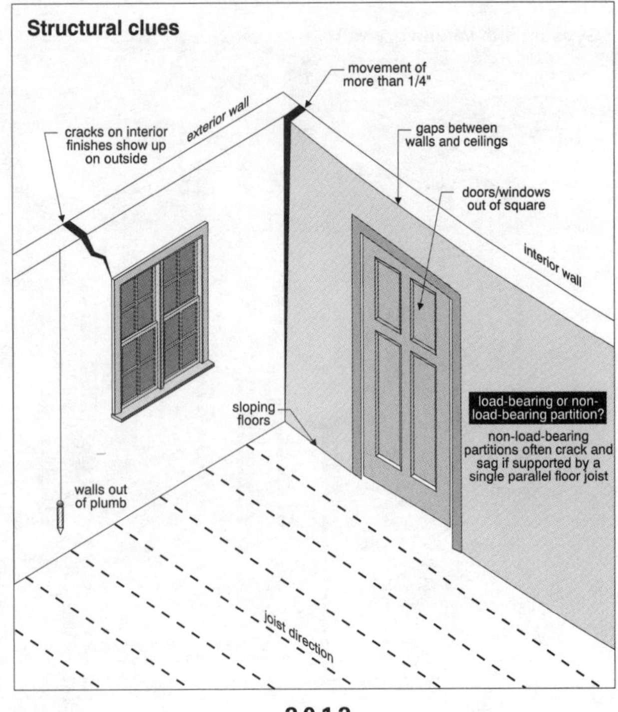

2012

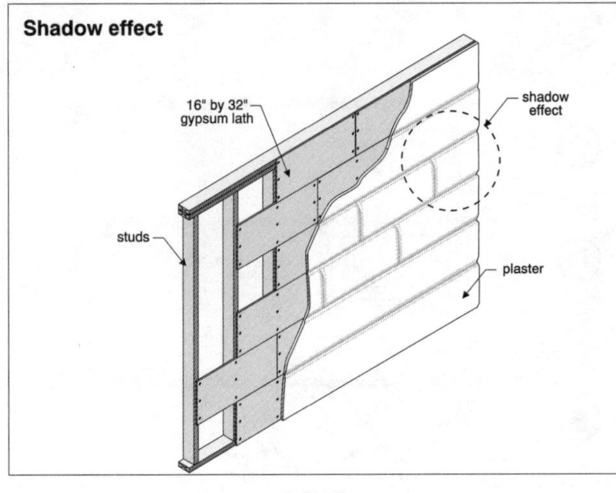

2013

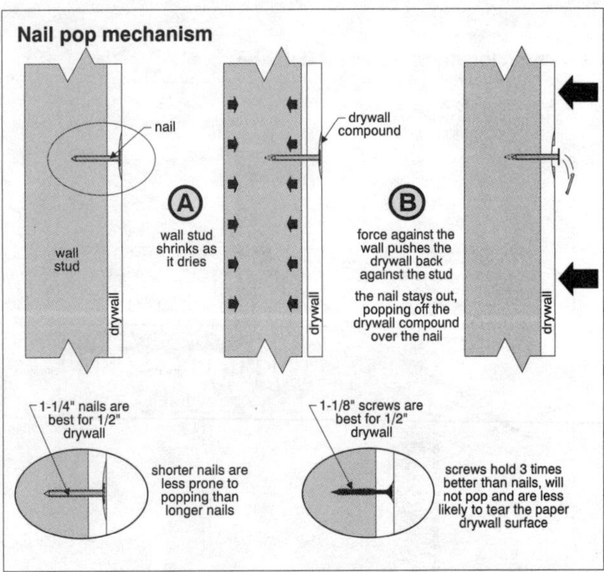

2014

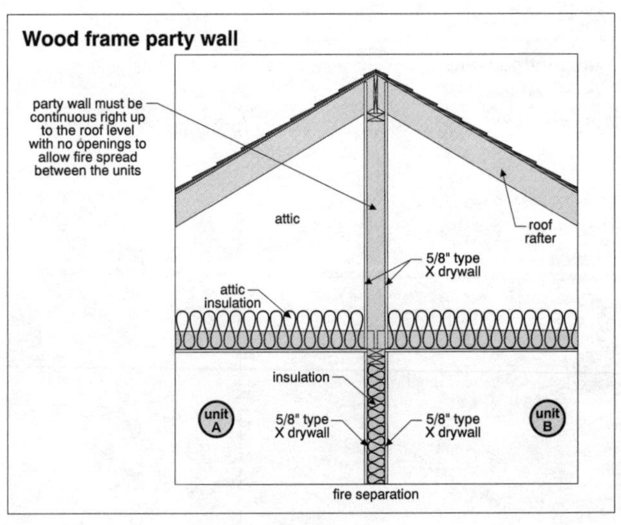

2015

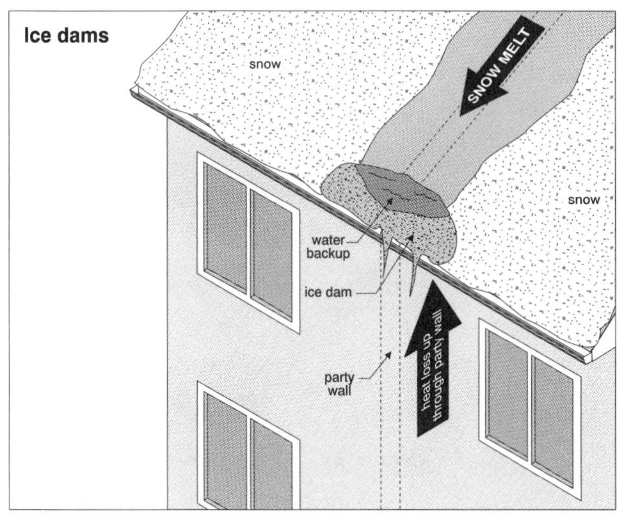

2016

Plaster with wood lath

layer 3: finish coat
layer 2: brown coat
layer 1: scratch coat
stud wall
plaster oozes through gaps in lath and hardens
note: key width exaggerated for clarity
"keys" secure the plaster to the lath
lath is nailed to the studs

2017

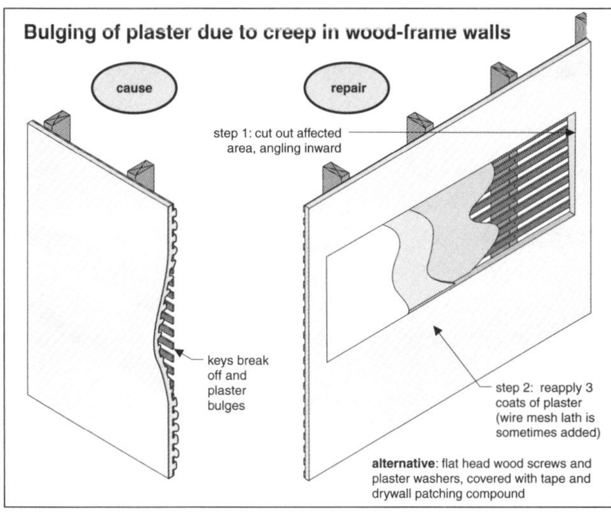

2018

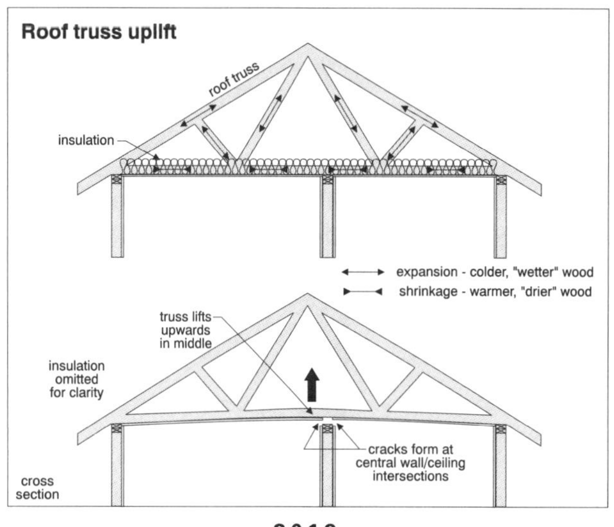

2019

Roof truss uplift - remedial action

1x6 installed between trusses to anchor edge of drywall (clips are also available for the same purpose)
A
OR
B
bottom chord of truss
drywall
install first ceiling fastener about 18" away from wall to allow the drywall to flex
bottom chord of truss
drywall
top plate
wall stud typ. 2x4
molding secured to ceiling (not wall) can float up and down with truss movement

2020

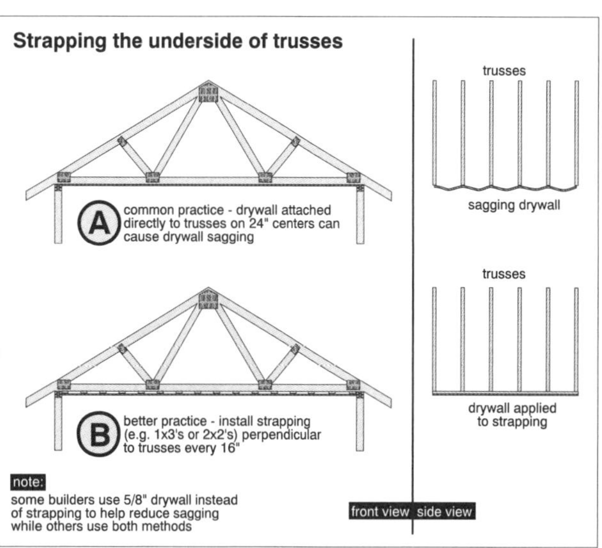

2021

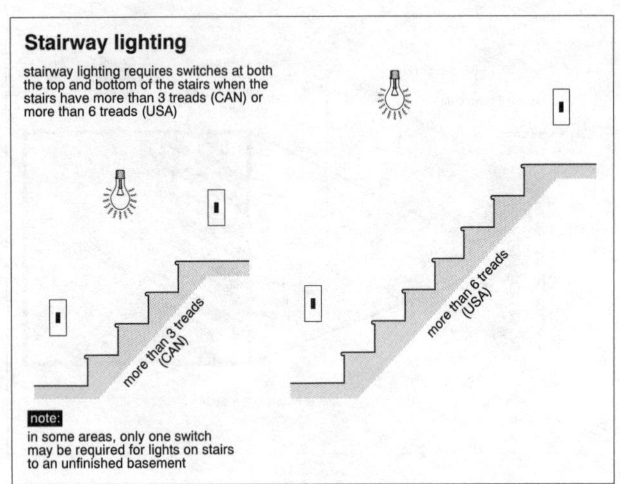

2022

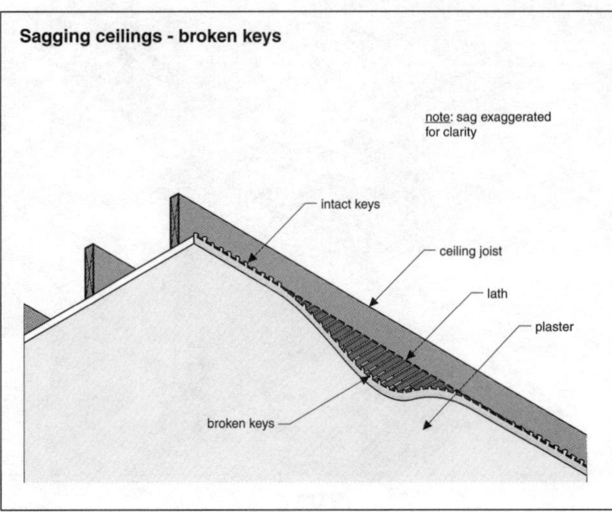

2023

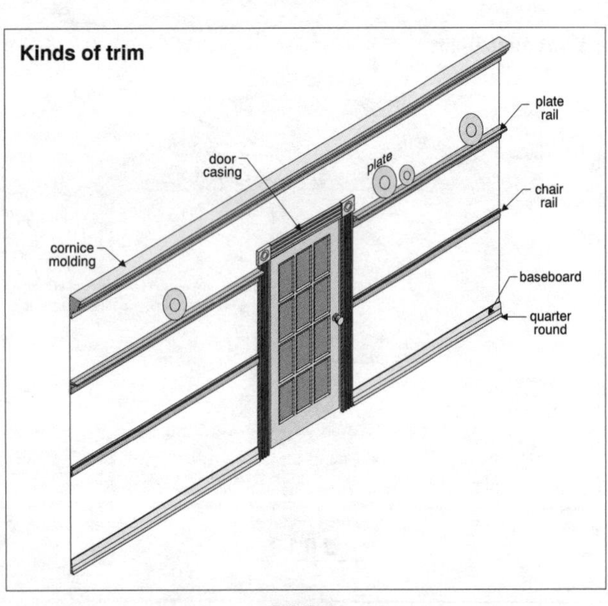

2024

Counter problems

stains or rust

burns

cuts

loose, missing or cracked tiles (or grout) on ceramics

mechanical damage

loose or missing pieces

2025

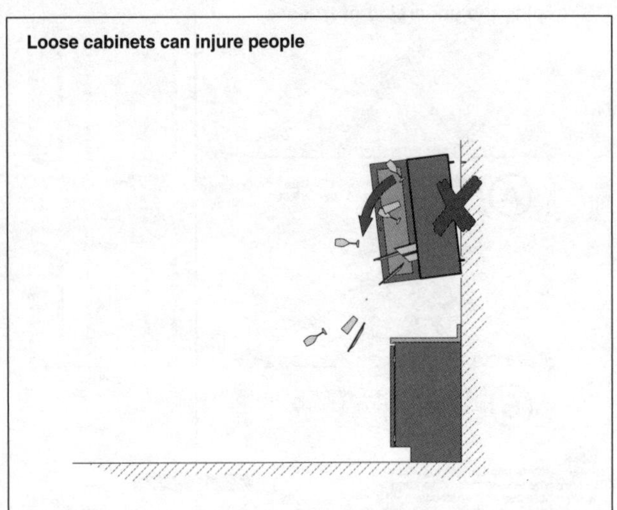

2026

Cabinet defects

check that cabinet is not loose or pulling away from wall

check underside of cabinet over stove for damage

check side of cabinet for scorching, grease

check edge of countertop

check edge of cabinet for peeling veneer, scorching, and warpage

test cabinet doors; do they open and close easily, or are they warped or racked?

2027

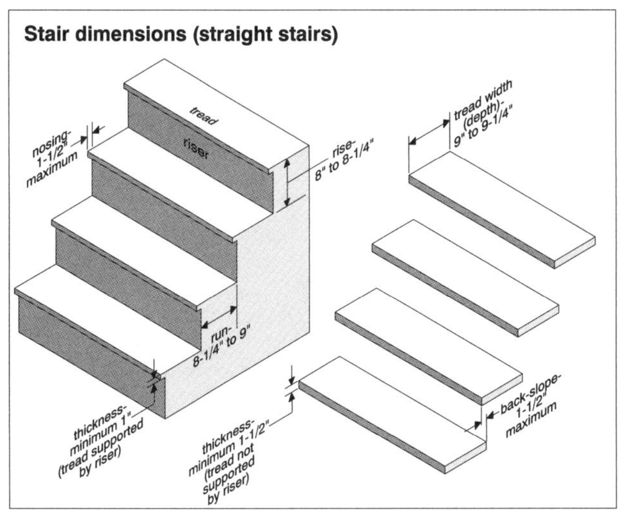

2028

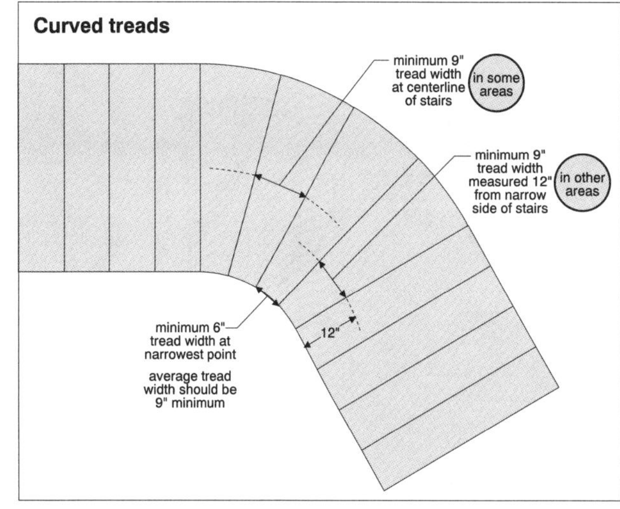

2029

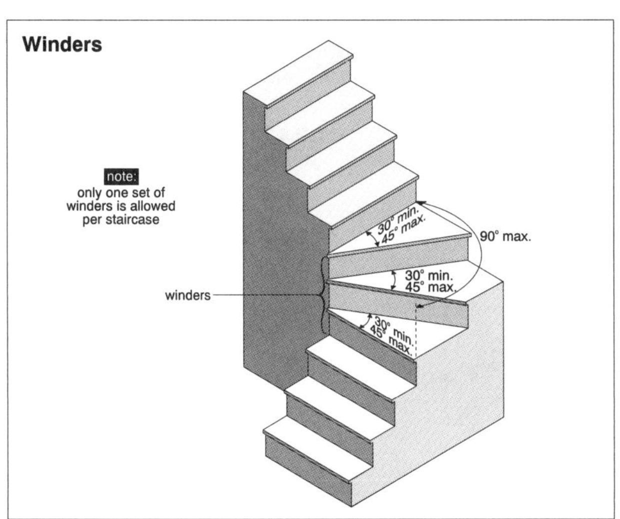

2030

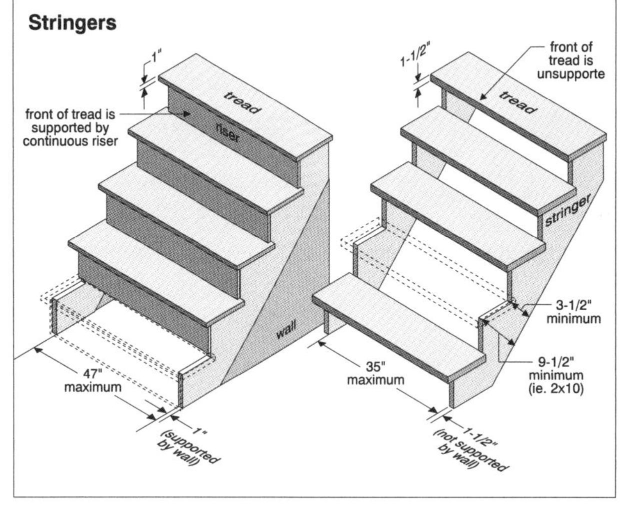

2031

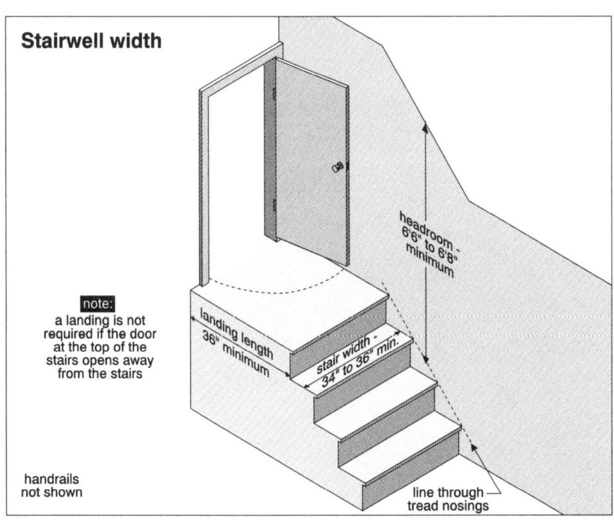

2032

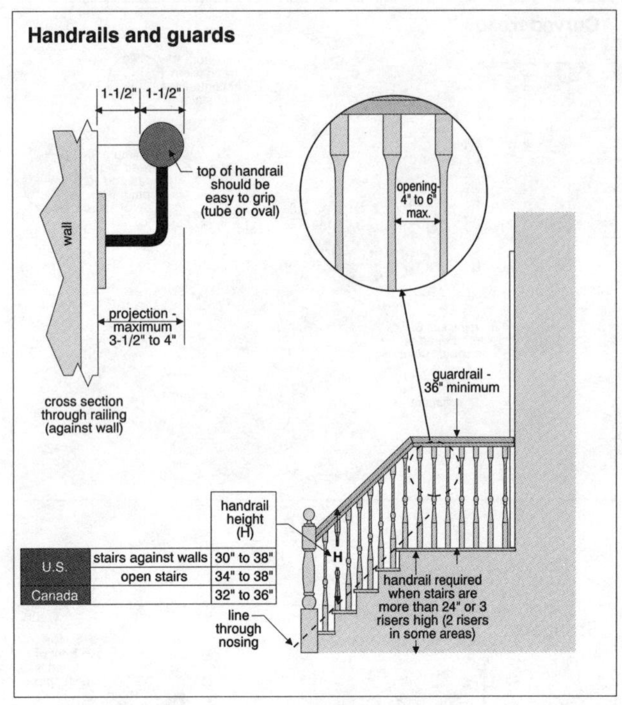

		handrail height (H)
U.S.	stairs against walls	30" to 38"
	open stairs	34" to 38"
Canada		32" to 36"

2033

Rot in wood stairs

stair stringers against exterior basement walls can be prone to rotting - check these carefully

stringer

exterior wall

watch for rot at the bottom of basement stair stringers (especially if they extend into the basement floor slab)

2034

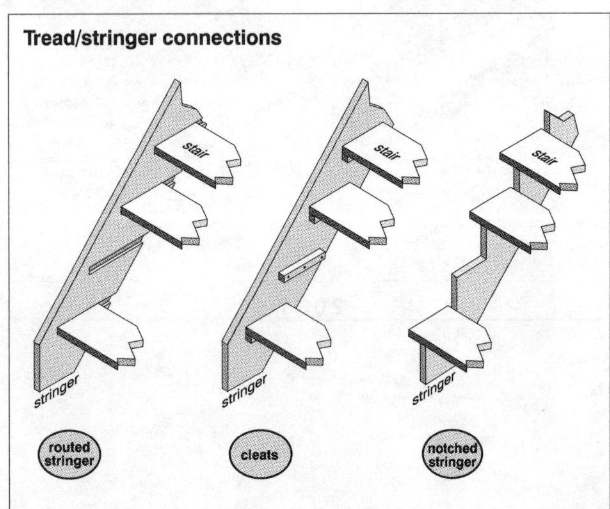

2035

Stringer movement

movement

stringer

top of stairs

wall beside stairs

these stair treads can lose their support

gap between stringer and wall may be concealed by trim

bowing

top of stairs

wall beside stairs

these stair treads can lose their support

bowing stringer

bottom of stairs

2036

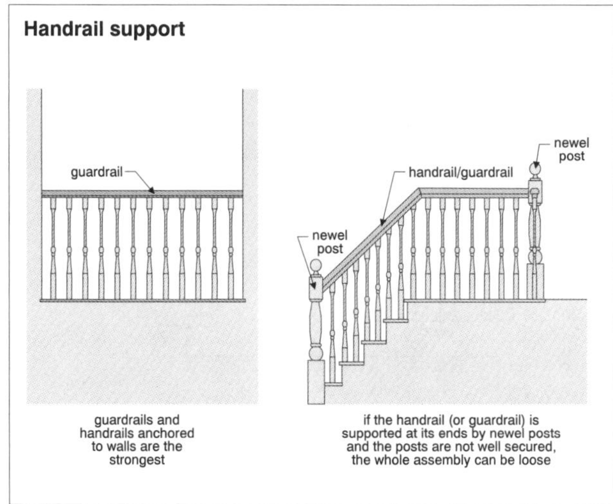

2037

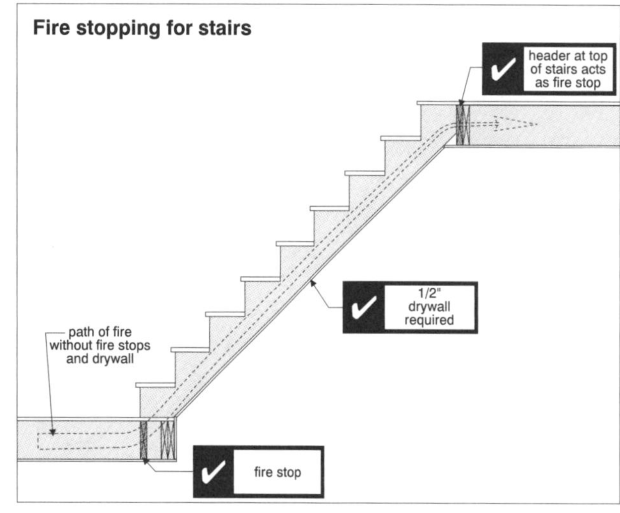

2038

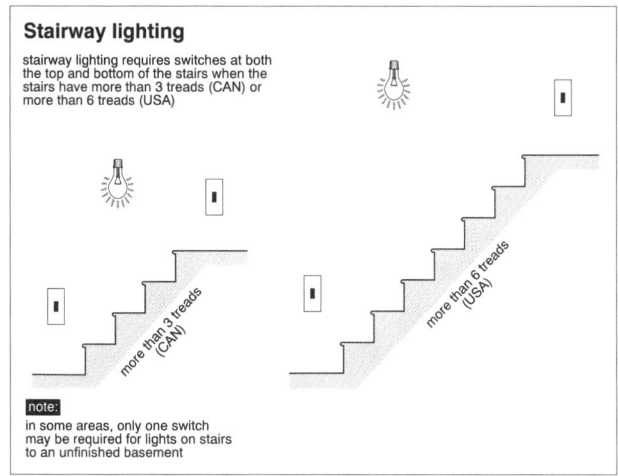

2039

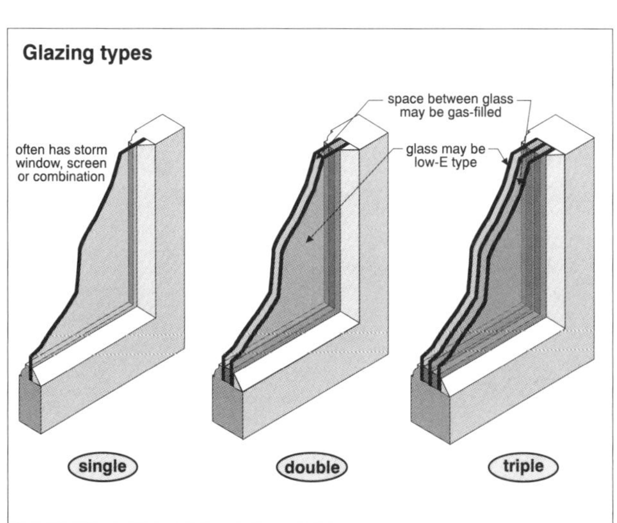

2040

Window types

single and double-hung: double-hung (warm air, cool air), single-hung, closed (inside, outside)

casement: opens out, opens out (pivot offset), opens in, closed (inside, outside)

horizontal slider (inside, open, outside)

awning (fixed, awning, inside, outside)

hopper (fixed, hopper, inside, outside)

fixed (inside, outside)

fixed (glass block)

jalousie (inside, outside)

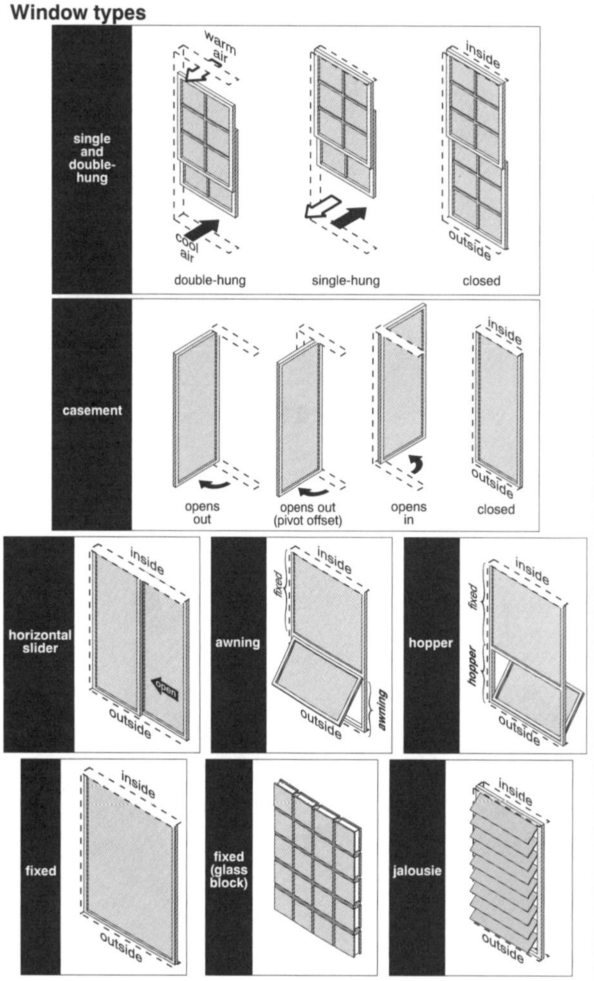

2041

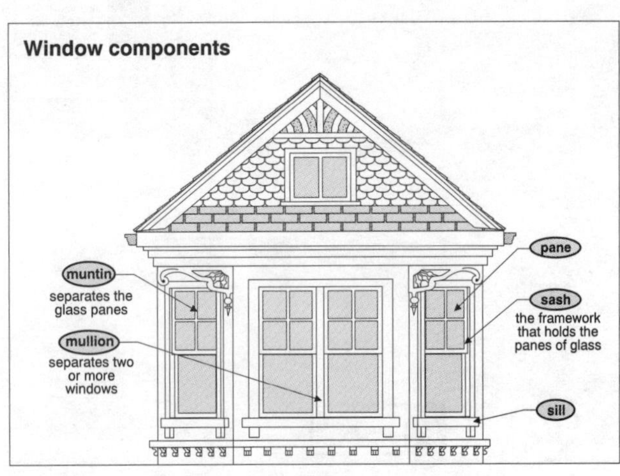

2042

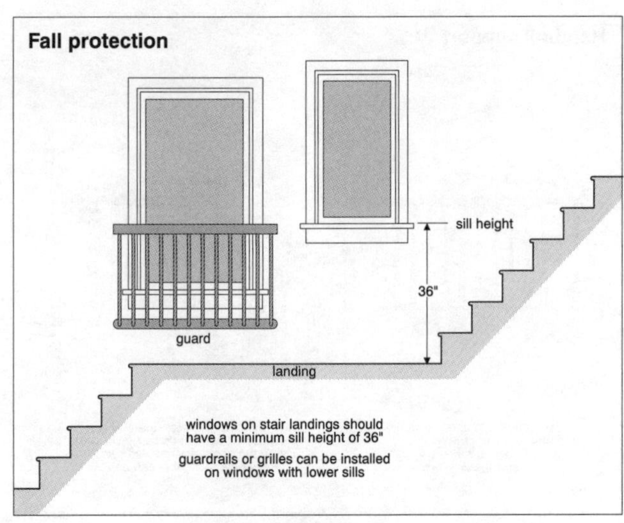

2043

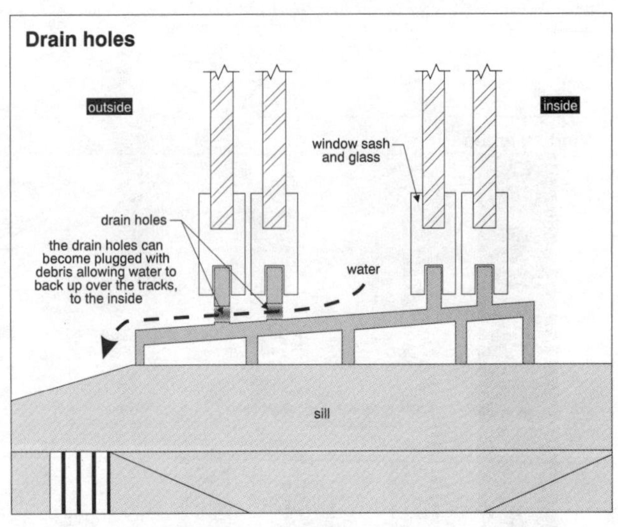

2044

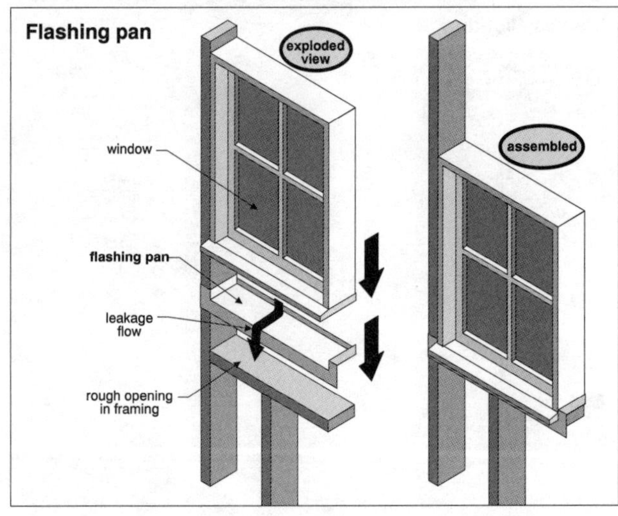

2045

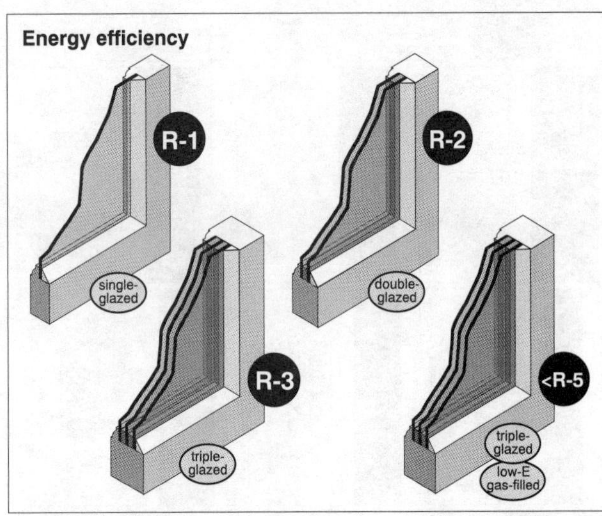

2046

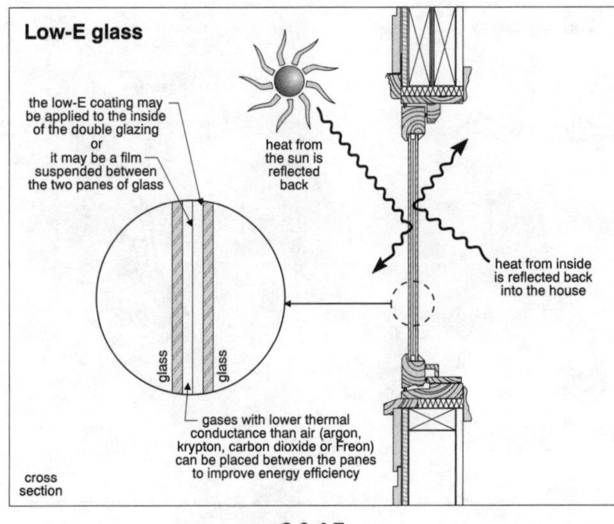

2047

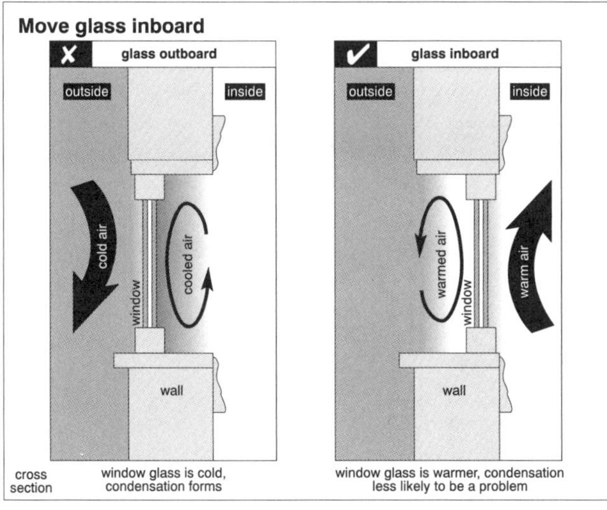

2048

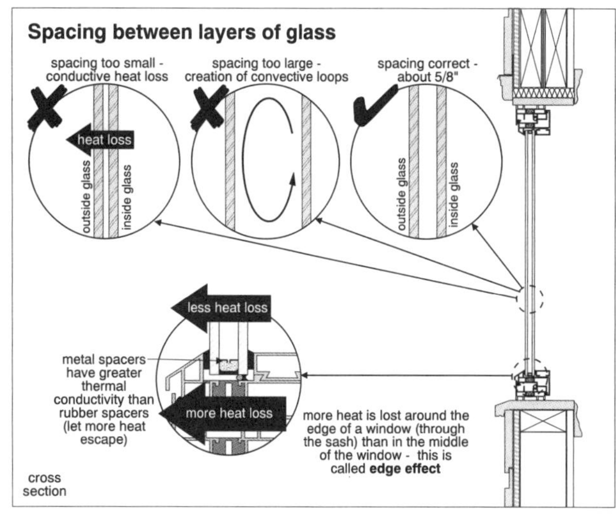

2049

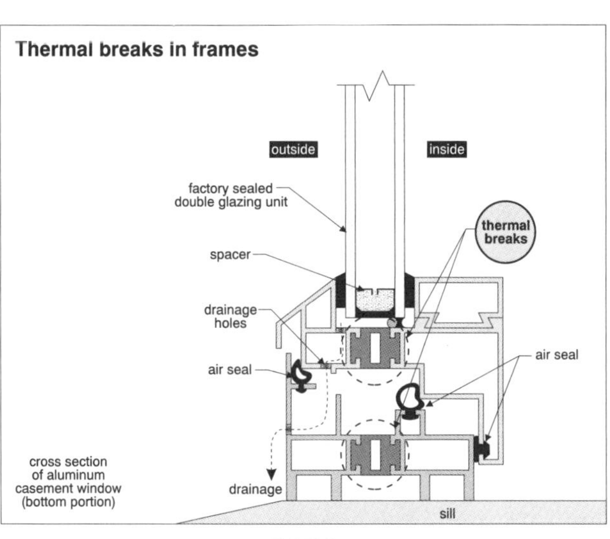

2050

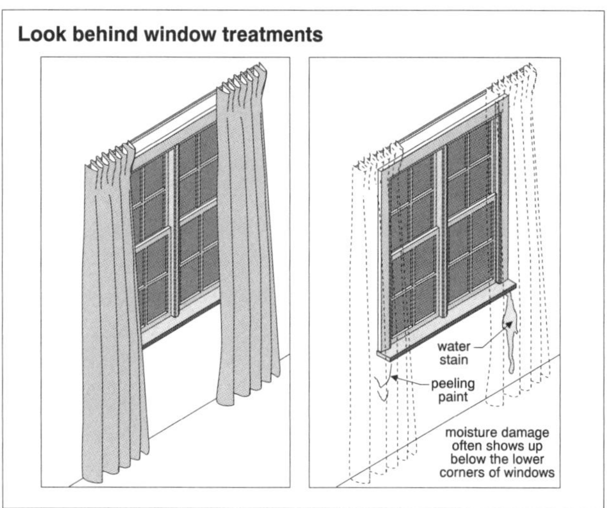

2051

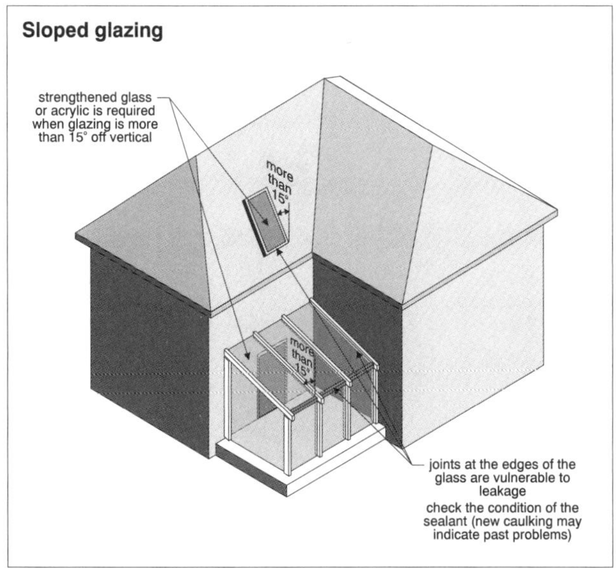

2052

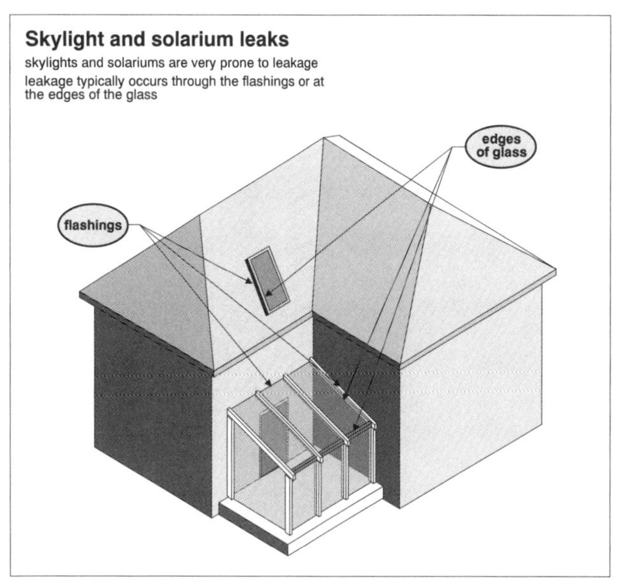

2053

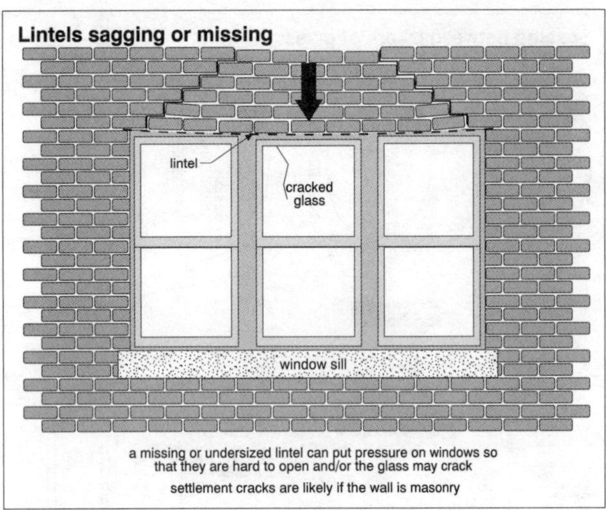

2054

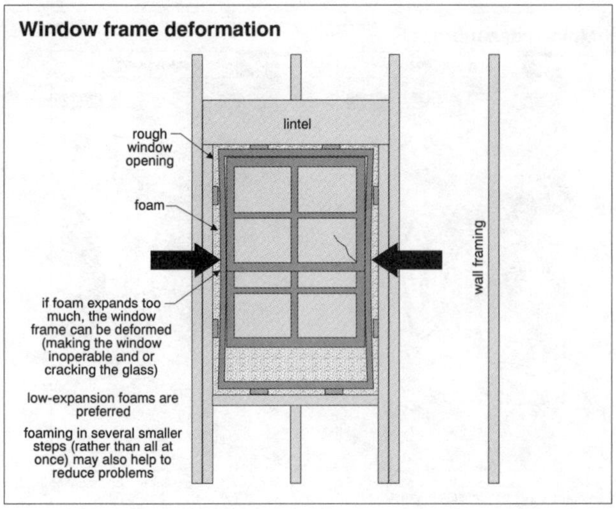

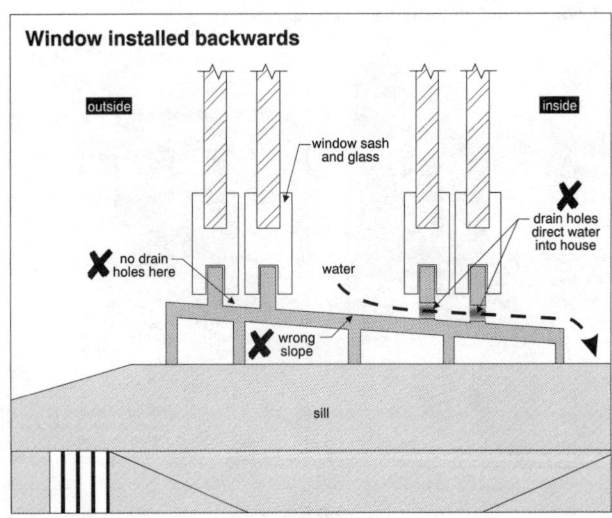

2056

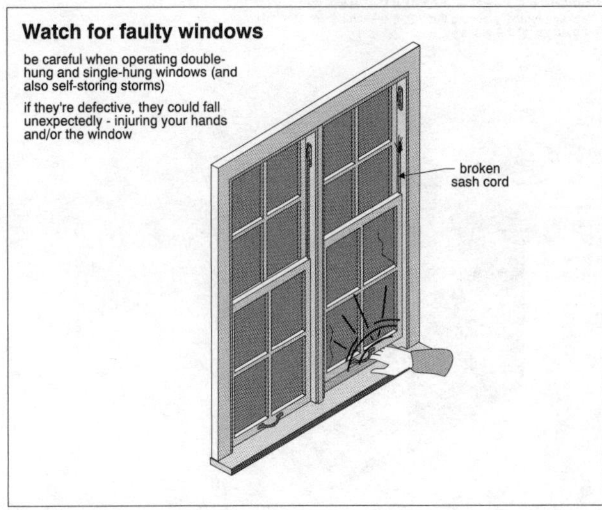

2058

Window frame deformation

lintel

rough window opening

foam

if foam expands too much, the window frame can be deformed (making the window inoperable and or cracking the glass)

low-expansion foams are preferred

foaming in several smaller steps (rather than all at once) may also help to reduce problems

wall framing

2055

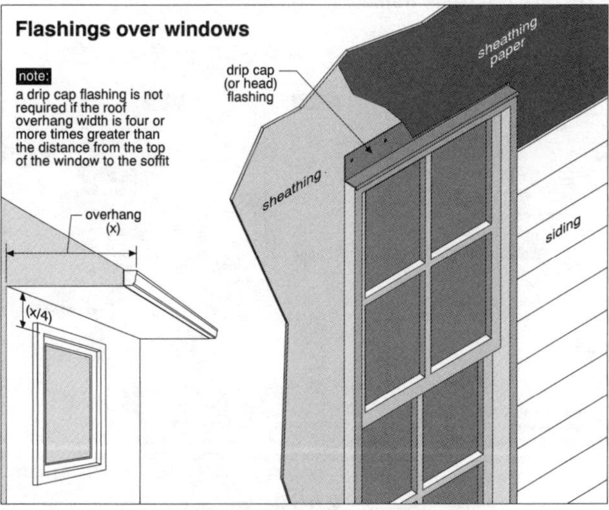

2057

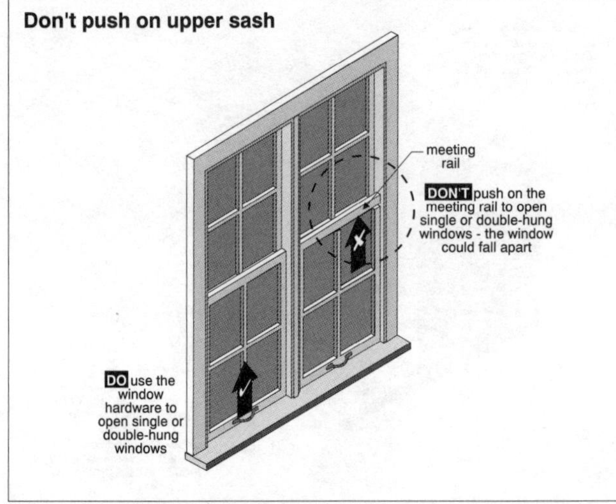

2059

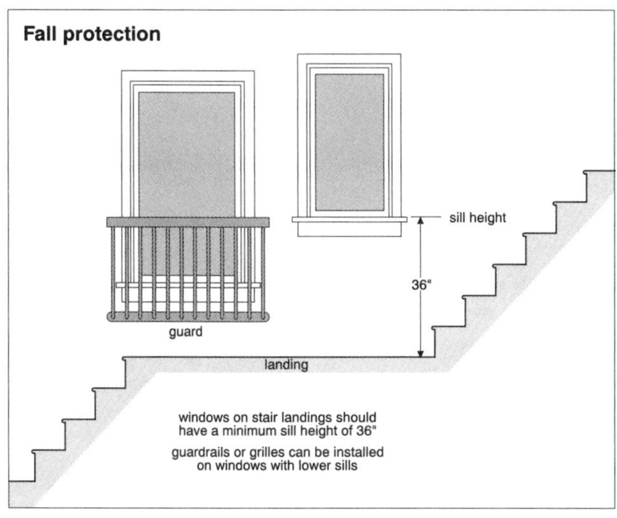

2060

2061

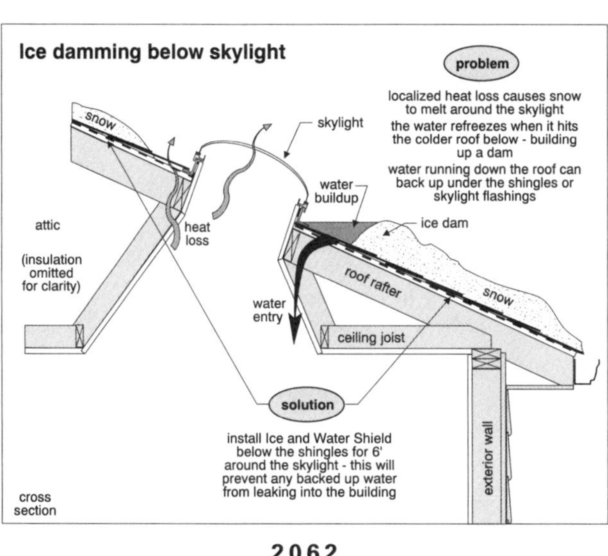

2062

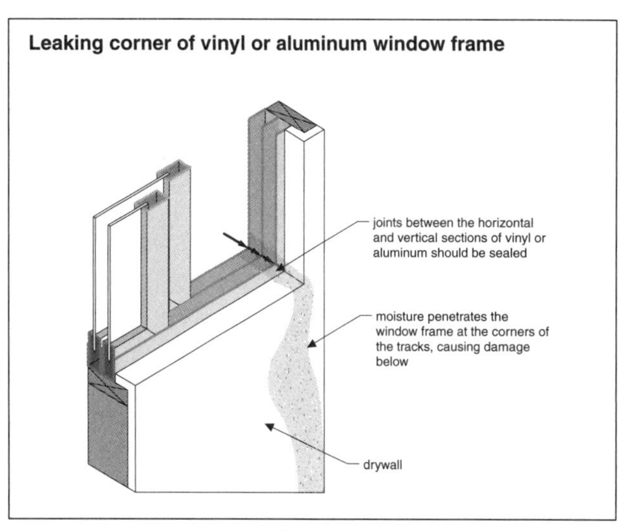

2063

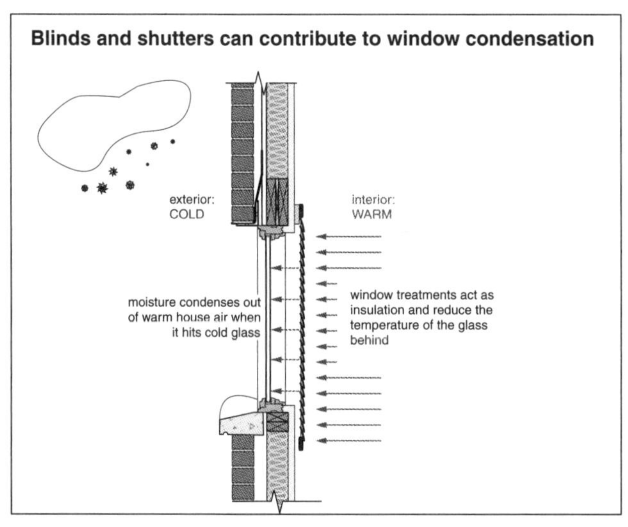

2064

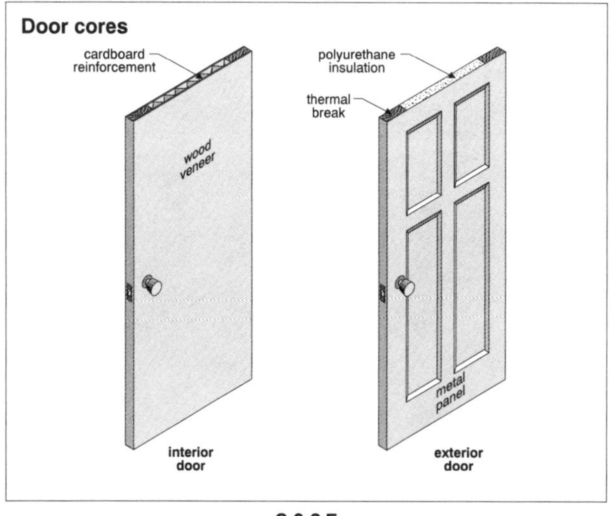

2065

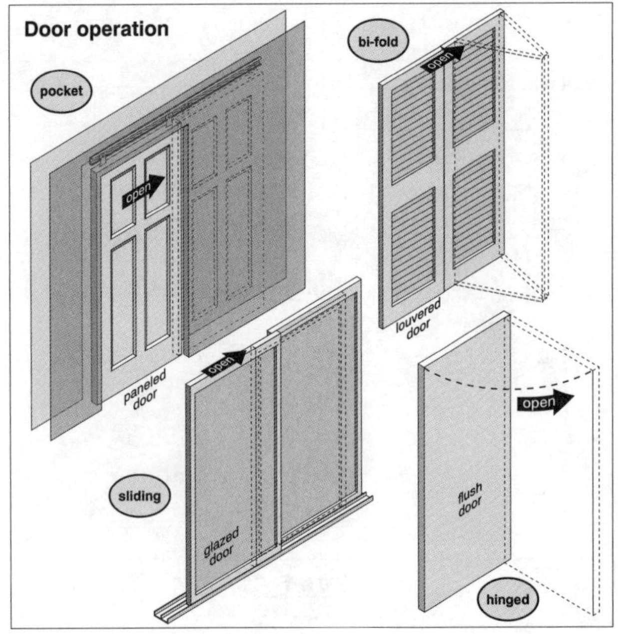

2066

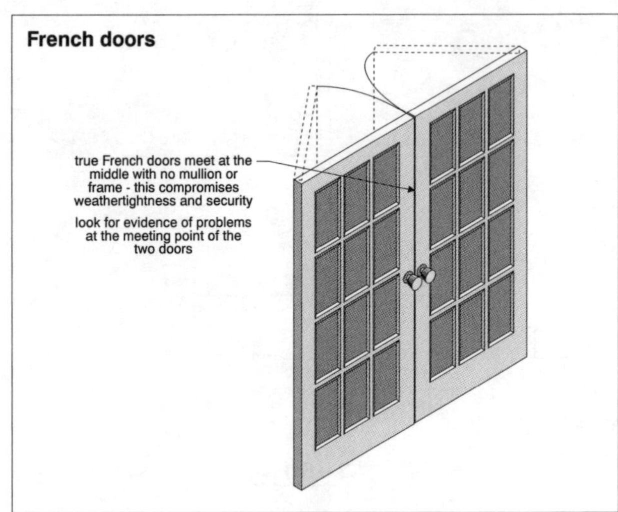

2067

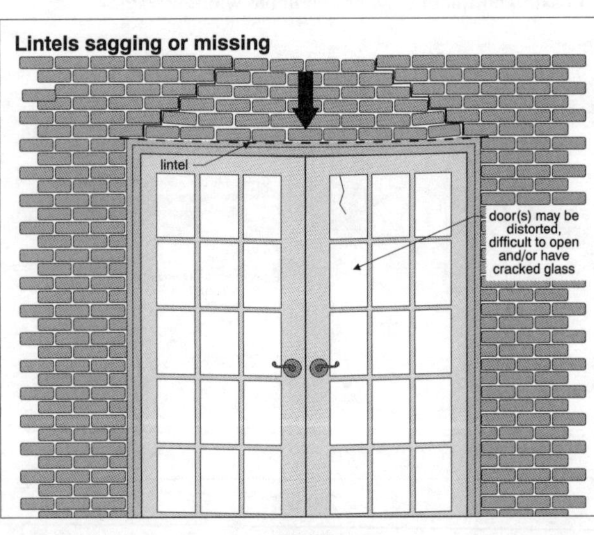

2068

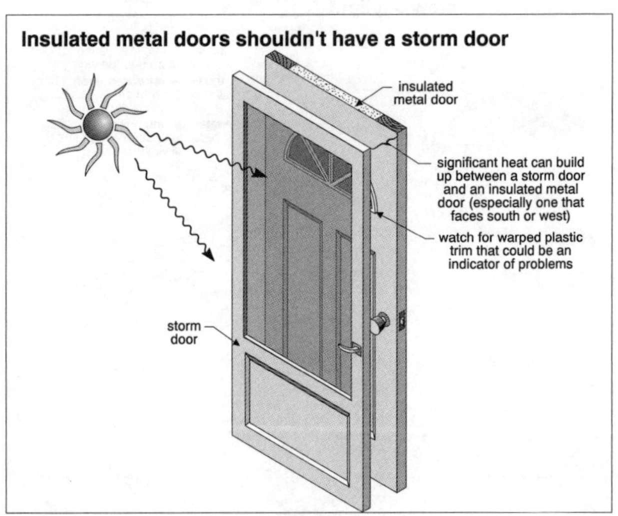

2069

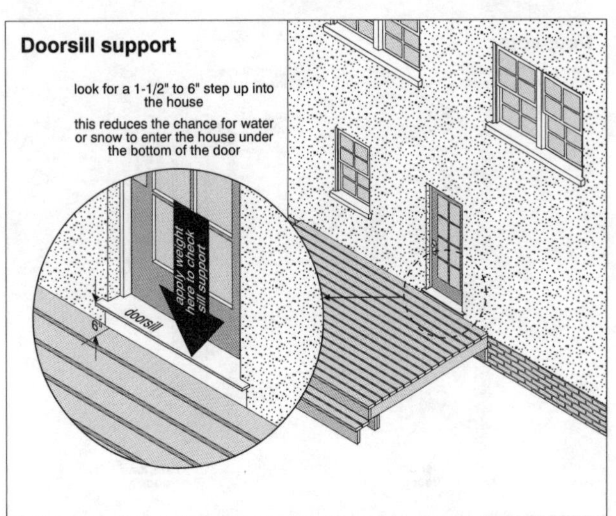

2070

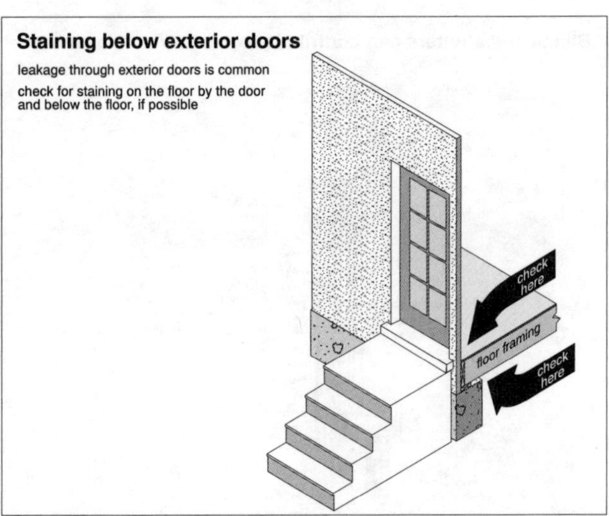

2071

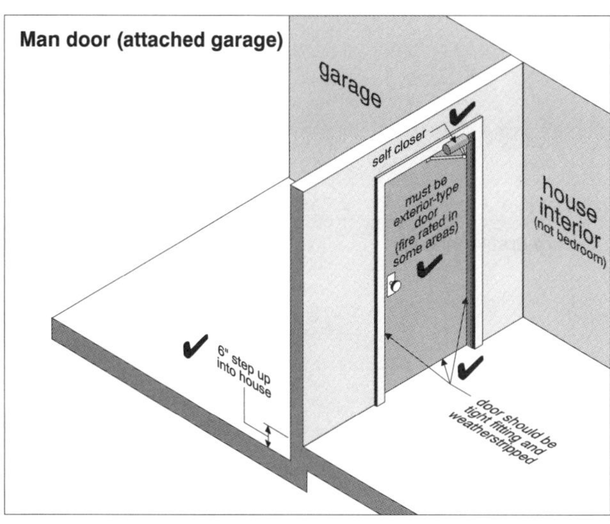

2072

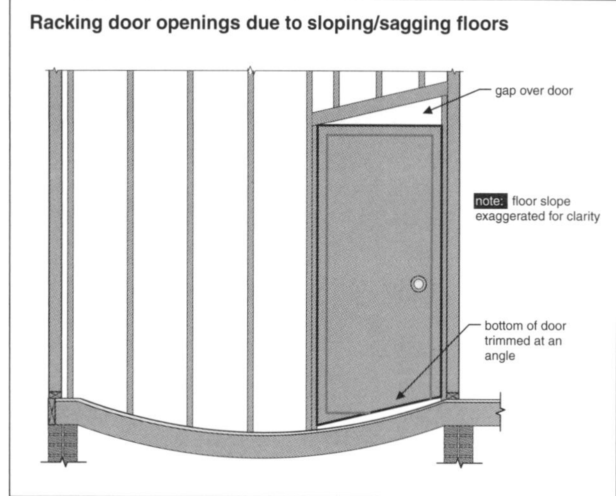

2073

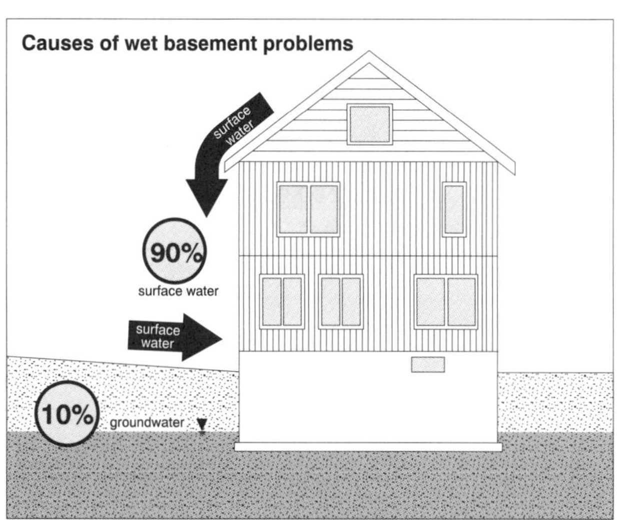

2074

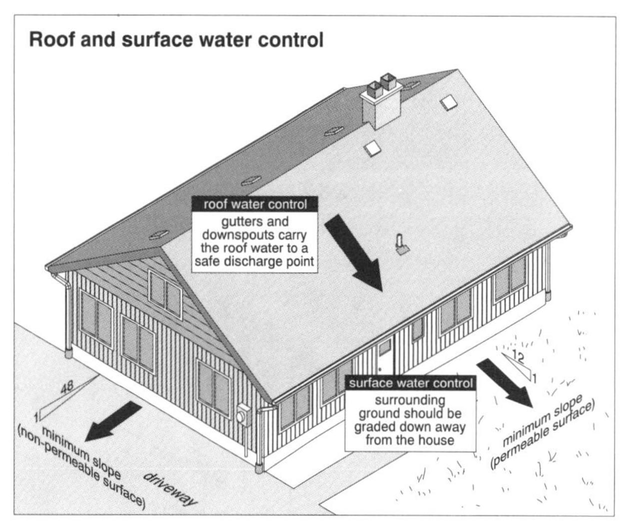

2075

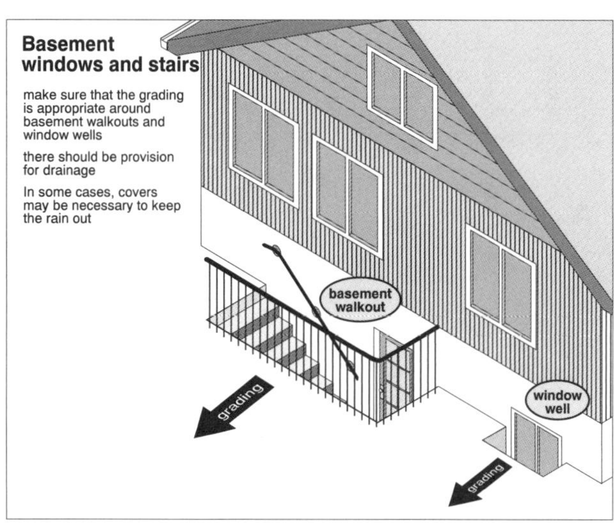

2076

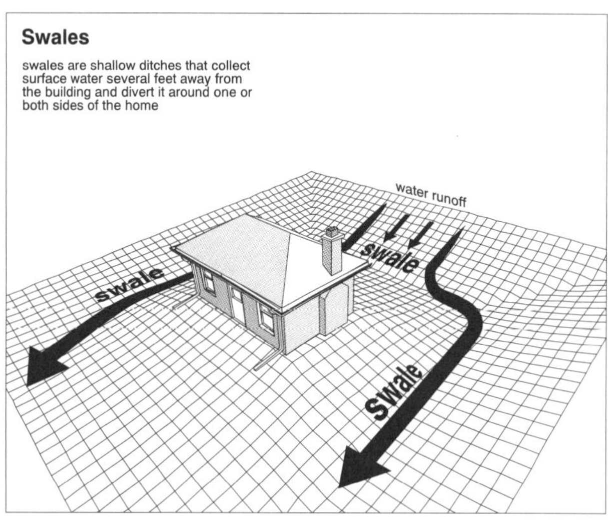

2077

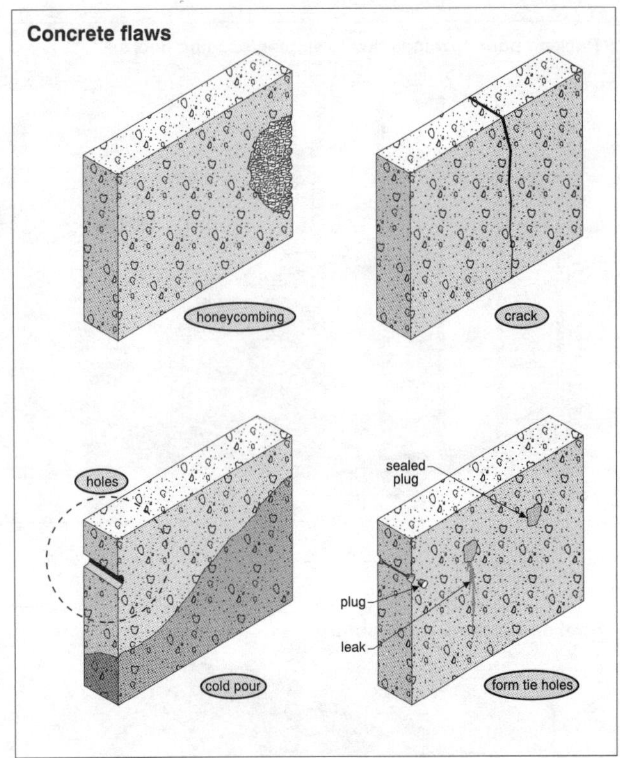

2078

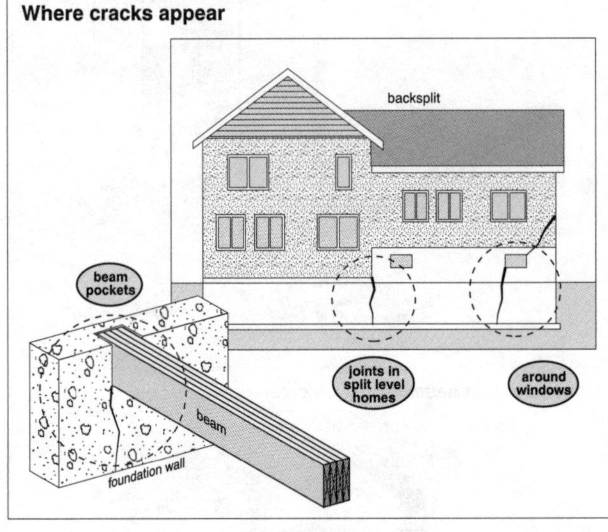

2079

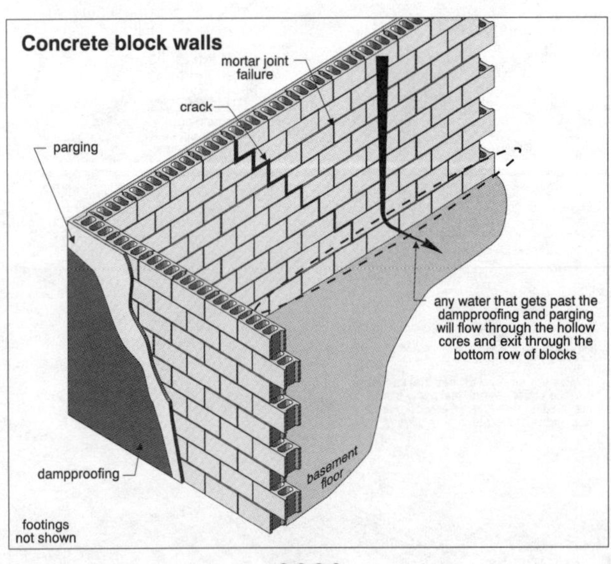

2080

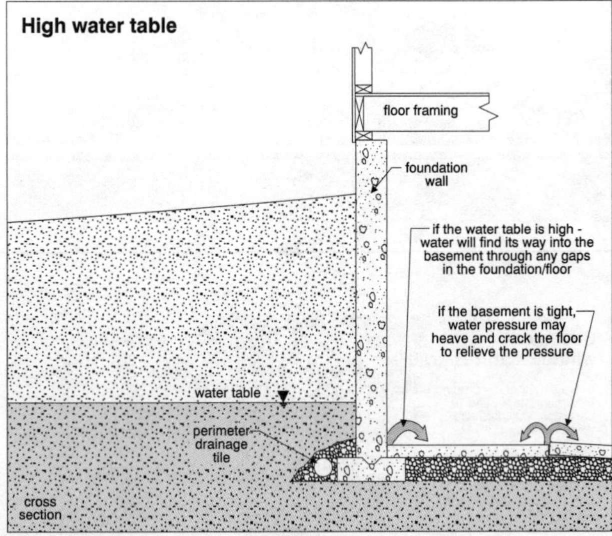

2081

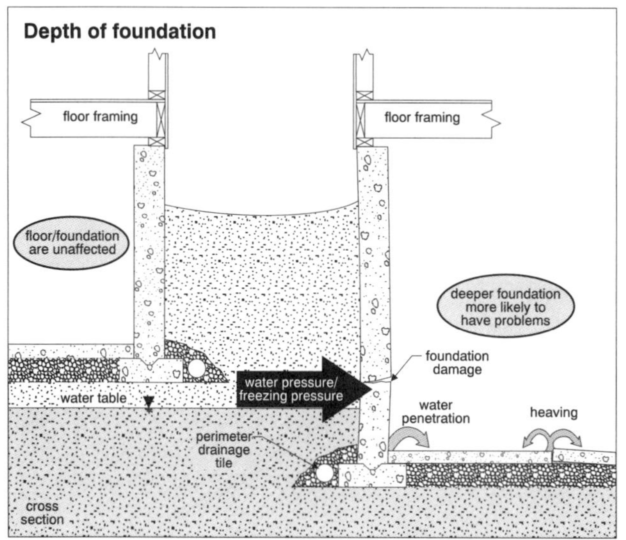

2082

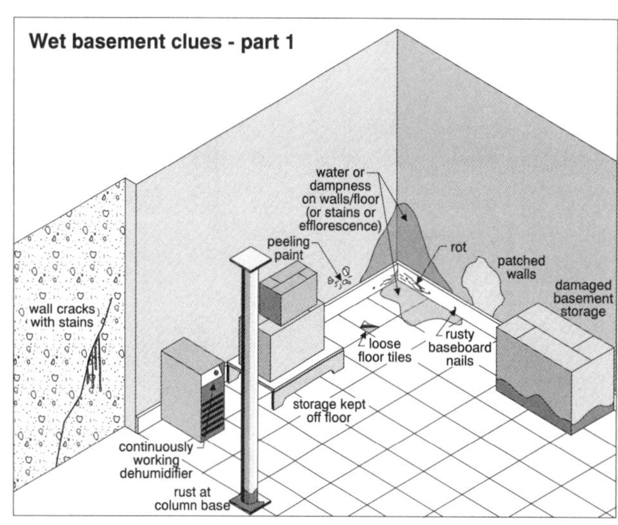

2083

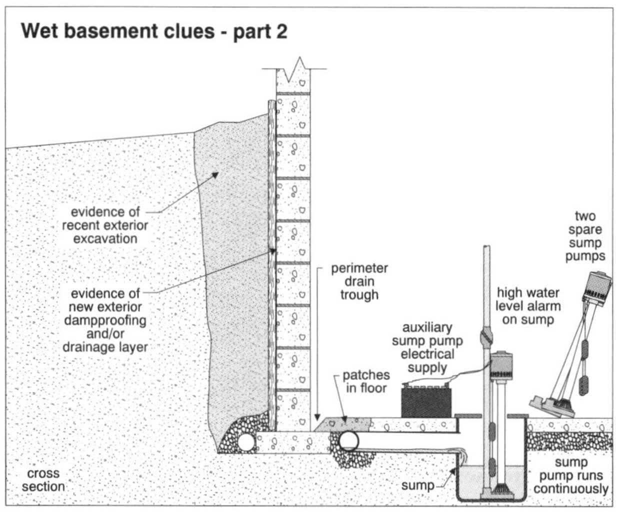

2084

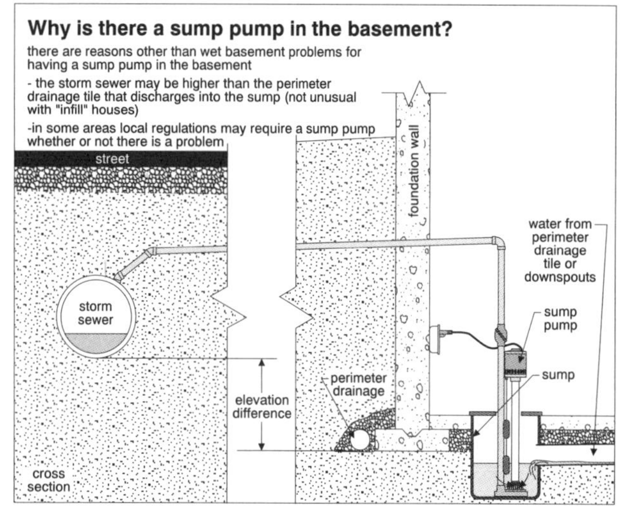

2085

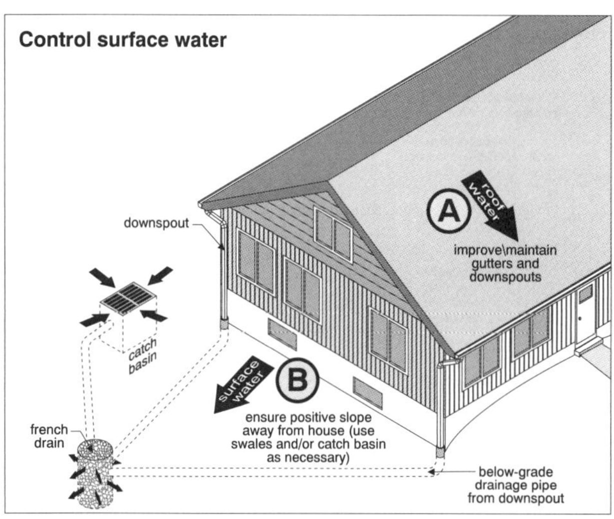

2086

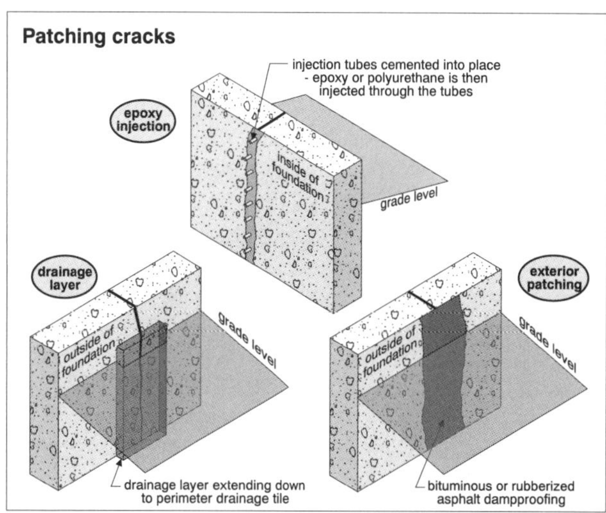

2087

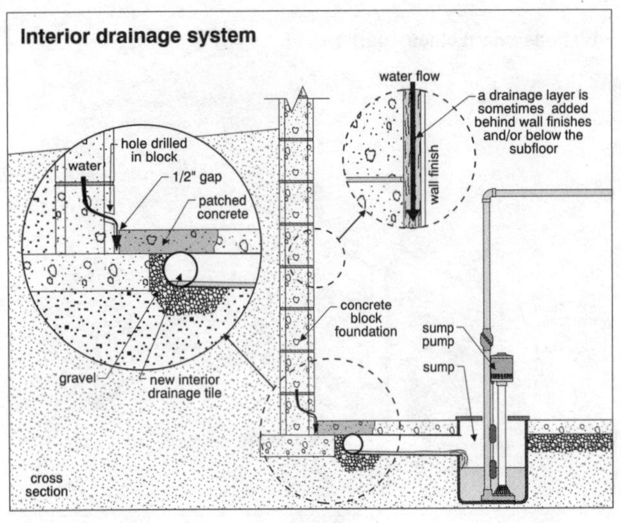

2088

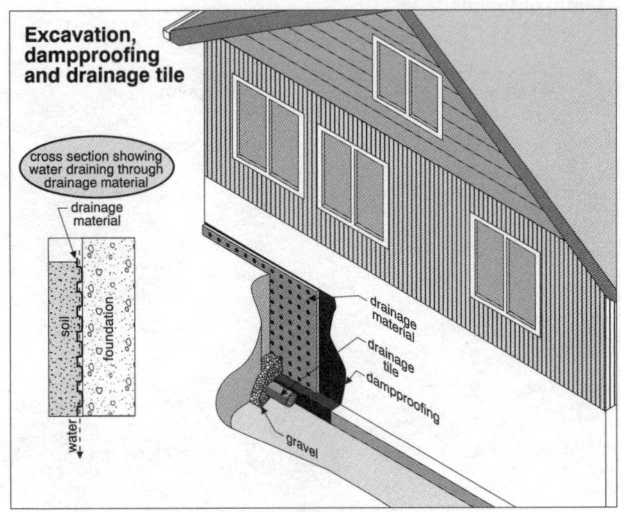

2089

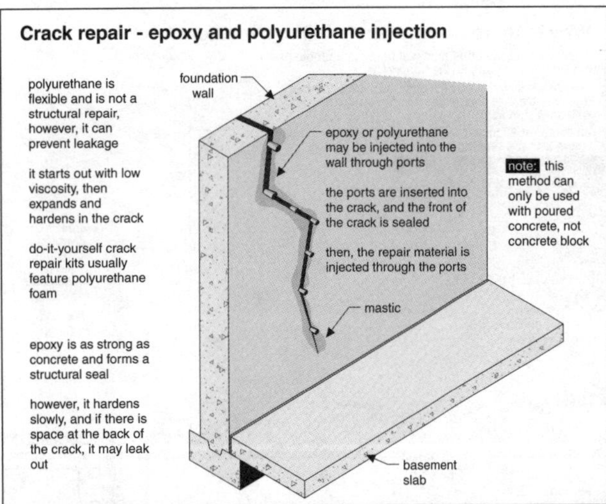

2090

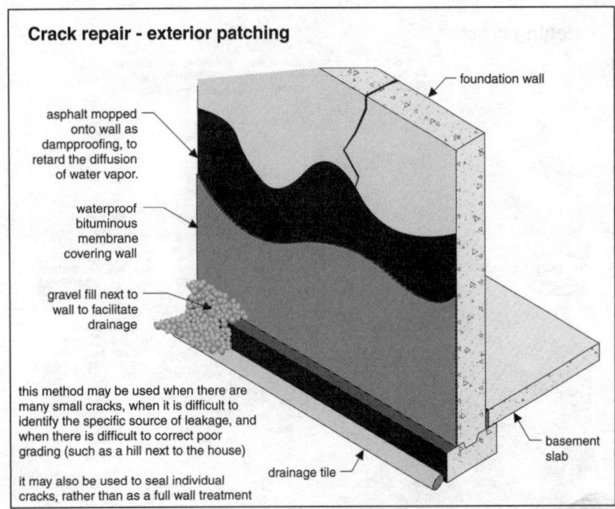

2092

Crack repair - drainage layer

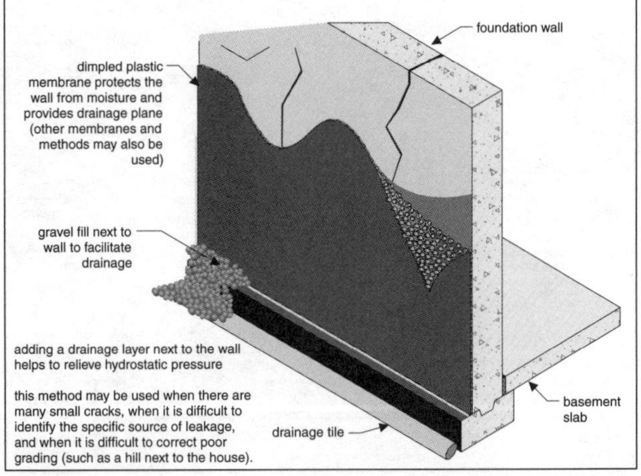

foundation wall

dimpled plastic membrane protects the wall from moisture and provides drainage plane (other membranes and methods may also be used)

gravel fill next to wall to facilitate drainage

adding a drainage layer next to the wall helps to relieve hydrostatic pressure

this method may be used when there are many small cracks, when it is difficult to identify the specific source of leakage, and when it is difficult to correct poor grading (such as a hill next to the house).

drainage tile

basement slab

2091

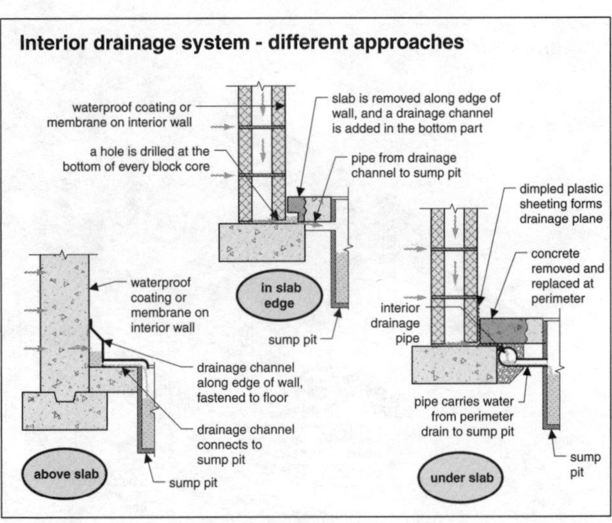

2093

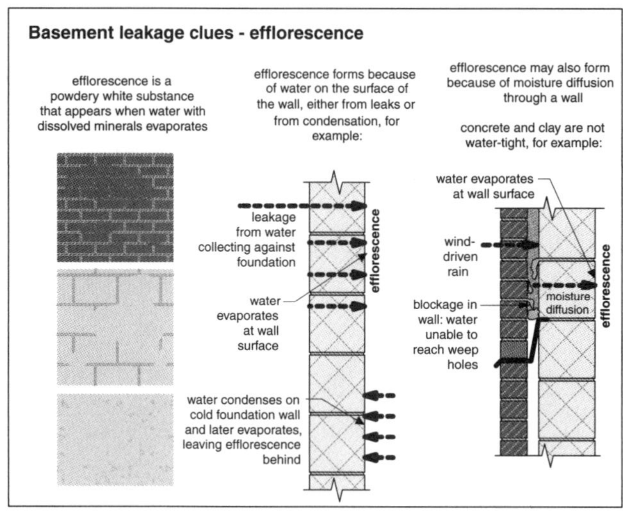

2094

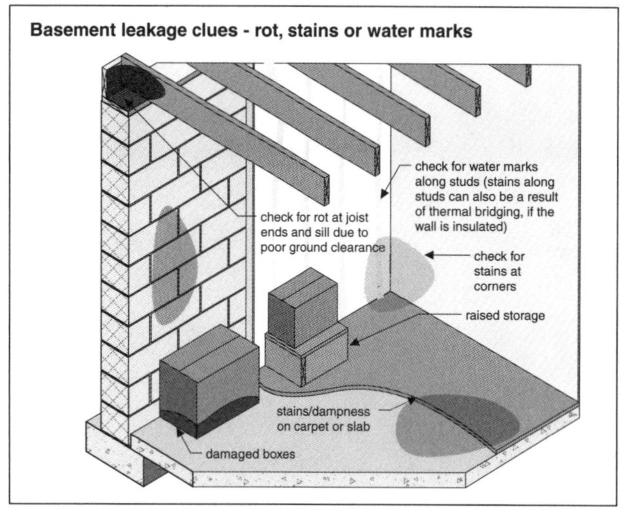

2095

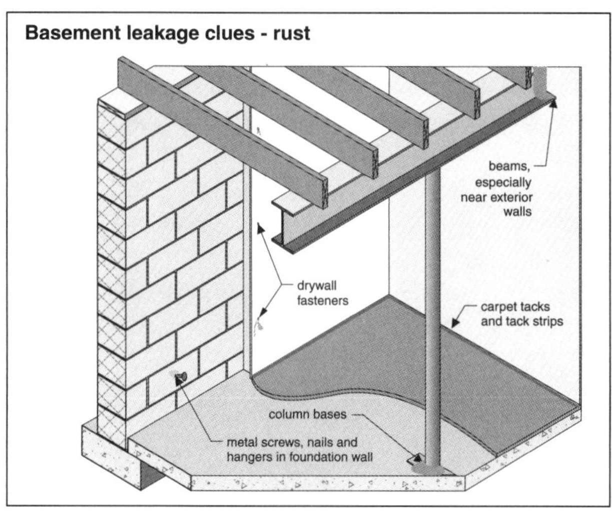

2096

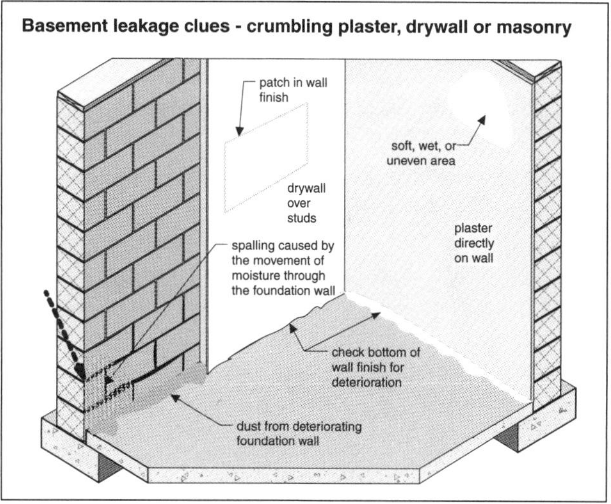

2097

CHAPTER 10

APPLIANCES

RANGES

360 ... 2100 Electric range components
360 ... 2101 Electric range defects
360 .... 2102 Gas range components
360 .... 2103 Gas range defects

MICROWAVE OVENS

360 ... 2104 Microwave oven components
360 ... 2105 Microwave oven defects

EXHAUST FANS

361 ... 2106 Exhaust fan components
361 ... 2107 Exhaust fan defects

DISHWASHERS

361 ... 2108 Dishwasher components
361 ... 2109 Dishwasher defects

WASTE DISPOSALS

361 ... 2110 Waste disposal components
361 ... 2111 Waste disposal defects

TRASH COMPACTORS

362 ... 2112 Trash compactor components
362 ... 2113 Trash compactor defects

CENTRAL VACUUM SYSTEMS

362 ... 2114 Central vacuum system components
362 ... 2115 Central vacuum system defects

REFRIGERATORS

362 ... 2116 Refrigerator components
362 ... 2117 Refrigerator defects

WASHING MACHINES

363 ... 2118 Washing machine components
363 ... 2119 Washing machine defects

DRYERS

363 ... 2120 Electric dryer components
363 ... 2121 Electric dryer defects
363 ... 2122 Gas dryer components
363 ... 2123 Gas dryer defect

DOORBELLS

364 ... 2124 Doorbell components

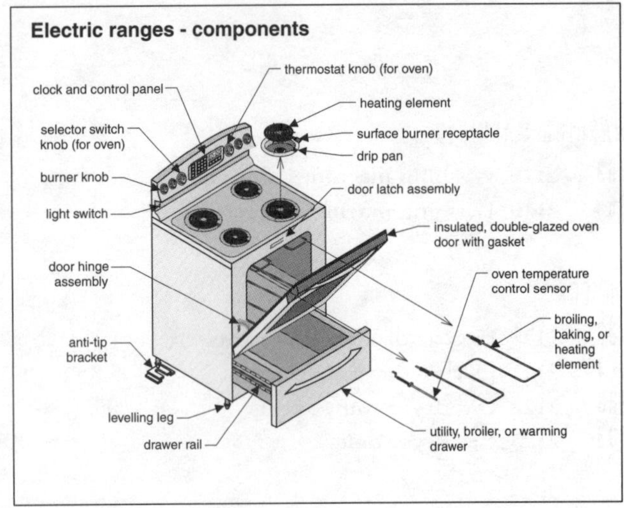

2100

Electric ranges - defects

worn, missing, inoperative controls/knobs
burners, oven or broiler inoperative
damage
gasket loose or damaged
overheating/insulation problems
drawer stiff
dirty
door handle, latch or springs damaged
out of level

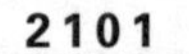

2101

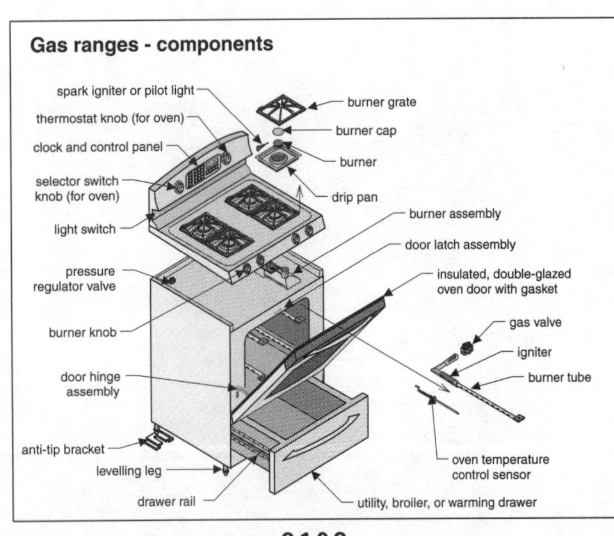

2102

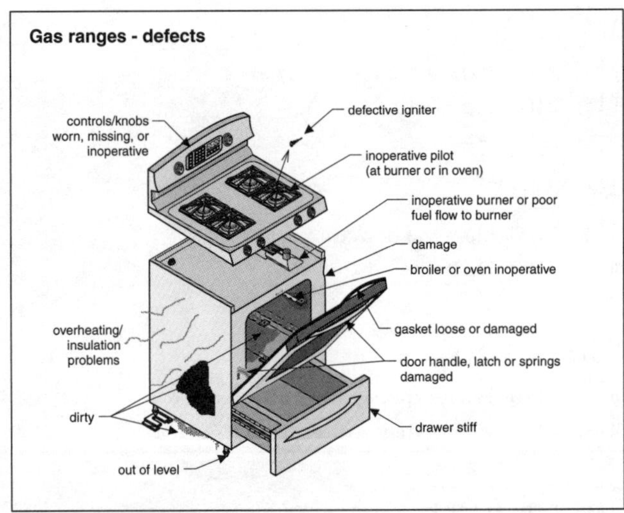

2103

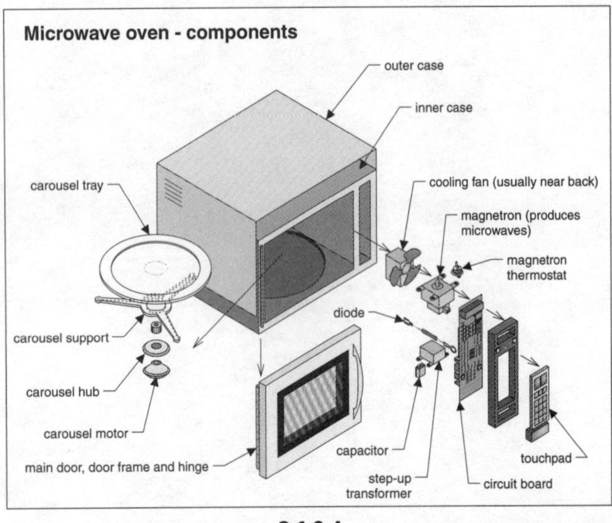

2104

Microwave oven - defects

mechanical damage - may affect containment, insulation
controls don't work - usually a faulty touchpad or circuit board
handle or latch damaged
gasket - poor seal
microwave oven inoperative - often an electrical problem

2105

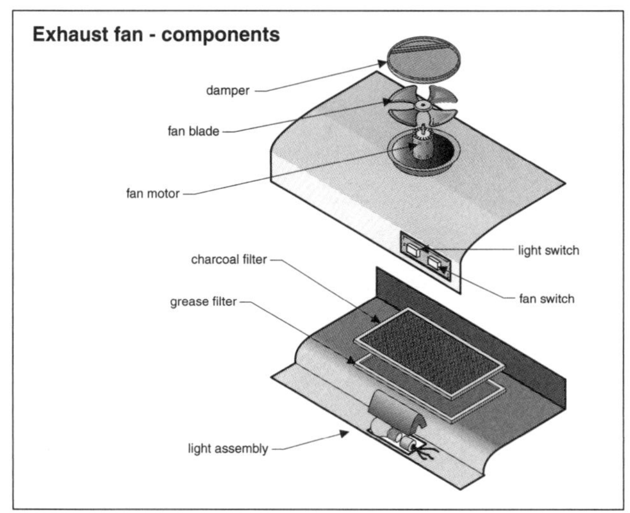

2106

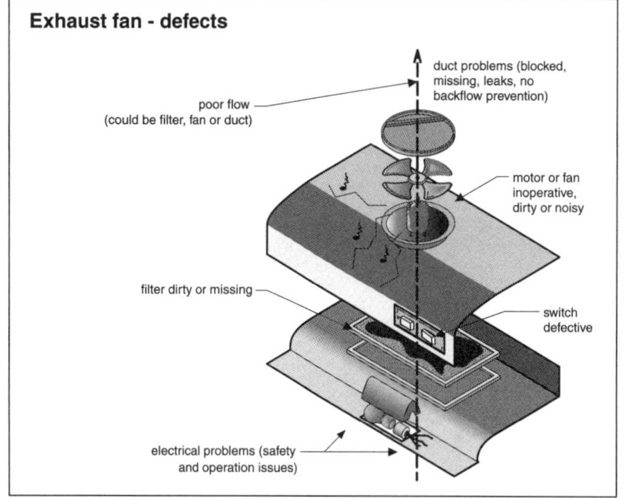

2107

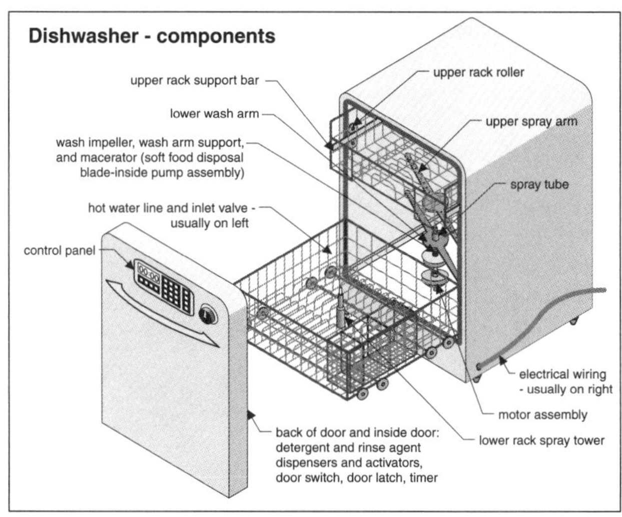

2108

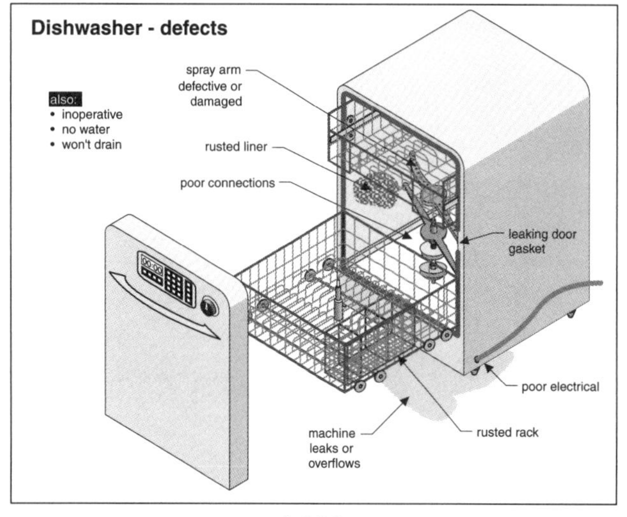

2109

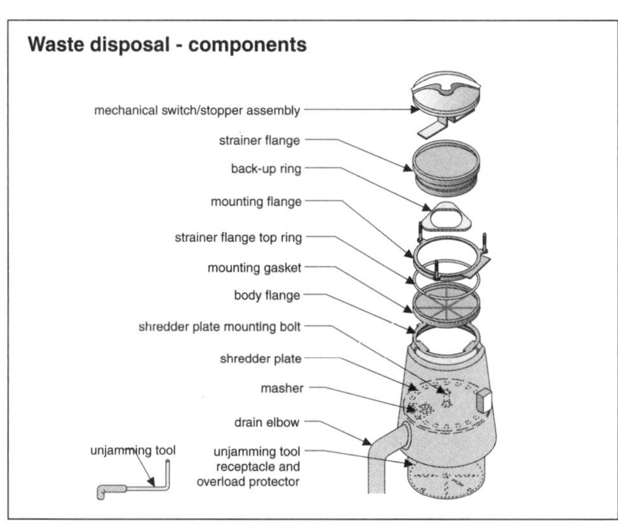

2110

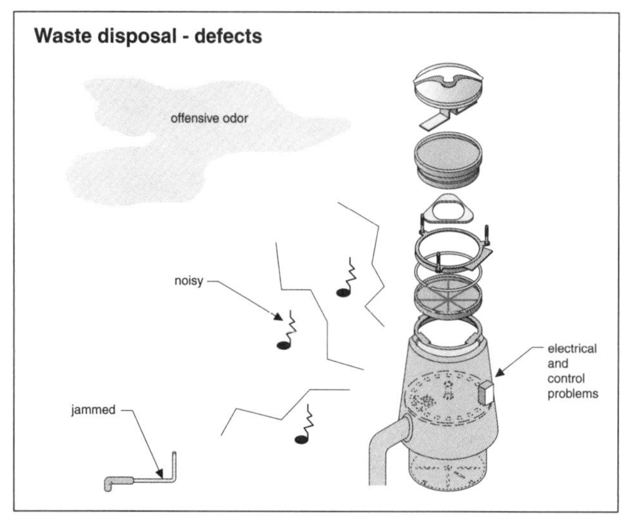

2111

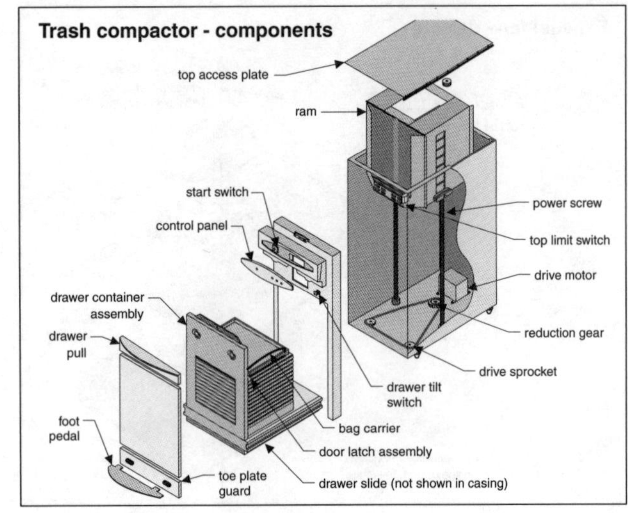

2112

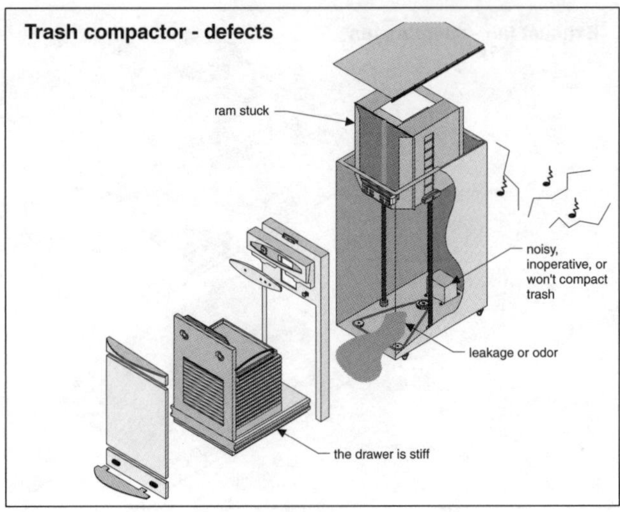

2113

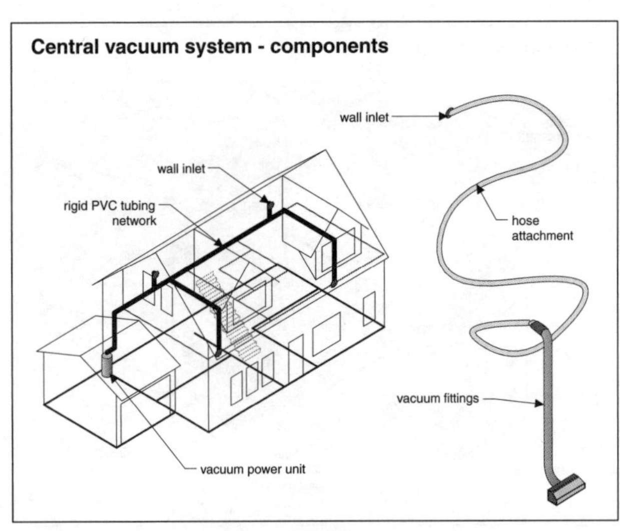

2114

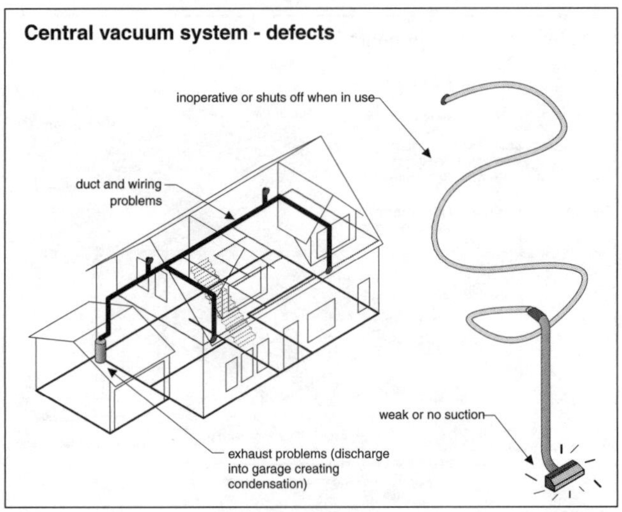

2115

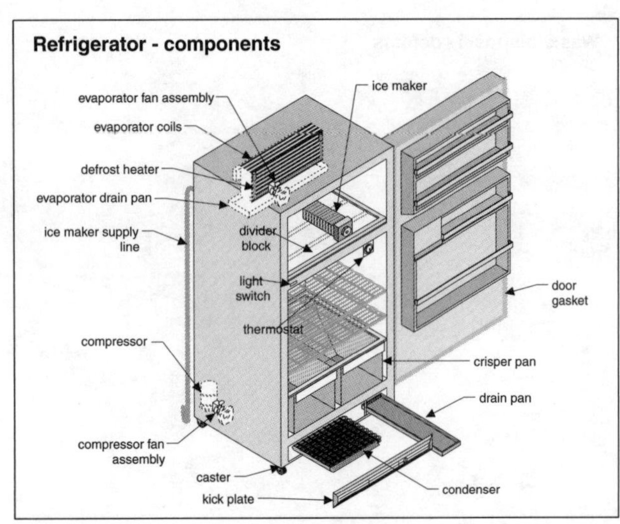

2116

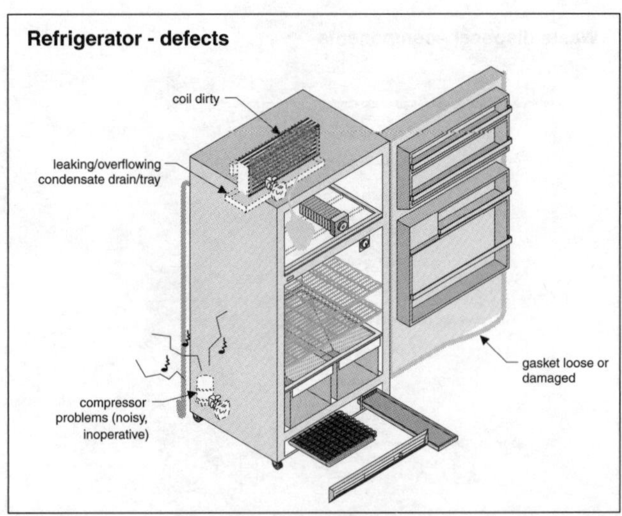

2117

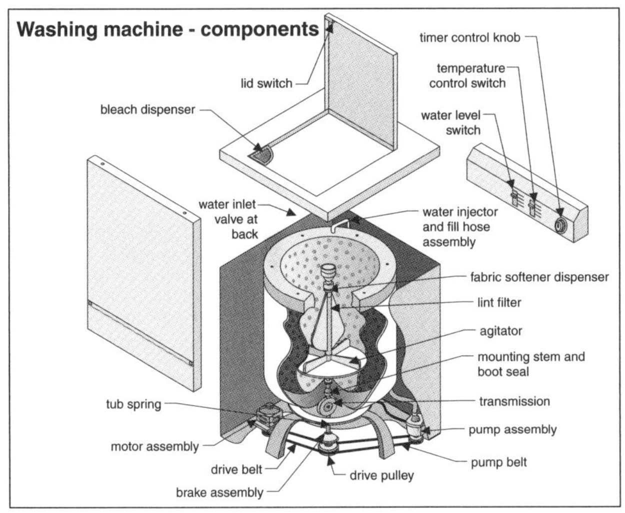

2118

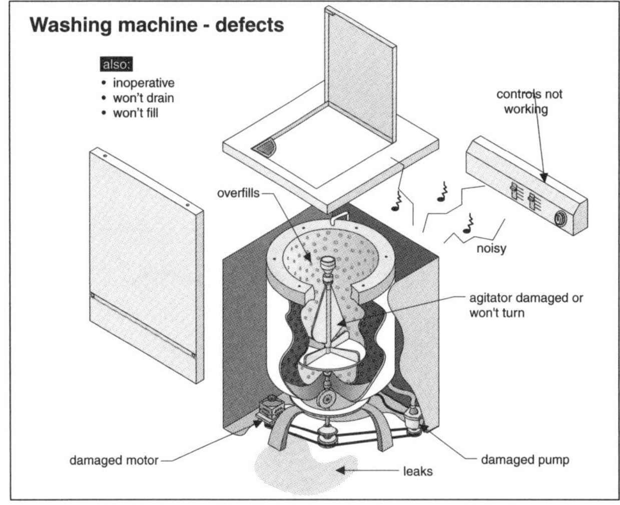

2119

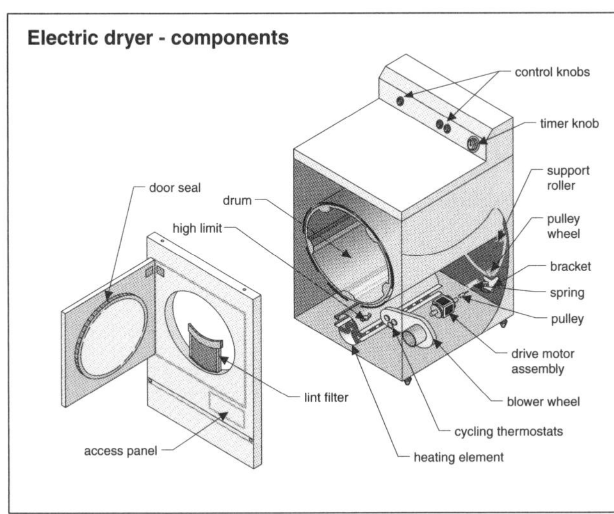

2120

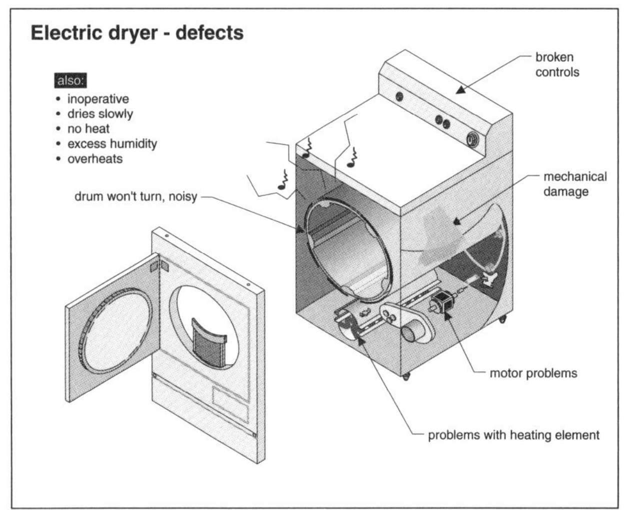

2121

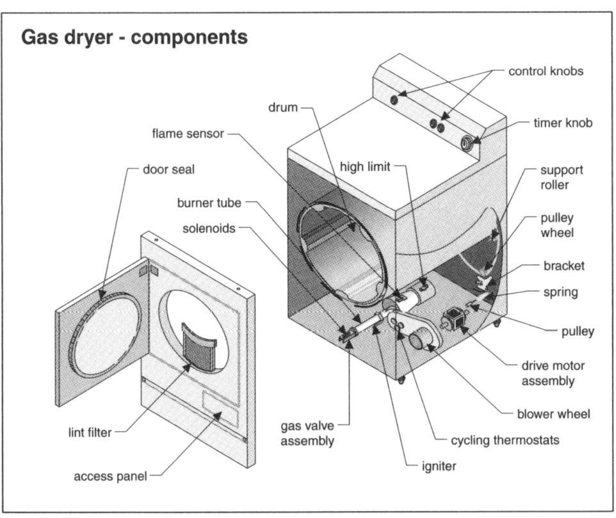

2122

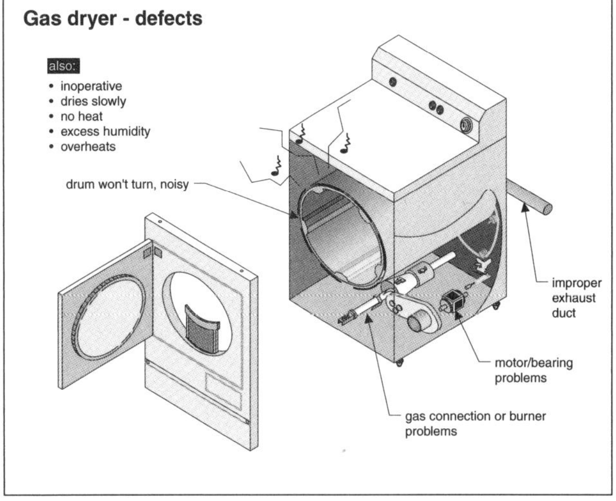

2123

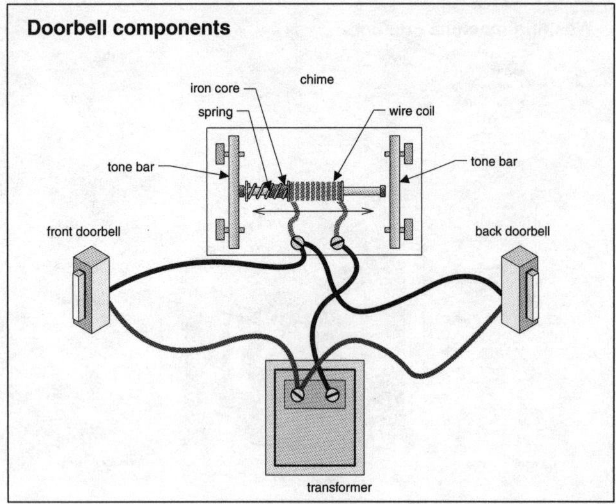
Doorbell components
chime
iron core
spring
wire coil
tone bar
tone bar
front doorbell
back doorbell
transformer

2124

A

Abandoned Chimneys – Removing 0969
Abandoned Flue Opening 0990
Above Ground Exterior Oil Storage Tank 0824
Absolute and Relative Humidity 1311
Access Hatch to Attic 1361
A-coil for Air Conditioner 1236
Adam Style Home 1726
Add or Extend Window Wells When Re-grading 1936
Adding a Drain to a Flat Roof 1934
Adding Insulation – Risks 1365
Additions to Masonry – Toothed-In 1760
Add-on Wood Furnace (Divider Plate Method) 1031
Add-on Wood Furnace (Downstream Series) 1030
Adfreezing 0244
Adfreezing and Deck Piers 0245
Adjacent Metal Chimneys of Different Heights 1010
Advanced Combustion Wood Stoves 1040
Air Barrier vs Vapor Barrier 1332
Air Bleed Valves on Radiators – Don't Operate 0869
Air Changes Balanced 1310
AIR CONDITIONING
A-coil 1236
Air Return Outside Room 1262
Attic Evaporator Coil 1238
Basics 1200-1216
Capillary Tube Defects 1242
Central vs. Ductless 1215
Close Humidifier Damper 1263
Coil Upstream of Heat Exchanger 1239
Compressor 1204, 1223-1230
Don't Test When Cold 1223
Life 1269
Scroll 1229
Scroll vs. Standard 1230
Slugging 1225
Wait Before Restarting 1224
Condensate
Discharge Locations 1246
from Attic Evaporator Coil 1244
Pump 1247
System 1243-1247
Condenser
Coil 1231-1233
Coil Exhausting Hot Air Outside 1205
Coil Location 1253
Dryer Vent too Close 1232
Fan 1252
Out of Level 1226
Units – Inspecting 1212
Water Heater Exhaust Fan too Close 1231
Discharging Condensate 1210
Ductless System 1216
Duct System 1219, 1256-1264
Ducts in Concrete Floor Slabs 1261
Evaporative Coolers 1267-1272
Single-Stage 1271
Two-Stage 1272
Evaporator Coil 1236-1242
Collecting Hot Air inside the House 1202
Inspection Procedure 1240
Evaporator Fan 1254
Excess Electric Current Draw 1227
Expansion Devices – Cooling Hot Liquid Freon 1207
Fan Belt, Pulley or Adjustment 1255
Filter/Dryer for Refrigerant 1249
Flexible Ductwork 1265
Freon Gas goes Outside 1203
General Rule for Ductwork Adequacy 1256
Guessing the Capacity 1221
Heat Transfer at the Inside Coil 1201
AIR CONDITIONING – CONTINUED
High and Low Returns 1259
High Pressure and Low Pressure Sides 1211
Hot Liquid Back to House 1206
How Much Area Can One Ton Cool? 1218
Larger Ducts Required 1219
Latent Heat of Vaporization 1209
Leaking Condensate Tray 1243
Leaking Refrigerant Lines 1251
Measure Temperature Drop Across Coil 1222
Modern Ductwork 1258
Moving Heat from Inside to Outside 1200
No Electrical Shut Off 1228
Older Style Ductwork 1257
One Ton of Cooling 1217
Refrigerant Lines 1248-1251
Schematic 1208
Sight Glass for Refrigerant 1250
Slab Coil 1237
Testing Air Returns 1260
Thermostat
Location 1268
Mercury Bulb 1266
Snap Action 1267
Thermostatic Expansion Valve 1241
Trap Required in Condensate Line 1245
Vapor Barriers and Air Conditioning Ductwork 1264
Water Cooled
Missing Backflow Preventer 1235
Schematic 1214
Testing 1234
Air Damper Arrangement for Wood Furnaces 1016, 1017
Air Filter Orientation and Forced Air Heating Systems 0784
Air Filters and Air Cleaners for
Forced Air Heating Systems 0784-0787
Air Flow through Humidifier 0790
AIR GAP
Dishwasher 1551
in Plumbing 1546
Air Gaps at Ends of Wood Beams 0278
AIR LEAKAGE
Potlights 1338
Locations 1373
AIR RETURN
Outside Room for Air Conditioning 1262
Outside Rooms 0800
in Ductwork – Testing 1260
Air Separators on Boiler 0871
Air Temperature Sensor – Outdoor for Boiler 0877
Air Vents on Steam Heating Systems 1100
Air/Vapor Barrier Incomplete or Wrong Locations 1372
Air/Vapor Barriers 1332-1340
All Electric Heat Pump System 1281
Alligatoring in Flat Roofs 0093
Alternate Application for Metal Valley Flashings 0060
Alternative Attachment Method for Counter Flashing 0111
Aluminum and Galvanized Steel Gutters – Identifying 1910
Aluminum Wire 0606
Amount of Attic Ventilation 1346
Amp Meter Testing of Electric Furnace 1148
Amperage Equals Current Flow 0504, 1132
Analyzing Crack Size 0225
Anchor Spacing for Wall Sill 0284
Anchoring Roofs to Walls 0424
Anchors – Helical 0229
Anchors for Wall Sills 0281
Anode – Sacrificial for Water Heaters 1559
Anticipator on Thermostat – Variable 0767
Appliance Connectors for Gas 0724
Appliances Chimney Height Above 0978
Appliances Direct Vent – House Air Pressure 1322
APPLIANCES
Central Vacuum Systems
Components 2114
Defects 2115
Dishwashers
Components 2108
Defects 2109
Doorbells
Components 2124
Dryers
Electric Dryer Components 2120
Electric Dryer Defects 2121
Gas Dryer Components 2122
Gas Dryer Defects 2123
Exhaust Fans
Components 2106
Defects 2107
Microwave Ovens
Components 2104
Defects 2105
Ranges
Electric Range Components 2100
Electric Range Defects 2101
Gas Range Components 2102
Gas Range Defects 2103
Refrigerators
Components 2116
Defects 2117
Trash Compactors
Components 2112
Defects 2113
Washing Machines
Components 2118
Defects 2119
Waste Disposers
Components 2110
Defects 2111
AQUASTAT
Primary Control on Boilers 0872
on Boiler Inoperative 0873
Arch Outside and Wood Lintel Inside 0360
Arches – Masonry – Cracking due to Lateral Thrust 0418
Arches and Lintels 0415-0421
Architectural Styles and Details 1700-1743
Architrave 1709
Arcing and Sparks – Electrical 0549
Arrangement of Panel Wires – Electric 0557
ASBESTOS CEMENT
Shingles 0048
Siding 1816
Ash Pit for Fireplace 1089
Asphalt and Concrete Driveways 1940
ASPHALT SHINGLE
Application – Roofing 0011
Composition 0010
Ridges 0018
Roofing Fastener Problems 0017
Siding 1818
Siding – Six Nails per Shingle 1818
Valley Flashings 0056
Atmospheric Vacuum Breaker 1547
Atomizing Oil Burner 0832
ATTIC
Access Hatch 1361
Ducts 1370
Electrical Wiring Exposed 0600
Heat – Reducing with Ventilation 1341
Power Vents 1377
Secondary 1364
Stairwells 1362
Ventilation – Recommended Amount 1346

Automatic Garage Door Openers 1881-1885
Automatic Reverse for Garage Door Openers 1874
Automatic Vent Dampers on Gas Furnaces 0815
Avalanche Guards – Roofing 0009
Awning and Hopper Windows 1716

B

B Vent 0996
Babies – Slate Roof Repair 0037
Back Up Heat for Heat Pumps – Testing 1290
Backdrafting 0736
Backer Rods for Caulking 1336
BACKFILL
  Height 0254
  Related Foundation Cracks 0257
  Settled Around Homes 1901
BACKFLOW PREVENTER
  Installed Backwards on Boiler 0864
  Missing on Water Cooled Air Conditioners 1235
  on Boilers 0862
Baffles for Soffit Vents 1345
Balance Point for Heat Pumps 1280
Balanced Air Changes 1310
Balancing Dampers and Flow Collars for HRVs 1404
Balancing Methods for Hot Water Heating 0885
Balconies 1838
Ball Valve for Plumbing 1536
Balloon versus Platform Framing 0378
Baluster Spacing for Handrails and Guards 1849
BAROMETRIC DAMPER
  (Draft Regulator) Problems 0840
  for Oil Furnace 0839
  on Wood Furnace 1022
  Schematic 1214
  Barrel Mission Style (Straight) Clay Tile 0040
BARRIER
  Air 1332
  Radiant 1331
  Vapor 1332
BASEBOARD
  Cast Iron on Hot Water Heating Systems 0898
  Finned Tube on Hot Water Heating Systems 0897
BASEMENT
  Bearing Wall 0387
  Crack Repair
    Drainage Layer 2091
    Epoxy and Polyurethane Injection 2090
    Exterior Patching 2092
  Cracks 2079
  Excavation, Dampproofing and Drainage Tile 2089
  Fireplaces 1064
  Floors Lowered with Bench Footings 0233
  Floors Lowering with Underpinning 0234
  Floors Provide Lateral Support 0258
  Heat Registers 0798
  Insulation – Adding Exterior 1388
  Insulation – Interior – Adding 1389
  Interior Drainage System 2088, 2093
  Keeping Dry by Controlling Surface Water 2086
  Leakage Clues
    Crumbling Plaster, Drywall or Masonry 2097
    Efflorescence 2094
    Rot, Stains and Water Marks 2095
    Rust 2096
  Moisture Control 1390
  Problems – Wet – Causes 2074
  Stairs – Exterior 1840
  Stairwell – Exterior – Side View 0241
  Stairwell – Exterior Insulated 0242
  Sump Pump 2085
  Walkouts 1840, 1887-1893
  Walls – Patching Cracks 2087
BASEMENT – CONTINUED
  Wet 2074-2089
  Windows and Stairs 2076
Basic Electrical Concepts 0501
Basins – Electrical Outlets Nearby 0621
Baskets/Strainers at the Top of Downspouts 1923
Bathroom Outlets and Switches 0620
Bay Window 1720
BEAM/JOIST CONNECTION 0309
  with Ledgerboard 0326
BEAMS
  Bearing Simply versus Continuous 0307
  Bolting of Wood Built-Up 0306
  Continuous and Simply Spanned 0299
  End Support 0301
  for Decks and Porches 1853
  Lateral Support for Steel 0311
  Lateral Support for Wood 0312
  Load Transfer 0297
  Mortise and Tenon Joints 0327
  Nailing of Wood Built-Up 0305
  Notches or Holes 0304
  Part of House Structure 0295
  Poor End Support 1855
  Punching through Foundation Wall 0250
  Rotated or Twisted 0303
  Rotation or Twisting – Exterior 1856
  Sag
    Exterior 1854
    Sight Along 0300
  Steel Attached to Joists 0298
  Stresses 0296
  Structural 0295-0313
  Wood – Air Gaps at Ends 0278
BEARING
  and Partition Walls – Identification 0391
  for Rafter 0429
  Strength of Soils 0203
  Wall Holes and Notches in Top Plates 0381
  Wall in Basement 0387
  Wall Metal Ties for Single Top Plates 0382
  Wall Offset 0400
  Wall Top Plate T-Connection 0380
  Wall with Lintel 0383
Bell-Cast Eave 1704
Below Grade Downspouts – Abandoned 1928
Below Grade Garages – Drains 1877
Belt Drive and Direct Drive Blowers for Furnaces 0782
Belt or Pulley Adjustment for Fan for Air Conditioning 1255
Belt-Course 1712
Bench Footings 0233
Bent Electrical Service Masts 0524
Bi-Metallic Thermostat 0746
Bivalent Heat Pump 1294
Black Label Wood Shingles 0020
Bladder Type Pressure Tank for Wells 1529
Blisters in Built-up Roofing Membranes 0092
Blockage Switches on Forced Air Furnaces 0804
Blocking, Strapping and Bridging for Joists 0321
Blocks and Bricks – Hollow Channels must be Vertical 0377
Blowers for Furnaces – Belt Drive and Direct Drive 0782
Blue Label Wood Shingles 0020
Board-and-Batten Siding 1791
BOILER
  Air Separators 0871
  Aquastat – Primary Control 0872
  Aquastat Inoperative 0873
  Backflow Preventer 0862
    Installed Backwards 0864
  Copper Tube Heat Exchangers 0856
  Electric 1150
  Feed Pump
    for Steam Heat 1113
    Location for Steam Heat 1112
  Flow Control Valves 0878
BOILER – CONTINUED
  Gas
    Conventional 0853
    High Efficiency 0854
  High Temperature Limit Switch 0860
  Hot Water, How They Work 0849
  Low Water Cut-Out (Hot Water) 0861
  Pressure Reducing Valve 0866
    Location 0863
    Relief Valve Installed Backwards 0870
  Pressure Relief Valves 0857
    Inspecting 0859
    Location 0858
  Pump Control 0874
  Temperature and Pressure Gauge 0865
  Water Pressure Set too Low 0868
  with Bypass Loop 0908
  with Combined Pressure Reducing Valve and Pressure Relief Valve 0867
  with Outdoor Air Temperature Sensor 0877
  with Series Loop 0881
  with Sidearm Heater 0906
  with Tankless Coil 0905
  with Zone Control
    by Pumps 0875
    by Valves 0876
  Wood 1012
Bolting of Built-up Wood Beams 0306
Bonding of Electric Service Box to Ground 0555
Bonding of Neutral and Ground Wires Downstream of Service Box 0554
Bored Wells 1514
Bow Window 1720
Bowed Brick Veneer Wall – Older Home 0370, 1764
Bowing Foundation Results in Excess Brick Overhang 0251
Bowing of Masonry Walls 0316, 0369, 1767
Bowing of Solid Masonry Wall due to Tie Failure 0372
Bracing for Metal Chimneys 1002
Bracing of Compression Webs in Trusses 0450
Bracket Chimneys 0973
Brackets and Dentils 1710
Branch Circuit Over-current Devices 0535
Breaker and Fuse-type Electrical Service Boxes 0536
Breakers and Fuses 0509
Breast for Fireplace Settled (Gap at Wall) 1087
Breast for Fireplace 0086
Brick Foundations with Masonry Walls 0212
Brick Mortar Joints 1761
Brick Overhang Excessive on Foundation 0251
Brick Repointing 1758
BRICK VENEER WALL 0353, 0402-0411
  Bowed – Older Home 1764
  Bowed in Older Home 0370
  Construction Detail 0402
  Detail 0280
  Masonry Tie Detail 0403, 1765
  Weep Holes 0406
  with Steel Lintel 0358
BRICK WALL
  Bowing 1767
  Flashing with Roof Intersection Below 0077
  Mortar Joints 1762
  Needs Lateral Support 1766
  Terminology 0354
Bricks and Blocks – Hollow Channels must be Vertical 0377
Bridging, Strapping and Blocking for Joists 0321
British Thermal Unit 0701, 1300
Broken Concrete Tiles 0046
Broken Pediment 1719
BTU 0701, 1300
BTUs per Hour vs. Kilowatts 1133
Buckingham Slate 0030
Buckling of Columns 0292
Building a Chimney 0709
Building Crack Shapes 0227

Building Crack Size Analysis 0225
Building Paper vs Housewrap 1333
Building Settlement – Types 0221
Building Settlement due to Cut and Fill Excavation 0224
Building Shapes and Details 1700-1743
BUILT-UP ROOFING 0089-0096
Membrane – Curbed Edge 0108
Membrane – Edge Details 0107
Membrane – Four-ply 0090
Membrane Blisters 0092
Roof/Wall Flashing 0104
Roof/Wall Flashing – Low Quality 0112
BUILT-UP WOOD BEAM
Bolting 0306
Nailing 0305
Buried Oil Storage Tank 0823
BURNER
Atomizing Oil 0832
Crossover Igniter 0743
Gas Supply 0742
Monoport – Gas 0741
Natural Draft Gas 0734
Scorching 0749
BURNER – OIL
Barometric Damper Problems 0840
Clearance From Oil Storage Tanks 0825
Flame Retention Head 0833
Flame Sensor 0838
Inspecting 0835
BUS BARS
Electrical Wires should not Cross 0585
in Fuse Panels 0580
Butt Joint Detail on Vertical Siding 1800
Butterfly Roof 0002
BUTTRESS 0259
Pulling away from Wall 0270
Bypass Damper on Catalytic Wood Stove 1042
Bypass Loop on Hot Water Heating System 0908

C

Cabinet Trim – Types 2024
Cabinets – Loose 2026
Cabinets, Trim and Counters 2024-2026
Cable Support – Electrical 0593
Cantilevered Concrete Retaining Wall 1947
Cantilevered Decks 1861
Cantilevered Joists 0331
Canvas Duck for Exterior Decks 1862
CAP FOR CHIMNEY 0967
Drip Edge 0985
Improper Slope 0984
Cap Missing for Metal Chimney 1005
Cape Cod Style House 1742
Capillary Tube Defects for Air Conditioning 1242
Caps for Fill and Vent Pipes on Oil Storage Tanks 0829
Carports and Garages 1839
Casement Windows 1714
Casings for Drilled Wells 1516
Cast Iron Baseboard on Hot Water Heating Systems 0898
Catalytic Combustors 1041
Catalytic Wood Stove Bypass Damper 1042
CATCH BASINS 1905
Drain Pipe Face Down 1878
CATHEDRAL AND FLAT ROOFS
Evidence of Insulation Added 1381
Insulating 1380
Two Insulation Strategies 1382
CATHEDRAL ROOF VENTING 1347
Channeled Vents versus Cross Ventilation 1383
CAULKING
Backer Rods 1336
Indoors or Out 1337
Causes of Chimney Settling 1067
Cavity Wall – Masonry 0352
CEDAR SHAKE
Application 0024
Nailing Details 0025
CEDAR SHINGLE
Application 0021
Application Spaced Plank Sheathing 0023
Application Synthetic Ventilation Layer 0028
Nailing Details – Roofing 0022
Nailing Details – Siding 1796
CEILING JOIST
Overlapped Splices 0427
Splices – Plywood 0428
with Walls that Extend Above 0357
CEMENT ASBESTOS
Roofing Shingles 0048
Siding 1816
Centrifugal Pump for Well 1523
Ceramic Tile Installation 0340
Ceramic Tiles – Alternatives for Installing 2008
Channeled Vents versus Cross Ventilation Roofs 1383
Channels and Rods to Stabilize House Movement 0231
CHIMNEY 0951
650 Degrees C 1000
Class A 0998
Metal
Adjacent Chimneys of Different Heights 1010
Combustible Clearances 1003
Excessive Offset from Vertical 1008
Not Continuous through Roof 1009
Rusting and/or Pitting 1006
Triple Wall 0999
and Fireplace Components – Masonry 0959
Bracing – Metal 1002
Bracket 0973
Cap 0967
Details 0116
Drip Edge 0985
Improper Slope 0984
Missing – Metal 1005
Clay Tile Flue Liners 0962
Clearances 0965
Connections for Wood and Oil Appliances
on Same Floor Level 0994
on Same Flue 0994
Creosote Deposits 0986
Damper for Fireplace at Top 1080
Decorative 1707
Deterioration 0968
Clay Chimney Liner – Masonry 0995
due to Condensation 1755
Extender 0956
Flashings 0065-0070
Head Flashing detail 0068
Overview 0065
Side Flashings Detail 0066
Things to Look for 0069
Flue Liners – Miter 0964
Height 0977, 1007
above Appliance 0978
Insulation too Close 1371
Leaning above Roof Line 0975
Liner Incomplete 0980
Liners for Fireplace Inserts 1038
Masonry 0957
Lateral Support 0961
not a Supporting Structure 0953
Offsets 0963
Rain Caps on Spark Arresters 0983
Removing Abandoned 0969
Saddle Flashing 0067
Settling
Causes 1067
or Leaning 0970
CHIMNEY – CONTINUED
Supporting Framing Members 0966
Tall Masonry 0971
Walls 0960
Warm is Best 0954
with Abandoned Flue Opening 0990
with Flue Divider Missing 0974
with Three Sides 0972
with Vent Connector
Extending too far into 0987
with Vent Connector Loose 0988
Chimney/Vent Connection
for Wood Stoves 1058
on Gas Furnaces 0775
CIRCUIT
Short 0508
Simple Electrical 0507
Circuit Breaker Panels with Staggered Bus Bars 0579
Circulating Pump on Hot Water Heating System 0890
Class A Chimney 0998
Clay Brick Expansion Causes Wall Cracks 0373
Clay Shingles for Siding 1817
CLAY TILE
Barrel Mission 0040
Flue Liners for Chimneys 0962
Interlocking Shingle 0042
Roof/Side Wall Flashings 0075
Roofing 0039-0044
S Type 0041
Securement 0043
Tapered Mission 0039
Cleanout Door for Fireplace too Close to Combustibles 0979
CLEARANCE
for Chimneys 0965
for Electrical Panels 0538
for Exhaust Flues on Oil Furnaces 0846
for Service Drop (Canada) 0516
for Service Drop (United States) 0515
for Unlisted Wood Stoves 1049
for Vent Connectors and B-Vents 0773
for Vent Connectors for Wood Stoves 1050
from Combustibles
for Combustion Air Duct for Fireplaces 1093
for Ducts on Wood Furnaces 1028
for Floor Furnaces 1160
for Gas Fired Room Heaters 1162
for Gas Fireplace 1168
for Metal Chimneys 1003
for Metal Firebox 1075
for Vent Connector on Wood Furnace 1023
for Wall Furnaces 1154
from Fireplace Opening 1088
of Electric Wires
around Windows 0517
from Draperies for Electric Baseboard Heaters 1143
from Edge of Studs and Joists 0597
of Wood from Soil 0393
over Roofs 0519
Requirements for Fireplace Cleanouts
from Combustibles 0979
Requirements from Combustibles
for Wood Fireplaces 1063
Cleats for Metal Valleys 0059
Close Nipple Missing on Hartford Loop
in Steam Heating 1123
Closed Cut Valleys 0063
Closed Hot Water Heating System 0880
Closed Hydronic System 0880
Closed Roof Valleys 0053
Closed Valley – Fully Woven 0064
Coal Burning Fireplaces 1077
Co-efficient of Performance for Heat Pumps 1279
Coil Location Outdoors for Heat Pumps 1288
Cold Floors in Homes 0703

COLD JOINTS
along Edge of Concrete Slabs 0342
in Poured Concrete 0271
Cold Pours 0271
Cold Wall Effect 1386
Cold-Side Ducts not Insulated in HRV 1400
Collar Ties 0446
Colonial Revival Style 1727
Color Coding for Typical 120-Volt Circuit 0506
COLUMN 1722
Buckling 0292
Connections 0293, 0308
Crushing 0289
Hinge Point Porch 1852
Hinged Affect Roof Structure 1866
Materials – Exterior 1851
Rising Damp 0294
Settling 0288
Sizes 0291
Structural 0287-0294
Types 0287
Combination Furnaces 0821, 0822
Combination Heating System with Tempering Valve 0822
Combination/Furnace/Water Heater System 0821
Combined Pressure Reducing Valve and Pressure Relief Valve on Boiler 0867
COMBUSTIBLE CLEARANCES
for Chimneys 0965
for Floor Furnaces 1160
for Furnaces 0761
for Gas Fired Room Heaters 1162
for Gas Fireplace 1168
for Metal Chimneys 1003
for Metal Fireboxes 1074
for Unlisted Wood Stoves 1049
for Vent Connector on Wood Furnace 1023
for Vent Connectors and B-Vents 0773
for Wall Furnaces 1154
for Wood Stove Vent Connectors 1050
from Fireplace Opening 1088
Requirements
for Chimney Cleanouts 0979
for Wood Fireplaces 1063
COMBUSTIBLE INSULATION
Exposed in Basements and Crawlspaces 1395
in Garages 1872
Combustible Return Ducts for Wood Furnaces 1029
COMBUSTION AIR
Damper Arrangement for Wood Furnaces 1016, 1017
Duct Clearances for Fireplaces 1093
Ducts for Fireplaces – Insulating 1091
for Gas Appliances 0732 –0739
Openings in Furnace Room 0737
Supplies from Outside 0738
Combustion Chamber for Wood Furnace 1019, 1020
Comfort Strategies – Two 1306
Common Electrical Wire and Fuse Sizes 0561
Common Mortar Joints 1761
Common Wire Sizes 0529
Components of Wood Furnaces 1014
Components of Wood Stoves 1035
Composite and Plywood Siding 1804
Compound, Saltbox and Four Square Plans 1701
Compression Fitting for Polybutylene Pipe 1557
Compression Fitting on Copper Plumbing Pipe 1541
Compression Web Bracing for Trusses 0450
COMPRESSOR
Air Conditioning 1223-1228
Heating Up Freon Gas 1204
Life of Air Conditioners – Typical 1269
Slugging on Air Conditioning 1225
Concealed Nails on Siding 1793
Concentrated Loads in Structures 0313
CONCRETE
and Asphalt Driveways 1940
CONCRETE – CONTINUED
Block Foundation Walls 2080
Cold Joints 0271
Flaws 2078
Floor
Control Joints 2002
Hollows 2006
Problems 2005
Slabs Cold Joints Along Edges 0342
Slabs Pre-Stressed and Post-Tensioned 0341
Slabs with Ducts 0796
Honeycombing 0272
Retaining Wall
Cantilevered 1947
System – Precast 1946
Steps – Exterior 1841
Tile Securement 0047
Tiles 0045, 0046, 0047
CONDENSATE
Discharge Location for Air Conditioning 1246
Drain Trap for HRV 1408
from Air Conditioning – Discharging 1210
Line from Attic Evaporator Coil 1244
Line Requires Trap in Air Conditioning 1245
Pump for Air Conditioning 1247
Pump for Steam Heat 1111
Pump for Steam Heat – Location 1110
System for Air Conditioning 1243-1247
Tray for Air Conditioning Leaking 1243
CONDENSATION
Damage to Chimney 1755
in High Efficiency Furnaces 0807
in Walls 1747
CONDENSER – AIR CONDITIONING
Coil
Exhausting Hot Air Outside 1205
for Air Conditioning 1231-1233
for Heat Pump 1277
Location for Air Conditioning 1253
Fan 1253
Out of Level 1226
Dryer Vent too Close 1232
Water Heater Exhaust Fan too Close 1231
Inspecting 1212
Condensing Gas Furnaces 0806-0819
Conductance – Thermal 1305
Conductivity – Thermal 1304
Conductors – Number of Electrical 0589
Cone-Style Plumbing Stack Flashing 0119
Connecting Downspout Sections 1921
Connections – Joist to Beam 0309
Connections – Metal Ties for Single Top Plates in Bearing Walls 0382
Connections – Types of Electrical 0591
Connections of Electrical Knob and Tube Wiring 0603
Connections of Metal Vent Pieces 1001
Containment of Fire 0708
Continuous Pilot Light for Gas Burner 0747
Continuous versus Simply Spanned Beams 0299
CONTROL JOINTS
and Concrete Floors 2002
in Foundation Walls 0217
Control Surface Water to Keep Basement Dry 2086
Controlling House Moisture in Hot Climates 1325
Convection Heating with Hot Water Radiators 0850
CONVECTIVE LOOP 1307
and Insulation Voids 1327
Convective Wood Stoves 1039
Convectors on Hot Water Heating System 0896
Conventional Expansion Tank On Hot Water Heating System 0889
Cool Spots in Homes 0702
COPPER
Pipe Hangers – Plumbing 1544
Supply Plumbing Pipe 1538
COPPER – CONTINUED
Tube Heat Exchangers in Boilers 0856
Corbelling 0375
Core Missing or Dirty on HRV 1407
Corinthian Column 1722
Cornice Terms 1709
COUNTER FLASHING
Alternative Attachment Method 0111
Two-piece 0106
Counter Problems 2025
Counters, Trim and Cabinets 2024-2027
Countertops or Floors with Electrical Outlets 0623
Cover Crawlspace Floor 1340
Covering Radiators on Heating Systems Reduces Efficiency 0895
Covers for Furnaces 0759
Covers or Roofs for Exterior Basement Stairwells 1893
Crack Shapes 0227
Crack Size Analysis of Buildings 0225
Cracked Concrete Tiles 0046
Cracked Joists – Causes 0330
CRACKING
Common Locations 0237
Foundation due to Driveways 0255
in Masonry Arches due to Lateral Thrust 0418
in Walls – Planes of Movement 0362
Retaining Walls 1951
Stucco 1771
CRACKS
due to Clay Brick Expansion 0373
Foundation and Tree Roots 0256
Horizontal in Foundations 0247
Horizontal Movement – Three possibilities 0249
in Basement 2072
in Foundation due to Backfill 0257
in Foundations – Repair Methods 1900
in Walls – Lintel Related 0368
in Walls – Types 0361
in Walls caused by Surfaces Sliding 0362
Rotational Settlement 0236
Vertical Foundation 0253
Cradle Repairs for Slate Roofs 0038
Craftsman Style Homes 1737
CRAWLSPACE
Cover Floor 1340
Insulation 1391
Insulation – Clues 1392
Wet 2074-2089
Creosote Deposits in Chimneys 0986
Cricket Flashings on Chimneys 0067
Crimp Fitting for Polybutylene Pipe 1556
Cross Connections and Plumbing 1545
Cross Ventilation versus Channeled Vents for Cathedral Roof Venting 1383
Crossover Igniters 0743
Crown up on Joists 0318
CuAl Designation for Aluminum Wiring 0606
Cupping Wood Shingles 0029
Curb Mount Skylight in Sloped Roof 0080
Curbed Edge on Built-up Roof Membrane 0108
Curbless Skylight in Sloped Roof 0081
Curling Wood Shingles 0029
Current Flow Equals Amperage 0504, 1132
Curved Stair Treads 2029
Cut and Fill Excavation Causing Settlement 0224
Cut Back Bottom of Wood Siding 1798
CUTTING THE POINTS
on Asphalt Shingles 0014
on Valley Flashings 0062

D

Damaged Flat Roofs 0091
Damaged Wire 0512

DAMPER
Barometric for Oil Furnace 0839
for Firebox in Fireplace 1079
for Fireplace at Top of Chimney 1080
DAMPER - CONTINUED
for Fireplace Low 1082
for Fireplace Missing 1081
not Fixed Open in Gas Fireplace 1165
on Wood Stoves – Testing 1060
DAMPPROOFING, EXCAVATION AND DRAINAGE TILE
around Foundations 1904
for Basements 2089
DECK 1837
Beam 1853
Poor End Support 1855
Rotation 1856
Sag 1854
Board Installation Details 1863
Cantilevered 1861
Joist Support 1857
Ledgerboard 1859
Flashing 1860
or Porch Boards Sagging 1864
Pier Heaving 0246
Piers and Adfreezing 0245
Skirting 1867
Decorative Chimneys 1721
Deflections – Allowable for Floor 0276
Defrost Control for HRV 1357
Defrost Cycle in Heat Pumps 1287
Delaminating Roof Sheathing 1378
Dentils and Brackets 1710
Depressurization of Houses 1324
Depth of Foundation 2082
Design Problems in Wood Fireplaces 1064
Deterioration of Chimneys 0968
Determining Height of Backfill 0254
Dew Point 1315
Diagonal Brick Bond in Masonry Wall 0355
Diaphragm Tank on Hot Water Heating System 0889
Dielectric Union for Supply Plumbing 1543
Differential Settlement Caused by Soils 0222
Diffusers, Grills and Supply Air Registers 0793
Dimension "A" on Steam Heating Systems 1101
Dimensions for Straight Stairs 2028
Dip Tube on Water Heater 1564
Direct Drive and Belt Drive Blowers for Furnaces 0782
DIRECT VENT
Appliances and House Air Pressure 1322
Gas Fireplace 1167
Wall Furnace 1158
Dirty or Missing Filters on HRV 1406
Dishing, Spreading and Sagging of Roof 0425
Dishwasher Air Gap 1551
Distribution Components for Forced Air Heating 0780
DISTRIBUTION PANELS – ELECTRICAL 0557- 0585
Wire Arrangement 0557
Disturbed Soil under Garage Slab 1875
Don't Confine Wood Stoves 1037
Don't Operate Air Bleed Valves on Radiators 0869
DOOR
Cores 2065
Flashings 1830
French 2067
Garage Problems 1880
Glass for Fireplaces 1094
in Garage – Man 1871, 2072
Insulated Metal 2069
Interior 2065-2072
Lights – Windows 1721
Lintels Sagging or Missing 2068
Openers – Garage 1881-1885
Operation 2066
Raking Door Opening due to Sloping Floors 2073
Staining Below Exterior 2071
Threshold – Exterior 1865
Thresholds for Exterior Basement Stairwells 1892
Types – Garage Overhead 1879
DOORS AND WINDOWS
Capillary Break 1827
Frame Deformation 1829
Putty (Glazing Compound) 1826
Doorsill Capillary Break 1827
Doorsill Support 2070
Doric Column 1722
DORMER
Flashings 0086, 0087
Framing 0438
Gutters 0003
Siding Flashings 0086
Types 1708
Double and Single Hung Windows 1713
Double Check Valve Assembly – Plumbing 1549
Double Lugging on Electrical Systems 0576
Double Tapping of Electrical Systems 0576
Double Taps on Electrical System – Pig-tailing 0577
Downflow and Upflow Furnaces 0756
DOWNSPOUT
35 Feet of Gutter Maximum 1922
and Gutter 1907-1934
and Gutter Installation 1916
Baskets/Strainers 1923
Below Grade – Abandoned 1928
Common Leakage Areas 1920
Discharge into Floor Drain 1925
Draining into Floor Drain Traps 1926
Extension too Short 1924
Missing on Secondary Roof 1917
Omitted on Small Roofs 1919
Proper Connection of Sections 1921
Running across Roof 1918
Draft for Burners – 3 Kinds 0733
Draft Hoods 0735
Draft Regulator Problems 0842
Drafty Houses 1317
Drain Clogged on Flat Roof 1932
Drain Holes in Windows 2044
Drain in Modified Bitumen Flat Roof 0122
Drain Pipe in Catch Basins Face Down 1878
Drain Problems for Window Wells 1939
DRAINAGE
in Garage Floor 1874
Layer for Exterior Foundation 1899
of Retaining Wall 1950
Systems for Flat Roofing 0088, 1929
Tile, Excavation and Dampproofing
around Foundations 1904
for Basements 2089
for Below-grade Garages 1877
for Flat Roofs – Adding 1934
in Columns and Walls 1933
Walk/Patio Sloping toward House 1944
Drawbands or Adjustable Connectors for Wood Stove Vent Connectors 1057
DRILLED WELLS 1515
Casing 1516
DRILLING AND NOTCHING
of Joists 0329
Studs 0390
Drip Edge on Chimney Cap 0985
DRIP LEG IN GAS PIPING 0730
on Water Heater 1572
Drip Loop – Electrical 0520
Drip Screed for Stucco 1770
DRIVEWAYS
and Foundation Cracking 0255
Asphalt and Concrete 1940
Dropped Ceiling – Missing Insulation 1367
Drum-Type Humidifier 0788
Drying Potential of Walls 1387
Drywall vs Gypsum Lath 2009
Dual Fuel Furnace (Wood/Oil) 1033
Duck – Canvas for Exterior Decks 1862
DUCTS
Adequacy for Air Conditioning 1256
and Pipes – Electrical Wire Clearances from 0595
and Vapor Barriers for Air Conditioning 1264
Arrangement for Wood Furnace Allows Reverse Flow 1033
Clearances for Wood Furnaces 1028
Cold side not insulated in HRV 1400
in Attics 1370
in Concrete Floor Slabs 0796
in Concrete Floor Slabs for Air Conditioning 1261
in Garages 1870
Modern for Air Conditioning 1258
Older Style for Air Conditioning 1257
Sizes for High Efficiency Furnaces 0814
System for Air Conditioning 1256-1264
Dug Wells 1513
Dutchlap Method for Slate Roofing 0034

E

Early Classical Revival Style 1723
Eave – Bell-cast 1704
Eave Closures for Spanish or Mission Tiles 0044
EAVE PROTECTION 0006, 0008
for Asphalt Shingle Roofs 0011
Edge Details on Built-up Roofing Membrane 0107
Edge Grain Wood Shingles 0019
EIFS 1774
Inspection Strategy – Exterior 1788
Inspection Strategy – Interior 1789
Insulation Details 1775
Stucco Exterior
Above Grade Termination 1782
Common Problems at Decks 1778
Drainage Layer 1786
Flashings around Decks 1783
Hosebib or Railing Attachment Detail 1785
Ideal Caulking Configurations 1787
Light Fixture Detailing 1784
Reinforcing Mesh Layout around Window Openings 1777
Window Flashing Detail (fully flashed) 1779
Window Flashing Detail (simple) 1780
Wire Penetration 1781
Elastomeric Roofing 0100
Electric Aluminum Wiring 0606
Electric Arcing and Sparks 0549
ELECTRIC BASEBOARD HEATERS
Clearance to Draperies 1143
Electric Outlets Above 0622
Wattage 1142
with Outlets Above 1144
Electric Boiler 1150
Electric Box Enclosures to Control Air Leakage 1334
Electric Box Gaskets 1335
Electric Branch Circuit over Current Devices 0535
Electric Bulbs for Potlights – Proper 0610
Electric Bus Bars in Fuse Panels 0580
Electric Cable Support 0593
Electric Circuit – Simple 0507
Electric Conductors – Number 0589
ELECTRIC CONNECTIONS
for Garage Door Openers 1883
Pig-tailing to Avoid Double Taps 0577
Types 0591
ELECTRIC CURRENT DRAW
Excessive on Air Conditioning Compressor 1227
Testing for Electric Furnace 1148

Electric Distribution Panels 0557-0585
ELECTRIC FURNACE
Fan Limit Switch 1146
Sequencers 1145
Temperature Rise 1149
Testing Current Draw 1148
Electric Fuse Panels with Bus Bars 0580
Electric Fuse Types 0564
Electric GFIs Protect Ordinary Outlets Downstream 0617
Electric Ground Wires – Location 0551
Electric Ground-Fault Interrupter 0616
Electric Grounding Equipment 0533
ELECTRIC HEAT
Watts per Square Foot Required 1135
Wire Fuse and Heater Sizing 1136
ELECTRIC HEATERS
Best Location 1140
Floor Mount 1137
Toe-kick 1138
Wiring 1141
Electric Heating Systems 1132-1152
Electric Inspection – Where Does It Start? 0500
ELECTRIC KNOB-AND-TUBE WIRING 0602-0605
Connecting a New Circuit 0604
Connections 0603
Electric Light Fixtures –
Importance of Correct Polarity 0614
ELECTRIC LIGHTING
Stairways 0607
in Insulated Ceilings 0609
Electric Lights need Isolating Links on Pull Chains 0612
Electric Load Miser 0619
Electric Meter Location 0537
ELECTRIC OUTLETS
above Electric Baseboard Heaters 1144
and Switches in Bathrooms 0620
in Floors or Countertops 0623
in Garages – 18 Inches off the Floor 0624
near Basins 0622
Protection by GFIs 0617
should not be above Electric Baseboard Heaters 0622
ELECTRIC PANEL 0534
Clearances 0538
Mounting 0541
Openings 0540
Securement 0539
Wires with Excess Sheathing 0583
for Ground and Neutral Wires 0547
Electric Plenum Heater 1147
Electric Polarity Importance on Light Fixtures 0614
Electric Potential 0502
Electric Potlights – Proper Bulbs 0610
ELECTRIC RADIANT HEAT 0714
Ceilings 1151
Floors 1152
Electric Receptacle – Wrong Type 0615
Electric Resistance 0503
Electric Reversed Polarity 0613
ELECTRIC SERVICE
Box 0532 –0545
Box and Panels – Inspecting 0565
Boxes – Breaker and Fuse-type 0536
Entrance – Areas of Potential Water Entry 0526
Entrance Cable should not be Covered by Siding 0528
Entrances – Support Requirements 0525
Equipment 0532
Masts – Bent 0524
Panel 0532
Size 0529-0531
Determining by Service Entrance Wires 0530
Determining by the Main Disconnect 0531
Underground 0514
Wires 0520-0528
Electric Shut Off Missing on Air Conditioning 1228
Electric Subpanel Wiring 0571-0573
ELECTRIC SWITCHES
for Furnaces 0626
for Garbage Disposal 0628
Push-button Obsolete 0625
Three-way 0608
ELECTRIC SYSTEM
Double Lugging 0576
Double Tapping 0576
Grounding 0546-0554
Electric Taps – Illegal 0543
Electric Wall Heater Fan Operated 1139
ELECTRIC WATER HEATER 1567
Element Sequencing 1568
ELECTRIC WIRE
and Fuse Sizes 0561
Clearance over Roofs – Inadequate 0519
Clearances around Windows 0517
Clearances from Ducts and Pipes 0596
Exposed 0599
Exposed in Attics 0600
in Studs and Joists – Clearance from Edges 0597
Securing 0584
Shouldn't Cross Bus Bars 0585
Sizes – Common 0529
Support with Steel Studs 0595
ELECTRIC WIRING
Arc Fault Circuit Interrupter 0586
for Garbage Disposals 0629
for Multi-Wire Branch Circuits 0618
Wire Support below Floors 0594
Electricity – Basic Concepts 0501
Electronic Air Cleaner 0785
ELECTRONIC AIR CLEANER
Installed Backwards/Parts Missing 0787
Problems 0786
Element Sequencing on Electric Water Heater 1568
Embedded Joist – Don't Insulate 1394
Emergency Shutoffs for Oil Furnace 0831
END BEARING
for Joist 0323
for Rafters 0429
for Steel Lintel 0420
for Wood Lintel 0421
Poor for Exterior Beam 1841
Energy Efficiency of Windows 2046
Energy Recovery Ventilator 1323
Engineered Wood for Floors 0333
Entablature 1709
EPDM ROOFING 0100
Wall Flashing 0113
EQUALIZER
and Hartford Loop Details for Steam Heat 1122
and Hartford Loop for Steam Heat 1117
Pipe for Steam Heating 1102
Equivalent Furnaces – Electric 1134
Erosion of Gravel on Flat Roofs 0094
ERV and HRV Heat Exchangers 1353
Evaporative Coolers 1270
EVAPORATOR COIL
Collecting Hot Air Inside the House 1202
for Air Conditioner in Attic 1238
for Air Conditioner Upstream of Heat Exchanger 1239
for Air Conditioning 1236-1242
for Air Conditioning – Inspection Procedure 1240
for Heat Pump 1276
Evaporator Fan for Air Conditioning 1254
EXCAVATION
Dampproofing and Drainage Tile 2089
Dampproofing and Drainage Tile
around Foundations 1904
Excess Brick Overhang of Foundation 0251
Excess Sheathing on Electrical Panel Wires 0583
Excess Shingle Overhang of Gutters 1911
Excess Temperature Rise on Electric Furnace 1149
Excessive Joist Overlap Causes Floor Bump 0322
Excessive Offset from Vertical on Metal Chimney 1008
Exhaust and Intake Locations for Heat Recovery
Ventilators 1401
Exhaust and Intake Locations for HRV 1355
Exhaust Breech through Cold Air Return 0754
Exhaust Fan Problems 1399
Exhaust Fans for House Ventilation 1321
EXHAUST FLUE
Clearances for Oil Furnace 0845
Extending too Far into Chimney 0987
Length for Oil Furnace 0844
Loose at Chimney 0988
Obstructions in Oil Furnaces 0846
Slope on Oil Furnace 0842
Support for Oil Furnace 0843
Exhaust Grill Locations for HRV 1403
Exhaust System Components for House Air 1350
Exit Window Sizes 2061
EXPANSION DEVICES
Cooling Hot Liquid Freon 1207
in Air Conditioning – Cooling Hot Liquid Freon 1207
Two in Some Heat Pumps 1286
EXPANSION TANK
on Hot Water Heating System 0888
Overflow Pipes for Hot Water Heating Systems 0887
Water Levels for Hot Water Heating 0886
Exposed Combustible Insulation 1395
EXPOSED ELECTRICAL WIRING 0599
in Attics 0600
Extender for Chimney 0956
Extending Hot Water Heating Systems 0889
Exterior above Ground Storage Tank 0821
EXTERIOR
Basement
Insulation – Adding 1385
Stairs 1873-1879
Stairwell – Insulated 0242
Stairwell – Side View 0241
Beam 1853
Poor End Support 1855
Rotation or Twisting 1856
Column Hinge Point 1852
Door Threshold 1865
Doors Staining Below 2071
Grading 1894 -1906
Inspection 1744
Insulating and Finishing Systems (EIFS) 1774, 1775
Insulation on Foundations 1898
Joist Support 1857
Stairs Handrails and Guards 1847
too Low 1850
Steps Settled or Heaved 1844
Support for Concrete Steps 1841
Trim, Flashings and Caulking
Diverter Flashing 1832
Kick-out Flashing 1831
Missing Kick-out Flashing 1834
Walkway Steps 1941
Wall Assemblies 1745
Wood Stairs – Rot 1845
Tank Water Heater 1563

F

Factors affecting Air Supply in Forced
Air Heating Systems 778
Factory Built Fireplaces – Hearth Extensions 1072
Failures of Fiberglass Shingles 0015
Fall Protection for Windows 2043
Fan Cover Missing on Furnace 0759
Fan Exhaust – Problems 1399
Fan Exhaust for House Ventilation 1321
Fan Operated Electric Wall Heater 1139

Fan Switch for Furnace 0762
FAN/LIMIT SWITCH 0762-0764
for Electric Furnace 1146
for Wood Furnaces 1027
Set Wrong or Defective 0764
Fanlight 1721
Fascia and Soffits 1824, 1825
Fastener Problems – Asphalt Shingle Roofing 0017
Faulty Windows 2058
FIBER CEMENT
Roof Shingles 0048
Siding 1816
Fiberglass Shingles – Premature Failure 0015
Fill and Vent Pipes on Oil Storage Tanks – Caps 0829
Fill and Vent Piping for Oil Storage Tanks 0828
Fill Lines – Undersized For Oil Storage Tanks 0830
Filter Orientation in Forced Air Heating Systems 0784
Filter/Dryer for Air Conditioning Refrigerant Lines 1249
FILTERS
and Condensate Drains for HRV 1356
Dirty or Missing on HRV 1406
Finned Tube Baseboard on Hot Water Systems 0897
Fire and Gas Proofing in Garages 1860
Fire Comes Inside 0705
Fire Cut Joists 0317
Fire Gets Contained 0708
Fire Outdoors 0704
Fire Triangle 0712
Firebox Clearance – Metal 1075
Firebox Damper for Fireplace 1079
Firebox for Wood Furnace 1019, 1020
Firebrick on Fireplace Walls 1074
FIREPLACE
and Chimney Components – Masonry 0959
Ash Pit 1089
Basement 1064
Breast 1086
Breast Settled (Gap At Wall) 1087
Cleanout Door too Close to Combustibles 0979
Coal 1077
Combustible Clearance Requirements 1063
Combustion Air Duct
Clearances 1093
Insulating 1091
Components – Masonry 1062
Damper 1079
at Top of Chimney 1080
Low 1082
Missing 1081
not Fixed Open in Gas Fireplace 1165
Design Problems 1065
Firebox Damper 1079
Footings 1066
Gas
Combustible Clearances 1168
Direct Vent 1167
Igniters 1096
Location Restrictions 1166
Glass Doors 1094
Hearth
Extension Dimensions 1070
Extension Forming Boards – Removed 1073
Materials 1068
Spark Strips 1069
Heat Circulators 1095
Insert Flue Connections 950
Inserts Need Chimney Liners 1038
Intake Screening for Combustion Air 1092
Lintel Rusting, Sagging or Loose 1078
Opening Combustible Clearances 1088
Outdoor Combustion Air 1090
Smoke Chamber – Wall Slope 1084
Throat, Smoke Shelf and Smoke Chamber 1083
Two on One Flue 992
Walls – Firebrick 1074
FIREPLACE – CONTINUED
with Raised Hearths 1071
Wood 1012
Wood – Three Kinds 1061
Firepot/Refractory 0744
Firestop Spacers for Wall Furnaces 1156
FIRESTOPPING 0981
for Stairs 2038
Firewood is Combustible 1053
Fish Mouths on Flat Roofs 0095
Flame Retention Head for Oil Burner 0833
Flame Rollout Shield 0750
Flame Sensor for Oil Burner 0838
Flare Fitting on Plumbing Pipe 1540
Flashing Pan for Windows 2045
FLASHINGS
below Windows with Metal and Vinyl Siding 1816
Chimney 0065, 0066, 0067, 0068, 0069, 0070
Chimney – Overview 0065
Deck Ledgerboard 1860
Kickout 1832
over Windows 1830, 2057
Roof/Walls 0073, 0074, 0075, 0076, 0077, 0078
Skylights 0080, 0081, 0082
Through Wall 0114
FLAT AND CATHEDRAL ROOFS
Evidence of Insulation Added 1381
Insulating 1380
Two Insulation Strategies 1382
Flat Grain Wood Shingles 0019
FLAT ROOF 1702
Alligatoring 0093
Damaged 0091
Erosion of Gravel 0094
Fish Mouths 0095
Drainage Systems 0088, 1929
Draining onto Sloped Roof 0123
Drains
Adding 1934
Interior 1907
Interior – Clogged 1932
Modified Bitumen 0122
in Columns and Walls 1933
Flashings 0104-0124
Ponding 0096
Ridging 0095
Skylight 0117
Weight of Water 1931
FLAT ROOF/WALL FLASHING
Built-up 0104
Built-up – Lower Quality 0112
Flexible Copper Tubing for Gas Piping 0726
Flexible Gas Appliance Connectors 0724
Float and Thermostat Trap for Steam Heating 1109
Floating Slab – Slab-on-grade 0206
Floating Tank Water Heater 1563
Floor Allowable Deflections 0276
FLOOR
Causes of Rot 2007
Cold 0703
Concrete – Hollows 2006
Crawlspace – Cover 1340
Deck – Installation Details 1863
Drainage – Garage 1874
Drains in Exterior Basement Stairwells – No Traps 1891
Engineered Wood 0335
Furnace
Clearances 1160
Inspection Cap Missing or Damaged 1161
Interior 2002 -2008
Inspecting for Termites
Protective Measures to Combat Subterranean Termites 0350
Vulnerabilities to Subterranean Termites – Exterior 0348
FLOOR – CONTINUED
Vulnerabilities to Subterranean Termites – Interior 0349
Joists 0314-0336
Types 0314
with Return Ducts for Heating Systems 0792
Wood "I" Joist Notching and Drilling 0336
Load Distribution 0277
Mounted Electric Heaters 1137
Old Homes
Creep Leading to Sag in Floor Joists 0347
Excessive Sagging around Poorly Framed Stair Openings 0345
Hump in Floor due to Joists Extending over Solid Masonry Wall 0346
or Countertop with Electrical Outlets 0623
over Unheated Area – Insulation 1397
Problems – Concrete 2005
Protection for Wood Stoves 1044-1048
Provides Lateral Support for Foundations 0248
Sag at Porch 1858
Slab
Pre-stressed and Post-tensioned Concrete 0341
Settling in Garages 1875
with Heating Ducts 0796
Steel-Framed Floors
Typical Assembly/Components 0343
Typical Details 0344
Structural in Garage 1873
Structure Openings 0332
FLOORING
Rot around Plumbing Fixtures 2003
Sources of Interior Water Damage 2004
Flow and Pressure of Water in Supply Plumbing 1500-1511
Flow Collars and Balancing Dampers 1404
Flow Control Valves for Boiler 0878
FLUE
Connections for Fireplace Inserts 0950
Divider Missing in Chimneys 0974
Liner
Clay Tile 0962
Miter 0964
Shouldn't Rest on Metal Firebox 1076
Openings Abandoned 0990
or Vent Connector Obstructed 0989
Foot Valve for Well 1521
FOOTINGS
and Foundations 0200-0273
for Fireplaces 1066
Frost Heaving 0226
Lowered around Basement Walkout 1888
Pad and Spread 0209
Stepped 0232
FORCED AIR
Ducts Removed During Renovations 0794
Heating
Air Filter Orientation 0784
Distribution Components 0780
Factors Affecting Air Supply 0781
High and Low Returns 0795
Supply and Return Registers Poorly Located 0798
Forced Draft for Wood Furnaces 1018
Forms of Insulation 1329
FOUNDATION
and Footing 0200-0273
Bowing – Excess Brick Overhang 0251
Brick with Masonry Walls 0212
Concrete Block with Masonry Exterior Walls 0219
Cracks
due to Backfill 0257
Horizontal – Three Possibilities 0249
in Tree Roots 0256
near Driveways 0255
Repair Method 1886
Vertical 0253

FOUNDATION – CONTINUED
- Depth 2082
- Drainage Layers 1899
- Excavation, Dampproofing and Drainage Tile 1904
- Floors Provide Lateral Support 0248
- Height above Grade 1820
- Horizontal Cracks 0247
- Insulated Concrete Forms 0220
- Pier 0211
- Pile 0210
- Poured Concrete with Wood Frame Exterior Walls 0218
- Preserved Wood 0216, 1822
- Problems on Ravine 0223
- Raft and Mat 0215
- **Repairs**
  - Adding a Sister Wall Outside 0264
  - Adding Interior Walls 0263
  - Buttress 0259
  - Pilaster 0260
  - Reinforcing Inside 0261
  - Steel Tie-backs 0262
- **Stone**
  - with Masonry Walls 0213
  - with Wood Frame Walls 0214
- **Wall**
  - Concrete Block 2080
  - Control Joints 0217
  - Lateral Support 0252, 0253
  - Parging 1823
  - Soil Pressure 0201
  - Spalling 0265
  - too Short 0273
  - with Beam Punching Through 0250

Four Square, Saltbox and Compound Plans 1701
Four-ply Built-up Roof Membrane 0090
Frame Deformation of Doors and Windows 1829

FRAMING
- Balloon versus Platform 0378
- for Dormers 0438
- Members Supported by Chimneys 0966

Freezing Water Spalls Bricks 1757
French Doors 2067
French Drain 1903
French Method for Slate Roofing 0035
Freon Gas goes Outside in Air Conditioning 1203
Fresh Air Supply Systems 1351
Frieze 1709

FROST HEAVING
- Evidence 0202
- in Unheated Houses 0205
- of Footings 0226
- Unlikely 0204

Fuel Oil Storage Tanks 0823-0831
Fuels – Heat Content of Various 1013
Fully Woven Closed Valley on Roof 0064
Furnace Blowers – Belt Drive and Direct Drive 0782
Furnace Clearances 0761
Furnace Covers 0759
Furnace Ducts – HRV Connection 1402
Furnace Electric Switches 0626
Furnace Equivalent Electric 1134
Furnace Fan Cover Missing 0758
Furnace Fan not Interlocked with HRV 1405
Furnace Fan Switch 0762

FURNACE FAN/LIMIT SWITCH 0762-0764
- Set Wrong or Defective 0764

FURNACE
- **Components Overview**
  - Conventional Furnace 0717
  - High Efficiency Furnace 0719
  - Mid-efficiency Furnace 0718
- **Gas**
  - Automatic Vent Dampers 0815
  - Condensing 0806-0819
  - Conventional 0717

FURNACE – CONTINUED
  - High Efficiency – Safety Devices 0811
  - Mid Efficiency 0718, 0801-0805
- Gravity 0710
- **Heat Exchanger**
  - with Heat Pump Coil Upstream 0755
  - with Humidifier Above 0791
- **High Efficiency**
  - Components 0719
  - Inspecting 0816
  - and Duct Sizes 0814
  - Gas – Improper Sidewall Venting 0810
  - Gas – Maximizing Temperature Differences 0808
  - Gas – Venting 0810
- Horizontal Gas Fired 0757
- **Oil**
  - Barometric Damper 0839
  - Emergency Shutoff 0831
  - Exhaust Flue Clearances 0845
  - Exhaust Flue Length 0844
  - Exhaust Flue Slope 0842
  - Exhaust Flue Support 0843
  - Mid Efficiency 0847
  - Obstruction in Exhaust Flue 0846
  - Sidewall Vent Location Problem 0848
  - Spillage from Barometric Damper 0841
- **Pulse**
  - How It Works 0812
  - Heat Exchanger Components 0813
- Room Air Openings 0737
- Room with Return Air Grills 0799
- Upflow and Downflow 0756
- **Wall**
  - Gas Fired 1153
  - Venting 1155
- with Exhaust Breech Passing through Cold Air Return 0754
- **Wood 1012**
  - Add-on (Divider Plate Method) 1031
  - Add-on (Downstream Series) 1030
  - Barometric Damper 1022
  - Combustible Return Ducts 1029
  - Combustion Air Damper Arrangement 1016, 1017
  - Combustion Chamber 1019, 1020
  - Components 1014
  - Duct Arrangement Allows Reverse Flow 1033
  - Duct Clearances 1028
  - Fan/Limit Switch 1027
  - Forced Draft 1018
  - Heat Exchangers 1021
  - Joining Vent Connector Sections 1024
  - not Downstream 1032
  - Thermostat Conditions 1026
  - Vent Connector Combustible Clearances 1023
  - Vent Connector Support And Slope 1025
  - Ventilation/Cooling Air 1015
- Wood/Oil 1034

Furnace/Water Heater System – Combination 0821
Fuse Blocks – Pull-out Type for 240-volt Circuits 0559
Fuse Types – Electrical 0564
Fused Neutrals and Old Wiring Systems 0566
Fuses and Breakers 0509, 0535
Fuses Provide Protection 0510

G

Gabion Retaining Walls 1945

GABLE
- Details 1706
- Overhang Less than 16 Inches 0436
- Overhang More than 16 Inches 0437
- Roof 0002
- Wall for Roof 0435

Galvanized Steel and Aluminum Gutter – Identifying 1896
Galvanized Steel Pipe in Plumbing System 1504
Gambrel and Mansard Roofs – Venting 1348
Gambrel Roof 0002
Gaps under Wall Sill 0285

GARAGE
- and Carport 1839
- Below-grade – Drains 1877
- Combustible Insulation Exposed 1872
- Door Openers 1881-1885
- Door Problems 1880
- Door Types 1879
- Electrical Outlets – 18 Inches off the Floor 0624
- Fire and Gas Proofing 1869
- Floor Drainage 1874
- Floor Structural 1873
- Heating Ductwork 1870
- Man Door 1871, 2072
- Settlement 0367
- **Slab**
  - on Disturbed Soil 1875
  - Settling 1875
- with Water Heater 1886

GARBAGE DISPOSAL
- Switches 0628
- Wiring 0629

GAS APPLIANCE
- Connectors – Flexible 0724
- Two on One Flue 0993
- with Improper Sidewall Venting 0805

GAS BURNER 0740-0750
- Continuous Pilot Light 0747
- Crossover Igniter 0743
- Monoport 0741
- Natural Draft 0734
- Relighting Pilot Light 0748
- Scorching 0749

GAS FIRED FLOOR FURNACE
- Clearances 0160
- Inspection Cap Missing or Damaged 1161

GAS FIRED SPACE HEATER
- Combustible Clearances 1162
- Unvented 1164

GAS FIRED WALL FURNACE 1153
- Clearances from Combustibles 1154
- Unvented 1159

GAS FIREPLACE
- Combustible Clearances 1168
- Direct Vent 1167
- Location Restrictions 1166
- not Fixed Open 1165

GAS FURNACE
- Automatic Vent Damper 0815
- Chimney/Vent Connections 0775
- Condensing 0806-0819
- **High Efficiency**
  - Duct Sizes 0814
  - Maximizing Temperature Differences 0808
  - Venting 0809
- Horizontal 0757
- Mid Efficiency 0801-0805
- Sidewall Venting 0818
- **Vent Connector**
  - Length 0771
  - Size 0774
  - Slope 0770
  - Support 0772

Gas Igniters for Fireplaces 1096

GAS METER
- Location For Water Heater 1570
- Poor Location 0722

GAS PIPING
- Connections with Teflon Tape 0725
- **Drip Leg 0730**
  - on Water Heater 1572
- Electric Grounding 0548, 0728

GAS PIPING - CONTINUED
Flexible Copper Tubing 0726
Support 0026
Support for Water Heater 1571
Terminology 0723
Gas Proofing Garages 1869
Gas Regulator – Ice 0721
GAS SHUT OFF VALVE 0727
Gas Shut Off Valve for Water Heater 1573
Gas Supply to Burner 0742
Gas Water Heater 1562
Gaskets – Sill 1334
Gaskets for Electrical Boxes 1335
Gate Valve for Plumbing 1535
Georgian Style 1725
Glass Doors for Fireplaces 1094
GLASS
Location for Windows 2048
Low-E 2047
Spacing in Windows 2049
GLAZING
Compound (Putty) 1826
Sloped 2052
Types for Windows 2040
Globe Valve for Plumbing 1534
Gothic Revival Style Home 1730
Gothic Windows 1719
Grade Clearance for Siding Inadequate 1748
Grading – Exterior 1894-1906
Graduated Slate Roof 0031
Gravel Erosion on Flat Roofs 0094
Gravity Furnace 0710
Greek Revival Style Home 1724
Grill in Furnace Room – Return 0799
Grills, Diffusers and Supply Air Registers 0793
Ground and Neutral Wires – Electrical Path 0547
GROUND SOURCE HEAT PUMP
Horizontal Closed Loop 1283
Vertical Closed Loop 1293
Ground Wires – Location 0551
Ground Wires let Fuses Blow 0546
Ground-Fault Circuit Interrupter 0616
Ground-Fault Interrupter Electrical 0616
Ground-Fault Interrupters Protect Ordinary Outlets Downstream 0617
Grounding Equipment – Electrical 0533
Grounding of Electric Service Box 0555
Grounding the Gas Piping 0548, 0728
GUARDS AND HANDRAILS
for Exterior Stairs 1847
for Stairs 2033
GUTTER AND DOWNSPOUT 1907-1934
Installation 1916
GUTTER
Attachment Methods 1914
Common Leakage Causes 1912
Discharging onto Roof 0003
Excess Shingle Overhang 1911
Identifying Aluminum and Galvanized Steel 1910
Integral 1908
Repairs 1913
with Screen 1915
Yankee 1909
Gypsum Lath vs Drywall 2009

H

Half Woven Valley 0063
Half-timbering 1711
HANDRAIL
and Guards for Exterior Stairs 1847
and Guards for Stairs 2033
Design 1848
HANDRAIL - CONTINUED
or Guards too Low 1850
Support 2037
Handsplit and Re-sawn Shakes 0020
Hangers for Copper Plumbing Pipe 1544
Hardboard Siding 1805
HARTFORD LOOP
and Equalizer Details for Steam Heat 1122
and Equalizer for Steam Heat 1117
Close Nipple Missing on Steam Heat 1123
on Steam Heating 1104
Hatch – Attic Access 1361
H-clips for Roof Sheathing 0461
Head Flashing Details on Chimney Flashing 68
Headlap on Asphalt Shingles 0011, 0013
HEARTH
Extension Dimensions for Fireplaces 1070
Extension Forming Boards – Removed 1073
Extensions for Factory Built Fireplaces 1072
Materials 1068
for Fireplaces – Raised 1071
Heartwood 0019
HEAT
Circulators for Fireplaces 1095
Content of Various Fuels 1013
How It Is Generated 0700
People Releasing 1303
HEAT EXCHANGER 0751-0755
and Hot Water Boilers 0855
Components for Pulse Furnace 0813
Copper Tube in Boilers 0856
for Wood Furnaces 1021
Heat Flow 0751
HRV and ERV 1353
in High Efficiency Gas Furnaces – Long 0806
on Furnace with Humidifier Above 0791
with Heat Pump Coil Upstream 0755
HEAT PUMP
All Electric 1281
Balance Point 1280
Bivalent 1294
Co-efficient of Performance 1279
Coil Upstream of Furnace Heat Exchangers 0755
Condenser Coil 1277
Defrost Cycle 1287
Evaporator Coil 1276
Ground Source
Horizontal Closed Loop 1283
Vertical Closed Loop 1293
Outdoor Coil Location 1288
H Principles 1275
Schematic – Summer Mode 1278
Testing Back Up Heat 1290
Triple Split System 1285
Two Expansion Devices 1286
Water Source – Open Loop 1282
HEAT RECOVERY VENTILATOR 1323
Cold-side Ducts not Insulated 1400
(Basic Components) 1352
Core Missing or Dirty 1407
Defrost Control 1357
Exhaust Grill Locations 1403
Filters and Condensate Drains 1356
Filters Dirty or Missing 1406
Flow Collars and Balancing Dampers 1404
Furnace Duct Connection 1402
Intake and Exhaust Locations 1401
not Interlocked with Furnace Fan 1405
Trap in Condensate Drain 1408
Heat Registers in Basements 0798
Heat Shield or Flame Rollout Shield 0750
HEAT TRANSFER
Methods of 0713
at the Inside Coil – Air Conditioning 1201
from Inside to Outside During Air Conditioning 1200
Mechanisms 1302
Heaters – Wood Space 1035-1060
Heating Cables to Prevent Ice Damning 0006
Heating Distribution System – Forced Air 0778-0800
Heating Ductwork in Garages 1870
Heating Requirements for Electric Heat 1135
Heating System – House Air Flow 0711
Heatlamp – Poor locations 0611
HEAVING
Frost – Evidence 0202
Frost – Unheated Houses 0205
Frost – Unlikely 0204
of Deck Piers 0246
of Footings due to Frost 0226
Sources 0239
HEIGHT
of Chimney 0977
of Chimney above Appliance 0978
of Metal Chimney 1007
of Adjacent Metal Chimneys 1010
Helical Anchors 0229
High and Low Returns for Forced Air Systems 0795
HIGH EFFICIENCY FURNACE
and Duct Size 0814
Condensation 0807
Have Long Heat Exchangers 0806
Inspecting 0816
Maximizing Temperature Differences 0808
Safety Devices 0811
Venting 0809
High Temperature Limit Switch on Boiler 0860
High Water Table 2081
High-hat Lights in Insulated Ceilings 0609
Hinged Pillars Affect Roof Structure 1866
Hip and Valley Rafter 0430
Hip Roof 0002
Hole in the Roof – Before Chimneys 0706
HOLES AND NOTCHES
in Beams 0304
in Joists 0329
in Top Plates of Bearing Walls 0381
Hollow Concrete Floors 2006
Hollow Masonry – Channels must be Vertical 0377
Homes Built with Holes for Chimneys 0707
Honeycombing in Concrete 0272
Hopper and Awning Windows 1716
HORIZONTAL CRACKS
on Foundations 0247
and Movement – Three Possibilities 0249
Horizontal Gas Furnace 0757
Horizontal Projection of Rafters Determine Span 0431
Horizontal Wood Siding 1790
Hot Climate Moisture Control 1319
Hot Climates – Controlling Moisture 1325
Hot Surface Ignition 0802
HOT WATER
Radiant Heat 0903
Boiler
Controls and Mixing Valve Layout for Radiant Floor Heat 0904
Conventional Gas Boiler 0853
Copper Tube Heat Exchanger 0856
Heat Exchanger 0855
High Efficiency Gas Boiler 0854
How It Works 0849
Heating
Balancing Methods 0885
Cast Iron Baseboard 0898
Circulating Pump 0890
Closed System 0880
Convectors 0896

HOT WATER – CONTINUED
Conventional Expansion Tank 0888
Covering Radiators Reduces Efficiency 0895
Diaphragm Tank 0889
Expansion Tank – Overflow Pipe 0887
Expansion Tank Water Levels 0886
Extending 0894
Finned Tube Baseboard 0897
Mixing Systems 0899
One Pipe System 0882
Open System 0879
Pipe Corrosion 0893
Radiant with Water Blender 0905
Radiator Covers 0851
Radiator Valve Leaks 0901
Radiators On Ceilings 0900
with Bypass Loop 0909
with Series Loop 0881
with Sidearm Heater 0907
with Tankless Coil 0906
with Two Pipe System (Reverse Return) 0884
House Air Changes with Exhaust System Components 1350
House Air Flow in a Forced Air Heating System 0711
HOUSE FAN – WHOLE 1273
Inadequate Attic Venting 1274
House Structure – Overview 0200
House Ventilation – Three Approaches 1349
Household Wiring in Parallel 0511
Housewrap vs Building Paper 1333
How Hot Water Boilers Work 0849
HRV
Attic Insulation 1360
Basic Components 1352
and ERV Heat Exchangers 1353
Cold Side Ducts not Insulated 1400
Components 1354
Connections to Furnace Ductwork 1359
Core Missing or Dirty 1407
Defrost Control 1357
Exhaust Grill Locations 1403
Filter and Condensate Drains 1356
Filter Dirty or Missing 1406
Flow Collars and Balancing Dampers 1404
Furnace Duct Connection 1402
Intake and Exhaust Locations 1355, 1401
Integrated Intake and Exhaust 1358
not Interlocked with Furnace Fan 1405
Trap in Condensate Drain 1408
HUMIDIFIER
above Heat Exchanger 0791
Air Flow 0790
Dampers Closed – Air Conditioning 1263
Drum-Type 0788
Trickle Type 0789
on Forced Air Heating Systems 0788-0791
HYDRONIC HEATING
Balancing Methods 0885
Circulating Pump 0890
Closed System 0880
Convectors 0896
Conventional Expansion Tank 0888
Covering Radiators Reduces Efficiency 0895
Diaphragm Tank 0889
Expansion Tank – Overflow Pipe 0887
Expansion Tank Water Levels 0886
Extending System 0894
Finned Tube Baseboard 0897
Mixing Systems 0899
One Pipe System 0882
Open System 0879
Pipe Corrosion 0893
Radiant 0903
Radiant with Water Blender 0905
Radiators on Ceilings 0900
Two Pipe System (Direct Return) 0883
HYDRONIC HEATING - CONTINUED
Two Pipe System (Reverse Return) 0884
with Bypass Loop 0909
with Sidearm Heater 0907
with Tankless Coil 0906
I joists – Wood 0458
ICE DAM 0006, 0007, 0008
at Skylight 0083
below Skylight 2062
on Party Walls 2016
Preventing with Ventilation 1342
ICE ON GAS REGULATOR 0721
for Water Heater 1569
IGNITERS
Crossover for Gas Burners 0743
Gas for Fireplaces 1096
Ignition – Hot Surface 0802
Illegal Electrical Taps 0543
Improper Sidewall Vent Locations for High Efficiency Gas Furnaces 0810
Improper Sidewall Venting of Gas Appliances 0805
Improper Slope on Chimney Cap 0984
Inadequate Wire Clearance over Roofs 0519
Incomplete Chimney Liner 0980
Indoor Caulking 0341
Inoperative Aquastat 0873
Inserts for Fireplaces – Flue Connections 0950
Inside and Outside Corners on Siding 0786
Inspecting an Oil Burner 0835
Inspecting High Efficiency Furnaces 0816
Inspecting Pressure Relief Valves on Boilers 0859
Inspecting the Service Box and Panels 0562, 0565
Inspection Cap Missing or Damaged for Floor Furnace 1161
Insulated Ceilings with Potlights 0609
Insulated Exterior Basement Stairwell 0242, 1889
Insulated Metal Doors 2069
Insulating Cathedral and Flat Roofs – Two Strategies 1382
Insulating Combustion Air Ducts for Fireplaces 1091
Insulating Cover Missing on Whole House Fan 1379
INSULATING CRAWLSPACES 1391
Clues 1392
Insulating Embedded Joists 1394
Insulating Flat and Cathedral Roofs 1380
Insulating Knee Walls 1368
Insulating Skylight Wells 1369
INSULATION
Added to Flat and Cathedral Roofs – Evidence 1381
Adding Exterior Basement 1388
Adding Interior Basement 1389
Adding to Solid Masonry Walls 1385
Behind Radiators 0715
Combustible in Basements and Crawlspaces 1395
Combustible in Garages 1872
Forms 1329
Holes in Siding 1752
in Floors over Unheated Areas 1397
Levels – Recommended 1309
Missing at Dropped Ceiling 1367
on Foundation Exteriors 1898
Rim Joist 1393
Risks of Adding More 1365
Short Circuits in Walls 1384
the Basics 1300-1325
too Close to Chimneys 1371
Voids and Convective Loops 1327
Wet below Roof Vents 1366
Insulbrick 1819
Intake and Exhaust Locations for Heat Recovery Ventilators 1355, 1401
Integral Curb Skylight on Sloped Roof 0082
INTEGRAL GUTTER 1908
Repairs 1913
Interior Basement Insulation – Adding 1389
Interior Ceilings 2019-2023
Interior Doors 2065-2072
Interior Drainage System for Leaky Basements 2088
INTERIOR FLAT ROOF DRAIN 1907
Clog 1932
Interior Floors 2002-2008
Interior Lintel – Sagging 0401
Interior Stairs 2028-2039
Interior Stairwell Lighting 2022
INTERIOR WALLS 2009-2016
Bulging Plaster due to Creep in Wood Frame 2018
Common Locations for Water Damages 2011
Inspecting 2010
Plaster with Wood Lathe 2017
Shadow Effect 2013
Structural Clues 2012
Used to Repair Foundations 0263
Interior Water Damage Source to Flooring 2004
Interlocking Shingle Clay Tile 0042
Intermittent Pilotlight 0801
International Style 1739
Inverted Roof Membrane Assembly 0089
Ionic Column 1722
Isolating Links Needed on Pull Chains for Electric Lights 0612
Italian Renaissance Style 1728
Italianate Style 1729

J

J Molding around Windows – Metal and vinyl siding 1815
JACK STUD SUPPORT 0386
on Wide Openings 0399
Jalousie or Louver Windows 1717
JET PUMP
Two Line for Well 1525
with Single Line for Shallow Wells 1524
Joining Vent Connector Sections for Wood Furnaces 1024
Joints – Mortise and Tenon 0327
Joints in Metal Valley Flashing 0058
Joints in Siding Boards 1801
Joist/Beam Connections 0309
JOISTS 0314-0334
Attached to Beams with Ledger Boards 0326
Attached to Steel Beams 0298
Cantilevered 0331
Ceiling – Overlapped Splices 0427
Ceiling – Plywood Splices 0428
Crack – Causes 0330
Crown up 0318
don't Insulate if Embedded 1394
End Support 0323
Fire Cut 0317
Floors – Types 0314
Notching and Drilling 0329
Overlap – Excessive 0322
Rim 0319
Roof 0426
Sagging Correction 0320
Strapping, Bridging and Blocking 0321
Support 1857
Wood I 0458
Jumper Wires for Electric Grounds 0552, 0553

K

KICKOUT FLASHING 1832
for Stucco 1776
Kilowatts vs BTUs 1133
KNEE WALLS 0446
Insulating 1368

KNOB AND TUBE WIRING 0602-0605
Connecting a New Circuit 0604
Connections 0603

L

L Vent 0997
Landings for Stairways – Exterior 1843
Latent Heat of Vaporization 1209, 1301
Lateral Foundation Support by Floors 0248
LATERAL SUPPORT
by Basement Floors 0258
for Exterior Masonry Walls 0315, 0360, 1766
for Foundation Walls 0252
for Masonry Chimneys 0961
for Steel Beams 0311
for Wood Beams 0312
Lateral Thrust Causing Cracking around Masonry Arches 0418
Leaking Downspouts 1920
Leaking Gutter – Causes 1912
Leaking Windows – Look Behind Window Treatments 2001
Leaks – Oil Storage Tanks 0826
Leaks in Skylights and Solariums 2053
Leaning Chimneys 0975
LEDGERBOARD
Flashing 1860
for Joist to Beam Connections 0326
Length of Exhaust Flue for Oil Furnace 0844
Length of Vent Connector on Gas Furnace 0771
Light Fixtures – Importance of Correct Polarity 0614
Lighting for Stairways 0607, 2022
Lights Need Isolating Links on Pull Chains 0612
Linear Plan vs Massed Plan 1700
LINER
for Chimney Incomplete 0980
for Chimney Flue for Fireplace Inserts 1038
for Flues – Clay Tile 0962
Links – Isolating for Pull Chains on Electric Lights 0612
LINTEL
and Arch 0415-0421
in Load Bearing 0383
Interior Sagging 0401
Loads in a Masonry Wall 0415
Loads in Wood Frame Walls 0416
Related Wall Cracks 0368
Rusting in Masonry Wall 1759
Rusting, Sagging or Loose on Fireplace 1078
Sagging or Missing for Window 2054
Sagging or Missing on Door 2068
Steel
End Bearing 0420
in Brick Veneer Wall 0358
Wood
End Bearing 0421
Solid Masonry in Wall 0359
Load Bearing Wall with Lintel 0383
Load Distribution on Floors 0277
Load Miser – Electrical 0619
Load Transfer in Houses 0297
Loads – Concentrated in Structures 0313
LOCATION
for Heat Lamps – Poor 0611
Issues for Gas Fireplaces 1166
of Air Leakage in Homes 1373
of Boiler Feed Pump for Steam Heat 1112
of Electric Meter 0537
of Pressure Reducing Valve on Boilers 0863
of Pressure Relief Valves on Boilers 0858
of Supply and Return Registers 0779
of Vapor Barriers 1339
Problems with Supply and Return Registers on Forced Air Systems 0797
Long Heat Exchangers in High Efficiency Gas Furnaces 0806
Longitudinal Shrinkage in Wood 0019
Lot Grading 1894-1906
Louver or Jalousie Windows 1717
Low and High Returns for Forced Air Systems 0795
Low Quality Built-up Roof/Wall Flashing 0112
LOW SLOPE
Roof – Defined 0001
Shingle Application – Roofing 0016
LOW WATER CUT-OUT
for Steam Boiler 1114, 1119
on Hot Water Boilers 0861
Low-E Glass 2047
LOWERED BASEMENT FLOORS
Bench Footings 0233
Underpinning 0234

M

Main Air Vent on Steam Heating 1125
Main Electrical Panel 0532
MAIN FUSES
Downstream of Disconnect Switch 0545
must be Properly Sized 0542
Main Panel – Electric 0532
Main Shut Off Valve for Plumbing – Stop and Waste 1533
Making Babies for Slate Repairs 0037
Man Door in Garage 1871, 2072
Mansard and Gambrel Roofs – Venting 1348
Mansard Roof 0002
Marks on Walls due to Thermal Bridging 1326
Masonry Arches – Cracking due to Lateral Thrust 0418
Masonry Block Retaining Walls need Rebar and Cap 1952
Masonry Cavity Wall 0352
MASONRY CHIMNEY 0957
and Fireplace Components 0959
Components 0958
Lateral Support 0961
Settling 1067
Tall 0971
MASONRY DAMAGE
due to Freezing 1757
Rising Damp 1756
Masonry Fireplace Components 1062
Masonry Mortar Joints 1761
Masonry Piers – Hollow Channels must be Vertical 0268
Masonry Repointing 1758
Masonry Roof/Side Wall Flashings 0076, 0077
Masonry Tie Detail in Brick Veneer Wall 0403, 1765
MASONRY VENEER WALL 0390-0399
Bowed 1764
Construction Detail 0402
Masonry Tie Detail 0403
vs Solid Masonry 1753
Weep Holes 0406
MASONRY WALL 0351-0377
adding Insulation 1385
Bowing 0316, 0369, 1767
Extending above Ceiling Joists 0357
Lateral Support 0315, 0356
Lintel Loads 0415
needs Lateral Support 1766
on Brick Foundation 0212
on Stone Foundation 0213
Solid 0351
with Diagonal Brick Bond 0355
with Rusting Lintels 1759
with Wood Lintel 0359
Massed Plan vs Linear Plan 1700
Mat and Raft Foundations 0215
Maximizing Temperature Differences in High Efficiency Gas Furnaces 0808
Mercury Bulb Thermostat 0746
Metal and Vinyl Siding 1811-1815
METAL CHIMNEY 0996-1010
Adjacent – Different Heights 1010
Bracing 1002
Cap Missing 1005
METAL CHIMNEY 0996-1010 – CONTINUED
Class A 0998
Combustible Clearances 1003
Height 1007
Not Continuous Through Roof 1009
Offset From Vertical 1008
Pitting or Rusting 1006
Triple-Wall 0999
Metal Clad Parapet Wall 0115
Metal Doors – Insulated 2069
Metal Drip Edge – Roofing 0011
METAL FIREBOX
Flue Liner Issue 1076
Clearance 1075
Metal Flashing Joints 0058
Metal Shingles 0049
METAL SIDING
Flashing below Windows 1814
Mounting Blocks 1813
Nailing too Tightly 1812
Metal Spark Strip for Fireplace Hearths 1069
Metal Ties for Connections in Single Top Plates 0382
METAL VALLEY FLASHING 0057
Alternate Applications 0060
with Upstand Up 0061
Secured With Cleats 0059
METAL VENT 0996-1010
B Vent 0996
L Vent 0997
Piece Connections 1001
Meter for Gas – Poor Location 0722
Meter Location – Electric 0537
MID EFFICIENCY
Gas Furnace 0801-0805
Oil Furnace 0847
Minimum Vent Height for Wall Furnace 1157
Miser – Electrical – load 0619
Missing Chimney Cap – Metal 1005
Missing Insulation at Dropped Ceiling 1367
Mission Style Home 1741
Miter Flue Liners 0964
Mitered Corners on Wood Siding 1799
Mixing Systems for Hot Water Heating 0899
Modernistic Style 1738
MODIFIED BITUMEN ROOF 0097-0099
Single-ply 0097
Staggering Side Laps in Single-ply 0099
Two-ply 0098
Modified Bitumen Roof/Wall Flashing 0105
MOISTURE
Control in Basements 1390
Controlling in Hot Climates 1319, 1325
How it Moves 1312
Reducing 1398
Trapped behind Siding 1318
Monolithic Slab – Slab-on-grade 0208
Monoport Gas Burners 0741
Mortar Joints – Common 1761
Mortar Joints in Brick Walls 1762
Mortise and Tenon Joints 0327
Mounting Blocks for Metal and Vinyl Siding 1813
Mounting of Electrical Panels 0541
Movement of Moisture 1312
Movements of Retaining Wall 1951
Mud Jacking 0228, 1876
Mud Sill 0283
Mullion 1718

MULTI-WIRE BRANCH CIRCUITS
Electrical Wiring for 0618
Over-current Protection 0578
Pull-out Fuse Blocks 0581
Muntin 1718

N

Nail Details – Slate Roofing 0033
NAIL POPPING 2014
on Stucco 1773
Nailing Controversy on Siding 1792
NAILING DETAILS
for Cedar Shakes 0025
For Wood Shingle Roots 0022
for Wood Shingle Siding 1796
Nailing of Asphalt Shingles 0011, 0013
Nailing of Wood Built-up Beams 0305
Nails – Good in Shear 0279
Nails in Joist Hangers 0310
Natural Draft Burners 0734
Need for Ground in Subpanel Feeder Wires 0556
Neoprene Plumbing Stack Flashing 0071
Neutral and Ground Wires should not be Bonded Downstream of Service Box 0554
Neutral Pressure Plane 1314
Neutral Wires Bypassing the Service Box 0544
Nogging 1711
Non-load Bearing Walls 0333
NOTCHES AND HOLES
in Top Plates of Bearing Walls 0381
in Beams 0304
Notching and Drilling in Joists 0329
Notching and Drilling Studs 0390
Notching of Studs 0396
Number of Electrical Conductors 0589

O

Obsolete Electrical Push-button Switches 0625
Obstructed Flue or Vent Connector 0989
Obstruction in Exhaust Flue on Oil Furnaces 0846
Offset Bearing Walls 0400
Offsets in Chimneys 0963
Oil and Wood Appliances Connected to Chimney on Same Floor Level 0994
OIL BURNER
Atomizing 0832
Barometric Damper Problems 0840
Clearance from Oil Storage Tanks 0825
Flame Sensor 0838
Inspecting 0835
with Flame Retention Head 0833
Oil Fired Water Heaters 1561
OIL FURNACE
Barometric Damper 0839
Emergency Shutoffs 0831
Exhaust Flue
Clearances 0845
Length 0844
Slope 0842
Support 0843
Mid Efficiency 0847
Obstruction in Exhaust Flue 0846
Primary Control 0834
Sidewall Vent Problems 0848
Sidewall Vented 0847
Spillage from Barometric Damper 0841
Stack Controller 0834
Stack Relay 0834
OIL STORAGE TANK 0823-0831
Buried 0823
Caps for Fill and Vent Pipes 0829
Clearance from Oil Burner 0825
Clearances from Wood Stoves 1054
Exterior above Ground 0824
Fill and Vent Piping 0828
Leaks 0826
Underground 0827
Undersized Fill Lines 0830
Oil/Wood Furnace 1034
Old and New Construction Re-insulating 1320
Old Wiring Systems with Fused Neutrals 0566
ONE FLUE
Serving Two Fireplaces 0992
Serving Two Gas Appliances 0993
One Pipe Hot Water Heating System 0882
One-Third Rule for Wall Stability 0266
One-Twenty Volt Circuit – Color-coding 0506
One-Twenty/Two-Forty Volts 0505
Open Hot Water Heating System 0879
Open Hydronic System 0879
Open Roof Valleys 0053
Openers for Garage Doors 1881-1885
Openings in Electric Panels 0540
Openings in Roofs 0445
Oriel Window 1720
Oriented Strandboard (OSB) Siding 1806
Oriented Strandboard Sheathing 0389
Outdoor Air Temperature Sensor for Boiler 0877
Outdoor Caulking 1337
Outdoor Combustion Air for Fireplace 1090
Outdoor Combustion Air Supplies 0738
Outdoor Fire 0704
Outdoor Intake Screening for Combustion Air for Fireplaces 1092
OUTLETS
and Switches in Bathrooms – Electrical 0620
in Floors or Countertops 0623
near Basins 0621
should not be above Electric Baseboard Heaters 0622
Over-current Protection for Multi-wire Branch Circuits 0578
Overflow Pipe for Expansion Tanks on Hot Water Heating Systems 0887
OVERHANG FOR GABLE
less than 16 Inches 0436
more than 16 Inches 0437
Overhangs of Wall Plate 0385
Overhead Electrical Wire – Stranded 0588

P

Pad Footings and Spread Footings 0209
Palladian Window 1719
PANEL
Electrical 0534
Clearances – Electric 0538
Mounting – Electric 0541
Openings – Electrical 0540
Roof Sheathing 0460
Securement – Electrical 0539
Siding – Vertical Joints 1807
Wires – Excess Sheathing on Electrical 0583
Parallel Circuits for Household Wiring 0511
PARAPET WALL
Metal Clad 0115
Prone to Damage 1754
Parging on Exterior Foundation Walls 1823
PARTITION
and Bearing Wall Identification 0391
Studs – Straightening 0397
Walls 0333
PARTY WALL
Ice Dams 2016
Wood Frame 2015
Patched Flat Roofs 0091
Patched Roofing 0004
Patching Cracks in Basement Walls 2087
Patios – Raised 1943
Pediments 1719, 1721
Pellet Stoves 1043
Pennsylvania Slate 0030
People Releasing Heat 1303
Perimeter Drainage Tile around Exterior Basement Stairwells 1890
Photo-eye for Garage Door Openers 1885
Pier Foundations 0211
PIERS
Heaving of Deck 0246
Hollowed Channels must be Vertical in Masonry 0268
on Deck – Adfreezing 0245
Things to Watch for 0267
Wooden – Things to Look for 0269
Pig-Tailing of Electrical Connections to Avoid Double Taps 0577
Pilaster 0260, 1721
PILE
Foundations 0210
Retaining Walls 1948
Piles to Stabilize Foundations 0230
Pillars – Hinged – Affect Roof Structure 1866
PILOTLIGHT
Continuous 0747
Intermittent 0802
Re-Lighting 0748
Pipe Connection – Soldered 1539
Pipe Corrosion in Hot Water Heating System 0893
Pipe Replacement in Plumbing System – Downstream vs Upstream 1505
Piston Pump for Well 1526
Pitch Pans (Pockets) for Roof Penetrations 0120
Pits for Wells 1517
Pitting or Rusting Metal Chimneys 1006
Planters or Gardens against Walls 1751
Plaster – Shadow Effect 2013
Plastic Roofing 0101, 0102
Plastic Supply Pipe Clearances to Vent Connectors 1554
Platform versus Balloon Framing 0378
Plenum Heater 1147
PLUMBING
Air Gap 1546
Atmospheric Vacuum Breaker 1547
Ball Valve 1536
Bending Radius for Polybutylene Pipe 1558
Compression Fitting 1541
Constant Water Flow can wear out Pipes 1508
Copper Supply Pipe – Types 1538
Correcting Water Hammer 1553
Cross Connections 1545
Dielectric Union 1543
Dishwasher Air Gap 1551
Double Check Valve Assembly 1549
Downstream vs Upstream Pipe Replacement 1505
Elbows and T's Reduce Pressure 1506
Flare Fitting 1540
Galvanized Steel Pipe 1504
Gate Valve 1535
Globe Valve 1534
Hangers for Copper Pipe 1544
Issues with Old Clay Pipe Sewer 1636
Larger Diameter Pipe to Water Heater 1510
Main Shut Off Valve 1533
Pinholing and Cracks in Cast Iron Stacks 1635
Plastic Supply Pipe Clearances to Vent Connectors 1554

PLUMBING – CONTINUED
- **Polybutylene Pipe**
  - Compression Fitting 1557
  - Crimp Fitting 1556
  - 18 Inches from Water Heater 1555
- **Pressure**
  - Decreases with Height 1509
  - Drops as Flow Rate Increases 1501
  - Regulator Required 1507
  - Type Vacuum Breaker 1548
  - Private Water Sources 1512-1530
  - Reduced Pressure Principle Device 1550
  - Separate Water Service from Sewer Pipe 1532
  - Services Piping 1531
  - Soldered Pipe Connection 1539
- S-traps Can Lead to Siphoning 1648
- **Stack Flashings 0071, 0072**
  - Cone-Style 0119
  - Stack Jack 0118
  - Stretched or Buckled 0072
- Static Water Pressure 1502
- Warning Signs for Tile Beds – Septic Systems 1669
- Water Heaters 1559-1615
- Water Supply Factors 1500

PLYWOOD
- and Composite Siding 1804
- Ceiling Joist Splices 0428
- Roof Sheathing 0460
- Subflooring 0338

POLARITY
- Importance on Light Fixtures 0614
- Reversed – Electrical 0613

POLYBUTYLENE PIPE
- Bending Radius 1558
- Compression Fitting 1557
- Crimp Fitting 1556

Polystyrene Insulation – Types 1330
Ponding on Flat Roofs 0096
Poor Electrical Seal at House/Wall Penetration 0527
Poor Gas Meter Locations 0722
Poor Vent Connection at Chimney – Wood Stove 1058

PORCHES 1836
- Beam – Poor End Support 1855
- Beam Rotation 1856
- Beam Sag 1854
- Beams 1853
- Column Hinge Point 1852
- Column Materials 1851
- Floor Sag 1858
- Joist Support 1857
- or Deck Board Sagging 1864
- Skirting 1867

Post-tensioned and Pre-stressed Concrete Floor Slabs 0341
Potential – Electrical 0502
Potential Air Leakage Location 1373

POTLIGHTS
- and Air Leakage 1338
- in Insulated Ceilings 0609
- Need Proper Bulbs 0610

Power Vents in Attic 1377
Prairie Style Home 1736
Precast Concrete Retaining Walls System 1946
Premature Failure of Fiberglass Shingles 0015
Preserved Wood Foundations 0216, 1822
Pressure Drops as Flow Rate Increases 1501
Pressure Grouting 1876
Pressure Plane – Neutral 1314

PRESSURE REDUCING VALVE
- Location on Boilers 0863
- on Boiler 0866

Pressure Reducing/Relief Valve Installed Backwards on Boilers 0870
Pressure Regulator for Supply Plumbing 1507, 1537

PRESSURE RELIEF VALVE
- for Steam Heat 1115
- Location on Boilers 0858
- on Boilers 0857
- on Boilers – Inspecting 0859

Pressure Set too Low in Boiler 0868

PRESSURE TANK
- and Pump Controls for Well Water 1528
- Bladder Type for Wells 1529
- Water Logged – Short Cycling 1530

Pressure Type Vacuum Breaker 1548
Pressuretrol for Steam Heat 1116, 1121
Pre-stressed and Post-tensioned Concrete Floor Slabs 0341
Preventing Ice Dams 0007
Primary Control – Aquastat on Boiler 0872
Primary Control for Oil Furnace 0834
Private Water Sources for Plumbing 1512-1530
Projection for Masonry Veneer 0376
Proper Sizing of Main Electrical Fuses 0542
Properties of Wood 0019
Protected Roof Membrane Assembly 0089
Public Water Supply for Plumbing 1531-1537
Pull Chains Need Isolating Links on Electric Lights 0612
Pull-down Attic Stairs 1363

PULL-OUT FUSE BLOCKS
- for 240-volt Circuits 0559
- for Multi-Wire Branch Circuits and 240-volt Circuits 0581

PULSE
- Combustion 0910
- Furnace Heat Exchanger Components 0813
- Furnace How It Works 0812

PUMP
- Centrifugal for Well 1523
- Control for Boilers 0874
- Controls for Well 1528
- for Well – Types 1522
- Piston Type for Well 1526
- Single Line Jet with Shallow Wells 1524
- Submersible for Drilled Well 1527
- with Zone Control on Boiler 0875

Purlins 0446
Purpose of Fuses 0510
Push-Button Electrical Switches are Obsolete 0625
Putty (glazing compound) 1826

PVC
- Roof Membrane 0101
- Roof Membrane Problems 0102
- Roof/Wall Flashing 0113

Q

Queen Anne Details 1733
Queen Anne Style Home 1732
Quoining 1712

R

Racking Resistance of Wood Frame Wall 0388
Radial Shrinkage of Wood 0019
Radiant Barriers 1331

RADIANT HEAT
- at Ceilings – Electric 1151
- at Floors – Electric 0714
- Electric 0714
- Hot Water 0903

Radiant Hot Water Heating with Water Blender 0905

RADIATOR
- Air Bleed Valves – Don't Operate 0869
- Covering Reduces Efficiency 0895
- Covers on Hot Water Heating Systems 0851
- Heats the Air through Convection 0850
- Insulation Behind 0720
- on Ceilings or High on Walls 0900
- on Hot Water Heating Systems 0850
- Valve Leaks 0901

Radius of Bending for Polybutylene Pipe 1558
Raft and Mat Foundations 0215

RAFTER
- End Bearing 0429
- Hip and Valley 0430
- Span Determined by Horizontal Projection 0431
- Spans – Reducing 0446

RAFTER – CONTINUED
- versus Roof Joist 0426

Rain Caps and Spark Arresters for Chimneys 0983

RAIN SCREEN PRINCIPLE – VENTED 1763
- Weep Holes 0405

Raised Hearth for Fireplaces 1071
Raised Patios 1943
Ravine Lots and Foundation Problems 0223
Receptacle – Wrong Type of Electrical 0615
Recessed Light Fixtures in Insulated Ceilings 0609
Recommended Amount of Attic Ventilation 1346
Recommended Insulation Levels 1309
Recovery Rate for Water Heater 1566
Red Label Wood Shingles 0020
Reduced Pressure Principle Device – Plumbing 1550
Reducing Moisture Levels 1398
Refractory/Firepot 0744

REFRIGERANT LINE FOR AIR CONDITIONING 1248-1251
- Filter/Dryer 1249
- Leaks 1251
- Sight Glass 1250

Registers for Heating Systems in Basements 0798
Regulator for Gas – Ice 0721
Reinforcing Foundation from Inside 0258
Relative Humidity 1311
Re-lighting Pilot Light 0748
Remedial Action for Roof Spreading 0441
Removing Abandoned Chimneys 0969
Removing or Altering Walls – Concentrated loads 0313
Renovations Remove Forced Air Ducts 0794
Repointing 1758
Resistance – Electric 0503

RETAINING WALL 1945-1954
- Cantilevered Concrete 1947
- Drainage 1950
- Gabion 1945
- Inspecting 1953
- Masonry needs Rebar and Cap 1952
- Moving or Cracking 1951
- Pile 1948
- System – Precast Concrete 1946
- Weep Holes 1954
- Wood 1949

RETURN AIR GRILL
- in Furnace Room 0799
- High and Low for Air Conditioning 1260

Return and Supply Register Locations 0779

RETURN DUCTS
- Combustible for Wood Furnaces 1029
- in Floor Joists 0792

Reverse Flow through Duct Arrangement for Wood Furnace 1033
Reverse Polarity – Electrical 0613
Reversing Mechanism for Garage Doors 1884
Ribbons in Slate 0032
Ridge Board not Required 0434
Ridge Boards 0433
Ridge Shingles – Asphalt Shingle Roofing 0018

Ridge Support for Roof 0432
Ridging on Flat Roofs 0095
Rim Joist Insulation 1393
Rim Joists 0319
Rise – Roof 0001
Rise, Run and Tread Width for Stairs 1842
RISING DAMP 1756
in Masonry Column 0294
Risks of Adding More Insulation 1365
Rods and Channels to Stabilize House Movement 0231
ROLL ROOFING 0051, 0052, 103
Problems 0052
ROOF
and Surface Water Control for Building 2075
Board
Insulation 0459
Sheathing 0459
Cathedral
Channeled vents versus cross ventilation 1383
Venting 1347
Details 1705
Dormer Framing 0438
Drainage Systems – Flat 0088, 1929
Drains – Interior on Flat Roofs 1907
EPDM 0100
Flat 1702
Flat and Cathedral – Evidence of Insulation Added 1381
Gable Overhang
less than 16 Inches 0436
more than 16 Inches 0437
Gable Wall for 0435
Insulating Flat and Cathedral 1380
Intersection
with Brick Wall above Flashings 0077
with Siding above – Flashing 0078
Joists versus Roof Rafters 0426
Membrane Assembly – Inverted or Protected 0089
Openings 0445
or Cover for Exterior Basement Stairwells 1893
Plastic 0101, 0102
PVC 0101, 0102
Rafter
Horizontal Projection Determines Span 0431
Span Reduction 0446
Ridge
Board 0433
Board not Required 0434
Support 0432
Sheathing 0459-0471
Delaminating 1378
H-clips and Spacing 0471
Panel Type 0460
Sheathing Boards 0459
Slopes 0001, 0423
Soffits 0439
Spreading 0440
Dishing and Sagging 0425
Remedial Action 0441
Steel-Framed Rafters, Roof Joists, and Ceiling Joists
Typical Assembly/Components 0447
Typical Details 0448
Structure affected by Hinged Columns 1866
Thermoplastic 0101, 0102
Truss 0451-0456
Overview 0451
Sag or Damage Caused by Drifting Snow 0453
Strapping the Underside 0451, 2021
too Long 0456
Types 0452
Uplift 0454, 2019
Uplift Remedial Action 0455, 2020
Turbine Vents 1344
Two Strategies for Insulating Flat and Cathedral 1382
Types 0002, 0422
ROOF – CONTINUED
Valleys – Open and Closed 0053
Ventilating Mansard and Gambrel 1348
Ventilation 1341-1348
Helps Prevent Ice Dams 0007, 1342
Helps Reduce Attic Heat 1341
Vents
Type and Location 1343
Wet Insulation Below 1366
with Bell-cast Eave 1704
with Downspout Running Across 1918
Roof/Masonry Sidewall Flashing 0076
ROOF/SIDEWALL FLASHING 0073
Clay Tile 0075
Roof/Siding Clearance too Small 1750
Roof/Wall Anchoring 0424
ROOF/WALL FLASHINGS 0073-0078
EPDM or PVC 0113
in Built-up Flat Roof 0104
Modified Bitumen 0105
ROOFING
Asphalt Shingle Fastener Problems 0017
Low Slope Shingle Application 0016
Membrane
Blisters in Built-up 0092
Four-ply Built-up 0090
Metal 0049, 0050
Shingles 0049
Patched 0004
Sheet Metal 0050
Slate Types 0030
Room Heaters – Gas Fired – Combustible Clearances 1162
ROT
in Exterior Wood Stairs 1846
in Flooring around Plumbing Fixtures 2003
in Floors – Causes 2007
in Wood Stairs 2034
Location in Walls 0380
Rotated or Twisted Beams 0300
Rotational Settlement Cracks 0236
Run – Roof 0001
Run, Rise and Tread Width for Stairs 1842
Rusting and/or Pitting Metal Chimneys 1006
Rusting Lintels in Masonry Walls 1759
R-value per Inch 1308

S

S Type Clay Tile 0041
Sacrificial Anode for Water Heaters 1559
Saddle Flashings on Chimneys 0067
Safety Devices for High Efficiency Gas Furnaces 0811
SAGGING BEAM 0300
Exterior 1854
SAGGING
Deck or Porch Boards 1864
Interior Lintel 0401
Joists – Correction 0320
or Missing Door Lintels 2068
or Missing Window Lintels 2054
Porch Floor 1858
Spreading and Dishing of Roof 0425
Saltbox Style Home 1743
Saltbox, Four Square and Compound Plans 1701
Sapwood 0019
Sash 1718
SCORCHING AT GAS BURNER
on Furnace 0749
on Water Heater 1575
Scouring of Gravel on Flat Roofs 0094
Screening for Combustion Air Intake for Fireplace 1092
Screens on Gutters 1915
Scuppers 1930
Secondary Attics 1364
Secondary Roof Missing Downspout 1917
Securement Methods for Concrete 0047
SECURING
Clay Tiles 0043
Decks to Buildings 1859
Electrical Panels 0539
Electrical Wires 0584
Gutters 1914
Ledgerboards on Decks 1859
Self-Flashing Skylight 0082
Self-Sealing Tabs – Asphalt Shingles 0012
Selvage Roofing 0103
Sequencers for Electric Furnaces 1145
Sequencing of Element on Electric Water Heater 1568
Series Loop on Hot Water System 0881
SERVICE BOX
and Panels – Electrical 0565
and Panels – Inspecting 0562
Breaker and Fuse-type 0536
Bypassed by Neutral Wires 0544
SERVICE DROP 0513-0519
Clearances (Canada) 0516
Clearances (United States) 0515
SERVICE ENTRANCE
Areas of Potential Water Entry 0526
Cable 0523
Cable should not be Covered by Siding 0528
Wires 0520-0528
Service Equipment 0532
Service Masts – Bent 0524
Service Panel – Electric 0532
Service Piping for Plumbing 1531
Service Size 0529-0531
Service Size Determining by the Main Disconnect 0531
Settled Backfill around Homes 1904
Settled or Heaved Exterior Steps 1845
SETTLEMENT
Cracks – Rotational 0236
Differential caused by Soils 0222
due to Cut and Fill Excavation 0224
of Buildings – Types 0221
of Garages 0367
Settling or Leaning Chimneys 0970
Shadow Effect on Plaster Wall 2013
SHAKE ROOFING
Application 0024
Nailing Details 0025
SHEATHING
Delaminating Roof 1378
Excess on Electrical Panel Wires 0583
Roof – H-clips and Spacing for Panel Type 0461
Strandboard 0389
Shed Roof 0002
Sheet Metal Cradle Repairs for Slate Roofs 0038
Sheet Metal Roofing 0050
SHINGLE
and Shake Siding 1795
Application Low Slope Roofing 0016
Application – Wood 0021, 0023, 0028
Shingle Style Home 1734
Shingles – Metal 0049
Shingles at Ridges 0018
Shoring Type Retaining Walls 1948
Short Circuit 0508
Shower Stalls 1692-1693
Shrinkage of Wood 0019
Shrubs and Trees too Close to House 1942
Shut-Off Valves for Gas 0727
Shutoffs – Emergency for Oil Furnace 0831
Side Laps – Staggered, in Modified Bitumen Roofs 0099
Sidearm Heater on Hot Water System 0907
Sidelight 1721

SIDEWALL VENT
Locations for High Efficiency Gas Furnaces – Improper 0810
Oil Furnace 0847
Problems with Oil Furnaces 0848
Sidewall Venting of Gas Appliances – Improper 0805
SIDING
Asbestos Cement 1808
Boards – Joints 1801
Butt Joint Detail on Vertical 1800
can Trap Moisture 1318
Clay and Slate Shingles 1817
Concealed Nails 1793
Cut Back Bottom 1798
Flashings at Dormers 0086
Hardboard 1805
Identifying Inner-Seal® 1810
Inside and Outside Corners 1794
SIDING – CONTINUED
Insulbrick 1819
Metal and Vinyl 1811-1815
Flashing below Window 1814
J Molding around Windows 1815
Nailing too Tightly 1812
Mitered Corners 1799
Mounting Blocks 1813
Nailing Controversy 1792
OSB 1806
Plywood and Composite 1804
should not Cover Electric Service Entrance Cable 0528
Strapping for Vertical 1803
Support 1746
too Close to Grade 1748
too Close to Roof 1750, 1808
Vertical Joints in Panels 1807
Wood
Horizontal 1790
Shingle 1797
Shingles and Shakes 1795
Wood/Soil Contact 1821
Z Flashings 1809
Inner-Seal® Siding – Identifying 1810
Sight Glass for Refrigerant on Air Conditioning 1250
SILL
Anchor Spacing 0284
Anchors for Walls 0281
Capillary Break 1827
Crushing – Wall 0286
Gaskets and Electrical Box Enclosures 1334
Mud 0283
should be above Grade 0282
Wall 0280-0286
Wall – Gaps 0285
Simple Electrical Circuit 0507
Simply Spanned versus Continuous Beams 0299
Single and Double Hung Window 1713
Single Flue Serving Two Appliances 0993
Single Top Plates – Metal Ties in Bearing Walls 0382
Single-ply Modified Bitumen Roof 0097
Sister Wall Outside Foundations for Repairs 0264
Six Hundred and Fifty Degree Celsius Chimney 1000
Six Nails per Shingle – Asphalt Shingle Siding 1818
Size of Vent Connector on Gas Furnace 0774
Sizes of Columns 0291
Skirting for Decks and Porches 1867
SKYLIGHT
and Solarium Leaks 2053
Flashings 0080, 0081, 0082
Ice Damming 0083
Ice Damming Below 2062
in Flat Roof 0117
in Sloped Roof – Curb Mount 0080
in Sloped Roof – Curbless 0081
SKYLIGHT- CONTINUED
in Sloped Roof – Integral Curb 0082
Wells – Insulating 1369
Window and Solarium from the Inside 2040-2064
Slab Coil for Air Conditioner 1237
SLAB-ON-GRADE
Monolithic 0208
Supported Slab 0207
Slate Hooks 0036, 0037
SLATE REPAIR
Method with Slate Hooks 0036
by Making Babies 0037
Using A Sheet Metal Cradle 0038
Slate Ribbons 0032
SLATE ROOF
Graduated 0031
Installation – Dutchlap Method 0034
Installation – French Method 0035
Nailing Details 0033
Typical Life 0030
Slate Types 0030
Slider Windows 1715
Slope and Support for Vent Connectors for Wood Furnaces 1025
Slope of Exhaust Flue on Oil Furnace 0842
Slope of Roof Valleys 0054
Slope of Vent Connector for Wood Stoves 1055
Slope of Vent Connector on Gas Furnace 0770
Slope on Chimney Cap 0984
Sloped Glazing 2052
SLOPED ROOF
Draining onto Flat Roof 0124
Shapes 1703
Slopes for Grading Recommended 1894
Slopes of Roof 0001, 0408
Small Roofs with no Downspouts 1919
SMOKE CHAMBER
for Fireplace 1083
Wall Slope 1084
Smoke Shelf for Fireplace 1083
Snap-Action Thermostat 0766
Soffit Vent Baffles 1345
SOFFITS 0439
and Fascia 1824, 1825
SOIL CONDITIONS
Causing Differential Settlement 0222
Causing Water Leakage 1895
Soil Level too High at Foundation Wall 0273
Soil Pressure on Foundation Walls 0201
Soil Strength 0203
Soil/Wood Clearances 0393
SOLARIUM 0084
and Skylight Leaks 2053
and Window and Skylight from the Inside 2040-2062
SOLID MASONRY
versus Veneer Walls 0407
Walls 0351
Walls – Bowing due to Tie Failure 0372
Solid vs Veneer Masonry 1753
Sources of Heaving 0239
Space Heater – Unvented 1164
Spaced Planked Sheathing for Wood Sheathing 0023
Spacing between Layers of Glass and Windows 2049
Spacing for Panel Type Roof Sheathing 0461
Spacing for Wall Sill Anchors 0284
SPALLING
of Brick due to Freezing 1757
of Foundation Wall 0265
Span of Rafter Determined by Horizontal Projections 0431
Spanish Colonial Style Home 1740
Spanish or Mission Tiles – Eave Closures 0044
Spans – Methods of Reducing for Rafters 0446
Spark Arresters and Rain Caps for Chimneys 0983
Special Circuit Breakers for 240-volt Circuits 0560
Spillage from Barometric Damper on Oil Burner 0843
Spillage Switch on Hot Water Heating System 0908
Spindle Spacing for Stairs 1849
SPLICES IN CEILING JOIST
Overlapped 0427
Plywood 0428
Splitting Wood Shingles 0029
Spread Footing and Pad Footings 0209
SPREADING ROOFS 0440
Remedial Action 0441
Dishing and Sagging of Roof 0425
Springy Steps 1846
Stack Controller for Oil Furnace 0834
Stack Effect 1313
Stack Flashings from Plumbing Systems on Roofs 0071, 0072
Stack Jack – Plumbing Stack Flashing 0231
Stack Relay for Oil Furnace 0834
Staggered Bus Bars on Circuit Breaker Panels 0579
Staining below Exterior Doors 2071
STAIR
Dimensions 2028
Exterior – Handrail Design 1848
STAIR – CONTINUED
Exterior – Handrails and Guards 1847
Handrail Design 1848
Handrail or Guard too Low 1850
Handrails and Guards 2033
Interior 2028-2039
Pull-down 1363
Rise, Run and Tread Width 1842
Rot in Wood 2034
Spindle Spacing 1849
Stringer Movement 2036
Stringers 2031
Tread/Stringer Connections 2035
Treads Curved 2029
Winders 2030
Wood Exterior – Rot 1846
Stairs that aren't Springy 1846
STAIRWELL
Exterior Basement – Side View 0241
Firestopping 2038
Insulated Exterior Basement 0242
Landings – Exterior 1843
Lighting 0605, 2022
to Attic 1362
Width 2032
Starter Course on Asphalt Shingles 0011, 0013
Starter Strip on Asphalt Shingles 0011, 0013
Static Head at Wells 1518
Static Water Pressure 1502
STEAM HEAT
"F" and "T" Trap 1109
Air Vents 1100
at Rest 1098
Boiler Feed Pump 1113
Call for Heat 1099
Condensate Pump 1111
Dimension "A" 1101
Equalizer Pipe 1102
Hartford Loop 1104
and Equalizer 1117
and Equalizer – Details 1122
Close Nipple Missing 1123
How It Works 1097
Location of Boiler Feed Pump 1112
Location of Condensate Pump 1110
Low Water Cut-out 1114, 1119
Main Air Vent 1125
One Pipe Counter Flow System 1105
One Pipe Parallel Flow System 1106
Pressure Relief Valve 1115
Pressuretrol 1116, 1121
Systems 1097 – 1131
Thermostat Satisfied 1103

STEAM HEAT - CONTINUED
Thermostatic Trap 1108
Two Pipe System 1107
Water Hammer 1118
Water Level Gage 1120
STEEL BEAM
Attached to Joists 0298
Lateral Support 0311
STEEL LINTEL
End Bearing 0420
in Brick Veneer Wall 0358
Steel Studs with Electrical Wires Running through 0594
Steel Tie-backs to Repair Foundations 0262
Steep Roof Types 0002
Step Rise, Run and Tread Width 1842
Stepped Footings on Sloped Lots 0232
STEPS
Exterior – Settled or Heaved 1844
Exterior Concrete Support 1841
in Exterior Walkways 1941
Stick Style Home 1731
STONE FOUNDATION
with Masonry Walls 0213
STONE FOUNDATION – CONTINUED
with Wood Frame Walls 0214
STOVES
Pellet 1043
Wood 1012, 1035-1060
Straightening Partition Studs 0397
Straightsplit Wood Shakes 0020
Strainers/Baskets at the Top of Downspouts 1923
Strandboard Sheathing 0389
Stranded Electrical Wires for Overhead Runs 0588
Strapping for Vertical Siding 1803
Strapping the Underside of Roof Trusses 2021
Strapping Underside of Trusses 0451
Strapping, Bridging and Blocking for Joists 0321
Strategies for Comfort 1306
Strengths of Soils 0203
Stretched or Buckled Plumbing Stack Flashing 0072
Stringer Movement in Stairs 2036
Stringer/Tread Connections in Stairs 2035
Stringers for Stairs 2031
Structural Clues on Interior Walls 2012
Structural Garage Floor 1873
Structure – House – Overview 0200
Structure – Openings in Floors 0332
STUCCO
Cracking 1771
Drip Screen 1770
Kickout Flashing 1776
Nail Popping 1773
Problems on Tudor-style Homes 1772
Synthetic – EIFS 1774
Three Coat Process 1768
Two Coat Process 1769
Wall 1768-1789
STUD
Notch and Drilling 0390
Notching 0396
Sizes and Spaces affect Wall Strength 0384
Straightening Partition 0397
Support for Jack 0386
Support for Jack Studs on Wide Openings 0399
SUBFLOORING 0337-0340
Edge Support 0339
Plywood 0338
Types 0337
Submersible Pump for Drilled Well 1527
SUBPANEL
Feeder Wires need Ground 0556
Wiring Disconnect by Main Panel 0573
Wiring Disconnect by Subpanel 0572
Wiring Electrical 0571-0573
Wiring No Separate Disconnect Switch 0571
Sump Pump in Basement 2085
Super Heated Water 0852
SUPPLY AIR
Registers, Diffusers and Grills 0793
Systems 1351
Systems for House Ventilation 1351
Supply and Return Registers Poorly Located 0797
SUPPLY PLUMBING
3/4 Inch Pipe 1503
Constant Water Flow Can Wear Out Pipes 1508
Downstream vs. Upstream Pipe Replacement 1505
Elbows and T's Reduce Pressure 1506
Factors Affecting Supply 1500
Flow and Pressure 1500-1511
Galvanized Steel Pipe 1504
In-house 1538-1558
Larger Diameter Pipe to Water Heater 1510
Pressure Decreases With Height 1509
Pressure Regulator Required 1507, 1537
Static Water Pressure 1502
Support and Slope for Vent Connector Section for Wood Furnaces 1025
Support for Beam End 0301
Support for Edges of Subflooring 0339
Support for Exhaust Flue for Oil Furnace 0843
Support for Gas Piping 0729
Support for Handrails 2037
Support for Jack Studs 0386
Support for Joist 1857
Support for Roof Ridge 0432
Support for Siding 1746
Support for Vent Connector on Gas Furnace 0772
Support Requirements for Service Entrances 0525
Supported Slab – Slab-on-grade 0207
Surface Water and Roof Runoff Control 2075
Swales 1896
SWITCHES
and Outlets in Bathrooms – Electrical 0620
Blockage for Forced Air Furnaces 0804
Electrical for Furnaces 0626
for Garbage Disposal 0628
Three-way 0608
Synthetic Rubber Roofing 0100
SYNTHETIC STUCCO 1774
Inspection Strategy – Exterior 1788
Inspection Strategy – Interior 1789
Insulation Details 1775
Synthetic Ventilation Layer for Wood Shingles 0028
System Grounding – Electrical 0546-0554

T

Tabs-Self Sealing on Asphalt Shingles 0012
Tall Masonry Chimneys 0971
Tangential Shrinkage of Wood 0019
TANK – OIL STORAGE
Caps for Fill and Vent Pipes 0829
Clearance from Oil Burner 0825
Exterior above Ground 0824
Fill in Vent Piping 0828
Leaks 0826
Underground 0827
Undersized Fill Lines 0830
Tankless Coil Water Heater on Boiler 0906
Tapered Mission Style Clay Tile 0039
Tapersawn Shakes 0020
Tapersplit Shakes 0020
Taps – Illegal Electrical 0543
T-connection in Top Plate of Wood Frame Bearing Wall 0380
Teflon Tape at Gas Piping Connections 0725, 1574
Temperature across Inside Coil of Air Conditioner 1222
Temperature and Pressure Gauge on Boiler 0865
Temperature Differences in High Efficiency Gas Furnaces 0808
Temperature Limit Switch on Boiler 0860
Temperature Rise on Electric Furnaces 1149
Tempering Valve on Combination Heating System 0822
TERMITES
Exterior Inspection for 0348
Interior Inspection for 0349
Measures to Combat 0350
Thermal Breaks in Window Frames 2030
Thermal Bridging Causing Marks on Walls 1326
Thermal Conductance 1305
Thermal Conductivity 1304
Thermoplastic Roofing 0101, 0102
THERMOSTAT 0762-0765
Bi-Metallic (Mercury Bulb) 0746
Conditions to Watch for on Wood Furnaces 1026
Mercury Bulb – Air Conditioning 1266
must be Level 0768
Poor Location for Air Conditioning 1268
Snap Action – Air Conditioning 1267
Snap Action 0766
Thermostatic Expansion Valve for Air Conditioning 1241
Thermostatic Trap for Steam Heating 1108
Three Approaches to House Ventilation 1349
Three Kinds of Draft for Burners 0733
Three Sided Chimneys 0972
Three-way Electrical Switches 0608
Threshold – Exterior door 0856
Throat, Smoke Shelf And Smoke Chamber For Fireplace 1083
Through-wall Flashings 0114
Tie Failure causing Bowing of Solid Masonry Wall 0372
Tile – Ceramic Insulation 0340
Tile Flue Liners 0962
Tiles – Ceramic – Alternatives for Installing 2008
Toe-kick Electric Heaters 1138
Toothed-in Masonry on Additions 1760
TOP PLATE
Holes and Notches in Bearing Walls 0381
T-connection in Wood Bearing Wall 0380
Transom Light 1721
Trap – Thermostatic For Steam Heating 1108
Trap in Condensate Drain for HRV 1408
Trap Required in Condensate Line for Air Conditioning 1245
Tread Width Rise and Run for Stairs 1842
Tread/Stringer Connections in Stairs 2035
Treads – Curved on Stairs 2029
Tree Roots Causing Foundation Cracks 0256
Trees and Shrubs too Close to House 1942
Triangle – Fire 0712
Trickle Humidifier 0789
Trim Flashings and Caulking – Macro Approach 1835
Trim, Counters and Cabinets 2024-2027
Trimmers with Wall Above 0334
Triple Split System Heat Pump 1285
Triple-Wall Metal Chimney 0999
TRUSS
Sag or Damage caused by Drifting Snow 0453
Types 0452
Uplift 0454, 2019
Uplift – Remedial Action 0455, 2020
TRUSSES
Bracing of Compression Webs 0450
Overview of Roof 0449
Roof 0449-0457
Strapping 0451
Strapping the Underside 2021
Tudor Style Home 1735
Tudor Style Stucco Problems 1772
Turbine Vents 1344
Tuscan Column 1722
Twisted or Rotated Beams 0303
Two Comfort Strategies 1306
Two Fireplaces on One Flue 0992

Two Gas Appliances on One Flue 0993
Two Pipe System (Direct Return) on Hot Water Heating 0883
Two Pipe System (Reverse Return) for Hot Water Heating 0884
Two-Forty Volt Circuit Pull-out Fuse Blocks 0559
Two-Forty Volt Circuits – Special Breakers 0560
Two-piece Counter Flashings 0106
Two-ply Modified Bitumen Roof 0098
Types of Roof 0002, 0422
Typical Supply and Return Register Locations 0779

U

UFFI Insulation Holes in Siding 1752
Undercoursing – Wood Shingles 0020
Underground Electrical Service 0514
Underground Oil Storage Tank 0827
UNDERPINNING 0234
  Timing of Concrete Pours 0235
Undersized Fill Lines for Oil Storage Tanks 0830
Unheated Areas – Insulation in Floors Above 1397
Unheated Houses – Frost Slab-on-Grade – Floating Slab 0206
Unvented Space Heater 1164
Unvented Wall Furnace 1159
Upflow and Downflow Furnaces 0756
Upper Sash Problems on Windows 2059
Upstand on Metal Valley Flashing 0061

V

Vacuum Relief Valve for Water Heaters 1560
Valley – Closed Cut or Half Woven 0063
Valley and Hip Rafter 0430
VALLEY FLASHING 0053-0064
  Asphalt Shingles 0056
  Metal 0057
  Cutting the Point 0062, 0087
  On Roofs 0053-0064
Valleys Roof Slope 0054
Valve for Zone Control of Boiler 0876
VALVE GAS SHUT-OFF 0727
  for Water Heater 1573
Valve Leaks on Radiators 0901
Valve Tempering on Combination Heating System 0822
VAPOR BARRIER
  and Air Conditioning Ductwork 1264
  Incomplete or Wrong Location 1372
  Location 1339
  vs Air Barrier 1332
Vapor Diffusion 1316
Vapor Retarders 1332-1340
Vaporization – Latent Heat of 1301
Variable Anticipator on Thermostat 0767
Variable Thermostat Anticipator 0767
Vehicle Doors for Garages 1879
Veneer Masonry vs Solid Masonry 1753
Veneer versus Solid Masonry Walls 0407
VENEER WALL 0402-0411
  Brick 0353, 0404
  Masonry Tie Detail 0403
  with Steel Lintel 0358
Vent and Fill Piping for Oil Storage Tanks 0828
Vent Connection at Chimney for Wood Stove 1058
Vent Connection for Wood Stoves 1056
VENT CONNECTOR
  and B-Vent – Combustible Clearances 0773
  Clearance from Plastic Supply Pipe 1554
  Clearances for Wood Stoves 1050
  Combustible Clearances – Wood Furnace 1023
  Extending too far into Chimney 0776, 0987
VENT CONNECTOR - CONTINUED
  for Wood Stove 1056
  Length for Gas Furnace 0771
  Loose at Chimney 0988
  or Flue Obstructed 0989
  Section Joints in Wood Furnaces 1024
  Size on Furnace 0774
  Slope – Gas Burner 0770
  Slope for Wood Stoves 1055
  Support and Slope for Wood Furnaces 1025
  Support for Gas Furnace 0772
  Wall Shields for Wood Stoves 1051-1052
Vent Dampers – Automatic on Gas Furnaces 0815
Vent Height – Minimum for Wall Furnaces 1157
Vent Location Problems for Oil Furnaces 0848
Vent Metal – Connection of Pieces 1001
Vent/Chimney Connections on Gas Furnaces 0775
VENTED RAIN SCREEN PRINCIPLE 1763
  Weep Holes 0405
Ventilating Roofs to Prevent Ice Dams 0007
VENTILATION
  Attic – Recommended Amount 1346
  Helps Reduce Attic Heat 1341
  Layer for Wood Shingles 0028
  Prevents Ice Dams 1342
Ventilation/Cooling Air for Wood Furnaces 1015
Ventilator – Heat Recovery 1323
Venting Cathedral Roofs 1347
VENTING
  for High Efficiency Furnaces 0809
  for Wall Furnace 1155
  Gas Furnaces 0769-0777
Venting Homes 1349-1357
Venting Living Spaces 1349-1357
Venting Mansard and Gambrel Roofs 1348
Venting Roofs 1341-1348
VENTS 0952
  Power – Attic 1377
  Roof – Types and Location 1343
  Turbine 1344
  Wet Insulation Below 1366
Vermont Slate 0030
Vertical Foundation Cracks 0253
Vertical Joints in Panel Siding 1807
VERTICAL SIDING
  Butt Joint Detail 1800
  Strapping 1803
VINYL SIDING
  Flashing below Windows 1814
  J Molding around Windows 1815
  Mounting Blocks 1813
  Nailing too Tightly 1812
Vulnerable Areas – Roofs 0005

W

Walkouts from Basements 1887-1893
Walkway Steps – Exterior 1941
WALL
  Bearing – Holes and Notches in Top Plates 0381
  adding Insulation to Solid Masonry 1385
  Analyzing Crack Size 0225
  Assemblies 1745
  Bearing and Partition – Identifying 0391
  Bowing of Masonry 0369
  Brick Veneer 0353, 0404
    Bowed in Older Home 0370
    Construction Detail 0402
    Detail 0280
    Masonry Tie Detail 0403
    with Lintel 0358
  Cavity 0352
  Condensation 1747
WALL – CONTINUED
  Crack Shapes 0227
  Cracking
    caused by Surfaces Sliding 0362
    Common Locations 0237
    due to Brick Expansion 0373
    Lintel-related 0368
    Planes of Movement 0363
    Rotational Settlement 0236
    Types 0361
  Drying Potential 1387
  Extending above Ceiling Joists 0357
  Furnace
    Clearances from Combustibles 1154
    Direct Vent 1158
    Firestop Spacers 1156
    Gas Fired 1153
    Minimum Vent Height 1157
    Unvented 1159
    Venting 1155
  Gable for Roof 0435
  Knee – Insulating 1368
  Lateral Support for Masonry 0315
  Lintel Loads
    in Masonry 0415
    in Wood Frame 0416
  Loading Bearing with Lintel 0383
  Marks due to Thermal Bridging 1326
  Masonry
    Lateral Support 0356
    Bowing 0316
    Bowing due to Tie Failure 0372
    Veneer 0402-0411
    with Diagonal Brick Bond 0355
    with Wood Lintel 0359
  Non-load Bearing 0333
  of Chimney 0960
  Offset Bearing 0400
  over a Trimmer 0334
  Parapet – Prone to Damage 1754
  Partitions 0333
  Plate Overhang 0385
  Retaining 1945-1954
  Rot Location 0392
  Shields – For Wood Stove Vent Connectors 1051-1052
  Sill
    Anchor Spacing 0284
    Anchors 0281
    Crushing 0286
    Gaps 0285
    should be above Grade 0282
  Slope for Smoke Chamber and Fireplace 1084
  Solid Masonry 0351
  Stability – The One-third Rule 0266
  Steel-Framed
    Bearing and Bracing Details for Light-gauge Steel 0414
    Lintels and Bridging for Light-gauge Steel 0413
    Typical Assembly/Components for Light-gauge Steel 0412
  Strength – Stud Sizes and Spaces 0384
  Terminology – Brick 0354
  Veneer versus Solid Masonry 0407
  Weep Holes in Brick Veneer 0406
  with Arch Outside and Wood Lintel Inside 0360
  with Planters or Gardens against it 1751
  Wood Frame 0378-0401
    Racking Resistance 0388
Wall/Roof Anchoring 0423
Warm Chimneys are Best 0954
Water – Super Heated 0852
Water Blender on Radiant Hot Water Heating 0905
WATER COOLED AIR CONDITIONER
  Missing Backflow Preventer 1235
  Testing 1234

Water Entry at Electrical Service Entrances 0526
WATER FLOW
and Pressure in Supply Plumbing 1500-1511
can wear out Plumbing Pipes 1508
WATER HAMMER
in Plumbing System 1553
in Steam Heating 1118
WATER HEATER
18 Inches from Polybutylene Pipe 1555
Dip Tube 1564
Drip Leg on Gas Piping 1572
Electric 1567
Element Sequencing 1568
External Tank 1563
Floating Tank 1563
Gas 1562
Piping Support 1571
Poor Location of Gas Pressure Relief Valve 1582
Shut Off Valve 1573
Ice on Gas Regulator 1569
in Garage 1886
Oil Fired 1561
Plumbing 1559-1668
Poor Gas Meter Location 1570
Recovery Rate 1566
Sacrificial Anode 1559
Scorching at Gas Burner 1575
Teflon Tape at Connections for Gas Piping 1574
Vacuum Relief Valve 1560
WATER LEAKAGE
at House/Wall Penetration of Electrical Service Conduit or Cable 0527
due to Soil Conditions 1895
Water Level Gauge for Steam Heat 1120
Water Level in Expansion Tank for Hot Water Heating 0886
Water Pressure in Boiler Set too Low 0868
Water Services Piping Separated from Sewer Pipe 1532
Water Sources Heat Pump – Open Loop 1282
Water Supply Factors 1500
Water Supply Pressure Drops as Flow Rate Increases 1501
Water Table – High 2081
Water-cooled Air Conditioning – Schematic 1214
Waterlogged Pressure Tank – Pump Short Cycling 1530
Watts per Square Foot Required for Electric Heat 1135
Web – Bracing of Compression Members in Trusses 0450
WEEP HOLES
Vented Rain Screen Principle 0405, 1763
below Grade 1749
for Retaining Walls 1954
in Brick Veneer Walls 0405
Weight of Water on Flat Roofs 1931
WELL
Bladder Type Pressure Tank 1529
Bored 1514
Casings for Drilled 1516
Centrifugal Pump 1523
Deep and Shallow 1520
Draw Down Test 1512
Drilled 1515
Drilled with Submersible Pump 1527
Dug 1513
Foot Valve 1512
Location 1519
Piston Pump 1526
Pits 1517
Pressure Tank Components and Pump Controls 1528
Pumps – Types 1522
Shallow with Single Line Jet Pump 1524
Static Head 1518
Two Line Jet Pump 1525
Water Logged Pressure Tank – Short Cycling 1530
WET BASEMENT
and Crawlspaces 2074-2089
Clues – Part 1 2083
Clues – Part 2 2084
WET BASEMENT – CONTINUED
Interior Drainage System 2088
Problem Causes 2074
Wet Crawlspaces and Basements 2074-2089
Wet Insulation below Roof Vents 1366
WHOLE HOUSE FAN 1273
Inadequate Attic Venting 1274
with no Insulating Cover 1379
Wide Selvage Roofing 0103
Width of Stairwell 2032
Wind Scouring on Flat Roofs 0094
Wind Washing of Insulation 1328
Winders on Stairs 2030
WINDOW 1713-1720
and Door Capillary Break 1827
and Door Frame Deformation 1829
and Door Putty (Glazing Compound) 1826
and Stair in Basement 2076
Awning and Hopper 1716
Bow, Bay and Oriel 1720
Casement 1714
Components 2042
Curved Tops 1719
Double and Single Hung 1713
Drain Holes 2044
Electrical Wire Clearance Around 0517
Energy Efficiency 2046
WINDOW 1713-1720 – CONTINUED
Exit Sizes 2061
Fall Protection 2043
Fanlights 1719
Faulty 2058
Flashing over 2057
Flashing Pan 2045
Flashings 1830
Frames – Thermal Breaks 2050
Glass Locations 2048
Glazing Types 2040
Gothic 1719
Installed Backwards 2056
Jalousie or Louver 1717
Leaks – Look behind Window Treatments 2001
Lintels Sagging or Missing 2054
Moves 1828
Mullion 1718
Muntin 1718
Palladian 1719
Sash 1718
Shapes 1719
Sill – Capillary Break 1818
Slider 1715
Terms 1718
Types 2041
Upper Sash Problems 2059
Well Drain Problems 1939
Wells 1935-1939
Damage 1937
Extend or Add when Re-grading 1936
Skylight and Solarium from the Inside 2040-2064
Wire – Damaged 0512
Wire and Fuse Sizes – Electric 0561
Wire Arrangement in Electrical Distribution Panels 0557
WIRE CLEARANCES
around Windows 0517
from Ducts and Pipes – Electrical 0595
Wire Fuse and Heater Sizing for Electric Heat 1136
Wire Sizes – Common 0529
Wire Support – Electrical within Steel Studs 0595
Wires not Well Secured to the House 0518
Wires Securement to the House 0518
WIRING
Exposed Electrical 0599
for Electric Space Heaters 1141
for Garbage Disposals 0629
for Multi-wire Branch Circuits 0618
Wood Appliance Below Oil Appliance on Same Floor Level 0994
WOOD BEAM
Bolting through Built-up 0306
Air Gaps at Ends 0278
Lateral Support 0312
Nailing of Built-up 0305
Wood Engineered for floors 0335
WOOD FIREPLACES 1061-1096
Combustible Clearance Requirements 1063
Design Problems 1065
in Basements 1064
Three Kinds 1061
Wood Floors – Allowable Deflections 0276
Wood Foundations – Preserved 0216, 1822
WOOD FRAME
Bearing Wall – Top Plate T-connection 0380
Bearing Wall in Basement 0387
Party Wall 2015
Wall 0378-0401
Wall Lintel Loads 0416
Wall on Stone Foundation 0214
Wall Racking Resistance 0388
WOOD FURNACE 1014-1034
(Downstream Series) – Add-on 1030
Add-on – (Divider Plate Method) 1031
Barometric Damper 1022
WOOD FURNACE 1013-1033 – CONTINUED
Combustible Return Ducts 1029
Combustion Air Damper Arrangement 1016, 1017
Combustion Chamber 1019, 1020
Components 1014
Duct Arrangement Allows Reverse Flow 1033
Duct Clearances 1028
Fan/Limit Switch 1027
Forced Draft 1018
Heat Exchangers 1027
Joining Vent Connector Sections 1024
not Downstream 1032
Thermostat Conditions 1026
Vent Connector
Combustible Clearances 1023
Support and Slope 1025
Ventilation/Cooling Air 1015
Boiler, Fireplace and Stove 1012
Wood I Joists 0458
WOOD LINTEL
End Bearing 0421
in Solid Masonry 0359
Inside and Arch Outside 0360
Wood Piers – Things to Look for 0269
Wood Retaining Walls 1949
Wood Roofing Application – Synthetic Ventilation Layer 0028
WOOD SHAKE
Application 0024
Nailing Details 0025
Typical Lengths 0020
Typical Thickness 0020
Wood Sheathing Application – Spaced Planked Sheathing 0023
WOOD SHINGLE
and Shake 0020
and Shake Siding 1795
Application 0021
Application – Synthetic Ventilation Layer 0028
Curling, Cupping and Splitting 0029
Edge Grain 0019
Flat Grain 0019
Nailing Details 0022
Nailing Details – Siding 1796
over Plywood Sheathing 0021
Siding 1797
Typical Lengths 0020
Typical Thickness 0020

WOOD SIDING 1790-1803
Cut Back Bottom 1798
Horizontal 1790
Wood Space Heaters 1035-1060
WOOD STAIRS
Rot 2034
Rot – Exterior 1845
WOOD STOVE 1035-1060
Advanced Combustion 1040
Catalytic – Bypass Damper 1042
Catalytic Combustors 1041
Clearance from Oil Tanks 1054
Components 1035
Convective 1039
Dampers – Testing 1060
Don't Confine 1037
Floor Protection 1044-1048
Unlisted – Combustible Clearances 1049
Vent Connector 1056
at Chimney 1058
Clearances 1050
Drawbands or Adjustable Connectors 1057
Slope 1055
Wall Shields 1051-1052
Wood/Oil Furnace 1034
WOOD/SOIL
Clearances 0393
Contact 1938
contact for siding 1821
Woven Valley 0063, 0064

Y

Yankee Gutter 1909

Z

Z flashings 1809
ZONE CONTROL
with Pumps on Boiler 0875
with Valves on Boiler 0876